JOURNALISM'S ROVING EYE

BOOKS BY JOHN MAXWELL HAMILTON

Main Street America and the Third World

Edgar Snow: A Biography

Entangling Alliances: How the Third World Shapes Our Lives

Hold the Press: The Inside Story on Newspapers
(coauthor George Krimsky)

*Casanova Was a Book Lover: And Other Naked Truths and Provocative
Curiosities about the Writing, Selling, and Reading of Books*

EDITED VOLUMES

Journalism of the Highest Realm: The Memoir of Edward Price Bell
(coeditor Jaci Cole)

*From Pigeons to News Portals: Foreign Reporting and the
Challenge of New Technology*
(coeditor David Perlmutter)

JOURNALISM'S ROVING EYE

A HISTORY OF AMERICAN FOREIGN REPORTING

John Maxwell Hamilton

LOUISIANA STATE UNIVERSITY PRESS

BATON ROUGE

Publication of this book is made possible in part by the support of the John and Virginia Noland Fund of the Baton Rouge Area Foundation and by the V. Ray Cardozier Fund.

Published by Louisiana State University Press
Copyright © 2009 by John Maxwell Hamilton
All rights reserved
Manufactured in the United States of America
First printing

Designer: Laura Roubique Gleason
Typeface: Minion Pro, Myriad Pro
Printer and binder: TK

Library of Congress Cataloging-in-Publication Data

Hamilton, John Maxwell.
    Journalism's roving eye : a history of American foreign reporting / John Maxwell Hamilton.
        p.   cm.
    Includes bibliographical references and index.
    ISBN 978-0-8071-3474-0 (cloth : alk. paper) 1. Foreign news—United States—History. 2. Foreign corespondents—United States—Biography. I. Title.
    PN4888.F69H36 2009
    070.4'3320973—dc22

                                                                    2008055651

The author is grateful for permission to reprint excerpts from the following:

Jack Belden, "Hey Soldier, Wounded," *Life.* Copyright 1943 Life, Inc. Reprinted with permission. All rights reserved.

James Bowen report on the sinking of the *Graf Spee.* December 17, 1939. Reprinted with permission of NBC.

Walter Cronkite, "Report from Vietnam," February 27, 1968. Reprinted with permission of CBS.

Brooks Egerton and Reese Dunklin, "Safe harbor," *Dallas Morning News,* June 23, 2004. Reprinted with permission of the *Dallas Morning News.*

John Gunther, "*Inside* England," *Atlantic Monthly,* March 1937. Reprinted with permission of Jane Gunther.

Richard Halliburton, *New Worlds to Conquer* (Indianapolis: Bobbs-Merrill, 1929). Reprinted with permission of Simon & Schuster.

Paul Scott Mowrer, "On Retiring from Active Newspaper Work," *On Going to Live in New Hampshire* (Sanbornhill, N.H.: Wake-Brook House, 1953). Reprinted with permission of Richard S. Mowrer.

Harrison E. Salisbury, "A Visitor to Hanoi Inspects Damage Laid to U.S. Raids," *New York Times,* December 25, 1966. Reprinted with permission of the *New York Times.*

Vincent Sheean, *Personal History,* 1935. Reprint, with new introduction, Boston: Houghton Mifflin, 1969. Reprinted with permission of Ellen Sheean.

Edgar Snow, "Will China Become a Russian Satellite?" *Saturday Evening Post,* April 9, 1949. Reprinted with permission of Lois Wheeler Snow.

Juan O. Tamayo, "What to pack in Middle East? You'd be amazed," *Miami Herald,* November 29, 1987. Reprinted with permission of the *Miami Herald.*

Dorothy Thompson, "I Saw Hitler!" *Cosmopolitan,* March 1932. Reprinted in Dorothy Thompson, *"I Saw Hitler!"* (New York: Farrar and Rinehart, 1932). Reprinted with permission of Dorothy Thompson estate.

Acknowledgement, as requested, is made here, too, for permission to quote from collections (see "A Note on Sources") at the Newberry Library in Chicago, the Howard Gotlieb Archival Research Center at Boston University, the Lilly Library at Indiana University, the Princeton University Library, and the Butler Library at Columbia University.

The paper in this book meets the guidelines for permanence and durability of the Committee on Production Guidelines for Book Longevity of the Council on Library Resources. ∞

This book is dedicated

To

Two Louisiana Ladies
Adrienne Moore and Mary Ann Sternberg

And a Yankee
Peter Shepherd

From Our Special at the Front

Roving knights of the pencil,
    Jolly smooth blades are we,
In ruck and luck of camp and march,
    On intravenal sea.

Ping of wire in our rifles,
    Boom of mail from our mounts,
We fire at sight, and sight to fire
    World echoes from our 'founts.'

Old World's a monstrous gossip,
    A babbling dame o' the town;
"O say!" "D'ye hear?" "What's that?" It's from
    Our labial godown.*

Blest and curst of the nations,
    Strife sentinels are we,
Of royal tilts as Moltke† bred
    To slink of Soudanee.‡

At the far-flung drama's crux,
    We hardily hold stalls,
Critical, erudite, eager,
    As a nation rises or falls,

Grim in the clash of epochs,
    We mask all cringe at fight;
Nor check nor laud; tell and let tell
    Of Nihon and Muscovite,

Wait in capital eddy
    The stride of epaulette;
O, rasp and gash, ye censor blade;
    Earn the silence ye get!

Up, away in the morning;
    Pick of peoples at eve;
Under the stars, with salt of blood,
    We sniff the grub they leave.

What grub for hallow hillsides,
    Ghastly, common and sore:
What purge of the rank earth's sourness
    In sacramental gore!

Soldierly dash and danger,
    None of a soldier's pay;
We dare and risk, we flare and flout,
    All we can do is—say!

RICHARD BARRY, correspondent for *Eastern Illustrated War News,* 1904

* Hindi for *warehouse.*
† Prussian Field Marshal Count Helmuth von Moltke, 1800–1891.
‡ Sudan.

CONTENTS

ILLUSTRATIONS

TABLES

MAPS

ACKNOWLEDGMENTS

As this book grew, so did the list of people who helped one way or another.

Jaci Cole, who was more involved than anyone else, appeared in my office at the Louisiana State University just as I started work on the book. She was a freshman eager to do a little research. The book was completed about the time she was finishing her master's degree more than seven years later. Jaci unearthed valuable information, thought through the implications of what we found, and edited. Together we wrote articles based on our research and brought to publication the memoir of one of the characters in this book, Edward Price Bell, whose autobiography lay forgotten in the Newberry Library in Chicago.

A number of other students with promising careers ahead of them provided valuable assistance: in particular Raluca Cozma and Eric Jenner—doctoral students with whom I also collaborated on articles—as well as Jodi Bannerman, Angela Broussard, Madeline Casey, Tristi Charpentier, William Gillis, Foad Izadi, Marisa Joelson, Adrien Martin, Nicole Marshall, Emily Metzger, Lindsay Newport, Jessica Perez, Casey Rayburn, Shearon Roberts, Karen Rowley, Mario Scherhaufer, and Rebecca Strobach.

LSU colleagues critiqued sections of the book, came up with ideas, or worked with me on related research: Jinx Broussard, the late Timothy Cook, William Dickinson, Gaines Foster, Ronald Garay, Emily Erickson, Regina Lawrence, George Lockwood, Robert Mann, Adrienne Moore, and Charles Zewe. Renee Pierce cheerfully solved the many computer problems that arose. In a class by herself is Angela Fleming, my assistant, who helped with research, editorial suggestions, and unfailing enthusiasm for this undertaking.

I am equally grateful to two longtime friends. Alex Jones, who directs the Shorenstein Center on the Press, Politics & Public Policy at Harvard's Kennedy School of Government, invited me to spend fall 2002 as a fellow. This propitious fellowship came early in the writing of the book and helped me think through some of the major issues I had to confront. Peter Shepherd, my agent before he retired and an editor at heart, dove into this book with gusto. He came to the surface with the best and most terrifying editing I have ever had.

William Schmick and Seymour Topping reviewed not only the chapters in which they are mentioned but others. Other useful comments came from Jim Amoss, David Binder, John Carroll, Charles Clark, James Hamilton, James Hoge, George Krimsky, Stuart Loory, Marcy McGinnis, Richard Moose, Donald Shanor, Robert A. Signer, John H. Sullivan, Susan Tifft, Andrew Tyndall, and William Wheatley. My friend Pamela Howard arranged for me to stay at the New York Yacht Club, where I could admire the painting of publisher (and commodore) James Gordon Bennett Jr.

A large number of archives were useful, but three were in particular because of their wealth of information and the people involved. One was the Newberry Library in Chicago, which holds important collections related to the *Chicago Daily News*. I especially thank Martha Briggs of the Newberry staff. The second is the *New York Times* archive, which was located in the printing press foreman's former office in the bowels of the old *Times* building when I used it. Much of the material has since been placed in the New York Public Library. Michael Golden assisted me in getting access to the papers, and Frederick Brunello, Laura Lihach, and Lora Korbut made it easy to use these materials and in other ways helped navigate the *Times*. The third collection is the Associated Press archive, which is taking shape under the competent and friendly hands of Valerie Komor and her assistant, Sam Markham. Although I relied on the following collections to a lesser degree, these staff deserve thanks: Laurel S. Wolfson, Klau Library, Hebrew Union College–Jewish Institute of Religion, Cincinnati, for copies of Dorothy Thompson's stories in the *Jewish Daily Bulletin;* Debra Bade of the *Chicago Tribune* News Research and Archives and Eric Gillespie of the Cantigny First Division Foundation's Colonel Robert F. McCormick Research Center for help on James Keeley; and Roberta Saltzman, Dorot Jewish Division, New York Public Library, for tapes of Sigrid Schultz.

I give no thanks at all to our federal government whose assiduous efforts in recent years to impede requests under the Freedom of Information Act frustrated my research. Episodes recounted in this book illustrate the evils that grow out of government that does its best to block the sunshine of facts.

I have been fortunate to work at a university with a superb publishing house. The director of LSU Press, MaryKatherine Callaway, has been a faithful champion of this book, for which I am very grateful. As with previous books, I had the pleasure of working on design issues with Assistant Director Laura Gleason.

I am indebted to LSU Foundation, which has supported me for more than a decade with the Hopkins P. Breazeale Professorship.

Finally, I thank Wendy Schmalz, my loyal agent; my son, Maxwell, for his ideas; and my wife, Regina, for her patience.

John Maxwell Hamilton

JOURNALISM'S ROVING EYE

INTRODUCTION

This is not the first book on foreign news with "Roving Eye" in the title. A 1957 paperback novel with that same name told the story of foreign correspondent Robert Adams. Adams travels with "guts, wits and typewriter in hand." On the book's cover a dark-haired beauty massages the correspondent's back while he drinks wine and hammers out a story on his typewriter in a Paris hotel room. "Robert Adams' adventures as he hunts down the real story—and the real truth—make a sensationally thrilling novel of one of the world's most exciting professions," proclaims a promotional blurb.

Foreign correspondents swoop into our imaginations with flash and gravitas. Here, in white tie, they dine with European royalty, trading bon mots and information. There, with sinister native guides, they slip through battle lines to find and interview rebel leaders.

Jules Verne, famous for his travel fantasies, wrung literary mileage out of foreign correspondents. "Mentally, I offer a last prayer to the God of reporters," says one of his heroes, Claudius Bombarnac, at the outset of a train journey to the Far East, "and ask him not to spare me adventures." "While the city beat might have its exciting side," wrote historian Bernard Weisberger, "the peak in reporting circles was reached when a writer could don a felt hat, riding boots, and a knapsack and swagger off to cover a war or a revolution."

Journalists have done their part, and more than their part, to burnish the image of the "roving knights of the pencil," as the poem that opens this book put it. "The special correspondent must be 'to the manor born,'" observed a *Scribner's* author in 1893. "He must be as sanguine as a songbird, and as strong and willing as a race horse." The *Chicago Tribune* defined "Foreign News" this way in an encyclopedia for readers in 1928: "What romance there is in the very words! . . . If to this business of getting out a great daily newspaper there still clings any of the aura of romance which once surrounded all newspapers and all newspapermen, it is the foreign correspondents who get the greater share of it."

This *Roving Eye* promotes this view of foreign correspondence—up to a point.

Some of the best talents in the profession *have* filled the ranks of foreign correspondents. Correspondents have plied their trade with élan. How gainsay the aplomb with which G. W. Steevens of the *London Daily Mail* succumbed to enteric fever while covering the Boer War in 1900? In his last moments he sipped a glass of champagne and sighed, "This is a sideways ending to it all."

But there are other sides to foreign reporting, sides that appear when one gets past the cover of that first *Roving Eye*. Robert Adams does not report high politics or revolutions for the *New York Times, Newsweek,* or CBS News. He writes for a second-rate vacation magazine, *Traveller,* and anonymously on the side for *Eyewitness,* a tawdry gossip-exposé magazine. "No journalist with any self-respect liked *Eyewitness,*" Adams confesses. The magazine's chief virtue is its circulation, 2 million. The villain in this tale is a depraved editor.

A cavalcade of characters parades through the history of American foreign news-gathering. Correspondents, noble and ignoble, are the most conspicuous. But they alone do not account for the news that reaches us. Owners of news media, publishers and network news executives, and editors march in the procession. So do journalism's technicians, who invented ways to transmit news quickly through the ether, and political leaders who "make" the news. So, too, does the public, whose interests as perceived by editors influence what is covered and not covered, for journalism is a business with customers as well as a public service for citizens. In the words of English poet Humbert Wolfe:

> The world goes on outside. No paper flinches,
> > however much the case may pain or shock it,
> from giving it the space in feet and inches
> > dictated by its public and its pocket.

Since the first days of colonial newspapering, when printers hustled down to the wharfs to collect mail and European periodicals from incoming ships, the processes of gathering foreign news have been a work in progress, although not every step has been a step forward. Despite their excellence, first-class foreign services have disappeared. The golden age of foreign correspondence is not today, as one might expect in view of growing global interdependence. It was in the period between the two world wars, when outlets for foreign news swelled and a large number of experienced, independent journalists circled the globe. Radio, which emerged during that golden age, and later television made news more immediate, more dramatic, and more personal. The voices and images of correspondents became as familiar as one's neighbors. The long-sought annihilation of space and time also led to journalism that favored speed over depth in reporting.

In this evolution troubling mutations appeared. Richard Harding Davis, whose talent for reporting and flair for self-promotion solidified the image of the knowledgeable, swashbuckling correspondent during the Spanish-American War, morphed into Fox News's buffoonish Geraldo Rivera, who covered the post-9/11 U.S. invasion of Afghanistan toting pearl-handled pistols and looking for any opportunity to appear macho on camera. If he found Osama bin Laden, he promised to

This is the front page of the *Baltimore Evening Herald* the day that editor and armchair foreign correspondent H. L. Mencken made up a story on the decisive naval battle of the Russo-Japanese War. The account, with its fictional Shanghai dateline, ran on the second column from the left, under the headline "FIRST STORY OF THE FIGHT." The cartoon, equally cobbled together but more weird, shows a Japanese sailor and the recent winner of an Atlantic Ocean race—a Captain Barr—each holding victory trophies. The incongruous cutline reads "Strike up the band! Here comes a sailor!"

"kick his head in, then bring it home and bronze it." And to this gene pool is added poet Edna St. Vincent Millay, who went to Europe for *Vanity Fair* to escape her mother; United Press correspondent Robert Best, who was imprisoned for making more than three hundred propaganda broadcasts for the Nazis during World War II; Jim McKay, who in an instant switched from ABC sportscaster to award-winning news anchor when Arab terrorists killed Israeli athletes at the 1972 Munich Olympics; and tobacco fortune heiress Doris Duke. Duke worked for the International News Service in Rome for twenty-five dollars a week after the liberation of Paris in World War II and dipped into her bank account to help finance the *Rome American,* one of the many English-language dailies overseas that served as incubators for would-be foreign correspondents.

Publishers and editors have their own quirky pasts. During his brief time as managing editor of the *Baltimore Evening Herald,* H. L. Mencken lost patience with the slow pace of news about the outcome of the decisive naval battle of the Russo-Japanese War in 1905. Taking matters into his own hands, he made up a dispatch.

It described in detail a victory by the Japanese: "The big Asama and the battleship Fuji bore down upon the Borodino and raked her from stem to stern with their twelve and ten-inch guns." It was full of good guesses. Mencken considered the story "my masterpiece of all time, with the sole exception of my bogus history of the bathtub."

Since then we have had Allen Neuharth, chairman of Gannett Co. and founder, in 1982, of *USA Today*. Aspirations to be a national newspaper typically prompt serious original news-gathering overseas, and *USA Today* had an added incentive because it circulated internationally soon after it launched. Ignoring these traditions, Neuharth's paper contained little foreign news reported by its own staff. The Ugly American, Neuharth said, was no longer the "wealthy, camera-carrying tourist in bermuda shorts. He or she is the arrogant, Nikon-carrying reporter from a big U.S. newspaper." Exempting himself, Neuharth stepped into retirement in 1988 with a thirty-nation "news-gathering" tour. He traveled like a maharaja in his corporate jet, stopping here and there to interview heads of state in order to acquire a better understanding of "people and governments." This same hands-across-the-sea spirit sent his staff into a tizzy on another trip. When Neuharth expressed unhappiness with the scratchy toilet paper he found in his St. Petersburg hotel room, an aide arranged to have softer stuff flown in from Finland.

The *New York Times,* the "good gray lady," has a colorful history. Its correspondents have come in shades as varied as the relentless, meticulous, stuttering Homer Bigart, who during the Algerian War commanded a stringer to "bring me someone who's been tortured," and Sarah Lyall, a talented member of the London bureau of the modern *New York Times,* who favors stories about bog snorkeling. The paper takes itself too seriously to be really funny very often, but behind the scenes reporters have cut up. In a little game diplomatic correspondents in the Washington bureau played in the 1970s, the Saturday duty officer left behind the name of a country, the more obscure the better, that a Sunday staffer was to write about for a Monday story. Nor is steamy romance à la Robert Adams a stranger at the *Times.* When Frederick T. Birchall gave up his job as managing editor in 1931 to become chief European correspondent, it was whispered around the newsroom that he was interested in a particular German baroness, not his wife. While driving with a busy hand on the woman's knee one day, he smashed into a German bus. "Foreign correspondents," he said afterward, "should be eunuchs."

The great *Times* publisher Adolph Ochs, who resolutely kept the paper on an upright course after he bought it in 1896, was no match for Allen Neuharth in ego or flamboyance. The self-effacing owner didn't even put his name on his personal stationery. Nevertheless, his foreign news-gathering operations gave him an opportunity to express himself. By 1925 Ochs had plastered five *New York Times* signs on the facade of the building housing his Paris bureau. A picture of rectitude at home, he liked to visit the City of Light to chase women.

None of this is what the *Times* promotions department had in mind when it produced a pamphlet in 1950 stating, "Our chronicler beyond the seas is a dashing, romantic fellow."

Correspondents have been cosmopolitan, unflinching in seeking facts, and perceptive as well as provincial, blinkered, untutored, and frivolous. Editors have valued astute coverage that scans distant horizons for impending crises, and they have jumped from one blurry breaking story to another. Wars have brought sharp increases in the numbers of correspondents, who have had to endure the "rasp and gash" of the censor's blade. Certain parts of the globe have enjoyed lavish attention while the roving eye of foreign news-gathering has only glanced at others.

This is the history this book endeavors to present. Personalities figure in this story. These characters are interesting in themselves, but the primary purpose in introducing them is to illuminate the major currents and crosscurrents that have shaped foreign news-gathering. For perspective, the reader may appreciate a few words of background about the previous study of foreign correspondence and the methods used in this book.

The best place to start, perhaps, is with a 1959 speech by Allan Nevins, then president of the American Historical Association and a student of the press. "Sound historical works on the press and its leaders are as important to the United States as sound works on president and cabinet officers, generals and admirals, investors and industrialists," he said. "Of such history we have as yet the barest beginning."

Few scholars of any sort examined foreign news-gathering at the time Nevins spoke, and much of what was written reinforced the romantic one-dimensional view of correspondents. One of the rare books around that time by a political scientist was Bernard Cohen's *The Press and Foreign Policy,* in which he noted that literature on the subject was "generally arid." Exceptional as his book was, Cohen did not waver from the standard view of the foreign affairs reporter as "a cosmopolitan among cosmopolitans, a man in gray flannel who ranks very high in the hierarchy of reporters." The most dedicated glorifiers were journalism professors. They went about their task like the faithful writing about the church. The rest of the literature came from the typewriters of foreign correspondents themselves. While their memoirs offered insights into the development and limitations of foreign news-gathering, this information was often served on a silver platter of personal adventure. Like the stage, the ballet, motion pictures, and the circus, Nevins noted, journalism history is "invested with a romantic aura and encrusted with legends. As a result, the typical newspaper historian . . . hangs nothing but spotless linen on the line."

Since then, progress has been made in the study of news generally. Journalism schools are more objective about their profession thanks to the influx of trained scholars. Political scientists as well as a few anthropologists, sociologists, and economists have begun to treat journalism as a vital organ in the body politic. Such work has taken on greater urgency due to the emergence of new media technologies such as the Internet, the rise of ever-greater expertise in media manipulation, the decrease in audiences for traditional news, and the accumulation of well-publicized journalistic transgressions. "The past year has been, I think, the worst

In 1925 a fifth *New York Times* sign was affixed to the facade of the building holding its Paris bureau. Although publisher Adolph Ochs agreed with his bureau chief, Edwin James, that they might have too many signs, he was in no hurry to take one down. What bothered him more, after examining this photograph, which James sent to him, were the slanted letters on the latest embellishment: "I think it would look better if they stood perpendicular. I am furthermore of the opinion that it might have been better to have taken down the sign above the windows and put it across the building along the cornice at the bottom of the windows, using the same sign or one with somewhat larger letters of the same character." Arrows mark the five signs in this photo. This attitude about adorning foreign bureaus did not die with Ochs. To the merriment of staff, his grandson, Arthur O. Sulzberger, micromanaged the furnishings in overseas outposts of the *Times*. Another example of Ochs's interest in signs is from a letter to him from a correspondent, Charles Grasty, who was delegated to look into quarters for the Paris bureau: "The great value of its location is that it is one of the very best corners in Paris, and, with electric signs, we could put the Times in evidence at a point where perhaps more Americans pass than any other." Adolph S. Ochs to Edwin L. James, July 6, October 26, 1925; and James to Ochs, July 22, 1925; Grasty to Ochs, April 19, 1922, NYT Archives. Copyright for photo © *The New York Times*.

year for American journalism since I entered the profession forty-four years ago," said former *New York Times* foreign correspondent David Halberstam in 1999. Most journalists would say there have been pretty bad years for journalism since.

Still, bookshelves are not about to collapse under the weight of volumes about foreign news. Furthermore, the books that sit there are mostly studies of contemporary or near-contemporary events such as the Vietnam War, the Cuban missile crisis, or the second Iraq War, although a few take up earlier subjects, for instance coverage of the Chinese Communists or of Europe during the first part of the twentieth century. The value of these studies lies in their depth. Their weakness is a lack of historical perspective. Readers are encouraged to come away with the impression "this is how foreign reporting works," instead of "this is how reporting worked at that time." Meanwhile, the ever-glamorous Richard Harding Davis and a few other correspondents have enjoyed the attention of biographers. Although their life stories are full of history, these books are not focused on the changing dynamics of foreign news-gathering, a central theme of this book.

Only three broad historical surveys of foreign news-gathering are in print. John Hohenberg's *Foreign Correspondence: The Great Reporters and Their Times* is a name-date-place history of "a small and tough-minded band." It was originally published in 1965 and reissued thirty years later with modest updating. Written in the same spirit but limited to a handful of twentieth-century events is Michael Emery's brief *On the Front Lines.* Phillip Knightley's *The First Casualty: The War Correspondent as Hero and Myth-Maker from the Crimea to Kosovo,* published in 1975 and slightly revised twenty-five years later, critically examines one aspect of correspondence, war reporting. Of value for basic facts, but dated and out of print, are Robert W. Desmond's five descriptive histories, beginning with *The Press and World Affairs,* published in 1937, and ending with *The Tides of War: World News Reporting, 1931–1945,* published in 1984.

It would have been difficult to write this history without Hohenberg's and Desmond's compilations of *who* covered *what, when,* and for *whom.* Bringing their work up to date in a new book would be a contribution, but less satisfying than writing a history that combines depth with breadth. In this latter approach, two options present themselves. One is to take a single line of attack, such as Knightley so effectively did in arguing that war correspondence is a constant and generally losing battle against patriotism and censorship. I have chosen, instead, to comprehend many themes in an effort to provide a multidimensional view of foreign correspondence. Although the result is not a seamless history, the reader can observe the evolution of American foreign news-gathering in the episodes strung across this book.

Much of my research was done the old-fashioned way. I have drawn on the memoirs of foreign correspondents, conducted scores of interviews, and excavated journalism archives, many of them underused. In 1956 Nevins sagely advised Arthur Sulzberger, one of a long line of family members to carry on from Adolph Ochs, to create a *Times* archive of "confidential materials." This and other such troves yielded a tremendous amount of valuable information.

At the same time, I have taken to heart an admonition more than forty years ago by Bernard Cohen, whose *The Press and Foreign Policy* was mentioned earlier: "How useful it would be if there were increased areas of collaboration between students of journalism and of political science." Sadly, journalism historians and political scientists have not linked arms, nor has there been anything approaching the collaboration that should exist with other disciplines. I have tried to do my part by incorporating studies by a variety of scholars and through research with colleagues having special expertise. These joint endeavors—for instance using quantitative analysis to draw new conclusions about the impact of the press on the Spanish-American War—appeared in shorter form as journal articles. I hope this book demonstrates the value of employing the full range of research tools to understand the evolution of foreign reporting.

Taking a cue from Robert Adams's fictional escapades, this *Roving Eye* diverges from standard approaches to the study of foreign correspondence in another way. With rare exception, the study of overseas reporting has focused on a small number of esteemed news outlets. Scholarly article after scholarly article carries a title along the lines of "*New York Times* and Network TV News Coverage of Foreign Disasters" and "Foreign News in Four U.S. Elite Dailies: Some Comparisons." Concentration on the so-called prestige media occurs because they tend to provide the best foreign news coverage and because they are the ones scholars tend to read for their news. This elite approach has serious limitations. Only a small number of ordinary Americans read the *New York Times.* The great majority rely on local journals with no foreign correspondents and modest amounts of wire service reports from abroad. Broadcast networks, which are included among prestige media, provide foreign news to a wider audience, but the amount is limited and is supplemented by national media that approach news from widely varying angles. Although elites don't think about it much, the public picked up foreign news from *Ms.* magazine, which in 1972 ran "Women of Bangladesh," one of many such stories during that period. More recently *People* magazine, MTV, and the trade publication *Engineering News-Record* covered the invasion of Iraq in 2003, as did Comedy Central's *The Daily Show with Jon Stewart,* which faked news more honestly than H. L. Mencken did and included guest interviews with people who knew what they were talking about.

In this same spirit of broadening the inquiry, I have attempted to correct the tendency to recycle a few well-known journals and journalists at the expense of others whose impact on foreign news-gathering was equally profound. Many journalists remember and revere Homer Bigart. Very few can identify Paul Scott Mowrer, Vincent Sheean, or Jack Belden, whose careers partly overlapped Bigart's and who were among the most accomplished foreign correspondents at bon mots and getting behind enemy lines. Neither Mowrer, who won the first Pulitzer Prize for "correspondence"; nor Sheean, whose *Personal History* established the benchmark by which other memoirs at the time were measured; nor Belden, who brilliantly conveyed the mechanics and emotions of war, has received the full biography he deserves. Likewise, whereas plenty of histories have been written about the *New York Times,* not one has been written about the *Chicago Daily News,* where Mowrer worked, although it led the way toward modern journalism and foreign correspondence. I have also sought to reach farther back into history than is usually done. As primitive as early news-gathering abroad was, it set the stage for what came later and in some respects is reappearing via new technologies today.

Although the eye of this book freely roves over many episodes, I have worked within limits. Modern editors often refer to the work of correspondents as "international" reporting, rather than foreign reporting. CNN, to give one example, does this because it has a global audience; its correspondent in Germany is reporting for Germans as well as Americans. This book uses *foreign* because that is the term employed historically and because this is a history of the coverage of news that has been foreign to Americans. This does not mean all the correspondents in the book were Americans. Henry Stanley and Lafcadio Hearn, who feature prominently, were foreign born. They are included because they wrote for American readers. Likewise, while each episode involves news from abroad, the action sometimes takes place in the United States, where we see government officials and editors interact with the news. The most extreme case is the Battle of New Orleans. The battle was fought in the United States but would not have occurred if news of the peace treaty signed in Europe had arrived in Washington sooner—which is the point of the story. I refer to reporting by foreign journalists when it is useful to understanding the evolution of the American history of news-gathering.

This book occasionally casts its gaze on China and, as such, is forced to make choices about the spelling of Chinese ideographs. Romanization has changed almost as frequently as American attitudes about the country. In the twentieth century, the Chinese capital was called Peiping, Peking, and Beijing. I have made some use of the pinyin system, for instance with the thoroughly established *Beijing* and other Chinese names that are well known in our time. Mostly, though, I employ the older Wade-Giles system because I quote extensively from reporting using that form of romanization. Thus, the reader will find Mao Tse-tung instead of Mao Zedong, Chou En-lai instead of Zhou Enlai, Kuomintang for Chiang Kai-shek's Guomindang party, and Chungking (his Chinese capital during World War II) instead of Chongqing.

Finally, I have combined description and analysis with actual news reports that exemplify what appeared in print or was broadcast. These excerpts are longer in early sections of the book because the style of writing during that time there is less familiar to us. It is impossible to understand the news in any period without reading some of it—printers' errors, stylistic peculiarities, and all.

All the problems of journalism are magnified in foreign news-gathering. For owners of media, this is the most expensive reporting. For editors, it is the most difficult to second-guess, because they have little intimate knowledge of what is happening. For journalists, it is the most demanding. Correspondents must acquire expertise that is taken for granted when covering news at home—facility with the local language, for instance, or an understanding of the social system. While at-home reporters typically have a narrow beat, such as education, the legislature, or the arts, foreign correspondents cover all these subjects and more. Adding still further to the challenges, they must put this news in context for an audience with a limited appetite for foreign affairs, which makes the high cost of foreign correspondence particularly vulnerable to cost cutting.

Also, the stakes in journalism are nowhere higher than in foreign news-gathering. At the end of the century just passed, the Newseum in Washington, D.C., listed the most significant news events of the previous one hundred years. Forty-five of these were foreign stories by any definition, and this number doesn't include the development of the atomic bomb, the creation of jet travel, or the discovery of AIDS, which also were on the list.

Paul Scott Mowrer of the *Chicago Daily News* anticipated such a development. In *Our Foreign Affairs,* published in 1923, he wrote:

> The first thing to be understood is that the United States has interests to-day everywhere. Our raw products are sent out to all manufacturing countries; our manufactures to all agricultural countries. We are exporting billions of dollars in the form of foreign investments. Our banks are everywhere establishing branches. Our vast organized charities are at work wherever there is suffering on a large scale, from the valley of the Hoang-Ho to Smyrna and Samara. Our energetic, inquisitive, money-making citizens are to be found traveling or trading, for business, science, art, education, or pleasure, in every corner of the six continents and all the islands of the oceans.

In the new century, Americans continue down the path Mowrer mapped. That path will bring them increasingly into contact and conflict with other nations, many of which have become more rather than less hostile.

In such a world as this, foreign news-gathering is a matter of national security and, like all matters of national security, requires constant reassessment. A romantic history is of little value in any serious consideration of foreign news. If this book has a steady gaze in any respect, it is in seeking to understand the vicissitudes of foreign news-gathering in order to better see what lies ahead.

1

THE MANNERS AND CUSTOMS OF ALL NATIONS

The Author of a Gazette *(in the Opinion of the Learned) ought to be qualified with an extensive Acquaintance with Languages, a great Easiness and Command of Writing and Relating things cleanly and intelligibly, and in few Words; he should be able to Speak of War both by Land and Sea; be well acquainted with Geography, with the History of the Time, with the several Interests of Princes and States, the Secrets of Courts, and the Manners and Customs of all Nations.*

From "Account of the Method we design to proceed in," *Pennsylvania Gazette,*
September 25–October 2, 1729

In early October 1729, twenty-three-year-old Benjamin Franklin and a partner who soon dropped out bought a foundering nine-month-old Philadelphia newspaper, *The Universal Instructor in All Arts and Sciences; and Pennsylvania Gazette.* Franklin shortened the newspaper's name to *Pennsylvania Gazette,* abandoned the previous owner's plan to reprint serially Ephraim Chambers's *Cyclopaedia* from A to Z (the *Gazette* was still on the letter *A* when Franklin took over), and, as projected in his "Method" above, set his sights on news from abroad.

The *Pennsylvania Gazette*'s orientation remained transatlantic for the nearly forty years that Franklin retained his financial interest in the newspaper. Diplomacy, war, and military matters dominated the *Gazette,* with reports on royalty, nobility, and illustrious personalities second in importance. Together those two foreign categories took up two-thirds of the total news hole in the *Gazette* from 1728 to 1765. News of local and provincial politics accounted for less than 2 percent.

The *Gazette*'s attention to foreign news was not unusual. Although the United States is today's dominant world power, with interests and responsibilities around the globe, the high-water point of foreign news—as measured by the amount of space given to it—was in the eighteenth century when America was a colonial appendage.

One common explanation for all the emphasis on foreign news is that it did not offend officials or alienate readers. The very first newspaper in the colonies was Benjamin Harris's *Publick Occurrences* in Boston. It lasted only one day, September 25, 1690. The local Colonial government objected to its contents, community news written in a relatively lively style. John Campbell, whose *Boston News-Letter* was the sole Colonial newspaper for fifteen years and continued after competitors appeared, followed a policy that "has always been to give no offense." The maiden issue of the *News-Letter,* when it appeared in 1704, devoted three of its four pages to foreign news. Campbell typically tucked local news in the back of the paper, just before the advertisements; local affairs rarely constituted more than one-fourth the total news.

As was the case with many Colonial newspaper publishers, Campbell was the local postmaster. If fear of losing that royal appointment was not enough to make him wary of irritating officials, there was the not-so-little matter of needing government approval to publish. Prior censorship ended in 1723, but prosecution after the fact remained a real threat.

Angry readers, who might shun a paper that irritated them, also were a concern for newspapermen. Franklin's famous "Apology for Printers," published in the *Gazette* in 1731, was not unusual. Printers all over the colonies took pains to remind their readers that they strove, as one New York publisher vowed, "*not to be any Ways concerned in Disputes.*"

While Campbell, Franklin, and others did not want to forfeit government positions, lose government printing contracts, or drive away readers, however, these factors do not adequately explain why they favored foreign news. A fundamental truth about journalism of any kind is that it cannot succeed financially by avoiding all unpleasant information. If that were not the case, printers' apologies would not have been common. As Franklin acknowledged in his mea culpa, "The Business of Printing has chiefly to do with Mens [*sic*] Opinions."

The strongest reason for providing foreign news lay in a simple calculus that continues to exist right up to the present, the need to offer information that people want. This is where foreign news came into play. As historian Charles Clark has noted, Campbell believed his first "duty to his readers. . . was to supply news from abroad."

Foreign news was newsier than local news. Boston, New York, and Philadelphia, the largest cities in North America, were little more than towns. Philadelphia had only ten thousand people in the 1740s. A weekly Boston newspaper rarely trumped firsthand observation or word-of-mouth transmission of local news in the early eighteenth century, when the ratio of Bostonians to Boston taverns was one hundred to one. After a Boston demonstration, the *New-England Courant* observed, "There were too many spectators there to make it now a piece of public news."

Foreign news, on the other hand, was not personally unobtainable, and yet it was personally relevant. The colonists may have enthusiastically settled a New World, but they had strong ties to the Old World, especially to England, which dominated the foreign news. When the Continental Congress convened in 1774, more members had previously seen London than Philadelphia. Campbell's emphasis on foreign news reflected a growing appreciation on the part of Bostonians that they were less an isolated colony than a province of England. "There never was a dark age that destroyed the cultural contacts between Europe and America," historian Bernard Bailyn observed. "The sources of transmission had been numerous in the seventeenth century; they increased in the eighteenth."

Ties were practical as well as emotional. Businessmen needed to know the "Price Currant" of imported and exported goods. Economic and political policy made in

London, Paris, Vienna, and Madrid shaped life in the Americas. The Seven Years' War in Europe, as just one example, spilled over to the colonies in the form of the French and Indian War; a central issue in that conflict was which European nation would control North America. Americans celebrated the English victory, signed at the 1763 Treaty of Paris, and rued the news about the resulting English taxation policy implemented to defray war debts. British newspapers themselves provided extensive coverage of foreign affairs for much the same reason American newspapers did: their readers in that island nation with global interests saw foreign news as relevant.

Another advantage of foreign news was that it was cheap. Newspapers in those days did not have reporters at home, let alone abroad. A printer was publisher, editor, copy editor, reporter, and typesetter rolled into one. The first foreign correspondents were literally that, friendly souls in London or Paris who wrote letters home. Supplementing them were passengers and crew who arrived in port with newspapers from abroad as well as their own stories to tell, some quite sensational. As John Campbell's *Boston News-Letter* noted in 1720, the seas teemed with "those Hell-hounds the Pirates," and these marauders generated lurid tales. Franklin acknowledged the importance of free help in his "Account of the Method we design to proceed in." "There are many who have long desired to see a good News-Paper in Pennsylvania," he said, "and we hope those Gentlemen who are able, will contribute towards the making This such." European newspapers and journals brought by ship were the equivalent of today's overseas wire services. Colonial newspapers freely reprinted official government pronouncements and other news found in those publications. The *Gazette* obtained more than four-fifths of its news about the British Isles directly from other newspapers. When harsh winter weather disrupted shipping or someone lost precious printed cargo, news dried up. "The Delay of Ships expected in and want of fresh Advices from *Europe*," Franklin once observed, "make it frequently very Dull; and I find the Freezing of Our River has the same Effect on News as on Trade."

This system of foreign news-gathering fit conveniently into the larger economic structure of publishing. Newspapers were nearly essential by-products of the Colonial printer's trade. Three-fourths of the Colonial printers between 1700 and 1765 published newspapers. Most could not make enough money otherwise. In addition to job printing (and using spare space in his shop to sell codfish and patent medicines), the entrepreneurial Franklin printed almanacs and other books, Pennsylvania's currency, *and* his *Gazette.* His appointment as royal postmaster was a cog in his business machine. Newspaper publishers cum postmasters sat comfortably at the center of the information flow into and out of their communities. Franklin, who was not only a Colonial postmaster but also the first postmaster of the United States, used his post riders to distribute the newspaper. With more circulation came more advertising.

Filling up their newspapers any way they could (and needing to edit purloined stories to fit the available space), printers didn't any more feel obliged to note when they lifted a story from another journal than they did to follow a rigid stylebook dictating uniform use of commas or capitalization. When Franklin reprinted the story below (improving on the spelling of Sardenia), he did not mention that it had appeared originally in the *London Gazette* in a somewhat longer version, also reproduced below.

Turin, June 2, N.S.

The two Armies continue still in the same Posture, and by the Accounts from the French Camp, it appears that the Imperialists had not yet made any Motion towards Parma. The Report of the Finalese having revolted against the Republick of Genoa is confirmed, and that the Inhabitants throughout the whole Marquisate of Final had set up a Standard with the Arms of France, Spain, and Sardenia.

London Gazette, June 8–11, 1734

Turin, June 2.

The Report of the Finalese having revolted against the Republick of Genoa is confirm'd and the Inhabitants, throughout the whole Marquisate of Final, had set up a Standard with the Arms of France, Spain, and Sardinia.

Pennsylvania Gazette, September 5–12, 1734

As suggested by the publication of this pair of stories three months apart, timeliness did not play the same role in newspapers that it does now. The *London Gazette*, after which the *Pennsylvania Gazette* and others patterned themselves, prioritized foreign news starting with events that occurred farthest away. The most remote events tended to be the oldest. Such an approach allowed newspapers to present information in more or less chronological order, thus ensuring that readers did not have gaps in their knowledge of events abroad. This made sense at a time when timeliness was impossible. Word of the death of Queen Anne in 1714 reached the North American colonies forty-six days after the fact, and that was considered fast. James Parker's *Weekly Post-Boy* in New York labeled its foreign news "The History of Europe, &c." John Campbell was so committed to his role as historian that in 1718 he was thirteen months behind in his chronological reporting. The next year he tried to catch up by printing an extra sheet of foreign news every other week. "Now we are less than five months behind," he proudly informed readers. Little wonder Cotton Mather spoke of Campbell's news as "the antiquities of our *Boston News-Letter.*"

Below is a "letter" from an anonymous foreign correspondent, a physician, to a Mr. John Weake in London. Written on September 8, 1720, it found its way into the August 7–14, 1721, issue of the *New-England Courant*. In addition to the time lag, the article is remarkable for its vivid reporting of a bubonic plague that struck Marseilles. The plague began in 1720 when the *Grand-Saint-Antoine* arrived from Syria with silk, cotton, and disease. Normally ships were quarantined if any disease was aboard. But Marseilles merchants hurried the ship through without inspection. In the next two years, ninety thousand people perished in and around Marseilles. The ship was eventually burned to the waterline and its captain imprisoned for years.

THE
Pennſylvania GAZETTE.

Containing the freſheſt Advices Foreign and Domeſtick.

Turin, June 2.

THE Report of the Finaleſe having revolted againſt the Republick of Genoa is confirm'd, and that the Inhabitants, throughout the whole Marquiſate of Final, had ſet up a Standard with the Arms of France, Spain, and Sardinia.

Paris, June 16. ' The Death of the Marſhal de Berwick at this Criſis, may poſſibly prove a bad Stroke to us, but no News from the Rhine is good News, and whether Prince Eugene is beaten or kept at a Diſtance, 'tis much the ſame thing to our Army. The laſt Advices from Philipsburg immerg'd us in Tears, whilſt they inform'd us of the unhappy Accident to our General; but on the other hand, the Succeſs which the Beſiegers gain daily in their Advances before that Place, gives ſome little Alleviation to our Sorrow.

' Our Letters from Italy, if you believe them, and believe them, no doubt, all true Frenchmen do, ſpeak of nothing but Triumphs and Victory, on the part of ourſelves and Friends, and of Diſtreſs and Flights on the part of the Enemy; they ſay that of the 9000 Imperialiſts which were in the Trenches near Bitonto when the late Action begain, 3500 had been already taken Priſoners, and 'twas believ'd, not a living Man of them would eſcape. Our Correſpondent writes thus from Parma. " A large Body of Imperial Troops, commanded by M. " de Ligneville, having thrice attempted to enter the " Village of Colorno, were as often repuls'd, by a Party " of no more than 400 French, who, at laſt, overcome " with Shame to ſee ſuch a heavy Corps of Troops make " no better head againſt a handful of Men, quitted the " Place to them, having firſt taken off the Imperial Ge- " neral, and 300 Soldiers, to ſhow what they could have " done if they had not choſe to withdraw."-

From the Ruſſian Camp before Dantzick, June 12.

Our Fleet having waited ſome time at Cronſtadt for a favourable Wind, ſet ſail from thence the 24th of laſt Month, and on the 5th Inſtant arriv'd at Pillau, and landed there the Artillery and Ammunition deſign'd for this Camp. This Morning the ſaid Fleet appear'd in the Road of Dantzick. It is commanded by Admiral Gordon, and conſiſts of 14 Ships of the Line, viz. The Peter of 100 Guns and 1000 Men, containing 700 Seamen, 200 Soldiers and 100 Matroſſes, for the Service of the Artillery. The St. Alexander, Marlborough, and five others of 66 Guns and 489 Men each, viz. 321 Seamen, 127 Soldiers and 41 Matroſſes. The Devonſhire and 5 others of 54 Guns and 393 Men each, viz. 271 Seamen, 87 Soldiers and 35 Matroſſes. Eight Frigates of 32 Guns and 217 Men each, one Snow of 16 Guns and 75 Men, one Fire-ſhip and two Bombſhips, carrying in the whole 1190 Pieces of Ordnance, and 8808 Men. All the French Ships, except one ſmall Frigate that lies under the Cannon of Wechſellmunde, have quitted theſe Seas; but the Troops continue encamp'd under the Cover of the Fort. They conſiſt of 3 Regiments, of 17 Companies in each Regiment, and 50 Men in each Company, making together 2550 Men. We are extremely diligent to perfect our Works for rendering their Communication with the City impracticable; nor are we leſs induſtrious in carrying on our Approaches before the Garriſon, in order for a general Aſſault, which we ſhall attempt the Moment our Artillery arrives, and the ſame is expected here in two Days at fartheſt, being already far advanc'd on its way hither.

From the Ruſſian Camp before Dantzick, June 14.

' The Arrival of our Fleet has given new Spirits to the whole Camp; 'tis eaſy to diſcern the Joy that glows in every Countenance upon ſo happy an occaſion; for the Truth is, we were reduc'd to the laſt Extremity for want of Ammunition and Proviſion, and we are inform'd that a large Supply of both is on board the Ships. We keep a Correſpondence with the Fleet by means of ſmall Shalops, which paſs ſafe under the very Cannon of the Fort Wechſellmunde, but they are not of a Burthen fit to convey any thing but Intelligence. Admiral Gordon has drawn up his Ships in ſuch a manner, as to flank the Battery which annoys the River, and we doubt not of having a free Communication in a few Days. We now begin to date ourſelves Maſters of Dantzick. This Afternoon, as General Munich rode through the Lines, his Excellency call'd out thus to the Soldiery, *Keep up your Courage, my Lads, your Fatigues are nigh at an end, I'll provide Quarters for you next Week in Dantzick.*'

Extract of a Letter from the French Camp under the Cannon of Wechſellmunde, June 15.

' The Men of War which brought us hither are ſail'd for Copenhagen, it being improper to expoſe them to a Force ſo ſuperior as is the Ruſſia Fleet, but we doubt not to ſee them ſoon again, with a Reinforcement ſufficient to chaſe the Enemy in their turn. The Capture they made of the four Ruſſian Ships bound from Libau with Artillery and Ammunition for the Ruſſian Camp, was an Incident of great Importance to us; There was found on board theſe Veſſels no leſs than 4000 Bombs, 3000 Bullets, 900 Carcaſſes, 30 large Cannon, 13 Mortars, 2 Pateraroes, 6000 Muſquets, a conſiderable Quantity of Gunpowder, the like of Proviſions, 300 Suits of Cloaths for the Soldiery, and 100,000 Rubles in Species, ſome of which Articles we very much wanted: But ſeeing the Ruſſians are at ſuch a Loſs for Ammunition, we purpoſe to ſend them their Ball and their Bombs, and have for that End planted the Artillery on ſuch Batteries as we are able to erect in our preſent inconvenient Situation. The Veſſels, as ſoon as unladen, were ſunk in the Sight of our Camp; their Crews being brought on Shore, were ſacrific'd to the Manes of Count Plelo, and their Bodies afterwards thrown into the Sea: But perhaps this laſt Particular would be more properly told by the Enemy, ſince 'tis poſſible ſuch an Action would favour of Inhumanity at any other Time but whilſt the Blood of his Excellency Count Plelo lay reeking from the Muſcovite Trenches.

Frankfort,

This front page of the *Pennsylvania Gazette,* in which appeared the excerpt on page 16 about the Finalese revolt "against the Republick of Genoa," is an example of Colonial printers' heavy use of foreign news. Every word on the page was devoted to that topic. The Library Company of Philadelphia.

Although tardy, the report was of particular interest to Bostonians. The city had spent the summer dealing with an epidemic of smallpox brought by the HMS *Seahorse*. More than half of the Boston population was infected; one in thirteen died. James Franklin, Benjamin Franklin's brother, was the *Courant*'s publisher. Happy to stir up trouble, he started one of the first American press crusades by vigorously opposing the new idea of protecting people through inoculation. Benjamin Franklin was his brother's apprentice at the time the story ran. The letter is as follows.

Abstract of a Letter from a Physician at Marseilles, to
John Weake Esq: at London.

SIR,   *Marseilles,* Sept. 8, 1720.
I arriv'd here the 8th, and enter'd the Gate of Aix esteem'd one of the most pleasant Prospects in the Kingdom, but that day was a dismal Spectacle to me. All that great Place, both on the Right and the Left, was fill'd with dead, sick, and dying Persons. The Carts were continually employ'd in going and returning to carry away the dead Carcases, of which there were that day above four Thousand. The Town was without Bread, without Wine, without Meat, and without Medicines, and in general without any Succours.

The Father abandoned the Child, and the Son the Father; the Husband the Wife, and the Wife the Husband; and those who had not a House to themselves, lay upon Quilts in the Streets and the Pavements. All the Streets were fill'd with Cloaths and Houshold Goods, strew'd with Dead Dogs and Cats, which made an insupportable Stench.

Meat was sold at 18 to 20 Sous per Pound, and was only distributed to those who had Billets from the Consuls. This, Sir, was the miserable State of this City at that time, but at present, things have a better Appearance. Monsieur le Marquis de Langeron, who commands here, has caused the Dead to be buried, the Cloaths and Goods to be burnt, and the Shops to be open'd, for the Sustenance of the Publick.

Two hospitals are prepar'd where they carry all the Sick of the Town; good Orders are daily re-established, and the Obligation is chiefly owing to Monsieur Langeron, who does Wonders. However, there is not any Divine Service celebrated, nor are there any Confessors. The People die, and are buried without any Ceremonies of the Church; But the Bishop, with undaunted Courage, goes thro' the Streets, and into Publick Places, accompanied with a Jesuit and one Ecclesiastick, to exhort the Dying, and to give them Absolution; and he distributes his Charity very largely. The Religious Order have almost all perish'd and the Fathers of the Oratory are not exempt. It is accounted that there have died 50000 Persons. One thing very particular is, that Monsieur Monstier, one of the Consuls of the City, who has been continually on Horseback, ordering the slaves who carried away the Dead in Carts, or those that were sick to the Hospitals, enjoys his Health as well as he did the first day he began; the Sickness seems at present to abate, and we have the Satisfaction to see several whom we took under our Care at the Beginning of the Sickness, promise fair towards a Recovery.

The Sickness however is of a very extraordinary Nature, and the Observations we have in our Authors, have Scarce any Agreement with what we find in this: It is the Assistance of Heaven we ought to implore, and to wait for a Blessing from thence upon our Labours.

I am, &c.

Benjamin Franklin resided in London almost continuously from 1757 to 1775. Long before he left Philadelphia to become a Colonial agent, he had taken David Hall as a partner in the printing business. With Hall responsible for day-to-day operations of the *Pennsylvania Gazette,* the wealthy Franklin had time to pursue his varied interests. According to prearranged terms, the ownership of the newspaper passed to Hall in 1766, while Franklin was in Britain. Notwithstanding that he no longer had a financial interest in the newspaper, Franklin's enthusiasm for newspapering was far from over. He was a prolific foreign correspondent.

Journalism afforded an outlet for Franklin's creative energies. It also was a convenient vehicle for shaping public opinion at home about matters of policy as well as about himself. Franklin was the consummate self-promoter, and he had critics at home—firebrands like Sam Adams—whose views he wanted to refute. Finally, Franklin used journalism to influence the English. A foreign correspondent in reverse, he introduced assembly documents from Philadelphia into the British press and wrote scores of articles for the *London Chronicle,* the *Gazetteer and New Daily Advertiser,* the *Public Advertiser,* and other London newspapers. Franklin knew that Colonial newspapers picked up his articles. Although he employed at least forty-two different pseudonyms, Franklin also knew that colonists knew he was the author. One of his regular signatures, "N.N." for *non nominatus,* seems to have been reserved for him by other Colonial printers.

As Franklin's time in London wore on, tensions between the British and the colonies mounted. Like a good diplomat, Franklin sought to mediate as well as inform, as the two articles below show. The first of them, directed to his fellow colonists, describes Prime Minister George Grenville's outrage over an American press commentary and the Parliament's decision not to take the action Grenville urged. The article appeared in the *Pennsylvania Chronicle,* February 29, 1768, and was widely reprinted by other Colonial publications, including the *Boston Gazette,* which had caused the row in the first place.

Feb. 22.—Feb. 29.

PHILADELPHIA.

Extract of a Letter from a Correspondent in London, to the Printer hereof, dated December 1, 1767.

"Mr. G——le's *Enmity against the Colonies still continues as violent as ever.— When the Debate on the King's Speech happened, he tired even his Friends with*

*a tedious Harangue against America. Last Friday he produced a Boston Gazette,
which he said denied the legislative Authority of Great-Britain, and was treason-
able, rebellious, &c. and moved it might be read, and that the House would take
Notice of it---but it being moved, on the other Hand, that the Consideration of it
should be postponed for six Months---it was carried without a Division. And, as
it was known that this Parliament will expire before that Time, it was equivalent
to a total Rejection of the Motion.—The D--- of B—d moved in vain for the Consideration of the same Paper in the House of Lords.---*These are favorable Symptoms of the present Disposition of Parliament towards America, which I hope
no Conduct of the Americans will give just Cause of altering."

The second article responds to a letter in the *London Gazetteer* that was critical
of the colonists. Many Britons thought the colonists should happily pay increased
taxes after having received so much from the Crown. They were outraged when
Boston, and then other cities, responded to the duties by embargoing trade with
Britain. Franklin answered "OLD ENGLAND," as the letter-writing critic called himself, with a letter signed "OLD ENGLAND *in its senses.*" Franklin's defense in the *Gazetteer* ran on January 8, 1768. Four months later, on April 7, 1768, it appeared in the
Virginia Gazette.

From the G A Z E T T E E R .

To the P R I N T E R

INSTEAD of raving (with your correspondent of yesterday) against the Americans, as "diggers of pits for this country, lunaticks, sworn enemies, false, un-
grateful, cut-throats," &c., which is a treatment of customers that I doubt is not
like to bring them back to our shop, I would recommend to all writers on American affairs (however *hard* their *arguments* may be) *soft words,* civility, and good
manners. It is only from a redress of grievances, and equitable regulations of
commerce, with mild and reasonable measures of Government, permitting and
securing to those people the full enjoyment of their privileges, that we may hope
to recover the affection and respect of that great and valuable part of our fellow subjects, and restore and confirm the solid union between the two countries, that is so necessary to the strength and stability of the whole empire. Rail-
ing and reviling can answer no good end; it may make the breach wider, but can
never heal it.

OLD ENGLAND *in its senses.*

As the transatlantic breach widened, American newspapers became less reti-
cent about offending authorities and helped unite the colonists in rebellion. Franklin, who initially tried to accommodate the British, changed course and threw his
weight behind the Revolution. "It was by means of News papers," the proprietor of
the *New-York Journal* told Samuel Adams, "that we receiv'd & spread the Notice of
the tyrannical Designs formed against America, and kindled a Spirit that has been
sufficient to repel them." This sort of politically driven journalism continued after
independence. Franklin's grandson was one of the most partisan.

2

I RISE TO BE USEFUL

Benjamin Franklin Bache was his grandfather's protégé. When Benjamin Franklin went to France on behalf of his nascent nation in 1776, grandson Bennie accompanied him. Franklin taught the boy the printing trade while attending to his general education in France and Switzerland. Bache subsequently went into the printing business with his grandfather in Philadelphia and, upon Franklin's death, inherited from him typefounding and printing equipment. When Franklin lay on his deathbed, Bache held his hand.

Bache, however, belonged to a new era of newspapering. His grandfather was inclined to seek middle ground when he ran the *Pennsylvania Gazette*. Lightning Rod Junior, as some called the grandson of the inventor of the lightning rod, was openly partisan on matters domestic and foreign in his own Philadelphia newspaper.

The Stamp Act of 1765 marked the turning point. The tax required American printers to pay a halfpenny or more duty on each copy of a newspaper or pamphlet, depending on the dimensions of the paper, and additional duty on each advertisement. Newspapers aggressively fought back until Parliament rescinded the tax. Publishers, historian Arthur Schlesinger Sr. wrote, became "acutely conscious of a new political and social force that they controlled: the power of the press." Emboldened printers fanned revolutionary sparks and, prodded by the Sons of Liberty, remained aggressively patriotic when the Revolution blazed. Partisanship, along with a proliferation of newspapers, continued after independence. The founding fathers divided over preferred policies for the new republic and financially supported the newspapers that sided with them.

Bache started the *Philadelphia General Advertiser* very shortly after his grandfather died in 1790. Four years later, in one of his efforts to refashion the paper and make it profitable, he renamed it *Aurora*. Printers like Bache still worked at a primitive level of journalism. They printed large amounts of foreign news lifted from overseas newspapers along with letters from travelers. Bache's paper drew directly from liberal English-language newspapers such as the *London Star* and the *London Morning Chronicle,* and he translated articles from such newspapers as the *Paris Moniteur* and the Dutch *Leyden Gazette.* His paper, in turn, was widely reprinted by other American newspapers, who freely borrowed from each other to fill their pages.

Much of the foreign news was reportorial, but much, too, was selective and slanted, and supplemented by the printers' own editorial comment. The *Aurora*'s motto was *"surgo ut prosim,"* "I rise to be useful," and the side to which Bache chose to be the most useful was that of Thomas Jefferson and the Republicans. The newspaper, as Jefferson acknowledged, "unquestionably rendered incalculable services to republicanism through all its struggles with the federalists and has been the rallying point for the orthodoxy of the whole Union." One of those struggles, which especially roiled with emotion, was over the meaning of the French Revolution.

The French Revolution marked the first in a long line of American love-hate relationships with foreign revolutions that carried through to the rise of communism in the twentieth century. Made heady by their own recently successful Revolution, eighteenth-century Americans initially felt a strong kinship with French revolutionaries. France had supported the colonists against the British, and its subsequent Revolution was widely viewed as evidence of the spread of an "American fever" threatening "the thrones of enlightened Europe," as one newspaper put it. It seemed fitting that the marquis de Lafayette, who had been a hero in the American Revolution, sent George Washington the key to the Bastille. In 1789 the Bastille prison, a grim symbol of the ancien régime, had been stormed in an outburst of revolutionary fervor. In Boston and other cities, Americans gave a respectful nod to the French revolutionaries by wearing their red cockade and addressing each other with the equally revolutionary French greeting "citizen." Elites as well as farmers and laborers joined hands, for here was a way to show one was truly American.

As chaos and violence increased in France, American public opinion split. On one side was Republican Thomas Jefferson, on the other Federalist Alexander Hamilton. The secretary of the treasury thought the French "sullied a cause once glorious." The Revolution, he and party fellows averred, aimed to destroy all that was sacred—property, the institution of marriage, female modesty, and all "ALTERS OF GOD." These subversive ideas allegedly infiltrated the United States through French agents, whose insidious influence helped instigate the Whiskey Rebellion in the West. The differences between Jefferson and Hamilton and their Republican and Federalist supporters were magnified by disagreements over their preferred future course for the fledgling democracy. Jefferson opposed Hamilton on the need for a centralized financial system; on the value of trading with the old enemy Britain, which declared war on revolutionary France; and on what he perceived to be Hamilton's interest in creating an American monarchy, which was just what the French were getting rid of. "The liberty of the whole earth was depending on the issue of the contest [in France]," Jefferson wrote after the execution of Louis XVI, "and was ever such a prize won with so little innocent blood?"

Bache did not waver in his support of Jeffersonian views. Strong emotional and intellectual ties to France emanated from his nearly ten years there as a student. Voltaire, whom French revolutionaries treated after his death as a "precious relic," had "blessed" young Bache at a ceremony; when Bennie was ten years old, Benjamin Franklin wrote home that the boy spoke French better than English. Contemporaries of the adult Bache viewed him as typical of those who supported the French Revolution, a biographer said, "but in terms of naïve infatuation, romantic rage, and stubborn insistence, he had no equals."

Bache's prejudices and hopes manifested themselves in his treatment of the aborted flight of the French royal family in 1791. On the night of June 20, Louis XVI, Marie Antoinette, and their two children slipped out of Paris in an attempt to escape an increasingly hostile city. They planned to make the two-hundred-mile trip to Montmédy on the Belgian border, where they could enjoy the protective embrace of the queen's brother, Austrian emperor Leopold, and friendly military forces. They got as far as Varennes, about three-fourths of the way, where they were apprehended. The next day they returned to Paris under escort.

The failed escape provoked violent reaction among the French public. When news of the flight initially spread throughout Paris, the *London Morning Chronicle* reported, "people had burst into the palace, and the royal apartments were filled by a troop of men and women. When we came, the National Guards had blocked the doors, but we might have entered at the window, with others, if we had chosen." Lafayette, suspected of aiding the king, was "immediately surrounded by the mob," the *Boston Gazette* reported. He and a companion were almost lynched. "The Duke D'Aumont," said another paper,

> was likewise stopped by the mob, and the clothes torn off his back.—The people were conducting him to the *Place de Greve*, with an intention of hanging him *a la lanterne*, but he was fortunately rescued by the National guard. . . . The mob, ever ready to exercise the uncontrolled rights of men, made a mockery of the King's Arms in the Market Places, and, dashing them and the figure of a crown to the ground, they trampled upon them, crying out—"Since the King has abandoned what he owed to his high situation let us trample upon the ensigns of royalty!"

The crowd at Varennes, where the royal party was apprehended, was no more forgiving. They gathered outside a grocery store where the king was being held and shouted, "To Paris! To Paris or we'll shoot him in his carriage!" When Louis and his family finally left the village, seven thousand angry townspeople, peasants, and national guardsmen followed their carriage. In Sainte-Ménehould, the Comte du Val de Dampierre, a local landowner, approached the king's carriage in a show of respect; citizens pulled the aristocrat from his horse and hacked him to death. Peasants spat on the king in the village of Chouilly. At Châlons, they threatened to "make cockades out of the bowels of Louis and Antoinette and belts out of their skins."

When the carriage finally rolled down the Champs-Elysées, armed national guards held back the vast crowd. The *London World* described the scene this way: "They were surrounded by immense multitudes of exasperated people, and . . . the National Guards found some difficulty in preserving order . . . nothing but distrust and horror reigned throughout the city." The *London Chronicle* reported that when the king returned, "the populace burst into groans, expressive of such disgust, contempt, and malignity, as were horrible even to those who knew themselves not to be the objects of them." Both the *London Morning Chronicle* and the *London Star* reported an ugly incident: "The three couriers who had attended the KING, and who were now on the KING's carriage, were surrounded by the people, who threatened to hang them. Twenty Commissioners went out, by order of the Assembly, to restore order." One of the couriers was severely beaten.

Bache regularly received the European newspapers that carried these accounts, which history has borne out, of rowdy French crowds threatening to disembowel the king and the queen. He was extremely selective, however, in what he reprinted. Sometimes his version was misleading, as when he reported the "absolute tranquility which reigned in Paris when the news of [the king's] flight was universally spread, and the perfect order preserved upon his entry into the capital." Below is one of the many stories in this vein that Bache ran between August 24 and September 1, 1791, on the royal escape.

Account of the KING's RETURN to PARIS.
[LONDON, *July* 1.]

In expectation of the King and Royal Family, the Police of the day left . . . [in] the Garden of the Thuileries,* some Deputies, and the National Guards, between whom the procession was to pass. An immense multitude occupied the Square of *Louis XV* and the Champs-Elysees—the ground—the roofs—the trees. But this multitude remained silent and immoveable.

The escort of the King and Royal Family, which, during the whole of the journey, had been numerous, became at last a considerable army, divided into detachments of infantry and cavalry. This army spent some time before it could be ranked in the most convenient order.—When the carriage of the Royal Family advanced to the garden of the Thuileries, not one cry or mark or confusion prevailed; all was the most profound silence, the most undisturbed regularity; the only murmur which could be heard, proceeded from the extreme eagerness of the Guards, who were entrusted with the care of the carriage, with regard to the safety of the Royal persons, whom it contained. The persons in the carriage were the King, the Queen, the Dauphin, Madame Royale, Madame Elizabeth, two of the four Commissioners of the Assembly, M. M. Petion and Barnave, and Madame de Tourzelle.

Upon the seat of the carriage, with one or two guards, were three persons

---

* Generally spelled Tuileries, this old palace in Paris became home to the royal family after the family left Versailles in 1789 during the onset of the revolution. The National Assembly wanted them under closer scrutiny.

bound, or chained, habited as couriers, and who had been apprehended assisting in that capacity the escape of the King and Queen. At some distance followed a cabriolet, with the two Ladies of the bed-chamber of Madame Royale and Madame Elizabeth. Last of all came an open chariot covered with laurel, on which, as a triumphal char,* was placed the soldier of the National Guard, who had with so much courage and address intercepted at Varennes the progress of the Royal Family.

At the moment when the carriage of the King and Queen stopped before the palace, the utmost steadiness of demeanor was observed by the people whom two years of liberty had taught how liberty ought to be maintained, and how the sovereignty of nations ought to be exercised. Nothing but the cry, *La Loi, La Loi,*† resounded on every side. In the manner and circumstances of this invocation, there was something indeed very awful, and which, to the breasts of the guilty, must have conveyed peculiar terror.

The noise, however, by degrees became more violent, and reached the Assembly, who were then engaged in deliberation, and who immediately dispatched Deputies for the sake of security. No danger, however, was to be apprehended. Indignation was peculiarly excited by the appearance of the three couriers, who had been assisting to the escape, and who, in spite of their visages covered with dust, and their hats drawn over their faces were distinguished as persons sufficiently known. The tumult was completely quelled by the authority of the Deputies, and when the gate of the Palace was shut, all subsided.

General Advertiser, August 24, 1791

Bache was not alone in his bias. Bias flowed wherever in the new Republic there was printer's ink. One of the strongest voices on the opposite side was John Fenno's *Gazette of the United States.* Alexander Hamilton, who financially supported the *Gazette,* enlisted Fenno to start it "with the object of propagating the Federalist faith." In the case of the French Revolution, Fenno opposed the "raging madness of Jacobinism."

This was clear in his coverage of the French chaos of September 1792. As more Parisians left the city to fight the French revolutionary war, newspapers and citizens' clubs excited popular fears that imprisoned refractory priests and loyalists would escape and take over the city. Republican leaders exhorted citizens to ensure that would not happen, and they executed royal sympathizers in prisons throughout the city. Fenno played this up for all it was worth and then some. He emphasized French mob violence in gory terms: "new massacres in Paris"; "hellish factions" of Republicans; France "drenched in blood." He sometimes ran several such stories in a single issue of the *Gazette* to make his point clear. Whereas

* Translation, wagon.
† Translation, the law, the law.

Bache preferred to draw from the minutes of the revolutionary National Assembly, Fenno tended to rely on letters and declarations coming from the royal family and its sympathizers. He reported as fact the observation of one informant that "6000 people were absolutely murdered by one pretended jury of twelve, sitting in one of the prisons." In reality, about fifteen hundred were killed.

Bache preferred a theme highlighted in an October story: "The city was never in a more flourishing situation, and that the whole kingdom of France never experienced more prosperous days." His *General Advertiser* ran two short articles mentioning the September mayhem. Neither one gave any indication of how many died.

Bache was never so one-sided that he offered no opposing views. In one of the above-mentioned short articles on the September massacres, his newspaper noted that "heads were carried through the streets." He published pro and con opinions concerning Louis XVI's execution in early 1793. Nevertheless, for most of the decade his newspaper was one of America's leading Republican voices, or, depending on one's point of view, "the most noted engine for spreading filth." William Cobbett, editor of another Federalist newspaper, *Porcupine's Gazette,* called Bache an "abandoned liar" and thought he should be dealt with like "a Turk, a Jew, a Jacobin, or a Dog."

Bache's support for the French continued. He was a close friend and counselor of Edmond Genet, the French envoy to America, and in 1795 did his best to torpedo the treaty John Jay negotiated to stabilize relations with the British. The Republicans viewed the agreement as a tilt away from France, which had seen continued Anglo-American tension to be in its interest. At first the Senate pondered the treaty in secret, a method of deliberation that lent itself to speculation of perniciousness and which Bache described as undemocratic and monarchical. When a senator sold a copy of the treaty to a French envoy, the Frenchman slipped it to Bache. Bache had a field day. He published a summary in the *Aurora,* as his paper was now called, and printed the entire document in a pamphlet shortly afterward. Bache shipped bundles of the pamphlets to New York and other cities and set out for Boston, where he distributed copies of the incendiary document. His timing, immediately before Independence Day, was ideal. The celebrations gave ample opportunity for citizens to denounce the treaty. Bache organized a protest rally in Philadelphia. The Senate barely ratified the agreement. Several months after President Washington signed the treaty, the House nearly passed legislation to nullify it.

The Republicans rewarded Bache's loyalty. Thomas Jefferson urged them to subscribe to his newspaper. James Monroe lent him six hundred dollars. Still, he was not so well supported as other Republican and Federalist newspapermen, and he could not compensate by deploying his grandfather's business instincts, for these he did not have. Although Bache may have viewed strident partisanship as a way to attract readers, it was the political combat he relished. His pro-French sentiments were genuine and boundless. Ignoring his grandfather's concerns over the

This politically charged cartoon depicts the domestic political clashes in the United States during the French Revolution. The French are coming from the left and beginning their executions; under their leader, carrying a Pole of Liberty, are the words, "The cannibals are landing." An American eagle hurls thunderbolts. While Jefferson and his political allies vainly try to hold them back, George Washington and his troops march forward, trampling Benjamin Franklin Bache. Near Bache's outstretched arm is a copy of is newspaper, the *Aurora*. A dog is urinating on it. The New York Historical Society.

tendency of postrevolutionary newspapers to launch personal attacks on leaders, Bache excoriated the departing president for insufficiently supporting France. ("If ever a nation was debauched by a man, the American nation has been debauched by Washington.") Some historians argue that virulent press criticism prompted Washington to surrender his office after two terms. If that is true, the most powerful single influence on Washington's decision was Bache, who once likened the president to Benedict Arnold.

This war of words brought on sticks and stones. In an early example of the donnybrooks that characterized newspapering through the middle of the nineteenth century, Bache was assaulted by the son of a leading Federalist he had insulted. Following another common journalism practice, he wrote an account of the altercation for his newspaper. The Federalist's son was fined by the local authorities and given a diplomatic mission to Europe by Federalist president John Adams. Political mobs broke the windows in Bache's house at night. In 1798, by which time he had lost between $14,700 and $20,000 on the *Aurora*, he was charged under the just-passed Sedition Act, which screamed out its partisanship. The law was directed at "malicious writing" done during Adams's term; it did not cover commentary on his Republican vice president, Thomas Jefferson. Only Republicans were convicted and jailed. Prosecution was persecution. The act's flagrant bias drove citizens to the side of the seditionaries.

Bache escaped the dock for a worse fate. Before his case went to trial, yellow fever swept through Philadelphia. The thirty-year-old editor, who had once recommended lightning rods as preventive for the disease, succumbed. So did his Federalist opposite, John Fenno. In Bache's case, a French physician attended.

3

TOMORROW'S MAIL

It was a battle that changed the course of American history; a battle that convinced
Americans they had earned the right to be independent and that their sovereignty
would be respected once and for all around the globe; a battle that thundered a
once-poor, wretchedly educated orphan boy into the White House.

Robert V. Remini

The Battle of New Orleans gave confidence and a president to the infant American Republic. But more than great generaling was involved. When Andrew Jackson asked the head of the Louisiana diocese to arrange for a Te Deum celebrating the victory, he should have told Abbé Guillaume Dubourg to offer a special prayer of thanks to the news—or, rather, to the delay of it. For had the news traveled quickly, there would have been no battle in which he could distinguish himself.

Before the Battle of New Orleans, Jackson had assured himself only a minor place in American politics. He was Tennessee's first congressional representative to Washington, but stayed just one term. He later accepted an appointment as senator, but came home after one year. While in the House, he spoke out forcefully on a single issue, to defend a Tennessee general's claim to compensation for leading an offensive against Indians in the state. Jackson's "senatorial record is nearly blank," his most dedicated biographer, historian Robert Remini, observed; "his participation in debate was nil." Jackson's interests were local. Shortly after his stint in the Senate, he was appointed a state supreme court judge and subsequently won election as major general of the Tennessee militia. In this capacity he led his troops against the Creek Indians, allies of the British during the War of 1812. Following his crushing victory at the Battle of Tohopeka in Alabama, fellow Nashville citizens gave Jackson a frenzied hero's welcome. Somewhat reluctantly, Washington officials made the backwoodsman a major general in command of the U.S. Army of the Southwest.

At the time Jackson took command, the war with Britain was widely considered a disaster. The young American Republic's soldiers were unpaid. Taxes had doubled. The British blockaded the East Coast, disrupting business, and burned public buildings in the capital itself. President James Madison's standing was low. Unwilling to fight "Mr. Madison's war," the governors of Connecticut, Rhode Island, and Massachusetts refused to provide troops. People feared more bad news in late 1814 when mail was delayed and rumors circulated about a British fleet carrying a wildly inflated number of troops to invade New Orleans. "We have cause of apprehension," the editor of the *New York Evening Post* wrote, "that to-morrow's mail will bring tidings of the winding up of the catastrophe."

Jackson surprised the British and his fellow Americans on the Plain of Chalmette, five miles outside New Orleans. On January 8, 1815, his raw militiamen withstood the attack of the far superior British force. Within a half hour, the battle was over. By their count, the British casualties totaled some 2,000. Two of their four generals were killed; another was severely injured. American casualties amounted to fewer than 340. Across the country Americans sang the newly written "Star Spangled Banner" and toasted the rough-hewn General Jackson.

So much jubilation. And yet, the victory was irrelevant. On December 24, 1814, two weeks before the Battle of New Orleans, envoys from the United States and Britain had signed the Treaty of Ghent in Belgium.

This episode in American history is an object lesson in the glacial pace of news transmission in this age—and of the consequences.

Here is how the news of the victory and the peace treaty unfolded ever so slowly and chaotically before the eyes of Americans.

"We are grievously disappointed at the present very interesting moment, by the failure of the Mail from Louisiana," reported Washington's authoritative and increasingly nervous *National Intelligencer* in its issue of January 16, 1815, about a week after Jackson's victory. In this environment people could imagine anything they wanted to imagine. An anti-Federalist newspaper speculated that the British had already won and that the Republican Madison knew it. Among the "various probable causes" for the slow mail, opined the *National Intelligencer,* were "high waters, bad roads and casualties." Two weeks later the newspaper was still impatiently wringing its hands: "The tremendous snow storm of Sunday last has greatly impeded, and almost entirely interrupted the transmission of mails over the rough, mountainous and *bridgeless* roads" between the capital and New Orleans. Finally, on February 4, the *National Intelligencer,* which was closely tied to the administration, exultantly reported Jackson's triumph. Not having professional correspondents in the field, for such did not exist, the *Intelligencer* relied for its news on after-action dispatches by Jackson as well as other official letters and reports.

News of the treaty, signed in Ghent on Christmas eve, arrived even later. The treaty went to London for ratification by the prince regent. That done, the document was put on board a British war sloop, the *Favorite,* which pulled out of harbor on January 2. It arrived in New York on February 11, where the news of peace swept through the city. The *Mercantile Advertiser* printed an extra and heaved copies from an office window in order to get the news out as fast as possible. Rumors of the peace reached Washington around mid-day on February 13, but these could not be confirmed. As the *Intelligencer* noted years later in a story recounting the momentous news, "Steam conveyances and Electric Telegraphs had not then been invented to realize the lover's prayer to the gods 'to annihilate both time and space;' and all classes in Washington had, with the President, no choice but to await the comparatively slow process of travel by horses and carriages from New York to Washington for confirmation or contradiction of the report." The *Intelligencer* re-

I MUST CLOSE

In keeping with the poor communication systems of the time, journalists were not seized with the need to get the news to readers as quickly and completely as possible. This is apparent in the work of the one person on the scene of Jackson's battle who could be deemed a correspondent.

James M. Bradford filed an on-the-spot report on the Battle of New Orleans for the *Time Piece,* a newspaper he published 110 miles north in St. Francisville, Louisiana. Like many contemporary journalists, Bradford was engaged in other endeavors besides the news. In addition to having started another newspaper, the *Gazetteer* in New Orleans, he was a lawyer, a plantation owner, a political appointee, and a two-time losing candidate for Congress. He also was a private in Jackson's forces in the Battle of New Orleans.

Bradford's reporting achievement is overlooked for a variety of reasons: His paper, of which only a few copies have survived, was insignificant nationally. He did not help his reputation before the war by seeming to side with Aaron Burr's intrigues to join western parts of the United States with Spanish Mexico in order to create a new country under Burr. (As a result, Bradford's New Orleans newspaper lost its government printing contract, and he moved to St. Francisville.) But the main reason Bradford is forgotten as a journalist is that he was more intent on fighting in the Battle of New Orleans than on reporting. As he frankly noted in his account for the *Time Piece,* "I must close—for as I write, I am informed our squadron is engaged with the enemy's piquet, and I must hasten to join them."

A local New Orleans newspaper was equally representative of the harum-scarum nature of journalism at the time. When it got around to publishing a story about the victory eight days after it was achieved, the quaintly named *Friend of the Laws* led with this disclaimer: "The editor and others employed in this office, at the moment of the invasion, joined their fellow-citizens in the camp, and thought themselves more useful as well as more honourably employed in defending their country than in satisfying the public appetite for news."

ported the rumors of peace in its February 14 edition. Not until the next day did it run a substantiated story on the peace treaty.

News of the victory in New Orleans and the treaty signed in Belgium appeared in New York and Washington newspapers piecemeal, but it appeared all at once in the February 15 issue of *Thomas's Massachusetts Spy, or Worcester Gazette,* a weekly owned by Isaiah Thomas Jr. Thomas inherited the paper from his father, a Colonial printer who distinguished himself during the American Revolution by reporting on the American stand against the British at Lexington and Concord, although he did not publish the story until nearly two weeks after the fact. The elder Thomas had been a participant in the event. (A reason for the long delay in publication was that Tory threats forced him to move his newspaper out of Boston to Worcester, where it remained permanently.) With its coverage of the end of the War of 1812, the *Spy* employed the still-common approach of using secondhand news. Borrowing from the *National Intelligencer,* which was widely reprinted in the country, the

Spy reprinted correspondence from Jackson and people in the field with him. The treaty news came from New York newspapers.

We cannot know precisely what Thomas was thinking when he decided on the placement of the news for his February 15 edition of the *Spy*. But we can guess. The *Spy* was a Federalist newspaper and, as such, opposed to Madison. Had Thomas run the treaty news first, he would have highlighted the administration's success. By running the victory story first, his paper would highlight the general's accomplishment. And so, although news about treaty negotiations in Ghent typically had led the news section of the paper up to this time, Jackson's victory took precedence on this day. Because page 1, as usual, was devoted to advertisements, this meant Jackson's triumph dominated page 2. News of the treaty was on page 3.

Thomas's newspaper unfurled its partisan colors by observing that the "successful opposition at New Orleans" demonstrated "in a still more convincing and striking manner, the extreme imbecility and guilt of the [Madison] government in not being able to save Washington from the grasp and violence of the enemy." Jackson, in contrast, was a leader of "sagacity prudence and vigilance."

Here are two of the stories from *Thomas's Massachusetts Spy, or Worcester Gazette,* February 15, 1815. The first reports Jackson's victory as if it won the war.

BY THE MAILS.

NEW ORLEANS.
From the National Intelligencer Extra.
Washington, Feb. 4, 9 o'clock, A.M.

Almost Incredible Victory!

. . . Second Intelligencer Extra.

Copy of a letter from Maj. Gen. Jackson to the secretary of war, dated H.Q. 7th Military District, Camp, 4 miles below New Orleans, Jan. 13, 1815.

SIR—At such a crisis, I conceive it my duty to keep you constantly advised of my situation.

On the 10th inst. I forwarded you an account of the bold attempt made by the enemy on the morning of the 8th to take possession of my works by storm, and of the severe repulse which he met with. That report having been sent by the mail which crosses the lake, may possibly have miscarried; for which reason, I think it more necessary briefly to repeat the substance of it.

Early on the morning of the 8th, the enemy, having been actively employed the two preceding days in making preparation for a storm, advanced in two strong columns on my right and left. They were received, however, with a firmness which, it seems, they little expected, and which destroyed all their hopes. My men, undisturbed by their approach, which indeed they had long anxiously awaited for, opened upon them a fire so deliberate and so certain, as rendered their scaling-ladders and fascines, as well as their more direct implements of warfare, perfectly useless. For upwards of an hour it was continued with a briskness of which there have been but few instances, perhaps, in any country. In justice to the enemy it must be said, they stood it as long as could have been expected from the most determined bravery. At length, however, when all prospect of success became hopeless, they fled in confusion from the field—leaving it covered with their dead and wounded. Their loss was immense. I had at first computed it at 1500; but it is since ascertained to have been much greater. Upon information, which is believed to be correct, Col. Haynes, the inspector-general, reports it to be equal to 2600. His report I enclose you.—My loss was inconsiderable, being only seven killed and six wounded.

Such a disproportion in loss, when we consider the number and the kind of troops engaged, must, I know, excite astonishment, and may not, every where, be fully credited; yet I am perfectly satisfied that the account is not exaggerated on the one part, nor under-rated on the other.

The enemy having hastily quitted a post which they had gained possession of, on the other side of the river, and we having immediately returned to it; both armies, at present, occupy their former positions. Whether, after the severe losses he had sustained, he is preparing to return to his shipping, or to make still mightier efforts to attain his first object, I do not pretend to determine. It becomes me to act as though the latter were his intention. One thing, however, seems certain, that if he still calculates on effecting what he has hitherto been unable to accomplish, he must expect considerable reinforcements, as the force with which he landed must undoubtedly be diminished by at least 3000. Besides the loss which he sustained on the night of the 23d ultimo, which is estimated at four hundred, he cannot have suffered less, between that period and the morning of the 8th instant, than 300; having, within that time, been repulsed in two general attempts to drive us from our position, and there having been continual cannonading and skirmishing, during the whole of it. Yet he is still able to show a very formidable force.

There is little doubt that the commanding general, Sir Edward Pakenham, was killed in the action of the 8th, and that Maj. Gens. Keane and Gibbs were severely wounded.

Whenever a more leisure moment shall occur, I will take the liberty to make out and forward you a more circumstantial account of the several actions, and particularly that of the 8th, in doing which my chief motive will be to render justice to those brave men I have the honour to command, and who have so remarkably distinguished themselves.

I have the honour to be, most respectfully, your obedient servant,
ANDREW JACKSON,
Major-General Commanding.

P.S. A correct list of my killed and wounded will be forwarded you by the adjutant-general.

Here is the second story, reporting on the peace treaty. Note the reference to the gentleman who brought the New York newspapers to the *Spy*.

Delightful Tidings of

PEACE!

———

From Yesterday's Palladium

We are indebted to the politeness of Dr. Still for the delivery of our New-York papers from the post-office in the night, immediately after the arrival of the mail.

· ·

———

Mercantile Advertiser—Extra.

NEW YORK, SATURDAY EVENING, 9 O'CLOCK, FEB. 11.

PEACE.

The great and joyful news of PEACE between the United States and Great Britain reached this city this evening by the British sloop of war Favorite, the Hon. J.U. Mowatt, Esq. commander, 142 days from Plymouth.

Henry Carroll, Esq. secretary of the American legation at Ghent, is the welcome bearer of the treaty, which was signed at Ghent, on the 24th of December, by the respective commissioners and ratified by the British government on the 28th of Dec. Mr. Baker, late secretary to the British legation at Washington, has also arrived in the sloop of war, with a copy of the treaty, ratified by the British government.

Both of these gentlemen proceed immediately for the seat of government.

We understand that the treaty is highly favourable to our country.

The Favorite sailed from Plymouth on the 2d day of January, and has brought London papers to the 31st of December.

Mr. Hughes, one of our secretaries, sailed in the Transit from Bourdeaux for the U.S. on the 30th of December.

Our ministers were to remain in Europe until spring.

We learn, verbally, that the congress in Vienna have not finished their important business.

We understand that London letters of Dec. 31 represent the affairs of the continent to be yet unsettled.

The treaty is said to have given great satisfaction in England, as there was no doubt it would be acceptable to our government. As soon as it is approved by our government, hostilities cease. Mr. Baker is to act as charges des affaires.

Historians have argued that more than the Battle of New Orleans would have been avoided if news traveled faster. Timely news months before could have headed off the entire war.

One of the chief causes of the war was the British "Orders of Council," which sought to restrict trade with the French and their allies. Among other harsh measures, the British stopped American ships and impressed sailors on the grounds that they were deserters from the British Royal Navy. The United States retaliated with commercial measures of its own. Reconsidering its approach in light of this, the British Parliament rescinded the "Orders of Council," but the following day— well before that news reached Washington—the American Congress declared war. Had he known that the British had backtracked, President Madison later said, "war would not have been at that time declared, nor is it probable that it would have followed."

For similar reasons the dearth of news prolonged the war in New Orleans *after* Jackson defeated the British. Although he was laureled by young girls and the good Abbé Guillaume Dubourg celebrated the victory mass, the general refused to lift martial law. How, he argued, did he know whether the war itself was over? Because Jackson insisted upon substantiated fact, he did not alter his policy when rumors of the peace treaty reached the city. On the contrary, he tried to stop newspapers from publishing the "inflammatory" report.

The entire misunderstanding should have been resolved by a courier who left Washington, D.C., on February 15, the day the treaty was ratified. Realizing the value of this news, the U.S. postmaster general provided the courier, one Charles Bell, with a letter asking local postmasters to give all help necessary to reach New Orleans expeditiously. Bell was to carry news of the treaty and orders for Jackson to discharge the militia. Unfortunately, due to some snafu, Bell arrived in New Orleans nineteen days later with the wrong document. When the seal on the letter was broken, Jackson found inside an old order calling out the militia. Bell showed Jackson the postmaster's letter, which mentioned "the state of peace which has taken place between the United States and Great Britain." Jackson also had Bell's own word of the treaty, which had been fully approved by the Senate and President Madison, as well as a report from the British that the treaty had been ratified. The general would have none of it. He still wanted explicit confirmation of the treaty's ratification. Martial law continued.

This brought on a new, internecine Battle of New Orleans between the intransigent Jackson and angry local citizens. Each attack met counterattack. When the legislature voted thanks to the officers of the victorious army, it listed all the names except Jackson's. Jackson's French soldiers became restive and sought release from their work by claiming the protection of their consul. Jackson responded by ordering out of the city all French citizens who claimed this exemption, and he sent the consul with them. Louis Louailler, a leading legislator who had never been enthusiastic about martial law, wrote an article criticizing Jackson's continuing military authority in the city. The angry general had Louailler arrested and charged him with being a spy. The federal district judge, Dominick Augustine Hall, himself fed up with martial law, ordered Louailler to be freed. Jackson responded by arresting Hall as well, putting him in the same barracks with Louailler and then expelling him from the city. The U.S. district attorney, John Dick, applied to Judge Joshua

THE VALUE OF ECONOMIC NEWS

The most obvious consequence of the slow news of the Treaty of Ghent lay on the field of battle, where the cost in life and limb was high. Less often discussed is a related incident pointing to the financial disruptions that come with delayed news.

Advance information is the mother's milk of speculators. The Rothschilds established an elaborate European communications system that employed private couriers and carrier pigeons. Their network was so effective that Queen Victoria used it for her banking and to make hotel reservations.

The outcome of the Battle of New Orleans was of intense interest in financial circles, as well as political ones. New Yorkers, for instance, owned a large share of the $3.2 million worth of cotton stored there. One merchant, the brother of a congressman, had advance word of the peace treaty. He proposed that the postmaster general delay the mail from New York by one day to give him time to speculate in southern commodities like cotton, tobacco, and sugar. The postmaster declined and reported the incident to James Monroe, the secretary of state and war, who informed the president. Large sums were made and lost when the news finally arrived. The prices for sugar and tea plummeted, and the value of U.S. treasury notes soared.

Jockeying for advance commercial information continued after the war, as the country became more prosperous. When cotton speculators developed a private mail system over parts of the post route between Washington and New Orleans, beating regular mail by an entire day, the U.S. postmaster general created a public express system, although it was not as efficient as he hoped. When telegraph lines were put in place on the eastern seaboard of the United States in midcentury, they hummed with commercial business news that arrived by ships in seaports. Dishonest speculators cut lines to give themselves an advantage.

The eager and wealthy audience for commercial news was an engine for the creation of news services. Around 1850 Israel Beer Josaphat—who had recently taken a new name, Paul Julius Reuter—started a news agency in Aachen, a German city that had long been a European crossroads; his agency supplied financial information to merchants, bankers, and eventually newspapers. According to lore, Reuter insisted on fair play by locking his Aachen clients in his office so that all of them would receive stock market prices at the same time. He soon moved his headquarters to an even more important crossroads, London. The Associated Press was organized in the United States about the same time. One of its chief selling points, a historian has noted, was that it provided "a consolidated digest of telegraphic data collected from all the country's major markets. And because it served the newspaper press, the service greatly expanded the circle of those who transacted business guided by common knowledge of market conditions." In 1871, the board of directors of the Western Associated Press noted "continuous pressure on the Executive Committee from members of the Association for more extended commercial reports." In 1904, the AP instructed reporters that only dramatic breaking news trumped commercial news for transmission: "Markets and sporting matter must be given precedence, except against *must* matter, and should be expedited on all circuits."

"Speculators should not have the advantage of earlier news than the public at large," proclaimed James Gordon Bennett, whose genius at democratic newspapering is recounted in the next chapter. A Rothschild made roughly the same admission: "People are too well informed and there is therefore little opportunity to do anything."

Lewis for a writ of habeas corpus seeking the release of Hall. Jackson ordered the arrest of Dick and Lewis, although only Dick ultimately went to the barracks. Finally, in mid-March official notification of the peace arrived.

Jackson had been foolish. He had very good reasons to believe the war was over and yet trampled on legal authority as well as constitutional rights. For this he found *himself* in the dock. With the end of martial law, Judge Hall took his own liberties with the law. He ordered Jackson to show why he should not be in contempt for refusing his order to release Louailler. Although Hall was anything but impartial, he presided over the trial himself on March 24 and found Jackson guilty. "The only question is whether the Law should bend to the General, or the General to the Law." Hall levied a $1,000 fine.

More than two and a half months after the American troops defeated the British on the plains of Chalmette, this little war-within-a-war in New Orleans finally came to an end.

If the Battle of New Orleans was unnecessary for the United States, it was a godsend to Jackson. Not even his foolish martial law could alter the fact that he was the hero of the Battle of New Orleans. A subscription was taken up to pay the fine Judge Hall imposed on him. Jackson covered his own debt and, noblesse oblige, gave the donated one thousand dollars to the orphans of soldiers who died in the battle. He wanted to do nothing to tarnish his victory, the greatest United States military feat up to that time.

A few die-hards continued to complain about Jackson's disdain for the law. A newspaper published a cartoon that depicted a leading local lady squeezing Jackson's rotund wife into an elegant dress. But the city generally returned to its adoration of Jackson and his family. In the coming months Jackson traveled about the country to receive accolades and speak. The press cooperated by reporting his appearances for those who could not witness them firsthand.

From the point of view of establishing winners and losers, the Treaty of Ghent achieved little. It dodged most of the issues that drove the countries into war. Neither the British nor the Americans acquired or lost territory. Both sides simply wanted the fighting to stop. The United States, however, gained a psychological boost. The mere fact of the stand-off established the United States as an independent nation to be reckoned with and legitimated the Louisiana Purchase in the eyes of other nations. And Jackson's victory gave Americans a satisfying dose of self-esteem. "Now," said legislator Henry Clay, one of the commissioners negotiating the peace treaty, "I can go to England without mortification!" Until the Civil War, January 8 was celebrated like the Fourth of July.

When Jackson ran for the White House, his campaign literature used press clippings about his generalship. Quotes from these stories appeared in eulogies when he died in 1845. By that time, Congress had refunded the $1,000 he was fined for contempt, with interest.

4

DISHING THE FOREIGN NEWS

We published yesterday the principal items of the foreign news, received by
the *Sheffield*, being eight days later than our previous arrivals. Neither the *Sun*
nor the *Transcript* had a single item on the subject. The *Sun* did not even know of its
existence. The large papers in Wall Street had also the news, but as the editors are
lazy, ignorant, indolent, blustering blockheads, one and all, they did not pick out
the cream and serve it out as we did. The *Herald* alone knows how to dish up the
foreign news, or indeed domestic events, in a readable style.

James Gordon Bennett, *New York Herald*

On September 3, 1833, twenty-three-year-old Benjamin H. Day launched a newspaper based on a radically new business model. The long-established mercantile daily papers were sold mostly by subscription, for as much as ten dollars a year, or, if a customer wanted to come by the office, for six and one-quarter cents a single copy. Day hired boys to sell his *New York Sun* on the streets for a penny. In addition to the *Sun*'s low price, he gave readers something else they had not had before. Politically oriented and catering to narrow commercial interests, the "sixpenny sheets" were not in the business of providing lively, broadly informative reporting. But the *Sun,* in its inaugural issue, promised just that, "all the news of the day." Within four months, the *Sun*'s circulation outran that of all other New York newspapers and had not stopped climbing.

Day's brilliant idea capitalized on a change in the American social equation, the emergence of a broad urban middle class that wanted news directed to its varied interests. He was helped still further by another mid-nineteenth-century development, improved printing technology. Old hand-operated presses printed 125 copies an hour; in 1835 Day employed a steam-powered press that printed 4,000 an hour. Other manufacturing innovations sharply reduced the price for paper, which Day was now using in great abundance to meet the public demand for his novel paper.

None of those who followed Day's lead better understood what readers wanted than enterprising, cross-eyed James Gordon Bennett, the self-styled "NAPOLEON of the press." His *New York Herald* began in 1835 with the proclamation "We shall support no party—be the organ of no faction or COTERIE," and then set out on an independent course to lure as many readers as possible. Bennett's reporting of the ax murder of the beautiful prostitute Helen Jewett and the trial of her young client, the scion of a respectable Connecticut family, was a tour de force for its vivid, crusading, gossipy, investigative, and often suspect reporting. His coverage included publication of a verbatim conversation with Rosina Townsend, the madam at Jewett's brothel. Some historians credit it as the first formal newspaper interview ever printed; some say he fabricated the story.

Either way, people read the *Herald*. Circulation soared as Bennett relentlessly covered suicides, murders, and fires; exposed landlord conspiracy and railroad corruption; campaigned for prison and police reform; published the first Wall Street stock market reports; and, despite all this attention to the local angle, went after foreign news, rather than waiting for it to come to him.

When Bennett left his native Scotland in 1819, most foreign news in the United States was still the scissors-and-paste journalism of Benjamin Franklin's time. Newspapers in port cities acquired their foreign news from periodicals aboard incoming ships. As coastal newspapers traveled through the mail to inland American cities and towns, their plagiarized reports from abroad were, in turn, plagiarized.

Bennett's first newspaper job was with one of the nation's best papers at the time, the Charleston, South Carolina, *Courier*. The *Courier* had been the very first in the country to report the Treaty of Ghent; the paper's owner had gained the scoop by rowing out into Charleston harbor to meet a schooner. At the *Courier*, Bennett participated in that enterprising tradition by translating incoming articles from French and Spanish newspapers. In the process he developed a lifelong interest in Latin America.

In New York, where Bennett subsequently reported for various newspapers, the competition for foreign news was especially keen among mercantile papers. Although tied closely to political parties, which could give them government printing contracts, they served readers whose livelihoods depended upon up-to-date financial information. The news pages listed ship arrivals and departures; foreign-exchange rate, stock, and bond tables; offerings of importers; and commodity prices abroad, along with other foreign economic news. Particularly competitive in this field were two newspapers started in the 1820s, the *Journal of Commerce* and the *Courier and Enquirer*. In 1831 the two newspapers' news schooners raced one hundred miles beyond Sandy Hook to greet ships and rushed the foreign news to the home office. Estimates of the cost of this "news-gathering" go as high as $15,000 to $20,000 a year for each paper.

Bennett eventually went to work for the *Courier and Enquirer*, which had some of the best foreign coverage in the late 1820s and early 1830s. He was an assistant editor, occasional local reporter, and out-of-town correspondent in Washington, D.C., and elsewhere. His writing was lively, enterprising, and controversial. He was, it was later said, the paper's "most efficient hand." He also was not an easy man to get along with, and neither was James Watson Webb, who owned the *Courier and Enquirer*. Inevitably, the two men parted company.

When Bennett started his own newspaper, he did not hesitate to compete with his old employer for foreign news. The *Herald*'s first issue contained two columns of "LATE AND IMPORTANT FROM EUROPE." He sent news boats to meet ships farther out than his competitors did; the boats took the news to Montauk Point, where news messengers boarded a locomotive bound for New York. "They would arrive at the *Herald* office covered with perspiration and glory," said Frederic Hudson, whom Bennett hired to collect harbor news. Hudson became the *Herald*'s managing editor and at the end of his career wrote one of the earliest histories of American journalism.

Hudson considered Bennett the originator "of organized European correspondence." Not content to win at the established game of collecting ship news, Bennett enlisted correspondents to secure firsthand information about events in Europe and elsewhere, just as others did about Washington politics and New York society balls. With the role of reporter, domestic or foreign, still ill-defined, these early foreign correspondents were part-timers with other jobs. Many, Bennett boasted, were volunteers. The *Herald*'s Jamaica correspondent was a local journalist who wanted to exchange newspapers with Bennett. Early correspondents from Liverpool and Le Havre worked in brokerage firms, which was in keeping with the *Herald*'s emphasis on commercial foreign news. Bennett buttressed this reporting with the established practice of running letters from American travelers as assorted in occupation as naval officers and actors.

Bennett's first trip to England as the *Herald* proprietor was in 1838 aboard the *Sirius,* which was making the first west-to-east Atlantic steamship crossing. His mission, he proclaimed, was to establish "a corps of correspondents, such as have never been attached to a New York paper." This he did, hiring six experienced newsmen to write for him from time to time from Glasgow, Berlin, Brussels, London, Rome, and Paris, among them an Irishman named Dr. Dionysius Lardner, who was in Paris for the *London Morning Chronicle.* Meanwhile, not being one to keep his own pen idle, he became a foreign correspondent himself in London, where an event full of journalistic possibilities spread out before him, Queen Victoria's coronation.

The dispatch below from July 27, 1838—the first of two he wrote on the glorious spectacle—is vintage Bennett, whose storytelling skills are on display. It is brassy, detailed, and personal, filled with flattering references to himself and unflattering ones to Col. James Watson Webb, his old employer at the *Courier and Enquirer,* who also was in town in search of correspondents and stories.

The Coronation.
LETTER NO. XVIII.

London, 29th June, 1838.
I have seen the Coronation of Victoria from beginning to end—in Westminster Abbey and out of the Abbey. It was, without exception, the most splendid sight I have ever yet seen—full of poetry, beauty, nonsense, sublimity, superstition, sense, and grandeur—a perfect *pot pourri* of the ceremonies and observances of Christianity, Catholicity, feudalism, and the classic ages. In all the London papers,* will be found correct and verbose descriptions of the ceremonies and festivities of yesterday, but this account which I shall give will be entirely different from these. It will be a narrative of what befell myself—of the impressions made

---

* Errant punctuation, such as this comma, remained commonplace in Bennett's time.

upon me—of the thoughts the strange scenes called forth—and the reflections they produced.

By the Royal Williams steamer, I send this letter and also several engravings representing the interior of Westminster Abbey, the sacred Chair, the Crown and other pageants. The engraving of the Abbey represents the crowning of a king—a small mistake caused by a drunken vagabond of an engraver, though a genius. By altering in the mind's eye that figure—the rascal told me as an excuse, that he was a democrat and opposed to she kings—into a little girl, and putting robes about her, with a sufficient expanse of petticoat, a tolerably accurate idea may be conceived of the magnificence and grandeur of the interior of Westminster Abbey during the ceremony.

I have already written to New York that I had a probability of getting an admission into the Abbey. It was successful and I have been there and saw the whole affair. In order that my readers may know the position I had, I refer them to the gallantry close to the peeresses on the right hand of the sovereign. It is called the Nightingale Gallery. To this gallery, contiguous to that which contained the foreign ministers, I had a blue ticket of admission.—Through the politeness of Mr. Stevenson, our very popular minister, I received this admission. The Duke of Norfolk, who officiated as the Earl Marshal of England, sent Mr. Stevenson two tickets, for the use of the American press. I believe such a favor was not extended to the press of any other country, but the popularity of the American republic with the British government is singularly strong and marked. Perhaps no minister has created this feeling to a higher and deeper extent than the personal conduct and fine, manly open, bold old Virginian manner of Mr. Stevenson. They recognize in him a chip of the old block—sprang from the old English race which settled Virginia.

Back to the Coronation. On the Wednesday morning I called on Mr. Stevenson and received the following, printed on a species of light blue hot pressed paper.

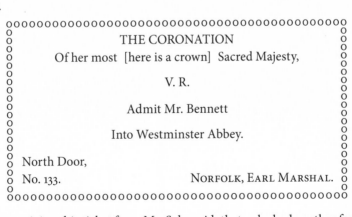

THE CORONATION
Of her most [here is a crown] Sacred Majesty,

V. R.

Admit Mr. Bennett

Into Westminster Abbey.

North Door,
No. 133.   NORFOLK, EARL MARSHAL.

On receiving this ticket from Mr. S. he said, that as he had another for a like purpose, he would give it to any other American editor, if I knew one being in London. I replied that I understand Mr. Webb was in London; for notwithstanding the many foolish things that my old associate had done, I would never allow personal feelings to interfere with such occasions as the present. Not only would I facilitate his entrance, as I did, into Westminster Abbey, but if I could I would open the kingdom of heaven for him, provided that he would repent of his sins, although I fear he would not be long there without making a riot, or challenging some one.

Be that as it may, having got my ticket, I now began to deliberate about the costume in which I was to make my appearance at the Abbey. On inquiry, I found that there was no necessity for a full court dress, although that is the verbal order of the program. I therefore made no other alteration in my usual simple black dress then varying it with a white vest and a white stock.

On the Wednesday night previous, I prepared my self at the cost of half a crown to visit the Abbey on the succeeding morning. Next morning, I had to get up early, for as soon as daylight begins to dawn, the avenues to the venerable pile are besieged by any rank and fashion. The doors were opened as early as five o'clock in the morning although the Queen does not enter 'til near twelve o'clock. I got up at five o'clock and had breakfast ordered; but the difficulty was in procuring a carriage. The one I had ordered the night previous did not come—accordingly I had to take pot luck, and the considerate hackman demanded 25 shillings in advance before he would budge an inch. I forked out the money, and was glad to get one at any price, for by this time it was wearing towards seven o'clock, and at eight o'clock the barriers were all to be closed.

But another important affair was arranged before I started. A young friend provided me with a small flask of choice sherry and a couple of crackers. "If you do not take these," said he, "you will get faint, and when you get into the Abbey, the crowd is so great that there will be no getting out again." I thought this very good and well considered advice—accordingly I took it, although I seldom do take any advice. I took the flask and put it in one pocket—then the crackers into the other. In my hand I carried the "Book of the Coronation" as a guide to the ceremonies when inside the Abbey. With these preparations I mounted the carriage and drove to the street leading to the North Entrance.

We entered the line of carriages at Charing Cross and proceeded bit by bit, up Whitehall, along Parliament street, 'till we reached the Abbey. Along the whole line, it was thronged with carriages—the side walks with pedestrians. The fronts of houses on each side were dressed up like the interior of a theatre, tier above tier, to the roof, and each tier already nearly filled with spectators, although five or six hours had to elapse before the procession would pass.

On reaching the entrance of the Abbey, I was set down and passed in. "Have you any ticket, sir?" "Yes," replied I—pulling it out. "You are not required to deliver it up," said he, "keep it and pass along." I did so. I passed a number of policemen and officers, in a very zig-zag direction, under the galleries and cloisters of this famous building. Coming from the light, it seemed so dark when I passed the great entrance that I could not find my way.—One of the attendants gave me his arm, led me through a dark passage, which took me to the ascending staircase, leading to the Nightingale Gallery.

On changing from darkness to light, I was for a moment dazzled by the splendid *coup d'oeil* which the interior of the magnificent structure presented. It was a few minutes after seven o'clock in the morning, and yet every seat, except those belonging to the peeresses, and the foreign ministers, was crowded with the beauty and splendor of this mighty Kingdom. It was impossible to conceive any scene more truly gorgeous. But amusing enough, the object that struck me on entering was the variable figure in full costume, of my particular friend, Colonel Webb, who had received a ticket of Mr. Stevenson, and was very securely ensconced in the center of two dozen very beautifully dressed ladies. There were three behind him—three before him, and four on one side, and a dozen on the left, each one of them a Hebe* or a Venus de Medecis. Heretofore it has been my pride and passion to be considered a ladies' man—an adorer of the sex—a passionate lover of the delicious petticoat. At last, I must admit that a greater in that line than I am, illuminates this nether world. I shall take my proper rank in a taste for the ladies and dueling—and that is second to Col. Webb. He certainly has outstripped me completely, and I acknowledge beat, but not done over.

But to return from this digression. It took me a full hour to look round, and mark out the most remarkable sights in the interior of the Abbey. The venerable grey columns of this Gothic structure, contrasted beautifully with the gold and silver decorations of the galleries. The newspapers here will give you the best descriptions—I confine my observations to the exact impressions made on me throughout the whole ceremony.

In a short time, that is to say at eight o'clock, the peers and peeresses began to enter. I got a seat very contiguous to that portion of the northern transept which was devoted to the accommodation of the female nobility, and I was quite interested in watching the appearance, and looks, and dress of each fair dame as she entered. They all appeared in similar costume—in white dress, with a crimson robe ornamented with ermine. Each peeress carried her coronet in her hand, and when she took her seat she put it in her lap or placed it before her. On the opposite side was the place for the peers, but I took less interest in the he creatures than in the she. What struck me most on the approach of the peeresses, was the singular degree of personal beauty, which, as a body of women, they generally possess. I do not think they reached so many as three or four hundred, as there were many seats vacant, but of such as were present, I can safely say that I have never seen, in one single collection, so many beautiful, graceful, and dignified women as they presented. They are generally over the ordinary stature of females—approaching the majestic in their height and appearance. The forms are full-rounded well, and present finely developed busts of remarkable classic beauty. Few are thin, lean, or meager in appearance—many on the contrary rather inclining to *en bon point*. But in complexion, benignant expression of face—and graceful movements, they are very superior. Hereafter it must be admitted that the higher female ranks of England are a beautiful race—

---

* Greek goddess of youth and spring; wife of Hercules.

and perhaps, on no other occasion, has been an opportunity to see this so superior as that of the coronation.

Around the galleries, in every direction, the crowd of beauty was immense. These were no peeresses although the great proportion belonged to the highest and most refined order of society. Among them I observed whole beaches of beauty—vast shoals of female elegance. The Abbey contained 18,000 persons and probably out of this number 7000 were females—generally beautiful and all gorgeously dressed. Such another sight I never expect to see as long as I live, and I am devilish glad I went there, although I had some intentions at the time to omit the chance.

But I had almost forgot the peeresses, sweet souls. It was quite amusing to see them enter. They sailed up the main isle, or nave of the Abbey, until they came to the center, where the ceremony was to be performed. There the officers of the Earl Marshal took hold of their crimson trains, three or four feet long, and conducted each to her seat, which was marked out and labeled for her. Each one of them rolled up her train around her, just as a pretty little kitten, tired of playing in the sun, curls up her tail in front, and licks her lips as a preparation for the next impulse of human life. The gentlemen in waiting, each with his baton, announced these ladies as they appeared. The Duchess of Richmond created a sensation—so did Lady King (the daughter of Byron.)

"Ada sole daughter of my house and home."

The Countess of Essex, the late actress, Mrs. Stephens, was beautiful and dignified—but none seemed so splendid as the beautiful Marchioness of Londonderry, and the equally lovely Countess of Shrewsbury, I think it was.

I must not forget another sight which struck me as connected with the peeresses. As they began to muster pretty thick, the sun through the eastern window shot through a brilliant beam. What do you think, gentle fair ones of New York, became of that beam? It was reflected and refracted in a dozen beautiful colors by the profuse brilliants, diamonds, and precious stones which ornamented their hair. I observed one peeress, not the most beautiful of the parterre, but the fattest by all odds. Her head dress was an incrustation of diamonds and other jewelry, and every moment she turned to look this way or that way, my eyes were dazzled with all the beautiful colors of the rainbow.

I shall never forget the fair peeresses of England. Their jewelry, ornaments, and decorations were profuse and rich, but their fine forms, exquisite complexions, and particularly their full, classic busts, heaving with loyalty and love, I presume will be found impressed on my memory as long as it can tag one idea after another.

The entrance of the foreign ministers was another object of great interest and splendor. Their costumes were as various as they were splendid. The Turkish ambassador looked well—but the veteran "old Soult," as he is familiarly called, brought forth the most attention. He created a sensation on his entrance. There was very peculiar propriety in this sentiment. Marshal Soult had thrashed the

English, and had been thrashed by them, during the last war. Two brave men, and two brave nations, always esteem each other. Soult won the populace.

The entrance of Duke of Nemours, the second son of Louis Philippe, also made a rustling. It is said that a number of second sons of the Kings of Europe have been present, besides several lots of German princes, all looking forward to have a chance for the fair hand of Victoria.

But of all the signs in the Abbey the entrance of the young Queen was the most beautiful and splendid. Here she was walking up the steps leading to the royal platform, where stood the holy St. Edward's chair, the throne, etc. She looked quite short in stature, but nevertheless she bore herself with much dignity. On her fair brow she wore a dazzling circlet of gold and precious stones. Her crimson train, ten or twelve yards in length, was borne by eight young ladies of the highest rank. The eight trainbearers were tall and majestic, and also very beautiful. Their head-dresses were adorned with lofty white plumes. It was really quite interesting to see the little girl bearing herself so well. In that part of the building where I stood, the ladies expressed a deep interest in her appearance. "Poor thing, they will smother her"—"sweet little girl, they will kill her with grandeur."

In truth, the accession of Victoria seems to have changed the nature of men and things in this land of sturdy liberty. The nation has gone back to the ancient days of tilt and tournament—and loyalty has become entwined with the sentiment of love. England never had before a young, delicate, rather pretty, rather sensible, chaste maiden for her sovereign. The very populace, up to the highest ranks, seem to consider her as a beautiful plaything—an elegant doll—and enchanting little idol, which creates in this bosom all the feelings naturally excited by youth and beauty. There never was in the world such another empire—an empire on which the sun never sets—met in that place to express love and devotion to a weak young woman. It was altogether a different scene from that presented by the coronation of an old, ugly, gouty, grasping old rascal. Perhaps the self-willed and majestic coronation of Napoleon, a representation of which I have sent for publication, is the only one that can produce equal effect—though different in purpose—to that of Victoria.

Colonel Webb served as an entertaining foil for Bennett, who frequently used him to show the *Herald*'s own superiority. In his second story, which appeared the following day, Bennett ridiculed Webb for not being able to find a decent meal while watching the coronation, as Bennett boasted he had done. Webb, however, was not his only victim. The *Herald* attacked rival editors individually and en masse.

While Bennett was sending reports home from London in 1838, the *Herald* ran an editorial maligning the competition for being deceitful "in making it appear they had received full files of the late British papers." It described the *Journal of Commerce*'s David Hale, a deeply religious man and a vigorous competitor, as "the pilferer, the quibbler, the liar, the branded liar, the hypocrite, the consummate scoundrel, the gallows looking scape grace . . . whose hang-dog look—unsightly cheeks and villainous eye [—] would alone convict him at the Old Baily. . . . This rascal was rogue enough to detain the letter bag with the property of others in it, and then told lies to Captain Marshall—we have beat him and his hypocritical crew, and will beat him again." Bennett described Park Benjamin, editor of the *Evening Signal*, as "half Jew, half infidel, with a touch of the monster." He went after his own Roman Catholic religion, criticizing the Mass as an occasion for "eating our own divinity." He said that the original penny newspaper, the *New York Sun*, had a "brace of blockheads for editors."

James Gordon Bennett's unabashed enthusiasm for heralding his *Herald* contributed to the upstart newspaper's success and made him an object of scorn. *Vanity Fair* was particularly fond of ridiculing the cross-eyed editor. Here Henry Louis Stephens, a *Vanity Fair* founder and one of the best cartoonists of his time, depicts Bennett trumpeting the *Herald*'s foreign news. The cartoon appeared in the magazine's February 18, 1860 issue. *Vanity Fair* itself showed an interest in foreign affairs from time to time, once publishing a series of articles that burlesqued war correspondence. The nineteenth-century *Vanity Fair* went out of business in 1863, although the magazine's name was revived in the next century. Frank Luther Mott, *A History of American Magazines, 1850–1865* (Cambridge, Mass.: Harvard University Press, 1967), 2:520–29.

If these editorials were not enough to make New York publishers hate James Gordon Bennett, there was his success as a journalist. The *Herald*'s bombastic journalism was winning the circulation war.

Webb, who had a penchant for dueling and other violence, throttled Bennett twice. Other editors gave him beatings as well. Once a letter-bomb arrived, addressed "For Mr. BENNETT (only). Should he be out of Town, KEEP FOR HIM." It failed to explode. Trying another tactic to counter his lurid, ax-murder-style reporting, publishers in league with ministers, stockbrokers, and leading politicians started a "moral war" against him. They asked hotel owners to bar patrons who arrived with the *Herald* tucked under their arms. "The creed of *all*," Webb said of the *Herald*, "should be—*purchase* not, *read* not, *touch* not." Bennett would die an upright man, said Benjamin Day, only if he were hung "perpendicularly from a rope."

Bennett also made transatlantic enemies. One was William Howard Russell, who achieved fame for himself and his paper, the *Times* of London, in covering the Crimean War. When Russell came to the United States to report on the Civil War, the *Herald* criticized him for showing the weakness of the Union forces. Later, it embarrassed Russell with a story hinting that the great war correspondent used inside news to speculate in financial markets. Russell, who was never able to put across a good case that he had done nothing wrong, wrote to his editor as well as his editor's brother-in-law to discourage the *Times* from quoting the *Herald* "so frequently as that most infamous paper was then made prominent in the eyes of Europe. . . . The fact is that its information is frequently false and when it is true the other papers [are] about as well informed."

The *New York Times* described the *Herald* as "a quasi obscene publication edited by a Scotchman as hideous in mind as ill shapen in body and who ere long earned for himself the surname of Mephistopheles of the Press." Perhaps stung by the "ill shapen" comment, the cross-eyed Bennett sued the *Times* for $50, according to a document in the *New York Times* files. The results of the suit are not to be found there.

No real damage was done to Bennett or his newspaper by any of the assaults on him. On the contrary, he turned abuse into entertaining and self-promotional news, as in this story written around the time of the *Herald*'s first anniversary:

> The Courier & Enquirer, and the Evening Sun, not daring to enter the lists with me on any public topic, gallantly and fearlessly sent out their *bravos* to knock me down in the street. . . . I never quailed—I never feared—I never saw the man I dreaded to meet face to face—or the obstacle I would not attempt to surmount. I have entered on a course of private enterprise, but also of public usefulness. I will show the people of this city the utter worthlessness of journals conducted as the *Courier & Enquirer,* without honor, talent, principle, or patriotism. Before I have done with it, I shall reduce that concern to a mere shipping and commercial list.

Circulation dipped during the moral war only temporarily. By the beginning of the Civil War, the *Herald* was the most popular newspaper in America as well as the most widely read American newspaper in Europe. Bennett was not the only newspaperman to boast about his product, for that was common in those days. The difference was that on most days the cross-eyed newspaperman had more to boast about than his competitors.

The profound idea that underlay the success of the penny press was the commercial value of paying close attention to local news, the magnet for the great mass of readers whom local advertisers wanted to reach. Accordingly, the amount of space devoted to foreign news generally declined in these new newspapers. In 1705 news items from abroad made up more than four-fifths of Campbell's *Boston News-Letter;* in 1856, the *Boston Post,* a comparable newspaper, contained 27 percent foreign news. The share of foreign news in the average metropolitan newspaper dropped well below this as the years rolled on.

Bennett was an exception in this as well as in many other ways. He attended to foreign news even as he prospered with rambunctious local coverage. In 1859 more than 60 percent of the *Herald* was given to foreign coverage. During a typical four-day period in the mid-1850s, it ran letters from China, France, Great Britain, Austria, Hawaii, Peru, Uruguay, Nicaragua, New Granada, Havana, and Mexico City. *Herald* correspondents, *Harper's New Monthly Magazine* reported in 1867, "were ever present with such expeditions as the American squadron in the Mediterranean, the allied army in Paraguay, the armies in Candia and Corea, and the Collins Telegraph Company in Kamtchatka!" Shortly after Bennett's death in 1873, *Frank Leslie's Illustrated Newspaper* proclaimed, "You can find a *Herald* man in every nook and cranny of the Earth."

Bennett's foreign news machinery was, by any modern measure, crude. The *Herald* still gleaned news from incoming ships. Although Bennett recruited additional correspondents on return trips to Europe, his reportorial network remained filled with part-timers, many of whom still did not qualify as journalists. A correspondent in Mexico confessed that he was not "a very expert hand at giving sketches in foreign countries." Much of the *Herald*'s "news" amounted to announcements that there wasn't any, an obvious ploy to show readers that someone was on the spot in case something important happened (and a sign to us of just how undeveloped the idea of "getting" news still was). An American envoy probably supplied this story from Shanghai: "I scribble you a few lines, simply to inform you what we are up and doing in this part of the world; also that our Minister, Hon. R. M. McLane, is going to see what the country is made of. . . . Everything is quiet here at present. Occasionally the rebel and imperialist forces have a small skirmish, but it does not amount to anything, except to injure trade and impoverish the country."

Yet, the *Herald*'s shortcomings do not stand out from our vantage point so much as Bennett's innovation. He was well ahead of others in conceiving of foreign news-gathering as a serious and worthwhile undertaking for a newspaper with broad appeal. Bennett's decision to separate the *Herald* from the penny newspapers with aggressive foreign news coverage contributed to circulation increases. The average penny readers got a little more for their money with the *Herald*. Meanwhile, the paper credibly competed for the upscale readers of the stodgy mercantile newspapers, which, as Bennett boasted, were not nearly as good at dishing up news in a "lively style." His European correspondence was "diversified in topic and interest, and elegant in point of narrative and detail."

In courting business readers, Bennett represented himself as an emissary of overseas commerce. (He added further to his credibility by adopting the thoroughly modern practice of not speculating in any stocks, thus allaying concerns he was using the press to make unfair profit.) Bennett, managing editor Frederic Hudson observed, "did not lose sight of Wall Street, the financial centre of the nation. . . . The public, those with money to invest, as well as the bulls and bears, have derived great benefit in having the financial affairs of the world daily spread before them." The strategy was profitable. A yearlong advertising contract in the *Journal of Commerce* cost $60. In the *Herald* it cost $1,000.

Bennett in his genius understood that foreign news coverage was a mark of excellence in a mass-market newspaper, making it a member of what came to be called the "prestige press." As a commentator put it at the end of the century, "The position of a paper may be gauged, generally, by the extent and quality—specially the latter—of its foreign matter."

This grand vision of newspapering was not one that Bennett fully conceived and developed by himself. The mercantile newspapers, speeding to meet ships bearing foreign news before they landed, were Bennett's classroom. Contemporary editors and reporters were only a few steps behind him in refining the concepts and mechanics of foreign news-gathering. Among those who put telling marks on foreign news were two of the first celebrated professional foreign correspondents, George Kendall of the *Picayune* in New Orleans and George Smalley of the *New York Tribune,* and Bennett's own son—men who populate the next three chapters. As an admirer wrote of Bennett in his heyday, "The mission of Bennett is not at an end. It is a continuous work."

5

MR. KENDALL'S EXPRESS

Louisiana produced a remarkable share of early war correspondents. We have already had a look at James M. Bradford, who filed a report for his St. Francisville newspaper on the Battle of New Orleans as an afterthought. But the most famous Louisiana war correspondent of all—in fact he may rank as the world's first true war correspondent—is George Wilkins Kendall, whose commitment to getting news far outdistanced anything Bradford did or probably could imagine doing.

Kendall began newspapering in Amherst, his New Hampshire hometown. In the itinerant fashion of printers, he subsequently worked in New York, Detroit, Mobile, and Washington. In 1837 he and Francis Lumsden, with whom he had worked at the *National Intelligencer,* pooled their resources to start their own New Orleans newspaper, the *Picayune,* which was soon renamed the *Daily Picayune.*

Kendall was a restless man with a taste for politics and adventure. As a correspondent for the *Picayune* in 1841, he joined a Republic of Texas–sponsored expedition whose ostensible purpose was to open a trade route to New Mexico. Aware that Texas coveted New Mexico and seeing the expedition as a step toward eventual usurpation, Mexican authorities arrested Kendall and his colleagues and marched them to a Mexico City prison. Kendall's book chronicling the adventure brought him a measure of fame. He became a leading spokesman for Texas. When the United States and Mexico went to war in 1846, he was all too happy to combine war reporting with military service. He offered advice to commanders, carried dispatches, and fought alongside the regular troops. Two generals cited him for gallantry. Kendall was wounded in the knee while covering the Battle of Chapultepec, which gave Mexico City to the Americans.

The Mexican War was the first to receive timely, comprehensive coverage from reporters who accompanied troops into battle. The competition was stiff. The *Picayune* itself had other correspondents besides Kendall. What distinguished Kendall—and underpins claims to his authentic firstness as a bona fide war correspondent—was his remarkable journalistic focus and ingenuity in trouncing rivals with authoritative news accounts that arrived ahead of others.[*]

[*] Other journalists have a claim on being the first war correspondent. Henry Crabbe Robinson covered the Napoleonic wars in northern Europe in 1807 for the *Times* of London; Charles Lewis Gruneisen was in Spain in 1837 to cover the Carlist War for a rival British newspaper, the *Morning*

✳

Correspondents from New Orleans dominated news-gathering in Mexico. When Kendall founded the *Picayune,* the thriving city was the country's third largest in population and the second in commerce and soon became the first in per capita wealth. It had as many newspapers as London did, among them the first Spanish-language daily in the United States. New Orleans's population and outlook were decidedly cosmopolitan. In the words of one poet,

> Have you ever been in New Orleans? If not, you'd better go,
> It's a nation of a queer place; day and night a show!
> Frenchmen, Spaniards, West Indians, Creoles, Mustees,
> Yankees, Kentuckians, Tennesseans, lawyers and trustees. . .

This population was eager for foreign news. In 1838, the year after its founding, the *Picayune* filled about 55 percent of its total news hole with reports from abroad, an extraordinary amount compared to most other newspapers. The *Charleston Courier,* which had made a name for itself in foreign news in another coastal city, devoted only 16.5 percent of its news hole to such coverage. Being located on the rim of the Gulf of Mexico, New Orleans had special interest in the war with Mexico and was well positioned as a conduit for news from the front. About forty-five hundred Louisianans fought in the Mexican campaign. One company of Louisiana soldiers had twenty printers, four of whom became notable correspondents for the *Delta* and the *Picayune.*

Even before the war, Kendall's upstart newspaper stood out. The *Picayune* took its name from a silver coin worth 6¼ cents, which was the street price of the newspaper. The name of the *Picayune*—which has been attributed to the French, Italian, and Caribbean languages as well as Spanish—was a nod to the international flavor of the city; the newspaper's price was a nod to New Orleans's competitive commercial environment. If the *Picayune* was not literally a penny paper, that was a mere technicality. It was the first newspaper to sell for less than a dime in New Orleans, a city that had a higher cost of living than New York; and whatever its cost, the *Picayune*'s temperament was that of Bennett's penny press *New York Herald.* Kendall's instinct was to "interest and amuse." His paper paid attention to local happenings, crusaded against dueling and other social evils, and ridiculed competitors. Reminiscent of Bennett's beating by one of his competitors, the publisher of the rival *Bee* thrashed Kendall's partner.

Kendall also put a premium on providing news quickly. He chafed particularly at the slow, uncertain pace of mail, which sometimes brought five days worth of news from the north all at once or delivered it soaked through despite the use

---

Post. Although Robinson preceded Kendall, he never actually saw a battle, which would make him less of a *war* correspondent. Gruneisen's reports lacked urgency, which undermines his candidacy. Other candidates have also been mentioned in passing. Historian Robert Desmond suggested that the *Swedish Intelligencer* sent the first war correspondent into the field with the forces of King Gustavus Adolphus in 1807; the reporter's name, alas, is forgotten.

THE PICAYUNE.

[NO. 72, CAMP STREET.]

By F. A. LUMSDEN & G. W. KENDALL.

Friday Evening, October 20, 1837.

Our Horse.

Just look at him—see how he bounds o'er hedge and stile—see how his legs fly and never touch the ground —observe how the Bee and Bulletin are in pursuit of him—see how our printer's devil hails him with the greeting of "go it Pic.!"—look what a good humored rider he has—see how he cracks his whip and leaves his pursuers in the lurch—observe his look of independence—scan his eye glistening with fun and pleasure—now just look at the flush of conscious victory which plays upon his brow as he lets fly the streamer bearing the words "you're all too late—my news is for the Picayune!" And that is the way the Picayune will do business this winter. It will be the first to publish all news, commercial, political, and foreign. Our horse is a capital animal—we are delighted with him. Mr. Gibson's horse used to run last winter an *hour* in thirty minutes; our horse will go it in 22 minutes precisely. It is thus that we will outrun all our neighbors and instil new life and vigor into the press of New Orleans.

"Our Horse," a woodcut, was published October 20, 1837, the year George Wilkins Kendall and his partner started the *Picayune,* a newspaper that earned considerable fame for the speed with which it brought the news to its readers. Courtesy of *New Orleans Times-Picayune.*

of rubber bags. Of the U.S. postmaster general, a distant cousin, he wrote, "Amos Kendall, from whom great things were hoped, treats us in the same scurvy manner as did his predecessor." As early as 1837, the *Picayune* arranged its own private express, which it later advertised with a large illustration, "Our Horse." "Our animal," Kendall wrote the following year, "got in last night about 12:30, leaving cousin Amos's horse nowhere. The news brought by our high pressure conveyances is of tremendous importance."

When the Mexican War broke out, the *Picayune* created a relay system to get news from the battlefields. "Mr. Kendall's Express" began with riders carrying dispatches to the Mexican coast. Regular mail boats carried the news onward to New Orleans. When the newspaper was especially eager to get a jump on competitors, it sent a small, fast steamer fitted out with typesetting equipment to meet the mail boat. By the time the steamer reached New Orleans, the dispatches were ready for the printing press. Kendall's system was hazardous and, as he ruefully reported in the *Picayune* in August 1847, expensive.

> I wrote to you a short time since that I had dispatched a man to Vera Cruz with letters, and that after his departure I was obliged, in virtue of a verbal contract, to pay all the expenses of his family during his absence, to keep a candle continually burning and have a *función* performed in one of the churches for his safety and *buen viaje*. I have just learned that the fellow was captured on the road by the guerrilleros, stripped, beat most unmercifully, his horse—I paid for the animal—taken from him, and was then turned loose to make the best of his way back to Puebla. The story of his adventures and capture is most amusing, and I will give it if ever I live to get home; at present I will only say that I thought the family made too much fuss from the first.

The rider was luckier than some. "Mr. Kendall," the *Picayune* reported a few days before, "perseveres in sending couriers to Vera Cruz, though he has had three captured. One has been killed."

Toward the end of the war, correspondent James L. "Mustang" Freaner set up an express service for the *Delta*. It could not best Kendall's, whose reports reached New Orleans from Monterrey, deep inside Mexico, in the amazing time of eight days.

From New Orleans the *Picayune*'s accounts leaped northward, sped along by other newspapers eager to be first with the news. The *Baltimore Sun*, whose work was especially noteworthy, had its own Special Overland Express, which made the trip from New Orleans to Washington in six days. The newspaper made good use of a fledgling technology, the telegraph, whose first experimental line was strung between Washington and Baltimore in 1844, thus allowing the *Sun* to acquire war news virtually as quickly as the capital did. "Neither wind nor weather, tide, or storm, or the heat of the Southern sun, it seems," boasted the *Sun*, "can dampen the spirits or clog the heels of our 'go-ahead' team of 'express ponies.'"

In the run-up to the war and through the conflict, a variety of other alliances took shape. The *New York Sun* took the lead in creating a cooperative arrangement with the *Charleston Courier* and three other papers. The *Herald* combined with the *New York Journal of Commerce* and the *New Orleans Crescent City*. Later the *Herald* joined with Baltimore's paper. The *New York Sun* paid a seven-hundred-dollar bonus for every successful express run between Mobile and Montgomery. Thanks to the ponies, fast boats, and telegraph lines, news reached New York one or two days ahead of the mail.

Because Kendall was so far ahead of the competition in Mexico, Yankee newspapers reprinted *Picayune* reports more frequently than those from any other New Orleans newspapers. As the *Charleston Courier* put it, the *Picayune* was the best informed "on all matters" about the war. Meanwhile, the ever-eager *Picayune* had New Orleans's most up-to-date market quotations and commercial news from the north.

Kendall's family considered him "a law unto himself." Never shy about his opinions, he displayed intense nationalism in his reports. Nevertheless, he did what the best war correspondents do: saw the action for himself and reported it. The general public did not have to rely on official reports to know what happened. His accounts of the Battle of Cerro Gordo, fought in mid-April 1847, listed casualties and, as evidenced by the May 1 dispatch below, provided colorful detail. Kendall supplemented one report with a map that sketched the battle. Lithographers in New York, competing to produce timely current-events prints on the fighting, drew on Kendall's descriptive reporting.

Another Glorious Victory ! ! !

Battle of Cerro Gordo.

. . . .

CAMP NEAR PLAN DEL RIO,
April 18—1 o'clock, P. M.

The American arms have achieved another glorious and most brilliant victory. Outnumbering Gen. Scott's force materially, and occupying positions which looked impregnable as Gibraltar, one after another of their works have been taken to-day, five generals, colonels enough to command ten such armies as ours, and other officers innumerable, have been taken prisoners, together with 6000 men, and the rest of their army driven and routed with the loss of every thing, ammunition, cannon, baggage train, *all*. Nothing but the impossibility of finding a road for the dragoons to the rear of the enemy's works saved any part of Santa Anna's grand army, including his own illustrious person.

Among the prisoners is our old friend La Vega, who fought with his accustomed gallantry. The other generals are Jose Maria Jarero, Luis Pinzon, Manuel Noriega, and Jose Obando. The names of the colonels I have not been able to gather. Nothing saved Santa Anna but the want of dragoons on the other side of their lines. As it is, his traveling coach, together with all his papers, valuables, and even his *wooden-leg,* have fallen into our hands, together with all the money of his army. No one anticipated, when they arose from their hard bivouack this morning, such a complete victory.

The loss on both sides has been heavy—how could it have been otherwise? The rough and rocky road, cut through rugged defiles and dense chaparral by our troops is now lined with our wounded. The Rifles, Col. Haskell's Tennessee volunteers, the 1st Artillery, the 7th Infantry, and Capt. Williams company of Kentucky volunteers have perhaps suffered most. Gen. Shields was severely wounded, and I am fearful, mortally wounded, while gallantly leading his brigade to storm one of the enemy's farthest works. Gen. Pillow was also wounded, all though slightly, while storming a fortification on this side commanded by La Vega. All the field officers of Col. Haskell's regiment were wounded at the same time, save himself. Of the Rifles, Capt. Mason has lost a leg, Lieut. Ewell has been badly wounded, Lieut. McLane, slightly. I have already mentioned the gallant Maj. Sumner and other officers wounded yesterday.

I have specified some regiments above which signalized themselves: it happened to be their fortune, in the disposition of the battle, to fall upon what all good soldiers may term pleasant places—the most difficult works to storm—and bravely and without faltering did they execute the perilous duties assigned them. At 1 o'clock this afternoon Gen. Twiggs, whose division has been in the hardest of it, was pursuing the flying enemy towards Jalapa. Pinzon, who commanded the forts nearest the Plan del Rio, asked of Gen. Worth time to consider before he capitulated. Desirous to come to terms, Gen. Worth gave him *fifteen minutes,* and he surrendered unconditionally! Had he not done so the slaughter would have been terrible.

I write in great haste, and have no time for particulars. The names of the killed and wounded I will ascertain as soon as possible. I think that five hundred will cover our entire loss. Had it not have been for the positive cowardice of Santa Anna and Canalizo, who ran, before the battle—at least in brave men's hands—was half lost, it would have been far greater. No one, at present, can estimate the loss of the Mexicans—they are scattered on the hills, in the roads, everywhere.

What disposition Gen. Scott is to make of the prisoners is yet unknown. He may set them all at liberty on their paroles, from the difficulty of feeding them, and to accelerate his own advance movements. We shall hear by tomorrow. I wish he could send the officers at least to the United States, for there is a fine string of them.

It is now impossible to name officers who have distinguished themselves. I cannot however omit to mention Cols. Harney, Riley, and Childs, of the regulars; Cols. Baker, Forman and Haskell, of the volunteers, as every one is talking of them.

I write this in great haste, and with noise, confusion and every thing else around me. You cannot appreciate the victory. To describe the ground and fortifications of the enemy, the difficulty of turning their outer works, and the toil and peril undergone by the troops were impossible.

No time to say another word. I shall send this off by express. It is Gen. Scott's intention, I know, to push on towards the city of Mexico with all haste. To-morrow I will write more fully, and send by Gen. Scott's express.

Yours, G.W.K.

In the Treaty of Hidalgo ending the war, Mexico ceded its claims to Texas north of the Rio Grande as well as to California and New Mexico territories. The United States grew by more than 1 million square miles. With the war over, Kendall pledged never again to "put myself in the way of whistling bullets in foreign countries," but he soon broke his vow. On an extended vacation in Europe, where he arranged for publication of his heavily illustrated account of the war, he could not resist covering political upheavals in England, France, Hamburg, and Brussels. Upon returning with a French wife, Kendall bought a Texas ranch that introduced sheep farming to the state. Before his death in 1867, the Texas legislature named a county after him. G.W.K. maintained his financial interest in the *Picayune,* temporarily returning to New Orleans to edit the paper and continuing to file stories from Texas.

Kendall's energetic, firsthand graphic reporting in the field with U.S. forces "was new to American journalism," wrote James Gordon Bennett's managing editor, Frederic Hudson. So was the premium placed on speedy transmission. Jour-

George Wilkins Kendall. From Bullard, *Famous War Correspondents.*

54

nalism was becoming a business, not a politically subsidized enterprise. The market value of news—and newspapers—was increasingly tied to how *new* the news really was. The fresher, the more readers and the more profit. "Rapidly as our press works," the *Picayune* proudly wrote during the Mexican War, "throwing off between five and six thousand sheets a hour, we began to despair of ever satisfying the demand for it."

Bennett and others enthusiastically talked about "the annihilation" of time and space. In Bennett's mind, the far-reaching communications validated the American impulse to acquire more of the North American continent, starting with Texas. At the same time editors had to face the reality that moving news over long distances was expensive. The *Baltimore Sun* is believed to have spent $1,000 a month on its Overland Express. Newspapers could have avoided the costs if all had agreed to be slow. But once speed became possible, speed became imperative as well. The only way to reduce costs—and avoid being beaten—was to pool resources for much of the routine distant news, leaving it to individual newspapers to deploy their own reporters to cover selected stories or regions of importance to their readers.

Some date the beginning of the Associated Press with the cooperative agreement started by the *New York Sun* to get news from the front during the Mexican War. In 1848, another date given for the AP's founding, newspapers agreed to share telegraphic transmission of foreign news received from ships arriving at Boston. In these early arrangements, the AP did not station correspondents overseas. All its foreign news efforts were devoted to dominating the dissemination of such news within the United States by organizing schemes to meet ships in Halifax, to move the information onward with such traditional tricks as carrier pigeons, to hook up with telegraph lines whenever possible, and to develop sharing arrangements with similar services overseas.* The goal in its foreign news was speed and reliability, not original news-gathering.

The prospect for accelerating the overseas news flow took a giant leap forward with the completion in 1858 of a transatlantic cable. The first news story carried on August 23 over the wires to the United States was addressed to the AP and printed in the *New York Sun*: "Emperor of France returned to Paris Saturday. King of Prus-

---

* In 1870 three European news agencies—the British Reuters, the French Havas, and the German Wolff—divided up the world into cartels in which each had a monopoly over selling its services in its country and its country's colonies. Each service placed bureaus in its regions and made its reports available to the other cartels. The AP became part of the arrangement, with its domain being the United States. It was regarded as a decidedly junior partner by the European threesome, who had less interest in news from the United States than AP did in their news fare. After the Spanish-American War, when the United States became a world power, the AP began to extend its global reach. By 1905 it had 6 overseas bureaus (which during this time it called "foreign offices," and which does not include places where it may have had a smaller presence as a result, say, of using stringers), in 1915 the number reached 11, and in 1930 it was 19, according to AP annual reports in its archives. Not until the 1930s did the AP break the cartel entirely and begin to sell its services abroad, a move that opened the way to establishing an even greater overseas presence. In 2009 it had 102 bureaus abroad. Background on the news cartel with Havas, Wolff, and Reuters is in Read, *The Power of News*, 53–58, 80–82.

sia too ill to visit Queen Victoria. Her majesty returns to England August 31st. Settlement of Chinese question. Chinese empire opens to trade; Christian religion allowed; foreign diplomatic agents admitted; indemnity to England and France. Gwalior insurgent army broken up.* All India becoming tranquil."

Soon afterward that cable line went permanently dead. Eight years later, however, a new "ocean greyhound" hummed with foreign news that was retransmitted inside the United States. The planet was about to be crosshatched with cables. Lines were strung between Dover and Calais (these were the very first submarine lines, completed in 1851), between Sweden and Denmark, between Ceylon and India, between Java and Port Darwin in Australia, and, in 1874, between Europe and Brazil. From 1868 to 1890, the miles of wire on Western Union poles inside the United States increased from 97,594 to 933,153, and by 1900 some fifteen hundred "brass pounders" tapped out news for the Associated Press. The *Picayune* averaged fourteen thousand words of telegraph copy every day by 1892.

The terms of foreign reporting had changed. Quasi-correspondent James M. Bradford had distinguished himself journalistically during the Battle of New Orleans by taking a break from fighting to report what he had seen. In this new era such half measures were passé. George W. Kendall, a transition figure, might hanker to fight as well as write, but the latter was his priority. And soon correspondents accepted as a matter of course that they should train every ounce of energy on reporting news as quickly and resourcefully as Kendall had.

As with all revolutions, there was much more to do after the old system was pronounced dead. In order to achieve serious foreign coverage, newspapers had to hire their own staff correspondents who could write lively, fact-based accounts that people wanted to read and who possessed ingenuity and organizational skills to run permanent bureaus that took advantage of modern communications. The AP did not establish overseas bureaus until decades later, but the full-time correspondents sent abroad by individual newspapers began to set them up on a limited basis. None of the "specials"—as such representatives of individual newspapers were called—was more a master of "methods," as he called them, than George Smalley of the *New York Tribune,* a daily that led the way in creating specialized reporters.

* This refers to the final stages of the Indian Mutiny, which began the previous year and ended with a final rebel stand at Gwalior.

6

FOREIGN COMMISSIONER FOR THE *TRIBUNE*

Mr. Smalley sails for Europe today to act as Foreign Commissioner
for the *Tribune,* resident in London.

New York Tribune

In late 1866 George Washburn Smalley returned from covering the Austro-Prussian War for the *New York Tribune.* In this, his first overseas assignment, Smalley displayed characteristic enterprise by obtaining a rare interview with Chancellor Bismarck of Germany. The story caused a sensation in the United States. Fresh from that triumph, Smalley proposed the novel idea that the *Tribune* post someone in London to manage all its foreign news out of Europe. London, he argued, was the ideal spot because it "must become the distributing centre of European news for America." John Russell Young, the managing editor, at first demurred. He thought such an outpost would be too independent of New York. On reflection, though, he agreed that having a reporter in London would give the *Tribune* an advantage over its rivals. Young offered Smalley the job. On May 11, 1867, the newspaper printed the announcement above that he was sailing for London.

G.W.S., as his dispatches were signed, represented another advance in foreign news-gathering. Unlike Kendall, Smalley became a career foreign correspondent, permanently based abroad. As what would be called today a bureau chief, he brought his expertise and pluck to bear on the task of organizing coverage of the news abroad, a challenge that has remained with journalism right up to the present day.

"The duties of Mr. Smalley in this position are no sinecure," reported the *Tribune* in 1869, eager to make the most of having installed its own man in Pall Mall offices in London.

He has to make himself familiar with the course of public events, not only in England, but throughout Europe. Every important point is to be watched by him as carefully, as are the proceedings of the New-York Common Council by your city reporters. He has even to anticipate the progress of affairs, and dispatch one of his staff of correspondents to the spot, wherever a significant movement or disclosure may be expected. His knowledge of American politics is, of course, highly valuable to our friends among the public men of England, who amid the clamor of parties and the collision of opinions, often find it difficult to obtain a comprehensive view of the situation, and are thankful to receive more light from an authority which they have learned to rely on with greater confidence than on either the dispatches of the Atlantic telegraph, or the anonymous American correspondence of the London press. Mr. Smalley is on intimate terms with several of the British statesmen and journalists, who have been most prominent in their support of American interests, and they make his office a place of frequent and familiar resort.

Horace Greeley founded the *Tribune* in 1841 as an alternative to the more sensationalist penny papers of the time. Although not above using a good murder to raise circulation, he set a relatively lofty tone and in other respects pointed toward greater professionalism. Greeley had an eye for newspaper organization and specialization. By the mid-1850s, the *Tribune* had ten editors and more than a dozen reporters, as well as staff members devoted to editorial writing and book reviewing. Greeley is credited with hiring the first American managing editor, Charles A. Dana, who is singled out sometimes as the first syndicated foreign correspondent. In 1848 and 1849, Dana reported for the *Tribune* and four other newspapers from Paris, Berlin, and London.

Greeley had an eye for newspaper organization and specialization, as it clear from this Mathew Brady photo. Seated from left to right are George M. Snow, financial editor; Bayard Taylor, who was a correspondent overseas while on the staff; Horace Greeley; George Ripley, literary editor. Standing, left to right, William Henry Fry, music editor; Charles A. Dana, who was a foreign correspondent during his long career; and Henry J. Raymond, who went on to co-found the *New York Times*. Library of Congress.

Greeley's staff was considered brilliant, in many cases transcending pure jour-nalism. This assessment held for those whom he paid to provide news and com-ment from abroad. Dana was a serious linguist, with some command of French, Gaelic, German, Russian, Norwegian, and Italian, the latter sufficient to read Dante in the original. Poet and inveterate traveler Bayard Taylor disengaged from wan-derings in Egypt to report Matthew Perry's opening of Japan to trade in 1853. He later covered the thousandth anniversary of Iceland. Taylor eventually became a U.S. minister to Germany. Englishman Thomas Hughes, the author of *Tom Brown's School Days* and a member of Parliament, wrote for Greeley's newspaper from time to time, as did novelist Thomas Trollope, the brother of the more famous writer Anthony. American novelist Henry James reported from Paris during one period; George William Curtis, who with others on the staff was a member of the utopian Brook Farm experiment, sent stories from Italy. He later became editor of *Harper's Weekly* and one of the country's most respected "liberal reformers."

Margaret Fuller was a star, literally, as Greeley used that symbol for the byline at the bottom of her stories. She was one of the first women to work on an Ameri-can newspaper, writing on social, political, and literary issues. Her star, as one bi-ographer has noted, "signaled the first serious book review section in the country." In 1846 she became America's first female foreign correspondent, having an un-derstanding with Greeley that she would write occasional articles for the *Tribune* while she was in Europe. Her first-person European "letters" spanned subjects as diverse as art galleries and slums. In Italy she was swept up in the revolution to cre-ate a unified republic independent of Austria. "What shall I write of Rome in these sad but glorious days?" she told readers when the infant republic fell. "Plain facts are the best; for my feelings I could not find fit words." With her infant son and the son's Italian father (it was never clear whether they had married), she died in a shipwreck on a trip home in 1850.

Karl Marx, based in London and toiling on *Das Kapital,* was a regular contrib-utor, or so the *Tribune* thought. Marx sent in almost five hundred articles during the decade he was attached to the *Tribune,* and cashed all the checks that came in return mail. But his colleague Friedrich Engels was the author of about one-fourth of the stories. The *Tribune* published some of this work as its own editorial com-ment, for Greeley was not a tool of capitalism. He supported cooperatives, labor unions, free homesteading, socialist community experiments, and vegetarianism. Over time, though, he grew disenchanted with Marx (and Engels), and the feeling was mutual. Complaining that Greeley did not give him more money, Marx called the *Tribune "Das Lauseblatt,"* "that lousy rag."*

---

* A century later, when the *New York Tribune* had become the *Herald Tribune,* its Moscow corre-spondent Stuart Loory thought it would be a nice touch to hang a poster of his fellow correspondent Karl Marx in the foyer of his office. When Loory arranged a small party to celebrate the arrival of a telex machine to his office, the deputy director of the Foreign Ministry's press operation showed up and admired the picture. Too bad Greeley hadn't given Marx a five-dollar raise, Loory told the official visitor; it would have saved the world from Communism. The official was not amused. Stuart Loory, interview by author, January 13, 2005.

One of Greeley's social causes, the abolition of slavery, attracted Smalley to the paper. Smalley had fallen "under the spell" of abolitionist Wendell Phillips and married his adopted daughter. Not interested in practicing law, for which he was trained, and eager to see the Civil War, he used his father-in-law's connections with the *Tribune* to find a position as a reporter.

When Smalley became a *Tribune* foreign correspondent, Greeley instructed him to write on "social movements and other matters beside politics and literature." While Smalley made politics an indispensable part of his job, he was happy to have a broad canvas on which to work. He wrote widely admired personality profiles of politicians, explorers, clergymen, and educators and of artists, actors, and musicians. In a pair of articles that appeared on the same day, he commented on the unveiling of a statue in London, government concessions to the Irish church, failures of the British press in business reporting, a woman's suffrage meeting, a meeting of representatives from Britain's Pacific colonies, and a British publisher's plan to expand book sales in the United States. The latter ended with Smalley's observation that the United States should honor international copyright instead of allowing its publishers to pirate foreign books.

Although adept at an unhurried letter style of reporting for routine news, Smalley thought "time is everything in journalism." He deemed the *Times* of London correspondent William Howard Russell's celebrated reporting on the Crimean War in the 1850s "not exactly journalism. It had little to do with that speed and accuracy in the collection and transmission of news which, after all, must be the chief business of a correspondent."

Smalley's intense determination made him famous early in his career, when he covered the Civil War. After the Battle of Antietam, a bloody affair in which the Union eked out a victory, he rode thirty miles through most of the night to the nearest telegraph office. The telegraph operator agreed to send a short dispatch but could not promise when—or even if—it would arrive at the *Tribune* since the military controlled the wires. The exhausted correspondent hopped a train to Baltimore and fell asleep en route. When he pulled into Baltimore, he had not yet written his full dispatch and, still not trusting the wires, decided to take a second train to New York. Standing under the light of a dim oil lamp that night, he wrote his full narrative of the battle in pencil. As it turned out, Smalley's original brief story had been delayed reaching New York. When he showed up the next morning in the *Tribune* offices at 152 Nassau St., cheering compositors were waiting for his copy. Just two mornings after the battle, *Tribune* customers read what many historians consider the best battle account of the war.

Smalley's vision of quality correspondence was not limited to the reliable delivery of news by a lone reporter. He appreciated the need to organize foreign newsgathering by teams to achieve depth and breadth in reporting as well as speed. A notable example of these "methods," as Smalley called them, came early in his tenure as London bureau chief. At the outbreak of the Franco-Prussian War of 1870–71, Smalley balked at instructions from New York sending him to Berlin, where he would have been a reporter. He elected, instead, to stay in London, where he was able to coordinate reporting. He hired two good correspondents—a Frenchman to cover the French side and an Englishman to cover the German side. Smalley told his correspondents they could telegraph news of preliminary engagements; but when it came to news of major battles, they were not to trust the telegraph. After sending no more than a summary report by wire, the correspondents were to hurry immediately to London, writing while they traveled as he had done with his Antietam report. "There was never much chance of sending the full story by wire from the battlefield or from any town hard by," Smalley said, "nor, indeed, from any capital; even from a neutral capital. Only when once in London was a correspondent master of the situation." Smalley further added to his method by establishing a pool arranged with the *London Daily News,* whose correspondent Archibald Forbes also was crafty. Forbes carefully mapped out a communication system involving field-post wagons, trains, and telegraph transmission, ensuring that any story he filed near Paris reached London within twenty-four hours. The *Tribune* and the *London Daily News* bested the *Times* and its great reporter William Howard Russell.

The *Tribune*'s cable fees for the Franco-Prussian War mounted up to a whopping $125,000. "It was the cable which first taught us to condense," Smalley said of the high cost of cable transmission. The *Tribune* urged reporters to use cable only for the most urgent stories, a refrain that echoed down the years at other newspapers as well. Smalley's discursive letter-style reports came to New York the cheap way, by mail. But it was not wars alone that merited the expense of cabling. Answering a letter from Smalley, who had expressed concern that foreign news was becoming less important to the newspaper, editor Whitelaw Reid acknowledged that he did "not wish to enlarge our correspondences from Europe in a more routine way." Smalley, however, was not to hesitate "whenever a good thing can be had at extra expense." One such good thing, Reid noted, was the upcoming Harvard-Oxford boat race for which "we will depend on you for our regular and full account."

The "war on the Thames," as it was called, was a foretaste of the 1974 Muhammad Ali–George Foreman "fight of the century" in Zaire and other international media extravaganzas involving sport in the twentieth century. An estimated 1 million people lined the Thames to watch the race. The pre- and post-race reporting went on for days. Smalley, who had been a member of the first Yale crew to challenge Harvard and therefore something of an authority on the sport, held forth with the rest of them, speculating on fair play, rowing styles, and athletes' diets. Reporters ruminated on each of the countries' respective characteristics, at least as viewed by the other. One commentator thought the Harvard rowers "resembled North American Indians." When the race was over and the British had won, the *Times* of London exulted, "The surrender of BURGOYNE or CORNWALLIS, the reluctant recognition of the United States, becomes a trifle in comparison with what our defeat would have been."

In covering the race, Smalley employed the ingenuity and "method" that characterized his war reporting. He rehearsed telegraphic operators and hired William Blaikie, secretary of the Harvard Boat Club, and English novelists Charles Reade and Thomas Hughes to supplement his own reporting. Unfortunately for Smalley, all his organization and precaution fell apart because of a weak link that he did not foresee.

As a matter of policy, the bureaucratic Anglo-American telegraph office refused to take copy directly; all dispatches had to pass through one of two inland British telegraph offices. Accordingly, after the Friday race, Smalley brought his full story on the event to the British and Magnetic office on Threadneedle Street himself and left it with a boy at the counter—the weak link. The boy was to copy the report and walk it to the Anglo-American office two minutes away for transmission. Not sharing Smalley's sense of urgency, he delayed making the copy until early the next morning. Smalley's story did not arrive in New York in time for the Saturday newspaper, forcing the *Tribune* to use news association dispatches. Not having a Sunday edition, the *Tribune* was unable to run Smalley's story until Monday, August 30, by which time its value as news had diminshed. The *Tribune* editorial page described the dispatch as "an interesting and animated account."

This was not the end of Smalley's woes. He complained that *Tribune* editors "mutilated" his copy. He had problems with the local talent he had hired—as, indeed, many bureau chiefs had in the coming years. (See "Managing Local Correspondents," p. 60.) In this case, Smalley complained that Blaikie, whose hiring was Reid's idea, "behaved badly" by not coming through with the stories he was supposed to write. Reade failed too. An enthusiastic Harvard supporter, he claimed he was too despondent over the race to put anything on paper and, anyway, figured the *Tribune* really wouldn't want anything from him in view of the defeat. "You may laugh at me if you like," Smalley wrote to Reid, "but the disaster was a blow to me which I have not got over. It left me unfit to do anything but sit on the beach at Dieppe* and curse the idiot who caused it."

In the letters that flew back and forth across the Atlantic for some weeks, Reid had complaints of his own. He was not happy that the British cable office gave Smalley only a credit, not a cash refund, for its "outrageous blunder." He told Smalley to threaten that the *Tribune* would write unflattering stories "concerning drunkenness in their office." Perhaps this tactic worked, for the money was returned. Reid also was angry with Smalley for airing his gripes about the editing of his copy to the British press and, to add insult to injury, wondered if Smalley's long dispatch should have been longer.

With all this, Reid considered the dispatch "incomparably greater to anything furnished in any of the New York papers." And it was, truly, a tour de force. Smalley's stroke-by-stroke recap of the race—written quickly—was stirring, vivid, and filled with the statistical detail and second-guessing that consumes sports fans.

* A French town on the English Channel whose eight miles of beach made it a fashionable resort spot.

MANAGING LOCAL CORRESPONDENTS

After the Spanish-American War, when the Associated Press began to venture overseas to do its own reporting, it encountered difficulties lining up local correspondents who could fill in the holes, especially when important news broke. The AP's in-house organ, the *Service Bulletin of the Associated Press,* often focused on the problem. Here is an excerpt from a 1912 letter from a correspondent in Mexico City to the home office.

COVERING THE NEWS IN MEXICO

One of the greatest difficulties encountered in covering news throughout the republic of Mexico is the almost complete absence of men with any newspaper training or news sense, as viewed from an American standpoint.

Mexican correspondents, who appear to serve well enough Mexican newspapers, invariably miss the point of a story, or bury it in such a mass of verbiage that one is left in doubt as to what actually occurred. If not this, then their reports are so biased by their prejudices that they are likely to represent their personal views.

As an example of the latter, an intelligent appearing Mexican was furnished by the Mexico office with credentials to represent THE ASSOCIATED PRESS in Sinaloa and Sonora, soon after the close of the Madero revolution. He was given explicit instructions as to the class of matter wanted, and particularly warned against sending anything in the nature of propaganda for any political fraction or party.

In due time this correspondent began filing matter from various points in Sinaloa, which at first appeared to be legitimate accounts of clashes between Maderista rurales and insurrectos against the Madero government. Later his despatches aroused suspicion by taking on a viciously partisan tone, and from the fact that notes were appended asking that they be passed along to a certain cabinet minister.

Then his despatches ceased to come. Later, by mail, a letter was received, written by the correspondent from a prison in Mazatlan, stating that he had been arrested as a Reyista spy and agitator, had been beaten, condemned to death twice and twice reprieved at the last minute, tied to a cart-wheel all day in the broiling sun, at Culiacan, and conveyed to the prison at Mazatlan.

After several weeks he wrote again from a prison at Aguas-Calientes, asking for a folding bed, some underwear, and a few minor comforts.

Early in March he called at THE ASSOCIATED PRESS office in Mexico City, relating a long tale of heart-breaking experiences, and had no hesitancy in admitting that he was all that he had been charged with being. He left, intending to return the following day for some clothing that was promised him, and has not been heard from since.

---

* The revolution started by Francisco I. Madero, who served as president for fifteen months beginning in November 1911.

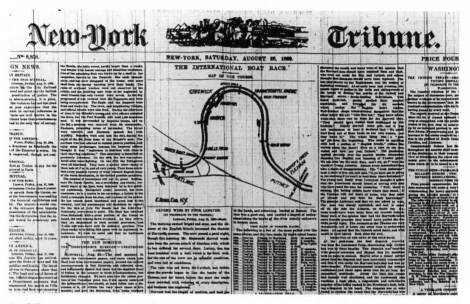

As if illustrating a military battle, the *Tribune* ran a front-page map of the Harvard-Oxford race along the Thames. It appeared on a Saturday, the day after the race, along with a news association account of the event because Smalley's was delayed.

THE INTERNATIONAL RACE.

◆

[The general story of the great International Race was graphically told in THE TRIBUNE of Saturday. The following dispatch, however, in which (though now forty-eight hours old) the American public will still receive the first coherent and satisfactory detailed account, should have reached us in ample time for Saturday's paper, having been filed in the London office—with wires clear for its reception—at 7 o'clock (N.Y. time) Friday evening. We await the result of investigations now in progress, before informing the public whom they have to thank for this wretched delay.—Ed.]

———

[BY TELEGRAPH TO THE TRIBUNE]

LONDON, Friday, Aug. 27—MIDNIGHT.

The defeat of the Harvards in the international boat race was less than reported. As reckoned on the press boat it appeared to be four lengths, and so I telegraphed; but the judge at Mortlake, Sir Aubrey Paul, personally informs me that the actual difference at the finish was but one length and a half. The time, too, given in my first dispatch was incorrect. The true time was 20 minutes 20 seconds and three-fifths, as taken by Frodaliam's chronograph,* registering independent fifths of seconds. This is nearly 21 seconds less than the time given by the London reporters, but I took it myself, and am confident it is accurate.

At noon the crowds began to collect, and at 3 o'clock were streaming densely over Putney Bridge and along the river sides. Fleets of steamers and small boats

* A stopwatch.

passed up stream with the tide, gay with flags and glancing oars—flags, unhappily, nearly all dark blue.* It was rare that Harvard's crimson colors enlivened the monotony. The morning was clear and hot, but the wind came sweeping far too freshly up from below the bridge. Luckily, however, it blew in the best direction, coming aft for the boats; yet still in one or two reaches it threatened mischief. Before the start it died partly away, and the race was rowed on good water throughout.

The vicinity of the White House, Harvard's head-quarters, was early thronged with Americans, but the morning was left judiciously quiet, only a few old Harvard oars—prominent among whom were Caspar and Crowninshield—a few official representatives like Moran and Dudley, and a few personal friends of the crew, being admitted; no others were allowed access. The crew lounged restlessly about, enduring as best they might a trial harder than the race—the suspense of the last few hours. Their condition was less perfect than three days ago. Simmons had been for some time suffering from diarrhea—slight, yet sufficiently alarming in a man soon to pull as for dear life in a desperate struggle. Loring was still troubled with boils, and was sallow-face, but clear-eyed and confident as ever. Fay and Lyman were both overtrained. There was too much work during the whole of last week for all the crew, and as a consequence they went into the boat only half fit.

Before 5, all London had gathered on the river banks. Both crews came out promptly, Oxford showing first three minutes before 5, and Harvard following.

The crews and weights were:

OXFORD

1. F. Nillan, Exeter, 164 pounds.
2. A. C. Yarborough, Lincoln, 170 pounds.
3. J. C. Tinne, University, 190 pounds.
3[*sic*]. G. D. Darbishire, Balliol, stroke, 160 pounds.
J. H. Hall, Corpus, coxswain, 100 pounds.

HARVARD

1. J. G. Fay, Boston, 159 pounds.
2. F. O. Lyman, Hawaain [*sic*] Islands, 157 pounds.
3. W. H. Simmons, Concord, 171 pounds.
4. A. P. Loring, Boston, stroke, 156 pounds.
A. Burnham, Chicago, coxswain, 112 pounds.

Harvard was much the lighter, and, as it proved, was much deficient in what had been thought it excelled—its staying power. Tom Hughes† was the referee. Chitty was Oxford's umpire; Gulston of the "London Rowing Club," Harvard's, and Blaikie acted as starter. The arrangement of the Thames Conservatory

* Oxford's colors were blue; Harvard's were crimson, derived from brilliant red silk handkerchiefs worn by a rowing crew in 1858.

† This is the same Hughes who was a novelist and special correspondent for Smalley.

Board and police for a clear course were admirable, and there was no trouble except with one row boat for a moment, which was finally got away. No steamers were allowed to follow the crews, but those containing the umpire and representatives of the press.

Sixty tickets were issued by each crew. Harvard invited Mr. Motley, but too late. Mr. Motley was at the time in Devonshire, ten miles from a railway station, and much regretted his absence. All the American tickets of invitation were sent out late, and there were, consequently, many disappointments. Among those on board were Charles Reade, who has invited Harvard to Oxford next week, the London Rowing Club officers, Moran Sturgis, Dudley, Morgan, Wilkes, Crowninshield, Shattuck, Bowditch and Ticknor.

On the press-boat no fewer than fifteen American journals were represented. Dickens* was invited, but was compelled to decline. Cox, Conway, Dicey, and other well-known journalists were on board, the arrangements being excellently managed by Wormalds of *Bell's Life*. Oxford limited their invitations to personal friends, and refused to ask the Prince of Wales.

To avoid possible difficulties, the whole of the course to be rowed over was planned and discussed in advance, between Referee, Umpires, and Coxswains, and a perfect understanding arrived at. To this is probably due the fact that no foul occurred at any one critical point. Oxford's conduct was fair on all points. Mr. Chitty is a most accomplished oarsman, and the umpires conciliated everybody by their good sense and good will. The start was made well in mid-stream, the umpire and press boats hugging the Middlesex shore. Harvard having won the toss, chose the Middlesex side, which is always reckoned an advantage.

Both crews were cheered as they came out, and there was an unmistakable popular liking for both. Harvard, with bronzed faces and arms, contrasted strangely with Oxford's fair or ruddy complexions. In paddling down into the place, the style, as always, was all on the side of Oxford, but the American physique excited universal admiration.

The boats started abreast of the umpire's steamer. Blaikie gave the word "Go" at exactly five hours, fourteen minutes forty-one seconds and two-fifths. The tide had almost ceased running up and the whole race was rowed on nearly slack water. Harvard jumped away almost immediately to lead, drawing away from Oxford amid loud cheers and rowing well together and in better form than ever before. At Craven Cottage they were full half a length ahead, and thence to Crab Tree kept steadily gaining. Both crews were doing all they wanted; but Oxford, which was never under any stress, increasing its measured stroke of forty to the minute, rowed with precision beyond all praise. Darbishire is like a machine, and is never flurried by an opponent's lead.

Long before Hammersmith was reached, Harvard, having a clear lead, Burnham should have taken Oxford's water; but trying to do so, he grew nervous,

---

* Charles Dickens did, however, agree to be toastmaster at a banquet following the race.

sheered wild, seemed then to lose his head, and never after regained his composure. He lost at least a length on the whole course. Oxford steered admirably well, making a straight line from Crab Tree to the center of Hammersmith Bridge, and thence did not lose an inch to the end.

At Crab Tree, Harvard was a good length ahead, the time being five minutes and fifteen seconds. But here the pace began to tell. The stroke had fallen from 46 to 44 and 40, and then went up again to 43. Flesh and blood could stand it no longer.

Beyond Crab Tree, Oxford began to creep up, and at the soap works were alongside. This Loring would not suffer, but drove on his boat with spirit, and shot Hammersmith Bridge a length ahead once more, Darbishire impressively pulling 40 to the minute, and never getting many inches astern of Harvard's rudder.

The bridge was a bedlam of varying shouts and cheers for the two struggling crews. Harvard passed under it in an unprecedented time—eight minutes and thirty seconds—but alas, the effort had been not only tremendous but desperate. To critical eyes the race was lost while Harvard was still a good length ahead. Their rowing grew wild, their form hitherto good, was lost, their time forgotten, and saddening symptoms of distress in the American boat became evident not far beyond Hammersmith. Oxford a second time began to draw up on the leading boat, never accelerating their stroke, but rowing with that final test of perfect oarsmanship, a spirit without haste. It was the last real struggle of the race. Harvard had little left to answer Oxford's challenge, the dark blue drew swiftly level, then ahead, then a full length ahead, and off Chiswick Church took Harvard's water. From that moment Oxford had a clear lead. The race was over.

There remained two miles and more to row, but the last chance and hope of Harvard was gone. Thence they rowed on, as brave men will row, a hopeless race—a race they know to be hopeless, and yet contest with heroic courage. Burnham frantically threw water over Loring, checking the boat without relieving the crew, and his wild steering still went on.

Barren's Bridge was passed in 18 minutes, Oxford apparently several lengths ahead, and Harvard vainly spurting before and beyond the bridge. To tell the plain truth, Oxford won as they liked after passing Hammersmith. To the passionate efforts of Harvard, Darbishire was content to respond with just effort enough to keep the lead undiminished; and so the two brave fours rowed on.

At the final moment, Loring, in no hope of success, but for honor's pure sake, rallied the last energies of his exhausted crew, and they drew to within a length and a half of that still vigorous, indomitable, terly [*sic*] Oxford four. And within a length and a half of opponents whom they were bound to respect in defeat, Oxford rowed steadily past the judge's boat as the signal gun heavily boomed out victory to St. George and defeat to the Stars and Stripes.

From beginning to end the race was fairly rowed. There was no suspicion of a foul and no real trouble. The course was kept perfectly open and no attempt was made to obstruct either crew. The umpires, referees, starter, and police all did their work perfectly. Neither from spectators nor from the crews was there any hint of unfairness. Harvard frankly own themselves fairly beaten.

Why were they beaten? For many good reasons. The hour of their defeat and chagrin is no time to say harsh things, nor would any one wish to do so; but the truth must be told. What carried them so well through such a race was their unparalleled physique and endurance. In style, form, knowledge of rowing, diet, method of training, and method of instruction, Harvard was utterly inferior to Oxford.

Had the race been won by them the credit would have belonged to Loring, the captain and despot of the crew. Being lost, he must equally bear the blame. A man of extreme self-reliance which partially neutralizes his high qualities of intelligence, generous devotion, and real capacity, but experience limited by knowledge of American rowing only, he persisted in adhering to American methods.

He would coach the crew himself from the inside of the boat, a thing radically impossible to do. He would not change the diet of the crew, although the climate required a change, and the diet manifestly impaired his own and Simmons's powers. It was sheer madness to go on eating currants and milk in this or any climate; but even diarrhea and other symptoms could not effect a change in the captain's stubborn opinion.

To have taken Blaikie or any other good coach on a steamer during that last three weeks would have added 20 per cent to Harvard's chance. Blaikie is not responsible for my opinion, and probably disagrees with it, but it is true nevertheless. Harvard upon arriving had nearly every fault a young crew could have, and retained many at the last moment. Good coaching would in three weeks have eradicated most of them.

Loring to the last believed that rowing could be taught inside the boat. I still think Harvard were the finest men, physically, and had it in them to beat Oxford. They had marvelous stamina, endurance, and force. Oxford was the heavier, doubtless, but weight alone is not an advantage: mere strength will not win a race. To row in a modern out-rigger demands most exact scientific application of force. Strength unskillfully applied is wasted, and there is no more delicate machine than a racing boat and crew—none where power goes for so little if wrongly exerted.

Harvard's stroke was fatally quick and fatally irregular. During the race it varied from 46 to 38—varied often twice in 60 seconds. With a coxswain, no living crew could have pulled the stroke with which Loring led off through four miles. In fact, the crew was rowed to a standstill. In less than two miles their power was gone. After that it was only heroic courage and resolution that carried them through; and a system that exhausts the crew at the end of two miles in a four-mile race cannot be sound.

I cannot too often reiterate any admiration of the marvelous pluck Harvard showed in their efforts during the last two miles to redeem a lost race. It was beyond praise. In many years' experience I never saw a losing crew row on with such unflinching determination. They more than atoned for all faults by their chivalrous fidelity and bravery.

Although the race is lost, it is no discredit to them. All England admires their gallantry, simplicity, and quiet good sense. In the behavior which Harvard has shown, nothing could be better than their demeanor from the beginning of the project. I opposed their enterprise as Quixotic, but after their defeat I acknowledge my mistake, and affirm that no American need regret their attempt. Laurels of victory do not crown their daring, but universal applause rewards their sincere endeavor.

Oxford, in my judgment, rowed within themselves during the last half of the race; the first half they had all they wanted to do, yet the race was never in doubt after Chiswick Church, and they won as they liked. For a short distance only their stroke varied from 38 to 40; from Chiswick to the end it was 40 steadily.

Harvard has been beaten by the finest four ever seen on the Thames. So perfect was their condition that Oxford could have rowed the race again half an hour afterward. In fact, after that race was over, they rowed down to Putney, keeping pace with the Press steamer. Harvard came down on the umpire's boat, and an hour's rest brought them round. In the Oxford's boat, as they rowed down, no distress was discoverable. To have led such a crew over nearly half the course was in itself an honor touching the highest. Harvard accept their defeat manfully, make no complaint and no apology, but bravely admit themselves fairly beaten. G. W. S.

In his memoirs, Smalley claimed that some good came out of the delayed-cable fiasco. To mollify him, the head of the Anglo-American telegraph office agreed to take his dispatches directly, a privilege not granted to his competitors. This, he said, gave him "a great advantage" when he organized his acclaimed coverage of the Franco-Prussian War. The secret arrangement with the Anglo-American became known in late 1870, but by then a two-step process was no longer necessary for cabling stories. Any British telegraph office was authorized to send dispatches over the transatlantic cable. Meanwhile, Smalley devised other "methods." To report on the Vienna Exposition of 1873, he rented a suite of rooms for five months and organized the filing of stories by special reporters.

Smalley seems never to have used the grand title foreign commissioner mentioned when his appointment was first announced in 1867. He didn't need to. No one—including Smalley—doubted his status. He was "an oracle with the peers and publicists of Mayfair," said one English writer. His salary reached a munificent fourteen thousand dollars in the 1880s. He spent weekends at the country homes of the rich and famous.

Smalley's editors gave him wide stylistic latitude, but over time clashes mounted. He became inclined toward the British view and less in touch with the temper of the newsroom. Editors, who in accord with the times increasingly favored fact-laden reporting, complained that Smalley did not often enough cite sources for his information and was too free with his opinions. When it came to those opinions, one in particular annoyed Whitelaw Reid, who took financial control of the newspaper after Greeley's death in 1872. Like Greeley, who ran for president, Reid held political aspirations. He wanted the Irish vote, not to mention Irish readers, and Smalley did not help by writing against Irish Home Rule.

Smalley had fallen into a common trap for correspondents in Britain up to our own day. London is considered a plum post. The *New York Times* has a history of awarding the bureau chief job as a consolation prize to someone who missed getting a big job or giving it to a rising star who is standing in line for a top position. Among the attractions of the post are that language is no problem, Americans are naturally interested in the country, Britain respects press freedom, and life is comfortable, if not always sunny. A correspondent can more easily identify with an English man or woman than, say, with a sheik. In our own times British broadcast media are forever inviting American reporters to serve as commentators, a phenomenon that has print antecedents well over a hundred years old. The rub is that reporters, in their comfort with the British, begin to identify with them, wearing braces and colorful dress shirts and fancying themselves part of the upper crust with whom they socialize. The tug on reporters' copy can be subtle, but it isn't always. In 1982 *Washington Post* London correspondent Peter Osnos conducted the first interview ever by an American reporter of Prince Charles. The prince, Osnos wrote in his account, "is only a few years younger than I am. Some people even say we look alike. I longed for the opportunity to say directly, 'Look, let's be friends. Tell me how it really feels to be the Prince of Wales. Would I like it?'"

Smalley, who began as a critic of royalty, became increasingly enamored with it. He collected autographs of lords and ladies, recommended court dress for American ministers, wrote stories with titles along the lines of "From Epsom to Ascot—the Gospel of Invitations," and gave splendiferous dinners at his Chester Square home. His Anglophilia proved fatal. A pugnacious man with the look of "a professional bruiser," he did not use much finesse in allaying home office concerns about his British leanings. He answered complaints from editors with criticism of his own. He refused to admit to a pro-British bias. Finally, in 1895 the editors decided that the only solution was to dismiss him as a permanent correspondent. Smalley returned to New York as the correspondent for the *Times* of London and later represented the *Times* in Washington, D.C. His career ended in 1905 after a falling-out with his British editors.

"Should a history of international journalism be written," Smalley wrote at the end of his illustrious career, "the historian will perhaps remember that as agent of *The Tribune* I set up in London that European news-bureau which all other great American journals after some years copied." Newspapers deep in the midwestern United States adopted his approach. In 1880 *Chicago Times* journalist Franc B. Wilkie proposed establishment of a London bureau along the lines of the one started by Smalley. "Just the thing!" said Wilbur Storey, the *Times*' eccentric, com-

George Washington Smalley, looking both a proper British gentleman and every bit the "professional bruiser" that made him a formidable journalistic foe. Frontispiece photograph from George W. Smalley, *Anglo-American Memories,* 1911.

bative owner. "All the great American newspapers have bureaux of news in the old world!" Wilkie's network extended to North Africa. During the brief time the bureau operated (it became an expendable luxury when financial problems overtook the paper at home), Wilkie secured an advance copy of the revised New Testament and beat competitors with results of a Cambridge-Oxford boat race.

Smalley's boast that he made journalism history was legitimate. His London bureau helped establish the concept of foreign outposts as organizing elements for the collection and transmission of the news for Americans on a broad scale. He did not, though, have the last word. The future was marked by expansion of his method and constant tinkering to make it work better.

At the end of the nineteenth century, London remained "*the* center of news-collecting for America" abroad, noted *Lippincott's Magazine,* and it stayed that way no matter whether the medium was newspapers, broadcast, or magazines. In 2006 *Reader's Digest* had its only bureau outside North America there because, its international editorial director said, it is a crossroads. As time marched on, however, London was not the only place correspondents congregated. American correspondents fanned out across the planet, establishing bureaus in Shanghai, Tokyo, Buenos Aires, Nairobi, and other cities for the same reason London was selected as a center. These cities provided relatively comfortable living conditions; they had good communications and transportation facilities; and they were where the news was—often in a way that keyed to local interests with the home newspaper. The *Los Angeles Times,* for instance, has paid considerable attention to news of Asia and Latin America because of its large readership with ties to those regions. In the early 1990s, the *San Jose Mercury* opened a Vietnam bureau, along with Vietnamese- and Spanish-language editions, to better serve its immigrant community.

When the focus of the news has swerved, as it has done from time to time, bureaus have closed and new hubs opened. With the end of the cold war and the rise of fundamentalist Muslim terrorism, bureaus shifted from Moscow to the Middle East. In some instances bureaus were established the way Smalley signed up correspondents, on a temporary basis. Following the Daimler-Benz takeover of Detroit-based Chrysler in 1998, the *Detroit News* operated a bureau for several years in Stuttgart, Germany. The *Portland Oregonian* opened a Tokyo bureau in 1989, a time when the community was experiencing considerable Japanese investment. It closed the bureau in 1996 when Japan was less important to the economy.

Similarly, Smalley's idea of pooling news-gathering with other papers has continued. The *Christian Science Monitor* and *USA Today* shared a bureau in Mexico City for a time in the early 2000s. Later *USA Today* joined forces with the *Arizona Republic,* owned by *USA Today*'s parent company, Gannett. Around the same time, a news exchange arranged by the Scripps News Service, which has no foreign correspondents, gave it access to the *Toronto Globe and Mail* coverage, which was a good source of foreign news. As we shall see later in a discussion of radio and television, broadcasters also have organized elaborate partnerships. "The concept," said CBS vice-president for news Marcy McGinnis in 2004, "is you can't be everywhere, so you need friends."

The experimentation has been endless because every method has a flaw, as an example from the 1990s illustrates. For some time each of the larger newspapers in the Knight Ridder group oversaw two correspondents who were supposed to report for all the other newspapers as well as their own. The *Miami Herald,* with its strong ties to South America, had day-to-day control of reporters in that region, for instance, while the *San Jose Mercury* looked toward Asia. The system was excellent in theory. In practice, it did not always work. Correspondents tended to write chiefly for their home papers. Occasionally individual newspapers duplicated coverage. To correct this problem, Knight Ridder brought all the centrally funded correspondents under the direct control of the Washington, D.C., bureau. Smaller newspapers, the Washington foreign editor noted, had a central gatekeeper to call for guidance "when they don't know the value of a story." The downside was that the Washington editor was less closely in touch with readers in communities with special foreign interests. "This was an especially big blow to the [*Miami*] *Herald,*" said Douglas Clifton, the editor at the time of the change, "because of its outsized interest in Latin American, an interest unmatched by any other paper in the group." The Knight Ridder scheme continued when most of its newspapers were acquired by the McClatchy Company of newspapers in 2006, which worked on its own special collaborations. In one of these, started in late 2008, it shared news from its bureaus in Caracas and Nairobi with the *Christian Science Monitor,* which in turn gave them its stories from New Delhi and Mexico City.

The management challenge is not limited to placing and coordinating permanent correspondents. News often breaks far from a permanent bureau. This makes it necessary to have part-time print and broadcast reporters or producers—often called stringers—in strategic secondary locations or to have local cameramen, drivers, or fixers who can assist staff correspondents who fly in. "We don't have the financial resources to have permanent correspondents in scores of countries," said Andrew Alexander, the Washington bureau chief for Cox newspapers, which ran its foreign service centrally along the lines of Knight Ridder. "Stringers often allow us to tackle a breaking story faster than it would take for one of our permanent correspondents to get there. In addition, our permanent correspondents often are juggling multiple assignments for our 17 newspapers. In cases where we can't call on a stringer, we may be able to turn to a freelance photographer or a fixer who can get us critical information. One of our goals is to have multiple ways of getting at the story." Table 1 shows the system used in 2004 by Cox Newspapers. The system became obsolete in 2009, after the parent company, Cox Enterprises, sold most of its newspapers and closed its Washington bureau; its three remaining newspapers, including the *Atlanta Journal-Constitution,* thereafter did whatever foreign reporting they chose to do independently.

TABLE 1. Overseas news-gathering "method" in use by Charles W. Holmes, foreign editor of the Cox News Service's Washington Bureau, Friday, February 19, 2004

Location	Staff correspondent[a]	Office assistant	Stringer[b]	Fixer[c]	Driver
Amman, Jordan				!	
Ankara				*	
Athens			*		
Baghdad	!			!	!
Baku				*	
Bangkok			!	*	
Beijing	!	!	!		
Beirut				*	
Belgrade				*	
Berlin			*		
Bogotá				*	
Brussels			*		
Buenos Aires			*	*	
Cairo				*	
Caracas				*	
Damascus				*	

TABLE 1 *(continued)*

Location	Staff correspondent[a]	Office assistant	Stringer[b]	Fixer[c]	Driver
Gaza Strip				!	
Guatemala				*	
Islamabad				*	
Istanbul			*		
Jerusalem	!		!(contract)[d]		
Johannesburg			*		
Kabul				*	
Kandahar				*	
Lima				*	
London	!		!		
Madrid			*		
Managua				*	
Manila			*	*	
Mexico City	!	!	*		
Miami[e]	!				
Milan			*		
Moscow			!	*	
Nairobi			!		
New Delhi			*		
Nicosia				*	
Paris			!		
Port-au-Prince				*	
Prague			*	*	
Pristina				*	
Rio de Janeiro				*	
Rome			*	*	
San Salvador				*	
Sarajevo				*	
Seoul			!	*	
Shanghai			*		
Skopje				*	
St. Petersburg				*	
Tbilisi				*	
Teheran			*	*	
Tel Aviv			!		

TABLE 1 (*continued*)

Location	Staff correspondent[a]	Office assistant	Stringer[b]	Fixer[c]	Driver
Tokyo				*	
Toronto			*		
Vladivostok				*	
Warsaw				*	

! = people actively working that day; * = other people available to Holmes.

[a] Staff correspondents are full-time.

[b] Stringers are part-time, freelance reporters, typically working for other news organizations as well.

[c] Fixers help correspondents and are especially useful when a reporter "parachutes" into a country to cover a story. Fixers translate, arrange interviews, etc. They sometimes gather information and file stories themselves. Some fixers are part-time or on an as-needed basis, but in Baghdad at the time of this survey the fixer was full-time.

[d] Contract stringers have a more formal agreement than stringers do and file more frequently. They often work nearly full-time.

[e] Covering Latin America and the Caribbean.

Behind the quest for the better method was something else that Smalley pointed to, the quest for original factual reporting. On a routine day during the time he was in London for the *Tribune,* newspapers were only slightly ahead of Benjamin Franklin's in their reliance on Europeans for much of their news. Even the few American correspondents who were posted permanently in London offices mined local newspapers for tidbits they could rewrite. The foreign correspondent, as *Lippincott's Magazine* explained in its article singling out London as a prime location for a bureau, can "cull from the great London dailies any special news or editorial comment of interest to America. And this is one of the main reasons why London is *the* center of news-collecting for America: the London dailies contain the largest and best collection of European news, which is all at the disposal of the American cable correspondents at the English capital." Smalley's mailed reports, in which he wrote a good deal *about* English journalism, obviously used this approach.

George Smalley's boat race story, however, was pure enterprise. Despite the snafu that held up transmission, he distinguished himself by applying his own powers of observation to the event. Even more creative in realizing the potential for such firsthand reporting was James Gordon Bennett Jr., the great impresario of news-making.

FIND LIVINGSTONE

On October 16, 1869, James Gordon Bennett Jr. telegraphed Henry Morton Stanley in Madrid, "Come to Paris on important business." The next night Stanley entered Bennett's room in the Grand Hotel. The publisher climbed out of bed, pulled on his robe-de-chambre, and got right to the point. He had an assignment in Africa for his young reporter. Stanley was to look for Scottish missionary-explorer Dr. David Livingstone "wherever you may hear that he is, and to get what news you can of him, and perhaps"—Bennett paused for a moment, thoughtfully—"the old man may be in want:—take enough with you to help him should he require it. Of course you will act according to your own plans, and do what you think best—BUT FIND LIVINGSTONE." When Stanley pointed out that this was a costly venture, Bennett waved him off. Draw a thousand pounds and then a thousand pounds more, ad infinitum, "—BUT FIND LIVINGSTONE."

Stanley and Bennett were the same age and, each in his own way, a prime candidate for psychobiography. Their combined peculiarities made them an ideal, if not always harmonious, match. The famous romanticized story of their Grand Hotel meeting—told in Stanley's memoir *How I Found Livingstone,* which he dedicated to his boss—fittingly marked the beginning of this collaboration. Before the insecure Stanley and the extravagant Bennett were through, they did far more than find Livingstone. They put their flags atop a new genre of foreign reporting.

Bennett was volatile, dictatorial, and wildly wealthy thanks to the newspaper legacy left by his father. He liked being called Commodore, a title derived from his three terms as head of the New York Yacht Club, where his oil portrait continues to hang. Boundlessly creative in making himself the center of attention, he drunkenly celebrated one New Year's Eve by urinating into his prospective parents-in-law's fireplace (or possibly it was the grand piano; accounts differ). The engagement was called off.

Bennett was as casual about international travel as a man hailing a taxicab. He was raised largely in Paris, where his mother had retreated to escape the social opprobrium resulting from her husband's raucous style of journalism in New York.

As an adult, the younger Bennett shuttled back and forth between the two cities, with additional homes on the Riviera and in Scotland. He cruised the Mediterranean in his yacht, *Lysistrata,* and occasionally ventured farther to Ceylon (now Sri Lanka) and New York. The *Lysistrata,* said the managing editor of his Paris newspaper, the *Herald,* "carried a crew of one hundred, a Turkish bath and a Alderney cow."

The peripatetic publisher's enthusiasm for travel apparently inspired a story by another travel enthusiast, Jules Verne, author of *From the Earth to the Moon, Twenty Thousand Leagues under the Sea,* and other such fantasies. Verne's hero in his final version of "The Day of an American Journalist in 2889" is "Francis Bennet," publisher of the *Earth Herald,* who barrels around the planet in aero-cars and submarine tubes. His reporters send in stories from other planets, something the real-life Bennett would have commanded if he could have.*

This photo of the *New York Herald* staff appeared in *Cosmopolitan Magazine* in 1886. The Bennett family is conspicuous in the image: on one wall is a painting of the elder Bennett, and on the other wall a painting of a sailing ship, a reflection of the junior Bennett's interest in yachting. The editor's chair is empty, for James Gordon Bennett Jr. was typically away from New York when the meeting took place.

* Verne's son may have written an initial version in English that was published in an American magazine and later reworked by the master himself. In any event, the story, as fantastic as it was then, is not today: "If they recalled the erratic working of the steamers and the railways, their many collisions, and their slowness, how greatly would travelers value the aero-trains, and especially those pneumatic tubes laid beneath the oceans [think the Chunnel], which convey them with a speed of a thousand miles an hour? And would they not enjoy the telephone and the telephote [which carried a caller's image as well as voice] even better if they recollected that our fathers were reduced to that antediluvian apparatus which they called the 'telegraph?'" Verne, "In the Twenty-ninth Century," 142.

Bennett dreamed up all manner of adventures for his harried staff, who in the words of one biographer often scampered "about the earth only to find themselves on fools' errands." On one occasion he sent a pair of reporters to search the French seacoast, between Mentone and Cannes, for a pair of swans. Another time he summoned two employees from the United States; upon their arrival in Paris, he curtly asked, "What in the hell are you doing here?" He told them to "go back to New York." The constant back-and-forth travel between the United States and Europe that Bennett was forever ordering was known as the "Atlantic Shuttle." "I worked for Bennett and his 'Herald' almost ten years," reporter Albert Crockett reminisced, "and I quit because of my inability to lead a really sane, normal, orderly life with the alternations between wildest hope and gloomiest foreboding that began to characterize my existence from the time I was first obtruded upon the attention of the Commodore."

Stanley's insecurity complemented Bennett's egomaniac manias, for his lack of confidence contributed to a defining idiosyncrasy, a casual attachment to truth. Writing a story to flatter his employer was as natural for him as making up names for himself. The Welsh-born journalist initially carried the name of his supposed father, John Rowlands. Working as a cabin boy, he landed in New Orleans and met Henry Stanley, a cotton merchant who employed him briefly. Young Rowlands adopted Stanley's name and made up a story that the merchant had adopted him. After he earned a measure of fame, Stanley practiced with several middle names—Morley, Morelake, and Moreland—before deciding on Morton. Stanley wore both gray and blue in the Civil War, became a U.S. citizen, and fell into journalism on the *Missouri Democrat*. In 1867, he secured a freelance assignment with the *Herald,* reporting on a British expedition against the emperor of Ethiopia, which led to a staff position. The year before Bennett sent him to find Livingstone, Stanley filed a thrilling story telling how he arduously linked up with guerrillas in the mountains of Crete and accompanied them in an attack against Turkish forces. As satisfying as the story was for *Herald* readers, Stanley doesn't appear to have been in Crete at the time.

Stanley's account of his 1869 Grand Hotel meeting with the great Bennett, the only description we have of the encounter, is dubious. The dates are wrong, besides which the story is a good deal more complicated than Stanley's simple tale suggests. Good evidence indicates that someone other than Bennett dreamed up the "Find Livingstone" idea. That someone may have been Stanley, who is recorded as having mentioned an interest in the adventure as early as 1866. The honor also may belong to Finlay Anderson, the *Herald*'s London representative. In 1868 Anderson sent Stanley with Bennett's permission on an errant mission to Aden to interview Livingstone, who was mistakenly thought to be to be exiting the interior there. When Stanley returned empty-handed, he found that Bennett had sacked Anderson and installed a new man, Douglas Levien. Levien also is a candidate for at least some of the credit for the quest to find Livingstone, because he sought to rekindle the scheme in Bennett's hot-then-cold mind right before the decision was made. The story is dodgier still because Bennett seems to have toyed with sending the mellifluously named De Benneville Randolph Keim instead of Stanley. Keim had had an action-packed career, covering twenty-three Civil War battles and chronicling the army's dealings with the "refractory savage" in the American West. He was a better writer than Stanley. Keim's assignment to the story may have foundered because a Bennett letter to him in Ceylon miscarried.

One wonders how serious Bennett really was about finding the Scotsman. The Commodore's full instructions, as Stanley related them, were to cover the inauguration of the Suez Canal, look into an expedition in Upper Egypt, write up a practical guide for Lower Egypt, check out "some interesting discoveries" in Jerusalem, visit Constantinople and "the Crimea and those old battle-grounds," investigate "a Russian expedition bound for Khiva," and "then, when you have come to India, you can go after Livingstone." Perhaps Bennett cannily hoped to build suspense. Perhaps he was hedging his bets in the event that Livingstone surfaced before Stanley could "find" him. Perhaps the idea for the trip was just another Bennett whim, a distinct possibility suggested by the fact that the mercurial publisher for a time refused to pay Stanley's bills in Africa. Bennett's instructions for desultory travel certainly suggest he wasn't all that concerned if Livingstone was "in want."

What is certain is the underlying journalistic principle at play in sending Stanley to find Livingstone: a reporter didn't have to sit around waiting for news to happen. Bennett, one of his reporters reminisced, "knew how to make news, not by the simple and unsatisfying process of manufacture out of whole cloth, but by starting something that should find an echo in popular imagination and stimulate a demand for more." In this case he and Stanley built on the technique of the interview, used so effectively by Bennett *père* with the madam of the murdered prostitute Helen Jewett. This seemingly innocent American invention was a brilliant answer to the journalistic problem of a slow news day. A reporter could generate interesting news by getting important people to talk. When the prospective interviewee was difficult to reach, the news value went up from interesting to sensational. In this sense, it was almost impossible to top Livingstone. He was a world-famous celebrity long out of sight, maybe dead, somewhere on the Dark Continent, Stanley's term for Africa.

Once Stanley was fully launched into Africa, the *Herald* gushed with self-promotional zeal that would have made the Commodore's father proud: "An African exploring expedition is a new thing in the enterprise of modern journalism, and in this, as in many other great achievements of the 'third [*sic*] estate,' to the NEW YORK HERALD will belong the credit of the first bold adventure in the cause of humanity, civilization and science." When word filtered back that Stanley might have been lost, the *Herald* did not flinch: "In the service of a journal like the HERALD men must give their lives, as they have, time and again, serving the great news in scenes of war and discovery and disaster." Not believing it possible to have too much of a good thing, the *Herald* that same day carried a story of a new Bennett expedition, this one undertaken by Alvan S. Southland to find Sir Samuel Baker, an explorer serving in the Sudan as a representative of the khedive of Egypt.

While the *Herald* trumpeted this "new era in journalism," Stanley drove his two hundred plus men 975 miles, over 236 days, into the perilous interior. The two white men he had recruited did not survive the trip; before succumbing, they tried to murder him. Men caught "the terrible fever of East Africa," Stanley noted in a dispatch to the *Herald*. Smallpox and dysentery raged. Others died in skirmishes with locals. There was attempted mutiny and desertion. Stanley used his dog whip energetically. He told *Herald* readers he would "never travel again in Africa without a good long chain" for securing his men to him.

In November 1871, nine months after leaving Zanzibar and more than two years after his Grand Hotel meeting with Bennett, Stanley stood on a hill overlooking Lake Tanganyika. As he descended into the village of Ujiji, his men fired guns in the air to announce their coming. Hundreds of villagers turned out to line his path, as Stanley recounted in the *Herald*.

> As I come nearer I see the white face of an old man among them. He has a cap with a gold band around it, his dress is a short jacket of red blanket cloth, and his pants—well I did not observe. I am shaking hands with him. We raise our hats, and I say:
> "Dr. Livingstone, I presume?"
> And he says, "yes."
> Finis coronat opus.*

Stanley's improbable greeting "Dr. Livingstone, I presume" was very likely as made-up as his name, a clumsy effort to seem the understated British gentleman he was not. Stanley later ripped the page out of his diary describing this part of their meeting. Also in keeping with his insecurity, Stanley did not divulge to Livingstone that he was a journalist until the second day, when he asked the Scotsman if he had heard of the *Herald*. "Oh," Livingstone replied, "who has not heard of that despicable newspaper?" Told that the *Herald* was the agent behind the trip, Livingstone's attitude brightened up, and he wrote a letter thanking Bennett for the badly needed supplies of food and medicine. Stanley developed a close relationship with Livingstone. When Livingstone resumed his explorations, he took the correspondent with him. They established that Lake Tanganyika was not the source of the White Nile. (As was later determined, the headstreams flow from Lake Victoria and Lake Albert.)

Stanley set out for the coast in March. On May 7, 1872, he reached Zanzibar. There he recuperated for a spell while news of his success raced ahead. He wondered if Bennett wanted him to go on to China, but he learned by cable that he was to forward his dispatches and public letters from Livingstone and come home. On July

---

* The end crowns the work.

15 the *Herald* ran a spread of Stanley's reports describing his encounter with Livingstone and their subsequent travels. The stories appeared under the main headline "LIVINGSTONE," followed by nineteen subheads such as "A STORY MORE ROMANTIC THAN ROMANCE." Additional lengthy reports ran in August, by which time Stanley had returned triumphantly to London. The story below, among the dispatches published on July 15, is one of the shorter ones but typical in its first-person style focused on the adventure as much as on the object of his quest.

Christmas at Ujiji and Livingstone's March for Unyanyembe–Fifty-four Days' Travel and Adventure.

KWIHARA, UNYANYEMBE

February 21, 1872

After spending Christmas at Ujiji Dr. Livingstone, escorted by the NEW YORK HERALD Expedition, composed of forty Wanguana soldiers, well armed, left for Unyanyembe on the 26th of December, 1871.

In order to arrive safely, untroubled by wars and avaricious tribes, we sketched out a road to Unyanyembe, thus:

Seven days by water south to Urimba.

Ten days across the uninhabited forests of Kawendi.

Twenty days through Unkonongo, direct east.

Twelve days north through Unkonongo.

Thence five days into Unyanyembe, where we arrived without adventure of any kind, except killing zebras, buffaloes and giraffes, after fifty-four days' travel.

The expedition suffered considerably from famine, and your correspondent from fever, but these are incidental to the march in this country.

"THE MAN OF IRON" MARCHES ON FOOT—THE ROLL OF THE DEAD

The Doctor tramped it on foot like a man of iron. On arrival at Unyanyembe I found that the Englishman, Shaw, whom I had turned back as useless, had about a month after his return succumbed to the climate of the interior and had died, as well as two Wanguana of the expedition who had been left behind sick. Thus during less than twelve months William Lawrence Farquhar, of Leith, Scotland, and John William Shaw, of London, England, the two white men I had engaged to assist me, had died; also eight baggage carriers and eight soldiers of the expedition had died.

ADVICE WELL TAKEN

I was bold enough to advise the Doctor to permit the expedition to escort him to Unyanyembe, through the country it was made acquainted with while going to Ujiji, for the reason that were he to sit down at Ujiji until Mirambo was disposed of he might remain a year there, a prey to high expectations, ending always in bitter disappointment. I told him, as the Arabs of Unyanyembe were not equal to the task of conquering Mirambo, that it were better he should accompany the HERALD expedition to Unyanyembe, and there take possession of the last lot of goods brought to him by a caravan which left the seacoast simultaneously with our expedition.*

The Doctor consented, and thus it was that he came so far back as Unyanyembe.

"YOU ARE NOW FAMOUS AS LIVINGSTONE HAVING DISCOVERED THE DISCOVERER," Bennett cabled his correspondent. The phrase "Stanley and Livingstone" was on everyone's lips. With his made-up name joined with Livingstone's, Stanley had the fame he craved. When Livingstone died little more than a year after the *Herald* expedition, Stanley assumed the famous explorer's work. The *Herald,* with the *London Daily Telegraph,* agreed to sponsor a new search for the headwaters of the Nile. The venture began in the usual jumping-off place, Zanzibar, on the east coast of Africa. It ended on the Atlantic Coast with Stanley becoming the first white man to trace the length of the Congo River. He undertook two more expeditions before he was through. One resulted in creation of the Congo Free State under the control of Belgium, whose king had funded the trip. After being renaturalized as a British subject, Stanley ran successfully for a seat in Parliament. Queen Victoria knighted him. *How I Found Livingstone* sold thousands of copies. Years afterward young reporters in the *Herald*'s New York newsroom gazed reverentially at the wooden desk Stanley had supposedly used.

In the hotly competitive news environment of the time, Stanley's success generated personal attacks from other newspapers. Those rivals impugned his character, an endeavor facilitated by a wealth of good material, and questioned the veracity of his work. The *New York Sun* claimed his discovery of Livingstone was a hoax— not a far-fetched charge, considering that Bennett was capable of devoting the entire front page of his newspaper to a fabricated story headlined "The Wild Animals Broken Loose from Central Park/Terrible Scenes of Mutilation/A Shocking Sabbath Carnival of Death." The phrase "Dr. Livingstone, I presume" became a common joke line among journalists and others. When Stanley received an honorary doctorate at Oxford, one waggish student shouted out the greeting.

"I have been taught to see how the scavenger-beetles of the Press contrive to pick up an infinitesimal grain of fact, like the African mud-rolling beetle, until it becomes so monstrously exaggerated that it is absolutely a mass of filth," Stanley confided in a private notebook. "In Africa, where I am free of newspapers, the mind has scope in which to revolve, virtuously content." If he had not been so thin-skinned, Stanley could have taken comfort in the fact that discrediting him was not nearly so satisfying to his competitors as emulation.

Among those editors keen to emulate Bennett and Stanley was Joseph Pulitzer. His *New York World* was in the vanguard of a "new journalism" marked by easy-

---

* Stanley's expedition stepped into the middle of a war between Arabs and the powerful Nyamwezi chief Mirambo.

to-read, bright news effervescing with uplifting crusades, attention-getting stunts, and interviews. One of its overseas reporters claimed the first interview with a pope in 1871.* "The Roman Catholic Church is the oldest, as the interview is almost the youngest, of the institutions of mankind," the *World* announced of its interview of Pius IX. "And they are this morning presented face to face." The *World* funded expeditions to rescue hostages from "oyster pirates" and to save twenty-four white slaves from bondage in the Yucatán.

One of the most sensational of all the *World's* news concoctions, which set others in motion, was Nellie Bly's brainstorm to eclipse in real life the record set in Jules Verne's novel *Around the World in Eighty Days*. Bly was a *World* ace at dreaming up stunts. Her undercover reporting promoted insane asylum reform. She posed as a sinner in order to get dirt on the Magdalen Home for Unfortunate Women. Her around-the-world trip in 1889–90 became the most memorable of all her stories, although not as original as the *World* and Bly would have had their readers think. Verne had drawn the idea for his book from reading about madcap millionaire George Francis Train's 1870 circumscription of the globe in eighty days (discounting his two-month layover in France). It was Verne's book, however, that most people remembered when Bly set out nineteen years later.†

The public's attention was aroused all the more when another comely journalist, Elizabeth Bisland with *Cosmopolitan* magazine, headed in the opposite direction with the same goal in mind. The trip now became a race, and the *World* made the most of it, among other things sponsoring "The Nellie Bly Guessing Match," in which readers predicted the number of days and hours her trip would take. Bisland finished second, although the runner-up status did not prevent her from getting a book as well as articles out of the adventure. Bly's book was *Around the World in Seventy-Two Days*.

Train, who made his money in shipping and railroads and wrote occasional travel articles for the *New York Herald,* was furious. He asked the *World* to sponsor him on a new trip. When the newspaper declined to show up its star reporter, Train secured support from the *Evening Ledger* in Tacoma, Washington, a town that owed him a favor because he had suggested locating the terminus of the Northern Pacific Railroad there. He made this second trip in sixty-seven days and, still

---

* Considerably later, James Creelman with the *New York Herald* inaccurately claimed to be the first newspaper reporter to interview a pope. His account of meeting Leo XIII is amusing nonetheless.

> The Pope looked at me intently for a moment.
> "You are not one of the Faithful?" he said.
> "I am what journalism has made of me."
> CREELMAN, *On the Great Highway,* 22

† Verne, however, did not forget the zany Train. One of the characters encountered by Verne's journalist hero in *The Adventures of a Special Correspondent* is Baron Weisschnitzerdörfer. Weisschnitzerdörfer is attempting to beat the around-the-world records set by Train, Bly, and Bisland. "I shall be much surprised if this German beats an American at globe trotting," says special correspondent Claudius Bombarnac. Verne, *The Adventures of a Special Correspondent,* 41.

eager to be the champ, a third one two years later in sixty days. To his dismay, Bly remained the remembered one.

Around-the-world derbies coincided with another travel craze in Europe and the United States, bicycling. The fad inspired new journals that pedaled along to the benefit of both the periodical's owners and the cycling industry. Two enterprising newsmen, Lord Northcliffe, the eventual founder of the *London Daily Mail*, and magazine publisher S. S. McClure, began their careers with cycling magazines eager to glorify the sport. The most enduring contrived bicycle event of all occurred in 1903. A struggling upstart sporting magazine, *L'Auto*, backed by French investors with interests in automobiles and bicycles, decided to attract attention to itself by staging a race. Holding a race was not at all unusual. A competitor, *Le Vélo*, had been holding them for some time. This one, however, had a twist. The self-styled "newspaper of ideas and action" designed it to take place in stages so as generate fresh newspaper stories day after day. *L'Auto*'s circulation soared from 20,000 before the race to 65,000 during it. *Le Vélo* folded. The race became the Tour de France.

Less well remembered, but exciting at the time, was the discovery by the outdoor sporting magazine *Outing* of an intrepid English biking enthusiast named Thomas Stevens. Stevens had just started out from San Francisco to pedal an ungainly big-wheel-little-wheel penny-farthing bicycle around the world. *Outing* made him a foreign correspondent assigned to covering himself. His trip began in July 1884 and ended in January 1887. Afterward he did what any enterprising journalistic adventurer did; he wrote a book, *Around the World on a Bicycle*.

Once publishers spotted a traveling talent like Stevens, they hung onto his coattails. With Stevens's journalistic credentials established, the *World* sent the indefatigable Englishman on a surefire news-making errand in 1889—Find Stanley! For two years Stanley had been leading an expedition to rescue Emin Paşha, the governor of the Equatorial Province of Egypt, who had been cut off by a revolt. "Here was a grand opportunity: the one chance mayhap, of a lifetime, to spring into fame on the stage of African exploit," Stevens recounted in a memoir. Stevens fantasized how *How I Found Stanley* would look alongside *How I Found Livingstone* on library shelves.

Stevens's leap at fame stumbled on Edward Vizetelly. Vizetelly, who hailed from a British family famous for fielding foreign correspondents, was an accomplished adventuring reporter. When Bennett sailed into Alexandria, Egypt, he summoned the journalist, who was then working for English-language newspapers in the country. Vizetelly accepted a "find Stanley" proposal and, in a kind of celebration, dove into the shark-infested water around the boat. Then he was off to Zanzibar, whence he plunged into the interior of Africa. Closing in on their famous quarry, Stevens and Vizetelly found themselves in the same retinue. Stevens devised a clever plan to leap ahead at the last moment, a meaningless achievement from a journalistic point of view, since neither reporter could file a story for days. Victory went to the man who was in print first, and that was Vizetelly. This earned him a bonus of two thousand pounds sterling. Stevens's reward was the pleasure of boasting that he had introduced Vizetelly to the great journalist-explorer. He also had the benefit of a long-winded sermon from Stanley on life's lessons, one of which was that "truth always triumphs over falsehood and deceit."

Upon returning home, Vizetelly retired. Stevens had one last book-producing assignment, this time in Russia. He acquired a horse named Texas from a Wild West show in Moscow and rode him to the Black Sea. After writing *Through Russia on a Mustang,* Vizetelly married the widowed mother of British actresses Violet and Irene Van Brugh and went into a new line of work, managing London's Garrick Theater.

"The instant you see a sensation is dead," Bennett said, "drop it and start in on something new." While some sensations were frivolous, some were not. Taking his own advice to look for new opportunities for news, the Commodore turned his ambitions on the Arctic, the locus of considerable exploration at the time. In another one of his famous meetings, this time in the Voltaire Hotel's Café Voisin in 1875, Bennett assigned Januarias MacGahan to an expedition seeking the Northwest Passage, the elusive Arctic water route from the Atlantic to the Pacific. For the journey Bennett helped finance the voyage of the *Pandora,* which in keeping with the "Find Livingstone" formula searched for the vestiges of a lost expedition by Sir John Franklin. The *Pandora* found some traces of Franklin's party but failed in its main objective.*

While MacGahan was writing his memoir, *Into the Northern Lights,* he received a letter from Bennett instructing him to prepare for a new Arctic adventure. "'Gird up your loins' for the fight," the letter said. "If you succeed you will eclipse Stanley, Livingstone and any former explorers whether African or Polar." MacGahan was one of Bennett's most intrepid special correspondents, someone he also may have considered for the "Find Livingstone" mission. This time, though, Bennett did not have his way. MacGahan wisely declined to do any loin-girding.

Bennett's new Arctic exploration, which set sail in 1879, sought to reach the North Pole via the Bering Strait in the same ship MacGahan had used, now renamed the *Jeannette* after Bennett's sister, who christened it. With no MacGahan to send, Bennett dispatched the *Herald*'s weatherman, Jerome Collins, an Irishman whose interest in technology was wide-ranging, to say the least. He had previously created a system for cabling storm warnings to Europe and dreamed of launching a submarine attack by U.S.-based members of Sinn Féin against the British. Collins brought electrical lighting, telephone, and photographic apparatus on the *Jeannette.* The equipment failed to work, although this was of minor significance compared with the tragedy that unfolded. The *Jeannette* was trapped in the ice and crushed. The weatherman, a whiny insubordinate, died of exposure along with many of the crew.

* The Northwest Passage was not traversed until 1906, when, sailing secretly to avoid creditors, Norwegian Roald Amundsen completed the voyage in three years. The first single-season crossing did not occur until 1944.

Collins's behavior did not reflect well on the *Herald;* nor did Bennett's meddling. Among other things, Bennett had diverted the *Jeannette* to find a lost vessel captained by a Swede who turned out not to be lost at all. When hints of the *Jeannette*'s disaster filtered back, Bennett dispatched two reporters, one from Europe and one from another Arctic expedition, to find out what had happened. Here was another opportunity to make news by finding people, but another element of self-interest was mixed in. Bennett wanted his reporters to intercept any damning papers about his involvement. He also instructed them not to air "soiled linen." Nevertheless, the *Jeannette* fiasco led to a congressional investigation that did his reputation no good.

Meanwhile, other journals in other countries were in hot pursuit of discoveries. A Russian newspaper, *Noyoe Vremya,* sent out an expedition to Franz Josef Land. True to their island's colonizing heritage, the British journals were especially ardent promoters of exploration. After Lord Northcliffe moved beyond bicycling, but before he created his *Daily Mail,* he started the magazine *Answers to Correspondents.* Although it could not equal a daily newspaper as a vehicle for maximizing the publicity value of sponsoring an expedition, it sponsored a British run at the North Pole that failed. No British paper was more aggressive than the *London Daily Telegraph.* Stanley's discovery of Livingstone "bore fruit," as the *New York Tribune* put it, when the *Daily Telegraph* gave one thousand guineas to the British Museum for a new expedition to Nineveh. George Smith, keeper of the British museum, brought back Assyrian artifacts that completed the story of the Flood. Later the newspaper financed Sir Harry Johnston's exploration of Kilimanjaro and Lionel Decle's journey from Cape Town to Cairo. Stanley wrote an introduction for Decle's *Three Years in Savage Africa.* The *Daily Telegraph*'s enthusiasm for discovery continued for decades. It supported expeditions on Everest in the 1930s.

The *New York Times,* established in 1851 as a respectable alternative to the likes of the *New York Herald,* also succumbed to the allure of adventurous travel. In 1908 it paid four thousand dollars to Commander Robert E. Peary for story rights to his upcoming expedition to reach the North Pole first, with the condition that he would receive nothing if he did not reach his destination. Before Peary returned, Dr. Frederick A. Cook emerged to announce he had accomplished the feat. The *Herald,* which had funded Peary's earlier unsuccessful attempts, paid twenty-five thousand dollars for Cook's story. When Peary reappeared, he claimed that the title was his and that Cook was lying. The *Herald* and the *Times* aggressively defended their men. The *Herald* described Peary's welcome in New York as "cheerless"; the *Times* called it "triumphal." Peary, who also enjoyed the moral and financial support of the National Geographic Society and its magazine, *National Geographic,* eventually won out in the contemporary court of public opinion. Since then, evidence has emerged that both men were lying, in the fine tradition of Henry Morton Stanley.

※

The foreign adventures Bennett and others launched were pseudo-events, to use historian Daniel Boorstin's term. Yet publishers' zeal to build circulation and make money created tangible progress. The frenzy of exploration at the end of the nineteenth century owed much to journalism in the same way that social and political reforms emerged from newspaper crusades undertaken to drive up circulation. One could scarcely think about exploration without a popular media outlet attached to it. Within the first year of its creation, the exploration-minded National Geographic Society had its own magazine. Admiral Peary was a contributor well before he became famous. "Other than the flag of my country," said Admiral Richard Byrd, who worked hard to court patrons, "I know of no greater privilege than to carry the emblem of the National Geographic Society."

"Newspapers are getting to be much more than mere transcripts of the news and gossip of the day," the *New York Tribune* proclaimed in an 1873 editorial praising the *Daily Telegraph*'s sponsorship of George Smith's Nineveh expedition. "They are pioneers in learned exploration; they are foremost in geographical and historical discovery; they are the teachers of social science."

The contributions of the press in subsequent years were apparent on newly drawn maps, where explorers penciled in names, some of which became permanent. Lt. Frederick Schwatka repaid press support for his Alaskan explorations by naming a river after George Jones, one of the three founders of the original *New York Times,* and a lake "after Mr. James Gordon Bennett, a well-known patron of American geographical research." A river flowed out of Lake Bennett, which Schwatka called Flynn River in honor of Edward Townsend Flynn, the *Herald*'s managing editor. Although the *Jeannette* polar expedition ended badly, it added new knowledge about the region. It put Bennett, Jeannette, and Henrietta islands on the

Newspapermen supported Lt. Frederick Schwatka's Alaskan explorations. He repaid them by naming rivers, lakes, and islands after them. Here is a woodcut of Lake Bennett that appeared in *A Summer in Alaska,* Schwatka's book-length account of his explorations.

map, the last of these named after Bennett's mother. The name Grosvenor, from the family that created the National Geographic Society and its magazine, was all over the map as well: on a glacier in Peru, an island in the Arctic, a natural arch in Utah, and a mountain in Norway, just to name a few locales.

The *New York Times* was a sponsor of Admiral Byrd's exploration of Antarctica in the 1920s. Byrd named a glacier after owner and publisher Adolph Ochs. In the near vicinity is Mount Iphigene, named for Ochs's only child; Birchall Peaks, named after a *Times* managing editor; and Marujupu Peak, a name that requires explanation. When Byrd gave Ochs the opportunity to name the peak on Ochs Glacier after one of his grandchildren, the publisher made up a name combining the first names of all of Iphigene's children, Marian, Ruth, Judy, and Punch. (The family later created the Marujupu/Sulzberger Foundation.) Southwest of the glacier is Arthur Hays Sulzberger Bay, named after Ochs's son-in-law, who eventually became publisher of the *Times*. These landmarks are found in the "*New York Times*" sector of a larger area named after a member of yet another sponsoring family, Edsel Ford. *Times* reporter Russell D. Owen, who accompanied the Byrd expedition, won a 1930 Pulitzer Prize for the stories he sent by radio from the Adolph S. Ochs Radio Station in Byrd's "Little America" encampment. "Without the assistance of the newspapers," the director of the American Geographic Society observed shortly after Byrd's success, "the well-equipped expeditions of recent years could not have been undertaken."

Stanley, awarded two medals by the Royal Geographical Society, was not bashful about playing the naming game. He put Livingstone Falls on the map; named an African hill after Sir William Mackinnon, the chairman of the British India Steam Navigation Company and sponsor of the Emin Paşha relief expedition; and royally named Lake Albert Edward (later called just Lake Edward). After himself, he created Stanley Falls and Stanley Pool. He did not forget the Commodore. Stanley put a Bennett Mountain and a Bennett River on the African maps he brought home.

Bennett was not so generous in the credit-giving department. Stanley's dispatches were written in the first person, but in keeping with journalistic custom at the time, his name appeared sparingly in them, which no doubt suited Bennett just fine. Associates remembered that Bennett broke into a rage when Stanley's name showed up in the news. When Stanley came to New York in 1872 after finding Livingstone, the *Herald* proprietor gave him a mere ten-minute audience.

"If there was anything the Commodore hated," remarked one of his star reporters, "it was to have anybody single out for praise any particular member of his staff." Sensing that the Commodore enjoyed seeing his correspondent put down, one *Herald* reporter panned a lecture Stanley gave in New York. He called it, among other things, "intolerably dull." Stanley's next talk was canceled. When the *New York Sun* revealed that Stanley's name really was Rowlands, Bennett used his paper to help spread the news for a couple of weeks. Some years later Bennett dispatched a reporter to investigate rumors that Stanley beat his wife. "Who was Stanley before I found him?" Bennett asked angrily.

8

A MINUTE . . . OVER THE NEWSPAPER . . . BEFORE BREAKFAST

This is a tale of two telegrams. One is as famous as the story of Bennett's summoning Stanley to his Paris apartments and equally apocryphal. The other is rarely recalled and has the virtue of being both true and revealing.

The source of the first telegram tale is James Creelman, who developed his flashy news-making skills under Bennett and went on to use them in Cuba for both Joseph Pulitzer's *New York World* and William Randolph Hearst's *New York Journal*. In his memoirs Creelman tells of Hearst's sending artist Frederic Remington to Cuba. "Presently Mr. Remington sent this telegram from Havana":

> W.R. HEARST, *New York Journal*, N.Y.:
> Everything is quiet. There is no trouble here. There will be no war. I wish to return.
> > REMINGTON.

Here, said Creelman, was Hearst's reply:

> REMINGTON, HAVANA:
> Please remain. You furnish the pictures, and I'll furnish the war.
> > W.R. Hearst.

The second telegram, dated December 7, 1897, is found in President William McKinley's papers. The day before, the president's annual message was read to Congress. It concentrated on what to do about the Cuban insurgency against their Spanish masters. The message's formulation was quintessentially McKinley. The president wanted to sound forceful without acting. Spain, he told Congress, should have time to make reforms. Failing that, he said vaguely, "action by the United States will remain to be taken." McKinley was at his home in Canton, Ohio, when the message was read. Aware that he was eager to know the reaction, John Addison Porter, his secretary, sent him a four-page telegram summarizing editorial comment from newspapers (to wit, "The Philadelphia Inquirer says editorially:- 'Like all of President McKinley's public utterances, the message is vigorous and able.'")

Creelman is the only source for the Remington telegram story. God only knows where he came up with it. No copy of the telegram has ever been found. Hearst never said anything about it.

This is not to say Hearst was unhappy when scholars repeated the canard in making the case that he started the Spanish-American War. Although he later disclaimed responsibility for the war, he did everything he could to make Cuba a big story. After the war was declared in April 1898, he twice printed this on the top of the *Journal*'s front page: "How do you like the *Journal*'s war?"

Looking down from some journalistic heaven (or up from its hell), Hearst probably is disappointed in equal measure that recent scholarship has absolved him of responsibility. Modern historians widely agree that a confluence of political and economic forces pushed the United States into war with Spain. Journalism scholars themselves have fallen in line with these explanations. "There is no evidence," one of the most prominent has written, "that Washington decision makers were influenced by media sensationalism or, for that matter, public opinion in general."

This, however, should not stand as the last word on the subject. It is one thing for modern historians to blast the myth that the Spanish-American War was "the *Journal*'s War" or, for that matter, the war of the yellow press generally. It is quite something else to shove the press out of the picture altogether. Ignoring the press creates a distortion of its own.

No clear understanding of the power of the press in the Spanish-American War is possible without examining news in a larger context than the yellow press provides. All the legends notwithstanding, Hearst and other yellow journalists were not acting alone. Newspapers of all stripes, along with magazines and books, drew attention to the plight of the Cubans and to U.S. economic interests on the island. While that broader coverage did not by itself "furnish" the war any more than stories in the yellow press did, pervasive news sympathetic to the insurgents helped move the country in the direction of war. The enabling environment created by the press was not just a matter of what journalists reported, but how policymakers perceived that those reports worked on the national psyche. That is where Porter's revealing telegram comes in. The president went to war with one keen eye on the press, his barometer for public opinion.

Inspiration for the Cuban insurrection lay with the romantic poet and journalist José Martí. In 1869, at age sixteen, he founded his first newspaper, the prorebel *Patria Libre*. After imprisonment and expulsion, he ended up in the United States, where he started another prorevolution newspaper, *Patria,* and helped create a prorevolution lobby called the Junta. While building his movement, he wrote for the sensationalist *New York Sun* as well as for many Latin American newspapers. Martí returned to Cuba in early 1895 to launch the revolution. His death in an early skirmish did not stop the insurrection. In the next months, the Spanish sent two hundred thousand troops to Cuba, the largest military force to cross the Atlantic up to that time.

In his farewell address as president, George Washington had inveighed against foreign entanglements. Jeffersonians opposed standing armies. America, John Quincy Adams had said, "does not go abroad in search of monsters to destroy." So, why did the United States break with tradition to intervene in Cuba? Why did intervention lead to a spate of American offshore annexation and colonization? Historians have offered a number of answers that arguably worked collectively.

One deals with commerce. The United States had run out of continental frontier. It had to look abroad for raw materials and customers. The depression from 1893 to 1897, triggered by a trade imbalance and a sharp decrease in foreign investment in the United States, further heightened American interest in overseas markets. McKinley, a foursquare probusiness Republican, understood this sentiment very well. "No subject can better engage our attention than the promotion of trade and commerce at home and abroad," he told the Commercial Club of Cincinnati shortly after his election in 1896. Although business leaders did not at first embrace the idea of armed intervention to further these goals, arguments for the expansion of trade were a regular feature in business journals.

The United States had strong economic ties to Cuba. Shortly after the Cuban insurgency began in 1895, President Grover Cleveland and his secretary of state Richard Olney estimated that American investment in the island exceeded $30 million. As strife continued unabated, Cleveland complained about the Spanish-imposed measures that threatened to ruin "the industrial value of the island." Another Spanish colony, the Philippines, offered a foothold in the Far East, where the United States saw enormous potential for trade expansion.

A powerful ally of commercial expansion was Capt. Alfred Thayer Mahan, president of the Naval War College and author of the landmark book *The Influence of Sea Power on History, 1660–1783*. Although the book was chiefly a history, Mahan's first chapter argued for developing a strong navy to promote commercial shipping. Key to this strategy was the establishment of overseas bases where naval vessels could lay in for fuel and supplies and where commercial vessels could store merchandise. Among Mahan's influential supporters were Senator Henry Cabot Lodge and Theodore Roosevelt, whom McKinley reluctantly appointed assistant secretary of the navy in 1897. Roosevelt gave Mahan's book an enthusiastic review in the *Atlantic Monthly*.

Humanitarian concerns were another force pushing Americans to intervene. The great majority of Cubans were poor to start with. In the last half of the nineteenth century, Cuba's death rate averaged twice that of England and Wales. The civil war made life far worse. Spanish general Valeriano Weyler imposed a *reconcentración* policy that herded civilians into "military areas." Such policies increased food shortages and illness. Although many Americans considered taxpayer-supported relief assistance to other peoples unconstitutional, McKinley issued an appeal for funds and supplies to be administered by the Red Cross. One of the principals in the Central Cuban Relief Committee was Dr. Louis Klopsch of the *Christian Herald*. When deciding to go to war in Cuba, McKinley emphasized the need "to put an end to the barbarities, bloodshed, starvation, and horrible miseries now existing there."

The Cuban fight for independence touched other emotions. One was Americans' itch to celebrate their own revolution, as most of the nation had done for a time through vicarious support for the French Revolution. This natural inclination to identify with struggles for freedom was easily aroused in the 1890s because of another emotion at work, insecurity. The end of the frontier and the rise of large cities populated by immigrants challenged the old ideas of agrarian America. The Spanish-American War, one proponent of this logic has noted, "expressed yearnings across the whole society for a way out of the tensions between the modern industrialized world and the earlier rural culture."

Emotions surged everywhere. They surged in the halls of Congress, where senators declaimed that "God was the author of the Monroe Doctrine." They surged in schools, where flag ceremonies such as the new Pledge of Allegiance became a daily ritual. They surged in homes, where average Americans employed "Spanish flag" toilet paper. And they surged in the press, where news and editorial opinion made Cuban independence a national cause.

The sensationalist New York press has commanded historians' attention for the most obvious reasons. It worked as hard at making a spectacle of itself as it did of Spanish rule in Cuba. In good showmanship fashion, it even had a mascot, a comic-strip character called the Yellow Kid. The history of the cartoon, and the way the Yellow Kid came to symbolize the sensational press, says something about the forces at work on these newspapers.

The Yellow Kid was born into a cutthroat environment. In those days, cities had a large number of newspapers, all vying for attention. In their search for reader-grabbing gimmicks, publishers took cartooning in a new direction with the comic strip. One of the most famous comics, which appeared in Joseph Pulitzer's *World,* was *Hogan's Alley.* Cartoonist Richard Outcault's leading character in that comic was an urchin with slightly Asian features, jug ears, and a toothy grin. Outcault dressed him in a yellow gown. Confronted by this wildly popular competitor, Hearst used one of his favorite tactics to undercut Pulitzer. He hired away Outcault. Pulitzer responded by assigning another cartoonist to draw the Yellow Kid, who appeared in both papers.

The crazed-looking urchin became the symbol of the sensational press in a round-about way. Before he hired Outcault, Hearst staged yet another one of those bicycling adventures so common at the time, this one the "Yellow Fellow Transcontinental Bicycle Relay." The rider who left San Francisco was clad entirely in yellow. Perhaps Hearst was trying to cash in on Outcault's creation, which he coveted; perhaps he simply liked the color. Anyway, Hearst's objective was to set a new coast-to-coast speed record for mounted riders and to generate readership. Dismissive of the Yellow Fellow cyclists and their news-making, the editor of the *New York Press* pejoratively called Hearst's style "yellow journalism." The term stuck.

The sensational competition for readers transformed the "Find Livingstone" craft of news-making into an irresponsible assembly line of distortions and outright falsehoods. At times Hearst's and Pulitzer's newspapers jumped their journalistic tracks altogether. Instead of covering government, they acted as though they were the government. Hearst's motto was "While Others Talk the Journal Acts!" When the daughter of a Cuban leader was thrown in jail, Hearst mobilized two hundred correspondents across the United States to get signatures on a petition asking the Spanish queen regent for the release of the "Cuban Joan of Arc." McKinley's mother signed it. When the petition failed, Hearst sent a reporter named Karl Decker to Cuba to engineer her escape, which critics described as "jail-breaking journalism." On other occasions Hearst sent a two-thousand-dollar sword and medical supplies to the commander-in-chief of the Cuban rebels, organized a delegation of congressmen to visit Cuba as "*Journal* commissioners," and ordered Creelman to make plans for purchasing a tramp steamer that could be sunk in the Suez Canal to block the Spanish fleet if it attempted to reach Manila—a ridiculously illegal scheme that was never executed. The *World* and its staff were not bashful about entering into the fray either. At the end of the war an uninvited *World* correspondent named Sylvester Scovel joined three officers in taking down the Spanish flag from the governor's palace. When Gen. William Shafter objected, Scovel hit him, or at least tried to; accounts differ.

A factual story involving Remington's visit to Cuba is a showcase for yellow news distortion. Hearst sent the Wild West artist with that most dashing of all correspondents, Richard Harding Davis, to the island in late 1896. Beset by logistical problems (and never receiving the famous Hearst telegram), Remington returned to New York. Davis soldiered on through more frustrations. He was on the verge of reaching the insurgents when Hearst ran a front-page story prematurely announcing that he had made contact with them. Davis was now a marked man as far as Spanish general Weyler was concerned. The correspondents with whom he was supposed to travel refused to take him along. Coming home aboard the *Olivette,* Davis met Clemencia Arango, who was being expelled for suspected aid to the insurgents and whose brother was an insurgent leader. Señorita Arango told him that she and two other women were searched three times before leaving the country. In writing up this story, Davis did not dwell on Spanish suspicions that the three women were taking secret dispatches to the Cuban Junta—which they had done previously and, as Arango subsequently admitted, did this time as well. With Victorian rectitude, Davis wrote instead about the supposed indignities of the searches, vaguely suggesting they involved stripping in front of men. Although Remington was in New York and nowhere near the scene, the artist provided an imaginative illustration showing a lithe woman standing naked before a semicircle of uniformed men. The drawing stretched two-thirds of the way across an inside page of the *Journal.*

The first uproar came from a public offended by Spanish brutishness; the second from the *World,* which interviewed Arango upon her arrival in the United States and learned that women had done the searching. Other newspapers howled. "Mr. Davis and Mr. Remington," editorialized the *New York Evening World* three days later, "should be well quarantined before they are allowed to mingle again

ILLUSTRATING THE WAR

Frederick Remington, who inaccurately sketched Spanish officials searching Señorita Clemencia Arango, was one of many who made Cuba a war of images as well as words.

Editors hired artists and experimented with sending photographs from Cuba by wire. The pictorial coverage in *Collier's* was the best ever by a magazine up to that time, a factor in its rise to national prominence. The size of *Journal* headline type grew 400 percent from February to April 1898, causing editor Arthur Brisbane to comment that "the greatest blessing" was that the word "war" had only three letters. "Had we had the French 'guerre' or even the German 'Krieg' to deal with, we would have been lost."

Meanwhile, a whole new visual genre of reporting emerged thanks to Albert E. Smith and J. Stuart Blackton. The two moving picture tinkers hit pay dirt with a dramatization of the sinking of the *Maine*. In it the Spanish flag was ripped from a flagpole and the Stars and Stripes hoisted in its place. The public responded enthusiastically. "With nationalistic feeling at fever pitch," Smith later recalled, "we set out to photograph what the people wanted to see." They filmed the funeral for the *Maine*'s victims at Arlington National Cemetery, the charge up San Juan Hill by Teddy Roosevelt's Rough Riders, and later "a violent segment of the Boer War with Richard Harding Davis." The newsreel was born.

Images have since become essential in human rights reporting. *Newsday* correspondent Roy Gutman learned this lesson when editors showed little interest in his coverage of the Serbian assaults on Croatian civilians in 1991. To get their attention, he came up with a new formula for covering human rights abuses in the Bosnia War the next year: "There had to be images to back up and support the story; there should be a mainbar [story] built around a hard news lead, and a sidebar built around the victims or some related topic. I stuck with that formula for years thereafter. Pictures were absolutely indispensable to convincing the reading public of the facts of the story on day one."

This is the imaginative (and inaccurate) Frederic Remington illustration that accompanied Richard Harding Davis's story in the *New York Journal* on Clemencia Arango.

with reputable newspaper men." The embarrassed Davis disingenuously put all the blame on Hearst and Remington. He vowed never again to work for the *Journal*.

The New York yellow journals wanted to steal the show. In terms of the way historians have focused on them, they succeeded. But for all their spectacular antics, they were hardly acting alone. Collectively journalists came down where Richard Harding Davis did. However much he disliked Hearst, he returned from Cuba favoring U.S. intervention. "No man, no matter what his prejudices may be," Davis said in a book recapping his assignment, "can make this journey and not go home convinced that it is his duty to try to stop this cruel waste of life and this wanton destruction of a beautiful country."

Just as Cuba was tinder for a burst of American imperialism, it ignited unprecedented news coverage from journals across the country. By one count, about seventy-five correspondents reported from the island between February 1895 and the start of the war in April 1898; fifteen reached insurgent forces. A conservative estimate puts the number of reporters covering the war after the United States intervened at two hundred; other estimates are more than twice as high.

Sensationalism was not confined to a few newspapers in New York City. Newspapers throughout the country leaned that way. Eager to attract readers, dailies in Cincinnati and St. Louis tended to be more yellow than those in New York, concluded one study of the press shortly after the war. If these newspapers could not afford their own correspondents, they were eager for reports from the *Journal*, the *World*, and the sensational *Sun*, which organized syndicates through which their often far-fetched stories circulated nationally.

More significant still, biased and often outright irresponsible coverage favoring the Cubans was not confined to the yellow press. The dignified newspapers did their part, as the *New York Herald* illustrates. The *Herald* had shed some of its extravagant ways to become a favorite sheet of wealthy conservative readers. Like a number of other relatively respectable newspapers, it did not swing editorially toward intervention until a few days before war was declared. Nonetheless, its news pages carried story after story showing the plight of the Cubans. In early 1897, *Herald* correspondent Stephen Bonsal reported impending famine and disease without "parallel in the history of human suffering." After the sinking of the *Maine*, the *Herald* joined the *World* and the *Journal* in sending in its own diving team to investigate the cause of the explosion. Also like the *World* and the *Journal*, its reports were syndicated.

Correspondents' reports were recycled in congressional testimony, quickie books, and magazines. "In these leaking huts, where the dead and the dying lie huddled together," Bonsal wrote melodramatically in *Harper's Weekly* upon his return, "unceasing prayers are being offered up to Our Lady of Pity, whose shrine in the far-off Cobre Mountains they have all visited and in happier days decked out bright with flowers. And I believe these prayers will be heard in these United States." Bonsal testified before Congress and wrote a book about his experiences.

In 1895, *Cosmopolitan*'s editor John Brisben Walker ran an article on the Cubans' suffering and proclaimed: "The time is ripe for interference of the United States in the affairs of Cuba." Quite happy to do the interfering himself, Walker sent a writer to Madrid to propose the purchase of Cuban independence for $100 million. The bylines of proexpansionist strategists filled magazines during this period. As early as 1895, Senator Lodge wrote about "Our Blundering Foreign Policy" of not annexing Cuba or the Spanish West Indies. The *Citizen,* a Philadelphia educational magazine, observed in mid-1898, "Certainly it is no fault of the editors if the public is not thoroughly conversant with every possible phase of the present war. . . . *McClure's,* indeed, is wholly given over to belligerency from cover to cover."

In their own ways, the Spanish colonizers and the Cuban insurgents created the circumstances for such reporting. Spanish brutality was a fact. The Spanish concentration camps lent themselves to human-rights-abuse stories. The Spanish made a bad situation worse by their treatment of reporters, whom they censored, arrested, and expelled. "The American newspapers . . . poison everything with falsehood," Weyler told Creelman. "They should be suppressed." On the other side was José Martí's Junta, which minimized news about insurgent transgressions while systematically influencing coverage in their favor. The Junta published its own newspapers and planted sympathizers on at least two journals, the *New Orleans Times-Picayune* and the *Washington Star.* Most effective of all, it spoon-fed stories to reporters in Washington, Chicago, New York, and the Florida cities where the Spanish forced reporters to congregate. The daily four o'clock Junta press meeting in New York was known as the Peanut Club. "No matter what the leanings of his paper," said Horatio Rubens, a New York lawyer who brought the peanuts and early on assisted Martí, "I know of none who was not personally sympathetic to Cuba in her trouble." Ironically, Rubens's complaint was that reporters "were not as careful about verifying rumors they should have been."* Respectable organs

* The Junta's relationship with correspondents is apparent from the congressional testimony of one of the most notorious exaggerators, Frederick Lawrence. The *Journal* correspondent pretty much confined himself to the Inglaterra Hotel in Havana while writing stories involving, among other things, "Amazon" insurgent leaders. After being expelled with Creelman, he testified under oath to a Senate committee that the Spanish version of events could not be believed, and that the insurgents could.

LAWRENCE: I found that in the reports of skirmishes the military censor invariably reported that the Spanish had killed from three to a dozen, or perhaps more, men, and had captured so many horses or had killed so many horses and had wounded so many, while communication from the ranks of the insurgents to their friends in Habana [a contemporary spelling of Havana] would be entirely the reverse. . . .

Q: The result, then, was you could not know which was nearest the truth?

A: Personally I have no knowledge of it. I did not go outside the lines and did not count the dead and dying or anything of that kind; but the gentlemen who would bring me information—and I did not have to seek for it, they were only too willing to give it to me—were men of the very highest character. They were men whose word is certain to be believed, at least on an equality with that of any man who walks the earth. . . . .

of journalism could be as flagrantly irresponsible as their yellow sisters. Relying on second-hand reports out of Cuba and Key West, the Boston bureau of the Associated Press reported in early 1896 that rebels had captured Havana. "Strangely enough," the *New York Times* noted, "this startling announcement did not come direct from Havana, as it naturally and very promptly would if the insurgents were really in possession of the Cuban capital, but it was projected upon the public from Boston." The Associated Press, said the *Times*' headline, was "IN PERIL OF REPORTING KURDS IN SANTIAGO."

Irritated with bogus reporting, as well as his treatment by an insurgent general, *Herald* correspondent George Bronson Rea assembled a book full of press transgressions, *Facts and Fakes about Cuba.* Among his examples was the self-righteous *New York Times.* Notwithstanding its "Kurds in Santiago" slam, the financially struggling paper relied largely on the object of its scorn, the AP, for foreign news and occasionally supported its own imaginative correspondents in the field. One of these reporters, William Francis Mannix, also represented the *Philadelphia Press* and wrote under the bylines William G. Leonard and the single-inital W. Mannix is vaguely remembered today as a literary forger. Rea exposed an article by Mannix that reprinted letters he had supposedly received from Cuban leaders. The letters, Rea noted, put the insurgent president in a city that did not exist and used made-up names for some of the central characters.

The following year, 1897, the *Times* ran a story with prose every bit as purple as that which flowed from Creelman's pen. The reporter, whoever he was, allegedly reached a camp belonging to insurgent "patriots." He recounted gruesome scenes of machete-hacked innocents left behind by the Spanish and quoted at length the Cuban general-in-charge, putting lines in his mouth from a recent Gilbert and Sullivan production, *The Pirates of Penzance:*

> Tears were rolling down the bronzed cheeks of the brave soldier as he proceeded.
>
> "Go back and tell them, Señor," he continued, "that every Cuban patriot stands with breast bared for the foeman's steel;* that he will spill the last drop of blood in his veins to win this fight. Say for them that men robbed of their homes, whose children and wives have been butchered in cold blood, burned in

---

Q: Were these gentlemen on the side of the insurgents?

A: Yes, sir.

Q: So for that reason you were inclined to give their accounts greater weight than that of the censor?

A: Yes, sir; and for this reason I found the sympathizers with the insurgents were more conservative than the other; that is, they were willing to concede a battle now and then to the other side, while the Spanish side of the news was that of a Spanish victory.

Lawrence also observed that 60% to 70% of the Spanish soldiers had syphilis; "they are a corrupt people, you know." "Conditions of Affairs in Cuba," *Hearing before a Subcommittee of Foreign Relations,* May 20, 1896, 54th Cong., sess. 2, serial no. 3471, 4–5, 29.

* Sergeant and Chorus of Police: "When the foeman bares his steel, / Tarantara! Tarantara!" Gilbert and Sullivan, *The Pirates of Penzance.*

the funeral pyre of their homes, and some doomed to a much worse fate, men whose nightly dreams are of homes that are homes no more. Autonomy and reform! No; a thousand times, no. Think you there is a Cuban in all this band of mine so mean and low that he would stand where we are now and cast his eyes over this desolate waste and ask of Spaniards terms of peace? No, Señor, there are a hundred bullets for every traitor and a thousand machetes for a single coward. He who dares to plead the Spaniard's cause will be considered now a Judas, and as such would reap reward. Back in the face of Spain we cast her reforms. Bring back our wives and children and our homes and then we will listen to reforms, and not until then."

George Bronson Rea admitted that he was not above reproach. His reporting "omitted many events that would have hurt the [insurgent] cause."

Every congressman, said a Maine representative arguing for war, "had two or three newspapers in his district—most of them printed in red ink . . . and shouting for blood." Looking back, Ernest May, one of the few modern historians to appreciate the power of press coverage of the war, came to the same conclusion: "Staid dailies like the Boston *Herald,* the Buffalo *Courier,* the Newark *Advertiser,* the Cleveland *Plain-Dealer,* the Omaha *World-Herald,* and the Portland *Oregonian* whetted sympathy for the rebels just as much as did the fiery New York *Journal* or *World.* The press as a whole, not just the 'yellow press,' aided the Cuban cause."

A study done in conjunction with this book builds on May's observation by examining coverage of the Spanish-American War in the seven months leading up to the war. The ten newspapers in the study ranged from the sensational or yellow (characterized by large headlines, flashy illustrations, rampant self-promotion, emphasis on entertaining news, and relative lack of concern for attribution) to the conservative ones on the opposite end of the spectrum. Mixed newspapers exhibited features of both. The study looked at what scholars call valence (whether news was generally pro-Spain or pro-Cuba) as well as the frames in which the newspapers presented the conflict. All editorial fare was studied: news stories (81% of the total), editorials (18%), and letters to the editor (1%).

Contrary to common assumptions about the yellow press's taking the lead in hammering away at Cuba, table 2 shows that conservative newspapers ran almost three times as many stories about Cuba (on average 8.1 stories) as the yellow sheets (3.13 stories). Mixed papers fell in between. The conservative papers were more balanced in the valence stories than the mixed or the yellow sheets, but this was only a matter of degree. Pro-Cuban items outnumbered pro-Spanish items in the yellow journals about 6 to 1 and in the mixed papers about 5 to 1. In the conservative press the ratio was a still considerable 2.5 to 1.

The yellow press was so flamboyant that it was sensational in every direction. When it came to issues of humanitarian abuses, promotion of conflict, and national rights, the yellow press ran more than twice as many stories as the conservative papers presenting Spain in a positive light. Again the mixed newspapers fell in between.

TABLE 2. Average daily editorial fare about Cuba

Newspaper	Daily average no. of items	Pro-Cuba %	Pro-Spain %
Conservative		14.7	6.0
Washington Post	8.0		
Los Angeles Times	9.4		
Seattle Post-Intelligencer	8.6		
New York Times	6.4		
Mixed		26.8	5.0
Atlanta Constitution	6.2		
St. Louis Post-Dispatch	3.5		
Chicago Tribune	6.3		
Yellow		38.5	6.2
Denver Post	3.4		
New York World	1.5		
New York Journal	4.5		

Coverage varied from paper to paper, time to time. The yellow *Journal* hollered for war when the *Maine* exploded, but the yellow *World* counseled moderation pending an investigation. Newspapers generally lost interest in Cuba during the 1896 presidential campaign. Still, a consistent message ran through the pages of newspapers and magazines, which reached a crescendo in the months leading up to the war. Day after day, the news reported Spanish insults to American citizens and property and recounted the abuses inflicted on the Cubans.

A great many stories were short items. Here is an example from E. L. Godkin's *New York Evening Post,* whose editorials counseled moderation in dealing with Cuba. The story, which appeared on February 25, 1897, presented a poorly attributed report on the imprisonment and death of a Cuban-American dentist accused of helping the insurgents derail a train.

> KEY WEST, Fla, February 25—A passenger from Havana who has just landed here from the steamer Olivette states that Dr. Ricardo Ruiz, the American citizen who was found dead in a cell of the prison of Guanabacoa, was killed by Fonsdeviela, the Spanish governor of Guanabacoa. The passenger explained that Gov. Fonsdeviela visited Dr. Ruiz in his place of confinement and violently questioned the prisoner. The latter resented the Governor's manner, and this so angered Fonsdeviela that he seized a club, struck the unfortunate man on the head, and so caused his death.

Editorials in conservative journals often ran along the lines of this long one-paragraph piece in the *Los Angeles Times,* which appeared on October 5, 1897.

The brave and resolute Cubans are standing out for absolute independence with a spirit of vigorous determination that promises to win for them sooner or later the glorious meed of liberty. When a people make up their minds to break loose from the monarchical system in this age of enlightenment, they are sure to find a solid backing that goes far to win battles and a moral support that is almost as hard to combat on the part of the monarchists, as the frowning muzzles of guns and the shining points of cold steel. Spain is evidently going to try hard to save something from the wreck in Cuba, but if the insurgents stand fast and insist upon independence they will achieve it. As in the old slavery days it is perhaps better to buy freedom than to fight for it, but if a price cannot be agreed upon it is surely a boon worth fighting for. The Cubans have made a gallant struggle and win they must eventually. God speed the day when those beautiful islands shall have a flag and a government of their own and be freed forever from a domination that has been bloody, cruel and inhuman to the last degree!

At the time of the Spanish-American War, the aggregate circulation of dailies matched the number of households and in urban areas exceeded the number. Literate Americans—and more than 90 percent were literate—could scarcely avoid Cuba, even if they read only the cartoons. The Yellow Kid showed up in a prewar comic series in which the Huckleberry Volunteers set out to address Cuba's ills. In one scene Cuban women embrace their ragtag liberators. Says the kid, "No wonder Cuba ought to be free." Those who never picked up a paper could get a little of the news simply by walking down the street. When the *Maine* sunk, the *Chicago Dry Goods Reporter* had as a suggestion for retailers: "The window dresser who is ever alert for novelty will not allow the disaster to the battleship *Maine* to pass without getting an idea out of it for a window display." An inspired ad copywriter came up with "We would like to C-U-B-A purchaser of a pair of our stylish fitting shoes."

In a sentimental *McClure's* article, the young Kansan editor of the *Emporia Gazette,* William Allen White, painted a picture of the heartland's march to intervention: the proliferation of flags, the little boys who stopped playing "cowboys and Indians" to play "war with Spain," and the drip-drip-drip of news stories about Cuba. "The Yankee did not gather in hoarse-voiced mobs," he wrote. "He did not lose time from his work. A minute or two with a bulletin board at noon, and another over the newspaper before supper and before breakfast, were lost—but that was all."

Shortly after President McKinley sent his fence-sitting message to Congress in December 1897, Enrique Dupuy de Lôme, the Spanish minister to Washington, wrote to the editor of Madrid's *El Heraldo*. The speech, he said, "shows once more McKinley for what he is, weak and popularity-seeking and in addition a hack politician who wants to keep all his options open and stand well with the jingoes of his party." The letter fell into the hands of the Junta, which passed it to New York newspapers as well as the *Washington Post*. It appeared on the front page of the *Journal* under the headline "THE WORST INSULT TO THE UNITED STATES IN ITS HISTORY."

" A minute . . . over the newspaper . . . before breakfast."

In his sentimental *McClure's* article, William Allen White described the American heartland's steady march to intervention in Spain. This drawing, which was in the article, suggested the drum beat of the news.

The embarrassed minister resigned his post. Moved to greater restiveness, both the House and the Senate passed resolutions calling on the administration to release U.S. consular reports from Cuba believed to be damning of the Spanish. Then, on February 15, the battleship *Maine* exploded in the Havana harbor, giving another opportunity for jingoes to call for action.

President McKinley ordered a naval inquiry and continued to seek a way to avoid war. Some scholars suggest that he was playing the public like a fiddle, skillfully letting support for war build while buying time to explore options for settling the Cuban problem. More likely, the Spanish minister's assessment was correct, the president was "weak and popularity-seeking." Asked about Cuba before his run for the presidency, he responded, "I most politely decline to go on record." Senior political appointees in his administration thought "he lacks backbone." Whatever the case, the press weighed heavily in his thinking, as well as the public's, and created an enabling environment for his decision to go to war.

The measurement and analysis of public opinion has come a long way in recent years. Social science research has underscored the power of the media to focus the public's attention. Journalists shape public attitudes through their selection of what gets covered, a phenomenon called agenda-setting, and how they tell, or frame, the story. Studies of agenda-setting and framing have concentrated on modern news occurrences, which allows researchers to verify that news coverage correlates with public opinion polls. We have no public opinion polls to validate that press coverage and American attitudes were aligned during the Spanish-American War. But given what we know about the way agenda-setting and framing work in current settings, given that newspapers were the dominant news source at the time, and given the enormous amount of coverage and its lopsided nature, we have every reason to suppose that the press influenced the public.

As already noted, the amount of coverage and its lopsidedness were extraordinary not only in the New York yellow press but also in journals of all kinds across the country. This coverage was particularly powerful because it resonated with insecurities and enthusiasms at large in the country. Resistance rooted in the traditional American aversion to overseas adventures still existed, but it was less powerful than usual. The foreign policy elite supporting that tradition was temporarily in disarray while at the same time the public was unusually engaged in foreign policy, Ernest May has argued. "Emotionalism increased dramatically as leadership dispersed to men who ordinarily deferred to the establishment."

News reports from abroad led to congressional hearings, which were covered by the press and produced more news stories. The day after Richard Harding Davis's story appeared about Clemencia Arango, the *Journal* ran this headline: CONGRESS WILL HEAR TO-DAY OF THE SEARCH OUTRAGE ON THE OLIVETTE. "We have a newspaper press in the United States," jingo senator John Morgan told his colleagues, "and I am very glad that we have, because through that agency we have acquired knowledge of what goes on in Cuba and elsewhere in the world, even in Armenia.* In the main it turns out that the consensus of statements made by the American press in respect to a matter occurring in a foreign country is true."

The same dynamic occurred outside Washington. The Junior Order of United American Mechanics, the Sons of the American Revolution, the Galveston Farmers Alliance, and the Bryan Silver Club of Spokane condemned Spanish oppression. Anti-Spanish rallies erupted in cities and small towns, where General Weyler was burned in effigy. The press covered these events, too. Such news, we may suppose, gave additional impetus to intervention in the same way that newspapers emboldened far-flung colonists in the years leading up to the American Revolution. As one historian of Colonial America has argued, newspaper stories about local boycotts of British imports "encouraged men and women who perhaps had never given much thought to what was happening in neighboring communities, let alone in distant colonies, to situate themselves within a larger community."

Even if one dismisses evidence that journalists influenced public attitudes, something else shows the power of the press to move the country toward war. Rightly or wrongly, national leaders attributed great powers to the press and paid considerable attention to it. These powers, as noted by William Randolph Hearst's *New York Journal,* were to both "form and express public opinion." Hearst described this as "government by newspaper." E. L. Godkin, the antiwar editor of the *New York Evening Post* and the *Nation* magazine, described this dual ability to create and reflect in an article on public opinion in January 1898. "That the newspaper's mode of presenting facts does seriously affect the way in which people perform the pro-

---

* The plight of the Cubans was not the only human rights concern to receive press attention at the time. Reports of the massacre of Armenians under Turkish rule in 1894 also triggered widespread sympathy in the United States. Walker's *Cosmopolitan* sent a "special commissioner" to cover famine in India in 1897 and published the following articles about India, both by Julian Hawthorne: "The Horrors of the Plague in India," July 1897, 230–46; and "India Starving," August 1897, 369–84.

cess called 'making up their minds,' especially about public questions, can hardly be denied. The nearest approach we can make to what people are thinking about any matter of public interest is undoubtedly by 'reading the papers.'" The prospect of war loomed over Godkin's analysis. Newspapers, he complained, "have to maintain their place in the estimation of their readers, and, if possible, to increase the number of these readers. Unhappily, in times of international trouble, the easiest way to do this always *seems* to be to influence the public mind against the foreigner. . . . The applause and support of the newspapers seem to be public opinion."

A keen appreciation of the power of the press to shape the debate animated the Cuban Junta public relations program. The Cubans had plenty of evidence that their strategy worked. "In my daily business I have clipped out for me reports in the papers from all over this country," said railroad president, politician, and sought-after public speaker Chauncey Depew to a Republican gathering. "Every morning they are placed before me, so that I may see how things that may have some bearing on the railroad business are going. I can't help seeing what a strong feeling is spreading over the whole land in favor of colonial expansion."

The number one close reader of the press was President McKinley, who broke with White House tradition. His predecessors were largely uninterested in courting public opinion, except at election time, and paid little attention to press relations. "President McKinley has always been friendly to newspaper men," said the *Ohio State Journal*. "He recognizes the power of the press." As Ohio governor, he appointed two journalists as assistants. Once in the White House, McKinley admitted journalists to the second floor of the east wing, where a table and writing materials were available. His secretary, John Porter, held a press briefing at ten o'clock in the evening, handing out news releases and answering questions. Porter's assistant, George B. Cortelyou, wrote many of these releases and supplied journalists with advance copies of speeches. When Porter retired, the press-conscious Cortelyou replaced him. The president himself regularly met with the White House press corps. Whenever McKinley left town on an extended trip by train, the staff attached a car for journalists. As war approached, he directed that press notices be given to journalists throughout the day.

McKinley, wrote Cortelyou in his diary, carefully read the press to glean "the drift of public sentiment." In a *McClure's* article describing the run-up to the war, journalist Ida Tarbell described the president as "a reader of newspapers, and scarcely a day has gone by, even in the hottest of the war excitement, that he has not found time to run through a large number, including five or six New York dailies, the Washington evening and morning papers, one or two from Chicago, and perhaps half a dozen others from large cities." McKinley's "chief gauge of public opinion," concluded a historian of his media management, was "Current Comment," a digest of press clippings assembled by his staff. Although McKinley's inner circle said he did not read the yellow journals, Current Comment carried clips from sensational papers, including the *Journal*. Even if it had not, McKinley's regular diet of reading material contained plenty of stories showing that Cuba was a major issue for the public, that the public empathized with the Cubans, and that enthusiasm for war was mounting.

The month after Enrique Dupuy de Lôme's incendiary letter and the *Maine* tragedy, Vermont senator Redfield Proctor gave a speech describing his recent trip to Cuba. Proctor's remarks about conditions on the island caused a sensation. Ida Tarbell reported, "The 'Maine' was for the moment forgotten in the realization that all the horrors of which the country had been hearing through the newspapers for months were not only true, but actually fell short of the truth." Other press accounts told of "war fever" in one community or another. The issue was no longer whether the Cubans deserved support. Noninterventionist businessmen worried that inaction would drag down markets. Republicans worried that it would tear apart their party.

By early April, most journals had made peace with war. Business publications that had previously stopped short of martial intervention became resigned to it. The *Chicago Times-Herald*, owned by McKinley's conservative confidant H. H. Kohlsaat, declared intervention "inevitable." In the fall of 1897, the *Washington Post*'s first-ever foreign correspondent had gone to Cuba and found the Spanish "the most kindly and courteous and gentleman beings I have ever seen in military uniforms." Following the sinking of the *Maine*, its headlines grew belligerent in bigger and bigger type. One front page of the *Post* carried a cartoon with Uncle Sam pointing to a sinking *Maine*. Underneath ran the words: "Stout hearts, my laddies! If the row comes, remember the Maine, and show the world how American sailors can fight." Another anti-interventionist newspaper owner friendly with the president, Whitelaw Reid, told his managing editor at the *New York Tribune*, "it would be unwise for us to be the last persons to assent to [war], or to seem to be dragged into the support of it." One historian has suggested that the most "influential note" McKinley received came in a March 25 telegram from W. C. Reick, "a trusted political adviser" and city editor of the *New York Herald*, whose editorials had resisted intervention. "BIG CORPORATIONS HERE NOW BELIEVE WE WILL HAVE WAR," the telegram read. "BELIEVE ALL WOULD WELCOME IT AS RELIEF TO SUSPENSE."

War had not been inevitable when the Cuban insurrection first broke out. "We want no wars of conquest," said McKinley in his inaugural speech; "we must avoid the temptation of territorial aggression." The forces for intervention gathered momentum with the help of the press, which kept Cuba on the public's mind and ultimately the president's agenda. The unfolding of events in this climate eventually left the president without any choices. From his reading of the press, McKinley had no doubt where the public stood when he sent his war message to Congress on April 11.

"The past few months have witnessed one of the most remarkable developments of public opinion ever observed in this or any other country," a scholar wrote in the *Annals of the American Academy of Political and Social Science* in September 1898. "A year ago we wanted no colonies, no alliances, no European neighbors, no army, and not much navy. Our relations with foreign nations were to be of the simplest. . . . Today every one of these principles is challenged, if not definitely rejected."

Following the quick defeat of the Spanish, the once war-reluctant president led the country on a spate of empire-building never again to be repeated. In addition to occupying Cuba, whose freedom was the objective of the war, the United States acquired the Philippines, Guam, and Puerto Rico, all from Spain, as well as Hawaii and uninhabited Wake Island. When a Cuban government was finally established in 1902, the United States retained a naval base at Guantanamo Bay, which it still holds.

People who spoke to the president during this acquisitive time noted his continuing preoccupation with public opinion. An article describing McKinley's routine said he "breakfasts at eight and reads the papers until shortly before ten." When he made a Midwest speaking trip to sell his postwar imperialistic foreign policy, his stenographer recorded how hard people clapped and for how long. The president didn't have to listen too hard to know jingoism continued to run high. When Europeans criticized U.S. aggression, newspapers across the country called for a boycott of imported fashions. "Patriotic Women," read an *Indianapolis News* headline, "They Will Not Buy Anything that Is Manufactured in France." The president had not wanted the Philippines initially, he said, "but in the end there was no alternative."

Issues central to this chapter remain in play today. They illustrate the complicated interplay of news and foreign policy that continues with varying outcomes.

Human rights reporting. The Spanish-American War was the first in which the United States invoked human rights as a rationale for intervention. Since then human rights have become a distinct feature of international relations. "Protecting individual rights, advancing the rule of law, preventing genocide, and the like have become an inescapable part of arguments over policy," wrote the president of the Council on Foreign Relations in 2003. The press can alert the world to human rights abuses and sometimes stop them by embarrassing perpetrators. Describing the creation of the United Nations International Criminal Tribunal for the former Yugoslavia, prosecutor Richard Goldstone credited the "visual and written reports of the plight of the victims of ethnic cleansing in Bosnia" with jolting "the Security Council into taking the unprecedented step of creating a court as its own sub-organ."

News media attention to human rights, however, has been uneven. While the excesses of coverage in the Spanish-American War dominate this chapter, journalists often come late to human rights stories or barely show up at all. "In 1993, when approximately 50,000 people were killed in political fighting between Hutus and Tutsis in Burundi," political scientist Steven Livingston noted, "American broadcast networks ignored the story." Americans were shocked when the conflict subsequently spiraled out of control in Rwanda, where more than 10 percent of the country's 7.7 million population were killed in just one hundred days. Between January

1995 and May 1996, Livingston added, print and broadcast news media concentrated on the plight of 3.7 million in Bosnia and gave little attention to twelve other humanitarian crises involving more than 25 million others. The first genocide of the twenty-first century, in Darfur, went largely uncovered for two years. "NBC had only five minutes of coverage all last year," commented Nicholas Kristof of the *New York Times* in 2005, "and CBS only three minutes—about one minute of coverage for every hundred thousand deaths."

McKinley's secretary of state John Hay called the Spanish-American War a "splendid little war." Certainly, from the point of view of the press, it was an ideal foreign story. The war was short. Getting to Cuba, only ninety miles from Florida, was relatively easy. U.S. interests appeared to be at stake. But the increases in circulation did not cover the costs of coverage. "Should a war reported as this has been continue two years, it would bankrupt the resources of every first-class newspaper in New York city," wrote Arthur Brisbane, the *New York Journal*'s managing editor. While newspapers are still willing to lose money covering major conflicts or wars, especially those involving the United States, they are less enthusiastic about paying for roving correspondents who may (or may not) find a distant human rights story no one knows about in a place where the interests of the United States are not clear.

As a result, nongovernmental organizations are often the first to spot human rights abuses. A good example of the process occurred in the mid-1970s. While in the Philippines to cover repatriation of American prisoners being flown out of North Vietnam, William Mullen of the *Chicago Tribune* filled down time by investigating a Muslim insurrection in the southern provinces, where there also happened to be a drought. United Nations relief workers told him conditions were even worse in Africa and India and that this was getting little press attention. For months Mullen unsuccessfully urged editors to let him cover the story. He might never have done so, except that he became miffed about being passed over for an overseas post he wanted. When Mullen threatened to quit, his editors placated him by agreeing that he could do the drought story. Mullen and a photographer, Ovie Carter, traveled for three months through West and Central Africa, Ethiopia, and India to put together a comprehensive, in-depth five-part series that won the Pulitzer Prize.

Lobbying the press. U.S. aggression in the Spanish-American War was not matched again, many thought, until the early twenty-first century, when the United States once again defied "Old Europe," as the secretary of defense called America's traditional Continental allies, to invade Iraq. The Iraq War had striking parallels with the earlier adventure in Cuba. Some of the similarities were merely silly, for instance Americans' strident anti-French sentiment. Some were serious. In the earlier war, the battle cry "Remember the Maine!" presumed that the Spanish had sunk the U.S. battleship, an unsubstantiated charge much later proved false.* In the

---

* A 1976 investigation by Adm. Hyman Rickover, commander of the U.S. nuclear submarine program, concluded that the ship had blown up from the inside, not from a Spanish mine on the outside.

latter conflict, the argument for invasion rested on inaccurate reports that Saddam Hussein had weapons of mass destruction and connections to anti-American terrorists. In both wars, the United States ended up at odds with the very people it set out to save.

Of particular relevance to this chapter, an organization eerily similar to the Cuban Junta paved the road to war in Iraq by subverting the modern media. That organization was the Iraqi National Congress (INC), made up of Iraqi exiles and defectors and led by Ahmed Chalabi. The U.S. government provided some $33 million in financial support to the INC between March 2000 and May 2003. Contrary to congressional intent, the INC used those funds to propagandize in the United States, assembling bogus evidence on weapons of mass destruction, and coached reporters just as Horatio Rubens did at the Peanut Club. Among these tutored reporters was Judith Miller of the *New York Times,* who for many years had relied on information from Chalabi, although she was not alone. The INC provided a congressional committee with a list of 108 articles it said were based on information that it provided. These stories appeared in the *Washington Post, USA Today,* and Fox News, among many, many others.

Successors to the Cuban Junta have shown up in many other guises. After the Communist triumph in China, Chiang Kai-shek and his exiled-to-Taiwan government spent substantial sums to lobby against U.S. diplomatic recognition of the Communist People's Republic of China. Henry Luce, founder of *Time* and other magazines as well as being a strong anti-Communist proponent of Chiang, was a dedicated supporter of Taiwan. On the other side of the political coin were the leftist Sandinistas, who overthrew the Somoza regime in Nicaragua. The Sandinista foreign ministry hired Agendas International to monitor U.S. press coverage and help arrange direct meetings with news executives. (The foreign minister was a member of the Maryknoll missionary order, and the owners of Agendas International were two former Maryknoll priests.) The Sandinistas needed the help, said one of the partners in Agenda International, because they were "losing the war of words in the United States."

The United States engages in its own opinion molding abroad. Some is covert, such as disinformation campaigns by U.S. intelligence services. Some is direct. The government launched the Voice of America (VOA) during World War II to ply Germany with propaganda. The modern VOA has its own foreign correspondents and a mandate to win hearts and minds with balanced news projecting "significant American thought and institutions." During the cold war, the CIA established Radio Liberty and Radio Free Europe to provide domestic news in Communist countries with no independent national broadcast stations. Those two networks, which no longer receive funding from the intelligence budget, continue to function along with newer ones, Radio Free Asia, Radio Sawa and Alhurra in the Middle East, and (in a direct nod to the Cuban Junta) Radio Martí and TV Martí. The 50,000-watt Radio Martí transmitter sits at the jumping-off spot for American reporters covering Cuba during the Spanish-American conflict, the Florida Keys. After the invasion of Iraq, the U.S. military initiated a covert campaign to plant news stories in local media. This involved secretly paying money to newspapers and local journalists, as well as funding a Baghdad Press Club—an approach that struck some as contradicting the U.S. claim that it was laying the foundation for an open democratic society.

The media as a proxy for public opinion. Concerns have mounted in recent years over the power of media to shape policy. One common term for this is the *CNN Effect,* which is used to argue that television, with its vivid pictures of human suffering during famines and other calamites, can force policymakers to take action. The reality is that broadcast and print journalists sometimes have such power and sometimes don't, depending on a variety of circumstances. In Vietnam in the 1960s, when the White House had a clear agenda underpinned by a strong national consensus, it set the course for a great deal of the coverage, as we shall see. Nevertheless, as their interest in using the media suggests, officials turn to the news media for clues to what the public is thinking. Ernest May writes, regarding this trend, that newspapers, newsmagazines, radio, and especially television have formed "more and more of the environment in which foreign policy decisions were made and diplomatic negotiations conducted."

About 75 percent of presidential appointees and 85 percent of senior career officials, in one study, identified the media as their principal sources of information on public sentiment, ranking journalists as far more valuable than any other public opinion vehicle, including polls. While members of Congress reported relying on a number of sources for opinions, such as telephone and mail communication, almost one-third noted the importance of the media, again placing it ahead of opinion polls. Legislative staffers in Illinois, according to another study, did not view media as merely a "conduit for public opinion expression: In their view it is the very essence of public opinion and can support or destroy legislative initiatives."

"The press is the leading point of contact between State Department officials and the external public," observed Bernard C. Cohen, a longtime student of the interaction of foreign-policy decision-makers and the press. These officials follow the news, mix with reporters, and listen carefully to their questions. As in McKinley's day, the media is both an expression of public opinion and a shaper of it. An aide to Secretary of State Alexander Haig estimated that staff members spent 80 to 90 percent of their time thinking about the news media.

Right up to end of his life, President McKinley monitored public opinion about foreign affairs. The day before he was felled by an assassin's bullet at the 1901 Pan-American Exposition in Buffalo, he gave a speech against commercial wars and for "a policy of good will and friendly trade relations." James Creelman thought McKinley's remarks "the greatest act of statesmanship of his life."

The yellow journalist was among the reporters who stood the eight-day death-watch. In his memoirs, Creelman described the president's final hours.

Mr. Cortelyou entered the room and stood beside the stricken chief.

"It's mighty lonesome in here" said the President.

"I know it is."

The President's eyes brightened, and the old familiar wrinkles appeared in his face as he turned eagerly to his assistant.

"How did they like my speech?" he asked.

9

THINKING WITH THEIR THOUGHTS

In 1889 a dark-skinned little man, with one blind eye and scant resemblance to the swashbuckling correspondents who covered the Spanish-American War, prepared for a reporting trip to Japan. Lafcadio Hearn's intention, he wrote in a proposal to *Harper's,* was frankly "romantic." He planned "to create in the minds of the readers, a vivid impression of living in Japan,—not simply as an observer but as one taking part in the daily existence of the common people, and *thinking with their thoughts.*" This was a common theme for Hearn. "One must be Egyptian," he said, "to write of Egypt."

Comments like this traditionally have set editors to wondering if it is time to recall reporters, not send them abroad. The concern, in the lingo of the home office, is that the reporter has "gone native," the charge eventually leveled against George Smalley. An extreme example of guarding against this pitfall occurred in a Paris meeting of *Chicago Tribune* correspondents in 1927. The imperious, xenophobic editor and publisher of the paper, Robert McCormick, asked who spoke French, German, or Italian. Only one, Larry Rue, didn't put up his hand. McCormick appointed him to the enviable position of roving correspondent. "I don't want my fine young American boys ruined by these damn foreigners," McCormick said.

Today news media often provide specialized training. More than one-half the correspondents representing U.S. media in China and over one-fourth of those in Japan possessed high proficiency in the local language, according to a 1990s study. In France and Argentina, countries with tongues more akin to English, over 90 percent of the U.S. correspondents had "high proficiency." "We should not hire men for foreign correspondence who do not have at least one or two basic languages such as Spanish, German and French," a *New York Times* editor commented in 1965. "We must increase our recruiting, particularly in the field of Russian language specialization." But editors remain wary of reporters' becoming too steeped in the countries they cover. As a matter of policy, the *Times* posts correspondents in one place for only four or five years, preferring four. That, commented a modern foreign editor of the paper, helps avoid the problem that comes around year five when "people have the tendency to go native." Editors also like to call reporters home for a spell so they can take the pulse of the audience for whom they write.*

The potential for going native accelerated around the turn of the twentieth century. The Spanish-American War brought America's status as a world power as well as its first offshore colonies. Merchants and missionaries went abroad in increasing numbers, and journalists were swept across the seas with them. Many sank roots and became a part of the foreign landscape. Although these journalists transplanted themselves because they relished the exotic, they often found themselves the exotic ones, living precariously on foreign soil.

Such a person was Lafcadio Hearn, a self-described "civilized nomad."

Hearn's adventures abroad coincided with and were at times sustained by the rise of expatriate newspapers. Such papers first appeared early in the century. The ever-enterprising James Gordon Bennett Sr. started the *Herald for Europe* in 1846. The *Tribune for Europe* and the *Times for Europe* followed. These were printed in New York and transported by steamer. The next step came when Americans began publishing abroad, either as extensions of their U.S.-based journals or as independent news entrepreneurs. Many a wandering youngster became hooked on foreign reporting after picking up a job on one of these newspapers. Besides being incubators for foreign correspondents, the newspapers served as way stations for out-of-work veterans.

Paris was the capital of American expatriate publishing. The *Chicago Tribune* created an army edition in Paris for American troops during World War I and continued publishing it afterward, with special editions on the Riviera and in Berlin. A wealthy expatriate American, Courtland Bishop, started the *Paris Times,* and another expatriate, a racehorse enthusiast named Jefferson Davis Cohn, started the *Paris Evening Telegram,* which lasted three years. A member of the Vanderbilt family financed the *Boulevardier,* a magazine that one correspondent described as "a feeble imitation of the *New Yorker.*" Other magazines included the *Paris Comet* and *Gargoyle,* as well as little periodicals that owed much to journalists who came to Paris with a literary bent: *This Quarter, Exile, transatlantic review,* and *transition—*

---

* We have examples of extreme cases in which the reporter could not write well in the newspaper's language. The great correspondent for the *Times* of London, Henri de Blowitz, was expert at hanging around—and getting scoops from—the corridors of power. German chancellor Bismarck, Blowitz commented with pride, once looked under a table "to see if Blowitz is not underneath." Blowitz did all of his reporting in French. For thirty-five years editors back at Printing House Square translated his copy. Edward Vizetelly, the reporter who tracked down Stanley in East Africa, tells of a war correspondent for the *Standard,* also a London newspaper, who was a German doctor of philosophy and also wrote in his native language: "When his dispatches reach the office in Shoe Lane, a clever English lady, with perfect knowledge of German, who resided in one of the London Suburbs, was immediately telegraphed for." Today, noted A. M. Rosenthal, a former editor of the *New York Times,* "the de Blowitzes can't get past the door." See Giles, *A Prince of Journalists,* 60, 105; A. M. Rosenthal's comment is in the introduction, 8; Vizetelly, *Reminiscences of a Bashi-Bazouk,* 193.

the lack of capitalization in the latter two cases expressing their avant-garde bent. The U.S. military published the *Stars and Stripes* for the American Expeditionary Force during World War I.

The most successful of the lot was the *Paris Herald,* which James Gordon Bennett Jr. started in 1887 the way he did much else, on a whim. It gave the Paris-based newspaper baron a little amusement—and eventually marked his finest and last hour. When French newspapers in Paris decamped for Bordeaux at the outset of World War I, Bennett stayed. He paid the salaries of staff members who went into the military and put aside his playboy ways to help put out the shorthanded newspaper. For the first time the *Herald*'s Paris edition became profitable. Bennett died in 1918, but his newspaper lived on. In 1934 it acquired the *Chicago Tribune*'s Paris edition. For nine months the new hybrid newspaper carried the full names of both its parents. After that it became the *Herald Tribune,* bringing its masthead in line with its parent's, for ten years before, the *New York Herald* had merged with the *New York Tribune,* becoming the *Herald Tribune.*

Other nations besides the United States created newspapers abroad. Establishing a newspaper was akin to planting a national flag in a foreign outpost. This was particularly true in colonized nations, where expatriates often introduced modern journalistic practice. The first Egyptian newspaper, *Le Courrier de l'Egypte,* appeared during Napoleon's campaign there in 1798. The Dutch started newspapers in the East Indies (today Indonesia); the British in China and India; the Spanish in the Philippines. When the United States took control of the Philippines in 1898, a natural evolution took place: first came U.S. military newspapers, such as the *Bounding Billow,* printed on Admiral George Dewey's flagship, and the *Official Gazette,* published by the military government; next was a private U.S. newspaper, the *American Soldier,* published by enlisted men from the 13th Minnesota Volunteers; finally a general circulation daily, the *Manila Times,* appeared. By 1902 the Philippines had five American dailies. One of them, the *Manila Bulletin,* is still publishing, under Philippine ownership.

The American newspaper presence in China was led by the cantankerous Thomas F. Millard, a veteran of the *New York Herald.* Enthusiastic about enlarging American trade with China, the Missouri-bred Millard nevertheless was deeply imbued with Midwest populist sympathy for revolution and self-determination. British imperialism particularly irked him. Millard started the *China Press* in 1911 with the heretical intention of making the Shanghai-based newspaper "substantially Chinese in backing and sympathy." A British advertising boycott forced him to bail out of the *Press* in 1915, but he soon afterward reappeared with *Millard's Review of the Far East.*

Millard was a magnet for like-minded journalists. Carl Crow, who worked for Millard, shared his boss's enthusiasm for the revolution that toppled the Qing Dynasty in 1911 and enjoyed special access to the architect of the revolution, Sun Yat-sen. Crow went on to other newspaper and advertising ventures. He claimed that his Shanghai advertising agency "placed the first lip-stick and vanishing cream advertising in Chinese papers," that he published the first Chinese fashion book, and that he wrote the first Chinese-language book of poker rules. Millard eventually sold out to John B. Powell, who renamed the paper the *China Weekly Review* but did not deviate from Millard's anti-imperialist policy. To the British, Powell was "a mischievous man from Missouri."*

Japan also attracted American journalists. One of the first was Edward Howard House, once part owner of the *Boston Courier*. He established the *Tokyo Times* in 1877. In addition to stringing for U.S. newspapers, House was said to have "prepared and conducted the first orchestral concerts" in Japan. Many journalists were introduced to Japan through the *Japan Advertiser,* which had been founded by an American printer and was passed to a Unitarian missionary and later to B. W. Fleisher, the son of a Philadelphia yarn manufacturer. Fleisher later helped Millard start the *China Press*.

National lines were often crossed in English-language newspapers. Americans worked on British-owned papers in China and Japan. Lafcadio Hearn, whose entire life was an exercise in crossing national lines, worked for a time on the *Kobe Chronicle,* which was edited by a Scotsman.

Hearn was born an outsider. His Irish father, Charles Hearn, was a physician with the British army; his mother, Rosa Cassimati, a young Greek woman whom Charles met while stationed in the Ionian Islands. Their first child, born before they wed, died. The second was named Patrick Lafcadio, the middle name deriving from the Greek island Levkas on which he was born in 1850. Charles kept his marriage a secret from the military for several years, because he was afraid it would hurt his career, and then took the boy and his mother to Dublin. Rosa was unschooled and, equally appalling to the Anglican Hearn family, zealously Catholic. Rosa returned to Greece, and the marriage was annulled. Lafcadio stayed, albeit on the fringe of the family. His one warm relationship, with his father's Catholic and childless aunt, disintegrated when she realized the youngster did not share her religious enthusiasms. She sent him off for rigorous Catholic schooling in France and England, which did no good, and switched her affections (and plans for her estate) to a gold-digging relative who gave Lafcadio a one-way ticket to the United States in 1869. The nineteen-year-old boy was told to locate relatives in Cincinnati. Instead he hung around New York City for awhile. Hearn never said why. Perhaps he had an inkling of what awaited him in Ohio. Upon his arrival there, his relatives gave him five dollars and, in the words of one biographer, "shoved him out the door."

Hearn was painfully aware of being an outsider, yet he thrived on it. In the

* The Missouri reference to Powell was not incidental. In the period between World War I and World War II, people spoke of the Missouri News Monopoly in China. The University of Missouri's journalism school and its dean, Walter Williams, abetted this old-boy network. By one incomplete count, 47 University of Missouri–educated journalists worked in Asia by 1927, more than half of them in China. Missourians also contributed significantly to journalism education in China. In the 1930s Dean Williams was mentioned as a candidate for the post of U.S. minister to China; it was probably an idea hatched by admiring alumni there.

United States, he dropped the American-sounding Patrick in favor of the foreign Lafcadio. He stood only five feet three and had a disfigured, sightless left eye as a result of a childhood accident. The vision in his "good" eye was so bad that he had to put his face within inches of a page to read, an act that made him all the more conspicuous. Hearn's insecurities made him suspicious and sullen—and gave him a peculiar perspective. "I think a man must devote himself to one thing in order to succeed," he said, "so I have pledged me to the worship of the Odd, the Queer, the Strange, the Exotic, the Monstrous." This was just the thing for the sensationalist *Cincinnati Enquirer,* where the bookish foreigner found work. Hearn's stories about ghastly murders, clumsy hangings, and life in the shady Tallow District made him one of the city's most compelling reporters.

His sojourn on the *Enquirer* abruptly ended in 1875 when the editor learned of his marriage to a half-black former slave. Although the rival *Commercial* picked him up, the outsider was ready to leave for New Orleans. Variously on the staffs of the *Item* and the *Times-Democrat,* Hearn wrote about things that naturally interested him and were abundant in New Orleans, suicides and murders, "voodoo charms," and dark-skinned women. He frequented the city's demimonde of brothels and opium dens. "I eat and drink and sleep with members of the races you detest," he wrote to a colleague. On the side, he read and wrote about Asian and Middle Eastern art, religion, history, mythology, and folktales. His Creole cookbook still is considered one of the best of its kind.

Given his interest in the outlandish as well as his own status as an interloper, Hearn was a *foreign* correspondent even when inside the United States. But in 1887 the title became literally correct. Tired of both New Orleans and newspapering—a mutual feeling, as his editors considered him "quite impossible"—he set his sights on the Caribbean. After a brief get-acquainted voyage in the region, he settled in Creole Martinique, living much of the time in St. Pierre with a young native woman.

In addition to writing a novel called *Youma: The Story of a West-Indian Slave* and a memoir, *Two Years in the French West Indies,* Hearn contributed to American magazines, which, in line with growing American world power and ties, had become interested in foreign topics. Some publications had a regional slant, for instance *Artistic Japan* and the *Journal of the American Asiatic Association* (later simply called *Asia*), *Modern Mexico, Pan-American Magazine,* and *Armenia.* Others had broad international interests: *National Geographic Magazine* (which showed its enthusiasm for Japan by publishing no fewer than eleven articles about the country in 1904 and 1905), *Chicago International,* and *International Monthly.* The newly founded Catholic Foreign Mission Society had its own magazine, *The Field Afar.* (The order survives as the Maryknoll Missioners, and its magazine as *Maryknoll.*) It was not unusual, Frank Luther Mott concluded in his monumental history of magazines, for general-interest monthlies "to devote half their space to material bearing on foreign affairs." *Cosmopolitan's* irrepressible editor and owner, John Brisben Walker, took up such crusades as the creation of a "World's Congress" composed of one hundred of "the most important peoples of the globe" and promotion of an international language.* The issue of *Harper's New Monthly Magazine* that carried Hearn's first article from Japan also published stories about Chile, Italy, Switzerland, and the Bavarian town of Rothenburg.

It was *Harper's* that pointed Hearn in the direction of Japan. After Martinique, Hearn figured he would inevitably "wander off to someplace else," but exactly where he did not know until he talked with William Patten, *Harper's* art editor, on a visit to New York City. Patten suggested he go to Japan and, to finance the trip, arranged for Hearn and artist W. C. Weldon to travel free on the Canadian Pacific's rail and steamship lines in exchange for writing promotional travel articles.

W. C. Weldon, who was ditched by Lafcadio Hearn shortly after they reached Japan, drew this sketch of the little man. From Edward Larocque Tinker, *Lafcadio Hearn's American Days.*

Harper's was ideally suited to Hearn. In the words of its editor, the magazine was interested in "interpretive sensibility," which allowed Hearn to satisfy his preference for "the prose of small things" instead of politics and economics. Likewise, it did not require him to travel at the breakneck speed of Nellie Bly and her around-the-world competitor Elizabeth Bisland of *Cosmopolitan*, who began her career working with Hearn at the *Times-Democrat* in New Orleans and remained a fast friend. "The more I work," Hearn wrote to *Harper's* editor, Henry Alden, "the more

* "The necessity of a world-language has long been apparent," a *Cosmopolitan* editorial said. "The increased communication between all parts of the globe, the opening up of Africa to settlement and Central Asia to commerce, the formation of states composed of men from many lands—all these have created a demand for a new language which can be used by all the nations of the world, and so scientifically constructed that it may eventually displace the illogicalities and barbarisms that had their derivation from uneducated and unreasoning peoples." "An International Language," *Cosmopolitan*, March 1898, 570.

the conviction grows upon me that no study of life can be written in less than the actual time required to *live* the scenes described."

Japan, too, ideally suited Hearn, the professional Ishmael who loved the exotic. Japan, ethnically and culturally homogeneous to an extraordinary degree, preferred to keep foreigners at arm's length. No longer did Hearn have to seek the weird in order to write about the exotic. Mysticism and spiritualism manifested themselves in everyday Japanese life. "I want to die here!" Hearn enthused upon landing in Yokohama. Within a day he separated from Weldon to wander around on his own. He never wrote any of the stories he had promised to the Canadian Pacific.

Hearn acquired a complete Japanese family. Through one of his few acquaintances, he found a job as a professor of English at a boys' high school in Matsue. When he fell ill during the cold winter, the school's dean proposed that Hearn take a wife, Setsu Koizumi, a twenty-two-year-old woman from a samurai family. Although Hearn had never divorced his Cincinnati wife, he assented.

The marriage bargain was not one-sided. Western intrusion in Japan had undermined the old shogunate and the elite samurai, who were essential to its functioning. Many Japanese were now impoverished. The much-diminished Koizumi family saw in this diminutive Western teacher with a salary the family's salvation. He accepted life to a large extent on Japanese terms. He lived with his extended family, which eventually included his own four children. Despite feeling awkward at first, he let his wife carry out her traditional Japanese duty of helping him get dressed in the morning. When not teaching and writing, he contemplated insects in his Japanese garden.

Life was not entirely tranquil. Hearn's eldest son remembered his moody father's frequent lamentation, "Money! Money! Money!" This kept Hearn on the move. He left Matsue to take a better-paying job teaching at the government university in the dull garrison town of Kumamoto. For a time he returned to newspaper work, writing editorials for one of the English-language papers in Kobe, the *Chronicle,* and freelancing for the *New Orleans Times-Democrat.* As in the past, he warred with editors. Angry over inadequate payment and sloppy typesetting by *Harper's,* he informed his one-time mentor Henry Alden that the editor's views had "less than the value of a bottled fart, and your bank-account less consequence than a wooden shithouse struck by lightning." He began to write frequently for the *Atlantic Monthly,* which took him a step up without forcing him to change his style. As Oliver Wendell Holmes Sr., one of its famous contributors, gushed about America's literary jewel, "All read the *Atlantic* as persons of culture do!" Hearn's essays about Japanese life became the basis for his first book on the country, the acclaimed two-volume *Glimpses of Unfamiliar Japan.*

Hearn quit the *Kobe Chronicle* after only a few months. The newspaper grind strained his good eye, and he did not like the work very much. He did his *Chronicle* writing quickly, reserving his energies for the evening, when he worked on the artistic writing for which he is best remembered. Even so, Hearn fit in at the *Chronicle* as well as he fit in anywhere. The *Chronicle* was "distinguished by the virility of its editorial comments, usually critical in character," in the view of the internationally minded dean of the University of Missouri Journalism School, Walter Williams. Although the *Chronicle*'s editor, a Scotsman named Robert Young, had mixed emotions about Hearn, whom he considered a not wholly "trustworthy guide," Hearn considered Young "liberal," by which he seemed to mean the editor gave him relatively free rein to express his opinions.

Hearn's commentary for the Kobe foreign community was thus a good barometer of his views. Writing about America, Hearn decried race relations and prize-fighting. Writing about local affairs, he inveighed against foreign missionary zeal and supported the Japanese in their "competitive struggle" with the West. In the editorial below, which appeared in the *Chronicle* on October 30, 1894, Hearn praised the Japanese for the patriotism they displayed in waging war against China; the war had begun over an incident in Korea. The editorial does not display his evocative literary style or his eye for the details of everyday Japanese life and culture, talents that established his fame. It does display his sympathies for the Japanese.

NATIONAL INDIVIDUALITY
Tuesday, October 30th, 1894

Perhaps most of us can remember the impression produced upon us in schooldays by the story of those antique women who cut off their hair to furnish bowstrings for the archers who were defending their city.* Such a fact seemed quite romantic to us in those times; but we are now living, as foreign settlers, in the midst of exhibitions of patriotism much more extraordinary. At no one time in history did the old Greeks or Romans or Carthaginians or Hebrews show more loyalty or love of country than the Japanese are showing to-day. Yet it is but little noticed by us. Why? Probably because we have all learned that most of what we were taught in European schools to consider exemplary as heroism, as self-abnegation, as patriotism, is regarded by the Japanese as simply duty— commonplace duty. We have become so familiar with Oriental feeling and acting in these matters that we have almost forgotten how remarkable a spectacle we are now privileged to watch. Each day new examples are being furnished which merit perpetual record as moral evidence of the Japanese national character.

Perhaps many of our readers have not as yet even given a thought to what has been going on all through this Empire since the declaration of war. Nevertheless very singular things have been, and still are, going on. Everybody in the country has been contributing something to the war-fund, or to the support of the wives and children of absent soldiers, or to the physical comfort of troops in Korea. We say everybody, in the largest sense of the word. The poorest peasant who has nothing in the shape of money to give,—who cannot spare even a handful of rice or millet,—gives straw. Hundreds of thousands of straw sandals (*waraji*) are being contributed by the poor of the great cities. Little bunches of toothpicks are given by those who cannot even afford to offer many *waraji*.

* Perhaps from Appian's description of the defense of Carthage against Rome.

Others give matches. Those a little better off furnish provisions, tobacco, pipes, fruits, small luxuries of a thousand kinds. The quantity in each individual case may be very trifling; but the aggregate is so large that there has been considerable difficulty in transporting it to the seat of the campaign. Merchants give casks of wine, clothing,—large quantities of valuable and costly supplies. Ordinary citizens,—mercantile employees, teachers, etc.,—aid by small subscriptions. All the schools throughout the country have been contributing something. Children offer their pocket money; and their pathetic little gifts cannot be refused without causing unnecessary pain. And in every separate street of the various garrison-towns other special subscriptions are being constantly collected for the support of the families of the men of the reserves called out; and supplies of food and all necessary comforts are given regularly to the households of the absent soldiers. It would be simply impossible in a single article to state all that has been or is being done in this patriotic way. The entire nation is behind the army—supporting it with all possible affection,—encouraging the humblest trooper to do even more than his duty by every kindness that can excite human gratitude.

To us the action of the Japanese child contributing two or three *sen* to the help of the soldiers is not less morally beautiful than the action of the aristocratic houses of Satsuma and Mito whose gifts to the war-fund aggregate many tens of thousands of *yen*. Perhaps indeed we must confess the trifling gifts of children more significant;—for the little ones cannot be charged with any of those complex motives usually assigned to adult generosities. But one particular donation on the part of a Japanese nobleman is really amazing, and betrays an individual patriotism and loyal enthusiasm of most exceptional nature. That donation included 100,000 *yen* presented to the Army and Navy (50,000 *yen* to each), 6,000 *yen* to support the families of the men of the first reserves already called out in Kaga, Etchu, and Noto;—2,700 yards of the best flannel for underwear to the Imperial marines; and 450 yards for underwear to the Army. Furthermore he has pledged himself to pay sums varying from five *yen* (in the case of a private) to fifty *yen* (in the case of an officer) to the family of every man killed in battle, who belonged to any one of the three provinces above mentioned. This nobleman is the Marquis Mayeda.

Probably thinkers of the type of Mr. Percival Lowell* would say that this immense unanimity of enthusiasm on the part of a whole nation implies lack of individuality. It is easy from a distance to make such a judgment, but no one who takes the pains to investigate Japanese sentiments among the Japanese them-

---

* A highly successful businessman from a famous Boston family, Lowell had wide interests that included Japan, to whose study he devoted a decade of his life. His book *The Soul of the Far East* helped inspire Hearn's interest in Japan. In addition to maintaining his enthusiasm for polo, Lowell spent the last part of his life trying to prove that there was life on Mars. It was he who established the Lowell Observatory in Arizona.

selves could possibly sustain it. And whatever might be said of personal individuality in the race, we have now startling evidence of the enormous strength of the national individuality. We fear that much of what has been termed in the West "the cultivation of the individual" means little more than the cultivation of pure egotism. However characterized by psychological theorists, the present phenomena of national sentiment in Japan are strangely beautiful. They afford also a lesson to those Occidental statesmen who have fancied Japan weak, because they have estimated her power by her material resources only. In the hour of a national peril, spirit counts for much more than matter.

Japan defeated China in the war. The resulting Treaty of Shimonoseki conferred on the Japanese all the treaty port rights enjoyed by Western powers in China. Around the same time, Western powers relinquished extraterritorial privileges in Japan. Although uncomfortable that this new, militant Japan was supplanting the ancient Japan that attracted him most, Hearn cheered its victories. He described a naval defeat of Russia several years later as the "killing off of the devils!"

Hearn became to Japan what the French-Canadian Hector Saint John de Crèvecoeur, the Frenchman Alexis de Tocqueville, and the Britisher Alistair Cooke were to the United States in the next two centuries. He was a foreigner who appreciated what the Japanese wanted him to appreciate. His admiration for traditional Japan reassured a people who idealized their old culture even as they were modernizing. Aware of the popularity of his writing in the United States, Tokyo Imperial University awarded Hearn a prestigious chair. From this vantage point and with the publication of more articles and books—twelve volumes on Japan in all—he achieved still more fame among the Japanese.

Not that Hearn became an insider. He never learned to read a Japanese newspaper. He developed a special Japanese-English language to communicate verbally with his wife and could write only simple notes to her in Japanese. Little boys emboldened by mounting anti-Western sentiments taunted him in the streets. From time to time he considered going back to the United States. He understood that his prestige derived from Japanese insecurities. "I fear—I suspect," he said about his appointment at Tokyo Imperial University, "that this position has been given unto me for a combination of reasons, among which the dominant is that I may write at ease many books about Japan."

Hearn worried that he could be deported. Furthermore, by retaining his British citizenship, which he had not given up, he knew he imperiled his wife's property rights when he died. To protect his family, he underwent the lengthy process to become a naturalized Japanese. To meet the requirement that he belong to a Japanese family, his wife's Koizumi family adopted him. Taking a surname ("eight clouds") from an ancient Japanese poem, he became Koizumi Yakumo.

The decision to become Japanese, at least legally, made him vulnerable in a different

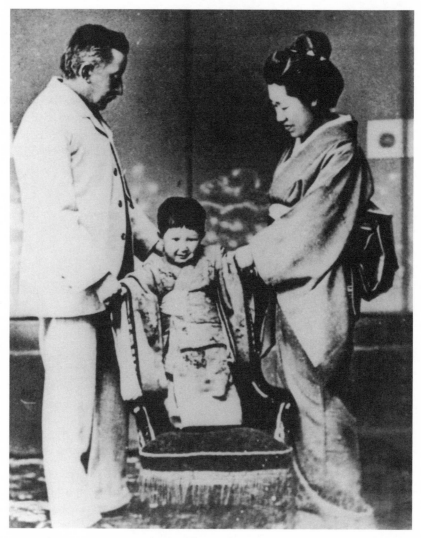

Hearn poses for a picture with his wife and eldest son. In a discourse on Japanese gardens, written around the time he was married, he ruminated on Japanese women. "It is a great mistake to affirm, as some writers have done, that the Japanese never think of comparing a woman to trees and flowers. For grace, a maiden is likened to a slender willow; for youthful charm, to the cherry-tree in flower; for sweetness of heart, to the blossoming plum-trees. Nay, the old Japanese poets have compared women to all beautiful things. . . . Japanese comparisons of women to trees and flowers are in no wise inferior to our own in aesthetic sentiment." From Lafcadio Hearn, *Glimpses of Unfamiliar Japan* (Houghton Mifflin, 1894), 2:358–59. Photo: Tulane University Library.

way. In 1903 the new, anti-Western president of Tokyo Imperial University changed his pay status to the lower amount given to native Japanese teachers. Hearn, who viewed himself as a Westerner deserving Western pay, resigned. Although some students protested, the university did not relent.

When Hearn died the next year, at age fifty-four, his bones were buried in

Tokyo. A memorial was erected in Yaizu, a small fishing village where he vacationed because it had no other summer visitors. He liked to swim naked in the sea. The marker read, in part, "In commemoration of the place where sang Professor Koizumi Yakumo."

Japanese eulogists hailed Hearn as "a spokesman of Eastern ideas." Japanese wrote books about him. They put his picture on advertisements for patent medicines. Hearn's reputation declined in the United States during the 1930s, when Japanese aggression mounted. He is not widely known among Americans today, although American foreign correspondents in Japan occasionally do retrospective essays on him.

In Japan, he remains a famous figure. His Matsue home is a museum, and around town he appears on park statues and street signs, as well as on local brands of beer, sake, and instant coffee. A Japanese society devoted to him publishes a journal called *Hearn*. Students read Hearn's ghost stories in English-language classes. He has been the subject of television docudramas, and a Japanese director has made a movie based on three of his stories.

Hearn, one Japanese scholar concluded, was "the most eloquent and truthful interpreter of the Japanese mind."

Hearn is not the only correspondent to become entrenched and then disappointed. Thomas Millard, the veteran foreign correspondent who founded the two English-language newspapers in Shanghai, served as an adviser to the Chinese government during the Versailles Peace Conference at the end of World War I. The *New York Times,* which made Millard its first China correspondent in 1925, wearied of his persistent advocacy for ending the unequal treaties that gave Western powers extraterritorial rights. It eventually replaced him. He had short stints with the *New York World* and *Herald Tribune.* In 1929 he again became an adviser to the Chinese government, which grew worried that his outspoken criticism of Japanese aggression would provoke the aggressors more. In the 1930s he was given the Order of the Jade and eased into retirement.

"I am not invited to any functions that are being given and none of my former friends have called on me," Millard complained. Unmarried and belonging in China as much as anyplace else, he stayed in Shanghai and kept speaking his mind to anyone who would listen. On the eve of the Japanese attack on Pearl Harbor, he broke his shoulder in a fall in front of the American Club and went to Seattle to recover with family. He died there of cancer on September 7, 1942.

Flamboyant Earnest Hoberecht, yet another example of overstaying, built up United Press International's Asia Division after World War II and made himself into an institution in Japan. To satisfy the Japanese hunger for American novels after the war, he wrote *Tokyo Romance* by dictating after work to a Japanese secretary who passed the text to a translator who had recently rewritten *Gone with the Wind* in a Japanese setting. Although called by *Life* magazine "an unfortunate specimen of U.S. culture," the book sold "like rice cakes." Hoberecht followed up with more fiction, a book of etiquette, and a collection of short stories that he filled out with several essays he had written years before as class assignments in college. Fan clubs sprang up across the country. He taught movie star Hideko Mimura how to do a kiss, which had never before been shown in a Japanese film. On a visit to Japan, novelist James A. Michener found that "Asia Earnie" ranked with Ernest Hemingway. Hoberecht got his comeuppance in 1966 when management decided he was throwing his weight around Japan too freely and fired him. Hoberecht returned home to Oklahoma, where he ran several family businesses that included an insurance company.

For many correspondents, returning home is more jarring than leaving it in the first place. No longer do they have big expense accounts. The stories they cover are often less dramatic. And everything is different. After a quarter of a century of reporting abroad for newspapers and radio, William Shirer felt like a stranger in the United States. His homeland, he thought, had changed "almost beyond recognition."

Our highly interdependent planet, interlaced by global commerce and jet travel, can heighten the sense of estrangement. Pico Iyer is an Indian born in England, who moved to California as a little boy. He writes travel books, which have touched on Japan. "I fly back to California every now and then to pay my bills, and sometimes I can't resist turning on the computer to see how the Lakers are doing," he wrote in *The Global Soul*. As smoothly as he moves about the planet, he finds the homogeneous habitat of the World Citizen—with its Holiday Inns, look-alike restaurants, interchangeable steel-and-glass structures, and ubiquitous Internet connections—an alien environment, "the equivalent to living in a wilderness." The citizens of Matsue keep Hearn's memory and writing alive, its mayor told a *New York Times* reporter in 2007, in order to combat the chain stores and malls that pave over traditional Japanese culture.

And yet, journalists continue to thrust themselves into foreign cultures.

Richard Critchfield, who died in 1994, became a legend among fellow journalists for his willingness to live among peasants for long stretches, often reporting on a freelance basis. In 1981 he received a prestigious $244,000 "genius" fellowship from the MacArthur Foundation to continue his work in the developing world. Kremlinologist Victor Zorza began his wandering at an early age. He was deported from his native Poland to Russia during World War II, escaped from Siberia, served with the Polish contingent of the Royal Air Force in the Middle East, and became a journalist in London and Washington, D.C. Independent and perceptive—and, like Hearn, prickly about editors changing his copy—he predicted the Soviet invasion of Czechoslovakia in 1968. He also foretold, far ahead of the event, the rise of democracy in Communist countries.

In 1982, when a doctor told him he had only a year to live as a result of a heart condition, Zorza set out to establish "a new genre of journalism," which actually had its roots in Hearn's. After several months of travel, he settled into a Himalayan village several hours by foot from the nearest Indian highway. Writing for the *Washington Post* and British papers, Zorza chronicled the village untouchables' struggle for economic and political rights. His intimacy with those about whom he wrote forced him into the uncomfortable role of adviser and spokesman. "The simple dramas of my village reflect, I believe, the sorrows and jobs that all men share," he wrote at the outset, "the common humanity of us all."

Zorza did not die until 1996. By that time he had moved on to developing hospice care in Russia.

10

A BELL-RINGER

"Your daddy has caught a man," James Keeley of the *Chicago Tribune* wrote to his family in 1906 from Tangier, Morocco. Reporters on the Chicago police beat had a special vocabulary for scoops. A good one was a *pippin*. A great one was a *bell-ringer*. Keeley's letter described a bell-ringer.

Although English-born, Keeley "knew little or nothing of international politics or European affairs. Chicago was his field," noted his generally admiring biographer. To the marrow of his bones, he was a police reporter. What propelled Keeley beyond the Chicago city limits to Morocco in 1906 was his "nose for news." He was relentless when on the scent of a hot story. Not even his desk job as the *Tribune*'s managing editor kept him home.

The greatest significance of Keeley's bell-ringer lies not in the oddity that this was his first overseas assignment or that he was supposed to be exhorting reporters, not doing their work. Strip the yarn down to its basic element, and it contains something all editors relish in a foreign story, a local connection—in this case an embezzling Chicago banker on the lam.

The Spanish-American War showed that the American press could devote considerable resources to foreign affairs, if so inclined. "It was tremendously expensive, and very few of the newspapers got their money back," said one correspondent for *Harper's Weekly* in 1901, "but it set up a standard which must be maintained whenever the United States are concerned in a contest of arms." The standard when there was no contest of arms, however, had not improved.

If anything, the press was less inclined to pay attention to foreign news than it had been when the United States was in its infancy. As noted in chapter 4, in 1856 foreign events accounted for slightly more than 25 percent of the news in the *Boston Post,* a paper fairly representative of its time. Fifty years later, when Keeley was hanging around the souks of Tangier, less than 10 percent of the news in a similarly representative Boston newspaper, the *Globe,* was foreign.

The pattern in the Spanish-American War repeated itself throughout the twentieth century. News media expended considerable resources to cover war. They put their wallets and correspondents away once peace was achieved.

The E. W. Scripps Company, which consists of the Scripps Howard Newspapers as well as broadcast stations, has a tradition of fielding outstanding war reporters, among them Ernie Pyle and Raymond Clapper, both of whom perished in the Pacific theater covering World War II. After the Japanese surrendered, Scripps recalled its correspondents. It repeated the process with the Korean War—where its correspondent Jim Lucas won the Pulitzer Prize—and again with the Vietnam War. When the United States attacked Iraq in 2003, Scripps had no permanent staff correspondents abroad. True to its past, it put thirteen reporters into the action, two of them representing the company's television stations. All were back home by the time President George Bush declared victory a few months later. When it turned out that Bush's declaration was premature, Scripps sent several reporters back. "We have never missed a conflict," said Peter Copeland, general manager and editor of the Scripps Howard News Service. "That is the threshold."

Following the U.S. invasion of Afghanistan in 2001, the Pew International Journalism Program commissioned a study to assess the attitudes of editors with medium-size and large newspapers toward foreign news. The underlying question was whether or not the September 2001 terrorist attacks on the United States increased editors' appetite for foreign news. Well over half of all foreign editors—presumably the gatekeepers with the most commitment to foreign news—thought foreign news should not increase "over the long run."

Two deterrents led editors to this conclusion. Cost was one. "The most serious item of expense is the collection of news from all parts of the world," the *New York Evening Post*'s E. L. Godkin lamented about newspapering around the time of the Spanish-American War. The *New York Tribune*'s first transatlantic dispatch by cable in 1866, a forty-nine-word cable, cost nearly $200. "The item of cable tolls is able alone to chill the ardor" of any owner for foreign news, said an editor in assessing the costs of covering the Spanish-American War. The perennial question was whether to file by mail, which was slow and cheap, or by cable, which was fast and expensive. In the 1930s the rate for "urgent" messages from Shanghai to New York ran as high as ninety-nine cents a word. During World War I, a New York newspaper put an editor in London for the sole purpose of cutting needless words from cable messages, which was said to "much more than cover" his salary.

Correspondents no longer cable stories. But new technology for direct transmission is expensive. Office space and office help add up, especially when a bureau is placed in Japan or some other expensive-to-live-in country, and correspondents often travel, which lays on another expense. More than half the newspaper foreign editors in the Pew study mentioned above cited cost as the "major obstacle" to increased foreign coverage. A 2004 study by the Radio and Television News Directors Association (RTNDA) of local television managers had the same result: 75 percent considered expense a large or very large barrier to covering foreign news.

The second deterrent to foreign news coverage showed up in a slogan over the desk of the *Brooklyn Eagle*'s editor in the 1920s: "A DOG FIGHT IN BROOKLYN IS BIG-GER THAN A REVOLUTION IN CHINA." The message, expressed in various ways in newsrooms elsewhere,* is that the public simply doesn't care much about distant news.

Proponents of foreign news argue against this proposition, as in this exchange some years ago between James Reston of the *New York Times* and Sol Linowitz, a former U.S. ambassador to the Organization of American States. "The people of the United States," Reston said, "will do anything for Latin America except read about it." Americans, responded Linowitz, will read about Latin America; the problem was "reporters will do anything for Latin America except write about it."

On Linowitz's side of the argument are surveys in which the public says it wants more foreign news. On Reston's side is the reality of what the average citizen does when such news is presented. When *Newsweek* made the assassination of Israel's prime minister, Yitzhak Rabin, a cover story in 1995, the number of newsstand sales was in the bottom 20 percent for that year. This is a typical response unless a weekly magazine's cover story is about war. Similarly, when NBC's *Today* show broadcast from Africa for a week some years ago, its audience grew smaller each day, complained Tom Brokaw of the *Nightly News*. Studies find that local news is "recalled and understood significantly better than information about more distant places." Editors suspect that survey respondents say they want more foreign news because they know they should or are embarrassed to admit they don't—just as *Reader's Digest* subscribers also fib about not reading stories about losing weight.

When the public actually does pay increased attention to foreign news during crises, editors don't perceive the dawning of a new era. They see a continuation of the status quo of local interest extended abroad. Increased public foreign news interest in the spring of 2004 was tied to the American occupation of Iraq. "International stories that are perceived to have little direct impact on American lives and security," a study concluded, "attract scant interest from the public."

One of the first studies of the amount of foreign news in American newspapers reached much the same conclusion (see table 3). "The average newspaper editor of an American morning daily," Cornell University professor Julian Woodward concluded in the 1920s, "is convinced that at least in peace times an increase beyond 5 or 6 percent in the proportion of news space devoted to foreign dispatches will not pay its costs in terms of increased circulation." We can call this observation Woodward's Law of Foreign News: Foreign news goes up when the United States is at war, but what goes up must come down. With the resumption of normalcy, to use a word made up by the inarticulate Warren Harding during his 1920s presidency, foreign news takes up a small share of the news hole.

In providing foreign news during normalcy, editors take reader interest into account in three ways. These may be stated as corollaries to Woodward's Law.

---

* To wit, this from a Missouri editor: "The farther it is from Kansas City, the less it is news." And this from a network television executive, speaking of his local experience: "The further we get from our town, the faster we lose viewers." Hamilton, *Main Street America and the Third World,* 1; John Frazee, interview by author, May 3, 2003.

TABLE 3. News space devoted to articles under foreign datelines in American newspapers, 1927

Newspaper	Avg. % (margin of error)
New York Times	8.95 (.38)
Baltimore Sun	8.05 (.67)
Chicago Tribune	7.92 (.55)
Washington Post	7.26 (.84)
New York Herald-Tribune	6.45 (.36)
Washington Herald	6.12 (.57)
New York World	5.89 (.30)
Detroit Free Press	5.88 (.55)
New York American	5.26 (.42)
Atlanta Constitution	5.18 (.45)
Kansas City Times	5.09 (.59)
Memphis Commercial-Appeal	4.90 (.60)
Kansas City Journal	4.87 (.46)
Los Angeles Times	4.86 (.36)
St. Louis Globe-Democrat	4.85 (.44)
Louisville Courier-Journal	4.84 (.76)
Philadelphia Inquirer	4.69 (.36)
Chicago Herald and Examiner	4.61 (.41)
Boston Herald	4.60 (.45)
Philadelphia Public Ledger	4.50 (.20)
Omaha World-Herald	4.46 (.56)
Daily Oklahoman	4.29 (.57)
Cincinnati Commercial-Tribune	4.26 (.50)
Buffalo Courier	4.16 (.41)
Dallas News	4.05 (.44)
Milwaukee Sentinel	4.02 (.65)
Cincinnati Enquirer	4.00 (.45)
Rochester Democrat and Chronicle	3.97 (.44)
Los Angeles Examiner	3.90 (.29)
St. Paul Pioneer-Press	3.81 (.62)
San Francisco Chronicle	3.80 (.36)
San Francisco Examiner	3.72 (.22)
Des Moines Register	3.68 (.60)
Boston Globe	3.50 (.37)
Portland Oregonian	3.50 (.57)
Indianapolis Star	3.34 (.44)
Houston Post-Dispatch	3.30 (.54)
Boston Post	3.09 (.36)
Cleveland Plain Dealer	3.07 (.37)
Pittsburgh Post	2.42 (.39)

Source: Woodward, *Foreign News in American Morning Newspapers.*

WOODWARD'S LAW OF FOREIGN NEWS

Julian Woodward set out to study one thing but stumbled onto something else that tells us a great deal about foreign news. His goal was to explore a method for "quantitative analysis of the daily press." He chose foreign news simply because it was a convenient category to examine. He used a ten-month time period in 1927 because it contained "no great world cataclysms or other factors which would have a pronounced effect upon the printing of foreign news." What Woodward found, as shown in table 3, is that foreign news is scarce in newspapers during times of peace and stability.

In Woodward's study, the average share of foreign news in forty nontabloid newspapers was 4.7 percent. Subsequent studies have consistently reached the same conclusion about the normal scarcity of foreign news. A Carnegie Endowment for International Peace study found that 3 to 5 percent of the news hole was devoted to foreign news in 1956. An *American Journalism Review* sample that did not include any prestige newspapers found foreign news averaging 5 percent of the news hole in 1963–64, when the Vietnam conflict had not yet ramped up, and 3 percent in 1998–99, another relatively peaceful time. A study of coverage in late 1987 and early 1988, another tranquil period, found that "ten leading American papers collectively devoted only 2.6 percent of their non-advertising space to news from abroad."

The exception comes in the exceptional times of wars, coups, earthquakes, or other crises. An earlier study than Woodward's—and one that was far less rigorous—showed, for instance, that "war news" in 1899 (apparently defined as news about negotiations after the Spanish-American War, about the Philippine insurrection against the United States, and about the Boer War) accounted for 17.9 percent of the total space (including advertising) in 110 newspapers, whereas other foreign news accounted for 1.2 percent. A modern study of nine dailies during May 1970, when the Vietnam War was raging, found that foreign news accounted for 11 percent of the news hole. Television coverage follows the same pattern.

One study explicitly tested Woodward's thesis over four separate years (1927, 1947, 1977, and 1997) in three newspapers (the *Memphis Commercial Appeal,* the *Cleveland Plain Dealer,* and the *Portland Oregonian*). Using different measurement techniques as well as different definitions (Woodward did not count stories from Mexico and Canada as foreign news), it found a slightly higher, but still modest, average for foreign news in 1927 (8.5 percent). This held for two other years of normalcy: 1977 (8.2 percent) and 1997 (9 percent). The one exception was 1947 (15.2 percent), the year that saw the inception of the cold war and the end of British rule in India and Palestine, among other dramatic foreign events.

The first—to keep foreign news simple and amusing—was summarized by editors at a Topeka, Kansas, newspaper in the 1950s. "*The State Journal* attempts to weed out what is not immediately important, and what is confusing without a full background," the telegraph editor said. Readers must get the big world stories, the city editor added, "plus the exceptional telegraph stories—those with the odd quirk or the human touch." Jay Allen, one of the *Chicago Tribune*'s star foreign correspondents, kept a photograph over his desk of "Simple" Willie Stevens, a retarded man implicated in Chicago's sensational 1922 Hall-Mills murder case. "That's my average reader," Allen said. "I try to write up to him."

A second corollary is to find equivalents to war, a tendency that has appealed to journalists since the day the penny press surfaced in the 1840s. "We newspaper people thrive best on the calamities of others," Benjamin Day proclaimed two days after launching the *New York Sun* in 1833. This approach is described around modern newsrooms as "coups and earthquakes," and it is literally true.

Six major dailies with correspondents in Latin America published a grand total of two features and three short news items on Guatemala in January 1976. When an earthquake hit the country the next month, initially knocking out almost all of its communications facilities, those papers published eighty-eight stories. Editors, another study found, favor "episodic stories about life-or-death situations." Two-thirds of the front-page banner stories dealing with foreign news in the *Chicago Tribune* during the peaceful period of 1926–1928 as well as in 1935, one historian found, "contained one of these words or a synonym: war, battle, revolution (rebellion or revolt), riot (massacre or 'hundreds slain'), armed forces, crisis (peril, threat, menace), hands-off-warning (curb), break (in diplomatic relations), and save (guard or protect)."

Similarly, on both radio and television, "If it bleeds, it leads." An ABC radio correspondent was on hand to cover a nationwide Peruvian strike in the mid-1970s. The protest presaged far-reaching political difficulties. Enlisted military personnel ineptly filled in for telephone-company employees who did not show up for work, making it nearly impossible to get a telephone line to New York. When the reporter finally got through (via phone patches to Panama and Miami), an ABC editor said he did not want the story. The next day the reporter telexed New York with a new story idea that mentioned that one protester had perished. An editor called back immediately to say ABC wanted the story. "Budgets and airtime are allocated to foreign stories with edge and blood," commented ABC television correspondent Jim Bittermann. "Editors share a common belief, supported by marketing surveys, that audiences are not interested in foreign news unless it has violence or direct relevance to Americans."

The third corollary, which picks up the thread of Bittermann's comment about direct relevance, argues for foreign stories that obviously intersect Main Street. Let a plane crash in some foreign land with one hundred people aboard. The lead of the story will mention the vacationing couple on board who happened to live in the newspaper's readership area. (Although the British like to sniff at such American provincialism, their hometown press is equally guilty.* Consider the headline over a story about a coup in the Maldives, which appeared in the *Hebden Bridge Times*, a

---

* This way of thinking generated a possibly apocryphal note in a London newsroom: "One Englishman is a story. Ten Frenchmen is a story. One hundred Germans is a story. One thousand Indians is a story. Nothing ever happens in Chile." An American version was made up by a network's journalists in the 1960s to shame their bosses into using more foreign news. The so-called Racial Equivalence Scale determined the minimum number of people who had to die in an airplane crash for it to be news on the air: "One hundred Czechs were equal to forty-three Frenchmen, and the Paraguayans were at the bottom." The shaming did not work. Jonathan Power, *New York Times*, November 7, 1975; Gans, *Deciding What's News*, 338.

newspaper in a small West Yorkshire town: "MILITARY COUP MARS COUPLE'S HONEYMOON.")

The *Chicago Tribune* was subject to Woodward's Law and its corollaries. Joseph Medill, who laid the newspaper's foundation, established a London presence in 1877 and sought foreign news elsewhere. Neither he nor his heirs, however, were about to let foreign affairs get in the way of business. "Devote your main editorial efforts to the discussion of home topics and furtherance of home interests," he admonished fellow editors and publishers in an 1869 Indianapolis speech. This remained a strong consideration for the *Tribune* newsroom at the end of the twentieth century, when the newspaper possessed a creditable foreign service. "We're still a hometown paper," explained the editor, Howard Tyner; the Chicago reader "is a subject we have gone over and over and over. . . . We have to make ourselves relevant."

This may be called the Keeley Corollary.

Keeley's first journalism experience was in his birthplace, London, selling newspapers. At age sixteen he came to the United States and worked for newspapers in Kansas City, Memphis, and Chicago. He began in Chicago in 1889 as a night police reporter on the north side. He was enterprising and, said critics and admirers alike, ruthless.

A famous early bell-ringer resulted from his out-of-town assignment to cover an 1892 range war. The conflict in Wyoming did not amount to much, but it had a strong local angle. Chicago was the nation's leading meatpacking city, and one of the Wyoming ranchers was from Chicago (he returned to the city after receiving death threats). Part of Keeley's success in Wyoming lay in finding an alternative way to transmit his stories after the telegraph service went dead because of a snowstorm or, as many thought, because of Keeley. Keeley had a reputation at police headquarters for disrupting rivals' telephones. One of his favorite tricks was to puncture the transmitter diaphragm with a lead pencil.

Keeley soared through the *Trib*'s ranks, becoming assistant city editor in 1894, city editor in 1895, and managing editor in 1898, when he was barely thirty years old. The news philosophy of the cigar-puffing editor was simple: "News is a commodity and for sale like any other commodity." He printed "what people want to read." In the hard-fought Chicago newspaper wars of the time, this meant local vice, murder, and robbery, mixed liberally with affairs of the heart—weddings of the high and mighty, interesting honeymoons, breach-of-promise proceedings, and messy divorces. One can imagine the sheer joy *Tribune* editors experienced the day they had a story about newlyweds who were counterfeiters.

"As far as war was concerned," one student of the newspaper observed, "the *Tribune* was internationally minded." Keeley's *Tribune* prominently displayed Remington's pictures from Cuba, reprinted dispatches from other papers, sent its own reporter to interview insurgent general Máximo Gómez, and broke the news of Admiral George Dewey's victory in Manila even though the paper didn't have a reporter on the scene. The latter was a major bell-ringer. Keeley made arrangements to use the *New York World*'s reports and stationed a reporter in its newsroom with strict orders to stay all night, every night. News of Dewey's victory came in on a Friday night around three o'clock Eastern time, when the *World* had gone to press and the few staffers around were playing poker. As the *Trib*'s man did not have a hand in the game, he answered the telephone. The operator read the cable reporting Dewey's victory. The reporter, Keeley later recounted, "took it down, hopped to our leased wire, and we had it about five minutes later. I stopped the presses, yanked back about 30,000 copies of the city edition, locked the doors, and got out an extra." Keeley telephoned the sleeping President McKinley with the news.

Energized by the Spanish-American War, the *Tribune* sprinkled a few correspondents abroad. The bureaus languished, however, and foreign coverage generally was erratic, except perhaps for a constant interest in the local angle. When Lord Northcliffe, owner of the *London Daily Mail,* sent a note to the *Tribune* by special messenger to show how fast it could be done, Keeley played along with the promotional stunt (the note itself was of such little importance that histories do not record what it said) and immediately dispatched his chief copy boy, James "Durk" Durkin, with a return missive, thus making him something of a recreational foreign correspondent. Keeley also made a foreign correspondent out of "a former dean of a women's college and an expert in dietetics as well as cookery," whom he sent overseas in search of "tasty and thrifty recipes." Chicago's great commercial emporium was Marshall Field's, and it was big news when the daughter of the department store's cofounder married into Britain's titled Curzon family. The *Tribune* assigned a woman correspondent to accompany the couple to India, where George Curzon became viceroy.

When hostilities erupted with Mexico in 1914, the *Tribune* found local connections aplenty. "One hundred and fifty former residents of Chicago are in peril in two inland Mexican towns, according to a letter received here [Chicago] today," said an April story. "Chicago Bride in Mexico City and Bank Cashier Are Safe," announced a nearby headline over two large photos of the pair.

Keeley's Morocco bell-ringer of 1906 started as a strictly local story, the closing in July of the Milwaukee Avenue State Bank, the largest state bank in Chicago. Both the bank's president and its cashier had disappeared. One of Keeley's tipsters told him where cashier H. W. Hering was hiding in Chicago. Keeley went there personally, got Hering's confession that he and the bank president had embezzled money, and turned him in to the police. Paul Stensland, the bank's president, a man of stolid Norwegian stock, was one of Chicago's most respected citizens and thus a bigger story. Leads to Stensland's whereabouts ranged from Duluth to Honduras. All petered out. Staying with the story, Keeley got a tip that Stensland had headed for Morocco via Europe. The editor set out after him, covering his tracks by saying he was taking "a fishing trip" to Canada. With him on this supposed vacation was assistant district attorney Harry Olson.

When Keeley reached Morocco, he learned that the banker had gone to Spain on a vacation of his own. Keeley followed, just missing him in Gibraltar on September 2. Stensland, Keeley was told, was now on a boat headed up the coast of Africa. The good news was that the vessel might make a stop in Tangier. Keeley hired a "filthy little Spanish steamer with a crew of ten" to take him to Tangier and, if necessary, follow Stensland to a farther destination. The captain said he was willing to go beyond the law, "even to forcibly kidnapping the old man."

Confident that he would soon have his man and eager to ring the bell with his scoop, Keeley filed his first *Tribune* story at the enormous cable cost of $1,200. The 2,500-word article was splashed over the front page on September 3. The pages of the paper brimmed with more of the same in the coming weeks. An abridged version of that first story—which turned out to be overly optimistic about how easy it would be to bring Stensland home—follows.

STENSLAND TO BE CAUGHT IN 24 HOURS.

Tracked to England, Gibraltar, and Tangier, Which He Left Yesterday.

HAS $12,000 CASH LEFT.

Tribune Representative and Assistant State's Attorney Olson Locate Wrecker.

UNDER ALIAS OF P. OLSEN.

Pursuers Miss Him by Less than 2 Hours and Follow in Torpedo Boat.

MOROCCO WILL GIVE HIM UP.

[BY CABLE TO THE CHICAGO TRIBUNE.]
[BY A STAFF CORRESPONDENT.]

GIBRALTAR, Sept. 2.—Paul O. Stensland, president and wrecker of the Milwaukee Avenue bank, left Gibraltar for the eastern coast of Africa at 5 o'clock this afternoon, just one hour and forty minutes before the representative of THE TRIBUNE and Assistant State's Attorney Harry Olson arrived, after trailing him from America to England, thence to Gibraltar, to Tangier, Morocco, back to Gibraltar, and thence to Ronda, where he saw a bull fight, to Bodadella, Granada, Seville, and other Spanish towns.

Stensland is traveling under the alias of P. Olsen of Norway.

Either Stensland is absolutely sure that he is not being followed or he has become extremely careless, for he is leaving a trail as wide as one made by a herd of buffalo on the plains.

Capture Practically Certain.

His capture practically is certain. We leave in the morning on a private torpedo boat and will either come up with the quarry in twenty-four hours or arrive at the farthest point ahead of the fugitive.

Grummere, the American minister to Morocco, is on watch, and the moment he receives instructions from the state department he will send a detail of the sultan's soldiers to make a captive of the biggest financial brigand in the history of Chicago.

Morocco Will Surrender Him.

Stensland chose Morocco as a permanent residence, thinking he is safe because there is no extradition treaty with that country. There isn't any treaty, but it is less safe than anywhere. The sultan at Fez, to whom Mr. Grummere is going on his first official mission in two weeks, will do anything for his great, good friend, President Roosevelt, and he will be delighted to chop off Stensland's head if required. The mere matter of throwing a bad man in jail and keeping him there indefinitely is so small a request that it is granted before it is asked. Two weeks in a Moorish prison would make a man willing to go anywhere else.

Warships May Aid.

If Stensland decides to return as a gentleman instead of as a handcuffed prisoner, well and good. Otherwise one of the United States warships that will be in Gibraltar in ten days probably will cross to Tangier, the fugitive will be thrown on board, and headed for Milwaukee avenue.

The bank wrecker is on the German tramp steamer Oldenburg. He went on board at noon. At first, it was thought the Oldenburg would not sail until tomorrow, and if it had not we would have pulled him off at daylight.

We missed him by an eyelash. We went to Tangier yesterday and he arrived at Gibraltar two hours after we sailed. The boat on which we were returning passed the boat on which he was going six miles out of Gibraltar. We passed so close that we could distinguish the passengers on the deck.

Doesn't Suspect Pursuit.

The fact that he thinks he is not being followed is shown by the directions he left at the Grand hotel, telling the clerk where to forward his mail for the next two months. He figured on spending the month of October at Teneriffe, in the Canary islands. He has some correspondent or friend in London, for he ordered his mail sent to the Metropole hotel.

If he should elude capture for the next few days he will come to a sudden halt in his travels because of a lack of money. We

discovered that he had $12,000 in a bank in Tangier. Steps have been taken by Assistant State's Attorney Olson to tie this money up, and if possible restore it to the swindled depositors. . . .

Arrives in Tangier July 28.

Stensland arrived in Tangier July 28 by the steamer Gibel from Gibraltar. He apparently made previous inquiries regarding the hotels, avoiding the large and prominent ones, such as Villa de France, Cecil, and Continental. He climbed the hill on which the quaint Moorish town is built and entered the city gate, and walked to the Grand Hotel Oriental. This small, second rate place is on a narrow street, so narrow, in fact, that two small donkeys cannot pass abreast. It is perched on top of a hill and is the most prominent building in the ranks of dazzling white and light blue structures that rise, terrace on terrace, till the summit is crowned. It is the resort of Europeans, and, by a strange coincidence, is the place where an absconding railway man of Atlanta, Ga., was captured through the efforts of United States Minister Grummere six years ago.

Phillip Sterwind, the proprietor, answered the Arab porter's hail and terms were soon agreed upon. Stensland registered as "P. Olsen, Norway." He was given a room overlooking the sea with a view of the Spanish shore in the distance. For one day he kept to his room, complaining of a cold on the lungs. The affliction was real, and for a few days he was a sick man.

Displays Big Sum of Money.

Stensland evidently thought himself absolutely safe from pursuit, or, like the majority of fugitives, became careless as soon as he set foot on foreign soil. The day after his arrival he amazed Proprietor Sterwind by exhibiting, as Sterwind said last night, "an awful lot of money and a great number of big bills." As a banker Stensland knew which was the best bank in Tangier, and, mounting a mule, with a small satchel in hand, rode to the Comptoir National d'Escompte, where he said he wanted to make a deposit and open an account.

When he dumped $12,000 on the counter the eyes of the clerk bulged out and he called M. Gaurant, the governor, who questioned the prospective customer. The money was in American bills, English bank notes, and French notes. Stensland, in answer to M. Gaurant's inquiries, said he came from America, and when further questioned as to why he carried money in such shape and had no letter of credit, said he thought he would get the worst of exchange and concluded it was best to carry currency.

Arouses Suspicion at Bank.

The deposit was accepted, but only provisionally, as M. Gaurant was suspicious. Stensland's explanation of his reason for carrying cash was puerile, and M. Gaurant thought he was doing business with a criminal of some kind. The French notes especially were regarded with suspicion, the banker suspecting they might be counterfeits. He was too polite to say so, but shipped them to Marseilles and Paris. They came back in ten days guaranteed genuine, and then were placed to Stensland's credit.

As soon as Stensland left the bank M. Gaurant sent for Hotelkeeper Sterwind and asked if he knew anything about his guest, saying he thought there was something wrong. Sterwind said his suspicions also had been aroused, but that he had looked through all the police circulars asking for arrest of fugitives and found nothing that would fit his guest. . . .

Stubby Mustache His Only Beard.

Stensland soon became a conspicuous figure in Tangier. This is not the height of the season, and, though the tri-weekly boats from Gibraltar bring some visitors, the stranger who tarries over three or four days is the object of some interest. Stensland was smooth shaven except for a stubby gray mustache, which had been growing since last March. The southern sun had given his face a brick tint. His blue suit of a particularly bright hue and patent leather shoes, the only ones seen in this Moorish town in years, made him a marked man.

The Oriental hotel stands just between the Mosque Dramakebir and the Café Française. Stensland gave the mosque the cold shoulder, though awakened every morning by the muezzin in the tower ringing the bell as he faced Mecca and called on Allah. But the Café Français, the Café Imperial, and the Café Turkesque found a good customer in him. Every night he climbed the hills and wound his tortuous way through alley-like streets, from one to the other. Mme. Yvette at the Français, was his favorite chanteuse, and between risque songs she chummed with him at a small table.

Becomes Arab's Rival for Danseuse.

But his real favorite was Senorita Vittoria, a Spanish dancer from Seville, who performs with exceptional abandon the fandango at the Café Imperial. Her partiality for him aroused a feeling of jealousy in the breast of an Arab chief who enjoyed the smiles of the danseuse until Stensland appeared on the scene. In the first few nights Stensland saw all that was to be seen in Tangier by moonlight and otherwise and then settled into a round of café visits. . . .

On August 14 Stensland . . . left for Gibraltar, Stensland's final act being to arrange with the Comptoir National d'Escompte for a credit of 2,500 pesatas, or about $400 at the Anglo-Egyptian bank in Gibraltar.

❋

Before Keeley left Chicago, he had Stensland's son watched. One of Keeley's spies came up with a copy of an apparently harmless business cable in Norwegian from Tangier, signed P. Olsen. On a hunch, Keeley sent a cable back, "Imperative await letters papers Tangier." This proved to be a shrewd move.

As luck would have it, the ship Stensland took from Gibraltar did stop, as Keeley hoped it would, in Tangier before heading up the coast. Stensland might have stayed on board except, as per the Keeley cable, he wanted to check his mail at the British post office. As Stensland was writing "P. Olsen's" forwarding address, Keeley got his man. "I hit him on the back and said, 'Write your own name, Stensland, and write Chicago.'"

At first Stensland resisted. Some of his shipmates, Germans, took his side, while a number of Moroccans gathered round. Keeley was forced to pull out warrants and other papers, which persuaded the Germans. He tried several arguments on Stensland—that his ways of escape were now cut off, that his money was tied up, that he had been living the high life with sultry dancers while poor Chicagoans were penniless, that Stensland's son would have to take his place in jail. Just as this latter point sunk in, a group of Moroccan soldiers arrived with a valet from the American consulate. The posse had been called out when the British minister complained to his American counterpart about the fracas in the British post office disrupting business. Stensland, Keeley, and the rest of the party were taken to the American consulate.

Keeley hoped to convince Stensland to come along voluntarily, but that was no longer possible now that the American and Moroccan authorities were involved. Furthermore, contrary to what he had suggested in his story, he was not sure how much cooperation he would receive from American officials. One of them expressly said he would make no promises. The envoy seemed irritated to have his pleasant routine ruined. Also, there was no prospect of an American warship arriving soon, as Keeley had reported was the case. It could take as long as two months for a ship to reach Tangier, since much of the fleet was in Asia.

Meanwhile, the *Tribune* was working the angles back in the United States. Anticipating problems, Keeley had cabled Clifford Raymond, the *Tribune* man in Washington, shortly before he captured Stensland. Judging from the stories that appeared as a result, Raymond relished his assignment to prod the government into action. He first went to the top ranks of the State Department. Even though it happened to be a Labor Day Monday, he found the acting secretary of state, Alvee A. Adee, fresh from a canoe ride on the Potomac. Adee made it clear that the lack of an extradition treaty was a major problem. Although reluctant to enter into any arrangement that would give Moroccans reciprocal rights against the United States, Adee did promise to cable the American envoy in Tangier, asking him to sound out the government on giving Stensland up. He also suggested that the Illinois governor make a formal request to have Stensland sent home. "It was unofficially sug-

J. K.'S FISHING TRIP.

This cartoon celebrating Keeley's pursuit of Stensland appeared in the *Tribune*'s in-house publication. The artist was John T. McCutcheon, who had distinguished himself as a foreign correspondent. McCutcheon, colleague Will Irwin wrote, was "the most original and human American cartoonist. But whenever he heard the preliminary rumbles of a war he took a leave of absence from his drawing board." The "fishing trip" in the cartoon headline refers to Keeley's ruse to keep his pursuit of Stensland secret. Irwin, *Making of a Reporter*, 209. Illustration: © 1906, Chicago Tribune Company, All rights reserved. Used with permission.

gested," Raymond reported, "that while the governor of Illinois may not be so gorgeously appareled as the sultan of Morocco he was the head of quite as important a state and such would be the view of the sultan." The Illinois governor agreed to make such a request.

In the course of these conversations, the matter of "an amicable kidnapping" arose, the idea being that the Moroccans should look the other way while Stensland was taken out of the country. Adee had been involved in such an incident years before. In 1876 New York's boss William Tweed fled custody and eventually ended up in Spain, where Adee was a diplomat—and where there also was no extradition treaty. The Spanish released Tweed, and Adee spirited him onto a U.S. Navy ship that happened to be in the vicinity. This tale appealed to Raymond, no doubt, because it, too, had a journalism twist. Tweed was apprehended thanks to a Thomas Nast cartoon with a likeness of the fugitive that appeared in *Harper's Weekly*. Adee gave the drawing to Spanish authorities with the request that they be on the lookout. Soldiers spotted Tweed disguised as a sailor. So now Raymond suggested that a warship should be sent to Morocco to collect Stensland, as it had Tweed, rather than taking a chance of passing "the wily banker" through the jurisdiction of other countries on a more conventional trip home. The idea irritated Adee, whose day of rest was already complicated enough. Raymond was unable to find anyone at the Navy Department willing to discuss the possibility.

Two days later, on Wednesday, the Moroccans agreed to release Stensland. Not yet done with his work, Raymond hied himself off to Oyster Bay, New York, where on Thursday he called on President Theodore Roosevelt. He found that Roosevelt "is not merely strenuous but is exceedingly rapid in comprehension and in action." TR had made political hay two years earlier when a tribal chief named Ahmed ben Mohammed el Raisuli kidnapped Ion Perdicaris, a wealthy American retired in Morocco. Roosevelt's ultimatum—"We want Perdicaris alive or Raisuli dead"—evoked cheers from Republican convention delegates who happened to be nominating him president for a second term at the time. Faced with this new episode, the president immediately dictated a note urging the State Department to get on the case. He made Keeley and Olson "official representatives" authorized to bring Stensland home. Raymond noted that Roosevelt's instructions may have been unconstitutional. "It was refreshing, to say the least, to find a man, and that one for the time being the greatest in the country, who was instantly willing to take the desired action in the interests of the people without the slightest regard to diplomatic traditions." The next day, Keeley and his deputized sidekick Olson took custody of Stensland. Keeley liked to refer to himself as the high commissioner in charge of Stensland.

Reporting from his post in Washington, Raymond announced that the banker was in American hands. The problem of transportation was subsequently solved when the Hamburg-American steamship *Prinz Adalbert* agreed to make a special stop in Tangier to pick up Stensland. From there it was a straight shot to New York. There was no risk that Stensland could claim his freedom during a layover in another country.

Not that Stensland, by this time, was averse to going home. Far from being a hardened criminal, the banker had used bank money to cover bad investments that he expected to pay back but found himself in the clutches of his cashier, whose illegal designs were more far-reaching. In addition to being contrite, he was aware that a prolonged stay in Tangier might easily lead to confinement in a Moroccan prison. Only by the grace of Keeley had he avoided this fate. Keeley was given the opportunity to throw the old man in the Kasbah prison, as local authorities wanted to do in order to avoid any problem with escape, which might arouse Roosevelt. Not wanting to see the banker condemned to such treatment, Keeley worked out a deal whereby he would rent a house and create a "private penitentiary." He hired "25 Moorish soldiers to guard the place day and night." But who knew how long Stensland would be so fortunate?

While the wheels of diplomacy ground along, Keeley milked the story for all the human interest he could: Stensland had planned to go to Russia. He "wrestled with the problem whether to blow his brains out or run." He considered staying in Tangier and opening "a big Deutsche bierhalle and building a brewery. He thought the Arabs could be taught to drink beer." Keeley reported his efforts to arrange special incarceration of the elderly banker in order to keep him out of the infamous Kasbah. "The Moorish official was greatly astonished when told that under no circumstances must a man be flogged," Keeley reported. "He said he did not see how on earth the ends of justice were attained without a morning and evening flogging."

Large, provocative photos showed the hotel where Stensland stayed. Readers could admire Stensland's supposed love-interest Señorita Vittoria, over whose comely portrait was the headline: "Spanish Danseuse for Whose Affections Stensland Became Rival of Arab Chief." They shivered at the scene of an "an Execution Before the Sultan," in which a swarthy Moroccan with a sword stood over a crumpled body.

The *Tribune* also ran synopses of previous stories, reported what local ministers said in their pulpits about Stensland, and reprinted salutes from other newspapers. Both the *Peoria Journal* and the *Union* of Springfield, Massachusetts, observed a connection with a previous scoop. "Not since James Gordon Bennett issued his mandate to Stanley to 'Find Livingstone' at that time in darkest Africa," said one, "has a great newspaper undertaken such a task of discovery."

Apart from observations on the Oriental propensity for flogging, Keeley showed little interest in Morocco itself. None of his stories carried bylines, for bylines were still not customary even for first-person reporting; we can guess that he probably wrote two short articles about the revolution under way in the country. One of them was five paragraphs long; the other consisted of this: "The pretender to the throne has been defeated near Muluya. His two principal chiefs were killed." In his letter to his family, Keeley recounted an encounter with a young "cockney" smuggling rifles into the country apparently for sale to these revolutionaries. This he did not report.

Keeley, Olson, and "the greatest fugitive from justice the city by the lake has ever known" reached Chicago by train on September 24 at 8:55 A.M., twelve days after leaving Tangier. Stensland pled guilty that morning and was on his way to the Joliet penitentiary so fast his son missed the train. The *Tribune* covered every move of prisoner number 9902: "The man who had sat at the banquet board at many a feast, who had been hailed in Chicago as the uncrowned king of the Norsemen, and foremost financier, was walking to a prison bathhouse."

When all the accounting was done, the Milwaukee Avenue State Bank was not in such bad shape as news reports had suggested. Stensland, quickly paroled, assisted in sorting out the bank's affairs and returning money to depositors. Keeley, who had described Stensland in his family letter from Tangier as a "fine, lovable old man . . . not a criminal by intent," sent money to him in Joliet and found him a job investigating investment opportunities in South America.

"In Chicago," as one chronicler put it, "every reporter tried to be a Keeley." Having the real article, Medill's heirs gave this journalistic whirlwind overall control of the paper in 1909. He carried the triple title of editor, general manager, and second vice president. "My authority," he stated, "is absolute." Two years later Keeley coined the *Tribune*'s extravagant slogan, "The World's Greatest Newspaper." It appeared on the masthead until 1977 and inspired the WGN call letters for the *Tribune*'s affiliated radio and television stations.

To the surprise of many, Keeley abruptly left the *Tribune* in early May 1914 and arranged with a group of investors to buy the ailing *Chicago Record-Herald* and the *Chicago Inter-Ocean,* which were combined into the *Herald.* Keeley may have been chafed because, for all his authority, he had not been able to acquire *Tribune* stock from the Medill family. He also may have sensed that the new generation of owners would curb his authority. If so, he would probably have been right.

After Keeley left, Joseph Medill's two strong-willed grandsons, Robert McCormick and Joseph Patterson, began to exert their influence over the newspaper. Patterson, who started the *New York News* in 1919, eventually became less of a force than his cousin, who imposed his own simplified spelling system on the paper (e.g., "frate" for "freight") and fired reporters even when they were superb at their work. McCormick's early responsibilities included foreign news, which was about to feature prominently in the *Tribune.* On June 28, 1914, little more than a month after Keeley jumped ship, a Serbian nationalist assassinated Archduke Ferdinand of Austria.

No American reporter was in Sarajevo to cover the assassination, which was reported by an Associated Press stringer whose name is lost to history. On the eve of World War I, the typical foreign correspondent had become "mainly a purveyor of gossip about Americans abroad," wrote Will Irwin, a press critic who was soon to be a war correspondent. "A Pittsburgh playboy who broke the bank at Monte Carlo or a young blood of the Four Hundred who entangled himself with a showgirl in London was worth more space in Chicago and New York than Asquith's social legislation or the rise of Social Democracy in Germany."

An editorial writer for Keeley's *Herald* observed of the assassination that "the fortunes and calamities of the House of Hapsburg are far away from us and of little interest." Not until July 24 did the *Herald* run a front-page story on the Austrian-Serbian mess. Even after war was declared in August, much of the press thought it would not amount to much. "During the next twelve months *Harper's Magazine* refrained from publishing so much as a single paragraph about the unpleasantness of the Western Front," recalled a later editor of that periodical. Correspondents were riveted on the sensational trial of the beautiful blonde wife of the former French premier, M. Caillaux; she had murdered the editor of *Le Figaro*, which had published private correspondence between her and her husband.

Although the *Tribune* had not been any better than other newspapers at anticipating trouble in Europe, it was at the head of the pack once trouble erupted. It splashed the assassination across its front page and soon had reporters in Europe. Showing all the enthusiasm Keeley had evinced in assigning himself to the Morocco bell-ringer, both McCormick and Patterson covered the early years of the conflict when the United States maintained its neutrality.

Keeley's spirit carried on nowhere more obviously than in Floyd Gibbons. Like his old boss Keeley, Gibbons had a nose for news, zeal in exploiting stories, and little interest in examining underlying causes. Fellow *Tribune* correspondent George Seldes described Gibbons as a "police reporter of Chicago in excelsis, covering the world as he would a ward."*

When the *Tribune* assigned Gibbons to London in 1917, the United States had just broken diplomatic relations with Germany over its announcement of unrestricted submarine warfare. The *Tribune* arranged expensive passage for Gibbons aboard the SS *Frederick VIII*, which was carrying home the German ambassador to the United States and was therefore immune to U-boat attack. The headstrong Gibbons decided to take the SS *Laconia* instead and packed a special light, nonsink vest. Two hundred miles off the Irish coast, the Germans torpedoed the liner. It sank in forty minutes. Gibbons survived in a lifeboat. Thirteen perished.

Gibbons's story appeared under the *Tribune*'s biggest headline type: "TWO CHICAGOANS DIE ON LINER. GIBBONS WIRES THAT HE IS SAFE; SENDS STORY TO TRIBUNE." "I have talked with a seaman who was in the same lifeboat with the two Chicago women," Gibbons reported in his long account, "and he has told me that he saw their lifeless bodies washing out of the sinking lifeboat." He also reported the name of "a former Chicago woman" who survived. The scoop had Keeley written all over it.

The "question being asked of the Americans on all sides," Gibbons reported,

---

* George Seldes also described Gibbons as "the best reporter of his time, one of the best of all times, in the old sense. That meant graduation from the city ward route, police court news, and stealing pictures from the homes of suicides and murderers, or pennies from the eyes of the dead if for some reason they were needed for a story." This from a colleague who "always liked Floyd." Not everyone did. Seldes, *Tell the Truth and Run*, 126.

was whether the sinking of the *Laconia* was "the *casus belli*." Judging from his memoir, Gibbons actually heard this question from a single person, a British survivor, shortly before dashing to his typewriter. It was not a nuance he or the *Tribune* worried about. The newspaper sounded the war trumpets. Five weeks later President Woodrow Wilson obliged, and America was in the fight. So were McCormick and Patterson, who picked up the rank of colonel and captain, respectively, before the war was over. True to its local focus, the *Tribune* published the names and addresses of each Midwesterner killed, wounded, or missing in action.

Keeley was in the fight too. The *Herald* didn't have the resources to compete with the mighty *Tribune* he had built. After four years of struggle, Keeley gave up. With the announcement that Hearst had merged the *Herald* with his *Examiner,* the feisty editor headed for Europe. There he joined the ranks of a new profession that sought not to provide the news, but to manipulate it. His business, Keeley wrote to his family from Paris, was to "propagand the enemy."

11

L'HOMME ENCHAÎNÉ

"We have the right to demand to be told everywhere and always the truth," Georges Clemenceau wrote early in World War I. The Tiger, as the elderly politician was called, had long championed press freedom and had vigorously used it when he was a journalist. His first foray as a newsman was as a correspondent for the liberal *Le Temps* in the United States at the end of the Civil War. Back home in France, Clemenceau combined journalism and politics: speaking up for the poor; crusading for Alfred Dreyfus, the Jewish officer falsely accused of selling military secrets; and toppling governments—by one count, eighteen in a sixteen-year period. (Displaying his government-toppling proclivities while a correspondent in the United States, he favored impeaching President Andrew Johnson.) With the outbreak of the Great War, Senator Clemenceau launched an opinion-laden newspaper, *L'Homme Libre*. The minister of the interior suspended the journal when it exposed miserable medical care for wounded soldiers. Undeterred, Clemenceau started *L'Homme Enchaîné*.*

In 1917, as French morale wilted and rumors of mutiny among the French troops circulated, Clemenceau moved from the political periphery to the center. Politicians who had suffered abuse at his editorializing hand acknowledged that they needed his leadership. The Tiger was named premier and from this new vantage point did a volte-face on press freedom. Now he opposed it. "Why should you think I want to make my task harder?" Clemenceau said with a laugh to a correspondent with the *Christian Science Monitor*. "The French press is irresponsible. Do you suppose I'm going to have it filled with defeatist articles? No, the newspapers must walk warily, or I shall close them down without mercy."

Clemenceau's dedication to an unfettered press was limited after the war as well, when he was president of the Versailles Peace Conference. Allowing correspondents to cover the negotiations, he said, was "veritable suicide." British prime minister Lloyd George agreed with the old Tiger and proposed a joint statement to

---

* This was not the first time a French journalist tried such a bon mot. Some years before, after a newspaper named *La Lune* was suppressed, it became *L'Eclipse*. Salmon, *The Newspaper and the Historian*, 49.

the press saying that the discussions would be sensitive and that it would not help to promote controversy. President Woodrow Wilson for the most part went along. Official communiqués, they all also agreed, should stick to bare "established facts, suppressing all matters under consideration."

"The war had brought to attention a new method in politics and diplomacy," later observed Will Irwin, who turned from war reporting to brief service as a propagandist for the Wilson government. "Governments had proved that the press could be gagged and the news slanted, biased or juggled to produce almost any temporary effect they wished; and that in time of war at least, people would endure the process. Here was a weapon of statesmanship too useful to abandon in time of peace."

Censorship was not new. In the Civil War Gen. William Tecumseh Sherman court-martialed a reporter for writing that Sherman would have won the Battle of Vicks-burg if he had "acted as earnestly and persistently against the enemy as against the press." Upon hearing that three reporters might have been killed, Sherman said, "That's good! We'll have dispatches now from hell before breakfast." Several decades later, in a stinging article for *Scribner's,* anti-imperialist Thomas Millard criticized British censorship during the Boer War. The enemy "England wished to keep in ignorance," he said, "was civilization." Lord Herbert Kitchener deported Millard. The Japanese were even more effective at sidelining correspondents during the Russo-Japanese War early in the next century. After having his camera confiscated and being court-martialed for knocking down a Japanese groom who he thought had pilfered his equipment, Jack London gave up the assignment for William Randolph Hearst and went home. He was not alone in beating a retreat from that battle in Japan for news.

World War I, however, marked a sharp departure from the past. The contest of wills between government and press was unprecedented because of the sheer magnitude—and newsworthiness—of the war and the Peace Conference, and because the censors and the censored brought so much more organization and sophistication to their jobs.

By the time of the Great War, journalists had developed a conscience and formal institutions to go with it. Publishers and editors no longer horsewhipped each other. They drank together at meetings of state editorial associations and at gatherings of the grander American Newspaper Publishers' Association. They created press codes, wrote journalism textbooks, and explored their shortcomings. Muck-raking *Collier's* assigned Irwin to investigate daily journalism. The *Chicago Tribune's* James Keeley, that feisty graduate of the school of hard knocks, frequently visited Notre Dame to talk to students and in 1913 was named honorary dean of its new "college of journalism." While that college did not amount to much before it disappeared, other university programs became established. Joseph Pulitzer, whose *World* was one of the most flagrant yellow sheets during the Spanish-American War, made so much money that he could afford to become a press statesman. He gave $250,000 to Columbia University for Pulitzer Prizes recognizing journalistic excellence and $2 million to help establish a school to teach would-be journalists to "exalt principle, knowledge, culture, at the expense of business if need be." "I wish to begin a movement," he said before he died in 1911, "that will raise journalism to the rank of a learned profession." The school would be most useful, one correspondent observed, if it taught "the opposite of everything that the *World* has been or now is."

Although journalism remained uneven and too frankly commercial to qualify as a profession like medicine or law, journalists viewed themselves as a special class with obligations and rights. As has been the practice in other wars, accredited war correspondents in World War I wore officers' uniforms, in this case with a green brassard on their sleeves bearing a *C* or a *P* for correspondent or photographer. When Gen. John Pershing, commander of the American Expeditionary Force (AEF), suggested that correspondents carry officer rank, they balked. "We felt it could hamper our work of collecting facts," one correspondent recalled. "In my line," Edwin L. James of the *New York Times* told a colonel, "I rank as a brigadier general."

No matter what rank correspondents thought they had, they were still subordinate to the government rules imposed on them. Ten days after declaring war in 1917, President Wilson issued a proclamation making publishers liable for treason if they printed information giving "aid or comfort to the enemy." Congress passed legislation giving Wilson considerable power over news. The Espionage Act contained broad language outlawing false reports that promoted enemy success; the Trading-with-the-Enemy Act authorized censorship of messages between the United States and any foreign country; the Sedition Act imposed fines and imprisonment for "disloyal, profane, scurrilous, or abusive language about the form of government of the United States, or the Constitution of the United States, or the military or naval forces of the United States, or the flag of the United States, or the uniform of the army or navy of the United States."

In administering press censorship and propaganda, Wilson created the Committee on Public Information (CPI) and placed journalist George Creel at its head. Many of those whom Creel hired were also journalists. An AP executive thought journalists-turned-censors would be less likely to "antagonize the press at every turn." He was wrong. "There can be no broader chasm than that between an army headquarters and a city editor's room," said Frederick Palmer, a veteran of war reporting. He patriotically gave up an assignment to cover the war for the *New York Herald* (for the princely sum of $40,000 a year) to take the rank of major (salary $2,400 per year) and oversee censorship and propaganda for General Pershing. Given the state of the war, Palmer found "a great deal to censor and very little to propagandize—so very little that if there had been no censorship officially applied or self-applied by the patriotism of the correspondents we might have lost the war."

Editors printed large amounts of the material coming out of the CPI. As remains the case today, correspondents understood the need to censor reports that put troops at risk. Occasionally they picked up weapons. One day fifteen German soldiers mistook a *Collier's* reporter for an officer and surrendered. He marched them to the American lines.

American reporters, however, were less compliant than their European counterparts and, to their credit, less likely to report atrocity stories concocted by propagandists. Occasionally they outfoxed censors with seemingly innocent cables that, thanks to a prearranged code or use of a clever reference, tipped off editors to big stories. Sometimes they found a loophole in the rules. When British censors did not pass reports about the Germans' first Zeppelin raid on London, United Press's William Shepherd wrote about the heroic Londoners coping with the aftermath of the bombing, a topic not banned.*

From the early days of the war, when it still was strictly a European conflict, American correspondents felt unduly constrained. Frustrated because he could not secure French permission to go to the front, *New York Times* reporter Wythe Williams joined an ambulance unit for several months. Others simply went home. As time went on, it was easier to reach the front lines, but correspondents were on a short leash. Notwithstanding his military rank and duties with the American Expeditionary Force, *Tribune* publisher Robert McCormick described censorship as "a lie factory."

The AEF arrived with a long list of rules for correspondents. One was that newspapers had to post a ten-thousand-dollar bond, which would be forfeited in the case of any infraction by their correspondents. One infractor was Heywood Broun. Broun learned of scandalous supply shortages affecting American troops. Unable to get the story past censors, he went home to write it. His newspaper, the *New York World,* paid the fine; he lost his accreditation as a war correspondent.

Correspondents grumbled that censors worried more about protecting the army's reputation than the public's right to know, especially when stories like Broun's had the potential for prompting corrective action. The censor's credo, Palmer acknowledged after the war, was: "When in doubt—kill it!" No reporter, United Press correspondent Wilbur Forrest said, could hope to repeat George Smalley's legendary scoop on the Battle of Antietam. There was not only military censorship, Wythe Williams complained, "but political, diplomatic, financial, personal, and even social censorship as well." Censors stopped the trivial news that a few American troops received a French gift of wine for fear folks back home would think the troops were drinking. Palmer even censored correspondents' expense accounts.

When it suited their interests, censors opened information spigots. The English allowed reporting of Germany's first use of poison gas on the Western Front in hopes of building sympathy among the American public. At the Peace Conference,

---

* In this war and later, stratagems to circumvent the censorship did not always work, of course. Isaac Don Levine of the International News Service devised a code to alert his editors in London that Lenin had died: "Send me £50." When the momentous event occurred, the editor on duty put aside the cable so he could query Levine on why he needed the money. Desmond, *Crisis and Conflict,* 41.

officials publicly decried breaches of information while promoting their agenda by privately helping to leak information to favored journalists. In one stratagem, an official conveniently arranged to be out of the office so a correspondent could snatch a document. At times it was hard to know what an official's agenda was. When Wythe Williams wrote a negative story about Clemenceau, the crafty French premier let it pass the censors and printed it on the front page of his own journal, now back to its old name, *L'Homme Libre*. Williams could not resist asking why. "It may be useful!" the premier said cryptically, laughing. Williams, who was charmed by Clemenceau, wrote a laudatory biography of the old man after the war.

None of the reporters at the Peace Conference were more creative in getting news or had better inside connections than the loud, flamboyant redhead representing the *New York World*. Herbert Bayard Swope was not a professional foreign correspondent steeped in overseas affairs, but he had distinguished himself as a correspondent for the same reason he had distinguished himself exposing police corruption in New York. Swope, said fellow reporter Damon Runyon, "carried the power of the press like a flaming beacon when he was a reporter, and fairly intimidated his way to news."

Swope's foreign correspondence began in 1914 as an afterthought tagged on to a frivolous assignment. When he was in the Azores to cover one stop of the first flight from the British Isles to North America, the *World* redirected him to Europe, where war was erupting. From his German-Jewish parents, who had immigrated to St. Louis, Swope had learned the German language and imbibed German culture, which gave him an advantage in the assignment. During his five-week stay in Germany, he secured a sensational interview with a German submarine captain who had sunk three British cruisers, drowning fifteen hundred men.

In 1916, after a stint as city editor, Swope returned to Germany for two months. The *World* wanted him to get a more balanced picture than the paper's permanent man-on-the-scene was able to provide. To avoid problems with the German authorities, Swope smuggled his notes out through a diplomatic pouch. His nineteen-part series, written in New York, portrayed a determined, anti-American Germany. That year the first Pulitzer Prizes were given, and Swope won in the "reporting" category. A book-length compilation of the articles, *Inside the German Empire*, appeared in January 1917, one month before the United States declared war. Long a Wilson supporter, Swope left the paper to work for Bernard Baruch at the War Industries Board. He rejoined the *World* when the armistice was signed and headed to Paris to cover the treaty negotiations with a shipload of fellow reporters.

Swope's entrance into the press corps in Paris was, in the words of Arthur Krock, then representing Louisville newspapers, "magnificent. . . . Somehow his voice and manner dissipated the drabness of the environment." When correspondents organized themselves as the United States Press Delegation, they elected him president. Swope's connections to the Wilson administration were an asset for the correspondents. When Wilson's state visit to Belgium did not make provisions for a press entourage, Swope managed to get a press car attached. In Paris he was in the forefront of a correspondents' grievance committee that won minor concessions. Among these was permission for a limited number of reporters to observe plenary sessions where the victors discussed the treaty.

Swope's interventions brought only minimal progress. Observing plenary sessions was small beer. France, Great Britain, Italy, and the United States—the big four—did all the important negotiating work in the inner sanctum of the French Foreign Ministry on the Quai d'Orsay. Surviving among Swope's personal papers is a letter to President Wilson—it is unclear whether Swope sent it—in which he protested that press restrictions were "rather more drastic than any heretofore undertaken." He considered it a "lack of good faith."

This letter may have followed a bitter experience in which a scoop Swope engineered came a cropper as a result of government restrictions. He acquired the first summary of the secret German reparations clauses. Eight hours after sending it to the *World* via London, he shared the document with a *New York Sun* reporter, thinking his own report would surely arrive first. Despite Lloyd George's assurances that censorship was over, the British delayed his story. The *Sun* story, sent from Paris, arrived promptly, scooping Swope's scoop. "HEARTILY DISGUSTED," he advised his editors to "MAKE A BIG EXPOSURE OF DELIBERATE DECEPTION REGARDING NO CENSORSHIP."

Swope was more successful with advance reports on the League of Nations Covenant. He secured both an exclusive verbatim report of proceedings in which the covenant was introduced and an exclusive summary of the near-final revised draft of the covenant. The *Paris Herald* called the latter "the greatest journalistic success of the Conference." In this latter scoop, Swope was helped by the president himself. Wilson suggested that if the reporter dropped in at the office of his adviser, Col. Edward House, no one would be in. Taking the hint, Swope showed up and found the draft.

Swope's most ingenious circumvention of authorities—and arguably his brashest—came when he joined their ranks surreptitiously. This was the occasion when the Allies presented their peace treaty to Count Ulrich von Brockdorff-Rantzau, the German representative, and a press pool was created to permit a limited amount of coverage. The pool system is a technique for managing hordes of reporters, who draw lots to see who will make up a small group allowed to observe an event. After the event, the pool reporters brief their colleagues. In the case of the treaty presentation, Swope was unlucky and did not draw a place in the pool. Undeterred, the fast-talking reporter borrowed an American army sedan with a general officer's flag at its prow and sailed through all checkpoints to the Petit Trianon in the park of Versailles. Swope was a notoriously snappy dresser, right down to his monogrammed socks, and he looked every bit the confident diplomat when he stepped out of his sedan arrayed in cutaway coat, striped pants, and top hat. Inside Petit Trianon, he took one of the front-row seats reserved for envoys and watched the

"At the Peace Conference, easily the most impressive person was Herbert Bayard Swope," fellow journalist Stanley Walker wrote in the *Saturday Evening Post*. "In top hat and cutaway, he received military salutes and crashed the gate to places where reporters were supposed to be barred. It was all highly effective." Here Swope is pictured with colleagues at the Peace Conference. True to form, he is the natty one, at the far left end of the front row, wearing the spats. Kahn, *World of Swope*, 8.

proceedings from a far better vantage point than the official press pool reporters, who had to come in the back door. No one spotted him.

When the pool reporters gathered afterward to report to their colleagues on what they had seen, Swope interrupted to correct the account. This irritated *New York Times* reporter Charles Selden. "Swope, can't you keep your damned mouth shut for five minutes?" Selden exclaimed. "How the hell would you know what was going on? You weren't even there." "Who says I wasn't?" Swope replied.

The Germans had agreed the year before to the armistice ending the fighting because they believed the idealistic Wilson would give them a just peace. Drawing on what he saw from his ringside seat at the Petit Trianon, Swope vividly conveyed German disappointment in his dispatch, published on May 9, 1919. Count Brock-dorff-Rantzau's response foreshadowed how the harsh terms imposed by the Allies would inflame German indignation, paving the way for a second grim world war. (The boldface type in the text is as in the original.)

RANTZAU'S FLASH OF DEFIANCE HID HIS HOPELESSNESS

———◆———

Germans, Heads Erect, Tried to Give Impression of a Nation With Spirit Unbroken—Challenge Rings False.

————

ALLIED ENVOYS AMAZED AT AUDACITY OF SPEECH.

————

Effect of Foe's Foreign Minister's Words Electrical, Cementing Anew the Bonds Between Nations Against Him.

————

By Herbert Bayard Swope.
(Staff Correspondent of The World.)
Copyright, 1919, by The Press Publishing Co.
(The New York World)
(Special Cable Dispatch to The World)

PARIS, May 7.—Germany came to agreement to-day, not in sackcloth and ashes, but with head up and with spirit unbroken. Her representatives came to hear sentence pronounced, and they remained in utter defiance. Instead of asking clemency they demanded justice, that should not find them alone guilty but should discover that other European nations, bitten by imperialism, also took part in the destruction of the world's peace.

So ran the German theme, but beneath it was to be felt the impotence that had overtaken that nation. The challenge rang false, for it followed a confession that fell haltingly from the lips of her spokesman, in which Germany appeared as physically powerless.

Dramatic Moment.

History never recorded a more dramatic moment, or a moment of deeper meaning to civilization. Brilliant sunshine flooded the room in the Trianon Palace, but the life and gayety befitting such weather were strangely absent. The atmosphere was somber and funereal. Few strolled, and those not often.

When the Germans filed in, led by Count Brockdorff-Rantzau, who looked like a death's head and could scarcely walk, one had much the same feeling as in court when the Judge pronounces sentence of death upon a murderer. In the agony of suspense trifles were greatly magnified, and there was a general sense of the embarrassment which often attends great occasions.

Response Unexpected.

It had not been expected that the Germans would speak. In fact, it had been said that there would be no response from those who resembled nothing so much as prisoners at the bar.

When the Premier Clemenceau had finished his brief and formal utterance, Count Brockdorff-Rantzau indicated that he wished to be heard. There was a questioning look on "The Tiger's" face, and he frowned as he nodded assent; whereupon the German chief began to read an address which, with the translation into French and English, occupied precisely thirty-five minutes.

The audacity of the speech left the hearers breathless. Their eyes turned to Premier Clemenceau, who for the first time, seemed uncertain what course to pursue. For an instant it looked as if the old man would peremptorily order the speaker to desist. Testily and sneeringly he commanded the interpreters to pitch their voices louder. He squirmed in his chair but finally, after whispering with President Wilson, he dropped into a posture half-attentive and half-bored, and listened.

Rantzau Remains Seated.

Count Brockdorff-Rantzau startled the delegates by remaining seated while he spoke. That act, combined with a tardy arrival of about six minutes, led some of those present to infer that deliberate insults had been studied. Others more generously attributed the act to the fact that the count has been very ill and has difficulty in standing. **But there was evident breach of courtesy in failure to request permission to remain seated,** especially after the members of the conference had risen to receive him and his associates as they had entered.

In a strained and tragic voice he read a document that history will regard as Germany's defense and palliation. Doubtless much was written with reference to the future; **more was written for reading in his home country,** and part was intended to apply to the matter in hand. But he failed to have in mind the impression such a speech would make upon those before him, and it was before this conference that his country was arraigned.

Effect Was Electrical.

Stunned at first, startled into attention, and fearing an unexpected denouement, the delegates sat straining their ears, lest they should miss some of the words or their import. The effect was electrical.

Here was a common enemy asserting himself in a defiant manner. In that situation differences among the delegates were sunk, and the one dominant thought was that against such an enemy all must be united. **One could feel the intensity of the union that German opposition had instantly recreated, and the fact was at once recognized that the union existed and had not been shattered, as had been believed.**

Into the fabric of his address Count Rantzau wove certain admissions which stand out boldly, such as confession of guilt toward Belgium and acceptance of reparation for that violation of treaty and other international engagements. He denied that similar guilt existed in German treatment of other European nations. According to his declaration peace can be made only on the basis of President Wilson's fourteen points, justly applied and the League of Nations, in his view, embodies the greatest advance that has been made for the benefit of mankind.

Accuses the Allies.

In tones of passion he delivered what he intended to be his hardest blow when he said crimes committed in the heat of war might be palliated, but asked what was to be said of the guilt of the Allies, who had permitted hundreds of thousands of noncombatants to be killed by the prolongation of the blockade six months after the signing of the armistice. A sharp intake of breath among the delegates showed the effect of his attempt to make out an indictment on this score.

Dryly and curtly, as the Count closed, Premier Clemenceau asked if the Germans desired to make further remarks, and Count Rantzau, rising feebly from his chair and bowing, said, in perfect French, "For my part, no." The Premier thereupon declared the session adjourned, waving to the Allied delegates to remain in their places, to permit the Toutons to file out alone. The final chapter of the war had begun.

Swope was not the only infiltrator among the press corps. Earlier Burnet Hershey of the *New York Sun* had disguised himself à la Swope except with a Tyrolean hat and insinuated himself among the German press corps, which was housed off on its own. He made friends with these reporters, who gave him the German perspective, and with their help slipped into the German-only press conference Count

Brockdorff-Rantzau gave after the treaty presentation meeting Swope attended. Although trying to avoid attention, Hershey ended up next to the count, who told the assembled journalists he had purposely remained seated when presented with the treaty. "We are Germans," he said. "We will not forget. We will rise from this shame."

It was a mark of Swope's pyrotechnic presence that he made the most ripples. Charles Selden of the *New York Times* was so angry about his gate-crashing that he posted a notice at the American press headquarters: "Members of the organization of American correspondents attached to the peace conference who resent the action of Mr. Swope in violating the rules for attendance at the Versailles meeting and who think that Mr. Swope should not continue to be a member of the organization's committee may indicate their feelings by signing this paper." Selden signed. So did Swope, right below him in red crayon. No other correspondents put their names to the paper, which Swope kept as a souvenir.

Swope went home to become executive editor of the *World,* a powerful title that had not existed on the paper before it was given to him. He is remembered for creating the first newspaper op-ed page, a selection of lively opinion opposite the editorial page that became a staple in American journalism. He retired in 1928, shortly before the *World* folded as a result of uninspired stewardship by Pulitzer's heirs. In his last years Swope was New York State racing commissioner, a consultant to political leaders, a member of various corporate boards, and a sought-after New York toastmaster. Swope helped create the World Room at the Columbia University Graduate School of Journalism in the early 1950s. In 1961, three years after he died, the school dedicated the room to him.

Wilson failed to secure Senate support for the Treaty of Versailles and his beloved League of Nations. He would have fared better if he had not seemed to violate his own high-minded pronouncements during the negotiations in Paris, if he had been as open to compromise with American legislators as he was with his European counterparts, and if he had courted the press and public opinion during the conference as vigorously as his administration had managed the press during the war.

In laying out his stirring Fourteen Points for the peace, Wilson promised "open covenants, openly arrived at."* To the disappointment of the 150 reporters who came to Paris to cover the conference, he did not mean journalists could look over negotiators' shoulders. Wilson meant that no treaties would be created without citizens knowing that negotiations had taken place and having a chance to discuss the terms later. Whatever might be said about Wilson not living up to his high-minded rhetoric in Paris, the fact was that to negotiate behind closed doors made very good sense. As one historian noted, "News of disagreement would encourage—and in

---

* The actual words were, "Open covenants of peace, openly arrived at, after which there shall be no private international understandings of any kind but diplomacy shall proceed always frankly and in public view." *Congressional Record,* 65th Cong., 2nd sess., January 8, 1918, 680–681.

fact did encourage—the enemy to resist the prospective terms." Although Wilson could have explained all this and worked with the press to build support for his goals and the treaty, he didn't. The American president, editorialized the *New Republic,* "has again and again insisted that it must be a people's peace. Neither of those conditions can be fulfilled if the machinery of censorship be extended to the period of the Peace Conference." The saying circulated among correspondents covering the treaty conference, "Wilson talks like Jesus Christ and acts like Lloyd George."

Although Wilson had created the Creel Committee on Public Information to promote the war, he did not personally like to interact with the press. He had said on an earlier occasion, when it was suggested that he do a better job of communicating with Congress, "I am not in the message business as a profession." In Paris he did not bother to tell reporters that he had argued behind the scenes to let a pool witness the peace terms being presented to Count Brockdorff-Rantzau. "It is astonishing, but it is true, that neither the correspondents themselves nor the public in America ever knew what a fight the President had made" for more openness, wrote Ray Stannard Baker, the former muckraking journalist who ran Wilson's press bureau in Paris.

Wilson's aides were poorly informed, with the result that press conferences were "dismal affairs," said William Allen White, who had left his *Emporia Gazette* to cover the conference for the McClure Syndicate. In another letter Swope drafted, he suggested that the president should appoint an informed subordinate who had his confidence to liaise with the press or, "if the prescription calls for too large an order, may we not ask, with all respect and in all earnestness, that you fill the bill as nearly as possible." The problem with this latter solution was that when Wilson did speak, he did not help himself much. The president, Swope admitted in a confidential memorandum, "is not a good Press Agent for himself because he talks best about abstract things."

"No group of men can be more fully trusted to keep a confidence or use it wisely than a group of experienced newspaper correspondents—if they are honestly informed and trusted in the first place," Baker wrote regretfully of the failure of Wilson's delegation to work constructively with the press. "But when the American press representative [for Wilson] arose to speak he could not promise the primary condition, real frankness, and could not therefore ask caution." Left to grope around in this information void, the American correspondents, self-described "ambassadors of public opinion," reported wild rumors and were susceptible to carefully planned leaks by envoys with competing interests, to whom they turned for information.

One competing interest was China's. The Chinese were angry that Wilson was prepared to honor a pre-armistice secret treaty to hand German control of the Shantung Peninsula to the Japanese. Chinese delegate Eugene Chen arranged to come to the *Chicago Tribune* office when no one was there. He left a complete copy of the not-yet-released Versailles Treaty. This was tantamount to giving raw meat to a wolf. As much as McCormick relished the fighting of World War I, he wanted the United States to have no part in postwar responsibility and was all too happy to help sink Wilson's league. In addition to publishing one-third of the treaty, the *Tribune* passed the full text to Republican senators irate with Wilson for refusing to give them a copy. After an intense debate, the Senate voted 47 to 24 to publish the document in the *Congressional Record*. Later, on two attempts, the treaty failed to achieve the needed two-thirds majority for ratification.

Wilson's loyalists tried a bit of leaking themselves, for instance of the documents that gave Swope his scoops. But this did them little good. The welter of information confused and alarmed Americans. Wilson lost the peace because he lost the battle of what is today called spin control. "The Peace Treaty has been attacked from many sides as a 'failure in advertising,'" said the Committee on Public Information's George Creel. "I agree."

Wilson's Creel committee spawned a cadre of experts eager to use the skills they had acquired. Edward Bernays, nephew of Sigmund Freud and considered the father of public relations, worked for Creel during the war and afterward in Paris, which he called "a training school without instructors in the study of public opinion and people." James Keeley, former *Chicago Tribune* editor, returned home after his propaganda efforts during the war and became a press agent. He put words in the mouth of presidential candidate Warren Harding and assisted a group of Chicago meat packers, who were accused of price fixing and faced trust-busting federal legislation. Swope's brother, Gerard, was tutored in public relations while serving on Wilson's War Industries Board. As president of General Electric, he presided over one of the first sophisticated corporate-image campaigns.

"Propaganda has become a profession," political scientist Harold Lasswell wrote after the war. "The modern world is busy developing a corps of men who do nothing but study the ways and means of changing minds or binding minds to their convictions." Having learned from Wilson's failure to win approval for the League of Nations, Franklin Roosevelt put poet and propagandist Archibald MacLeish and the promising young politician Adlai Stevenson in charge of a national PR campaign in support of the creation of the United Nations after World War II. Where Wilson failed, Roosevelt succeeded.

Newton's Third Law of Motion was at work: For every action, there is an equal and opposite reaction. No sooner had journalism become a profession than an equally professional adversary arose with the purpose of manipulating it—often using the press's tricks to its own advantage. When Stanley found Livingstone, James Gordon Bennett Jr. made the interview into a journalistic art form. Now press agents, masters of pseudo-events, arranged interviews and, dispensing with the old formalities, made up quotes if their bosses were too busy to meet with a journalist. The press agent, Swope lamented, "gives out a statement and says this is what Mr. Blank wants to say."

Wherever journalists turned, a press agent seemed to be on hand to greet them. "The great corporations have them," said *World* editorial writer Frank I. Cobb in a talk at the Women's City Club of New York in 1919, "the banks have them, the railroads have them, all the organizations of business and of social and political activity have them and they are the media through which news comes. Even statesmen have them."

Sir Harold Nicolson, who had been part of the British delegation in Paris, began his diplomatic career in a genteel environment without press attachés. Although charmed by Swope, "the star turn in the American journalistic world," he was overwhelmed by his rambunctious, intrusive style of news-gathering and distressed about the lengths to which diplomats now went to manage the press. "Until the war of 1914–1918 came to degrade all international standards," Nicolson observed in a handbook he wrote for diplomats, "it was still considered unfitting and unwise for a statesman to make public pronouncements to his own people which public opinion in other countries would know to be totally untrue." Nevertheless, Nicolson's handbook offered instruction on the role and use of the press attaché. The attaché, advised Nicolson, is "one of great usefulness and considerable importance, and the system should be extended to every important mission."

By the time of the invasion of Iraq in 2003, the military's management of the news included a $250,000 television set for military media briefings at Camp As Sayliyah in Qatar. George Allison, most recently art director of a Michael and Kirk Douglas movie, designed the slick, high-tech stage. "We use the latest technology in our military operations," said Col. Ray Shepherd, director of Central Command public relations. "It's only fitting we use it here." Central Command public affairs officers barred photographs of the set while it was under construction. "It's not part of the communications message yet," Shepherd said. Meanwhile, to guard against leaks, the CIA added a new question to those that they asked employees taking their standard polygraph examination: "Do you have friends in the media?"

Among the early observers of manufactured consent, as he called it, was a fretful Walter Lippmann. When the United States entered the war, Lippmann turned in his press credentials to work for the government. "Certain experiences with the propaganda machine," he said on his return from Paris, when he became an editorial writer for Swope's *World,* set him to questioning the democratic ideal of truly informed public opinion. "The private citizen today," he concluded, "has come to feel rather like a deaf spectator in the back row. . . . Public affairs are in no convincing way his affairs. They are for the most part invisible. They are managed, if they are managed at all, at distant center, from behind the scenes, by unnamed powers. As a private person he does not know for certain what is going on, or who is doing it, or where he is being carried."

In retirement Georges Clemenceau, who wrote books and articles, including a series for Swope's *World,* also worried about the future. "The world crisis has not yet been met," he said in a speech in New York, "and the sad part about this is that it means another world war." The Germans, he told a reporter, were waiting for a new leader to "shackle them into line." Like Lippmann, he doubted the capacity of citizens in democracies to form sound judgment, so susceptible were they to demagogy. Nor did he have much faith in the press to help. "All my life I have fought for what they call the freedom of the Press, freedom of speech, *et caetera*," the Tiger said shortly before he died in 1927. "Now I have come to believe that all these freedoms end in the worst form of slavery and degeneration."

12

THE HIGHEST REALM

Great corps of foreign correspondents, like great newspapers, come and go. At the end of the twentieth century, the *New York Times,* the *Washington Post,* the *Wall Street Journal,* and the *Los Angeles Times* fielded the premier foreign services. In an article on foreign reporting written shortly before World War II, Carroll Binder, the *Chicago Daily News* foreign editor, had an almost entirely different four-newspaper A-list.

Only one paper on Binder's list, the *New York Times,* was on the modern one as well. Having gained a measure of financial security, the *Times* began to pay serious attention to foreign news around 1908. It added overseas staff and special sections during World War I. On a 1922 trip to Paris, publisher Adolph Ochs asked correspondent Edwin James what it would cost to expand the staff in Europe so the *Times* would have the most comprehensive coverage. James said five hundred thousand dollars. Ochs directed him to draw up a plan for how to spend it.

Another New York newspaper on Binder's list was the *New York Herald Tribune.* It fielded outstanding correspondents during the 1930s, into the war, and afterward—all the while suffering a gradual decline. In the 1930s cost cutting crimped the ability of correspondents to write at length. After World War II, the owners did not reinvest in news as the *Times* did, and their paper gave ground across the board to its competitor. When it closed in 1966, the *Herald Tribune* had only two foreign bureaus. The Moscow bureau sold its equipment and handed over its lease and three Russian staffers to the *Christian Science Monitor,* the third paper on Binder's list.

The *Monitor* had an unusual pedigree. A victim of sensational newspaper coverage, church founder Mary Baker Eddy applied her theology of clean living to "clean journalism" with the founding of the paper in 1908. With a new twist on missionary work, the *Monitor* gave its readers extensive news about the world. Christian Science distaste for medicine, tobacco, and spirits led to idiosyncratic editorial rules that barred references to wine in travel stories on France. Because of Christian Science's skittishness about discussing death, the paper listed the survivors, not the victims, when the *Titanic* sank. Still, the extraordinary amount of cable news from the *Monitor*'s reporters, the perspective and balance of its coverage, and its willingness to look at the underreported developing world made the paper's foreign coverage superior until about 1990, when it lost momentum due to internal church wrangling about the newspaper's direction and identity.

The fourth paper Binder listed was his own and rightly so. The *Chicago Daily News,* under the guiding hand of its owner, Victor Lawson, virtually invented the ideal of a high-quality American newspaper foreign service. Lawson's predated the *Times'* and the *Monitor's*. While the old *New York Herald* and the old *New York Tribune* separately ventured abroad earlier than the *Daily News,* their excellence was mostly episodic and rooted in individual accomplishments of men like George Smalley, who helped establish the bureau concept. By the time the *Herald* and the *Tribune* combined into a single paper in 1924, the *Daily News's* foreign service had been consistently superb for years.

Lawson's foreign service was grounded in the idea that American correspondents should gather original news for American readers, which marked one kind of breakthrough. Another was its mission of supplementing the wires, which came to mean less emphasis on the routine and more on background and analysis. At the high point more than one hundred North American newspapers subscribed to the *Daily News* service in order to use its stories in their pages. Behind this success lay yet another factor that may be attributed to Lawson's vision, the expertise of its correspondents, who spent years abroad and came to view themselves on a par with ambassadors in their interpretive skills and power. "Our men," noted Edward Price Bell, Lawson's first important standard-bearer abroad, "are journalistic intellectuals, with definite personalities, with considerable personal reputations, and charged with duties in the highest realm of newspaper work."

The *Daily News* foreign service, now long gone and virtually forgotten, contained some of the most respected names in foreign reporting, none more so than Paul Scott Mowrer. Mowrer went to Paris in 1910, plucked from the ranks of local reporters. His maturation paralleled the maturation of the foreign service, whose statesman-like qualities he personified. He won the first Pulitzer Prize in the category of "correspondence" and became editor of the newspaper in the 1930s. At each step, including his last days at the paper, Mowrer was acutely aware of the fragility of the foreign reporting enterprise. Those last days came after World War II when he, along with Binder, abruptly resigned. As Mowrer saw it, the new owners, three times removed from Lawson's proprietorship, were putting "bobby sox on the Madonna."

Robert Casey, a pudgy leprechaun of a journalist, covered local politics, revolutions, and wars for the *Daily News* and on the side wrote more than thirty books. Two were newsroom memoirs. The *Daily News,* he said in one of them, was "probably the strangest newspaper in the world."

When Casey joined the staff in 1920, one's first sight upon entering the building on North Wells Street was graying women clerks who had begun working for the paper as girls. They worked under ancient gas fixtures wired for electric lights.

The building had expanded willy-nilly by breaking through firewalls into adjoining buildings, which were entered by stepping up or down to the varying floor levels. The reporters and the editors—some of the most brilliant in the profession—worked under similarly disconcerting circumstances. The paper trumpeted its successes with as much modesty as a carnival barker, all the while showing how profit and responsible reporting could be harmoniously married. The *Daily News,* Casey recalled, was "not only the only paper I had ever worked on but the only paper I had ever heard about that threw ads into the hellbox to make way for news." Although the staff included eager tipplers, the paper took no liquor ads.

The *Daily News* was a writer's paper. Eugene Field, who joined eight years after its founding in 1875, wrote the first popular American newspaper column, chronicling the human condition with verse, humor, and other snippets of comment. The column's name, *Sharps and Flats,* was borrowed from the title of a popular play written by Slason Thompson, also on the news staff. Later came columnists Finley Peter Dunne, creator of the homespun, nationally famous philosopher "Mr. Dooley," and playwright George Ade.

Henry Justin Smith, a revered news executive at the *Daily News,* saw "the newspaper as a daily novel written by a score of Balzacs," said Ben Hecht. Hecht's local reporting experiences on the *Daily News* were grist for the coauthored comedic play and movie *The Front Page.* Smith himself wrote two novels about "a certain famous and fascinating newsroom." At Hecht's suggestion, Smith hired poet-historian Carl Sandburg, ostensibly as a labor reporter; Sandburg mostly worked on his own stuff while in the office. Others who toiled at one time or another on the long, sagging floor of what was called the "local room" included Ray Stannard Baker, later chief of President Woodrow Wilson's Paris press office and his biographer; Robert Hardy Andrews, author of the Jack Armstrong radio serials; theater critic Lloyd Lewis, who doubled as a Civil War historian and coauthored a play with Sinclair Lewis; Brand Whitlock, who became a novelist, the mayor of Toledo, and an envoy to Belgium; and Edward P. Morgan, who served overseas with CBS radio during World War II. Henry Luce, who built the Time-Life media empire, was once a legman for Hecht.

The single most powerful force at the *Daily News* was "an invisible but omnipotent entity" adorned in a black frock coat, a top hat, and a Prince Albert beard. Victor Fremont Lawson was the son of a Norwegian-born immigrant who made a fortune in Chicago real estate and other investments. One of those holdings was a Norwegian-language daily called the *Skandinaven,* which was edited by young Lawson's granduncle. Victor Lawson's father suffered financially from the 1871 Chicago fire and died shortly afterward. Looking for ways to rebuild what was left to him, twenty-five-year-old Victor Lawson found an opportunity in his own newspaper building. Melville Stone, Lawson's Chicago High School classmate, had rented railed-off space in one room to start an evening daily he called the *Daily News.* When Stone's investors lost interest, he turned to Lawson for capital. In the deal they struck, Lawson acquired financial control and became business manager. Stone remained editor.

Victor Fremont Lawson, a picture of respectability. When he died, newspapers across the nation eulogized him and his "clean journalism." Frontispiece photo in *World Chancelleries,* a collection of interviews conducted by Edward Price Bell and published by the *Chicago Daily News* to promote world peace.

The *Daily News* started out as a penny paper with a penny paper's penchant for excitement. "All our fine theories would be of little avail," Stone observed, "unless we could compel attention of the public." Long before James Keeley perfected the catch-a-thief school of foreign reporting in Morocco, Stone personally tracked a local embezzler until he found him in Germany. The paper was a leader among Chicago papers in graphics, using red ink for "extras" with the latest sports scores, and it was quick to pick up on the potential for engaging photography.

Despite the *Daily News*'s enthusiasm for fires, earthquakes, murders, scandals, and other entertainment, Stone eschewed "the silly so-called 'human-interest stories' of cats born with two heads." He aimed to supply reliable news on a range of serious subjects. So did Lawson, who became editor as well as publisher in 1888, when Stone sold his interest and went on to lead the Associated Press. "We do not want to fool our readers with sensational stories that have little or no foundation in fact," admonished Lawson, in one of many instructions to his editors during the Spanish-American War. "In all editorials and news," he said in another missive, "be enterprising but conservative in expression and tone."

Few of the newsroom rank and file knew Lawson, except to see him on the elevator. None called him by the familiar "Fremont." The turkeys the patrician owner dispensed at Thanksgiving did not offset complaints about the low wages he paid. But Lawson gave his reporters just what they wanted in the way of journalism. Unlike many flamboyant publishers of the era, Lawson remained in the shadows. He never desired elected office. He expressed his views through the pages of his paper, which exposed corporate greed and official corruption, promoted good government associations such as Chicago's Municipal Voters' League, argued for the nation's first juvenile court and for regulations to improve health and reduce pollution, and championed the creation of the Chicago Symphony Orchestra. The *Daily News,* as one historian noted, was the first newspaper "to articulate a vision of public community."

Lawson was a tough businessman, sharp about collecting what was owed him, creative in gimmicks that promoted sales, and demanding of his lieutenants. "I note your miserable failure to keep the circulation of the Daily News at the 280,000 mark," he wrote ominously to managing editor Charles Faye from Europe, where he was traveling in 1898. "When I get back you will have to answer for this. Anybody can get out a paper that nobody will buy." But many of Lawson's best business practices lay in his high-mindedness. He charged one rate to all advertisers, rather than making side deals the way other publishers did. He rejected advertisements that promised more than they delivered. These policies enhanced the credibility of the newspaper to readers and made it more attractive to advertisers. In 1895 the evening *Daily News* circulation—then at 200,000—was more than twice as large as any other Chicago paper except for the morning *Record,* which Lawson also owned. During the early 1900s, *Daily News* circulation reached 400,000, which was 100,000 more than any other American daily.

No publisher stood higher in making journalism a respectable business. When the impecunious Adolph Ochs wanted to establish his credentials in order to buy the faltering *New York Times* in 1896, one of the people to whom he turned for a recommendation was the admired Lawson.

Lawson showed an early, if episodic, interest in foreign news. In 1879 his readers had regular front-page foreign news roundups. A decade later, what foreign news existed in the paper was on the inside pages. Lawson sent reporters to less-well-covered regions: Latin America, Australia and New Zealand, and Sweden. The work of Ross Raymond, an occasional correspondent in these early years, typified the *Daily News*'s sketchy foreign reporting. In his wanderings from place to place, and from newspaper to newspaper, Raymond worked on the local staff of the *Daily News* and subsequently, out of the blue, cabled Stone from Cairo with a story about an important battle. It scooped the British newspapers.*

The Spanish-American War prompted Lawson to undertake a more concerted effort at foreign news-gathering. Amid early rumblings with Spain over Cuba, Lawson put reporters in Key West and Havana and with the insurgents. After the sink-

---

* Ross Raymond was a nom de plume, although it was closer to the mark to call it an alias. Besides passing himself off as a foreign correspondent, Raymond was variously a college professor, a clergyman, and a scientist. In one of his scams, he pulled off a jewelry heist in Paris by impersonating the representative of the Khedive of Egypt. Toward the end of his life he edited the *Star of Hope,* the Sing Sing prison newspaper.

ing of the *Maine,* he instructed his editors to "send all men possible to war reducing number later if advisable." Lawson's *Record* was his primary vehicle for foreign news. At one point during the war, foreign news consumed more than 40 percent of the *Record's* news hole. The *Record's* bureau in Key West received eyewitness dispatches carried from Cuba by the *Hercules,* a yacht Lawson hired. At the height of the conflict, Lawson had fourteen correspondents stretched from Cuba to the Philippines.

Before the war was over, Lawson announced he was starting a permanent foreign service. The United States had become a world power. It needed, Lawson thought, its own reporters abroad to represent American interests and points of view. "It is no longer desirable, or even safe," he told one of his editors, "for public opinion in this country to rely, as it now does, almost exclusively on foreign agencies, most of them subsidized by foreign governments, for their news of foreign countries."

Lawson considered his fledgling foreign service "largely an experiment." Initially he did his experimenting in the morning *Record.* When he sold that paper in 1901, he kept the service for the *Daily News.* There it stayed when Lawson reacquired an interest in the then hyphenated *Herald-Record* for a time. Not certain how best to make foreign news a financial success, he briefly tried a syndicate partnership with Bennett's *Herald* and equally briefly supplemented his supplementary service with one started by the *London Standard.* In 1902 Lawson and Ochs explored the possibility of running a foreign news service jointly. The discussions with the *Times* came to nothing, as Lawson was unwilling to cede adequate control to his New York junior partner. Lawson's plan to sell a *Daily News*–owned service to other newspapers temporarily faltered when escalating prices for newsprint prompted his eight clients to cut costs and withdraw.

Lawson did not want his correspondents to rewrite stories from foreign newspapers, as was routinely done by the few correspondents stationed permanently abroad. Because most of this trolling for news was done from offices in London, the British angle predominated in American media. Lawson's correspondents were to do original reporting. They also were enjoined not to duplicate the Associated Press, which Lawson helped reorganize and, under the leadership of his old partner Melville Stone, was keen to expand beyond its single permanent foreign bureau in London. This, nevertheless, left a broad open field in which to search for a journalistic mission.

A stream of decisive, ever-changing instructions issued from Lawson's office in Chicago. His Paris correspondent, Theodore Stanton, started out in July 1898 with an admonition to create a "brief cable service covering important matters" that did not duplicate the AP; it was to contain "opinions statesmen American questions, foreign relations, continental happenings, not more than 300 words daily, much less ordinarily." Six months later, Lawson redirected Stanton to mail "short, concisely written news notes on matters of recent occurrence and special interests"; "short stories on royalty"; "a terse and carefully written letter once a month, giving a general 'bird's-eye view' of matters of most important general interest in the country at date." A year later, Lawson shifted gears again. "What I want to empha-size is to be particularly on the lookout for short, bright, novel, interesting bits of news and story-telling gossip of interest to Americans."

Lawson also struggled with the question of who should do this reporting. At first, he relied heavily on foreigners—for instance, a German-American reporter in Berlin, "whom we especially engaged and trained here before sending him over," and an Englishman stationed in Vienna, who spoke German and helped the *Daily News* cover the Spanish-American War. Many newspapers took this approach be-cause foreigners had an intimate feel for local customs and politics, possessed local language ability, and were convenient to hire (and if things did not work out, easy to let go).* Lawson continued to use foreigners, especially as stringers, of which he had scores. Gradually, though, he laid the foundation of his foreign service with full-time, homegrown talent such as Edward Price Bell, who in 1900 replaced a British journalist manning the London bureau and served as a chief of correspon-dents.

Raised on Raccoon Creek in Indiana, where he started his journalism career, Bell was one of the *Daily News*'s best reporters. His stories on local corruption would have won national awards if such honors had been given at the time, recalled Frederic William Wile, a younger Hoosier who was soon sent to assist Bell in Lon-don and who went on to have a long overseas career. Good local reporters like Bell and Wile, Lawson reasoned, could develop foreign expertise on the job and "judge news from the point of view of the average American newspaper reader."

Chicago was simultaneously international and provincial. With Germans, Irish, English, Poles, Scandinavians, and Bohemians pouring in, it was the second-most-populous city in the country. By 1890, when one thousand trains came or left the city daily, four out of five Chicagoans had been born abroad or had foreign-born parents. Ten years later, more than one in five Chicago journalists was foreign-

---

* The *New York Times,* in contrast, was heavy with "foreign" foreign correspondents for years. At one point in the late 1920s, Wythe Williams was the only *Times* bureau chief in a Continental capi-tal to carry a U.S. passport. Three of the first four *Times* reporters to win Pulitzer Prizes in the "cor-respondence" category for work abroad were two Englishmen, Walter Duranty (1932) and Frederick Birchall (1934), and German-born Otto Tolischus (1940). The fourth reporter, Anne O'Hare McCor-mick (1937), was born in England of American parents. In a "Report on London Office, February 1925," Paris correspondent Edwin James told Adolph Ochs, "It is a conservative estimate that seventy-five per cent of all words cabled to the New York Times is taken directly from the London Times ser-vice at night. . . . Under existing conditions it seems that the most valuable addition which could now be made to the London staff would be a live reporter with a good knowledge of the United States, with rewrite ability, and with some knowledge of copy reading. He should above all be an American, for emphasis is to be placed on the fact that the three members of the London staff are all Englishmen." As late as World War II, *Times* publisher Arthur Sulzberger was troubled that so many of his corre-spondents were British. He thought "an American paper should be served primarily by Americans." The James report to Ochs is in the NYT Archives; for Sulzberger's comment, see Tifft and Jones, *The Trust,* 209.

born. Chicago coveted international recognition, earning the sobriquet "windy city" from New York editor Charles Dana for the aggressive boosterism that led Congress to select it to host the 1893 World's Columbian Exposition. To find foreign exhibits for that extravaganza, the exposition executive committee sent an emissary to fetch a tribe of Pygmies that Henry Stanley had recently found in one of his explorations (the emissary died in Zanzibar). At the same time, Chicago was still very much attuned to its agrarian roots and possessed a populist wariness of foreign influences. In 1927 Mayor Big Bill Thompson launched a crusade to purge the city's libraries and schools of pro-British books.

The *Chicago Tribune,* a chief rival of the *Daily News,* was a microcosm of this schizophrenia. The *Tribune* created a permanent foreign service after World War I, headed up by swashbuckling Floyd Gibbons of SS *Laconia* fame. Some press watchers would have put the *Tribune*'s service on Binder's list of the best, but one factor prevented unanimity, the *Tribune*'s quirky Col. Robert McCormick. McCormick had his suits made on Savile Row and yet was an avowed Anglophobe. His orders ranged from the spectacular ("FLY INDIA," he cabled William Shirer, who was in Vienna) to the trivial (he ordered Shirer to find a pair of binoculars he had left in a French barn during the Great War, nine years before). Some of McCormick's communications, said correspondent Edmund Taylor, "seemed to possess a kind of cosmic irrelevance that suggested the indecipherable cliff-writings of some vanished civilization."

Although McCormick sustained a money-losing Paris edition of the newspaper for some time after World War I, his enthusiasm for foreign news was peculiar at best and often perverse. His outlook, readily apparent in the paper because of his micromanaging style, was reactionary and jingoistic. Gibbons advised John B. Powell, who in addition to owning the *China Weekly Review* served as the *Tribune*'s China correspondent, how to satisfy the home office: "You must always 'write down'—don't be 'intellectual,' the people who buy the *Tribune* in Chicago don't understand or give a damn about Far Eastern politics—they want hot stories about battle and bandits." Later, with Japanese aggression mounting in Asia, the meddling McCormick closed Powell's bureau. "The Colonel," he was informed, "thinks China is no longer important as a source of news." From 1937 to 1941, the *Tribune* had just one correspondent in Asia, a Japanese national based in Tokyo.

Parochialism was more pronounced at other Chicago newspapers. Before he worked for the *Daily News,* Ben Hecht worked at the old but not distinguished *Chicago Journal.* An editorial writer hired to comment on foreign affairs, Hecht thought, "was out of place on the newspaper. Who the hell wanted to read about Greeks, Bulgarians, Englishmen, and Russians, when they could read about Chicagoans!"

Lawson, a director of the World's Columbian Exposition, hoped to appeal to and nurture Chicago's more open-minded, international side. Because of his experience with the family's Norwegian-language newspaper, the *Skandinaven,* he saw potential for readers in the foreign-born audience "who would be glad to get news from home directly instead of through foreign sources." Another set of readers was to be found among the prominent Chicagoans who traveled abroad for business and pleasure, as Lawson himself did. Some of these individuals were distinguished internationally. Chicago banker and businessman Charles Dawes, who served as vice president under Coolidge, became ambassador to London; plumbing manufacturing heir Charles Crane became ambassador to China. Crane, who considered Lawson "a most valued friend," financed Thomas Millard's Shanghai weekly—the successor to Powell's—and, with Walter Rogers, who had worked on the *Daily News,* established the Mutual News Service to bring articles by European correspondents to Americans and vice versa.

The Chicago Council on Foreign Relations, one of America's first local foreign affairs organizations, was for many years a dividing point between the likes of McCormick and Lawson. The *Daily News* had strong ties to the council, whose founders stated in their first meeting, February 20, 1922, that "it was the duty of all intelligent" Americans to provide leadership in addressing the problems emerging out of World War I. Clifton Utley, appointed the council's executive director in 1931, worked for the *Daily News* and was a well-known commentator on WMAQ, a station that Lawson and a local department store started in 1922. In his broadcasts, Utley warned of the impending war and, after 1939, argued for supporting England. McCormick forbade the use of Utley's name in the *Tribune,* an edict not broken until the early 1950s when one of Utley's sons, who played local basketball, showed up in the *Tribune* sports pages.* When a new council president came aboard in 1974, he was told not to expect invitations to dinner parties that included Chicago *Tribune* people.

Chicago's internationalists and its immigrant population could not by themselves justify the creation of a foreign service. The public's interest in foreign news was neither so big nor so intense that it would raise circulation appreciably, especially considering that the *Daily News* was enormously successful without a foreign service. What counted most in Lawson's calculation in creating a foreign service was that it was a public service, a view that was held by the newspapers that followed him in this approach to news-gathering.

Lawson's courage was all the more remarkable because of the resistance he encountered from his own staff, who considered his interest in foreign news eccentric. Bell's assistant, Frederic William Wile, visited the home office in 1903 and reported back to Bell that managing editor Charles Faye considered the foreign service "a delusion and a snare." Were it not for orders from Lawson, Faye would "kill large slabs" of foreign news. In 1901, when Lawson sold the *Chicago Record,* his primary vehicle for foreign news, Bell and other correspondents waited for the service to be abandoned and to be called home to cover Chicago again.

The *Daily News*'s legendary editor Henry Justin Smith considered correspondents puffed up and useless. The foreign correspondent in one of his novels was John Goode, nicknamed Sinful and derisively described as "Young-Man-Going-Somewhere."

* Another of Utley's sons, Garrick, became a well-known television correspondent abroad.

"Goode's going to Mexico," the Old Man told the city editor.

"Glad of it. Hope he croaks," replied the [city editor], whose nerves had also been worn a bit thin by having Sinful Goode in barracks.

The rest of us were more benevolent. We gave Goode a farewell dinner, at which and to which our doggerel experts did great execution. Next day we inspected his new riding breeches, his camera, and horrendous revolver. And then we forgot him.

The kind of journalist Smith liked was young Paul Scott Mowrer, who was born in downstate Illinois and thrived in the local room. The cub reporter tracked down a local murderer whom neither the police nor reporters from other Chicago newspapers could find. He rewrote police stories into ballads. Long after his colleagues had cleared out at the end of the day, Mowrer stayed at his desk and filled up wastebaskets, "trying to perfect a style," as he told Smith one evening.

Smith sourly greeted the news of the twenty-two-year-old's overseas assignment in Paris in 1910. "A fellow goes to Europe to stay a few months and he stays for years," he warned his protégé. "He may be a pretty fair newspaperman when he leaves. He comes back at last, wearing spats and carrying a cane, too good for reporting, no good as an executive, no place for him anywhere, his career wrecked." Fellow reporters and editors signed a petition urging Lawson to keep Mowrer in Chicago, where he could do more good. Lawson ignored the advice.

Lawson, who never forgot that he ran a business as well as a public service, put a lot of money at risk with his foreign "experiment." His expenses for the service at the end of 1899, its first full year of operation, were $122,155.79, he precisely noted to potential newspaper customers for his foreign stories. With this and the tug of his staff's ambivalence weighing heavily on his mind, he promoted tried-and-true approaches to coverage that appealed to a broad range of readers.

The quaint and the amusing—a theme in those early letters to his Paris correspondent—was one such approach. Before Bell was sent abroad, the paper ran a column from London, "Queer Sprigs of Gentility." Lawson sent this as a promotional piece to prospective subscribers to his budding news service. Although the column was mercifully abandoned, the concern persisted that too many readers greeted stories on European politics "with a yawn or not at all." In 1911 the home office asked for a weekly summary of the best jokes from the European press—a challenge for Mowrer since the funniest Parisian humor was too risqué for the Chicago reader.

Another approach was to cater to local interests. Editors pestered Bell for stories that awakened a "responsive thrill in the minds" of Chicago readers. "For circulation purposes," he was reminded, "cables from Berlin, Vienna, Denmark, Sweden and Norway are distinctly of more value than from Paris and London, so far as The Daily News is concerned, owing to the very large foreign population in Chicago who are interested in the Teutonic and Scandinavian nations." Localism also showed up in the way Lawson made his foreign news bureaus hospitable to visitors. A reading table held the latest home papers. Visiting Chicagoans also were attracted to the offices because they could secure tourist information, collect their mail, and leave their names, which the *Daily News* dutifully printed on its front page.

In contrast to the *Daily News*'s decrepit Chicago quarters, the London and Paris offices were fitted out like clubs, with potted palms, oriental rugs, and stuffed leather chairs. "Please remember," Lawson instructed Bell, "to spare no expense to have the decorating and the furnishing and big, outside, gold, wall-sign just as good as money can buy. In the matter of color for wall treatment avoid the dead white and use the white with a light cream tint or an 'old ivory' white, but the latter should not be too dark." When Bell was conspicuously planting the *Daily News* flag on Trafalgar Squarer, the *Chicago Tribune* was nowhere to be found in London, the *New York Sun* and the *Herald* occupied inauspicious, out-of-the-way offices, and a successor to the *New York Tribune*'s George Smalley, whose office had catered to tourists, wrote at home or in the smoking-room of the National Club.

Bell understood the logic of Lawson's ostentatious bureaus. They augmented the prestige of the service and its attractiveness to newspapers who might subscribe, an important ingredient to making the service financially sustainable. Other correspondents, however, were inclined to think them a sign of Lawson's superficial in-

Paul Scott Mowrer described his Paris bureau: "My office was right across from the Café de la Paix, at the corner of the Place de l'Opéra, one floor up, with a private entrance on the Boulevard des Capucines. No tourist could come to Paris without seeing our big sign." Mowrer can be seen in the second-story window. Mowrer, *The House of Europe,* 135. Photo: Newberry Library.

terest in foreign news. In 1906 Frederic William Wile, by then the paper's Berlin correspondent, told Bell that he had "the firm impression" that Lawson's bureaus were "*the* reason, of all reasons, for his continuing to keep the service up. I have the feeling that news is only an incidental feature of the enterprise." A later Berlin bureau chief, Raymond Swing, thought Lawson "did not care a hoot about foreign news."

Such frustration was understandable, if ungenerous. True, Lawson favored news that he thought a broad segment of Chicago readers would appreciate, but it could not be said fairly that he did not care about serious news. Early on, under Bell, articles about the significance of upcoming French legislative sessions were mixed in with stories about Chicagoans in Norwegian boat crashes. Over time the service took on more gravity, as table 4 shows. In Bell's first year in London, 1901, more than 60 percent of the foreign news in the paper from all sources, including the Associated Press as well as the *Daily News* staff, was hard news rather than lighter fare such as human interest articles. The share of such news rose to 84 percent by 1921. Story length also increased through 1918, as did the proportion of stories that went beyond straight facts and provided background, analysis, and color—the category defined in the table as news analysis. Although the amount of this analysis dropped off overall in 1921, *Daily News* correspondents filed twice as much analysis after the war as in 1901. According to data not in the table, they accounted for more than 80 percent of all the foreign analysis in the paper. This was to be the forte of the *Daily News* correspondents.

TABLE 4. Development of foreign reporting at the *Daily News*

	1901	1913	1918	1921
No. of all foreign stories in *DN*[a]	98	169	329	184
Filed by *DN* correspondents	31	59	118	65
Percent of all foreign stories on pages 1 and 2[a]	62.2	75.7	70.1	70.9
Percent filed by *DN* correspondents	87.1	76.3	78.8	90.8
Percent of all foreign stories more than 6 paragraphs long[a]	12.5	19.8	26.7	23.1
Percent filed by *DN* correspondents	16.7	29.3	47.4	48.4
Percent hard news/percent soft news[a]	63.3/36.7	72.2/27.8	90.9/8.6	83.7/15.8
Percent filed by *DN* correspondents	64.5/35.5	55.9/44.1	90.6/9.4	83.1/16.9
Percent straight news/percent news analysis[a]	89.7/10.3	75.6/15.5	76.5/16.5	88/11.4
Percent filed by *DN* correspondents[b]	90.0/10.0	47.5/27.1	60.7/37.6	76.9/21.5

Note: These findings are based on a sample of two randomly constructed weeks for each year tested. Because the *Daily News* did not publish on Sundays, these weeks had six days each.

[a] Figures includes reports from all sources, Associated Press and other services as well as *Chicago Daily News* correspondents.

[b] Percentages do not equall 100 because there was a third category for reproduction of documents and speeches.

World War I was a catalyst for this serious reporting. All the foreign expertise that Lawson had built up in that corps of talented reporters, all the experience his staff had developed in working with and supporting those reporters, was primed to swing into action. As *Chicago Tribune* editor-turned-war-propagandist James Keeley said in a London speech, Lawson's "harvest was at hand."

Recognizing his advantage, Lawson deposited gold coin in strategically located overseas banks. The funds were used by the thirty-odd correspondents he deployed "at the places of impact." Some were veterans—in addition to Bell and Mowrer, for instance, there was John Bass, who had covered the Boxer Rebellion in China for the *New York Journal* and the Russo-Japanese War in 1904–5 for the *Daily News,* and Oswald F. Schuette, a Chicagoan on the staff who had reported from Germany for other newspapers just after the turn of the century. Some were foreign stringers who had regularly supplied copy to the *Daily News,* among them Constantine Stephanove, a University of Chicago–trained professor living in Sofia, and Elizabeth Christitch, a Serbian writer. Still others were raw recruits from Chicago with specialties: Chicago aeronautics writer Percy Noel; Anthony Czarnecki, "a leading spirit among the young citizens of Chicago of Polish descent and a newspaper writer of wide experience," who was to study conditions for Poles; and Eunice Tietjens. Tietjens, who had traveled widely and had been an editor of the internationally distinguished Chicago magazine *Poetry,* coaxed the editors into sending her to write "the woman's side of the war"; once in France, she shunned stories about socks knitted by Chicago women and wrote human interest features on American soldiers, refugees, and the French.

In Paris, Mowrer hired his younger brother, Edgar Ansel Mowrer, who had come to Europe to study; A. R. Decker, an American engineer whose work in France gave him rare access to frontline action; two French friends who scoured camps, hospitals, and towns for information; and an American who had been medically discharged from the French army. Although he got off to an ungainly start by beginning his first dispatch in Latin, Edgar Mowrer went on to cover the war in Italy; Decker became the Vienna correspondent after the armistice.

After the war, Ben Hecht took his writing flair to the Berlin bureau. ("GERMAN BOLSHEVIK REVOLUTION TO DATE CONSISTS NINETY PERCENT RUMORS TEN PERCENT BAD SHOOTING," he wrote in a clipped cable.) Charles Dennis, who had risen from foreign editor to managing editor, helped Mowrer cover the Paris peace talks, where the *Daily News* placed seven accredited correspondents, three more than the *New York Times.*

In 1918 Lawson foresaw that the year's expenses would "considerably exceed $200,000," a substantial sum at the time. This cost was only partially offset by the newspapers that bought his foreign service. Lawson reckoned the fifteen current subscribers would bring in between $50,000 and $60,000. The expense, however, did not diminish his enthusiasm. Accolades poured in. The *London Chronicle* called the *Daily News* "by far the best evening newspaper in the world." In a special article on Lawson's foreign service, the trade magazine *Editor and Publisher* said the *Daily News* scored "more beats on the war in its special foreign service than perhaps any other paper in the world." "The comment of other publishers is very common," Lawson told Bell in 1918: the *Daily News* had "the best special service coming to America." A sign of the service's stature was that Bell was the acknowledged dean of foreign correspondents in London as well as dean of Lawson's correspondents. Newspaperman Lord Northcliffe called him "the best American newspaperman London has ever had." Wrote Lawson to Bell, "We were never more satisfied with the wisdom of maintaining a foreign service than now, and we shall continue to maintain one 'forever.'"

The acknowledged excellence of the foreign service was something on which its correspondents could build. They had time to gather news and room to report it. The paper ran fifteen foreign stories a day in 1921, one-third of them by staff correspondents. Whatever was on the front page, day after day page 2 was devoted to these reports. Correspondents also had access to a larger audience than Chicago alone. In the four-year period ending in 1922, the number of newspapers subscribing to the *Daily News* foreign service more than doubled to thirty-one. And correspondents knew they were journalistic stars, none more so than Mowrer, who soon eclipsed Bell, his mentor.

Mowrer arrived in Paris in 1910 with a jejune bias against the social convention of evening dress and an awkward feeling of being "dumped into a great strange city whose language I speak none too fluently, whose methods are entirely different from those I have been accustomed to work in." A little defensive over Bell's familiarity with "the fascinating intricacies of international politics," Mowrer told the elder correspondent such reporting was fine in London, but not in Paris. "My situation is different," he wrote. "I was educated in features. My eye is trained to them. For a long time I wrote one a day for the front page of the paper in Chicago. Thus I feel I know something about what the *local* management wants in this respect. . . . I say we are both right. Let the dignified, enlightening, really-worth-while cables come from London, and let Paris effervesce the freakish, the far-fetched and the fantastic."

This attitude did not last long. As much as Mowrer enjoyed covering Chicago, as sincerely as he assured Smith that he would stay only a year in Paris, he was too restless, too much the intellectual, to have been happy permanently in the *Daily News* local room. He had taken a break from the *Daily News* to attend the University of Michigan for two and one-half years as a "special student." Special students forewent credits toward graduation in order to study what interested them. He used money from editing the student newspaper to travel to Europe one summer. Shortly after he returned, the prestigious literary magazine *Forum* published his first poem. He considered becoming a full-time poet or novelist, except he needed the steady income a newspaper job afforded.

"Although it made me feel inferior," he said of his first visit to London, "I much admired Ed Bell's incessant, often brilliant conversation. A man who can talk like that, I thought, will go far." Mowrer acquired the veteran's serious tastes in foreign news as well as a dinner jacket and full dress, essential if he was to accept invitations to dine with people who could keep him informed. He also bought the cane and spats that Smith despised. During the early years of the war, he grew a Vandyke beard to add further gravitas.

Mowrer's first major foray into serious reporting—as well as his first byline, something editors still awarded sparingly—began in late 1912. The Balkan states formed an alliance against Turkey. Mowrer urged that the *Daily News* not ignore the fighting as other papers were doing. Bell told Mowrer the task was his. With the help of Bulgarian stringer Constantine Stephanove, he braved the wintry mountains of Macedonia and Albania on horseback to reach the front.

World War I seasoned Mowrer more. He covered the fighting at the front. As his Paris bureau grew, he had his first experience managing often-unruly reporters. Although French authorities temporarily kept Mowrer off the front lines as punishment for writing unfavorable reports, he was later awarded the Legion of Honor. His first books appeared: *Hours of France,* which contained his poetry, and *Balkanized Europe,* the first analytic book by an American correspondent on postwar Europe. Convinced that the Paris treaty negotiations had not solved global problems, only put them off, Mowrer set out to visit the "small, weak, jealous, afraid, economically dependent" new countries oddly drawn by the victors. He took exception to the postwar analysis of British economist John Maynard Keynes. In his popular volume *The Economic Consequences of the Peace,* Keynes argued for canceling German reparations. Mowrer asserted that Europe's problems were chiefly political, not economic. If the dry volume enjoyed limited sales, *Balkanized Europe* confirmed him as an expert, although he was probably too ambitious in saying his title coined the term.

When Mowrer was on a home leave after the war, Lawson surprised him with a raise and a five-thousand-dollar bonus. In 1922 Bell gave up his London post and returned to Chicago, where he wrote about foreign affairs, and Lawson made Mowrer chief of the foreign service in Europe. Mowrer remained in Paris, which was in second place to London as a hub for foreign correspondence. He contributed to the *Atlantic Monthly* and to the French political weekly *L'Europe Nouvelle.* He wrote another book of poetry. During an interlude in the mid-1920s, when he briefly stepped down as European chief to serve as a roving correspondent, he went to Morocco. Tribes in the northern Rif Mountains were revolting against the Spanish colonial authorities. With all the bravado of the most derring-do correspondents, he penetrated Spanish lines to reach the Riffian rebel leader Abd el-Krim and described his experience to Chicago readers.

> I have visited the unknown Riff. During fifteen days dressed in flowing robes and turban, burned brown as an Arab by the noonday African sun, harried by the howling night winds of the wide bare places, sleeping on the ground in caves or under the tents of the Sons of Bou Yahi, among donkeys, goats, chickens, fierce wolfish dogs and men scarcely less wolfish, drinking muddy water and native tea, eating rancid oily messes with my fingers from a common wooden

bowl, conversing as best I could by signs and picked-up words of the strange Berber dialect, overcoming unaccustomed fatigues, having vermin, discomforts and Spanish airplane bombs, averting ill will with smiles, meeting suspicions with friendly confidence I have lived the life of a native North African.

Mowrer fit into the *Chicago Daily News* literary tradition without embracing the hard-drinking, prank-prone ethos described by Robert Casey. To the local room's irreverent delight, as Carl Sandburg noted, Mowrer's pallor, "dark zeal," and beard made him look like Christ. Ernest Hemingway, who had a special relationship with Mowrer, picked up on the religious theme; he considered Mowrer "a little too saintly for me." The special relationship sprang from the fact that Mowrer, whose first marriage had failed in the early 1930s, married Hemingway's first wife, Hadley, shortly after her divorce from the novelist. "There was something so tranquil, so solid, about Paul," Hadley said. If he were casting a movie, said a newspaper colleague, he would pick Mowrer to be a British diplomat, a Morgan partner, or "most likely a general."

Mowrer considered journalism "the newest of the great public professions." He was not impressed with the *Chicago Tribune*'s enterprise in smuggling a complete copy of the Versailles Treaty out of Paris and presenting it to the U.S. Senate. He had acquired his own copy from a member of Wilson's staff and cabled the essential parts home. The *Tribune*'s undignified grandstanding degraded "our profession—playing cheap politics, to no constructive purpose!" In building up the *Daily News* foreign service, Mowrer wanted more people like himself. Writing Bell with his impressions of Raymond Swing, who was being considered for a job before the war, Mowrer sounded as though he were vetting someone for the diplomatic corps: "He's rather serious minded—sociologist, student of politics, etc., etc. But the dangerous side of that will soon be knocked out of him. I'll bet his morals are O.K. and that he'll be faithful. . . . He's tried to write fiction and plays without success—naturally!—and has just finished a magazine article on industrial housing in Vienna."

Junius Wood fell into a distinctly different class. Robert Casey remembered him as "the greatest correspondent who ever lived" and "the sort of acid gent with whom no stuffed shirt could ever be friends." During the war the *Daily News* reporter raised the ire of officers handling press relations. A little uncertain of his own authority and a bit of a stuffed shirt himself, Mowrer took the side of the military. "He is socially unfit because of his loud, rough manner, his general uncouthness, his constant criticism and complaints, his lack of general culture, his inability to associate pleasantly with cultivated men," Mowrer wrote Charles Dennis. "He is morally unfit, because of his excessive drinking, and his public association with immoral women. . . . It hurts our standing, and our whole profession." Among Wood's sins were not letting censors read his outgoing mail and spending a wild night with some news pals. "The other evening, I am informed on reliable testimony, a number of them got drunk," Mowrer reported, "and going along the corridor of the hotel late one night, put the cards of various houses of prostitutes they had visited into the shoes of supposedly respectable women, these shoes having been placed outside the door to be cleaned."

Mowrer made no pretense that he was plebeian or that he wanted to write for plebeians. His ideal Chicago readers, he once suggested, were members of a local committee made up mostly of business executives who drafted a report on foreign policy for the Chicago Association of Commerce. "If public opinion is to conduct our foreign affairs wisely, it must be rightly informed, by expert observers," he wrote in a 1920 internal memo. "It is better to give a first-class service to those who can appreciate it than to aim to please all, and succeed in pleasing none."

In his diplomatic reporting. Mowrer worked hard to understand complex international political maneuverings. Lilian Mowrer, Edgar's wife, described the scene when the two brothers covered an international conference together: "Edgar and Paul would sit together piecing out their story. Each had contacts with half a dozen delegates and observers, each worked with certain foreign correspondents; their 'lines' were always out."

In the mid-1920s, Paul Mowrer persuaded the *Daily News* to let him write a weekly article that synthesized such broad issues as "The Reorganization of the British Empire" and "Real Uses of the American Diplomatic Service." "I had to keep up on international politics everywhere, by constant reading of reports, by personal contacts and a system of files," Mowrer said. "I got so I felt competent to write a speech for almost any foreign minister, expressing his country's views."

In 1929 the Pulitzer Prize board gave the first awards exclusively for "correspondence." (Swope's Pulitzer for coverage of Germany a decade earlier had been in the general category of "reporting.")* The *Daily News* had two nominees, Mowrer in Europe, and Bell, who had accompanied President Hoover on his trip to South America. While covering the Young Commission on German reparations, Mowrer received word that he was the winner. His reports, the jurors said, "most closely approximate the ideals" expressed in the award criteria: "fair, judicious, well-balanced and well-informed interpretive writing, which shall make clear the significance of the subject covered in the correspondence or which shall promote international understanding and appreciation."

The stories that won Mowrer's Pulitzer Prize were written in the manner of an insider writing for insiders. The focus was on diplomatic maneuverings. Attribution was minimal. The dominant voice was Mowrer's, which was knowledgeable, slightly pompous, and opinionated. On the surface was his belief that the United States needed to shed the isolationist tendencies that prompted it to refuse mem-

* The new category in which Mowrer won, "correspondence," was not exclusively for foreign reporting either; it included "correspondence" from Washington, although foreign reporting dominated. In 1942 a prize for International Telegraphic Reporting was added. In 1947, jurors recommended the single international category that exists today. This, of course, does not preclude stories with overseas datelines winning in other categories, as Swope's did.

bership in the League of Nations. The reports were well suited to the diplomatic pouch.

Ex cathedra analysis was common for Pulitzer Prize–winning "correspondence" during the early years of awards in this category, which were won successively by Leland Stowe of the *New York Herald Tribune* (and later the *Chicago Daily News*), H. R. Knickerbocker of the *New York Evening Post,* Walter Duranty of the *New York Times,* and Mowrer's brother Edgar. Today such stories would not be considered seriously by Pulitzer jurors, let alone printed in daily newspapers. While interpretation continues to win Pulitzers, judges' tastes now run toward livelier reporting intelligible to average readers.

Below is one of the articles by Mowrer that was considered by the Pulitzer Prize committee. It was published on March 17, 1928. Note the significant role he assigns to journalists in the third paragraph.

U. S. PROPOSAL TO BAN WAR IS GAINING GROUND ABROAD

Europe's Acceptance of Multilateral Treaty Now Believed to Be Only Question of Time; Influential Members of League Favor It.

BY PAUL SCOTT MOWRER.

SPECIAL CABLE

To The Chicago Daily News Foreign Service,
Copyright, 1928, The Chicago Daily News, Inc.

Paris, France, March 17.—Careful inquiry among the chancellories of Europe leads to the belief that adoption, by virtually all the nations, of the United States' proposal for a multilateral treaty outlawing war is now only a question of time. Europe's first reaction to this proposal was unfavorable, but gradually the view is gaining ground that the present moment is perhaps decisive in the relations between the United States and Europe.

Rejection of our proposal would, in the words of one foreign diplomat, be nothing less than catastrophic, for it would tend to keep Europe and the United States apart and might perilously aggravate the incipient United States-British naval rivalry. Acceptance, on the other hand, probably would lead to close permanent co-operation between the United States and the league of nations, thus ending a decade of unfortunate misunderstandings between the two great branches of the white race peopling opposite shores of the Atlantic.

League Favors Acceptance.

All influential members of the league secretariat are in favor of such acceptance. So do Germany and Japan, and probably Great Britain and the Soviet Union favor it. Canada is using its good offices for acceptance by both Great Britain and France. Aristide Briand, French foreign minister, has been influenced in these circumstances in the course of the recent private conversations at Geneva, and French opinion, which had been greatly confused during the negotiations, is slowly being somewhat enlightened by a few farseeing journalists and such American utterances as Secretary of State Kellogg's speech on Thursday and Senator William E. Borah's recent article. But even if France unexpectedly tries to let the proposal drop this will be impossible because the United States has already communicated the documents to Germany and Spain and will soon communicate the proposal to Great Britain also.

A vastly important situation underlies these negotiations. The United States after refusing to join the league plan for peace has gradually evolved a complete peace policy of its own. The time is therefore come to compare these two plans and see to what extent they are similar and can be reconciled and to what extent they fundamentally differ.

Plan Provides for Arbitration.

Both plans provide for the conciliation of all international disputes but by a special commission in one case and the league council in the other. Both favor arbitration of all justifiable disputes or reference to the international court. Both favor regional peace agreements, but in one case merely for common consultation in the event of danger, and in the other case for armed aid in the event aggression is committed. Both tend toward disarmament, but in one case regional without international supervision, and in the other case general and interrelated with international supervision.

None of these points offer insuperable obstacles to co-operation between the United States and the league. Real difficulty emerges from divergent methods of trying to end war. The league provides for common causes against an aggressor; the United States' multilateral declaration allows no resort to war and is without sanctions.

U. S. Opposes Sanctions.

The United States is strongly opposed to the idea of sanctions. Secretary Kellogg clearly implied in his speech Thursday that he considers treaties prearranging sanctions are military alliances, dangerous and ineffective for keeping peace. However, the United States is protected against aggression by two oceans. The continental European states, especially France and its allies, which have common frontiers with discontented neighbors, feel insecure without promises of mutual aid and they refuse to disarm except in proportion to such aid as is promised.

The divergence would be less serious were it not for the fact that the United States, as the world's strongest power, can, if it likes, render the league's plan of sanctions against a pact breaker ineffective simply by refusing to recognize the league blockade. The belief is widespread in Europe that the projected increase in our navy is due mainly to our desire to protect our commerce against interference from blockaders acting for the league.

Was this the condition of affairs which led M. Briand to make his original offer of a dual outlawry treaty with the United States?

French Suspicions Unjustified.

In the French mind a Franco-American treaty outlawing war could be followed by similar treaties between the United States and other powers, and the neutrality of the United States in case of league action against an aggressor would have been insured. The French were somewhat piqued when we rejected this offer and proposed instead a multilateral treaty. The French became suspicious immediately and scented a sort of plot against the league and also against France and its allies.

Now, however, thanks to Secretary Kellogg and Senator Borah, it is being made clear that these suspicions are unjustified. Since all nations may sign the treaty, Poland will be as much protected from Germany as will France, and, since breach of the treaty by one signatory restores freedom of action to all, the league covenant and regional treaties, like the Locarno pact, can immediately be enforced against the pact breaker.

Unfortunately Senator Borah's explanations on this last point remain unofficial. If and when they are confirmed by Secretary Kellogg, the chief cause of France's present hesitation doubtless will be removed.

Our proposal, says the British statesman, Gilbert Murray, "is an extension and not a contradiction of the league covenant."

Briand Still Doubtful.

With the French elections at hand and the domestic campaign in full swing, M. Briand is still meditating, but it is significant that on the left, Leon Blum, influential socialist leader, is outspoken for acceptance of the American proposal, while on the right the influential journalist, Jacques Bardoux, has begun in the newspaper Le Temps an even franker series of articles on the Franco-American relations.

"France's suspicions," says M. Bardoux, "betray its smallness of view. The preponderance of the United States since the world war changes the outlook of world politics, and it is to France's interest that the United States should be associated as closely as possible with European affairs. By the acceptance of Mr. Kellogg's proposal, the United States would be bound morally if not legally to act sympathetically toward any common action taken against a possible pact breaker. Great Britain would be reassured and the league covenant would at last become effective."

M. Bardoux's view seems to be gaining ground. The outlook for permanent political reconciliation of ourselves with Europe has never been brighter than it is now.

Simply by being a bridge between the people they cover and the people for whom they report, correspondents are envoys. But at times they go beyond reporting to become moving parts in the machinery of diplomacy. Brash yellow journalist James Creelman, apparently acting for Hearst, proposed that the president of Haiti join his country to the United States. The more serious George Smalley worked behind the scenes to help defuse a dispute between the United States and Britain over Venezuela's border with British Guiana. During the 1962 Cuban missile crisis, John Scali of ABC News carried messages between the Kennedy administration and the Soviet KGB station chief in Washington; the communication helped bring about a peaceful settlement. (Scali later became a real ambassador to the United Nations.) Closer to our own times, Ted Koppel's *Nightline* television program served as an "electronic negotiating table" by bringing together opposing sides in overseas hot spots to discuss their differences. In 2002 the *New York Times*' Thomas Friedman— strangely criticized by Koppel for "journalism-fueled diplomacy"—floated a Saudi proposal for Middle East peace, which he acquired in a dinner with Saudi crown prince Abdullah.

While by no means unique in the willingness of its correspondents to play envoy, the *Daily News* was exceptional in the extensiveness of its involvement and the seriousness of purpose with which it pursued those tasks. A glimmering of its interest in diplomacy was evident as early as the 1880s, when a *Daily News* correspondent helped establish the forerunner to the Organization of American States. By the 1920s, such journalistic statesmanship was a habit. "The right kind of foreign correspondent," said Charles Dennis, "is, in fact, an unofficial envoy who frequently performs services of value to the American people." During his three-plus years in Constantinople, Constantine Brown "helped the embassy again and again," he told Dennis in 1927. He passed information to American diplomats that he could not report without compromising his sources and, vice versa, served as a backdoor channel for unofficial overtures to foreign governments. "While the embassy could not officially be in touch with the Nationalist rebels, we—who were not official people—were in constant touch with them, and we were able to tell the state department all the moves of Kemal [Atatürk] and his confederates."

"More than any other writer of his time, Edward Price Bell was a newspaper reporter on the ambassadorial level," said the undiplomatic Junius Wood. With the bright conversation Mowrer admired, Bell cultivated the powerful. They, in turn, came to view him as an important interpreter both of Great Britain to America and of America to Great Britain. During early stages of World War I, he privately urged the British to undertake more aggressive war propaganda in the United States, which had yet to take sides militarily. In letters to the *Times* of London in 1917, Bell explained to impatient British subjects why Wilson had not entered but would. He considered his exclusive wartime interviews with British statesmen to have the status of official state papers.

Lawson worried that Bell's pro-British sentiment did not go down well with the largely stay-out-of-the-war Chicago audience. "If the reader thinks the correspondent is a partisan," he cautioned his correspondent, "the correspondent's influence is distinctly impaired, regardless of how faithful may be his presentation of the truth as he sees it." Bell, however, did not desist. And after the war, Lawson was all for his world tours to interview leaders for a frankly diplomatic purpose. Lawson and Bell were "afraid the consequences of the war are going to be worse than the war itself." They hoped Bell's interviews would foster international understanding and "jar" the American public into appreciating its global responsibilities. Lawson called it "Our Great Adventure." The *Daily News* published Bell's reports in two books. A number of statesmen supported his nomination for the Nobel Peace Prize.

Other *Daily News* reporters took on diplomatic roles. Col. Edward M. House in President Wilson's kitchen cabinet enlisted Raymond Swing to quietly lobby left-of-center French politicians to embrace the president's Fourteen Points. Paul Mowrer endorsed the mission. In the 1930s, after moving on to the *Philadelphia Public Ledger*'s foreign service, Swing found himself a serious candidate to be the U.S. ambassador to Ireland. Just before World War II, the *Daily News* assigned Paul Scott Mowrer's brother Edgar to work with William Donovan, who was asked by President Roosevelt to design and run the wartime intelligence agency, the Office of Strategic Services (OSS). They coauthored a series of articles on fifth columnists in Europe, which the *Daily News* offered free to any newspaper that wanted it. Edgar Mowrer subsequently made an undercover fact-finding trip to Asia for Donovan while maintaining his status as a correspondent, something that would be considered inappropriate today but was not at all unusual at the time.* He quit the *Daily News* during the war to work for the Office of War Information, resigning from that position after being denied a mission to North Africa because he was "too emotional" and out of step with Roosevelt's pro-Vichy policy. After the war, Carroll Binder served on two UN commissions on press freedom. *Daily News* corre-

---

* An example of the change in attitude can be seen in journalistic involvement with the Central Intelligence Agency. Investigations in the 1970s revealed that the CIA had recruited correspondents to work as agents or to assist agents, or had used news media as cover for its agents. The foreign correspondent role was ideal for such purposes since persons in that profession are expected to travel widely, mix with officials of all kinds, and ask lots of questions. By one count, compiled by Carl Bernstein in *Rolling Stone* in 1977, some four hundred journalists had ties to the CIA during the previous quarter century. Many were with major news media like CBS and the *New York Times*.

Some of the help given by foreign correspondents came as patriotic favors, with no expectation of remuneration. Sometimes the correspondents were engaged in casual back-and-forth in which information useful to both the journalist and the American officials were exchanged. Sometimes the involvement was much deeper. At one point in the 1950s, the CIA had formal training programs to teach agents to be journalists.

The embarrassing revelations about this involvement were not the only reason journalists drew back from this work. Journalists came to see that they could not be independent of officialdom and part of it simultaneously, something that became less desirable as the cold war consensus disintegrated and evidence of government mendacity increased. Journalists also put themselves at serious physical risk abroad if they were perceived as arms of government, rather than as independent observers.

Legislation has since made it more difficult, but not impossible, for intelligence agencies to employ journalists representing U.S. news media organizations. The president or the director of the CIA can waive this rule in the event of "overriding national security interests of the United States." House and Senate committees on intelligence must be notified of the waiver. The law also does not bar a correspondent from volunteering to cooperate. See Carl Bernstein, "The CIA and the Media," *Rolling Stone*, October 20, 1977, 55–67.

spondent William Stoneman was for three years an adviser to the first UN secretary general, Trygve Lie.

One member of the staff, the charming, aristocratic Paul Ghali, joined the newspaper *after* diplomatic service. Ghali was unusually well connected to international politics. His family on his mother's side had come to Avignon with the popes in the thirteenth century; his father was an Egyptian judge at the International Court. After graduating from Oxford, the Paris School of Political Science, and the Sorbonne, he joined the Egyptian Diplomatic Service. In 1939 he became a *Daily News* correspondent. During the war, he helped Donovan's OSS acquire the diaries of Count Galeazzo Ciano, Mussolini's son-in-law and foreign minister, whom Mussolini had executed for disloyalty. Portions of the diaries, embarrassing to Mussolini and the Germans, were published in the *Daily News,* which paid twenty-five thousand dollars for the rights. They were used later in the Nuremberg war crimes trials.

An American ambassador to France told Dennis that Paul Mowrer "never forgets his country and he is ever ready to help it in any way he can." Mowrer did not share Bell's enthusiasm for long verbatim interviews with leaders, which left misleading statements unchallenged. (The wisdom of Mowrer's criticism can be seen in Bell's flattering portraits of Hitler and Mussolini.) Mowrer's preferred method of diplomatic intervention took a step beyond the approach in his Pulitzer Prize–winning articles. In the manner of many European journalists, who considered themselves intellectuals, and a few American journalistic public intellectuals, such as Walter Lippmann, Mowrer sought to provide expert advice in writing.

Our Foreign Affairs was his most important contribution. Although not written with the verve of Lippmann's book-length musings on foreign affairs, the 1924 volume deserves to be remembered for its forward-looking analysis. Mowrer foresaw the global depression, the increasing importance of arms-limitation agreements, the disruptiveness of rapid communications for diplomacy, the need for better White House foreign policy coordination among a wide array of government agencies, and Americans' growing dependence on foreign petroleum and other minerals. "Diplomatically, the principal trait of the new era is the henceforth unavoidable political, economic, and moral interdependence of the nations." Nearly thirty years later political scientist Hans Morgenthau told Mowrer he was still assigning the book to his students.

Daily News correspondents acquired expertise rivaling that of any diplomat. Their reports ranged widely, touching regions and issues most Americans otherwise did not think much about. *Daily News* series in 1928 and 1929 included Stoneman on Schleswig, Binder on the Calabria region of Italy, and John W. White on the reasons for South American ill will toward the United States. "See that glint!" exclaims a character in Sir Arthur Conan Doyle's 1928 Professor Challenger short story, a tale of the mad British scientist's secret drilling in Sussex to reach the earth's life force. "That's the telescope of the Chicago *Daily News.*" The foreign service, judged journalist and press critic Oswald Garrison Villard, was "as distinguished a corps of correspondents as has ever been assembled by an American daily." With scores of newspapers including the *Washington Star* subscribing, *Daily News* correspondents were read in the White House and across the nation.

On the strength of this, the mood in the local room at the *Daily News* changed from the days when Mowrer apologetically set out for Europe on his first assignment. Instead of ridiculing foreign news, ambitious reporters clamored for a chance to go abroad, too. Stoneman hadn't waited to be asked. Learning of an opening in Sweden, he left Chicago for Stockholm and cabled home. Since he was already there, he said, he might as well have the job.

Mowrer stood at the top of this distinguished heap. In typical "Timestyle" pretentiousness, *Time* dubbed him "a journalist panjandrum." When a League of Nations body assembled a report on the educational role of the press, it turned to him for one of the essays. Putting aside his concerns about the spats and cane, the discriminating Henry Justin Smith held him up as a model. Mowrer's style, he told journalism students, "whether he employed it upon 'human interest' topics or upon analysis of diplomatic tangles, is among the most brilliant, well-poised and flexible media of expression wielded by a journalist."

The *Daily News* was not about to forget the average reader, who might not care much about foreign affairs. Sports stories were a fixture on the front page, sometimes the banner story. Serialized fiction and Hollywood news entertained readers. "There are more romances told or suggested in a single issue of a metropolitan daily," Lawson believed, "than you will find in a dozen novels." Whatever he might say about the success of the experiment in foreign news-gathering, home considerations and foreign ones clashed. There were constant reminders that the foreign service, as brilliant as it had become, could not be taken for granted.

Foreign reporting was an expensive undertaking, and Lawson, parsimonious to start with, never let correspondents forget it. In the first days of the service, when it was housed in the *Record,* Lawson was painfully aware of the costs of cabling, which in the first year of operation, 1899, were more than double all of his correspondents' salaries plus stories he paid for on an as-used basis. When a cable seemed trivial (and some indubitably were), he pasted it to a form letter that he sent to the correspondent. The letter ended with the words, "the attached cable should *not* have been sent. It is worth neither the cost of cabling nor the necessary space" in the paper.

Imperatives to keep costs down, correspondents complained, were self-defeating. They said editors pressed for mailers but treated them with little respect, sometimes not running them at all or giving them second place to AP stories by wire. The discord reached an absurd level when cost-conscious Chicago editors barred correspondents from using the word *stop* in their cables. This command generated a years-long debate on the merits of the little word. Junius Wood complained in 1917 that excluding "stop" or "period" from cables led to "bad results in printed copy, sentences split, joined together wrongly, entire sense changed. . . . Even the U.P. which gets a half page out of a 50 word cable, requires 'stop' in its cables." At one point Bell wrote a three-page defense of "stop." To make sure Dennis was getting the message, Bell raised the issue in a letter two months later: "Re the use of the word 'stop' in cables, I have just heard from [Percy] Noel. He says he has suffered 'shockingly' at times from the omission of this word. Indeed he goes so far as to state that in his opinion commas should be cabled."

Other expenses were scrutinized as well. Junius Wood, who was notorious for circumventing *Daily News* auditors, was reduced to writing a plaintive memo justifying his expenses during twenty-two months in Asia: "I had a single room without bath or running water, so dark that artificial light was needed in daytime, which was both workroom and living quarters."

The tension over money crackled with intensity when Hopewell Rogers in the business office got involved with expense accounts. Rogers was "Mr. Lawson's efficiency man in all departments of The Daily News. He has a genius for detail," Dennis informed Mowrer in 1924, explaining that foreign correspondence was the last branch of the paper's activity to be given to Rogers "for his expert consideration." Among Rogers's ideas for improvement was elimination of the category "incidental" from expense forms. Bell in Chicago advised Lawson that just the opposite was called for: "There should be no detailed scrutiny as to how our men spend their money." Paul Mowrer proposed taking over Rogers's accounting functions for the foreign service. Getting nowhere and finding Rogers's hectoring "humiliating and demoralizing," Mowrer resigned. Lawson placated Mowrer by disclaiming any knowledge of Rogers's enthusiastic cost cutting and promising it would not happen again.

Correspondents complained that Lawson's view of foreign news—and often the view of his managing editor, Dennis—was not always theirs. In 1920 Lawson still urged correspondents to look for human interest angles. "Mr. Lawson's last order is perfectly impossible, and is simply going to kill our foreign service," Paul Mowrer wrote. Chimed in his hyperbolic brother, "To write about silly visitors and businessmen, at a time when Europe is going to pieces, is sheer fiddling." In 1926 Dennis suggested to Mowrer that readers wanted fewer political stories and more stories like one from Rome about a bird that sang at night in the Coliseum. Likewise, Lawson turned aside suggestions to expand the service. "Our efforts to broaden the service," Dennis wrote to Mowrer in 1923 almost apologetically and somewhat cryptically, "do not meet with Mr. Lawson's approval, because he says truly that more correspondents make more cable dispatches and more cable dispatches are merely an embarrassment, as well as an added expense."

These frustrations notwithstanding, Lawson was not about to let Rogers drive off Mowrer, and he and his editors rarely second-guessed the substance of correspondents' stories. Lawson's editorial philosophy, expressed through men like Dennis and Smith, was "the man on the spot is always right." "No argument by cable," said Edgar Mowrer; "no tampering with his copy." The *Daily News* foreign service, they all understood, was secure as long as the gentlemanly owner in the frock coat was taking the elevator to the top floor of the *Daily News* rickety building. When Lawson died in 1925 and uncertainty gripped the newspaper, Edward Price Bell put all the disagreements with the home office behind him. He thought Lawson's "journalistic genius was near to a perfect thing."

Lawson's death was a blow. He carried his business around in his head and, with the expensive enterprise of foreign news, in his heart. While he micromanaged the office furnishings for his foreign bureaus and meddled in other details, he made no provision at all in his will for the *Daily News*. The will simply lumped the newspaper with his other property. Because his wife predeceased him and he had no children, the proceeds went to charities and a few close associates. Mowrer feared that the newspaper could end up in the hands of a grocer, a banker, or a lawyer with no interest in its traditions. "My deep conviction," said Bell, in the anger stage of grief, "is that Mr. Lawson while meaning well, wronged me unpardonably, and wronged others much more than myself. He torpedoed the good ship on which we were sailing. It was our ship, in the sight of right, as much as it was his."

To everyone's relief, Walter Strong stepped in with a solution. A distant relative of Lawson's wife, he had worked on the business side of the *Daily News* for years and now organized a group to buy the newspaper, with himself owning a controlling interest and becoming publisher. Although his group did not submit the top bid, its $13.5 million purchase price was the highest for an American newspaper up to that time. The trustees and beneficiaries of Lawson's estate accepted it in order to ensure that the newspaper continued along familiar lines.

This was no guarantee that nothing would change, for change was essential. Circulation had been flat for the past decade, "despite the fact that hundreds of thousands of dollars have been spent on promotion," management consultants told Strong. The facilities needed modernizing. Victor Lawson's inefficient patrician management style was equally outmoded. "It is a marvel to all persons outside the News and many inside," the consultants also noted, "that the staff is able to produce a daily Newspaper of the size and quality of the Daily News." Strong tightened the budget, raised salaries, and ordered construction of a twenty-five-story art deco skyscraper at 400 Madison St., along the Chicago River. Radio station WMAQ broadcast from the top floor. For the first time in anyone's memory, the furniture matched.

The *Daily News* foreign service was secure—for the time being.

A second test of the Lawson tradition came in 1931 with Strong's untimely death. This time a will made provisions for the *Daily News*. It directed that the paper should be sold to someone who would preserve "The Chicago Daily News or its successor as a semi-public institution, with substantially the character it may have at my death." Strong provided a grace period to allow employees to arrange purchase of his controlling interest. But the staff could not marshal the resources, which may have been just as well. Strong had taken on heavy debt to acquire the newspaper and build its new quarters. An experienced financial manager was needed to satisfy creditors and cope with the Depression economy. The search for such a person led to Col. Frank Knox, who purchased the paper with financial support from a New England newspaper supplier. Knox had long newspaper experience, most recently as general manager of Hearst's twenty-seven newspapers. Strong's family claimed that he was the man to carry on *Daily News* traditions. A *New York Times* editorial thought Knox "may be counted upon not to depart from the high standards set by his predecessors." In an editorial of its own, the *Daily News* promised to uphold "its priceless heritage."

The transition, nevertheless, was again jolting, this time more so than with Lawson's passing. The retiring Lawson had claimed he never voted in a primary. Knox, an extrovert, had charged up San Juan Hill with Teddy Roosevelt's Rough Riders and had risen to the rank of lieutenant colonel in World War I. As publisher and owner of the *Manchester Union Leader,* he unsuccessfully campaigned for governor of New Hampshire. His political aspirations did not end with his purchase of the *Daily News.* In 1936 he ran for vice president on Alf Landon's ticket. Nor was Knox the kindly patrician Lawson and Strong had been. Upon becoming owner of the newspaper, he ordered a pay cut and sold its half interest in WMAQ. Strong had made a loan to help Mowrer prop up his investments during the stock market crash. Knox wrote to ask when he was going to pay it back and, in line with other cost-saving steps, slashed his pay by 15 percent. "I should like to have word from you as to what you think is going to happen to all of us," correspondent John Gunther wrote to Carroll Binder. "Being remote here, and off the main currents, we are a bit worried."

The future of the foreign service was probably as unclear to Knox himself. His knowledge of foreign affairs was limited to the battlefield. Critics said his geography was shaky. Correspondence with Bell suggests he did not know much about the history of the newspaper's foreign coverage or Bell's role. Although the *Daily News* already had released part-time correspondents in Oslo, Madrid, Ireland, Milan, and elsewhere to cope with the bad economy, rumors had it that Knox still considered the foreign service too expensive. He recalled Junius Wood from Moscow and closed the bureau. Constantine Brown, who had become the *Daily News*'s diplomatic correspondent in Washington, got the ax. The reason, Brown thought, was that he did not check stories against the Hoover administration foreign policy line. In addition to forcing his resignation, Knox refused to honor a contract that, Brown said, entitled him to severance. Knox sent him downstairs to get "his week's pay" and dared him to sue. (Brown became foreign news editor and columnist at the *Washington Star.*)

Knox initially reassured Edward Price Bell. He said he supported the foreign service's interpretive tradition. Unlike McCormick, the new owner liked the British. (When Knox died, his widow endowed a Harvard educational exchange in his name between the United States and the British Commonwealth.) But the embryonic comity between Bell and Knox died in a matter of weeks. Knox's British sympathies notwithstanding, he was disenchanted with Bell's strong pro-British viewpoint as well as, possibly, his Olympian approach to news analysis. For his part, Bell disliked Knox's overt Republican sympathies and what he seems to have regarded as pressure "to deflect me from the line of conscience." Bell wanted freedom and deference that Knox was unwilling to grant. Whether Bell was fired, as Mowrer believed, or resigned, as Bell's papers suggest, he and the paper severed ties. In his twilight years Bell scrounged magazine assignments abroad, toiled over an autobiography he could not get published, and at the very end wrote a column for the *Saturday Spectator* in Terre Haute, Indiana.

"Bell's attitude," Knox told fellow republican Charles Dawes, "is only an exaggerated illustration of the difficulties I am encountering in handling the staff of the foreign news service." In addition to "difficulties" keeping costs down, Knox may have felt intimidated by the foreign correspondents, a feeling he was not used to. He certainly did not want to be pushed around by reporters who fancied themselves on a par with presidents and prime ministers and were likely out of touch with readers.

Mowrer, second to none on the staff in his elitist views, had good reason to apprehend that Knox's housecleaning could sweep him unceremoniously out the door. He knew Knox diagnosed in him a different strain of the Bell disease, Francophilia. Besides that, soon after Knox acquired the paper, a brief letter arrived to say that Mowrer was no longer head of European correspondents. Management of all foreign news was being brought back to Chicago. When Mowrer asked to come home to discuss this decision, the request was denied. Meanwhile, word reached him that Knox was keeping an eye on him for any reporting mistakes he might make. A worried Mowrer toyed with the idea of accepting a job as an adviser to the Chinese government.

Catching Mowrer in a mistake was not easy. Fellow correspondents considered him "an almost fanatical stickler for accuracy." When Mowrer scooped an impending armament agreement with detailed—and correct—figures, Knox sent congratulations. The two men subsequently met in London and hit it off. Knox wanted to bring him home to oversee editorials and eventually replace Dennis as editor. On a trip to Berlin, Knox was similarly won over to Edgar Mowrer's tough reporting on Hitler (although Knox briefly brought him back to Chicago to reacquaint him with his own country). "Colonel Knox arrived in Europe an isolationist ('we must keep out of that dogfight')," Edgar Mowrer said, "and returned to America a resolute antifascist."

After almost a quarter of a century abroad, Paul Scott Mowrer returned to Chicago as associate editor. In 1935 he became editor. He was known to impose "his will around the office on foreign affairs," although he was scarcely alone in his expertise in foreign affairs. The front office was full of such talent. Mowrer's managing editor was a longtime foreign correspondent, Hal O'Flaherty. Carroll Binder, a reserved, thoughtful internationalist who came home to serve as Knox's assistant, became foreign editor the year after Mowrer took the top job.

The staff had been rattled during the first years of the new regime. Good correspondents were lost. Knox's commitment to the paper was in doubt not only in the minds of his reporters and editors, but in his own as well. He confided to his wife, shortly before acquiring the *Daily News,* "Just as soon as I know a deal [to buy the paper] can be consummated I will renew discussions with Roy Howard [of Scripps

Howard] with a view to eventually sale [*sic*] to them when they are ready to take on another big paper and this property has been made to earn what it should earn. That is where and how I can expect to make our fortune."

Knox understood the majesty of the *Daily News,* "easily among the first half-dozen papers in the country." When Prohibition was repealed in 1933, Knox held true to Lawson's teetotaling rule of not running liquor ads. Once the foreign service shake-up was over, the paper settled in for a new strong run in which it ended the less-than-grand tradition of publishing the names of Chicagoans who visited its overseas bureaus. Mowrer respected the new owner as a thoroughgoing newspaperman. On politics, they were in general sympathy. Knox ran as a Republican; Mowrer voted that way. Knox was "Critic Number One" of Roosevelt, when it came to the New Deal. When it came to international affairs, he endorsed FDR's assertive foreign policy. If Mowrer wished that greater sophistication about foreign affairs underpinned Knox's internationalism, he appreciated that his boss did not meddle, even when he ran for vice president or when Roosevelt reached across the aisle to appoint him secretary of the navy. Press critic Villard had roughly the same view: Knox did not measure up to Lawson and Strong; but he "was wise enough not to interfere with this [foreign] service or to change the fundamental character of the paper."

If anything, the *Daily News*'s feud with the *Tribune* became more intense. Knox and McCormick belonged to the same political party, which might have made them allies, except that they both had an interest in being at the head of Illinois Republicans. On the journalistic front, Knox was critical of the practices of "our chief competitor." The *Tribune,* he told John Gunther, "doctors its news from abroad and from Washington to fit its editorial views. I do not regard that as honest newspaper work."* The *Daily News* crusaded against the *Tribune*'s isolationist view of the world, often explicitly, as when cartoonist Cecil Jensen wickedly lampooned McCormick in a series of cartoons called "The Adventures of Col. McCosmic." In 1941 the *Daily News* ran a daily feature called "Famous Sayings of History," consisting exclusively of silly comments by McCormick. McCormick used his pages to repay the insults. "You will be interested to hear, by the way, that the Tribune has not attacked you personally for more than a week," Mowrer wrote to Knox in the spring of 1942, when the *Daily News* owner was in Washington serving as navy secretary. A new, serious controversy flared up a few weeks later when McCormick's paper recklessly published a story about a naval battle, revealing that the United States had broken the Japanese code. Knox wanted to prosecute, an idea that was ditched only when the navy realized this would draw Japanese attention to the story.

Knox attempted to manage the *Daily News* while serving in Washington, an arrangement that was not optimal from a business point of view. Circulation in 1943 was slightly below the mark of 1930. Nevertheless, the paper remained prestigious

---

* One occasion on which McCormick combined editorializing and reporting was his failed campaign to put Chicago on summer daylight time year round, which would have made it more difficult for the *Daily News* to run end-of-day stock market results.

and profitable, and from the point of view of the foreign service, strength built on strength during the 1930s. Not happy with the *Herald Tribune,* John Whitaker jumped to the *Daily News* overseas staff. He was joined later by his Pulitzer Prize–winning colleague Leland Stowe, to whom the *Herald Tribune* denied an overseas assignment at the outbreak of the war in Europe in 1939. Stowe was "delighted to be a member of the recognized highest-quality foreign correspondent team of any U.S. news media." George Weller, a future Pulitzer Prize winner who had worked at the *New York Times,* joined too. At the outset of the war, journalists praised the *Daily News* foreign service as "the crowning glory of the newspaper world."

Knox sent a note to Binder with a one-thousand-dollar bonus at the end of 1943. "I want to congratulate you on the fine progress we have made during the year in the Foreign News Service," Knox wrote. "It continues to be what I have always regarded it—the best foreign news service in the country—and that means in the world."

Four months later Knox died.

A group of employees, including Paul Scott Mowrer, tried to buy the paper. Leading the effort was future presidential candidate Adlai Stevenson, an international-minded local attorney who had worked with Knox at the Navy Department. The deal fell through when the overly cautious Stevenson wouldn't take the bidding one notch higher. From among the many suitors who showed an interest in buying the paper, Knox's heirs chose John Knight, whose budding newspaper chain included dailies in Miami, Detroit, and Akron.

The new owner offered the usual platitudes about maintaining the foreign service, which Binder telegraphed, in cablese, to the foreign service: "IN MY ANNOUNCEMENT OWNERSHIP PAYING SPECIAL TRIBUTE TO VICTOR LAWSONS VISION GENIUS BUILDING SERVICE WHICH IS PREEMINENT IN ITS FIELD STOP PLEASE BE ASSURED THERELL BE NO CURTAILMENT SERVICE IN ANY RESPECT." Other signs were less promising. On his first day in the office, Knight declared an end to the war with McCormick's *Tribune.* Cartoonist Cecil Jensen's "Adventures of Col. McCosmic" never appeared again. On October 21, 1944, two days after Knight's cabled message about a bright future, Binder sent a second cable announcing his resignation. Mowrer followed with his own, "for reasons of incompatibility."

"It seemed to us as if the world were falling about our ears," said Binder's wife. The new editor, Basil "Stuffy" Walters, possessed enormous energy and a mandate to boost sagging circulation. Knight correctly considered Walters ahead of his time. Foreshadowing the relentless search for strategies and simple tricks to keep readers interested, Walters spun theories about RPUs (reader pulling units) and emphasized bright layouts and story condensation, which made him unpopular with correspondents who were accustomed to being left alone—and with sophisticated Chicagoans, who enjoyed the newspaper as it was. "What can you expect us to do in education when the press is in the hands of men like Stuffy Walters?" University of Chicago president Robert M. Hutchins asked.

Colonel McCormick, the isolationist, and Colonel Knox, the internationalist, reflected Chicago's two attitudes toward the world. The "battle of the colonels" spilled over into *Daily News* cartoons with Cecil Jensen's portrayal of Colonel McCosmic, "the world's greatest military, economic and political expert." In one cartoon Jensen ridicules McCosmic's Anglophobia; in the other he depicts McCormick throwing darts at FDR; Henry Stimson, FDR's secretary of war; and Colonel Knox, who was navy secretary.

William Stoneman, a veteran of the foreign service, tried to educate Knight on the paper's great foreign reporting legacy with which he was entrusted. The *Daily News,* he emphasized, was the only one that had "fully and intelligently reported the situation which led up to the Second World War." That accomplishment, he added, meant more to reporters in the foreign service than huge salaries. Knight, who earned a reputation as a news-oriented owner, sought to reassure Stoneman even as he revealed his worries about the expense of upholding the Lawson tradition. "A quality newspaper is nice to have if you can afford it," Knight said; "frankly I am interested in popular journalism."

Bylines that seemed as much a part of the newspaper as the *Daily News* masthead disappeared. Robert Casey, whose writing had for many years graced the paper he loved, left as unceremoniously as Edward Price Bell had fifteen years before. "So, mighty Casey went under, before our startled eyes—fired, to tell the truth," said a colleague, "because he no longer could fit in, or wouldn't." Carroll Binder, courted by the *New York Times* editorial page, accepted an offer in his wife's home state, Minnesota. *Minneapolis Tribune* owner John Cowles, who distributed the *Daily News* foreign service material through his syndicate, was broadening his newspaper's perspective. Binder edited the editorial page and wrote a foreign affairs column. Arch Steele, a respected China Hand on the *Daily News* foreign staff, went to the *Herald Tribune.*

The *New York Post* was a singular beneficiary of this talent drain. In a media buying spree, Dorothy Schiff, the *Post*'s owner, and her new husband, journalist Ted Thackrey, had made a bid for the *Daily News*. When Knox's heirs opted to sell to the more Republican Knight, Schiff and Thackrey recruited Mowrer, whom they had come to know in the process and whose brother Edgar was now a syndicated columnist for them. Although Thackrey thought a man like Mowrer more suited to the *New York Times,* Mowrer was just the sort of person needed if the *Post* was to become a prestige newspaper. Mowrer was to report from Paris for the *Post* and its Brooklyn radio station, WLIB, as well as build a foreign service and start a Paris version of the paper, the *Paris Post*. This heady time at the *Post* was as brief as the Schiff-Thackrey marriage, and Mowrer soon retired altogether from journalism. While the *Post*'s foreign interests still bloomed, however, Mowrer helped recruit his son, Richard Mowrer, as well as *Daily News* correspondent Helen Kirkpatrick. Kirkpatrick decided to quit the *Daily News* when stuffy Walters cabled instructions to concentrate on "the Chicago angle" in an important diplomatic meeting in Moscow.

Walters elevated circulation to an all-time high. His crusading local news won awards. And, as it turned out, the *Daily News* foreign service continued to shine. "Walters didn't waste any time," the dislodged Robert Casey observed in a book about the good old days. "He booted out most of the foreign service before which the customers had stood in awe for so many years, and booted it back in again when the awe got overloud." George Weller, Paul Ghali, and William Stoneman stayed. Stoneman told Binder he could not afford to leave because of alimony and his investment in the *Daily News* retirement fund. Some new talent, such as Georgie Anne Geyer, joined. Keyes Beech and Fred Sparks shared the 1951 Pulitzer for coverage of the Korean War with correspondents from three other newspapers. The service still sought, as its Tokyo correspondent wrote in the mid-1950s, to do original reporting, not rewrite the wires, with an emphasis on interpretation of the "big developments of the day and elaborate the spot developments with material that the agencies do not include in their reports." The momentum of the past carried these correspondents forward. They had sources that went back for decades and used those contacts, Mowrer-fashion, to provide context. In 1952, 31 newspapers subscribed to the *New York Times* foreign news service, 45 to the *Daily News*'s.

To the schooled eye, nevertheless, all was not well. Walters spoke of the virtues of quality over quantity, which sounded good enough, until one understood that he meant less room for foreign news, fewer correspondents, and more direction from the home office. In late 1952 and early 1953, a study showed, the *Daily News* carried about one-fifth of the foreign news found in the *New York Times*. At least half of the best stories, Walters boasted, came from the newsroom, offered up by "editors, copyreaders, editorial writers, reporters and even office boys." Although this may have been an overstatement, the exuberance in his comment was a long way from the time when Edward Price Bell confidently protested to Lawson about second-guessing in Chicago: "a man of my experience—I see no virtue in modesty that is dishonest—should [not] be turned over to some sub-editor." Walters could fuss all he wanted when the respected broadcaster Eric Sevareid lamented "the break-up of

ON RETIRING FROM ACTIVE NEWSPAPER WORK

The *Paris Post* launched on July 4, 1945, with Paul Scott Mowrer as editor and publisher. Like a Fourth of July rocket, it disappeared as abruptly as it started.

Due to shortages caused by the war, paper and ink were in short supply and expensive. American servicemen were leaving Europe and there was no corresponding influx of tourists. The old *Paris Herald Tribune,* which bounced back after being shut down during the war, put up a strong fight. Mowrer was willing to hang on, he told Ted Thackrey, the *New York Post* editor, but "it is a question of what you are willing to pay for the prestige, good will, good deeds." On January 28, 1946, seven months after it started, the *Paris Post* suspended publication.

Still proud to have Mowrer on its staff, Thackrey retained him as associate editor and chief correspondent for European affairs, based in Paris. This, too, was short-lived. "Much as I regret to write it," Thackrey informed Mowrer in early 1948, "I am not at all sure at this time whether we can continue the foreign service on its present basis." Six weeks later he shut the London bureau. Mowrer was instructed to close the Paris office by the end of the year. A final contract kept Mowrer on the *Post* until the end of 1949. During this last stint in Paris, his byline occasionally appeared in the *Chicago Daily News.*

Mowrer and his wife retired to Chocorua, New Hampshire. There he indulged his passion for fishing and the outdoors, played chess by mail with his brother, and devoted himself to his early love, poetry. He defended traditional verse against the "modern" variety in the *Saturday Review of Literature* and produced so much of his own that he was named New Hampshire's first poet laureate. For good measure he wrote a book of short plays. Below is one of his poems.

ON RETIRING FROM
ACTIVE NEWSPAPER WORK

> A hated tyrant falls; a fierce plot tears
> The webs of power; war rumors cross the sea
> A crisis—yet my fingers tap no key.
> After a life well crammed with public cares,
> How strange to stand apart from world affairs
> And let, like other men, what is to be
> Occur without one warning word from me!
> No more to deal in daily threats and scares,
> Cluck round events like anxious, brooding hen;
> Dash comment out, explain, or analyse!
> I sit and muse at last, like other men,
> Read books, walk forth and watch the clouds take shape.
> The great may do or die; I poetize.

once-great foreign staffs, as happened with the Chicago Daily News." The service was losing steam at the same time that the newspaper generally faced an uphill financial struggle.

Social and economic forces worked against afternoon newspapers. In the *Daily News*'s heyday, homebound commuters boarded a train or bus with the newspaper tucked under their arms. With the postwar rise of sprawling suburbs, more and more readers drove their cars to work. They listened to their radios on the road and to their televisions in their living rooms. Getting newspapers to inner-city projects was perilous; getting them to the suburbs on time was increasingly difficult because of the distances involved and the congested expressways. The morning papers, in contrast, were delivered when most motorists were in bed.

That was not all. Under Lawson, who strictly observed the Sabbath, the *Daily News* was a six-day-a-week paper, and it remained so. Without a Sunday edition, it missed out on lucrative weekend advertising; faithful readers who wanted a Sunday newspaper had to split their loyalties. This may have been less of a problem when Colonel McCormick imposed his peculiar views on the news from his office atop the *Chicago Tribune*'s gothic tower. With his death in 1955, the *Tribune* improved. Offended by the *Daily News*'s aggressive coverage of civil rights, its campaign to make birth control information available to Chicago families on welfare (which won a Pulitzer gold medal for public service), and other sensitive issues, middle-class readers had an alternative, and many of them took it. Advertisers, meanwhile, became highly selective. In city after city across the country, they gravitated toward the newspaper with the largest circulation, a process that made the financially strong papers stronger and the weak ones weaker.

Although these factors worked against the *Daily News*, its circulation remained healthy, reaching a high point of 614,000 in 1957. In an effort to protect the financial viability of the franchise, Knight in 1959 tried to buy the afternoon *Chicago American*, a Hearst paper. By merging it with the *Daily News*, he would have a Sunday paper. The *Tribune*, however, made a stronger bid, converting the *American* to a bright tabloid. Thwarted, Knight decided to sell the *Daily News*. Once more the sale price, $24 million, was unprecedented. The purchaser this time was Marshall Field IV, a descendant of Chicago's department store magnate of the same name. Field owned the morning *Sun-Times* and wanted an evening paper to go with it. He moved the *Daily News* to North Wabash Avenue, where it was consolidated with its new stepsister paper.

Field named himself editor when Walters retired in 1961. Field's interest in the editorship was positive, in that it indicated his commitment to journalism, and negative, given his precarious mental health, which was characterized by wide mood swings. One day he could insist on putting someone in Moscow and the next day abruptly change his mind, remembered Milt Freudenheim, a correspondent and foreign editor with the *Daily News*. When Field died in 1965 at age forty-nine, the next in line was his son. Marshall Field V turned twenty-seven that year, roughly the same age Victor Lawson had been when he took over his father's newspaper interests.

Management tried all manner of schemes. "It seemed like we had a new vice-president every day," said Georgie Anne Geyer. Nothing seemed to help. By 1971, when the Society of Professional Journalists named the *Daily News* a historic site because it had the oldest continuous foreign service, circulation dipped to 327,000, roughly half of what it had been in 1957. *Daily News* accountants wrote in red ink.

The foreign service faded like a newspaper left too long in the sun. George Weller, Paul Ghali, and William Stoneman retired. Geyer left the paper to write a column for the *Los Angeles Times Syndicate.* Correspondent Donald Shanor spoke with Marshall Field V on home leave. Field seemed excessively adamant about keeping the paper open; Shanor decided the opposite was the case and quit. There were still moments of pride, such as when Bob Tamarkin, a superb reporter, was one of the very last reporters to leave Vietnam at its fall in 1975. But the paper's Vietnam bureau—one of the first to be established in the country after the *New York Times*' bureau—had been downsized when the war was raging. Tamarkin's predecessor, Larry Green, sold the office car, gave his office and staff to a reporter with the *Los Angeles Times,* and worked out of a hotel room. Correspondents elsewhere were urged to do the same, more or less as Bell's competitors had been forced to do at the beginning of the century in London. Milt Freudenheim, in Mowrer's old post in Paris, had a grand office at 23 Rue de la Paix. He rented most of it to two Lebanese businessmen, making an office for himself in the kitchen.

As a last-ditch effort in 1977, Field put James Hoge, editor of the *Sun-Times,* in charge of both papers. Hoge accepted the assignment with the understanding that he had two years to bring the *Daily News* back to life. Hoge had an interest in foreign news—later in his career he became editor of *Foreign Affairs* magazine. Even so, he saw no way to maintain the *Daily News* foreign news tradition. He called the newspaper's four remaining correspondents home. The *Daily News* relied on the *Washington Post–Los Angeles Times* syndicate and a few stringers for nonspot foreign news. Only once did the last foreign editor, Joe Geshwiler, get permission from Hoge to send a stringer on an assignment.

With advice from consultants, an increasingly common sight in newsrooms, Hoge concentrated on local coverage, advice and how-to features, and finance. Circulation increased the first year; advertising lagged. The result was increased printing and delivery costs without offsetting gains in revenue. Hoge argued that the rising circulation and improved content built in year one gave the paper the ability to woo advertisers in year two. Field's business lieutenants lost faith in this strategy before it had played out. They argued that it was time to cut their losses and kill the *Daily News.* Some later blamed Field for reneging on his two-year commitment for rejuvenating the *Daily News;* others thought he simply bowed to the inevitable.

In 1911 Will Irwin singled out the *Daily News* in a series of articles for *Collier's* on the state of journalism. "Even should it change hands, should a get-rich-quick policy destroy its character, the 'News' would go on paying for a generation by power of its old honesty," he wrote. The Lawson tradition carried the *Daily News* through more than one generation. But as perceptive as Irwin had been in one sense, he misjudged in another. "In the business of journalism," he declared, "it seems that virtue does get its final material reward."

On the same day in early 1978 that a *Daily News* reporter won the prestigious William Allen White Award for editorial writing, Field stood on a city room desk and announced the end of the paper. As the newspaper prepared to close, editors from around the country flew in to recruit the bereaved staff for their newspapers. In a final burst of self-promotion that would have gratified Lawson, the staff devoted most of the final edition on March 4 to recalling the *Daily News*'s accomplishments. "May the spirit of the writer's newspaper survive," wrote one staffer in his eulogy, "somewhere in newspaper heaven."

13

MY OWN JOB IN MY OWN WAY

"About eight o'clock one evening in April 1927," Waverly Root recalled, "it occurred to me that I was out of a job, that I had a little money, and that I had long wanted to go to France. At noon the next day I was aboard the SS *President Harding* steaming down the Hudson, outwardbound. I had no definite plans. If anyone had asked me how long I expected to be away, I suppose I would have said a few weeks, possibly a few months." Once in Paris, Root made the rounds of local English-language newspapers and found a place on the *Chicago Tribune*'s. He fell in love with France and its women, four of whom he married. Root died in Paris in 1982.

Over and over, young Americans with journalistic aspirations went into the world this way. Hallett Abend "planned only a vacation jaunt" when he headed for Asia. He ended up overseas on the *New York Times*. So did Tillman Durdin, a young Houston newspaperman, who "decided I had to see the world." An Ohio college boy, Cecil Brown, stowed away on an ocean liner to South America one summer and on his next break "shipped out as an able-bodied seaman on an American Export freighter to Black Sea ports." After graduation he freelanced magazine articles in Europe until he was hired by the International News Service and CBS. Another soon-to-be CBS broadcaster, Howard K. Smith, after graduation from Tulane worked his way on a ship from New Orleans to Bremen in order to take advantage of a German-sponsored tuition-free summer German language program for Americans at Heidelberg University. F. McCracken Fisher went to China on a trip sponsored by the American Cultural Expeditions of the Orient, took a job helping with the tours, and enrolled in the journalism school at Yenching University in Beijing. After graduation, he worked first for the *Peiping Chronicle* and later for the United Press. Mary Knight, who also worked for United Press, said, "I went to Paris for two weeks and stayed five years."

When the economy boomed during the Roaring Twenties, young journalists and a few veterans went abroad confident that another job and more money awaited their return. When the Depression hit and work was scarce, there was no point in hanging around at home. "Prices in Europe were down to rock bottom," wrote Albion Ross of his first trip in 1930 as an itinerant student. "In addition, Mussolini's government, for some inscrutable Fascist reason, was offering students a fantastic third-class railway ticket that took you from the Channel ports round and about through France and Italy for next to nothing." Upon returning home, Ross lucked into a slot on the *New York Evening Post* but quickly was out on the street with the great mass of unemployed. He headed to Berlin, where he got a job in the *Evening Post*'s bureau.

When world war was in the offing, would-be foreign correspondents had another reason to head overseas. Thirty-seven-year-old Robert St. John, who had worked domestically for the Chicago *Daily News* and the Associated Press, was a farmer in New Hampshire when the idea struck him. He and his wife left for Europe in 1939 with $1,005.50 in their pockets. On the day Germany invaded Poland, he wandered into the AP office in Budapest. The wire service, which had refused to send him to Europe, hired him instantly.

As far as it was away and as strong as the social conventions about a woman's place were, China was a destination for a few young ladies. Edna Lee Booker went there in the early 1920s to work for the English-language *China Press;* she arrived with credentials to represent the International News Service. Through family connections, Helen Foster secured a clerk job in the American consulate in Shanghai in 1931; on the side she wrote travel stories for the Seattle-based Scripps-Canfield League of newspapers. Later, after she married Edgar Snow (a stowaway to China), she wrote about the Chinese Communists under the pen name Nym Wales. The most daring of all was Emily Hahn, who traveled in Africa before arriving in China in 1935. Hahn wrote for Shanghai's *North-China Daily News,* became the mistress of a Chinese intellectual who had a Chinese wife and a brood of children, and acquired an opium addiction. She went on to a nearly seventy-year association with the *New Yorker.*

Root's destination, Paris, was especially enticing to young Americans, who, led by journalists, "began to roll up in waves about 1924," said an editor at the *Paris Herald.* The franc was depressed. In place of Prohibition, there was good, cheap wine plus the promise of sexual and other freedoms. "Nobody cared a damn what you did, how you dressed, or what you said," said Arnold Sevareid, who dropped his first name and picked up his middle one, Eric, around the time he found a job on the *Herald.* Paris offered aspiring novelists the tonic of culture and, when funds ran low, a job in a lower form of authorship as a reporter. "The dream of becoming a 'writer' had helped lure me to Paris," said Edmund Taylor, who ended up with the *Chicago Tribune*'s Paris newspaper. "The hope of becoming a foreign correspondent held me there."

How could a would-be correspondent possibly get a job in Paris when so many were bent on the same course? Yet they could and did, with experiences like William Shirer's. Shirer worked his way to Europe on a cattle boat after graduating from Coe College in Iowa in 1925. He fruitlessly reconnoitered American newspaper offices in Paris. The day before he was to go home, an editor at the *Paris Tribune* called him in. Apparently needing a warm body and misled about the extent of Shirer's newspaper experience, the editor hired him as a night copy editor, starting right away. At the desk next to his was James Thurber, who initially thought he could live by freelancing alone while turning out "verse, short stories, and my Great American novel." "Newspapermen returned and talked of how easy it was to get a job there," remembered Kenneth Stewart, who, thus emboldened, went to Europe with "only a one-way ticket and a little money."

In the vanguard of this diaspora was Vincent Sheean, who reached Paris on a dreary October day in 1922 and went to the *Chicago Tribune* office. "In a click of time," he said, "I became what was called a 'foreign correspondent'"—but, as it soon became clear, not one to be tied down to a single newspaper or to conventional ideas about keeping news at arm's length. He was too passionate to assume "professional indifference to the material of journalism," he wrote in *Personal History,* a book that came to define a new genre of eyewitness foreign correspondence. His motto, he noted in his private journal in 1946, was "My own job in my own way."

The years between the two world wars were a golden age for foreign correspondence. News was momentous. News outlets were plentiful. Living costs abroad were low. Americans were well liked. In no era have so many correspondents traveled so widely and so freely, many as highly independent freelancers.

Newspapers were active abroad and their reports widely available. Six newspapers besides the *Chicago Daily News* ran syndicated news services: the *New York Times,* the *New York Herald Tribune,* the *Chicago Tribune,* the *New York World,* and the *Philadelphia Public Ledger–New York Evening Post,* which had a joint service. Although the *Christian Science Monitor* did not syndicate, it circulated nationally, and the *Baltimore Sun* began to have a greater interest abroad in this period. The Associated Press and the United Press, the latter operated by Scripps Howard Newspapers, now rivaled the great European wire services. Hearst's International News Service, the Consolidated Press Association, the North American Newspaper Alliance, and other smaller services came along as well. Many of these took freelance material or contracted with reporters who took on short-term assignments.

Magazines interested in foreign affairs abounded. Many paid well even in the Depression and gave reporters plenty of room to write long reports. *Collier's,* which had been around for years, was a prime outlet. Martha Gellhorn, in Spain during the civil war in 1937, sent an article to the magazine "not expecting them to publish it." *Collier's* accepted that story and after the next one put her name on the masthead. "It began like that," said Gellhorn. "I could go where I wanted, when I wanted, and write what I saw." About the time the foreign affairs–interested *New Republic* started in 1914, the *New York Times* created *Current History* to take overflow material from its correspondents; the magazine carried on. Along the same lines as *Current History* were *Literary Digest, Review of Reviews,* and *Current Opinion.* The *Saturday Evening Post*'s reputation for conservative isolationism belied its notable range and depth. It serialized Leon Trotsky's *The Russian Revolution* and published liberal, world-minded correspondents. Robert McCormick and his cousin Joseph

Patterson started *Liberty* in 1924. Harold Ross launched the *New Yorker* a few years later. Henry Luce cofounded *Time* in 1923 and created *Life* in 1936. Both soon had rivals, *Newsweek* and *Look*. These magazines gave correspondents large national audiences. In a famous mid-1930s study of an average American community, so-called Middletown, subscribers to *Collier's, Liberty,* and the *Saturday Evening Post* accounted for more than one-third of the households.

Another vehicle for foreign news emerged with the advent of an entirely new medium, radio, which took root and then burst into flower when overseas crises erupted and the public wanted up-to-the-minute reports. By the end of the 1930s, millions of Americans had their ears turned toward their radio sets. Some print correspondents became full-time broadcasters. Others did broadcast reporting as a sideline.

Enterprising independent correspondents parlayed their work into multiple outlets. The *Saturday Evening Post* sent Vincent Sheean to Europe in 1941 with a $3,500 advance and a commitment of $2,500 more when he produced two articles, which were grist for a book he was writing. During these years, Sheean's voice could be heard from London alongside that of CBS's Edward R. Murrow.

The paradoxical place of the United States in the world also was an advantage. The country was deeply isolationist. It supported protectionist trade and opposed being drawn into overseas conflict, a sentiment reflected in the passage of the neutrality acts. America, President Calvin Coolidge declared, was not about to get embroiled with "the terrible political intrigues of Geneva," where the League of Nations limped along. In another way, however, Americans were enthusiastically internationalist, as Paul Scott Mowrer had observed in his book *Our Foreign Affairs,* "traveling or trading, for business, science, art, education, or pleasure, in every corner of the six continents and all the islands of the oceans." As counterproductive as it was for the United States to avoid taking a greater role in managing the increasingly interdependent world—a folly lamented by many correspondents—Americans were generally admired abroad precisely because America had steered clear of foreign entanglements on the scale of the great colonizing European powers. While correspondents found it increasingly difficult in the 1930s to work in places like Nazi Germany, they could expect to be welcome and were not surprised to be invited to lunch with a foreign head of state.

Another liberating factor was the strong dollar. It seemed to stretch endlessly. CBS correspondent Cecil Brown's expenses totaled only $264.73 for March 1941, when he made a trip to Belgrade from his base in Rome. That amount covered food, hotels, transportation, entertainment, and all the rest. Graham Peck, who won an around-the-world trip in an art contest sponsored by Ivory Soap after graduating from Yale, stopped in China. He lived in "Oriental luxury for as little as sixty dollars a month." In the countryside, he needed only half that much. Domestic help was so cheap in Moscow that a wire service reporter could afford to have two cooks, a butler, a secretary-interpreter, and a chauffeur.

Finally, this was a golden age because the news took on grand, urgent proportions. Fascism rose in Germany, Italy, Spain, and Japan; communism emerged in

Russia and China; the seeds of independence germinated in India and other colonized lands. The issues were sweeping, the consequences for people everywhere staggering. "The phenomenon of contemporaneity is one that has never been experienced by the world as a whole until now," Sheean wrote in the late 1930s, "and there are still many parts of the inhabited earth where events are not known until long after they have taken place; but in the alert and anxious countries of Europe and the Americas, part of Africa and Asia, the countries which make up our conscious world and are responsible for its possible courses of historic development, there is only the slightest lapse of time between an occurrence of importance and a general dissemination of the news to the innumerable varieties of minds that are prepared to receive it."

James Vincent Sheean—"Jimmy" to his friends and Vincent to the *Tribune* editors who nixed the idea of a "J.V. Sheean" byline—was born on the eve of the twentieth century, December 5, 1899, in the small south-central Illinois town of Pana. He left as soon as he could and spent the rest of his life on the move.

In his books, Sheean wrote at length about his British wife's distinguished family. He had so little to say about his own Irish Catholic parents that his two daughters did not know what their grandfather did for a living. (William Sheean's obituary in the local *Daily Palladium* says he "followed the occupation of traveling salesman, and was a manufacturer of flavoring extracts and sundries of this class.") What Vincent Sheean's children did know was that their father did not like his authoritarian, often absent father or the dogmatic Catholicism instilled in him and his three elder brothers. Other dominant features of his childhood also predicted a speedy exit from Pana: a love of reading and a vivid imagination about the world beyond. Sheean devoured German tourist magazines at the drugstore run by the Bavarian-born father of boyhood chums. He also had an aptitude for language. He was acquainted with French, German, and Italian by the time he headed to the University of Chicago.

Sheean's mother, who had been a schoolteacher and recited Shakespeare "in her deep beautiful voice," took on extra jobs to help him through college. When she died in January 1921, he was dispirited and too poor to complete his studies. For reasons Sheean never specified, he was quickly fired from a job at the *Chicago Daily News* and left for New York. For less than a year, he worked on the *New York Daily News,* the spicy tabloid financed by the *Chicago Tribune.* "When I came in possession of enough money to be off," he said of his decision to go to Europe in 1922, "I went on my way."

His initial impulse was to follow the familiar path of F. Scott Fitzgerald, Ernest Hemingway, and other budding expatriate novelists of the "Lost Generation" seeking release from puritanical, materialistic America. "In those days publishers were looking for future authors," said Malcolm Cowley in his memoir of the period, *Exile's Return,* "and the authors insisted that their books would have to be finished in France, where one could live for next to nothing." After three months in northern France, writing a never-published novel, Sheean found a spot on the *Paris Tribune*. Very quickly he became a roving correspondent in the *Tribune*'s foreign service, where he had a tutorial in world news. He covered the Separatist uprising in the Rhineland, the League of Nations Assembly in Geneva, the early days of Mussolini's fascist state in Rome, and Primo de Rivera's Spain. His Spanish dispatches led to his temporary arrest.

Sheean's biggest break came when he reported on the Riffian revolt in Morocco. The uprising against the Spanish authorities started in the north and spread south, where the French had control. Riff rebel leader Abd el-Krim was willing to talk to any correspondent who managed to make the hazardous trip across Spanish or French lines to reach him. By the time Sheean arrived in Morocco in late 1924, a *London Daily Mail* reporter had found Abd el-Krim, as had Paul Scott Mowrer, who came back with a thrilling story in which he narrowly avoided being held ransom by a group of renegades. Mowrer's trip—which the *Chicago Daily News* aggressively promoted as "Extraordinary adventures in African deserts"—may have spurred the *Tribune* to put its own reporter into action.

Donning a turban and a loose-fitting robe called a jellaba, Sheean finagled passage through the French lines. A petty tribal chief waylaid him. When orders for his release arrived from Abd el-Krim, the chief relieved Sheean of his money and other valuables. After Sheean interviewed the rebel leader, he was given a tour of Abd el-Krim's dominion. He returned to Tangier in February under a hail of Spanish bullets. Rumors that Sheean had been killed in the Riff improved the story.

Although the *Tribune* did not give Sheean's stories quite the send-up the *Daily*

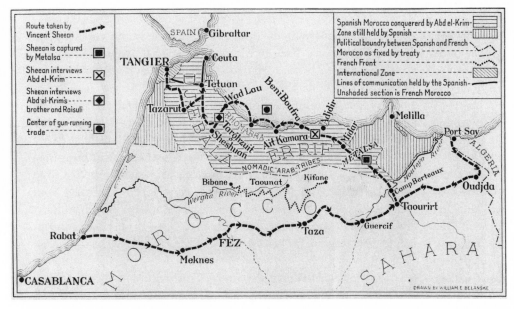

This map traces the course of Sheean's first journey into the Riff to interview rebel leader Abd el-Krim. It appeared with an article by Sheean in *Asia* magazine, September 1925.

News gave Mowrer's, they had color: "The battlefields of western Morocco are piled high with Spanish dead, which lie all along the road from Sheshuan to Tetuan, bearing evidence of the piteous, useless sacrifice." Sheean found himself cast as a latter-day Richard Harding Davis. In a memoir, William Shirer said Sheean's dispatches kindled his own dreams of being a foreign correspondent.

Sheean received typical *Tribune* treatment in Paris. Colonel McCormick took him to dinner at the Ritz to celebrate his triumph and safe return. Not long afterward, Sheean was fired. As with his earlier dismissal from the *Chicago Daily News,* the specifics are vague. Sheean said it was because a Paris boss thought he took an overlong dinner break one evening. In a letter to his cousin, Joseph Patterson, the temperamental McCormick pronounced Sheean "a liar, disloyal and dishonorable. When he was in Italy he so conducted himself as to be suspected of bad practices. I have forgotten whether he left the Foreign News Service or was fired." Next to the phrase "bad practices" McCormick penciled in the word "perverted."

The colonel may have been referring to an incident that occurred several months before the Riff adventure, when Sheean was in Rome. As colleague George Seldes told the story, Sheean reported that the pope was determined to proclaim a new dogma, the bodily assumption into heaven of the Virgin Mary, "against the opposition, open or tacit, of more than half of the Cardinals." The Assumption became doctrine some twenty-five years later. At the time it was considered heresy by faithful Chicago readers. The *Tribune* sent in Seldes to relieve their sinning reporter.

Sheean did not search for another full-time job. He returned to New York in the spring of 1925 to write his first book, *An American among the Riffi.* Displaying a lifelong characteristic, Sheean wrote in a white heat and had little interest in revision or checking proofs. By September *Asia* magazine was running a series of articles drawn from the book, which it advertised as "the first graphic, face-to-face story of the most romantic international drama now going on in the world." When the book came out, Sheean was back in Morocco on special assignment for the North American Newspaper Alliance, commonly referred to as NANA.

By now French forces, under the command of Marshal Pétain, had joined Spain's. With the conflict magnified, legions of correspondents, among them such marquee names as Floyd Gibbons and Larry Rue of the *Chicago Tribune,* Webb Miller of the United Press, and Wythe Williams, then of the *Philadelphia Public Ledger,* swooped into the country. Sheean again slipped into the Riff, suffering hostile fire nearly every day for two months, outwitting a nefarious guide who liked to finger the knife he carried, contracting malaria, and carrying back a message from Abd el-Krim. The rebel offered to have a representative meet with French authorities. (The offer was refused, and ultimately the Riffian revolt was put down. Abd el-Krim was sent into exile.) Again, Sheean's arrival in Tangier was news. This time he supposedly had been shot as a spy.

Sheean stayed on the move after his second Riff adventure: to Persia for the installation of the new Shah, Reza Pahlavi, who had knocked his predecessor off the Peacock Throne; to China, where Chiang Kai-shek's Nationalist forces consol-

Vincent Sheean was the picture of the footloose foreign correspondent. This is one of several photographs taken at the time of
his Riff adventure in the 1920s. It appeared in *Asia*.

idated their hold on the country and ousted their Communist partners; to Moscow for the tenth anniversary of the Revolution, an event marked by Stalin's arrest
of Trotsky; and to British-controlled Palestine, where in August 1929 Arabs clashed
with Jews bent on creating their own state.

NANA, which sold its service to a number of American dailies, and *Asia* used
Sheean extensively, but without monopoly. His reporting, along with short fiction
stories, appeared in the *Atlantic Monthly, Harper's, Woman's Home Companion,
Collier's, Century,* the *Saturday Evening Post, Commonweal,* and the *New Republic.*
In France between assignments, he worked for the *Paris Times,* which lacked circulation and revenue but not talented journalists. The newspaper appeared to have
correspondents everywhere, while in fact its clever staff was imagining what was
happening abroad. After work *Times* reporters joined colleagues with other Paris
newspaper allegiances for long nights of drink and talk. Shirer sometimes accompanied the handsome, six-foot-two Sheean to a little Italian restaurant. When the
customers cleared out, Sheean and the husband-and-wife owners played the piano
and sang arias far into the night. "Jimmy," Shirer thought, "seemed to have memo-
rized them all."

In between all of this roving, Sheean also wrote *The New Persia* and his first published novels—and then a memoir that transformed his notoriety into genuine fame.

Personal History, Sheean wrote in a preface to one of the many later editions of the book, "is, I suppose, a hybrid form, and is neither personal nor historical but contains elements of both." The book's skeleton was that of a familiar adventure story, a journalist on the trail of news. The difference was that Sheean did not observe like a neutral bystander called upon to testify. He was an emotional participant, searching for the meaning of what he experienced. Similarly, the autobiographical tone was deceptive. Much of his life was omitted or obscured. As intensely personal as the book was at one level, at another it was not about him at all. From its beginning (with his entrance into the University of Chicago as an uncertain small-town boy) to its end (when measuring himself against the beautiful young revolutionary Rayna Prohme, who tragically died of encephalitis after committing herself to the Communist Party), Sheean's persona was that of a self-deprecating guide. He could have been any American searching for answers to the sweeping questions of the day.

The antecedents of *Personal History* were more *The Education of Henry Adams* or Lincoln Steffens's *Autobiography,* both of which included foreign reflections, than Richard Harding Davis's *A Year from a Reporter's Notebook,* which found coronations and wars "interesting" but not life-changing. "Even if I took no part in the direct struggle by which others attempted to hasten the processes that were here seen to be inevitable in human history," Sheean wrote at the end of the book, "I had to recognize its urgency and find my place with relation to it, in the hope that whatever I did (if indeed I could do anything) would at last integrate the one existence I possess into the many in which it had been cast."

The chapter reproduced below occurs at the point when Sheean arrives in the Chinese city Hankow, one of the intensely emotional stopping places in his saga. The inland industrial city was the base for Communist operations after Chiang Kai-shek gained control over most of China and purged leftist elements from his government. Here Sheean met and fell platonically in love with Rayna Prohme and talked at length with Mikhail Borodin, an agent of the Comintern, the Soviet Union's organization for promoting revolution abroad. Borodin, who was directing the soon-to-fail Communist stand in Hankow, was "a large, calm man with the natural dignity of a lion or a panther. . . . As I knew him better I perceived—or, rather, he showed me—how his political philosophy made breadth and elevation inevitable in the mind that understood it."

I was not, to begin with, a "sympathizer" in Hankow. It was part of the middle-class dilettante view of life that I had half adopted, to accept experience of this kind much as the translated experiences of art (a play or a poem) are accepted, and to value them, what is more, as separate parts of a continuous process of education. To the dilettante the Chinese Revolution might have been of interest as an exciting spectacle, like a new ballet of Diaghilev's, and of value as a contribution to his own education, like the acquirement of a new language. By 1927, after constant exposure to the atmosphere of London and Paris, such ways of receiving experience, although not natural to me, had ceased to be altogether alien, and it was in some such frame of mind as that of your plain seeker-after curiosity that I first went to Hankow.

To Hankow, then, I brought the mind and character of an American bourgeois, twenty-seven years old, who had divided his adult years between the subjects to which this book has been chiefly devoted—living history of the time—and the preoccupations of personal taste. In these preoccupations, which had assumed greater importance in the last two years, influences of a powerful order had deflected what must originally have been a nature of considerable vigour and simplicity into channels where it was not wholly at ease. The character of the American bourgeois—let us call him Mr X—had been tinged with the colour of his surroundings, had taken on some of the flavour of Paris and London, and disengaged, no doubt, a light aroma of decay. The American character is not made to withstand, over long periods of time, the influence of older cultures in their self-conscious forms. Our Mr X was almost—and could in time have become—a dilettante. That is, he already possessed by nature, and had fertilized by experience, those tastes by which a man could live through sensation alone. Books, pictures, music and the satisfaction of physical appetites constituted this world of sensation, and although it had always existed in some degree for our Mr X—as it exists for everybody—it had only recently shown signs of taking over the whole of his life.

He was preserved, then and afterwards, from this fate. Aside from any possible reasons that might be sought in deeper regions of the personality, he was preserved by two rather obvious circumstances. The first was that he had no money at all except what he could earn. The second was that, independently of the first, he wanted (why, God knows) to "write"—that is, to put into words whatever he could learn about the mysterious transaction of living. His attitude towards work was neither consistent nor serious; he was capable of writing the most undisguised piffle to make money when he needed it; but he did possess, at the core, a determination to do some little work of which he need not be ashamed before he was finished. These two circumstances fought against the world of sensation at every point. A man who has to earn his living cannot spend his whole time, or even much of it, in pursuit of the experiences in art and life that might yield sensation; and a man who wants to do good work at some time or other can only learn how to do it by working.

The second circumstance was the really powerful combatant. Money, in the world in which Mr X lived, could be come by in various ways. For instance, it was not wholly impossible (however unlikely) that somebody might die and leave him a million dollars. But even with a million dollars in pocket and all the pleasures of the world at hand for the taking, he would still have been harassed by the thought that his time, the most precious and the most precarious of his possessions, evaporated with terrifying speed; that he had done nothing with it, was doing nothing with it; and that he must learn how to light the light before darkness descended.

Mr X was thus, through no effort of his own, and indeed almost automatically, protected against the worst results of his own laziness and self-indulgence. But he was lazy and self-indulgent, just the same. He preferred the line of least resistance, avoided conclusions that might be troublesome to himself, and was tending, more and more, to treat the whole of the visible universe as a catering firm employed in his service. The mind he directed upon people and things in China, and upon the whole drama of revolution, had been originally a good one, acquisitive, perceptive, and retentive, but it was softened and discoloured beneath later influences, which constantly suggested that fundamental questions were not worth bothering about. The shock of general reality was what he needed, and he was about to receive it—a seismic disturbance of greater intensity and duration than he would have believed possible a few months before.

So much for Mr X.

Personal History appeared in early 1935. The timing could not have been better. The questions Sheean raised were on the minds of an uneasy American public. The Great Depression brought doubts about capitalism. Fascism was a growing menace. In an essay in the *Saturday Review of Literature,* editor Henry Seidel Canby perused popular new books for clues to the public's frame of mind. "I believe it to be fear," he concluded, "although fear is too strong a word for its quiet margins, and panic would better describe some of its hurrying tides. . . . Sometimes the unrest which spreads through a book is a reflection of the author's belief that democracy is bankrupt; sometimes jubilantly or fearfully he hails the rise of the proletariat, or the reappearance of the strong arm and submission to the state." Of the books by journalists that resonated with these sentiments, Canby singled out *Personal History* as the exemplar.

Critics everywhere agreed. "A remarkable achievement in synthesis," said the *New York Times;* Sheean was "something of a landmark, and somebody that even those who disagree with him rather vigorously on the subject of communism or Zionism will have to take account of." Mary McCarthy, known for her acid-tongued reviews in the *Nation* and elsewhere, pronounced Sheean "a human being of extraordinary taste and sensibility, who throughout fifteen years of turbulent experience has been primarily interested in moral values." Malcolm Cowley reviewed *Personal History* in the *New Republic,* where he was literary editor: "To me the most impressive feature of the story is that besides being an extraordinarily interesting personal document it is also, by strict standards, a work of art . . . [T]his autobiography, with a few names changed to give it the appearance of fiction, would certainly rank among the good novels of this decade."

Personal History was the fourth-best-selling nonfiction book the year it appeared, according to *Publishers Weekly,* which kept the most authoritative list at the time. It was a selection of the Literary Guild, one of the two major book clubs. When the National Book Awards were inaugurated in 1935, *Personal History* won in the biography category. The acclaim continued. In the 1940s it appeared in a Modern Library edition. Years later, when it was less well remembered, it was discussed in the *New Yorker* as a "classic of intelligent and involved reporting." "There has never been a better book about what journalism is really like and what it should be when it is very, very good," commented a *Life* magazine critic of a 1969 reissue of *Personal History.*

For decades correspondents had written colorful books about chasing news or dry tomes analyzing foreign affairs. None brought together such a volume of intellectual adventure abroad as Sheean did at that pregnant moment in world affairs. Those earlier books were candles compared to *Personal History*'s beacon scanning a world careening toward war. "Sheean established, as had nobody before him, that what counts is what a reporter thinks," observed fellow correspondent Kenneth Stewart, noting the many books that followed as "extensions and refinements" of Sheean's. "I should guess that no book published in our time had a greater direct response from the working press itself or gave the public better insight into a newspaperman's mind." *Personal History,* said Canby in his *Saturday Review of Literature* essay on 1930s books, was the "type book" of a new genre trying "to break through the crust of the news to see what lies underneath."

In 1936, the year after *Personal History* appeared, three memoirs by foreign correspondents made it to the *New York Times* best-seller list and showed up on *Publishers Weekly*'s list of the ten most successful nonfiction books of the year. One was by the *New York Times*' Walter Duranty, the doyen of the Moscow correspondents. Duranty recounted his experiences, particularly in Russia, in *I Write as I Please.* Reviewers made comparisons to Sheean, one noting that the book was "full of adventure, of hairbreadth escapes, of drama and tragedy—enough for a dozen novels." The author of the second was Negley Farson, a gifted writer whom colleagues on the *Chicago Daily News* called a combination of "Childe Harold and Captain from Castile." In early 1935, when he was chief of the paper's London bureau, Colonel Knox recalled him, in the belief that he was no longer a "detached American observer and commentator." Farson quit instead and went to Dalmatia to write about his adventures in *The Way of the Transgressor.* His replacement in London was John Gunther, another young man who went abroad as a hand on a cattle boat. Having been used as a fill-in at several *Daily News* bureaus in Europe, Gunther acquired a good feel for those countries. When he arrived in London, he was in the final stages of writing a book on contemporary Europe applying that knowledge. A few months after his book, *Inside Europe,* appeared, Gunther left the *Daily News* for a life of freelance reporting and book writing.

In the books that piled up in the wake of *Personal History,* the book remained *sui generis.* None matched Sheean's intensively emotional style or his literary talent. "No other American correspondent of this century (if ever?) has sustainably produced such peerless evocations in English," his colleague Leland Stowe reminisced at the end of his long career. "He writes like a God." But Sheean's patrimony could be seen even in impersonal books that took on weighty subjects, as did Marquis W. Childs's scholarly *Sweden: The Middle Way.* The dry volume on the success of the Swedes' mixed economy "through the grim years of the depression" appeared on the *New York Times* best-seller list in 1936.

The list of titles that nodded, one way or another, to Sheean during the next decade into World War II would be stupefying if it weren't full of so many good books: Mary Knight, *On My Own* (she "joined the parade," as one reviewer put it, after Sheean "set so many worn portable typewriters clacking"); John T. Whitaker, *And Fear Came* ("Mr. Sheean, Mr. Duranty, and now Mr. Whitaker," said John Gunther in a review of the book); William Henry Chamberlin, *The Confessions of an Individualist;* United Press's Webb Miller, *I Found No Peace: The Journal of a Foreign Correspondent* (the dust jacket proclaimed, "Like Vincent Sheean's *Personal History,* another absorbing biographical record of an American newspaper correspondent"); Carleton Beals, *Glass Houses: Ten Years of Freelancing* and a sequel, *The Great Circle: Further Adventures in Freelancing;* Pierre van Paasen, *Days of Our Years* ("only Vincent Sheean's prose," said one reviewer, approached this 1939 memoir by the Dutch-born roving correspondent for the *New York Evening World*); Robert St. John, *Foreign Correspondent;* Quentin Reynolds, *A London Diary;* Howard K. Smith, *Last Train from Berlin;* Cecil Brown, *Suez to Singapore;* Larry Lesueur, *12 Months That Changed the World;* Louis Fischer, *Men and Politics: An Autobiography;* William L. Shirer, *Berlin Diary* (the number one nonfiction best seller in 1941); Richard Tregaskis, *Guadalcanal Diary* and *Invasion Diary* (both best sellers); Paul Scott Mowrer, *House of Europe;* and Eric Sevareid, *Not So Wild a Dream* (a best seller written at the end of the war). In 1938 the *New York Times* published *We Saw It Happen,* a collection of first-person accounts by its reporters, which Stewart considered ungenerous in not mentioning its obvious connection to *Personal History.*

And the books kept coming after the war. Negley Farson made a career out of personal history books, producing, among others, *Transgressor in the Tropics, Caucasian Journey,* and *A Mirror for Narcissus.* Shirer followed *Berlin Diary* with *Midcentury Journey* and the three-volume *Twentieth Century Journey.* Others used the technique more sparingly, but often effectively: Herbert L. Matthews, *The Education of a Correspondent;* Edgar Snow, *Journey to the Beginning: A Personal View of Contemporary History;* Albion Ross, *Journey of an American* (worth much more attention than it gets); Edgar Ansel Mowrer, *Triumph and Turmoil: A Personal History of Our Time* (an exception to the good-book rule); Harrison Salisbury, *A Journey for Our Times* and *A Time of Change: A Reporter's Tale of Our Time;* Theodore White, *In Search of History* (the title was the title of the British edition of Sheean's *Personal History;* White's subtitle was *A Personal Adventure*).

"It has now been 30 years or more since Vincent Sheean wrote his *Personal History,*" commented *Saturday Review of Literature* editor Norman Cousins when reviewing one of Shirer's books in 1977. "Many of the foreign correspondents have tried to convey the same sense of an intimate, interactive relationship with events and people that gave such luster to Sheean's book."

Vincent Sheean, John Gunther acknowledged, "is the father of us all."

Toward the end of the war, Eric Sevareid was with British commando troops outside of Wesel. "I say there, correspondent," a Cockney sentry said, "ye wouldn't be Mister Vincent Sheean by off chance, would ye?" Sevareid set him straight. "I read his book," the sentry said. Sheean, Sevareid thought, "was the golden boy."

By the mid-1930s, Sheean was no longer a mere journalist seeking out the famous. He was famous. *Personal History* was required reading in a freshman English class at Dartmouth. Young people read the book and decided they, too, wanted to be foreign correspondents. Sheean could be found weekending at Long Barn, the country place of diplomat Harold Nicolson and his literary wife Vita Sackville-West, whom he first met in Persia; at the Connecticut home of Henry Luce; or at Albert Einstein's house in Princeton. He became a permanent guest at Twin Farms, the Vermont retreat of journalist Dorothy Thompson and her novelist husband, Sinclair Lewis. The couple gave Sheean and his family use of the "old house" on the property, which he decided to buy until financial troubles forced him to stop making payments and reverted him back to the visitor mode. At Twin Farms he became friends with presidential aspirant Wendell Willkie.

Sheean's marriage to Diana Forbes-Robertson in 1935 broadened his contacts still further. Dinah, as she was familiarly called, was the daughter of distinguished actor and theater manager Sir Johnston Forbes-Robertson. Sheean struck up his friendship with George Bernard Shaw at Sir Johnston's Bedford Square home in London. Dinah's mother, an American by birth, had an actress sister, Maxine Elliott, whom Sheean called "the most famous of American beauties." The Sheeans were regular guests at her coastal summer Château de l'Horizon, not far from Cannes. There he mixed with the duke and duchess of Windsor, other lords and ladies, and another frequent guest, prime-minister-to-be Winston Churchill. Aunt Maxine pressed *Personal History* on Churchill. Sheean's British publisher, Hamish Hamilton, was for a time an in-law.

Sheean also became an object of attention in Hollywood. Producer Walter Wanger purchased the film rights to *Personal History* for ten thousand dollars in 1936. Wanger, who became interested in films while working in World War I propaganda, wanted to do a movie that highlighted the political crisis in Europe. After overcoming investor resistance to a film that might undermine U.S. neutrality, he arranged for Alfred Hitchcock to direct. At one time or another more than a dozen writers worked on the script, which was constantly revised to keep up with events in Europe. The last, already-filmed final scene was rewritten when it was clear that Nazis were about to begin bombing England. When the movie finally appeared in 1940, the title had been changed from *Personal History* to *Foreign Correspondent*, and events depicted in the story had no resemblance to Sheean's *Personal History* experiences. The hero correspondent Johnny Jones, played by Joel McCrea, was far more naïve than Sheean had been—although as happened with Sheean, Jones's editors fashioned a byline, Huntley Haverstock, to impress readers. Still, the broader theme—the independent journalist willing to take sides in a conflict between good and evil—was pure Sheean. The movie was nominated for an Academy Award for Best Picture.

Sheean took advantage of the interest in him to expand beyond journalism. He wrote more novels. He translated Eve Curie's biography of her mother, *Madame Curie,* from French to English; it hit the best-seller lists in 1938. His Italian-to-English translation of Benedetto Croce's *Germany and Europe: A Spiritual Dissension* appeared in 1944. He wrote a play, *An International Incident,* for actress Ethel Barrymore. It drew from his experiences. In it a young reporter (one supposes Sheean) tries to make a distinguished English lady of American birth (Aunt Maxine?) socially conscious. "It is not much better than a first play by anybody else," *Time* noted. Unlike most flops by first-time playwrights, however, a number of publications besides *Time* paid attention to it, and Sheean wrote a story about his playwright experience for the *New York Times.* Meanwhile, his journalism appeared in an ever-widening circle of magazines—the highbrow *Virginia Quarterly Review,* the liberal *Nation,* and the middlebrow *Reader's Digest.* In 1940, the year *An International Incident* appeared briefly on stage, his writing, royalties, and lecturing brought in thirty-eight thousand dollars—equivalent to nearly six hundred thousand dollars in 2008.

The genesis of his relationship with the *Herald Tribune* illustrated how far Sheean's reputation and blue-ribbon contacts took him. At a party of arts and letters glitterati in New York in 1938, he told Dorothy Thompson he wanted to cover the Spanish civil war. "You must go for the Herald *Tribune,*" declared Thompson, who was a columnist for the newspaper. Although it was the middle of the night, she called Helen Reid, the wife of the publisher and a force at the newspaper, which she officially ran after her husband's death. Reid agreed to meet Sheean the following day. Thus began his long freelance association with the leading Republican newspaper in the country. With other assignments for NANA, whose reports were published in the *New York Times* and elsewhere, and with magazine work and radio broadcasts, Sheean reached millions of Americans.

Able to write his own ticket, Sheean thrust himself into some of the most dramatic moments of news during the period. Besides covering the civil war in Spain, Sheean was in Austria after the *Anschluss,* when Jews were violently persecuted; in Czechoslovakia when France and Great Britain acquiesced in Hitler's demands for the Sudetenland; in London during the blitz; in Chungking, where the nationalists had retreated from Japanese aggression. He no longer wore Arab garb or crept past sentries, but there was danger just the same. In Spain he, Herbert Matthews of the *New York Times,* and photographer Robert Capa continually hurled themselves to the ground as shells landed only a few yards away.

From these experiences, Sheean produced three more in-search-of books. He wanted to entitle them *Personal History II, III,* and *IV,* but they ended up as *Not*

Peace but a Sword (1939), *Between the Thunder and the Sun* (1943), and *This House against This House* (1946). Sequels rarely measure up to the fresh spontaneity of the original. Critic Malcolm Cowley, who had so lavishly praised *Personal History,* wondered if Sheean fit the story in *Between the Thunder and the Sun* to his personal history literary style, rather than the other way round. Also, with so many foreign correspondents writing books, the novelty had worn off. Yet Sheean's three books had much to commend them, which was what critics generally did. In addition to the urgency with which he pointed to global threats to peace, Sheean brought to the books his literary power. It was displayed in his discursive, evocative descriptions, some of them not centered at all on the places where news was made, but where it was ignored by those who would not face the reality of imminent war. Edmund Wilson, who had initially dismissed Sheean as just another journalistic scribbler, called attention to his "special Irish facility for seeing people in their most human, and sometimes in their comic aspects, and yet making them walk the earth like the creatures of heroic legend."

Between the Thunder and the Sun, which made it to the *New York Times* best-seller list, ended with the Japanese attack on Pearl Harbor. By this time Sheean had come to see journalism, as he wrote in the book, "a petty thing to do in comparison to the effort of those who fought, or the suffering of those who were driven into exile." While gathering material for the book, he may have contributed to a little behind-the-scenes work for the U.S. government—or so recalled F. McCracken Fisher, a United Press correspondent in wartime China. When Edgar Mowrer landed in Chungking on his intelligence-gathering trip for U.S. intelligence chief William Donovan in 1941, he and Sheean took Fisher for a ride in the U.S. naval attaché's car and talked him into heading the government information and propaganda program in China if the United States entered the war.

Twelve days after the Japanese attack on Pearl Harbor, Fisher was sworn into service. Mowrer joined the Office of War Information. For his part, Sheean tossed aside journalism and took a captain's commission in the intelligence branch of the Army Air Corps, an ideal assignment for someone with his language ability and analytical powers. He served in North Africa, Italy, India, and China.

Sheean started out enthusiastically. For Gen. John Cannon, his commander, "I was quite ready to do any job that might be considered useful." Inevitably, though, his independence of mind took over. He was especially angry that the Allies installed Fascist leaders in Italian government positions, a policy Sheean considered "a contradiction of what I had conceived to be the meaning of the war." He secured early discharge (he was a lieutenant colonel by this time) at the end of 1944 and returned to foreign correspondence.

When Sheean got himself in trouble over his 1924 Virgin Mary story, his replacement, George Seldes, arrived to find his *Chicago Tribune* colleague "celebrating his recall with splashing of champagne and a round of dance amidst upset furniture, a score of guests tearing dozens of roses to pieces and throwing the petals into the air." A reveler stuffed some of Sheean's shirts and fine crystal into a suitcase and jumped up and down on the bag to make it all fit.

Everyone who knew Sheean had a story like that to tell. "Sheean is perhaps the most remarkable American of my generation I know," John Gunther wrote in 1937. "I met him when we were both at the University of Chicago. He was bizarre in those days. He hummed Mozart, wore green pants, and spoke better Italian than the Italian professors." "Nobody could call him tranquil," said his daughter Ellen. He drove cars the way he wrote, like the wind. During a Vermont drought, Sheean enlisted his daughters and others in the neighborhood for a Hopi rain dance. A deluge followed. He and "Protestant sister" Dorothy Thompson could carry on through the night discussing politics, reciting poetry, and drinking. "I could work at night after dinner," he noted in his diary in 1946, "but I always go to Dorothy's instead. And argue hotly. And drink."

Sheean called himself "a socialist materialist." He traipsed around for days in sloppy clothes and then all of a sudden dressed like a dandy. He liked champagne and enjoyed having crisp bills in his wallet but was ashamed about living comfortably and was casual about material possessions. Once, when checking into the London airport, Sheean could not pay the excess baggage charges for the pile of luggage he had brought along. He was not about to leave behind either of his two typewriters (he was forever breaking them), and he wanted his books. That left the clothes. Lady Diana Cooper, a friend who had come to see him off, began to hand out the garments to people waiting in line.

Sheean's emotions occasionally spun out of control. Sheean wept and drank disconsolately when Rayna Prohme died. In *Personal History,* he described imaginary conversations with her. These may have seemed to readers like a literary device. To friends, they were real. "I see her, Bernie," Sheean blurted out to his *Paris Times* colleague Hillel Bernstein, while they sat drinking in a bistro. "There she is. There's Rayna." Sheean conversed with her while Bernstein looked on.

This emotional fragility expressed itself in his ambivalence about journalism. In Palestine in 1929, when the Jewish-Arab confrontation led to more than two hundred deaths, Sheean "could not go on. My nerves had fallen to pieces altogether, so that I could not hit the right keys on the typewriter and indeed could scarcely pick up a pencil. I had seen too many dead and wounded Arabs being carried silently through the street in front of the Hospice [where he lodged]; my ears were ringing with the sounds I had heard in the Jewish hospitals." He did not get out of bed for four days and swore he would never again send a news cablegram. The pattern was repeated in 1938, when Sheean was covering Czechoslovakia for NANA and the Germans occupied the Sudetenland in the western part of the country. Hitler's triumphal speech at Carlsbad made him "so sick and weary and angry that I was incapable of writing a story fit to be printed in a newspaper. I fixed on Carlsbad as the last occasion on which I could bear to cable, telephone or otherwise communicate anything about the horror of this vivisection while it was still going on."

Sheean had experienced a particularly serious breakdown in Ireland two years before. It coincided with the outbreak of the Spanish civil war, although that was not the only thing on his mind. A new responsibility was thrust upon him when his wife gave birth to their first child. He was disappointed that his novels weren't more successful. There was drinking. He may have felt guilty about living in a grand house in a country where his ancestors had lived humbly. Perhaps, too, the setting forced him to reflect on his Catholic upbringing, which he carried around like a weight. In a particularly unpleasant moment, Sheean descended a staircase wielding a knife. "I have come down to save you," he said. News of his breakdown appeared in the *New York Times,* which reported that a "bad infection" complicated his condition. Sheean was flown to a hospital on Lake Geneva for several months of rest. He finished recuperating at St. Germain outside Paris. Ernest Hemingway visited Sheean at St. Germain en route to reporting on the Spanish civil war. NANA was paying him more than a dollar a word, which *Newsweek* described as record-breaking for a newspaper war correspondent. Hemingway told Sheean not to worry about staying behind, "I'll go to Spain for you." Fuming because he was not near the action, Sheean drank too much and had a relapse.

Although a fallen-away Catholic, Sheean was a believer, as he told a friend, "in heroes, saints, and prophets"—or wanted to be. He saw UFOs and was surprised when others did not. "People never do look up," he told Dorothy Thompson. When his Hopi rain dance exceeded his expectations, he called Vermont authorities to apologize. Sheean's search for something to replace the Catholicism he had lost drew him to Rayna Prohme and Mikhail Borodin in China and to others with life-defining convictions. "I could have stayed on with Abd el-Krim almost indefinitely," he said. The rebel's singleness of purpose "was a proof of greatness."

Unfulfilled longing for a Messiah was the theme of Sheean's 1933 novel *The Tide.* A female reporter named Ann Howard decides to quit her job and become a follower of Menachem Honotzri, a latter-day prophet with mystical powers who is visiting the United States. In the end she returns to journalism. As much as she wanted to stay in the prophet's retinue, which was returning with him to the Middle East, she confessed, "I'd have been a fish out of water." "Mr. Sheean," said a reviewer of *Personal History,* "went through that process of rebirth, of being 'saved,' which can be brought about in all sorts of ways outside those of what ordinarily is known as religion."

Sheean's friends found his wild imaginings entertaining and eerie. "If some people really are psychic," Eric Sevareid said, "Sheean was." Sevareid recalled the day the conversation at John Gunther's apartment turned to Sinclair Lewis, known to his friends as Red. "Sheean looked grave. No, he said, Red Lewis is dead. Only hours later the news came from Rome." Sheean turned from being "bright, sober and catty" to "violently sick" during a party in Italy at the very moment Gunther, back in the United States, died in 1970. Dinah Sheean described the event as another one of her husband's "queer things of prescience."

Although Gunther and Sheean obviously had a little fun in an interview Gunther did of his friend for the *New York Herald Tribune,* the back and forth captured Sheean's personal, mystical approach to religion.

JG: Are you a Christian?

SHEEAN: No.

JG: Are you an atheist?

SHEEAN: No.

JG: Are you an agnostic?

SHEEAN: Yes, but much more religious than most agnostics . . . .

JG: Are you a socialist?

SHEEAN: Of course! In my own way.

JG: Do you believe that there is any life in the hereafter?

SHEEAN: I *hope* not!

JG: Have you ever feared it?

SHEEAN (pensive): I would welcome it, but not do anything to bring it about.
I have taken every possible risk, but nothing has ever happened to me. I
can walk through a swarm of bees. They will not touch me. They are my
brothers.

Sheean's emotional state was especially precarious after World War II. Money
problems mounted to serious proportions. He owed $16,000 in back taxes. One
month he received a single check for a mere $46. He became disillusioned over the
United Nations, which had not brought comity between superpowers, and worried
about nuclear conflagration. When the very Catholic Clare Boothe Luce invited him
to go to a Christmas Eve mass, he begged off. Clare could not possibly appreciate,
he said, "that one midnight mass might produce a month's turmoil." Drinking, as
he said of an evening with Dorothy Parker, was one of his "main occupations." His
benders became grim. After a party, Gunther, novelist Erich Remarque, a British
Labor M.P., and Sheean carried on drinking. When the others went home, Sheean
visited a speakeasy. "When I awoke Friday," he noted in his diary, "I had no money
at all and no wallet. And, of course, no memory at all of what had happened."

Making matters worse, Sheean did not have his wife to nurse him, as she had in
the past. Their marriage broke down during the war, and they divorced. Dinah was
attracted to his "charm and gaiety and intellectual fascination" but found little ten-
der love. Puritanical about women, Sheean's passions were mostly for ideas, and he
was patronizingly domineering of his much younger wife. While in the military in
1943, he was horrified to get word that she might have a small role on stage. How, he
lectured, could she take part in the "semi-brothel conditions of musical comedy"
while he was fighting fascism? Breaking free, Dinah worked for Donovan's Office
of Strategic Services (OSS), wrote her own books, and sought love elsewhere.

In this agitated state of mind, Sheean made his greatest prediction of all. He announced to Dorothy Thompson in September 1947 that he was leaving for India,
which had just achieved independence from Great Britain. "I am at the end of my
tether in search for meaning of life. I feel I shall find it through Gandhi. But the
time is short, for Gandhi is going to be assassinated within six months and by a
Hindu. You don't know that, do you?" He went to his old friend William Shirer
with the same message. Shirer had covered Gandhi, and Sheean asked for a letter

of introduction. He made the same prediction to the editor of *Holiday* magazine, a new periodical that was far more serious than its name suggested. In addition to its travel and tourism fare, it commissioned big-name novelists and journalists to tackle big themes, some of them political. In mid-November Sheean left for India with *Holiday* credentials in his pocket.

Sheean's premonitions of impending catastrophe did not deter him from indulging his life-long peripatetic inclinations. He stopped in Paris, Prague, Vienna (for the music), and Cairo. His resolution to purify himself for Gandhi by giving up smoking was conveniently forgotten. He reached Pakistan, puffing away, the day after Christmas and decided to hang around to learn more about the country, which had been hived off from India and was wracked by horrendous communal violence. While in Karachi, he met a fellow journalist, Serge Fliegers, in the Palace Hotel. It was midday, and Sheean was drinking Singapore Slings. After lunch they hurried to the scene of a melee between Muslims and Sikhs. They had to lie in a deep gutter to avoid flying stones. After another meal and more drinking (they found champagne in a shop that had escaped being wrecked by rioters), Sheean arranged for them to go to a hashish parlor. Sheean passed out, and Fliegers lugged him to a taxi. The next morning Sheean banged on Fliegers's door, brimming with enthusiasm for the next leg of his trip to India and Gandhi. Fliegers suggested they first go to the bar for "a hair of the dog that bit us." "Liquor!" responded Sheean indignantly. "What would the Master think of me if I came to him with the smell of liquor on my breath!"

Writing in his diary on January 14, Sheean chided himself for having dawdled: "Considering the strength of my premonition about this whole thing, I should have followed my instinct." The following day he was in New Delhi. To get his bearings, he dined with his old friend Edgar Snow, who was covering Indian independence for the *Saturday Evening Post*. Jimmy, Snow wrote in his diary, was "on the edge of getting religion and wants to join Gandhi's *ashram*." Nevertheless, they went sightseeing and ended up "singing Italian songs at the piano until all hours."

Sheean first saw Gandhi at his Birla House residence in New Delhi on January 21. He stood at the back of the crowd at evening prayers. On the 27th, with the help of Jawaharlal Nehru, he met the Mahatma. Gandhi invited him back: "You can move into the house if you like." Sheean returned for a second conversation the next day and traveled out of town with Nehru on the 29th. The next day he attended prayers in anticipation of speaking to Gandhi afterward. While Sheean stood a few paces away, a fanatic Hindu fatally shot the diminutive leader.

Sheean leaned against the wall, doubled over, in a semidazed state. He felt stinging in his right hand; blisters appeared on his third and fourth fingers. At the time he apparently regarded them as stigmata. He later described this reaction as psychosomatic. Sheean wandered in the garden for about an hour and a half, passages from the Bible and Shakespeare floating through his mind. "I've lost my only *guru*," he told Snow, who hurried over to Birla House.

Sheean retreated to his room. The next day Margaret Parton with the *Herald Tribune* forced him to get out of bed to write something for the newspaper. She reduced it to cablegram form. The article, which he wrote with "such pain and suffering," recounted his reaction to the assassination: "The sacred drama which came to an end Friday night toward sunset in a garden in Delhi will be subject to cogitation for the Western man for whatever period he continues to exist." Far more personal than reportorial, it was not the sort of story a newspaper normally ran. But Sheean's stature was such that it appeared on the front page.

His subsequent book, *Lead, Kindly Light,* took its name from a Christian hymn Gandhi liked. Subtitled *Gandhi and the Way to Peace,* it carried Sheean further than ever beyond normal reporting. His experiences took up less than one-fourth of the book. The rest explored Gandhi's life and spiritual beliefs, often in highly technical terms. One appendix was titled "Caste, Karma, and Darshan."

Lead, Kindly Light, a Book-of-the-Month Club selection in 1949, was Sheean's last hurrah as a personal historian of world affairs. America and foreign correspondence were changing.

After World War II, young Americans still struck out on their own to go abroad and became correspondents. Jonathan Schell went to Vietnam in 1966 about as casually as Sheean had gone to Paris. With a little help from resident journalists, he acquired press credentials on the preposterous claim that he represented his alma mater's student newspaper, the *Harvard Crimson.* Schell accompanied reporters covering the largest undertaking in the war up to that time, Operation Cedar Falls, designed to pacify the troublesome Iron Triangle region. "Up to a few months ago, Ben Suc was a prosperous village of some thirty-five hundred people," he began his lengthy report. At the end of the account, which painted a bleaker picture of the war than was common at the time, he described how the military completed its obliteration of Ben Suc with bulldozers. "I wasn't writing for anyone but myself," Schell said of the article, which appeared in the *New Yorker* (and later as a book) and resulted in his joining the magazine full-time.

Correspondents were still colorful characters, none more so than the drug-fortified Hunter Thompson. In 1959 Thompson went to work for a Puerto Rican magazine with a special interest in bowling. Later he wandered around South America, sending freelance articles to the *National Observer,* a short-lived but highly literate weekly newspaper published by Dow Jones. He covered the end of the Vietnam War for *Rolling Stone.* Thompson's assignments, wrote an appreciative critic of the Gonzo journalist, "always became quests." His writing, said Tom Wolfe, was "part journalism and part personal memoir admixed with powers of wild invention and wilder rhetoric."

Although a few people like Schell and Thompson sprouted from time to time, however, the soil of modern journalism had fewer nutrients to sustain correspondents who wanted to do their own job in their own way. Significantly, for both Schell and Thompson, foreign correspondence marked phases in their careers, not the career itself. "Rio was the end of the foreign correspondent tour," Thompson wrote after a year in South America. "I found myself at the point where I was twenty-five years old and wearing a white suit and rolling dice at the Domino Club—the foreign correspondents' club—and here I thought, 'Jesus Christ, what am I going to do now?'" Thompson's zaniness outstripped Sheean's, without in any way matching the elder correspondent's depth or sense of responsibility.

In a search for explanations for this change, Thompson's "what am I going to do now?" is a good place to start. Correspondents in Sheean's time rarely asked that question in Thompson's nihilistic way. As frustrated as many were by American reluctance to act globally, this gave them a mission: their job was to awaken their country to a world beset by evil and to the possibilities for redemption. Furthermore, admiration abroad for the United States and its democratic values gave correspondents confidence in their pursuits as well as entrée to peoples abroad.

That is not so any longer. When Sheean wanted to get in and out of the Riff, he had to slip by Spanish and French sentries. Today, the American military, with some seven hundred overseas installations, stands guard around the world. When Sheean visited Teheran in the mid-1920s, he found a handful of American advisers helping the shah manage his empire. The advisers stood largely apart from the British and the Russians; their work, Sheean said, "can only be admired." Since then Iran, as Persia is now called, has tacked in a different direction. Whereas it once issued a postage stamp honoring "Eleanor Roosevelt defender of Human Rights," Iran followed its 1979 revolution with stamps commemorating the takeover of the U.S. embassy and the failed American military attempt to rescue American hostages. One of those stamps showed a dead American serviceman splayed on the ground in front of a downed helicopter.

"Anti-Americanism is on the rise throughout the world," the Council on Foreign Relations noted in 2003. This was "unlikely to change anytime soon in much of the world," a study of international attitudes noted around the same time. American youngsters no longer grow up, as Sheean said he did in Illinois, believing that their citizenship "was a kind of insurance against misfortune." Once representing a solution in the minds of many peoples, Americans became the problem. "Now when we go out," said *Washington Post* correspondent Molly Moore in 2008, people "wouldn't want to talk to us. They would want to kidnap us."

While all this has transpired, other changes have combined to make it more difficult to be an independent foreign correspondent such as Sheean was. One of these is the dearth of mainstream media outlets eager for foreign news. The *New Yorker* continues to make effective use of the "letter from" format and other personal reporting by talented journalists. "My approach to the problems of foreign correspondence," said William Finnegan, a member of the staff, "has leaned heavily on the analysis of my own preconceptions as a way to communicate something about difference in culture and experience." But *Asia*, the *Saturday Review of Literature*, *Woman's Home Companion*, *Holiday*, and the *Saturday Evening Post*—magazines that paid Sheean well and gave him space to write at length—have disappeared along with *Collier's*, *Liberty*, the *Literary Digest*, *Look*, and *Life*. NANA succumbed as did the Consolidated Press. The International News Service and the United Press joined forces in 1958 to become United Press International, which has weakened to the point of insignificance.

"I was indeed lucky in having a platform," said Eric Sevareid, who had written for magazines, in 1977. "I often wonder what in the world I would do were I a free lance writer these days. Not only have the big general magazines vanished but those that remain pay no more for words than they did twenty or thirty years ago." The *New Yorker* and a few other magazines that continue to pay well are exceptional. Just before it died in 1969, the *Saturday Evening Post* averaged $2,500 for a lengthy article, less than it paid Sheean in *nominal* dollars in 1941. When the magazine came back briefly in an abbreviated nine-times-a-year version in the 1970s, its top rate was $1,000. Freelance newspaper correspondents have fared accordingly. Referring to the $200-per-story payment she received in the mid-1990s, the part-time Paris correspondent for the *San Francisco Chronicle* called her reporting "charity." "In real dollars," the National Writers Union reported in 2002, "freelance rates have declined by more than 50 percent since the 1960s."

Economics work against journalistic independence in other ways. The cost of living abroad has increased as countries have developed, and food and lodging have become even more dear as the value of the dollar has declined. The attraction of a full-time job is now much more powerful because of the need for benefits. In Sheean's day, health insurance wasn't a concern. In 1940, less than 10 percent of Americans were covered by some sort of health plan. Fifty years later, with the costs of health care escalating, only 14 percent of Americans did *not* have health coverage—and 71 percent of those who did acquired their insurance through an employer. "There's probably a limit to how long I'll be interested in coming to places like Iraq," said Charles Crain, a freelancer for Cox News Service, in mid-2004. "There's also a part of me that wants to have a normal life; an apartment in a cool American city, a job with health benefits, and the rest of it."

Finally, the news media, to use the anodyne modern term, have become more corporate. The foreign correspondent, concluded the author of a 1967 study of correspondents' work habits, is unlike his dashing predecessors "in at least one significant respect: he is not a loner but an organization man." No matter how insistent foreign editors are about wanting to give correspondents plenty of latitude, large organizations run by executives with MBA's, boards of directors, and mission statements inevitably place a high value on control. Worldwide communications that facilitate instant daily communication with correspondents give added muscle to this managerial discipline. The technological force is so transformative that a full chapter (chapter 23) is devoted to the subject in this book.

"It's a corporation, and it's a business; it's a brand," said *USA Today* world editor Elisa Tinsley, sitting in the conference room of *USA Today*'s sprawling headquarters outside Washington, D.C., "and there is less tolerance for the kind of eccentricities that you used to always see in our profession." Her newspaper has issued a written "USA TODAY OVERSEAS JOURNALIST SAFETY POLICY." "You must obtain permission from your editors before entering a hostile environment," it states. "You must routinely advise your editors of your movements."

Most pernicious of all are policies that increasingly caution reporters to rely heavily on the pseudoscientific artifices of attributing insights and opinions to others and of balancing unequal points of view to avoid seeming biased. Readers typically don't have the background to put the various sides into a meaningful context. More than domestic news, foreign news requires context and explanation. The difference is between a local reader's response to a snowstorm in Miami (no one has to point out that it is a freak) and a story on juju medicine by "witch doctors" in Nigeria (which without explanation may well be regarded not as a curiosity but as the therapy of choice for the entire nation). "In domestic news," Latin American correspondent Carleton Beals commented in the 1930s, "we can often supply our own background; in foreign news false analogies with the foreign scene throw the whole picture out of focus."

Curtis MacDougall, one of the great journalism teachers of the mid-twentieth century, praised Sheean and others like him for their reporting during the interwar years. "In the reporting of foreign news, the objective ideal didn't work," he said. "It was not enough to present the factual day-by-day news of what was happening in the great capitals of the world, leaving the reader to make up his own mind with or without the assistance of editorials written by unknowns thousands of miles away from the scenes of action."

Although Sheean was uncomfortable within the traditional norms of journalism, he still was essentially a reporter. He searched for facts and introduced alternative points of view into his correspondence. The difference was that he took objectivity to a level that approached real science. Sheean brought expert observation skills to this reporting. He told the reader what he saw, the conditions under which he saw it, and what it meant.

Readers did not have to wade through a thicket of equivocations when they read a lead, front-page story by Sheean in the *Herald Tribune* in mid-1938. The dateline was Vienna, the subject the aftermath of the *Anschluss.*

> The various elements of opposition, scattered through jails and concentration camps, or paralyzed with fright at home, are powerless to impede the triumphant progress of National Socialism through the mind and institutions of what once was Austria. Liberals, intellectuals, Communists, Jews, aristocrats and Catholics are the oddly assorted enemies—or, at least, victims—of the new regime. . . .
>
> Just the same, fear does not altogether account for the phenomenon. Sufferers from the Nazi revolution and those who sympathized with them are much given to the opinion that National Socialism rules by terror alone. I believe this to be a fantastic distortion of the truth.
>
> The regime is, indeed, a tyranny and imposes the bitterest humiliation and suffering upon hundreds of thousands of people. But it is much more than that. It is also a mass movement which appeals very powerfully to the whole lower middle class and to a great part of the workers. To the youth of the masses its appeal is practically irresistible, and it is among these—the very young uneducated and non-political poor—that it finds the real sources of power. . . .
>
> I am unable to name any sources or any authority for what I say, since nobody in Vienna is willing to be quoted, but investigations in the last ten days

have given me one firm belief—that nothing will shake the power of national socialism here until it has completed its historic functions and has reached its natural and inevitable conclusion in general war.

Sheean did not believe the Allied victory in World War II settled international relations any more than the Versailles Treaty after World War I had. The new challenge was the perilous arms race and the corresponding need to reach an accommodation with the Soviet Union. This message and Sheean himself did not fit postwar America, whose citizens had renewed self-confidence in their way of life and its material rewards.

Sheean searched for answers to questions that few readers were asking. Not one of the ten books on the *Publishers Weekly* best-seller list in 1949, the year Sheean's *Lead, Kindly Light* appeared, was by a journalist, let alone a foreign correspondent. Three of the ten were how-to books about winning at canasta, a pastime that was the rage; one was by Norman Vincent Peale, *A Guide to Confident Living*. "One wonders," commented a reviewer of Sheean's postwar *This House against This House*, "if this type of intimate, first-person journalism hasn't about outlived its usefulness as a serious contribution to world thought."

Sheean's subsequent novel *Rage of the Soul* received modest reviews but enjoyed strong sales. *Harper's* excerpted *Dorothy and Red*, his dual biography of Dorothy Thompson and Sinclair Lewis, whose stormy marriage ended in 1942. Westinghouse Broadcasting hired him for overseas and domestic reporting. But Sheean's name did not automatically open the publishing doors he had previously entered easily. The public relations firm Hill and Knowlton, which represented the Saudi Arabian government, arranged for him to write a biography of King Faisal, an experience fraught with frustrations. Promised access to the monarch was slow in coming; when they did talk, the king did not seem to approve of the idea of writing the biography. Worse, no publisher wanted the book, until several years later when it was brought out by the shadowy University Press of Arabia.

With political subjects less open to him, Sheean wrote *First and Last Love*, subtitled "an autobiography of his life in music," as well as books on other musical subjects. His byline was now more likely to appear in *Opera News* and *High Fidelity* than in the *Atlantic Monthly*, which published him for the last time in 1951. In 1953 he wrote a biography of Thomas Jefferson for Landmark Books, a Random House imprint aimed at children.

His personal life remained tumultuous. He remarried Dinah in 1949, and they separated again. One day he came down to breakfast with his children and commented that he had just talked to "Jesus of Nazareth." "I hope you gave him some nuts," the nanny said laconically. He broke out of his funk and laughed, but he often did not make a soft landing so quickly. On the anniversary of Gandhi's assassination, he fasted alone in his New York flat and not long afterward shot off an angry cable to his old friend Nehru: "Your insufferable arrogance and bad temper have alienated the whole world from India." Sheean professed frustration that Nehru was straying from the Mahatma's path, but he was equally frustrated with his own impotence.

Before the war, *Commonweal* labeled Sheean a "Communist fellow-traveler." That errant accusation did not mean much then, when the immediate threat was fascism, but it carried weight by 1946, when Sheean took a break from foreign reporting to cover the trial of twenty-five blacks accused of killing a policeman in Lawrenceburg, Tennessee. The chief of the state Highway Patrol called Sheean a "lying, Communistic son of a bitch." Sheean was spared an appearance before congressional committees investigating domestic communism, but it did not help to be lumped in with that carelessly defined group of liberals, many of whom were his friends. Frustrated and angry—and having had too much to drink—Sheean occasionally tried to call red-baiting Senator Joseph McCarthy's staff to ask to testify.

Sheean was a burden to friends. At a 1968 Washington dinner party hosted by Eric Sevareid, he was in a dark mood because of the assassination of Robert Kennedy, which led to too much drink, which led him to offend Alice Roosevelt Longworth, the daughter of Theodore Roosevelt and the wife of a former Speaker of the House. Longworth, known as an elegant, witty Washington conversationalist, did not approve of excessive drinking. John Gunther and his wife were afraid to invite Sheean to parties. Dorothy Thompson lost patience and for a time banned him from Twin Farms. She complained of the disruptive hours and his vast consumption of food and liquor, all a bad influence on other guests. In February 1955, she rebuked him for running up long-distance telephone bills and not paying them. In its files on Sheean, the FBI noted, "His credit rating was poor, there were indications that while in Vermont he was plagued with process servers and bill collectors."

In the 1920s, Sheean confidently went abroad to stretch his intellectual legs. In the 1950s, when the United States turned inward, his trips abroad were still an escape, but much grimmer. Sheean's destination was a favorite place, Lago Maggiore in northern Italy, where he had written *Personal History*. Italian art and music attracted him. "India is a country of the soul," he said, "Italy of the heart." Dinah joined him there in 1970, and they settled into a more tranquil relationship than at any time before. She had a small inheritance from her Aunt Maxine. Their close friend, author Thornton Wilder, helped with money when Sheean was diagnosed with cancer of the mouth.

Sheean never realized his plan to write a final sequel to *Personal History*, which he had pledged to undertake upon reaching the age of seventy-five. In January 1975, after unsuccessful cancer treatment in New York, he returned to Lago Maggiore and passed away in March. At the end, when he was mostly confined to his bed, Sheean "played in orchestras and traveled all in his own head." Occasionally he awoke and asked his daughter Ellen, "Do you have my passport?"

14

WHO'S WHO

Has interviewed Lloyd George, Pres. Masaryk of Czechoslovakia, King Carol
of Rumania, Gandhi, Trotsky, De Valera, Dollfuss, Generalissimo and Madam
Chiang Kai-shek, President Quezon of Philippines, presidents Cárdenas and Avila
Camacho of Mexico; Vargas of Brazil; Marshal Tito of Yugoslavia, Pope Pius XII,
Premier de Gasperi of Italy, Nehru, Emperor Hirohito of Japan, General
MacArthur, and many other contemporary statesmen.

Who's Who in America, on John Gunther

In the early 1930s Drew Pearson and Robert Allen anonymously wrote *Washington Merry-Go-Round.* The book's dust jacket juicily announced that this was the "inside story of Washington society, politicians and politics." The gossipy, venomous, and hugely successful book set others wondering how they, too, might profit from such a theme. "At about this time," said Cass Canfield, president of Harper & Brothers, "it occurred to me that if I could find someone to write intimately about personalities and events in Europe, the resulting book should be useful as well as salable."

Canfield's first choice for an author was H. R. Knickerbocker with Hearst's International News Service. Knickerbocker declined and suggested John Gunther, the *Chicago Daily News*'s Vienna bureau chief, who had much to commend him for the job. The ambitious young correspondent had acquired wide experience filling in for *Daily News* correspondents in various European capitals. A veritable writing machine, he had churned out magazine articles and five novels that Canfield had published. But Gunther wasn't interested in the project either. Like Sheean and many other correspondents, he aspired to make a name for himself as a novelist; it was a dream only a few of them, most notably Hemingway, achieved. When Canfield came calling, Gunther was working on a new novel he thought had promise.

As Gunther told the story, Canfield pressed his book proposal, asking what size advance might change his mind. Seeking to put the matter to rest, Gunther proposed "the largest sum I had ever heard of—$5,000." Canfield agreed and still had to badger Gunther into signing the contract.

Gunther started the book in 1934 in Vienna and continued working on it the next year when he was transferred to London. Given his regular *Daily News* chores, he wrote evenings and on weekends. On a three-week vacation, he traveled around the continent, quizzing friends and colleagues from a list of twenty-six questions about political leaders: "Attitude to sex," "What does he believe in most?" "Tastes in food and drink," and so forth. The heart of the book was profiles of Hitler, Stalin, and Mussolini. Gunther toyed with such titles as "The Age of Dictators," "Men over Europe," and "Doomed Europe" until he hit on one that borrowed, without his realizing it, from a book published nearly twenty years before, Herbert Bayard

Swope's *Inside the German Empire.* In early December 1935, Gunther sent his man-uscript to Canfield, who rushed *Inside Europe* into print as though it were a news story.

Inside Europe sped to the best-seller lists in the United States as well as Britain. Within six months Gunther quit the *Daily News* and wrote a revised, updated edi-tion. Five more editions appeared in the next four years. Canfield, who initially fig-ured sales might reach five thousand copies in the United States, pushed the book with a gimmick used by automobile dealers: trade in your old *Inside Europe* and get fifty cents off the new model. After the book became an alternate selection of the Book-of-the-Month Club in 1939, total sales in both the United States and Britain exceeded a half million copies.

By that time Gunther was relishing the five-hundred-dollar-a-week lecture cir-cuit, appearing on Rudy Vallee's nationally broadcast Thursday evening radio show, and extending his *Inside* formula to other parts of the planet. The potent combina-tion of being attractive in the limelight and working hard at his craft made Gunther a national figure. "A hulking (6 ft. 1 in., 238 lbs.) legman in seven-league boots," *Time* wrote in a cover story in the late 1950s, "he has at once traveled more miles, crossed more frontiers, interviewed more statesmen, earned more money (more than $1,000,000), written more books and sold more copies (more than 2,000,000) than any single other newsman." Gunther did not have the "stylist graces" of Neg-ley Farson or Vincent Sheean, *Time* noted. His gift lay in the ability to popularize "remote places and difficult subjects."

Gunther relished the attention, courted it, and deserved it. Yet his significance is not limited to his own fame. Like Mowrer and Sheean, as well as correspon-dents discussed in later chapters, Gunther vivifies an aspect of the golden age of foreign correspondents. From the time *special correspondent* entered the argot of journalism, stay-at-home reporters and editors regarded their far-flung colleagues as a breed apart. Some early correspondents parlayed this reputation into celebrity. But in the interwar years, carrying through World War II, the urgency of foreign news, combined with other factors, turned scores of foreign correspondents into household names and (thanks to radio) household voices. Because of *their* special talents, honed in foreign reporting, Ernest Hemingway, Dorothy Thompson, and Ernie Pyle also found their faces on the cover of *Time* and, like Gunther, were pur-sued by autograph seekers.

In a classic statement, written nearly a century ago, sociologist Vilfredo Pareto de-fined elites as those who achieved "the highest indices in their branch of activity." Although this definition left out such variables as heredity, which brings financial fortune or royal titles, the definition fit foreign correspondents in their golden age so well that George Seldes dubbed them "the nobility of American journalism."

Publications that fielded foreign correspondents ranked high in many of the in-dices that traditionally matter to journalists. The Associated Press, for instance, excelled in trustworthiness, while the *New York Herald Tribune* and the *Chicago*

Daily News had superb writers and analysts. Those newspapers as well as the *Christian Science Monitor* and the *New York Times* also attracted audiences with higher income and education. The same could be said for magazines. Although many viewed the *Saturday Evening Post* as middlebrow, it had high standards for writing and reporting, published respected foreign correspondents, and reached an enormous audience. Furthermore, because the number of correspondents working in these organizations was relatively small, these journalists became an elite within an elite.

Foreign correspondents also had power, another indicator of elitism. What the great mass of Americans learned about the world came from that small group of journalists. Americans who traveled and worked abroad extensively—themselves elites—were, if anything, more reliant on correspondents. Diplomats or business executives with overseas financial interests could not by themselves know all there was to know about world affairs, and such knowledge about the direction of events was practically important because it translated into concrete decisions.

For media organizations, foreign news-gathering and elite status were mutually reinforcing. The best organizations gathered news abroad and thereby affirmed their excellence. A similar reinforcing process existed for individual correspondents, who enjoyed privileges and trappings that enhanced their status.

Specialization and Education. "Whereas formerly, only men half educated but possessed of good 'horse sense' and a keen scent for news, were employed as special correspondents," *Cosmopolitan* observed in an 1897 article on the growing sophistication of journalism, "now the ablest men . . . are chosen as ambassadors of the great dailies to every part of the world. . . . They are at once men of knowledge and men of the world, capable of holding their own with the ablest."

Correspondents acquired their expertise on the job, but in many cases they were well educated to begin with. It was a relative matter, of course. Early in the twentieth century, college education was a rarity among journalists of all kinds, as among Americans generally, and many regarded it as a disqualification for the newsroom. Mowrer earned $20 a week before he left the *Daily News* for the University of Michigan. When he returned to the newspaper, the managing editor reduced his pay to $15 a week, observing, "You won't be worth as much to us now as you were before."

Mowrer was not the only *Daily News* correspondent who sat in a university classroom. Edward Price Bell had a degree from a liberal arts college, Wabash, in central Indiana. Like Mowrer, William Stoneman attended the University of Michigan. Mowrer's brother, Edgar Ansel, studied there as well as at the University of Chicago and the Sorbonne. Carroll Binder and George Weller graduated from Harvard. Weller, a member of Phi Beta Kappa, also pursued graduate study at the University of Vienna. John Gunther was a classmate of Vincent Sheean at the University of Chicago and also a Phi Beta Kappan. Constance Brown earned a doctorate in political science from the University of Munich.

These correspondents often had strong ties to their universities. In the twilight of his career, Gunther wrote a short history of his alma mater, "the most exciting university in the world." Weller set his 1933 novel, *Not to Eat, Not for Love,* in Harvard undergraduate life. "A Harvard man," one of his characters says, "is deeper marked."

Compensation. After the Civil War, *Herald* foreign correspondents averaged "$40 gold" per week, *Harper's* noted in an article on the evolution of the news business; "home correspondents" were paid less, thirty to thirty-five dollars. And so it remained. In addition to better salaries, correspondents acquired elastic expense accounts that city beat reporters could not dream of. These covered office automobiles, memberships in associations where they could meet news-makers, and travel and tickets to cover theater performances or festivals.

Correspondents' creative use of expense accounts added to their legends. Carleton Beals recalled that a correspondent covering Pancho Villa kept filing "flim-flam sheets" to recoup alleged expenses for shoeing his horse. Finally a message came back from the home office: "What are you riding? A horse or a centipede?" Even at the parsimonious *Chicago Daily News,* correspondents developed reputations for expense account evasion. When Robert Casey came home from covering a revolution in Cuba, he asked how much money he had been advanced. Told it was $3,286.22, he wrote a note: "I spent $3,286.22. I wish to God I knew where." Colonel Knox approved it, telling the comptroller, "They were shooting at him with machine guns." After the *Daily News* accounting department insisted that correspondents itemize food expenses, they questioned Junius B. Wood's caviar breakfast. The cantankerous reporter replied, "Eggs is eggs."

Air travel, when it came along, added to correspondents' glamour and status. It was standard policy at many newspapers and magazines for correspondents to buy tickets for the front of the plane. "After you cross the Susquehanna River," one *Baltimore Sun* correspondent advised a colleague who was about to head overseas, "start traveling first class." Richard Clurman, chief of *Time* magazine's correspondents, had two first-class seats, one for his briefcase, although he claimed the second was courtesy of the airline. The perquisite was so firmly established at the *New York Herald Tribune* that on the eve of the paper's demise, the editor advised a Moscow correspondent to prepare for impending doom by buying "yourself a first class ticket around the world."

Autonomy. Home-based reporters sat within a few feet of copy editors, city editors, news editors, and managing and executive editors, all of whom usually knew the reporter's beat as well as the reporter did. Correspondents worked alone. Even if they had been on the job only a few weeks, they were likely to be far more knowledgeable than any out-of-sight editor. The correspondent decided what to cover and how.

The correspondents' "work never can be measured by the clock," said one, "and therefore is not held to the elementary principle of routine that would make it comparable with some professions." The foreign correspondent, Paul Scott Mowrer wrote at the end of his newspaper career, "can lie abed as long as he likes. He can stay in or go out. He can wait until evening to have his first drink, or can start be-

fore breakfast." Little wonder correspondents who were recalled home often resisted or quit. Once free, they no longer could endure "the kindergarten discipline
of the city desk."

Lifestyle. "The social origins and allegiances of most journalists are, by and large,
middle class," observed Leo Rosten in a 1930s study of the press. But once abroad,
correspondents joined a different class. They routinely socialized with news-makers, who regarded them, more or less, as equals. Newspaper proprietors made the
most of this. They called their correspondents "ambassadors" and, as illustrated by
the attitudes of Ochs and Lawson, viewed their bureaus as embassies to be adorned
much more lavishly than the city room back home. There were good reasons for el-
evating foreign correspondents. Foreign news-gathering was an expensive undertaking. One might as well wring as much prestige out of it as possible. If correspondents were envoys, owners might fancy themselves heads of state. And building up
correspondents helped those news-gatherers get access to news-makers.

"The Special Correspondent of a great newspaper possesses for the time being
something of the influence of an Ambassador from one nation to another," James
Gordon Bennett Jr. said in one of his grand summonses and send-offs of a correspondent from Paris—this one to dispatch Sidney Whitman to find the truth about
Turkish atrocities against the Armenians in 1896. "Now, according to an axiom of
Machiavelli, an Ambassador should endeavor to make himself *persona grata* with
those to whom he is accredited, if only thereby to gain the best opportunities for
obtaining every possible information."

For their own self-interested reasons, foreign news-makers were receptive to
the idea of socializing with correspondents. In the implicit bargain that shaped
their relationships, the correspondents acquired *inside* news, and news-makers, in
turn, acquired the correspondents' knowledge and perspective, as well as a vehicle for enlarging their own influence. "News gathering in Europe," John Gunther
commented in a 1935 *Harper's* article, "is largely a collaboration whereby men who
know and trust one another exchange gossip, background, and information."

Dress. Judges are identified with black robes, doctors with white coats, and foreign correspondents, in an oft-used image, with "trench-coats," although their
wardrobe bulges with getups. War correspondents wore the uniforms of officers;
those in the savannas of Africa pith helmets; and those in Britain fancy dress.
"Imagine a reporter wearing a tall silk hat," said Wythe Williams, who began his
overseas career in pre–World War I London for the *New York World.* "We wore
them, with long-tailed morning coats, striped trousers and spats, and we carried
sticks and gloves. This was necessary regalia for the West End. Otherwise we would
not have impressed the immaculate reception clerks at the great hotels where we
call daily in our search for news." Raymond Clapper, a United Press reporter with
little enthusiasm for dandified dress, covered the 1930 Naval Conference. "Listen—
don't tell anybody," he wrote to his wife, "but I had to get a silk hat for last night.
It cost $7.50. Over here everybody wears silk hats at night. . . . I just couldn't go to
Lady Astor's and the French Embassy in that old soft one so I went and done it. I
won't wear it in Washington."

In an autobiographical sketch, Associated Press correspondent James Mills described the dress requirements foisted on him: a full-dress evening suit, a high silk hat, white gloves, and patent-leather spats for Haile Selassie's wedding, which began at four in the morning in Addis Ababa; similar attire—overcoats forbidden—for Henry Pu-Yi's open-air coronation in thirty-below-zero Manchurian weather (the Japanese enthroned the former Chinese emperor to legitimate their conquest of that part of China). Mills had particular difficulty suiting up for the state funeral of King Ferdinand of Romania. He arrived in town with only the clothes on his back, a soiled white linen suit. He scrounged much of the formal dress he needed from the attic of a friendly prince; the headwaiter at his hotel supplied the stiff shirt, collar, and black tie. Mills afterward described the scene as he walked behind the coffin: "In one hand I carried my portable typewriter, and with the other I held up my buttonless trousers."

Honors. Correspondents received honors above and beyond those that journalists bestowed on themselves. The process can be said to have begun with William Howard Russell. He returned from the Crimean War "in a blaze of glory," as his paper, the *Times* of London, put it, "to be lionized as no journalist had ever been before." Queen Victoria knighted him. After the Prussians' victory over the French in 1871—a war Russell also covered—they awarded him the Iron Cross. On an 1856 trip to Paris, he complained in his diary, "I find I am unpleasantly well known principally by my portrait." Nevertheless, he dressed up for painters and photographers. A late-in-life photograph shows him in a resplendent military uniform, medals cascading down his chest. Other English reporters followed in his footsteps, receiving knighthood for helpful coverage of World War I. The *Times'* Dr. George Ernest "China" Morrison had a Beijing street named after him.

Americans were not far behind. Januarius MacGahan, who appears in chapter 7 as one of James Gordon Bennett Jr.'s correspondent-explorers, distinguished himself covering the Bulgarian uprising against the Ottomans for the *London Daily News* in the 1870s. MacGahan's sympathy for the insurgents and his reporting of atrocities committed against them brought him lasting fame in Bulgaria. Streets were named after him. His portrait still hangs in museums and public buildings throughout the country, and his bust is displayed in a small Balkan village where he did some of his most powerful reporting on Turkish cruelties. When John Reed died in Russia in 1920, he was given a hero's burial under the Kremlin Wall; the Chinese Communists buried in the Babaoshan Cemetery of Revolutionary Martyrs two journalists who devoted themselves to the cause, Anna Louise Strong and Agnes Smedley. In 1920, according to Edgar Ansel Mowrer, Albania's acting foreign minister devised a plan to help achieve national independence. He proposed that Mowrer become king.

"The French, Italians and Greeks offer the journalists something that they themselves would like to be given—decorations," wrote an anonymous correspondent after World War I. "There are few American newspapermen in Paris who haven't at least one of the little ribbons Frenchmen wear in their button holes. Most of the Americans have the purple ribbon of the order of l'Instruction Publique, conferred on school-teachers and French journalists; a few selected American correspondents wear the red ribbon of the Legion of Honor." The awards, the author noted, served everyone's interests. Governments gave them to warm up relations with correspondents. Correspondents accepted them because they were "an actual boon in gaining entrée" to the corridors of power.

Floyd Gibbons, the *Chicago Tribune* correspondent who presciently boarded the ill-fated *Laconia* before U.S. entry into World War I, was amply draped with awards. He received three wounds, including the loss of one eye, while trying to save a marine major during the Battle of Belleau Wood in France. The French awarded him the Croix de Guerre with Palm. Before he died in 1939, Gibbons was further decorated by the Polish government, the Sultan of Morocco, and hyperactive French medal-givers who pinned two more on him. Nor was he forgotten in death. On the eve of World War II, the United States began to manufacture cargo-carrying Liberty Ships. One was christened the *Floyd Gibbons*.

Gibbons was not the only one of his brethren to be placed on the same plateau as iconic Americans Paul Revere and Carole Lombard, whose names were also painted on the hulls of Liberty Ships. Many of the characters who appear in this book—and a few journalists who contributed substantially to foreign newsgathering but did not make it onto these pages—joined him. A very partial list includes printer-publishers Benjamin Franklin, Adolph Ochs, Cyrus Curtis, Joseph Pulitzer, and Victor Lawson; mid-nineteenth-century pioneering correspondents Margaret Fuller and George W. Kendall of the *New Orleans Daily Picayune;* James Gordon Bennett and Henry Stanley; Asia hands Lafcadio Hearn and John B. Powell; Frederic Remington, Stephen Crane, Richard Harding Davis, Heywood Broun, William Allen White, and Irwin S. Cobb, who had been correspondents in previous wars; John Reed, whose reporting also gave him the niche in the Kremlin Wall; Richard Halliburton; and University of Missouri Journalism School dean Walter Williams, known for sending many would-be foreign correspondents on their way.

At times, correspondents bemoaned getting too much attention. After William Stoneman took a break from the *Chicago Daily News* to work for the UN secretary general, Norwegian statesman Trygve Lie, he rued "a tin medal given by the Norskis to civil servants and odds and strays." He considered it, he told a colleague, "a dirty trick played on me by Trygve Lie in order to ingratiate himself with me and to carry on the fiction that we never had any trouble about anything. Had my Norwegian friends had the decency to tell me what was up I would have made them stop it."

Correspondents also benefited from the general change in status that occurred for journalists around the end of the nineteenth century. The famous reporter began to eclipse the famous newspaper owner-editor in the public's imagination.

One reason was the changing nature of the news business. No longer did an entrepreneur launch a newspaper with a few thousand dollars. In 1894 Charles Dana, editor of the *Sun,* estimated start-up costs for a daily at $1 million, whereas fifty years before the price tag had been $5,000 to $10,000. From 1900 to 1905, according to government figures, the capital invested in publishing doubled. Publishers and editors increasingly focused on the effective use of their assets. "The executive heads of some two-score of the great newspapers in America, 'talking shop' on a railway train last spring, spoke of their properties as factories, and when the editorial department was mentioned discussed 'their traffic in news,' and likened the management of it to that of a department store," Lincoln Steffens wrote in an 1897 *Scribner's* article, "The Business of a Newspaper."

One of the most valuable assets for news executives was their reporters. A respected and well-known reporter was an advertisement for a newspaper or magazine. This led to increased use of bylines. "Newspaper proprietors have encouraged signature for the sake of increasing circulation through the éclat given by distinguished names," one student of the press noted. The greatest beneficiaries of the trend were foreign correspondents. In 1925 the Associated Press began to use bylines; one of the first to get one, an AP history notes, was its handsome foreign correspondent James A. Mills. At the *New York Times,* Adolph Ochs originally disdained bylines, thinking "the business of the paper must be absolutely impersonal." But *Times* editors gave them with increasing frequency in the interwar years, with the largest numbers going to those overseas, as indicated by table 5. Turner Catledge, who joined the *Times* in 1929 and eventually became executive editor, explained the powerful consequences of bylines: "The by-line gave the reporter increased prestige. He became a star and could command a greater salary." The *Chicago Daily News* "seldom acknowledged its photographers," notes a history of its picture-taking. "The foreign correspondents, who took news photographs during their travels, were the only staff members consistently credited in the paper for their photography." This was a long way from the time James Gordon Bennett Jr. begrudgingly gave credit to Henry Stanley for finding Livingstone.

Richard Harding Davis, the first American correspondent to be lionized on the scale of Britain's William Howard Russell, found that his name brought him princely sums. Shortly after acquiring the *New York Journal,* William Randolph Hearst paid Davis five hundred dollars to cover the 1895 Yale-Princeton Thanksgiving football game. It was said at the time to be the largest fee ever paid to a reporter for a story about a single event. He subsequently persuaded Davis to take on a foreign assignment of his own choosing, on his own terms. "They are trying to get all the well known men at big prices," Davis commented in 1895.

Davis was far from passive in these transactions. His secret, if it could be called that, lay in hard work and his frankly admitted enthusiasm to "sell the goods." His first foray abroad was to Central America in 1895. The trip resulted in a book as well as magazine articles. He elevated his status further by writing about what it was like to be a correspondent. Mindful of how he looked to his audience, Davis complemented his square-jawed manliness with specially tailored uniforms and was never shy about being photographed or handing photos out.

Davis, said Will Irwin, who worked alongside him, "seemed to me to have cre-

TABLE 5. Front-page bylines in the *New York Times*

Year	% stories with byline	% foreign stories with byline	% other stories with byline
1920	7	19	0
1921	6	12	3
1923	4	12	0
1927	8	24	6
1930	12	31	6
1931	14	33	6
1933	18	40	8
1935	18	41	10
1939	35	56	25
1940	43	56	27

Source: Jessica Perez.

Note: This table is based on a sample of front pages of the *New York Times* from 1920 to 1940. The total number of stories on the front pages = 3,404. The study examined ten randomly selected years and four randomly selected weeks within each year to arrive at the above averages. As can be seen, foreign news consistently carried bylines more often than any other kind of story. In 1920 all the stories in the study with bylines were foreign; by 1940, when bylines were more frequent, the percent on foreign stories was still twice as high as for all the others.

ated a picture of himself and to be trying to live up to it." He owned a sprawling country home in Mount Kisco, New York, Crossroads Farm, and married the much-ogled Bessie McCoy, the "Yama Yama Girl" of the Ziegfeld Follies. Once in motion, Davis's celebrity built on itself, gaining size and velocity like a snowball rolling down a hill. Improbably handsome, he served as the model for the male counterpart to the dazzling, long-necked beauties sketched by his friend Charles Dana Gibson. Even a glitch could become good publicity. When German soldiers apprehended Davis during the early stages of World War I, he convinced them he was not a British spy by showing the label in his hat, "Knox, New York." "If I were an Englishman," he told his captors, "would I cross the ocean to New York to buy a hat?" After Davis wrote about the episode, Knox produced an ad in which two German soldiers surrounded the reporter: "The hat saved him." An American novelist named Winston Churchill modeled the hero of one of his books after Davis. The novel was entitled *The Celebrity*.

When Davis died of a heart attack in 1916 at the relatively young age of fifty-one, he was the yardstick by which correspondents' fame was measured. Whenever adventurous reporters with a little talent and flair came along, they were likened to Richard Harding Davis. Davis, literary critic Van Wyck Brooks thought, "was one of those magnetic types, often otherwise second-rate, who establish patterns of living for others of their kind. . . . Davis made the reporter a hero whose life was all

Dashing correspondent Richard Harding Davis was always careful to dress the part. In this photograph he is wearing his well-fitted military uniform while covering the Greco-Turkish War for the *Times* of London. The inscription is to John Bass, who was with him in the trenches for the *New York Journal*. Newberry Library.

glamour and romance." As a young, impressionable reporter in Baltimore, H. L. Mencken considered Davis "the hero of our dreams." When Mencken grew up, he revised his opinion and said Davis was "a cheese-monger."

As successful as Davis was at self-aggrandizement, his publicity tool kit was primitive by the standards of what was about to come. His fame began in the days

of buggy whips and gaslights. The names of the next generation of stars were electrified.

"In all the history of inventing," said an editorial in *Outlook,* "nothing has approached the rise of radio from obscurity to power." The radio craze began in 1922.
Customers stood in long lines to buy the new devices. By 1924, the year of the *Outlook* comment, Americans owned 3 million of them. By 1936, the year Gunther's
first *Inside* book appeared, the number of radio sets had climbed to 33 million, giving journalists a mass audience with whom they had unprecedented intimacy.

As personal as a byline was, it was not nearly so intimate as the human voice,
with its individual timbre and cadence. On the air, a journalist became a recogniz-
able person. "The microphone makes the lesser journalist well known," said Raymond Swing, who graduated from the *Daily News* and other newspapers to full-
time radio work in 1936. "He becomes a factor of value to the radio industry, to
advertisers, to newspapers, to the general public, and, inescapably, to himself."

The fledgling broadcast networks made extensive use of print journalists, who
provided reporting and commentary as a sideline to their regular work. Like many
colleagues, Gunther found talking easy. "Did my broadcast about India—in two
hours and 10 minutes of actual writing time," he noted in his diary in October 1939.
"And the research was not difficult. All out of my head, except for a few bits of current news, in fact."

With the lure of big audiences and big paychecks, some print journalists jumped
almost entirely to broadcasting. Floyd Gibbons's maiden broadcast was on Christmas night 1925 on the *Tribune*'s WGN radio station. His mother had just died, and
he was home on leave. He told his audience of the various far-flung places where he
had spent Christmas and how he would trade it all for a Christmas tree and kids
romping around it. The broadcast was a sensation. The *Tribune* followed up with an
experiment in which Gibbons broadcast some of his experiences and the paper reprinted them the next day. Chicagoans were invited to say which version they preferred. Letters poured in, showing that the majority favored radio. Gibbons left
the *Tribune* the next year, and NBC gave him a program of his own, *The Headline
Hunter,* in which he related personal experiences. Contracts and sponsors for other
programs followed.

With his signature eye patch over his World War I wound, his rapid-fire announcing (he was clocked at as many as 245 words a minute), and his homely commentary style, Gibbons developed a persona that was at once identifiable and appealing. Another tear-jerking Christmas broadcast brought him five hundred
invitations to Christmas dinner. According to his brother, "His fan mail was running almost a thousand letters a day." A baby and an American Legion post were
named after him. A Floyd Gibbons School of Broadcasting trained announcers. In
addition to working the lecture circuit, he wrote a column for the *New York Evening World* in the same breezy style as his broadcasts: "Hello everybody: wonder
what's doing in Russia?" He narrated short films about his adventures and historic
news events. As a result of Gibbons's colorful travels, cartoonist Stookie Allen fea-

tured him in his 1933 book for boys, *Men of Daring,* along with Richard Harding Davis, globe-trotting cameramen Merle LaVoy and Nick Cavaliere, Henry Morton Stanley, and broadcaster Lowell Thomas, who wrote the book's introduction.

When radio became a serious medium for news reporting during the war, broadcast journalists did not become less human, nor did they try to. They spoke intimately. "The air raid is still on," said CBS News pioneer Edward R. Murrow during German nighttime bombing of London in 1940. "I shall speak rather softy, because three or four people are sleeping on mattresses on the floor of this studio." Radio not only made Murrow and other broadcasters into public figures; it also helped elevate print journalists, as another Murrow report suggests:

> Before eight, the siren sounded again. We went back to the haystack near the airdrome. . . . Huge pear-shaped bursts of flame would rise up into the smoke and disappear. The world was upside down. Vincent Sheean lay on one side of me and cursed in five languages; he'd talk about the war in Spain. Ben Robertson of *PM* lay on the other side and kept saying over and over in that slow South Carolina drawl, "London is burning, London is burning."

While radio worked its magic, the star-making power of the movie industry enhanced the image of the foreign correspondent. Richard Harding Davis had a brief encounter with the new medium late in his career when filmmakers started to think about finding good stories and stars to act them out. His novel *Soldiers of Fortune,* successful as a play, became the subject of one of the first full-length feature films, produced by the All-Star Feature Corporation. The movie was filmed in Cuba. Davis came along to advise and, ever true to his goal of making himself news, subsequently wrote "Breaking into the Movies" for *Scribner's,* noting that when it came time to dress the part of the hero, leading man Dustin Farnum wore Davis's clothes. The 1914 release was a mixed success. Critics liked the scenery but not the confusing scenario.

Hollywood, a sleepy village when Davis died, quickly grew into a movie metropolis. The orange grove on the corner of Hollywood and Vine disappeared. Newly built studios dotted the city's map. Journalists came to work as accomplices to the hyperactive studio publicity departments that orchestrated the star system. The first movie fan magazine, *Photoplay,* started in 1919 and others followed. In the 1930s, Hollywood was the third-largest news source in the United States. Some of the three hundred Hollywood reporters, including one from the Vatican, were foreign journalists. These correspondents attracted attention to themselves by organizing the Hollywood Foreign Correspondents Association and creating the Golden Globe movie awards. For their own reasons, American foreign correspondents also found their way to Hollywood's luxurious boulevards.

Some came to imbibe the atmosphere, which then as now was heavily laced with interest in politics. At the time those interests were fixed on the rise of militant fascism and leftwing solutions to social ills. Several years after the publication of *I Write as I Please,* veteran Moscow correspondent Walter Duranty severed his ties with the *New York Times* and migrated to Beverly Hills to work on other writing projects, enjoy the balmy weather, and socialize. The lively raconteur was in his element with adoring actors, writers, and émigré intellectuals like Thomas Mann.

While Duranty entertained Hollywood stars, other correspondents wrote for them. Irwin S. Cobb, a versatile journalist, humorist, and occasional foreign correspondent, wrote screenplays, eventually acted in movies, and in 1935 was master of ceremonies at the Academy Awards. When Edgar Mowrer vocally predicted the coming war, a producer invited him to "Come to Hollywood and write about it." Although he declined to uproot himself, he wrote a screenplay that was never produced. Radical American journalist Anna Louise Strong was hired to work on a movie about Russia in 1941. For the first time in her life, she acquired a Social Security number. "For many years Hollywood held this double lure for me," said former *Daily News* correspondent Ben Hecht, "tremendous sums of money for work that required no more effort than a game of pinochle." Hecht was one of the script surgeons called in to work on *Foreign Correspondent,* the film version of Sheean's *Personal History.*

Foreign Correspondent, among many other films, featured foreign correspon-

---

FOREIGN CORRESPONDENTS AT THE MOVIES—THE GOLDEN AGE

Feature films with foreign correspondents as prominent characters:

War Correspondent (1932)	*Confirm or Deny* (1941)
Clear All Wires! (1934)	*A Yank in Libya* (1942)
Four Frightened People (1934)	*Berlin Correspondent* (1942)
I'll Tell the World (1934)	*China Girl* (1942)
Viva Villa! (1934)	*Cairo* (1942)
Paris Interlude (1934)	*Dangerous Moonlight* (1942)
Next Time We Love (1936)	*Once upon a Honeymoon* (1942)
Love on the Run (1936)	*Somewhere I'll Find You* (1942)
Exiled to Shanghai (1937)	*The Day Will Dawn* (1942)
Fly Away Baby (1937)	*Behind the Rising Sun* (1943)
I Cover the War (1937)	*Desert Song* (1943)
Last Train from Madrid (1937)	*Guadalcanal Diary* (1943)
Barricade (1939)	*The Lady Has Plans* (1943)
Espionage Agent (1939)	*They Got Me Covered* (1943)
Everything Happens at Night (1939)	*Passage to Marseille* (1944)
Stanley and Livingstone (1939)	*Blood on the Sun* (1945)
Arise, My Love (1940)	*The Story of G.I. Joe* (1945)
Comrade X (1940)	*Objective, Burma!* (1945)
Dispatch from Reuters (1940)	*Sing Your Way Home* (1945)
Foreign Correspondent (1940)	*Lover Come Back* (1946)
Affectionately Yours (1941)	

dents during the 1930s and the war years. These movies ran the gamut. *They Got Me Covered,* with Bob Hope, and *Lover Come Back,* with Lucille Ball, were frivolous; *Desert Song* was a musical. In *Everything Happens at Night,* Sonja Henie figure-skates for nearly five minutes. Many of the movies contained the glibly humorous repartee popularized in the play and movie *The Front Page,* which Hecht co-wrote. One of the best of these often lame efforts was *Comrade X,* in which Hecht also had a hand. Another play-movie comedy was *Clear All Wires!* written by former *New York World* Moscow correspondent Samuel Spewack and his wife Bella. At least nine foreign-correspondent films received Oscar nominations in one category or another (*Foreign Correspondent* was nominated in six categories); and *Viva Villa! Arise, My Love,* and *Blood on the Sun* produced winners.

Serious or light-hearted, these movies almost always tracked the grim political landscape abroad—the Spanish civil war in *Last Train from Madrid* and the London blitz in *Confirm or Deny.* Things turned serious even in *Everything Happens at Night,* where two competing correspondents joined forces to save Henie's father from Nazis. If correspondents were naïve and ill-equipped when an editor whimsically sent them on their first overseas assignment, they matured into heroes by the time the credits rolled.

"The public's taste," *Variety* noted, was "educated to accept its newspaper characters as brittle and cynical, but ever staunch personalities." In *Blood on the Sun,* James Cagney played a tough American editor of a Tokyo newspaper who defiantly publishes the Japanese plan to conquer the world. Among the memorable scenes, *Variety* observed patriotically, was "one showing Cagney beating the yellow low-lifes at jiu-jitsu." In *Espionage Agent,* the foreign correspondent—in this case a bit part—uses his expense account and connections to help an undercover American diplomat root out spies.

Moviegoers could discern real occurrences in the celluloid correspondents and their adventures. In *Clear All Wires!* Buckley Joyce Thomas, the Moscow correspondent for the *Chicago Globe,* has a three-barrel name like Paul Scott Mowrer and, like Mowrer and Sheean, penetrated enemy lines in the Riff. The 1932 film *War Correspondent* starred Ralph Graves as a radio reporter in China. *Variety* described Graves as "a la Floyd Gibbons," who that year covered Japanese military incursions into China for the International News Service and made news with a broadcast interview of a Japanese general. *The Story of G.I. Joe,* whose screenplay Arthur Miller worked on, was a tribute to war correspondent Ernie Pyle, who was killed by a Japanese machine gunner in 1945. The book *Guadalcanal Diary,* by International News Service correspondent Richard Tregaskis, became the basis for a 20th Century Fox movie by the same name. Twice in his career Tregaskis wrote screenplays for Hollywood.

It didn't hurt correspondents' images that matinee idols played their parts.* At

* In one case an authentic correspondent acted with one of these beauties, although it was not in Hollywood. When he was studying in Vienna, George Weller played American bit parts in movies by Otto Preminger and Max Reinhardt, "danced with Hedy Lamarr in her Viennese speaking debut,"

one time or another, foreign correspondents Don Ameche, Cary Grant, Joel Mc-Crea, Jimmy Stewart, John Wayne, Ray Milland, Errol Flynn, Robert Mitchum, Dana Andrews, Humphrey Bogart, Ralph Richardson, George Montgomery, George Brent, Spencer Tracy, and Clark Gable (who had four such roles) embraced, variously, Lana Turner, Dorothy Lamour, Hedy Lamarr, Laraine Day, Joan Crawford, Nancy Kelly, Deborah Kerr, Margaret Sullavan, Gene Tierney, Ginger Rogers, Claudette Colbert, Virginia Gilmore, and of course Sonja Henie, whose parts ranged from sultry spy to pretty, eyeglass-wearing geography teacher from Chicago. Although on screen, as in life, the role of reporter was chiefly a man's part, Paulette Goddard was a foreign correspondent in *The Lady Has Plans* and Benita Hume in *Clear All Wires!*

Real correspondents' love lives intertwined with the entertainment world the way Richard Harding Davis's did when he married the Yama Yama Girl. Radio broadcasters were particularly notable in this way, especially those who belonged to the outstanding CBS corps of correspondents. The suave and always impeccably dressed Charles Collingwood broke off an engagement to a British aristocrat to marry actress Louise Allbritton; after she died, he married a Swedish singer with whom he had had an affair years before. Sevareid divorced his wife to marry a professional singer, the daughter of two opera singers, one of whom was Italian. After the war, Gunther dropped by William Shirer's CBS office one day with movie directors Frank Capra and Anatole Livak and Viennese prima ballerina Tilly Losch in tow. They wanted to watch his broadcast and then go out for a drink. That evening at "21," Shirer began a long affair with the beautiful dancer. (Other CBS correspondents also found themselves in the bedrooms of the politically powerful, which also spoke to their cachet. Winston Burdett married the daughter of a prominent Rome banker, who also was the granddaughter of a former Rome mayor. Edward R. Murrow had an affair with Pamela Churchill, the prime minister's daughter-in-law.)

The movie-journalistic connection could be played in reverse. Annalee Whitmore was a successful screenwriter in Hollywood with MGM before she set her mind to going to China in the late 1930s and, through her connections, became a *Time* correspondent. She married *Time* colleague Mel Jacoby. After he died in a plane accident, she married Theodore White, another *Time* reporter in Asia. And Hollywood inspired news stories. In 1923 the *Chicago Tribune* dispatched Floyd Gibbons on this assignment:

GIBBONS

CHITRIB

ORGANIZE AND EQUIP CAMEL CARAVAN CROSS SAHARA DESERT OBTAIN TRUE PICTURE OF SHEIKS AND THEIR APPEAL ANGLO-SAXON AND AMERICAN WOMEN.

---

and was a spear carrier in the movie *Ben Hur,* as the *Daily News* once bragged of its star reporter. *Chicago Daily News,* May 8–9, 1971.

MRS. HULLS BOOK THE SHEIK CREATING WIDE INTEREST HERE AMONG WOMEN-
FOLK WELL AS RUDOLPH VALENTINO'S CHARACTERIZATION IN MOVIES. CABLE
WHEN CAN LEAVE.

EDITOR

With a photographer, Gibbons traveled two thousand miles over more than
three months across the broiling desert, ending up in Timbuktu. His American
flag was said to be the first carried across the Sahara. Gibbons, who had a reputation for running up expenses in keeping with his star status, presented the *Tribune*
with a bill for twenty thousand dollars, which exceeded even his outsized fame and
according to one account hastened his departure from the paper—and thrust him
in the arms of NBC radio.

The star system built on interlocking and mutually reinforcing media. Publicists sought to get their stars mentioned in newspapers and on radio, and newspapers and radio cooperated because stars attracted readers and listeners. Foreign
correspondents enjoyed similar synergies. Articles led to books, which led to lucrative lecture tours, which led to radio appearances and maybe a Hollywood gig
of some kind. All this generated more demand for the correspondents' writing.
At a lunch in New York, an editor offered to publish anything CBS's Eric Sevareid
wanted to write. He wanted the journalist's name in his magazine. Sevareid also
was induced to take a stab at script writing. Nothing came of this, but he appeared
in a publicity trailer for a Warner Bros. war film. The studio's publicity department
urged theaters to put a poster with Sevareid's photo in the lobby.

Many news organizations besides CBS had promotion departments to organize
lectures for their correspondents on home leave. Independent lecture bureaus set
up speeches for freelance correspondents like Vincent Sheean. Sheean disliked the
press agentry. "The lecturer was, *ipso facto,* a 'celebrity,' and the more celebrated he
could be made to seem the better it was for the business." After his maiden lecture
tours in the 1920s, Sheean forswore the podium, with the same effect as his for-
swearing newspaper reporting from time to time. From 1939 to 1942 he lectured
"from one end of the United States to the other." The money was good, and it put
him in touch with his readers.

Outgoing, handsome Quentin Reynolds was more enthusiastic about his fame.
Few people in London were better known, Sheean believed, than Reynolds, a *Collier's* correspondent who frequently spoke on the BBC during the war. Reynolds's
"autograph was valued like that of a film star." When another pal told Reynolds he
was a celebrity at home as well, he doubted it—until *Collier's* helped book him for
a countrywide lecture tour for British War Relief. His Hollywood stop, he thought,
was the best of all. He spoke at "an actor's hundred-dollar-a-plate affair" and raised
twenty thousand dollars. He hobnobbed with old friends who had settled in Hollywood and with the famous actors who sought him out. Yet another sign of his fame
came shortly afterward, when Reynolds got married. Averell Harriman, the millionaire diplomat with whom he had traveled on assignment, lent his Sun Valley,

Idaho, home for the honeymoon. Reynolds had a wartime biography, *War Correspondent,* written about him.

Celebrity-making also found an accomplice in book publishing. Mail-order book associations sprang up in the 1920s. The Book-of-the-Month-Club, the first, started in 1926 and within the first year had forty thousand members. Publishers and authors crafted their product to meet the needs of this market. "The book clubs were a vital point in the expanded literary circuit of the 1920s," one scholar has noted; "more specifically, between 1920 and 1925, as the number of titles published increased twofold, club adoption not only spawned monumental publicity for a featured book but, finally, often produced a quick and lucrative Hollywood sale for the author."

John Gunther was a Book-of-the-Month Club favorite. The BOMC selected all eight of his *Inside* books as well as others he wrote. Several times it suspended usual practice to select an *Inside* book based on a few chapters and an outline. The club's confidence in Gunther rested on his tried-and-true formula, ideal for the large audience that relied on the BOMC to pick books they would like to read.

The *Inside* books were extraordinarily fresh, thanks to rapid manuscript-to-book production and rewriting right up to the last possible minute. Although full of facts and figures, which Gunther collected through prodigious research, his books focused on personalities. This and his knack for seemingly effortless prose made the books accessible to readers with little or no background on a geographic region. An added attraction for the BOMC was the brand name "*Inside.*" No matter where in the world Gunther applied his technique, the resulting book was sure to have instant public recognition. When he tackled Europe anew for a book published in 1961, the title was changed only slightly from the first time. It was *Inside Europe Today.* Every one of his *Inside* books was a best seller.

Gunther's personality contrasted with that of his University of Chicago classmate and friend Vincent Sheean. Sheean was moody, mystical, undisciplined, puritanical about the opposite sex, interested in large philosophical issues, and (as Gunther and Shirer thought) the most erudite of all foreign correspondents. Gunther was straightforward and focused. "It is not in me to be profound," Gunther confided in his diary in 1931. He never mastered a foreign language. As he did for *Inside Europe,* he created a list of questions for each book and systematically asked them everywhere he went. "One of the most indefatigable workers," according to Canfield, Gunther revised material several times before he was satisfied.

Unlike Sheean, Gunther never felt guilty about using his royalties to live well. His love of the good life was apparent in his magazine writing while he was in Vienna for the *Daily News,* a task that allowed him to combine business with pleasure. He wrote a series of articles for *Esquire* on food and eating throughout Europe, contemplated writing a restaurant guide, and produced a *Saturday Evening Post* article titled "Cabbages for Kings," in which the central character was one of the city's great headwaiters. One Viennese restaurant, he noted, served "a hashed breast of goose ($.70) that leaves me practically delirious." Once asked his favorite color, he replied, "smoked salmon—Prunier's, of course, not Reuben's." Between marriages in the 1940s, he always had a beautiful woman on his arm. One romance was with actress Miriam Hopkins, and another especially passionate affair was with the wife of his colleague H. R. Knickerbocker, the correspondent whom Canfield had initially approached about writing *Inside Europe*. In 1951 Truman Capote invented a parlor game, the International Daisy Chain, in which inebriated guests linked people by their affairs they had. Gunther figured in one that started with his involvement with Leonora Schinasi, who became the wife of a Hollywood producer.

Gunther had a troubled childhood, fraught with money problems and, like Sheean, had a distant father and an adoring mother. When he was courting his second wife, Jane, she asked about his father. Gunther brushed off the question. She thought being an outsider as a boy made him all the more interested in being an *insider* as a man—a response opposite to Sheean's. Sheean liked to mix with influentials who had something interesting to discuss; he cared little for partying per se and disdained "famosity." Gunther craved both. One motivation to supplement his *Daily News* reporting with prodigious magazine and book writing was, by his telling, a 1932 *Vanity Fair* photo spread of a dozen of the best-known foreign correspondents. Walter Duranty, H. R. Knickerbocker, and Paul Scott Mowrer were shown. Gunther was not. Gunther was, he confessed, "ravenously interested in human beings." For his *Who's Who* entry in 1956, from which the quote at the beginning of this chapter is taken, he listed the heads of state he had interviewed much as someone might list the awards they had received. (Possibly embarrassed when *Time* quoted the list in its profile of him, Gunther eliminated it in future editions of *Who's Who*.)

Tall, broad-shouldered, and attractive, unassuming and generous, an inveterate socializer, Gunther attracted notable friends. Parties at his apartment on New York's East Sixty-second Street attracted as many as seventy-five people, and among them could be found Audrey Hepburn, Marlene Dietrich, and other movie stars, as well as princes, concert pianist Arthur Rubinstein, fashion designer Valentina, diplomats and politicians, John Steinbeck, Irwin Shaw, and Edward R. Murrow.

Gunther did not bring anything approaching Sheean's personal intensity to his journalism, but he did write about himself as a journalist in the style of Richard Harding Davis. In the mid-1930s, as his fame was opening its petals, he considered writing a little book about "the inner and outside life of a journalist" in London. Although he did not follow through, he recounted his daily activities for the *Atlantic Monthly* and wrote "An Autobiography in Brief" for *Story Magazine*. Toward the end of his life, he wrote *A Fragment of Autobiography: The Fun of Writing the Inside Books*. *Harper's* excerpted the short book. Below is a portion of one of his autobiographical *Atlantic Monthly* articles. It appeared shortly after publication of his first *Inside* book in 1936.

John Gunther in an author's promotional photo taken around the time his first *Inside* book appeared.

INSIDE ENGLAND
BY JOHN GUNTHER

Tuesday, December 3, 1935.—Finished the damned monstrous thing last night! It runs about 190,000 words and I have done the actual writing in five months. I woke Frances* up when I tottered in at five in the morning and we celebrated. The last section I wrote, on England, was the hardest, and I don't like it, but it's too late to do much about it now. I wrote the last chapter and a half, Hoare, British Foreign Policy, Eden, Simon, the Tories, and the whole "Left and Right" chapter, in one final desperate spurt: about 8500 words in twelve or fourteen hours. It absolutely had to be done because Jamie Hamilton, my publisher, was sailing for New York, and, since the book is to be published before he returns, he wanted at least a glance at the English chapter, if only in first draft. His boy called for the MS. at 8 A.M., and took it to the boat train.

I felt very empty and exhilarated. I slept till noon and we had lunch at Lady Oxford's. Margot was a joy to listen to; she described some pianist—Horowitz, I

* Gunther's first wife.

think—playing a pianissimo passage like a mouse darting across the keyboard, and she said of one of her friends that, although his jokes were good, his humor as a whole didn't hang together: it was like a string of beads without the string. I like it best when she reminisces. Once she told me that she had met Lord Curzon, when he was foreign secretary, in Fortnum and Mason's buying a ham. He couldn't depute authority even in the smallest things.

F. and I left at 3.15, she to shop, while I walked slowly to the office. It was hard for me to believe that the whole gigantic script was done. There wasn't much to do in the office. I met F. again at Harry Flory's, where a large cocktail party was going on. Guest of honor was Hugh Baillie, the new chief of the United Press. Process of noisy conversation with many friends. I told a few that the book was finished. We left, late, to join Antony Asquith* and Margot—the arrangement had been made at luncheon—at the ballet at Sadler's Wells;† I haven't the faintest idea what the ballet was. We saw the leading lady after the performance. Then to Rule's‡ for supper and drink. Talk about music, sanctions, politics. I had about a dozen beers.

Friday, December 6.—This was a big day. I sent a 600-word cable about Italy, the war, and the possibility of oil sanctions. Then luncheon at Lady Oxford's to meet the Prince of Wales. There were only eight at table: Lady Oxford, the Prince, Lady Violet Bonham-Carter, Princess Elizabeth Bibesco, General Arthur Asquith, one of her late husband's secretaries (Sir Roderick Meiklejohn), Mrs. Simpson, and myself. I was annoyed because I had been told to wear only a lounge suit, and everybody else was in striped trousers. However, I imagine it is better to be under- than over-dressed on such occasions.

The Prince, whom I hadn't seen close up for years, was smaller than I remembered him, blonder, and in much better physical shape than his pictures show. He was extremely brisk, charming, and vivacious; during the first twenty minutes he and Margot talked incessantly, the Prince laughing a great deal. He drank only iced water. The food was simple and perfect: silverside of beef and a lot of vegetables. Margot brought me into the conversation by asking if I skied. Apparently she and H. R. H. had been talking about vacations. I said that I skied a little, but that on the last occasion, the Semmering, a landslip had taken place in the adjacent Alps the next day. He asked me if I knew Vienna well; Margot explained for me how long I had been there. The Prince asked if I worked for the *Chicago Tribune* or the *Chicago Daily News*. I explained the difference. Then he said, very vivid and brisk, that he had had one disappointment in Vienna last year; he could find no restaurant that served *Lachs-schinken*. I burst into enthusiasm on the subject of *Lachs-schinken* (which, as the name indicates, is a sort of ham that both looks and tastes like salmon) and said that, unfortunately, the only places in Vienna where it might be procured were not the places he would be likely to visit. . . .

* A British Film director.
† A London theater.
‡ A fashionable restaurant known for its beef.

Wednesday, January 15.—We dined at Schmidt's, on Tottenham Court Road, with Aneurin and Jennie, full of life and beans.

Aneurin Bevan, compact and powerful, should be Prime Minister of England some day. Some people think he will. But he is an inveterate lone wolf, and often wrong-headed. And he lacks elasticity. Aneurin was born in Wales and worked underground in the mines for years. The courage and resourcefulness by which he managed to educate himself are remarkable. He got a job in the miners' union and is now so impregnable in his constituency, Ebbw Vale, that ordinarily the conservatives don't bother to put up a candidate against him. In the last elections, however, they did, in order to tie him up, keep him from speaking in other parts of the country. In drawing-room or platform, he is contagiously brilliant. His rich laugh and Welsh accent help. Aneurin, hot, humorous, impish, frank, forward, vivacious, has given us some of the best times we've had in England.

F. and I decided on the way home to give up parties for a while. They are too expensive. A dinner party costs $30 to $35, a cocktail or evening party $40 to $50, depending on how much people drink. We are very broke. We have by modest standards, a decent enough salary; but we cannot live on it. In Vienna we did; here it is impossible. This is because, of course, we like to do nice things, buy books, see people, go out a lot. The last two or three years I have made a good deal each year by outside writing, and while we were in Vienna we saved this; here at about a rate of $100 a month, we have to cut into it. The office allows me £10 per month for all entertainment, taxis, and so on, which is very little indeed. I spend at least six to eight shillings a day on taxis alone, and nine out of the ten for *Daily News* purposes. . . .

Gunther's *"Inside"* brand name became so potent that he could not go anywhere without someone's making a lame joke. "You can imagine what happens when I need an x-ray," he told an interviewer. "It's ghastly." Evelyn Waugh's famous spoof of foreign correspondents, *Scoop,* contains a character suspiciously Guntheresque; he is writing a book, *Under the Ermine.** Gunther's first wife annoyingly kept after him to write about world religions to be called *Inside God.* Getting nowhere, she finally considered writing it herself with Vincent Sheean as a coauthor.

Gunther experienced what many celebrities do, pressure to keep themselves in the public eye. His publisher wanted more books, and maintaining his lifestyle de-

---

* Writes Gunther's doppelgänger, Wenlock Jakes, in *Scoop:* "I shall never forget the evening of King Edward's abdication. I was dining at the Savoy Grill as the guest of Silas Shock of the *New York Guardian.* His guests were well chosen, six of the most influential men and women in England, who are seldom in the news but who control the national pulse. . . . I at once raised the question of the hour. Not one of that brilliant company expressed any opinion. There, in a nutshell, you have England, her greatness—and her littleness." Evelyn Waugh, *Scoop* (Boston: Little, Brown, 1999), 111–12.

"Isn't it about time another one of John Gunther's 'Insides' came out?"

John Gunther was the object of cartoons spoofing him, a sign of his celebrity status. ©The New Yorker Collection 1944 Helen E. Hokinson, from cartoonbank.com. All Rights Reserved.

manded it. "I have eaten every book before it's written," he joked. To support himself during the long months of travel to research his books, he wrote magazine articles. Gunther complained that he spent much time writing in hotel rooms, when he could have been interviewing people.

"Being a journalist," Gunther jotted in his diary in 1931, "is like being a chorus girl. There are few 'pure' journalists, just as there are few chorus girls who expect to *stay* chorus girls. Each profession is essentially a step to something beyond." Gunther wrote other books (his lifelong total was thirty-six); a not-very-good novel based on Vienna was a Literary Guild selection.* An account of his son's tragic ill-

---

* The novel, *The Lost City*, was a love story involving a foreign correspondent. This self-referential approach was used by many journalists who tried fiction over the decades. Stephen Crane in *On Active Service*, Ernest Hemingway in *The Sun Also Rises*, Walter Duranty in *The Search for a Key*, Henry

ness, *Death Be Not Proud,* was turned into a made-for-television movie. Buried under a mountain of bills, he agreed to write an annual report for the drug company Pfizer. It was called *Inside Pfizer.*

At the invitation of director Frank Capra, Gunther made the obligatory trip to Hollywood. During the first visit he worked on documentaries to support the war effort. During the same period he pocketed five thousand dollars for movie rights to one of his novels. He returned to Hollywood when reclusive movie star and close friend Greta Garbo contemplated a movie comeback. She encouraged Gunther to write a script for a romantic movie about a foreign correspondent and a beautiful German spy. Given her dramatic retirement at age thirty-six, the movie would have been a sensation, but she changed her mind about the film.

Gunther was suited to broadcasting. He had a good voice and was the sort of engaging expert NBC wanted. As a panelist on *Town Meeting of the Air,* he was introduced as "a famed foreign correspondent." He filled in on-air for Raymond Swing and Walter Winchell and appeared on *Information Please,* a question-and-answer program. During the war, he broadcast from North Africa while filing stories for the North American Newspaper Alliance and *Reader's Digest.* In the late 1950s he had his own television show, *John Gunther's High Road to Adventure.* "There was no better name to get," said a network executive.

Whereas most reporters struggle to secure interviews with heads of state, leaders courted Gunther when he was abroad doing research. In the Philippines working on *Inside Asia,* he and his wife were entertained on the private yacht of President Manuel Quezon and his wife. Chiang Kai-shek gave him a rare interview. The generalissimo's media-savvy wife had read *Inside Europe.* Gunther marveled at having "virtually a semi-official status" when he traveled to collect material for *Inside Latin America.* Nicaraguan dictator Anastasio Somoza put on a military review in his honor. Wishing to advertise itself, Pan American Airways provided free plane tickets. When he researched *Inside Africa,* he and his wife "were put up at Government House in every British territory we visited." While researching *Inside U.S.A.,* he was asked to address the Texas legislature; in Minnesota the politically ambitious Minneapolis mayor and future vice president Hubert Humphrey called to ask for a meeting.

Others perpetuated Gunther's fame, the ultimate sign of celebrity. In the feature film *Once upon a Honeymoon,* one of the characters tells broadcast correspondent O'Toole (Cary Grant), "You might even write a book called 'Inside Something.'"

Miller in *Tropic of Cancer,* Elliot Paul in *The Amazon,* Pamela Sanders in her Vietnam War–era novel *Miranda,* and others drew on their overseas journalistic experience for themes and characters. When Gunther wrote *The Lost City* in the 1930s, his publishers in the United States and Great Britain worried that the too-close-to-authentic characters invited a lawsuit. Gunther refused to make changes. The roman á clef was eventually published in 1964, with some updating by Gunther. A character based on UP correspondent Robert Best throws his lot in with the Nazis, as Best did when the war broke out. The hero in *The Lost City* is a correspondent for a Chicago paper who has a love of food and women.

Composer Arthur Schwartz bought the title to *Inside U.S.A.* for a musical show that contained nothing else from the book. In 1939 Norman Cousins coined the term "Guntherize" (to condense enormous subjects into digestible prose). A Baghdad bar was named after him. King George II of Greece conferred on Gunther one of the country's highest peacetime awards, the Virgin Eagle. When Gunther died in 1970, his obituary ran on the front page of the *New York Times*. His popularity lasted long after Sheean and other foreign correspondents had dropped off the best-seller lists.

As famous as Gunther was, he remained a serious journalist. His books were enormous in breadth and length (*Inside Africa* and *Inside U.S.A.* ran nearly one thousand pages each) and were timely. Deadline-oriented, he sought to quickly bring this vast material to market "before things changed," his wife Jane commented in an interview after his death. He called it "book journalism," and it was exhausting. One could almost hear a sigh of relief in one book's last line, which came at the end of many pages listing sources: "So now *Inside Africa* is done."

In that book and others later in his career, Gunther now and then expressed an opinion. He criticized the overall U.S. policy on Africa, "which was to sympathize in the abstract with colonial peoples in their desire to be free, but to do nothing that will embarrass their European masters. Nothing, obviously, could be more self-nullifying." But mostly he reported. He was clinical in his description of the philosophy and workings of *apartheid*. "I have little messianic blood in my veins," he said, "and I seldom editorialize. On most issues I take a somewhat detached, even cold, old-fashioned middle view, although I stand more to the left than to the right." "He remains the newshound," said a commentator of an earlier book. "I have read the 600 pages of his *Inside Asia*, but I doubt whether I could tell you what he thinks."

If this approach was in many respects admirable, the scale on which he worked was too vast to avoid superficiality. "My kind of book would never get done at all if I allowed myself unlimited time," Gunther said defensively. "Besides, you can see an amazing lot in a country in a day or two if you really use your legs, eyes and ears. And what you observe is supplemented by intensive reading and other research." He had to generalize, and this produced stunningly naïve observations. When he wrote "Asiatics are generally less competent than Westerners," critics ridiculed the statement. Because of Gunther's journalistic approach, his *Inside* books, like daily newspapers, had short shelf lives.

Knowing his limitations, critics still found John Gunther irresistible. In the late 1940s, journalist Richard Rovere thought "someone ought to show him up for what he was." But after starting on an article about Gunther for the *New Yorker*, he couldn't follow through. Gunther's young son was terminally ill, and Gunther found obvious relief talking to Rovere, who discovered the self-deprecating journalist to be "extremely modest." Rovere considered his resulting profile of Gunther mildly critical. Actually, it was glowing. "In an age that has elevated its journalists above its poets and philosophers, he is perhaps the world's foremost journalist. He is certainly the foremost world journalist." After the release of *Death Be Not Proud,* Gunther's moving book about his son's death, Rovere wrote to congratulate him.

Contemporary surveys of overseas correspondents persistently reaffirm the elite image of the foreign correspondent. "Twice as many foreign correspondents as Main Street journalists have attended private colleges and four times as many have graduate degrees," according to one such examination. "Increasingly, younger foreign correspondents have two professional or managerial parents." Thanks to our ever more pyrotechnic star system, a few correspondents have been propelled to preposterous levels of celebrity. In 2005 actress Renée Zellweger interviewed CNN's Christiane Amanpour for one of the Sundance Channel's *Iconoclasts* segments, which looked at "ground shakers who have transformed our culture through their passions." With some frequency in recent years, the U.S. Postal Service has featured journalists on stamps. Such honorees have tended to be those with experience as foreign correspondents—Martha Gellhorn, Marguerite Higgins, Edward R. Murrow, Ernie Pyle, Eric Sevareid. Combat reporter Pyle's fame is so durable that he also entered the modern-day pantheon of children's toys as a Hasbro G.I. Joe action figure, complete with typewriter and trenching tool.

But Pyle and most of the others on postage stamps belong to a bygone era. Contemporary correspondents, even if lionized on the Sundance Channel, do not as a group seem quite so elite or so heroic.

One place to look is the movies, a mirror of society as well as a magnifier of heroic images. Alfred Hitchcock opened *Foreign Correspondent* with a dedication "to those intrepid ones who went across the seas to be the eyes and ears of America . . . To those forthright ones who early saw the clouds of war while many of us at home were seeing rainbows . . . To those clearheaded ones who now stand like recording angels among the dead and dying." As time has marched on, movie correspondents have become less self-assured, less majestic. When figuring in a feature film—and that does not happen with the same frequency as before—they are more likely to be angst-ridden and out of synch with those they cover. John Wayne, the fearless newsreel cameraman who put down an Arab revolt in *I Cover the War* in 1937, was Col. Mike Kirby in the 1968 movie *The Green Berets.* He and his men disdain the war correspondent who accompanies them. In *The Killing Fields,* a movie based on the experience of the *New York Times'* Sydney Schanberg in Cambodia during the Vietnam War, the frustrated correspondent laments, "It's not a fucking forties movie. You can't just get on a goddamn plane and make the whole world come out right."

The trends that have made it more difficult to spawn independent, knowledgeable, confident correspondents like Sheean also have made it difficult for correspondents to reach Gunther's hero status, which also was founded on a sense of journalistic mission to illuminate a world sliding into darkness. Although his *Inside Europe* in 1935 had a flashy title, its true intent lay in the working title "Doomed Europe." In a later book on the Soviet Union, Gunther boldly avoided cold war rhetoric to illuminate the human side of the Soviet Union. "Correspondence has somewhat lost its glamour, and its career appeal," said British correspondent Alexander Cockburn in 1974. "Gone are the great days of a Shirer or a Farson, when European correspondents were cocks of the walk, face-to-face with Fascism, or watching bombs fall from the roof of the Savoy."

Also chipping away at the statuary of foreign correspondence is the lack of exclusivity in that line of work. Would-be special correspondents for daily newspapers no longer have to start their careers by competing for a spot on the *Paris Herald,* where they get a little schooling in the craft. Virtually anyone can board an airplane to anywhere. And when they land, they can flip open a laptop and begin to blog. Correspondents are not so *special* anymore.

In this modern journalistic world, correspondents rarely recline in first class. Sitting with them in tourist class is their audience, Americans bent on seeing the world for themselves. Asked why foreign correspondents aren't on the lecture circuit the way they once were, *Chicago Daily News* alumna Georgie Anne Geyer observed that average Americans don't feel they need knowledgeable intermediaries to help them understand the world. "They've been on a cruise in the Volga and they think they know Russia."

This did not happen all at once. The roots of easy travel are found in the interwar years, as we shall see in the next chapter with journalist-adventurer Richard Halliburton, whose fame was spectacular if much more superficial than Gunther's. But the full consequences were not apparent until Gunther and others passed from the scene.

In a requiem to these correspondents, the *Nation* noted there was no longer "magic to the moniker" *foreign correspondent.* "Since World War II, Americans, particularly students, have traveled abroad in unprecedented numbers, becoming amateur correspondents complete with their own photography-illustrated stories. Then, too, television, with its global reach, has demystified, if not deepened, the reporting of foreign news. Traveling reporters, although too often lazy carriers of cliché in their work, now can be there when it happens, transmitting the news instantaneously, making us on-the-spot spectators, only dimly reflecting the glamour of the old Marco Polos of the news."

As sociologist Vilfredo Pareto said in his seminal sociological treatise in 1916, the most entrenched elites are fluid: "Aristocracies do not last."

15

NEW WORLDS TO CONQUER

"By 1925 there remained no considerable portion of the earth's surface that had not been explored," Mark Sullivan observed in his up-to-the-minute chronicle of the century. Journalists, however, were not about to fold their tents. The easily accessible horizons that spread before them offered more riches than the unknown alone ever could.

Previously travel had been reserved for those with lots of time and resources. Travelers pushing into unlit corners of the planet also needed plenty of courage. Now the same forces that had facilitated overseas jaunts by Vincent Sheean, John Gunther, and so many other young journalists set average Americans in motion as well. "Never before in the history of the world has so large a part of the population of any nation gone sightseeing in strange lands," *Harper's* reported in 1931. Every institution seemed determined to help. Employers shortened work weeks and offered paid holidays; banks let Americans pay for vacations on the installment plan; steamship companies created tourist third-class passage "to meet the demand for steerage prices without the accompanying odor of garlic." And urging all of these along were the organs of journalism.

Traveling Americans needed Baedekers if they were to enjoy a well-mapped world. Journalists wrote them as stories in magazines and newspapers and in book form. These travel guides were sometimes written in flights of literary style. More often they consisted of down-to-earth advice on what to see, how to get there, and where to stay and to eat. In 1933, the *Nation* published a series of travel articles "designed to give practical information to persons of moderate means and liberal interests." Around the same time the *New York Times* initiated a separate Sunday travel section, rather than run travel stories in the drama section.

Journalists also found new ways to have adventures. Some of their horizon-chasing was significant, such as that promoted by *National Geographic*. The magazine's parent company, the National Geographic Society, came as close to making a science out of such journalism as was possible with a popular magazine. A stream of botanists, anthropologists, archaeologists, oceanographers, and naturalists filled the periodical's pages, either writing the stories themselves or having their tales told by a journalist. Many more journalistic adventures were as contrived and zany as the 1920s crazes of flagpole-sitting and marathon dancing—and likely to involve the same sort of collegian looking for a thrill. The corner on this market was held by a perpetual college boy, Richard Halliburton.

In 1895 a teacher named Annie S. Peck became the third woman to climb the Matterhorn. Supporting herself through lecturing and writing for *Harper's,* the *Boston Herald,* and other publications, Peck became a professional traveler particularly known for scaling South American slopes. In 1929 the seventy-nine-year-old Peck demonstrated the possibilities of air travel south of the border by flying the entire continent on local carriers. The last leg of her twenty-thousand-mile trip, recounted in *Flying over South America,* was aboard one of Pan-American Airway's new Clipper airboats, which had the comforts of home and then some. "Clipper Ships contain a ladies' lounge, smoking-salon, buffet fitted to prepare meals in the air, with electric range and refrigerator. With real couches and easy-chairs they afford vastly more luxurious comfort than the finest Pullman, room to circulate easily, stewards to wait upon the guests, so to speak, and no tips essential." It was an exciting story and a common one. Ordinary Americans, Peck said, could think of "flying as now in the day's work."

Everywhere new travel opportunities materialized, journalists were on hand to record them, participate in them, or promote them. Of the eight passengers on the first *China Clipper* flight from San Francisco in 1936, three were senior newspaper executives, brought along for the obvious reason of generating good publicity.* *Cosmopolitan's* John Brisben Walker staged a race between his old and new offices in New York City, bought the Stanley Automobile Company, became the first president of the American Automobile Manufacturers' Association, and organized the National Highway Commission. Later he sponsored an essay contest on "aerial navigation." Pulitzer's *World* offered a $10,000 purse for the first flight between Albany and New York and, with its sister paper the *St. Louis Post-Dispatch,* put up $30,000 for the first flight between New York and St. Louis. Neither the *Post-Dispatch* nor any other newspaper was willing to pay for the $25,000 prize for Charles Lindbergh's sensation-making first nonstop flight between New York and Paris on the *Spirit of St. Louis.* "We have our reputation to consider," a *Post-Dispatch* editor told Lindbergh regarding the paper's concern that the danger was too great. The *New York Times,* however, secured exclusive rights to Lindbergh's account, which their reporters wrote for the aviator after he landed in Paris. The *Chicago Tribune's* Colonel McCormick grew so excited about having his reporter Larry Rue in the air in search of news that he ordered him to buy his own plane. Rue's memoir was titled *I Fly for News.* For all its seriousness, the *National Geographic* was not left out. Its first permanent foreign correspondent, Maynard Owen Williams, participated in a

---

* Journalists have always been found on maiden voyages. As noted in chapter 4, James Gordon Bennett Sr. was aboard the first steamship from New York to England. Twelve journalists were aboard the first steam passenger train from Albany to Schenectady over the Mohawk and Hudson Railroad in 1831.

ten-month-long expedition jointly financed by the society and French automobile maker André Citroën to retrace by car Marco Polo's trip to China.

Dignified Victor Lawson of the *Chicago Daily News* had a penchant for these locomotions. In the mid-1920s he agreed to a proposal by Negley Farson, a freelancer at the time, "to cruise down the Danube, stopping over wherever I see the chance to secure good material." The trip resulted in Farson's first book, the lyrical *Sailing across Europe,* and a place for him in the *Daily News* Foreign Service, which later sent him to drive a motorcar to the Arctic Circle. Lawson personally headed a more complicated venture as president of the Wellman-Chicago *Record-Herald* Polar Exploration Company. The Wellman in the title was Walter Wellman, Lawson's Washington correspondent. After Wellman twice failed to reach the North Pole by dirigible, he attempted the first transatlantic dirigible trip in 1910, this time with additional backing from the *New York Times* and the *London Daily Telegraph.* An internal *Times* memo noted that Wellman had "no faith in the utility of airships of any type, within our day and generation, for purely commercial pursuits, such as carrying passengers and freight." He thought the value of this transatlantic flight, the first time an aircraft was equipped with a wireless radio, was scientific and military. The dirigible crashed off Cape Hatteras.

Around-the-world antics, inspired by George Francis Train and Nellie Bly from an earlier generation, continued to consume oceans of printer's ink. Journalists covered trips by a Chicago police chief (40 days) and by a New York theatrical producer (36 days), the latter traveling the last forty miles of his 1913 trip sitting on an airplane wing. Associated Press reporter Linton Wells stowed away for the India leg of the first-ever globe-girdling done strictly by air, a nearly six-month enterprise undertaken by American military pilots in 1924. William Randolph Hearst underwrote the dirigible *Graf Zeppelin*'s twenty-one-day circumnavigation in 1929. In 1931, when Wiley Post and his navigator Harold Gatty cut that time by more than half, the *New York Times* syndicated the pilot's in-flight reports. NBC radio sponsored a lecture tour afterward. A *Boston Globe* reporter ghosted their story, *Around the World in Eight Days.*

Eager to set a record, not just report one, Wells teamed up in 1926 with a wealthy Detroit businessman and aviation enthusiast to "reduce the girth of the globe" by the judicious use, where possible, of airplanes. The trip, under the auspices of the *New York World* and the North American Newspaper Alliance, cost forty-two thousand dollars and set a new record. "Verily," the *World* editorialized, "we have come a long way since Jules Verne." Wells afterward wrote *Around the World in Twenty-Eight Days* and married Fay Gillis, a pioneering aviatrix who reported with him overseas and in Hollywood for the *New York Herald Tribune.* More exciting still was a three-way race around the earth launched in 1936 by the *New York World-Telegram.* This was Nellie Bly's old newspaper, the *World,* which had undergone a merger and was now owned by Scripps Howard. (See "Gallantly Ignoring Stomach Aches," p. 247.) The journey showed that the world could be circled so fast by commercial airplane that passengers could scarcely know that they had been abroad. "I would recommend," wrote the *New York Times* reporter who competed in the race,

GALLANTLY IGNORING STOMACH ACHES

Imbued with the news-making instincts of Joseph Pulitzer, the former owner of the *New York World*, Roy W. Howard instructed H. R. Ekins of the now hyphenated *New York World-Telegram* to "demonstrate without loss of time that any person with funds sufficient for the purchase of tickets could fly completely around the world and entirely by commercial airlines." While Ekins was preparing for the trip, the *New York Times* and the Hearst-owned *New York Evening Journal* announced that they were sending Leo Kieran and Dorothy Kilgallen, respectively, on the same mission. The twenty-three-year-old Kilgallen, whose primary qualification for the trip was being the same gender as Bly, had never been out of the United States. All three left on the same day, from the same place—Lakehurst, New Jersey, aboard the dirigible airship *Hindenburg*. Just before takeoff, Ekins was given a dainty flask owned by Bly.

Kilgallen and Kieran got along together. Misery loves company. On the first leg of the flight on the *Hindenburg*, Ekins wrote: "Gallantly ignoring a stomach ache that may have been caused by the egg Miss Kilgallen fried in the ship's kitchen, Leo Kieran wanders about trying to get other passengers to write stories for him. Finally, his brow wrinkled, he sits down and thrashes away at a typewriter (borrowed)."

After landing in Europe, Ekins rushed ahead on a carefully planned schedule, upon which he had to improvise. He had coordinated the trans-Pacific leg of the trip with the first eastbound commercial flight of the *China Clipper* from Manila. As a result of delays caused by a typhoon, the *Hawaii Clipper* happened to be in Manila. Although the *Clipper* was not yet taking paying passengers—and hence could not give him a commercial flight per se—Ekins caught a ride on it as a "crew member." The first of the trio to reach New York, he set a new record of eighteen days, fourteen hours, fifty-six minutes, and two-fifths of a second, went on the lecture circuit, and wrote *Around the World in Eighteen Days: And How to Do It.*

Each newspaper played the story its own way. The *Times* ran Kieran's short reports inside. A story announcing his return appeared on page 13. The *World Telegram* splashed Ekins's stories on the front page, along with photos and maps. Difficult as it was to do, the tabloid *Journal* went even further. Kilgallen's stories, as well as scores of stories about her, dominated the front page and nearly filled a full page inside on most days. One day the *Journal* lowered its masthead and ran above it a picture of one of the airplanes in which she flew. Large photos of her accompanied the stories.

When the trip was over, the *Times* primly noted that its man was the only one to follow the rules. Not above cheating any more than Ekins was, Kilgallen had taken a private plane from California to New York. In any event, the female runner-up came out the biggest winner. The *Journal* gathered her dispatches into a book, *Girl around the World*; a songwriter created "Hats Off to Dorothy"; she appeared on Kate Smith's coast-to-coast radio show; and Camel cigarettes used her in a full-page ad: "I snatched meals anywhere, ate all kinds of food. But Camels helped me keep my digestion tuned up." When Kilgallen went to Hollywood as a columnist for the paper, she took with her a screenplay based on the trip. The Kilgallen character is the hero. The Ekins character is anything but. "In umpty-ump years of screen-viewing," said a reviewer of the film, *Fly Away Baby*, "we've never before come upon a fourth-estater who was such a bad man."

"that, on a duplication of my trip, longer stops be made to see the wonders of the world."

While Annie Peck engaged in more serious quests (a peak in Peru is named after her), other careers that hyphenated journalism and adventure yielded escape literature. Before the war, Burton Holmes, who wrote for the *Ladies' Home Journal* and lectured widely, and Harry A. Franck, author of *A Vagabond Journey around the World,* glamorized travel as easy and fun. After the war, Everests of saccharin travel books piled up. E. Alexander Powell, who once sold typewriters in London and fought in World War I, was best known for such books as *By Camel and Car to the Peacock Throne.* William Seabrook turned out *Adventures in Arabia, Jungle Ways,* and *The Magic Island,* which introduced the word *zombie* to American conversation. In the 1920s South African novelist Ethelreda Lewis took in hand a hard-living Englishman, Alfred Aloysius Horn, and coauthored his memoir of fifty years in Africa. "Romance will run amuck," proclaimed an ad for *Trader Horn,* which soon became a movie. In the flesh at New York cocktail parties, Horn was a prosaic drunk; his real surname was Smith.

A long-shining star in this part of the journalistic firmament was Lowell Thomas, whom *Literary Digest* called "the world's foremost globe trotter." On the eve of World War I, the young newspaper reporter filmed an Alaska travelogue. When the war came, Thomas Travelogues latched onto Col. T. E. Lawrence in the Arabian Desert. Thomas embroidered his *With Lawrence in Arabia* and went on fabricating a colorful public "adventure" personality for himself while developing a reputation for privacy (always a good technique if one really wants attention). In the 1930s he took over on of Floyd Gibbons's radio programs and, with the arrival of television, hosted CBS's *High Adventure with Lowell Thomas.* With the help of a longtime ghostwriter, Thomas wrote more than fifty books, several of which reflected his passion for aviation. He was reputedly "the first reporter to broadcast from a ship at sea, a mountaintop, a jungle, a plane, and a helicopter."

Although some made a career out of adventure-journalism, virtually anyone could fashion the odd escapade. Mary Knight posed as a TWA stewardess in order to "describe the sensations of the new feminine profession in the clouds." Lasso-twirling humorist and newspaper columnist Will Rogers undertook a six-month tour of Europe for the *Saturday Evening Post* in 1926, "vaulting from cloud to cloud . . . air is the thing." His travel articles resulted in *There's Not a Bathing Suit in Russia and Other Bare Facts.* In 1931 Rogers flew to the Far East with Gibbons. On the 1936 best-seller list with books by Gunther, Farson, and Duranty was *Around the World in Eleven Years,* putatively written by the three young offspring of photographer John Abbe and actress Polly Platt. Hearst Publications sponsored *Your True Adventures,* a radio program in which Gibbons paid twenty-five dollars for the best story submitted by a listener.

College students were not to be denied these pleasures. In 1923 the University of Delaware started the first junior-year-abroad program for students; Smith, a women's college, followed two years later. "A trip to Europe, either during or just after college," commented the *Atlantic Monthly* in 1930, "is coming to be as much a mat-

Will Rogers, a sometime foreign correspondent, was another devo-
tee of flying. This drawing is from the endpapers of his book *There's
Not a Bathing Suit in Russia and Other Bare Facts*.

ter of course to the average American student as the Continental Grand Tour was
to the young aristocrat of eighteenth-century England."

While they were at it, these wanderers itched to take a fling at giddy writing,
which also stood a chance of appearing in the *Atlantic Monthly*. "When the diploma was safely clutched in the hand, a profound feeling of emptiness, of task officially completed but actually undone, enveloped the celebrant, . . ." wrote a recent
Yale graduate in the magazine in 1932, "June, and the customary romances of com-
mencement; and speeches and no job. . . . The only thing to do was to go far away,
swing into some new tide, find a further world, perhaps win a diploma more worth
having."

The Yalie's breathless, lo-the-wonder prose was as common as a college boy on
the Champs Elysées. Youngsters widely mimicked it in articles and letters home.
Its originator, right down to the liberal use of ellipses, was Richard Halliburton,
whom *Vanity Fair* archly described as "that hardy perennial. . . responsible first for
bringing the gospel of impetuous youth to the hinterlands."

Halliburton's jumping-off point was Princeton University, a school F. Scott Fitzgerald described in his first novel as "the pleasantest country club in America." Halliburton and his classmates, who matriculated when Fitzgerald was still a student there, fed on the glamorous Richard Harding Davis and the English poet Rupert Brooke, who died in 1915, the year before Davis did, at the even younger age of twenty-seven. One of Brooke's idealistic poems about search and failure gave Fitzgerald the title of his novel *This Side of Paradise.* The working title of the book fit Halliburton perfectly. It was *The Romantic Egoist.*

When Harry Franck, author of *Vagabond Journey around the World,* lectured near campus, Halliburton wheedled a dinner invitation and plied the famous author with questions about the travel writing career he had confected after graduating from the University of Michigan. "The *romantic*—that was what I wanted," Halliburton said of his decision to travel abroad upon graduation in 1921. "I hungered for the romance of the sea, and foreign ports and foreign smiles. I wanted to follow the prow of a ship, any ship, and sail away, perhaps to China, perhaps to Spain, perhaps to the South Sea Isles, there to do nothing all day long but lie on a surf-swept beach and fling monkeys at the coconuts." Unconscious of any presumptuousness, he sent a telegram to Gilbert Grosvenor, editor of the *National Geographic,* "PLEASE WRITE ME AT EARLIEST CONVENIENCE REQUIREMENTS FOR CONTRIBUTIONS TO GEOGRAPHIC SAILING THURSDAY FOR A TWO YEAR SEMIVAGABOND [*sic*] AROUND THE WORLD TO COLLECT MATERIAL AND PHOTOGRAPHS FOR A BOOK."

Halliburton's traveling companion was one of his roommates, a Kansas City boy named Irvine "Mike" Hockaday. The pair bicycled through Germany and climbed the Matterhorn in Switzerland, Hockaday delighting "I can actually spit a mile." They split up in Paris, Hockaday to complete his around-the-world trip on a schedule and Halliburton to follow at a more leisurely pace, piling up adventures. He rode through part of Andorra on a rented donkey and spent an evening chatting with the country's head of state, or syndic, in his simple home. He was arrested for violating the no-picture rule at the British fortifications in Gibraltar. He swam the Nile at Luxor. He slipped inside the Taj Mahal at night and slept there until dawn. He climbed Mount Fujiyama in the midwinter.

Halliburton's freelance writing during the trip was a mixed success, at best. His hometown newspaper, the *Memphis Commercial-Appeal,* published his stories. *Travel* magazine accepted an article on Malaysia and rejected others. *National Geographic* did not use either of the stories he submitted, although it paid him for one of them—a well-written piece on Ladakh, in Tibet, that carefully described a remote, interesting culture. This anthropological approach had been a staple of the best nineteenth-century travel literature. By the time he returned home, however, Halliburton had decided that old-fashioned genre was not for him. He accentuated the lighthearted in his book *The Royal Road to Romance,* which he dedicated to his four Princeton roommates.

Mike Hockaday, whom Halliburton visited in Kansas City upon his return, became a successful stockbroker. He did not travel to Europe again for thirty years.

Halliburton never stopped moving. Although he had struggled to find a publisher for *The Royal Road* and more than a few reviewers were unimpressed with its jejuneness, the public loved it. "*The Royal Road to Romance,*" one reviewer noted, "is the best substitute available for those unable to make a similar trip." Halliburton's next book, *The Glorious Adventure,* loosely retraced Ulysses' *Odyssey.* In one of those feats that authors dream of, both *The Royal Road* and *The Glorious Adventure* were on the top-ten list of nonfiction books in 1927. After that came *New Worlds to Conquer,* which recounted his adventures in Latin America. During that journey, he had a three-thousand-dollar-per-article contract with *Ladies' Home Journal.* His book royalties in 1930, the year after the stock market crash, totaled $38,657, the equivalent of a half million dollars in 2008.

Halliburton, a "gorgeous, clean-cut, 110 per cent red-blooded, all-American boyish hero," was made for the lecture circuit. His book contract for *The Royal Road* materialized when two Bobbs-Merrill editors attended a talk he gave at the Princeton Club in New York. He claimed the book did not sell well until he managed to get in front of the booksellers' convention in St. Louis. No matter where he spoke, his theme was the same. "A middle aged audience crowded in Orchestra hall last night," the *Chicago Tribune* noted in 1926. "Romance was the young lecturer's favorite word." (Halliburton had insisted on the title *The Royal Road to Romance;* "romance" was a word "women can't resist.") Halliburton typically arrived in town wearing a derby hat, spats, and a flamboyant necktie and carrying a black silver-tipped cane. "Had an audience of 3,000 last night at Rockford," he told his parents; "6,000 teachers in Columbus," he said in another letter. Two thousand people were turned away from a talk in Dallas because of a full house.

Halliburton's adventures in the 1920s followed the pattern set by his first around-the-world trip: climbing mountains (Mount Olympus in Greece, Popocatépetl in Mexico, and Cerro Pirre on the Colombia-Panama border), swimming (the Hellespont and the Panama Canal), and trespassing (in the Parthenon at night). When these adventures became threadbare, he decided that "an adventure not in the air is obsolete." He acquired a plane and a pilot and left Paris on a two-year series of flights that ended in Asia. En route he marched with the French Foreign Legion and, unable to resist an old trick, swam the Sea of Galilee. He named the plane and the resulting book *The Flying Carpet.*

Halliburton was "one of the greatest press-agents of his time," *Time* said; "his only client was himself." His Hellespont swim only *seemed* original. His hero Lord Byron had done it, and so had others. He made it newsworthy by arranging for word to get to the *New York Times* that he had drowned. The attention he received "triggered almost a mass bathing invasion of the tricky current," which included foreign correspondent Leland Stowe as well as college boys and girls, who informed their hometown newspapers.

The Panama Canal was perfect for a Halliburton swim. Built to speed up shipping, the waterway was an alluring symbol of the shrinking planet. In the prewar years, travel author Burton Holmes's most popular lecture was about the canal. When Halliburton arrived in Panama in 1928, *Pan-American Magazine* noted, the

In a typical look-at-me pose, Richard Halliburton stood with legs apart in front of the Taj Mahal in India. Princeton University Library.

canal had been "enjoying its greatest tourist season in many years. . . . Shriners, Elks, Chambers of Commerce and a host of other organizations have made the Isthmus their Mecca." Again, Halliburton was not the first swimmer. Two professional swimmers—a man and a woman from New York—had made a partial transit through the canal in 1913. Shortly after the canal officially opened the next year, two workers swam the entire fifty miles from the Caribbean to the Pacific by stages in their spare time. Halliburton, too, did the swim by stages. What made his trip singular was that he wrangled permission from the governor of the Canal Zone to go through the locks as a ship would. No one had done that before. The trip attracted press attention as far away as the Natal *Mercury* in South Africa.

Halliburton's account of the swim in *New Worlds to Conquer* is typical: his purple, excited prose; his guise as an average young man with no special physical powers; and his buildup of the story with a love interest, the "undeniably pretty" Isabella. He met the bar girl at an all-night party at the American Cabaret before starting his swim; in his telling, she became Queen Isabella to his Christopher Columbus. Halliburton's swim began on the Caribbean side of the canal. The excerpt below begins with his arrival at the locks that open on to Gatún Lake. Accompanying him in the rowboat *Daisy* is Quentin, a Jamaican familiar with the canal, and "the sharpshootingest sergeant on the isthmus," lent by the commander of the American forces to guard Halliburton against barracuda and other perils.

Armed with my omnipotent letter from the governor, I knocked on the colossal outer gates and demanded entrance. The gate-keeper looked down from the control house and would have shooed me away with a rock, if I had not waved my imperial order.

"What nonsense is this?" he asked, seeing I insisted on standing by my rights.

And when he read my letter he could not decide which was the more insane, me or the governor.

"Do you realize what you're asking?" he said. He led me into the vast and awesome control room. "Do you see all this machinery?" It looked to me as if all the engines in the world had been collected in this place. It made me dizzy to try to comprehend the power it represented, and the silent, gleaming magic with which the greatest ship on earth, once this terrible power spoke with its deep-rumbling voice, was lifted like thistledown from the mud of the Atlantic channel into the fairy seas and fairy isles beyond the magician's shining castle.

"Do you see all this?" the magician repeated. ". . . It will take nine million cubic feet of water three times displaced to raise you into the lake. It will take just as much horse-power as it takes to lower the *California*. And most important of all, it will take twice as long. For three hours you will hold up ship traffic in the Gatun locks. Do you think you are worth it?"

Did I think I was worth it! Was a microscopic earthworm justified in assaulting the gates of heaven and loudly demanding that they swing ajar?

Did I think I was worth it!

"Y-yes, sir!"

There was nothing else for the superintendent to do but acquiesce. The governor had commanded.

"Very well. But I have this to say, young man. You certainly have your nerve."

Even so, the lights were beginning to twinkle in his eyes.

"One other thing," he added, "before you start blocking the Canal. Don't think the locks are free toll. The governor doesn't say anything about waiving charges."

"Quite right, sir. Governor Walker and I agreed I was to pay like all other ships—according to my tonnage. I'm the S. S. *Richard Halliburton,* registered in Memphis, Tennessee. Length, five feet ten inches; beam, one foot; tonnage, one hundred and forty pounds—that's one-thirteenth of one ton."

"One-thirteenth of one ton, eh." He got down his tables. "You're the smallest ship in the history of the Panama Canal." And then after a bit of calculation: "You owe me thirty-six cents."

Meanwhile several hundred people had lined the edges of the locks, for the newspapers had announced that this unique event would take place, and the curious had flocked, many from Colon, to see the first swimmer locked through.

Pushing past these spectators I rejoined the sergeant and Quentin who had been waiting in the rowboat before the haughty gates.

We gave the signal. Those Titanic steel jaws, each leaf seventy feet high, seventy feet wide and seven feet thick, weighing eight hundred thousand pounds each, peeped apart, and slowly swung wide to admit me.

I dived from the rowboat and swam into the over-towering chamber, with the *Daisy* not a foot away. I looked up and back and saw the monstrous doors silently swing closed, imprisoning me at the bottom of this sunken thousand-foot lake. It was a long thousand feet to swim. I should have liked to have one of the electric "mules" that tow ships through tow me, but I had no hooks or stanchions on which the hawsers could make fast.

As I moved along, great numbers of fish, sucked into the lock system from Gatun Lake, splashed all about me, frantic with alarm over the violent adventure of being swirled so unexpectedly from fresh water into salt. Innumerable hell-divers attracted by the hysterical fish scurried over the surface of the water glutting themselves on the unwary perch. Small alligators, water snakes, tarpons, every kind of life that inhabits the tropical lake, caught in the descending flood were now jumping and swimming about me.

Reaching the second set of gates, holding back the water in the lock above, we found everything ready for the magic elevator. . . . Three times this process was repeated until I'd reached the level of the lake and swum out upon its calm blue waters.

Here, the first thing I encountered was the exasperated glances of the captains on the line of ships who had been killing time as best they could until the

S. S. Richard Halliburton paddled out of their way and permitted traffic through the locks to resume its normal flow.

There was one glance however that was kindly, sympathetic—even proud for me. It came from a girl half-hidden by a parasol, one of the people who had lined the locks and watched me struggle through. This girl had followed me on out to the end of the breakwater that jutted into the lake, and when I swam around it, seeking the dock at the lakeside town of Gatun, she shouted down:

"Buenos días, Señor Cristóbal. I am here."

This greeting came at a very opportune time. Of the gallery of five hundred or more people scarcely one had any sentiment for me other than ridicule. They had gathered expecting a sensational swimmer to rip across the waters, to give an exhibition of perfect form that would shame the sea lions.

And instead of a sea lion they had seen an amateur, with no swimming form whatsoever, sideswipe his way into the Olympian locks. The gallery had been let down, cheated. I was an imposter and a fraud. They all marched home indignant.

All—but Isabella.

She seemed to understand that I was a land animal doing my utmost to be a dolphin, and she appreciated the difficulties I was having.

"Isabella," I said, crawling up beside her and hiding under her parasol to escape the scorching sun, "I'm a disgrace to the Panama Canal."

"Disgrace—?"

"Sure. Rotten—bum—punk."

"Ah no! Not punk. Not very good—not very bad. You reach Panama by and by."

"And when I do will you be there to meet me? I probably won't arrive till next year."

"*Sí.*"

"And we'll go to Kelly's Ritz and dance?"

"Sí, sí!"

Then I'm on my way, my little wag." And I stood up to dive off.

"*Momentito, Señor Cristóbal. Mucho sol,*" she said, pointing to my shoulders and face scarlet from the sunburn that had begun the day before to torment me. "*Aquí*—have my parasol."

I accepted it laughingly and gave it for safe keeping to Sergeant Wright, who, as I plunged in for the twenty-four-mile grind across the lake, raised Isabella's pink sunshade above his pine-tree frame and settled back into the boat to watch for crocodiles.

Halliburton was a perfect target for *Vanity Fair.* The sophisticated magazine poked fun at him in two articles, "The Adventure Racket" and "New Ladies' Clubs to Conquer"; another time it nominated him for "oblivion" "because his books are marvelously readable, transparently bogus, extremely popular, and have made their author a millionaire; because his invariable picture of himself (patent pending) is that of a diffident, romantic boy; because he is the most popular ladies' club lecturer in America, and every knock *Vanity Fair* gives him is just a boost." In a *Collier's* cartoon, a matron proudly shows off her tiny garden pond. "We're very proud of this pool," the woman says. "Richard Halliburton jumped over it."

Skeptics said Halliburton's feats were hoaxes. Whatever the merits of other criticism, this one missed the mark, and Halliburton worked hard to prove that was so. One of the most common charges against him was that he could not have swum in the Taj Mahal pool. It was too shallow. The swim had actually taken place in a deep lily pond at the center of the garden, Halliburton explained; on a 1930s trip to India, he repeated the stunt, though without the same joie de vivre. The pool, no longer "clean and clear," crawled with "strange life." The day after he dived seventy feet into the Well of Death in the Yucatán, he returned with an audience and did the trick a second time. "In the presence of newspaper representatives," said one newspaper account, "[Halliburton] today shattered centuries of superstition by jumping into the sacrificial well at the Chichen Itza ruins and clambering out alive. The well was employed by the ancient Mayans to sacrifice maidens and war prisoners, part of their religious rites. Mr. Halliburton is probably the first person in the 1,000 years history of Chichen Itza who ever took the great dive and lived to tell the tale." "When I say I did something," Halliburton told his father, "I actually did it. But I splash a little red paint on it to make it more interesting."

This was one of Halliburton's few understatements. He displayed genuine courage in launching himself over the Yucatán precipice. He was a faker in the way he slathered on the color afterward. Annie Peck disappointed her *New York World* editors when she climbed Popocatépetl. "It wasn't a difficult climb at all," she reported. Halliburton described his ascent as "climbing to the moon up a ladder made of ice." In addition to exaggerating, he made virtually no attempt to get his facts straight and turned them all around when it suited his story. He could not make up his mind whether the Panama Canal held alligators or crocodiles (it was really caimans). He was especially cavalier in recounting his next Panama adventure, his climb of Cerro Pirre in the Darién region bordering Colombia.

The Darién is one of the least-traveled spots in Latin America. The Pan-American Highway, whose construction was approved in 1923, is still uncompleted in a sixty-odd-mile stretch there. Naturalists who study Cerro Pirre's diverse cornucopia of butterflies, birds, snakes, and other species consider it unusually inhospitable. Halliburton's putative reason for climbing Cerro Pirre was that "the foremost historian in Panama" had told him Vasco Núñez de Balboa, the first European sightseer to spy the Pacific, did so from that vantage point. Quite possibly he really did say this, for some romantics thought Balboa's lookout was on a high peak in the Darién. But that was wrong. Cerro Pirre, five thousand feet high, lies in a difficult-to-traverse wilderness that would have taken the conquistador far out of his way. Besides, a chronicler with Balboa said he saw the ocean from a "bare high hill"; the mountains of Darién, in contrast, are cloaked with thick jungle foliage.

More inquiries would have informed Halliburton that the true sighting probably took place nearer to San Miguel Bay, although the precise location is still disputed. Halliburton, however, was not long on detailed inquiries. In a small town a few miles from the mountain, he simply found an old black man "who thought he knew the best way to the top." Indians and not blacks are most familiar with the heavily vegetated route, which is elusive even if one is familiar with the climb. In addition, the sketchy details in Halliburton's account do not match the on-the-ground reality. Although this may be one of the few cases when Halliburton did not do what he said he did, he probably didn't know any better. The best explanation is that Halliburton reached a high point, and the exhausted guide suggested they were at the summit. Halliburton could not have disputed him. Even at the real summit, the canopy is too thick to see much of anything, let alone the distant ocean.

Halliburton's red paint also covered up the grim scenes that he encountered. "Burning current events are poison in book form" he told his publishers. Everything was a lark. He was forever the teenager who would rather race to the top of the Eiffel Tower than ponder its significance. Where others saw poverty or simmering revolution, he saw an opportunity for self-gratification. His attitudes about darker races belonged to the nineteenth century. "As always happens among Negro populations," he observed in Ethiopia, "the [Christian] religion has been degraded until it consists chiefly of superstitions, fasts, incantations and the wearing of charms. There certainly are no Christian moral standards." In India, he insisted on riding in first class even though he had purchased a cheaper ticket that put him in a car uncomfortably full of "natives." "You buy third-class—you go third-class," said an angry train guard. "You not sit with Indians—why come to India?" Halliburton struck the guard "as hard as I could. And that was the end of that." The story was reminiscent of an episode in F. Scott Fitzgerald's *This Side of Paradise*. A college boy rips up the restaurant check in front of a waiter, explaining to his friend, "He'll think we're the proprietor's sons or something."

Life in this make-believe world was not as satisfying as Halliburton's writings suggested. Two Richard Halliburtons lived side-by-side. The public Halliburton wrote an article titled "Where I'll Spend My Honeymoons" and was named as a co-respondent in a divorce case initiated by a Los Angeles physician whose wife had a crush on Halliburton. The *Philadelphia Inquirer* ran a full-page spread on his love life: "Richard Halliburton, who has been everywhere and seen everything including the lovelies of every clime and country, wants to get married . . . but he can't find a bride!" A girl from his Princeton days thought he wanted to marry her. The other Halliburton was gay. When his father sent a "serious" letter of concern about his son's failure to make a firm female attachment, Halliburton replied, "The woman situation is no cause for alarm. They play a very small part in my life, chiefly because their minds and natures bore me worse than words." When Halliburton's family published a posthumous collection of his letters, they left out this comment and others like it.

Halliburton was trapped in the persona he created. He knew what would happen if he declared himself gay. In 1920 Harvard expelled a group of students for homosexual behavior. Halliburton, noted a historian of sexual identity in America, had to hide "behind the mask of the dashing, unattached adventurer" if he "wanted to make a lot of money." As deft as he was at creating a gossamer pleasure world for readers, Halliburton chafed at it. He could be as rude off the stage as he was engaging on it. He offended bookstore clerks at book signings. "What are all you silly people doing?" he said to a group of people who came to see him at a Waterloo, Iowa, hotel lobby. It galled him that he was not much appreciated in the precincts of Princeton: "It's becoming the vogue there to discredit my books."

Halliburton's way out of triviality was to write a biography of Rupert Brooke, "my first and last love." He interviewed people who knew the poet and collected his correspondence. The rub was Brooke's mother. She could not imagine Halliburton writing a satisfactory biography of her son and forbade him to do so until after her death. Any idea of turning to another style of writing than the one that made him a celebrity also had to face the hard reality of money. Halliburton was always run-

"Youse is lettin' a second Halliburton slip t'ru yer fingers!"

Who knew when the next Halliburton would show up? It wasn't all that hard anymore to hit the international highway and have adventures. This cartoon appeared in the *Des Moines Register* on June 21, 1936. William L. Chambers of Bobbs-Merrill liked it so much he had it framed and hung over his desk. William Chambers to Richard Halliburton, July 5, 1938, Bobbs-Merrill Mss.

ning out of it. In 1933 he told his editor at Bobbs-Merrill that he "was down to my last dollar" and kiting checks besides. He was accustomed to living well and was generous to friends and his parents. The construction of Hangover House, a dwelling overlooking South Laguna Beach in California, particularly drained his coffers. "NEED ONE THOUSAND DOLLARS URGENTLY QUICKLY," he cabled Bobbs-Merrill in 1937, when he was behind on construction payments. He had to stay on the treadmill of his tried-and-true genre of writing. When Brooke's mother died, Halliburton did not undertake the biography. Someone else wrote Brooke's life for Bobbs-Merrill in the 1940s, using Halliburton's notes. "I want to write about the world as it is, and as I see it, instead of these adolescent romantic tales spun from a few bare facts," Halliburton said privately, "but I know my readers won't accept anything else."

The atificial world of Hollywood, not far from Laguna Beach, seemed a more likely venue for Halliburton. He was welcome as a lecturer and in social circles. He sold *The Royal Road to Romance* to Fox, although the studio never produced the movie. He starred in *India Speaks*. The movie mixed film clips from South Asia with a romantic story line built around Halliburton and an Indian-looking actress, Rosie Brown. Though not a financial success, it kept him in the public eye. As befitted a star, he endorsed Chase & Sanborn Coffee and began to rely on the help of a ghostwriter, longtime companion Paul Mooney.

In the mid-1930s, the Bell Newspaper Syndicate commissioned Halliburton to write fifty stories, which were subsequently published as *Seven League Boots,* a title borrowed from the fairy tale "Hop o' My Thumb." For the most part, his stories kept to such whimsies as crossing the Alps Hannibal-style on an elephant rented from the Paris zoo, an enterprise that failed when the pachyderm's feet blistered. In the Soviet Union, however, Halliburton fell into the middle of a real news story.

On a tip from the *Chicago Daily News* Moscow correspondent William Stoneman, Halliburton, and an interpreter took a train to Yekaterinburg in the Ural Mountains, the site of the 1918 execution of the czar and his family, the details of which were so murky that sightings of Anastasia and other "surviving" family members were an international sport. In Yekaterinburg he found one of the executioners, Peter Zacharovitch Ermakov. Although spitting up blood as a result of "cancer of the throat," Ermakov was willing to talk. He insisted that the czar's entire family was killed, which investigations after the fall of the Soviet Union showed to be true. In other respects Ermakov was inaccurate. His motivation for the interview was to establish that he personally had killed the czar, a dubious claim. Even his "deathbed confession" was a fabrication. Ermakov lived twenty more years. Oblivious to all this, Halliburton described his story as "one of the most extraordinary encounters that ever befell a journalist." Stoneman considered Halliburton "the worst kind of phony."

Soviet authorities refused to extend his visa because, Halliburton said, they opened a letter to his parents in which he described his Ermakov interview. Whatever the reasons that his visa was not renewed, Halliburton cast himself as a victim of Communism and extolled the virtues of "Freedom! I'd never known what it was before, because I'd always had it and taken it for granted. But my adventures in the U.S.S.R. made me, for the first time, fully realize the meaning of the word."

This liberated feeling was short-lived. Halliburton was soon back on the adventure treadmill, which had become progressively treacherous as he sought new ways to hold the public's attention. Whereas the worst that could befall him in the Panama Canal was sunburn, inasmuch as he had a sharpshooter along, it was something else to inadvertently put his plane *The Flying Carpet* into a stall while trying to get a good picture of Mount Everest (he wanted proof that he had flown closer to the peak than anyone else) or to take an unseaworthy junk across the Pacific Ocean, for which he made preparations in 1939.

The junk was the *Sea Dragon*. Halliburton planned to sail it nine thousand miles from Hong Kong to San Francisco, where the Golden Gate International Exposition was being held that spring. With all the fanfare his trip would generate, he figured fairgoers would pay a dollar apiece for a ride around the bay. The voyage was to be a spectacular, if weird, beginning to an adventure that would produce his next book, *The Royal Road to Romance in America*.

Apart from its colored sails and the wild dragons on the hull, the *Sea Dragon* had little to commend it. In an aborted first attempt to make the voyage, the vessel rolled dangerously and had other problems, a few of which Halliburton tried to address. His choice of captain was a "regular Captain Bligh," who threatened to deny bread and water to two members of the first crew, who quit. The Chinese sailors he recruited to take their place told him the junk's name was bad luck. A dragon was a land animal.

Halliburton set sail again for San Francisco on March 4. He radio-telegrammed Bobbs-Merrill from the *Sea Dragon* to report he was in "HIGH SPIRITS." Eighteen days later a storm began to brew and soon reached typhoon proportions with forty-foot seas. On March 24 radio contact was lost. Halliburton and his crew were not heard from again. In 1940 a rudder was found with what appeared to be a year's worth of barnacles on it.

"Perhaps we're wrong, but it seems to us that a great change has come over adventure recently," the *New Yorker* observed shortly after Halliburton's Panama Canal swim. "Many of the paths of adventurous living have been surfaced with concrete, and mapped. No matter where a young man might turn, he would find fresh tracks in the dust—the marks of Richard Halliburton's boots; and he would find signposts pointing down side-roads to publishing houses."

The canal authorities never let another swimmer go through the locks and had no particular interest in seeing Halliburton eclipsed in any other way. In 1962 Albert H. Oshiver, an oceanographer from Washington, D.C., swam for twenty-nine hours nonstop. For safety reasons, he was required to strap a flashing red light to his forehead. He paid a forty-five-cent toll. When Oshiver learned that Halliburton had paid nine cents less, he appealed for a dime refund so he could have the record. Canal officials turned down his request on the grounds that he wore a headlight, which meant he had to pay the laden-vessel rate. So eager was the public-relations staff to fence off Halliburton's feat, they forgot the whole thing was a gimmick to start with. Elaborate toll computations for ships don't work for something as small as a swimmer. The fee, said a modern-day chief of the canal's assessment unit, was "just an accommodation for publicity." In 1992 a freelance public radio reporter asked to recreate Halliburton's full swim, locks and all, saying it would show that some romance was left in the old waterway. The answer was no. A public-relations official directed the reporter to the visitors' center at Miraflores Locks on the Pacific side, where he could watch a film that included footage of Halliburton's swim. As for romance, an official noted that an episode of "Love Boat" had been filmed on a passing cruise ship.

Halliburton was not the only journalist-adventurer to perish on the job during the 1930s. Will Rogers, who wrote an introduction to Wiley Post's around-the-world memoir, died with the pilot in a 1935 crash. Their Siberia-bound plane went down in Alaska. Two years later Amelia Earhart set out on her own around-the-world flight. She, too, had journalism credentials—articles in newspapers and books and the title of aviator editor for *Cosmopolitan*. Her variation on the familiar theme was to be the first to follow the thick waist of the planet along the equator. Her two-engine Lockheed Electra disappeared in the Pacific.

In the coming war, Rogers would have bucked up the public with his homely sayings. Earhart, a genuine inspiration for women, may already have been involved with war work when she went down. Some suspected her flight was a secret mission to take pictures of Japanese installations. How would Halliburton have fit in during the coming years? "Few careers afford a better cartoon of their period," wrote George Weller, who early in his career at the *Chicago Daily News* was assigned "to retrace Stanley's trail" in Africa and now was about to distinguish himself in covering World War II for that paper. Halliburton, he wrote in *Esquire,* "was an Ariel left over from the summer of the Jazz Age. . . . It is hard to think of him dying, but to imagine him accompanying the century into its forties is painful."

Halliburton belonged to a carefree world. With the war gaining attention in the final months of his life, attendance at his lectures fell off. Americans were at home listening to Edward R. Murrow and other radio broadcasters describe the deteriorating peace in Europe. "Gone are the holidays abroad," wrote a journalist-traveler a few days after Germany invaded Poland. "Is Your Journey Really Necessary?" asked a British railway poster once the war was under way. By acting as if nothing had changed, Halliburton would have mocked the dangers that beset the world as well as his fellow journalists.

Halliburton would have been equally out of place after the war, when tourism rebounded. He was a transitional figure between a world out of reach to most people and a world overrun with tourists—and with adventurers vying for literary attention. In 1947, humorist S. J. Perelman and cartoonist Al Hirschfeld wrote and drew a multipart series for *Holiday,* "Westward Ha! Or Around the World in Eighty Clichés." Nellie Bly's sort of travel had become a joke. At the end of the twentieth century—when the world was replete with theme parks and organized "extreme" adventure trips, when traffic jams were a hazard on the slopes of Mount Everest, and when readers thumbed the newspaper travel sections and travel magazines that had proliferated—one of the latest circumnavigation books scaled the purely silly, *Around the World in Eighty Dates.* When a freelance adventurer walked across the Atlantic on canoe-like skis, it earned only a squib inside the newspaper and had little chance of being remembered in record books, which were trying to weed out some of the meaningless human achievement in their pages. One of those to lose out was Mihir Sen. In 1966 the native of Calcutta came up with a new angle on the Panama Canal. He swam it plus the Palk Strait, the Strait of Gibraltar, the Dardanelles, and the Bosporus. After a few years, the *Guinness Book of World Records* dropped his entry without replacing it with anyone else's. Meanwhile, Halliburton's authentic props for adventure travel disappeared. One could no longer duplicate his 1921 trip across Andorra atop a mule. The tiny country had become a giant shopping mall with no mules to rent. Descendants of the innkeeper who gave Halliburton a room in the village of Soldeau now ran the Soldeau Sport Hotel, a ski lodge. That they could remember Halliburton's visit suggested how singular his trip was then—and how unlikely now.

It was true, as an editorial adviser to Bobbs-Merrill noted, that Halliburton did not compare "with some of the young writers who came out of college about his time, say Vincent Sheean, John Gunther, or even Negley Farson, to mention a few at random." And yet, Halliburton was significant not only as an artifact of insouciant travel. In a way that is often overlooked, he also was a gateway to the serious side of international affairs. William Harlan Hale, the young Yale graduate who had mimicked Halliburton's voice in the 1932 *Atlantic Monthly* article mentioned earlier in this chapter, went on to write serious novels and history, held positions at *Vanity Fair* and the *New Republic,* and served in the 1940s in the Office of War Information. Edgar Snow, whose career as a China Hand ended up being nothing but political, went to China in 1928 with visions of becoming another Halliburton. His first idea for a book was to write a travel account. The Japanese incursion into China in the early 1930s preempted the effort. "The first travel books I read, and surely among the most important books of my life, were by Richard Halliburton," said writer Susan Sontag, who became political in a way that Halliburton could not approach. "The point was: the faraway world was full of amazing sites and edifices, which I too might one day see."

The difference was that these people grew up, and Halliburton didn't. Slipping into the oblivion that *Vanity Fair* proposed for him, he became in his last years what he had been all along, a children's author. *Richard Halliburton's Book of Marvels,* a rehash of his earlier adventures written expressly for kids, sat on shelves across the country. It was republished after his death. His following became increasingly small but was devoted. Princeton, once a source of ridicule, bestowed a Distinguished Service Award upon him in 1946: "From the beginning of his all-too-brief period of seventeen years as a loyal Princeton alumnus, Dick developed the enviable knack of making play his work." A periodical in his hometown of

Memphis ran—and several years later reran—"Richard Halliburton: The Forgotten Myth." An online computer "adventure game" revolved around "the mysterious disappearance of the famous archeologist/explorer Richard Haliburton [*sic*]." It is called "The Forgotten."

When Halliburton was lost at sea, diehard admirers wrote letters to local newspapers expressing doubt that their hero was gone for good. He had "died" before. "The late (?) Richard Halliburton," read a *Time* picture caption. The coast guard refused to conduct a search. The navy delayed for six weeks. One speculation had Halliburton living on an island with Amelia Earhart. His college traveling chum, Mike Hockaday, who had turned down Halliburton's invitation to join the *Sea Dragon* voyage, didn't buy that farfetched idea. He had to admit, though, that hiding on an island was the sort of thing Halliburton would do.

16

SEND THE WHOLE BUNCH OF THEM PACKING

In 1975, Edith Lederer became the first woman to head an Associated Press bureau overseas. She was based in Lima, with responsibility for news coverage of Peru, Ecuador, and Bolivia. Shortly after arriving, she hosted a get-to-know-you Sunday brunch for diplomats and fellow journalists, timing it to coincide with a news event. The Peruvian Air Force was holding its first public military display in years just offshore from Lima. Lederer's apartment in suburban Miraflores, which overlooked the water, was an ideal vantage point from which to watch. When the air force bombing runs were over, she went to the office and filed a story that began this way in the *Washington Post,* one of the many newspapers that uses the AP:

> Peru Meets Match
> In Show of Force
> LIMA, Peru July 21 (AP)—Thirty Peruvian air force fighter-bombers, in full view of tens of thousands of spectators, attacked 14 decoy fishing boats yesterday in an exercise celebrating Air Force Week. None of the boats sank.
> Peru's French-built Mirage fighters, U.S.-built Sabre jets and British-built Canberras carried out more than 60 bombing runs on the target vessels. Ten of the boats were hit and burned, but remained afloat. Peruvian-made surface-to-surface missiles also failed to sink the boats.

This report amused readers of the *Post* on Monday. Peruvian diplomats in Washington and the country's leaders in Lima, however, were not laughing. The Peruvians had meant to show their manhood with a little saber-rattling as the one-hundredth anniversary of their humiliating defeat by Chile in the War of the Pacific approached.

On Tuesday plainclothes internal security police picked up Lederer at her office. At headquarters, the head of internal security informed her that she was being expelled for interference in sovereign relations between Chile and Peru. When denied permission to stop at her apartment to pack a few things, the five-foot-one-inch-tall reporter turned on the tears. The police let her go home for thirty minutes to pack a single suitcase. When officers held up clothes for her to select, she thought it comical, but when they drove in the dark onto a side road at the airport and kept her there for thirty minutes before going onto the tarmac and escorting her to the plane, it was terrifying.

As the plane took off for Ecuador that night, Lederer became the newest member of an exclusive but growing club of journalists whose patron saint—as much as anyone could be said to have that distinction—was Dorothy Thompson. In 1934 the Nazis expelled the flamboyant Thompson from Germany. She was hardly the first to get the boot. But peacetime expulsions were rare and uncelebrated until Thompson's; afterward they became systematic and regarded as an occupational hazard.

"Nowadays the expulsion of a foreign correspondent from almost any country causes no astonishment, but thirty years ago it was an event almost unknown," Thompson's good friend Vincent Sheean wrote in 1963, three years after her death. Thompson's expulsion, he said, "caused a great deal of excitement and anxiety. It seemed a foretaste of the future, as indeed it was."

Women are today a common sight in the top ranks of modern foreign correspondents. Lederer rose to the exalted position of AP United Nations bureau chief. But when AP president Wes Gallagher sent her to Vietnam in 1972, she was only the second female AP reporter to cover the war and the first assigned full-time to the Saigon bureau (the first was only on special assignment). In sending Lederer abroad, Gallagher bucked the AP's informal assignment system. Under normal procedures, reporters did a stint on the foreign desk in New York before going overseas. This arrangement worked against women, because the foreign editor at the time refused to put any of them on the desk. Gallagher sidestepped the problem by sending Lederer directly to Vietnam on a putatively short assignment of six months, which in fact stretched to nine.

Although women went as far as China in Thompson's time, few rose to the top ranks of foreign reporting. Those who did stood out thanks to their small numbers and the gumption it took to succeed in this almost all-male corner of journalism: glamorous Martha Gellhorn, who wrote for *Collier's* and the British *Guardian*; adept interviewer and insightful foreign affairs commentator for the *New York Times* Anne O'Hare McCormick, the first woman to win a Pulitzer Prize; and multilingual, pipe-smoking Sigrid Schultz, appointed the *Chicago Tribune*'s Berlin bureau chief shortly after Thompson arrived in the city to assume her own bureau chief assignment in 1925 for the *Philadelphia Public Ledger*.

As a student, Thompson was strong-willed and outspoken. Going on a date with her at Syracuse University was considered an act of courage, according to legend. After graduation in 1914, she was an organizer for the suffrage movement and a publicity director for an experimental social work project in New York City. She wrote occasional newspaper articles. Interested in the fate of postwar Europe, she became in 1920 yet another young aspiring journalist to go abroad with little money and boundless self-confidence.

Upon arriving in London, Thompson was given assignments by the International News Service, which was heavily dependent on freelance material. She sold stories directly to the *Christian Science Monitor, Outlook,* and other publications. On the side, she did public relations writing for the Red Cross. Thompson had a knack for landing in the right place. On a visit to family in Ireland, she interviewed Terence MacSwiney, a Sinn Féin leader who an hour later was thrown in jail, where he died after a long hunger strike. In Paris, she interviewed Baroness Wrangel, the wife of an anti-Bolshevik Russian leader. "This was the first real story of Russian refugees, Czarists at menial labor," recalled Wythe Williams, the *Public Ledger* Paris bureau chief, who paid Thompson twenty dollars for the story and eventually hired her.

The *Public Ledger*'s foreign service was a brilliant conception that burned out quickly. The owner was Cyrus H. K. Curtis, whose media holdings included the highly profitable Philadelphia-based *Saturday Evening Post, Ladies' Home Journal,* and *Country Gentleman.* He purchased the *Public Ledger* in 1913 and stoked it with extravagant amounts of money in hopes of creating a national newspaper that he envisioned as "the *Manchester Guardian* of America," a British paper with a strong interest in foreign news and one that was often held up as a model of journalism by Americans. He bought and killed Philadelphia's *Evening Telegraph* for the sole purpose of obtaining its Associated Press contract, which he transferred to the *Public Ledger,* and hired Wythe Williams, who had reported abroad for the *New York World* and the *New York Times,* to organize from Paris a European foreign service. Curtis, Edward Price Bell reported to a watchful Victor Lawson in 1922, "has bought many full pages in The Times [of London] and the Daily Mail, telling the people here what a wonderful city Philadelphia is, and what a journalistic masterpiece it has turned out in The Public Ledger. . . . He aspires to make The Public Ledger a household word in both America and Europe." After the death of Victor Lawson in 1925, Curtis made an unsuccessful bid for the *Daily News,* a move that may have been motivated by the idea of joining its service with his own.

Engineering a foreign service to rival the *Chicago Daily News*'s was no small task. The *Public Ledger*'s audience, in the words of one historian, was more interested in "a warehouse fire or a Phillies' baseball game than in the quality of a story from Paris." An added disadvantage was Curtis himself. He was a genius in magazines, not newspapers, and sustained his newspaper with money, not execution of his vision. As one critic noted, he was not disposed to stray from the path of his friends in the Union League Club. When he died in 1933, the foreign service was discontinued.

Still, it was a good run during the brief time it lasted. "We had *carte blanche* in purchasing news features, sending men on far distant assignments, and hiring writers with big names," Williams recalled. At a high point in the late 1920s, when Curtis had added the *New York Evening Post* to his media empire, scores of newspapers used syndicated *Evening Post–Public Ledger* stories.

The idea to hire Thompson was more hers than Williams's. He remembered her continually "buzzing into the office always with excellent copy, and informing me that she fully intended being on the staff." Paul Scott Mowrer, who was so impressed with Thompson that he invited her to dinner, advised her to relocate to a city with less journalistic competition than Paris, and she pressed Williams to appoint her the newspaper's correspondent in Vienna, which was covered out of the Berlin bureau. He agreed, after a fashion. Thompson could call herself a special correspondent for the *Public Ledger;* he would pay her on a per-story basis. She arrived in Vienna in the winter of 1921. By the spring, Williams had her on the full-time payroll, responsible for all of Central Europe. "Dorothy had filed so many stories already on space rates," biographer Peter Kurth observed, "her editors decided they could save themselves some money by offering her a regular job." Four years later, in 1925, the resourceful, energetic reporter was given the prestigious post of chief of the Berlin Bureau.

Thompson, a colleague said, "was Richard Harding Davis in an evening gown. Nothing prosaic ever happened to her." It was this way in both her professional and her personal life. In Vienna she married a handsome Hungarian intellectual and sometimes correspondent for the AP, Joseph Bard. She stuck with him through his extravagant affairs with other women, many of them Thompson's friends, until she moved to Berlin. One lonely, drunken night, she slept with Floyd Gibbons. Her regrets were temporary. Over the years she had other one-night flings as well as love affairs with both sexes. On the day in 1927 when her divorce with Bard was final—also her thirty-fourth birthday—she met Sinclair Lewis, himself in the throes of ending a marriage. He proposed to her.

That November Thompson was in Russia writing a series on the tenth anniversary of the Russian Revolution. Lewis followed her there. The next spring they married. She gave up her Berlin post and moved with Lewis to Twin Farms in Vermont, a quiet setting where he could write. Thompson was not yet as famous as her husband. Lining up reporting assignments and lectures in the United States, she found it useful to use "Mrs. Sinclair Lewis." Tying herself to Lewis and Vermont for the long haul, however, was out of the question, even after they had a son. Fascism was emerging in Germany, and she could not sit on the sidelines.

When Thompson had arrived in Berlin in 1925, the country seemed "full of promise." Previous years of destabilizing inflation were under control. The arts flourished. Political troublemakers like Adolf Hitler and the Nazis had little traction. Correspondents enjoyed an endless round of parties until dawn. The annual press ball brought out professors, artists, and politicians. "For a foreign newsman," wrote *Daily News* correspondent Edgar Ansel Mowrer, "it was a unique opportunity to talk with the people who made the news." Friday press conferences in the Foreign Office, Thompson remembered, often brought the chancellor or the foreign minister. Correspondents asked questions freely, and "answers were freely given, sometimes in confidence, sometimes for publication. Criticism, even the most hostile, was received in dignified silence or openly discussed."

Beneath this journalistic paradise, however, lay a totalitarian volcano. George Seldes, who enjoyed a long—albeit not lucrative—career exposing threats to press freedom while criticizing journalism, was among the first to spot the impending crackdown on journalists.* A magnet for such trouble, Seldes had been expelled from the Soviet Union and Italy. On his train out of Italy in 1925, he narrowly escaped a gang of Mussolini's "Blackshirt" thugs, armed with sticks and blackjacks, shouting "*Dove* Seldes? Where is Seldes?" As he saw it, World War I tactics to control the press and public opinion had continued into the peacetime. "Government agencies of suppression in many countries continue to function with unrelenting thoroughness," he reported, and the suppression virus was spreading. "Germany has been a land of almost absolute freedom," Seldes observed in the conclusion of *You Can't Print That!* published in 1929, the year after Thompson left Berlin. "It is only lately that the big propaganda funds have been revived and that an attempt to control foreign correspondents has been made."

By the time Thompson returned to Germany for a visit at the close of 1930, Seldes's fears loomed larger. The Weimar Republic was careening toward economic and political disaster. To mollify political factions, the government spent lavishly on unemployment and medical benefits as well as subsidized housing and resorts. As the bills came due, banks and industries failed; unemployment soared. The Nazis were not in power, but they were aggressively campaigning to get there. Their propaganda machine never stopped. At a rally, Thompson saw halls hung with swastikas and huge pictures of Hitler. Upcoming elections, she wrote in an article for the *Saturday Evening Post,* "may throw the republic into the bitterest inner conflict of its history."

At the time Thompson thought the Nazis were hampered by the "stupidity of their demagogic leadership." But on a subsequent visit in late 1931, as they continued to gain momentum, she wanted a chance to size up the leadership for herself. In late 1931 Hitler, who had kept his distance from correspondents, obliged. His prospects on the rise, he thought it time to court international opinion. Ernst "Putzi" Hanfstängl, the clownish chief of the Nazi's Foreign Press Department, congratulated himself on arranging the Thompson interview. He shouldn't have.

Here is an excerpt from the article Thompson wrote about the encounter. "I Saw Hitler!" was published in *Cosmopolitan* and subsequently appeared in a quickie book by the same title.

> When I finally walked into Adolf Hitler's salon in the Kaiserhof Hotel, I was convinced that I was meeting the future dictator of Germany. In something less

---

* Will Irwin, Oswald Garrison Villard, A. J. Liebling, and George Seldes, four of the twentieth century's leading press critics, had service as foreign correspondents. None topped Seldes in longevity and self-sacrifice. He wrote *You Can't Print That!* his first book of press criticism, after resigning from the *Chicago Tribune* in a huff. Seldes had prepared a series of articles on Mexico, some showing the American point of view and some the Mexican side. The *Trib* killed the pro-Mexican articles, which conflicted with Col. McCormick's editorial policy. Seldes continued his press criticism, as well as his fearlessly independent journalism on other subjects, almost until 1995, when he died in Vermont. Seldes had been friendly with Thompson and especially Sinclair Lewis, who gave him money to buy a Vermont home near his own in 1933.

than fifty seconds I was quite sure that I was not. It took just about that time to measure the startling insignificance of this man who set the world agog.

He is formless, almost faceless; a man whose countenance is a caricature; a man whose framework seems cartilaginous, without bones. He is inconsequent and voluble, ill-poised, insecure—the very prototype of the Little Man.

A lock of lank hair falls over an insignificant and slightly retreated forehead. The back head is shallow. His face is broad in the cheekbones. The nose is large, but badly shaped and without character. His movements are awkward. There is in his face no trace of any inner conflict or self-discipline.

And yet, he is not without a certain charm. But it is the soft, almost feminine charm of the Austrian! When he talks it is with a broad Austrian dialect.

The eyes alone are notable. Dark gray and hyperthyroidic, they have the peculiar shine which often distinguishes geniuses, alcoholics, and hysterics.

As I saw him, I thought of other German faces.

The President, von Hindenburg. A face cut out of rock. No imagination in it; no light; no humor. Not exactly an appealing face, but one revealing character.

Chancellor Brüning. The head of an eighteenth-century cardinal—statesman. A high-bridged, sensitive nose. A finely cut mouth. Quizzical, wise, humorous. A man who will hold on forever. A little too sensitive, perhaps.

I thought of this man before me, seated, as an equal, between von Hindenburg and Brüning, and involuntarily I smiled. Looking at Hitler, I saw a whole panorama of distinguished German faces. And I thought: Mr. Hitler, in the next election you may get the fifteen million votes which you expect.

But fifteen million Germans CAN be wrong.

The interview was difficult, because one cannot carry on a conversation with Adolf Hitler. He speaks always as if he were addressing a mass meeting. His voice rises sometimes almost to a scream. He gives the impression of a man in a trance. He bangs the table.

"Not yet is the whole working class with us . . . we need a new spirit . . . Marxism has undermined the masses . . . Rebirth in a new ideology . . . Not workers, not employers, not socialists, not Catholics—but Germans!"

This, in answer to the question: What will you do for the working masses when you come to power?

It is an important question. Millions of Germans follow Hitler because he has proclaimed war upon the banks, upon the trusts, upon "loan-capital." He has asserted time after time that he will abolish the rule of one class by another. What, actually, do these statements mean in terms of practical politics?

I couldn't find out. When I dared to interrupt the stream of eloquence by bluntly repeating my question, Hitler replied (rather coyly) that he didn't intend to hand his program over to his enemies (the German chancellor) for them to "steal." Later on, however, from one of his adjutants, I got a clearer answer to the question. . . .

[Hitler's] social and economic theory is a tale told by an idiot. Beside it

Lenin's consequent Communism and revolutionary program glitters with intellect. But reason never yet swept a world off its feet, and Hitler, an agitator of genius, knows this. Self-interest, expressed in pathetic terms, does. Hitler is the most golden-tongued of demagogues.

"One must judge a public speech not by the sense it makes to scientists who read it next day, but by the effect which it has on the masses," says Hitler himself in "My Fight."* Openly and guilelessly Hitler asserts that the function of speech-making is not the telling of the truth. He does not shrink from lying, or from advocating the use of the lie.

"It was false," he says, "to treat the war-guilt question from the standpoint that Germany alone should not be made responsible for the outbreak of the catastrophe. We should have shifted the *entire* guilt upon the shoulders of the others, even if the truth were not so." This is an actual quotation from his book.

Above all, he appeals to the invisible realities, to the emotions, to faith rather than to reason. His speeches are full of talk about Honor, Folk, Fatherland, Loyalty, Family, Sacrifice, Revenge.

This is the way Hitler writes—but he cannot write: his book is one long speech. Eight hundred pages of Gothic script, pathetic gestures, inaccurate German and unlimited self-satisfaction.

You must imagine the crowds he addresses. Always remember: Little People, weighted with a feeling of inferiority. Hitler, too, is weighted with it. . . .

Adolf Hitler's tragedy is that he has risen too high. In the seats of the mighty the Little Man, lusty for power, nevertheless feels insecure. He needs money for this vast organization which he has built up—banks and great trusts give it to him. (*Let him come in, they say. Then we shall see who really runs things.*) What becomes, then, of his brave words against them?

Once in power, will he want to risk another French invasion? What becomes, then, of his sonorous calls to arms?

He will have to maintain law and order. What becomes, then, of his promises to a revolutionary working class?

He has promised to win back all that the Germans handed by the peace treaties to other countries. But diplomacy demands concessions, and already he has abandoned the mountain Germans of the South Tirol.

And the Jews? Bismarck's first speech in the Reichstag was against the Jews, but he lived to have a Jewish banker as his most intimate adviser.

If Hitler comes into power, he will smite only the weakest of his enemies. And German intellectuals, disgust in their faces, will move to Liechtenstein, to Switzerland, to Paris. They are beginning to do so already, fearing, not revolution, but banal and unendurable reaction.

But perhaps the drummer boy has let loose forces stronger than he knows.

If so, who will come after him?

---

* The reference is to Hitler's book *Mein Kampf.*

Foreign correspondents live with fear of getting a scoop that turns out to be wrong. Roy Howard goes down in history for his skill at news management, which resulted in becoming a partner in E. W. Scripps's media empire, *and* for prematurely reporting the armistice ending World War I. The errant scoop took place when he was president of Scripps's United Press news service. Howard blamed German secret agents, although no one has definitively explained the origin of the false telegraphic message upon which he relied. When the bogus story appeared, Howard recalled ruefully, "new records were established for newspaper sales." When the story was discredited, competitors called him "a traitor to his country and to his profession."

Thompson had made a class-A mistake in her article on Hitler. It was not that other good reporters hadn't underestimated the German demagogue. The difference was that Dorothy Thompson had been conspicuously and unequivocally dismissive. She was annoyed to be reminded of her error afterward. Yet, she did not go down in journalistic infamy. The interview had quite the opposite result. It showcased journalistic qualities that catapulted Thompson into a special journalistic role.

Thompson found her voice in the 1930s. Sheean described it as "more like a call to arms than like anything normally known in journalism." This was in pace with the "personal history" reporting common at the time but was done in her own way—blunt, highly opinionated, combining reporting with admonishment. This style, which John Gunther described as having a "peculiar quality of argument and conclusion," had not been possible when she wrote for daily newspapers. In magazines it was welcomed. Of those for which she wrote, the most important was Curtis's widely circulating, well-paying *Saturday Evening Post*. Many of Thompson's articles for the *Post* took months to write and ran more than eight thousand words. For the first time, her powerful personality was on full display to average American readers, who became an enthusiastic audience for her work.

Instead of losing her self-confidence after her Hitler interview, Thompson hammered away. Hitler described his rearmament program as defensive; Thompson said he was making "Germany safe for war." The Nazis, Thompson explained in another article, exploited German emotions, especially their sense of humiliation as a result of the Versailles Treaty. "In this atmosphere every citizen must reiterate his patriotism in the most fervid terms, or be suspect," she wrote. "Hence—a Jew is a member of an alien race, therefore potentially a traitor."

When the Nazis passed official anti-Semitic laws in early 1933, Thompson was one of the first and loudest to reveal the brutal consequences, which were denied by officials and by large numbers of Americans, as opinion polls showed—and overlooked by large elements of the news media. From 1939 to 1945, by which time persecution had turned into extermination, the *New York Times'* front page mentioned "Jews as Hitler's unique target for total annihilation" on only six occasions, a *Times* editor recalled sorrowfully a half century later. In 1941, the death of 450 Dutch Jews in the Mauthausen concentration camp ran as a thirteen-line article on the bottom of page 10 of the *Baltimore Sun;* and the announcement that year that German

Jews were stripped of their citizenship appeared on page 30 of the *New York Journal American.* Thompson's articles in the early 1930s went beyond reporting individual episodes, a safe approach correspondents tended to take, to explain that the abuses were systematic, that violence and discrimination were a central feature of Nazi ideology. "First of all," she wrote in the first of a three-part series for the *Jewish Daily Bulletin* in New York, "it must be said, it must be re-iterated, that there has been and still is a widespread terror, which extends throughout the whole of Germany, and which has been, and still is, accompanied by individual atrocities." Hitler's press aide, Herr Hanfstängl, denied that terror existed, she said, but such denials "were all untrue."

Thompson continued belittling Hitler. Going for the jugular, she even challenged his right to be a German. For all his accumulation of power, she wrote, he was not representative of Germany; he was not even as "manly" as his countrymen. "No one less like a non-German's conception of a dictator can be imagined," she observed in 1933, after he became chancellor. A few months later Thompson focused on Hitler's perverse determination to get elected in order to kill democracy, "to destroy law and public opinion as the real sovereigns of the state, and substitute for them force and propaganda."

Nazi suppression of free speech weighed heavily on correspondents. Joseph Goebbels, in charge of the almost amusingly named Ministry of Popular Enlightenment and Propaganda, organized massive book burnings and put German newspapers out of business. By John Gunther's 1935 count, "no fewer than fourteen hundred" disappeared in the previous two years. "No one who has not lived for years in a totalitarian land can possibly conceive how difficult it is to escape the dread consequences of a regime's calculated and incessant propaganda," observed William Shirer, who became an authority on the subject. In dealing with the foreign press corps, the Nazis used the unsubtle technique of *Zuckerbrot und Peitsche. Zuckerbrot,* sugared bread, came in the form of evenings in which Nazi officials plied reporters with beer and propaganda. When the country was on a war footing, the Nazis gave reporters double rations and good living accommodations. *Peitsche,* the whip, was a public tongue-lashing or worse.

Thompson's friend and neighbor in the 1920s, Edgar Mowrer, got the *Peitsche.* Like Thompson, he criticized the Nazis and underestimated Hitler in news reporting that won a Pulitzer Prize in 1933 and in a popular book, *Germany Puts the Clock Back.* A volatile personality, he added insult to injury by making fun of the Nazis at a luncheon hosted by the Foreign Press Association. Hanfstängl retaliated by spreading rumors that Mowrer was a "secret" Jew. Plainclothes police followed him. Goebbels tried to oust him as chair of the press association. Fellow correspondents staved this off for a time by giving Mowrer an overwhelming vote of confidence. He eventually agreed to step down in exchange for the release from prison of an elderly ailing Jewish correspondent for a Viennese newspaper. The deal received international attention, which infuriated the Nazis even more. Told the government could no longer guarantee his safety and scheduled to take up a new *Daily News* post, he left several days early. British and American correspondents pre-

Dorothy Thompson in a photo taken when Hitler booted her out of Germany. AP/Wide World Photos.

sented him with a silver rose bowl inscribed to a "gallant fighter for the liberty of the Press." When a new edition of *Germany Puts the Clock Back* came out later in that year of 1933, Thompson wrote a short introduction endorsing it.

As she moved in and out of Germany, Thompson remained much on the Nazis' minds. It was bad enough that a woman, whose place according to Nazi ideology was at home, cut down Hitler. According to reports circulating, they were irked, too, that she, a non-Jew, had written on Nazi anti-Semitism in the *Jewish Daily Bulletin*. A well-connected journalist with the *Vossische Zeitung*, Bella Fromm, heard that the Nazis had created a "Dorothy Thompson Emergency Squad that rushes translations of every word she writes."

The time to settle scores came in the summer of 1934. After tracking down information about the Nazis' failed attempt to engineer a putsch in Vienna, Thompson went to Germany. President Paul von Hindenburg had just died, leaving Hitler undisputed chief of state. Thompson observed the sham plebiscite ratifying Hitler's new position. Nowhere, she noted, could anyone dare to put up a poster saying "Hitler is a big stiff. Vote No!" From an acquaintance, Thompson heard about a bloody purge of Hitler's opponents. Friends warned her away from using hotel phones.

Five days after the plebiscite, a member of the secret police "in a trenchcoat like Hitler's" called on Thompson at the Hotel Adlon in Berlin and presented a letter. "In view of your numerous anti-German publications in the American press," the letter read, "the German authorities, for reasons of national self-respect, are unable to extend to you a further right of hospitality." She could leave on her own within forty-eight hours or be escorted to the border. From the U.S. embassy, Thompson learned that an appeal would be fruitless. She had violated a law against expressing an opinion that was "detrimental to the interests of the Reich" or disrespectful of officials. Exhibit A in this crime, the secret police told an embassy official, was her 1931 "I Saw Hitler!" article in *Cosmopolitan*. The Führer himself had given the expulsion order. Journalists suspected that Putzi Hanfstängl also was behind the act of revenge.

Thompson's expulsion was the first for a western correspondent from Nazi Germany. Nearly all the American and British correspondents in Berlin gathered to see her off at the train station. The journalists, reported the *New York Times* in a widely reprinted story, "gave her a great bunch of American Beauty roses as a token of their affection and esteem." She "waved a cheerful farewell."

Thompson gave a statement to reporters before leaving and kept talking all the way home. In Paris she spoke on a radio broadcast heard in the United States and wrote an article for the *New York Times*: "My offense was to think that Hitler is just an ordinary man, after all. That is a crime against the reigning cult in Germany, which says Mr. Hitler is a Messiah sent by God to save the German people—an old Jewish idea. To question this mystic mission is so heinous that, if you are German, you can be sent to jail. I, fortunately, am an American, so I merely was sent to Paris. Worse things can happen to one." New York gave her a hero's welcome. *Time* and *Newsweek* ran stories on her. She wrote "Good-Bye to Germany" for *Harper's* and "The Age of Propaganda" for the *Saturday Evening Post*.

Thompson had been wrong about Hitler's staying power in her 1931 interview. But the expulsion by a bullying Hitler made her appear to have been right about his insecurities. Instead of being remembered as a sinning journalist, she was a Joan of Arc. The reporters asked about the Nazis, not about the state of her marriage, as had been common in the past. Thompson's expulsion, Sheean recounted, made her "a heroine within twenty-four hours and propelled her into that national and international celebrity—not as Red's wife but as herself—which was to be her native climate." Her fame as well as the intensity of her political interests irritated Lewis. He derisively called her "the senator." "If I ever divorce Dorothy," Lewis said in anticipation of the breakup of their marriage, "I'll name Adolph Hitler as co-respondent."

Thompson framed the Nazi expulsion order and hung it on the wall of her office at the *Herald Tribune,* which hired her to write a thrice-weekly column that appeared next to Walter Lippmann's. By 1940, her syndicated *On the Record* column had 7.5 million readers. Her lectures packed in as many as three thousand people at a time. She did commentary on NBC. "She is read, believed and quoted by millions of women who used to get their political opinions from their husbands, who got them from Walter Lippmann," proclaimed a *Time* cover story on Thompson.

Staying in character, she showed up at a 1939 Nazi rally in Madison Square Garden and laughed so loudly at the proceedings that "Storm Troopers" escorted her out, creating yet another Nazi expulsion that attracted press attention. She decried German persecution of the Jews in her columns and pressured President Roosevelt to broadcast appeals directly to the German people to stop the atrocities. She herself broadcast a series of anti-Nazi radio programs directed at Germans in their own language. Hitler, she said, was a "conceited ass." The talks were published in the United States in a book called *Listen, Hans.*

Thompson's "liberal conservatism," initially anti-Roosevelt and anti–New Deal, fit with the *Herald Tribune*'s philosophy until the 1940 election, when she endorsed FDR over his Republican opponent Wendell L. Willkie, whose victory she believed would set back the war effort. The *Herald Tribune* management wanted her to rein herself in. This was as likely as her staying home and darning socks for Lewis. When her contract was not renewed, she moved her column to the *New York Post,* where she again raised hackles with the owners. Despite her early sympathy for Zionism and criticism of Nazi treatment of the Jews, the independent-minded columnist supported Palestinian Arabs and opposed the Nuremberg trials. The *Post* decided to drop her column, which nevertheless continued to be carried by the Bell Syndicate.

"Quite possibly," Sheean wrote after Thompson's death, "she was the greatest journalist America has known since the first batch, Hamilton and Jefferson and Madison." The effusion was characteristic of Sheean, but Thompson had this effect on many. John Gunther, another close friend, thought her 1930s articles on Germany secured her reputation as "the best journalist this generation has produced in any country." He said Thompson was "an activist, a positivist. She believed in free will. She believed that she could exert command, that she could control events."

William Shirer, assigned to Berlin by the Universal Service in 1934, arrived by rail a couple of hours after Thompson left the city. Two Gestapo agents stopped him as he got off his train and closely checked his passport. The next day H. R. Knickerbocker of the International News Service told him the agents probably thought he was attached somehow to Thompson. Knickerbocker said he was in trouble himself on account of articles he had written about Joseph Goebbels, the Nazi propaganda minister.

Except in the Soviet Union, where George Seldes and others were ejected,* expulsion in Europe was a rarity until Dorothy Thompson's abrupt departure from Germany. Then it became a real, constant, spreading threat. "I ought to send the whole bunch of them packing," the Führer told Hanfstängl in a moment of pique. "All through my years in Berlin," wrote Shirer, who jumped from print journalism to become the CBS correspondent posted, "I was conscious of walking a real, if ill-defined line. If you strayed too far off it you risked expulsion. . . . One by one over the next few years many of my colleagues—and they were usually the brightest and the best—would get the axe."

By one count, twenty-seven correspondents from various countries had departed from Germany by mid-1935 because of "real or imagined compulsion." The German Foreign Office told S. Miles Bouton, reporting for the *Baltimore Sun,* to change his "style of reporting or leave." Bouton, along with his German-born wife and Germany-educated sons, chose leaving. Sigrid Schultz of the *Chicago Tribune,* because she had a hand in arranging Thompson's interview with Hitler, was "highly unpopular with the Nazis for quite awhile." Once the Nazis came to full power, the Gestapo often called her in and threatened expulsion. When she wrote a series of articles on the Nazi dictatorship, the *Tribune* protected her by publishing them under a pseudonym, John Dickson. Advised by Col. McCormick that she could leave whenever she felt too much endangered, Schultz went home in early 1941. The ride out in a train full of drunken Nazis frightened her. The German government turned her down when she applied for readmission later in the year. Similarly treated was Otto D. Tolischus, one of two *New York Times* correspondents to win Pulitzer Prizes covering the Nazis in the 1930s.[†] (Tolischus subsequently became the *Times'* Tokyo bureau chief and was arrested the day the Japanese attacked Pearl Harbor.) Shirer left Germany in 1939, after threats of expulsion and fear that he would be accused of espionage.

Each ejected correspondent had a slightly different story to tell. Emlyn Williams of the *Christian Science Monitor* had to leave when Germany went to war with Great Britain because he was a British subject. Nervous about being a reporter in Germany, Janet Flanner of the *New Yorker* did not ask to interview Hitler for her long profile, "Führer," published in 1936. G. E. R. Gedye, whose reports from Vienna appeared in the *New York Times* and the *London Daily Mail,* was ejected after

---

* When Seldes was sent out of Russia in 1923, three others left with him: Samuel Spewack of the *New York World,* Percy Noel of the *Philadelphia Ledger,* and Francis McCulough of the *New York Herald* and the *Manchester Guardian.* Two other *Chicago Tribune* reporters were expelled later in the 1920s, John Clayton (the second time for him) and Larry Rue.

† The other was Frederick T. Birchall, whose story on Nazi book burning in 1933 is a classic piece of reporting.

the Nazi occupation of Austria in 1938. The Germans expelled Ralph Barnes of the *New York Herald Tribune* for forecasting Hitler's breakup with Stalin after their joint invasion of Poland. In March 1941 the United States suppressed the German agency Transocean News; the Germans, in turn, arrested a United Press reporter, Richard C. Hottelet, for espionage. He was released four months later in exchange for German nationals arrested in the United States.

Those it could not confront directly, Nazi officials dealt with in other ways. John Gunther's four-thousand-word profile of Hitler in *Inside Europe*—the Nazi leader had an "Oedipus complex as big as a house"—so infuriated the Nazis that they banned the book. The Gestapo put Gunther on a "death list." Also banned were all of Vincent Sheean's writings, as decreed in January 1940 by Heinrich Himmler, head of Germany's police. Sheean and Gunther were "honored" to be thus singled out, much as later generations of journalists considered it a badge of honor to have been on President Richard Nixon's Enemies List.

Thompson was not only materfamilias for such honors in Germany. Her expulsion marked the beginning of heavy-handed press relations elsewhere.

Although George Seldes early on wrote about Mussolini's strong-arm tactics, most others had seen a different side of Il Duce, who charmed the foreign press. Mussolini accumulated a large number of journalistic admirers, among them William Randolph Hearst, *Time* magazine founder Henry Luce, the *Chicago Daily News*'s Edward Price Bell, and *Times* correspondent Anne O'Hare McCormick. Pro-Bolshevik Lincoln Steffens called Mussolini the "divine Dictator." In an interview with muckraking journalist Ida Tarbell, he "chatted as naturally, simply and cordially as a friend you had come across at a tea party," she wrote for *McCall's* in 1926. "Mussolini has one of the loveliest smiles I ever saw—it is not only on his lips but in his eyes; and to finish the conquest of one who sees him in this mood for the first time—he has a dimple!"

Seldes had difficulty finding a publisher for his unfavorable biography of Mussolini, finished in 1932. In 1935, however, public opinion shifted. Italy invaded Ethiopia and began to move into the Nazi orbit. The following year Seldes's *Sawdust Caesar* appeared. Seldes, the only correspondent bounced out of Italy from the time Mussolini came to power in 1922 until 1935, was now in a growing company of reporters. "It must be remembered," CBS's Cecil Brown observed from Rome, "that constantly over every correspondent hangs the sword of Damocles of expulsion from the country, and of other penalties for 'errors of judgment.'"

The first to go in the mid-1930s was *Tribune* correspondent David Darrah. From the start of his assignment in Rome, which began in 1927, he "knew that the Seldes affair still smoldered in the minds of the Fascist Foreign Office officials." Despite occasional censorship, he managed to remain until 1935. In one story, headed by the notation *"Telephoned to London to avoid Censor,"* he reported that Mussolini's invasion of Ethiopia was "meeting with the disapproval of Italians. . . . Foreign correspondents here are being subjected to added difficulties as the Fascists seek to project their favorable picture of events." He subsequently reported the war was worsening Italy's economic situation. Not long afterward, Darrah was escorted out of the country. Later he wrote the critical *Hail Caesar!* which was published within months.

The *Tribune* prudently chose not to replace Darrah. After Frank Smothers of the *Chicago Daily News* was ejected, the editors sent in Paul Scott Mowrer's son Richard. He lasted only a few months, by his own count becoming the sixteenth reporter tossed out of Italy. One historian put the total number expelled between 1936 and 1939 at twenty-four, with others leaving later. Cecil Brown himself was expelled in 1941 for his "continuing hostile attitude toward Fascism."

Similar tactics were used elsewhere. Hubert Harrison, the *New York Times* correspondent in Yugoslavia, was expelled for a story about the banning of Mickey Mouse comic strips. The Spanish government could not expel Edmund Taylor of the *Chicago Tribune* for his accounts of nationalist atrocities during the civil war because he had already left. So, instead, they booted the reporter who had replaced him. During the failed coup in Austria in 1934, officials did their best to intimidate reporters. Two AP photographers were arrested, one for nine days.

Being expelled was especially a problem for the Associated Press. The AP franchise stood on two legs. One of those was straight factual reporting, rather than the opinionated journalism of Dorothy Thompson. The other was being wherever news broke. No one expected the *New York Times* to have a correspondent everywhere a coup might break out, but they did expect the AP to have someone there. As is still the case, special correspondents for daily newspapers relied on the AP as well as other wire services for basic facts on events they were covering themselves; and if a special correspondent was sent packing, the editors relied on the AP as backup. "The basic point about a wire service like the AP is that we are there; we're always there. We have always been there, we are there now, and we will be there," declared AP foreign editor Nate Polowetzky, who oversaw AP foreign coverage for seventeen years beginning in 1973. "There isn't anywhere that the sparrow falls that the AP doesn't report it in some way or another."

Under threat of expulsion, the AP's two legs of reporting facts and staying on the job sometimes tripped over each other. "After nineteen ejections of foreign correspondents, caution seemed to be in order for most foreign countries," wrote Louis Lochner, who was threatened with expulsion several times and faced a dilemma. "Our orders from our bosses were to tell no untruth," Lochner wrote of coverage of Nazi Germany, "but to report only as much of the truth without distorting the picture as would enable us to remain at our post." He described his predicament to the AP management in a 1933 letter.

> Believing as I do that you want us to try in every way to keep our hold in Germany, rather than risk being expelled, we have passed up things that have come to us from trustworthy sources which, however, refused to be quoted because they are afraid for their lives. Some of these things are hair-raising. . . . Some of the "specials," I understand, do send stories of this kind, but they are people whose offices don't care whether or not they stay, as they know the A.P. will protect them anyway. Several of the "specials" have told me that the best thing that

could happen to them would be to be ejected, as they would then be martyrs in the eyes of their papers and their countrymen.

Even though daily newspapers did not suffer as much as the wire services if their correspondents were expelled, expulsion was not desirable for them either or for a broadcast correspondent. The list of reasons was long, and it led correspondents to be careful in their reporting.

For the special correspondent, being expelled meant being removed from a big story and uprooting the family, if the correspondent had one. Seldes sympathized with correspondents in Italy who did not want to risk expulsion over a small story. "If I had had a three-year lease on a house in Rome, or a wife and children and other obligations there, I too should have waited for bigger news." For the home office, it meant the expense of bringing a reporter home and sending a new one out. The new reporter was unlikely to have as much expertise or as many contacts.

Yet another factor led correspondents to rein themselves in. When their stories ran counter to heavily censored reporting and intense German propaganda, editors—and audiences—back home often raised doubts, not plaudits. When he was expelled over his stories about the impending Hitler-Stalin rift, which no one else was reporting at the time, Barnes confessed to his close friend William Shirer of his worries about the consequences of *Herald Tribune* editors' reactions. Correspondents, the *Evening World*'s Pierre van Paassen wrote in the same vein, "discovered only too soon that if we did speak out, we did not last very long, either in the countries in which we were stationed or in our jobs. For when a correspondent is expelled from one country after the other suspicion soon ripens that there is something wrong, not with the place he is forced to leave, but with himself."

Correspondents also were concerned about protecting their sources. Lochner spoke German like a native and was married to the daughter of well-connected German family, in whose spacious house he and his wife lived and entertained. They could seat twenty-six people for dinner. He accumulated especially good informants during his seventeen years in the country. He estimated that, because he feared Nazi reprisals against his sources, he used less than 40 percent of the information they gave him. "The difficulties under which we work here," Thompson said at the time of her expulsion, "are made most acute by the fact that in our search for all information except that put out by the Propaganda Ministry we are aware that we are endangering the comfort and freedom of the people who may give us information or who may be suspected of having done so."

Correspondents used a variety of ploys to avoid incriminating others. Lochner delayed stories for weeks in order "to wipe out any traces that might lead to my contact with an informant." Resorting to a time-honored technique, he smuggled stories out by diplomatic pouch or through informal couriers. When reporting negative information, he and other correspondents sought truth through indirection. Correspondents thought Gen. Wilhelm Keitel arrogant and sycophantic. In print Lochner described him as typifying "the best in Prussian military tradition."

Holding back information and writing in euphemisms impeded reporting. As the foreign editor at a midwestern newspaper commented to Lochner, interpreting his dispatches required "some imagination." Most readers didn't have the time or the experience to figure out what a correspondent might be saying between the lines.

The end of World War II did not usher in a new era of openness. Every reporter working in Moscow in the 1950s remembered the green curtain through which stories were passed to censors. When mildly unhappy with correspondents, Soviet officialdom might tamper with their food shipment from Finland. "I always knew I was hostage to them," says Marvin Kalb, a CBS correspondent based in Moscow. In 1977, the Soviet government expelled AP reporter George Krimsky, who seemed too aggressive in reporting on dissidents. (See "The Expulsion of George Krimsky," p. 281.)

Nor did the subsequent collapse of Communism in Russia and Eastern Europe and the rise of democracies in Latin America change conditions for correspondents. In 2004 Brazil announced the expulsion of a *New York Times* correspondent who reported on the prodigious drinking of its democratically elected president, Luiz Inácio Lula da Silva. The government reversed itself when the *Times'* Brazilian lawyers apologized to the Ministry of Justice: the reporter had not meant to offend and was sorry for any embarrassment. Four years later, in 2008, a *Times* reporter was jailed while covering a presidential election in Zimbabwe that deviated from democratic norms. He was charged with "committing journalism."

Thompson's rather benign expulsion morphed into a myriad of horrors. In the early 1960s German-born AP photographer Horst Faas was captured by rebels in the Congo, who decided by his accent that he was Belgian, the country that had colonized them. He talked his way out of the terrifying experience, which seemed destined to end in death, although he was forced to eat his press pass. In 1977 Emperor Jean-Bedel Bokassa I of the Central African Empire personally clubbed and kicked another AP reporter. The emperor's police thought the journalist's garbled telex message was code and therefore that he was a spy. In 1985 the Shiite terrorist group Hezbollah abducted AP reporter Terry Anderson in Beirut. He was not released until 1991. While in Pakistan following up stories about the September 11, 2001, terrorist attacks, Daniel Pearl of the *Wall Street Journal* was abducted and beheaded. Women correspondents have been raped, although just how often this occurs is unclear; the women sometimes don't say much about sexual assaults for fear of seeming less able than men to cope with the dangers of foreign reporting.

The threat of violence weighs heavily on reporters. "A common device in Africa's socialist countries," *Washington Post* correspondent David Lamb reported in 1978, was "The Program," which ensured that correspondents stay packed in a tight, easily supervised group. "I must insist that you do not deviate from The Program," an Ethiopian Information Ministry official told Lamb, "or we will take revolutionary measures against you." The official said he was joking, Lamb noted, "but it still had a troubling ring. In Ethiopia, 'revolutionary measures' means death."

THE EXPULSION OF GEORGE KRIMSKY

When Soviet Union officials had expulsion on their minds, Associated Press correspondent George Krimsky was an ideal candidate. He covered Soviet dissidents, whom the authorities did not want in the news. They couldn't say that publicly, so they accused him of espionage. Here is the story of his 1977 expulsion in his own words:

AP had one mission in the USSR and everywhere else—to keep major news flowing to its worldwide clientele. For that reason, my employer needed to staunch the crisis caused by my expulsion. When the time came for me to actually leave, my bureau chief was a very nervous fellow. He didn't want me carrying anything out that could be used to further jeopardize AP's status in the country—no souvenirs or anything that could be considered "contraband."

When we—I, my wife Paula and our baby daughter—got to Sheremyetovo Airport, the place was crawling with soldiers outside and strange men with scarves covering their faces inside. There were no passengers we could see, but there were a couple dozen friends who came to say good-bye.

As we headed toward the stairs for our final exit, we heard shouts: "Wait, wait." Turning back, we saw [dissident] Andrei Sakharov and his wife Yelena Bonner stumbling through the parted crowd. They came up to the turnstile barrier, but could not cross, so we went up to them and reached across the divide for our final goodbyes. Sakharov thanked us, planted a wet kiss on me and took a book from his pocket. He said he wanted me to have this inscribed copy of his work, *My Country and the World.* I was about to take it, when I saw the AP bureau chief hovering in the distance with a horrified expression on his face.

Recalling my promise to "leave clean," I looked back at Sakharov and said: "Andrei Dimitryovich, you are very kind. But please understand that I cannot take this book now, because we have already been cleared through Customs. Give it to one of my associates, and he will make sure I get it later." Sakharov looked crestfallen. It was the measure of this man that such a tactical compromise was unthinkable. One did the decent thing, whatever the cost. But, frankly, my only concern at that moment was to take myself and my family out of this country. . . . We muttered our farewells, climbed the stairs and left the Soviet Union for good. I eventually got the book.

A small postscript: As we were being processed through Passport Control, a vigilant young soldier noticed that my exit visa had my name misspelled—"Krinsky" instead of Krimsky. "You cannot leave," he said. I asked how old he was, and when he answered with a puzzled frown, I said: "Check with your boss." He left the booth for a few minutes and returned at a gallop. *Whomp, whomp, whomp* went the stamp on our passports, and without looking at us, he hoarsely whispered, "Go." You see, the KGB chief, Yuri Andropov, had personally ordered my expulsion.

"How many journalists in this environment have tried seriously to probe beneath the surface of Hizbullah, exploring its link to Islamic Jihad, its financing, the directives it receives from Tehran or factions of the PLO?" asked the *Washington Post's* Nora Boustany shortly after Anderson's abduction. "For those who try to report these issues, there is always the danger of getting killed." When the Iraq War broke out in 2003, CNN news executive Eason Jordan made a confession on the op-ed page of the *New York Times.* His reporters had withheld "awful things" about Saddam Hussein's regime for fear of jeopardizing "the lives of Iraqis, particularly those on our Baghdad staff."

Expulsion and censorship can achieve just the opposite of what is intended by thrusting a repressive regime into the news even more, thereby increasing international pressure on it to reform. And of course, some stories are simply too big to suppress. One such case in the annals of the *New York Times* occurred when Frank Kluckholm reported evidence of Nazi-Fascist intervention in the Spanish civil war. After he was thrown out of the country, Arthur Hays Sulzberger, president and publisher of the *Times,* put the episode down as "an excellent example of where the sending of a single story is worth the expulsion that may follow it."

The costs and benefits of Peruvian coverage were on the minds of AP executives when Edith Lederer was expelled in 1975. Five years before, the military government had ordered AP correspondent Joseph McGowan to buy a one-way ticket out of the country. McGowan was covering an earthquake that killed sixty-six thousand Peruvians. The government objected to his "unreal and offensive" description of the aftermath, in particular his implication of widespread promiscuity by Peruvian women with foreign relief workers. McGowan later heard that the government's real concern was that he had an excellent anonymous source inside the government. The source tipped him off that official statements egregiously played down the death toll.

When Lederer returned to New York after her expulsion, AP president Wes Gallagher put on a lunch for her at the Rainbow Room, the elegant restaurant atop Rockefeller Center then favored by AP executives. Gallagher, a gruff journalist, knew what it meant to be a foreign correspondent under trying circumstances. During World War II, the Germans had detained him in Athens for several months; in Tunisia, he was severely injured in a jeep accident. Recognizing Lederer to be a tough, competent reporter, he okayed a new, plum assignment as bureau chief in the Caribbean. But something else was on his mind at the lunch, too. "Edie," he said in a toast, "the next time you get kicked out of a country, will you please do it for a good story?"

17

GIMME THE AIR!

When foreign correspondents leaped from the printed page to broadcasting, they couldn't be certain where they would land. The wireless, which Guglielmo Marconi brought to life at the end of the nineteenth century, was still inventing itself. Journalism, especially journalism broadcast from abroad, was on uncertain footing. Some thought no news of any kind had a place on the air. But when Americans became eager for reports of the mounting international crisis of the late 1930s, and radio proved able to deliver those reports in real time, that attitude changed. Virtually overnight, a new breed of broadcast foreign correspondent took the medium to its pinnacle. This chapter tells this story and shows why radio and its offspring television found it difficult to scale the same peaks as time went on.

The Italian-born Marconi brought his wireless to the United States in 1899. To publicize his invention, which transmitted messages by Morse code, he teamed up with accomplished attention-getter James Gordon Bennett Jr. The two engineered an experiment involving an event dear to the "Commodore," the America's Cup yacht race, and employed a piece of equipment the *New York Herald* had long been accustomed to using, intermediary ships. This time, though, the vessels did not intercept ships carrying newsy mail from abroad. Outfitted with wireless equipment, they transmitted news of the race's outcome to shore. Although "unparalleled in the history of journalism," as the *Herald* put it, the feat was not aimed at changing news-gathering in any profound way. Bennett was simply looking for another news gimmick. Nor did Marconi anticipate a mass audience for news. He hoped the trick would interest the U.S. Navy in using his invention for point-to-point communication. As the inventor quickly discovered, however, the tradition-bound navy was a difficult customer. Its vastly different ideas about the deployment of the technology led to endless squabbles.

While the navy dragged its feet, the press had flights of fancy. Writing in *McClure's,* Ray Stannard Baker speculated that wireless might be effective over land and imagined "the great banking and business houses, or even families and friends" with their own wireless systems, each having "its own secret tune." "What developments will be made on ethereal telegraphy hereafter can hardly be foreseen," observed the *New York Times,* concluding its little editorial with:

—I come
To answer thy best pleasure; be 't to fly,
To swim, to dive into the fire, to ride
On the curl'd clouds; to thy strong bidding task
Ariel and all his quality.

A major advance occurred when Reginald Fessenden, who helped the U.S. Weather Bureau develop early warning systems for storms, invented technology to transmit the human voice. On Christmas Eve 1906 he made the first "radio" broadcast to a handful of ships, whose crews were accustomed to the dots and dashes of Morse code. Although he did a violin solo on the air, Fessenden thought this new technology was best used as a means of practical communication to ships at sea. Unsuited to government bureaucracy, he went off to start a private wireless company, a task for which he was equally ill equipped.

Another early innovator, Lee De Forest, developed a vacuum tube that facilitated transmission of the human voice. He combined a talent for tinkering with a con man's instincts for promotion. He "looked forward to the day when opera may be brought into every home. Someday the news and even advertising will be sent out over the wireless telephone." A press-release-happy partner boldly predicted that automobiles would have radios. Meanwhile the United Fruit Company invested in wireless in hopes of improving communications with its remote Latin American agricultural holdings, and amateur radio operators chatted away, often heedless of government regulation. In 1917 licensed operators totaled 13,581; estimates of unlicensed stations reached 150,000.

Around 1912, the U.S. Navy began to work more constructively and enthusiastically with commercial wireless entrepreneurs. The war further heightened its awareness of the vast potential of this communications medium and sharpened the realization that it could be used to undermine national security. The navy took control of all the country's privately owned radio stations and ordered amateur operations to shut down. In addition to using radio for military communications, the navy broadcast "Home Stuff" propaganda as far as Europe.

As hard as it tried, the navy failed to maintain control of wireless after the war. Radio emerged from the postwar tussle in the hands of a government-sanctioned monopoly in which General Electric, Westinghouse, American Telephone and Telegraph, and United Fruit pooled their wireless patents in a company called the Radio Corporation of America (RCA). The trust quickly fell victim to the competitive instincts of its members and new rivals. At the end of 1922, the Ford Motor Company; the Omaha Grain Exchange; St. Matthew's Cathedral in Laramie, Wyoming; Gimbel's; and the Alabama Power Company, as well as seventy-four colleges and universities and sixty-nine newspapers, all owned radio stations.

Still, radio was a question mark. Should it be educational? Could it be? Should it provide entertainment? Should wealthy patrons endow stations the way industrialist Andrew Carnegie supported libraries? Should local governments support stations, or should operating funds come from a tax on each radio set, not unlike the way Great Britain later charged citizens a license fee for television receiving equipment and used the funds to support the BBC? Should radio carry advertisements? Was it fit to be heard in the home? The trade publication *Printer's Ink* thought commercial radio would "prove positively offensive to great numbers of people. . . . the family circle is not a public place."

Victor Lawson of the *Chicago Daily News,* who had financed Walter Wellman's failed transoceanic dirigible flights, started WMAQ in Chicago with similarly limited expectations. "You are quite right in condemning the broadcasting of news," the progressive publisher wrote to his old partner Melville Stone. Sounding like a modern newspaper publisher justifying an investment in the Internet that might never be profitable, he continued: "I have gone into the broadcasting proposition merely on the ground that it is a new and undefined development which may, or may not, have some permanent relation to the newspaper, and I felt it was the part of wisdom to be in the front rank, so that if any such unexpected development came we should not be behind any of our competitors. As the matter now stands, the only value we get out of this considerable expenditure is an undefined 'good will.'"

Coincidentally, one of the first journalists on the air was one-time *Chicago Daily News* foreign correspondent Frederic William Wile, whom Lawson had sent to help Edward Price Bell in 1900. After working overseas two decades for various newspapers, Wile returned home and became a columnist with the *Washington Star.* As a sideline in 1923, he started a weekly local radio program of commentary, to which he gave the awkward title *The Political Situation in Washington Tonight.* Wile worked on the air without pay.

Like Benjamin Franklin and other Colonial printers who lifted news from other publications, early broadcasters read from newspapers and magazines. In 1926 RCA created the National Broadcasting Company, the first national network, as a subsidiary to its electronics business. NBC had little enthusiasm for news-gathering. "The radio can never be a substitute for the newspaper," Merlin Aylesworth, the president of NBC, said in a 1931 speech. "The broadcast news flashes are simply glorified headlines that whet the appetite of the listener and make him buy the newspaper for amplification." After considerable newspaper experience, Abel Schechter joined the network's publicity department in 1932: "So I, having probably the most experience with press associations and newspapers, was told I was the news department." His office was a cubbyhole.

At first newspapers were attracted to radio's potential to give them a small edge in news-reporting and public attention, as Bennett had had in using wireless to enhance coverage of the America's Cup. During the Russo-Japanese War, Lee De Forest established a wireless telegraph station on the Shantung coast, which was "in easy communication" with a cable office from which he supplied news to the *Times* of London and the *New York Times.* The station received signals from a boat that plied the sea looking for battles and other naval maneuverings—until Japanese officials put it out of business. In the early 1920s, the *Brooklyn Daily Eagle* arranged for associate editor and former foreign correspondent H. V. Kaltenborn to discuss current events on the radio. The newspaper's management thought the publicity would build circulation.

Not all publishers were enthusiastic about having radio provide regular news reports, which aired well before their newspapers hit the streets. "If radio is to be the means of distributing news," wrote a Minot, North Dakota, publisher to a colleague in 1924, "the newspaper of the United States will soon have very little to offer." Radio appeared more and more to be a Trojan horse. Newspapers questioned why they should publish listings for NBC and CBS, which were gaining attention from the papers' advertisers, or why they should let announcers breathlessly read the news that the papers had gathered. It was also disturbing to see print journalists become full-time broadcasters, as Kaltenborn did when he left the *Daily Eagle* in 1930 to join the Columbia Broadcasting System, the second U.S. national network to be created.

As the Great Depression began to weigh on newspapers, the American Newspaper Publishers' Association, in league with the wire services, declared a press-radio war. The intensely self-interested publishers prosecuted this war with moral righteousness. One of its leaders was Edward Harris, an Indiana publisher and an ANPA leader, who raised the specter of government licensing that could lead to "the suppression of legitimate news and the substitution of Government propaganda." This tactic played on fears that radio in America could go the way it had in Germany, where the Nazis used it to shape public opinion. Newspapers demanded fees for publishing radio schedules and pressed advertisers to choose between the two media. Wire services refused to sell news to radio stations (except to those owned by newspapers, and those had to pay an additional assessment). When CBS responded by setting up the Columbia News Service, newspapers stopped publishing its program listings.

A peace treaty was signed at the Hotel Biltmore in New York in 1934. CBS killed its news service and, along with NBC, agreed to limit news to two five-minute daily summaries based on bulletins provided by the newly created Press-Radio Bureau. The newspaper publishers and wire services ran the bureau; the two networks paid the expenses. NBC and CBS could not sell ads around the two news broadcasts, and they were to stay out of the news-gathering business. In return, newspapers agreed to run their daily radio schedules.

The agreement was unrealistic. Though news was verboten, news commentary over the networks by journalists like Floyd Gibbons and Lowell Thomas wasn't. Independent stations ignored the Biltmore agreement and gathered their own reports. The International News Service and the United Press broke ranks first and started to sell their services to radio. In 1938 CBS and NBC stopped paying for Press-Radio Bureau bulletins. Soon AP surrendered.

Newspapers, meanwhile, found that the publication of radio schedules was in their interest as much as in the interest of the stations. Readers bought newspapers in order to know what was on the air, where foreign events were attracting increased attention.

❈

Kaltenborn was traveling in Europe when the Spanish civil war broke out in 1936. As an experiment, CBS sent him to Hendaye, on the French side of the border with Spain. Kaltenborn and a French technician found a telephone in an abandoned farmhouse and contacted New York. In a live broadcast, he described the fighting in the distance. Listeners heard the whiz of bullets and the rumble of artillery. Kaltenborn won a prestigious National Headliner Award. Even so, CBS's permanent representative in Europe, César Saerchinger, did not see much future in such broadcasting. "The idea of broadcasting a 'running commentary' on the cruelest kind of war, just as you would do with a football game, was grotesque but perfectly feasible," he predicted, "though the opportunity is not very likely to occur again."

The sort of foreign reporting the networks initially favored was delivered by the likes of Boake Carter. The foreign-born but stridently isolationist Carter broadcast from Philadelphia as the Hearst Globe Trotter in the City of Brotherly Love. Unlike George Smalley, who wrote his stirring, though delayed, account of the Harvard-Oxford boat race based on what he saw, Carter covered an Oxford-Cambridge boat race by imagining what happened. Crowd noises were piped in. Frederick William Wile, who went on to full-time paid broadcasting, claimed to be "the first transatlantic radio reporter of a great international news event" when CBS sent him to the Five-Power Naval Conference in 1929. He recruited dignitaries to speak on the air, which was the norm on radio, and provided a once-a-week news review, which was unusual.

In 1935 NBC listed the year's eleven milestones, six of which originated overseas. None involved reporting. The broadcasts included the first broadcast ever from Mount Vesuvius ("The actual sounds of the flowing lava and the hissing steam were heard as a microphone was dropped within"); the canonization ceremonies of Sir Thomas More; and a salute to Marconi "via radio by ships at sea, by Admiral Byrd at the South Pole and by the Graf Zeppelin flying across the Atlantic." Earlier, NBC carried a speech from Germany all in German. CBS followed the same pattern. One of its broadcasts in the early 1930s consisted of a nightingale singing from a Surrey woods for thirty minutes. Radio editors on American newspapers voted it the most interesting program of the year.

CBS lagged NBC overseas. European countries, which had a strong tradition of state ownership of radio, initially thought of NBC as *the* national broadcasting company of the United States and were therefore more eager to work with it. Fred Bate, its representative in London, moved in elevated social circles and forged close relations with the BBC. Working on the continent was Max Jordan. Ubiquitous Max, as he was known, had been born and educated in Germany (he held a Ph.D. from Jena University); he had worked for Hearst newspapers in the United States and abroad before joining NBC. When he heard that CBS was sending a new man to Europe in 1937, Jordan scurried around Europe arranging exclusive deals with state radio stations from Stockholm to Budapest. The new "European Director"

CBS sent to replace César Saerchinger—Edward R. Murrow—was at a disadvantage in other ways as well. Whereas Saerchinger had been a newspaper correspondent before joining the network, the twenty-nine-year-old Murrow had no journalism experience at all. Rumors circulated at CBS that his overseas assignment was a maneuver to get him out of the way.

Like NBC, CBS was not eager to air real reporting when it dispatched Murrow. Doing so might compromise the network. "Broadcasting has no role in international politics," said one of the network higher-ups. Murrow was a glorified booking agent. The American Foreign Correspondents' Association in London, populated by print journalists who also thought radio had no place in news-gathering, rejected his application for membership. Murrow couldn't even attend the meetings. When he wanted to hire out-of-work journalist William Shirer to help him, New York agreed even though the veteran print reporter did poorly on his voice test. Why not? Shirer, whom Murrow transferred from Berlin to Vienna, was to use his considerable contacts to compete with Jordan in the race to get "talks," interviews, and other such events on the air. If a real journalist occasionally was called for, Murrow and Shirer could put Vincent Sheean, Edgar Ansel Mowrer, or one of their print colleagues on the air. A New York Times pal of Shirer's predicted that he would soon return to newspapering.

Not long after Shirer took up his job in Vienna, Hitler began the series of moves that forced Austrian unification with Germany in 1938. Shirer, straining at the CBS reins, proposed a short broadcast explaining what was afoot. Instead he was sent to Bulgaria to arrange for a children's choir to appear on the CBS School of the Air. When he returned to Vienna, the final stages of the Anschluss were under way. This was "the most important story of my life," Shirer thought. Besides, NBC's Max Jordan wasn't in town. Shirer raced to the Austrian state radio station and found it occupied by storm troopers. He couldn't broadcast. With Murrow's permission, he finagled a plane ride to London in hopes that he would be allowed to tell the story from there. CBS put him on the air.

Jordan nevertheless beat Shirer. He hustled back to Vienna and used his contacts to broadcast from the occupied country before Shirer could air his story. But CBS sensed it had an opportunity to leap ahead of its rival. CBS president William Paley, the cigar manufacturer who had acquired the then-faltering network in 1928, directed his staff to arrange a half-hour broadcast in which foreign correspondents in various European capitals weighed in on the significance of the Anschluss. This had to be done live, since networks at the time did not use recorded broadcasts.* CBS raced to lease lines and assemble correspondents who could comment. Shirer remained in London while Murrow, who had been in Warsaw organizing another children's choir presentation, went to Vienna and contributed analysis to the roundup. In that instant, he became a foreign correspondent.

"The crisis has done one thing for us," Shirer wrote hopefully in his diary. "I

---

* Networks forbade taped broadcasts because they feared that entertainers would produce their own programs and sell them to stations, cutting networks out of the production business.

think radio talks by Ed and me are now established. Birth of the 'radio foreign correspondent,' so to speak." When Hitler made his run on the Czech Sudetenland in September 1938, CBS and NBC again went head to head. At first, Shirer noted in his diary, CBS "let me talk five minutes daily—revolutionary in the broadcasting business!" Soon he broadcast much more. For the first time, the two American networks carried news throughout the day—from Shirer and Jordan in Munich, from Murrow and Bate in London, and from elsewhere. CBS commentator H. V. Kaltenborn, who slept on a cot in his New York studio, delivered eighty-five broadcasts by himself over eighteen days; he recounted the broadcasts in a quickie book, *I Broadcast the Crisis*. Again showing his edge, Jordan had a forty-six-minute beat announcing the agreement that sold out Czechoslovakia. According to one often-used count, CBS carried 151 broadcasts and NBC 147. An internal NBC report to its board of directors scored the competition differently. Including all of Kaltenborn's reports, it said, "We had 41% more bulletins and summaries." In addition, it noted, NBC had 49 press notices in New York newspapers, and CBS had only 28.

"Radio's performance in the current turmoil," *Newsweek* reported afterward, "has proved it the fastest agency yet devised to flash world-shaking events into every home that can afford a receiver." People were glued to their radios. When power was lost after a hurricane ripped through New England, people went out to their cars and turned on the radio (the wild prediction about automobiles being connected to the ether had come to pass). Aware of heightened listener interest, advertisers bought more time on news programs. A Midwestern radio station that previously did not have sponsors for all of its eight scheduled news programs now had advertisers standing in line, even though it was airing more news than before.

"For the first time history has been made in the hearing of its pawns," observed a writer in the *Nation*. "The radio coverage of the crisis was good not only because of the professional competence, sense of public responsibility, and devotion of the journalists and network executives who did the job but also because the radio networks and individual stations seized a glorious opportunity. . . . it is quite possible that the dissemination and interpretation of news will now be recognized as the most important function of the industry."

Great Britain and France declared war on Germany in September 1939. Officially neutral Americans were tethered to their radios. "Passionately though we may desire detachment," President Franklin Roosevelt said in a radio broadcast, "we are forced to realize that every word that comes through the air, every ship that sails the sea, every battle that is fought does affect the American future." Radio's great attraction was its immediacy and, to use one of the medium's terms, its ability to convey *actuality*. The radio reporter was on the scene telling the eager listener what "*is* happening."

Radio's advantage in covering on-the-spot episodes of war electrified listeners at the end of 1939, when Talbot G. Bowen picked up a microphone in Montevideo, Uruguay. In keeping with the harum-scarum nature of broadcasting at the time,

Bowen was an accidental foreign correspondent. Not only was he unfamiliar to listeners; his identify was vaguely confusing to his temporary bosses at NBC. Possibly working backward from his nickname, Jimmy, they referred to him on the air as James. Bowen's route to broadcasting was haphazard. He had served in the armed services in World War I. Afterward, according to a contemporary magazine story, he "knocked around considerably," managing the American Club in Buenos Aires and drifting to Montevideo, where he represented Metro-Goldwyn-Mayer pictures and on one occasion arranged the broadcast of a Montevideo opera for NBC radio. When Nazi Germany's *Graf Spee* took refuge in the neutral Montevideo harbor on December 14, following a sea battle with British cruisers, the network asked Bowen to keep a watch on the pocket battleship in case any news developed.

The heavily gunned warship was a symbol of the resurgent Germany navy and, as such, a considerable prize. It had sunk nine merchant vessels in a little over three months. While the *Graf Spee*'s captain, Hans Langsdorff, buried his dead in Montevideo and tried to complete repairs, the British pressed Uruguay's government to force the ship to leave. On December 15, Uruguayan authorities informed Langsdorff that the hobbled ship must depart by the evening of Sunday, December 17, or it would be interned. NBC had Bowen on the air throughout that day, talking about the coming and goings on the ship, which left the harbor at 3:15 P.M. When not broadcasting, he kept an open line to the New York studio (a link that ran by a telephone landline from Montevideo to Buenos Aires and thence to New York by shortwave radio). At 5:55 Bowen yelled over the phone, "Hello, New York! Hello, New York! Gimme the air, gimme the air! She's exploding, blowing up!"

Believing his damaged ship could neither prevail in battle nor escape, and not wanting it to fall into British hands, Langsdorff had sunk the *Graf Spee*. Print correspondents watched the ship go down, taking notes for stories to appear in the next day's newspaper. Relatively untutored in broadcasting and struggling to keep his balance on the crowded dock, Bowen peered at the *Graf Spee* through binoculars and described what he saw. His thirteen-minute broadcast went far beyond Kaltenborn's recording of battlefield sounds during the Spanish civil war. Bowen's account was the first "major war episode" reported live. Here is an excerpt:

> It looks now that the War of Nerves is absolutely over. We just gave you the Flash News Report since the *Graf Spee* had scuttled the ship—as we call it—had blown itself up. What method was used we can't tell you at the moment. The ship is 5 miles out, and all we can see at the present moment at the shore here is a lot of smoke and flame. The launches leaving the ship—we tried to get it with the glasses. The smoke seemed to overcast the action. She's still afloat; pieces of her have gone up; the hull is still afloat, and the *Tacoma* which left,* as we wired you a short time ago, left shortly after the craft, is trying to stand by her. It's without

---

* Before sailing, most of the *Graf Spee*'s crew transferred to the German cargo steamer *Tacoma*. The *Tacoma* did not go down, as Bowen speculated that it might. Those on the *Tacoma*, along with the rest of the crew on the ship, were transferred to Argentine tugs and a barge, which took them to Buenos Aires.

doubt that the *Tacoma,* also being loaded with fuel oil, will very possibly take fire and also go up. . . .

The ship is moving—rolling from side to side. There goes another explosion! The bow is brought up. Evidently, the powder magazine has caught fire. She's going down! She's going down by the stern! The stern is completely under water! Flames are still shooting up in the air! Smoke! Evidently, this wasn't what we call exactly scuttling the ship, because the nautical term "scuttling a ship" is opening the sea valves and letting in the water. These boys evidently are making a good job of it and leaving nothing but the pieces. They aren't going to leave anything anyone can reclaim whatsoever.

Without a doubt there'll be no reclamation for any of the sailors. This afternoon in our broadcast we told you of the transfer of some of the sailors to the hospital, a transfer of 31 sailors to the hospital. It may be possible that those are the only sailors who'll remain of the pocket cruiser *Graf Spee.*

She's going down by the fore part. The bow is under! She seems to raise a little at the stern. That is possibly due to seeing it from here. Naturally, that would throw her bow a little bit in the air. Now she seems to be settling—going down a little bit. She's just about where we can see the aft-stern gone completely. Part of the superstructure is gone. The stack is still there. She's down in the water due to the low depth of water. Her superstructure is out of the water. She is absolutely on the bottom. Only thing showing now is her superstructure, her stack, and part of her battle tower above water.

We have just received information which is not official and will probably need a long time to be confirmed. The confirmation or rumor is, or the advice which we'll have to accept as the rumor at the moment, the advice is that the explosion of the *Graf Spee* was done at the dictation of Mr. Hitler—absolutely. That of course will have to be proven in time like a number of things in the last war that we waited 20 years to find the truth.* However, the first naval battle in this war fought in South American waters has probably come to its conclusion. . . .

We are unable at the moment to determine what is happening to the crew even with glasses, due to the movement of launches and the movement of two or three tugs which left the harbor here after the *Graf Spee* had gone out. All the launches seem to be getting to the *Tacoma.* Whether the *Tacoma* is unloading the sailors that were transferred to her to the launches, it's impossible to define at the moment even with glasses. There's a lot of action, and the crowd around here are just about crowding us into the water. We are in a very bad way. However, we'll do the best we can. It's awfully hard to describe this. We know more or less what is going on, but we don't want to tell you what we think is going on. We want to tell you what we can see, and we can't see a great deal, due to the excessive action and movement. At least 300,000 people are here on the "rambler"

---

* Newspaper accounts the next day reported that Hitler had ordered Langsdorff to sink the *Graf Spee.* Historical records show that Langsdorff was ordered to negotiate for more time, to attempt to break through to Argentina, or—if those two failed—to sink the ship.

as we call it—a wide highway wider even than the boardwalk at Atlantic City—and it's absolutely blocked—it's impossible to move. . . .

The *Graf* seems to be settling a little bit at the moment. It may be possible that the rest of her may go.

ANNOUNCER: This is NBC in New York. You've been listening, ladies and gentlemen, to another in the series of the NBC On the Spot broadcasts. James Bowen, NBC's representative in Montevideo, Uruguay, has told us of the sinking of the *Graf Spee* and of the condition of the German supply ship *Tacoma.* The voice of Mr. Bowen was heard in the United States via RCA Communications.

Keep tuned to your favorite NBC station for the latest news. This is the National Broadcasting System.

The network interrupted programs on 175 network stations as well as on international shortwave to broadcast Bowen's report. A United Airlines pilot picked up the NBC signal while flying over Nebraska and piped parts of it to his passengers. Foreshadowing the time when White House officials would watch CNN to follow an overseas crisis, President Roosevelt listened on a radio in his Hyde Park home. FDR, reported NBC to its board of directors, "telephoned in to say it was the most thrilling broadcast he ever heard." Bowen was heard as far away as Timbuktu and Berlin, said *Time. Newsweek* chronicled the "blow-by-blow feat." "In international matters," said Lenox Lohr, who had become NBC president, "there has been no question of our superiority."

Yet, even while it basked in all of this glory, NBC was far from convinced that there was much of a future in foreign news. A few months before the *Graf Spee* went down, the network had temporarily halted news broadcasts from Europe. "We are cutting our coverage to the bone," NBC executive John F. Royal had said in an interdepartmental note. "The hysteria is off and finished, and we have grabbed about all the glory we can get." The network feared that coverage of the war might drive the public into a war mood, and it did not want to jeopardize its broadcast license by seeming to violate the U.S. Neutrality Act. Besides, such coverage abroad was a drain on profits. Speaking of transmission costs, Royal observed that NBC paid its parent RCA "approximately $8,100 in facilities costs during the crisis. There is little satisfaction in this—that the Telephone Company did not get all the money, but they got too much." NBC's Abel Schechter questioned whether advertisers would be interested in offsetting these costs by sponsoring war news. "What sponsor," he asked, "would want to sponsor death?"

John Royal sent Bowen a five-hundred-dollar check to reward him for his spectacular report. No one at the network seems to have thought of hiring him on the staff. "It is unfortunate that we didn't have a better announcer than Mr. Bowen," Royal observed. His pronunciation "was only one stage removed from 'dese, dose and dems.'" Besides this, Royal was irritated by Bowen's continual descriptions of his difficulties seeing the event. "There were times," Royal said in an internal memo, "when I wished the crowd *had* pushed Bowen into the water."

Bowen disappeared from the network's collective memory as completely as the *Graf Spee* disappeared when it sank into the Atlantic. Twenty years later, when Royal recounted "probably one of the most dramatic Radio pick-ups of the War," he remembered Bowen as an "American clerk from a local club." By the turn of the century, his name "did not ring any bells" at NBC, a producer acknowledged. "It certainly seems as if James Bowen has, indeed, been entirely forgotten."

Not so for Murrow. For him and the hungry CBS network, the mounting crisis in Europe was an opportunity to move out of perennial also-ran status to fame. "Your name is as well-known as that of any home commentator," Kaltenborn wrote to Murrow in November 1939. And when he came home, CBS could "sell you for as many lectures as you care to deliver, and you'll get twice as much for them as you did last time." For the first time, Kaltenborn wrote, "The News Department is paying for itself with sponsored news broadcasts."

The rise of mass communication research coincided with the rise of commercial radio. Radio stations and networks needed to measure audience size and impact for their advertisers. Scholars were eager to apply their new social science tools and theories to a medium with great potential for shaping attitudes.

One of the most important early systematic studies was the Radio Research Project. It was the brainchild of Princeton professor Hadley Cantril, an early student of public opinion, and Frank Stanton, a young Ph.D. in industrial psychology who was responsible for audience research at CBS. The Rockefeller Foundation funded the project and Viennese-born Paul Lazarsfeld directed it. Lazarsfeld, who knew little about radio news, described himself variously as a mathematician, a social psychologist, a sociologist, and a social scientist. Radio appealed to him, he said, because "it is a topic around which actually any kind of research method can be tried out and can be applied satisfactorily." Among Lazarsfeld's contributions were two methods for measuring communication effects. One was the focus group interview, and the other a mechanical device called the Lazarsfeld-Stanton Program-Analyzer that was installed in radio receivers. "The Lazarsfeld Radio Research Project," one scholar later said, "virtually created the field of mass communication research."

Among Lazarsfeld's findings was the public's keen interest in foreign news broadcasts during periods of tension. A survey conducted immediately after the Nazis occupied the Sudetenland in October 1938 asked respondents, "In the European crisis, were you more interested in the radio reports or the newspaper reports?" The answers were compared to a similar question asked the preceding year (see table 6). "The profound significance of radio in a period of tension is made clear by these figures," Lazarsfeld observed. "Each new crisis, one might argue (and there seem to be more crises every year), puts radio more in the lead." Asked if they usually learned about an important event first on the radio or newspaper, 68 percent of respondents picked radio in March 1939, 77 percent picked radio in March 1940, and 82 percent picked radio in mid-1942 and mid-1944. On the afternoon after the Japanese attack on Pearl Harbor in 1941, half of all Americans had turned on their radios.

Edward R. Murrow, destined to become the Tennyson of the ether, did not have the pedigree of many journalists. He compensated by doctoring his résumé when he put his first foot on the career ladder. In addition to adding years to his age, he switched his alma mater from Washington State University to the more prestigious University of Washington and tossed in for good measure some education at Stanford University. He also said he had been a political science major, when his field really had been speech. His education, nevertheless, served him well. Speaking in a reassuring baritone, he was understated and steady in the midst of chaos. His prose, even when conjured up extemporaneously, was vivid and personal. Listeners hung on his words. "Ed didn't know how to write like a newsman, which freed him to write with his own fresh eye and ear," said a colleague.

In August 1940, with the German Blitz of London hot and heavy, Murrow did his first *London after Dark* broadcast from Trafalgar Square. Air raid sirens wailed in the background.

A searchlight just burst into action off in the distance, one single beam sweeping the sky above me now. People are walking along quite quietly. We are just at the entrance of an air raid shelter here, and I must move this cable over just a bit so that people can walk in. There's another searchlight just square behind Nelson's statue. Here comes one of those big red busses around the corner, double deckers they are, just a few lights on the top deck. In this blackness it looks very much like a ship that's passing in the night, and you just see the portholes.

TABLE 6. Preference for radio as source of news at a normal time and at a time of crisis

	Percentage preferring radio[a]	
	In 1937 (normal)	In 1938 (crisis)
Rural population		
Low income	46.5	67.4
Middle income	48.3	76.9
High income	34.9	70.4
Urban population		
Low income	33.8	74.9
Middle income	28.8	79.6
High income	18.6	71.9

Source: Lazarsfeld, *Radio and the Printed Page,* 259.

[a]Only people who had a choice between radio and other sources of news are reflected in these percentages.

Washington State University professor Ida Lou Anderson, an enthusiastic mentor who introduced Murrow to music, poetry, and the classics, stayed in touch. She suggested his famous sign-on, "This is London," instead of the stodgy "Hello America. This is London calling." Soon similar salutations—"This is Berlin," "This is Rome," "This is Paris"—were uttered by the correspondents Murrow recruited and molded for CBS.

The CBS News staff grew overall from 4 in 1939 to more than 60 by 1941. Murrow took advantage of this hiring spree to recruit aggressively to his ranks. The tradition in print journalism was—and to a large extent remains—that a reporter started at the bottom, writing obituaries, chasing fire engines, covering the cops, and earning the right to move up to better assignments. That was not the model Murrow adopted in his recruiting. Nor did he care much about voice quality. He could just as easily hire Eric Sevareid, whose voice test was worse than Shirer's, as Larry LeSueur, who sounded good on air. What commended Sevareid was that he wrote beautifully. Thomas Grandin had two strikes against him, a bad voice and no journalism experience. His compelling credential was being a scholar at the Geneva Research Center. Mary Marvin Breckinridge, the first woman from Maine to receive a pilot's license, had filmed a documentary on Appalachia and wandered to Europe with freelance commissions from *Town and Country* and several other publications. After she showed a good touch with freelance stories, Murrow made her the CBS Amsterdam correspondent. Charles Collingwood and Howard K. Smith joined Murrow after only a few months' experience with United Press, jobs

Edward R. Murrow with one of his boys, William Shirer. CBS.

they landed after being Rhodes Scholars at Oxford. Murrow's magnetic personality bound together these journalists and others he brought into the fold. Although not all were men, they came to be known as "Murrow's Boys."

NBC and, to a lesser extent, the Mutual and ABC networks (the latter had been hived off of NBC's second-string network) had glory moments during the war. Mutual was the first to report the Japanese attack on Pearl Harbor. Max Jordan, as NBC noted in a press release, "gained a six-hour best on the Nazi invasion of Denmark" and was the first to report the Japanese reply to the Allied peace terms. But Murrow's Boys outshined them all. They vividly described the fall of Paris and chronicled what it was like to make a bombing raid over Germany. Collingwood's scoops in North Africa left newspaper correspondents "quoting him increasingly," *Newsweek* reported. Only twenty-eight of the five hundred American correspondents in London were selected to accompany troops on the D-Day Invasion. Five were CBS reporters. At the war's end, Paley noted in his autobiography, six hundred radio editors voted that CBS had done the "Best News Job in Radio" in its coverage of V-E Day, V-J Day, the Japanese surrender, and the death of Franklin D. Roosevelt.

Murrow, who put all this together, went from arranging attractions on the air to being the attraction. Advertisers wanted to sponsor his programs. In 1944 the American Foreign Correspondents' Association in London, which had refused to admit Murrow in the 1930s, elected him president. When he returned home, Paley appointed him vice president for public affairs. After Murrow tired of the desk job and went back on the air, Paley took the highly unusual step of naming him to the corporate board of directors. Having established himself as a voice of integrity and authority, Murrow corrected the false statements in his resume. The year he died, 1965, his alma mater, Washington State University, named its journalism school after him.

CBS emerged from World War II as the premier broadcast news operation. Its bureaus around the world, staffed by journalists with education and skill, rivaled the foreign services of the great newspapers. Murrow and his correspondents were the standard against which excellence in foreign broadcast reporting was measured. "There were no precedents," Sevareid said. "We had to create tradition."

Radio had matured in what seemed like a flip of the switch. "In twenty years," said the author of a report in the *New Republic* in 1940, "radio has nearly reached the goal toward which print has been working for five hundred: to extend its audience to include the whole population." Broadcasting "put on long pants" faster than any other form of journalism in history, said Frank Stanton, who became CBS president in 1946. The question was how long that excellence would last—and what would happen with the new medium close on its heels, television.

After the war, NBC and CBS radio maintained their overseas bureaus, broadcast *Our Foreign Policy* and other interview programs that paid attention to foreign affairs, and produced documentaries on the atom bomb, famine, and the plight of children overseas. Correspondents doubted that the upstart medium of television could improve on this. The emphasis on makeup and lighting had little to do with the printed word, the milieu from which many radio journalists emanated. They didn't like all the equipment or taking instructions from a cameraman. London-based Howard K. Smith complained that reporting for both television and radio was "about as absurd as asking a surgeon to fill a few of his victim's teeth after an appendectomy—medicine and dentistry being about the same thing." Stanton had to beg Murrow and Sevareid just to appear on television during the 1948 presidential convention. "I wish God damned television had never been invented," Murrow complained.

In 1951 Murrow's *Hear It Now* radio program morphed into *See It Now,* a weekly magazine-style television news program. But cooperation from correspondents abroad remained "spotty—good in some areas; weak in others; non-existent in still others," observed Sig Mickelson, who headed the network's television news efforts. When radio correspondents made their traditional end-of-year visits to New York in 1953, most of them found ways to duck invitations to mingle with television staff. Because television depended particularly on radio for foreign news, the radio broadcasters' intransigence was a major cause of concern. Faced with this, CBS executives decided they had to take a different course of action.

In August 1954 a frustrated Stanton assembled his correspondents in Paris to announce that he was creating two parallel news operations, one for radio, in which they would work, and the other for television, for which he would bring in new talent. To his surprise, the correspondents asked that radio and television be combined. The reason was not their sudden love of the new medium. It was their recognition of its growing power. CBS was the largest carrier of commercial advertising on the entire planet. Its television programs were the chief reason why. The nightly fifteen-minute news on CBS television drew a bigger audience than the network's most popular radio programs. Television was destined to become American's primary source of news.

Several factors gave impetus to foreign news over the air in the coming years: the quality of the correspondents, who had amassed years of experience abroad in radio and were authorities on foreign affairs; the cold war generally and the hot war in Vietnam particularly, which kept foreign policy in a crisis mode; Federal Communications Commission regulations that made local licenses contingent on public-interest broadcasting and indirectly encouraged networks to be public service oriented; and the prestige foreign news brought. Every year throughout the 1950s, the network brought home a half dozen or so correspondents to do a joint *Years of Crisis* broadcast. The expense was "considerable," but so was the publicity and goodwill it generated, thought Sig Mickelson, the impresario of CBS television news and the first to carry the title of CBS News president: "It was an invaluable opportunity to showcase a superior reporting staff and promote the entire news and public affairs function."

No one valued the prestige more than CBS board chair William Paley. At a dinner meeting in Paris with correspondents in 1962, he outlined plans for the coming year. "Bill," said Charles Collingwood, who as one of Murrow's most celebrated boys had the right to call Paley by his first name, "that's going to cost you a lot of money." "You guys cover the news," Paley responded. "I have Jack Benny to make money for me."

Murrow did for infant television what he had done for infant radio: he gave it credibility. CBS News was "the House that Murrow built." Anyone who aspired to a similar journalistic mansion was expected to follow the same general floor plan. When ABC decided to establish itself on a par with its two rivals in the 1970s, it enhanced foreign coverage. When CNN started its twenty-four-hour cable news operation in 1980, it carried considerable foreign news, for which it was heralded.

During the 1960s, 1970s, and early 1980s, the networks continued to maintain bureaus in the great capitals of Europe, in the Middle East, in Asia, in Latin America, and in Africa. Along with CNN, they maintained the Murrow tradition of outstanding crisis reporting during the three-year period that began in 1989, when one earthshaking story after another erupted abroad—the Tiananmen protests in China, the fall of the Berlin Wall, the toppling of Communist regimes in Romania and Czechoslovakia, the dissolution of the Soviet Union, and the first Iraq War. And there were moments of courageous reporting when correspondents covered the second Iraq War at considerable peril. ABC's new anchor, Bob Woodruff, was severely injured during the conflict. "I believe the coverage of the war in Iraq has been every bit, if not more challenging for American networks as covering World War II," commented Bill Wheatley, vice president for news at NBC when the war began.

Advanced satellite and communications technology, analog and digital, made the gathering and delivery of information, images, and sound practically instantaneous. Because viewers and listeners were expecting live or nearly live coverage of events, news organizations had to find ways to satisfy that demand without going broke in the process. They subscribed to video services such as Reuters and Associated Press Television News (APTN) and to organizations like the European Broadcasting Union (EBU), which gave them access to video shot by reputable news crews spread around the world. In the early 1990s CBS News executives John Frazee and Marcy McGinnis organized a news consortium of private broadcasters in Europe whose purpose was to share information, personnel, and facilities in addition to video while gathering, reporting, and disseminating news with a deadline of "now." The consortium, which became known as ENEX (European News Exchange), grew to a membership of more than thirty private European broadcasters by 2006. "When a story breaks just about any place in Europe," said McGinnis, Wheatley's counterpart at CBS, "we have instant access to video, satellite uplinks, reporters, camera crews and technicians through our ENEX partners." Individual partnership deals, driven by the need to have access to news quickly, also grew throughout the broadcast world. "In the USA we rely on our affiliates to be our 'first line of defense' on many stories in over 200 local markets," said McGinnis. "Similarly our broadcasting partners around the world supplement our own news-gathering operation by serving as additional reporters and photographers on a daily basis."

CNN led in providing live coverage abroad by making use of new, lightweight equipment. Now a correspondent working with what CNN news executive Sid Bedingfield called a "techno-producer" could fly into a country and set up in a few hours. "Suddenly," he said, "live TV was available the way local stations were live." "Foreign coverage was no longer an updated version of the newsreel (filmed footage shipped to a land line studio and then put on air)," observed Andrew Tyndall, whose *Tyndall Report* tracks television news. "Roone Arledge [ABC] and Ted Turner [CNN] deserve as much prominence for the way they opened up TV to new technology as Murrow does for the way he opened up radio."

Over the years, nevertheless, broadcasters complained that the Murrow tradition was under assault or had disappeared. Murrow himself said as much—repeatedly. In 1958 he lamented that top network management was trained in "advertising, research, or show business," not news. Shortly before he left the network in 1961 to become the director of the U.S. Information Agency, Murrow decried an industry "bloated with statistics . . . indifferent to what our words and pictures are doing to the mind of America." It seemed at times as though the most secure aspect of the Murrow tradition was broadcast journalists' criticism of it. Frank Stanton, who stepped down in 1973, called CBS "just another company with dirty carpets." When CBS anchor Dan Rather left CBS thirty-three years later, he bemoaned the "'corporatization' of news and its effect on content." He "sought solace" watching *Good Night, and Good Luck,* a movie celebrating Murrow; Rather said in an interview that he had seen it five times.

One of the topics that most troubled veterans was foreign news coverage.

As we saw in chapter 10 with Woodward's Law, the amount of foreign news rises and falls in newspapers depending on whether it is a time of crisis or peace. The same pattern holds for television with a particularly pronounced downward trend in recent years. The fall-off in stories filed from abroad was dizzyingly steep during the 1990s "peace dividend" after the collapse of Communism in the Soviet Union. The rebound during the Iraq War of the early 2000s did not reach the levels of 1989–1991 (see table 7) and tapered off as the decade wore on, notwithstanding the fact that 135,000 American servicemen remained in an active war zone as of early 2009. Similar declines occurred in the time networks gave to international stories that did not directly involve U.S. foreign policy (see table 8). As a result, television was less likely to anticipate events that would someday affect the United States.

The number of broadcast correspondents who had deep knowledge abroad decreased. When NBC's Wheatley retired in 2006, he calculated that the number of foreign correspondents stationed abroad had fallen by about 50 percent from the high point in his thirty-year tenure at the network. CBS had experienced a similar decline. For almost a year in the middle of the mid-1990s, Jim Bittermann found himself "the only full-time, on-air correspondent for ABC News based between London and Antarctica."

Critics of this decrease focused on executives who were said not to care about news as their forerunners did. To make their case, they often pointed to the example of real estate developer Lawrence Tisch, who set CBS back when he bought it in 1986. Twenty years later the news division still suffered from his layoff of three hundred people, cutbacks that CBS anchor Dan Rather decried in a *New York Times* op-ed article with the headline "From Murrow to Mediocrity?"

Yet, network executives were not the root of the problem. Many labored to maintain high-quality news. The problem arose from the nature of television itself. The medium's structural problems were masked in times of crisis, when broadcasters gave a lifeline to audiences eager for foreign news. But the further networks progressed from the Murrow years, the more obvious television's inherent limitations became.

TABLE 7. Minutes on network television devoted to stories filed from foreign datelines

Year	ABC	CBS	NBC	Total
1988	1,158	1,090	1,013	3,257
1989	1,397	1,454	1,181	4,032
1990	1,414	1,377	1,081	3,872
1991	1,417	1,132	1,217	3,766
1992	1,037	736	749	2,521
1993	1,057	752	543	2,352
1994	992	974	768	2,733
1995	784	740	467	1,990
1996	577	692	327	1,596
1997	609	666	356	1,631
1998	513	647	304	1,464
1999	654	687	457	1,799
2000	481	479	422	1,382
2001	588	628	451	1,667
2002	667	779	657	2,103
2003	848	1,007	917	2,772
2004	711	890	823	2,424
2005	718	894	746	2,358
2006	654	837	700	2,191
2007	574	592	690	1,856
2008	473	354	589	1,416

Source: Tyndall Report.

TABLE 8. Minutes on network television devoted to overseas stories not involving U.S. foreign policy

Year	ABC	CBS	NBC	Total
1988	1,410	1,310	1,221	3,941
1989	1,675	1,660	1,490	4,828
1990	1,575	1,391	1,265	4,230
1991	1,493	1,183	1,263	3,939
1992	1,156	788	827	2,771
1993	1,270	862	712	2,843
1994	1,182	1,028	830	3,044
1995	998	789	616	2,403
1996	918	824	528	2,270
1997	998	926	609	2,533
1998	885	887	605	2,377
1999	1,021	892	695	2,608
2000	856	740	531	2,127
2001	925	861	671	2,458
2002	1,026	978	933	2,937
2003	1,019	902	949	2,871
2004	951	780	861	2,592
2005	1,062	965	1,004	3,030
2006	1,053	1,051	955	3,059
2007	742	659	863	2,264
2008	658	516	755	1,929

Source: Tyndall Report.

The contrast with newspapers is instructive. Foreign news is precarious even at the best newspapers. The saga of the *Chicago Daily News* shows that, as does the recent decline in the numbers of full-time foreign correspondents abroad for newspapers. But an elite newspaper like the *New York Times* is far better equipped to provide in-depth, routine foreign news than is an elite network like CBS.

Television, noted Garrick Utley, who reported for NBC, ABC, and CNN, "is the most expensive medium for news, and production costs for international reporting are particularly high." Print correspondents can travel alone, picking up a fixer, a translator, or a driver as necessary. Television correspondents travel mostly in teams, with a producer as well as sound and camera technicians and other helpers to deal with equipment. Television correspondents, the most visible component of the team, are akin to stars; and, starlike, they have agents to negotiate their salaries, which are loftier than those of newspaper correspondents.

Even with lighter equipment as technology miniaturizes, broadcasters have more to lug around than print reporters do. Their equipment slows them down, makes them more intimidating to interviewees, and puts them at greater risk when it is useful to be inconspicuous. In a radio commentary from London in 1952, Howard K. Smith complained on air that a television assignment had kept him from preparing adequately for the program. "I have been far too occupied . . . satisfying the requirements of up-to-date, streamlined, jet-propelled electronically operated, plastic-insulated, modern journalism." The equipment, he said, was more important than the journalist. Television correspondents also are less nimble when it comes to using interviews. Sound bites on television work best if they are in English. A print reporter can translate a good quote without jolting the reader at all.

Radio and television have advantages over newspapers. Newspapers come out at intervals. Broadcasters can report news as it occurs, the way Bowen did from the docks of Montevideo. Also visual images on television convey the look and feel of a place more vividly than a newspaper story can. As television has become better and better at exploiting these advantages, it has learned to package news reports with denser information, poignant video content, and faster-paced stories. Television excels as a headline service and in capturing emotion—all of which, however, is a relative disadvantage in other important ways.

Newspapers can carry more news than broadcasters. In 1995 the national and international news hole for the *New York Times* was 6.5 times greater—and the news hole for the *Atlantic Constitution* and the *Des Moines Register* 2 times greater—than the *total time* available for news on the evening network newscasts. "When I hear some character on television reporting some foreign news story with a 30-second sound bite," said Robert St. John, who switched from print to NBC during World War II, "I think of the Chicago *Daily News*," its inside pages packed with stories from overseas. When Walter Cronkite began in broadcasting, he acknowledged the discrepancy by proposing that he end his broadcasts with "For more information, read your local newspaper." CBS nixed the idea.

Also, the printed word is better suited to providing context and analysis. Sig Mickelson was a hardheaded realist about the medium he was inventing. "Ideas are not easy to translate into sound and pictures," he mused in notes that he prepared on the orientation of CBS News in 1957. "Print, in a sense, is easier because there is more time for reflection and re-reading. Ideas, sometimes, cannot be pictured." In 1985, after CBS did a fortieth-anniversary retrospective, Sevareid complained that one of his famous war reports had not been used. A new CBS executive rejoined that it was "too literary and reflective." News on television, in the words of Andrew Tyndall, has "plenty of action but little meditation." (Television did not offset this limitation by achieving anything approaching the great photojournalism found in *Life* and *Look*. Photographers Robert Capa and Margaret Bourke-White deserved to be famous; television cameramen and camerawomen are anonymous technicians.)

It was something of an exaggeration to say, as Charles Collingwood did when he retired, "Today's correspondents so often are limited to writing captions for pictures." Nevertheless, over time words were generally devalued, and correspondents more often ended up reading what others wrote for them. In 1998 Peter Arnett, a Pulitzer Prize–winning AP correspondent who went to work for CNN, appeared in a report that the American military secretly had killed American defectors during the Vietnam War with sarin nerve gas. The story, for which he did interviews, proved incorrect. "They gave me the list," Arnett said. "I asked these questions. The producers took the tape, and I was gone. I was the face. I hope they don't saddle me with the blame." Two producers were fired. This was far from the authoritative reporting that made Murrow and his colleagues famous.

Another point of comparison is the way consumers use newspapers and television. As Paul Lazarsfeld observed in 1940, newspaper readers select what they want to read and skip over the rest. Not every story must please consumers. Broadcast listeners or viewers don't get to choose. When they skip a story, it is as if they put the newspaper down and walked away. To keep people tuned in, Lazarsfeld noted, radio had to rely on its strengths capturing "the dramatic and the emotional." In line with this, broadcasters employed increasingly sophisticated techniques to figure out what kept audiences from flipping the dial—something consumers could easily do with the advent of the television remote control. The audience measurement company Nielsen installed "Audimeters" in a sampling of household television sets to keep track of what was watched and later developed "people meters" that tracked who in the family was doing the watching. Eventually, minute-by-minute measurements were possible.

In addition to his news-oriented *See It Now,* Murrow anchored *Person to Person,* a weekly half-hour program that peered at celebrities in their homes. The latter program, which he did not enjoy anchoring nearly as much, achieved higher ratings. The ratings book, Mickelson observed, "became the Holy Grail and the product began to soften." In 2006, as Ted Koppel was leaving the anchor chair at *Nightline,* a thoughtful, long-format program interested in foreign affairs, he decried the "dictatorship of the demographic."

The audience that advertisers most wanted to attract—women in the 18–34 age range—was the one least interested in foreign news. And the audience most interested in foreign news—men of 50 and older—was the one many advertisers considered the least valuable. The one exception, which harked back to radio's great success during the war, occurred "when something important or interesting is happening" abroad. "There is great interest in global perspectives during time of crisis," a local television journalist commented in 2004, "but not at all most of the time. Besides, consultants keep telling us to keep stories local." If he tried to put more foreign news on the air, Dan Rather said, executives would tell him that NBC had more viewers and that it did "the least" foreign news.

The impact of audience measurement was felt in cable as well. In the early years, as producer Steve Redisch once noted, CNN did not pay much attention to ratings. But eventually the network laid off employees to cut costs and reformatted itself with more lighter, personality-driven programming along the lines of its cable competitor Fox News, whose formula did not require much foreign news-gathering.

Fighting entertainment with entertainment, networks and cable incorporated foreign news into soft news programs. These attracted large audiences, but the depth and breadth of the information communicated was diminished. "Soft-news media," as scholar Matthew Baum has noted, "self-consciously frame issues in highly accessible terms—which I call 'cheap framing'—emphasizing dramatic and sensational human-interest stories." During U.S. military interventions in the Middle East following the September 11, 2001, terrorist attacks, soft news stories focused on "the travails of American prisoners of war, the threat of terrorism in the United States, and the effects of the war on celebrities, family, and children."

The differences between print and broadcast do not stop there. Newspapers are *news*papers. News is fundamental to what they do. "Unlike every newspaper in America," said Grant Tinker, NBC chairman in the 1980s, "the fundamental business of a television network is not news. Television networks, whose only income is from advertisers who want to reach the largest possible number of viewers, are in the mass-appeal business."

Successive waves of acquisitions accentuated this difference. Newspapers tended to be owned by companies whose chief business was news. General Electric and Disney bought NBC and ABC. For those companies and for Viacom, the international media and entertainment empire that eventually bought CBS, news was a small part of the total operation. CBS, said Richard Salant, president of the news division in the 1960s and 1970s, passed "from the Paley-Stanton era to a new era in which nonbroadcasting businesspeople, experienced as executives in very large, and very different, lines of business, were now at the top." This did not mean that news executives didn't care about foreign news. It did mean corporate CEOs had less appreciation for the prerequisites of high-quality news-gathering and news ethics, and that they derived less psychic reward from a high-quality foreign-news operation than Paley did, although he had not been oblivious to economic considerations.

Even during the early years of broadcasting, when radio often provided foreign news on a sustaining basis, the potential for profits was in the back of people's minds. "While I think the showing that you have made is excellent," an NBC executive commended the News and Special Events Department in early 1941, "I am always anxious to see the revenue producing units operating at a profit. I do not know whether it is possible for the Special Events Department to accomplish this requirement, but if you can work towards that end, I would like to see it done."

Paley's reassurances that foreign correspondents only needed to worry about the news, not the news business, were as unrealistic as they were noble. No matter what he said about the revenue comedian Jack Benny brought in, the TV news divisions were at a disadvantage at budget time. They could not bolster their case for more money with the most compelling argument of all: that they could thereby make more money. "We must," Mickelson noted, "compete with attractive entertainment shows." In 1955 Alcoa, wanting something along the lines of Ed Sullivan's variety program, dropped its sponsorship of Murrow's *See It Now*. A quiz show took the program's time slot. *See It Now* appeared intermittently before disappearing altogether. Finding that public affairs programming on Sunday afternoons had a small following, CBS substituted football games.

By and by, the inevitable happened. News divisions were expected to be profit centers just like every other network operation. CBS News presidents, said Andrew Heyward, shortly before he was ousted from that job in 2005, are "expected to generate profits and not just prestige." When it came to radio, the Murrow tradition of foreign news prevailed only on nonprofit public radio.

Other factors worked against foreign news on television. In the beginning, CBS and NBC enjoyed hegemony over foreign images. "A ninety-six-hour-late film story had just about as much impact as a much more recent one," said Mickelson of Korean War coverage, "if it provided pictorial coverage that had not previously been seen by viewers." This incentive to air foreign news disappeared when cable television and independent producers supplied video to whoever wanted it.

Meanwhile, the FCC deregulation softened public service requirements for both local radio and television license renewals. "Television is just a toaster with pictures," said an FCC chairman in the 1980s. Radio did not have to carry any news at all. Stations could play music all day long. This relaxation of rules did not have a direct impact on network or national cable operations or their foreign news-gathering, but it validated the idea that television didn't have to care as much about serious news.

Newspapers had advantages in reporting foreign stories that television found difficult to match unless moved by some outside force. Murrow's tradition was born in crisis and thrived there afterward. Said Marcy McGinnis, shortly after she stepped down as the senior vice president for news coverage at CBS, "You'll often see individuals rise to the top covering a crisis. There's something about crisis coverage that separates out the extraordinary people even from the good or very good ones."

Evaluating radio's triumphs in a post–World War II series of articles for the *Atlantic Monthly*, historian Dixon Wecter noted, "The higher circles of radio [resemble] the world of the theater—with its dazzling salaries, fan mail, dramatic flair, log-rolling, and personal éclat—rather than the world of pressrooms." For all Murrow's brilliance of mind and for all his belief that Shirer's voice quality wasn't what really mattered, a large part of the Murrow mystique came from his resonant tones on the radio and his dark good looks on television. In the words of the *New York Times'* Scotty Reston, he was "a very decorative man, a theatrical man." Many years after he started NBC radio news from his cubbyhole office, Able Schechter thought back on broadcast's beginnings. It is more than "just news knowledge that is important," he said. "It is the show business."

The decorative qualities of newspaper reporters count for little in judging them for advancement, whereas foreign news experience is an asset when moving up the newspaper ladder. At the *New York Times* it is virtually required for the top editor. In television looks and likability are important. The latter quality is rated through yet another measurement of audience attitude, called "Q scores." Foreign news experience is less important, as changes at the anchor desks show.

CBS anchor Walter Cronkite was a United Press war correspondent in Europe and after the war the UP bureau chief in Amsterdam and Moscow. His successor, Dan Rather, had less experience abroad. In 1965 and 1966, Rather took a break from being White House correspondent to report from London, where he jumped off to cover other stories, and subsequently Vietnam. He had not wanted to go abroad, but an overseas tour, he was told, was essential to being "a fully rounded correspondent." In London he broadcast from Murrow's old studio. Rather was followed in the anchor chair by Katie Couric, who had been a host on the entertainment-heavy

---

YOU'LL GET USED TO IT

During World War II, CBS's *World News Roundup* acquired a sponsor for the first time, Sinclair Oil. From now on, Murrow told his team, they would get a seventy-five-dollar bonus each time they reported on the program. Sevareid questioned if it was right to take money from an advertiser when they were covering a story with such human travail. After thinking a moment, Murrow said, "You'll get used to it." They did, along with relishing their star quality. At the end of his career, Sevareid was disappointed when people didn't recognize him in restaurants.

"The networks," commented senior CBS foreign correspondent Tom Fenton in a bitter end-of-career memoir, "discovered early that the presence of a fair and comely reporter among scowling tribesmen and falling bombs could add *frisson* to the broadcast." Mixed into Fox News's corps of correspondents in recent conflicts was Geraldo Rivera, who like movie star Cher is known by his first name and who is about as journalistically credible. "Showbiz invokes showbiz in the guise of news," quipped a *Wall Street Journal* editor about Rivera's reporting of the war in Afghanistan in 2001.

Turning journalists into celebrities makes economic sense. It enhances the brand for viewers and advertisers. Television news anchors, the most conspicuous on air and thus virtually the brand itself, need to be constantly hyped. That is why they, and not a foreign correspondent, are likely to do a head-of-state obituary and why the networks send anchors and their retinues to the scene of a crisis.

Unfortunately, as media economist James T. Hamilton has noted in the careful lexicon of his profession, "Time spent in developing reporters as celebrity may reduce the resources available for covering hard news." Reuven Frank, president of NBC News on two occasions, put this concept another way: most of the budget cuts in the mid-1980s "came out of getting the news and almost none from the costs of presenting it. News bureaus were closed as anchormen's salaries rose."

Salaries for anchors such as Cronkite and Chancellor were the equivalent of 28 ads per year in 1976; in 1999, anchors' salaries equated with 149 ads per year. According to various reports, Peter Jennings, Dan Rather, and Ted Koppel offered to give back part of their celebrity-sized salaries if their networks would plow the money into news, especially foreign news-gathering. The answer was always the same. "That's generous, even noble," Rather was told, "but it's not the way the system works."

NBC *Today Show.* Her major foreign experience, some years earlier, had been a short-term assignment to cover the Iraq invasion of Kuwait.

NBC anchor John Chancellor was a correspondent in Vienna, London, Moscow, Brussels, and Berlin before becoming the network's anchor. Tom Brokaw, never a foreign correspondent, came after him. Brokaw made his name covering the White House and, like Couric, as a *Today Show* host. Brokaw's successor, the first new anchor of the millennium, was Brian Williams, who came from the lesser anchor job on the cable MSNBC and had only episodic overseas experience. Williams's biography noted, as a highlight of network experience overseas, his being the sole White House television correspondent to accompany President Clinton to the funeral of Yitzhak Rabin.

Peter Jennings was an exception. He won the prized ABC anchor seat in his twenties. Realizing he was not ready for the job, he asked to go abroad instead. Jennings had "everything but authority," said Howard K. Smith, who became an ABC anchor after Jennings left. In addition to postings elsewhere, Jennings was for seven years the NBC bureau chief in Beirut, the first American television news bureau in the Arab world. In 1983, with his authority very much established, he became the anchor and senior editor of *World News Tonight.* Not one of the anchors who have succeeded him has been a foreign correspondent. The most recent, Charles Gibson, was a host on *Good Morning America.*

Foreign correspondents, Peter Jennings commented not long before he died in 2005, are "very hard to recruit. They are told, first of all, it's not the hottest thing. It's not the way to get to the top."

18

HEY SOLDIER, I'M WOUNDED!

> This is probably my last message. I'm staying with General Stilwell and a
> small command post directing the rear-guard action on approaches to India
> and northernmost Burma. The Japanese are driving with incredible speed,
> swinging wide of both our east and west flanks and somehow we have
> to get the troops out of this closing-in trap.
>
> Jack Belden, *Time*

On May 1, 1942, Gen. Joseph Stilwell was at Shwebo, seventy miles north of Mandalay, hoping for a plane to evacuate three Anglo-Burmese women, his wounded, and some of his staff. With him was Jack Belden, a *Time* reporter in his early thirties. Stilwell, Belden, and two others were playing gin rummy when Japanese planes were heard overhead. One officer suggested that Belden in particular should make haste to the trenches outside. The reporter had had two close calls already. "Your number's about up. They always get you the third time, you know."

Once the danger had passed, it dawned on Belden that if a friendly plane did come, he could send out a dispatch to *Time* as well as the *London Daily Herald*, for which he also reported. He went down to the code room and pounded out an account that began with the words printed above. When a green transport plane landed, Stilwell asked Belden if he wanted to take his message out personally.

Belden had plenty of reasons to climb aboard the airplane. He had courted danger for weeks. Just a few days before, he had escaped another Japanese encirclement. "We had to break through or die—die of either thirst or hunger while being slowly cut to bits by an enemy whose campfires were at the very moment drawing in around us." The plane was a way to avoid hardship and more terror, and besides, he would reach India before his correspondent colleagues, who were on their way out of Burma by foot.

"Are you going?" Belden asked Stilwell.

"No." The general intended to march out.

"I guess I better stay then," Belden said.

Of all the groups leaving Burma, Stilwell's was extraordinary because of the arduous route it was forced to take and because of its composition, a queer mixture—just over 100 strong—of British, Chinese, and American officers and enlisted men, 2 doctors, 19 native nurses, 7 Quakers belonging to an ambulance unit, an American missionary, servants, 2 women refugees, and Belden, the lone foreign correspondent. The trip began by truck and jeep over congested roads, but most of the two-week journey was on foot and by river raft. Malaria and dysentery, lack of sleep, and half rations weakened the travelers. Leeches and thorns, the blazing sun and the blinding rain, slippery jungle paths, and seemingly endless waves of mountains—all were a torment. They were ever fearful of encountering the Japanese. Before they were done, Belden threw away his typewriter in favor of carrying a rifle.

Fourteen days after leaving Shwebo, they reached Imphal, India. "I claim we got a hell of a beating," the blunt-talking Stilwell told correspondents several days later. "We got run out of Burma, and it is humiliating as hell." Belden, who shared a blanket with Stilwell on the march and was every bit as direct as the doughty general, had said as much in his final dispatches from Shwebo. Although he complained of being "caught in the fog of war," he brilliantly reported what went wrong. His report contradicted American newspaper stories, based on Chinese government communiqués, of Allied victories. Burma, Belden accurately predicted, was about to fall to the Japanese. The Allies were losing because they did not understand the political situation among the Burmese. Tired of being a British colony, many of them helped the Japanese. Meanwhile, Allied supplies and communications were inadequate and reinforcements should have been sent but weren't.

Belden amplified his analysis in a personal-history-style book, *Retreat with Stilwell*. Nowhere had the Allies "attempted to lighten the yoke of economic slavery over the natives of the Asiatic colonies, and they could not think of the war as a struggle to better the lot of the colonial peoples. . . . The Japanese force was inherently stronger materially, psychologically, and politically." Advocating Asia for the Asiatics, the Japanese rallied support among the Burmese.

Time China correspondents Annalee Jacoby and Theodore White, who had helped Belden get a job with the magazine, said, "The best description of the Burma campaign, indeed the best political analysis of the entire war in the South Seas, is the opening chapter of Jack Belden's *Retreat with Stilwell*." Writing in the *Saturday Review*, Asia hand Hallett Abend called the book "as gripping as a piece of fiction." Diplomat John Paton Davies considered Belden "the Homer of the Stilwell odyssey."

Belden claimed, defensively, that he did not care about the reviews. When his mother, whom he had not seen for years, wrote to say he had become a hero among her friends in Summit, New Jersey, he replied, "This sort of thing is a bubble celebrity and something you should not concern yourself with." He hadn't felt triumph even at the moment when he realized he had survived the trek out of Burma: "It was as if some meaning, some excitement, some drama, though there had been little enough of all these, had suddenly gone out of life—as if a castaway on some lonely isle should suddenly see a ship—a rescue ship—steaming toward him and he didn't want to be rescued, didn't want to go back to all the horrors of civilization, didn't want to leave his enchanted isle."

Jack Belden was exceptional—in his knowledge of military tactics and strategy, in the intensity and honesty of his writing, and in his dark attraction to battle. Because that darkness led him to quit journalism early, because he fell into oblivion for the rest of his life and stayed there in death, more is the reason to tell his story. But to show how Belden stood out, this chapter begins by looking at the physical and emotional perils that commonly confronted war correspondents.

Jack Singer of the *Los Angeles Times* realized every sports writer's dream, a chance to write his own column, after the Japanese attacked Pearl Harbor. "Sports, everything, lost all their meaning to me, in that moment. So, I tore up the contract and became a war correspondent," he told a colleague after joining the International News Service foreign staff. "I wanted in on the biggest story." Singer was killed when the *Wasp* was torpedoed and sunk. The officers of the *Wasp* finished Singer's story for him and filed it. The colleague to whom he explained his reason for becoming a war correspondent was UP correspondent Joe James Custer. When the ship Custer was aboard in the Pacific came under attack, he lost an eye.

More journalists went in harm's way during World War II than ever before. The United States had the most correspondents in the field, more than sixteen hundred. By one count, 37 were killed and 112 wounded. The casualty rate (killed 2.2%, wounded 6.8%) was higher overall than for military personnel (2.5% killed, 4.2% wounded). The figures did not include combat reporters working for *Stars and Stripes, Yank,* and other government-run periodicals, or correspondents who perished covering China, Ethiopia, and Spain in the 1930s.

Becoming a battlefield casualty was only one of the risks. "My own motto has always been, 'A dead correspondent sends no dispatches,'" said the *New York Times'* Harold Denny, who had covered six previous wars and served in the army in World War I. The cautious reporter hadn't given much thought to being captured until Germans nabbed him during the fighting in Libya. He was the first U.S. prisoner of war taken to Germany. There he was interned with American correspondents in Berlin who, as AP's Angus M. Thuermer recalled, were "jerked out of bed between one and two o'clock in the morning before the official declaration of war, hustled to the notorious Alexander-platz secret police headquarters, and held." Thuermer and Denny, along with twenty-one other correspondents, were repatriated from Germany, Italy, and Romania several months later.

On the other side of the world, John B. Powell continued publishing his *China Weekly Review* in Japanese-occupied Shanghai despite an assassination attempt on him that had failed because the grenade pin was not completely pulled. In December 1941, he and other American journalists were imprisoned. Held initially in a twelve-by-eighteen-foot cell in the infamous Bridge House Prison with forty others, Powell was beaten, deprived of food, and forced to sit on his feet, which became gangrenous and had to be amputated before he was repatriated. A broken man, he died in 1947. The AP's Joe Morton was captured along with a small OSS force behind the lines helping the Slovak partisans in the final months of the war. Three months earlier he had told his Rome bureau chief he was embarked on "the story of a lifetime." He was executed at the Nazis' Mauthausen concentration camp in Austria.

One of the most harrowing escapes was the flight of four correspondents from Yugoslavia after the Nazi invasion in 1941. Robert St. John of the AP, Leigh White of CBS, Russell Hill of the *New York Herald Tribune,* and Terrence Atherton with the *London Daily Mail* traded a car for a twenty-foot sardine boat on the Adriatic coast at Budva. By the time they reached Pátra, Greece, over storm-tossed seas, Atherton had been wounded in a German air attack. While they were on a troop train to Athens, another air attack left White and St. John wounded. They hitched a ride on a military truck that was bombed. All but White managed to get out of Greece. His wounds required him to stay in German-held Athens, where he was imprisoned.

When Gen. Douglas MacArthur waded ashore at Leyte, reporters were on hand to cover the story. In the foreground of this photo, carrying a typewriter is UP correspondent William Dickinson, whose famous dispatch reported that the general had fulfilled his pledge to return to the Philippines. According to Dickinson family lore, the photo was taken by Frank Prist, who became yet another casualty of the war when a Japanese sniper on Leyte killed him. Three other war correspondents—one representing both the *Fort Worth Star-Telegram* and the *Houston Chronicle,* one with the *Chicago Daily News,* and one with the Associated Press—sustained fatal wounds on Leyte. A fourth, an NBC correspondent, was wounded.

While MacArthur liked the picture-taking and any adulation, he did not brook criticism from the press, which he tried to control after the war as well as during it. One of his censors wrote, as George Weller ruefully noted, "We believe that a correspondent has a certain duty towards the Commander of the Forces whom he represents, and it is the Commander-in-Chief's desire that nothing of a political nature be released as coming from his staff of correspondents, and nothing that may be in any way criticizing the efforts of any Commander of any of the Allied nations." Weller, *First into Nagasaki,* 275–76. Photo courtesy of William Dickinson.

Those who were not killed, wounded, or captured had to endure the daily rigors of the front line. Charles Corte of Acme Newspictures was hospitalized for shell shock in North Africa. It didn't help, said Joe James Custer, that correspondents tended to train on "beer and cigarettes" and had no special military instruction. Nearly everyone in the Southwest Pacific, he reported, "has had malaria, dysentery, and feet and leg sores."

The government named Liberty Ships after fallen correspondents, including sports-columnist-turned-INS-correspondent Jack Singer. Like the GIs they covered, correspondents received Purple Hearts for their wounds and decorations for valor. In 1946, when the war was over, thirty-six of them were awarded Bronze Stars, Silver Stars, Air Medals, and other military honors. The AP's Larry Allen, who survived eight sinkings and two imprisonments, received the Bronze Star and the Order of the British Empire from King George VI, as well as the Pulitzer Prize. Gen. Dwight Eisenhower pinned the Medal of Freedom on a score of correspondents at a National Press Club ceremony in November 1947.

In the ongoing debate whether World War II was one of the worst- or the best-reported wars, correspondents (and historians) could point to instances when journalists produced enterprising stories that the authorities found inconvenient. *Chicago Daily News* correspondent Leland Stowe's scoop on the German invasion of Norway was one of the most notable examples. While Allied newspapers were full of optimistic reports, if not triumphant ones, about Norwegian valor, Stowe reported that Norway was decisively defeated because of bungling by the British expeditionary force and because the Norwegians put up little resistance. "Norway's capital of nearly 300,000 inhabitants was occupied by a German force of approximately 1,500 men . . . without dropping a bomb, without firing a shot within the city limits." The *New York Herald Tribune*'s Homer Bigart reported that the invasion of the Anzio beachhead in Italy was a disaster of military leadership. It was disheartening, he reported, "to hear correspondents who have never been within 20 miles of the front speak glibly about our success."

But military restrictions on correspondents' movements and the heavy hand of blue-pencil-wielding censors put limits on them. As a condition of military accreditation, correspondents were required to agree in writing that they would file only stories passed by censors. Stowe's reports had come from neutral Sweden, where he was not subject to censorship. Cecil Brown, who had constantly worried about being thrown out of Italy and eventually was, railed against the Allied censors in Singapore who blocked his stories predicting that the city-state was defenseless against the Japanese. In January 1942, a fed-up British major directed him to "surrender your license . . . and discontinue wearing your uniform. . . . Your broadcast tomorrow is your final one." A *Chicago Tribune* correspondent was expelled too. A little more than a month afterward, Singapore fell to the Japanese. In May 1945, when the war ended, *New Yorker* war correspondent and acerbic press critic A. J. Liebling observed, "'Horror stuff,' by which the censors meant any mention of ugly wounds or indecorous deaths, was for a long time forbidden, but recently it has been found compatible with security."

The military did not shake the censorship habit after the war. Not unlike Gen. Andrew Jackson's prolonged martial law after the Battle of New Orleans, Gen. Douglas MacArthur kept censors in place when he occupied Japan; flexing their muscles, they killed a story by *Chicago Daily News* correspondent George Weller reporting the continuation of censorship. The exasperated Weller removed the brass "War Correspondent" insignia from his uniform, passed himself off as a colonel, and slipped into Nagasaki, which was officially off limits. There he found an important story, that radiation from the atomic bomb continued to kill Japanese. Weller naïvely figured that by the time he finished it would be possible to get his reports home. The stories never ran in the *Daily News*.

Although Belden wrote an unvarnished, wide-angled account of the Burma fiasco, it was not easy. Chinese censors killed stories that forecast the impending disaster. He and two colleagues told visiting *Time-Life* correspondent Clare Boothe they wanted to leave the country. "You can't say how *badly* you're losing," she recounted of their frustration, "because that just depresses everybody and you can't say *why* you're losing because that's either comfort or information to the enemy. All you can do is wait until the whole thing is lost and then you file one big exciting story on the blowup, and then go to some other front."

"The worst form of censorship," Liebling thought, was perpetuated by public relations personnel. To discourage reviews of strategy as well as of failures, they kept correspondents as busy as possible on small-bore stories. Typical was a pamphlet for "war correspondents who want ideas" prepared by the public relations unit with the U.S. Pacific Fleet. The unit promised to "arrange for you to visit any of its commands, line up interviews, arrange picture coverage, send you to sea on its ships, or, in short, do anything for you that will help you get your yarn."

One of the best ways to tell a yarn was to zero in on the local angle in the form of individual soldiers, sailors, and air force personnel in the thick of the action. "Correspondents acquired the habit of giving in their dispatches the names, address, and favorite 'girl friends' of the G.I.'s to whom they talked," observed historian Joseph Mathews. "Public relations officers set up special units to see that a steady flow of accounts went to home-town papers about local boys." Some thought of this as democratic, but as Mathews noted, totalitarian regimes employed the same technique. The conventions of this reporting, said novelist-turned-*Herald-Tribune*-war-correspondent John Steinbeck, were that generals were geniuses and that soldiers were brave and not interested in sex. GIs, he facetiously commented, really only used the condoms issued to them to keep moisture out of the barrels of their weapons.

The *Milwaukee Journal,* a beautifully written and edited newspaper not known for its foreign reporting, sent Robert Doyle to the Pacific. When he came up to a unit, Doyle asked, "Anybody here from Wisconsin?" On one occasion he won a coveted seat on an airplane taking reporters to watch Gen. Douglas MacArthur landing and chose instead to do his duty: he went to see if anyone from his state

"Fresh, spirited American troops, flushed with victory, are bring-
ing in thousands of hungry, ragged, battle-weary prisoners . . ."
(*News item*)

Staff Sergeant Bill Mauldin was a cartoonist on the armed forces newspaper *Stars and Stripes*. Soldiers loved—and General Patton hated—his irreverent drawings, which American newspapers
reprinted. He received a Pulitzer Prize in 1944. The Pulitzer Prize selection committee singled out
this one when giving the award. "Newspapers at home have to print the news as it appears on a
world-wide scale," Mauldin said, "but if they would clamp down a little harder on their enthusiastic rewrite men who love to describe 'smashing armored columns,' the 'ground forces sweeping
ahead,' 'victorious, cheering armies,' and 'sullen supermen,' they wouldn't be doing a bad job."
Mauldin became another casualty of the war when he suffered a shrapnel wound in the shoulder in Italy. Bill Mauldin, *Up Front* (New York: W. W. Norton, 2000), 21. Cartoon used with permission from the Stars and Stripes ©1944, 1945, 2006 Stars and Stripes.

was on a nearby ship. The plane he would have taken crashed, killing two reporters. Hal Boyle of the Associated Press won a Pulitzer for his stories of American
foot soldiers, recounted in his column *Leaves from a War Correspondent's Notebook*. The *New York Sun*'s Gault MacGowan "always had his pad and pencil out,
and was a fiend for writing down names and addresses of New York soldiers," Ernie
Pyle noted admiringly in a story from North Africa. "One day we saw him right

up among the men who were firing, writing down names." Pyle, a journalistic Everyman known for his simple dress, colorful swearing, and hypochondria, was the epitome of the genre, in the military's mind as well as everyone else's. Here is a typical passage that he wrote for Scripps Howard: "Lieutenant Jack Ilfrey was a fine person and more or less typical of all the boys who flew our deadly fighters. He was from Houston, Texas, and his father was cashier of the First National Bank there. The family home was at 3122 Robinhood Street. . . . It was hard to conceive of his ever having killed anybody."

Pyle could be negative. He criticized the U.S. policy supporting Vichy officials in North Africa. But his chief cause was the individuals in the trenches. He was their champion. He argued that soldiers should be allowed to wear stripes on their sleeves to mark their overseas service and receive extra combat pay. Legislators passed these measures in what they called "the Ernie Pyle bill." A *Time* cover story about him was entitled "Ernie Pyle's War." The magazine called him "a sort of national conscience." Pyle identified so closely with GIs, the *Saturday Evening Post* said, that just by covering himself he covered "the war both accurately and dramatically."

After surviving North Africa and the European theater, Pyle would have liked to stay home. "I have to fight an inner depression over the ghastliness of it all," he wrote a friend, "that almost whips me a good deal of the time." Feeling a sense of duty, he shipped off to the Pacific Theater. While traveling in a jeep on the small island of Ie Shima, a Japanese machine gunner opened fire. Pyle and his colleagues jumped into a ditch. He was shot in the left temple when he raised his head.

Ernie Pyle. This AP photo was taken shortly after the Scripps Howard correspondent was killed by enemy machine-gun fire on the Pacific island of Ie Shima. AP/Wide World Photos (courtesy of Richard Strasser).

Not all correspondents approved of the surfeit of down-home combat news. "The American way of writing about war," Vincent Sheean complained, "was . . .—partly under the influence of Ernie Pyle—to get as many names of infantry and artillery soldiers into print as possible, and thus to establish a channel of communication between the soldier and his family at home. The trick was much overdone." This war, complained another correspondent, "was well reported in the sense that never before had so much attention been given to the individual soldier or sailor with his home address and next of kin, but in that sense alone. Of the larger issues of the war, of the way it was fought, of what actually happened both on the home and military fronts, most Americans—in the service or out—remained profoundly ignorant."

Most editors liked this news because they were patriotic and so were their readers. Reporters who in other circumstances eagerly bucked authority also were inclined in that direction. "I'm going to use you fellows," Eisenhower frankly told a group of correspondents in London. "You are the links between our GIs and the home front, and the people at home have a right to know how their sons are being trained and cared for." The correspondents were not offended. This was their war, too. They didn't want to do anything to derail Allied victory.

When Gen. George Patton slapped an enlisted patient whom he accused of faking an injury during the Sicilian campaign, correspondents did not run with the story even though Eisenhower said it would have passed the censor. "Our conclusion is that we're Americans first and correspondents second," Demaree Bess of the *Saturday Evening Post* told Ike. "Every mother would figure her son is next." Merrill Mueller of NBC expressed a similar view: the correspondents would deny the story if any of their colleagues reported it. When the story finally did break, the author was a columnist in Washington, D.C., Drew Pearson.*

Shared danger with GIs and the need to find good stories that passed the censor led correspondents to write about themselves. Correspondents had done the same in other wars. The *New York Journal's* Edward Marshall wrote accounts of his being wounded during the Spanish-American War for both *Scribner's* and *Cosmopolitan,* which published them the same month. The difference this time was that so many of the correspondents wrote so many such stories in space normally reserved for third-person news. In its typical fashion, the *Christian Science Monitor* instructed its reporters not to "soup-it-up." Nevertheless it had plenty of stories like this one by Ronald Stead: "As I am writing this, with the shells of our artillery batteries rushing overhead . . . "

When a correspondent with a Canadian newspaper, the *Montreal Standard,*

---

* Pearson, who had been a foreign correspondent early in his career and later a diplomatic correspondent for the *Baltimore Sun,* disliked the pretentiousness of the State Department and relished needling the powerful. After he criticized the Roosevelt administration's cover-up of the damage done by the Japanese at Pearl Harbor, officials threatened him with loss of press privileges. FDR called him a "chronic liar." Pearson responded with the Patton story. It was embarrassing to the administration but came after Patton had diffused the situation for himself through profuse apology, including one to the entire 93rd Evacuation Hospital staff where he had hit the soldier.

took shrapnel in his buttocks, he burst out, "What a story! What a story!" An Australian correspondent wrote a parody of such reports and sent it to his paper, the *Melbourne Herald*. His editors thought the story was the real thing and published it. After Byron Darnton of the *New York Times* was killed in northern New Guinea, a fellow journalist praised him for his fearlessness, for his expertise, for his accuracy, and for breaking from the pack and not making "unrelenting use of the first person singular."

Thus readers were bombarded with the word *I*.

"I am now able to tell the full story how I escaped from the Germans and joined the Maquis* in what is now liberated France."—Gault MacGowan for the *New York Sun*

"The torpedo did not make as loud a crash as I had expected, nor did the ship list as much as it does in the movies. But somehow everyone on the sleeping transport knew almost instantly that this was the end of her. Tossed out of my upper bunk, I snapped on the light switch."—*Life* photographer and reporter Margaret Bourke-White

"It was a hell 26,000 feet above the earth, a hell of burning tracer bullets and bursting flak, of crippled Flying Fortresses and flaming German fighter planes. I rode a Flying Fortress into the midst of it."—Walter Cronkite for the United Press

"The first shell of the barrage hit me—and then when consciousness came back, and I knew I had been badly wounded, I came to realize something I had long suspected: that there was absolutely no sensation of pain in such a situation. It was like a movie without the sound."—Richard Tregaskis in Italy for the International News Service

"On the dying cruiser's quarterdeck I clung tenaciously to the starboard rail until the list of the ship flung me into the cold, choppy sea."—Larry Allen for the Associated Press

Tregaskis had book and movie deals; Allen a Pulitzer Prize. Robert St. John's escape from Yugoslavia became a book, *From the Land of the Silent People,* that was serialized in *Cosmopolitan,* selected by the Literary Guild for its members, and dramatized over NBC. But it was not only the need for a story or the quest for accolades that motivated correspondents. Some seemed to court danger. Perhaps it was the rush of adrenaline or the chance to test one's self—or maybe something darker. It was hard to pin down.

A British reporter who abhorred war in the beginning confessed that he "came to adore the whole business and had a wonderful time." Barred from covering the D-Day Invasion of France because she was a woman, fearless Martha Gellhorn stowed away on a hospital ship crossing the channel. "Where I want to be, boy, is where it is all blowing up," she told John Gunther. Many who knew the ambitious Edward R. Murrow believed he had a death wish. He flew some two dozen combat missions, many more than were necessary to tell the story and prove himself. On a

---

* The Maquis were mostly rural guerrilla bands belonging to the French Resistance.

bet with Sheean, he once stopped his car so Quentin Reynolds could read a paper by the light from buildings set afire during an air raid. Said a CBS colleague, Larry LeSueur, "There was a perverse exhilaration to it all."

Jack Belden was another American for whom youthful travel led to foreign correspondence. But his journey to the front line of war was more aimless, more desperate than most. He told and retold the story in angry late-in-life autobiographical notes and to those who would listen to him in Paris bars.

Although Belden was named after his father, Alfred Goodwin Belden, he did not use the name. The senior Belden left the family fold when his son was an infant. When recalling his father, Jack Belden had little to say apart from the fact that he and his older sister had formal Sunday lunches with him from time to time. After graduating from Colgate University in 1931 at the height of the Depression, Belden drifted from a job on a ship to one with a tobacco company and back to the sea to escape "the rat race." While standing night watch at sea, Belden "imagined myself being lured to death by the ocean's hypnotic eye. I often imagined I was in the ocean for various reasons; saving someone's life or getting cut up by the propeller."

Belden considered jumping ship in Hamburg, he wrote in one of his autobiographical screeds: "We used to get in fights with Hitler brown shirts, prostitute talked me out of it, said I would starve." He again thought about jumping ship in Tokyo and in Hong Kong, where he finally did. In China he lived precariously: "Broke for nine months, slept on ferry boats, Salvation Army—very hungry, lonely, begged on streets." Belden gambled with the sailors, and the winnings kept him going at times. His first newspaper job was on the English-language *Evening Post & Mercury* in Shanghai. In Beijing he studied the Chinese language, taught English at a night school (a job he lost when it "was given to the nephew of a famous missionary"), and house-sat for a Chinese general. "Feel a little bitter how fellowships and funds given to people [with] far less background than me to study Chinese—nothing ever given me."

During these years, the Japanese made incursions into China economically and militarily, creating a puppet state in Manchuria. The conflict escalated on July 7, 1937, at the Marco Polo Bridge, about ten miles outside Beijing. The Chinese won the initial skirmish, but the fighting continued. A few weeks later the Japanese marched into the old imperial city. Full-scale national war had begun.

The Marco Polo Bridge Incident, considered by many to be the first battle of World War II, set in motion Belden's career as a war correspondent. Reporting for the United Press, he flung himself into the action. With Tillman Durdin of the *New York Times,* he drove a car past the fighting armies outside Shanghai to reach Nanjing, the Nationalists' new capital. When the Nationalists abandoned the city in December 1937 and retreated further to Hankou, Belden moved too. He was one of the "last ditchers" who hung on there despite incessant Japanese air raids. While many reporters stayed inside the cities, he ventured into the countryside with Chinese forces, where conditions were tougher and more precarious. He drew detailed maps of the fighting and, Durdin marveled, "gained an encyclopedic knowledge of the Chinese armies." Stilwell, with whom he sometimes traveled into the Chinese interior, and other military advisers consulted him.

United Press made the most of Belden's eyewitness accounts. Some newspapers offered them under an editor's note emphasizing—as the *Portland Express* did on November 20, 1937, for this one—that "he was the only foreign newspaperman who followed the Chinese armies":

> WITH CHINESE ARMIES, NEAR TSINAN, Shangtung Province, Nov. 20. (U.P.)— For nearly two weeks I have followed the wake of the great Chinese retreat southward from Taiyuan, and in that time have seen more Hell than I thought there was on earth.
>
> I have passed wounded men, groaning with agony, lying in ditches with shattered arms and legs.
>
> I have seen men running through fields like maniacs, their skins seared off with the splash of acid from sulfur bombs.
>
> I have knelt beside men almost unconscious from infection and pain and smelled the foul odor of rotting flesh on their living bodies.

Covering frontline fighting, Belden verified rumors that the Japanese were using gas in combat. After the fall of Hankou, he gathered information on Shanghai's underground, riven by terrorist conflict between Nationalist secret agents and Japanese gangsters. In 1940 he went to the new capital of Free China, Chungking, and

Jack Belden in China in the 1930s. Courtesy of David Belden.

again traveled out in the countryside. After breaking with UP over a policy dispute, the details of which have been lost, Belden joined the International News Service and later, in 1942, signed on with *Time-Life* and went to Burma with Stilwell.

Belden's life on the edge set him apart from colleagues, to whom he was "the man who knew the seamy side of China, where the lice lurked." Edgar Snow called him "mad and gifted." Diplomat John Paton Davies described him as "a sad, ragged, torn, incredible character." Belden was intense and suspicious at times and, alternately, could be funny, fun-loving, and warm. Durdin asked him to be his best man when he was married in Shanghai. Hugh Deane of the *Christian Science Monitor* recalled his long drinking bouts alone in his room at the mud-and-wattle Press Hostel in Chungking. When Belden opened the blinds, Deane recalled, he was ready to socialize again. He always seemed to be looking for love. "I think of him as my teacher," said Deane of his capabilities as a war correspondent. In Durdin's words, Belden had "an in-born capacity to see and depict the inner sense of what he observed and was almost indifferent to danger in his search for material."

As much as Belden was admired for his honest reporting on the nature of war and on failed war policies, that uncompromising quality made him a trial to editors. He "often ruffled feathers by his forthrightness," Durdin said, "even with friends." "As for Jack's four-letter words," Teddy White wrote to a *Time* editor in Belden's defense, "well, Jack is Jack. If he wants to say fuck, shit and piss, that's his business. If you can't publish them because of law, I should suggest substituting the Chinese equivalent which gives it an oriental flavor and means nothing to the American reader. For example. Wherever he says 'fuck,' say 't'sao!'; where he says 'his mother' say 'ma ti pi.'"

Belden's *Retreat with Stilwell* was woven from the various threads of his personality: There was the angry idealist who disliked the "gangster imperialism" engineered by nations that called themselves democratic. There was his fascination with the strategy and tactics of war, and the confusion and roiling emotions experienced on the ground during battle. There was Belden's "mixed and unknown longing" as he watched the Burmese nurses when he made his retreat with Stilwell.

War, as he later said, had become "a sort of emotional drug."

After only a week's rest from his Burma retreat, Belden returned to China. He covered the American Flying Tigers' air war against the Japanese. "Down below us on the river was a large ship, and out of it came bursts of fire; balls of red flecked with white began shooting toward our plane," he wrote in one *Time* account. By the end of the summer, he was in a hospital in Srinagar, in India's Vale of Kashmir, for a badly needed rest. His pulse was jumping between 110 and 130.

When he was on his feet again, Belden headed to North Africa to replace a *Time* correspondent injured in a plane accident in Cairo. *Time* billed Belden's accounts from this new theater as "a soldier's eye view of war" and "battle as it looks to the soldier in battle." As in China, Belden periodically disappeared, leaving his colleagues wondering where he was. One day Don Whitehead, a green correspondent with the AP, asked him outright. When Belden said he had been on the front lines, Whitehead realized he himself had not been covering the war the right way. He decided to "use the Belden approach to reporting and get as close as I possibly could to the fighting." Belden flew with American bombers over Tunisia, visited British-controlled Malta immediately after its long siege, accompanied British forces counterattacking Gen. Erwin Rommel along the Mareth Line in Tunisia, and made two separate American amphibious landings, wading ashore in Sicily to cover the fall of Troina.

Belden's third landing was in September 1943 south of Salerno. The Italian campaign ranked in hellishness with the fighting he witnessed in Burma, and Salerno marked an especially grim chapter. Although he had boarded the ship with a bad cold and another recurrence of the malaria contracted in Burma, Belden went ashore with advance reconnaissance. He was under fire during the landing, crawled through barbed wire along the beach, and tumbled into a ditch filled with sewage. His unit stumbled onto a highway. While attempting to climb over a wall, he took two bullets in his leg and lay "on the battle field alone and in pain, as so many have done before me."

Belden wrote a fifty-four-hundred-word account of the experience while in the sick bay of a ship. It appeared in *Life*. *Time* ran a shorter version. The story is one of the best of its kind, although it does not appear in any of the many anthologies of war reporting. Unlike most first-person stories, it combines superb reporting of overarching military strategy with vivid description of the terrifying chaos on the ground.

The story began this way:

"HEY, SOLDIER, I'M WOUNDED!"
A LIFE correspondent, going ashore with the Fifth Army at Salerno, becomes a casualty in bitter fighting
by JACK BELDEN

In sick bay aboard ship

The Germans knew we were coming and waited for us. All they had to do was study the map and see the obvious place for us to strike was south of Naples. Even correspondents who were not briefed before the operation and who possessed no special information guessed, on the basis of logic, that was where we would land. While we were steaming toward our objective the Swiss radio announced that an Allied invasion fleet was carrying the Fifth Army toward Naples. The day before our landing our LST's were bombed continuously. Probably the German Air Force had us under observation at all times. The enemy knew not only approximately where we were going to land but when.

As late as 5:30 on the afternoon of Sept. 8 the naval commander of the forces I was with said that a bombardment was scheduled. Yet it never came off. Perhaps the Army, wishing to rely on surprise, didn't want the bombardment. If that is so, it was a repetition of tactics that already had been used in landings in Sicily. A repetition of tactics as a general rule is bad. It plays into enemy hands.

Perhaps the announcement of the Italian surrender made the authorities change their minds. Maybe neither of these reasons is correct. But whatever the reasons we had little or no supporting fire on the American part of the beach. That announcement of the Italian surrender which we heard at 6:30 on our radios had an unfortunate effect on the troops. We all cheered the news and shouts from the whole fleet echoed over the Mediterranean. Too many officers and men thought it was all over but the shouting. Some of them had not been in combat before and some complained that they wouldn't have a chance to fight.

Here is the portion of the story that describes his experiences after being wounded:

. . . To get rid of the pain I closed my eyes. When I opened them again there were four medics standing in front of me.

"Morphine," I said.

"You're talking," said a dark-haired boy and he jabbed me in the arm. Then two of them grabbed my shoulders, a third pulled on my leg, and the dark-haired fellow prepared a splint.

"The wounded aren't supposed to cry," I said, disgusted with myself.

"Aw, you ain't done so bad," said one kindly.

They were pulling hard on me now so I had to keep talking.

"What's your name, where you from?" I said to the dark-haired fellow who was sliding a splint under my leg.

"John Fleischman, Philadelphia," he said, yanking my foot down toward the bottom of an iron frame.

He almost had me now, so I said: "Philadelphia. Hell, the Athletics are 36 games behind."

"Yeah." He yanked hard. My teeth chattered.

"Let's give him another shot of morphine," said a medic. They laid me on a stretcher and tied my leg to it and carried me out on the road and headed up toward the halted German truck.

A wild panic flared inside me.

"No, no. Don't take me there. Only Germans are there."

"Take it easy," said the medics, as if they were speaking to a delirious child. "The ambulance will come up here and get you."

"The ambulance can't get here. None of our soldiers are here. Take me away."

"Take it easy. Our soldiers are all up here."

"Why don't you believe me?" I sort of wailed in desperation.

They laid me on the side of the road near the truck and then they laid a wounded German boy near me and then they went away.

I heard a car approaching and I lay there listening. The Chinese have a saying: "Fear a devil and there is a devil." I had been afraid of a devil and here it was coming now. It snorted and poked its head around the truck and stopped 20 yards away.

It was a German *volkswagon* [*sic*]. There were six men in it. One got out.

Can he be coming at me, I thought. Suppose the wounded German cries out. Will he come over here then and take me prisoner or will he kill me in a fit of anger?

The German soldier looked at the dead body [of a German soldier] in the road and then got back in the *volkswagon*. I grinned all over. I knew exactly what he was feeling. He was afraid. He talked to the five other men and soon the *volkswagon* turned around and went away.

The medics, excited and out of breath, ran up from the opposite direction.

"Gosh, that was a German car, wasn't it? We better get you out of here."

Picking up the stretcher, they hustled me away from the truck and the stretcher was jostled as shells arched overhead toward the beach and the bearers quickened their pace.

I saw a two-story stone building some 25 yards from the road and I said, "Put me behind there for shelter." They set me down behind it among a flock of chickens and put a stone under my head and went away.

After a while I heard a clanking on the road. Nearer and louder, louder and nearer it came. Can our tanks have at last got here, I thought. Then the clanking ceased.

They've stopped and maybe they'll pick me up, I hoped. Heavy machine guns burst sharply on the other side of the house. Clearing the road, I thought.

Once more the clanking started. And now it was passing by the front of the house. Propping myself in a sitting position I watched with popping eyes a column of tanks, with turrets clamped down, moving slowly down the road, their guns revolving round and round.

They don't look like ours, I thought, and then I saw they were yellow-brown and not green and I knew they weren't ours.

It's a strange thing to be wounded and watch the enemy's tanks go by and not be able to take cover or get up and run away or help yourself in any manner. I think if I had been in the same position but not wounded I would have been more frightened than I was then. As it was, I couldn't influence matters—I had no will and no responsibility. Anything that happened was just up to fate . . .

Pretty soon some of our jeeps—I forgot to mention that they had passed by an hour before—raced back from the direction which the tanks had taken. As they went by, the occupants yelled something to the group by the house next door and those men, to my astonishment, suddenly started running toward the beach, looking back over their shoulders in anxious alarm at the road.

When I saw them running away I called as loud as I could: "Hey, Yankee soldier, Yankee soldier, I'm wounded! Hey, I'm wounded!"

One or two paused and turned around as if they would come back to me and I yelled again but after hesitating for a moment they turned back and went the other way. . . .

Plasma drips into your veins drop by drop. A bottleful takes an unbearably long time to get in. With my eyes I watched the line of liquid in the bottle; with my ears I listened for the approaching tanks. The brown line in the bottle didn't seem to move at all, but the tanks were coming in fast, throwing shells as they came.

One of the shells flew over with a quick whistle and fell a few yards away by the corner of a building. A small black cloud showed where it fell and exploded. In the opposite direction, through the grapevines, I could see one of our heavy guns coming up the road. So this gun and the tanks were about to duel with each other at close range and we were right in the middle.

At this time there were two Italian officers wandering around in the garden and I was idly watching them, wondering if they had heard about the armistice, when I thought they could very well carry me toward the beach if they were willing. I made the appropriate signs and motions and they quickly signified they would.

The tanks were coming nearer and nearer and a shell flew uncomfortably close. By now two-thirds of the bottle of plasma was inside me and with the medics' consent I decided to forego the rest.

The Italians picked me up. I had been vomiting off and on for the last hour and I did so again and the Italians looked at me with sorrowful eyes. The Italians weren't very strong and they set me down to rest every hundred yards or so but they were willing bearers and they kept going toward the sea, though shells were now coming down faster in the vicinity of the beach.

After a mile I saw an artillery unit under some trees and a man with a red cross on his arm.

Belden was evacuated to a military hospital in Oran, Algeria. The experience led to a second highly personal article about the long, lonely process of convalescing. He wrote in *Life* that, coming to the hospital, he dreamed of a nurse who would "press her lips against mine and say: 'Hurry up and get well; I'm waiting for you.'" A shapely young nurse with "golden silk hair," Beatrice Weber, materialized. He referred to her in the article as "Miss Beautiful Body." When he joked with her about marriage, she sensed he was serious. Far younger and "not ready to get involved with such a man in need of security and such psychological help," she did not encourage him. He was angry when his fellow reporters ribbed him about the article.

The articles generated considerable mail. A secretary thanked him for his accurate picture of war, "a long cry from all the glamorous bally-ho that is sponged into our minds." Nurses said they had the same experiences. A woman said she was jealous of Miss Beautiful Body. A camouflage officer said he posted the first story to illustrate the importance of not climbing over walls in combat. Also came criticism—that Belden was too graphic about the war, too negative about hospital life, too sentimental, too personal, that he was a "weeping wolf."

In a response to one critic, Belden wrote, "I should like to write about War and not battles; about the meaning of war, not its spectacle, not its shot and shell, and certainly not gossip about Joe Smith or John Doakes (326 W42nd St. Phil. Pa.)." Under the circumstances, he continued, "what better way could I choose to tell how the battle was going than through myself and what was happening to me. There is such a thing as censorship, you know. Even that message, personal as it was, took three days for a fellow correspondent to get through the censors." If he could have written the hospital story over again, Belden said, "I should lay myself open even more."

Say what he would, Belden's style of reporting was not merely one of professional convenience. He craved sympathy, understanding, love. Of his time in the hospital, he said, "I was very lonely, very woman longing." While recovering in New York, Belden finished another book, *Still Time to Die.* The title was from a line by military theorist Karl von Clausewitz, whom he quoted liberally throughout. The book, which his previous publisher, Knopf, turned down, eschewed war correspondents' "sports reporting" description of the feats of ace pilots and privates who charged pillboxes. Mostly, he confessed, "it is about myself in the midst of battle. . . . My life, more than that of anyone I know, has been spent in lonely wanderings among the dreary wastelands of war."

"I learned early on that war forms its own culture," wrote *New York Times'* Chris Hedges. "The rush of battle is a potent and often lethal addiction, for war is a drug, one I ingested for many years." Hedges covered wars in El Salvador, Sudan and Yemen, the West Bank and Gaza, Algeria, Bosnia, Kosovo, and elsewhere before he sat down to make sense of it all in his 2002 book, *War Is a Force That Gives Us Meaning.* If he was aware of Belden, he did not say so. Yet the kinship is there.

"Everything was bathed in a blurry radiance," Belden wrote of his sensations during a shelling in China. "But most curious of all, I was not only tingling with delirious excitement, but, to my great astonishment, I realized that I was almost panting with a sexual kind of pleasure, and I found myself leaning against the wind, surrendering to the rough caress of the sand, pulsing and throbbing and thrilling to the crashing, tumultuous orchestration of the shells which were now beating the earth about us with a punishing, orgiastic frenzy."

Wrote Hedges: "Casual encounters are charged with a raw, high-voltage sexual energy that smacks of the self-destructive lust of war itself. The erotic in war is like the rush of battle. It overwhelms the participants. . . . Sex in war is another variant of the drug of war."

There is a tie with many other war reporters also. Martha Gellhorn confessed that she did not derive much pleasure in sex, but a great deal in covering war. "I plunged into that." When the Vietnam War was over, Peter Arnett with AP could have moved on to a safe assignment, but "war reporting was what I did in my life." A colleague, John Laurence with CBS, used liquor and drugs to keep from dreaming of the "daily miracle" of his survival and, when he returned home, as a substitute for the excitement he lost. "Drink and drugs," he wrote, "were other means of risk taking." "War and smack: I always hope for some kind of epiphany in each to lead me out but it never happens," wrote Anthony Loyd, a British freelance correspondent who came home from Bosnia addicted to war and drugs. Said an American television cameraman, Jon Steele, "Whole scene went down like good drugs. Walking through the valley of death and coming to the other side over and over again. Man, what a rush." "When reporting or traveling you feel so young," wrote Robert Kaplan, an *Atlantic Monthly* correspondent who had experienced his share of war; "the moment you stop you feel old."

The trench-eye view remains a staple of war correspondence. The term for it when the United States invaded Iraq was "embedded" reporting. These correspondents wrote in the first person and used themselves as the focus of reporting, often at considerable personal risk. Michael Weisskopf, a correspondent for *Time* in Iraq in 2003, had his writing hand blown off when he tried to throw a grenade out of his Humvee. He told the story of his recovery in Ward 57 with other wounded servicemen in *Blood Brothers*. Altogether, 136 war correspondents from a host of countries had died in Iraq as of the end of 2008. The risk on the battlefield, where a reporter could be confused for a soldier, was combined in that war with the risk of being targeted precisely because one was a journalist. During the siege of Sarajevo in the early 1990s, an ABC producer was killed while riding to the airport. The bullet entered the sign on the back of the van right between the letters "T" and "V."

This was another sign of the perilous progression for journalists that had gathered momentum since Dorothy Thompson's expulsion from Nazi Germany. Killing a reporter was a way to make a political point. The danger of death or abduction—or both—was so great in Baghdad during the war in Iraq that correspondents were "under virtual house arrest," wrote *Wall Street Journal* correspondent Farnaz Fassihi in a private e-mail that became public and raised concerns about whether reporters could do their jobs. In the spring of 2003, the death rate among corre-

TABLE 9. Confirmed deaths of journalists (all nationalities) covering armed conflicts through December 2008

Conflict	Journalists killed
World War I (1914–1918)	2
World War II (1939–1945)	68
Korean War (1950–1953)	17
Vietnam (1955–1975)	66
Algerian Civil War (1991–2002)	64
Yugoslav Wars (1991–2001)	61
Afghanistan War (2001–2008)	17
War in Iraq (2003–2008)	136

Sources: Compiled from data provided by the Freedom Forum and the Committee to Protect Journalists.

spondents covering the war in Iraq was about 1 percent; for the military it was 0.1 percent.

Until 2002 the only studies "on the psychological health of war reporters" came from the correspondents themselves in memoirs, observed Dr. Anthony Feinstein and two colleagues that year in the *American Journal of Psychiatry*. Feinstein found that war correspondents were more likely than other journalists to experience emotional numbness, unwanted recollections, and depression. They were reluctant to mix with others and found it difficult to readjust to a normal life. They drank more. They typically were not aware of what afflicted them. Although almost 25 percent suffered from posttraumatic stress disorder, their parent organizations had no real understanding of their problems either. Many correspondents were eager to return to fields of battle, and their bosses were equally happy to send them. "The standard practice," wrote one war correspondent, "has been to go forth with bottle of Scotch, absorb the pain and fear, and never tell your editors."

Since then, a few news organizations have begun to provide counseling for reporters and trauma-training sessions for their editors. The University of Washington operates the Dart Center for Journalism and Trauma, whose mission is to improve coverage of conflict and tragedy and to address "the consequences of such coverage for those working in journalism." To help journalists avoid the more obvious physical wounds, the Committee to Protect Journalists publishes guides. Media boot camps, offered by the military or private companies, prepare journalists for combat assignments.

It is doubtful that Belden would have accepted counseling even if it had been available. Shortly before he came home to recover from the wounds he suffered in Italy, he warned his mother "not to be hurt if I am gloomy, despondent or absent-minded. And I also wish you to know that I shall probably wish to be left alone a great deal."

In April 1944, after Belden completed treatment in New York, *Time-Life* sent him to its London bureau in time for the D-Day landing in Normandy that June. He crossed the channel and moved westward along with advancing military forces. As usual, his reporting—long dispatches, written in shorthand cablese, and expanded in New York—was vivid: "first sun seen in weeks on german front shown like dirty penny through overcast which broke apart in places like gray icefloe showing patches of forgotten blue sky stop half hour later fighter and medium bombers shot in and out of grayness like wraiths stop." Also as usual, Belden felt wronged. He believed his editors had promised him the number-one reporting position and was angry when it didn't work out that way. "They say he's a prima donna," Annalee Jacoby, who worked for *Time-Life,* told Teddy White. The following January, Belden was fired. *Harper's* gave him credentials but did not use any of his material or pay him.

In Europe, Belden looked, almost frantically, for affection. His dispatches often turned to pretty women he encountered. "A ravishing blond," Belden wrote in a cable about the liberation of Paris, "one of the most beautiful women eye* ever saw rushed up to our jeep and threw her arms around me and pressed me and hugged me and kissed me until she finally dissolved in tears." Another girl, he reported, "said in surprise quote all alone unquote and then kissed me." Several months later, in a German town occupied by American troops, he and William Stoneman of the *Chicago Daily News* found quarters in a private residence. When they went to bed, Belden asked Stoneman to roll over, facing the wall, while he romanced a German girl.

At the end of the war, Belden married a "very lovely" French woman who jumped on his fiacre during Gen. Charles De Gaulle's triumphant return to Paris. After the war Belden unsuccessfully tried freelancing from Paris, where cold weather and recurring malaria nagged him. He and his wife, with whom he had a son, separated in 1946 (and divorced in 1954). He returned to China to cover the civil war between the Jiang Qing's Nationalist forces and the Communists, slipping back and forth across the battle lines. Belden was disenchanted by the corrupt Nationalist government, which did not do much to improve the lives of the Chinese, and hopeful about the Communists, who developed support in the countryside while brutalizing landlords. *China Shakes the World,* the resulting book, would by itself make Belden worth a chapter in the history of foreign correspondence, for it was an outstanding behind-the-lines account that revealed the viability of the Communists. Many reviews were positive, but its success was hampered by a political climate that froze out anything positive about Communism. Eminent China Hand Owen Lattimore, himself a victim of the Red Scare, later called the book "a neglected masterpiece." The embittered Belden left uncashed a $28.07 royalty check, which he considered "a reminder of the folly of writing books."

Belden's wars—the formal, declared kind between countries—were over. His personal battles continued to rage. "There is nothing out there any more," Belden told Keyes Beech of the *Chicago Daily News* one evening in Shanghai before the Communist takeover in 1949. He sounded bitter, Beech thought, "but then Belden was always bitter." His friend Teddy White spotted the problem. Jack Belden, "perhaps the ablest of all war correspondents," could not give up the war. He "went on forever listening to the echo of the combat sounds that had stirred his heart."

Publisher Michael Bessie at Harper offered Belden a contract to write a novel set in contemporary China. Bessie thought he wrote about war in "an almost novelistic way" and was encouraged by the opening chapters Belden wrote of this fictional story about the civil war. The rest of the chapters did not come, though. Finally Belden made a confession. He did not know China after the Communist takeover. He couldn't write about what he hadn't seen.

In the 1930s, Belden had retreated from the Japanese all across China, from Beijing to Nanjing, to Hankou, to Chungking. In the 1940s he retreated with Stilwell

---

* Cablese for *I.*

in Burma. When the Allies had a setback in the final months of the war in Belgium and had to retreat, he was with them. "I believe I know more about defeat and retreat than almost any living American," Belden wrote in *Still Time to Die*. Now, after a spectacular but brief career of war reporting—only a dozen years really—he retreated from journalism. He drove a taxi and a school bus, sold aluminum siding, and worked for a time in a post office. He gambled. He wrote poetry, which his friend Jack Egle, a former INS reporter, thought was a form of retreat, too. The poems were sonnets, and sonnets didn't have much of a market. As Belden told a friend, one publisher turned them down on the grounds they were "archaic."

In 1969 Belden left the United States for France, in part to get away from his second wife, with whom he had another son. There had been ugly courtroom scenes. Alimony was a problem. Belden returned to the United States once, in 1985, for his mother's one-hundredth birthday. After U.S.-Chinese rapprochement in 1972, Belden was one of the China Hands to return for a visit. He came back with "a great set of notes" and "a fine set of slides," thought Durdin, who saw him in Paris. Durdin suggested that he send the material to *Life*. Nothing came of it.

Those who saw Belden in Paris found a man who could still be playful and funny. He told Edgar Snow's widow, Lois Snow, he couldn't recite his poetry because "a nice echoing whistle" came through his false teeth; he thought it better to go on stage "as a bird imitator." Mostly, though, he appeared "crazed, wild, intense"—and vulnerable. In the bars he frequented, he told his life story to women almost as a form of seduction, although as he grew older it proved less effective. He constantly worried about being stopped in the street because he did not have a residence card. His quarters were shabby. He wore a long Chinese coat Lois Snow gave him as both a bathrobe and a street coat. What little savings he had came to almost nothing. "Survival is an overwhelming problem," he confessed to his niece.

Belden liked to play in a regular Saturday night poker game organized by American expatriate James Jones, author of *From Here to Eternity*. Fellow novelists William Styron and Irwin Shaw could be found there from time to time. But Belden didn't fit in. He was too intense, thought Egle, who watched Belden win twenty thousand dollars at chemin de fer one night in Montparnasse. Other nights, of course, he lost. Belden received support from his mother, from friends, and from the Correspondents Fund, which was created with proceeds from the sale of the old limestone building that once held the Overseas Press Club in New York. "I wouldn't mind having a place to live," he noted in one of the sketches he wrote of his life. "Or a fellowship or even free lessons with support money that French govt. gives out to some foreigners. I suppose the old can go fuck themselves." Finally through a friend, who was close to the wife of then president François Mitterrand, he managed to secure a residence card and move into a retirement home.

Belden's Salerno wounding and recovery had a final chapter. In October 1988, the pretty nurse from Oran, Beatrice Weber, came across his *Life* article about her in an antique shop. Weber, who had married and divorced in the intervening years, had thought of Belden often. Finding the old article seemed providential to the spiritual woman. "He still needs me," she thought. Weber wrote *Time* for information. No one replied. She telephoned Knopf, which said Belden died in 1975. Months later, through Monthly Review Press, which had reissued *China Shakes the World* in 1970, she located him in Paris, where he was terminally ill with lung cancer. She telephoned Belden immediately.

Weber was at Belden's side in the hospital for about three weeks, almost to the end. When she found the experience emotionally overwhelming, she returned home. Belden died on June 3, 1989.

19

TWO WARRING IDEALS IN ONE DARK BODY

On January 31, 1942, just a few weeks after the Japanese attack on Pearl Harbor, one of the nation's leading black newspapers printed a letter from a Wichita cafeteria worker named James G. Thompson. "Should I sacrifice my life to live half an American?" this reader wrote the *Pittsburgh Courier.* "Let we colored Americans adopt the Double VV for double victory. The first V for victory over the enemies from without, the second V for victory over our enemies from within." Probably no letter in a black newspaper ever reverberated so intensely through black society.

The front page of the next edition of the *Courier,* which circulated nationally, carried a large "Double V." "Black America may not emerge victorious in its war at home," wrote a *Courier* editor. "Our two wars are inextricably intertwined." For weeks the *Courier* kept up the Double V campaign, hiring Thompson to head it for eight months. It filled its pages with pictures of Double V beauty queens and reports about Double V dances, songs, gardens, and flag-raising ceremonies.

Across the country other black newspapers echoed the Double V slogan. "We must stand united against this common enemy and beat him away from our shores," the *Chicago Defender* wrote. "But we have some internal problems of our own to settle before we can present a solid united front." "Our own people," proclaimed the *Norfolk Journal and Guide,* "cry out in anguish: 'This is no time to be conservative; to stick to a middle-of-the road policy; help us get some of the blessings of Democracy here at home first before you jump on the "free other peoples" band wagon and tell us to go forth and die in a foreign land; speak out with courage and decision.'"

Still fresh in the minds of black Americans was their experience in World War I. The black press had urged race members to "close ranks" and support the war effort. In return, blacks hoped to be fully enfranchised. They were disappointed. Discrimination in the military was rampant. Black troops were not allowed to march in the victory parade down the Champs-Elysées. At home, the lynching of blacks increased. In some cases, as one black newspaper noted, returning soldiers "were not allowed to wear their uniforms on the streets, even when those uniforms were decorated for bravery in preserving the ideals of this government."

When a new world war loomed in the late 1930s, black newspapers openly questioned whether the Japanese and the Germans were really that much worse than the British and the French, whose histories were replete with aggressive colonization. "Tokio is as heartless as London, Paris, Rome and Berlin," editorialized the *Journal and Guide* in 1939. That same year the *Baltimore Afro-American* wrote, "It is plain now that the objective of the Japanese government is to boot the white races out of China, and set up an Asiatic Monroe Doctrine through which Japan can control the destinies of the Far East. The *Afro-American* fully believes Japan is justified in the foregone objectives."

Once the United States was in the war, the black press patriotically showed little sympathy for the Japanese or the Germans. Blacks, including James G. Thompson, enlisted in the war effort, their totals reaching about seven hundred thousand by the war's end. Nevertheless, the frustration that gave rise to his Double V letter continued. In mid-1943, blacks rioted in Mobile, Detroit, Beaumont, Los Angeles, and New York. By one count, at least 242 "major incidents" occurred from March 1 to the end of the year. Just wanting to put on a military uniform was a challenge to the status quo, for the military did not welcome blacks to their ranks. And blacks wanted more than the uniform—they wanted a frontline combat role, not a support one in the rear. "We cannot defend America with a dust brush, a mop and a white apron," said the *Afro-American*. "We cannot march against enemy planes and tanks, and challenge armed warships armed only with a whiskbroom and a wide grin." Blacks, said another slogan, had to "fight for the right to fight."

The black press sought its own equality. It insisted that blacks have the opportunity to fight *and* that black correspondents go into combat with them. The result was black newspapers' first concerted effort to field foreign correspondents. In keeping with the Double V campaign, these black correspondents had a split-screen perspective that made them both similar to and different from their white counterparts. They employed established conventions of war reporting but used those conventions to crusade for their race as well as report progress in the war abroad. This, it was later said, was the "Golden Age" for the black press.

"It is a peculiar sensation, this double-consciousness, this sense of always looking at one's self through the eyes of others, of measuring one's soul by the tape of a world that looks on in amused contempt and pity," black intellectual and journalist W. E. B. Du Bois wrote movingly in *The Souls of Black Folk*. "One ever feels his twoness,—an American, a Negro; two souls, two thoughts, two unreconciled strivings; two warring ideals in one dark body, whose dogged strength alone keeps it from being torn asunder."

The black press was conceived in this "peculiar sensation" of black duality. The first black newspaper, founded in 1827, is said by some historians to have been a response to the *New York Enquirer*'s proposal that freed blacks should be removed from the streets of New York and sent to Africa. In addition to objecting to colonization, *Freedom's Journal* set out to serve the "five hundred thousand free people of colour" who were not enjoying the privileges of the American Constitution, "our polar star." The newspaper promoted education and good conduct and highlighted black achievements. It lasted two years. Before it folded, one of its editors accepted money from the Colonization Society and moved to Liberia, where he started the Liberian *Herald*.

Subsequent newspapers sought, as the *Freedom's Journal* had, to elevate blacks and protest white discrimination. The *Pittsburgh Mystery* was founded in 1843 because local journals refused to print letters written by blacks. Four years later William A. Hodges started the *Ram's Horn* in New York after the editor of the local *Sun* told him the newspaper's slogan was now revised. "The *Sun* shines for all white men," the editor said, "and not for colored men." During the Civil War, Frederick Douglass prefigured the Double V when he editorialized in his journal, *Douglass' Monthly*, "We shall be fighting a double battle against slavery in the South and against prejudice and proscription in the North."

Colorful newspaper names like *Mystery* and *Ram's Horn* (a reference to the biblical story of a horn's sound bringing down Jericho's walls) were common at this time, and not just with black newspapers. A white Massachusetts newspaper had the improbable name *Give 'Em Jessie!* In Washington, D.C., one could find the *Hickory Tree* and the *Cotton Plant*. Where black newspapers differed was in their tendency to use titles along the lines of *Freedom's Journal,* which spoke to their readers' being both part and apart. Before the Civil War, there were the *African Sentinel,* the *Colored American,* the *Emancipator and Free American,* and the *Palladium of Liberty;* afterward the *40 Acres and a Mule,* the *Race Pride,* the *Black Dispatch,* the *Colored Tennessean,* the *Colored Citizen,* and the *Freeman.** The widely circulating monthly operated by the National Association for the Advancement of Colored People, edited by W. E. B. Du Bois, was called *The Crisis: A Record of the Darker Races.*

From 1865 to 1900, nearly 1,200 African American newspapers sprouted up. Most wilted and died. But a few survived as blacks began to congregate in urban areas and editors employed the sensational techniques of Hearst and Pulitzer to attract readers. On the eve of World War II, the total number of black newspapers—all but one appeared weekly—reached 210. From 1933 to 1940, their circulation more than doubled to 1.27 million, and this figure understated their reach. One-third of the newspapers did not report circulation numbers, and individual copies passed from person to person. The Office of War Information reckoned that 4 million blacks read an African American newspaper each week. In addition some 130 monthly and quarterly publications served blacks. "The press, more than any other institution, has created the Negro group as a social and psychological reality to the

---

* Two-thirds of American dailies in 1928 had names with these words: News, Times, Journal, Herald, Tribune, Press or Free Press, Star, Record or Recorder, Democrat, Gazette, Post, Courier, Sun, Leader, and Republican or Republic. During Colonial times, when the United States was alive with thoughts of revolution, there was more likelihood of getting a Centinel of Liberty or Centinel of Freedom (the unusual spelling being usual then). In time, the black press began to pick up conventional names like Courier and Journal, although even today a number have names like *Chicago Defender*.

individual Negro," Swedish socioeconomist Gunnar Myrdal concluded in his monumental 1944 study of the plight of blacks in America, *The American Dilemma.*

Although black publishers and editors possessed enormous influence, they had to navigate crosswinds that sometimes kept them from entirely setting their own course. They did not enjoy the levels of advertising that white newspapers did. As a result they were heavily dependent on circulation for revenue and, consequently, particularly sensitive to pleasing readers. At the same time, they could not ignore the opinions of whites, who held the keys both to freedom and to jail. During World War I, a *Chicago Defender* cartoon depicted black soldiers facing the Germans while white American soldiers shot them in the back. The owner avoided a prison sentence as well as suspension of his second-class mailing permit by buying fifty thousand dollars worth of Liberty Bonds and urging readers to do likewise.

Given its focus on blacks' own foreignness at home, as well as the shallowness of its coffers, the black press did not assemble corps of foreign correspondents the way the white press began to do at the turn of the century. When black editors ran foreign news, it usually was because the news directly intersected some aspect of black life. Africa held particular attraction. Said a poem in the *Negro World,* Marcus Garvey's Back to Africa movement weekly, "O Africa, sweet Africa! All Negroes turn to thee." Likewise, in the 1890s, the black press paid attention to the Cuban insurgency, in which its readers initially saw their own struggle for freedom reflected.

In the case of the Spanish-American War, black editors considered pooling their resources to send a correspondent to Cuba. When the scheme fell apart because they couldn't agree on who should represent them, individual newspapers made extensive use of letters written by the ten thousand blacks who signed up to fight in Cuba and the Philippines. Some of the more prolific ones became virtual special correspondents. By the end of the war, when the United States replaced Spain as colonial master in the Philippines, many blacks sympathized with the Filipino insurgents, who distributed posters reminding "The Colored American Soldier" about lynching at home. "I must confess," a black soldier wrote to the Wisconsin *Weekly Advocate,* "they have a just grievance."

A few nineteenth-century black Americans traveled abroad more or less independently. One of the most remarkable of these quasi-correspondents—for they often combined political work with journalism—was George Washington Williams. Williams had been a Union soldier during the Civil War, a clergyman, the author of the first comprehensive history of African Americans, and a columnist for the white-owned *Commercial* in Cincinnati. He journeyed to the Congo in the 1880s to investigate the potential for sending African Americans there as workers. He also had credentials as a representative of S. S. McClure's syndicate, the Associated Literary Press of the U.S.A. Contrary to what he expected, conditions for workers in the Congo Railway Company were "equal to anything in the slave trade." All that was missing was "chains about their necks!"

In an "Open Letter to His Serene Majesty Leopold II," Williams decried Belgium's "deceit, fraud, robberies, arson, murder, slave-raiding, and general policy of cruelty." He singled out Henry Stanley, who had been an agent of Belgium in the Congo, as especially abusive of the natives. The *Boston Globe* and the *New York Tribune* ran Williams's stories, and James Gordon Bennett's *Herald* commented favorably on the "Open Letter," perhaps as another way to put Stanley in his place. Historians have called Williams's reporting "a milestone in the literature of human rights and of investigative journalism."

Williams died in 1891 at age forty-one. In his footsteps came the first black American missionary, William Sheppard. Sheppard wrote articles for the *Kassai Herald,* a newsletter for church supporters back home, and other magazines that revealed white brutality in the Congo.

Two of the first bona fide foreign correspondents for black newspapers were Roscoe Conkling Simmons and Ralph Tyler. They gave highly contrasting performances in World War I. Simmons was an accomplished Republican speaker and politician and one of the highest-paid journalists in the country. The *Chicago Defender* sent him to cover frontline black troops during World War I, an assignment the publisher came to regret. The flashy orator, the publisher's biographer noted, "somehow never got beyond the Paris fleshpots." His greatest accomplishment from the *Defender*'s point of view seems to have been a spectacular speech upon his return to Chicago. Thousands of people turned up and paid a dollar each to hear him. The other correspondent, Ralph Tyler, started out on a black newspaper in Columbus, Ohio, where he was city editor, and jumped to the white-owned *Evening Dispatch,* where he began as a janitor. He eventually became a *Dispatch* reporter, columnist, and cashier; made shrewd personal business investments; and was appointed the navy's auditor. During the war, the government was concerned that blacks would be susceptible to German propaganda, and in that frame of mind George Creel's Committee on Public Information agreed to a request by black journalists to accredit a black war correspondent. Tyler was an obvious choice. Although the National Negro Press Association paid his expenses (he worked for free) and distributed his stories, he reported to the CPI. Tyler recounted "the splendid endurance and valiant fighting of the Colored soldiers." He did not report the discrimination he witnessed—not that he had much choice. The CPI spiked stories in which he reported French women's willingness to fraternize with blacks.

Black newspapers also picked up stories from the mainstream press that were favorable to race men and embraced those who wrote them. Irwin Cobb, a southerner who relished telling stories in which black characters said "dis" and "dat," praised black troops in the *Saturday Evening Post.* Today Cobb would be viewed as condescending at best. Then, when he returned home to Paducah, Kentucky, local blacks invited him to speak at their church and asked him if he would like to be driven there in a limousine.

Blacks joined in the general American travelfest after the war and, like other Americans, wrote about it. Blacks' sense of liberation was especially exhilarating. Whites merely escaped American materialism and provincialism. Blacks escaped segregation. Europe offered "a sense of freedom that is almost alarming," wrote Joel Rogers in *The American Mercury.* "Trained to resist race prejudice or to submit to it, [the black] now finds himself without an enemy to attack or a fetish to bow to." France was especially welcoming. In 1919 the *Chicago Defender* ran a story called "Why French Girls Adore Our Men." By the mid-1920s, there were enough blacks in Paris that it made sense for the *Defender* to circulate there.

During these interwar years, much of the foreign news in black newspapers was cribbed from other papers or came from letter-writers and part-time correspondents. The Associated Negro Press (ANP), which found it difficult to deliver on its early promise "to scour the world for race news," scrounged news where it could. Rudolph Dunbar, a noted West Indian musician and orchestra leader living in London, was a correspondent. Thyra Edwards, a social worker from Chicago, wrote ANP feature stories while conducting European tours in the 1930s. Another black woman, Fay Jackson, covered the coronation of King George VI while in Europe on a six-month tour. Poet Langston Hughes, a young American writer who had worked his way abroad on ships, later covered the "Colored Volunteers" who joined the Loyalist side of the Spanish civil war. He sent his dispatches to the *Afro-American* as well as the ANP. John C. Robinson, a volunteer black aviator in the Ethiopian air force when the Italians invaded in 1935–36, filed stories to the ANP under the byline Wilson James.

Ethiopia evoked a powerful response from blacks. While European colonization swept across Africa, this country kept its freedom. Its rulers traced their ancestry to King Solomon and the Queen of Sheba. Black associations and churches in the United States put *Ethiopia* or *Abyssinia,* an alternative name for Ethiopia at the time, in their names.* Like many other black newspapers, the *Chicago Defender* was keenly interested in the Italian invasion of Ethiopia in 1935 but not keen to pay the freight for a foreign correspondent to cover the story. Instead, the weekly pieced together news from a variety of sources, including an on-the-scene "correspondent" codenamed "Operative 22." The *Defender* told readers it could not use Operative 22's real name "because of censorship difficulties that might be encountered in getting FACTS out of Ethiopia," a strange explanation inasmuch as it was accompanied by a photograph of the man whom the *Defender* was supposed to be protecting. The explanation is even murkier because the biographer of Robert Abbott, the newspaper's publisher, said Operative 22 was the foreign editor, who rewrote stories from other newspapers and put an Ethiopian dateline on them. (Abbott favored this approach. When the foreign editor suggested sending someone to cover Emperor Haile Selassie's personal appeal for help from the League of Nations, Abbott responded, "Before a Negro could get to Geneva, the *Chicago Tribune* would have the full story, and for two cents we can get the story.") Whoever Operative 22 was, many of the foreign stories in "The Chicago Defender Foreign News Section" were of uncertain provenance.

The *Pittsburgh Courier,* whose national circulation reached a quarter million in the 1930s, was one of the most prosperous black newspapers and, accordingly, es-

---

* The Rastafarian movement that began in Jamaica took its name from Haile Selassie's precoronation name, Ras (Prince) Tafari. Rastafarians consider the Ethiopian emperor divine.

tablished the best overall record on foreign news. Its editor, Robert L. Vann, covered the Berlin Olympics, where Jesse Owens was showered with medals. George Schuyler wrote a much-heralded series on the continuation of slavery in Africa. Jamaican-born Joel Rogers, who first worked in the United States as a Pullman car porter and wrote the *American Mercury* article mentioned above, often visited Africa as well as Europe beginning in the 1920s. In the next decade, Vann sent him to cover the coronation of Emperor Haile Selassie and the Italian invasion. Rogers was the first correspondent to have an exclusive interview with Selassie. When Rogers's initial stories appeared, the *Courier*'s circulation jumped by twenty-five thousand. Rogers incorrectly predicted the Ethiopians would prevail.

One of the most adventurous independent black correspondents of this period was Homer Smith, who in retirement told his story in *Black Man in Red Russia*. Smith earned a journalism degree from the University of Minnesota in the early 1930s. The journalism department was in its heyday at the time, turning out the likes of Harrison Salisbury and Eric Sevareid. Smith had little hope of finding a job on of the mainstream newspapers where his classmates went to work; he looked forward unhappily to a career at the post office, where he worked while in school. After an altercation over seating in a restaurant, Smith wrote to authorities in the Soviet Union asking for a position in the Moscow post office. The Soviets, who saw propaganda value in courting blacks, gave him a job as well as citizenship. He initially did occasional reporting for black American newspapers under the name Chatwood Hall. By the mid-1930s he was a full-time correspondent and soon after acquired a Russian wife. Smith stayed throughout the world war, at the end working in the Moscow bureau of the Associated Press as well as for the ANP. He thus participated in the first and only systematic effort to field African American foreign correspondents.

At least twenty-seven black journalists, one of them a woman, were war correspondents in World War II. They represented the *Pittsburgh Courier,* the *Chicago Defender,* the *Baltimore Afro-American,* and the *Norfolk Journal and Guide* as well as the National Negro Publishers Association and the Associated Negro Press. They reported from all theaters. The nationally circulating and influential *Norfolk Journal and Guide*—which was neither the most strident nor the most accommodating—spoke for virtually all of them when its editor published the "Credo for the Negro Press" in 1944. The editor, P. Bernard Young Jr., who had gone abroad for the papers and was one of the newspaper founder's sons, wrote: "I shall be a crusader and an advocate, a mirror and a record, a herald and a spotlight, and I shall not falter."

Although none were killed or wounded, black correspondents went into action when they could and, like white correspondents, wrote dramatic first-person accounts of what they experienced. Also like their white counterparts, they put the names and addresses of military personnel in their stories; they were patriotic; they tangled with censors. John "Rover" Jordan with the *Journal and Guide* had trouble with Col. B. O. Davis, the son of the first black general. "I'm not the kind of reporter to report whatever I'm told," the reporter said defiantly. But to these conventions shared with white correspondents, they applied Young's chronicle-and-crusade credo. The names and addresses in their stories were the names and addresses of blacks, whom the *Journal and Guide* called "the forgotten men." The black press's patriotism expressed itself in defense of blacks discriminated against as they fought for their country. Although correspondents endured the usual aggravation of censorship, black issues overlaid that, too. A censor in India refused to pass a story about a segregated military swimming pool in which whites could swim one day and blacks the next. When the reporter threatened an investigation of both pool and censorship practice, the censor gave in. Shortly afterward, the pool was integrated. While the white press was looking for an American victory, black correspondents were on the front lines of their race championing a double one.

Those front lines lay stateside as well as abroad. Black journalists chronicled the progress of blacks joining the military and their treatment once in uniform. Much

In this cartoon, the *Norfolk Journal and Guide* highlighted one of its crusading missions, to destroy "anti-Negro influences."

of the news was bad. The government reneged on promises for proportional representation in the military. When the army announced an appeal for 3,000 nurses, it said that only 56 could be black and that the black nurses could treat only black soldiers. The *Journal and Guide* decried military athletic programs: "Top-ranking Negro college coaches are being taken into the Army as privates or as low ranking, non-commissioned officers and are having to serve under young men who they coached, and taught." Reporters visited military posts and found that blacks enjoyed few recreational amenities on-base and were often unwelcome off-base. Incidents of MPs beating blacks led to riots and in a few cases deaths. The War Department promulgated a policy of nondiscrimination that was not uniformly honored. The commanding officer of a reception center at Fort Benning, Georgia, told soldiers he would make no changes. "This is Georgia," the colonel said. "When in Rome, we do as the Romans do." The *Journal and Guide* reported the officer's comments.

A *Negro Digest* poll in 1943 found overwhelming support for black press militancy. The white establishment had a radically different view. Virginius Dabney, the liberal editor of the *Richmond Times-Dispatch,* criticized black journalists for pressing too hard for "an overnight revolution in race relations." "The country," he concluded in an *Atlantic Monthly* article, "is sitting on a volcano." Seven different federal agencies investigated the black press for evidence of subversion. It was "a rare day" when the FBI did not call on a black paper, said the founder of the *Journal and Guide,* P. B. Young Sr. Had it not been for the intervention of the attorney general, Francis Biddle, black publishers and editors would almost certainly have been indicted for sedition. "The most important job an Attorney General can do in a time of emergency is to protect civil liberties," Biddle said. Even so, the Post Office revoked second-class permits for some black newspapers. Copies of black newspapers were sometimes kept out of military camps on the grounds that they were "agitational."

Black correspondents overseas also experienced discrimination. In North Africa, a white colonel refused to let Ollie Stewart of the *Afro-American* stay with him or the white correspondents he was billeting. "No black sonofabitch is going to sleep under the same roof with me," the officer said. No blacks were among the seventy-seven correspondents who went along on the Normandy invasion. But the closer one got to the battle front, the less discrimination one was likely to find. "Strange as it may seem," noted a black correspondent who had covered the treatment of black troops stateside, "I had a greater sense of security with our military forces in combat areas than I had at times during the eighteen months I spent touring the South." Each time blacks' roles expanded, black correspondents treated it like the major victory it was. After the predominately black crew of the destroyer USS *Mason* was in combat, Thomas W. Young (another son of the *Journal and Guide*'s founder) wrote, "Tan Yanks in Navy blue have taken their place beside Uncle Sam's fighting men of the Army Air Forces who are now battling Nazi pilots in the skies over Europe and of infantry and armored regiments of the 93rd Division fighting Japs through the jungle of the Pacific Inlands. Now it can be said accurately that Negroes are fighting 'on land, on sea and in the air' in combat units of United States forces engaged in the world-wide struggle for democratic principles."

Journal and Guide correspondents used every occasion to report the awards blacks received, as with this item about the pilots in the 99th Pursuit Squadron, the famed Tuskegee airmen: "Twenty six of the intrepid sky warriors, first in American history, have been decorated with the Air Medal." When black servicemen were overlooked by military authorities, as was often the case, the black press took up their cause. For twelve weeks it pressed the U.S. Navy for the name of a black sailor who, though a messmate, had gone onto a burning deck to man an antiaircraft gun during the Japanese attack at Pearl Harbor. The *Courier* subsequently led a campaign to award the Congressional Medal of Honor to the hero, Dorie Miller, who ended up with the second-highest combat award, the Navy Cross.

Black correspondents did not shut their eyes to negative news about their race. The *Journal and Guide*'s Rover Jordan wrote two stories, side-by-side, challenging inflated stories of the accomplishments of black aviators. Mostly, though, the correspondents countered criticism of black military personnel. When the black 92nd Division performed poorly in southern Italy, military leaders attributed the problem to race. Jordan as well as Collins George of the *Courier* pointed to other factors: that the units had met stiff resistance, that many blacks acquitted themselves well, that they were leaderless because many of the officers were killed, that the "race problem" also involved white officers who may have shown "prejudice on certain occasions."

The black newspapers went out of their way to highlight the exploits of their correspondents. The *Journal and Guide* sometimes put the names of its "genuine war correspondents" in headlines and often ran thumbnail head-and-shoulder photos of them in military uniform along with their bylines. When correspondents returned home or relocated on the battlefront, the newspaper ran stories about them and full-length photos. Correspondents cooperated by seeking out the action. Rover Jordan, who had a reputation for insisting "upon going where the story was," covered the aerial invasion of southern France from a glider tow plane (discovering in the air that he didn't have a parachute). The next week he reported, "I was one of the first three war correspondents to enter Toulon after it had been taken by the French invasion forces and I found myself caught in the cross fire of two street battles."

Here is an excerpt of a *Journal and Guide* story about black quartermaster drivers. It captures the tenor of much of the coverage—the focus on individual blacks, in this case blacks toiling in nonglamorous support roles; the correspondent's use of the first person; and the overall black pride. The original story, published June 19, 1943, was more than twice as long as the excerpt here.

Soldiers Volunteer
For Advance Action
With U.S. Rangers
One Colored Lieutenant Found Near

Battlelines; Sergeant Refuses To
Leave Officer In Mine Field Danger
By THOMAS W. YOUNG
Journal and Guide War Correspondent
(By Air Mail. Delayed. Passed by Censor)
(Copyrighted. Reproduction Expressly Forbidden)

. . .

SOMEWHERE IN NORTH AFRICA—Battles, and wars, have been won, and have been lost, because supplies—the ammunition, food, replacement parts, equipment, fuel, and all the countless thousands of little items required to keep a fighting force in condition to transact the business it is trained for—were, or were not at the place required, or at the time needed.

When you've been mixed up with the Army for a few weeks, as I have since I started my duties back in the States as a war correspondent attached to a group of Negro fighter pilots about to embark for this theatre of operations, you begin to understand the importance of supplies in military operations.

It is the job of the Quartermaster Corps to "deliver the goods," so to speak, to the fighting men at the front. In battle areas where boats are "sitting ducks" for enemy aircraft, and where railroads can be rendered inoperative by one well placed bomb on a bridge or tressle [sic], or where, as this theatre, the railroads are notoriously ancient and slow most of the delivery must be done by motor trucks.

In a recent cable I told of meeting some of the colored truck drivers who had faced many of the hazards of front line fighting. These drivers of trucks have been called by some competent observers the "unsung heroes of this war."

They must push forward as long as the front lines are advancing. Delivery, as far as they are concerned, means delivery to the spot where the supplies are required. Frequently that is in an area the enemy has picked for shelling, bombing, or strafing.

Whenever there are missions of this kind they are to all intents and purposes front line soldiers. They are in the thick of the fight. In a sense they are in a less desirable spot than the infantryman who has dug himself into a foxhole opposite enemy lines. The truck driver must get shot at, bombed or strafed, but he cannot fight back. He can only take cover if it can be found, or keep on driving.

NO DRAMATIZATION

You can't make heroes out of truck drivers, no matter how much they have to go through. Their occupation just does not submit to dramatization. But you can understand the kind of work these boys do for their country, and you can appreciate the hardships they have suffered as courageously as any of their fellow countrymen if you just listen to some of the experiences they have been through.

One particular company had been carrying supplies up to the front lines relentlessly for a long spell. All along the road the Military Police knew them well. They had the reputation for getting the goods there, come hell or highwater.

The commanding officer of this company, a white captain from the Midwest, was leading a convoy one day. He stopped to identify himself and his unit.

"All the trucks following me," he told the MP, "will have the same number as you see painted on my front bumper."

The guard took a look at the unit number. His face lighted up as he told the officer.

"I know all about them, Captain. They are those 'Spitfire' drivers.". . .

COLORED OFFICER

In another company, quartered nearby, I saw the only Negro commissioned officer encountered on this trip to the front. He is 2nd Lt. Robert H. Simms, 929 Edgemont street, Indianapolis, Ind.

There are other colored soldiers commissioned in this theatre, of course. There are, for instance, all the pilots and ground officers of a squadron of fighter pilots who recently came across. And there are other Quartermaster commissioned officers in North Africa.

In fact, there were several on the transport that brought the fighter squadron over. And recent reports which may be considered very reliable are that coast artillery (AA) and infantry units with Negro officers are now in North Africa.

But up in the combat zone—at least, during the final stages of the Tunisian campaign when I was there—they just weren't present. The colored soldiers I saw were either Quartermaster units, airfield security battalions or other service groups under white commissioned officers.

SON OF MINISTER

It was, therefore, a refreshing and inspiring experience to meet Lt. Simms. Son of a retired minister, the Rev. L. C. Simms of the same Indianapolis address, he had gone to Lane College in Tennessee after completing his high school course in Indianapolis. His majors were French and English. He also played varsity football, and graduated in 1941.

For the next six months he worked in a defense plant in Indianapolis. After joining the Army he went to Officer Candidate School and gained his commission.

One of the unusual situations to be found in this regiment is the inclusion of one company of white truck drivers among the several colored companies.

They are not really a part of the battalion, according to the officers, but are, rather, attached to it, similar to the arrangement for the Aviation Squadrons (separate) in the Army Air Forces. These, it will be recalled, are the labor or service detachments attached to training fields and air bases in the United States.

"PROVISIONAL" COMPANY

These white drivers are known as "Company P" a designation derived from the character of their organization—a "provisional" company.

[Editor's note: Here the censor deleted a paragraph.]

When a convoy of trucks is needed, equipment and personnel from any of the companies in the battalion are called on. If there are 15 or more trucks a commissioned officer goes along in charge of the group. Sometimes, when it is Lt. Simms' time to lead the convoy, the drivers are all white. So far as this reporter could learn, no bad reaction nor reaction of any kind had set in.

"It doesn't make any difference; there's no time now for differences," said Maj. James T. Stewart, Winifred, Mont., white, commanding officer of this outfit. It was he, incidentally, who arranged for the transfer of Lt. Simms to his unit, because he believed it would work.

Working side by side with Lt. Simms is 2nd Lt. Albert Steiner Jr., white, of Lancaster, Ohio, who has a high regard for the colored drivers under his and Lt. Simms' command. . . .

Among the hazardous missions given a detachment of these truck drivers was one of hauling a unit of Rangers—the American equivalent of the British Commandos—during several days of advance patrol activities.

One night during operations the Rangers asked some of the drivers if they would like to go along on a mission. The question was put obviously in jest, but 15 of these Quartermaster truck drivers volunteered to tag along.

Among them was T-3 Willie B. Morris, 903 East Olney road, Norfolk, Va., son of Mrs. Amanda Morris of the same address. At the time he went into the Army in June, 1941, Morris was a clerk in the Brown Derby Grill at 835 Church street.

The object of the patrol was to locate an 88 mm. gun that had been firing on American forces during the day. That night they located the cannon. The Rangers crept close enough to learn that it was being operated by six Italians. They returned to report their findings.

GUN DESTROYED

The next night the same party, including the volunteer truck drivers, went out to destroy the gun. The Rangers killed four of the Italians, wounded one and captured another uninjured. The gun was destroyed with ten half-pound boxes of TNT to which they set a fuse.

This was an operation for the Rangers, of course, but the colored soldiers who went along for the excitement were close enough at all times to see every move made by these specially trained troops. On this same mission, the trucks driven by these boys were dive bombed while parked near the Ranger headquarters. . . .

The success and good name enjoyed by this particular company can be credited in a large measure to the excellent group of non-commissioned officers it has.

The white commissioned officers who command the company think they are the best in the entire regiment, and have to keep their eyes on the boys to keep the other companies from taking them over, either singly or as a group. . . .

But the spark plug for this organization is a natural leader of men, 1st Sgt. Willie Johnson, 1308 Hercules street, Mobile, Ala., a "veteran" of 21 years, who is the youngest first sergeant in the regiment. He volunteered for the Army in July, 1941 shortly after finishing Dunbar High School in Mobile, and within a few weeks was acting first sergeant. After six months in that capacity he was made a full sergeant.

He runs the administrative machinery of the company, is truck-master, and in general furnishes a dynamic and responsive leadership for the men. He performs a liaison function between the men and the white officers, who cannot, in the normal course of their activities, get a really sympathetic view of the peculiar problems of these soldiers.

HAS TWO BROTHERS

Sgt. Johnson has two brothers, one in Mobile and another in Birmingham, as well as a sister who teaches in Meridian, Miss. Their parents, Mr. and Mrs. Connie Johnson, live in Meridian.

Sgt. Johnson is saving almost all of the money Uncle Sam is paying him to be a soldier. He hopes to have enough when the war is over to purchase a nice large farm in one of the border states and raise poultry for a business.

These truck drivers are not the glamour boys of this war, but often the hopes of victory by some unit on the front lines hangs on their ability swiftly and well to carry out their appointed missions.

"The record of the Negro war correspondents in World War II stands as a monument to the progress of the Negro Press," wrote the *Pittsburgh Courier*. "And when the history of this war is written they will have their share of glory."

This glory came largely in serving as a counterweight to the unbalanced white press.

A few liberal journals like the *Nation,* the *New Republic,* and *PM* wrote sympathetically about black war contributions and published black journalists. Walter White, executive secretary of the National Association for the Advancement of Colored People and a sometime columnist for black newspapers, went overseas to assess the war in light of race with accreditation as a correspondent for the *New York Post. Life* magazine published a generally favorable story on blacks in the military, and radio networks broadcast a few positive programs on blacks. But for the most part the white press paid little attention to blacks or black perspectives; when it did, it depicted blacks in stereotypically depreciative ways. Blacks were either comic—as in Irwin Cobb's use of "dis" and "dat" in his stories—or dangerous. When military police abused black troops, the headlines read "race riots."

Journalism conventions perversely worked against blacks. By reporting "both sides," journalists inherently legitimated racist points of view. Virginius Dabney said as much in his article on the volcanic black press when he reported the comment of an Alabama attorney: If the NAACP had a place in America, the lawyer told him, so did a "League to Maintain White Supremacy." As was pointed out by

Rudolph Dunbar of the Associated Negro Press talks to men in a signal construction battalion somewhere in France, 1944. Dunbar, a West Indian, had once been a bandleader in London. The photo appeared in a U.S. Army volume, *The Employment of Negro Troops*.

the National Commission on Civil Disorders in the 1960s, the media reported and wrote "from the standpoint of a white man's world."

Black journalists counteracted this one-sidedness by emphasizing their side, as they had since the days of *Freedom's Journal*. The result sometimes was tendentious, over-the-top cheerleading, but it gave blacks their due. Anyone watching the newsreels would think "there were no Negroes in this war," a *Journal and Guide* columnist commented in 1944. "The American daily press and, to a lesser extent, the major weekly and monthly white magazines are guilty of the same tragic omission. Were it not for the Negro press, and especially those who at tremendous expense are maintaining their hard won war correspondents in the various theaters of war, the American public would be unaware of the contribution and sacrifices of our people in this global war."

In considering the wider meaning of the global war, the black press countered stereotypes of dark-skinned people abroad. A *Journal and Guide* story began, "African natives, naked but for their belts, from which hung wicked looking knives, acted 'not like savages but like gentlemen,' when 41 survivors of the United States ship, torpedoed late in June in the Indian Ocean, landed on a wild African beach, according to a report made by the skipper of the ship." Black reporting also reinforced the view that the war was a conflict about race everywhere. In 1944 the

American Negro Publishers Association sent a group to Africa. The White House facilitated the trip in hopes it would lead the black press to tone down criticism of conditions at home. Instead the tour gave the black press ammunition to assail conditions in both places. Every issue of major black weeklies, Gunnar Myrdal observed in his study of blacks in the United States, seemed to have an article about the perfidy of British colonization.

Walter White, executive secretary of the NAACP, returned from his fact-finding about race abroad to write a book on the subject, *A Rising Wind.* "The United States, Great Britain, France, and other Allied nations," he wrote, "must choose without delay one of two courses—to revolutionize their racial concepts and practices, to abolish imperialism and grant full equality to all of its people, or else prepare for World War III." "In the present conflict the Negro is finding the problems of the Chinese, the Indians, and the Burmese strangely similar to his own," a black journalist wrote in the *Nation* in 1943. "In this sense the Negro has become more international-minded than the rest of the population."

The black press foreshadowed massive postwar decolonization and the parallel civil rights movement in the United States. This reporting was *potentially* edifying for whites. "Almost everything in the Negro press will be new [to the white reader], or if not new, written in a strange new key," the *New Republic* said in 1943. "But the white reader must be careful about what he allows to anger him, for there is a vast amount of raw, solid fact which they handle well within the bounds of accuracy, and which the white reader simply has got to gulp down and let it educate him." Unfortunately, although the circulation doubled for black newspapers that tracked their readership numbers during the war, few of those new readers were white. A survey of congressional representatives in 1945 found that only half knew a black press existed. A mere five members of Congress remembered seeing a black publication.

The FBI scrutinized the black press for enlightenment on a narrow topic, signs of subversion. Its ambitious 714-page "Survey of Racial Conditions in the United States," which drew heavily on black newspapers collected around the country, set out "to determine why particular Negroes or groups of Negroes or Negro organizations have evidenced sentiments for other 'dark races' (mainly Japanese) or by what forces they were influenced to adopt in certain instances un-American ideologies."

Many educated northerners, Myrdal noted, "are well-informed about foreign problems but almost absolutely ignorant about Negro conditions both in their own city and in the nation as a whole. . . . There is no doubt, in the writer's opinion, that a great majority of white people in America would be prepared to give the Negro a substantially better deal if they knew the facts."

Still, the war and the black press provided impetus for change. "By the war's end," Eric Foner wrote in his history, *The Story of American Freedom,* "racism and nativism had been stripped of intellectual respectability and equated with pathology and irrationality." This gave blacks an opening, and the black press was prepared to push their cause for civil rights through it. When the Allies ended German race laws at the end of World War II, the *Journal and Guide* ran this headline: "Race Discrimination Ends—In Germany—*Not* America."

The war helped confirm that blacks were, after all, able to work side-by-side with whites. Toward the end of the conflict, the military began to integrate blacks into combat units. Although this policy was motivated by necessity, not the desire for social justice, a postwar study found that "the most successful employment of Negro units occurred when they were employed as units closely associated with white units on similar tasks." In such ways, the continuing black protest for equal rights blended with the growing conviction on the part of many white Americans that racial segregation was un-American. The signs of change were small, as when Rover Jordan and his black colleagues integrated officers' messes; and they were large, as when a march on Washington to protest discriminatory hiring practices by defense industries led President Roosevelt to create the Fair Employment Practices Commission.

"When the white Southern editors state flatly that the Negroes must always expect to be segregated in the South," the *New Republic* observed in its 1943 article on the black press, "then these editors must always expect to be confronted by a segregated Negro press." The opposite also was true. A black was accredited to the White House Correspondents Association for the first time in 1943, and soon after the black press integrated the State Department press room. With steps like this, said the *Defender*'s publisher, stories in the black press about the government became more factual and less sensational. Similarly, coverage of the army was less confrontational when the army brass worked constructively with black journalists.

There was, of course, still much more to be done. In the years after the war, blacks became increasingly impatient with what Martin Luther King called "the tranquilizing drug of gradualism." The black press, abetted by American socialist and Communist publications, was again in the vanguard. As late as 1955, only one national newspaper, the *New York Times,* regularly covered race in the South. "Negro reporters," observed a history of press coverage, "still went places white reporters wouldn't go, in search of stories white reporters didn't even know about."

This situation changed when the Supreme Court issued decisions that thwarted discrimination and southern whites fought back, often with violence. The establishment press began to pay attention to civil rights, tentatively at first, as if approaching an alien object, but with increasing determination. The civil rights movement and television, with its vivid images of discrimination, were said to reach maturity together. Racial strife across the country in the 1960s led editors to rethink not only coverage of race, but also their own hiring practices. No longer did a young black reporter as well trained as Homer Smith have little hope of securing a job on an establishment newspaper. Now mainstream newspapers sought out black reporters and promoted them to the top jobs. In the 1960s Carl Rowan, a black American who earned an advanced journalism degree from Smith's alma mater, the University of Minnesota, and received awards for his reporting from India, succeeded Edward R. Murrow as head of the U.S. Information Agency. Afterward he became a syndicated columnist.

Blacks, along with Asian-Americans, Hispanics, and other minorities on daily newspaper staffs, rose from less than 4 percent in 1978 to 13.5 percent in 2005 (blacks were the largest minority in 2005, at about 5.5%). On local broadcast news staffs, some 21 percent were people of color. By one count, 15 percent of American foreign correspondents were not white. Although these percentages were below the roughly 30 percent minority share of the national population and although many journalists were alarmed over the lack of progress, the advances and the belief that more should be done to recruit and cover minorities was a significant attitude change from the past.

"In a fully integrated society," black publishers speculated at the end of the war, "the black press would shrink and eventually vanish." This did not happen. Race pride and de facto separation of races dictated continuing black interest in black media, a tendency that shows up with other minority groups in the United States and their media as well. But by a margin of three to one, blacks rely more heavily on establishment media than their own for political and governmental news. "The state of the black press in World War II and the state of the black press now," said Gordon Jackson, managing editor of the *Dallas Examiner,* a black-owned newspaper, "are just two totally different situations." Most black newspapers struggle financially. None have permanent foreign correspondents abroad. Black foreign correspondents during World War II were an expression of a crucial time in the history of blacks, not a trend in foreign news-gathering.

In subsequent wars blacks were on the front line of the fighting and the front lines of coverage. "The Negro makes up 9.8 per cent of the military forces in Vietnam," reported Thomas A. Johnson, a black *New York Times* correspondent, in 1968, "but close to 20 per cent of the combat troops and more than 25 per cent of such elite Army units as the paratroops." At the beginning of the Iraq War in 2003, the chief spokesman at the Doha, Qatar, command center was a black general, Vincent Brooks (his brother commanded West Point); only one correspondent representing the black press was there to cover him, George Curry. The National Newspaper Publishers Association—the renamed National Negro Publishers Association—had to scrape together money to send him. Before going to work for the NNPA, Curry had a successful career with the *Chicago Tribune.* Black journalists from the *Washington Post,* the *St. Louis Post-Dispatch,* CBS, and NBC were embedded with troops in the war zone.

Race remains a multifaceted issue for blacks. In one of the better contemporary in-search-of memoirs, Keith Richburg of the *Washington Post* described the experience of being a black foreign correspondent in Africa. He was sometimes able to get news more easily than white reporters and sometimes not. He missed much of the fighting in the brutal Rwandan genocide of 1994 out of fear that he would be mistaken for a Tutsi and killed. Writing a negative story about blacks or Africa,

Richburg recounted, brought charges of betrayal by blacks. This did not stop him from calling attention to the tendency of many black American leaders to countenance human rights abuses in Africa that they would criticize elsewhere and "to offer tortured explanations as to . . . why reform must not be immediate but gradual, step by step. It's as if repression comes only in white."

Curious about their roots, blacks in mainstream media often were interested in being foreign correspondents in Africa. The pattern was repeated for South Asians and Hispanics, who might have been less enthusiastic about foreign correspondence than in having "a roots tour" of the lands of their ancestors, observed Richburg in 2005. This was particularly the case for blacks who grew up in the 1950s and 1960s, an important time for the civil rights movement in the United States and decolonization in Africa.

Jerelyn Eddings was one of the many black correspondents editors sent to cover the final days of apartheid in South Africa in the early 1990s. When the *Baltimore Sun* editors gave her the assignment, the local black community was clamoring for the newspaper to appoint a black in its foreign service. The real breakthrough, she points out, came when editors routinely posted blacks in non-African countries, as happened with Richburg, who also was bureau chief in Hong Kong and embedded with American troops during the Iraq War. The *New York Times'* Howard French was posted in the Caribbean and Central America before going to Africa, and Japan and Shanghai afterward.

Richburg noted how much attitudes had changed when, as the *Post's* foreign editor, he approached several blacks about taking an assignment in Nairobi. They demurred. They preferred Latin America, where they could use their Spanish.

20

THE STRANGE CASE OF EDGAR SNOW

In 1920 Walter Lippmann asked fellow journalist Charles Merz to join him in conducting a test. Like Lippmann, Merz had left the *New Republic* for government service during the war. The two of them worked together on propaganda, which proved itself a potent tool for manipulating the public's view of the world. Much on Lippmann's mind afterward was whether the press could counteract such influences. To test this, he proposed an experiment to evaluate *New York Times* coverage of "one great event in the recent history of the world. That event is the Russian Revolution."

"A Test of the News," which ran in a forty-two-page *New Republic* supplement, presented a severe indictment of one of the best newspapers in the country: *Times* reporting from the Czar's abdication in March 1917 through March 1920 "was nothing short of a disaster." "Hope and fear in the minds of reporters and editors," Lippmann and Merz concluded, had censored the news. The coverage of Russia was "a case of seeing not what was, but what men wished to see."

The *Times* had overestimated both the domestic strength of the provisional government that overthrew the Czar and its power to continue the war against Germany. When the Bolsheviks seized control and it appeared that they might fight on against the Germans, the wishful-thinking *Times* was largely uncritical of the regime. After Lenin took Russia out of the war, the newspaper served up a self-contradictory picture of worldwide Red Peril threatened by a government on the verge of collapse. "No less than ninety-one times was it stated that the Soviets were nearing their rope's end, or actually had reached it," Lippmann and Merz said of a two-year period. The *Times* falsely reported that Lenin and Trotsky had planned flight on four occasions and fled on three; that Lenin had been killed once and imprisoned three times.* At the very same time that the *Times* described the

---

* Lippmann and Merz were not the only ones to draw attention to this pattern. Five months earlier, Francis Musgrave observed in the *Nation,* "We find Lenin's life in considerable danger as a result of the activities of the Associated Press and the *Times. . . .* [Petrograd] has thus far fallen six times, been on the verge of capture at least three times more, has been burned to the ground twice, been in absolute panic twice, has starved to death constantly, and has revolted against the Bolsheviks on no

350

Bolsheviks as tottering, it reported they had advanced against Poland—when, in fact, the Poles had invaded Russia. One *Times* headline proclaimed: "Reds Raising Army to Attack India."

Lippmann and Merz attributed the false reports to lack of press standards. But their indictment did not extend far enough, as Lippmann later recognized. The American public and their officials also viewed the Russian Revolution, as they had viewed the French Revolution, through the lenses of hope and fear. These emotions distorted their reading of the news and created conditions that limited the flow of news and information that reached them.

As one historian noted, self-interest "magnified the Revolution's meaning" for the American public. Americans welcomed the new government, which promised to continue the war. The downfall of the Czar gave Americans a nonmonarchal ally, in the words of President Wilson "a fit partner for a league of honor." Americans looked benignly on the Bolshevik government when it seemed possible they, too, would be allies. When the Bolsheviks made peace with Germany and Austria-Hungary, Americans slipped into what became the default position in U.S.-Soviet relations, fear.

Broad generalizations inevitably run afoul of obvious exceptions. A few Americans—and American journalists—found great hope in the very idea of communism. Even before he arrived in Moscow in 1919, the muckraker Lincoln Steffens was practicing variants of his famous line, "I have seen the future and it works." But this was not the typical gut-level response. Communist revolution threatened Americans' most cherished beliefs about themselves. Americans believed their approach to government was superior and viewed other revolutions as referendums on that superiority. The Russian Revolution ratcheted up American emotions because its alternative state-controlled model was a direct challenge and because the Communists claimed they, not the United States, heralded for the rest of the world a brighter future, which they intended to promote.

These emotions reverberated in the information vacuum that followed the Czar's overthrow. In the early stages of the Russian Revolution, correspondents struggled to find reliable sources among unfamiliar groups vying for power, often behind the scenes. Much of the inaccurate news in the *Times* during the Russian Revolution came from American officials, who had their own agenda, or from dubious characters with an allegiance to the old regime, many of whom were outside the country. When Walter Duranty reported in October 1919 that "the days of the present Bolshevik regime are numbered," he was in Paris. "If the world wants to know what's happening in Russia at the present time," wrote a correspondent in *Everybody's*, "the world must wait until it stops happening."

After the Communists took power, Allied forces including American units advanced into Russia to promote counterrevolution. Not one American correspon-

---

less than six different occasions—all in the columns of the *Times*." Musgrave, "Lenin, the 'Times,' and the Associated Press," *Nation*, March 6, 1920, 293–94.

dent accompanied the anabasis in northern Russia, which produced so little news that Lippmann and Merz could not include it in their study. A British journalist eventually showed up, but he was anti-Bolshevik and, in any case, heavily censored by his countrymen. If Americans were (and to a large extent still are) unaware that they invaded Russia, the Communists were not. The incursions stuck in their minds for years and did nothing to decrease their distrust of Western governments or their natural inclination to manage the news.

Three times the Russians jailed Marguerite Harrison of the *Baltimore Sun,* who secretly passed information to U.S. Army Intelligence. Others were barred, expelled, and censored. "Eleven British and U.S. reporters did manage to reach Moscow in the 1918–1921 interval," historian Robert Desmond noted, "but only two or three were able to work professionally while there." For one stretch during 1920–21, not one Western correspondent was in the Soviet Union. In 1930 only six were. In order to get stories past censors and avoid expulsion, correspondents hid "behind softening euphemisms and compromise phrases," as one of them reported after leaving. Covering the Soviet Union from the outside was unsatisfactory, for doing so meant working in places rife with rumors promoted by anti-Soviet sources. The *Chicago Tribune,* always in the front anti-Communism ranks of the press, favored this approach. Its correspondent in Riga, Latvia, Donald Day, provided a steady stream of negative news, in time developing ties with the Nazis, for whom he later broadcast propaganda from Berlin during World War II.

The United States, the first great power to recognize the provisional government in 1917, was the last to recognize the Soviet Union sixteen years later. When solid firsthand news did arrive in the United States, it was not always welcome. John Reed, who helped to found the American Communist Party, had unparalleled access to the Bolsheviks during the days when they engineered the November revolution. He sent home the first complete report on their success. His full account, *Ten Days That Shook the World,* remains an important primary historical source. But Reed's initial on-the-scene reporting was confined to outlets with limited readerships, the socialist weekly *New York Call* and the radical *Masses.* The latter was put out of business when the government barred it from the mail and tried Reed with six associates for conspiracy under the Espionage Act. No convictions resulted, but the writing of *Ten Days* was delayed for a year because the U.S. authorities seized Reed's papers. Meanwhile, after Stalin came to power, the Soviet government banned Reed's book because it gave a prominent place to his rival Trotsky.

And so, the stage was set. In the coming decades, as Communist revolution spread, foreign correspondents could not work outside the environment of hope and fear. It influenced their reporting and their careers, none more than Edgar Snow's. Snow was the first correspondent to report on the Chinese Communists in the 1930s. His career rose and fell with American emotions about them. It hit rock bottom during the cold war when red baiters zeroed in on his "Strange Case" as an example of journalistic perfidy. Living a life of semi-exile, Snow struggled to open communication between China and the United States.

In their early beginnings, usually far from centers of existing power, revolutions and revolutionaries are wrapped in mystery. Reaching them makes journalistic reputations: Vincent Sheean made his way to Abd el-Krim in the Moroccan Riff; Carleton Beals found Augusto Sandino in Nicaragua; Herbert Matthews of the *New York Times* interviewed Fidel Castro in the Sierra Maestra; Leon Dash of the *Washington Post* spent seven months with the guerrilla forces of Jonas Savimbi's National Union for the Total Independence of Angola (UNITA).

In writing typical of this genre of reporting, Beals concentrated on the thrilling adventure of it all in the articles he wrote for the *Nation* in 1928. His first cable, banged out on a rented typewriter in Managua, read: "HIGH HOUR COLD NIGHT IN TEETH OF ICY WIND IN COMPANY THREE SANDINISTA OFFICERS WHEN EYE GALLOPED INTO MAIN SANDINO CAMP SAN RAFAEL MARKED CLIMAX MONTHS EFFORTS. . . HARDSHIP DANGER BEING SHOT BOMBED BOTH SIDES."

Edgar Snow's "discovery" of the Chinese Communists in 1936 contained standard dramatic elements. Driven into northwest China by Chiang Kai-shek's Nationalist forces, Mao Tse-tung and his followers had been out of sight and widely dismissed as "Red Bandits," just as Sandino was the "TERRIBLE QUOTE BANDIT UNQUOTE OF NICARAGUA." Sometimes Mao was reported dead; sometimes he was reported unhorsed as a leader. Reports in the English-language press in China described the Communists' promoting unchristian "naked body processions." Snow's trek to terra incognita was along a "lonely trail that wound over the interminable loess hills of the northwest," passed through Nationalists' lines, and delivered him "into the laps of those gods which the Chinese Marxists say do not, in fact, exist." Snow spent four months observing the Communists and interviewing their leaders. His return to Beijing was all the more dramatic because, according to reports relayed by the Associated Press, he had been murdered by the Communists when they spotted him writing in his notebook.

If these elements were standard, the effect of his reporting on political thinking was not. John Service, then an American diplomat in China, noted that Snow's report that the Chinese Communists were a viable political movement changed "the China equation." The *Daily Herald* in London gave front-page display to Snow's serialized reports. The *New York Times* and the *New York Sun* quarreled over exclusive rights in the United States. To Snow's surprise, *Life,* a new magazine published by Chiang Kai-shek supporter Henry Luce,* splashed forty-one of his pho-

---

* Luce, born in China of missionary parents, was strongly anti-Communist. *Time,* which he also published, was unenthusiastic about Chiang Kai-shek in the beginning because of his ties with Russian Communists. This attitude changed when Chiang broke with Communists in 1927 and killed thousands of them, and then married Mei-ling Soong, whose Methodist religion he adopted. Twice in the space of just several years, Chiang's picture was on the cover of *Time.* So much control did Luce exert over the content of his magazines that his wartime correspondent in China, Theodore White, posted this sign on his office door in Chungking: "Any similarity between this correspondent's dispatches and what appears in Time is purely coincidental."

tographs across eleven pages of two successive issues. Malcolm Cowley reviewed Snow's book-length account *Red Star over China* in the *New Republic*. "To Edgar Snow," he declared, "goes credit for what is perhaps the greatest single feat performed by a journalist in our century."

In *Red Star* Snow adopted a personal-history approach to enliven the story. The book shared with Reed's *Ten Days* the distinction of being a primary historical source. But unlike Sheean, who was broadly philosophical and self-absorbed, and unlike Reed, whose book was a history of the Bolsheviks' recent rise to power, Snow was an on-the-ground reporter chronicling a powerful force only emerging in China. That force, he was the first independent journalist to report, was willing to make common cause with the Nationalists against the Japanese, a proposal that Chiang Kai-shek was shortly forced to accept as a result of mounting Japanese aggression. Chinese translations of *Red Star* circulated in China before the American edition appeared in the January 1938. Inspired Chinese youngsters tucked the book under their arms and headed for the Communist base in Yenan. *Red Star,* as China scholar John Fairbank later put it, was "an event in modern Chinese history."

Snow was not partisan in anything like the way Reed was. Born in Kansas City, he attended the University of Missouri journalism school until wanderlust struck. He arrived in Shanghai in 1928 on a youthful around-the-world trip, part of the journey traveled as a stowaway. A letter home explaining his motives for travel read like a passage from a book by Richard Halliburton, whom Snow hoped to emulate: "Brooding over my stereotype style of living had to have a culmination. I determined it should be a happy one. And to me, fond ones, happiness at the moment meant but one thing. And that was travel!!! Adventure! And Experience!"

Offered a job on the *China Weekly Review* by fellow Missourian John B. Powell, Snow elected to stay for a while. He instinctively gravitated toward the views of Powell and his mentor Thomas Millard, who desired a modern China independent of the Western powers that enjoyed extensive extraterritorial privileges. "Strange, isn't it," Snow wrote home only three days after arriving in Shanghai, "that this, the most progressive, the wealthiest port in China should be controlled by foreigners! Yet the British and the Americans say it is all right; doubtless it is—for them."

Snow stayed in Asia, becoming a correspondent for the Consolidated Press and then a successful freelance correspondent. As the years rolled on, a gulf grew between Snow and his mentors. Yet in a fundamental way he continued to emulate them. They welcomed Sun Yat-sen and Chiang Kai-shek as the answers to imperial China's problems. Snow came to believe that the Nationalists could not "Lift China out of the Mud," as he had initially speculated they would, and wondered if the answers might reside with yet another political group, the Communists. The ongoing revolution, as he wrote to his brother, "is the people's thumbs down on the rulers of the realm."

Snow developed extensive contacts among the Left: Sun's widow, Mme. Sun Yat-sen, who broke with her husband's successor, Chiang Kai-shek (who also was her brother-in-law); students whom he met while teaching journalism at Yenching University in Beijing; and avant-garde Chinese literary figures who broke with tradition by writing in vernacular and whose books were burned by the Nationalists. Snow translated vernacular stories for a book he called *Living China*. He also read Marxist literature. But ideology was never his forte. Once asked what he thought about Snow, Communist leader Chou En-lai replied that he was "liberal and progressive," but he made the Chinese Communists nervous: "He sometimes tries to explain things in China by saying 'from the Marxist point of view. . . ' as if he had some Marxist authority for what he is saying. The point is that Snow is a man who, by temperament and by intellect, never in his whole life will understand what Marxism is."

Snow's insights lay in understanding the aspirations of the Chinese to shake off foreign domination and seek a better life, aspirations the Communists harnessed. Moreover, whatever Chou En-lai later said about Snow's shortcomings when it came to the "Marxist point of view," his ideological incorrectness was a plus from the Communists' point of view. Having survived Nationalists' attacks and established a base in the Northwest, they had a story to tell outsiders in 1936. They invited Snow because he was an independent journalist who would listen to them and was able to reach a broad audience through such mainstream publications as the *Saturday Evening Post,* the *Chicago Daily News,* and the *New York Herald Tribune.* The great strength of *Red Star* was Snow's faithful reporting of what he saw and heard and how it struck him.

As often happened when Western correspondents encountered revolutionaries, Snow was impressed by the leadership qualities he found in the Chinese Communists and presented them in ways with which readers could identify. Mao and his fellow leaders lived simply, they were informal, and they spoke to people in the people's own terms. The rural setting, with hardworking men and women getting better health care and education, resonated with Snow's Midwest populist instincts. Gaunt, high-cheek-boned Mao, he thought, was "rather Lincolnesque." Many poor farmers complained about the Communists, Snow noted in *Red Star,* "but most of them talked about the Soviets as *womenti chengfu*—'our government'—and this struck me as something new in rural China."

Mixed with this romantic image were unvarnished reports about the political objectives of the Chinese Communist Party. Although the CCP's project in the Northwest was more of a "rural egalitarianism than anything Marx would have found agreeable," they were, after all, Communists. "Every new step taken, every change made, was examined, debated, decided, and integrated in terms of Marxism." The people congregated in Lenin Clubs. The schools in which children learned to read were decorated with hammer-and-sickle emblems. Red propaganda, to Snow's irritation, was relentless. The goal was total revolution. "The Communist Party of China was, is, and will be ever faithful to Marxist-Leninism," Mao told Snow, who quoted him at length, "and it will continue its struggle against every opportunist tendency. In this determination lies one explanation of its invincibility and the certainty of its final victory."

At another time the American public might have seen a menacing power on the horizon. But when *Red Star* appeared, readers were themselves inclined to see

Mao as Lincoln, not Lenin, and along with Lincoln Steffens to think that communism "worked." One factor that prompted Americans to gaze in this direction was the Great Depression, which challenged their confidence in the political and economic system. Many Americans, as a *Baltimore Sun* editorial writer put it, "developed a new and decidedly critical attitude toward certain details of the capitalist system." While Americans were not about to embrace communism, they were open to government economic planning, the most advanced exponent of which was the Soviet Union. Walter Duranty, who in 1919 had reported the Bolsheviks' impending doom, became convinced as the *Times* permanent Moscow correspondent that "the U.S.S.R. is only just beginning to exercise its tremendous potentials." (See "You Can't Make an Omelet without Breaking Eggs," p. 379.) A *Washington Post* review of Duranty's *I Write as I Please,* published in 1935, noted that he "was in the midst of the most interesting social and political experiment of the century." "After all," Edmund Wilson had written in the same vein five years before, "the Communist project has almost all the qualities that Americans glorify—the extreme of efficiency and economy combined with the ideal of a herculean feat to be accomplished by common action in an atmosphere of enthusiastic boosting—like a Liberty Loan drive—the idea of putting over something big in five years." John Reed Clubs, sponsored by the American Communist Party, sprang up. In 1933 Roosevelt reversed the policy of the preceding Republican administrations and extended diplomatic recognition to the USSR. The USSR encouraged these positive feelings. The next year it became a member of the League of Nations and began determined efforts to build a barrier of collective security against the increasing power of Fascist Italy and Nazi Germany.

This cartoon depicting Lincoln Steffens and his famous comment appeared in the *New Masses* in 1932, a year when the Depression in the United States prompted Americans to look to the Soviet Union for possible solutions.

Americans worried about fascist military aggression in China as well as in Europe. With the Japanese-instigated Marco Polo Bridge incident outside Beijing in July 1937, war engulfed China. The subsequent Japanese attack on Shanghai produced one of the most searing images of the era, a *Life* photograph of a terrified Chinese baby sitting in the grim wreckage of a bombed rail depot. China's plight engendered widespread American sympathy. Only 2 percent of the public was pro-Japanese, poll data showed. But Americans were not interested in collective action to help the Chinese. They wanted to stay out of their war. After the Japanese sank the U.S. gunboat *Panay* in the Yangtze River in December 1937, killing three Americans, the share of Americans favoring total withdrawal from the Far East jumped from 54 to 70 percent. Humorist Will Rogers summed up American public sentiment (as he often did) while touring China in the early 1930s to collect material for his syndicated newspaper column. "The news of this war," he told a reporter, "is that WE WANT TO KEEP OUT OF IT."

Red Star, which appeared a few days after the *Panay* sinking, offered a reassuring message to the many Americans whose concerns Rogers summed up. The Chinese Communists were strengthening the Nationalists' ability to resist Japan. The cover of a revised and updated edition of the book that came out six months later proclaimed:

IS THE BOOK THAT TELLS WHY
JAPAN CAN'T WIN!

Red Star drew sharp criticism both from the Nationalists, who urged Americans in China to spread the word that Snow "was a Communist agent or spokesman," and from American and Russian Communists. According to the latter's ideological faith, Moscow was the vital center for all Marxist revolution. Snow challenged that doctrine and, to strengthen the point, emphasized his words with italics: *"The Soviet movement and the Chinese Red Army began spontaneously, under purely Chinese leadership."* What is more, he wrote, the Comintern could "be held responsible for serious reverses." Its Communist sensitivities offended, the *New Masses* refused advertisements for *Red Star.*

Reviewers in the mainstream press raved about the book and, reflecting the hope and fear of their readers, focused on Communists' anti-Japanese resolve, their short-term reforms, and Snow's adventures getting the story. Some short reviews did not even use the words *communism, Marxism,* or, except to note the book's title, *red.* "The 'Red bandits,'" a *New York Times* reviewer concluded, "bear a close resemblance to the people we used to call patriots." A *Milwaukee Journal* reviewer compared the Communists to "primitive Christians." "How Red are the Reds?" John Gunther asked in *Inside Asia,* published shortly after *Red Star* and drawing on it. "Not very, by our standards," he concluded. "What the Chinese Reds stand for is agrarian reform. The movement is not communism, in that it does not even advocate nationalization of the land; what it advocates is tremendous land reform."

Subsequently other correspondents made their way to the Chinese Communist headquarters in Yenan. They routinely returned with glowing reports. People were better fed than in the Nationalists' area. The Communists made do for themselves rather than living off the peasants. They were fighting the war, as evidenced by the presence of far more Japanese prisoners than reporters saw elsewhere. A 1944 story by *New York Times* correspondent Brooks Atkinson ran under the headline "YENAN, A CHINESE WONDERLAND CITY." Atkinson described a happy population that worked ten hours a day, had "a 100 per cent food surplus," and enjoyed free plays every night. Going from Nationalist to Communist areas was like going "from hell to heaven," later recalled Arch Steele, a hardnosed journalist who at one time or another reported from the Far East for the *Chicago Daily News,* the *New York Herald Tribune,* and the *New York Times.* "We were," he wrote, "reluctant to paint them as real Communists, though, because we knew that that would go against the American grain. If you took a favorable attitude toward the Communists, it would probably have created, in the eyes of the publisher, a feeling that the correspondent in question was maybe pro-Communist."

Snow visited the Communists again in 1939 and asked Mao if the Communists were "merely reformers." "We are always social revolutionaries," the leader replied, "we are never reformists." Snow attempted to set the record straight in his next book, *The Battle for Asia.* "My personal feeling in the matter," he wrote, "is that liberals who build up hopes that the Communists of China are 'different' and 'only reformers' and have abandoned revolutionary methods to achieve their program, are doomed to ultimate disillusionment." The Communists shed red stars from their military caps in concession to the United Front, Snow noted, only to pin the emblems "just inside their left breast pockets."

After Snow's second visit, the Nationalists effectively sealed off Yenan from visitors. Snow, the first foreign correspondent to reach Communists in the Northwest, was the last until the summer of 1944. His authority on the Chinese Communists was assured; full appreciation of his point of view was not. In a private meeting with President Roosevelt in 1942, Snow emphasized that the Communists were real Communists. FDR insisted on calling them "so-called Communists." When he met with Snow for the last time in 1945, the president said they aimed for agrarian reform.

Snow was at the top of his profession when he finally returned to the United States in early 1941. The *Saturday Evening Post* hired him with a handsome salary. In addition to having access to the *Post*'s large readership, he had wide latitude to roam and the time to report in depth. During the war Snow reported from China, Russia, India, and Europe. He and Jack Bell of the *Chicago Daily News* were the first correspondents to reach Vienna in 1944. He covered postwar Japan and the independence of India. Books based on these assignments were well received. In 1944 the *Post* named him associate editor. The Book-of-the-Month Club, which selected one of his wartime books, noted that a *Saturday Evening Post* poll placed Snow "first and way in the lead" as subscribers' favorite war reporter.

This fame, however, rested on shifting sands of public opinion.

During the war, the fascist Germany and Japan were feared enemies, the Communist Soviet Union a hard-fighting ally. Most newspapers and even conservative magazines such as *Life, National Geographic, Reader's Digest,* and the *Rotarian* accentuated the positive over the negative in reporting on the Soviet Union. *Time* named Stalin "the man of the year" for 1942. "He collectivized the farms and built Russia into one of the four great industrial powers on earth," the magazine reported. Given the similarities between the two countries, it added, the United States, "of all nations, should have been the first to understand Russia." The *New York Times'* performance was better than during the Bolshevik Revolution, but it, too, tended to report in a "Pollyanna fashion" when American and Soviet interests were aligned, concluded a scholar who brought the Lippmann-Merz study up to date. In a Gallup poll at the end of 1943, nearly twice as many Americans said the Russians could be trusted to cooperate after the war as those who said they could not.

With peacetime, however, interests diverged and fear took over once again. The Soviet Union sought to enhance its security through territorial acquisition and installation of governments that answered to it, setting in motion countermeasures and mutual distrust. In 1946, financier and statesman Bernard Baruch led a U.S. effort to put in place United Nations controls on nuclear weapons that at the same time allowed the United States to maintain its atomic weapons monopoly. The plan was unacceptable to the Soviets, who used their veto on the Security Council to kill the measure. The following year, Baruch gave a name to this era, the cold war. In a speech written by his feisty old friend Herbert Bayard Swope, whose retirement from journalism did not keep him out of politics, Baruch said, "Let us not be deceived—we are today in the midst of a cold war. Our enemies are to be found abroad and at home."*

China was one of the battlegrounds. As the Nationalists faltered, Americans foresaw that a Red tide would "smash across the Pacific Islands and cover the United States—all according to Soviet plan." To the insistent question Who lost China? Snow's name was often answered. With disregard for all that he had written, he was charged with insidiously promoting the myth that the Chinese were simple agrarian reformers. "One pro-Communist article in the *Saturday Evening Post* can do more damage than ten years of the *New Masses* or the *Daily Worker,*" wrote the author of a typical book of the period, *While You Slept: Our Tragedy in Asia and Who Made It.*

In *Post* articles republished in 1947 as *Stalin Must Have Peace,* Snow argued that the Soviets wanted security, not armed conflict, that the United States should help them rebuild with loans and credits—a policy that, as he put it, recognized that "external peace and the prosperity of other nations are inseparably linked with our own domestic peace and internal prosperity." He also challenged the popular con-

---

* To Swope's chagrin, Lippmann was widely credited with coining the term, which he used for his 1947 book *The Cold War.*

vention of monolithic communism. He described Yugoslavia's defiance of the Soviets in 1948 as offering "the first effective frontier against *the expansion of world communism as an extension of Russian nationalism*."

In April 1949, when the Communists were about to take control of China, Snow spelled out why the new regime would not become a pawn of the Kremlin. The *Saturday Evening Post* article, excerpted below, drew on Snow's many years of covering the Chinese.

Will China Become a Russian Satellite?
By Edgar Snow

. . . Will a communist-led government inevitably mean that China must fall under the absolute domination of the Kremlin?. . .

In some quarters I have been derided as the creator of "the exceptionalist theory" for China. It has never been my contention that the Chinese communists are "not real Marxists." But internal evidence did convince me that they will not give "absolute obedience" to the Kremlin—the basic test of anyone accepted as satisfactory by Moscow. After a dozen years of firsthand study of China I concluded that Soviet Russia would not hold effective domination over the extremely nation-conscious Chinese communists. . . .

First, consider some geopolitical facts of fundamental significance. China is an immense country—almost as large as the United States, and with two times Soviet Russia's population. It is rich in human and natural resources, with an ancient civilization that has survived 3000 years of catastrophes to keep its basic values intact. China is the first country among all the colonies and semicolonies in which communists have won power. From their beginnings, China's Marxist leaders have, in theory, been internationalists. In practice they have been nationalists continuing an independence movement.

Second, China is the first major power, outside Russia, to fall into the hands of avowed Marxists. Very important: it has, in contrast with Eastern Europe, a markedly lower standard of living than the U.S.S.R. as a whole.

Third, the Chinese Red Army—or People's Liberation Army, as it now calls itself—fought its major battles for survival long before the recent war, and without any Soviet aid. Excepting Yugoslavia, China has the only communists who actually came to power without direct political or military dependence upon Russian arms.

Fourth, the Chinese party alone in the world today is led by a communist who has never been to Russia. He is the only communist chieftain ever expelled from a party—not once, but several times—who remained in power despite a Comintern order for his removal. Mao Tse-tung and Chu Teh—now commander in chief of the Chinese communist forces—adopted an independent line in 1927–28, launched their own agrarian program and set up the Red Army, and first soviet, without party directives. Mao is the only communist leader— Tito excepted—who has publicly criticized Moscow's agents. . . .

Fifth, as a result of long isolation and independent development, the Chinese

Communist Party has acquired immense experience and self-confidence. Decades of civil war have trained great numbers of competent military and political leaders. China now has the largest Communist Party outside Russia—more than 3,000,000 members—and more than 2,000,000 troops backed by millions of armed peasants. It is one thing for Russian generals to push around military or political bosses in the small occupied states of Europe. It is quite another problem to manage a giant the size of China, run by a disciplined party in control of a great army—which knows it could make a good defense of its independence against any foreign power.

Sixth, Mao Tse-tung's personality is reflected in the internal structure of a party that is—whatever one may think of its methods or what it upholds ideologically—deeply Chinese in composition. It is doubtful if 10 per cent of the members of the central committee are Soviet-educated. In the rank and file not one in 10,000 has been to Russia. They have learned their Marxism largely from the history of the Chinese party, the Chinese revolution, the textbooks and doctrines worked out in the writings of Mao Tse-tung and other native leaders. Virtually all the veterans who form the hard core of this party, men now in their fifties and sixties, are products of more than twenty years of common history *made in China*. They could not now be seriously divided by outside critics.

Seventh, the Chinese communists were, until the Belgrade schism, the only non-Russian party which dared openly proclaim that it had made vital new contributions to the theory and revolutionary practice of Marxism. "Mao Tse-tung has created a Chinese or Asiatic form of Marxism," one of the Politburo members at Yenan told an American correspondent. "His great accomplishment has been to change Marxism from its European to its Asiatic form. He is the first who succeeded in doing so." A dangerous thought, of a variety unlikely to please the Kremlin. . . .

China now represents a long-range problem of "management" for the Kremlin, which can either be simplified or greatly complicated by American policy. So long as it is true that the United States is the main support of the old regime in China, and of any or all anticommunist parties, groups, politicians or war lords prepared to continue what is now clearly a lost war, Americans will easily hold their present position as Foreign Enemy No. 1. . . .

As it came to pass, American policy "simplified" matters for the Soviets. The United States withheld diplomatic recognition of China. The Chinese adopted a Soviet economic model that emphasized development of heavy industry.* Thousands of So-

---

* It is unclear why the Chinese chose the Soviet model. As China scholar Jonathan Spence has noted, it may have been the only possible choice in view of the failure of the Nationalists to succeed "at reform along Western lines, and after the Korean War and the mass campaigns against foreigners left China further isolated from Western power. China's use of the Soviet model was certainly one

viet technicians came as advisers. Moscow made military equipment available, including licenses to manufacture jet fighters.

As Snow foresaw, however, the ties between Beijing and Moscow did not bind. Mao visited Moscow only twice. On the first visit, in late 1949, he was none too happy with the stalling tactics Stalin used in negotiating formal agreements. The Kremlin, for its part, resented Chinese claims made for the brilliance of Mao's political theorizing, which called into question some of its own. Nor did it welcome Mao's subsequent call for continuous revolution, which was considered a Trotskyite concept and took Chinese development off the course dictated by the Soviet model. The Soviets were at odds in other ways as well. While the Chinese looked to the Soviets for support against an American nuclear attack, they wanted their own bomb, and the Soviets' nuclear assistance stopped short of providing a prototype. After Stalin's death, Nikita Khrushchev took both theoretical and policy lines at odds with the Chinese.

In 1960, with frustration mounting, the Sino-Soviet conflict came out in the open. The Soviets withdrew their advisers. When they called for a meeting of Communist parties from around the world several months later, Mao refused to attend. As he had said in mid-1949, the Chinese Communist Party "is no longer a child or a lad in his teens but has become an adult."

Snow was not entirely alone in his views. Colleagues like Vincent Sheean shared concern about policies that heightened Soviet feelings of insecurity. Walter Lippmann, whose syndicated column for the *New York Herald Tribune* was the nation's most influential, argued for giving loans to the Soviets and finding other ways to promote negotiation. Lippmann, Snow commented to a *Saturday Evening Post* editor in 1947, "seems to have been looking over my shoulder."

But few read off the same page as Snow, whose prophecies about China did not fit into the picture formed in the minds of the great majority of Americans—a picture the editors of the *Saturday Evening Post* were reluctant to tamper with. They did not want "strongly slanted Leftie articles," as they told Jack Belden a few months earlier when they did not use his eyewitness articles on the Chinese civil war. The editors ran a note at the top of Snow's story "Will China Become a Russian Satellite?" It read: "The Post is by no means as hopeful as Mr. Snow is that a Communist China can remain outside the orbit of Soviet Russia." The article was the only one Snow wrote for the magazine that year.

Snow never appeared before a congressional investigating committee on Communist influence. He was, however, scrutinized in articles with titles like "Red Star over Independence Square: The Strange Case of Edgar Snow and *The Saturday Evening Post*"—Independence Square being the address of the *Post*'s Philadelphia

---

way of emphasizing the anti-capitalist and anti-imperialist nature of the new Chinese state." Jonathan D. Spence, *The Search for Modern China* (New York: W. W. Norton, 1990), 541.

headquarters. The phrase "strange case," which was applied to others besides Snow, was ideal for its intended purpose.

A strange case did not have to stand up to serious scrutiny. Nebulous connections, vague inferences, selective evidence brought in a verdict. One victim of the sort of reasoning that prevailed was correspondent Robert St. John, who had his passport lifted while he was living in Geneva in 1954; among the reasons were his "contacts with representatives of Communist governments"—never mind that such contacts were hardly unusual for a foreign correspondent, especially one researching a book on postwar Yugoslavia. Similarly, something must be amiss, fearful Americans thought, if Communists read a correspondent's book. Similarly, Snow must be obedient to Moscow because of the changes he made to *Red Star* following American Communists' criticism of the book, even though the points Moscow found the most objectionable remained.* An FBI analysis of one of Snow's articles concluded that his reporting was not well founded because it deviated from stated U.S. policy. The fact that he wrote for the conservative *Saturday Evening Post* showed how devious he was. As the "Red Star over Independence Square" article averred, Snow was, "without a doubt, one of the cleverest, smoothest, and most subtle advocates the Kremlin has ever had on its side."

Congressional investigations gave impetus to a vast apparatus designed to root

* Snow did make changes in early editions of *Red Star* related to the role of the Soviet Union in China. He was not certain he fully understood the CCP-USSR relationship, much of which was below the surface when he visited the Chinese in the Northwest. He was concerned, too, about criticism from American Communists who reflected Moscow's point of view. He believed party squabbling deflected thinking from what really mattered, fascist aggression. Even so, Snow's minor revisions could hardly have satisfied the Soviets. For instance, he took out a reference to the "dictatorship of Stalin," which might have been viewed as positive, but he collaterally made a point of deemphasizing the influence of the Comintern in China, which was not. Still standing—and still emphasized—were the points that troubled Soviet Communists most of all, that the Comintern had made mistakes in China and that the CCP had arisen largely on its own, with little help from Moscow.

A similar pattern occurred in Snow's response to CCP concerns before *Red Star* appeared. Chou, who criticized Chiang as a bad leader who could not even ride a horse properly, subsequently asked Snow not to use the comments because they might hurt the nascent United Front. With some irritation, Snow agreed to take these out of the manuscript, which overall was remarkably free of criticism of Chiang. He did not, however, make changes on a more significant point: in articles written shortly after his return from the Northwest, Snow said the CCP would not abandon the class struggle during the United Front. Word subsequently reached him that Mao thought he should downplay this point. Nevertheless, *Red Star* made it clear that the class struggle remained an important component of CCP thinking.

Well before Snow had to insist to Red baiters that he was not a Communist, he found himself making the same point to the Communists themselves. "You know I am not a Communist," he told Earl Browder, secretary of the American Communist Party, expressing his concern about internecine political controversy over the book. "[It] was not expected that I should return with the report of a Comintern agent. . . . It is help for China that primarily interests me." With regard to Snow's changes to *Red Star,* see a fuller discussion in Hamilton, *Edgar Snow,* 86, 93–96, 198–99; also Edgar Snow to Earl Browder, March 20, 1938, Snow Papers.

out Communists and their influence. The State Department, which ousted superb foreign service officers in the interest of purification, removed and sometimes burned suspect books in embassy libraries. Special-interest groups such as the American Legion and the China Lobby, a network of Chiang Kai-shek supporters, pitched in. News organizations did their part. CBS administered loyalty oaths, did its own investigations, and maintained blacklists that kept questionable characters such as Theodore White from appearing on its programs. White, a former *Time* correspondent in China, was tainted because of his anti–Chiang Kai-shek comments, which made him, like St. John, a victim of the "Limitations on Issuance of Passports to Persons Supporting Communist Movements." Robert Hutchins, president of the University of Chicago and a promoter of media responsibility, scolded American newspaper editors at their annual meeting in 1955: "And what of freedom in the garrison state? Since most of you take the official line that the only important fact of life is our imminent dangers from the international conspiracy, most of you have watched the erosion of freedom without a twinge."

Snow ran into difficulties getting his passport renewed, an irony considering that the Soviets refused him a visa because they disliked his reporting. His books were among those removed from State Department libraries abroad. Alfred Kohlberg, a wealthy importer of Chinese lace who supported the China Lobby, described Snow as "a plain, unmitigated liar in attempting to make a case for the Communists." Snow's FBI files bulged with odds and ends of information and weird directives. In one an agent was instructed to "discreetly obtain" a copy of one of his books. Although Snow grew "sick to death" of defending himself from the "old canard" about agrarian reform, the habit of it made him reflexively defensive. When FBI agents called on him one day in 1951, he assumed they were interested in his alleged transgression. When they inquired instead about another journalist, he nevertheless volunteered about himself, as the agents later reported, "that in his writing concerning China for the past 15 years, he has stated on numerous occasions that the Chinese Communists are not agrarian reformers but are Communists in every sense of the word."

Old journalistic admirers became adversaries, sometimes working in the open, sometimes not. One of these was Henry Luce, who had written to Snow after *The Battle for Asia* appeared in 1941 to say "how deeply indebted I feel to you for that masterly book." Luce, however, was a strong supporter of the China Lobby. His magazine *Life* sounded the charge against spreading Communism in a 1946 editorial: "It has been rediscovered that the capitalist world is Russia's inevitable enemy." As Luce's biographer concluded, "Probably more than any other single force, the Lucepress channeled the groping and disorganized emotion of American distress into McCarthyism." The *Saturday Evening Post* suspected Luce was a source of rumors that Snow was a Communist, a label that surfaced, among other places, in a 1952 *New York Times* article by James Reston loosely and damningly lumping Snow with "a mixed crew of Communists and liberals."

McCarthyism silenced many journalists who made a name for themselves abroad. Carleton Beals, the journalist who discovered Sandino, had been outspoken in his left-leaning views about Latin America. His description of a U.S.-backed government in Guatemala as "a military dictatorship" prompted Vice-President Richard Nixon to request an FBI investigation, something the FBI already had done without turning up anything adequately "subversive." Still, in the climate of the times, few publications were interested in Beals's reporting. To put food on the table, he wrote New England history books for high schools.

Quentin Reynolds took a similar tack when Hearst columnist Westbrook Pegler tagged him as a Communist sympathizer and *Collier's* severed its ties with him. While waiting for the courts to reach a verdict on his libel suit (which eventually brought him a sizable financial settlement), Reynolds wrote biographies of Gen. George Custer and St. Patrick for Random House's Landmark book series for kids. J. B. Powell's son John kept the *China Review* alive as a monthly in Shanghai after 1949. Hopeful about the Communists, he criticized U.S. policy in Asia and charged that America had been involved with germ warfare during World War II and in Korea. American postal authorities occasionally banned the monthly from the mails. Upon returning to the United States in 1953, Powell and his wife were indicted for sedition. The government did not drop its case until 1961, by which time Powell had begun a new career in San Francisco restoring old homes. After Theodore White finally persuaded the State Department to give him a passport in 1954, he decided to find something else to write about. "From 1954 to 1972," he ruefully commented in his memoir, "I never wrote another article about the China I knew so well; and only four articles on Vietnam. . . . Too much danger lurked there."

Snow's editors at the *Post* urged him to take a similar approach. They liked him and wanted him to stay, not resign as he proposed. Snow begrudgingly wrote several articles on American cities and a piece on an acting troupe. But having been influential, not willing to give up his old freedom to write on foreign affairs, and earnest in the extreme about promoting a better policy toward China, he went about the tasks half-heartedly. With Independence Square inundated with critical mail and Snow troubled by the *Post's* cold war editorial politics, he and the editors gradually came to understand that they could not coexist. When Snow again offered his resignation, the editors sadly accepted it.

Snow's career went into a tailspin at a particularly bad time for him personally. After divorcing his first wife, Helen, he had married actress Lois Wheeler and soon had two young children to worry about. The ever-liberal *Nation*, where he could still be published, had a small audience and paid very little. Looking for other ways to make money, he tried a children's' book and a musical, the latter working with musician Sam Zimbalist, a neighbor in Sneden's Landing outside New York City. Neither project made it to the finish line. The family of Chicago plumbing manufacturer Charles Crane, who had been ambassador to China and a Thomas Millard supporter, paid Snow to work on a biography of Crane that was never published. Snow's autobiographical "personal history" appeared in 1958 as *Journey to the Beginning*. Despite some good reviews, readers' enthusiasm was not what it had been in an earlier era.

Eager to get abroad again, Snow accepted an offer to teach the next year in the

International School of America, a high school program that combined classes with around-the-world travel. Snow relocated his family to Switzerland for what he planned to be one year. The Swiss exile lasted the rest of his life.

Diplomat George Kennan is often credited with creating the framework for the aggressive postwar containment policy of the United States toward the Soviet Union through his anonymous 1947 "Mr. X" article in *Foreign Affairs.* Later he repudiated that policy. He had ineptly stated his position, Kennan said, and hardliners had run away with his concept. He meant to advocate policies much like those advocated by Walter Lippmann. Although he did not correct the record in the heat of the moment, in internal communications Kennan counseled against "hysterical anti-Sovietism," which would confound not only international relations but American democracy itself: "The greatest danger that can befall us in coping with this problem of Soviet communism is that we shall allow ourselves to become like those with whom we are coping." Kennan's fears materialized on the domestic front with the Red Scare, which in turn made it difficult to fashion a realistic policy toward China.

After the Chinese marched into Beijing, President Harry Truman's secretary of state, Dean Acheson, supported recognition of the People's Republic of China (PRC) to keep the Chinese from forming closer relations with Moscow. Three months later the president proclaimed that the United States would not intercede to prevent the Communist invasion of Taiwan, where the Nationalists established their much-diminished Republic of China. But the window of opportunity for the realistic, enlightened debate about policy that Kennan had advocated quickly slammed shut. The Korean War, which erupted shortly after the Communist takeover of China, was yet another sign to each side of the implacable hostility of the other. It fueled the witch hunt in the United States as well as parallel domestic emotions in China. The United States announced support of the Nationalists on Taiwan, where it positioned weapons that added to the menace from the Chinese point of view.

By the end of 1954, Senator Joseph McCarthy was discredited. The *Saturday Evening Post* was among the journals that had had enough of him. But as Kennan despairingly noted, "McCarthyism was never decisively rejected by the political establishment of the country." The charge of being a Red or a fellow traveler or soft on Communism remained politically potent. It broke careers and lost elections.

An emblematic moment in Sino-American diplomatic relations—or the lack of them—came in 1954 when Secretary of State John Foster Dulles encountered Chou En-lai during a Geneva conference. The Chinese premier held out his hand. "I cannot," Dulles said and left the room. He similarly turned aside information brought by an aide that the Chinese Communists were prepared to release American prisoners from the Korean War and talk about normalizing relations.

In Dulles's view, correspondents should not have contact with the Chinese Communists either, and his view prevailed. In October 1949, the new government in China had ordered the departure of correspondents from countries with whom it did not have diplomatic relations. In its determination to seal off the bacillus of communism, the State Department buttressed the wall that blocked the view of China by invalidating passports for travel to the PRC. Beginning in 1954, the Chinese periodically indicated they would welcome visits by U.S. journalists. At one point the Associated Press excitedly named a Beijing bureau chief, whom it sent out to buy office supplies. Still, the State Department refused to cooperate.

"There are many reasons for this," Dulles told *New York Times* publisher Arthur Sulzberger in 1957. Two of them were "the existence of a quasi-state of war" and the increased prestige that would come to the Communists if correspondents could visit. Under considerable pressure from Sulzberger and other journalists, Dulles changed his mind in 1957, but the Chinese rescinded their invitation because the State Department would not reciprocate with a parallel permission for Chinese journalists to enter the United States.

In 1956, David Lancashire, a Canadian working on a freelance basis for the Associated Press, entered China for three months. That same year three American correspondents defied the ban—William Worthy, a black reporter with the *Baltimore Afro-American* who worked out an arrangement to file for CBS; *Look*'s Moscow correspondent Edmund Stevens; and one of the magazine's photographers. The Cowles family, which owned Midwest newspapers as well as *Look* and were Republican in sympathy, were disappointed in Dulles's foreign policies. In Gardner Cowles's view, "the American people had a right to know what was going on behind the bamboo curtain." When the State Department learned that Stevens and the photographer were in China, it protested that their visit hampered negotiations over the release of ten Americans held in Chinese jail. Cowed, the magazine told the pair to leave. Back in Moscow, where he was based, Stevens was told his passport was now invalid for all travel except to return to the United States. After legal wrangling, a deal was struck in which his passport remained valid on the understanding that he would not return to China. His month-long trip resulted in just one substantial *Look* article. Worthy's trip took a similar turn. After his first broadcast from Beijing, which also disputed the view that the PRC verged on collapse, the State Department successfully pressured CBS not to air any more of his reports. When Worthy returned to the United States, he met with CBS correspondent Eric Sevareid, who wrote a report criticizing the State Department. CBS killed Sevareid's story.* In 1958, the State Department made an exception for a farm editor who was allowed to visit China. His reports were syndicated by a feature service, the Newspaper Enterprise Association. *Look*, still interested in China, carried a short article by him.

---

* Undeterred by having his passport lifted when he returned, Worthy continued to travel, visiting Hungary and Cuba, both forbidden countries. In an interview years later, Worthy noted, "We see only what is already in our eye. We learn only what we are already inwardly prepared to accept." From a profile by Phyllis Graber Jensen on the Web site of Bates College, which Worthy attended. http://abacus.bates.edu/pubs/mag/95-Fall/worthy.html (accessed July 24, 2007).

These diplomatic games frustrated Snow's aspirations to return to China. In addition, he needed someone to pay his way and was unwilling to accept Chinese financial favors. When he finally arranged to go in mid-1960, he had a book contract from Random House and magazine commissions from *Look*. The State Department as well as a few legislators tried to persuade Gardner Cowles to change his mind. When that failed, Snow was approved under the rubric of "journalist." The Chinese admitted him in a different category, "writer." In his conversations with Snow in China, Chou En-lai insisted he was admitted as a "writer and a historian, not a correspondent."

Snow's visit was the first by an American correspondent who had covered China before the revolution. During the five-month trip, he traveled to fourteen of the country's twenty-two provinces and interviewed scores of Chinese. His interview with Mao was the first the CCP chairman had given an American journalist since 1949. The journey had elements of Snow's 1936 trip to northwest China. He was visiting people not well known and largely misunderstood. There were errant reports that Mao was dead and that the Chinese were adopting the Russian alphabet.

This time, however, Snow worked under conditions that were far different in both China and America from those of the 1930s. No matter how determined Snow was to get information—and he went about the task with characteristic determination—it was difficult to gather facts independently. China was a tightly controlled society. A Western correspondent, let alone an American one, was a rarity. It was impossible for Snow to move about without being an event himself. Getting Chinese to speak frankly was problematic. "At formal interviews there was generally an official or interpreter present," he wrote in his book-length account, *The Other Side of the River: Red China Today*, "and nobody bares his soul to either one, especially with a foreigner around." Under these circumstances, no mine or factory quota was ever underfilled, and it was "difficult to get a well-trained Chinese Communist to answer a question which hypothesizes a situation he knows to be the incorrect outcome of reform." Even people he knew well were not always forthcoming.

"The limits of education by travel," as Snow put it, were apparent in his reporting on food production. Pursuing his idea of ongoing revolution, Mao launched the Great Leap Forward in 1958. This misguided program promoted disastrous farming practices and led to sharp drops in food production. The tragedy was compounded by inflated production figures reported up from the local level, which gave the government the confidence to export food. The real dimensions of the catastrophe were not yet known when Snow visited. Snow went to great pains to calculate production, reckoning the 1960 harvest at 152 million tons. That figure turned out to be less than 6 percent above the actual level of production—a good estimate and a credit to Snow's doggedness, considering that Chinese officials gave out a far higher number, as did many experts, and that the actual data were not available for decades. Yet, basing his conclusion on the small part of China he saw and what he heard, Snow greatly underestimated the impact of the food shortfall, concluding that there might be some "isolated instance of starvation due to neglect or failure of the rationing system. . . . Considerable malnutrition undoubtedly existed. Mass starvation? No." In fact, as many as 30 million may have perished.

In their conversations in 1960, Chou told Snow that he was admitted as a writer-historian because the Chinese did not want to set a precedent for dealing with American journalists. Snow brushed this mislabeling aside: "Who cared? The story was the thing." But the contrived title underscored that he was, after all, a special case, and that mattered a great deal.

Snow was heavily invested in the story. His discovery of the Chinese Communists in the 1930s had brought him fame, and now he was on the defensive both personally and in larger ways. Knowing that the news about the PRC was thoroughly negative and that his visit was a unique opportunity, Snow felt a special responsibility to correct American perceptions of the PRC.

These circumstances did not stop him from reporting that American freedoms did not exist in China or from expressing doubt about industrial and agricultural figures. When told that one of the Chinese writers he had worked with in the 1930s was enjoying himself in the countryside and "no longer interested in writing," Snow was dubious: this was "a change of character I could not at all imagine." He was as frank as the best social scientist in explaining the difficulties he encountered in his reporting.

But in seeking to balance the scales (and limited in what he could find out), Snow put more weight on finding the positive and offsetting the negative. He offered explanations and excuses that he would not have used before. Yes, Mao was brutal, but so was Chiang Kai-shek, and Mao was not as bad as Stalin. The efforts to glorify Mao rankled Snow, but he backed into his criticism: "In so far as the Mao 'cult' is reminiscent of the synthetic beatification of Stalin when he was alive, it is to any Westerner nauseating in the same degree." Snow didn't listen to the nagging voice inside him about the cult of Mao, which gave the Communist leader power to crush political opponents and cynically promote the destructive Cultural Revolution.

Nevertheless, Snow's reporting established that Communist China was firmly in place. Despite the CCP's tragic Great Leap, the country was making progress. "China's most remarkable achievement during the past three decades," a World Bank report noted in 1983, "has been to make low-income groups far better off in terms of basic needs than their counterparts in most other poor countries." Snow's interviews with Chou had diplomatic news value as well. China, said the premier, was open to discussions with the United States. Chou had two provisos: that disputes "should be settled through peaceful negotiations" and that the United States withdraw forces from Taiwan. But Chou said details on withdrawal could be worked out much later. The premier also gave Snow Beijing's first "official acknowledgement of any differences or dissimilarities" between China and the Soviet Union.

Snow was to remain a special link with the Chinese Communists. "You have made China practically a monopoly!" Harrison Salisbury of the *New York Times* congratulated Snow after his next trip in 1964–65. That visit was the last by an American reporter before the outbreak of the Cultural Revolution. And in 1970

Snow became the first to return afterward. Although the Chinese leadership gave him misleading information in interviews, they also sent important signals. In 1965 Snow left China with the first statement by a CCP official—Mao—that Chinese troops would not fight in Vietnam.

Getting these interviews in front of the American public remained difficult. Editors were wary of anything that came from Communists, and Snow felt an obligation to ensure that the Communist leaders' views were expressed in full, not chopped up by American editors whose preconceived sentiments might result in distortion. "The interviews," Snow said, in one of several standoffs with the *New York Times* that led to rejection, "were given to me with the understanding that I would secure intact publication and in sequences, and that they were official even if in part paraphrase. They could be edited or rearranged only if I myself could justify it.... If it had been my own story and not an official interview-cum-talk I could have been amenable to any reasonable Times' improvements."

Although Snow tried to dismiss Chou's point about his historian status and joked to his wife about the Chinese calling him a "friendly personage," these titles troubled him. As determined as he was to remain his own man, Snow could never extricate himself from their implications. When he met with Mao in 1970, the chairman wanted to interview *him*. In his diary, Snow fretted that he could not give "realistic answers." He did not speak for the American government. Yet, he added, "no one can entirely avoid responsibility for power. It bothers me greatly that I have not solved this contradiction in my lifetime."

Snow had not been passive in the 1930s and 1940s. "In this international cataclysm brought on by fascists it is no more possible for any people to remain neutral than it is for a man surrounded by bubonic plague to remain 'neutral' toward the rat population. Whether you like it or not, your life as a force is bound either to help the rats or hinder them. Nobody can be immunized against the germs of history." It was this that led him to translate patriotic Chinese fiction into English, rather than work on his own reporting. Although he disliked being diverted from journalism, he helped start cooperatives to keep the Chinese economy going during the 1930s. He withheld Communists' negative comments on the Nationalists in the interests of keeping the United Front intact.

Such self-censorship was unremarkable at the time. Vincent Sheean's *Personal History* appealed to journalists because his quest was a search for "my place in relation" to the human struggle then under way. In China, correspondents' win-the-war attitude prompted them to withhold negative information about the corruption and ineptness of Chiang's regime while promoting the view of a workable United Front with the Communists, who seemed far more patriotic and democratic than their sometime allies. In the late 1930s, concluded historian Kenneth Shewmaker, American correspondents "looked at the brighter side of the landscape and refrained from smudging their canvases with shaded pastels." Not until 1944, when the rift between Chiang and his American military adviser Joseph Stilwell led to the general's recall, did newspapers burst forth with a troubling picture of the Nationalists and the struggling war effort.

In the 1960s, when the wind was blowing with gale force against him, Snow's trip to the other side of the river was dismissed. Even before he set out for China, *Time* magazine ran a story on his impending trip with the headline "Snow Job." When he came back, one reviewer wrote that his reports constituted "a public danger." *Look*'s editor, Dan Mich, had a progressive publishing philosophy. He ran stories in the mid-1950s on racism in the South and stood by reporters even if he did not fully agree with them. But *Look* published only one of Snow's articles and begged off of the other two that were planned. The Communists, wrote a nasty British reviewer of *The Other Side of the River* in the *New York Times,* could not really be interested in improving relations, as Chou had suggested, because they spent three times as much time with a person like Snow as with Clement Attlee and "other British Labor party leaders" who visited the country.

Snow hoped the election of John Kennedy as president heralded a new day in Sino-American relations. Upon returning to New York, Snow arranged to see Kennedy's nominee for secretary of state, Dean Rusk. The early-morning meeting was in Rusk's office at the Rockefeller Foundation, where he was president. Snow uncharacteristically arrived on time, despite having to come on foot because a heavy snowfall had stopped traffic. After bolting down breakfast and taking calls while Snow talked, Rusk abruptly dismissed him on the grounds that he had a lot to do. Four months later, a friend of Snow asked Rusk with feigned innocence if it would be a good idea to talk with the China Hand. "We have nothing more to learn about those people," Rusk replied.

Having won by a whisker in an election that had forced him to take a strong stand on defending Quemoy and Matsu, tiny islands still in the hands of the Taiwan government, Kennedy was not about to court trouble by seeking to improve relations with China. Eisenhower warned that he would "return to political life" if Kennedy considered allowing the PRC to have membership in the United Nations. Chester Bowles, Kennedy's nominee as Rusk's deputy, backed away from his preelection view that it was time to seek change in the China policy. In his confirmation hearings, Bowles pointed to Snow's interview with Chou, just published in *Look,* as confirming that "the Chinese will not talk or negotiate with us on any rational basis until Formosa is controlled by the mainland Peiping Communist government." No one at the hearing pointed out that Chou, in Snow's interview, had said the Formosa question could be put aside. A few midlevel State Department officials later advocated small policy changes. About twice a year from 1961 to 1964, one State Department official recalled, a proposal to allow journalists and scholars to visit China would wend its way from the Bureau of Far Eastern Affairs to the secretary of state, who ignored it.

This same modus operandi carried into the Johnson administration, which viewed China through the prism of its intractable war in Vietnam. "The United

States fought in Vietnam in part to contain and compete with the People's Republic of China," historian Robert D. Schulzinger noted; "exaggerated fears of the influence of the revolutionary doctrines of Mao" probably incited policymakers.

Between 1960 and 1964, Snow wrote a single major article for an American magazine, his piece for *Look*. When he went to China in 1964–65, *Le Nouveau Candide* in France, *Stern* in Germany, and *L'Europeo* in Italy advanced him money for expenses. When he returned with Mao's statement about the Chinese not sending combat troops into Vietnam, he had no problem publishing it abroad. At home he had a struggle. When he finally placed it with the *Washington Post*, a misunderstanding with Snow's agent led the paper to do a major rewrite and, also counter to Snow's wishes, syndicate the truncated story. The *New York Times*, which had turned down the piece, picked up portions when they appeared elsewhere. After considerable effort, Snow managed to get the full interview out in one piece through the *New Republic*.

The chaotic Cultural Revolution and the unfinished war in Vietnam left Snow unsure what to conclude about events in Asia. "Too much going on," he wrote to a friend. "And too little reliable information." Getting back to China to see for himself was impossible. In addition to the chaos there, he had become one of those under attack in the Cultural Revolution for being an American spy. Stymied, Snow turned historian, after all. He put together a film, *One Fourth of Humanity*, based on footage from the 1930s as well as his two trips to the PRC. He also revised *Red Star*, a book he really had never stopped writing. Immediately after it first appeared in the United States thirty years before, he had tinkered with it in new editions, sometimes rewriting sections, sometimes adding an update. This time, in the 1960s, he undertook a major overhaul and added a long appendix with biographical sketches drawn from his notes.

In the late 1960s America experienced a crisis of confidence on the scale of the one in the 1930s. The morass of the Vietnam War, with its relentless casualties and lack of victory, raised questions about foreign policy and, combining reappraisals about lingering poverty and civil rights, brought into question the values of American democracy. Disillusioned Americans were intrigued by—and often glorified— the antiestablishment Cultural Revolution in China. In this environment Lyndon Johnson decided not to run for reelection, and Richard Nixon entered the White House on a pledge to end the war.

In Nixon's foreign policy calculus, the United States needed to shore up its strength by reaching out to other countries. China, no longer seen as part of a monolithic communism, could help cut American losses by putting pressure on North Vietnam and serve as a counterweight to the Soviet Union. Wanting their own lever against the Soviet Union, which was muttering about the use of nuclear weapons against them, the Chinese, too, were ready for a new era.

That this shift occurred in Nixon's administration was truy strange. How could a president who rode to power on the charger of anticommunism and sided fully with the China Lobby (even to the point of being willing for Taiwan to invade the mainland) come to think of his greatest achievement as opening the door to China? As was said often, only a Republican with such credentials could undertake a new China policy. Even then, Nixon had to proceed gingerly, given the many years each side had railed against the other. The diplomatic minuet between the United States and the People's Republic was so secret that in the early stages it wasn't clear to either side whether the other was dancing.

Snow's special status made him a go-between in this furtive flirtation. With the worst of the Cultural Revolution over, he secured permission to return to China and was in Beijing on October 1, 1970, when the PRC celebrated its twenty-first anniversary. Snow and his wife were invited to join dignitaries on the balcony of a huge gate building where the leadership presided over the festivities in Tiananmen Square. When the parade below was well along, Chou led Snow and his wife to the spot where Mao was standing at the center. In a separate talk with Snow, Mao said Nixon was welcome to visit. "He can just get on a plane and come," Snow quoted Mao in his notes.

Mao thought of all of this as "a trial balloon to test the senses of America" as well as a way to prepare his own country for change. The *People's Daily* ran a photo of Mao and Snow on Tiananmen Gate. Minutes of Snow's interview were distributed to party officials. Senior American officials, however, gave little heed to the trial-balloon photo. Henry Kissinger, Nixon's national security adviser, commented dis-

On October 1, 1970, Edgar Snow was invited to stand next to Mao Tse-tung during the national day celebrations. For the Chinese it was a sign of their willingness to open relations with the United States. For Snow, it turned out to be another case of being ignored by his own country. Courtesy Lois Wheeler Snow, who is standing on the far right.

ingenuously in his memoirs that "our crude Occidental minds completely missed the point." He was actually purposeful in looking the other way. When China scholar and former diplomat Allen Whiting called Kissinger's office with an offer to debrief Snow when he returned home, he was turned down. A quarter century after the fact, Kissinger said in a speech, "We suspected that the message conveyed by Snow was not reliable." Secretary of State William Rogers, who in mid-1971 still did not know of steps to take Nixon to China, dismissed Snow's reports, saying the Chinese comments did not amount to a "serious invitation."

One who did see value in Snow's "unparalleled opportunity for access in China" was Seymour Topping. Topping, who had admired Snow since reading *Red Star* as a young man, covered China in the late 1940s for the INS and the AP, later joining the *New York Times,* where he now was assistant managing editor. He urged the foreign editor "to make an energetic effort to try to tap some of the material" from Snow's trip and eventually called Snow himself. Notwithstanding Topping's enthusiasm, problems arose. The paper's top editor, strongly right-wing A. M. Rosenthal, did not trust Snow. When Snow would not agree to editorial changes, Rosenthal rejected the story. Topping had to call Snow with the turndown. Snow was infuriated and crushed, his wife recalled: "It meant a total refutation finally on top of all the years . . . of not being accepted, not being the bridge, not having the attention every important way in Washington."

Snow turned to the *New Republic* once again, which began running a five-part series by him in late March. The first, "The Open Door," recounted his interviews with Chou En-lai. Within a few days the Chinese sent a signal no one could miss by inviting the American Ping-Pong team to China. Snow thought it was time to come out with Mao's comment that Nixon was welcome to visit. Because it had been made under conditions that did not allow him to quote freely, he first had to confirm that the Chinese had no objection. The Chinese agreed, but they kept off the record information that messages had been exchanged between the two countries. Using standard journalistic practice to circumvent this restriction, Snow confirmed the exchange messages with other sources and included them in a story that *Life* ran along with an editorial stating it was time for rapprochement.

Whatever Kissinger thought of Snow, his staff read and reread Snow's *Life* interview. It "gave us a great encouragement," said one, who began to appreciate that Snow's "purpose was the same as ours, that is, to bring China and the United States together." When Nixon appeared on television in July to announce that Kissinger had returned from a secret visit to Beijing with an invitation for him to visit, Snow's phone rang constantly. Journalists wanted his comments. Television networks sent crews to Geneva to interview him. *Life* ran a second article by him, and *Time* excerpted part of the story in its next issue. A full-page ad in the *New York Times* promoted the article. The revised *Red Star* sold briskly.

Life proposed to send Snow to cover Nixon's visit to China. If his agent would say exactly what he wanted, a *Life* editor wrote to Snow, "he would get it for you from *Life* at the best price and without difficulty." But in one of those twists of history, Snow was diagnosed with cancer of the pancreas shortly before Christmas

1971. He died the following February, sixty-two hours before Nixon's plane left Andrews Air Force Base for Beijing.

Most of the eighty-seven correspondents who accompanied Nixon were ill-equipped for the assignment. In the past, confessed Jerald F. ter Horst of the *Detroit News,* all a reporter had to remember was "that every President has been against Red China, and that solved a lot of political problems and a lot of thinking on the journalistic side." Reporters turned to Snow's earlier reporting for clues to what the leadership was thinking and descriptions of Mao's home and other places that were off-limits to them.

"Your handshake," Chou said to Nixon when they met, "came over the vastest ocean in the world—twenty five years of no communication." The Shanghai Communiqué issued at the conclusion of the visit met the conditions Chou had laid out in his 1960 talk to Snow—that disagreements should be worked out peacefully and that the United States withdraw its forces from Taiwan, the details of this latter point to be worked out. In private, Nixon made an even larger concession: Taiwan was part of China.

Nixon's visit was a vindication of Snow's efforts to open communications with the Chinese during the cold war. But the question remained whether the lessons of the past had been learned. This new era in Sino-American relations rested on a shaky foundation of euphoria. In the words of one scholar, positive images were "more fresh but no less superficial than the earlier negative ones." The *New York Times'* James Reston, who had visited just before the Nixon visit, compared the Chinese spirit to that found on the American frontier in the nineteenth century. Although the *Times* had balked at publishing the entire text of Snow's interviews with CCP officials, it agreed to Chinese demands to publish the whole transcript of Reston's interview with Chou.

One of the most striking journalistic changes of heart was columnist Joseph Alsop's. With his brother Stewart, he had written a strident three-part series in the 1950s called "Why We Lost China" for the *Saturday Evening Post* and stayed in the vanguard of anti–Chinese Communist commentators. He remained particularly critical of Snow. Then Alsop went to China shortly after Nixon opened the door and found that everything "has changed, in truth, except the endlessly resilient, hard-working and clever Chinese people. The quality of life has changed, vastly for the ancient ruling class but for the better of everyone else." As for the Great Leap, "the destructiveness of those four years of seeming-chaos has been considerably exaggerated." Chou En-lai and Alsop, who had an exclusive interview with the premier, "got on like a house afire," recalled Alsop's wife.

Snow, in contrast, had become progressively concerned about the cult of Mao and uncertain what the next stage of development really held. He also worried that the pendulum of American public opinion might swinging wildly again, a point he made in *The Long Revolution,* published posthumously: "The danger is that Americans may imagine that the Chinese are giving up communism—and Mao's world view—to become nice agrarian democrats. A more realistic world is indeed in sight. But popular illusions that it will consist of a sweet mix of ideologies, or an end to China's faith in revolutionary means, could only serve to deepen the abyss again when disillusionment occurs. . . . [A] world of relative peace between states is as necessary to China as to America. To hope for more is to court disenchantment."

In Snow's final days, he received a letter from the president. "I can only hope that it will strengthen you to know that your distinguished career is so widely respected and appreciated. My best to you always."

"Should I respond?" Snow's wife asked.

"Don't bother," Snow replied.

At his death in 1975, Mao was glorified abroad as well as at home. An obituary by one of the foremost China scholars, Michael Oksenberg, compared him to Thomas Jefferson, Winston Churchill, Charles de Gaulle, and Franklin Roosevelt. Mao's successor, Teng Hsiao-p'ing, was *Time* magazine's "Man of the Year" twice—in 1978 and in 1985. Before his trip to China in 1984, President Ronald Reagan referred to "so-called Communist China," just as Roosevelt had forty years earlier.

Then came the Tiananmen Massacre in spring 1989. Young Chinese initiated antigovernment demonstrations, protesting corruption and calling for civil liberties—and carrying a look-alike Statue of Liberty. The government responded with brute force. The resulting number of deaths probably came to more than 700 and may have reached 2,700. While government control of information made firm numbers elusive, the impact on American audiences was enormous. The crackdown on Tiananmen Square marked the first time a major foreign news story was covered in real time around the clock. The images that flickered on the screen were as emotionally charged as *Life*'s 1936 photo of the Chinese baby sitting in Shanghai's smoldering ruins.

"It was not possible to be dispassionate," acknowledged Charles Kuralt of CBS News. "The most cynical journalists could not help but be caught up." Correspondents played up the protestors as American-style democrats. They played down less pleasant aspects of the demonstrators, for instance their heavy-handed methods of manipulating the news, the reluctance of some students to include workers, and the fact that some hunger strikers secretly ate. One reporter, John Pomfret of AP, fed one of the leaders. "I was put in a difficult situation over the meal. Here was a guy I had just started to work with and he asked me to keep certain things discreet, and then he asked me for a meal. What can you do?"

In the years after, a more complex picture of contemporary China took shape, one of a country that was repressive and yet energetically pursuing economic growth and trade. Even so, in the ongoing study of Mao's China, witch hunts occurred in which Snow was yet again presented as journalistically disreputable. It was said that he misled Americans about Mao's China, sometimes lying outright; that he was a leftist journalist, a fellow-traveler, a member of the Communist Party. When an article in *Foreign Affairs* called Snow a Communist Party member, a reader challenged the author for evidence. Quite right, replied the author, Bruce Gilley, a young political science professor; Snow was not a member of the American Communist Party. "'Loyal follower' or 'obedient servant' would have been better terms."

As during the McCarthy period, critics used history selectively and recycled misinformation. At each turn the "evidence" picked up more appearance of credibility. The charge that Snow had altered *Red Star* shortly after it first appeared "to please Moscow" resurfaced. This time the alleged support came from American Communist Party documents brought to light at the end of the cold war. The documents, said one critic, were "more shaming than the distorting account of China Snow wrote after he returned to Peking in the 1960s and 1970s to renew his relationship with Mao." These documents consisted of only two letters. One, without any citation of source, said that Snow, shortly after *Red Star* appeared in 1938, offered to "destroy the entire third part of the book and rewrite it to the satisfaction" of the American Communist Party. This he did not do. The author of the second letter confused Edgar Snow with British author C. P. Snow. The Communist documents on Snow had the same defects as the reports that filled the FBI's files on Snow.

It did not help Snow's image that while Western critics decried him as a propagandist, the Communist Chinese sought to use him for that purpose. Some of this Snow's widow was able to deflect. She turned down the offer to bury Snow in Beijing's Martyrs Memorial Park, a resting place like that of John Reed, who died of typhus in 1920 and was buried beneath the Kremlin Wall with heroes of the revolution. Knowing her husband would not have approved of such a burial, Lois Snow placed his ashes on the campus of Beijing (formerly Yenching) University, where Snow had taught in the 1930s, and on the bank of the Hudson River under a Missouri dogwood tree. Undeterred, the Chinese erected a white marble statue of Snow in an Inner Mongolian town, where he had reported an appalling famine in 1928 that heightened his concern for the Chinese, used him as a prop in films (one of which was *Mao Tse-tung and Snow*), and organized meetings of scholars to "discuss the contribution to Sino-U.S relations made by Edgar Snow." The Chinese Communists made of Snow just what he hated, a cult figure.

Lost in the selective portrayal of Snow by Communists and his Western critics was a telling parallel between present and past. That parallel was a student demonstration that erupted in Beijing more than a half century before the Tiananmen Massacre. In December 1935 students took to the streets to protest Chiang Kai-shek's foot-dragging in resisting the Japanese. As in 1989, demonstrators carried signs calling for civil liberties. Correspondents covering the event emotionally sided with the students. Snow helped them translate broadsides publicizing their goals. When one was being beaten, Snow and Victor Keen of the *New York Herald Tribune* rushed over, using their presence to shame police into stopping.

Many of the students in the 1935 protests became leaders in the Communist regime, which Snow's widow now condemned. "I cannot and will not remain silent while basic human rights are being trampled underfoot and I know that my husband would agree with the action I have taken," Lois Snow said of her own protest in support of Chinese families who had suffered. "The violation of these basic rights by the government, while Edgar Snow's ashes lie buried on the campus of Beijing University, makes a mockery of all that he stood for."

Like a modern-day Inspector Javert in relentless pursuit of Jean Valjean, Snow's detractors lost perspective in their concentrated effort to corner him. This tendentiousness appears generally in studies of correspondents sympathetic to Communist revolutions. The resulting analyses tend to be one-dimensional, with oversimplified black-and-white judgments. Critics often display the very same lack of balance they decry in offending correspondents.

Foreign correspondents who perceived positive qualities in Communist revolution have traveled by vastly different routes. John Reed, intensely ideological, and Walter Duranty, cynically intellectual, were both marked as apologists for Russian Communism, but they also were different in temperament, philosophy, and style of reporting. Snow was yet a third type, holding in his own way to the prorevolution sentiment of his early mentors Thomas Millard and J. B. Powell. Those two Missourians aligned themselves with Chiang Kai-shek, whose politics were at odds with communism. Snow parted company as he saw the failures of the Nationalist regime, but he always had in common with them the dream of a movement that would be responsive to the great mass of Chinese and able to establish China as a strong, independent nation. As Snow's case shows, high hope is an affliction shared widely among journalists. It sometimes grows out of views that are less on the political right or left than they may seem on the surface.

Snow's case also illustrates the pitfalls of inflated expectations. In the beginning revolutions are blank slates on which revolutionaries promise to write a better life than their fellow citizens are living. Over and over, starting with the beheading of King Louis XVI in 1793, revolutions have produced their own evils. "Human habits, sentiments, dispositions," wrote Crane Brinton in *The Anatomy of Revolution,* "cannot be changed all that rapidly." Correspondents do well to keep historical patterns in mind. Lincoln Steffens's "I have seen the future" comment became famous for being wrong.

And yet critics, in assessing what makes for better coverage, would do well to remember that something is lost in reporting without passion, reporting that does not care. Snow's hopefulness was tied closely to his understanding of the human aspirations to which the Communists appealed. That empathy accounts for much of his success as a correspondent.

Another dimension of Snow's strange case relates to the impact of his reporting. Detractors and admirers alike have made much of his influence on Americans. *Red Star* was a stunning scoop or a powerfully misleading document, depending on one's point of view. But much has to be made, too, of the selective attention hope-

YOU CAN'T MAKE AN OMELET WITHOUT BREAKING EGGS

Walter Duranty, an Englishman who became one of the most controversial figures in the history of foreign reporting, went to the Soviet Union for the *New York Times* in 1921. The *Times* was stung by the Lippmann-Merz critique and wanted someone on the spot to cover a major story in Russia. As he later said with a telling bit of callousness, "Luck broke my way in the shape of the great Russian famine" in 1921. Duranty stayed until the mid-1930s.

Although the *Times* management grew concerned with Duranty's overly bright picture of the Soviet Union, he was "one of the great institutions of Moscow," widely admired by colleagues for his entertaining evenings and interpretive abilities. He won a Pulitzer Prize and was lionized in the United States, where invitations to lunch came from Walter Lippmann and philosopher-activist John Dewey. His downplaying of a second famine in 1932–33 left a great blot on his record. In 2003 the Pulitzer Prize board resisted considerable pressure—especially from Ukrainians, who suffered during the famine—to rescind Duranty's honor.

Duranty's positive approach to the Soviet Union was at odds with his reporting during the revolution, when he described "the Bolshevik system as one of the most damnable tyrannies in history." In the debate over what motivated Duranty to pull his punches later, several factors get particular attention. He lived comfortably in Moscow, with a pretty Russian mistress and a chauffeur-driven car that flew through the streets with its horn blaring. This good life may have made him less energetic, something noted in a 1933 observation by Adolph Ochs: Duranty seemed to be "relaxing his attention to his duties." Also Duranty worried about filing reports that might lead to expulsion. Thanks to his extraordinary access, he twice had rare, exclusive interviews with Stalin. Harrison Salisbury, in his analysis, considered Duranty a "cynical man on-the-make." And, to be sure, Duranty possessed none of the ideological passion of John Reed. His was a hard-boiled philosophy that tolerated Stalinist policies on the grounds that they were necessary to create a modern state. This view applied particularly to the harsh measures that brought about the 1930s famine—the collectivization of the peasants, who were seen as backward. As Duranty liked to say of the crueler aspects of the revolution, "You can't make an omelet without breaking eggs."

Duranty was eager for the United States to recognize the Soviet Union, which also may have motivated him to explain away the grimmer aspects of the Soviet Union with a long view that foresaw progress. "Behind the facade of communism, the quarrels and confusion it produces inside Russia and abroad," he wrote to Adolph Ochs, "there is all the fret and turmoil of a great young nation, newly freed from Tsarism and feudalism, which stifled it before."

Although Duranty's record has undergone careful scrutiny in recent years, he was scarcely alone in excusing Stalin's tough policies. Because of travel restrictions, few correspondents covered the famine well. Many offered mea culpas for their reporting when time and distance separated them from the Soviet Union, as Duranty himself did, admitting lapses "in my critical faculty." William Stoneman, who showed considerable enterprise in reporting the famine for the *Chicago Daily News*, considered Duranty "the grand old man of Moscow correspondents." He was "simply amoral without any deep convictions about the rights and wrongs of Communism."

ful Americans gave the book. The public and its policymakers tended to see what they wanted to see. In the 1930s, they largely ignored Snow's reports that the Chinese Communists were, really, Communists. Later, when he was virtually America's sole journalistic link with Mao's China, he again was ignored.

As this illustrates, news does not exist in isolation from the forces of official and public opinion. Americans filtered correspondents' reports through their own hopes and fears, and the public's hopes and fears shaped the kind of reporting that could be done. Despite journalists' "self-image," observed James Thomson, a China Hand who worked in the State Department and later headed Harvard's Nieman fellowship program for journalists, "the U.S. press has usually been an accurate reflection of the country in its approach to revolution abroad—no better, no worse." A few might "fight the homeside tide," but "by and large the national press reflected the conventional wisdom of both citizen and policy-maker."

Americans have been particularly susceptible to imposing their emotions on China. But the pattern is not confined to the Chinese, as we can see with the Soviet Union and, to point to one more example, Cuba. When Fidel Castro professed not to be a Communist, Americans were open-minded toward the country and toward *Times* reporter Herbert Matthews, who had first interviewed him in the Sierra Maestra. Attitudes changed when Castro announced in a 1961 speech that he would be a "Marxist-Leninist . . . to the last days of my life" and moved into the sphere of the Soviet Union. The United States ended diplomatic relations in that year and supported the ill-fated Bay of Pigs invasion shortly thereafter. All this pushed the Cubans further into the arms of the Soviet Union.

In Walter Lippmann's continuing study of the interaction of press and public opinion after his 1920 *New Republic* article with Charles Merz, he came to understand that hope and fear worked on a larger scale than just among the news media. "Newspapers," he wrote in his landmark book *Public Opinion,* published in 1922, "necessarily and inevitably reflect, and therefore, in greater or lesser measure, intensify, the defective organization of public opinion." In mounting despair, he argued that the press could do nothing to cure its "own defects."

The next chapter takes another look at the problem Lippmann identified by examining the power of determined policymakers over foreign affairs reporting and also the power of determined journalists to resist those pressures. A fundamental lesson comes through there as well as here. Lippmann's despair notwithstanding, more news rather than less news remains the best medicine for the ills both of public opinion and of government. It was in restricting news, rather than in the failure of a few reporters, that Americans failed themselves in China.

The Chinese were partly responsible for the news blockade erected after 1949, at times barring reporters and assiduously managing them when they were inside the country. But the Chinese made opportunities for American reporters to visit. Had the American government not stood in the way, a greater flow of reporters would have pushed at the barriers imposed by the Chinese government. Firsthand observation is the most effective cure for the emotional fevers that take hold of journalists. It is instructive to remember that when John Reed returned to the Soviet Union in 1920 and had considerable freedom to see what was transpiring, his optimism began to fade. With news from China largely cut off, the vessel of public opinion was left to fill with fears, not facts.

Working under these cold war conditions, Snow became a victim of his own scoop. As hard as he worked to dig out facts, as much as he hated being "'guested' to death by the Chinese," Snow had become part of the story. With *Red Star* and other reporting held up as evidence of his un-Americanism, he was put on the defensive. His determination to use his access to correct the picture Americans held of Chinese Communists thrust him into a political role, whether he liked it or not. Snow was too stubborn, too earnest to follow the advice of his *Saturday Evening Post* editors who tried to point him toward other topics.

Had many correspondents filed from China after 1949, Snow's responsibilities for correcting errors of perception would have diminished. His reports would have counted for less and, without the constraints of his special role, likely would have been better. "Different reporters see different things, or the same things, differently," observed press critic and sometimes foreign correspondent A. J. Liebling; "the reader at home has a right to a diversity of reports. A one-man account of a crisis in a foreign country is like a Gallup poll with one straw."

As good a judgment as there is on Snow came from China scholar John K. Fairbank. "Edgar Snow," Fairbank said of his friend, "was set up by Mao and mugged by the Cold War. . . . Snow's factual reporting, even under the suffocating blanket of the guest-host relationship, made a useful contribution that we generally refused to accept. Snow did what he could as a professional journalist."

WHY DON'T YOU GET ON THE TEAM?

If there are any persons who contest a received opinion . . . let us thank them for it,
open our minds to listen to them, and rejoice that there is someone to do for us what
we otherwise ought . . . to do with much greater labor for ourselves.

John Stuart Mill, *On Liberty*

Neil Sheehan, a young UPI correspondent, had been in Vietnam for just two weeks
when, in May 1962, an American military officer gave him a tip. The colonel, whom
he met in an officers' club bar, told him the South Vietnamese had just won a military victory in which three hundred Vietcong were killed. Sheehan's scoop ran on
the front page of the *New York Times,* a newspaper that prefers to use its own correspondents' reports.

The next morning, Sheehan had a wake-up call from Homer Bigart, the legendary war correspondent for the *New York Herald Tribune* and, now, the *New
York Times.* Sheehan's story trumped Bigart's, which reported two occurrences
that cast matters in a quite different light: that "a small Communist force blew up
a troop train," killing 27 civil guardsmen, and that guerrillas had threatened an
American-sponsored resettlement project. This latter event was significant because
several days earlier Secretary of Defense Robert McNamara had visited the project
on the grounds that it was a model of improved security. Besides pushing Bigart's
account inside the paper, his editors cabled to ask why he did not have Sheehan's
story. The angry veteran ordered the young reporter to drive with him to the scene
of the "victory," seventy-five miles southwest of Saigon. They found that perhaps 20
Vietcong, but certainly not 300, had been killed. Sheehan's tipster colonel had been
drunk. During the month Bigart had remaining in Vietnam, Sheehan followed
him around as if going to journalism school. He called Bigart "the professor."

The soon-to-escalate conflict in Vietnam presented new challenges to correspondents and the officials with whom they interacted. Just as the battle lines in
this guerrilla war were not clearly laid out, as they had been in the world wars and
Korea, the rules governing correspondents were less formal. Except during one interlude, the South Vietnamese government—whose war this was supposed to be—
did not formally censor reporters; nor did the U.S. military, lest it seem to con-
tradict the Western-style freedom it was supposed to be fighting for. In addition,
television, a brand-new medium with untested power, debuted as a major source of
news for millions of Americans.

The war was different in other ways as well—ways that Sheehan was beginning to learn under Bigart. It started as a war in which the American government thought involvement, as far as the public was concerned, should be "minimized, even represented as something less in reality than it is." It became a war in which the White House and the military repeatedly promised victory that never came, in which boos and catcalls could be heard among the laughs and applause at Bob Hope's shows to bolster troop morale. It ended with government–news media relations at a level of antipathy not seen since the early years of the Republic when Bache-style journalism was regnant.

Michael Herr, an exemplar of a new style of journalism that used novelists' techniques to convey the inner truth of the story, went to Vietnam just before the 1968 Tet Offensive, when hundreds of thousands of North Vietnamese soldiers and Vietcong guerrillas launched attacks throughout the country that shocked Americans into the realization that the war was going to drag on. Writing in *Esquire,* home base for much of the New Journalism, Herr sounded nothing like Ernie Pyle. Instead of writing down the names and hometown addresses of soldiers, he used the names they gave themselves, "S---kick and Motherf---er." "Conventional journalism," he wrote, "could no more reveal this war than conventional firepower could win it."

Was the war being won? Was it winnable? Was it worth fighting? These questions cried out for attention as the conflict enlarged in the 1960s. They are still asked. In some minds, the explanation for America's defeat went beyond the strategy and prowess of the North Vietnamese and the Vietcong. "Our worst enemy seems to be the press," said Richard Nixon.

But was it? After 1968 journalists joined the great majority of the American public and their officials in viewing the war as unwinnable. Before that, only a handful of correspondents diverged from the government line, and their defiance was limited. The courage it took to oppose the government before 1968 belied Nixon's assertions about the press as enemy. A purposeful White House possessed considerable power to shape coverage of Vietnam, especially when a tight official consensus favored the policy.

This chapter is a study in the withering wind of determined officials and the journalistic intrepidity needed to tack into it. Tough as he was, Bigart confessed that reporting in Vietnam wore on him. The South Vietnamese government came close to throwing him out, and he would not have been disappointed if they had. "This," he said in the *Times* in-house newsletter, "has not been a happy assignment. . . . Too often correspondents seem to be regarded by the American mission as tools of our foreign policy."

Lippmann and Merz's "A Test of the News" article in the *New Republic* was a benchmark in the systematic study of the news media. Scholars built on it to analyze how journalists shape public and official attitudes, as we have seen in the Spanish-American War, and how the processes of media-government interaction work in the other direction, with officials influencing coverage of foreign affairs. One way of describing government influence is called indexing, a concept that emerged from the study of media coverage of the Vietnam War.

Indexing argues that the media have a bias toward power. The view is supported by analysis showing that coverage tends to trace the contours of official views. As one of the more important of the studies puts it, "Once officials engage with news events, the story frames generated by journalists are then generally 'indexed' to the range of sources and viewpoints that reflect levels of official agreement and consensus." When consensus within the government is strong, the range of views in the news media tends to be narrow. When the range of official views widens, coverage tends to widen with it.

The phenomenon of indexing is prevalent in the reporting of wars. The executive branch has strong constitutional power in foreign affairs, and legislators typically defer to the president in the midst of a national security crisis. The Vietnam War provides striking illustrations of this tendency. Rooted in the cold war consensus about the need to halt the spread of Communism, it was a liberals' war as much as it was a conservatives' war. Although Lippmann initially argued against the containment policy framed by George Kennan, from 1950 until 1965 he "essentially accepted the consensus" of the policymakers with whom he interacted, his biographer noted. The Tonkin Gulf resolution of August 1964, which legitimated escalation of the war by President Lyndon B. Johnson, passed with only two dissenting votes in the Senate and none at all in the House.

The American entry into the war began gradually after 1954, the year that France ended its fight against the Viet Minh led by Ho Chi Minh. Under the Geneva Accords, the country was divided, North and South, at the 17th parallel. National elections, which were to lead to unification, were not held because South Vietnamese leader Ngo Dinh Diem foresaw almost certain victory for the Communists. To protect Diem's regime from the North Vietnamese, the United States sent in military advisers. By 1961 the U.S. had more advisers in the country than permitted by the accords (which the United States did not sign but had pledged to honor) and was secretly planning to commit far more manpower and matériel.

In the early 1960s, the war was still a back-burner conflict that did not show up on the mental maps of most Americans, legislators included. When Bigart arrived in early 1962 for a half-year tour, he was the only full-time correspondent in Saigon representing a daily newspaper, a distinction he handed off to his successor, David Halberstam. Reporting was otherwise left to wire services and a few stringers. Much of what Americans knew about the country came from journalists in Washington, covering either the State Department or the White House or working as columnists.

Reporting from Washington is particularly susceptible to the process described by indexing, although indexing applies to correspondents abroad who are covering events where policymakers and policy implementers are on the scene in full force, as during the Vietnam War. One of the elemental journalistic imperatives that accounts for indexing is the need for sources. Reporters are supposed to suppress their own views, and one of the best ways to do so is by attributing facts and views to others. Some of the most attractive sources are elected and appointed officials: they make and implement policy; they are knowledgeable; and they tend to be relatively easy to reach. Reporters don't have to justify quoting an official. Quoting a source outside government circles is more subjective and more subject to second-guessing by editors and the public, particularly when the outside voice is a dissenting one. Accordingly, dissenting opinion gets more media attention when officials are doing the dissenting, as happened when the official consensus broke down after the Tet Offensive in 1968.

Two other factors lead to indexing. First, elite foreign affairs reporters and columnists have much in common with elite policymakers. They have similar educations and vacation preferences. They are less likely to bond with dissident non-establishment sources. Second, journalists and policymakers have a keen mutual interest in keeping lines of communication open. Reporters are better positioned to pick up news about government plans and action, and policymakers are better able to build public support for their points of view.

As powerful as all of these forces are, indexing is not found in all reporting. It does not apply when officials care little about an issue, when officials' attention lapses, or when officials don't know what position to take at a given moment. Nor do journalists always go along when policymakers are focused. African American reporters, who did not identify with government leaders during World War II, provided a different perspective on the news. Edgar Snow, a creature of the footloose 1930s, gave up his post at the *Saturday Evening Post* rather than reorient his reporting on China. And a few journalists inside the mainstream media challenged the government's portrayal of the Vietnam War, a difficult task because they had to resist not only government and public opinion, but their own editors as well.

American involvement in Vietnam rested on delusions, one historian has suggested. The government was deluded in believing that the war could be won militarily and that Diem was a genuine democrat. Officials deluded the public because they feared, correctly as it turned out, that a fully informed citizenry would not support their plans. President Kennedy lied when he said Americans weren't involved in combat. The Tonkin Gulf resolution, secured from Congress by President Johnson, was predicated on false reports of "naked aggression" by the North Vietnamese against U.S. warships on "routine patrol in international waters." The very day in 1964 that Johnson was elected president on a platform of "no wider war," an interagency working group planned to do precisely that. Officials consistently claimed the war was being won when it wasn't.

A January 1963 confrontation between South Vietnamese forces and the Vietcong near the village of Ap Bac was a case in point. Here, at last, was a chance for the Diem forces to show what they could do, for the enemy was this time to stand and fight, rather than use frustrating hit-and-run tactics. The battle turned out badly. Although outnumbering their foe almost three to one, the South Vietnamese commanders did not want to fight for fear of taking casualties, which would irritate Diem. Vietnamese officers delayed and faked mistakes to save face. Their men fired on their own troops. Five U.S. helicopters went down; three Americans were killed.

Gen. Paul Harkins, commander of the U.S. Military Assistance Command, Vietnam (MACV), called the encounter a victory. He reported that 101 VC had been killed, although only three bodies were found and his staff estimated that the VC had carried only a dozen or so bodies off the field. (VC reports captured later showed that eighteen had died.) One of Harkins's subordinates, Lt. Col. John Paul Vann, called the battle "a miserable fucking performance, just like it always is."

Buddhist protests soon afterward raised questions about South Vietnamese democracy. Diem was a strong Catholic in a largely Buddhist country. When he cracked down on the Buddhists for flying banners in celebration of Buddha's birthday (even though Catholics had been allowed to fly theirs), the Buddhists demonstrated. When Diem's police and military retaliated, Buddhist dissidents immolated themselves in protests, and grisly photographs appeared in the news. Diem's government briefly censored correspondents.

Three correspondents in particular riled Diem and American policymakers—Neil Sheehan, David Halberstam, and Associated Press bureau chief Malcolm Browne. They "seized on the Buddhist crisis," as they had on Ap Bac, Sheehan later said, "holding it up as proof that the regime was as bankrupt politically as it was militarily." In June 1963, during the Buddhist demonstrations, Halberstam boldly reported, "Some well-informed observers believe there will be an attempt to oust the Government. The question appears to be when?" Four months later, Diem was ousted.

Official irritation escalated along with the war into an "embittered confrontation," which Sheehan described as "the opposite of the experience of the World War II generation of journalists." When Halberstam finally was granted an interview with American ambassador Frederick Nolting, the conversation lasted only a few minutes. Nolting asked Halberstam if he was going to cover a press conference with a Vietcong defector. When the correspondent said he was leaving that to the wires, Nolting threw him out of the office. "Why don't you people do any of the regular things?" the irritated ambassador complained. Adm. Harry Felt, commander of the U.S. Pacific Fleet with overall responsibility for the U.S. military in Vietnam, was in Saigon shortly after the Ap Bac fiasco. "I'd like to say that I don't believe what I've been reading in the papers," Felt said. "As I understand it, it was a Vietnamese victory." After a probing question by Malcolm Browne, Felt shot back, "Why don't you get on the team?"

Browne stopped checking in with the embassy because officials refused to be helpful. He compiled a long list of dos and don'ts for his bureau. One read, "Don't believe any official statement." Halberstam called Harkins's operation "the great Saigon lying machine." At a cocktail party in the summer of 1963, he listened for a few minutes while a general talked to a visiting *Time* magazine editor. At six-feet-three, Halberstam was imposing just by standing around. He added to this by booming out his opinions, in this case breaking in, "You're standing there lying and feeding him full of bullshit!"

The defiance of these correspondents came by a different route from Bigart's. His came from experience, theirs from a lack of it. Bigart, who covered World War II and Korea, had distaste for war and for military misstatements about success. And with Pulitzer Prizes from both conflicts, he had standing. An institution within an institution, he disdained editors, whom he once likened to Nazi mass murderer Adolf Eichmann. Youth fortified the independence of Sheehan, Halberstam, and Browne. They had not worked for establishment media long enough to identify fully with it. The month before his wayward "victory" story for UPI in May 1962, Sheehan had been in the army, reporting for *Stars and Stripes* in Asia. Browne had also served in the army as a *Stars and Stripes* reporter before briefly working at a small New York newspaper. Halberstam began his career on a small Mississippi newspaper, which he left when his civil rights reporting went too far for the editor. After a stint at the *Nashville Tennessean*, he joined the *Times*' Washington bureau. He did not do well as a low man in an office of outsized egos and took a dislike to Washington insiders.

Yet, it was not correct to say Halberstam, Sheehan, and Browne were not on the team. While Bigart came to Vietnam hating war and distrusting cold war ideology, they arrived as believers, two of them fresh from military service. "We regarded the war as our war too," Sheehan said, "We believed in what our government said it was trying to accomplish in Vietnam." Halberstam later confessed that he had looked for victories, and it showed in the tenor of his initial reporting. State Department officials let the *Times* know how pleased they were. In predicting Diem's removal from power, Halberstam was pointing not only to a problem but a solution: installation of a better government. "The military effort against the Communists," he wrote in his June 1963 report on crumbling support for the South Vietnamese leader, "can be successful only in a favorable political climate."

For all his feistiness, Bigart had not reported that American "advisors" fired guns. Correspondents who came later self-censored information that might have helped the enemy under terms established by the military. And the military was not entirely without means to influence correspondents, whose ranks grew gradually. The February 1962 State Department Cable 1006 directed the military to keep reporters away from operations that might result in negative coverage. Building on this concept, General Harkins failed to notify reporters when operations were under way. Daily military briefings doled out information in such misleading ways that they eventually become known as the Five O'Clock Follies.

The briefings were more effective with less independent-minded correspondents than Halberstam, Sheehan, and Browne, who circled their wagons the way the officials did, creating two camps, each dedicated to proving the other wrong. But subtle and not-so-subtle forces operated like a flywheel on their work.

Although Diem only briefly used sledgehammer censorship, he aggressively wielded the stiletto. Dispatches disappeared or were held up at the telegraph office. Men in black jackets trailed reporters. Correspondents' phones were tapped. They were detained and questioned. Diem's police beat up Peter Arnett, who joined the AP bureau. At one critical moment toward the end of the Diem regime, a source told Halberstam and Sheehan that they were on a hit list. Even though expulsions were rare, correspondents were on guard. In watching Bigart, Sheehan marveled at "how Homer used his ammunition very carefully. He raised the temperature very slowly. As he reached the end, his stories got rougher and rougher. He was counting the days. So, we learned to calculate how far we could go without being thrown out."

No matter how aggressive they were, correspondents had a narrow range of sources. They could not get information from the North Vietnamese or the Vietcong. Even if they refused to go to the embassy for information, they had to rely on officials. Thus, while they might distrust flag-grade officers like General Harkins, they built much of their reporting on the views of field-grade colonels and company-grade captains and lieutenants. Some of these officers understood that the war was being lost by a corrupt regime out of touch with its people, yet they were conservatives who accepted the righteousness of the cause and questioned only the tactics.

Halberstam's report on the disastrous outcome of the battle at Ap Bac was heavily reliant on military sources:

> The Vietcong simply refused to panic and they fired with deadly accuracy and consistency. The Vietnamese regulars, in contrast, in the eyes of one American observer, lost the initiative from the first moment and never showed much aggressive instinct and consequently suffered heavier casualties than they might have had they tried an all-out assault of the Vietcong positions.
>
> "The Vietcong were brave men," one American officer said. "I think any officer would have been proud to have commanded that unit."

Correspondents' ties with John Paul Vann and other dissident officers became the deep and personal kind that grows out of shared life in real or metaphorical foxholes. These officers facilitated correspondents' ability to get into the field and to see classified documents. An American captain would phone Sheehan to say, simply, "get cracking." With this cue, Sheehan dashed to the captain's office, where a Vietnamese officer gave him a document and left the room. When Halberstam and AP photographer Horst Faas rented a house without hot water, a military friend sent over a water heater. Another source, Special Forces officer George "Speedy" Gaspard, bunked there once with his twelve-man Green Beret team. Halberstam patterned the hero in his war novel *One Very Hot Day* after Gaspard. Halberstam later thought it ironic that he and his colleagues were considered "a bunch of liberals" for relying on sources that were, in some cases, "almost reactionary."

Sheehan, Halberstam, and Browne also found themselves struggling against their establishment-oriented colleagues, whose ranks gradually grew. Keyes Beech of the *Chicago Daily News*, a former marine who wore a Marine Corps fatigue cap, won a Pulitzer covering the Korean War, where the traditional comity between officials and journalists tended to prevail. He was inclined to accept official estimates of progress and dismissed Halberstam, Browne, and Sheehan as "young and inexperienced." Visiting journalists, with little time and background, were more likely than not to buy into the official line and challenge the pessimistic correspondents. Richard Tregaskis, the World War II reporter famous for his *Guadalcanal Diary,* came to collect information for *Vietnam Diary.* As before, he wrote "about Americans fighting." Ap Bac occurred during his stay. Although Vann told him how badly it had gone, Tregaskis pronounced the defeat a simple case of "bad luck." He chided Halberstam, "If I were doing what you are doing, I'd be ashamed of myself."

This was gentle compared to the raking Marguerite Higgins administered. The *Herald Tribune* reporter was indomitable during World War II and Korea, in the latter war defying her then-*Herald Tribune* colleague Homer Bigart, who wanted her to leave the field to him. She was fearless under fire. Unlike Bigart, however, she was under the sway of official policy in Vietnam, a point of view fostered by her marriage to an air force general. After returning from a trip to Vietnam, she told colleagues in the Washington bureau that the offending reporters were "just little boys." In a six-part series entitled *Vietnam—Fact and Fiction,* she quoted liberally from senior American officials to conclude, "contrary to recent published reports . . . the war in Viet Nam is beginning to be won."

Hearst columnist Frank Conniff said the *New York Times'* reporting was "a political time bomb." Halberstam, he said, slickly used questionable sources, whereas Higgins's "byline carries authority." Columnist Joseph Alsop, who credited himself with coming up with *domino theory* to describe the danger of countries falling one after another unless a stand was taken against Communism, said the "young crusaders" warped the news. His reporting circulated widely among Washington officials seeking reassurance.

In addition, the dissident correspondents had their bosses to contend with. A Pentagon spokesman once blurted out to reporters, "Look, I don't even have to talk to you people. I know how to deal with you through your editors and publishers back in the States." Without prompting, editors sometimes removed alarming conclusions from stories rather than go against what they heard in Washington. When Martha Gellhorn wrote in 1966–67 about poor hospital care for civilian casualties and other horrors of the war, no U.S. newspaper published her articles except for two of the milder pieces, which appeared in the *St. Louis Post-Dispatch.*

Time editors in New York contorted the reports of their Southeast Asia correspondent Charles Mohr, who on his frequent trips to Vietnam reluctantly came to the same conclusions about the war as did Sheehan and his colleagues. Mohr began a 1963 story, "Vietnam is a graveyard of lost hopes, destroyed vanity, glib promises, and good intentions." The sentence was excised in a rewrite that proclaimed, "If last week's battles were any criterion, the government troops are fighting better than ever." In the same issue, pro-Diem *Time* repudiated Saigon reporting. "For all the light it shed," *Time* pronounced, "the news that U.S. newspaper readers got from Saigon might just as well have been printed in Vietnamese." After bitter staff response, the magazine ran a begrudgingly balanced follow-up story. By the time it appeared, Mohr and the *Time* stringer in Saigon had resigned.

In October 1963, after the *Time* article on the Saigon press, Sheehan's byline appeared only once in the *Washington Post*. It had been there and in other papers regularly during the preceding two months. Sheehan's boss, Earnest Hoberecht, stationed in Tokyo, had his own concerns about the tone of Sheehan's reporting, as did UPI headquarters in New York. Hoberecht insisted that Sheehan come to Tokyo for a rest, ignoring his pleas that a big story was in the offing. As a result, Sheehan was not in Vietnam when Diem was assassinated. Browne's AP bosses forced him into a vacation, too, but he had his out of the way by the time of the coup. Meanwhile, Halberstam was on his own bumpy ride with the *Times,* whose editorial policy supported the war and whose news editors were leery of anything that resembled crusading reporting.

The *New York Times* is a favorite target of both liberals and conservatives. Critics often lose sight of the fact that the *Times* makes a big target because it attempts so much more than other media. No newspaper is studied more closely for foreign reporting because none devotes so many resources to it. Moreover, criticism that the *Times* leans to one side or the other politically in its news pages detracts from its central feature as an establishment newspaper, not one bent on taking up causes to right wrongs. "A great newspaper is to some extent a political institution," said managing editor Turner Catledge; "to maintain its power it must use it sparingly." When a *Times* reporter learned of the impending CIA-supported Bay of Pigs invasion of Cuba in 1961, soul-searching set in. Would the story endanger national security? Would it arm those who condemned the paper for Herbert Matthews's sympathetic reporting of Castro? The cautious editors decided to run a watered-down story. Publicly, President Kennedy criticized the *Times* for going even that far. Privately, he told Catledge, "Maybe if you had printed more about the operation, you would have saved us from a colossal mistake."

Halberstam was a handful for the *Times.* The paper did not like having its correspondents call generals liars at cocktail parties. His long-winded, tortured prose required extensive editing. With more latitude than wire services, he could dig a bigger hole to fall into, and the government did what it could to push him in, detailing staff to scrutinize his copy. The foreign desk hectored Halberstam, asking him to be more explicit about his sources (quite difficult considering they were junior officers with careers on the line) and telling him to get off his "soap box." After *Time* ran its story critical of Saigon reporting, Robert Trumbull, senior *Times* correspondent in Asia, suggested a letter defending Halberstam. The editors said no. When one of Halberstam's stories conflicted with a report from Washington, the editors planned to put his inside the paper until Washington bureau chief James Reston intervened.* The stories appeared on the front page, side by side. Halber-

---

* James Reston, an influential columnist as well as bureau chief, was the quintessential establishment insider. Although this did not prevent him from decrying government secrecy in Vietnam in the early 1960s, his great strength—a strength that made him mandatory reading—was his close relationships with influential officials, who opened up to him. When it came to straying far from the

stam's turned out to be correct. He wrote long letters rebutting criticisms. If his editors queried him one more time on Marguerite Higgins's stories, he cabled home, "I WILL RESIGN REPEAT RESIGN AND I MEAN IT REPEAT MEAN IT." Clifton Daniel, who shortly became managing editor with the elevation of Catledge to the job of executive editor, thought Halberstam "should be brought home on charges of insubordination."

At one point the *Times* did consider recalling Halberstam, or at least that was the rumor among the staff. Ironically, a White House push led to the opposite outcome. The newly installed publisher, Arthur O. Sulzberger, made a courtesy call on President Kennedy, who turned it into a hectoring session aimed at getting Halberstam out of Vietnam. Afterward, Sulzberger discussed the conversation with Reston. It simply wouldn't do, they agreed, to let the White House dictate staffing.

Although Halberstam made occasional errors, his accuracy—and the accuracy of Sheehan and Browne—stands out. "For a while every time Halberstam did a story from the boonies," said a CIA officer detailed to check his facts, "I was asked to do a report. I was impressed." But the situation in Vietnam was complicated, the country was far away, and the government had the advantage in making the case for its policy. In a 1964 poll, conducted during the presidential campaign, in which the war was an issue, two-thirds of respondents said they "paid little or no attention to developments in South Vietnam." "It was relatively easy for Administration spokesmen to make a series of bland statements about Vietnam," complained Halberstam, "and to attack a handful of young newspapermen without established reputations."

Halberstam and Browne, both of whom subsequently wrote books on Vietnam, jointly won a Pulitzer Prize for their reporting; Sheehan might have shared in the award if he had been in the country to report Diem's overthrow. Browne, along with Sheehan and Mohr, joined the *Times,* yet another accomplishment. The war made their reputations. Yet, in hindsight, they realized that they had not gone far enough in challenging the assumptions about the war. Sheehan left Vietnam in 1964 and returned for a second tour, this time for the *Times.* As disillusioned as he was when he departed the second time in 1966, he still was not yet ready to stop prosecuting the war. Twenty years later, after obsessively ruminating about Vietnam, he finished *A Bright Shining Lie.* "We missed the big one," Sheehan concluded. "I always wrote stories as if we were engaged in a heroic, patriotic venture. How wrong I was."

The correspondents also agreed that they could not have written any other way. Even the solidly liberal *New Republic* framed solutions in terms of replacing Diem in order to engineer reforms. The dominant line of thinking, concluded Leslie Gelb, a State Department and Pentagon official who later became an editor and columnist at the *Times,* was "The United States could not afford to lose." To challenge the consensus about the validity of war aims, Halberstam told a friend later, would have made him "unemployable."

consensus, he preferred to champion young journalists like Halberstam and Sheehan, who eventually went to work in the Washington bureau. Reston, Sheehan noted, "didn't want to do this kind of reporting himself at this stage of his career. He wanted us to do it." Stacks, *Scotty,* 243–51.

To head in that direction, a reporter had to have much more solid journalistic credentials and be wrapped in a thick skin. Such a journalist was Harrison Salisbury.

In 1930 the University of Minnesota expelled Harrison Salisbury. His infraction was to have crusaded in the campus newspaper, which he edited, against a ban on smoking in the library vestibule during the subzero winter. In the journalism career that ensued, Salisbury continued to challenge authority. In addition he displayed an iron perseverance that got him into out-of-bounds locales where news was made and moved him up the ranks of establishment journalism. One of those places was North Vietnam, when he was associate editor of the *New York Times*.

Edgar Snow and Vincent Sheean nourished Salisbury's ambitions (he "gulped down" Sheean's *Personal History* and admitted to "a hero worship of Ed"), but he was more of an organization man than they were. He began with the United Press, which sent him abroad during World War II. In Europe, he encountered Homer Bigart, whose blunt reporting on the failures in the Anzio invasion he admired, and went on to be Moscow bureau chief. He achieved his dream of working at the *Times* by persistently visiting managing editor Edwin James, who finally made a deal. The *Times* had not been able to get anyone into Moscow since correspondent Drew Middleton was denied reentry. If Salisbury could secure a visa, he could have the job. This Salisbury did in early 1949.

During the Red Scare years of the late 1940s and early 1950s, Salisbury thought Snow should bide his time, writing about baseball or some other uncontroversial topic, as *Saturday Evening Post* editors hoped he would. When the furor died down, Snow could return to writing about China. Salisbury, after all, was willing to shift gears when he returned from Moscow in 1954 with a Pulitzer Prize. The *Times* editors gave him an assignment meant to bring him down a notch, New York garbage. This was a subject of particular interest to the publisher's wife. When the topic had earlier been handed out from time to time, a few modest inches of type resulted. In Salisbury's hands, the assignment took weeks of work and produced a three-part series that drew praise from Catledge: "Also, let me add we are all highly gratified at the way you are adjusting yourself to the local staff."

Salisbury, whose steel-rimmed glasses seemed a personal statement, was lean, energetic, organized, intense. He fell into dark periods and for a time checked into a psychiatric center. When he acquired and added to well-timbered property in Connecticut, he prowled around his holdings, commanding trespassers to leave. Back at the *Times* office, he filled mailbags with correspondence to people who might help him get into one or another off-limits country—Romania and Bulgaria in 1957, Albania the next year, Mongolia in 1959 (as well as Russia that year, after being barred by the Soviets for five years), and Burma in 1966. Adept at bureaucratic maneuvering, he became national editor and Clifton Daniel's most trusted assistant managing editor, responsible for making suggestions to improve coverage, especially in Washington, which Salisbury considered too close to official sources. Salisbury was a *Times* man—and, like Bigart, his own man.

In 1966 Salisbury's laser-beam determination was directed at securing an invitation to North Vietnam. He sent a blizzard of mail and telegrams, and talked to anyone who might be able to help. In the spring he made an extended trip on the periphery of China. While he reported, he unsuccessfully looked for an opening to Hanoi. The payoff came with a December 15 cable from Hanoi saying a visa awaited him in Paris. Salisbury called his eldest son to say he was sorry that he would not be able to attend his wedding in early January. He did not give a reason. Only six of his colleagues on the *Times* knew of Salisbury's trip.

Salisbury could have gone to Hanoi a month earlier, had a North Vietnamese invitation not been lost in the Paris office of the *Times* international edition. The delay gave a special focus to his visit. For months the American government had contended that its bombing of North Vietnam, begun two years before, was directed at strictly military targets and was highly accurate. Shortly before the congressional elections in November 1966, President Johnson said, "We have never bombed their population." Around the time Salisbury finally received word of his invitation, Communist news agencies reported that American bombs had hit residential neighborhoods in Hanoi. The administration stumbled around in response, admitting off the record at the State Department that mistakes were possible and reversing course the next day to say there was no basis to think mistakes were made. A week later, on December 22, the administration said, *obscurum per obscurius,* that the possibility of accidents could not be completely ruled out.

Salisbury touched down in Hanoi the next evening after a flight from Phnom Penh. The day after, Christmas Eve, he filed his first report, a vivid story reported and written on the fly that blasted the administration's contention that U.S. bombs did not hit civilians. The story arrived in New York too late for the first edition the next day, Christmas Sunday. Clifton Daniel overruled the assistant managing editor on duty, who wanted to hold the story for Monday. It ran on the front page of later Sunday editions and was rerun in the first edition of Monday's paper. Below is an excerpt.

A VISITOR TO HANOI INSPECTS DAMAGE LAID TO U.S. RAIDS

A Purposeful and Energetic Mood in Embattled Capital Found by a Times Man

The writer of the following dispatch is an assistant managing editor of The New York Times, who reached Hanoi Friday.

BY HARRISON E. SALISBURY

Special to The New York Times

HANOI, North Vietnam, December 24—
Late in the afternoon of this drizzly Christmas Eve the bicycle throngs on the roads leading into Hanoi increased.

Riding sidesaddle behind husbands were hundreds of slender young Hanoi wives returning to the city from evacuation to spend Christmas with their families. Hundreds of mothers had small children perched on the backs of bicycles—children being returned to the city for reunions during the Christmas cease-fire. . . .

But this random evidence of Christmas spirit did not convey the mood of North Vietnam's capital, at least not as it seemed to an unexpected observer from the United States.

The mood of Hanoi seemed much more

that of a wartime city going about its business briskly, energetically, purposefully. Streets are lined with cylindrical one-man air-raid shelters set in the ground at 10-foot intervals.

The shelters are formed of prestressed concrete with concrete lids left ajar for quick occupancy—and they are reported to have been occupied quite a bit in recent days with the sudden burst of United States air raids. There is damage, attributed by officials here to the raids, as close as 200 yards from this hotel....

Christmas Eve found residents in several parts of Hanoi still picking over the wreckage of homes said to have been damaged in the United States raids of Dec. 13 and 14. United States officials have contended that no attacks in built-up or residential Hanoi have been authorized or carried out. They have also suggested that Hanoi residential damage in the two raids could have been caused by defensive surface-to-air missiles that misfired or fell short....

This correspondent is no ballistics specialist, but inspection of several damaged sites and talks with witnesses make it clear that Hanoi residents certainly believe they were bombed by United States planes, that they certainly observed United States planes overhead and that damage certainly occurred right in the center of town.

Large, Sprawling City

Hanoi is a very large, sprawling city. The city proper has a population of 600,000 and the surrounding metropolitan area brings the total to 1,100,000.

The built-up, densely populated urban area extends for a substantial distance in all directions beyond the heavy-lined city boundaries shown on a map by the State Department and published in The New York Times of Dec. 17....

For instance, the Yenvien rail yard, which was listed as one of the targets in the raids

Dec. 14 and 15, is in a built-up area that continues south west to the Red River with no visible breaks in residential quarters. Much the same is true of the Vandien truck park south of the city, which was another listed target....

The first area inspected was Pho Nguyen Thiap Street, about a three-minute drive from the hotel and 100 yards from the central market. Thirteen houses were destroyed—one-story brick and stucco structures for the most part. The Phuc Lan Buddhist pagoda in the same street was badly damaged.

Five persons were reported killed and 11 injured, and 39 families were said to be homeless.

Says Bomb Exploded

Tuan Ngoc Trac, a medical assistant who lived at 46 Pho Nguyen Thiep Street, said he was just going to the clinic where he works when an air alert sounded, indicating planes 25 kilometers (about 15 miles) from Hanoi. He had stepped to the street with his medical bag in his hand when he heard a plane and flung himself to the ground.

He said that the next instant a bomb exploded just over a row of houses, collapsing nine on the other side of the street. Tuan Ngoc Trac displayed an American leaflet, which he said he had found in the street, warning Hanoi residents not to remain in the vicinity of military objectives.

The North Vietnamese say that almost simultaneously—also about 3 P.M. Dec. 13—about 300 thatch and brick homes and huts along the Red River embankment, possibly a quarter of a mile from Pho Nguyen Thiep Street and equally distant from the Thongnhat Hotel, were hit. The principal damage was again done by a burst just above the houses, but there were also three ground craters caused either by rocket bursts or small bombs.

This area, 200 by 70 yards, was leveled by

blast and fire. Four persons were reported killed and 10 injured, most of the residents having been at work or in a large well-constructed shelter....

Contrary to the impression given by United States communiqués, on-the-spot inspection indicates that American bombing has been inflicting considerable civilian casualties in Hanoi and its environs for some time past....

It is the reality of such casualties and such apparent byproducts of the United States bombing policy that lend an atmosphere of grimness and foreboding to Hanoi's Christmas cease-fire. It is fair to say that, based on evidence of their own eyes, Hanoi residents do not find much credibility in United States bombing communiqués.

Salisbury filed from North Vietnam for two weeks and wrote an eight-article follow-up series from Hong Kong. He appeared on television and radio to describe his trip and spoke to groups frequently after his return. His articles presented the North Vietnamese view of the war, which was sharply at odds with the statements of American officials. Whether intentional or not, bombs hit civilian targets like Phatdiem, a cluster of villages with "no visible military objectives." The bombing did not cripple North Vietnam materially. A highway, for instance, seemed "capable of operating almost continuously regardless of how many bombs are dropped." The country's fighting will was not crippled. "Little waitresses in their black sateen trousers and white blouses stood ready with rifles to fire at any low-flying planes." Also, in an exclusive four-and-one-half-hour interview with Salisbury, Premier Pham Van Dong reiterated conditions for settling the war, including "withdrawal of United States forces pending reunification of Vietnam." Clarifying a question debated at home, the premier said North Vietnam's so-called four points for ending the war did not have to be agreed upon before negotiations began.

Following Salisbury's first report, the Pentagon conceded that its bombs had hit civilian targets by mistake. Neil Sheehan, working for the *Times* in Washington, reported the story, which appeared on Wednesday, December 28. This was only a partial admission by the government that anything was amiss tactically or strategically. President Johnson insisted at a New Year's Eve press conference that this was "the most careful, self-limited air war in history."

Scores of analysts in the Pentagon and the Defense Intelligence Agency, some working nights and weekends, scoured Salisbury's reporting in search of errors. In a version of the old joke that no one should want to belong to a club that would admit them, officials held up North Vietnam's invitation to Salisbury as evidence that he must be biased. Pentagon officials referred to him as a "Hanoi-picked correspondent" and as "Ho Chi Salisbury of the *Hanoi Times*." The FBI, Salisbury learned later, looked for dirt on him.

Considering the zeal with which journalists reflexively defend their First Amendment rights, the media should have formed a solid phalanx around Salisbury when the Defense Department admitted hitting civilian targets. Instead, large elements of the news media attacked him. *Time*, which ran a photo of Salisbury

Salisbury not only took pictures in North Vietnam; he also saw to it that he had pictures of himself taking pictures. These were made available to organizations that wrote about him and served as evidence that he did firsthand reporting. The grease-pencil lines are cropping instructions for printers. Copyright for photo © *The New York Times*.

with the caption "Strictly one-dimensional," was particularly creative at putting the new wine of his reporting into old bottles justifying the war. True, the magazine conceded, Salisbury's accounts widened the "credibility gap," something that never would have happened if the administration had been honest. But in so reporting, *Time* said, Salisbury gave the enemy an opportunity to "stir up a virulent new round of anti-Americanism" abroad. An editorial in the *San Diego Union* pointed to another emerging "credibility gap." Thanks to Salisbury's dubious "reporting," the government might break faith in its own commitment to the war and prohibit "bombing within 5 miles of the center of Hanoi." A *Washington Star* columnist blamed the government for letting a correspondent go to Hanoi: "The seeming indifference of the government is matched by an utter lack of identification by an important segment of the press with what the government defines as the national interest." William Randolph Hearst Jr. likened Salisbury to World War II broadcast propagandist Tokyo Rose, who was tried for treason. The *St. Louis Globe-Democrat* compared his reporting to Heinrich Himmler's "rhapsodies on the Third Reich." A regional news service dug up the antiestablishment smoking editorials that led to Salisbury's expulsion from the University of Minnesota.

In another line of criticism, Howard K. Smith, now at ABC, warned viewers that Salisbury's reporting was "careless, erratic, and misleading." The criticism, cited by others as well, centered on sourcing: Salisbury did "not always indicate explicitly the source of his material." He was not sufficiently skeptical about North Vietnamese claims. He used himself as a source, by drawing conclusions about what he saw, rather than sticking to facts he could substantiate completely.

Salisbury had a reputation among his brethren for "nearly boundless confidence in his reporting and intuitions." These qualities, honed in Moscow while reading between the lines of *Pravda,* were put to use in North Vietnam under the pressure of time. This, Salisbury admitted later, led him to make a mistake in some early reports that he was taught to avoid in journalism school—he did not provide proper attribution. In his report on bombing in Nam Dinh, for instance, Salisbury stated without giving a source (which was the city mayor) that "forty-nine people were killed, 135 were wounded on Hang Thao [street] and 240 houses collapsed." Also without attribution and adding a bit of commentary, he reported, "The textile plant, whose most dangerous output from a military point of view would presumably be clothes for uniforms, has been bombed 19 times." To ensure that these problems did not occur in subsequent articles, Clifton Daniel instructed editors to insert attributions along the lines of "147 were said to have been killed" or "this correspondent was told. . . ." In a cable he urged Salisbury to exercise more care about attribution and editorializing; foreign editor Seymour Topping did likewise.

Salisbury's transgression, however, was not as damning as it was made to seem. The ease with which *Times* editors added attribution was a sign of the obvious. Whose point of view would a reader expect to find in a report from North Vietnam? Daniel asked in Salisbury's defense. Furthermore, Salisbury did not, as critics suggested, run amuck. Although he made factual mistakes, this, too, was hardly surprising considering the limitations of being the first reporter in an unfamiliar place writing daily stories. Besides, he was careful to hedge. Did Nam Dinh have military targets that justified bombing? Perhaps, he speculated, an agricultural implementation plant had been converted to military uses. "This reporter cannot say. Are there other war plants in town? This correspondent cannot say. He saw intensive destruction of civilian housing and ordinary business streets in considerable areas—damage so severe that whole blocks have been abandoned."

More significant than Salisbury's lapses was the journalistic double standard at work. His critics applied standards for sourcing and for making inferences that they did not apply to reporters' coverage of Washington officials. George Wilson, the *Washington Post*'s Pentagon correspondent, reported that unattributed statistics from the mayor in Salisbury's Nam Dinh account were identical to statistics in a Communist propaganda pamphlet—*Report of U.S. War Crimes in Nam Dinh City*—which was distributed to correspondents in Moscow. In making this accusation that Salisbury purveyed Communist propaganda, Wilson vaguely noted that his information came from "intelligence sources." He did not reveal that the Pentagon planted the story. The *Wall Street Journal* subsequently reported that the Pentagon had leaked the story, but the revelation was buried in a one-sentence note in its *Washington Wire* column, which did not mention Salisbury by name.

Far more visible was a *Washington Post* "news analysis" the day after Wilson's story. Diplomatic reporter Chalmers Roberts, who often took the official lead, observed that Ho Chi Minh, having failed to win militarily, had a new strategy:

> Now he is using another weapon, one as cleverly conceived as the poison-tipped bamboo spikes his men emplant underfoot for the unwary enemy. At long last he has opened his country, or part of it, to an American journalist. . . . Harrison Salisbury of the New York Times is Ho's chosen instrument.

Walter Lippmann did not agree. His doubts about the war had mounted as he realized President Johnson had co-opted him with disingenuous requests for advice and false assurances that he would not expand the war. In a letter to Arthur Sulzberger, Lippmann expressed "admiration" for Salisbury. In his column, which now originated with the *Washington Post,* he wrote, "What is said on the enemy's side of the front is always propaganda, and what is said on our side of the front is truth and righteousness, the cause of humanity and a crusade for peace. Of course, a reporter in Hanoi will be told what the authorities in Hanoi wish him to believe. But what is a reporter in Washington told when he talks to the State Department, the Defense Department, and the White House?" Thanks to such opinionating, Lippmann the insider was becoming an outsider. Establishment friends turned against him. In the spring he moved his home from Washington to New York.

It was much easier to kick Salisbury than explain why he deserved a pat on the back, as the work of editorial cartoonists showed. While a *Los Angeles Times* cartoon depicted government officials planning to bomb the *New York Times,* most

"Did You Say Bomb The New York Times?"

Harrison Salisbury's trip to North Vietnam was a boon to editorial cartoonists. Most drew him in dark unpatriotic poses. Patrick Oliphant, syndicated cartoonist with the *Denver Post,* was an exception. He focused on the administration's attitude. © 1967 Patrick Oliphant.

were along the lines of a happy Ho Chi Minh reading Salisbury's accounts (the *Hartford Courant*) or getting ready to pin a medal on his chest (the *San Diego Union*).

It would have helped Salisbury's image if the public had known that the Johnson administration sought his help, and that he gave it. While Salisbury was in Hanoi, Dean Rusk made a late-night call to *Times* publisher Arthur Sulzberger to express concern that his correspondent might not be asking the right questions. After hanging up, Sulzberger called Clifton Daniel and instructed him to contact Rusk to ascertain what questions he thought Salisbury should ask the North Vietnamese government. The list of questions reached Salisbury too late to be useful, but he met with Rusk immediately upon his return to give details of his conversation with Premier Pham Van Dong, some of which was off the record and more promising for negotiations than his *Times* report suggested. Pham Van Dong, Salisbury told Rusk, had said that if the United States stopped bombing and escalation, the North Vietnamese would reciprocate. "Obliquely but perfectly clearly," the premier signaled interest in secret talks in Paris.

Rusk had previous knowledge of Salisbury's meeting with Pham. While Salisbury was in Hanoi, the administration received a back-channel message from a Western diplomat who talked to the *Times* correspondent. Based on this report, the administration had initiated behind-the-scenes communication with Hanoi. That ongoing effort was not apparent to Salisbury when he met with Rusk, who used most of the time to lecture him. Embassies, meanwhile, were under instructions to consider Salisbury's interview with Pham "a clever, carefully prepared piece of propaganda, in which the adamancy of Hanoi's position on a settlement is partially camouflaged by an aura of reasonableness." The quiet diplomacy quickly petered out when President Johnson communicated to Ho Chi Minh that the bombing would continue until the Vietnamese de-escalated. Not knowing any of the details of Salisbury's behind-the-scenes efforts to help, columnist Joseph Kraft criticized Salisbury's reporting as "second rate" because he "gave no precise account" of what he was told by the premier "on the most crucial issues of war and peace."

Publicly the *Times* stood by its man. "It isn't necessary for him to cover 'our side of the story,'" Daniel wrote to a critical reader. "We have been doing that for many years in the most thorough fashion." Inside the paper, sentiments were mixed. The *Times* staff was made up of hawks and doves on the war and on Salisbury. His hard-nosed criticism as assistant managing editor was not universally appreciated. Some thought he went out of his way, in letters seeking visas and possibly in his reporting, to ingratiate himself with Communist countries. It was the sort of charge that concerned the paper's proprietors and editors, who worried about a *Times* credibility gap. In 1965 the editorial page tilted against the bombing, and the war, but only so far. An antiwar editorial the following year—by Herbert Matthews, who was writing most of the Vietnam editorials—was changed between the first and second editions because it seemed "too emotional" to the publisher and the editorial page editor, John Oakes.

The *Times* kept careful track of letters pro and con on Salisbury. Although the final count ran three-to-one in his favor, management emotions wavered. On December 28 Sulzberger sent a note on a blue-tinted sheet used for internal correspondence to "congratulate" Salisbury. A January 4 memorandum from Daniel to Catledge struck a different tone. Daniel noted, "The Publisher is perturbed about Salisbury's pieces." "Getting into Hanoi was a journalistic coup," Daniel concluded, although Salisbury's reporting "obviously gave comfort to North Vietnam by affording an outlet for its propaganda and point of view." Salisbury "complicated matters" by his weak attribution. Daniel said he had begun to read all Salisbury's stories himself before they went into the paper. In a subsequent postmortem, he reported that editors had had "qualms" about attribution beginning with Salisbury's first dispatch; they also were not as diligent as they should have been in complying with Daniel's directions to insert attribution, some apparently concerned about doing surgery on someone of Salisbury's rank. Daniel said he had killed one story because it was "not based on eyewitness reporting" and because it was "argumentative."

This internal drama spilled out on the pages of the newspaper. One who had no sympathy for Salisbury's reporting was Hanson Baldwin, the paper's military specialist for three decades. Baldwin had excellent sources inside the Pentagon. In the 1950s he knew that manned U-2 spy planes were secretly over flying the Soviet Union.* Like his military sources, he advocated expanding the war—a million troops if necessary. On December 27, he shot off a "Dear Clif" memorandum to Daniel. He was "extremely disturbed" by Salisbury's reporting and made his case, as he often did, by playing on the paper's concern for its good name. "I do not think it is fair or accurate to make judgments based on statistics from Communist sources and print them as gospel without some qualification. . . . My chief concern is the effect that these stories will have upon the country and upon The Times." Thanking Baldwin "for your excellent memorandum," Daniel gave him the go-ahead to write a story with a counter point of view, although he cautioned Baldwin not to make it look like an argument between two staff members.

When Baldwin's story appeared on the front page on December 30, it looked like an argument between three, since it also took a swipe at Sheehan's report on the Pentagon's admission of errant bombing. It also showed the double standard at work. All of Baldwin's sources were unnamed, some offered up in the most general way, as in "military officials in the Pentagon said yesterday." He inserted judgments without attribution: "Bombing or, for that matter, major military operations of any sort, have nearly always exacted a toll of civilians as well as of the military." Pentagon sources, he said, considered Salisbury's reports on casualties "grossly exaggerated."

* This secret reconnaissance came to light when Soviets shot down a U-2 plane in 1960. The Eisenhower administration, believing that the plane had disintegrated with its pilot, said it was a weather plane. When the Soviets trotted out the pilot, the administration had to admit it lied.

In another memorandum, Daniel encouraged editors to "do everything we can in the coming weeks to balance the Salisbury reports." One such story was a report by United Nations correspondent Drew Middleton. It suggested that Salisbury had been invited to Hanoi because the bombing was working. The editorial page sought to maintain balance in an editorial that repudiated Hanoi's claims that civilians were targeted on purpose. "We reject," it said, "the sweeping deductions and false conclusions many Americans seem to have drawn from the statistics of civilian deaths and the pictures of destruction reported from Hanoi last week by this newspaper's correspondent, Harrison Salisbury."

Catledge regretted Salisbury's lack of attribution and thought the *Times* should have done more to explain "the circumstances of Salisbury's visit, instead of simply shocking our readers with a Hanoi dateline." He also considered Salisbury's trip, which forced admissions from the Johnson administration on the bombing, a "triumph of American journalism." Salisbury had dropped into a "strange place," raised important questions, and "did what he did alone," a considerable accomplishment in this "age of the press officer, the handout, the junket, the press conference, the guided trip, the briefing and the team job."

When the *Times* nominated Salisbury for a Pulitzer Prize, competing emotions surfaced again. The Pulitzer jury, the first stage in the process, recommended his award of the prize by a vote of 4 to 1. At the next stage, in one of the most contentious moments in memory, the Pulitzer Board nixed the recommendation 6 to 5. The chairman, Joseph Pulitzer Jr., the publisher of the *St. Louis Post-Dispatch,* argued that Salisbury's work was distinguished "despite minor technical flaws" and "compelled the Defense Department to revise earlier claims about precision bombing." After Pulitzer called for a second vote, the result was the same. The trustees of Columbia University, which administers the prize and in that era had the final vote, agreed.

Among the letters Salisbury received afterward was one from Marvin Kalb, who was himself conflicted. When Salisbury's Hanoi reports began to appear in the *New York Times,* the CBS reporter dashed off a hasty note to foreign editor Seymour Topping to express his concern about sourcing: "I love Harrison, as you know, but I was just embarrassed at the way in which he ignored sources and conveyed an entirely one-sided view of the bombings and their effect. I wonder if he would have displayed that same wide-eyed innocence in reporting what a South Vietnamese military briefing officer would tell him." Weeks later, after the Pulitzer reversal, Kalb sent a condolence letter to Salisbury: "That Pulitzer belongs to you, if it ever belonged to anyone." Reflecting on the episode years later, Kalb recalled the mind-set of the time—the cold war and the out-and-out lying by the Soviet government, which he saw firsthand as a correspondent in Moscow. He preferred to use official American sources and add his own qualifications. Salisbury, he said, "was always open to the other side, and this was a mark of his greatness."

Salisbury's reporting was much more accurate than American bombing was, something the government knew. In October 1966 reconnaissance photographs showed that bombers had mistakenly hit civilians. "Over 75 percent of the casualties in 1966 were civilians," reported a top-secret CIA memo on the bombing in December. In January 1967 the CIA concluded that Salisbury's reporting on bombing damage was "good," although he "had not described the full extent of the bomb damage, which is 'everywhere.'" An intelligence report written before his trip noted that the air attacks had not "shaken the confidence of the regime."

One of the most startling such documents to dribble out accidentally fell into the hands of Charles Mohr nearly twenty years later. In 1984, Mohr came across a declassified CIA 1967 analysis estimating the bombing's heavy toll on civilians. In support of their estimates, the analysts drew on Hanoi's *Report of U.S. War Crimes in Nam Dinh City.* This was the document the same government had used to portray Salisbury as a retailer of red propaganda. "Success appears dubious, at least by means considered acceptable in many parts of the world," the CIA report said.

Salisbury was not the first Westerner to report the consequences of American bombing. *Le Monde* ran a series when he was still in North Vietnam. Wilfred Burchett, a radical Australian journalist with extraordinary access to North Vietnam who traveled with Salisbury during his visit, covered the bombing for the left-wing *Guardian* in the United States, among other publications. Nor was Salisbury the last. On his heels came Harry Ashmore, a former editor of the Arkansas *Gazette,* and William Baggs, editor of the *Miami News.* Later came Joseph Kraft for the *New Yorker,* novelist and critic Mary McCarthy, and Anthony Lewis and Malcolm Browne of the *Times,* and others. But Salisbury was the first journalist with an American establishment newspaper to make the journey. His reporting gave legitimacy to going behind the lines. Baggs's dispatches, which confirmed the bombing of nonmilitary targets, were "looked at primarily as news," the *Columbia Journalism Review* noted, not as treason. The AP carried Baggs's stories.

Salisbury would have had much less of a story if the government had been truthful about the bombing. Phil Goulding, a Defense Department spokesman, considered this "the biggest public affairs mistake" during the time Robert McNamara and Clark Clifford served as secretaries of defense. He devoted a forty-page chapter of his memoir to it. By leading the public to think it dropped bombs with "surgical precision," the government had created "a national disaster." The facts revealed by Salisbury, he believed, disillusioned many Americans.

At Yale, Dartmouth, Cornell, and other universities, faculty and administrators signed protest letters asking Johnson for a bombing halt. A group of corporate executives made the same plea. A month after Salisbury's return from Hanoi, Senator William Fulbright, chairman of the Committee on Foreign Relations, held a hearing in which the *Times* reporter was the sole witness. Years later, Salisbury's reporting was seen as an important marker on the road that led Americans out of an ill-conceived, unwinnable war.

Nonetheless, the weight of official opinion still favored the administration's position. Senator Fulbright, whose mounting disillusionment with Vietnam policy had led him to begin hearings on Vietnam the previous year, was in a distinct minority that had limited power and a decided preference, as Fulbright said, not to "embarrass the administration." A January 9 *Newsweek* article mentioned Fulbright's desire to investigate bombing policy in light of Salisbury's reporting, adding, "It was the hawks who made the most of last week's development." Later in 1967, a Senate subcommittee on military preparedness endorsed the bombing strategy. The *Times* devoted an entire page to printing its report.

"We face more cost, more loss, and more agony," President Johnson said in his 1967 State of the Union address. After a Vietnamese New Year pause, bombing resumed. U.S. troop strength continued its climb to more than 540,000. In May just 6 percent of the public favored withdrawal.

With the increase in American troops in Vietnam came an increase in the number of correspondents. By January 1966, the press corps numbered 282, of whom 110 were Americans. A year later the total exceeded 500, and it rose by another 100 with the Tet Offensive in 1968. Included in this media buildup were correspondents for network television.

The first network correspondent to open a full-time bureau was Garrick Utley of NBC in 1965. Soon Saigon was the largest overseas bureau for each network. The expansion of the evening news from fifteen to thirty minutes in September 1963 by CBS—and later others—further bolstered television news. In those heady times, the networks experimented with hour-long newscasts full of foreign coverage. Some broadcast reporting, vivified by the television camera, became iconic. In August 1965, CBS's Morley Safer filmed marines callously setting the village of Cam Ne ablaze with cigarette lighters, an act set against elderly villagers' pleas that their homes be spared. That same year Frank McGee of NBC criticized the government's lack of candor.

The surprise Tet Offensive in late January 1968 was perfect for television. Tens of thousands of Communists launched attacks throughout the country. Vietcong penetrated the U.S. embassy compound. Fighting pulverized the lovely ancient city of Hue. With combat this time in the open during daylight, television correspondents had what they craved, action shots. In a memorable scene that went down in news history, an NBC camera caught South Vietnamese general Nguyen Ngoc Loan putting a pistol to the head of a captured Vietcong and blowing out his brains.*

Vietnam was a high point for television news from abroad. Nonetheless, television was, if anything, more susceptible to indexing than print was. Network television was a massive, capital-intensive undertaking. Substantial revenue was at stake in retaining nationwide audiences and powerful advertisers. The networks' lifeblood, their broadcast licenses, was in the hands of the government. RCA, which owned NBC, had defense contracts that could be canceled. The networks' strength was a weakness. Officials ascribed enormous influence to network news, which reached a larger audience than any single newspaper. President Johnson was a regular viewer. When LBJ was pleased—or displeased—he picked up the phone to call CBS anchor Walter Cronkite. Broadcasters, recognizing the potential power of the

---

* An AP photo of the same event by Eddie Adams won a Pulitzer Prize and many other awards.

medium and their vulnerability as a result of that power, reined themselves in. As CBS chairman William Paley put it, television was a "consensus medium."

The official point of view dominated network news. Although networks built up large Saigon bureaus, their largest bureaus overall were in Washington. Correspondents in the capital were not only more likely to see events through the eyes of officials; they also had more clout to get their stories on the air. In the field, network policies called for deference to officials. In 1966 ABC advised its Vietnam correspondents, "The main source for hard news is the daily briefing given by the Joint United States Public Affairs Office." Before Tet, one study found, television journalists portrayed military operations as victories more than twice as often as they portrayed them as defeats. "Positive assessments of the overall military situation in Vietnam outnumbered negative assessments by ten to one." Similarly, another study found, "hawks" outnumbered "doves" as sources in network documentaries and news interview programs by a ratio of about nine to one before 1966; from then until 1970, when the consensus broke down, hawks still dominated two-to-one.

Some television documentaries offered nuance and context that might raise questions about the war for the discerning viewer. One of the best was *Morley Safer's Vietnam*, which had the honest personal perspective of Vincent Sheean's reporting. Much more of what appeared on television was along the lines of the ABC documentary "Operation Sea War Vietnam," which focused on the aircraft carrier *Kitty Hawk* off the coast of Vietnam and uncritically projected the government view. In 1965 CBS produced a series of "Vietnam Perspective" programs using interviews with administration officials, who were allowed to review and edit the tapes as well as to publish the transcripts in book form. The networks occasionally produced documentaries with film from Vietcong or North Vietnamese sources and superimposed the warning that it was Communist propaganda. With less apparent concern, they used Pentagon film from bombing missions. ABC ran stories in which no reporter was seen and the narrator was a military officer.

CBS president Frank Stanton hunted doves at President Johnson's Texas ranch and served as a member of his Advisory Commission on the United States Information Agency. Along with other favors, Stanton sent CBS technicians to install televisions in Johnson's bedroom. And he took LBJ's calls when the president was angry over CBS coverage. Although he might publicly defend negative reports aired on CBS, behind the scenes he could be critical. When correspondent Murray Fromson reported the use of bases in Thailand to launch bombing in North Vietnam, Stanton angrily told subordinates that Fromson gave away sensitive information, although the *New York Times* and *Time* had run detailed stories and the North Vietnamese were not in the dark. When Walter Lippmann was brought by for lunch in the CBS corporate dining room, Stanton made a point of eating at a separate table.

When a correspondent transgressed, as officials believed Morley Safer did in his story on the burning of Cam Ne, retaliation came in large wallops. In Saigon, a drunken marine major stood outside his hotel room shooting a revolver in the air and screaming "Communist Broadcasting System." Marine after-action reports sanitized the Cam Ne village-burning operation, while marine headquarters in Washington claimed Safer's film was faked. A Defense Department official called Fred Friendly, CBS president for news from 1964 to 1966, to demand Safer's recall. Officials hinted that because Safer was Canadian by birth, he was unreliable. Safer, Johnson told Stanton in a telephone call, "shat on the American flag"; if CBS did not get rid of Safer, the White House would reveal his Communist ties. Friendly defended his correspondents, wrote Gary Paul Gates, a CBS newsman, which "required no small measure of courage."

Friendly's courage notwithstanding, the network pressed Safer harder about his facts on Cam Ne than if he had reported government claims of a South Vietnamese military victory. Once they agreed to run his reports, CBS followed them with anchor-read reactions from the Johnson administration. Friendly resigned in disgust in 1966 when the network decided to air reruns of *I Love Lucy* and *The Real McCoys* instead of televising Senate hearings on Vietnam.

One of the great remembered moments of television courage was not one of images, but of words—Walter Cronkite's editorial against the war after the Tet Offensive in early 1968. The comments were a significant break from CBS policy. Equally significant, Cronkite's editorial brought him no opprobrium, for, as another example of the workings of indexing, it coincided with a breakdown of the official consensus on the war.

Cronkite, managing editor of *CBS Evening News* and television's first anchor, was anything but a bomb-thrower. For years he had viewed the Vietnam conflict the way it was viewed at the White House, where he had private briefings from the president and his staff. On his first visit to Vietnam in 1965, he had the full treatment of guided tours and a dinner at which he and senior officers swapped World War II stories. He was embarrassed by the cynicism of the younger correspondents who questioned military officers at the daily briefings. The older ones, who had a tradition of working with authorities, seemed more rational. Progress, he thought, was being made.

As time went on, Cronkite began to have some doubts. He said Salisbury's reporting from Hanoi put government credibility in a bad light. (He put in a good word with the Pulitzer board for Salisbury, for whom he had worked as a UP correspondent in London during World War II). But on the air, Cronkite generally was not contentious. Without blinking, he ran stories that gave credence to the administration's point of view. In February 1966, he reported that a bus loaded with refugees had hit a land mine: "The Johnson administration and Saigon have long insisted that the Communist domination of South Vietnam's countryside was based primarily on terrorism. Well, today the war provided a bloody example of that terrorism." As David Hallin noted in his history of coverage, Cronkite "had no way of knowing—so far as one can tell from the story—whether the Vietcong land mine was intended for a bus of refugees or a military convoy." Cronkite agonized over running stories such as Safer's about the torched village of Cam Ne.

Cronkite agonized again over Tet in 1968. "What the hell is going on?" he asked when news of the offensive first reached New York. "I thought we were winning the war." The disturbing turn of events, coupled with growing antiwar demonstrations, prompted Cronkite to propose a trip to Vietnam. This time the upbeat comments from flag officers were less persuasive than the glum stories from the trenches. On camera an earnest, all-American-looking junior officer admitted he was "discouraged." With the support of News President Richard Salant, Cronkite decided to violate the network's rule against mixing editorials with the news.

Cronkite's report aired on February 27, 1968, at 10:00 P.M. to an audience of 9 million viewers. It began with old-fashioned reporting. In Hue, with scenes of the Tet offensive in the background, he wore a combat helmet, slightly askew in the manner of a veteran. The report wound up with Cronkite in a business suit, behind a desk in New York, the sound of a teletype rattling away. He looked straight into the camera and over the next three minutes made these "personal observations":

> Tonight, back in more familiar surroundings in New York, we'd like to sum up our findings in Vietnam, an analysis that must be speculative, personal, subjective. Who won and who lost in the great Tet offensive against the cities? I'm not sure. The Viet Cong did not win by a knockout, but neither did we. The referees of history may make it a draw. Another standoff may be coming in the big battles expected south of the Demilitarized Zone. Khe Sanh* could well fall, with a terrible loss in American lives, prestige and morale, and this is a tragedy of our stubbornness there; but the bastion no longer is a key to the rest of the northern regions, and it is doubtful that the American forces can be defeated across the breadth of the DMZ with any substantial loss of ground. Another standoff. On the political front, past performance gives no confidence that the Vietnamese government can cope with its problems, now compounded by the attack on the cities. It may not fall, it may hold on, but it probably won't show the dynamic qualities demanded of this young nation. Another standoff.
>
> We have been too often disappointed by the optimism of the American leaders, both in Vietnam and Washington, to have faith any longer in the silver linings they find in the darkest clouds. They may be right, that Hanoi's winter-spring offensive has been forced by the Communist realization that they could not win the longer war of attrition, and that the Communists hope that any success in the offensive will improve their position for eventual negotiations. It would improve their position, and it would also require our realization, that we should have had all along, that any negotiations must be that—negotiations, not the dictation of peace terms. For it seems now more certain than ever that the

---

* Khe Sanh was a Marine outpost with strategic importance as a staging area for operations to cut supply routes from North Vietnam. In January the Communists moved seven regiments, amounting to some fifteen thousand troops, in position to attack. The administration secretly considered—but publicly denied—using nuclear weapons to defend the base. The Communists shelled but never attacked.

bloody experience of Vietnam is to end in a stalemate. This summer's almost certain standoff will either end in real give-and-take negotiations or terrible escalation; and for every means we have to escalate, the enemy can match us, and that applies to invasion of the North, the use of nuclear weapons, or the mere commitment of one hundred, or two hundred, or three hundred thousand more American troops to the battle. And with each escalation, the world comes closer to the brink of cosmic disaster.

To say that we are closer to victory today is to believe, in the face of the evidence, the optimists who have been wrong in the past. To suggest we are on the edge of defeat is to yield to unreasonable pessimism. To say that we are mired in stalemate seems the only realistic, yet unsatisfactory, conclusion. On the off chance that military and political analysts are right, in the next few months we must test the enemy's intentions, in case this is indeed his last big gasp before negotiations. But it is increasingly clear to this reporter that the only rational way out then will be to negotiate, not as victors, but as an honorable people who lived up to their pledge to defend democracy, and did the best they could.

This is Walter Cronkite. Good night.

Cronkite's editorial, said David Halberstam, was the first time that a war had been declared over by an anchorman. President Johnson was supposed to have switched off the TV afterward and said, "If I've lost Cronkite, I've lost middle America." His press secretary, George Christian, told CBS Washington bureau chief William Small, "Shock waves rolled through government."

Cronkite's courage was undeniable. A great deal was at stake. CBS, by breaking its own rule against editorializing, could damage its bottom line. Cronkite risked sacrificing his standing as arguably the country's most trusted journalist.

Circumstances and public opinion, however, had changed. By the weekend the network had received three hundred calls and letters. Only seven objected to the broadcast. Whereas members of Congress nine times inserted comments in the *Congressional Record* on Salisbury's trip to Hanoi, not one had such remarks for Cronkite's talk. Neither Johnson nor his staff called to complain. The shock value of Cronkite's broadcast came from the fact that it was, in effect, a needle registering the thoughts of others. Indeed, Cronkite might not have come out so strongly—or so it has been argued—if the White House had had a clear policy line to rally around. Instead, critics inside the government tent were debating what to do. Only 16 percent of the congressional speeches during Tet could be called hawkish. The wall of official consensus was crumbling. Within a few days of Cronkite's broadcast, a national survey for the first time showed that more Americans believed the commitment of troops to be a mistake than didn't.

Instead of piling on Cronkite, as they had on Salisbury, other journalists mirrored the widening debate among officials, a trend that had begun the previous year. The editorial pages of the conservative *Los Angeles Times* and a few other papers had started to move in a different direction. Henry Luce died in February 1967, and the new editor of Time Inc., Hedley Donovan, heard from conservative friends and businesspeople that the war was a financial and human waste. "Stalemate"—the word Cronkite used—appeared in weekly news magazine analysis. In October 1967 *Life* called for a pause in the bombing. Some of this talk was beaten back by LBJ's national security adviser, Walt Rostow, who went on the offensive with the selective release of encouraging information. *U.S. News and World Report* said shortly before Tet, "There is good reason to believe, as 1968 starts, that this year really is going to see the beginning of the end of the war here in Vietnam."

With Tet, officials found it harder to sell such statements. On February 1, nearly a month before Cronkite's broadcast, Joseph C. Harsch of the *Christian Science Monitor* said in an ABC commentary "that the enemy has not yet, and probably never will, run out of enough manpower to keep this effort going." The *Wall Street Journal*'s conservative editorial page concluded that the war "effort may be doomed." The Salina, Kansas, *Journal,* one of many newspapers to reprint the editorial, voiced its own view that the "only honorable and wise course is to de-escalate." Asked James Reston, "What is the end that justifies this slaughter?"

After Cronkite's broadcast, Frank McGee did an hour-long NBC report that juxtaposed reporting on Tet with positive official statements from the past. "In short," said McGee, "the war, as the administration has defined it, is being lost." McGee's statement, said the *New York Times* television critic, was "further evidence that the influential mass media are steadily adopting a harder line in questioning national policy in Vietnam." At *Newsweek,* editors decided it was time for a "searching reappraisal"; one editor worried that if they did not hurry, the magazine would lose its claim to being a pace-setter. Although the Washington bureau of *Newsweek* thought the magazine was overreacting, the March 11 edition said, "A responsible journal must at least explore alternatives to the Vietnam cul de sac." Even the *Washington Post,* one of Johnson's staunchest allies, began to slip away from the official fold.

The *Post* had been an administration stalwart. LBJ said its editorial page, which influenced the editorial pages of newspapers like the *Milwaukee Journal* and the *St. Louis Post-Dispatch,* was worth two divisions. The commander of those divisions was Russell Wiggins, the *Post*'s longtime editor, who also controlled the editorial page. Although a few young reporters were unhappy with attacks on Salisbury and diplomatic reporter Murrey Marder coined the term "credibility gap" in late 1965, Wiggins kept a firm grip on the paper's tiller. When the *Post* got around to sending a full-time reporter to Saigon in 1964, it chose a former air force officer in hopes that he would get along with the brass. Peter Braestrup, who was subsequently hired at the suggestion of Joseph Alsop to head the Saigon bureau, later wrote a book explaining how the media coverage of Tet lost the war. In 1965 Katherine Graham, the *Post*'s president, received a letter from prowar journalist Marguerite Higgins congratulating her on the paper's editorials.

Graham was a frequent guest at the nearby White House and, back at the newspaper, subject to similarly large doses of Wiggins's opinions on the war. She later acknowledged that she was a believer far too long. Even when she began to nurture some private doubts in 1967, when her son joined the army and went to Vietnam, she kept them to herself while putting in place the agent of change, Philip Geyelin. Graham urged Wiggins to hire Geyelin, a diplomatic reporter at the *Wall Street Journal,* as an editorial writer and heir apparent to head the editorial page. Geyelin, a Lippmann protégé, thought the war unwinnable, favoring a gradualist approach to exiting the conflict. After Tet, his voice helped make the editorial sessions loud and rancorous. The *Post*'s course, which was gradually shifting, became even freer of prowar views when Wiggins retired in September 1968 to become LBJ's ambassador to the United Nations. Wiggins's responsibilities were split: Ben Bradlee, who had been recruited in 1965 as deputy managing editor, was in charge of news, and Geyelin presided over the editorial page.

An especially vivid attitudinal change was apparent in the work of the *Post*'s editorial cartoonist Herblock, as Herbert L. Block signed himself. He had occasionally criticized the war's impact on LBJ's domestic agenda and the lack of respect for civil rights by the Saigon government. But he did not attack the overriding wisdom of the war until Tet. A February 1 cartoon showed a military general, his Saigon headquarters in rubble, grinding out statements of victory while speaking on the telephone: "Everything's okay—they never reached the mimeograph machine." Wrote Herblock in a memoir, "There had been too many victories in the offing, too many deceptions, too many lights at the end of too many tunnels and too many Americans brought home in flag-draped caskets."

The Tet Offensive, which lasted nearly a month, presented the United States with a metaphor for an endless conflict. It brought the war, one scholar noted, "into open political debate within established institutions." The previous November, Minnesota senator Eugene McCarthy had launched his campaign for president as a seemingly lonely antiwar dissenter. In March, he surprisingly garnered 42 percent of the vote in a New Hampshire primary; emboldened, New York senator Robert Kennedy announced his own candidacy on an antiwar platform. Secretary of Defense Clark Clifford channeled his own doubts about the war by arranging a meeting of a group of formidable statesmen who had turned from reassuring to pessimistic. Three days later, President Johnson announced in a surprising televised speech that he was calling a halt to bombing north of the 20th parallel and that he would not run for reelection. He was willing to pursue negotiations with the North Vietnamese. "The press," Reston wrote, "has great influence on American foreign policy when things are *obviously* going badly."

Many thought the visual impact of television on the public was powerful. Fearful that images of the fighting eroded public support, Pentagon officials complained to CBS's Bill Small that television was running too many battle scenes. Hans Morgenthau, an antiwar professor, thought the result of television coverage was "bound to be a revulsion against war." Journalists themselves made such claims, sometimes with pride, sometimes not. "For the first time in modern history," ruefully wrote

Robert Elegant, the prowar Asia correspondent for *Newsweek* and the *Los Angeles Times,* "the outcome of a war was determined not on the battlefield but on the printed page and, above all, on the television screen."

It was not surprising that television generated so much government concern. The effects of the new medium were an unknown. For policymakers eager to sell the war, it did not take much of a leap to imagine that viewers would not support a war that they actually saw. Concrete evidence for this supposition, however, was and is far from conclusive.

Broadcast correspondents, as well as those with print media, felt pressure to get "bang-bang." Still, not much blood flowed across television screens, as many studies later showed. Before Tet, only 22 percent of the film from Southeast Asia showed combat. And what was shown often amounted to little more than gunfire heard in the distance. Similarly, about 24 percent contained casualties, yet commonly only in brief shots. In a sample of 167 reports and voice-over stories, "only 16 had more than one video shot of the dead or wounded." From mid-1965 to mid-1970, 3 percent of Vietnam reports on the evening news had heavy fighting, and the trend continued through 1973. As a matter of policy, networks did not show casualties who could be identified by viewers. "We were very sensitive to the pictures themselves," Cronkite said. "We considerably limited those pictures that showed bloodletting and missing members and things of that kind."

When vivid footage did flicker on the public's television sets, as during the exceptional period of Tet, people were able to draw their own conclusions. After an estimated 20 million Americans watching NBC saw Gen. Nguyen Ngoc Loan execute the captured guerrilla with a pistol during Tet, the network received ninety letters. This mail did not focus on the injustice of an execution without a trial. Fifty-six thought the film in bad taste; the next biggest criticism was that children might have seen it. Film footage showing the torching of a village—with elders begging for their homes to be spared—was "evidence" for antiwar activists. For many of the viewers who flooded the network with calls, it was Communist propaganda.

Although the military disliked platoon-level stories by television, in-the-field images of routine patrols, punctuated by bursts of fighting with a hidden enemy, may have been much better for the administration than reporting that coherently examined military strategy or asked searching questions about Vietnamese governance. There was, believed Safer, "small appetite—at least among the networks—for the political story from Vietnam." Almost two-thirds of the public said in a 1967 poll that television led them to be supportive of American policy. "The evidence," concluded media scholar Lawrence Lichty, "shows that those whose opinions of U.S. involvement in Vietnam changed the most were those *least* reliant on TV."

Print reporters were caught up in the bang-bang, for their bosses, too, wanted combat action. Jay Reed of the *Milwaukee Journal* and Jim G. Lucas of Scripps Howard—both former marines—were straight out of the Ernie Pyle tradition with their in-the-mud reporting. Any reporter sent into the field with combat units or assigned to the daily military press briefing, where body counts were reported, had an episodic view of the war. While in Vietnam for the *New York Times,* Charles

Mohr complained of the emphasis on daily combat stories, calling them "largely meaningless scraps." Said Ward Just, in Vietnam for the *Washington Post,* "From the briefing came the war story."

Michael Arlen, the *New Yorker* media critic who wrote frequently and insightfully about the "television war," doubted the television camera's political impact. The figures on the screen were small and unreal; very little that was "Goyaesque" showed up. "For most of this undeclared war," Arlen concluded, "almost nothing resembling a flunking grade was given our military by television news, until the final phase when some nervous C-minuses were handed out, though by a television press confident that mainstream Americans felt pretty much the same way about it."

Tet, hawks rightly argued, was a military setback for the Communists. The Communists suffered huge loses. It would take them time to recoup. If the American public was patient, the South Vietnamese could prevail. But after years of expecting a better return on the investment of lives and money, the public lost heart. They no longer believed the claims of impending victory. They were tired of troops coming home in body bags. They came to see what Salisbury saw in Hanoi. The North Vietnamese would fight on and on.

Mainstream media reflected this perspective without stepping beyond the area officially made legitimate. The student demonstrations, which began in 1965 with the bombing of North Vietnam, were strictly a fringe activity from the point of view of the public and the media. After Tet, moderate antiwar activities were considered legitimate; militant protest was troubling. In mid-1969, Americans considered the war the country's largest problem and student protests the second-largest; 84 percent favored a crackdown on demonstrators. In the early years of the war, Eric Sevareid, who did a four-times-a-week commentary on CBS, thought it presumptuous to assume he knew more than the president. One of the first to display doubts, he was equally dubious of left-wing protest and chants of "Hey, hey, LBJ, how many kids did you kill today?" Reston and other journalists felt the same. At NBC, antiwar protesters were called "Vietniks." When Peter Arnett reported that troops attacking a Cambodian town engaged in looting, the AP removed the looting references for its U.S. distribution. They feared it would inflame protesters' passions.

"As protest moved from the left groups, the anti-war groups, into the pulpits, into the Senate . . . as it became a majority opinion, it naturally picked up coverage," *Times* Washington correspondent Max Frankel said. "And then naturally the tone of the coverage changed. Because we're an establishment institution, and whenever your natural constituency changes, then naturally you will too."

Cronkite's voice was a voice of moderation, calling for negotiation, not cutting and running. When he received an invitation to visit Hanoi after his Tet broadcast, he declined. That might seem a reward, and he did not want to veer too far from center. (Charles Collingwood made the trip instead.) Writing a book on television,

Edward Jay Epstein interviewed thirty-two correspondents in the late 1960s. Over two-thirds "seemed more in agreement with the Johnson Administration's post–March 1968 Vietnam policy for negotiating an end to the war than with the critics calling for unilateral withdrawal without conditions." After Tet, the number of war critics appearing on television almost equaled the number of proponents. But nearly half of all criticism originated with public officials. Only 16 percent came in journalists' commentary.

The *New York Times,* still one of the more aggressive in its coverage, found it easier to build alternative story lines now that those lines were furnished by dissident officials. One of its biggest such stories came on the heels of Tet in 1968. It began when a *Times* economics correspondent attended a social gathering with Townsend Hoopes, the undersecretary of the air force. Hoopes was distressed about a secret Pentagon request for an additional 206,000 troops. Without being specific, he told the reporter that he and others in the administration were opposed to enlarging the war. Seeing the split in the administration as newsworthy, the *Times* bureau assigned the story to two reporters, Hedrick Smith and Neil Sheehan. Over several days, they pieced together the military plan to increase troops as well as the internal debate. When the news broke under the headline "Westmoreland Requests 206,000 More Men, Stirring Debate in Administration," the *Post* and other papers scrambled to catch up.

In June 1971, the *New York Times* began publishing the Pentagon Papers, secret documents assembled at the request of McNamara to trace the history of U.S. involvement in Vietnam. The "Papers" revealed steps taken against the advice of members of the intelligence community and without full explanations to the public. Publisher Arthur Sulzberger, who was told by his lawyers that he risked prison, worried that the paper's "reputation was on the line." The Nixon administration obtained a temporary restraining order after three days of publication, which was lifted by a 6-to-3 Supreme Court vote. The news staff literally cheered the paper's courage, seen as "redemption" for downplaying the Bay of Pigs invasion. In addition to its display of courage, this act was yet another manifestation of the fragmentation of official views. The voluminous study was passed along to Neil Sheehan and other newspapers—which followed the *Times'* lead—by one of the officials who helped assemble the papers, a disillusioned former political appointee in the Pentagon during the Johnson administration, Daniel Ellsberg. More evidence of the fragmentation of views came when it was time to award Pulitzer Prizes. This time the Pulitzer board voted for the *Times* to receive the public service gold medal. The trustees of Columbia voted to reverse the decision after a four-hour debate but caved when the university president threatened to resign if they didn't.

Nixon, who came to office promising to end the conflict, pursued "Vietnamization"—his plan for gradual withdrawal—with deception worthy of previous administrations. The spring 1970 incursion into Cambodia was conceived, in the words of one admiral, as a "plausibly deniable covert" operation. When air strikes were ordered, a general instructed public affairs officers to lie; the official line was that the attacks were in response to a threat against U.S. forces. Nixon ordered that failure was to be described as success. From November 1971 through early 1972, the commanding general of the 7th Air Force encouraged his pilots to ignore constraints on the bombing of North Vietnam, which they did at least 147 times. Many pilots filed fake reports that they had been fired upon.

While using the IRS and the FBI to harass antiwar groups, Nixon kept the press at bay by various stratagems. During the Cambodian incursion, his appointees flooded the network talk shows, as did supporters in Congress. Political allies spent tens of thousands of dollars on a radio campaign promoting the military operation. Other times, as a form of retaliation, Nixon told his staff not to talk to reporters with the *Times* and the *Washington Post*. He put journalists on an enemies list. Before giving a speech on Vietnam in 1969, Nixon ordered that "a strike force is to be set up for each network." After Nixon's speech, the chairman of the Federal Communications Commission personally asked each network for a copy of its commentary, an unprecedented step that suggested threats against the networks' licenses. As a result of publication of the Pentagon Papers, Nixon encouraged the FBI to harass Neil Sheehan by inquiries into his finances. He unleashed his vice president, Spiro Agnew, to denounce the press as "nattering nabobs of negativism." A member of the Nixon staff noted that the goal was not simply to discredit individual journalists or their organizations. "What we are trying to do," he said, "is to tear down the institution."

The government mounted an intense counterassault when CBS ran *The Selling of the Pentagon* in February 1971. The documentary turned a lens on the military's massive propaganda apparatus to build support for prosecution of the war. In a high-minded and revealing demonstration of self-evaluation, CBS pointed to its own complicity: Cronkite, among other newscasters, had narrated military films on the spread of communism. A former information officer said on air that CBS had produced a report on bombers that was "as good as if we had done it ourselves." Agnew denounced the program as a "vicious broadside against the nation's defense establishment." A congressional subcommittee subpoenaed all CBS footage, used and not used. When Stanton refused to obey, a subcommittee unanimously cited him for contempt. This action was reversed by a 226-to-181 House vote. More than one CBS executive, including Cronkite, noted intimidation that made them more cautious. All of the networks declined the Pentagon Papers when Ellsberg made them available several months later.

The treaty with the North Vietnamese was not signed until January 1973. Although it was unfavorable to perceived U.S. interests, Nixon proclaimed "peace with honor." In the spring of 1975, Communist forces launched an offensive that swept through the South. On April 29, 1975, a helicopter airlifted the American ambassador from the roof of the embassy chancery as he clutched the embassy flag. It turned out in Vietnam as Bigart told Sheehan in 1962 that it would—"It doesn't work, kid."

With equal ignominy, Nixon had resigned half a year earlier. His undoing, the Watergate scandal, began with the investigative journalism of two young *Washington Post* reporters, who were relatively less susceptible to the indexing. Bob Wood-

THE *NEW YORK TIMES* OVERSEAS EDITION

Not long after he bought the *New York Times* in 1896, Adolph Ochs contemplated creating an international edition. Such a venture, he thought, would make little, if any, money. But there was prestige and promotional value, as well as a chance to express patriotism, a subject this son of German Jewish immigrants was sensitive about. Here was a way to give expatriates news of home and Europeans a better sense of America. His patriotism was so strong, however, that it worked in reverse, contributing to decisions to table the idea.

Ochs's first attempt overseas came in 1900. The *Times* printed an edition at the International Universal Exposition in Paris. Ochs thought of carrying on by creating a permanent newspaper in partnership with the *Times* of London. He gave up the idea because it was a distraction from a plan to invest in an evening newspaper in New York, an idea that also never got off the ground, and because he was concerned that the partnership opened him up to charges of being pro-British.

Following World War I, the idea flickered again. One short-lived possibility, raised in 1922, was a partnership with the *Paris Tribune*. Col. Robert McCormick, about as different from Ochs as one could get, suggested that they split the front page between them as well as divvy up sections inside. Another idea that year was a weekly newspaper in either London or Paris. When this move was postponed "indefinitely," Edwin James in the Paris bureau tried to rekindle Ochs's interest by appealing to his sense of civic duty. The *Times,* James argued, could "give a better idea of our motives and wishes to a Europe which at this time, as you know, does not love us and which may love us less." By 1926, Ochs was back on board, telling James, "We will . . . go right ahead." In May Ochs visited Paris and London to work out details.

The weekly was to be a tabloid, published in London, with at least forty-eight pages of news and photographs. It was probably James who drafted an announcement: "THE NEW YORK TIMES in establishing this periodical is actuated by a desire to perform what it regards as a needed public service to make the United States better known in Europe, and to give news other than that of crime, casualties, horrors and sensations."

Then, out of the blue, James received a telegram. Once again the project was "indefinitely postponed." It was not just that Ochs had been told losses the first year would be substantial. The *Times* editorial policy, he wrote to James, favored U.S. cancellation of war debts and membership in the League of Nations, positions at odds with the government policy. "When we find it necessary to review and criticize the action of our Government in such matters, and these differences of opinion are republished for circulation in foreign lands," he wrote, "we may subject ourselves to inferences and charges by malevolent people that our foreign publication is employed as a subtle means to misinform Europe and to embarrass our Government in its foreign relations."

Ochs's dream did not die with him in 1935. During World War II, his son-in-law Arthur Hays Sulzberger, who became publisher, launched an overseas weekly for military personnel. "The Publisher," wrote Turner Catledge, "was convinced that such a paper, giving world news and war background, would make for better understanding of war issues." That experience led in 1948 to creation of the International Air Edition, which was flown abroad. Later, when the newspaper was printed in Europe, it became simply the International Edition. For a time an edition was also printed in Lima, Peru.

By 1965 the *Times* decided to create an autonomous newspaper in Paris, going head to head with the Paris *Herald Tribune*. The *Herald Tribune* had passed into the hands of John Hay Whitney, who purchased the failing *New York Herald Tribune*. To compete with the *Times,* Whitney acquired a partner, the *Washington Post,* and made major investments. But as was happening so often in American cities, only one newspaper survived. That survivor was the now renamed *International Herald Tribune,* which in its new form had yet another partner, the *New York Times*. Within several years the *Times* and the *Post* were the sole owners. By 2002, the *Times* wanted full ownership and, to force the issue, offered the *Post* a deal: sell out or the *Times* would withhold additional funds and launch a new edition of its own. The *Post* sold, and Michael Golden, the great-great-grandson of Adolph Ochs, became publisher.

Profits have become important for the international edition, which also is less self-conscious about its patriotism. In a month taken at random, October 2005, more than half of the *International Herald Tribune*'s editorials on U.S. foreign policy disagreed with the Bush administration. "This needs to be a European paper for Europeans," said Golden.

ward and Carl Bernstein were on the metropolitan beat. Neither previously had covered official Washington.

In the 1920s Adolph Ochs decided against publishing a European edition because it would have resulted in running editorials critical of his own government. (See "The *New York Times* Overseas Edition," p. 414.) By the 1970s, that attitude was as antique as hand-set type. Salisbury marked the Pentagon Papers as a watershed. The *Times,* he said, was no longer a "handmaiden" of government. By the time of Nixon's resignation, relations between the press and the government were routinely described as adversarial. In a 1982 survey of Washington reporters, 90 percent said that the Vietnam War and Watergate were the chief causes of this state of relations. Said one respondent, Fred Graham of CBS, "There's a presumption now that they're lying." Max Frankel, later the *Times* editor, spoke of "the *habit* of *regular* deception."

At the same time, the old lopsided equation often prevailed. When the White House had a foreign policy agenda it was determined to pursue, it could carry the news media along. This power was exercised particularly effectively in times of crisis, when legislators and the public rally behind the president.

To manage reporters when launching the 2003 Iraq War, the Pentagon recreated Ernie Pyle camaraderie by embedding more than 650 correspondents with invading forces. The strategy produced stories more positive and episodic than those by nonembedded correspondents. Although correspondents chafed at military restrictions, their reporting during the run-up to the Iraq invasion was embedded in the official consensus engineered by the White House. ABC, NBC, and CBS ran

414 stories dealing with the impending war; only 34 of them originated outside the White House, the Pentagon, and the State Department. The *Washington Post,* lamented its ombudsman, Michael Getler, gave scant attention to speeches by such lonely skeptics in the Senate as Ted Kennedy and Robert Byrd. A central argument for the invasion rested upon Bush administration claims that Saddam Hussein possessed weapons of mass destruction and was in league with Osama bin Laden. These arguments, reinforced by Iraqi political interest groups, received prominent play in the *New York Times* and elsewhere. Editors relegated the few stories presenting dissenting views to positions inside their newspapers. The Washington bureau of Knight Ridder was an exception. Unfortunately, Knight Ridder did not own newspapers in Washington or New York, let alone Chicago or Los Angeles, which limited the impact of its reporting. After the United States became mired in Iraq, the editors of the *Times* and the *Washington Post* acknowledged their credulity. Meanwhile, the networks employed former military officers, many with ongoing ties to the defense industries and the Pentagon, for on-air analysis.

The Bush administration kept pressure on the media. When David Halberstam died in an April 2007 car accident, Dexter Filkins of the *Times* wrote a memorial with one eye on Vietnam and one eye on the present conflict: "During the four years of war in Iraq, American reporters on the ground in Baghdad have often found themselves coming under criticism remarkably similar to that which Mr. Halberstam endured: those journalists in Baghdad, so said the Bush administration and its supporters, only reported the bad news. They were dupes of the insurgents. They were cowardly and unpatriotic."

The power of the first amendment is strong, but the will of the establishment media to use that power is often weak. To some extent this is healthy. The best media are self-restrained, in the interest of both building credibility and letting officials do the jobs for which they were elected or appointed. At work is a kind of Hippocratic oath promising to do no harm. Equally fundamental to democracy, though, is the presentation of diverse voices and debate, especially in the event of misguided policies or outright deception. At those times independent journalists are needed most and, paradoxically, are rare.

A reporter can challenge officials even if acting alone. Important investigative pieces in Vietnam and Iraq came from Seymour Hersh. As a young reporter, he broke the story of the massacre by U.S. soldiers of hundreds of civilians in the South Vietnamese hamlet of My Lai. It was released through the small antiwar Dispatch News Service (*Life* and *Look* weren't interested). For the *New Yorker,* years later, Hersh brought to light the abuse of detainees by American military personnel in Abu Ghraib prison in Iraq.

Richard Moose, a young foreign service officer who worked for Rostow in the White House from 1966 to 1968, changed his mind on the Vietnam War because press accounts "seemed to make more sense to me than what I was reading in policy papers and cable traffic." Harry McPherson, LBJ's special counsel and speechwriter, said much the same thing. Harrison Salisbury's reports, Ellsberg recalled, "were the first accounts of civilian damage in the North that most Americans, including high officials, had read." They distressed McNamara, who was losing faith in his own pronouncements on the war. The pity was that more reporters did not get off the government team.

Salisbury relished his role. While under fire for his reporting from Hanoi, he wrote to Herb Klein, editor of the *San Diego Union*, to ask for the original of an editorial cartoon ridiculing him. It would go, he said, into his collection, which "seems to be growing day by day." He wrote a quickie book, *Behind the Lines—Hanoi*, a portion of which appeared in *Esquire* along with an article about him by Gay Talese, a former *Times* reporter who turned New Journalist. Salisbury, Talese noted, was supposed to step aside graciously as assistant managing editor—as *Times*men did when their time was up—to give a little elbow room to Abe Rosenthal, who was moving up through the ranks quickly en route to becoming managing editor and who had distaste for Salisbury's edgy reporting. Salisbury, however, was not one to go quietly into the night. Responsible for special projects and given independence to pursue stories that interested him, Salisbury stayed on until 1970, when he became the founding editor of the paper's op-ed page, an ideal job for someone who defied conventional thinking. The page gave "space to voices not often heard in the U.S. media," one press critic noted shortly after the page swung into action. In 1972, he and another *Times* reporter became the first Western journalists to visit North Korea since the end of the Korean War. After his retirement the next year, Salisbury remained a prodigious and peripatetic author.

Salisbury also remained a champion of speaking truth to power. "The true and the crusty ingredients of history are not apt to be thrust into our hands by the vested authorities," Salisbury said in a speech on Vietnam. "It should be engraved on our cortexes that men of prejudice and power will halt at nothing—nothing when that power is threatened or when political temperatures rise."

22

DOSSING DOWN

> Everyone decided to doss down in the [Hotel] Liberty. Mrs. Jackson recom-
> mended other lodging available from friends of hers in town. But, "No," they
> said. "We've got to doss down with the bunch."
>
> The bunch now overflowed the hotel. There were close on fifty of them. All
> over the lunch and dining-room they sat and stood and leaned; some whispered
> to one another in what they took to be secrecy; others exchanged chaff and gin.
> It was their employers who paid for all this hospitality, but the conventions were
> decently observed—"My round, old boy." "No, no, my round!"

This is from Evelyn Waugh's satire on foreign correspondents, *Scoop*, a novel
nearly every one of them reads, rereads, and recommends to newcomers. Waugh
is their "patron saint." The novel resonates because it rings true about the collective existence of foreign correspondents. In reminiscences and in other fictional accounts written in imitation of *Scoop*, correspondents set the same scenes, tell the
same stories. Here is *Baltimore Sun* correspondent Patrick Skene Catling's recollection of Seoul during the Korean War:

> In all that miserable city there were only a few men who were altogether free
> and reasonably content with what they were doing. They were the correspon-
> dents who lived in the United Nations press billets, a flat-roofed Japanese apart-
> ment house in a compound enclosed by a barbed-wire fence. In this place there
> was institutional security for which the inmates were not responsible; there
> were privileges without duties; there were interesting things to learn, when one
> felt like learning them; there was plenty of food and drink and service. Living
> there was like living in a pleasantly eccentric progressive boarding school, with
> unlimited pocket money, and without any teachers and rules.

Journalists at home are citizens of the community in which they live and about
which they report. Foreign correspondents are outsiders. This feeling of being apart
inevitably breeds camaraderie. Rudyard Kipling, who began his writing career as a
journalist in South Asia, picked up this theme in his first novel. He described "the
New and Honorable Fraternity of war correspondents." Those covering Gen. John

Pershing's 1916 expedition into Mexico created the "Pancho Villa Literary and Debating Society" and wrote their own song, inspired by a military one, which they
called "Old War Correspondents Never Die, They Merely Fade Away." In Coblenz,
after the Allied troops crossed the Rhine in World War I, correspondents organized the Razzberry Club in the parlor of the Risen Furstenhof Hotel. The club's
first rule, wrote Wilbur Forrest, was that "military rank shall not count." During
the Algerian War for independence, correspondents created the Maghreb Circus.
The "one essential criterion for admission was that one had to be able, on occasion, to add to a common pool of knowledge." In Vietnam AP photographer Eddie
Adams organized a club called the Terrified Writers and Photographers, complete
with secret signs, catchphrases, and a pledge to inform fellow members of the name
of anyone who gave them a case of VD. The one hundred or so correspondents covering the rebel insurgents in El Salvador in the early 1980s formed the Salvador
Press Corps Association, SPCA for short, and donned T-shirts with an inscription
designed to prevent cruelty to correspondents. Written in Spanish, it read: "Journalists! Don't Shoot!"

The pranks, too, smack of fraternity life. Will Irwin referred to correspondents
at the 1905 Portsmouth peace conference ending the Russo-Japanese war as "The
Lost Legion." To spoof a colleague who displayed on his lapel a Russian decora-
tion, the Order of St. Stanislaus, Irwin and his pals created the Order of St. Vitus
of Crete: "a bow tie of white ribbon representing the innocent public, bound at the
center with a narrow strip of yellow symbolizing the anaconda coils of the sensational reporter." When asked if he would consent to have his picture taken with
reporters, Russian count Sergei Witte unknowingly became part of the joke: He
agreed to the photo on one condition: "I'd prefer a select group. Suppose we say
only the members of the Order of St. Vitus of Crete?"

Moving like nomads from one big story to another, correspondents congregate
in caravansaries like Waugh's Hotel Liberty. During the Russo-Turkish War in the
1870s, Januarius MacGahan and his confreres compared notes in a private room in
Missere's, a Constantinople hotel. During the Russo-Japanese War, the Japanese
virtually confined foreign journalists to the Imperial Hotel, which the reporters
called the "Imperial Tomb." During the 1920s and 1930s, correspondents could be
found in the Hotel Regis in Mexico City, the Hotel Adlon in Berlin, the Café Lou-
vre and the Café Imperial in Vienna, the Savoy in London, the Hotel Crillon in
Paris, and the Majestic in Barcelona. During World War II, they stayed in the mud-
and-wattle Press Hostel in Chungking, built outside of town for correspondents so
the government could easily keep track of them, and the Hotel Metropol in Moscow. In this "museum of smells," as Harrison Salisbury remembered the Metropol,
plainclothes police lurked in the lobby. Negley Farson recalled, "We had no place
to go—we were animals in a hostile habitat—and a few of us stayed in the hotel so
long, for days on end, that we got what was known as the 'Metropole [sic] pallor.'"
It continued thus as the century rolled along. In Saigon during the Vietnam War, it
was the eighth-floor bar in the Hotel Caravelle; in San Salvador in the early 1980s,
it was the Camino Real Hotel, which had the only working telex in town; in Bei-

In 1904 correspondents from around the world gathered in Tokyo to cover the Russo-Japanese War. The restrictions the Japanese placed on them made this a frustrating assignment. To kill time while dossing down together at the Imperial Hotel, some decided to write short accounts of their experiences as correspondents. These were collected by Frederick Palmer of *Collier's* and George Lynch of the London *Daily Chronicle* and published by a Japanese printing house. The book *In Many Wars by Many War-Correspondents* contained this photo of the correspondents on the steps of their hotel as well as the poem at the front of this book.

rut during its civil war, it was the Commodore Hotel; in Sarajevo during the Bosnia war, it was the half-bombed-out Holiday Inn.

When veteran foreign correspondent G. Jefferson Price became the *Baltimore Sun*'s foreign editor in 1991, he frequently gave each new correspondent a copy of Waugh's *Scoop* as a reminder "never to take this stuff too seriously." In fact, though, interactions among correspondents, as well as with visiting editors and publishers, are serious. They shape and often enhance news-gathering. For a look at this socialization and its benefits, we turn chiefly to the *Sun,* a newspaper with an illustrious tradition that included first-rate foreign correspondence.

No less gimlet-eyed a press critic than Oswald Garrison Villard, editor of the *Nation,* called the *Baltimore Sun* a "venerable Maryland institution." Back in the early 1920s, when Villard wrote, the *Sun* was known for independence and integrity, qualities that emanated from the Baltimore families who owned it—principally the Abells and the Blacks—and the two families who managed it for most of the century. From 1919 to 1981, its publishers were Paul Patterson, William F. Schmick Sr., William F. Schmick Jr., and Donald H. Patterson.

At the time Villard wrote, the *Sun* was, if not the largest in Baltimore readership, the paper of choice for Baltimore's leading citizens. Its circulation reached Washington, D.C., where the local newspapers were inferior. This relatively elite audience and the desire to make a truly first-class newspaper underpinned the *Sun*'s decision in 1921 to provide superb coverage of the Naval Disarmament Conference in Washington. The publisher and one of his chief lieutenants traveled to Europe to get foreign perspective on the issues at stake and to arrange cooperative agreements with European journalists who would cover the conference. The *Sun* placed a correspondent in London to report views from there and arranged for commentary from philosopher John Dewey. Once the conference was under way, Villard noted, "it speedily appeared that this old-fashioned journal was printing so many exclusive stories that a journalist had to read it to be sure of being up to the minute on the Conference news."

Encouraged by this beginning, Patterson secured rights to the prestigious news service of the *Guardian* of Manchester, developed ongoing relationships with foreign journalists, sent some of his staff abroad (Felix Morley, later editor of the *Washington Post,* went to China for the *Sun* in 1925), and set up in London the *Sun*'s first overseas bureau. In the beginning, Patterson personally selected the London bureau chiefs and made a practice of rotating reporters frequently. His rotation philosophy, which became a *Sun* tradition, was partly the usual one of not wanting reporters to get out of touch with the audience for whom they wrote and partly inspired by the idea of giving a number of the staff an opportunity to report abroad. His approach enriched the international perspective in the home office and was a powerful recruiting tool. Good reporters sought jobs on the *Sun* because they had a shot at an overseas assignment and stayed because they might get another. As a modern *Sun* managing editor noted, overseas assignments are "absolutely core" in keeping good people longer. Other newspapers have seen the wisdom of this approach as well.

As many papers did, the *Sun* sent staff abroad to cover World War II. Afterward it continued to pursue major stories. In 1949 Patterson briefly opened a bureau in Paris to report on the new North Atlantic Treaty Organization and the then-turbulent French political scene. Reporters on special assignments chronicled the end of the British Empire. This became one of the first major assignments for William Manchester, a young reporter destined to be a prominent historian. Price Day won a Pulitzer Prize for his series "Experiment in Freedom—India and Its First Year of Independence." Paul Ward won a Pulitzer Prize for a series on life in the Soviet Union.

The prospect for regular long-term postings abroad increased sharply under William F. Schmick Jr. and Charles "Buck" Dorsey, his managing editor, in those days the top news job on the newspaper. The *Sun* opened bureaus in Bonn, Moscow, Rome, New Delhi, Rio de Janeiro, Hong Kong, Tokyo, Paris, and Saigon. Some closed as new ones were opened to focus on the most important news. The *Sun* was among the first to open a China bureau. In 1980 it opened another in South Africa to cover apartheid.

Other newspapers had larger foreign services and typically sought to defray costs and add to their prestige by syndicating their reporting. The *Sun* experimented with a syndicate made up of similar newspapers but soon gave up. The newspaper was remarkable for the expenses it was willing to incur in the interest of informing its local readers about foreign affairs.

Sun editors gave enormous leeway to their foreign correspondents. These reporters, said a 1937 history of the *Sun,* "are chosen with care, but once they are in service they are free to write whatever seems to them to be the truth." When a departing correspondent asked Buck Dorsey what he should do, the laconic editor replied, "I'm the editor. You're the reporter. You find out where the news is." One rare exception involved Dorsey's short-term interest in stories about foreign restaurants for the food page. When correspondents did not respond as he wished, he cabled: "Send food stories. Or else. Love, Dorsey."

But if the correspondents who gravitated to the *Sun* foreign service were smart, enterprising, and independent, they also learned the value of alliance.

Dossing down does not preclude competition. In some respects, it is an expression of it. At close quarters correspondents can conveniently watch each other. They also can conveniently toast those correspondents who figure out ways to score ahead of others on important news. "All was fair in love or war correspondence," observed a character in Kipling's *The Light That Failed.* Said a real-life correspondent for the *Times* of London, while covering the war between Russia and Japan in 1904, "As in love, so in war—and especially War Correspondence—all is fair."

The *Times* reporter proved his point by liquoring up a *Daily Mail* competitor and locking him in his room—all to prevent him from filing a story. Some seventy years later, in 1974, *Baltimore Sun* correspondent Jeff Price spotted Turkish troops parachuting into Cyprus while he stood outside the Ledra Palace Hotel in Nicosia. With the local communications system collapsing, the desperate Price saw Jim Hoagland of the *Washington Post* speaking on a hotel phone. Somehow, it seemed, Hoagland had gotten an outside line—a miracle not likely to be repeated easily. Perhaps, Price ventured to ask, Hoagland could ask the operator to patch him through to Baltimore when he was done? Hoagland finished his call, hung up, and flashed his signature Cheshire cat grin.

Rivalry has been cutthroat among journalists working for the same employer. One of the fiercest intranewspaper wars was between Marguerite Higgins and Homer Bigart, when they both covered the Korean War for the *New York Herald Tribune.* Bigart wanted Higgins to defer to him or, better yet, to leave the country. She refused. As each tried to outdo the other, both of them took more battlefield risks than they otherwise would have. For months they did not speak to each other. Once, when the pair happened to be in the same place, they noticed a *New York Times* reporter heading to the rear to file a story. Keyes Beech of the *Chicago Daily News* arranged a truce so they could decide which of them would go back to file too. "The two met in the middle of the road and conversed," Beech recalled. "I have often felt that a plaque should be erected on the spot suitably inscribed: 'Homer and Maggie spoke here.'"

However much correspondents glorify those who beat them in getting the news, this is only one side of foreign news-gathering and, really, not the dominant one on a normal day. Not only do correspondents huddle to drink and talk after filing their stories; normally they do so after having worked together, in one fashion or another, all day long. Hoagland may not have cooperated with Price, but Price was the cooperating sort. In fact, he was in Cyprus because of a plan he orchestrated with Donald Wise of the *London Daily Mirror.* With the Nicosia airport closed, the two men arranged for correspondents to pool their resources—about ten thousand dollars—to rent a freighter to ferry them from Beirut. Higgins and Bigart disliked each other, that was true, but they did talk when they had to, and Beech, who should have enjoyed the internecine warfare, helped. He and Higgins shared a jeep and a bed. Furthermore, both the competition and the romance produced good reporting. Bigart, Higgins, and Beech were among the six correspondents in Korea singled out in 1951 for the Pulitzer Prize. Although Bigart did not have a particularly good reputation for helping others, he did let Sheehan follow him around in Vietnam.* He spent many happy hours drinking with his fellow reporters. He was quite good, a friend remembered, at telling "the stories the journalists loved to tell and hear." Among those tales was his relationship with Higgins, for whom he nurtured considerable enmity. When he learned some years later that she had given birth to a baby, he asked, "Did she eat it?"

Waugh himself was yet another example of this phenomenon of being a misanthrope and a member of the fraternity. Twice in the 1930s he was a correspondent in Abyssinia—as Ethiopia was then commonly called. Once he was there to report the coronation of Haile Selassie for the *Times* of London and once to report on the Italian invasion for the *Daily Mail.* On both occasions, Waugh could not resist the centripetal force of the press hotel and didn't really want to. It was there that he acquired background for *Scoop*'s Ishmaelia. In two nonfiction books recounting those news excursions, as well as in *Scoop,* he ridiculed his colleagues. Waugh dubbed a correspondent for the *News Chronicle,* whose political views differed from his, the "Radical" and described him as a naïve pawn of the home office. "His editor had told him that he must wear silk pajamas under his clothes if he wished to avoid typhus; he never neglected to do so." Nevertheless, Waugh teamed up with the Radical and others to share resources and chase news. After Sir Percival Phillips of the *Daily Telegraph* and the AP's Jim Mills scooped all of their colleagues on a big

---

* In keeping with his reputation for avoiding cant or sentimentality, he was less kind to young R. W. "Johnny" Apple, who asked Bigart for advice on his upcoming assignment in Vietnam. Bigart disliked Apple's eager solicitousness and responded, "Kid, I couldn't give less of a shit where you go and what you do." As Arthur Gelb tells the story in his history of the *New York Times,* Bigart was no more cordial when Apple visited the city room three years later. "Where have you been?" he asked. Gelb, *City Room,* 352.

story—which overshadowed a scoop that Waugh scored at the same time—Waugh attended a banquet at the Imperial Hotel to celebrate their journalistic victory.

When Bradley Martin opened a bureau in New Delhi for the *Baltimore Sun,* he had a lesson in the dynamics of cooperation. The teacher was Michael T. Kaufman, the *New York Times* bureau chief. "I was bowled over by his generosity," Martin recalled. "He had me over to dinner at his house, advised me on how to get established, passed along sources. Finally, I pointed out to him that we were, to some extent, competitors. Why was he helping a competitor? That's when he told me about his news value scale." "I rank every story from one to ten nubes," Kaufman said, "with the Second Coming and the end of the world representing one. Most of the stories you and I work on are ten nubes, and nine and a half—eight at the most. There's no point in fighting over an eightnuber. We might as well cooperate and save the competition for the big ones."

Kaufman's scale was highly personalized, the word *nube* pure invention. But the underlying principles, which go like this, made very good sense:

Teaming up is a journalistic expression of the Golden Rule. "The people who survive in the newspaper business may be anonymous to the rest of the world but never to themselves. Whether or not they are a race apart or, as has been suggested, merely a convention of borderline cases, they understand each other and, what is even more remarkable, they know one another." So wrote one of the more likable of foreign correspondents, Robert Casey of the *Chicago Daily News.* In practical terms this means that correspondents, a relatively small group of people, repeatedly run into one another as they move around. One time the correspondent is the new person in town and needs pointers, as Martin did in New Delhi. The next time, the correspondent is the old pro, perpetuating the pattern of reciprocity. George Seldes called this activity "ear biting" and listed it as number one among the ways correspondents get information.

The great Polish correspondent Ryszard Kapuscinski once described how he was helped and how he, in turn, helped others. Being from a Communist country made it difficult for him to get into countries when a right-wing coup occurred unless he had help from colleagues. "And when it was a left-wing coup d'état," he said, "I was helping my friends from Western countries sneak in." When Michael Kaufman went on his first posting abroad for the *Times* in Africa in the mid-1970s, one of the very first people to help him was Kapuscinksi, who gave him inside dope on the Communist point of view for a story he was writing.

Yet another expression of the golden rule is this: Reporters try to scoop reporters who have rooms down the hall. But after they do, they give the competition a call to say that a "rocket" is probably on the way from their editor asking why they missed the story and what they are going to do about it.

Teaming up is efficient. Correspondents save money and time working together. During the Suez Crisis in 1956, when the Israelis sent troops into the Sinai Peninsula, Patrick Catling met up in Tel Aviv with Donald Wise, the same *London Daily Mirror* correspondent with whom Jeff Price worked eighteen years later in Cyprus. Wise, one of the most respected foreign correspondents and one of the wittiest, was known for helping others, although his motive was frank self-interest. As he told Catling, he was glad to see him back; he needed somebody to share the cost of keeping a taxi on call twenty-four hours a day. "This is a very expensive little war," he said. When *Sun* correspondent Gilbert Lewthwaite covered the Grenada invasion in 1983, the scene he found upon arrival was chaotic. He teamed up with an Australian journalist. "You get the hotel," Lewthwaite said. "I'll get a car."

Teaming up adds value. In Waugh's *Scoop*, the British correspondents roost near one another on the theory that it is easier to spy on competitors than to go out and get a story yourself: "As early arrivals Shumble, Whelper and Pigge might, like the Frenchmen, have had separate rooms, but they preferred to live at close quarters and watch one another's movements."

While it is true that cooperation offers possibilities for doing less, first-class correspondents work together for the opposite reason, to get more done. "I worked regularly, for instance, with an Englishman, a Frenchman, a Russian, and a Pole," said John Whitaker of the *Herald Tribune* of cooperating with correspondents from other countries, each of whom had special sources at a Geneva disarmament conference between the world wars. "We met every night before writing our dispatches. . . . Piecing together the several versions of the various delegations as to what took place in secret conversations or sessions, we were able to reconstruct the whole with astonishing accuracy."

During the treaty negotiations in Paris after World War I, Herbert Swope of the *New York World* and Arthur Krock, then representing newspapers in Louisville, joined forces. Correspondents were limited to four hundred words each evening for wireless transmission. Sending a joint dispatch, they could double the size of their report. Swope's contacts inside the Wilson administration and young Krock's legwork made those joint reports richer. Several times when Swope had a clean beat on a big story, he kept it to himself. But that stopped when Krock kept one for himself.

A more contemporary example of cooperation occurred in China during the late 1980s, when John Schidlovsky was the *Sun*'s Beijing correspondent. The Chinese government required correspondents to live in diplomatic compounds, where they could be monitored, and officials did whatever they could to limit access to information. "In an environment where the Chinese authorities were actively trying to prevent foreign journalists from learning about things they did not want us to know, it was natural for correspondents to trade rumors, tips, information about what was going on."

Teaming up gives correspondents added power against authority. A lone correspondent, even one representing a powerful television network or the *New York Times,* is a David next to the Goliath of a national government that is making newsgathering difficult. It is here that formal and informal press associations become, as it were, clubs to brandish against authorities.

"I dare to make a specific suggestion to American editors and news services," veteran correspondent Eugene Lyons once wrote. "It is that they relax, or even abandon, competitive journalism in countries where there is censorship and dictatorial control. With this one move they would multiply the self-respect and reinforce the courage of the entire American press corps in those countries. A correspondent could then insist on his rights, and even risk offending the powers-that-be by sending out an unpleasant truth, without the haunting fear of becoming *persona non grata* and therefore at a disadvantage as against the competition."

In addition to providing a framework for collective bargaining, associations provide a venue for meeting officials and breaking news. At a Foreign Correspondents Club of Japan luncheon, tough questioning of Prime Minister Kakuei Tanaka about his financial dealings set in motion a wave of national media investigations leading to his resignation in 1974. Japanese journalists, who had previously looked the other way, could not ignore the impact of the correspondents' action.

Teaming up also gives reporters greater sway over the editorial authorities in the home office. While in Vietnam for CBS, Murray Fromson came up with an important story that was not well suited for television. A general told him at a cocktail party in Saigon that General Westmoreland "just doesn't get it. The war is unwinnable. We've reached a stalemate and we should find a dignified way out." The general, Frederick Weyand, agreed to an interview on the condition of absolute confidentiality, which meant no film footage. Knowing that a pictureless story was a hard sell to his New York editors, Fromson won agreement for R. W. Apple of the *New York Times* to come along to the interview. "I guessed—correctly—that once it appeared in The Times," Fromson said years later, "the universal scream would be for me to match it."

Teaming up offers a measure of physical safety. Much overseas news, almost by definition, occurs where people are shooting at each other or where governments are repressive. Correspondents travel together in order to protect each other. Two or three reporters are less likely to be waylaid than is a lone reporter. And if you are arrested by drunken soldiers who think you are a spy, as *Sun* correspondent Weldon Wallace was in the Belgian Congo in 1963, you want, also like him, to be with two other correspondents. The greater the number of correspondents who are in trouble, the more conspicuous they are, and the more likely someone will notice and come to the rescue.

Teaming up maintains sanity. There is sanity as well as safety in numbers. Camaraderie fights against the loneliness and breaks the stress. It helps battle insecurities that extend homeward, where correspondents can imagine newsroom enemies furiously undermining them. Said one *Times* editor, Betsy Wade, "Even a message saying the sun came up this morning brings back a reply: 'What do you mean by that?'"

The *Washington Post*'s Keith Richburg wrote fondly of "the Al-Sahafi Hotel, our rather familiar redoubt," in violent Mogadishu in the early 1990s. "The rooftop became the site of our own regular nightly party sessions, which usually began with Paul Alexander, the Associated Press reporter, mixing up his particularly wicked batch of whisky sours, using lemon Kool-Aid bought from the U.S. military PX."

A tonic imbibed by correspondents everywhere is sardonic humor. When Jeff

Price covered the Turkish invasion of Cyprus, he shared a rental car with three other reporters, all veterans of the Vietnam War. While Price did the driving, they gave him advice. "If one of these planes takes a dive in our direction, pull over so we can all get out of the car." "When you see a tank coming, stick your hand out and wave to let them know you are friendly." When Price's waving grew a little frantic, one counseled, "Wave to them like a friend, don't shake your fist." Exasperated, Price lost his temper. "If you big war correspondents know so much about driving a car in a fucking war zone, why am I driving the fucking car?" "Because," one responded, "statistics show the driver's the last one to make it out of the car."

The informal rules of cooperation have infinite variations, and the relationships among journalists are fluid.

Cooperation works best with noncompetitors, which explains why the *Baltimore Sun*'s Patrick Catling typically paired up with a European correspondent. Higgins and Beech made a good team because she represented a morning newspaper and his hit the streets in the late afternoon. A wire service reporter is after straight news; a special correspondent for a newspaper emphasizes depth and color—so, why not rent a car together?

Personalities can get in the way of joint arrangements, to be sure. During the Vietnam War, Malcolm Browne of the AP coldly rebuffed David Halberstam's suggestion that they work together in Saigon. Halberstam joined forces with Neil Sheehan of the UPI instead. Their team grew to include Charles Mohr of *Time,* Nick Turner of Reuters, and a few others. Browne, something of a loner, nevertheless had his own camp of confederates, including *Newsweek* reporter Beverly Deepe, a broadcaster named John Sharkey, and François Nivolon of *Le Figaro.* When Browne married a Vietnamese woman, Nivolon was the best man.

In Moscow in the 1950s and 1960s, correspondents organized themselves into combines. These centered on large news services, which helped correspondents keep up with events by giving them access to their wires. Ernest B. Furgurson with the *Baltimore Sun* was grouped with the Associated Press and Reuters—wire services from different countries and therefore not at the time competitive—as well as the *New York Times.* The other combine was anchored by United Press International and Agence France-Presse, also not competitors. The reporters in each combine traded information among themselves. They took turns staking out major events to keep track of who was coming and who was going. When Stuart Loory of the *Herald Tribune* got a scoop on the ouster of Khrushchev, he gave the information to Reuters. From then on Reuters helped him. After he turned down an offer to cooperate with longtime Moscow correspondent Henry Shapiro, the UPI bureau chief issued orders to bar him from the office.

Combine solidarity could be overridden. Although NBC and CBS belonged to opposing combines, that did not stop John Chancellor of the former from holding the television camera for Marvin Kalb of the latter—and vice versa. "We were all outsiders," Kalb recalled, and that engendered back scratching. When Kalb had an exclusive story that he wanted to keep away from others, his wife did the camera work.

"You're all in it together," said the *Boston Globe*'s Curtis Wilkie, who frequently traveled with Jeff Price of the *Sun*. "You're trying to make sense out of a chaotic situation." Their "trench companionship," as Price called it, continued back at their permanent bureaus in Jerusalem, where they had offices next to each other. Alan Moorehead of the *Daily Express* and Alexander Clifford of the *Daily Mail* struck up a close relationship while covering the North African phase of World War II. "Mentally, by this time," Moorehead said, "I was more married to Alex than I was to Lucy." Such a feeling can carry over when one returns home. The Frontline Club was started in London in 2003. Its founder, Vaughn Smith, called it a "camp fire" for people who risk their lives as foreign correspondents.

Having been bound closely together in the field, correspondents fondly recall their colleagues afterward. In the heyday of "personal histories," journalists' memoirs become a roll call of mutual admiration. In one of his books, the highly independent Vincent Sheean spoke of the "fraternity or the club system" that binds reporters during war and in keeping with this praised "jovial and warmed hearted Quent." Quentin Reynolds, in one of his memoirs, returned the compliment. He recalled looking for a book one evening and spotting "an old favorite, Vincent Sheean's *Personal History*."

And even this does not test the limits of comradeship. When circumstances call for it, correspondents go a step further than writing *about* colleagues. They write *for* them.

Reviewing *Somewhere I'll Find You,* a feature film with a foreign correspondent theme, a *Variety* critic labeled as "tripe... that incident of [Clark] Gable cabling his own scoop to an opposition newspaper under the byline of an old, sick correspondent." The reviewer had never been a foreign correspondent.

In Cuba during the Spanish-American War, Edward Marshall of the *New York Journal* fell seriously wounded while covering the Rough Riders. His longtime friend Stephen Crane walked four or five miles along a difficult jungle trail in stifling heat to file Marshall's dispatches. All that Crane managed to send to his own newspaper, the *World,* was seven sentences. When a despondent Sisley Huddleston, who wrote for the *Christian Science Monitor* as well as various British newspapers, decided to leave a dead-end diplomatic conference even though it would jeopardize his career, Wythe Williams of the *Philadelphia Public Ledger* saved "me by sending cables in my name." A surfeit of such help came to a reporter covering President Herbert Hoover's postelection trip to Latin America. After several weeks of abiding by Hoover's Prohibition platform, the correspondent decided to go on a bender and asked a colleague to cover for him, "a request no newspaperman with a heart ever refused in such circumstances," said Will Irwin, who was on the trip. As the correspondent began to drink, he asked others for help as well just to be on the safe side. At least four correspondents cabled at considerable expense the full text of a speech by Argentina's president. A terse, sardonic cable came from the correspondent's home office—"SPEECHES RECEIVED."*

Then there is the case of William F. Schmick III. The son and grandson of *Baltimore Sun* publishers, Schmick had a special claim on the newspaper's tradition. As a correspondent for the paper in the late 1960s, he was accustomed to operating independently from his base in Rome. By his count, Schmick had bylines out of twenty-two countries and only two involved assignments suggested from Baltimore. In other cases, he cabled his intent "to go to xxxx unless I hear otherwise." In equally time-honored fashion, Schmick received help from colleagues and gave it, too, as illustrated by his partnership with John Wallis of the *London Daily Telegraph*, a newspaper with its own traditions.†

Like the *Sun*, the *Daily Telegraph* had been in the hands of two families for over a century. It was launched with an eye to mimicking James Gordon Bennett's freewheeling *New York Herald,* and like the *Herald* it became more responsible with maturity, at times seeming to be compulsive in its pursuit of precision. In the 1950s, when Elizabeth Taylor arrived in London and was asked how she was feeling, the *Telegraph* reported her response as "I'm feeling like a million dollars (£375,000)." One of its traditions was foreign news. Its first overseas bureau was opened in Paris the year after the paper was founded in 1855. In the 1930s, the *Telegraph*'s foreign service numbered more than sixty full- and part-time correspondents.

By the time Schmick met Wallis in the Middle East in the late 1960s, the fifty-nine-year-old Wallis was a *Daily Telegraph* veteran. He had covered Israel in the 1940s when it was Palestine. For Schmick, who occasionally went to Jerusalem from his base in Rome, Wallis was an ideal companion: He knew the terrain and its history better than did Schmick, who was still in his twenties. He also had a

---

* It is worth mentioning here, by way of filling out the sociology of foreign news-gathering, that correspondents, when in large groups, are notorious for being unruly around officials and inclined toward drink-laced high jinks. Diplomat George Kennan was the putative leader of Americans detailed in Germany at the outset of World War II. When the group was allowed to leave in 1942 for Spain, he wrote in a memoir, "We found it necessary to lock the doors of the trains to keep the more exuberant members of our party (primarily the journalists) from disappearing into the crowded, chaotic stations in search of liquor and then getting left behind." As a *Daily Mail* correspondent in Ethiopia, Evelyn Waugh persuaded a military attaché to pour gin into the fruit salad at a luncheon. When they mounted horses to ride home, the inebriated secretary to the British legation fell off his steed while it was standing still. George F. Kennan, *Memoirs: 1925–1950* (New York: Pantheon, 1983), 137; Deedes, *At War with Waugh*, 43–44.

† Not all *Daily Telegraph* correspondents had a reputation for being helpful. One of its most famous was Bennet Burleigh, who flourished in the late nineteenth and early twentieth centuries. He was described by a member of one of the newspaper's owning families as "immensely strong, tough, enterprising and, as I remember him and others found him, rather disagreeable. . . . Burleigh was never known to go out of his way to express good will to anybody or to bother unduly about his family." When it served his purposes, he hogged the telegraph wire by filing trivia so his competitors could not use it. Lord Burnham thought Burleigh "possibly the greatest of all war correspondents." Burnham, *Peterborough Court*, 8–9, 59–60.

reputation, as a biographer of the *Daily Telegraph* noted, for "always being astonishingly well informed, and usually at least one jump ahead of the competition."
(While Paris bureau chief in 1958, Wallis telephoned the night foreign editor to say
he had to leave immediately for Algiers; he was the only British correspondent the
next day to witness the coup that eventually brought down France's Fourth Republic.) Wallis's interest in Schmick was a mixture of the avuncular and the practical.
Schmick could help pay the taxi fares.

The duo made a habit of staying at the American Colony, an old Jerusalem
hotel. At dinner on a Saturday in June 1969, Wallis said, "Bill, we are going to have
a good story on Sunday morning." He had contacts among the Palestinian Arabs,
from whom he had learned that the Israeli Ministry of Religious Affairs had decided to demolish Arab dwellings that abutted what some argued was an extension
of the Wailing Wall. The two reporters showed up at eight o'clock. Within minutes,
armed military policemen and ministry officials roughly escorted Schmick off the
scene. His shirt was torn in the process. When Wallis was spotted, he, too, was
taken away. He hurt his arm when he stumbled. After protesting to government
press authorities, the men were allowed to return, albeit briefly. When Schmick
used his Brownie camera to take pictures of hysterical Palestinian women in front
of their doomed homes, the pair was taken away again.

The afternoon found Wallis and Schmick in a cinderblock press center run by
the Ministry of Public Affairs. Schmick wrote his story. Furious about being manhandled, Wallis went to the cafeteria to drink beer and cool off. The alcohol and
the heat had gotten to him by the time he sat down to write, and he dozed off. On
the advice of a stringer for Reuters who occasionally worked for the *Sun,* Schmick
strolled over to look at Wallis's unfinished story. It began with something about
"the so-called Ministry of Religious Affairs." British correspondents have greater
license to state their opinions and throw in provocative adjectives, but this went
too far. Taking matters in hand, Schmick wrote the story and filed it under Wallis's name. Schmick's story for the *Sun* was written entirely in the third person with
no mention of the correspondents' being manhandled (the *Sun* used a story from
the Reuters correspondent to report Schmick's treatment by government officials).
Schmick wrote Wallis's story British-style, which is far less constrained about use
of the first person, and included details of their confrontation. The *Daily Telegraph*
ran it on June 16.

REPORTERS BARRED

AS ISRAELIS

RAZE ARAB HOMES

By JOHN WALLIS in Jerusalem

The Israeli Ministry of Religious Affairs yesterday started to destroy a number of houses on what the keen Zionists believed to be the southern extension of the Wailing Wall—the western wall—of the Great Temple built by
Herod.

These nine houses immediately behind the Al Aksa, one of the oldest mosques in Jerusalem, belong, according to the Arabs, to a family religious foundation called the Waqf.

The Abu Saud, one of the oldest and best known families in East Jerusalem, has a stake in the foundation.

Yesterday's destruction was to remove the last remaining houses along the Wailing Wall, the holiest site in Jewry. Over 100 other nearby houses were destroyed and their residents evicted after the June 1967 war in order to create a broad plaza for the Wailing Wall.

The ostensible reason given for yesterday's destruction is that cracks had appeared in the Abu Saud homes and that they constituted a public danger. However, this finding by municipal engineers was made only two months ago.

Rabbi Dov Berla, director of the Ministry's Division of Holy Places, admitted that the Government had actually decided to clear and lay bare the wall.

Arabs conceded that the buildings were shaky. But they pointed out that Israeli archaeologists had been digging under the nearby Al Aksa mosque for months before.

Fear of publicity

Fearful of bad publicity and its repercussions abroad, the Israeli Religious Ministry yesterday attempted to bar foreign reporters from the scene. I was notified on Saturday by a member of the Abu Saud family that they had been warned their furniture would be removed.

With William Schmick, an American correspondent of the *Baltimore Sun,* I went round to the scene. Within seconds we were questioned by an Israeli military policeman who rejected Israeli Press passes.

Schmick was then seized by two members of the Ministry for Religious Affairs who hustled him across the Mosque compound, tearing his shirt, into the open piazza below.

I tried to adopt an inconspicuous position, but an Arab woman rushed up, sweat pouring off her face and tears in her eyes, as she regarded the home where she was born, crying "Allah Akhbar [God is Great]."

A few minutes later I, too, was seized by two members of the Religious Affairs Ministry who rushed me across the sacred soil of the Mosque courtyard, to which they paid no attention or respect, and then down the steps to the piazza in front of the Wailing Wall below.

Arab anger

Schmick and I then protested to the Israeli Press authorities and we were told that we could return without hindrance.

But when Schmick started to photograph Israeli workers demolishing the upper floors of the buildings and shouting with glee while Arabs were yelling in rage, the Religious Ministry authorities again ordered us to leave.

A member of the Abu Saud family later told us that his ancestors had for centuries used the Al Aksa Mosque. They enjoyed certain traditional rights like the other great Arab-Jerusalem Moslem families—the Husseinis, the Alamis, the Khatibs.

Correspondents' selflessness is not always fully appreciated by editors. On a trip to Cuba, where he was covering a sporting event for the *World-Telegram,* Quentin Reynolds filed for three drunken colleagues before wearily writing his own report, which was rather dull by comparison. Next day came a cable: "WHERE WERE YOU YESTERDAY? IN HAVANA? ALL THE OPPOSITION HAD LIVELY STORIES." Schmick once helped another British colleague who had missed a story by giving him a copy of the story he filed for the *Sun.* Back came a cable from the Brit's home office: his story was "insubstantial"; they used the wires instead. This time, though, Schmick fared better. Along with the satisfaction of helping Wallis, he got an apology from the Ministry of Religious Affairs and the offer of a new shirt to replace the one that was ripped.

For a publisher—or equally for an owner or editor—having a foreign bureau is like having a yacht—or a fleet of them, should they have several such outposts. Visiting them is a cherished perk, for a visit offers a pleasant outing as well as a chance to say to a peer, "I think I'll be visiting our Paris bureau next week. Need to see how our correspondent is doing. [Pensive pause.] Besides, I really need to have a chat with Prime Minister _____." A side benefit is the good excuse for a change of scenery on the company tab along with the guiding services of a well-informed resident foreign correspondent who doesn't expect a tip. "One of the rules," says Milt Freudenheim, whose career has included the *Chicago Daily News* and the *New York Times,* "is to entertain publishers."

The opportunity to doss with the boss is a mixed blessing. Correspondents, as one noted, serve as "friends, political counselors, and interpreters," which sounds like a fine way to fortify one's career until the visiting editor or publisher and their spouses turn out to be provincial, prejudiced, and ignorant as well as chronic complainers. How one handles a visit is often seen as a measure of reportorial competence: if you can get the car to the airport, observes *Sun* correspondent Gilbert Lewthwaite, you can get the news. A Rome bureau chief was forever tainted in the eyes of Henry Luce because he failed to meet the Time-Life founder at the airport. "It was more fun to be a member of an organization that didn't have their top editor on location," recalls Gordon Mott, who covered Mexico and Central America for AP and Knight Ridder, "and laugh at how much better dressed, or behaved, your competitor was with a boss in tow." While visits can induce gut-wrenching terror, however, they also can make a correspondent's job a bit easier and more productive.

Victor Lawson, the usually stately owner of the *Chicago Daily News,* was suffering from a breakdown when the publisher's London correspondent met him at Waterloo Station in 1908. Filled with "nervous dread," Lawson commanded Edward Price Bell to doss down with him, literally, by sleeping in the same bedroom.

When he left London, Lawson took Bell along without letting him go home to get a bag. Although Lawson was soon joined by his wife, he insisted on keeping the correspondent at his side for the next four months as the threesome traveled Europe. Once, when accused of not acquiring the proper tea quickly enough, Bell blew up at his boss. The biggest problem, though, was tedium. "The worst of it is, from my point of view, that I can do nothing," Bell wrote to editor Charles Dennis back in Chicago. "I merely hang about and wait for a call from Mr. or Mrs. Lawson." Nevertheless, the experience solidified their relationship. When Lawson finally allowed Bell to return to his family in London, he gave his correspondent an envelope with $1,000 in it. Lawson bequeathed Bell $25,000.

Col. Robert McCormick, always a sharp contrast with his rival Lawson, tormented his *Tribune* staff without giving commensurate reward. The imperious publisher never carried money when he traveled. While he wandered about a foreign city, a correspondent followed behind with a wad of cash to pay the bills—a challenging job because McCormick walked briskly. At one of McCormick's command dinners, a foolishly unguarded reporter mentioned some reckless artillery work during World War I, a fiasco that, it so happened, was attributed to the colonel, who had had a command. "Never fire that man," McCormick ordered, "and never give him a raise."

McCormick's family also required special attention on their visits. When his mother rolled into Paris, William Shirer recalled, local staff were "assigned to rent a special Pullman for her use, meet her at Cherbourg, get the special car attached to the boat train, accompany her to Paris, and put her up at the Ritz." Once, while having tea at the hotel, the dowager commanded the captive Shirer to take dictation for a lengthy cable to the long-deceased Abraham Lincoln. Weird as this was, helping family members was not unusual at other papers. At one point, correspondents in the *Daily Telegraph* Paris bureau were asked to bring expensive underwear and a whole ham to Lady Pamela, the publisher's wife in London.

No matter how laid-back the publisher wants to be, staff angst is inevitable. Katherine Graham, who presided over *Newsweek* as well as the *Washington Post,* enjoyed visiting her overseas bureaus. She used the trips to broaden her knowledge, worked hard to prepare herself, and discouraged the use of limousines. She wanted low-key travel, which was about as likely as the pope bicycling to work at the Vatican. She was owner and publisher of a prestigious newspaper whose offices were a short walk from the White House. As a result she had extraordinary access to heads of state (she was the first woman granted in her own right an audience with the emperor of Japan), along with considerable pomp and circumstance. On her 1965 trip to Japan she was greeted by eighty applauding people at a Tokyo advertising agency, which put up a sign, "Welcome Mrs. Philip L. Graham." Her entourage, which typically included editors as well as others, was large, and a prodigious amount of planning had preceded the trip. Correspondents did dry runs of her itinerary, visiting all the stops she would make and plotting out such details as the location of toilets. Tension mounted when *Post* and *Newsweek* bureaus in these countries competed to make arrangements.

Visits from *Baltimore Sun* executives were colored by the visitor's personality. *Sun* editor Buck Dorsey, not much for traveling, was nevertheless a bit of an Anglophile. When he sent word that he was going to visit London, bureau chief Russell Baker told his office assistant to lay on a Daimler, the type of car used by Queen Mary. "Our futures," Baker told his office assistant, "might depend on making Buck Dorsey happy for the next seven days." Dorsey also liked to drink, which Baker did with him the first night of his stay. When the young correspondent left shortly before dawn, he was calling his editor Buck.

Publisher William F. Schmick Jr. took considerable pride in the foreign service established during his tenure. When he traveled, often with his wife, he cared less about meeting with dignitaries than seeing how the reporters and their families were faring. Financially conservative, he would raise an eyebrow over an oriental carpet in the correspondent's apartment that seemed too expensive. Once, when flying with Schmick, a Hong Kong correspondent booked first class, only to find the publisher flying economy. When the Paris bureau chief asked Schmick's son how to handle the old man, the answer was, Don't try to impress him with fancy wines, just give him two martinis before dinner.

The chairman of the *Sun*'s board from 1956 to 1984 was far more flamboyant. Gary Black was the scion of one of the *Sun*'s two owning families. It was and is a custom among media owners who want to bring their offspring into the enterprise to send them to another newspaper for training. Black went for his training to the *Milwaukee Journal,* then considered one of the finest-run newspapers in the United States. Unlike most people with entry-level jobs, he brought his valet with him. Not familiar with such mundane matters as the shift key on the typewriter, he complained one day that no matter how hard he hit the keys none of the letters came out capitals. Later he was not ashamed to admit the story was true. Expecting to travel well when he rose in the ranks of the *Sun,* he grew huffy when things did not work out. He and his wife checked out of the swanky Claridge's in London when the butler came into his suite while they were having breakfast in bed and asked to borrow the salt and pepper. When Black and his wife visited Tokyo, she did not like their suite in the upscale but old Okura. Black asked the bureau to arrange rooms in the Imperial Hotel, which had been rebuilt to a Frank Lloyd Wright design since correspondents had been herded there during the Russo-Japanese War. The bureau's news assistant had to persuade the Imperial's management to move an Arab visitor to a lesser suite. Black also expected to drive in luxury. When he visited Beirut, Jeff Price hunted a couple of weeks for a suitable car, finally finding a bulletproof Fleetwood used two decades earlier by a president of Lebanon. He told the owner, who was to drive it, to wear a chauffeur's cap.

All the fuss and heartburn aside, these trips had value besides what they might do for a correspondent's career. For months, Rome correspondent Weldon Wallace wrote to the home office seeking permission to buy a new, bigger, and more dignified car to replace the bureau's beat-up, cramped Fiat 500. He had no luck until a visit by Schmick, who found it difficult to fold his six-foot-three body into the rattletrap. When Schmick returned home, Wallace was given the go-ahead to buy a new car. More important was one of Black's visits to Tokyo. The resident correspondent was never able to secure an interview with Prime Minister Takeo Fukuda until Black showed up. Then the prime minister agreed to a meeting, just as the emperor had agreed to meet with Katherine Graham. In a formula typical of such interviews, Black opened the door, and his employee wrote the story. Trips by the boss "required lots and lots of preparation," said the *Sun* correspondent Brad Martin. "But you get to see people you would not see otherwise."

One of the most dramatic examples of this sort of joint effort was the 1955 visit to Moscow by William Randolph Hearst Jr., who had two reporters along to do the real journalism. Nikita Khrushchev wanted to broach the concept of "peaceful coexistence." Rather than talk to American correspondents on the scene, he chose Hearst, who commanded a media empire and, adding punch to the news, was strongly anticommunist. Other leading Soviet officials also granted interviews. As a result, Hearst and his two reporters won a Pulitzer Prize for international reporting.

"The workings of the great newspaper," pronounced pompous Lord Copper, the owner of the *Beast* in Waugh's *Scoop,* "are of a complexity which the public seldom appreciates. The citizen little appreciates the vast machinery put into motion for him in exchange for his morning penny." But even those in news management, it sometimes seems, overlook how their vast machinery grinds away in tandem with their competitors' equipment.

In the mid-1980s, *Los Angeles Times* press critic David Shaw wrote a series of articles on foreign correspondence. Jim Hoagland, by this time the *Washington Post*'s assistant managing editor, told him, "I don't want our correspondents helping [the *New York Times*] out, and any of our correspondents who expects them to help us out is dreaming." The *Times* editor Abe Rosenthal was just as adamant decrying cooperation. From the reporters themselves, Shaw heard a different story:

> Foreign correspondents for both the Post and the New York Times say they cooperate with each other more often than Rosenthal and Hoagland think. Reporters from other papers agree.
>
> "With all due respect to [Hoagland] he's living in a dream world," says David Lamb, who was based in Nairobi, Cairo and Sydney for the Los Angeles Times. "I could give you six examples of the New York Times, the Washington Post and the Los Angeles Times sharing information. . . . With rare exception, you share everything with your colleagues. . . . And why shouldn't you? The readers are better-served if we share information. Who are we supposed to serve anyway— our readers or our editors' egos?

Editors' protestations to the contrary, they encourage collaboration. They post their reporters in the same places, such as London. "It is almost impossible to miss a major new story there," observed the *Sun*'s Catling, "unless everyone else misses it also, and then it really isn't news, because news is what is reported." Editors also force correspondents to retrace each other's steps. Peter Copeland, a correspondent for Scripps Howard Newspapers in El Salvador during the mid-1980s, outlined the process: The *New York Times* reporter goes to a village on, say, a Wednesday. The next day, the reporter's front-page story is faxed to the ABC correspondent, who also goes out to the village. That story airs Thursday evening. Copeland, taking a breather in Mexico City, is told to go to back to El Salvador. With two stories about the village, it must be hot.

Whether correspondents doss down together is not in question. It is not in doubt either that dossing down benefits readers when cooperation is mixed with the kind of independence the *Sun*'s management gave its reporters. But one matter is questioned these days: whether the tradition of experienced, autonomous, professional foreign correspondents' dossing down together will continue.

Improved communication technologies offer benefits, but fostering correspondents' independence is not one of them. Editors can stay in touch all day long. Meanwhile, the loss of audience and revenue is pressuring traditional news media to cut back on foreign correspondents. While this book was being written, the Chicago Tribune Company, which acquired the *Sun* in 2000, eliminated the newspaper's venerable foreign service. Henceforth the *Sun* was to rely for special overseas reporting on the correspondents of the *Tribune* and the *Los Angeles Times,* which the *Tribune* also owned. When Russell Baker learned that the London bureau, where he worked as a young man, was closing, he wrote in his diary, "The *Sun* has died."

"The Chicago *Tribune* wants synergy between its newspapers and television stations," wrote Jeff Price shortly before he left the paper. "If you had asked Gary Black what he thought of synergy, he might have responded 'straight up or on the rocks?'"

These changes in the vast machinery of journalism are the subjects of the final two chapters of this book.

23

THE CORRESPONDENT'S KIT

Anthony Beard joined the London bureau of the *New York Times* in 1955, fresh out of the British Royal Air Force. When he retired forty-six years later, he reckoned his career spanned three eras of news technology.

In the 1950s, London, as a *Times* promotional booklet put it, was "the principal 'post office,' or relay point of THE TIMES abroad." It had served this purpose for decades. When Edwin James suggested in the 1920s that Paris, where he was based, was a better hub, Adolph Ochs replied, "While it may be true that it is easier to get European news into Paris than into London, communication between London and New York is easier, quicker and slightly less expensive and there is not the element of a foreign language to hamper communication."

Ochs was not alone in this conviction. In the mid-nineteenth century, Paul Julius Reuter could have built his news service in his home country, Germany; he chose London instead. George Smalley successfully argued for putting the *Tribune*'s chief overseas office there a few years later. In addition to its other attributes, London was the capital of a political and commercial empire interlaced with the world's best communications network. As one of Edwin James's contemporaries put it, "The French telegraph system, which stops when a cigarette is to be lighted or a bite of lunch to be eaten, is so much slower than the British lines that London has been chosen by practically all American news-gathering organizations as the relay point for their Continental news. Even the Spanish and the Italian news takes the longer and more expensive but quicker way around, and passes through London instead of Paris." Thomas Stevens, who appeared earlier in this book as the around-the-world bicycling foreign correspondent for *Outing* magazine, marveled at the telegraph poles—"a solid reality in English iron"—he spotted on the Turko-Persian border. They stretched, he wrote in an 1888 article for the *Electrical Review*, "across the dead level wastes of the Persian plains . . . set up as evenly and perpendicularly as they might have been in Hyde Park."

When Beard appeared on the scene, the *Times* London bureau collected correspondents' reports from points as far away as China and, at various times, South America in a process that worked like this: A correspondent brought a dispatch to a postal-telephone-telegraph (PTT) agency in some distant land, where the story was typed into a telex machine. The telex version was sent to London over a telephone line, usually one operated by the British-owned Cable & Wireless. The Commonwealth press rate—called the "old penny" rate—was a penny a word (there were 240 pennies to a pound). To keep costs down, which was as constant a theme at the *Times* as it was with other newspapers, correspondents wrote in cablese, in which "untreaty smorning" meant "no treaty agreed upon this morning." The London news desk put the stories back into plain English—a task that was sometimes challenging (see "Cablese," p. 439)—and edited them.

At this point Beard came into play. He had been a radio telegrapher in the military. He and colleagues worked around-the-clock shifts keying the edited stories onto a perforated tape using a system called Murray code and pushing the tape into a transmitter box, which sent 66.6 words per minute. The stories traveled over the Reuters wire, unless the wire was down, in which case they went via the more expensive Commercial Cable wire. Reuters in New York forwarded the stories to the *Times* building.

The next era for Beard, beginning in the late 1970s, commenced with the introduction of computers. The *Times* was one of the first newspapers to use them abroad. In London, American "Megadata" computers were linked by local telephone lines to the Reuters master system, where a code automatically routed stories to the *Times* editors in New York. Eventually *Times* copy from around the world was sent directly to New York via the Reuters system—and later through the Associated Press system, and later still through the Internet without any intermediary.

These changes made the news desk and the communications room in the London bureau obsolete. The *Times* bureau moved to smaller quarters. Beard, dependable and resourceful, stayed on to help correspondents use the unfamiliar, often maddeningly finicky technology. He was there, for instance, when bureau chief R. W. Apple's computer lost a story because he wrote with his shoes off and his socks caused static on the carpet. Apple pounded a cabinet and threatened to throw the computer out the window.

In the third era, the 1990s, correspondents used satellite systems. The first were text only, no voice. Initially correspondents needed a south-facing hotel room to get an uplink to the appropriate satellite, which required compasses and satellite footprint maps. In Sarajevo during civil war in the 1990s, *Times* correspondent John Burns's south-facing bedroom window also faced the shooting. With no electricity, he wrote by candlelight in the bathroom and crawled on the floor to his generator-powered satellite system.

Beard carried on in this era, too. Although London was no longer the *Times'* post office abroad, it remained a jumping-off point for traveling correspondents because of its excellent air connections. As international telecommunications manager, Beard was the *Times* version of Q in James Bond movies. He outfitted correspondents, taking care that they did not "end up with the wrong bits and bobs." He also traveled abroad to help reporters use the sophisticated equipment.

When Beard retired in 2001, journalism's technicians had attained the long-dreamed-of annihilation of time and space. Correspondents filed directly to New

CABLESE

Cablese was an answer to the problem of high cable costs. Unfortunately, the elimination and condensation of words turned cables into puzzles that sometimes were not easily solved.

The letter below from *Chicago Daily News* editor Charles Dennis to London correspondent Edward Price Bell illustrates the hair-pulling that went into deciphering cablese.

August 24, 1904

Dear Mr. Bell:

... Mr. St. Clair [cable editor] is on his vacation just now and I am struggling with the cable. To-day your industrial societies cable gave me some puzzles and I fear I made some silly errors. I inclose [sic] what I made of it and also the cable as it reached me:

Thousands working men assembled crystal palace safternoon participate opening annual meeting societies seeking organize industrial principle all engaged sharing profit capital control responsibility Robert Yerburgh M.P. delivers opening address Richard Bell M.P. presides attractions include exhibition products copartnership workshops huge flower fruit vegetable show choir contests concert with orchestra twenty five hundred voices innumerable special general meetings leaders movement copartnership production which moving lines distinct those cooperative distribution becoming one strikingest examples collective enterprise Great Britain started twenty years ago but developed rapidly only past two years embraces hundred twenty six societies engaged agriculture clieping boot leather metal building wood printing various other trade capital counting shares loans reserves about two million sterling annual sales three million five hundred thousand profits last year two hundred thousand our movement says secretary Henry Vivian makes industrial peace securer prevents strikes lockouts elevates status worker that responsible unit scheme production this calls activity side character trades unionism leaves dormant makes workers take more pride homes stimulates interest education athletics music develops business capacity selfrespect selfreliance[.]

Now this is the simplest form of cable. Yet already—it being too late to correct it—I see that what I made "the worker who is responsible for the unit scheme of production" should have been "elevates the status of the worker to that of a responsible unit in the scheme of production." My only excuse for such stupidity is that I was much interrupted and harassed this morning. But the chief puzzle is as to whether or not "societies seeking organize industrial principle" is the name of the association. After much worry I concluded it must be, since if they were so organized individually they would not seek to be organized and, further, the organization has a secretary, since you quote him. Yet it is an example of peculiar nomenclature if my puzzlement has led to to [sic] the correct conclusion. The phrase "engaged sharing profit capital" puzzled me. How can one share capital? "Concert with orchestra twenty five hundred voices" must be as I have made it in the article, I suppose, since I can find no authority for calling voices an orchestra.

I am very rusty on cables, so my puzzles and awkwardness have some excuse. My experience, however, leads me to ask you to expand the cable for me so that I may see how far I was from getting your meaning. The missent word I could not make out ("clieping") and I omitted "leaders movement" so as to make the character of the meetings more general. I have no doubt that the cable would have been clear to Mr. St. Clair, who could have figured it out without interruptions. If, however, we are making many errors in your cables at this end of the line it may be that they should be sent a little more fully.

With regards, very truly yours,

C. H. Dennis

York. And yet, the achievement was not entirely satisfying. Journalists were like dogs that persistently try to bite their tails, finally succeed, and, still holding on tightly, wonder what, really, they have achieved. Speed and quality did not go hand and hand, a dilemma that became apparent to many correspondents when speed was still relatively slow. In 1937, after years of reporting for the *New York Times,* the *Saturday Evening Post,* and other news media, Wythe Williams complained that "Speed in transmission often seems more important than the news. The great volume of news, dispatched hastily, cannot maintain the high degree of accuracy that distinguished the reports of the old timers. Its analysis, so important for the reader, frequently is left to the home editor, who cannot always have a thorough understanding of the distant subject."

"Every age," historian Robert Darnton has observed, "was an age of information, each in its own way." One way, he noted, was in mid-eighteenth-century Paris, which at the time had no daily newspaper. Energetic word-of-mouth newsmongering took place around a large chestnut tree, the Tree of Cracow, and flowed through the apartment of Mme. Doublet. Mme. Doublet kept two books that were filled each day with news and gossip (a book for each). Visitors supplied this information, read it, and passed it on.

But if that was *an* information age, it was light years away from *the* Information Age in which we now live. This is nowhere more apparent than in up-to-date foreign news, little of which would have been found in Mme. Doublet's apartment. For obvious reasons, distance is a greater factor in foreign correspondence than in any other category of news, and the Information Age has brought enormous strides in moving news quickly around the planet.

For centuries, human beings traveled at more or less the same pace. In 1750, as in 1500, it took about three weeks for an ordinary letter or gazette to reach Venice from London. After the American Revolution, travel gradually sped up. As we have seen, nearly a month passed before news of General Jackson's victory at the Battle of New Orleans in 1815 reached Washington; fifteen years later, reports of President Jackson's State of the Union address reached New Orleans in less than a week. Between 1794 and 1817, the time lag between an event in Washington and its report in a Boston newspaper dropped from 18 days to 6.2; between 1817 and 1841, it dropped still further, to 2.8 days. Steamships such as the one James Gordon Bennett took to London in the mid-nineteenth century halved the average time required to make the voyage to well under three weeks.

With its zest for attracting readers, the penny press took advantage of any device at hand to transmit the news more quickly—steamboats and railroads as well as the old technology of carrier pigeons, although the birds' speed of 40 to 75 miles per hour was offset by the fact that they grew tired and undependable after four or five hundred miles. In a late-life interview, one of the owners of the first penny press, the *New York Sun,* remarked on his newspaper's use of "200 or 300 pigeons" as well as "telegraphing by lights or signals, but we never made much out of it." The same editor "had planned out a system of telegraphing by semaphore, and intended to get the steamer news from Boston in that way; but the electric system was perfected, and that revolutionized journalism altogether."

Although Congress was reluctant to fund Samuel F. B. Morse's telegraphy experiments, the value to journalism was obvious on the day in 1842 that his trial line was put in operation between Baltimore and Washington. The first sentence transmitted was "What hath God wrought?" The second was "Have you any news?" With this tool, the Tree of Cracow could spread its branches across the globe. "Village gossips," enthused James Gordon Bennett's managing editor, Frederic Hudson, "are magnified into world gossips."

By 1900, when the *Scientific American* recounted the past century's progress, it gushed about communications: "The railroad, the telegraph, and the steam vessel annihilated distance; peoples touched elbows across the seas; and the contagion of thought stimulated the ferment of civilization until the whole world broke out into an epidemic of industrial progress. . . . To-day two cents carries a letter to Manila, half way round the world . . . and the New York daily morning papers are distributed in Washington in time to be read at the breakfast table there on the same day of their issue."

Over the years the Associated Press, which existed to deliver news from distant places to its members, crammed its in-house *Service Bulletin of the Associated Press* with items on technological advances. "At present," a 1920 story reported, "there are eleven different methods by which the report is transmitted—leased wire, telephone, telegraph, cable, automatics,* wireless, trains, trolleys, boats, pneumatic tubes and messengers. . . . The most recent innovation in delivery of news is the automatic machines. THE ASSOCIATED PRESS is the pioneer in adopting this method and now has almost 100 of these machines in operation on city circuits and long distance lines."

As revolutionary as all of this was, distance was, really, not yet completely annihilated. In 1912, the *New York Times* received nearly all its foreign reports by wireless, but average transmission times from Europe were painfully slow and uneven by our standards, varying from one hour and fifteen minutes to three hours. Communications with other parts of the world were less certain. "Despatches [*sic*] from Tokio to New York before the war required an average time of transmission of about three hours," an AP correspondent moaned in 1919. "In the last year the average time of transmission for months at a time has been eight to ten days."

The sort of operator problems that bedeviled George Smalley in filing his Harvard-Oxford boat race continued. J. B. Powell, who was a stringer for the *Chicago Tribune* as well as editor of the *China Weekly Review* in Shanghai, wrote in 1927 of his frustrations with communications. Correspondents were reluctant to

---

* Wheatstone Automatic Morse transmitters—called automatic machines or automatics and invented by Charles Wheatstone—did not use human operators to key in Morse code. That was done by perforated tape that caused electronic impulses. The rate of four hundred words per minute on a good line was more than ten times greater than the average telegraphers could achieve. Operators, however, had to key Morse code into the tape in the first place and decode it at the other end.

Charles Whitney went to work as an Associated Press telegrapher in Boston in 1893. Here he is close to his retirement in 1933; the days of "brass pounders" transmitting news by Morse code also were numbered. Photo courtesy of his great-grandson Brian Connelly.

cable news from China because the rates were much higher than in Europe. The result, Powell complained, was that stories preparing the public for major events were less likely to be filed. Furthermore, "listless" and disinterested Chinese telegraphers garbled messages so badly they were worthless. A *Chicago Daily News* correspondent was tripped up by Turkish telegraphers who displayed the opposite problem by dutifully following government rules. "Operators were not required to know much English," Stanley Washburn said, "but were carefully drilled in a few important words, such as 'riot,' 'revolution,' 'disorders, 'bomb,' 'anarchist,' etc. The instructions were that any message containing any such dreadful word should be held pending an investigation." Washburn wrote about his experiences in a book called *The Cable Game.*

Frustrations like these persisted for decades. Henry Bradsher, in India for the AP in the late 1950s, found it "virtually impossible to get a workable phone line to Europe, the U.S., or Japan by which to dictate copy to someone." He handed his stories to telegraph operators in short "takes." In especially isolated parts of the country, telegraphers still tapped out Morse code. Only four Indian cities had the capability to send photographs back to the United States. Later, when he was a correspondent for the *Washington Star* in Asia, Bradsher sometimes became so antsy at the slowness of telex clerks that he climbed over the counter and keyed his copy himself.

For all its marvels, television had its own problems overcoming distance. Heavy equipment limited broadcasters' mobility. Getting the story home was a time-consuming chore. During the Korean War, CBS put film on a plane bound for Japan, whence it was flown to the West Coast of the United States and switched to a transcontinental flight to New York. "Rarely," reminisced CBS executive Sig Mickelson, "could a film story from the Korean battle front find its way to the air in less than ninety-six hours." Battle film from Vietnam in the 1960s was sometimes unusable "because the couriers bringing it into the West Coast studios were caught in late-afternoon traffic jams in San Francisco or Los Angeles."

The networks' determination to beat each other with coverage of Queen Elizabeth's coronation in 1953 was another point of progress engineered by journalism's technicians, who without apparently knowing it took a page out of George Wilkins Kendall's Mexican War strategy. Just as *Picayune* boats outfitted with typesetting equipment intercepted ships arriving from Mexico, CBS and NBC sent film back to the United States on airplanes rigged out with film-editing equipment. Pictured here is the CBS airplane. All sorts of glitches bedeviled the race. But, said CBS's Sig Mickelson, "the whole episode signaled what television would be able to do once it had videotape, electronic cameras, communications satellites, digitized video editing equipment, and experienced personnel." Mickelson, *The Decade That Shaped Television News,* 108. Photo courtesy of Elena Mickelson.

When Beard was in the twilight of his career at the *Times* London bureau, technology advanced on every front. In 1990 the cost of a telephone call in real terms was 1.5 percent of what it was in 1930. For television, speeds of new transmission quickened in a succession of phases: portable video instead of motion picture film in the 1970s; satellite communications with portable uplinks for live coverage in the 1980s; digital technology that facilitated rapid editing on computers and the creation of engaging graphics in the 1990s.

For broadcasters, lighter equipment permitted greater mobility and quicker setup in remote locations. When Fred Francis of NBC arrived in Panama on the eve of the American invasion in 1989, his team lugged eight hundred pounds of equipment: "Once we landed at Howard AFB in Panama [City], it took a large truck, two technicians and several airmen to get the gear up to Quarry Heights Headquarters. It took between five and seven hours to set everything up and make our first feed to the U.S. When I slipped into Iraq from Iran in January 2003, the two cases, 140 lbs, looked just like large luggage to Iranian airport customs and the border guards. Once we reached our base in Kurdistan, five days later, it took one technician just about 20 minutes to set up." The development of small digital equipment has made it possible for Kevin Sites, formerly of CNN and NBC, to become a one-person television crew who reported, edited, and transmitted stories for Yahoo! News while on the run all over the world.

The miniaturization of technology helped print correspondents, too. A satellite phone in Operation Desert Storm weighed 50–60 pounds and cost some $50,000. In the second Gulf War it was the size of a cell phone, weighed less than a pound, and cost $8,000. The smaller size, Tony Beard recalled, reduced the chances that foreign officials would spot the equipment and confiscate it—or that some military commander could (as happened in Operation Desert Storm) prevent correspondents from taking their satellite phones into the field. The phones become standard equipment like pencils and notebooks. It became a matter of routine for Keith Bradsher, Henry Bradsher's son and a *New York Times* correspondent, to dictate a story he was witnessing in India over his cell phone, providing new details right up to the deadline for the front page of the final Sunday edition.

These advances reversed the dynamic of filing news. At the beginning of television, broadcast correspondents waited while a crew set up equipment. Now, as one scholar noted, producers and technicians "were ready to present a story before the correspondent was ready to tell it."

Foreign correspondents relish spreading out their belongings for others to see. "A man's outfit is a matter which seems to touch his private honor," observed Richard Harding Davis in a characteristic display of Victorian sentiment. Reporters' kits suggest the size of the expense account that underwrites them, which is a measure of one's worth. The foresight and economy with which one packs is a sign of competence. And if one does manage to mispack, there is a good story for a slow news day.

RICHARD HARDING DAVIS'S "A WAR CORRESPONDENT'S KIT"

In importance after the bed, cooking kit, and chair, I would place these articles:

Two collapsible water-buckets of rubber or canvas.

Two collapsible brass lanterns, with extra isinglass sides.

Two boxes of sick-room candles.

One dozen boxes of safety matches.

One axe. The best I have seen is the Marble Safety Axe, made at Gladstone, Mich. You can carry it in your hip-pocket, and you can cut down a tree with it.

One medicine case containing quinine, calomel, and Sun Cholera Mixture in tablets.

Toilet-case for razors, tooth-powder, brushes, and paper.

Folding bath-tub of rubber in rubber case. These are manufactured to fold into a space little larger than a cigar-box.

Two towels old, and soft.

Three cakes of soap.

One Jaeger blanket.

One mosquito head-bag.

One extra pair of shoes, old and comfortable.

One extra pair of riding-breeches.

One extra pair of gaiters. The former regulation army gaiter of canvas, laced, rolls up in a small compass and weighs but little.

One flannel shirt. Gray least shows the dust.

Two pairs of drawers. For riding, the best are those of silk.

Two undershirts, balbriggan [knit cotton] or woollen.

Three pairs of woollen socks.

Two linen handkerchiefs, large enough, if needed, to tie around the throat and protect the back of the neck.

One pair of pajamas, woollen, not linen.

One housewife.

Two briarwood pipes.

Six bags of smoking tobacco; Durham or Seal of North Carolina pack easily.

One pad of writing paper.

One fountain pen, *self-filling*.

One bottle of ink, with screw top, held tight by a spring.

One dozen linen envelopes.

Stamps, wrapped in oil-silk with mucilage side next to the silk.

One stick sealing-wax. In tropical countries mucilage on the flap of envelopes sticks to everything except the envelope.

One dozen elastic bands of the largest size. In packing they help to compress articles like clothing into the smallest possible compass and in many other ways will be found very useful.

One pack of playing-cards.

Books.

One revolver and six cartridges.

Some of the most famous stories of errant preparation came during the Italo-Ethiopian war in 1935. Not knowing anything about Ethiopia, correspondents had to guess what to bring with them. Because Linton Wells and his aviatrix wife Fay, both reporting for the *Herald Tribune,* wanted to be prepared for any eventuality, they traveled with twelve cases, weighing twenty-nine hundred pounds and including horse hobbles. Laurence Stallings of Fox Movietone brought fifty thousand feet of film, a fleet of trucks and motorcycles, and a collection of American flags. "The flags are to warn bullets to 'keep off, this means you,'" reported the North American Newspaper Alliance, for which Stallings also was to file stories.

Davis's account, "A War Correspondent's Kit," was typically self-indulgent. He boasted of once having a train consisting of "an enormous cart, two oxen, three Basuto ponies, one Australian horse, three servants, and four hundred pounds of supplies and baggage." But behind his baggage bravado lay practical considerations revealing a good deal about the way he gathered foreign news abroad. His kit, described in "Richard Harding Davis's 'A War Correspondent's Kit'" on page 445, equipped him to stay in the field for months to *collect* news. That part of his luggage designed to *send* news back home was almost an afterthought—writing paper, "one fountain pen, *self-filling,*" ink, envelopes, and stamps.

It was the same with Webb Miller of UPI, who went to cover the Italian invasion of Ethiopia similarly loaded down with field gear. His memoir breezed past the subject of communication, merely noting he brought "enough writing materials to last several months." Linton Wells, in his account of covering the war, didn't even mention pens or paper—except toilet paper—in his outfit of "essentials for an eight months' stay."

"Kit" stories today, in contrast, emphasize communications equipment. Often they appear in the technology section of the newspaper, a section that did not exist until recently. "When foreign correspondents gather these days," wrote Eugene Robinson of the *Washington Post* in April 1990, "there's distressingly little talk about world affairs, or newly discovered restaurants, or even the old conventional staple that might be termed 'expense account management.' Undashingly, unromantically, we talk instead about the care and feeding of our computers." Even discussions of clothes swerve into this new theme. James Sterba extolled the virtues of a photographer's vest he wore on a reporting assignment to Indonesia for the *Wall Street Journal.* The vest was ideal for holding pens, his Recording Walkman and cassettes, and his handheld short-wave radio and batteries. The *New York Times*' Nicholas Kristof observed that his backpack had become a communications center.

The old stuff, like novels to read in downtime or a flashlight to see in the dark, is not obsolete, as illustrated in the following article by Juan Tamayo, a correspondent with the *Miami Herald.* Nevertheless, the change in emphasis toward news transmission, rather than news-gathering, is unmistakable. Tamayo's article was written in 1987, when he was based in Jerusalem. Many improvements in communications, such as the satellite phone, were yet to come.

Juan Tamayo, a correspondent for the *Miami Herald,* at work in Kandahar, Afghanistan, in late 2001. The two white matchsticks on the computer keyboard were needed to hold up keys that had stuck when someone spilled a glass of sweet Afghan tea on them. No technology, no matter how advanced, is perfect. Photo by Tom Pennington/*Fort Worth Star-Telegram.*

What to pack in Middle East? You'd be amazed
Juan O. Tamayo

Dubai, United Arab Emirates—One foreign correspondent never leaves home without his miner's headlamp. Two others pack their own telephones. Virtually all carry tiny computers half the size of a Miami phone book.

Once, being a foreign correspondent was a relatively straightforward job. They wore crumpled raincoats in lousy weather and bush jackets when the sun shone, and toted sturdy Olivetti 32 portable typewriters.

They rapped out stories with two-fingered tattoos, handed them to Telex operators and waited for their bosses' replies: a neutral "received," a laudatory "kudos" or the dreaded "others reporting." . . .

Today, technology has eased the mechanics of journalism, with correspondents using laptop computers to write their stories and transmit them to editors over telephone lines.

No more slothful Telex operators taking lunch breaks five minutes before deadline. No more "helpful" operators removing all punctuation marks from stories in misguided attempts to save the senders a few dollars.

But technology has brought its own burdens and correspondents, especially those assigned to the Middle East, must now lug hefty loads of equipment on assignment to glamorous and festering corners of the Third World.

Each correspondent's travel kit is now almost as distinctive as his byline, each item carefully selected with an eye toward making work easier in the Third World yet keeping the kit small enough to sling over a shoulder and carry aboard airplanes, even if it means busting a hernia.

Here, then, is a list of some of the items packed into the typical, and sometimes not-so-typical, shoulder bags of foreign correspondents.

Basics:

- Hefty phone book. A correspondent's heart and soul, listing hundreds of numbers for important people; background information such as a country's population; spelling of the ruler's name and good restaurants, and massive list of computer codes and passwords needed to transmit stories back home.
- Swiss Army Knife, including a screwdriver for opening telephone cable junction boxes (more on this later) and a razor-sharp knife, in case above phone book is lost and veins must be slit.
- Compact shortwave radio. A must in any country that has a Ministry of Information, to monitor foreign newscasts like the British Broadcasting Corp. and find out what's really happening across the street.
- Pocket Flight Guide, a paperback listing all commercial flights in the area. Essential when emergency travel is necessary, but never to be trusted when it lists Iraq Air flights.
- Assorted maps, large enough to show those towns always being flattened by natural or man-made disasters, but not big enough to arouse the suspicions of intelligence services.
- Small flashlight, for those not infrequent blackouts. New York Times Cairo Bureau Chief John Kifner carries a miner's battery-powered headlamp so that he can continue to type when the lights go out.
- Two paperback novels. One by a young author whose tortured first novel just got rave reviews, to flash in front of colleagues. And a good thriller to read.
- Letterhead stationery for requests to interview the local ruler. They are never approved, but it may impress the heck out of the Information Ministry pencil-pusher who's handling the request and just might win an interview with the assistant deputy vice minister for fishing.
- Tape recorder for interviews, extra batteries and cassettes and extra buttons for when clothes come back from the hotel laundry.
- Interview notepads, carefully selected to give the impression of organization, a quality rare among correspondents. Michael Ross, Cairo bureau chief for the Los Angeles Times, favors yellow legal pads; the Baltimore Sun's Robert Ruby brought with him a boxful of special French notepads when he moved from Paris to the Middle East this summer.

I use four-inch pads with pictures of saucer-eyed children on the cover for two reasons: the longer reporters' pads that are standard issue in most newspapers can catch on chairs and rip off back pockets, and that's what the office assistant bought.

There are special items needed for covering the Persian Gulf War. They include:

- Gulf navigational charts. The Chicago Tribune's John Broder bought an inch-thick Gulf pilot's navigation book giving detailed descriptions of shipping channels, ports and oil loading terminals in the combat zone, plus interesting tidbits to salt into stories, such as the presence of venomous snakes on Iran's Lesser Thumb Island.
- Dividers. Compass-like instruments used to measure distances on nautical charts. A length of paper or knuckles can serve the same purpose, but brass dividers are SOOOO much more professional.
- Binoculars. Great for reading the names on the transoms of stricken tankers, and oggling airline stewardesses at poolside. Not much more entertainment available on the Arabian Peninsula.

Computer equipment:

- Laptop computer for writing stories and transmitting them home over phone lines. Standard issue is Radio Shack's Tandy 100, a virtually indestructible little machine dubbed "The Ak-47 of the journalism world" by Newsweek Cairo Bureau Chief Christopher Dickey.
- Small telephone, the tips of its wires stripped bare. Credit Newsday's Middle East Correspondent Timothy Phelps for this innovation. To transmit stories over the phone, computers must be hooked up to the correct two wires within a four-wire line—a tough proposition when each country seems to have its own unique wiring system and when hotel telephones are wired to perform so many tasks, from automatic wake-up calls to message lights, that their cables can be as thick as a thumb. The correct two wires can be found by touching the extra telephone's bare wires to different wires on phone lines until a dial tone is heard.
- Jeweler's screwdrivers, and Swiss Army knife, to tear up telephones and wall junction boxes in hotel rooms in search of the above.
- Lengths of telephone cable ending in alligator clips, to connect the computer to the two correct wires.
- Electricity converters and adapters for the myriad plug shapes and voltages found around the world.

Health kit:

- Tetracycline pills for Egypt's King Tut Tummy, Iraq's Baghdad Belly, Israel's Jerusalem Jog and Syria's Damascus Dash and other such stomach disorders.
- Seasickness pills for the occasional boat ride from the Mediterranean island of Cyprus to the Lebanese Christian enclave of Junieh—Moslems control the Beirut airport—or bumpy rides aboard small airplanes chartered for emergencies.

Finally, there should be a large, lightweight duffle bag, stuffed into regular suitcase and ready to hold those on-the-road purchases that simply cannot be passed up.

Most Middle East correspondents buy regional handicrafts such as Persian carpets, antique coffee pots and Bedouin daggers. But those based in Cairo, where some Western food items are impossible to find, go in for more mundane fare.

They can be spotted on Cairo-bound flights lugging duffle bags stuffed with cans of catfood, bottles of ketchup and wine vinegar and containers of spices.

The star newspaper reporter of the future, *Chicago Daily News* editor Henry Justin Smith told journalism students at Northwestern University in 1923, "will be—as perhaps he is now—the man who has best mastered the control of the new servants of journalism and wields them most boldly. And the present stimulations that we get out of a taxicab race with another paper, or out of gaining a sixty second start on somebody with the 'flash' on a prize fight, may seem as antique as now seem the efforts of publishers in 1706 to beat each other across the Atlantic by a month or so with the news brought on sailing ships."

It has come to pass as Smith said it would. Bred to provide news as quickly as possible, modern journalists, like their penny press predecessors, instinctively grab onto every available technique to step up the pace of delivery. Because broadcast journalists can go live with their reports, they do. Weekly news magazines like *Newsweek* or *Time,* even the *Atlantic Monthly,* have Web sites on which they post news and information daily. "We now live in a nanosecond news cycle," said David Hoffman, the *Washington Post*'s assistant managing editor for foreign news in 2005. Correspondents must be "information warriors." He expected reporters to write first for the Web, then for the newspaper. That double process, he argued, makes the second story better organized and written with more flair, which is essential if a reader is going to pick up a newspaper when the main points of the story are already out via television or the Internet. "Technology," said Frank Governale, CBS vice president for operations, "has advanced to the point where the only limitation is in the imagination of the correspondent."

With assists from modern communications technology, stories arrive home faster and more reliably. No longer does a correspondent have the communications problems the *Christian Science Monitor*'s John Hughes coped with covering the attempted Communist coup in Indonesia in 1966. For a time he and two correspondents from other countries had the story to themselves, but the government did not allow them to transmit their dispatches. They had to ride a dilapidated DeSoto to the airport and search for outbound passengers willing to carry their stories to a cable office abroad. (Hughes's reporting won the Pulitzer Prize in place of Harrison Salisbury's stories from North Vietnam.) Today Hughes would employ the Internet or a satellite phone, which are also useful to search the World Wide Web for facts to fill out stories and to "interview" experts outside the country.

In Beard's early days, most *Times* correspondents informed London, not New York, of their day-to-day travel plans. This arrangement was far from perfect. At the end of World War II, three *Times* reporters filed a similar report on Pierre Laval, head of the Vichy government, who was soon to be tried. The problem, said Drew Middleton, one of the reporters, was "communications, pure and simple." A decade later, three *Baltimore Sun* correspondents self-assigned themselves to cover a Geneva summit meeting.

Now, by touching four little numbers on a phone connected to a satellite link, editors coordinate one correspondent's work with what others are doing, shaping coverage into "packages" that fit the interests of readers, viewers, and listeners. Whereas formerly correspondents might not know for weeks how their stories looked in the newspaper (at the *Sun,* tear sheets were sent by ship's mail; at the *New York Times,* they received a "fronting" cable that gave a rundown of the previous day's headlines and notice whether one of their stories had been held or used inside), they now participate in the editing process. In his reporting from northern Iraq, for instance, NBC's Fred Francis helped New York edit his stories. This helps preserve accuracy and nuance—and in Francis's case it gave him an opportunity to watch the *Today* show via his satellite connection.

The Internet also assists editors in checking whether a reporter has cribbed from someone else's story or made something up. Such transgressions are very much on the minds of *USA Today* editors, who were embarrassed in 2004 by revelations that the newspaper's foreign correspondent Jack Kelley had fabricated and plagiarized reporting over a number of years. Today, if a *USA Today* correspondent reports

Dexter Filkins of the *New York Times* in Iraq, satellite phone in hand. Photo by Ashley Gilbertson.

that university walls in Romania contain anti-Gypsy graffiti, the copy desk will ask an editor to ask the reporter if this was a firsthand observation or passed on by someone else. As World Editor at *USA Today,* Elisa Tinsley was in touch daily with most correspondents by e-mail or telephone. She preferred telephone. "I try to be in voice contact with the reporters two or three times a week whether they like it or not. Some don't."

Some do, of course. The absence of communication with the home office can bring fear of being forgotten or, as *Los Angeles Times* media reporter David Shaw once observed, of having "fallen from favor." With editors in direct touch, the home office more easily assures correspondents' physical safety and emotional security. Also, correspondents can keep up on newsroom gossip, one of the most entertaining kinds there is.

Morse's invention, in the mind's eye of Frederic Hudson, was a shortcut to journalistic paradise. As the *New York Herald* editor foresaw, "the newspaper reader will have a fresh photograph of the world twice a day, taken by electricity, and spread before him in all its amplifications morning and evening. Journalism will then be perfect." But just how much better is the technologically enhanced information warrior than the technologically challenged correspondent of the past? Not all correspondents have been as giddy as Hudson was about the stringing of the first telegraph wires.

While George Smalley of the *New York Tribune* thought "time is everything in journalism," the great war correspondent William Howard Russell of the *Times* of London was not so sure. The laying of the transatlantic telegraph cable, he said in his 1866 book on the subject, was "the greatest work of civilized man." On the other hand, he did not want to have much to do with such devices when it came to filing his news reports. When the London-Paris telegraph line opened in 1851, he complained, "The electric telegraph quite annihilates one's speculative and inductive facilities." He was still complaining twenty-five years later. In a note to his editor, he explained that he had finally gotten around to writing "a longish letter for the paper by mail. . . . I cannot explain to you the paralyzing effects of sitting down to write a letter after you have sent off the bones of it by lightning."

Ambivalence has mounted with each increase in the speed with which the home office can be in touch. The *Christian Science Monitor*'s veteran correspondent Sisley Huddleston, a Yorkshireman-turned-Bohemian who dictated stories for that paper and others from his bed in a rat-infested Paris building, ruminated in 1938 that "The very improvement of the mechanical side of journalism, the development of technique has, in my opinion, almost ruined the only kind of journalism that really matters." Said the *Los Angeles Times*' Robert Elegant at mid-century, "Marconi ruined foreign correspondence. I think Morse may have helped."

Although technology saves time in filing stories, it devours time in other ways. Meeting rolling deadlines means less time for reporting and reflection, as Marvin Kalb explained: While a broadcast correspondent in Moscow in the late 1950s and early 1960s, he filmed his television stories and afterward went to the airport to look for someone willing to carry the raw footage to the United States. With a wink at a nineteenth-century technology for moving news, he called these travelers "pigeons." During the time it took for the film to make its way to New York, Kalb had two or three days to think about how he would write the story, for which he could provide the voiceover via phone later. Modern correspondents, he commented, don't have that kind of time and therefore are less authoritative. With live stories they often say "I think" when describing events, as was foreshadowed by Jimmy Bowen's live coverage of the *Graf Spee*'s sinking: "We don't want to tell you what we think is going on. We want to tell you what we can see, and we can't see a great deal, due to the excessive action and movement."

Every broadcast veteran seems to have a story like Kalb's, including his brother, who was a correspondent in Vietnam. "Like executions," Bernard Kalb recalled, technological innovations coming "one after the other, did away with distance and time. . . . The cellular phone was the final nail. There was no escape. By then, New York had synchronized all this gadgetry into an art form. *Live! Live! Live!*" No longer could a correspondent "take days . . . to accumulate a story. *Days?* No complaints from New York, either, though print was more generous than television about our wandering off into the boonies." Lost, said broadcaster Garrick Utley, was "the editorial process of balance, thought, structure, and confirmation of facts." Live coverage, he argued, is more appropriate for sports events than serious news. Fred Francis confessed he was not certain that covering news "tied to a camera position" was really journalism.

"Going live"—which is much less expensive than highly edited and produced programming—accentuates the inherent weakness of television to emphasize images over words. Correspondents spend less time crafting scripts and more time speaking extemporaneously. This has been particularly the case with cable news. About one-half of all cable news amounts to a reporter in the field interacting live with an anchor. In addition, cable is loaded with talk shows and "anchor reads" of wire service news. Networks have been sucked in, too. With affiliates clamoring for live stories, especially when dramatic news erupts, CBS and the other networks have had to increase the number of times they interrupt regular programming to announce breaking news.

Print reporters are not exempt from the pressure to go live, for instance when they file for the Internet before doing a story for the ink-on-paper version of the paper, which will appear later. In 2006, a new editor for digital news at the *New York Times* declared that his staff would give readers the "stories they would expect to read in the printed newspaper if it were available from 6 a.m. to 8 p.m. or 9 p.m."

Although another *Times* editor enthused about "delivering quality stories on a second-by-second basis," speed is the enemy of depth. Even correspondents who do not file for the Web feel that speedy medium breathing down their necks. They are always competing with the Internet, said Roger Cohen, a correspondent and former foreign editor at the *New York Times*. "Almost every American correspondent I know," commented Alan Cooperman of the AP, "has had an editor back home phone, question—or even rewrite!—to 'match' CNN." Technology has made "rockets"—those messages to correspondents to chastise a reporter for not getting a story—all the more potent. Instructions "to match" what others are reporting used to land after some delay of time, not instantly like live coverage. "You're constantly getting feedback of what the AP reporters reported or the Reuters man has just put on the wire," said CNN's Jim Bittermann. "Have you seen the same thing, and can you match that?" "To be out of contact with the desk for two or three days," Cohen notes of contemporary journalism, "is almost inconceivable."

The benefits of close supervision are easily exaggerated. While it is true that *USA Today* editors can more easily keep tabs on reporters to prevent another Jack Kelley from playing fast and loose with the news, old-fashioned common sense works just as well. "Any appraisal of how Jack Kelley got away with years of fraudulent news reporting at USA TODAY, despite numerous, well-grounded warnings that he was fabricating stories, exaggerating facts and plagiarizing other publications, must begin with this question," an investigation concluded: "Why did newsroom managers at every level of the paper ignore, rebuff and reject years of multiple serious and valid complaints about Kelley's work?"

Meanwhile, this close supervision undermines one of the great traditions of foreign news-gathering, correspondents' ability to look under rocks that the home office did not know existed.

Correspondents' autonomy from the home office was a long-standing tradition, not only at the *Chicago Daily News* and the *Baltimore Sun,* but elsewhere as well. "Rarely does the telegraph editor find it necessary to give orders to these representatives," observed a 1907 primer on the news business. "They forward the news they think worth forwarding without waiting to ask questions, and most stories they write can be turned over to the printers just as they are received." Just as Buck Dorsey, managing editor at the *Sun,* instructed correspondents seeking guidance to "Please stop asking me to write letters. Love, Dorsey," a *Collier's* editor told correspondents who were exasperated with censorship in the Soviet Union during World War II, "YOU TWO GO WHEREVER YOU CAN FIND STORIES. IF YOU NEED MONEY, CABLE. MY ESTEEM AND AFFECTION."

On occasion *Times* editors scrutinized copy, as was the case with Halberstam's reporting from Vietnam. But its correspondents enjoyed considerable leeway. One of the paper's reporters went to the Far East in the 1950s without knowing who the foreign editor was. Edwin James, managing editor in the 1930s and 1940s, had a general policy of either printing correspondents' reports as they wrote them or throwing them away. His successor, Turner Catledge, called a correspondent home not long after Beard went to work in London. "Some people work better under an editor than on their own," Catledge wrote to the reporter, "and I feel you come in that category." Said foreign editor Craig Whitney roughly a quarter of a century later: "Correspondents make, in the field, many of the editorial judgments that editors make on local and national staffs. We don't tell our correspondents what the story is, and then send them after it, except in special series or projects; most of the time, 90% of the time, correspondents tell us what the story is, and file it, and it's our job to run it if our other editorial demands are satisfied."

Most correspondents considered such freedom a perk and fondly remembered the affection with which editors like Dorsey granted it. In reality, though, editors did not have much choice. They could not have controlled correspondents if they had wanted to. International telephone lines simply did not work well enough.

Whatever its satisfactions and origins, foreign correspondents' autonomy had practical value for the quality of their work. While greater control and efficiency is desired in assembly-line production, it is not ideal in journalism. News is not predictable. News-gathering entails a trial-and-error process of fretting out facts. Although all reporters need freedom to do their job, independence is especially important for foreign correspondents. Editors are much farther removed from overseas events than from the local or national scene, and accordingly less able to spot nascent trends abroad that deserve coverage. When they try to direct the news, they are much more likely to see it in terms of what other news agencies are reporting—as in "match their story"—and more likely to shape news to suit domestic expectations than to awaken the public to matters they have not appreciated before. Also editors are likely to be "much more subject to the conventional wisdom around Washington"—exacerbating the "indexing" problem that was so apparent during the Vietnam War.

It is essential—really, a matter of national security—for journalists to test government assumptions by independently gathering facts and analyzing trends that policymakers may have missed or may ignore. This is less likely to happen when editors drive coverage more than their correspondents do. Vincent Sheean pointed to the value of independent reporting during the 1920s and 1930s. When it came to foreseeing the impending Second World War, he wrote, "International journalism was more alert than international statesmanship."

The *Washington Post*'s Jonathan Randal described how, during the first Iraq War, his paper's "top brass . . . convinced themselves they had a better overall grasp of events than their men on the spot and wrote the overall lead story from Washington," among other things overstating the accuracy of so-called "smart" bombs. "I unashamedly pine for the old cable office or the telex in the Third World that shut down at nightfall in the 1950s and 1960s and allowed me to get drunk or read poetry without fear of an editor's intrusion until the next morning," added Randal. "That free time also allowed me time to meet and read about the people I was covering."

Live coverage from the field does not make journalists any less likely to pay attention to official views. As two scholars have noted, "the one predictable component of [live] coverage remains official sources." What has changed—and creates problems as far as government management of foreign affairs is concerned—is that fast-as-lightning communication accelerates and intensifies the interactions between policymakers and the media when crises erupt. With instant news, officials must react quickly, lest the government seem feckless. The time for "solemn and careful deliberation," which diplomat George Kennan favored, has collapsed into minutes.* Just as it is a problem when news arrives too slowly, as happened in the Battle of New Orleans, it can be a problem when it arrives too quickly.

Editors typically insist that correspondents still have plenty of freedom, that editors work collaboratively with their reporters. Such comments have a managerial gloss, as convincing as when the new owner of a venerable newspaper promises the staff that "nothing will change." While correspondents have not lost all their freedom, they are considerably less free than in the past.

Although technology inevitably brings more management, yet another factor makes editors even more determined to take advantage of communication. Correspondents' freedom was a sign of editorial confidence not only in the reporters themselves but also in the overall enterprise of news-gathering. That does not exist today when newspaper circulation is slipping and so is the audience for network evening news.

The *Washington Post*'s daily circulation dropped from 707,000 in 2005 to 624,000 in 2008. Newspapers, argue editors like the *Post*'s David Hoffman, must find ways to make themselves compelling in an age when readers can get news quickly from the Internet. Space is tight in the newspaper, foreign stories have to be carefully crafted, and Hoffman has to plan to get them in the paper. He is a sharp departure from Philip Foisie, who joined the paper in the mid-1950s and built up its foreign coverage without closely managing correspondents. Each day Hoffman tries to call two of his roughly two dozen correspondents. He also expects a Monday memo from them outlining their plans, which he will modify. A correspondent who just sends in a story is at a disadvantage. It's not like the old days, he says, when whatever a correspondent sent in was published.

Journalists who covet assignments abroad often are the sorts who relish working on their own. Of those Monday memoranda that Hoffman requests from his reporters, he acknowledges, "I ask them, but they don't always have the time or remember." Still, it is much more difficult to avoid the editor's pull when the chains of communication have few weak links. "Gone forever, I'm afraid, is the sense of isolation that used to come with a war," the *New York Times*' R. W. Apple lamented

---

* The increased ease of global communication has had an impact on overseas American diplomats similar to the one it has had on correspondents: loss of autonomy. In the past Washington policymakers depended on their envoys to act as intermediaries, reporting back to Washington and speaking to foreign leaders for their government. Diplomats have less clout now because CNN-watching White House officials follow events in real time and communicate their views directly to their counterparts abroad. "CNN is so good that it regularly beats our own embassies and consulates to stories," Nicholas Burns, at the time State Department spokesman, wrote in 1996; CNN's "jingles and theme music provide the backdrop in government offices and palaces from Santiago to Seoul." Nicholas Burns, "Talking to the World about American Foreign Policy," *Harvard International Journal of Press and Politics* 1 (Fall 1996): 12.

late in life, "that romantic feeling that you were at the end of the earth with nothing to sustain you but your wits and your expense account. Times have changed forever. Never again will the harried correspondent be able to explain that the hotel must have lost the cable ordering him someplace he doesn't want to go or requesting a story he doesn't want to write."

Some see worse ahead. Just as Tony Beard was not replaced after his retirement from the *Times'* London bureau, whose function had changed with technology, many woryy that traditional correspondents will disappear along with the annihilation of time and space. "When young men ask me for advice on how to become a foreign correspondent," wrote C. L. Sulzberger, the *Times'* chief correspondent, in 1969, during the twilight of his career, "I tell them: 'Don't.' It is like becoming a blacksmith in 1919—still an honorable and skilled profession; but the horse is doomed."

24

THE NATURAL HISTORY OF FOREIGN CORRESPONDENCE

Newspapers have evolved from the Colonial press, run by printers with little sense of urgency; to the party-supported partisan press with little pretense of fairness or unbiased reporting; to an independent press with both the yellow journalism epitomized by William Randolph Hearst's *New York Journal* and the monumental journalism exemplified by Lawson's paper. Both the *Journal* and the *Chicago Daily News* disappeared, and entirely new and varied species of news media emerged. From the wireless's uncertain beginnings, radio and television proliferated into hundreds of channels offered via cable and satellite. The Internet moved news from the mass media to one that is easily personalized.

In 1925, the year *Chicago Daily News* owner Victor Lawson died, Robert Park, a University of Chicago sociologist, published a seminal essay, "The Natural History of the Newspaper." That history, he wrote, "is the history of the surviving species. It is an account of the conditions under which the existing newspaper has grown up and taken form." Park's point was that individuals alone did not account for the development of journalism. He was right, as we have seen in this book. The changing economic structures of the news business, including forms of ownership and business management; the advent of new technologies; the rise of professional norms; interaction with government, which at times makes the news and at times feeds off it; war and peace and other developments abroad; the public's current interests and predilections, anything, as Park said, that will make people exclaim "Gee Whiz!": all of those conditions and more form the environment in which news has evolved. And still evolves, often with Darwinian drama.

At the beginning of the twenty-first century, media empires seemingly destined to grow ever larger entered a new phase characterized by the fate of Knight Ridder, which was second only to Gannett in the number of dailies it owned. Under pressure from shareholders, who were impatient with its lackluster stock price, Knight Ridder sold off its properties in 2006 and disappeared completely. The purchase of one of its premier newspapers, the *Philadelphia Inquirer,* by private local business interests fed hope that journalism pried loose from the clutches of Wall Street would flourish. But the new owners soon cut back on staff because they could not make enough money, thereby adding to widespread fears that mass-distributed newspapers were dinosaurs headed for extinction.

"The struggle for existence, in the case of the newspaper," as Park observed, "has been a struggle for circulation." Between 1950 and 2000, paid newspaper subscriptions fell from 353 to 202 per 1,000 population. Audiences for the three weekly newsmagazines—*Time, Newsweek,* and *U.S. News and World Report*—and for broadcast news declined as well. A 2007 study found that the networks' nightly news lost about a million viewers each year over the previous quarter century. In step with this, advertisers changed their preferences, often gravitating toward new media. "Not much imagination or boldness is required to predict that classifieds could completely disappear from newspapers," one student of newspapers observed of the trend to put those ads on the Internet. NBC, owned by General Electric, announced in late 2006 that it was cutting seven hundred jobs and shifting spending from traditional broadcast television to digital platforms. "The pace of change over the next five years is going to dwarf the pace of change over the last 50 years," said an NBC television executive, "and we're going to have to get out in front of it."

Foreign correspondence has a natural history of its own intertwined with this larger media history. As with that larger history, modern foreign news-gathering has entered a phase seized with agonizing concerns—and even doubts—about adaptation and survival.

The episodes in this book suggest eras in the natural history of foreign news-gathering.

In the Colonial beginning, when professional reporters did not exist, there were *The Casual Correspondents,* those unpaid travelers who wrote letters as well as homebound printers who shoveled news into their papers from the foreign journals that arrived by ship. In the mid-nineteenth century, when the partisan press gave way to a mass-market commercial one and news transmission began to speed up, journalists like George Wilkins Kendall and Henry Stanley appeared. These were *The Specials,* after whom the next era can be aptly named. They operated alone, with enterprise and verve, sending home timely and entertaining stories. Out of

TABLE 10. Changes in percentage of people who accessed news media

	1993	1998	2000	2002	2004	2006	2008
Watched nightly network news regularly	60	38	30	32	34	28	29
Read newspaper the day before	58	48	47	41	42	40	34
Listened to radio news the day before	47	49	43	41	40	36	35
Got news online three or more times per week	—	13	23	25	29	31	37

Source: Pew Research Center for the People and the Press, 2008.

this phase evolved *The Foreign Service,* staffed by professionals whose governing concept was systematic news-gathering over the face of the earth. George Smalley took one of the first steps with his "methods" for covering major events, by which he managed a team of reporters from his London bureau. After the U.S. victory in the Spanish-American War, Victor Lawson realized the concept on a grand scale—a corps of expert American correspondents routinely gathering original news for a nation that had joined the ranks of the great powers.

Although foreign news-gathering was never perfect, the next age came the closest to it. Here were *The Compleat Correspondents.* These knowledgeable journalists worked abroad through a wide variety of media, including upstart, exciting radio. They remained largely independent of the home office and, thanks to international goodwill toward Americans, were well received wherever they roamed. The news—two great world wars, Communist revolutions, the emergence of global interdependence—was of towering significance. The celebrity of correspondents was never greater.

The transition from one period to another never took place with one door slamming shut and another opening wide. Each was gradual, with vestiges of the past carrying forward. And so it was with the emergence of *The Corporate Correspondent.* More and more, the news fell into the hands of large companies that owned many other outlets and answered to Wall Street. Correspondents, in closer touch with editors and worried about declining credibility of their profession, were less eccentric, colorful, and independent. More than ever before, their work was subject to owners and chief executives who felt no special calling to journalism.

While the foregoing periods span decades, the seeds of sweeping change were typically sown in the day-to-day decisions of reporters and editors, who were constantly experimenting as Victor Lawson had done when creating his foreign service. "We should not expect the present re-organization of European staff to endure very long," said a *New York Times* editor in 1965, describing the view of Clifton Daniel on foreign news coverage. "Every two or three years a whole series of changes inevitably comes about." The following year the *Times'* new foreign news editor, Seymour Topping, announced, "I have begun an effort to improve the content of the foreign news report." As happened from time to time with such plans, Topping's marked bold shifts in foreign news that offer up an illuminating case study in incremental evolution. (See "A Case Study in Incremental Evolution," pp. 462–63.) But his was not the last word by any means. Those who followed Topping as overseers of foreign news addressed new questions in their own memoranda: "How to make the best use of the foreign staff in the post-Vietnam, post-Kissinger era we are now entering" and, later, "where we should be going in our foreign coverage in the post–Cold War environment. . . . The process, of course, is on-going."

As incremental as change normally has been, the latest phase in the evolution of foreign news has come with a wrenching swiftness not seen since the beginnings of the mass media penny press. A central element in this change has been driven by a problem we have seen in this book more than once: foreign news is one of the *most* expensive journalistic undertakings and one of the *least* rewarding in terms of audience interest.

Although advanced technology saves money, for instance by eliminating per-word cable charges, it is not unusual for a newspaper to budget well over $250,000 a year to support a single foreign correspondent with a salary, housing, office space, and the like. The salary alone of a network correspondent is two or three times that amount, and those correspondents often travel with retinues who also must be paid and supported. Moreover, major news events, such as the Olympics in China in 2008 or the war in Iraq, typically require news media to lay out large sums. After the U.S. invasion in 2003, a one- or two-reporter bureau in Iraq cost newspapers well over $1 million a year, largely because of security needs.

Evidence of the episodic nature of audience interest in foreign news was in full display in February 2004 at *U.S. News and World Report.* The covers of the past thirty-three issues of the magazine were arrayed on an office wall. Just three had international themes. Newsstand sales for those were among the lowest. Two other covers, one on Jesus and the other on weight loss, sold almost twice as well. *Time* and *Newsweek* were as wary of international covers as their competitor.

Gen. Charles H. Taylor, one of those who blew life into newspaper journalism in the late nineteenth century, understood the public's news appetites. When he became the publisher of the *Boston Globe* in 1873, Taylor built one of the country's largest circulations by ordering editors to do as much as possible to get each reader's name in the paper at least once a year. Told on one occasion that the competing *Boston Herald* had hired another London correspondent, he exclaimed, "Then, by God, we'll have to get another in South Boston!" Taylor's ghost has haunted newspaper newsrooms ever since. Although Herbert Bayard Swope made notable scoops for the *New York World* during World War I, he thought that foreign news should be given to the reader "in spoonfuls and damned small ones at that."

The exception, as per Woodward's Law, occurs when a war or some other crisis erupts abroad. Audience interest grows keener. "If it is terrorism, the Iraq War, or Middle East—someplace where we have soldiers," said the *U.S. News and World Report*'s assistant managing editor responsible for foreign news in 2004, "there is no question; we put the war on the cover." Similarly, with each drop-off following a crisis, proponents of foreign news become alarmed. "That the overseas press ranks should be thinned at the end of the war was only natural," a foreign correspondent lamented in the *Saturday Review of Literature* after World War II. "But that the dilution should be so complete as to eliminate eight out of every nine foreign correspondents is another matter." Twenty-five years later, another foreign correspondent writing in the same magazine decried the more-than-one-third decrease in the number of foreign correspondents from the high point of the Vietnam War in 1969. Coverage was so dismal, the reporter noted, that no Pulitzer Prize was given for international reporting in 1977.

The roller-coaster pattern of foreign news-gathering persisted as this book was being written. This time, though, the downward trend was accelerated by forces that simultaneously eroded the old economic models for news generally. One description of this came from Jack Fuller in a 2002 speech, when he was president of the Chicago Tribune Publishing Company: "The reason that we'll be challenged over the next decades is two-fold. The rapidly falling cost of computing power, and

A CASE STUDY IN INCREMENTAL EVOLUTION

When Topping assumed the job of foreign news editor, virtually his entire career had been devoted to foreign reporting. He began with the International News Service in the Far East after World War II and was soon hired by the Associated Press. He joined the *Times* in the mid-1950s and stayed abroad for the newspaper. The changes he brought as editor, however, were based on profound insights about the future of journalism at home.

The first of his departures from the past was from the convention that a newspaper should compete with broadcasters by beating them at breaking news. The emphasis on getting spot news first, Topping argued, was outmoded as a result of the "special challenge" of electronic journalism, with around-the-clock radio news and the early glimmerings of cable television news. "Foreign news dispatches on news agency printers," he noted, "are shown on TV screens at about the same time those dispatches come into the [*Times*] wireroom."

The second departure was from the paper's nearly unwavering spotlight on heads of state and high-level diplomacy, an approach championed early on by Edward Price Bell and Paul Scott Mowrer at the *Chicago Daily News* and widely employed by others. "There is a chilling suspicion that while *The Washington Post* as presently constituted would have reported what Russell and Palmerston said and did in 1848 and 1859 in Commons," *Post* managing editor Alfred Friendly wrote in a 1964 memorandum to his staff, "it might not have noted a publication by Marx and a book by Darwin in those years." At the *Times* home office, staff joked that C. L. Sulzberger, the newspaper's chief foreign correspondent and nephew of the publisher, "never spoke to anyone below the rank of prime minister unless it was to tell them where to put his luggage." In keeping with its Olympian perspective, the *Times* published complete diplomatic documents as well as stories that read like them, in order to maintain its status as the newspaper of record.*

Topping believed this approach no longer made sense. "For much of the detail of the daily developments, which we formerly reported," he wrote, "the historian will go in the future to the computer-regulated data bank rather than specifically to The New York Times." This observation—made when computers were still large, clunky machines owned by institutions, not individuals—was so far ahead of its time that someone scribbled "?" in the margin of the copy of the memorandum saved in the *Times'* files.

Topping's reorientation pointed his correspondents toward broader, deeper coverage: "We can be less preoccupied with the daily official rhetoric of the capitals. We should report more about how the people live, what they and their societies look like, how their institutions and systems operate. Our report should reflect more fully the social, cultural, intellectual, scientific and technological revolutions, which, more than the political, are transforming the world society. And to comprehend, our readers must have more sophisticated interpretive writing."

---

* These documents often appeared with none of the ponderous formalities edited out, like this one from January 3, 1951, relating to planning for a summit conference with the Soviet Union, the United States, France, and Great Britain, which began: "The Ministry of Foreign Affairs of the U.S.S.R. acknowledges receipt of the note of the Government of France of Dec. 22, which was a reply to the note of the Soviet Government of Nov. 3, 1950, on the question of the Council of Foreign Ministers, and, on the instructions of the Soviet Government, has the honor to state the following: The Soviet Government in its note of Nov. 3 proposed . . . "

One of Topping's innovations was the "takeout," a feature designed "to add perspective, depth and understanding to the reader's knowledge of a subject." This was a way to get trend stories into the paper about underreported countries in Africa, South America, and elsewhere. Topping urged his reporters to use other techniques, including "the Man or Woman in the News" ("a living portrait" of a figure whom "the reader may know only as a name") and the "Talker ("the loosest and most flexible story we have. We know it is still evolving. . . . Perhaps the closest we have come to a formula is a string of anecdotes or vignettes, which have a common element or which tend to make a common point").

As Topping swung foreign news in new directions, his title was changed from foreign news editor to the more commanding foreign editor. He wielded his power by recalling correspondents who did not abide by his new directives. His competence and steady hand elevated him to managing editor.

the rapid expansion of bandwidth, which causes . . . the cost of moving information from one place to another to fall precipitously. . . . Potential competitors will use the cheaper bandwidth and cheaper computing power to go after our advertising revenues and our audience. . . . The ongoing fragmentation of the information environment will put pressure on the business model that supports excellent journalism, including and perhaps especially foreign coverage."

As this new reality sunk in throughout the news business, one could routinely hear the gloomy Darwinian conjecture that "the genre known as 'foreign correspondent' is becoming extinct" and international news "an endangered species." Not only did the *Baltimore Sun* foreign service vanish. Gone, too, were esteemed news services of similar size run by *Newsday,* another newspaper owned by the *Chicago Tribune;* by the *Boston Globe,* acquired a few years before by the New York Times Company; and by the *Philadelphia Inquirer.* Piping the spirit of the patriarchal General Taylor, *Globe* managers talked about going "hyperlocal" in order to attract readers. Not long after the sale of the *Philadelphia Inquirer* by Knight Ridder in 2006, the new owner brought home its last foreign correspondent—from Jerusalem—and gave no hope that the foreign staff would rebuild to the half dozen correspondents the paper had had a few years before. "We don't need a Jerusalem bureau," said Brian Tierney, a local public relations man who engineered the purchase of the paper and became publisher. "What we need are more people in the South Jersey bureau."

A 2008 study of 250 newspapers found that foreign news "was rapidly losing ground at rates greater than any other topic area." Two-thirds of the surveyed papers had given less space to foreign news over the past three years; half had cut the resources dedicated to such coverage. The response rates were about the same for large and small newspapers. Meanwhile, other media slashed away at foreign news. In the years after Tom Fenton joined CBS News in 1966 (he broke into foreign reporting at the *Baltimore Sun*), its global presence reached 14 major bureaus and 10 smaller ones. When he retired in 2004, CBS had 8 foreign correspondents in all, 4 of them in London. In early 2007, ABC's bureau in Nairobi, Kenya, was the only outpost for any network in Africa, India, or South America. The next year, with audience interest waning in the protracted stalemate in Iraq, both NBC and CBS no longer had permanent correspondents in Baghdad. Among the weekly news magazines, *Time* had 26 bureaus in 1986, 20 in 1990, and 14 in 2008. At *Newsweek,* the number of bureaus dropped from 16 in the late 1980s to 11 in 2008, with 1 headed by a contract hire. The magazine enhanced coverage, said its chief of correspondents, by other means, for instance using contributing editors, some in the United States, to write on foreign affairs. "It's a mix between commentary, analysis, and reporting." *U.S. News and World Report* chopped away to the point that it had no foreign bureaus at all. It also abandoned the weekly print edition in 2009, concentrating instead on electronic delivery. In the years before the print edition disappeared, the type size of "*World*" on its cover gradually shrank in relation to that of "*U.S. News.*" In 1948, the *W* was 60 percent of the height of the *U;* sixty years later, in 2008, it was less than 20 percent as tall. Before 1948, *World Report* and *United States News* were separate freestanding magazines.

While foreign news could never be completely secure, even in a paper like the *Chicago Daily News,* it has had a relatively better chance of thriving when family owners answered to themselves. Although they made good livings, Victor Lawson and the Ochs-Sulzberger family received something else that they held precious in exchange for their aggressive foreign coverage: the psychic reward of praise from peers and the public for their civic virtue. During the difficult economic years of the 1970s, there was always an understanding that foreign news was important at the *Times.* While Topping was managing editor in that period, he had the authority to remove ads to make room for important news. As media companies have gone public and have grown larger, more diversified, and more corporate, in some cases becoming part of nonmedia companies (e.g., NBC is now owned by General Electric), their executives have sought their bragging rights on Wall Street. On that boulevard, few were impressed that an editor was spending more money on foreign news coverage.

One of the more arresting examples of this trend was the change of ownership that occurred at the Chicago Tribune Company. In 2007 unhappy shareholders sold the property, with its stable of thoroughbred newspapers,* to real estate investor Sam Zell. Zell had evidenced no previous interest in news or public service. Such motives, said a business colleague, "would have been totally out of character." Antediluvian in contrast was the 1933 purchase of the *Washington Post* by financier Eugene Meyer, whose character was different. Although he had amassed considerable wealth and enjoyed its benefits, he invested in the paper to achieve more than profit. Among his stated principles was this: "The newspaper shall be prepared to make sacrifices of its material fortunes, if such a course be necessary for the public good." Whatever one might say about Col. McCormick, that quirky potentate of the *Tribune* had a deep attachment to the social purpose of his newspaper that its new owner, Zell, would never approach.

---

* In addition to the *Chicago Tribune,* the *Los Angeles Times,* the *Baltimore Sun,* and *Newsday,* the Chicago Tribune Company at the time owned four other dailies, including one of the nation's oldest, the *Hartford Courant,* as well as twenty-three radio stations and the Chicago Cubs.

Although many prominent journalists decried cutbacks in coverage in the early years of the twenty-first century, support for foreign news was not overwhelmingly strong in newsrooms in light of the forces working against news-gathering generally. Washington bureaus were shrinking and being eliminated, as were bureaus in state capitals. Axing four or five people from a foreign service in a crunch saved three or four times as many less costly jobs at home. Staff members who favored foreign news were often the ones who wanted to go abroad themselves, but even they could be reluctant. Said one about the idea of his metropolitan newspaper putting a bureau in Asia, "I think we need to continue to do more locally before we do something like that. If the economy turns around we'll consider it."

Yet, for all the cutbacks and stygian forebodings, the adverse environment for old models of news-gathering spawned not just a new model, but new models, plural. In our progression of eras in foreign news-gathering, we may call this system *The Confederacy of Correspondents*. In this confederacy, serious foreign news-gathering by the traditional media continued, albeit with significant adaptations, while new species of foreign news-gathering and news distribution emerged. All these species carried the DNA of earlier forms. The overall result was a broader, more variegated class of foreign correspondents that, though still imperfect, ensured a continued foreign news flow and formed a basis for improvement.

The American foreign correspondent for the *New York Times* or CBS News—the familiar Traditional Foreign Correspondent—continues, but not alone. Three other types of correspondents have become integral to traditional mass media news-gathering abroad.

The first is the Foreign Foreign Correspondent, that is, the foreign national who operates as a correspondent for an American news organization. In the beginning of the penny press's overseas coverage, the use of foreigners as full-time correspondents or stringers was standard practice. Even in the twentieth century, one could find a foreign-born reporter like Paul Ghali on the staff of the *Chicago Daily News,* but the emphasis was increasingly on using American foreign correspondents. Now practice is changing once again. A survey conducted in 2000 found that 69 percent of foreign correspondents for American news organizations were not Americans; they outnumbered Americans in every news medium. Only about one-quarter of Associated Press byline reporters abroad were American. Editors may worry about American correspondents going native, but many of today's correspondents are native to start with.

The 2000 survey did not distinguish between Foreign Foreign Correspondents who were local citizens and those who were neither American nor local but hailed from a third country. But other evidence shows the role of locals increasing. CNN promoted its cable service abroad by telling foreign viewers that local correspondents were reporting from their home countries. The *New York Times* at one point employed seventy local reporters and translators in Iraq, as well as forty-five guards. Translators are of elevated importance journalistically as are other "fixers," a term for local dragomen who also help correspondents cut through foreign

TABLE 11. The Confederacy of Correspondents

Class	Definition
Traditional Foreign Correspondents	Americans who are sent abroad by an established news organization to maintain a permanent bureau or who work abroad for years as freelance correspondents for such media. These are the once-elite correspondents who for decades held sway in the public's mind as what it meant to be a foreign correspondent. The prototype was the foreign correspondent of the *Chicago Daily News* Foreign Service and is today a correspondent with the *New York Times* or CBS.
Foreign Foreign Correspondents	Non-American reporters, often citizens of the countries they cover. They work for established U.S. media but also are found among premium service foreign correspondents (see below). They are cheaper to maintain. They often can move more easily around the country than a traditional correspondent when there is danger, but they also are more vulnerable when the government has little patience for critical reporting.
Local Foreign Correspondents	Correspondents who cover the world from in the United States. Sometimes they are dedicated full-time to stories involving local ties to foreign events and trends. Sometimes they cover foreign news as part of their work on another beat; for instance, a business reporter may look at the impact of foreign competition on a local manufacturing concern. Local foreign correspondents are an expression of growing global interdependence, in which foreign affairs shape Americans' lives every day in tangible ways.
Parachute Foreign Correspondents	Reporters dispatched for short-term assignments, usually to cover major breaking news. They take several forms. News media find these reporters a cheap alternative to stationing correspondents permanently in the field. In some cases, though, media deploy parachute correspondents to supplement their permanent staff in the field. Often such correspondents have special expertise. Parachute correspondents also work for small- and medium-sized news media that previously never sent anyone abroad, but thanks to the ease of modern travel can now do some original foreign news-gathering of their own. These parachutists can be permanent roving correspondents based at home or reporters sent to cover one-time ad hoc stories.
Premium Service Foreign Correspondents	Correspondents who report from bureaus overseas for "gated," high-cost news services, for example, Bloomberg News and the Dow Jones Newswires. These correspondents are both foreign and local because the services for which they report have a global audience. A Bloomberg correspondent in Singapore is a foreign correspondent as far as a client in Minneapolis is concerned, but local for a Singapore subscriber.
In-House Foreign Correspondents	Employees of a nonnews organization whose exclusive job is to provide updated and high-quality news and information related to the organization's mission. Sometimes they do original reporting; often they aggregate news that appears in traditional and nontraditional media and distribute it over their own networks.

TABLE 11 (*continued*)

Class	Definition
Citizen Foreign Correspondents	Individuals without journalistic training or affiliation who become de facto journalists when they report on foreign events and issues, often by posting the information directly on the Internet. They can also function as their own foreign editor by accessing information without relying on the editorial function of a newspaper, a magazine, or a broadcast entity.
Foreign Local Correspondents	Non-Americans who work and report for a foreign news organization whose news is available worldwide on the Internet. An example is a Peruvian journalist reporting for a Lima newspaper or broadcast station, whose work is accessed via the Internet or satellite in the United States. One of the chief audiences for such news is Latin American emigrants.

bureaucracy, arrange interviews, drive the bureau car, take the odd photo, and the like. Again, fixers have been prized in the past. In a memoir, *New York Times* foreign correspondent Stephen Kinzer told how his multitalented fixer in Managua in the 1970s, a former bus driver named Luis López, was hired away by NBC News for a salary three times that of a Nicaraguan minister. Dith Pran, who helped the *New York Times*' Sydney Schanberg in Cambodia in the 1970s and eventually escaped from the Khmer Rouge–controlled country, became a photographer at the newspaper in New York and a hero in the movie *The Killing Fields*. Junnosuke Ofusa, a Japanese citizen, worked in the *Times* Tokyo bureau for nearly sixty years as a "fixer" who occasionally did reporting. At his retirement in 1987, the *Times* gave him its medal for service to the newspaper. But until recently, these were exceptions. Today more of them are employed in difficult-to-cover countries, and more of them are praised publicly for their work. A Baghdad bureau chief for McClatchy newspapers referred to local fixers as "journalists in their own right" and "the backbone of our coverage." In recognition of this, McClatchy set up an "Inside Iraq" blog exclusively for the use of its Iraqi staff. Many fixers now receive joint bylines. The *Washington Post* has brought fixers to the United States to get formal training as journalists.

Cost is a factor in using locals. The median salary for foreign nationals, according to the 2000 study, was about half that for their American counterparts. In addition, as one veteran correspondent observed, "they do not require the kind of plush housing and cost-of-living benefit packages that North Americans routinely received in the past."

Nearly one out of five Foreign Foreign Correspondents earned his or her highest degree in the United States, also according to the 2000 survey. Americans and foreigners had remarkably similar news priorities for politics, economics, culture, social programs, sports, religion, environment/energy, and human rights. They are not, however, the identical twins of American reporters. As a result, a number of trade-offs suggest themselves. Foreign Foreign Correspondents may have less appreciation for the needs of American news consumers and at the same time be better equipped to understand and interpret events abroad. They may have more appreciation of local circumstances and have a greater propensity toward bias. They may move around a country more easily and yet be more vulnerable. In heavy-handed countries like China, authorities have imprisoned citizens who serve as Foreign Foreign Correspondents. Because Foreign Foreign Correspondents are less expensive, editors may feel less need to use their reports.

What is certain is that Foreign Foreign Correspondents have at times distinguished themselves. For example, in 1999, when war broke out in Chechnya, the threat of being kidnapped kept Western reporters from stationing themselves in the capital, Grozny, to cover the Russian attack. Two Chechen reporters on the AP staff, Lyoma Turpalov and Ruslan Musayev, provided vivid firsthand reporting that exemplified the best journalism—revealing the truth when officials lie. The Russian government claimed it had neither attacked the capital nor suffered a defeat. Musayev reported walking "through the wreckage in Minutka Square on Thursday, counting the [115] dead. Seven burned Russian tanks and eight armored personnel carriers were also seen." The AP's coverage of the war was a finalist for the Pulitzer Prize for foreign reporting that year.

Another full-blown class of foreign correspondents that has emerged—and is thoroughly American—is made up of reporters who cover the world from their hometowns. This Local Foreign Correspondent, seemingly a contradiction in terms, has come about because of the development of global interdependence.

Human history has been a long march toward greater interaction between cultures and countries. The term *interdependence*, prominent in contemporary conversations about the new state of world affairs, actually dates from the nineteenth century. Vincent Sheean, along with other correspondents in the 1930s, was acutely aware that "'Near East' and 'Far East' and 'Adriatic' and 'Baltic' were coming nearer and nearer to each other with vertiginous speed." What has changed in our own time is that interactions have speeded up and proliferated, blurring the line between foreign and domestic affairs. Nearly every federal agency, no matter how domestic its agenda seems, has activities abroad, while foreign affairs are intertwined in the daily lives of cities, towns, and villages. "We're in a new era now in which the ambiguity in what is international and what is not international is very great," commented experienced *Washington Post* foreign correspondent Don Oberdorfer. "And I think that if we just . . . say that if the news isn't coming from overseas then it's not international, we're misleading ourselves."

American farmers and agricultural extension agents pay close attention to the ups and downs of foreign markets, which are sometimes the destination for their crops and in any event determine domestic prices. Local entrepreneurs, supported by community banks as well as state development authorities, invest and trade abroad. Communities declare themselves nuclear free zones and state development authorities send delegations to monitor and lobby federal trade negotiators. Young men and women dance to "world beat" music. Local physicians inoculate their patients against the influenza that travelers bring from Asia each winter. All of these are stories journalists can report locally.

Such reporting is still in the experimental stage. Sometimes local media run special series on local connections; sometimes they try to make a routine out of such news. The *Atlanta Journal-Constitution* tried a "Global Atlanta" section on Mondays in the first part of the newspaper, then tried a stand-alone "Atlanta & The World" section on Wednesdays, and finally, in 2006, decided to weave foreign stories inside the newspaper as it always had done. In a 2004 Radio and Television News Directors Foundation survey, two-thirds of local broadcasters said they integrated world and local news into their newscasts.

Journalism organizations have trained journalists to see and pursue local connections abroad. One project, funded by the Carnegie and Ford foundations and carried out under the auspices of the Society of Professional Journalists in the mid-1980s, worked with newspapers and some television stations around the United States to explore approaches for making foreign news local. The American Society of Newspaper Editors, with help from the Freedom Forum, mounted a similar project a decade later. The International Reporting Project and the International Center for Journalists, both located in Washington, D.C., sponsored fellowships to give reporters, many associated with smaller local media, a chance to travel abroad. Participants in the ICFJ program, said ICFJ president Joyce Barnathan, pursue a "global story of local importance."

Major media have tracked foreign-local connections, sometimes using their foreign correspondents as well as domestic reporters. In a particularly good example of this approach, the *Wall Street Journal* traced manhole covers in U.S. cities to their manufacturers in India and showed how the Chinese make money with American garbage.

The pursuit of transnational stories points to a third new class of foreign correspondence. The term Parachute Foreign Correspondent has been a pejorative. It describes a cost-cutting ploy through which a major news organization reduces the size of its staff of permanent foreign correspondents and covers foreign news only when a big story comes along by flying ill-equipped reporters to the scene. As valid as the critique of such economizing is, it overlooks the positive ways parachute journalism serves the public. The critique also is misleading in its assumptions about the way traditional correspondents function.

Most traditional foreign correspondents are to some degree parachutists. Henry Stanley was a parachutist when he found Dr. Livingstone. Paul Scott Mowrer left his Paris post before World War I to explore the conflict in the Balkans; his roving assignments after the war took him to the Riff. It is not unusual for modern-day correspondents to travel half the time away from their bureaus. In 2004 the *Los Angeles Times* had roughly thirty foreign correspondents, one of the largest corps of any metropolitan newspaper, but its Jakarta correspondent still had to cover virtually the whole of Southeast Asia. Individual newspaper correspondents often are responsible for much, if not all, of Latin America or of Africa. Assignments became particularly fungible after 2001, with many correspondents leaving faraway posts to cover the fighting in Iraq and Afghanistan. "Mike Hanna of CNN," noted anthropologist Ulf Hannerz, "described his outfit as a 'travel bureau': since CNN operates on the principle of extreme flexibility, unless he was busy with something in

Johannesburg, he might fly in wherever there was a staff shortage, whether it was Jerusalem, Cairo, Moscow, or somewhere else."

From time to time newspapers without foreign correspondents extended this concept to parachute reporters. After John Cowles Sr. acquired the *Minneapolis Tribune* in the 1930s (and hired Carroll Binder of the *Chicago Daily News* as his foreign editor), the paper sent reporters overseas "to explore and research situations that might underlie future crises and wars." The *Milwaukee Journal,* though less ambitious, sent reporters on trips that yielded impressive results. Thomas Blinkhorn and photographer Don Nusbaum went to the Middle East in the late 1960s to report on the growing tension between Israel and Palestine. They talked their way into one of Yasir Arafat's Palestine Liberation Organization training camps outside Amman, Jordan, where militant recruits were going through their paces. The Associated Press picked up Nusbaum's photos. Blinkhorn managed to get the first foreign journalist's interview with Golda Meir, the new prime minister of Israel. "The fact that she used to teach school in Milwaukee, and loved the experience," Blinkhorn recalled later, "turned the trick."

What is different today is that this approach to news-gathering is much more widespread and is routine. A 2004–5 survey of fifty newspapers—ranging in size from the fifty-thousand-circulation Burlington, Vermont, *Free Press* to the *Los Angeles Times,* whose Sunday circulation topped 1 million—found that forty-four of them at least occasionally sent reporters abroad. A survey of local television news directors around the same time showed that 64 percent of the stations had sent reporters outside the country to cover a story.

A key factor in this parachuting is the ease of modern air travel. In 1940 *Times* correspondent Frederick Birchall spoke of the "blessed invention" of the airplane, which "carried me from convention to revolution, from coronation to tragedy, always to great news." Since then, improvements in speed and cost have conferred more blessings on travelers. On its maiden flight in 1936, the propeller-driven *China Clipper* took six days to reach Hong Kong from the West Coast; by the turn of the twenty-first century, commercial jets made the trip in little more than half a day. The per-mile cost for individual passengers fell about 90 percent in real terms between 1937 and 2000. "Staff mobility has been enhanced tremendously by the jet airplane," wrote Seymour Topping in one of his 1960s memorandums. "Bureau chiefs will continue to have primary responsibility for coverage of their areas, but staffers who have specialized knowledge and experience will be moved with increasing frequency across bureau lines to add new dimensions to our reporting." After he was promoted to managing editor, he told the foreign editor, "I think you ought to set up some kind of system so that our correspondents in the field will have a variety of visas in their passports so that they can move quickly."

The use of parachute journalists gives editors at news organizations with permanent correspondents a chance to learn whether a promising reporter is up to the challenge of working permanently abroad in its foreign service. The prospect of parachuting also is a way to recruit reporters with international interests and to retain talented reporters when they return to the local staff after a foreign assignment. But the major advantage is that it allows editors to put more reporters in the field. The *Chicago Tribune,* as an example, sent a music reporter to Cuba, even though the paper had a correspondent in Havana, and a metro desk reporter to the South Pacific to investigate the disappearance of an American basketball star. When Pope John Paul II died, the *Tribune* created a team of two foreign correspondents, along with two staffers from the metro desk who had experience covering religion. "There are examples [of this] all the time," said the *Chicago Tribune's* associate managing editor for foreign news in 2005.

Permanent foreign correspondents and home-based reporters with special expertise, such as investigative skills, can be a powerful combination. An example of its use is the *Dallas Morning News* series on "runaway priests," one of whose stories began this way on June 23, 2004:

Safe harbor
By Brooks Egerton and Reese Dunklin
Staff Writers

ALBISSOLA MARINA, Italy—Inside a 16th-century Catholic church by the Mediterranean Sea, the priest dresses as a man of God and preaches about the Holy Spirit.

Outside, he tells lies.

"I'm not a functioning priest," he says, until he realizes a reporter has just seen him celebrate Sunday evening Mass. Then he says he only "occasionally" leads a service and isn't in active ministry. "Ministry means one has to be in a parish," he says.

In fact, the Pakistani has been serving here since last fall as associate pastor of Nostra Signora della Concordia. He has also been leading a smaller congregation in the nearby village of Ellera.

Italy, it turns out, is at least the third country in which he has worked in parishes since denying child molestation charges in England seven years ago and fleeing, before he could be tried. *The Dallas Morning News* tracked him down after Scotland Yard failed.

Church aid and law enforcement lapses have made the sojourn possible, as they have in many other cases that *The News* reviewed in its yearlong investigation of the international movements of priests accused of child molestation.

This story resembled a page out of the career of the *Chicago Tribune's* James Keeley, but unlike the lone editor's tracking down an absconding Chicago banker, the *Morning News* team investigated a significant trend. As the map on page 472 illustrates, the reporters sometimes flew to other countries, they sometimes did interviews overseas by phones, and they sometimes used the newspaper's stringers or found local journalists on the scene who could help.

The anchors of the series were two local reporters with strong investigative skills, Brooks Egerton and Reese Dunklin, and Brendan Case, a business reporter stationed in the newspaper's Mexico bureau. They worked on the project for more than a year, and their stories appeared over many months, clearly establishing that

RUNAWAY PRIESTS INVESTIGATIONS

O Places visited by reporters of *The Dallas Morning News* for *Runaway Priests* series

■ Places where freelancers were hired to help on the investigation

△ Places called outside the United States

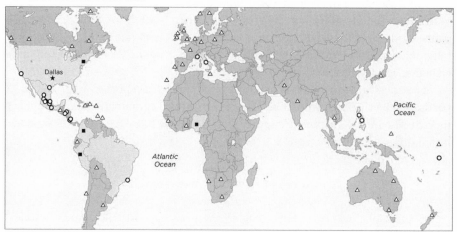

PLACES VISITED

BRENDAN CASE*

Mexico:
Mexico City
Tehuacán, Puebla
Cuacnopalan, Puebla
Puebla, Puebla
Toluca, Estado de México
León, Guanajuato
Tuxtepec, Oaxaca

Costa Rica:
San José
Alajuela
Buenos Aires de Pocosol
Ciudad Quesada

Honduras:
Tegucigalpa
Guinope

REESE DUNKLIN

Samoa:
Apia

Italy:
Rome
Albissola Marina

BROOKS EGERTON

Philippines:
Manila
Cebu

Brazil:
Rio de Janeiro

Mexico:
Matamoros

United States
California: Los Angeles
Texas: Edinburg, Pharr, San Juan

* Brendan Case was based in *The News'* Mexico City bureau at the time. Graphic by Sergio Peçanha, courtesy of *The Dallas Morning News.*

Catholic Church leaders were helping priests avoid justice. A priest featured in the series was deported from Samoa to Australia, where he subsequently pleaded guilty. Australian newspapers followed the story closely.

This was not the first time the *Morning News* put together an international team. The newspaper won a Pulitzer Prize in 1994 for a fourteen-part series, "Violence against Women: A Question of Human Rights." For that story, recalled editor Bob Mong, "We went all over the world." "You need to be thinking from an issue perspective, not a geographical one," says one of the reporters who worked on the series.

Parachuting also is a way to trace local stories abroad. KRON-TV in San Francisco produced a five-part series on Japan's economy and its ties to the local economy. The *Eugene Register-Guard* sent a reporter to do a story on a local nurse who ran an AIDS orphanage in Kenya and a coastal reporter to investigate Japan's approaches to tsunami preparedness. After Hurricane Katrina flooded New Orleans in 2005, the local newspaper, the *Times-Picayune,* sent a reporter to Holland to find out how the Dutch managed flood control.

In a few cases, a news organization has had a permanent parachuting correspondent based at home. It is usually a reporter who has had considerable experience abroad. Richard Read, who had opened the *Oregonian*'s Tokyo bureau, became that paper's roving correspondent when he came home in 1994. Describing his job in 2007, Read said he averaged two long trips each year and did others on an ad hoc basis. In most cases, the stories had "some relationship to Portland. . . . I am always looking for those links." He reported on sweatshops in Vietnam run by a local company, Nike, and traveled to Scotland to scope out an investor there who was making a play in Portland. He traveled to North Korea in 2007, though, for the old-fashioned journalism reason that he had a chance for a great story on an unknown place.

The ease with which correspondents can parachute has led, inevitably, to reconsideration of the concept of foreign bureaus by television. Although the Murrow years are remembered nostalgically because of the many bureaus CBS as well as NBC had abroad, those outposts had limitations as well as strengths. The correspondent in Rome acquired quite a lot of expertise on Italy. But how much news from Rome could a thirty-minute evening newscast use? Besides, observed Marcy McGinnis in 2004, when she was CBS's senior vice president for news coverage, stories rarely happen where you have a bureau. With the ability to travel far and fast, television employed a new arrangement with a few central locations staffed with mobile reporting teams. A handful of reporters, camera staff, fixers, and producers reside at strategic locations around the world, constituting a base to which ABC added in 2008 by setting up one-person bureaus at seven posts. Most of the work of these ABC bureaus was done for the Internet, but they provided a foundation when a big story demanding traditional air time broke. This strategy played to television's strength—breaking news—and left analysis to print journalism, which was doing its own rethinking of bureaus.

Newspapers have begun to see bureaus as bases for covering transnational issues as much as places. The *Boston Globe*'s experience with veteran correspondent John Donnelly, shortly before it ended its foreign service in 2007, was illustrative. Taking advantage of Donnelly's expertise in covering health issues, which were of special interest to Bostonians with their outstanding research hospitals, the *Globe* placed him in Cape Town, where he covered the normal run of stories but concentrated on river blindness, AIDS, and other such stories crucial to the future of Africa. When the tsunami struck in 2004, Donnelly flew to Asia to cover its aftermath. Similarly, after September 11, 2001, the *Washington Post*'s correspondent in Berlin became a terrorism correspondent and ranged widely, as did his successor. In transportation-easy London, the *Post*'s correspondents have been used as broad specialists, reporting on migration of people, on religion and spirituality, and on the impact of digitalization on people around the world. *USA Today* benefited from having Barbara Slavin, whom a foreign editor described as "our Empress of Rogue

States." Slavin, a former foreign correspondent who became the paper's diplomatic correspondent, specialized in Iran, North Korea, and Libya.

Parachuting is not an adequate substitute for posting foreign correspondents permanently in the field, where they can accumulate expertise, contacts, and perspective. Something is clearly wrong when a major metropolitan newspaper like the *Boston Globe* shutters its permanent foreign bureaus and, at the very same time, outsources in-house financial work to India, demonstrating how interdependent the world has become. More troubling still is *USA Today*. It has by far the largest national circulation, not to mention distribution overseas. But in 2005 the daily fielded only three permanent full-time foreign correspondents. To fill in the rest of the vast world, it relied on "firefighters," as an editor put it. If the paper has "one or two on the road all the time," said another editor, "then I think we're OK."

At the same time, the great majority of American news media—the hundreds of local dailies and weeklies and the hometown radio and television stations in towns and cities across the country—were never able to afford permanent foreign correspondents anyway. For these journalism entities, parachuting and local foreign reporting is a net plus on the balance sheet of foreign coverage. What's more, as surveys show, stories connecting the foreign to the local counter the old problem of low audience interest in international news.

In November 1981 the International Reporting Information Systems announced itself to the world. A London insurance broker and the founder of the *National Journal* in the United States conceived of IRIS. The prince of Liechtenstein, a Swedish shipping magnate, and others helped finance it. The idea was to arm advanced computers with special software to gather and sort political and economic information in eight languages from all over the world and to sell it to governments, bankers, and corporate executives. These clients would pay a hefty premium for this news, which was to arrive via their computers, and for related analysis by a staff of big-name journalists assembled in Crystal City, outside Washington, D.C. Among these journalists were John de St. Jorre, a former Africa correspondent with the *London Observer*; Richard Davey, who had covered Eastern Europe for the *Times* of London; and Juan de Onis, who had been a Latin America correspondent with the *New York Times*. Bureaus around the world were to fill out the operation.

That, at least, was the plan. The senior executives—mostly former American government foreign affairs bureaucrats with dollar signs in their eyes—hung fancy art on the office walls and hired a chef. Unfortunately, they knew nothing about what it takes to create marketing plans or make them work. The computer wunderkind who was to mastermind data collection using equipment that was originally designed for military and intelligence jobs fell months behind in delivering on promises. The journalists who signed up for the ride—accomplished questioners when it came to business and politics—displayed little skepticism when accepting well-paid positions at IRIS, which ended up with one client, who paid four hundred dollars for some advice. When IRIS was officially laid to rest at bankruptcy court, records showed it lost $15 million.

©1981 Daily Mail, London/Rothco

"Denis, bring in the flyspray—007 is at the window again."

The International Reporting Information Systems attracted respected journalists and government bureaucrats. Its advisory board included former defense secretary and World Bank president Robert McNamara and former British prime minister Edward Heath. The *London Daily Mail* spoofed IRIS when it was launched with great fanfare in 1981. The man outside Prime Minister Margaret Thatcher's window is Heath; the reference to James Bond's 007 came about because some of the government officials involved with IRIS had worked at the CIA. IRIS soon crashed, but others of this species of news succeeded spectacularly.

The concept, nevertheless, was brilliant. It combined advanced technology and modern journalism principles with the idea that inspired Paul Julius Reuter's mid-nineteenth-century information service for bankers and Charles-Louis Havas's newspaper-clipping and translation service for embassies and government agencies, banks and other businesses, and a few provincial newspapers. "It's a laudable objective," said former World Bank president and defense secretary Robert McNamara, who served on the IRIS advisory council. "We need more information. The average American industrialist doesn't know enough about the world."

Although Reuters and Havas expanded into news services reaching the general public—Havas morphed into Agence France-Presse—many news media have found it profitable to provide special services to sophisticated financial audiences willing to pay more for them. Reuters, which was acquired by Thomson Corporation in 2007, runs one of these services, as does the parent company of the *Wall Street Journal*, Dow Jones, through Dow Jones Newswires. In 2008 Dow Jones Newswires had about 900 reporters and editors, up from the previous year; about 525 were abroad in some sixty-five bureaus. This staff—the great majority of whom were from the countries in which the bureaus are based—provided news on a dozen English-language services and ten in foreign languages. This specialized service was among the fastest-growing areas of the entire Dow Jones operation. The *Economist* had an Economic Intelligence Unit, which promoted itself as "delivering vital business intelligence to influential decision-makers around the world." It had forty offices worldwide.

The journalists working around the world for these organizations—which serve narrow, not mass, audiences—constitute another new class, which can be called Premium Service Foreign Correspondents.

The operation closest to the IRIS model, and the most successful, is Bloomberg News, which began around the same time IRIS did. The founder, Michael Bloomberg, came to start his news operation by the same back door that Reuter used. When Salomon Brothers, where he was a partner, merged with the Philbro Corporation, Bloomberg received a large check and was pushed out. He struck out on his own to build a financial information company that began by offering sophisticated financial data to money managers and the securities industry via computer. His first client was Merrill Lynch, which eventually took an equity position in the business; others around the world signed up, among them the Bank of England and the Vatican. In 1990, with the company prospering, Bloomberg took the next step of venturing into news. In early 2009 Bloomberg had 1,089 journalists and support staff (television technicians and the like) inside the United States in some 40 bureaus and 1,284 outside in about 105 bureaus. For a single Bloomberg terminal, customers paid sixteen hundred dollars per month, slightly less if they had several.

From the beginning Bloomberg's approach was animated by a view similar to James Gordon Bennett's claim to democratizing financial information. Investors, Bloomberg noted, could use his data to "see which bonds were cheap and which bonds were expensive, without having to rely on the calculations and spiel of a bond salesperson with a vested interest in which securities he purchased." Before long Bloomberg News overcame the resistance of traditional news organizations, which at first had blocked accreditation of its reporters to cover Congress and other federal agencies on the grounds that it did not do real journalism. Going beyond dry business news, Bloomberg reporters won the same awards that mainstream journalists did.

Bloomberg News branched into traditional media as a way to add credibility and bring in additional revenue. It syndicated news to almost five hundred newspapers and magazines and more than one hundred radio stations, owned eleven television networks of its own around the world, and operated a twenty-four-hour radio station in New York, which could be heard outside the region on satellite radio. Translation was done into Chinese, German, Italian, Japanese, Portuguese, and Spanish. In its printed magazine, *Bloomberg Markets,* could be found such investigative cover stories as "The Secret World of Modern Slavery," a report on forced labor in Brazil that was worthy of the muckrakers of yore. Matthew Winkler, Bloomberg's editor-in-chief and once a London correspondent for the *Wall Street Journal,* hired outstanding traditional journalists such as Al Hunt, the *Wall Street Journal*'s executive Washington editor; Amanda Bennett, a refugee from the troubled *Philadelphia Inquirer,* where she was executive editor; and William Schmick, who won a Pulitzer Prize with the Gannett News Service after dossing down abroad for the *Baltimore Sun.*

More than fifty percent of Bloomberg's individual subscribers were outside the United States, making the concept of "foreign correspondent" meaningless. A report from China on soybeans is a foreign story to someone reading it on a computer terminal in Milwaukee and a local story to a Shanghai business executive. As a result, Bloomberg's journalists, no matter where they may be, were foreign and domestic correspondents simultaneously.* The firm's staff was rarely included in censuses of foreign correspondents, but it should have been.

A variation of the Bloomberg Premium Service Foreign Correspondent is the In-House Foreign Correspondent. Its antecedent is the House of Rothschild's private communication network, which allowed it to profit by acquiring financial information ahead of other financiers in the nineteenth century. This class of foreign correspondence is difficult to quantify, let alone assess. The people doing such work are not classified as journalists. They have no incentive for explaining to the public what they do or how they do it. They answer only to their superiors in the corporation. Their work is all the more difficult to pin down because it is often woven into public relations efforts.

At the most basic level, global companies have editors who produce what British Petroleum in 2007 called *BP News,* a daily summary of stories from around the world about the company, "published" in London. But activities could be much more sophisticated. At EDS, itself a business information company, staff constantly monitored Web sites to see who was blogging about the company and what they were saying. Alcoa's aerospace division hired a small firm headed by a former Associated Press reporter to cover the annual Paris Air Show: a reporter and a photographer sent material to London, where it was edited by a former Reuters reporter to be put on the Alcoa Web site. Federal Express operated FedEx-TV, which delivered video with news and information to staff. (Its "truth squad" tracked breaking stories in print and on the air and, when they spotted inaccuracies, they immediately got in touch with the offending journalist.)

Professional journalists of the old school dismiss In-House Foreign Correspondents as having nothing to do with real journalism, but in crucial ways they do. Like traditional journalists, In-House Foreign Correspondents care about timely, accurate information. In the words of an executive at a meeting of the Global Pub-

---

* The only time one hears the word *foreign* at Bloomberg, said editor Matthew Winkler, is in a sentence that says something like "this is a foreign concept." Similarly, when Ted Turner ran CNN, which broadcasts news around the world, he outlawed the word *foreign* in broadcasts and in "conversation and writing"; the word *international* was preferred. His memo to staff said, "The policy is in keeping with the Company's philosophy of promoting greater global understanding and friendship, and dealing positively with our international customers." Individuals below the management level were fined fifty dollars for each offense and managers one hundred dollars; the funds went to the United Nations Children's Fund. *Washington Post,* March 13, 1990.

lic Affairs Institute, an organization that brings corporate communications chiefs together, "It's all about 'I've got news.'"

Until recently, journalists had a virtual monopoly on news gathering and dissemination. Audiences gathered around whatever journalists gave them. The foreign correspondent was indispensable. In the words of Keyes Beech of the *Chicago Daily News,* the correspondent was "the eyes, the ears, and the brain of his readers . . . their only link with the outside world, with distant lands and strange people, and if the link is weak so is their source of information."

The weblogs or bloggers that now worry EDS are evidence that the monopoly no longer exists. The audience is fragmented and active. Everyone can be a foreign correspondent. "Today and in the future," veteran network foreign correspondent Garrick Utley observed, "anyone sending information from one country to another is a de facto foreign correspondent. The number of correspondents, accredited or not, will rapidly increase. Equipped with camcorders and computers, they will send out and receive more foreign dispatches." In fact, all an amateur correspondent needs is a cellular telephone with a built-in camera, a device that in 2004 outsold digital still cameras by a four-to-one margin.

These Citizen Foreign Correspondents are their own editors and publishers, who roll the presses and deliver their news simply by pressing the send button on their computers. Among these correspondents can be found:

SALAM PAX, a young Iraqi architect who anonymously posted personal dispatches on his Web site, *Where is Raed?* about conditions in his beleaguered hometown, Baghdad, before and after the invasion of Iraq in 2003. The reports were vivid and revealing, as was this one right before the fighting started: "The dinar is hovering around 2,700 per dollar and the hottest items after the 'particle-masks,' are earplugs—they can't be found in shops and you have to pre-order." After initial speculation that Pax was a fictitious character dreamed up by Mossad or CIA propagandists, he got respect. There were Salam Pax T-shirts and coffee mugs. Within eighteen months, the BBC estimated, "Pax had been joined by more than 70 other Iraqi bloggers."

L. T. SMASH AND SGT. STRYKER, ordinary American soldiers unconstrained by the convention that traditionally divided them from the press. Using their own Web sites early in the Iraq War, these war correspondents posted reports about the fighting. Their ranks swelled as the American military became bogged down in Iraq. By mid-2005, at least two hundred active-duty soldiers kept blogs in which they were their own Ernie Pyles.

AIDS ACTIVIST WAN YANHAI, who started his Web site, www.aizhi.org, in 1994 to "raise awareness about HIV/AIDS in China and support the rights of AIDS patients," according to the Committee to Protect Journalists. "Notably," reported CPJ, "his reporting for the project's Web site has exposed an AIDS epidemic in Henan Province. . . . Wan Yanhai's Web site has become one of the only independent sources of information on the epidemic in China." Wan came to journalism in a roundabout way. He was previously an employee in the Chinese Ministry of Health.

MARK RANKOV, one of the 750 people taken hostage by Chechen rebels in 2002 in a Moscow theater. Using his cell phone, Rankov contacted his friend Olga Brukovsky, who took down his words and published them on LiveJournal. com, a U.S.-based weblog service that allowed anyone to create a journal on-line.

THE ENVIRONMENTAL ORGANIZATION GREENPEACE, which used its Web site to carry news. Here a reader could find a story on Greenpeace's shutting down Luxembourg's Esso stations, an update on continuing health problems for victims of the Union Carbide plant explosion in Bhopal, and a report that an international commission was studying the implications for biodiversity of genetically engineered crops. Greenpeace preferred the loaded phrase *genetic contamination* when talking about genetically engineered crops, but the biodiversity commission study was not likely to get much attention in local newspapers. Alternatively, a reader could get news about Esso from Exxon-Mobil's Web site.

In do-it-yourself journalism, editing and publishing functions are not confined to one's own material. With new technology, Internet users can be much more specific about the international news that they want to read, view, or hear. MSNBC's site, for instance, allowed consumers to identify news they wanted by region and even city. The *New York Times* Web page had a similar feature, "My Times," where consumers organized their own pages, adding and shuffling *Times* content and outside "bookmarks." Through its "My Alerts" service, readers received messages on their mobile phones or by e-mail about breaking news of interest to them.

No longer forced to wait around for the news to appear on a television screen or in the pages of the newspaper tossed onto their front porch, homebound news seekers use their computers to pick up a foreign newspaper or tune in to a foreign television program. Thus has emerged yet another variant of foreign correspondence, the Foreign Local Correspondent, who, as an example, might be an Indian journalist reporting for a New Delhi newspaper or broadcast station that is accessed over the Internet or via satellite from Indianapolis. One of the chief audiences for such news is Indian emigrants. For the curious who cannot speak Hindi, specialized software translates. (This works another way, too, with Indians Google-searching Indian stories in the *New York Times* far more than Americans do.)

Immigrants pay special attention to their homelands, as the fictional ward-heeling mayor in Edwin O'Connor's novel *The Last Hurrah* wryly noted about the foreign policy interests of his Boston constituents: "When you come right down to it, there are only two points that really count. . . . One, *All Ireland must be free.* Two, *Trieste belongs to Italy.*" The foreign-born population of the United States is the largest it has been in the past hundred years, and Foreign Local Correspondents serve these immigrants and their offspring in the way African-American correspondents served their audience during World War II—by providing news specially tailored to their interests.

The news and information from such correspondents has grown from a trickle to a torrent, as is apparent from the fare available in 2006 to an Iranian living in the United States: Iran-centered content in Farsi as well as English via 21 satellite television stations (2 directly from Iran), 10 satellite and Web radio stations (3 directly from Iran), 39 newspapers (all from Iran and found on the Web), 65 periodicals (all on the Web and from all over the world), and 61 Web-based news sites. Writes a scholar who studies dual citizenship, which is allowed by roughly 150 countries: "Today's immigrants to the United States, not only *can* be more in touch with their home countries but *expect* to be and are."

Getting indigenous foreign news from afar will become easier over time, even routine. Thanks to an entrepreneurial cable operator in Burlington, Vermont, subscribers in that quiet community, beginning in 2006, tuned in to the controversial Qatar-based news channel Al Jazeera. Residents of Toledo, Ohio, were not far behind.

When Keyes Beech commented on the power of the foreign correspondent, his point was to underscore the responsibility that went with it. Self-appointed and unsupervised Citizen Foreign Correspondents, in contrast, possess the same features as those letter-writers who supplied information to Benjamin Franklin and other colonial printers. They work for free. No editor compels them to care about fairness or accuracy. Often they are highly partisan. They are unreliable in terms of delivery. They do pretty much what they want, when they want to, in the cut-and-thrust mode of Benjamin Franklin Bache.

Even so, Citizen Foreign Correspondents provide valuable information often available nowhere else. That is why mainstream American journalists use them. Foreign correspondents covering the U.S. occupation of Iraq found out about the latest terrorist attacks in the country from groups that monitored terrorist Web sites, for instance the Terrorism Research Center in Virginia. When suicide bombers struck London trains in 2005, passengers used their cellular phones to take photos, which newspapers and television stations passed on. Video taken by tourists who witnessed the Asian tsunami went on the air. In 2007, citizen journalists provided images of protesting Buddhist monks bloodied by Myanmar authorities. These pictures reached AP, CNN, and Reuters as well as new media like YouTube through media groups organized by exiles. In late 2008, when terrorists struck Mumbai in India, victims and onlookers became citizen journalists; during the heaviest violence, the short-message service Twitter carried more than one posting every second with the word "Mumbai." When offering a range of services that permitted customizing of news, CNN.com included "iReport," through which users could supply news. An "iReport Toolkit," a quick course for would-be journalists, told them how to make their stories newsworthy. Some of these stories end up on the air.

A particularly dramatic example of this sort of news-gathering occurred when Saddam Hussein was executed. A witness surreptitiously videotaped the hanging. Unlike the official version, which had no sound and did not show the actual moment the floor dropped from under the condemned man, this one, carried worldwide over the Internet, captured the frenzied yells and taunting that instructively gave the execution the feel of a lynching rather than of dignified state-administered justice. Network and cable news used the images and sound.

"Many of these [Web] sites seem to rely on their own distance from power for their credibility," one scholar has noted of the propensity of citizen journalists to defy authority. As hard as the Bush administration tried to restrict unpleasant news about the fighting in Iraq, video coverage of snipers hitting American troops appeared on YouTube and Google Video. When the Vatican banned cameras at the funeral of Pope John Paul II, it overlooked the fact that telephones often are "cameras." Church officials were no more able to stop this picture-taking than they had been able, centuries earlier, to prevent the publication of books after Gutenberg's invention of movable type. Governments worry that Google Earth software allows citizen reporters to zero in on places around the world as only intelligence-gathering agencies once could do.

Salam Pax was a good example of a Citizen Foreign Correspondent speaking truth to power. He insightfully observed that the aftermath of the invasion would go badly for the United States: "What will happen," Salam Pax wrote on March 16, 2003, "is something that could/should have been avoided. Don't expect me to wear a 'I ♥Bush' T-shirt." Pax was "better than the army of foreign correspondents in the country," said Peter Maass, a contributing writer to the *New York Times* magazine who used the Iraqi as a translator without knowing of his blogging.

When sociologist Robert Park wrote his essay in 1925, the newspaper was "a very recent manifestation." Measured against the sweep of human history, it still is. The concept of professional journalists governed by canons of responsibility has existed for less time than professional baseball and psychoanalysis. When this book was published, in 2009, the Internet was not as old as the wireless was in 1925. The term *Weblog* was coined in 1998. It still seems like a near miracle that ordinary citizens can use the cell phone tucked in their pocket to get video, take pictures, read snippets of news, check e-mail, watch short shows, surf the net, and, if time is left over, call home to say they'll be late for dinner. Journalism—and foreign news-gathering—is as yet only climbing the foothills of continuous change.

"We have a very large global independent laboratory right now," said Charles Lewis, who created the Center for Public Integrity, a nonprofit investigative journalism organization that has worked abroad as well as domestically, "and everyone should be testing models, testing ideas, and testing means of distribution and ways to create more substantive journalism in the online context, because there's clearly a need for it, and it will evolve. It's not a question, it's an inevitability."

Statements like this echo in the halls of the most respected traditional media.

"It is my heartfelt view that newspapers will be around—in print—for a long time," confessed New York *Times* publisher Arthur Sulzberger Jr. in 2007. "But I also believe that we must be prepared for that judgment to be wrong. My five-year time-frame is about being ready to support our news, advertising and other critical operations on digital revenue alone." The first national newspaper to leap in this direction was the *Christian Science Monitor*. In October 2008, almost one hundred years to the day after it was created, the newspaper announced that it would deal with the high costs of newsprint and delivery by killing its ink-on-paper daily and instead providing daily news electronically. In order to counteract falling revenue from traditional evening news programs, which works against foreign news-gathering, said Bill Wheatley shortly before retiring as NBC's vice president for news in 2006, television needs to develop new "platforms" such as providing news on cell phones or the Web. "I tell people, if there is a demand for it, I'll come to the house and sing the news to you."

Change has never come easily. Col. James Watson Webb beat up James Gordon Bennett, who strove for a mass medium in contrast to Webb's narrow commercial one. Victor Lawson's newsroom disdained the early experimentation of the *Daily News* foreign service. New technology has appeared to be particularly menacing. When typewriters first came to the *New York Times* in the 1890s, they were relegated to a "felt-covered table in a remote part of the newsroom," where the clatter would not irritate the "older men" who wrote the old way in longhand at slanted desks. When computers were first installed at the *Times* in the mid-1970s, the innovative Seymour Topping, then managing editor, stood watching with editor Abe Rosenthal. Both speculated whether the new machinery would make their journalists too facile.

As it turned out, their fears did not come to pass. But not every change has been a change for the better. As we have seen in this book, survival of the fittest has not always been survival of the best. Similarly, the changes currently under way are no more likely to produce uniformly high-quality news than did the golden age of foreign correspondence. Just as many Americans learned about the world from Will Rogers and Richard Halliburton, many learned about Prince Charles's involvement in the Northern Ireland peace process on the daytime television talk show *Live with Regis and Kathie Lee* and had reports on Iraq from Gideon Yago of MTV News.

Yet, the basis for high-quality reporting about the world is not over. The *Times* is as formidable in foreign news coverage as when Topping was foreign and managing editor. The McClatchy Company, which sold off a few of the properties it acquired when purchasing Knight Ridder, kept the foreign correspondents attached to the Washington bureau even as its stock price and the economy declined during 2008. Nor has foreign news stumbled at the *Wall Street Journal* after the long-time family owners, the Bancrofts, sold out to News Corporation, the news organization run by media mogul Rupert Murdoch in 2007. Despite Murdoch's reputation (among other things he turned the venerable *Times* of London into a tabloid), the number of front page *Wall Street Journal* stories on foreign topics jumped in the months after his purchase. Pages of foreign news were added inside the paper as

well. For this increase the paper drew on the vast resources of its Newswire operations. The Associated Press, which ensures that dailies have foreign news even if
they have no correspondents of their own, increased the number of bureaus abroad
to 102 in 97 countries in 2009, in part to make itself more attractive to its international customers. Its bureau chiefs spent less time selling the service abroad, turning that job over to specialized sales people, and more time perfecting reporting
online and with video as well as in the old print-based way. AP correspondents had
more scope for trend and investigative reporting, rather than concentrating only
on breaking news.

Meanwhile, in the style of George Washington Smalley and the *New York Tribune,* the *Washington Post* looked for ways to leverage its foreign coverage at a time
when the paper's circulation and revenue were decreasing sharply by using a time-
honored technique of partnering with other media. In 2008, it and National Public
Radio split the time of a correspondent in Colombia, and the *Post* had a similar arrangement in Iran with a correspondent for a Dutch newspaper. In a different kind
of swap, it received news from Southeast Asia from the *Financial Times* and gave
in return its prize-winning stories out of Iraq. Also in 2008, the *Post* purchased the
money-losing *Foreign Policy* magazine in hopes of making it profitable by linking it
with its online news. "In a world that is so big and complex," said David Hoffman,
the *Post*'s assistant managing editor for foreign news, "I don't cover it all. I am always looking to expand my resources."

Behind these developments lie several constants. One of them is that foreign
news-gathering continues to confer respectability. In its current iteration the
celebrity-focused *Vanity Fair* hired a foreign correspondent to help it get "meat."
The middlebrow *Reader's Digest* runs foreign stories even though its reader surveys
show that such articles get low readership. Said Jacqueline Leo, editor-in-chief of
the magazine's U.S. edition, the *Digest* must do international stories if it wants to be
a serious journal and because it is the responsible thing to do.

Also innovative new media migrate toward tried-and-true media. Many of the
most sought-after news Web sites are those run by the likes of the *New York Times,*
which regularly carried stories from Bloomberg News in its ink-on-paper news
pages. In a joint venture with Microsoft, the AP created "an ad-supported video
network." Salam Pax became a columnist for the respected *Guardian* in London,
and his online dispatches appeared in the old-fashioned format of ink-on-paper.
Yahoo! News deployed the one-man reporting crew Kevin Sites, who set out in
2005–6 to visit every war or conflict zone on earth and produced 600- to 800-word
stories, audio travelogues, slide shows of digital photographs, and video. His written reports were available to the Scripps News Service as part of its news-sharing
arrangements. This gave Yahoo! more credibility and Scripps more stories. Returning home, he did what correspondents have done for decades—he wrote a memoir.
Titled *In the Hot Zone: One Man, One Year, Twenty Wars,* it had the added modern
twist of a DVD showing footage from his travels. Pax, meanwhile, wrote *The Clandestine Diary of an Ordinary Iraqi.*

In the future we will see endless mixing of old and new models. When the

Christian Science Monitor ended its traditional daily in 2009, it devised a three-part strategy to carry on: a Web site supported by advertising; a subscription-based electronic edition; and a weekly print edition. All three carried content from *Monitor* correspondents abroad. Another experiment, started from scratch about the same time, was GlobalPost, which had many features found in The Confederacy of Correspondents. The Boston-based enterprise delivered foreign articles, photographs, video, and audio over the Web by drawing on the services of contract correspondents on the ground around the world. Some of these "super stringers," as it called them because of the expectations that they would file regularly, were Americans; some were Foreign Foreign Correspondents. The GlobalPost also saw the value of Foreign Local Correspondents and quickly developed a partnership with VietNamNet, which carried reports by local journalists in Vietnam. The brainchild of cable television entrepreneur Philip S. Balboni and former *Boston Globe* foreign correspondent Charles M. Sennott, GlobalPost expected to generate income from advertising on its Web site, by selling a specialized premium service to those willing to pay $199 a year, and through syndication to traditional news media. The editorial focus was on news that helped Americans "measure the impact of international events on their lives in an increasingly interconnected world." GlobalPost, said Sennett, was "banking on a shift of news to the Web." He and Balboni wanted to be on the ground floor.

As Seymour Topping noted at the end of his long career, newspapers that excel at foreign news usually have an elite readership (at least relative to other newspapers) as well as a commitment to foreign news by their owner-publishers. One reason the *Times* has carried on in its foreign news-gathering tradition is that Ochs's heirs control the majority of *Times* stock voting rights, and therefore the newspaper is less susceptible to the sentiment of investors who want bigger returns. The model exemplified by Bloomberg News is the ultimate expression of the elite-audience side of Topping's equation. Its subscribers have higher education levels and higher incomes than those of the *New York Times* subscribers. For these people, tracking the news is not simply an act of good citizenship. They follow it to protect and increase their assets. These customers, says Winkler, "take the view that what I don't know will kill me."

The *Times*' commitment to foreign news, however, cannot be taken for granted. As the sale of Dow Jones and the *Wall Street Journal* by the Bancroft family made plain, family priorities can shift and shareholder pressure can force change. Add to this basic truth the fact that profit margins make a big difference in the quality and quantity of foreign news no matter what an owner's inclination is. Similarly, the Bloomberg model has a major downside. Its democratizing powers are limited to those who can afford to pay a premium for the service. Few members of the general public have a Bloomberg computer connection at home. In view of all this, it has become clear that professional journalists committed to foreign news will have to think beyond the for-profit model for news. As Donald Graham, who succeeded his mother as chairman of the Washington Post Company, noted in 2007, "Sending those reporters overseas costs lots of money and doesn't add a penny to this year's circulation or advertising revenue."

A good place to start thinking about new models is with this concept: all news must be subsidized. The traditional subsidy in the case of a mass-market newspaper or network television newscast has come mostly from advertisers (they typically have accounted for 75 percent of newspapers' income). This approach supported foreign news relatively well when newspapers and broadcasters bundled together a wide array of news and entertainment in order to appeal to as many people as possible. Readers and viewers who didn't want foreign news got some anyway along with the stuff they did want. Advertisers liked this approach because it brought them large audiences of consumers for their products. But with the unbundling of news, the audience and the advertisers have migrated to whatever niches suited them best. This is the phenomenon the *Chicago Tribune*'s Jack Fuller described in his 2002 speech about "the ongoing fragmentation of the information environment." All traditional news delivery is imperiled because of this, but foreign news especially so, because it is costly and has a small constituency. Subsidies must come from elsewhere.

Although until recently dismissed as not worth serious attention, nonprofit models exist and point the way to concepts that can be followed in the future. The First Church of Christ, Scientist, started the *Christian Science Monitor* as an antidote to yellow journalism, not to make money. In fact, for most of the newspaper's history, the church subsidized it, something the church was still doing when the daily edition made the switch to electronic delivery. Financial projections for its new approach called for continued subsidies, essential if foreign news was to continue, as the newspaper's editors said it would. One of the most striking modern nonprofit examples is National Public Radio, the one broadcast entity that excels in original foreign news-gathering. NPR receives funding for overseas coverage from the German Marshall Fund and other charitable foundations. An expansion of bureaus came after a $235 million bequest by Joan Kroc, the widow of the entrepreneur who built McDonald's. Among other examples, Charles Lewis's philanthropically supported Center for Public Integrity has worked across borders with its International Consortium of Investigative Journalists. *Foreign Affairs, National Geographic,* and *Harper's*—all with overseas interests—are supported by nonprofit organizations; *Frontline* and the *NewsHour with Jim Lehrer,* which pay attention to events overseas, appear on the nonprofit Public Broadcasting Service.

On a smaller scale, foundations have supported reporting abroad for working journalists. The Fund for Investigative Journalism, set up by philanthropist Philip Stern, gave a boost to Seymour Hersh's pursuit of the My Lai story in the late 1960s with a one-thousand-dollar check. More recently, the Ford Foundation established Environmental Reporting Fellowships. After the Pulitzer family sold all their news properties in 2005, including the *St. Louis Post-Dispatch,* where their great ancestor Joseph Pulitzer began his empire, Emily Rauh Pulitzer and other family members donated more than $1 million in start-up funds to a former *Post-Dispatch*

Washington bureau chief for the Pulitzer Center on Crisis Reporting. Other donors came forward afterward. The center funded overseas travel by freelance as well as staff reporters who wanted to cover overlooked foreign stories. One of its early projects was to send two reporters to write about Ethiopia's repressive regime, a project that aimed to counter the one-dimensional view of Ethiopia as a liberator of Somalia from Muslim control. The Pulitzer Center was aggressive about getting stories on multiple media platforms, including the Internet and satellite television as well as establishment media such as the *New York Times*.

Much more of this can be done. For such efforts to be successful, donors will have to jettison a common assumption that funding should be temporary and that ventures can be self-supporting. Like parks, soup kitchens, local opera, and educational institutions (which is precisely what high-quality news media are) foreign news rarely pays for itself.

As thinking progresses about alternative ways to fund news, we also may see journalists press for government support. This, too, is not as heretical as it sounds. For more than two centuries the American government has supported the news, for instance with reduced postal rates and exemptions from unfair trade practices, the latter allowing financially troubled newspapers to share facilities so that a city does not end up with only one daily. One strategy to support foreign news would be to grant tax breaks to offset the expense of foreign correspondents or foreign bureaus in the way companies receive tax incentives for locating in urban areas needing development. Another possibility would be tax credits—say $2,500 a year—to individuals who purchase news from premium-service publications like Bloomberg. Yet another approach could build on an idea from France, where individual journalists receive a generous income-tax deduction; the United States could use this concept to encourage independent correspondents to go abroad. This is only a beginning. Much more creative thinking can be done along these lines.

While covering the Italian invasion of Ethiopia in 1935, a few correspondents gathered around an old Fitwarari, an Abyssinian general, to ask for an interview. The commander, one of the journalists recounted, "wanted to know exactly what our job was, and why we wanted to interview him. We explained that we were there to write all about him, and if he won a battle to describe it for our papers. He wanted to know why, so we told him because people all over the world wanted to read all about it. At this he just sat back and held his sides and roared with laughter. He thought it was the craziest thing he had ever heard of."

This scene is eons away from our own time. Petty commanders in desolate, isolated backcountries watch satellite television, rally followers via the Internet, and reach global audiences with video messages broadcast over networks sympathetic to their cause. If we have learned anything from the rise of global terrorism, it is that a small band of foreigners can mount a formidable attack on American soil. No longer can Americans assume, as they have, that they live apart, protected by oceans and self-sufficient in resources.

The terrorism of September 11, 2001, which occurred while this book was being written, revealed American vulnerability—and gross journalistic failures. Our news media had not prepared Americans for the rise of global terrorism and the threats it posed on their own soil. After the attacks it did not adequately probe the Bush administration's assertions about the role of Iraq, which became the basis for the U.S. invasion and occupation of that country. The lesson, as if we needed another one, is that journalists must report what policymakers have missed or don't want to acknowledge. The most valuable foreign news-gathering is that which tells us what we do not know or have been told incorrectly.

This is not easy. The task of covering the planet is not only the most expensive of journalistic enterprises; it also is one of the most daunting. "All the reporters in the world working all the hours of the day," Walter Lippmann famously observed in 1922, "could not witness all the happenings in the world." And yet, there is hope.

The history outlined in this book has illustrated the influence of government officials, audience interest, economics, and technology on foreign news coverage. Those all remain powerful and, often, limiting, as Robert Park suggested. Foreign news has been and will likely remain precarious. But it is also true that the roving eye of foreign news-gathering has seen clearly and far ahead at times. And when it has—and when it has not—the decisive force has generally been the one that Park sought to downplay, journalists themselves. *New York Sun* editor Charles A. Dana, who early in his career had been one of Horace Greeley's pioneering foreign correspondents, said as much in 1895 when commenting on the "comparatively new" profession of journalism. "The most essential part of this great mechanism," said the great editor, "is not the mechanism itself; it is the intelligence, the brains, and the sense of truth and honor that reside in the men who conduct it and make it a vehicle of usefulness or, it may be, of mischief."

The simplistically romantic view of foreign correspondents does not help us understand the future any more than it does the past. As Park said, "We must learn to look at political and social life objectively." But the entrepreneurial, principled, and courageous owners, editors, and correspondents who people this book show what can be done in informing Americans about the world. The new species of correspondents emerging from the bog of history can serve us well, and maybe even better.

Not the End . . .

NOTES

INTRODUCTION

1   **"guts, wits and typewriter in hand"** Michael Wells, *The Roving Eye* (New York: Ace, 1957), 1. **"Mentally, I offer"** Jules Verne, *The Adventures of a Special Correspondent* (Akron, Ohio: Superior Printing, n.d. [the book first appeared in 1892]), 33. Bernard A. Weisberger, *The American Newspaper Man* (Chicago: University of Chicago Press 1961), 161.

    "The special correspondent" Julian Ralph, "The Newspaper Correspondent," *Scribner's,* August 1893, 154. The term *special correspondent,* as Ralph used it, applied to any reporter outside of the newspaper's hometown, be it Washington, D.C., or Vienna; in time the foreign application became more firmly rooted in journalism terminology. *Pictured Encyclopedia of the World's Greatest Newspaper* (Chicago: Chicago Tribune, 1928), 257–58.

2   **"a sideways ending to it all"** Reginald Pound and Geoffrey Harmsworth, *Northcliffe* (London: Cassell, 1959), 253.

    "No journalist with any self-respect" Wells, *The Roving Eye,* 31.

    "The world goes on outside" Humbert Wolfe, *The Uncelestial City* (London: Victor Gollancz, 1930), 196.

3   **"kick his head in"** James Kirchick, *Yale Daily News,* posted online April 9, 2004. Many of the characters mentioned here in passing are treated at length later in the book. For those who are not, see Nancy Milford, *Savage Beauty: The Life of Edna St. Vincent Millay* (New York: Random House, 2001), 200–201; Stephanie Mansfield, *The Richest Girl in the World: The Extravagant Life and Fast Times of Doris Duke* (New York: Pinnacle Books, 1994), 224–42; and, on Best, Robert W. Desmond, *Tides of War: World News Reporting, 1931–1945* (Iowa City: University of Iowa Press, 1984), 399–400. A story on the wide range of media types covering the invasion of Iraq is in the *New York Times,* March 27, 2003.

4   **"The big Asama"** *Baltimore Evening Herald,* May 30, 1905. For background on the story, see H. L. Mencken, *Newspaper Days: 1899–1906* (New York: Knopf, 1941), 272.

    There was a good deal of faking during the Russo-Japanese War. The Japan *Daily Mail* in Yokohama had this to say about the reporting of the *London Daily Telegraph:* "It appears, therefore, that the *Daily Telegraph* employs as special correspondents spooks or spirits, omnipresent, since they can be simultaneously writing messages from Moji in Japan and taking observations on the coast of Korea, and omniscient since they can witness imaginary battles from a distance of over 100 miles. Stranger still is it to find that this wonderful correspondent saw a battle fundamentally different from that which really took place." This is quoted in "Feats of Reporting," *Service Bulletin of the Associated Press,* September 1, 1905, 4.

    Allen Neuharth On Neuharth, see George Garneau, "JetCapade Takes Off," *Editor and Publisher,* February 13, 1988, 15; *Washington Post,* January 3, 1988. The toilet paper incident is mentioned in "Neuharth Shows Russians the Good Life," *Washingtonian,* August 1992, 7.

Neuharth's glib assessments of the world can be found in his memoir, *Confessions of an S.O.B.* (Garden City, N.Y.: Doubleday, 1989), 274–80, as well as in a binge of post-JetCapade books whose publication was supported by his own company: Allen H. Neuharth with Jack Kelley and Laura E. Chatfield, *World Power Up Close: Candid Conversations with 31 Key Leaders* (Washington, D.C.: Gannett, 1989); Allen H. Neuharth, *Nearly One World* (New York: USA Today Books / Doubleday, 1989); and Allen H. Neuharth, *Window on the World: Faces, Places, and Plain Talk from 32 Countries* (Washington, D.C.: USA Today Books, 1988). This is reminiscent of the globetrotting of his predecessor, Frank Gannett, who with fifteen journalistic colleagues visited "17 cities and several islands" in thirteen days courtesy of Pan American World Airways in 1947 and republished his stories in a slim brown pamphlet: Frank Gannett, *Winging 'Round the World* (Rochester, N.Y.: Gannett Newspapers, 1947).

"bring me someone who's been tortured" Edward Behr, *"Anyone Here Been Raped and Speaks English?" A Foreign Correspondent's Life behind the Lines* (London: New English Library, 1985), 122–23. Sarah Lyall, interview by author, November 16, 2004. On Birchall, see Gay Talese, *The Kingdom and the Power* (New York: Dell, 1986), 44. On the diplomatic game played in the Washington bureau, Nancy Maynard Hicks, e-mail to author, February 7, 2006. Ochs's use of Paris as a playground and the absence of his name on his stationery are discussed in Susan E. Tifft and Alex S. Jones, *The Trust: The Private and Powerful Family behind the New York Times* (Boston: Little, Brown, 1999), 67, 130.

"Our chronicler" The *Times*' promotional brochure advertising its foreign correspondents is *Around the World . . . with The New York Times,* 1950, n.p., NYT Archives.

5 **"Sound historical works"** Allan Nevins, "American Journalism and Its Historical Treatment," *Journalism Quarterly* 36 (Fall 1959): 412.

"generally arid" Bernard C. Cohen, *The Press and Foreign Policy* (Princeton, N.J.: Princeton University Press, 1963), 3, 17. Cohen sought collaboration but did not think much of the ability of journalists to scrutinize themselves: "As a group [journalists] are not well equipped by their training to address themselves to substantive questions about the press and foreign policy, questions that at bottom concern the political order and the political system; while political scientists, who should be equipped to deal with these subjects, have not explored them with comparable determination" (3). Nevins, "American Journalism and Its Historical Treatment," 419.

"The past year" David Halberstam, introduction to Bill Kovach and Tom Rosenstiel, *Warp Speed: America in the Age of Mixed Media* (New York: Century Foundation Press, 1999), ix.

7 **"a small and tough-minded band"** John Hohenberg, *Foreign Correspondence: The Great Reporters and Their Times,* 2nd ed. (Syracuse, N.Y.: Syracuse University Press, 1995), xi. Emery's correspondents are "for the most part . . . men and women of stamina, heart, and healthy self-confidence." Michael Emery, *On the Front Lines: Following America's Foreign Correspondents across the Twentieth Century* (Washington, D.C.: American University Press, 1995), 280. Among the histories that focused on an era or a place, I particularly appreciated Morrell Heald's *Transatlantic Vistas: American Journalists in Europe, 1900–1940* (Kent, Ohio: Kent State University Press, 1988), which sparked my interest in the underappreciated *Chicago Daily News.*

"confidential materials" Nevins, "American Journalism and Its Historical Treatment," 415. The creation of the current archive is discussed in Richard F. Shepard, *The Paper's Papers: A Reporter's Journey through the Archives of the New York Times* (New York: Random House, 1996), 4–5.

"How useful it would be" Bernard C. Cohen, "Mass Communication and Foreign Policy," in *Domestic Sources of Foreign Policy,* ed. James N. Rosenau (New York: Free Press, 1967), 212.

8 **esteemed news outlets** Douglas A. Van Belle, "New York Times and Network TV News Coverage of Foreign Disasters: The Significance of the Insignificant Variables," *Journalism and Mass Communication Quarterly* 77 (Spring 2000): 50–70; Andrew K. Semmel, "Foreign News in Four U.S. Elite Dailies: Some Comparisons," *Journalism Quarterly* 53 (Winter 1976): 732–36.

"Women of Bangladesh" Joyce Goldman, "The Women of Bangladesh," *Ms.,* August 1972, 84–89. On Jon Stewart's interviews, see *New York Times,* February 25, 2007.

expense of others For examples of journalists whom correspondents remember, including Bigart, see Stephen Hess, *International News and Foreign Correspondents* (Washington, D.C.: Brookings Institution, 1996), appendix C; a version of this appendix appeared as Stephen Hess's "Who Is the Best Foreign Correspondent You Have Known?" *Media Studies Journal* 7 (Fall 1993): 65–72. Another survey carried out by journalism faculty at New York University identified the "top 100 works of journalism"; the survey is described by Felicity Barringer, *New York Times,* March 1, 1999. Sheean's name does not come up in the Hess study; his *Personal History* barely made the New York University list at number 96, more than 35 places below Bigart's account of being over Japan in a bomber when World War II ended and 67 places below Richard Harding Davis's coverage of the German march into Belgium. Edgar Snow and his classic *Red Star over China,* which get attention in this book, are not on either list.

10 **the most significant news events** The Newseum study is described in a press release of February 24, 1999.

"The first thing" Paul Scott Mowrer, *Our Foreign Affairs: A Study in National Interest and the New Diplomacy* (New York: Dutton, 1924), 308.

CHAPTER 1

11 **orientation remained transatlantic** Charles E. Clark and Charles Wetherell, "The Measure of Maturity: The Pennsylvania Gazette, 1728–1765," *William and Mary Quarterly* 46 (April 1989): 279–303.

"has always been to give no offense" Thomas C. Leonard, *The Power of the Press: The Birth of American Political Reporting* (New York: Oxford University Press, 1986), 18; Stephen Botein, "Printers and the American Revolution," in *The Press in the American Revolution,* ed. Bernard Bailyn and John B. Hench (Worcester, Mass.: American Antiquarian Society, 1980), 22. In *The Good Citizen: A History of American Civic Life* (New York: Free Press, 1998), 36, Michael Schudson says foreign news appeared in Colonial newspapers "primarily . . . because it afforded local readers and local authorities no grounds for grumbling." John Campbell's quote is from the *Boston News-Letter,* August 7–14, 1721. On foreign news in Campbell's paper, see Charles E. Clark, *The Public Prints: The Newspaper in Anglo-American Culture, 1665–1740* (New York: Oxford University Press, 1994), chap. 4.

12 ***"not to be any Ways concerned in Disputes"*** Stephen Botein, "'Meer Mechanics' and an Open Press: The Business and Political Strategies of Colonial American Printers," *Perspectives in American History* 9 (1975): 190.

"The Business of Printing" Ibid., 184. A good discussion of the way printers challenged authority—and defended freedom of the press—is found in Jeffery A. Smith's *Printers and Press Freedom: The Ideology of Early American Journalism* (New York: Oxford University Press, 1988).

"duty to his readers" Clark, *Public Prints,* 89.

"There were too many spectators" Frank Luther Mott, *American Journalism: A History of Newspapers in the United States through 250 Years, 1690 to 1940* (New York: Macmillan, 1947), 51.

"There never was a dark age" Bernard Bailyn, *Faces of Revolution: Personalities and Themes in the Struggle for American Independence* (New York: Knopf, 1990), 190; David A. Copeland, *Colonial American Newspapers: Character and Content* (Newark: University of Delaware Press, 1997), 29. The visits to London by delegates to the Continental Congress is from Schudson, *The Good Citizen,* 25. For other background, see Al Hester, Susan Parker Humes, and Christopher Bickers, "Foreign News in Colonial North American Newspapers, 1764–1775," *Journalism Quarterly* 57 (Spring 1980): 22; Richard L. Merritt, "Public Opinion in Colonial America: Content-Analyzing the Colonial Press," *Public Opinion Quarterly* 27 (Fall 1963): 368–69; Clark, *Public Prints,* 81. On British newspapers, see Jeremy Black, "The Press, Party, and Foreign Policy in the Reign of George I," *Publishing History* 13 (Spring 1983): 25–26.

13 **"those Hell-hounds the Pirates"** Copeland, *Colonial American Newspapers,* 33; Botein, "'Meer

Mechanics' and an Open Press," 195. On lifting news from other papers, Clark and Wetherell, "The Measure of Maturity," 295.

Three-fourths of the Colonial printers Botein, "'Meer Mechanics' and an Open Press," 147.

14 **"Now we are less than five months behind"** Kenneth Silverman, ed., *Selected Letters of Cotton Mather* (Baton Rouge: Louisiana State University Press, 1971), 219. Campbell's efforts to catch up are described by Whitelaw Reid in "Schools of Journalism," *Scribner's Monthly*, August 1874, 194. Details on the plague can be found in Charles T. Gregg, *Plague! The Shocking Story of a Dread Disease in America Today* (New York: Scribner's, 1978), 19–20; and Charles F. Mullett, *The Bubonic Plague and England* (Lexington: University of Kentucky Press, 1956), 266–306.

17 **the two articles below show** The excerpted articles are found in Verner W. Crane, ed., *Benjamin Franklin's Letters to the Press, 1758–1775* (Chapel Hill: University of North Carolina Press, 1950), 103, 107–8. Crane's introduction provides a good summary of the techniques Franklin used to transmit his journalism to the United States.

18 **"It was by means of News papers"** Arthur M. Schlesinger, *Prelude to Independence: The Newspaper War on Britain, 1764–1776* (New York: Knopf, 1958), 284.

CHAPTER 2

19 **grandfather's protégé** For a comparison of the two men and the different eras in which they practiced journalism, see James Tagg, *Benjamin Franklin Bache and the Philadelphia Aurora* (Philadelphia: University of Pennsylvania Press, 1991), 75; Schlesinger, *Prelude to Independence*, 58; Stanley Elkins and Eric McKitrick, *The Age of Federalism: The Early American Republic, 1788–1800* (New York: Oxford University Press, 1993), 459; Eric Burns, *Infamous Scribblers: The Founding Fathers and the Rowdy Beginnings of American Journalism* (New York: Public Affairs, 2006), 317.

"acutely conscious" Arthur M. Schlesinger, "The Colonial Newspapers and the Stamp Act," *New England Quarterly* 8 (March 1935): 81.

20 **"I rise to be useful"** Tagg, *Benjamin Franklin Bache*, 104; Thomas Jefferson, *The Writings of Thomas Jefferson*, ed. Paul Leicester Ford (New York: Putnam, 1892–1899), 9:316–17. For general background on foreign news at the time, see Tagg, *Benjamin Franklin Bache*, 100–101; Mott, *American Journalism*, 154.

"American fever" Davis R. Dewey, "The News of the French Revolution in America," *New England Magazine* 1 (September 1887): 87. For other such comment, see Beatrice F. Hyslop, "American Press Reports of the French Revolution, 1789–1794," *New York Historical Society Quarterly* 42 (October 1958): 329–48; David Brion Davis, *Revolutions: Reflections on American Equality and Foreign Liberations* (Cambridge, Mass.: Harvard University Press, 1990), 35–37; Elkins and McKitrick, *The Age of Federalism*, chap. 8, where this comment is made: "What the French did was viewed by Americans very selectively: through American eyes and with reference to American needs only" (309; also see 821*n*159).

"sullied a cause" Elkins and McKitrick, *The Age of Federalism*, 360. For the "ALTERS" quote, see Davis, *Revolutions*, 48, as well as 46–47 on fear of subversion. For the Jefferson quote, Thomas Jefferson to William Short, January 3, 1793, in Jefferson, *The Writings of Thomas Jefferson*, 6:153–56. Scholars are divided over the date of this split in American public opinion. David Brion Davis, for example, argues that American opinion was overwhelmingly positive well into the mid-1790s, through the kind of violence and tumult that came with the Reign of Terror. See Davis, *Revolutions*, 29–54. Others make the case that significant opposition arose as early as 1792 or 1793. See Tagg, *Benjamin Franklin Bache*, 172–75, as an example of this argument.

21 **"precious relic"** Simon Schama, *Citizens: A Chronicle of the French Revolution* (New York: Knopf, 1989), 561; Tagg, *Benjamin Franklin Bache*, 175. Bache's French childhood is discussed by Tagg on 27, 29, 42.

"people had burst" *London Morning Chronicle*, June 29, 1791; *Boston Gazette*, August 29, 1791;

London Chronicle, June 25–28, 1791. A similar report appeared in the *Diary; or, Woodfall's Register,* June 28, 1791.

"To Paris" Munro Price, *The Road from Versailles* (New York: St. Martin's Press, 2002), 183–84; Louis Madelin, *The French Revolution* (London: William Heinemann, 1928), 192.

22 **"They were surrounded"** *London World,* June 30, 1791; *London Chronicle,* June 28–30, 1791; *London Morning Chronicle,* July 1, 1791; and *London Star,* June 30, 1791.

"absolute tranquility" *General Advertiser,* August 26, 1791.

23 **"with the object"** Donald H. Stewart, *The Opposition Press of the Federalist Period* (Albany: State University of New York Press, 1969), 116; Geoffrey R. Stone, *Perilous Times: Free Speech in Wartime* (New York: Norton, 2004), 35. For a comparison of the coverage of the French Revolution by Bache and Fenno see Jaci Cole and John Maxwell Hamilton, "Another Test of the News: American Partisan Press Coverage of the French Revolution," *Journalism History* 34 (Spring 2008): 34–41.

"new massacres in Paris" *Gazette of the United States,* November 17, 21, 28, 1792. For background see Schama, *Citizens,* 627–39; and Albert Soboul, *The French Revolution, 1787–1799: From the Storming of the Bastille to Napoleon* (London: NLB, 1974), 262–66.

24 **"The city was never"** *General Advertiser,* October 15, 1792.

"heads were carried" Ibid., November 15, 1792; Edward G. Everett, "Some Aspects of Pro-French Sentiment in Pennsylvania, 1790–1800," *Western Pennsylvania Historical Magazine* 43 (March 1960): 36; Stone, *Perilous Times,* 36.

Bache's support for the French continued Bernard Fay, *The Two Franklins: Fathers of American Democracy* (New York: AMS Press, 1969), 182, 240–43; Elkins and McKitrick, *The Age of Federalism,* 418–20.

25 **"If ever a nation was debauched"** *Aurora,* December 23, 1796.

donnybrooks Paul Starr, *The Creation of the Media: Political Origins of Modern Communications* (New York: Basic Books, 2005), 79; Burns, *Infamous Scribblers,* 336; Jeffery A. Smith, *Franklin and Bache: Envisioning the Enlightened Republic* (New York: Oxford University Press, 1990), 161; Tagg, *Benjamin Franklin Bache,* 193, 396; Jerry W. Knudson, *Jefferson and the Press: Crucible of Liberty* (Columbia: University of South Carolina Press, 2006), 27.

CHAPTER 3

27 **"It was a battle"** Robert V. Remini, *The Battle of New Orleans* (New York: Viking, 1999), 5.

Jackson asked John William Ward, *Andrew Jackson: Symbol for an Age* (New York: Oxford, 1979), 101–2.

"senatorial record" Robert V. Remini, *Andrew Jackson and the Course of the American Empire, 1767–1821* (New York: Harper and Row, 1977), 109. See p. 100 for a summary of Jackson's "modest" previous term as a congressman.

"We have cause of apprehension" Allan Nevins, *"The Evening Post": A Century of Journalism* (New York: Boni and Liveright, 1922), 84.

28 **"We are grievously disappointed"** *National Intelligencer,* January 16 and 28, 1815. William E. Ames, *A History of the "National Intelligencer"* (Chapel Hill: University of North Carolina Press, 1972), 88, 92, 114, 127. The February 4 date for the *Intelligencer* article announcing the victory is tricky. Unfortunately, microfilm of the *Intelligencer* contains no extras from February 4. We know, however, that the *Spy,* a newspaper discussed in this chapter, reprinted a story on the victory *"from the National Intelligencer Extra, Washington, Feb. 4, 9 o'clock, A.M."* Because the *Intelligencer* was published Monday through Saturday—and because February 5 was a Sunday—it could be that extra editions appeared on Saturday, February 4, and some of the same stories from those extras appeared again on Monday, February 6. In any event, the reprinted *Spy* story is identical to a February 6 story in the *Intelligencer.* (It is also possible, of course, that the *Spy* headline reference to February 4 is incorrect.)

"**Steam conveyances**" *National Intelligencer,* August 25, 1849. For background on the battle and the treaty, see A. J. Langguth, *Union 1812: The Americans Who Fought the Second War of Independence* (New York: Simon and Schuster, 2006), 371–74. An "early warning" of the peace came on February 9. A privateer captured a British vessel and found a London newspaper dated November 28 reporting a speech by the prince regent that offered hope of an ending to the war. The privateer brought the news to Salem, Mass., and the news item was reprinted widely.

29 "**I must close**" James Bradford, *Time Piece,* January 17, 1815.

Mott briefly mentions James Bradford's accomplishments, in *American Journalism,* 196, and so does Robert W. Desmond in a footnote in *The Information Process: World News Reporting to the Twentieth Century* (Iowa City: University of Iowa Press, 1978), 174–75. John Hohenberg does not include him in his *Foreign Correspondence,* nor is he found in F. Lauriston Bullard's *Famous War Correspondents* (Boston: Little, Brown, 1914); Phillip Knightley's *The First Casualty* (Baltimore: Johns Hopkins University Press, 2004); Joseph J. Mathews's *Reporting the Wars* (Minneapolis: University of Minnesota Press, 1957); or Mitchel P. Roth's *Historical Dictionary of War Journalism* (Westport, Conn.: Greenwood, 1997). An attempt to correct this oversight is Karen M. Rowley and John Maxwell Hamilton, "A Missing Link in the History of American War Correspondents: James Morgan Bradford and *The Time Piece* of St. Francisville, Louisiana," *American Journalism* 22 (Fall 2005): 7–26. The best previously available description of Bradford is found in a publication held in the Louisiana State University Library: Elrie Robinson, *Biographical Sketches of James M. Bradford: Pioneer Printer,* published by the *St. Francisville Democrat* in 1938. The *Friend of the Laws* quote is from Robinson's book, p. 30.

A leading contender for the title of first professional journalist to serve as a war correspondent is the senior Isaiah Thomas. It can be argued that Thomas was less of a professional journalist than Bradford, which would give the Louisianan the title. For a thorough discussion of news about the American-British encounter at Lexington and Concord, see Frank Luther Mott, "The Newspaper Coverage of Lexington and Concord," in *Highlights in the History of the American Press,* ed. Edwin H. Ford and Edwin Emery (Minneapolis: University of Minnesota Press, 1954), 86–99.

30 **We cannot know** The *Spy* does not use a single discernible method of organizing news, for instance publishing the oldest reports first or the news from overseas first.

By the Mails Microfilm archives present a problem sometimes, and this is one such case. Words from newspapers occasionally are lost or smudged. I have had to guess, for instance, at some words—for instance, "Dr. Still"—and punctuation.

33 "**war would not have been at that time declared**" David Paul Nickles, *Under the Wire: How the Telegraph Changed Diplomacy* (Cambridge, Mass.: Harvard University Press, 2003), 20. This book contains a good discussion of the arguments why war could have been prevented with better communications.

lift martial law John Spencer Bassett, ed., *Correspondence of Andrew Jackson* (Washington, D.C.: Carnegie Institute of Washington, 1927), 2:170–71; Remini, *Andrew Jackson and the Course of American Empire,* chap. 20; Langguth, *Union 1812,* 376–79; James A. Padgett, "The Difficulties of Andrew Jackson in New Orleans Including His Later Dispute with Fulwar Skipwith, as Shown by the Documents," *Louisiana Historical Quarterly* 21 (April 1938): 367–419; Leonard Victor Huber and Clarence August Wagner, *The Great Mail: A Postal History of New Orleans* (State College, Pa.: American Philatelic Society, 1949), 22.

34 **The Value of Economic News** For background on this topic, see Niall Ferguson, *The House of Rothschild: Money's Prophets, 1798–1848* (New York: Viking, 1998), 234; Donald Read, *The Power of News: The History of Reuters* (Oxford: Oxford University Press, 1992), 9–13; Menahem Blondheim, *News over the Wires: The Telegraph and the Flow of Public Information in America, 1844–1897* (Cambridge, Mass: Harvard University Press, 1994), 29, 36–37, 72–80, 172–73; *Service Bulletin of the Associated Press,* October 15, 1904, 7; Winston Groom, *Patriotic Fire: Andrew Jackson and Jean Laffite at the Battle of New Orleans* (New York: Knopf, 2006), 236; Parton, *Life of An-*

drew Jackson, 2:251; Huber and Wagner, *The Great Mail,* 37–38; Jonathan Fenby, *The International News Services* (New York: Schocken, 1986), 31–32.

35 **"The only question"** Langguth, *Union 1812,* 378.

"I can go to England without mortification" James Parton, *Life of Andrew Jackson* (Boston: Houghton Mifflin, 1860), 2:257; Alexander Walker, *Jackson and New Orleans: An Authentic Narrative* (New York: J. C. Derby, 1856), chap. 19.

eulogies Ward, *Andrew Jackson,* 158, 254–55, describes the political power of Jackson's press clippings.

CHAPTER 4

36 **"We published yesterday"** Allan Nevins, *American Press Opinion: Washington to Coolidge: A Documentary Record of Editorial Leadership and Criticism, 1785–1927* (New York: Kennikat Press, 1928), 1:118–19.

a radically new business model Mott, *American Journalism,* 216, 222; James L. Crouthamel, "The Newspaper Revolution in New York: 1839–1860," *New York History* 45 (1964): 91–92. For an important discussion of the economic success of penny papers such as the *Sun* and the *Herald,* see James T. Hamilton, *All the News That's Fit to Sell: How the Market Transforms Information into News* (Princeton, N.J.: Princeton University Press, 2004), chap. 2. For a discussion of the various pricing of newspapers, see Blondheim, *News over the Wires,* 217.

a broad urban middle class A discussion of this is found in Michael Schudson, *Discovering the News: A Social History of American Newspapers* (New York: Basic Books, 1978), especially chap. 2; John Steele Gordon, "The Man Who Invented Mass Media," *Audacity* (Fall 1995): 35.

"NAPOLEON of the press" James L. Crouthamel, "James Gordon Bennett, the *New York Herald,* and the Development of Newspaper Sensationalism," *New York History* 54 (July 1973): 311. The famous murder is the subject of Andie Tucher, *Froth and Scum: Truth, Beauty, Goodness, and the Ax Murder in America's First Mass Medium* (Chapel Hill: University of North Carolina Press, 1994). Tucher suspects that Bennett fabricated the interview with the madam.

37 **Treaty of Ghent** James L. Crouthamel, *Bennett's New York Herald and the Rise of the Popular Press* (Syracuse, N.Y.: Syracuse University Press, 1989), 7. For a discussion of the ship-news system used by Bennett and his competitors, see Desmond, *The Information Process,* 88–90; Crouthamel, *Bennett's New York Herald,* 11; and Frederic Hudson, *Journalism in the United States from 1690 to 1872* (New York: Harper, 1873), 346, 451. For a discussion of the diffusion of foreign news among inland papers, see Allan Pred, *Urban Growth and the Circulation of Information: The United States System of Cities, 1790–1840* (Cambridge, Mass.: Harvard University Press, 1979), 32.

"most efficient hand" James L. Crouthamel, *James Watson Webb: A Biography* (Middletown, Conn.: Wesleyan University Press, 1969), 31–32, 83–84; Hudson, *Journalism in the United States,* 446–51; Ulf Jonas Bjork, "The Commercial Roots of Foreign Correspondence: The *New York Herald* and Foreign News, 1835–1839," paper presented at the annual convention of the Association for Education in Journalism and Mass Communication, Quebec, 1992, 8–10.

"They would arrive" Hudson, *Journalism History,* 446.

38 **"of organized European correspondence"** Ibid., 451; Bjork, "The Commercial Roots of Foreign Correspondence," 10–13.

"a corps of correspondents" Bjork, "The Commercial Roots of Foreign Correspondence," 7; Desmond, *The Information Process,* 92–93; Crouthamel, *James Watson Webb,* 54–55.

43 **"in making it appear"** *New York Herald,* June 8, 1838; Gordon, "The Man Who Invented Mass Media," 36; Crouthamel, "James Gordon Bennett," 301.

44 **"half Jew,"** Crouthamel, *James Watson Webb,* 85.

"For Mr. BENNETT (only)" Hudson, *Journalism in the United States,* 466–67; Crouthamel, *Bennett's New York Herald,* 98, 301; Oliver Carlson, *The Man Who Made News* (New York: Duell, Sloan, and Pearce, 1942), 131.

45 **"so frequently"** William Howard Russell to G. S. Dasent, September 15, 1861, Delane Papers. Background on Russell's run-in with the *Herald* is in Knightley, *The First Casualty,* 36–37; John Black Atkins, *The Life of Sir William Howard Russell* (London: John Murray, 1911), 2:75, 99–106.

"a quasi obscene publication" The *New York Times*' lambasting of Bennett is found in a suit he filed against the newspaper's principals. There is no date on the filing, but it seems to have been from about 1858. NYT Archives.

"The Courier & Enquirer" *New York Herald,* March 2, 1836.

the most widely read American newspaper in Europe Michael Emery and Edwin Emery, *The Press and America: An Interpretive History of the Mass Media* (Englewood Cliffs, N.J.: Prentice-Hall, 1992), 131.

foreign news generally declined Figures on foreign news over this two-hundred-year period are from Jurgen Wilke, "Foreign News Coverage and International Flow of News over Three Centuries," *Gazette* 39 (1987): 157. Other studies show a similar pattern for declining foreign news, for instance, Donald Lewis Shaw, "At the Crossroads: Change and Continuity in American Press News, 1820–1860," *Journalism History* 8 (Summer 1981): 38–50. Donald R. Avery has noted a decline in foreign news in the years before the War of 1812: see "The Emerging American Newspaper: Discovering the Home Front," *American Journalism* 1 (Winter 1984): 51–56; Donald R. Avery, "American over European Community? Newspaper Content Changes, 1808–1812," *Journalism Quarterly* 63 (Summer 1986): 311–14; and Donald R. Avery, "The Newspaper on the Eve of the War of 1812: Changes in Content" (Ph.D. diss., Southern Illinois University, 1982). He argues that foreign news declined because editors and readers began to think of themselves as American and thus were more oriented toward domestic affairs.

46 **"were ever present"** "How We Get Our News," *Harper's New Monthly Magazine,* March 1867, 518; Crouthamel, *Bennett's New York Herald,* 50; Bjork, "The Commercial Roots of Foreign Correspondence," 6; Giovanna Dell'Orto, *Giving Meanings to the World: The First U.S Foreign Correspondents, 1838–1859* (Westport, Conn.: Greenwood Press, 2002), 123.

not "a very expert hand" Dell'Orto, *Giving Meanings to the World,* 51; *New York Herald,* January 25, 1835.

"lively style" *New York Herald,* January 3, 1870. John C. Nerone argues that the penny press did not change journalism to the degree that many historians have suggested. See Nerone, "The Mythology of the Penny Press," *Critical Studies in Mass Communication* 4 (December 1987): 376–404.

"did not lose sight of Wall Street" Hudson, *Journalism in the United States,* 434–36, 441; Blondheim, *News over the Wires,* 25; Bjork, "The Commercial Roots of Foreign Correspondence," 11.

47 **"The position of a paper"** Theodore Stanton, "The Foreign Correspondent," *Lippincott's Monthly Magazine,* May 1893, 746.

"The mission of Bennett" Isaac Pray, *The Memoirs of James Gordon Bennett and His Times* (New York: Stringer and Townsend, 1855), 412.

CHAPTER 5

48 **a taste for politics and adventure** Background on Kendall is found in Fayette Copeland, *Kendall of the Picayune* (Norman: University of Oklahoma Press, 1943).

49 **thriving city** Thomas Ewing Dabney, *One Hundred Great Years: The Story of the Times-Picayune from Its Founding to 1940* (Baton Rouge: Louisiana State University Press, 1944), 5, 11. On newspapering in New Orleans, see Bullard, *Famous War Correspondents,* 356; Tom Reilly, "A Spanish-Language Voice of Dissent in Ante Bellum New Orleans," *Louisiana History* 23 (Fall 1982): 327. The size of the *Picayune* news hole for foreign reports is in Dell'Orto, *Giving Meanings to the World,* 52.

well positioned as a conduit for news Copeland, *Kendall of the Picayune,* 155. New Orleans printers also were in the vanguard of establishing newspapers in Mexico during the war. See Lota M.

Spell, "The Anglo-Saxon Press in Mexico, 1846–1848," *American Historical Review* 38 (October 1932): 20–31.

"interest and amuse" George W. Kendall, *Narrative of an Expedition across the Great Southwestern Prairies, from Texas to Santa Fé* (London: David Bogue, 1845; reprint, Ann Arbor: University Microfilms, 1966), 1:vi. For early background on the *Picayune*, see Dabney, *One Hundred Great Years*, 15, 23–24.

51 **"Amos Kendall,"** Huber and Wagner, *The Great Mail*, 38–41.

"I wrote to you" *Picayune*, August 7, 1847, 2.

"Neither wind nor weather" Harold A. Williams, *The Baltimore Sun, 1837–1987* (Baltimore: Johns Hopkins University Press, 1987), 30; Blondheim, *News over the Wires*, 49; Richard A. Schwarzlose, *The Nation's Newsbrokers*, vol. 1, *The Formative Years, from Pretelegraph to 1865* (Evanston, Ill.: Northwestern University Press, 1989), 65–66. Among the many references to Kendall's prowess at getting the news, see Richard B. Kielbowicz, *News in the Mail: The Press, Post Office, and Public Information, 1700–1860s* (New York: Greenwood Press, 1989), 171–72.

52 **"on all matters"** Ron Tyler, introduction to *The War between the United States and Mexico, Illustrated,* by George W. Kendall (Austin: Texas Historical Association, 1994), xv.

"a law unto himself" Rick Stewart, "Artists and Printmakers of the Mexican War," in *Eyewitness to War: Prints and Daguerreotypes of the Mexican War, 1846–1848*, ed. Martha A. Sandweiss, Rick Stewart, and Ben W. Huseman (Washington, D.C.: Smithsonian Institution Press, 1989), 17. Stewart describes how artists and lithographers drew on the reporting of Kendall and other correspondents to depict the war.

54 **"put myself in the way"** Copeland, *Kendall of the Picayune*, 224.

"was new to American journalism" Hudson, *Journalism in the United States*, 494, 599; Copeland, *Kendall of the Picayune*, 180.

55 **"the annihilation"** Hudson, *History of Journalism*, 610–11; Williams, *The Baltimore Sun*, 31; Mott, *American Journalism*, 251; Blondheim, *News over the Wires*, 49–50. For background on the AP's early foreign news-gathering, see Schwarzlose, *The Nation's Newsbrokers*, 34; Fenby, *The International News Services*, 35–42; Jean-Luc Renaud, "U.S. Government Assistance to AP's World-Wide Expansion," *Journalism Quarterly* 62 (Spring 1985): 10–16; Valerie Komor, "AP's Origin Revealed," *AP World*, Spring 2006, 20–21. The connection between continental communication and continental imperialism is discussed in Daniel Walker Howe, *What Hath God Wrought: The Transformation of America, 1815–1848* (New York: Oxford University Press, 2007), 697–98.

"Emperor of France" John Steele Gordon, *A Thread across the Ocean: The Heroic Story of the Transatlantic Cable* (New York: Walker, 2002), 138.

56 **"ocean greyhound"** The phrase is used in Theodore Stanton, "The Foreign Correspondent," *Lippincott's Monthly Magazine*, May 1893, 746. Figures on transmission line construction in the United States are in Donald L. Shaw, "News Bias and the Telegraph: A Study of Historical Change," *Journalism Quarterly* 44 (Spring 1967): 6; Dabney, *One Hundred Great Years*, 309. The laying of submarine cables around the world is described in Francis Williams, *Transmitting World News: A Study of Telecommunications and the Press* (Paris: UNESCO, 1953), 24; and W. H. Russell, *The Atlantic Telegraph* (1866; reprint, Brimscombe Port, UK: Nonsuch, 2005), 8, which focused on the story of the laying of the original transatlantic cable. The latter author is the W. H. Russell who was a famous British foreign correspondent. The figure of fifteen hundred Associated Press "brass pounders" is from J. Steven Smethers, "'Pounding Brass' for the Associated Press: A Press Telegrapher Recalls His Craft," list.msu.edu/cgi-bin/wa?A2=ind0101b&L=aejmc&T=0&P=14847.

CHAPTER 6

57 **"Mr. Smalley sails"** Harry W. Baehr Jr., *The New York Tribune since the Civil War* (New York: Dodd, Mead, 1936), 32.

"the distributing centre" The standard account of the genesis of this concept is in George W. Smalley, *Anglo-American Memories* (New York: Putnam's, 1911), 220–24. Smalley provided a slightly different version in George W. Smalley, "Chapters in Journalism," *Harper's New Monthly Magazine,* August 1894, 430–31. Smalley's Bismarck interview is in G.W.S., "An Afternoon with Count Bismark [*sic*]," *Tribune,* October 25, 1866.

"The duties of Mr. Smalley" R, "Ten Days in London . . . No. I," *Tribune,* August 3, 1869.

58 **eye for newspaper organization** Emery and Emery, *The Press and America,* 178; Mott, *American Journalism,* 270; Desmond, *The Information Process,* 93.

59 **staff was considered brilliant** Paul C. Wermuth, *Bayard Taylor* (New York: Twayne, 1973), 48–49, 72; W. Joseph Campbell, *The Year That Defined American Journalism: 1897 and the Clash of Paradigms* (New York: Routledge, 2006), 23; Joseph J. Mathews, *George W. Smalley: Forty Years a Foreign Correspondent* (Chapel Hill: University of North Carolina Press, 1973), 72; Sterling F. Delano, *Brook Farm: The Dark Side of Utopia* (Cambridge, Mass.: Harvard University Press, 2004), 83.

"signaled the first serious book review" Charles Capper, *Margaret Fuller: An American Romantic Life: The Public Years* (New York: Oxford University Press, 2007), 198, 271, 281; Margaret Fuller, *These Sad but Glorious Days: Dispatches from Europe, 1846–1850,* ed. Larry J. Reynolds and Susan Belasco Smith (New Haven, Conn.: Yale University Press, 1991), 285. On Fuller's star byline, see Catherine C. Mitchell, ed., *Margaret Fuller's New York Journalism: A Biographical Essay and Key Writings* (Knoxville: University of Tennessee Press, 1995), 39–40. For general background on Fuller, see Mitchell's book as well as Eve Kornfeld, *Margaret Fuller* (Boston: Bedford Books, 1997); Margaret Vanderhaar Allen, *The Achievement of Margaret Fuller* (University Park: Pennsylvania State University Press, 1979); and Richard Kluger, *The Paper: The Life and Death of the New York Herald Tribune* (New York: Knopf, 1986), 59–61.

Among the early women succeeding Fuller were Sara Jane Clarke Lippincott, who wrote under the name of Grace Greenwood for the *Saturday Evening Post,* and Nancy Johnson, who reported abroad for the *New York Times* and used the pseudonyms Anna Cummings Johnson and Minnie Myrtle. Dell'Orto, *Giving Meanings to the World,* 105–6.

"Das Lauseblatt" William Harlan Hale, "When Karl Marx Worked for Horace Greeley," *American Heritage,* April 1957, 20–25; Charles Blitzer, introduction to *The American Journalism of Marx and Engels,* by Karl Marx and Friedrich Engels, ed. Henry M. Christman (New York: New American Library, 1966), xvii–xxiv; John Lent, "Karl Marx: Greeley's Ace Foreign Correspondent," *Media History Digest* 11 (Spring–Summer 1991): 24–25; Karl Marx, *Dispatches for the New York Tribune: Selected Journalism of Karl Marx,* ed. James Ledbetter (New York: Penguin, 2007).

60 **"under the spell"** Mathews, *Smalley,* 15.

"social movements and other matters" George Smalley to Whitelaw Reid, July 8, 1869, Reid Papers. For background on this, see Mathews, *Smalley,* 4, 91–93; Ulf Jonas Bjork, "'Sketches of . . . Life and Society': Foreign Correspondence in the *New York Tribune,* 1841–1845," paper presented at the annual convention of the Association for Education in Journalism and Mass Communication, Kansas City, 1993, 1. The pair of articles, with the byline G.W.S., appeared in the *Tribune,* August 4, 1869.

"time is everything in journalism" George Smalley to Whitelaw Reid, March 27, 1870, Reid Papers; Smalley, *Memories,* 227–28.

he covered the Civil War Smalley's feat is described in Mathews, *Smalley,* 25; Smalley, "Chapters in Journalism," 427–30; Smalley, *Memories,* 151–52; Louis M. Starr, *Bohemian Brigade: Civil War Newsmen in Action* (Madison: University of Wisconsin Press, 1987), 143–48; J. Cutler Andrews, *The North Reports the Civil War* (Pittsburgh: University of Pittsburgh Press, 1955), 281–82.

"methods" Smalley, *Memories,* 223–31; Knightley, *First Casualty,* 48–50.

61 **"It was the cable"** Smalley, *Memories,* 264; Whitelaw Reid to George Smalley, July 11, 1869, Reid

Papers. Details on the cost of cabling are in John Lent, "The International Horace Greeley," *Media History Digest* 11 (Spring–Summer 1991): 23.

"resembled North American Indians" Newspaper quotes from Joseph J. Mathews, "The First Harvard-Oxford Boat Race," *New England Quarterly* 33 (March 1960): 74, 76.

62 **ingenuity and "method"** Details on Smalley's approach are found in Smalley, *Memories,* 167–68; Mathews, *Smalley,* 54–56; Mathews, "The First Harvard-Oxford Boat Race," 78–79.

Smalley's woes Reid to Smalley, August 29, 1869 (two letters sent on the same day), November 6, 1869; Smalley to Reid, September 11, 1869 (two letters on that date), September 12, 25, 1869, January 12, 1870, Reid Papers. Also Mathews, *Smalley,* 51–56.

63 **COVERING THE NEWS IN MEXICO** Walter C. Whiffen, "Covering the News in Mexico," *Service Bulletin of the Associated Press,* October 31, 1912, 27.

64 **THE INTERNATIONAL RACE** G.W.S., *New York Tribune,* August 30, 1869.

69 **"a great advantage"** Smalley, *Memories,* 168.

"an oracle" Mathews, *Smalley,* 32–33, 99. His salary is discussed on p. 79.

clashes mounted Kluger, *The Paper,* 119–20. Mathews, *Smalley,* 88–89, 103–7.

70 **"only a few years younger than I am"** Peter Osnos, *Washington Post,* August 29, 1982.

"professional bruiser" Mathews, *Smalley,* 75, 87, 98–99; Starr, *Bohemian Brigade,* 139–40.

"Should a history of international journalism be written" Smalley, *Memories,* 252; Franc B. Wilkie, *Personal Reminiscences of Thirty-five Years of Journalism* (Chicago: Schulte, 1891), 292. Wilkie's account, replete with invective for his often mad employer, includes interesting detail on Wilkie's first short-lived assignment abroad as well as on the foundation and functioning of the bureau he later organized. See especially "Part Second," chaps. 8 and 9, and "Part Third," chaps. 1 and 2. Additional background on *Chicago Times* coverage abroad is in Justin E. Walsh, *To Print the News and Raise Hell! A Biography of Wilbur F. Storey* (Chapel Hill: University of North Carolina Press, 1968), 205, 211, 261. The overseas presence of other Chicago papers is noted in Ernest R. May, *American Imperialism: A Speculative Essay* (New York: Atheneum, 1968), 92–93.

71 **"*the* center of news-collecting"** Theodore Stanton, "The Foreign Correspondent," *Lippincott's Magazine,* May 1893, 748. The continuing importance of London is documented in H. Denis Wu and John Maxwell Hamilton, "US Foreign Correspondents: Changes and Continuity at the Turn of the Century," *Gazette* 66 (December 2004): 524–26. Conrad Kiechel, Reader's Digest editorial director, international, interview by author, May 10, 2006. On the *Los Angeles Times* catering to its immigrant community, see Christopher E. Beaudoin and Ester Thorson, "LA *Times* Offered as Model for Foreign News Coverage," *Newspaper Research Journal* 22 (Winter 2001): 80–93; on the *San Jose Mercury,* see *New York Times,* March 20, 2006.

72 **When the focus of the news has swerved** On the Stuttgart bureau, Robert Giles, e-mail to author, February 23, 2006. On the *Oregonian,* Richard Read, interview by author, September 8, 2007.

Smalley's idea of pooling On Gannett and the *Christian Science Monitor,* Eliza Tinsley, interview by author, February 2, 2005; e-mail to author, July 14, 2008. On the Scripps News Service, Peter Copeland, interview by author, January 22, 2007; on CBS news, Marcy McGinnis, interview by author, May 19, 2004.

"when they don't know the value of a story" Joyce Davis quoted in transcript of "Why International News Matters," American Society of Newspaper Editors/Freedom Forum Roundtable, Arlington, Virginia, May 5, 1998, 21; Douglas Clifton, e-mail to author, March 30, 2004; Associated Press, December 1, 2008.

73 **"We don't have the financial resources"** Andy Alexander, e-mail to author, March 4, 2008. On Cox's sale of its newspapers, www.poynter.org Romenesko page posting, December 2, 2008.

The system became obsolete Associated Press, December 2, 2008.

75 **"cull from the great London dailies"** Stanton, "The Foreign Correspondent," 748; Mathews, *Smalley,* 33, 73.

CHAPTER 7

76 **"Come to Paris"** Henry M. Stanley, *How I Found Livingstone: Travels, Adventures, and Discoveries in Central Africa* (London: Sampson Low, Marston, 1872), 1–3.

Bennett was volatile For details on Bennett's life and manners, such as they were, see Don C. Seitz, *The James Gordon Bennetts* (Indianapolis: Bobbs-Merrill, 1928), 223; Kluger, *The Paper*, 144.

77 **"carried a crew of one hundred"** Eric Hawkins and Robert N. Sturdevant, *Hawkins of the Paris Herald* (New York; Simon and Schuster, 1963), 19.

"The Day of an American Journalist in 2889" This Verne story has a murky history and comes in many versions. One version is found in Jules Verne, "In the Twenty-ninth Century: The Day of an American Journalist in 2889," in *Yesterday and Tomorrow*, by Verne (New York: Ace, 1965), 141–59. Background on the story is found in Lawrence Lynch, *Jules Verne* (New York: Twayne, 1992), 77–79; Arthur B. Evans, "The 'New' Jules Verne," *Science-Fiction Studies* 22 (March 1995): 35–46; Herbert R. Lottman, *Jules Verne: An Exploratory Biography* (New York: St. Martin's Press, 1996), 269–71. In the French versions of the story, a Bennet is the hero. In the English-language version published in the United States, the hero is George Washington Smith.

78 **"about the earth"** Seitz, *The Bennetts*, 241; Richard O'Connor, *The Scandalous Mr. Bennett* (Garden City, N.Y.: Doubleday, 1962), 163; Albert Stevens Crockett, *When James Gordon Bennett Was Caliph of Baghdad* (New York: Funk and Wagnalls, 1926), 27, 230.

defining idiosyncrasy Stanley's names are discussed in John Bierman, *Dark Safari: The Life behind the Legend of Henry Morton Stanley* (New York: Knopf, 1990), 4, 24–29, 64. The fabricated story from Crete is discussed in Frank McLynn, *Stanley: The Making of an African Explorer* (Chelsea, Mich.: Scarborough House, 1990), 77–78.

79 **"refractory savage"** De B. Randolph Keim, *Sheridan's Troopers on the Border: A Winter Campaign on the Plains* (Philadelphia: David McKay, 1885), 4. Keim was a superior writer to Stanley, as his book shows. A discussion of Bennett's possible interest in sending Keim instead of Stanley is found in Bierman, *Dark Safari*, 77; McLynn, *Stanley*, 94; and Oliver Knight, *Following the Indian Wars: The Story of the Newspaper Correspondents among the Indian Campaigners* (Norman: University of Oklahoma Press, 1960), 69–70, 321. Keim had extraordinary access to Ulysses S. Grant's White House and carried out a special assignment for the president to assess overseas consulates.

A great deal of detail on the idea for the trip is found in Tim Jeal, *Stanley: The Impossible Life of Africa's Greatest Explorer* (New Haven, Conn.: Yale University Press, 2007), 65–85, 500. Jeal insists that the idea for the trip was Stanley's. For another discussion about the dubiousness of Stanley's account of the Grand Hotel meeting, see Bierman, *Dark Safari*, 65, 77.

full instructions Stanley, *How I Found Livingstone*, 3–4; Bierman, *Dark Safari*, 78, 120–21.

"knew how to make news" Crockett, *Caliph of Baghdad*, 7. As noted in chapter 4, there is debate about whether Bennett senior did the first interview. Some credit Horace Greeley's interview with Mormon leader Brigham Young in 1859 as the first. Neither Bennett nor Greeley used the term *interview* at the time. For discussion of early interviews and the importance of this technique, see Michael Schudson, *The Power of News* (Cambridge, Mass.: Harvard University Press, 1995), chap. 3; John Brady, *The Craft of Interviewing* (New York: Vintage, 1977), appendix; George Turnbull, "Some Notes on the History of the Interview," *Journalism Quarterly* 13 (September 1936): 272–79.

"An African exploring expedition" *New York Herald,* December 23, 1871; February 13, 1872; Henry M. Stanley, *Stanley's Despatches to the New York Herald, 1871–1872, 1874–1877*, ed. Norman R. Bennett (Boston: Boston University Press, 1970), xxii.

80 **"new era in journalism"** *New York Herald,* February 13, 1872; Bierman, *Dark Safari*, 97, 107.

"As I come nearer" *New York Herald,* August 10, 1872.

"who has not heard" Bierman, *Dark Safari*, 117. On the authenticity of Stanley's greeting, see Jeal, *Stanley*, 117–18.

81 **returned triumphantly** Details of Stanley's homecoming are found in Bierman, *Dark Safari*, 196–97, 203; Stanley, *Stanley's Despatches*, xxii.

82 **"YOU ARE NOW FAMOUS"** Bierman, *Dark Safari*, 127. On the wooden desk, E. J. Kahn, *The World of Swope* (New York: Simon and Schuster, 1965), 106.

    "The Wild Animals" Kluger, *The Paper*, 143–44; Bierman, *Dark Safari*, 111–12.

    "I have been taught" Henry M. Stanley, *The Autobiography of Sir Henry Morton Stanley*, ed. Dorothy Stanley (Boston: Houghton Mifflin, 1909), 288, 527.

83 **"The Roman Catholic Church"** Schudson, *The Power of News*, 79; Brian Denis, *Pulitzer: A Life* (New York: John Wiley, 2001), 155–56.

    Around the World in Eighty Days Brooke Kroeger, *Nellie Bly: Daredevil, Reporter, Feminist* (New York: Times Books, 1994), chap. 5. The race is also described in Jason Marks, *Around the World in 72 Days: The Race between Pulitzer's Nellie Bly and Cosmopolitan's Elizabeth Bisland* (New York: Gemittarius Press, 1993). Details on George Francis Train's trip are in Irving Wallace, *The Square Pegs: Some Americans Who Dared to Be Different* (New York: Knopf, 1957), chap. 3.

84 **"newspaper of ideas and action"** Geoffrey Wheatcroft, *Le Tour: A History of the Tour de France* (London: Pocket Books, 2003), 12–22. Background on the Tour de France is in Andrew Johnston, *International Herald Tribune*, July 3, 2003, 9; Christopher S. Thompson, *The Tour de France* (Berkeley: University of California Press, 2006), 17–18.

    Thomas Stevens Stevens is discussed in Thomas Pauly, introduction to *Around the World on a Bicycle*, by Thomas Stevens (1889; reprint, Mechanicsburg, Pa.: Stackpole, 2001), v–xv; Desmond, *The Information Process*, 278–79. McClure and *Outing* are discussed in Peter Lyon, *Success Story: The Life and Times of S. S. McClure* (New York: Scribner's, 1963), 32–45. On Northcliffe, see Pound and Harmsworth, *Northcliffe*, 55–61.

    "Here was a grand opportunity" Thomas Stevens, *Scouting for Stanley in East Africa* (London: Cassell, 1890), 5. Edward Vizetelly was author of a memoir that appeared before his Stanley exploration, *Reminiscences of a Bashi-Bazouk* (London: Bristol, 1878). Vizetelly's victory is recounted in Desmond, *The Information Process*, 279; and Bullard, *Famous War Correspondents*, 281–85.

85 **"truth always triumphs"** Stevens, *Scouting for Stanley*, 260.

    "The instant you see a sensation is dead" Hazel Dicken-Garcia, *Journalistic Standards in Nineteenth-Century America* (Madison: University of Wisconsin Press, 1989), 220. The Northwest Passage episode is described at length in Dale L. Walker, *Januarius MacGahan: The Life and Campaigns of an American War Correspondent* (Athens: Ohio University Press, 1988), chap. 9.

    "Gird up your loins" Walker, *Januarius Macgahan*, 164.

86 **"soiled linen"** Leonard F. Guttridge, *Icebound: The Jeannette Expedition's Quest for the North Pole* (Annapolis: Md.: Naval Institute Press, 1986), 271. Guttridge has a good discussion of the fiasco as well as of Collins, 59–60, 86; so does Fergus Fleming, *Ninety Degrees North: The Quest for the North Pole* (New York: Grove, 2001), chaps. 11, 12, 13.

    "bore fruit" "A New Field for Journalism," *New York Tribune*, February 11, 1873. Background is found in Fergus Fleming, *Off the Map: Tales of Endurance and Exploration* (New York: Atlantic Monthly Press, 2005), 291; Lucy Maynard Salmon, *The Newspaper and the Historian* (New York: Oxford University Press, 1923), 13. Salmon discusses news-making generally. The *Daily Telegraph* activities are also noted in Desmond, *The Press and World Affairs*, 28; and in Edward Frederick Lawson Burnham, *Peterborough Court: The Story of the Daily Telegraph* (London: Cassell, 1955), 138–39. Curiously, Lionel Decle's *Three Years in Savage Africa* (1900; reprint, Bulawayo, Zimbabwe: Books of Rhodesia, 1974), does not contain any reference to the *Daily Telegraph;* nor does H. H. Johnston, *The Kilimanjaro Expedition: A Record of Scientific Exploration in Eastern Equatorial Africa* (London: Kegan, Paul, Trench, 1886). On Northcliffe, see Pound and Harmsworth, *Northcliffe*, 72, 162–63.

    both men were lying Tifft and Jones, *The Trust*, 65–66. A full discussion of the war between the *Herald* and the *Times* is found in Fleming, *Ninety Degrees North*, chap. 21; and Pierre Berton, *The Arctic Grail; The Quest for the North West Passage and the North Pole, 1818–1909* (New York:

Viking, 1988), 567–612. On National Geographic Society support, see Robert M. Poole, *Explorers House: National Geographic and the World It Made* (New York: Penguin Press, 2004), 85–103.

87 **"Other than the flag"** Frank Luther Mott, *A History of American Magazines,* vol. 4, *1885–1905* (Cambridge, Mass.: Harvard University Press, 1957), 625; also *Great Adventures with National Geographic* (Washington, D.C.: National Geographic Society, 1963), 6. On psuedo-events, see Daniel J. Boorstin, *The Image: A Guide to Pseudo-Events in America* (New York: Atheneum, 1972).

"Newspapers are getting to be" "A New Field for Journalism."

penciled in names Meyer Berger, *The Story of the New York Times, 1851–1951* (New York: Simon and Schuster, 1951), 168; Frederick Schwatka, *Summer in Alaska* (St. Louis, Mo.: J. W. Henry, 1894), 100; William H. Gilder, *Schwatka's Search: Sledging in the Arctic in Quest of the Franklin Records* (New York: Scribner's, 1881), vii; Seitz, *The Bennetts,* 341–44, 350; Poole, *Explorers House,* 146–48; Walter Sullivan, *Quest for a Continent* (New York: McGraw-Hill, 1957), 81–153; Talese, *The Kingdom and the Power,* 195; Elizabeth A. Brennan and Elizabeth C. Clarage, "Russell D. Owen," in *Who's Who of the Pulitzer Prize Winners,* by Brennan and Clarage (Phoenix: Oryx Press, 1999), 554; Shepard, *The Paper's Papers,* 289–90.

The naming of places was a hit-or-miss affair; some names never became official. George Jones River, Lake Bennett, and Flynn River in Alaska did not stick. The Bennett, Henrietta, and Jeannette islands resulting from polar exploration did. Ochs-Sulzberger family names are found on maps of Antarctica. Livingstone Falls remains as named, as does Stanley Pool. Stanley Falls, an alternative name for Boyoma Falls, is not far from Kisangani, whose alternative name is Stanleyville, which lies in a country that itself has had a variety of names, including Congo and Zaire. In Kenya there is a Bennetts Road, whose pedigree is uncertain, as far as I can tell. The quirkiness of naming is revealed in an encounter between Stanley and Prime Minister William Gladstone. The latter took the explorer to task for putting the names of Bennett and Mackinnon on mountains; he maintained that those landmarks should retain the names given by Herodotus. Gladstone was mixed up, however: those mountains were not named by Herodotus. In any event, there are no Bennett and Mackinnon mountains in Africa at the moment. The author appreciates the help in understanding the naming game given by Roger L. Payne, executive secretary, U.S. Board on Geographic Names.

88 **"Without the assistance of the newspapers"** W. L. G. Joerg, *The Work of the Byrd Antarctic Expedition, 1928–1930* (New York: American Geographical Society, 1930), 2.

"If there was anything the Commodore hated" Crockett, *Caliph of Baghdad,* 282. Other details on the Commodore's irritation with Stanley's fame are found in *New York Herald,* December 22, 1871; Jeal, *Stanley,* 149–51; Stanley, *Stanley's Dispatches,* xxi; Seitz, *The Bennetts,* 299–301, which includes the "Who was Stanley?" quote.

CHAPTER 8

89 **"Presently Mr. Remington sent this telegram"** Creelman, *On the Great Highway,* 177–78. Creelman made weird and confusing use of quotation marks in his quote. I have altered them for readability.

"action by the United States" Ivan Musicant, *Empire by Default: The Spanish-American War and the Dawn of the American Century* (New York: Henry Holt, 1998), 115. The Porter telegram to McKinley, December 7, 1897, is in the McKinley Papers.

90 **"How do you like the *Journal*'s war?"** Charles H. Brown, *The Correspondents' War: Journalists in the Spanish-American War* (New York: Scribner's, 1967), 440. Hearst's welcoming credit for starting the war is in David Nasaw, *The Chief: The Life of William Randolph Hearst* (Boston: Houghton Mifflin, 2000), 125–28.

"There is no evidence" Michael Schudson, "Toward a Troubleshooting Manual for Journalism History," *Journalism and Mass Communication Quarterly* 74 (Autumn 1997): 464–65. Other scholars who argue against the power of the press in the Spanish-American War are W. Joseph Campbell, *Yellow Journalism: Puncturing the Myths, Defining the Legacies* (Westport, Conn.: Praeger, 2001); and, contrary to the misleading title of his book, Brown, *The Correspondents' War*. The scholarly arguments attributing the war to the yellow press took shape in the 1930s with Marcus Wilkerson, *Public Opinion and the Spanish-American War* (Baton Rouge: Louisiana State University Press, 1932); and Joseph E. Wisan, *The Cuban Crisis as Reflected in the New York Press, 1895–1898* (New York: Columbia University Press, 1934). Neither Wilkerson nor Wisan regurgitates the fictitious Hearst telegram to Remington. Similar arguments to theirs have been made more recently in Joyce Milton, *The Yellow Kids: Foreign Correspondents in the Heyday of Yellow Journalism* (New York: Harper and Row, 1989); and Emery and Emery, *The Press and America*, 198–204.

journalist José Martí Martí and conditions in Cuba at this time are discussed at length in Hugh Thomas, *Cuba: The Pursuit of Freedom* (New York: Harper and Row, 1971), chaps. 24–33.

91 **"does not go abroad"** Walter Russell Mead, *Special Providence: American Foreign Policy and How It Changed the World* (New York: Knopf, 2001), 193.

"No subject can better engage" A leading proponent of the commercial argument, from whom I have taken the quotes in this paragraph and the next, is Walter LaFeber, *The New Empire: An Interpretation of American Expansion, 1860–1898* (Ithaca, N.Y.: Cornell University Press, 1963), 296, 332, 371–73.

Alfred Thayer Mahan For a good discussion of the impact of Mahan, Roosevelt, Lodge, Elihu Root, and John Hay on the decision to go to war, see Warren Zimmermann, *First Great Triumph: How Five Americans Made Their Country a World Power* (New York: Farrar, Straus and Giroux, 2002).

Humanitarian concerns Ibid., 251, 262, 497–99. Visitors' reactions to misery in Cuba and the death rate are discussed in Thomas, *Cuba*, 284–85. Foreign aid is described in Merle Curti, *American Philanthropy Abroad* (New Brunswick, N.J.: Transaction Books, 1988), chap. 8.

92 **"expressed yearnings"** Robert Dallek, *The American Style of Foreign Policy: Cultural Politics and Foreign Affairs* (New York: Knopf, 1983), xv.

"God was the author" The senatorial quote is from Frederick W. Marks III, *Velvet on Iron: The Diplomacy of Theodore Roosevelt* (Lincoln: University of Nebraska Press, 1979), 25–26. On the Pledge of Allegiance, see John Higham, *Writing American History: Essays on Modern Scholarship* (Bloomington: Indiana University Press, 1970), 83. The Spanish-flag toilet paper is mentioned in Paul Scott Mowrer, *The House of Europe* (Boston: Houghton Mifflin, 1945), 25.

the Yellow Kid Campbell, *Yellow Journalism*, 26–32; Milton, *The Yellow Kids*, 40–43; Bill Blackbeard, *The Yellow Kid: A Centennial Celebration of the Kid Who Started the Comics* (Northampton, Mass.: Kitchen Sink Press, 1995), chap. 7.

jumped their journalistic tracks altogether Brown, *The Correspondents' War*, vi–vii, makes the point that the press acted as if it were the government. Hearst's antics are described in Nasaw, *The Chief*, chap. 7; and Thomas, *Cuba*, 371. The jail break is described at length in Campbell, *The Year That Defined American Journalism*, chap. 4.

93 **Remington's visit to Cuba** This famous story is told in Arthur Lubow, *The Reporter Who Would Be King: A Biography of Richard Harding Davis* (New York: Scribner's, 1992), chap. 6. Davis's story appeared in the *New York Journal*, February 12, 1897.

94 **Editors hired artists and experimented** Brisbane, "Great Problems in Organization," 545; Brown, *The Correspondents' War*, 133–35; Mott, *American Magazines*, 4:455.

"With nationalistic feeling at fever pitch" Albert E. Smith, *Two Reels and a Crank* (Garden City, N.Y.: Doubleday, 1952), 12, 54.

essential in human rights reporting Roy Gutman, interview by author, April 22, 2004; Gutman, e-mails to author, August 17 and 19, 2004.

95 **"No man"** Richard Harding Davis, *Cuba in War Time* (1897; reprint, Lincoln: University of Nebraska Press, 2000), 139.

By one count Good summaries of the amount of coverage are found in Brown, *The Correspondents' War,* 444–49; Marcus Wilkerson, "The Press and the Spanish-American War," *Journalism Quarterly* 9 (June 1932): 129–48.

Sensationalism was not confined D. F. Wilcox, "The American Newspaper," *Annals of the American Academy of Political and Social Science* 16 (July 1900): 71 and passim. This article discusses the difficulties of deciding just what is yellow or sensational. A more recent discussion is in Campbell, *Yellow Journalism,* chap. 5.

"without parallel in the history of human suffering" Stephen Bonsal described his *Herald* reporting in his book *The Real Condition of Cuba To-day* (New York: Harper, 1897), 107.

"In these leaking huts" Stephen Bonsal, "Starvation in Cuba," *Harper's Weekly,* May 29, 1897, 531; Brown, *The Correspondents' War,* 90–91; "Our Duty to Cuba, the Republic," *Cosmopolitan,* August 1895, 471. *McClure's* discusses its reporting in "McClure's Magazine in War Times," *McClure's,* June 1898, 206; and "McClure's and the War," *McClure's,* July 1898, 496.

96 **"The time is ripe"** Mott, *American Magazines,* 4:235–37, 485, all of which has background on magazine coverage of the war.

"The American newspapers" Creelman, *On the Great Highway,* 161; G. W. Auxier, "The Propaganda Activities of the Cuban *Junta* in Precipitating the Spanish-American War, 1895–1898," *Hispanic American Historical Review* 29 (April 1939): 268–305; Ernest May, *Imperial Democracy: The Emergence of America as a Great Power* (New York: Harcourt Brace, 1961), 70–71; Horatio S. Rubens, *Liberty: The Story of Cuba* (New York: Brewer, Warren, and Putnam, 1932), 202–5; Phillip Foner, *The Spanish-Cuban-American War and the Birth of American Imperialism* (New York: Monthly Review Press, 1972), chap. 9.

97 **"Strangely enough"** *New York Times,* January 8, 1896. The AP report is described in George Bronson Rea, *Facts and Fakes about Cuba* (New York: George Munro's, 1897), 149–54.

William Francis Mannix W., *New York Times,* March 29, 1896.

Mannix's relationship with the *Times* is a mystery. Neither standard histories of the *Times* nor the *Times* archives offer any clues about W. or Mannix. George Bronson Rea tells the "W" story and makes other observations in *Facts and Fakes about Cuba,* 25–26, 144–45, 163–64. Desmond, *The Information Process,* 388, mentions Mannix in passing. Wisan, *The Cuban Crisis,* 194, says the Spanish expelled Mannix, but his source for this assertion (microfilm of the *New York Times,* February 12, 1897) carries no such story. A letter from Mannix, November 14, 1900, is in the McKinley Papers. In this letter, written from Peking, China, Mannix requests discharge from the army: "Having accomplished the object of my enlistment, as stated to the President, in my communication of August 14, I am desirous of returning to the United States to resume my newspaper work." Mannix had enlisted in the army in order "to know the feeling of the rank and file of the army on exploded issue of 'imperialism.'" He represented a syndicate of six newspapers.

Mannix's literary forgeries cry out for a proper history. He seems to have forged the *Memoirs of Li Hung Chang* (1913) and may have been similarly involved with a collection of love letters supposedly written by Abraham Lincoln to Ann Rutledge, published by the *Atlantic Monthly* in 1929. Details on this can be found in the Ruth E. and Edward M. Brecher Collection on William F. Mannix, Princeton University Library. The Spanish claimed that they paid for Mannix's fare to Cuba and that he subsequently offered to work as a spy. When they turned this offer down, they claimed, he began to write negative stories. *New York Times,* February 7, 1896.

Talese, *The Kingdom and the Power,* 200, says the *Times* had two of its own reporters in Cuba. Elmer Davis, *The History of the New York Times: 1851–1921* (New York: New York Times, 1921), 230, says the *Times* had "a little mail correspondence, but that counted for nothing." More or less echoing Berger in his *Story of the New York Times,* Tifft and Jones, *The Trust,* 55, say the *Times'* coverage of the Spanish-American War was limited to AP stories. In reviewing their files in response to an inquiry for this book, Jones found evidence of one correspondent representing the

Times in Cuba, who is not Mannix but Stanhope Sams. Jones to Hamilton, e-mail, July 15, 2004. *Times* coverage of the Spanish-American War remains to be studied in depth.

"**Tears were rolling down**" *New York Times,* February 21, 1897.

98 "**omitted many events**" Rea, *Facts and Fakes about Cuba,* 330.

"**had two or three newspapers**" Thomas A. Bailey, *A Diplomatic History of the American People* (Englewood Cliffs, N.J.: Prentice-Hall, 1974), 461; May, *Imperial Democracy,* 71.

A study done in conjunction with this book John Maxwell Hamilton, Renita Coleman, Bettye Grable, and Jaci Cole, "An Enabling Environment: A Reconsideration of the Press and the Spanish-American War," *Journalism Studies* 7 (February 2006): 78–93. The definitions for "sensational," "mixed," and "conservative" come from Campbell, *Yellow Journalism,* 153–54. The study used a standard sampling practice of two constructed weeks. A much earlier and narrower qualitative study of Midwestern newspapers came to much the same conclusion: George W. Auxier, "Middle Western Newspapers and the Spanish-American War, 1895–1898," *Mississippi Valley Historical Review* 26 (March 1940): 524. Another qualitative regional study disagrees with our findings and Auxier's: Mark M. Welter, "The 1895–98 Cuba Crisis in Minnesota Newspapers: Testing the 'Yellow Journalism' Theory," *Journalism Quarterly* 47 (Winter 1970): 719–24. For yet another view, see Marvin N. Olasky, "Hawks or Doves? Texas Press and Spanish-American War," *Journalism Quarterly* 64 (Spring 1987): 205–8. Olasky's survey contends that the Texas press was more critical of the New York yellow journals early in 1898 than of Spain but later argued for war.

99 **paper to paper** Meredith W. Berg and David M. Berg, "The Rhetoric of War Preparation: The New York Press in 1898," *Journalism Quarterly* 45 (Winter 1968): 653–60; Brown, *The Correspondents' War,* 88–89.

100 **read only the cartoons** Rob Schorman, "Remember the *Maine,* Boys, and the Price of This Suit," *Historian* 61 (Fall 1998): 119–34; Blackbeard, *The Yellow Kid,* 124. On newspaper readership, see Thomas Leonard, *News for All: America's Coming-of-Age with the Press* (New York: Oxford University Press, 1995), 177–78; and Campbell, *The Year That Defined American Journalism,* 9; on literacy, Carl F. Kaestle, "The History of Readers," in *Literacy in the United States: Readers and Reading since 1880,* by Kaestle, Helen Damon-Moore, Lawrence C. Stedman, Katherine Tinsley, and William Vance Trollinger Jr. (New Haven, Conn.: Yale University Press, 1991), 24–25.

"**The Yankee did not gather**" William Allen White, "When Johnny Went Marching," *McClure's,* June 1898, 198.

editor of Madrid's *El Heraldo* Thomas, *Cuba,* 360–61.

101 **playing the public like a fiddle** H. Wayne Morgan, *William McKinley and His America* (Syracuse, N.Y.: Syracuse University Press, 1963). The opposite view, in which McKinley fiddled, is found in May, *Imperial Democracy,* 112. "Rightly or wrongly," Ernest May observed, McKinley "conceived that he had some justification for demanding a final end to the violence in Cuba, that his highest duty lay in keeping his own country united, and that the alternative to war might be a domestic crisis tantamount in his eyes to revolution. For these reasons he led his country unwilling toward a war that he did not want for a cause in which he did not believe" (159). The quote on McKinley's lack of backbone is from Thomas, *Cuba,* 379.

agenda-setting and framing For studies of framing and agenda-setting, see Robert M. Entman, "Framing: Toward Clarification of a Fractured Paradigm," *Journal of Communication* 43 (Autumn 1993): 51–58; Herbert J. Gans, *Deciding What's News: A Study of CBS Evening News, NBC Nightly News, Newsweek, and Time* (New York: Vintage, 1980); Alice S. Hornig, "Science Stories: Risk, Power, and Perceived Emphasis," *Journalism Quarterly* 67 (Winter 1990): 767–76; Shanto Iyengar, *Is Anyone Responsible? How Television Frames Political Issues* (Chicago: University of Chicago Press, 1991); Maxwell E. McCombs, David L. Shaw, and David H. Weaver, eds., *Communication and Democracy: Exploring the Intellectual Frontiers in Agenda-Setting Theory* (Mahwah, N.J.: Lawrence Erlbaum, 1997); Maxwell E. McCombs, Edna Einsiedel, and David H. Weaver, *Contemporary Public Opinion: Issues and the News* (Hillsdale, N.J.: Lawrence Erlbaum,

1991); Douglas M. McLeod and Benjamin H. Detenber, "Framing Effects of Television News Coverage of Social Protest," *Journal of Communication* 49 (Summer 1999): 3–23; Z. Pan and G. Kosicki, "Framing Analysis: An Approach to News Discourse," *Political Communication* 10 (January–March 1993): 55–75; Gaye Tuchman, *Making News: A Study in the Construction of Reality* (New York: Free Press, 1978); Wayne Wanta, Guy Golan, and Cheolham Lee, "Agenda Setting and International News: Media Influence on Public Perceptions of Foreign Nations," *Journalism and Mass Communication Quarterly* 81 (Summer 2004): 364–67.

102 **"Emotionalism increased dramatically"** May, *American Imperialism*, 224.

News reports from abroad May, *Imperial Democracy,* 78–81; *Congressional Record,* 55th Cong., 1st sess., April 6, 1897, 621; *New York Journal,* February 13, 1897.

"encouraged men and women" T. H. Breen, *The Marketplace of Revolution: How Consumer Politics Shaped American Independence* (New York: Oxford University Press, 2004), 250.

"form and express public opinion" The Hearst quote is in *New York Journal,* September 25, 1898; Ben Procter, *William Randolph Hearst: The Later Years, 1911–1951* (New York: Oxford University Press, 2007), 6. The Godkin quotes are in E. L. Godkin, "The Growth and Expression of Public Opinion," *Atlantic Monthly,* January 1898, 6, 9. Another contemporary article that touches on concerns over the press and public opinion is Richard Olney, "International Isolation of the United States," *Atlantic Monthly,* May 1898, 577–88.

103 **"In my daily business"** May, *Imperial Democracy,* 138 and 249.

"President McKinley" This was found in "Current Comment" in the McKinley Papers; it appears to have been from the *Ohio State Journal,* November 30, 1897.

"the drift of public sentiment" Campbell, *Yellow Journalism,* 120; Ida Tarbell, "President McKinley in War Times," *McClure's,* July 1898, 213–14. The entire Tarbell article is useful for McKinley's handling of the press, as is Robert C. Hilderbrand, *Power and the People: Executive Management of Public Opinion in Foreign Affairs, 1897–1921* (Chapel Hill: University of North Carolina Press, 1981), chap. 1, where observations on the importance of "Current Comment" can be found. See also Margaret Leech, *In the Days of McKinley* (New York: Harper, 1959), 229–30.

104 **"The 'Maine'"** Tarbell, "President McKinley in War Times," 218; May, *Imperial Democracy,* 144–45.

"inevitable" May, *Imperial Democracy,* 146, 152; LaFeber, *The New Empire,* 392; Chalmers M. Roberts, *In the Shadow of Power: The Story of the Washington Post,* rev. ed. (Cabin John, Md.: Seven Locks Press, 1989), 48–49.

"We want no wars of conquest" Zimmermann, *First Great Triumph,* 252. Public opinion also was a factor for the Spanish, as Ernest May has noted. Spanish opinion was "the reverse of America's. In Spain, it was conservatives who held that the nation should conduct itself as a major power. . . . Successive Spanish ministries judged it safer to get into a losing war than to have the Queen Regent bear the obloquy of having voluntarily abandoned Cuba." Ernest May, introduction to a new edition of *American Imperialism* (Chicago: Imprint, 1991), viii.

"The past few months" H. H. Powers, "The War as a Suggestion of Manifest Destiny," *Annals of the American Academy of Political and Social Science* 12 (September 1898): 173.

105 **"breakfasts at eight"** Albert Halstead, "The President at Work," *Independent,* September 5, 1901, 2082; Schorman, "Remember the *Maine,* Boys," 119–34; May, *Imperial Democracy,* 259.

human rights as a rationale for intervention Zimmermann, *First Great Triumph,* 497–98; Leslie H. Gelb and Justine A. Rosenthal, "The Rise of Ethics in Foreign Policy," *Foreign Affairs* 82 (May–June 2003): 5; Richard Goldstone, foreword to *Crimes of War: What the Public Should Know,* ed. Roy Gutman and David Rieff (New York: Norton, 1999), 14; Gary J. Bass, *Freedom's Battle: The Origins of Humanitarian Intervention* (New York: Knopf, 2008), chap. 2.

"In 1993" Steven Livingston, "Clarifying the CNN Effect: An Examination of Media Effects according to Type of Military Intervention," Research Paper R-18, June 1997, Shorenstein Center, Cambridge, Mass., 9. Nicholas D. Kristof's article was in the *New York Times,* July 26, 2005.

106 **"Should a war"** Arthur Brisbane, "Great Problems in Organization: The Modern Newspaper in

War Time," *Cosmopolitan,* September 1898, 542. Other stories written at the time in the same vein are Ray Stannard Baker, "How the News of the War Is Reported," *McClure's,* September 1898, 491–95; and John R. Spears, "Afloat for News in War Times," *Scribner's,* October 1898, 501–4.

the first to spot human rights abuses. William Mullen, interview by Nicole Marshall, the author's research assistant, September 2004.

was not matched again Thomas E. Ricks, *Washington Post,* May 31, 2004; Daniel Moran, "The Uprising," *Strategic Insights* 2 (September 2003), www.ccc.nps.navy.mil/si/sept03/middleEast.asp; John Maxwell Hamilton and Jonathan Schell, "An Imperial Moment," *Nation,* December 23, 2002, 16–18; and John Maxwell Hamilton and Jonathan Schell, "Tarantara!" *Nation,* November 1, 2004, 10.

107 **Ahmed Chalabi** Michael Massing, "Now They Tell Us," *New York Review of Books,* February 26, 2004, 43–49; Jane Mayer, "The Manipulator," *New Yorker,* June 7, 2004, 58–72; Douglas McCollam, "The List," *Columbia Journalism Review* 43 (July–August 2004): 31–37; Franklin Foer, "The Source of the Trouble," *New York,* June 7, 2004, from www.nymag.com/nymetro/news/media/features/9226, downloaded March 4, 2007. The list of 108 articles was reported first by two reporters with the Knight Ridder bureau, which also had the distinction of providing a counterpoint to the WMD stories that dominated the news: Jonathan S. Landay and Tish Wells, in a story posted on the Web March 15, 2004, www.realcities.com/mld/krwashington/news/special_packages/8184211 (accessed July 1, 2004).

shown up in many other guises W. A. Swanberg, *Luce and His Empire* (New York: Scribner's, 1972), 351–53; Darryl Hunt, interview by author, August 22, 2004.

The United States engages Alvin A. Snyder, *Warriors of Disinformation: American Propaganda, Soviet Lies, and the Winning of the Cold War* (New York: Arcade, 1955), 15, 305. On Radio Martí transmission, see *New York Times,* May 21, 1985. A good discussion of the politics of VOA is in Sanford J. Ungar, "Pitch Imperfect," *Foreign Affairs,* May–June 2005, 7–13. The secret payments to journalists and news media in Iraq are reported in *New York Times,* December 1, 2005.

108 **"more and more of the environment"** Ernest R. May, "The News Media and Diplomacy," in *Rethinking International Relations: Ernest R. May and the Study of World Affairs,* by May, ed. Akira Iriye (Chicago: Imprint, 1998), 170.

For a discussion of the various circumstances under which the CNN Effect works or does not work, see Piers Robinson, *The CNN Effect: The Myth of News, Foreign Policy, and Intervention* (London: Routledge, 2002); as well as Steven Livingston and Todd Eachus, "Humanitarian Crises and U.S. Foreign Policy: Somalia and the CNN Effect Reconsidered," *Political Communication* 12 (October–December 1995): 413–29; David Perlmutter, *Photojournalism and Foreign Policy: Icons of Outrage in International Crises* (Westport, Conn.: Praeger, 1998), chap. 4. For the argument that television drives policymakers, see Philip Seib, *Headline Diplomacy: How News Coverage Affects Foreign Policy* (Westport, Conn.: Praeger, 1997), chap. 3; Seib notes, however, that policymakers have learned ways to push back. A case study of the impact of press coverage on decision making regarding deployment of the neutron bomb is found in David Whitman, "The Press and the Neutron Bomb," in *How the Press Affects Federal Policymaking: Six Case Studies,* ed. Martin Linsky, Jonathan Moore, Wendy O'Donnell, and David Whitman (New York: Norton, 1986).

"conduit for public opinion expression" Pew Center for People and the Press, "Washington Leaders Wary of Public Opinion," Survey Report, April 17, 1998, Pew Center for People and the Press, Washington, D.C.; Susan Herbst, *Reading Public Opinion: How Political Actors View the Democratic Process* (Chicago: University of Chicago Press, 1998), 65, 187.

"The press is the leading point of contact" Bernard C. Cohen, *The Public's Impact on Foreign Policy* (Boston: Little, Brown, 1973), 107, 122; Bernard Kalb, foreword to *The Media and Foreign Policy,* ed. Simon Serfaty (New York: St. Martin's Press, 1990), xiv.

the president's final hours This quote and the one in the previous paragraph are from Creelman, *On the Great Highway,* 408–10.

CHAPTER 9

110 **frankly "romantic"** Edward Larocque Tinker, *Lafcadio Hearn's American Days* (New York: Dodd, Mead, 1924), 330; Lafcadio Hearn, *Life and Letters of Lafcadio Hearn,* ed. Elizabeth Bisland (Boston: Houghton Mifflin, 1923), 1:217.

"I don't want" Richard Norton Smith, *The Colonel: The Life and Legend of Robert R. McCormick, 1880–1995* (Boston: Houghton Mifflin, 1997), 300. George Seldes told it somewhat differently in his *Lords of the Press* (New York: Julian Messner, 1939), 284.

"high proficiency" Roger Cohen, foreign editor, *New York Times,* interview by author, September 17, 2003. On language training, see Hess, *International News and Foreign Correspondents,* 83. The 1965 comment on the need for more language specialization is in Harrison Salisbury to Clifton Daniel, March 1, 1965, NYT Archives. The low level of training in previous times is discussed in Ernest R. May, "U.S. Press Coverage of Japan, 1931–1941," in his *Rethinking International Relations.*

111 **"civilized nomad"** Lafcadio Hearn, "A Ghost," *Harper's New Monthly Magazine,* December 1889, 116.

the *Herald for Europe* The *New York Tribune for Europe* is discussed in Schwarzlose, *Nation's Newsbrokers,* 1:53; and in Richard A. Schwarzlose, "The Foreign Connection: Transatlantic Newspapers in the 1840s," *Journalism History* 10 (Autumn–Winter 1983): 44–67. On the *New York Times,* see Shepard, *The Paper's Papers,* 343; and Berger, *Story of the New York Times,* 6. Although Berger does not say so explicitly, it appears that the *Times* was printed in New York and shipped overseas. In addition to its *Europe* edition, the *Times* briefly published Spanish-language supplements for Latin America on three occasions in the nineteenth century. The name change for the *Herald* to the *Herald Tribune* is discussed in Charles L. Robertson, *The International Herald Tribune: The First Hundred Years* (New York: Columbia University Press, 1987), 172.

"a feeble imitation" Wythe Williams, *Dusk of Empire* (New York: Scribner's, 1937), 21. For background on U.S. newspapers in Europe, see Kluger, *The Paper,* 207–8; Seitz, *The Bennetts,* 376–77; David D. Kirpatrick, *International Herald Tribune,* January 2, 2003; Al Laney, *Paris Herald: The Incredible Newspaper* (New York: D. Appleton-Century, 1947), 151–52, 301–4; Robert W. Desmond, *Windows on the World: World News Reporting, 1900–1920* (Iowa City: University of Iowa Press, 1980), 379–80; Waverly Root, *The Paris Edition, 1927–1934* (San Francisco: North Point Press, 1987), 156. A good deal of background on Paris publishing can be found in Ronald Weber, *News of Paris: American Journalists in the City of Light between the Wars* (Chicago: Ivan R. Dee, 2006).

112 **in a foreign outpost** Desmond, *The Information Process,* 281–89; Desmond, *Windows on the World,* 179, 207–8; Denis L. Wilcox, *English Language Newspapers Abroad: A Guide to Daily Newspapers in 56 Non-English-Speaking Countries* (Detroit: Gale, 1967); Carson Taylor, *History of the Philippine Press* (Manila: Self-published, 1927). Taylor was the founder of the *Manila Daily Bulletin.*

Overseas military activity has spawned newspapers in the United States as well as in other nations. The French who came to fight against the British in the American Revolution started *La Gazette Françoise.* The history of this effort is found in *La Gazette Françoise, 1780–1781,* trans. and ed. Eugena Poulin and Claire Quintal (Newport, R.I.: Salve Regina University, in association with University Press of New England, 2007).

The history of expatriate newspapers deserves a volume all its own. Among the more interesting characters is one Gene Gregory, who bought the *Times of Vietnam* in Saigon in 1957. He established close and highly profitable relations with the ruling Nhu family. When the Nhus fell so did Gregory and his paper. Some of this story is found in "The Gregorys of Saigon," *Newsweek,* September 23, 1963, 40–41. Another interesting effort was the *Overseas Weekly,* established in Europe as an antidote to the government-financed *Stars and Stripes.* The tabloid, which folded in 1975, offered servicemen scantily clad women and reports that angered the military. See "Stars and Stripes Forever," *Newsweek,* July 18, 1966, for some of the details.

Thomas F. Millard For background on Millard and J. B. Powell, see J. B. Powell, *My Twenty-five Years in China* (New York: Macmillan, 1945); as well Mordechai Rozanski, "The Role of American Journalists in Chinese-American Relations, 1900–1925" (Ph.D. diss., University of Pennsylvania, 1974). Millard's prospectus is discussed in Rozanski's dissertation, 91–95.

"placed the first lip-stick" Carl Crow, *Four Hundred Million Customers: The Experiences—Some Happy, Some Sad—of an American in China, and What They Taught Him* (New York: Harper, 1937), 32, 42, 186. Crow talks about his coverage of Sun Yat-sen in Carl Crow, *China Takes Her Place: A Story of Struggle and Achievement* (New York: Harper, 1944), chap. 4. For a biography see Paul French, *Carl Crow: A Tough Old China Hand* (Hong Kong: Hong Kong University Press, 2006). The "mischievous man" quote is in Nicholas R. Clifford, *Spoilt Children of Empire: Westerners in Shanghai and the Chinese Revolution of the 1920s* (Hanover, N.H.: University Press of New England, 1991), 260. Powell writes about his China experience in *My Twenty-five Years in China*.

On the "Missouri News Monopoly," see John Maxwell Hamilton, "The Missouri News Monopoly and American Altruism in China: Thomas F. F. Millard, J. B. Powell, and Edgar Snow," *Pacific Historical Review* 55 (February 1986): 27–48; Edgar Snow, *Journey to the Beginning* (New York: Random House, 1958), 31; Stephen R. MacKinnon and Oris Friesen, *China Reporting: An Oral History of American Journalism in the 1930s and 1940s* (Berkeley: University of California Press, 1987). The forty-seven journalists are mentioned in Rozanski, "The Role of American Journalists in Chinese-Americans Relations," 375. Williams's candidacy for ambassador to China is mentioned in Roscoe B. Ellard, "In Memoriam, Walter Williams: 1864–1935," *University of Missouri Bulletin,* February 10, 1936, 75. A general discussion of Missourians in the Far East is found in John B. Powell, "Missouri Authors and Journalists in the Orient," *Missouri Historical Review* 41 (October 1946): 45–55. The Missouri influence in Japan is discussed in S. H. Wainwright, "Missourians in Japan," *Missouri Historical Review* 15 (April 1921): 481.

113 **"prepared and conducted"** Desmond, *The Information Process,* 287. On Fleisher, see Rozanski, "The Role of American Journalists in Chinese-American Relations," 20–21, 93–94.

"shoved him out the door" Jonathan Cott, *Wandering Ghost: The Odyssey of Lafcadio Hearn* (Tokyo: Kodansha International, 1992), 32. I have relied heavily on this book for details on Hearn's life. A brief description of Hearn's stay in New York is in Tinker, *Hearn's American Days,* 11–12.

114 **"I think a man must devote himself"** Lafcadio Hearn, *Lafcadio Hearn's America: Ethnographic Sketches and Editorials,* ed. Simon J. Bronner (Lexington: University Press of Kentucky, 2002), 9; Christopher Benfey, *The Great Wave: Gilded Age Misfits, Japanese Eccentrics, and the Opening of Old Japan* (New York: Random House, 2003), 213–14. Hearn's personality traits are discussed in Ellwood Henrick, *Lafcadio Hearn* (New York: New York Public Library, 1919), 7; and Arthur E. Kunst, *Lafcadio Hearn* (New York: Twayne, 1969), 127.

"voudoo charms" Cott, *Wandering Ghost,* 180.

"quite impossible" S. Frederick Starr, *Inventing New Orleans* (Jackson: University Press of Mississippi, 2001), xii.

"to devote half their space" Mott, *American Magazines,* 4:223–24; see also on Asian magazines, 232–34; on missionary activities, 237–38; on John Brisben Walker, 481–87. Mott drew from a thesis by one of his students, James C. Bowman, "Trends of American World Consciousness, 1890 to 1900, as Shown by Nine American Magazines" (University of Missouri, 1952). The quote from *Cosmopolitan* is in "A World's Congress," March 1902, 461. The quote from the editor, Henry Alden, is found in Lewis H. Lapham, "Hazards of New Fortune," *Harper's Magazine,* June 2000, 62. For more discussion of *Harper's Monthly,* see Mott, *American Magazines,* 2:398. Hearn's first article was "A Winter Journey to Japan," *Harper's New Monthly Magazine,* November 1890, 860–68.

The modern *Maryknoll* magazine, which has not received the historical treatment it deserves, evolved into a vehicle for serious overseas reporting on political, social, and economic issues as well as about the Maryknoll Missioners activity abroad. The magazine, which has a circulation of just under 400,000, is given to anyone who makes a contribution to Maryknoll. *Maryknoll* editor Frank Maurovich to author, February 2, 2006, e-mail.

115   **"wander off to someplace else"** Hearn, *Hearn's America,* 26.
       "the prose of small things" Ibid., 33; Cott, *Wandering Ghost,* 210.

116   **"I want to die here!"** Tinker, *Hearn's American Days,* 345. Tinker discusses Hearn's assignment
       to Japan at length in chaps. 15 and 16.
       "Money!" Kazuo Koizumi, *Father and I: Memories of Lafcadio Hearn* (Boston: Houghton Mif-
       flin, 1935), 12; Cott, *Wandering Ghost,* 260; Mott, *American Magazines,* 2:515.
       "distinguished by the virility" Walter Williams, "A New Journalism in a New Far East," *Uni-
       versity of Missouri Bulletin,* December 1, 1928, 8; Robert Young, "Lafcadio Hearn," *Living Age,*
       January–February–March 1907, 763; Elizabeth Stevenson, *The Grass Lark: A Study of Lafcadio
       Hearn* (New Brunswick, N.J.: Transaction, 1999), 272.

117   **"competitive struggle"** Lafcadio Hearn, *Lafcadio Hearn's Japan: An Anthology of His Writings
       on the Country and Its People,* ed. Donald Richie (Rutland, Vt.: Charles E. Tuttle, 1997), 36; Laf-
       cadio Hearn, *Editorials from the Kobe Chronicle,* ed. Makoto Sangu (Tokyo: Hokuseido Press,
       1960), 57–60.

119   **"killing off of the devils"** Cott, *Wandering Ghost,* 342.
       "I fear" Benfey, *Great Wave,* 227.
       adopted him Hearn's adoption and citizenship is discussed in Stevenson, *Grass Lark,* 278–82.

121   **"In commemoration"** Ibid., 321. Hearn's son devotes an entire chapter, "At the Sea," to Yaidzu
       in Koizumi, *Father and I.*
       "a spokesman of Eastern ideas" Benfey, *Great Wave,* 236.
       "the most eloquent" Cott, *Wandering Ghost,* xvii. Cott's introduction describes Hearn's last-
       ing fame in Japan, as do Koizumi, *Father and I,* 3; and *New York Times,* February 20, 2007.
       "I am not invited" Rozanski, "The Role of American Journalists in Chinese-American Rela-
       tions," 370–71. For a good discussion of the seductive powers of China, see Jonathan Spence, *To
       Change China: Western Advisors in China, 1620–1960* (New York: Penguin, 1980).
       "an unfortunate specimen of U.S. culture" Richard M. Harnett and Billy G. Ferguson, *Uni-
       press: United Press International, Covering the 20th Century* (Golden, Colo.: Fulcrum, 2003), 74–
       75; "Japanese Best-Seller," *Life,* April 7, 1947, 107; Hoberecht, obituary, *New York Times,* Septem-
       ber 26, 1999. Earnest Hoberecht's memoir is *Asia Is My Beat* (Rutland, Vt.: Charles E. Tuttle,
       1961).

122   **"almost beyond recognition"** William L. Shirer, *Midcentury Journey: The Western World through
       Its Years of Conflict* (New York: Farrar, Straus, and Young, 1952), 259.
       "I fly back to California" Pico Iyer, *The Global Soul: Jet Lag, Shopping Malls, and the Search
       for Home* (New York: Knopf, 2000), 287. The *New York Times* story was published February 20,
       2007.
       a legend among fellow journalists For details on Critchfield, see his obituary in Claudia Levy,
       Washington Post, December 14, 1994. One of his more important books is *Villages* (Garden City,
       N.Y.: Anchor/Doubleday, 1981). He was also editor and coauthor of a textbook for Indian jour-
       nalists, *The Indian Reporter's Guide.*
       "a new genre of journalism" Elizabeth Bumiller, *Washington Post,* May 15, 1986; unsigned ar-
       ticle in the *Washington Post,* March 7, 1982. For examples of Zorza's India reports, see Victor
       Zorza, *Washington Post,* January 30, March 13, 1983. For biographical details, see his obituary,
       Louie Estrada, *Washington Post,* March 22, 1996; and Geoffrey Taylor and Jonathan Stele, *Guard-
       ian* (London), March 22, 1996.

CHAPTER 10

124   **"Your daddy has caught a man"** James Keeley to "family," no date, files of Julie Potter, Kee-
       ley's great-granddaughter, Lake Forest, Ill. Portions of the letter, although not the quotation in
       the text, are found in James Weber Linn, *James Keeley: Newspaperman* (Indianapolis: Bobbs-
       Merrill, 1937), 130–36. The letter reproduced in the Linn book is not identical to the original; de-

tails are left out and altered. The *bell-ringer* term is found in the same book on 40. Unless otherwise noted, details of Keeley's life are drawn from Linn's account, which contains the only substantial discussion that exists of the capture referred to in Keeley's letter.

"knew little or nothing" Linn, *James Keeley,* 116–17.

"It was tremendously expensive" Oscar King Davis, "Reporting a Cosmopolitan War," *Harper's Weekly,* July 27, 1901, 748.

foreign events accounted for slightly more than 25 percent Jurgen Wilke, "Foreign News Coverage and International Flow of News over Three Centuries," *Gazette* 39 (1987): 157.

125 **"We have never missed a conflict"** Peter Copeland, interview by author, November 5, 2003. By the time Clapper died, he had switched from print reporting for Scripps to broadcasting for the Mutual Broadcasting System. The Scripps bureau was not alone in the way it covered the Iraq War. Cox newspapers had ten reporters in Baghdad, then cut back with Bush's (mis)declared victory. Charles Holmes, interview by author, February 12, 2004.

"over the long run" Dwight L. Morris and associates, "America and the World: The Impact of September 11 on U.S. Coverage of International News," 2002, Pew International Journalism Program, Washington, D.C., 4.

"The most serious item of expense" E. L. Godkin, "The Growth and Expression of Public Opinion," *Atlantic Monthly,* January 1898, 7; Baehr, *The New York Tribune since the Civil War,* 32; Arthur Brisbane, "The Modern Newspaper in War Time," *Cosmopolitan,* September 1898, 552; Morris and associates, "America and the World," 22; Oswald Garrison Villard, "The Press as Affected by the War," *American Review of Reviews,* January 1915, 79. J. C. Oestreicher, *The World Is Their Beat* (New York: Duell, Sloan, and Pearce, 1945), chap. 9, has an excellent discussion of transmission costs. The Radio Television News Directors study is *Global Perspectives in Local Television News Coverage* (Washington, D.C.: Radio and Television News Directors Foundation, December 2004), 15.

126 **"A DOG FIGHT IN BROOKLYN"** Quentin Reynolds, *By Quentin Reynolds* (New York: Pyramid, 1964), 22.

"will do anything for Latin America" Linowitz and Reston are quoted in John Maxwell Hamilton, "Ho-hum—Latin America," *Columbia Journalism Review,* May–June 1977, 10.

"recalled and understood" *Newsweek* sales for the Rabin assassination are mentioned in the *New York Times,* September 23, 1996. Brokaw is referenced in Max Frankel, "Beyond the Shroud," *New York Times Magazine,* March 19, 1995, 30. The local-recall quote is from Laura Donnelly, "Proximity, Not Story Format, Improves News Awareness among Readers," *Newspaper Research Journal* 26 (Winter 2005): 62. *Reader's Digest* readership's interest/disinterest in foreign news and dieting is from Jacqueline Leo, interview by author, May 10, 2006.

"International stories" "Online News Audience Larger, More Diverse," 2004, Pew Research Center for the People and the Press, Washington, D.C., 26. See also "Eroding Respect for America Seen as Major Problem," 2004, Pew Research Center for the People and the Press, Washington, D.C.; and "Worldviews 2002: American Public Opinion and Foreign Policy," 2002, Council on Foreign Relations, New York, 12.

Only 25 of the 218 editors in the Pew International Journalism Program study thought interest in foreign news would be permanent. Morris and associates, "America and the World," 13–14. Fifty-eight percent of local news managers in the RTNDA study thought the public didn't care about global perspectives; see *Global Perspectives in Local Television News Coverage,* 6–14.

"The average newspaper editor" Julian Laurence Woodward, *Foreign News in American Morning Newspapers: A Study in Public Opinion* (New York: Columbia University Press, 1930), 67. President Harding's quote on normalcy is "America's present need is not heroics but healing; not nostrums but normalcy; not revolution but restoration." It can be found in Frederick Lewis Allen, *Only Yesterday: An Informal History of the Nineteen Twenties* (New York: Harper, 1931), 41.

128 **"quantitative analysis of the daily press"** Woodward, *Foreign News in American Morning Newspapers,* 5, 46–47.

Subsequent studies Alfred O. Hero, *Mass Media and World Affairs* ([Boston]: World Peace Foundation, 1959), 79, quotes Carnegie findings; Carl Sessions Stepp, "Then and Now," *American Journalism Review* 21 (September 1999): 64; Michael Emery, "An Endangered Species: The International Newshole," *Gannett Center Journal*, Fall 1989, 151–64. Woodward calculated the average proportion weighted by circulation as 5.15%. It was derived by multiplying the average percentage of foreign news in each newspaper by its circulation; the grand total of all these numbers was divided by the total circulation of all the papers.

The exception comes in the exceptional times Wilcox, "The American Newspaper," 66–67; George Gerbner and George Marvanyi, "The Many Worlds of the World's Press," *Journal of Communication* 27 (Winter 1977): 52–66. Paul W. White, "Quarter Century Survey of Press Content Shows Demand for Facts," *Editor and Publisher,* May 31, 1924, 1–2, compares the Wilcox study with 1924 coverage. White found no "war news" in 1924; foreign news amounted to 2.3% of the total newspaper, including advertising. As might be expected, foreign news is even scarcer in weekly newspapers. For an early discussion of this, as evidenced in Connecticut weeklies in 1922, see Malcolm MacDonald Willey, *The Country Newspaper* (Chapel Hill: University of North Carolina Press, 1926). Almost no newspapers in his study devoted more than 1% of the news hole to foreign news.

explicitly tested Woodward's thesis Cleo Joffrion Allen, "Foreign News Coverage in Selected U.S. Newspapers, 1927–1997: A Content Analysis" (Ph.D. diss., Louisiana State University, 2005).

keep foreign news simple Oscar S. Stauffer, "World versus Local News," *IPI Report* (December 1952): 3–4 ; John T. Whitaker, *And Fear Came* (New York: Macmillan, 1936), 88.

129 **"We newspaper people"** James L. Crouthamel, "James Gordon Bennett, the *New York Herald,* and the Development of Newspaper Sensationalism," *New York History* 54 (July 1973): 297–98.

"episodic stories" The "life-and-death" quote is from Beverly Horvit, "Combat, Political Violence Top International Categories," *Newspaper Research Journal* 24 (Spring 2003): 33. On banner stories in the *Chicago Tribune,* see Jerome E. Edwards, *Col. McCormick's Tribune: 1929–1941* (Reno: University of Nevada Press, 1971), 38. Discussion of the Guatemala earthquake is in Hamilton, "Ho-hum—Latin America," 10. The focus on coups and earthquakes is an old concern. Here is Calvin Coolidge in a 1926 speech: "Some one has remarked there is a time when readers of our newspapers here might have imagined revolutions and volcanic disturbances were the chief product of Latin America." Calvin Coolidge, *Foundations of the Republic: Speeches and Addresses* (Freeport, N.Y.: Books for Libraries Press, 1968), 269. Reflecting the newsroom emphasis on covering calamities, one correspondent, Mort Rosenblum, chose as the title of his book *Coups and Earthquakes: Reporting the World to America* (New York: Harper, Colophon, 1981).

"If it bleeds, it leads" Jim Bittermann, "The Best of Times," in *Live from the Trenches: The Changing Role of the Television News Correspondent,* ed. Joe S. Foote (Carbondale: Southern Illinois University Press, 1998), 80. The Lima correspondent is myself, then a young stringer for ABC. "If it bleeds, it leads" is a local television news mantra. More study is needed of the relationship between televised foreign news and violence, but economist James Hamilton has found this interesting connection: local television news programs are ten times more likely to cover crime stories than foreign affairs stories, and stations that emphasize crime are more likely to cover foreign affairs stories that emphasize violence. See James T. Hamilton, *Channeling Violence: The Economic Market for Violent Television Programming* (Princeton, N.J.: Princeton University Press, 1998), 245, 251.

130 **"MILITARY COUP MARS COUPLE'S HONEYMOON"** *Hebden Bridge (UK) Times,* November 11, 1988.

"Devote your main editorial efforts" Lloyd Wendt, *Chicago Tribune: The Rise of a Great American Newspaper* (Chicago: Rand McNally, 1979), 223, 265; Howard Tyner, interview by author, January 2, 2004.

ruthless Wendt, *Chicago Tribune,* 342–44; Terry Ramsaye, "James Keeley," *Chicagoan,* July 1934, 19. Background on the stockyards at the time can be found in Julian Ralph, "Killing Cattle for

Two Continents," *Harper's Weekly,* July 9, 1892, 670. In 1890, Ralph noted, the Chicago stockyards slaughtered 2,219,312 cattle, more than 1 million sheep, and 5,733,082 hogs. Keeley mentions the ranch executive from Chicago in *Chicago Tribune,* April 19 1892.

"News is a commodity" Linn, *James Keeley,* 72, 166. Wendt, *Chicago Tribune,* 386–92.

"As far as war was concerned" Linn, *James Keeley,* 82–83, 201; Wendt, *Chicago Tribune,* 345–47. Linn tells the Manila victory story somewhat differently than Mark Sullivan does in *Our Times: The United States, 1900–1925,* vol. 1, *The Turn of the Century, 1900–1904* (New York: Scribner's, 1926), 319–21.

131 **local angle** The recipe and Durkin anecdotes are in Linn, *James Keeley,* 106, 183; the Curzon story in Wendt, *Chicago Tribune,* 315. For a discussion of bureaus at this time, see Edwards, *McCormick's Tribune,* 26–27; Wendt, *Chicago Tribune,* 352.

"One hundred and fifty" *Chicago Tribune,* April 30, 1914.

132 **"filthy little Spanish steamer"** Keeley to "family."

135 **"Imperative await letters"** Ibid. In his letter, Keeley spelled Olsen as "Olson."

"I hit him on the back" Ibid. The details in this section come from this letter, with some additional background from Linn, *James Keeley,* chap. 6; and from the reports that Keeley wrote for the *Tribune,* September 4–13, 1906. It should be noted that the various tellings of this episode are inconsistent. I have pieced them together as well as I could.

"It was unofficially suggested" *Chicago Tribune,* September 4, 1906. Although there is not a byline on this story, Clifford Raymond almost surely wrote it.

137 **"an amicable kidnapping"** *Chicago Tribune,* September 4 and 6, 1906. The boss William Tweed episode is recounted at length in Denis Tilden Lynch, *"Boss" Tweed: The Story of a Grim Generation* (New York: Boni and Liveright, 1927), 398–401. A news report of Tweed's capture is in the G.E.H.H. dispatch for the *Baltimore Sun* reprinted in the *New York Times,* October 21, 1876.

"is not merely strenuous" "Raymond," *Chicago Tribune,* September 7, 1906. Edmund Morris, *Theodore Rex* (New York: Random House, 2001), 335. As it turned out, Perdicaris had given up his citizenship to avoid taxation during the Civil War, but this did not mute Roosevelt's press coverage at the time.

138 **"25 Moorish soldiers"** Keeley to "family."

Keeley milked the story *Chicago Tribune,* September 4, 5, 6, 7, 8, 9, 11, 13, 1906.

"Spanish Danseuse" *Chicago Tribune,* September 4, 1906.

"Not since James Gordon Bennett" *Chicago Tribune,* September 9, 1906.

"The pretender to the throne" *Chicago Tribune,* September 4, 1906. The five-paragraph story appeared on September 8, 1906. Keeley also was probably responsible for a ridiculously trivial story that appeared after he had left Morocco. It described the difficulties the U.S. envoy encountered getting an audience in Fez with the sultan. Not only was there a spat over whether the German minister could make the trip to Fez at the same time, but in addition the envoy seemed to have lost an ironing board for his clothes. *Chicago Tribune,* September 26, 1906. One reason to believe that this is a story by Keeley is that he recounts the details in his letter to his family.

"the greatest fugitive" *Chicago Tribune,* September 7, 1906.

139 **"The man who had sat at the banquet board"** *Chicago Tribune,* September 27, 1906; Keeley to "family"; Ramsaye, "James Keeley," 20.

"In Chicago" Ramsaye, "James Keeley," 55; Wendt, *Chicago Tribune,* 361; Linn, *James Keeley,* 143.

Keeley abruptly left Smith, *The Colonel,* 149–50; Wendt, *Chicago Tribune,* 397–406, 568.

"mainly a purveyor of gossip" Will Irwin, *The Making of a Reporter* (New York: G. P. Putnam's, 1942), 244. A discussion of the ill-preparedness of American media is found in Emery, *On the Front Lines,* chap. 1. The *Tribune* ran a story about Austro-Hungary and "the European situation" the day before the assassination. Frederic William Wile, *Chicago Tribune,* June 28, 1914. It appeared next to another front-page article headlined "KAISER DECLINES TITLE TO BRIDE"— the bride was to be the morganatic wife of Prince Oscar.

140 **"the fortunes and calamities"** Linn, *James Keeley*, 201–2; Lapham, "Hazards of New Fortune," 64.

"police reporter of Chicago in excelsis" George Seldes, *Tell the Truth and Run* (New York: Greenberg, 1953), 126.

"TWO CHICAGOANS" Wendt, *Chicago Tribune*, 424, 439. Gibbons's dispatch is recounted in full in Edward Gibbons, *Floyd Gibbons: Your Headline Hunter* (New York: Exposition Press, 1953), 63–73. Floyd Gibbons retells the story in Floyd Gibbons, *"And They Thought We Wouldn't Fight"* (New York: George H. Doran, 1918), chap. 1; the *"casus belli"* quote is on 41. Gibbons does not say he took the *Laconia* because he thought it would sink (see his memoir); his brother, Edward, and many historians have made that claim. For background linking Gibbons and Keeley, see Wendt, *Chicago Tribune*, 385.

141 **"propagand the enemy"** James Keeley, note, November 8, 1918, files of Julie Potter. Keeley, who described the note as "a scrappy record of a rather interesting week," apparently sent it to his family. George Creel mentions Keeley in his memoir *How We Advertised America* (New York: Harper, 1920), 284. Keeley did not accomplish much in the propaganda field; the end of the war cut short a major propaganda effort he was responsible for mounting.

CHAPTER 11

142 **"We have the right"** Gregor Dallas, *At the Heart of a Tiger: Clemenceau and His World, 1841–1928* (New York: Carroll and Graf, 1993), 439; Charles L. Mee Jr., *The End of Order: Versailles 1919* (New York: Dutton, 1980), 21; J. Hampden Jackson, *Clemenceau and the Third Republic* (New York: Macmillan, 1948), 164–66; Dallas, *Heart of a Tiger*, 441. A summary of Clemenceau's efforts to thwart the press can be found in Robert A. Burnett, *"L'Homme Libre—L'Homme Enchaîné:* How a Journalist Handled the Press," *Journalism Quarterly* 50 (Winter 1973): 708–15.

"The French press is irresponsible" Sisley Huddleston, *In My Time: An Observer's Record of War and Peace* (New York: Dutton, 1938), 58.

"veritable suicide" Margaret MacMillan, *Paris 1919: Six Months That Changed the World* (New York: Random House, 2001), 57; Kahn, *World of Swope*, 218.

143 **"The war had brought"** Will Irwin, *Propaganda and the News* (New York: McGraw-Hill, 1936), 206. Irwin had given thought to public relations before the war, writing a short story on the subject called *Warrior the Untamed: The Story of an Imaginative Press Agent* (New York: Doubleday, Page, 1909).

"acted as earnestly" James M. Perry, *A Bohemian Brigade: The Civil War Correspondents* (New York: Wiley, 2000), 144, 159; Thomas F. Millard, "The War Correspondent and His Future," *Scribner's*, February 1905, 243; James R. Mock, *Censorship 1917* (Princeton, N.J.: Princeton University Press, 1941), 9; Lubow, *The Reporter Who Would Be King*, 237–38.

144 **"exalt principle"** Joseph Pulitzer, "The College of Journalism," *North American Review* 178 (May 1904): 655, 657. The comment on the new school ideally doing what the *World* didn't is in Katherine C. Aman, "Education and Journalism," *Nation*, August 27, 1903, 168. For general background on journalism education and professionalization, see Dicken-Garcia, *Journalistic Standards in Nineteenth-Century America*, 8; Mott, *American Journalism*, 388–91; 405–6, 727–28; Irwin, *Making of a Reporter*, 164; W. A. Swanberg, *Pulitzer* (New York: Scribner's, 1967), 347–50, 475; Linn, *James Keeley*, 165.

"We felt it could hamper" Wilbur Forrest, *Behind the Front Page: Stories of Newspaper Stories in the Making* (New York: Appleton-Century, 1934), 106; Seldes, *Tell the Truth and Run*, 38. A longer discussion on the problems of rank for correspondents is in Emmet Crozier, *American Reporters on the Western Front, 1914–1918* (New York: Oxford University Press, 1959), 141–43; and Cedric Larson, "Censorship of Army News during the World War, 1917–1918," *Journalism Quarterly* 17 (December 1940): 313–23. James was not the only correspondent to have such exalted feelings. In the next world war, the *Times*' Harold Denny was taken prisoner and accorded status as an officer until some Italian authority decided he should be treated as a private. Denny argued that he really was a civilian: "You are acting purely arbitrarily in classifying me as private. If you must give me an arbitrary rank, it would be much more logical, because of my age and associations, to consider me a general." Harold Denny, *Behind Both Lines* (New York: Viking Press, 1942), 184.

"aid or comfort to the enemy" Mott, *American Journalism,* 623–24; James R. Mock and Cedric Larson, *Words That Won the War: The Story of the Committee on Public Information, 1917–1919* (Princeton, N.J.: Princeton University Press, 1939), 45.

"antagonize the press at every turn" Mock, *Censorship 1917,* 45; Frederick Palmer, *With My Own Eyes: A Personal Story of Battle Years* (Indianapolis: Bobbs-Merrill, 1932), 342; Nathan A. Haverstock, *Fifty Years at the Front: The Life of War Correspondent Frederick Palmer* (Washington: Brassey's, 1996), 195–97.

145 **He marched them to the American lines** Knightley, *The First Casualty,* 135.

less compliant Ibid., 123–26.

"a lie factory" Smith, *The Colonel,* 194.

affecting American troops Knightley, *The First Casualty,* 139–40.

"When in doubt—kill it!" Palmer, *With My Own Eyes,* 339; Forrest, *Behind the Front Page,* 109; Williams, *Dusk of Empire,* 147. The wine and the expense account censorship are described in Knightley, *The First Casualty,* 140–41.

146 **"It may be useful!"** Wythe Williams, *The Tiger of France: Conversations with Clemenceau* (New York: Duell, Sloan, and Pearce, 1949), 145–46; also Williams, *Dusk of Empire,* 124–25; Jean Martet, *Georges Clemenceau* (Longmans, Green, 1930), 1.

"carried the power of the press" Kahn, *World of Swope,* 139; Alfred Allan Lewis, *Man of the World* (Indianapolis: Bobbs-Merrill, 1978), 37–38.

"magnificent" Arthur Krock, *Memoirs: Sixty Years on the Firing Line* (New York: Funk and Wagnalls, 1968), 51–52; Kahn, *World of Swope,* 213–14; and Lewis, *Man of the World,* 62.

147 **"rather more drastic"** Swope to Woodrow Wilson, n.d., Swope Papers. For a description of how great powers worked behind the scenes, see MacMillan, *Paris 1919,* 53–54.

"HEARTILY DISGUSTED" Swope to Tuohy, cable, April 15, 1919, Swope Papers.

"the greatest journalistic success" James Wyman Barrett, *Joseph Pulitzer and His World* (New York: Vanguard Press, 1950), 361–62; Kahn, *World of Swope,* 223; Hohenberg, *Foreign Correspondence,* 122–23; Louis L. Snyder and Richard B. Morris, eds., *A Treasury of Great Reporting* (New York: Fireside, 1962), 311.

snappy dresser Kahn, *World of Swope,* 26.

148 **"How the hell would you know"** Lewis, *Man of the World,* 73.

151 **"We are Germans"** Burnet Hershey, "German's Meekest Hour," in *How I Got That Story,* ed. David Brown and W. Richard Bruner (New York: Dutton, 1967), 26. Hershey obviously enjoyed telling this story, for it appears in an earlier collection, Robert Spiers Benjamin, ed., *Eye Witness: By Members of the Overseas Press Club of America* (New York: Alliance, 1940), chap. 22. Although not so well known as Swope's scoop, Hershey's is remembered: Knightley, *The First Casualty,* 144–45; and Desmond, *Windows on the World,* 424–25. In a file at the NYT Archives entitled "Jamesiana" and devoted to Edwin James, it is noted that he and Swope crashed the treaty signing. This is the only mention I have seen of this. It may have been assumed at the *Times* that such a coup as this could not have been done without the great James being somehow involved.

"Members of the organization" Lewis, *Man of the World,* 74. This was not the only time when Swope monkeyed around with the pool process. Before the treaty signing ceremony, he pocketed one of the pool passes, which he denied doing until it was revealed that the correspondents wanted to give it to the highly regarded journalist Lincoln Steffens. "Well, I'll be damned!" Swope said. "That's the man I swiped it for." Lincoln Steffens, *The Autobiography of Lincoln Steffens* (1931; New York: Harcourt, Brace, 1958), 787–88.

Correspondents can become testy when one of their number breaks the rules. Perhaps the most famous case is that of Edward Kennedy's refusal to play by the rules during World War II. While in midair in a C-47 flight to Reims, where they witnessed the German surrender, Kennedy, an AP correspondent, and several of his colleagues were told they must hold the story. By his reckoning, the bargain was off when the Germans announced their surrender over a broadcast he heard on the BBC. He told American military officials he was breaking the story and did, even though he knew it would outrage competing correspondents. Subsequently asked by AP management to ask forgiveness, Kennedy quit. Kennedy tells his side of the story in Edward Kennedy, "I'd Do It Again," *Atlantic Monthly,* August 1948, 36–41.

dedicated the room to him James Boylan, *Pulitzer's School: Columbia University's School of Journalism, 1903-2003* (New York: Columbia University Press, 2003), 135, 146.

"News of disagreement" Thomas A. Bailey, *Woodrow Wilson and the Lost Peace* (Chicago: Quadrangle, 1944), 129; Williams, *Dusk of Empire,* 180; "Censorship and the Peace Conference," *New Republic,* November 16, 1918, 63.

152   **"I am not in the message business"** August Heckscher, *Woodrow Wilson* (New York: Scribner's, 1991), 284; Ray Stannard Baker, *Woodrow Wilson and World Settlement,* vol. 1 (Garden City, N.Y.: Doubleday, Page, 1922), 151.

"dismal affairs" William Allen White, *The Autobiography of William Allen White* (New York: Macmillan, 1946), 566; Swope to Wilson, n.d., Swope papers (it is unclear whether this letter was actually sent); Kahn, *World of Swope,* 190.

"No group of men can be more fully trusted" Baker, *Wilson and World Settlement,* 149–50, 116. Irwin, *Propaganda and the News,* 205–6, discusses the various interests of subnational groups. A useful discussion on secrecy and censorship during the treaty deliberations is found in E. J. Dillon, *The Inside Story of the Peace Conference* (New York: Harper, 1920), chap. 4.

Chen arranged Smith, *The Colonel,* 218–19; Wendt, *Chicago Tribune,* 441–47. These accounts differ slightly.

153   **"The Peace Treaty"** George Creel, *How We Advertised America,* 401. Creel argued for openness.

Creel committee spawned Stephen L. Vaughn, *Holding Fast the Inner Lines: Democracy, Nationalism, and the Committee on Public Information* (Chapel Hill: University of North Carolina Press, 1980); Larry Tye, *The Father of Spin: Edward L. Bernays and the Birth of Public Relations* (New York: Crown, 1998), 22; Linn, *James Keeley,* chaps. 12–13. The impact of Swope's brother is discussed in Roland Marchand, *Creating the Corporate Soul: The Rise of Public Relations and Corporate Imagery in American Big Business* (Berkeley: University of California Press, 1998), 163.

"Propaganda has become a profession" Harold D. Lasswell, *Propaganda Technique in the World War* (New York: Garland, 1972), 34.

"gives out a statement" Erika J. Fischer and Heinz-Dietrich Fischer, *American Reporter at the International Political Stage: Herbert Bayard Swope and His Pulitzer Prize-winning Articles from Germany in 1916* (Bochum, Germany: Studienverlag Dr. N. Brockmeyer, 1982), 233.

154   **"The great corporations have them"** Cobb's talk is printed in Frank I. Cobb, "The Press and Public Opinion," *New Republic,* December 31, 1919, 144.

"the star turn" Lewis, *Man of the World,* 72; Harold Nicolson, *Diplomacy* (London: Oxford University Press, 1950), 168–69.

"We use the latest technology" Robert Hodierne, ArmyTimes.com, March 8, 2003; *USA Today,* March 10, 2003; Peter Weitzel, "A Zeal for Secrecy," reprint from *American Editor,* by the John S. and James L. Knight Foundation, n.d., 4.

"Certain experiences with the propaganda machine" Ronald Steel, *Walter Lippmann and the American Century* (New York: Vintage, 1980), 171; Walter Lippmann, *The Phantom Public* (Macmillan, 1927; New Brunswick, N.J.: Transaction 1999), 3.

"The world crisis" Williams, *The Tiger,* 221, 228; Jackson, *Clemenceau,* 249.

CHAPTER 12

156 **four-newspaper A-list** Carroll Binder, "The Role of the Foreign Correspondent in the Shaping of American Foreign Policy," 12, unpublished manuscript, n.d., Binder Papers (although the manuscript has no date, Binder's son David Binder, in an e-mail to the author, September 21, 2004, estimated that it was written in July 1941). The contemporary A-list is from Donald R. Shanor, *News from Abroad* (New York: Columbia University Press, 2003), 34.

For other background, see Hohenberg, *Foreign Correspondence,* 138–46, 151–52; Oswald Garrison Villard, *The Disappearing Daily: Some Chapters in American Newspaper Evolution* (New York: Knopf, 1944), 110; Kluger, *The Paper,* 233–37, 291–305, 361, 574, 633–35; Erwin D. Canham, *Commitment to Freedom: The Story of the Christian Science Monitor* (Boston: Houghton Mifflin, 1958), xxii, 14–15, 38–40, 121–22; Berger, *Story of the New York Times,* 249, which mentions the Ochs-James conversation and James's plan for expansion. Unfortunately, I could not find the plan in the *New York Times* Archives.

For a good discussion of the *Monitor*'s approach to news, see the comments of one of its correspondents during the interwar years, Sisley Huddleston, in *In My Time,* 175–82. I can attest to the strengths and weaknesses of the *Monitor,* having contributed regularly to the newspaper during part of my career—including writing a French travel story sans any mention of wine for the *Monitor*'s short-lived magazine, *World Monitor.* Stuart Loory, the last correspondent for the *Herald Tribune* in Moscow, recalls that the *Monitor* bought his Moscow assets. Loory, interview by author, January 13, 2005.

157 **"Our men"** Edward Price Bell to Victor Lawson, May 11, 1924, Bell Papers. For a comment on Lawson's pioneering syndicate, see Richard A. Schwarzlose, *The Nation's Newsbrokers,* vol. 2, *The Rush to Institution, from 1865 to 1920* (Evanston, Ill.: Northwestern University Press, 1990), 189. Desmond notes, "However perceptive other U.S. newspaper publishers may have been in 1898–1900, none matched Lawson in purposeful extension of foreign coverage until 1908 and later." Desmond, *Windows on the World,* 129.

"bobby sox on the Madonna" See Charles Whited, *Knight: A Publisher in the Tumultuous Century* (New York: Dutton, 1988), 122, for the "bobby sox" quote, and see Whited's chap. 10 for description of the purchase and changeover. The attribution of the "bobby sox" quote to Mowrer is in David M. Nichol to author, November 15, 1990.

"probably the strangest newspaper" Robert J. Casey, *Such Interesting People* (Garden City, N.Y.: Garden City, 1945), 162 and, for background, all of chap. 14. The "leprechaun" description of Casey is in the *Daily News* final edition, March 4, 1978; and in Quentin Reynolds, *By Quentin Reynolds* (New York: Pyramid Books, 1964), 179. Casey's other newsroom memoir is *More Interesting People* (Indianapolis: Bobbs-Merrill, 1947). The founding date of the *Daily News* is debated. A prototype appeared in December 1875; the first continuous issue was January 1, 1876.

158 **"not only the only paper"** Casey, *Such Interesting People,* 163.

"the newspaper as a daily novel" Ben Hecht, *A Child of the Century* (New York: Simon and Schuster, 1954), 208, 249–50; Ray Stannard Baker, *Native American: The Book of My Youth* (New York: Scribner's, 1941), 268; Mott, *American Journalism,* 465; Emery and Emery, *The Press and America,* 539; W. A. Swanberg, *Luce and His Empire* (New York: Scribner's, 1972), 48. The Henry Justin Smith quote is from the frontispiece of his *Deadlines: Being the Quaint, the Amusing, the Tragic Memoirs of a News-Room* (Chicago: Covici-McGee, 1923). His other book is *Josslyn: The Story of an Incorrigible Dreamer* (Chicago: Covici-McGee, 1924).

Victor Fremont Lawson Jason Rogers, *Newspaper Building: Application of Efficiency to Editing, to Mechanical Production, to Circulation and Advertising* (New York: Harper, 1918), chaps. 1 and 2; Benedict Karl Zobrist, "How the Chicago Daily News Covers the War," *Editor and Publisher,* September 2, 1916, 5–7. Melville Stone describes the early philosophy and history of the *Daily News* in his memoir, *Fifty Years a Journalist* (Garden City, N.Y.: Doubleday, Page, 1921). On

65–71 he also recounts the extraordinary tale of Ross Raymond. Equally useful is the biography of Lawson by his long-time managing editor: Charles Dennis, *Victor Lawson: His Time and His Work* (Chicago: University of Chicago Press, 1935). Also see Lawson's obituary, *Chicago Daily News,* August 20, 1925; and the recollections of two correspondents: Mowrer, *House of Europe,* 525; and Frederic William Wile, *News Is Where You Find It: Forty Years' Reporting at Home and Abroad* (Indianapolis, Ind.: Bobbs-Merrill, 1939), 70. Lawson's brilliance at the newspaper business is discussed in Donald J. Abramoske, "The *Chicago Daily News:* A Business History, 1875–1901" (Ph.D. diss., University of Chicago, 1963).

159 **"All our fine theories"** Stone, *Fifty Years a Journalist,* 77. The brilliance of *Chicago Daily News* photography is memorialized in a magnificent volume, Mark Jacob and Richard Cahan, *Chicago under Glass: Early Photographs from the Chicago Daily News* (Chicago: University of Chicago Press, 2007).

"the silly so-called 'human-interest stories'" Stone, *Fifty Years a Journalist,* 77; Benedict Karl Zobrist, "How Victor Lawson's Newspapers Covered the Cuban War of 1898," *Journalism Quarterly* 38 (Summer 1961): 325; Victor Lawson to Charles Faye, cable, April 2, 1898, Bell Papers.

160 **"to articulate a vision of public community"** David Paul Nord, *Communities of Journalism: A History of American Newspapers and Their Readers* (Urbana: University of Illinois Press, 2001), 109; David Paul Nord, *Newspapers and New Politics: Midwestern Municipal Reform, 1890–1900* (Ann Arbor, Mich.: University Microfilms International, 1979), 29–30, 64–65.

"I note your miserable failure" Victor Lawson to Charles Faye, September 7, 1898, Lawson Papers; Rogers, *Newspaper Building,* 17; Jacob and Cahan, *Chicago under Glass,* 11.

for a recommendation Lawson's letter of recommendation for Ochs, which is far from ringing, is in Lawson to Spencer Trask, the head of the committee trying to arrange a sale of the newspaper, April 8, 1896, NYT Archives. It reads, "He impresses me as a man who has a talent for hard work, and in the newspaper business hard work counts rather more than genius, although I do not mean to suggest that Mr. Ochs may not also possess qualities of the latter sort—I do not know him well enough to speak on that point."

Ross Raymond Dennis, *Lawson,* 57–59; Stone, *Fifty Years a Journalist,* 65–71.

161 **"send all men possible"** Zobrist, "How Victor Lawson's Newspapers Covered the Spanish-American War of 1898," 329; Dennis, *Lawson,* chap. 15; Desmond, *Windows on the World,* 110–11; Lawson to Charles Dennis and Charles Faye, April 26, 1898, Bell Papers; Brown, *The Correspondents' War,* 131.

permanent foreign service No complete published study has been made of the *Chicago Daily News* foreign news coverage, although several books have chronicled aspects of it: Dennis, *Lawson,* chap. 16, which includes Lawson's quoted rationale for starting it (264); *Editor and Publisher,* September 2, 1916, 5–7; James D. Startt, *Journalism's Unofficial Ambassador: A Biography of Edward Price Bell, 1869–1943* (Athens: Ohio University Press, 1979), 21–22; Wile, *News Is Where You Find It,* 65–71. A useful unpublished study of the early years of the service is in Benedict Karl Zobrist, "Edward Price Bell and the Development of the Foreign News Service of the Chicago *Daily News*" (Ph.D. diss., Northwestern University, 1953). Melville E. Stone describes how he began to build the AP's foreign service in "The Associated Press," *Century Magazine,* April 1905, 888–97.

"largely an experiment" Victor Lawson to Theodore Stanton, August 8, 1898, Lawson Papers. Background on Lawson's thought of cooperating with the *New York Times* is found in Lawson to Adolph Ochs, August 8, 14, 1899; January 4, 1902; and in Ochs to Lawson, January 7, 1902, all in NYT Archives.

ever-changing instructions Victor Lawson to Theodore Stanton, July 22, 1898; January 26, 1899; and January 13, 1900, Lawson Papers.

162 **"whom we especially engaged and trained"** Victor Lawson to Dexter Marshall, November 17, 1900, Lawson Papers.

"judge news" Victor Lawson to William J. Tucker, April 21, 1899, Lawson Papers. David Binder pointed me to the fact that the *New York Times* for many years favored foreigners for correspondents. David Binder, interview by author, August 2, 2004. Williams, *Dusk of Empire,* 8.

international and provincial Robert G. Spinney, *City of Big Shoulders: A History of Chicago* (DeKalb: Northern Illinois University Press, 2000), chap. 7; Eric Larson, *The Devil in the White City: Murder, Magic, and Madness at the Fair That Changed America* (New York: Vintage, 2003), 11, 14, 121, 209; Norma Green, Stephen Lacy, and Jean Folkerts, "Chicago Journalists at the Turn of the Century: Bohemians All?" *Journalism Quarterly* 66 (Winter 1989): 813–21; Denis B. Downey, *A Season of Renewal: The Columbia Exposition and Victorian America* (Westport, Conn.: Praeger, 2002), 8, 10; John E. Findling, *Chicago's Great World's Fairs* (Manchester, UK: Manchester University Press, 1994), 6–7.

163 **"FLY INDIA"** Edmund Taylor, *Awakening from History* (Boston: Gambit, 1969), 101; Wendt, *Chicago Tribune,* 298, 474, 517–18; Smith, *The Colonel,* 252, 303, 443–44; Edwards, *McCormick's Tribune,* 26–39, 44, 69, 138, 214.

"You must always 'write down'" Powell, *My Twenty-five Years in China,* 320–24. Emery and Emery, *The Press and America,* 313, which says that the four great foreign services in the 1930s were the *Daily News,* the *New York Times,* the *Herald Tribune,* and the *Chicago Tribune,* the latter in place of the *Monitor.* Robert W. Desmond, *The Press and World Affairs,* 301, had all five papers on his list.

"was out of place" Ben Hecht, *Gaily, Gaily* (Garden City, N.Y.: Doubleday, 1963), 6.

"who would be glad to get news from home" Abramoske, "The *Chicago Daily News*." For background on Charles R. Crane, a most interesting man deserving a full-fledged biography, see David Hapgood, *Charles R. Crane: The Man Who Bet on People* (Self-published, 2000), 26, 66–69, 86, 92; and "The Life and Letters of Charles R. Crane," ed. Edgar Snow, typescript, n.d., in possession of author. Another version of this manuscript can be found in the Hoover Institution Archives, Stanford University; it contains the comment on Lawson as "a valued friend," on 147. On Lawson's relations with the Exposition, see Dennis, *Lawson,* 160–61.

164 **"it was the duty"** Minutes, Chicago Council on Foreign Relations, February 20, 1922, files of Chicago Council on Global Affairs, as the organization has been renamed, Chicago, Ill. The new council president who was told not to expect invitations from *Tribune* staffers was John Rielly. John Rielly, interview by my research assistant Emily Metzger, September 17, 2004. Also see Garrick Utley to Emily Metzger, e-mail, October 4, 2004; David Binder, interview by author, August 2, 2004; *60 Years of International Understanding: The Chicago Council on Foreign Relations, 1922–1982* (Chicago: Council on Foreign Relations, n.d.); Clifford Utley obituary, January 20, 1978, *Chicago Daily News; RCA News* article from September 1931, reprinted at www.richsamuels.com/nbcmm/wmaq. The call letters WMAQ came to stand for "We Must Ask Questions," which is much more modest than the call letters that McCormick used for his broadcast operation, WGN—"World's Greatest Newspaper."

eccentric Startt, *Unofficial Ambassador,* 27; Casey, *Such Interesting People,* 188–89.

"Young-Man-Going-Somewhere" Smith, *Deadlines,* 71–72.

165 **"trying to perfect a style"** Henry Justin Smith, *"It's the Way It's Written" and "Writing Versus—Everything Else"* (Chicago: Chicago Daily News Reprints, 1923), 18. This reprint includes two addresses Smith delivered to the Medill School of Journalism, Northwestern University. Journalists everywhere would benefit from hearing this speech today.

"A fellow goes to Europe" Mowrer, *House of Europe,* 129–30; part 2 of his book provides good background on Mowrer's early years.

$122,155.79 Victor Lawson to A. H. Belo Messrs., February 9, 1900, Lawson Papers.

"Queer Sprigs of Gentility" The "Queer Sprigs" promotion can be found in Lawson to Edgar W. Coleman, December 22, 1898, Lawson Papers. Discussion of the paper in these early years is in Mowrer, *House of Europe,* 115, 135–37, 157, 221–22, 348; Paul Scott Mowrer to Edward Price Bell, September 21, 1911; March 9, 1909; September 5, 1910; August 4, 1914; Bell to Charles Dennis, May 26, 1901, all in Bell Papers; Edward Price Bell, *Journalism of the Highest Realm: The Memoir of*

Edward Price Bell, ed. Jaci Cole and John Maxwell Hamilton (Baton Rouge: Louisiana State University Press, 2007), 117–20; Mathews, *Smalley,* 67–68; Startt, *Unofficial Ambassador,* 40; Edgar Ansel Mowrer, *Triumph and Turmoil: A Personal History of Our Time* (New York: Weybright and Talley, 1968), 166; *Chicago Daily News,* March 23, 1927.

"responsive thrill in the minds" Charles Dennis to E. P. Bell, July 8, 26, 1901, Bell Papers.

166 **"Please remember"** Victor Lawson to Edward Price Bell, February 16, 1909, Bell Papers; Bell, *Journalism of the Highest Realm,* 119.

167 **"did not care a hoot"** Raymond Swing, *"Good Evening! A Professional Memoir* (New York: Harcourt, Brace, 1964), 37; Frederic William Wile to Edward Price Bell, January 31, 1906, Bell Papers.

took on more gravity The study on which this is based is Jaci Cole and John Maxwell Hamilton, "A Natural History of Foreign Correspondence: A Study of the *Chicago Daily News,* 1900–1921," *Journalism and Mass Communication Quarterly* 84 (Spring 2007): 151–66.

168 **"harvest was at hand"** Dennis, *Lawson,* 276, 352.

"at the places of impact" Ibid., 273–74; Eunice Tietjens, *The World at My Shoulder* (New York: Macmillan, 1938), 140–58. The quote on Czarnecki is from a promotional piece in the *Daily News* about its correspondents, December 31, 1915, which includes a rundown on many of the *Daily News* correspondents. The number of correspondents is from "List of American Correspondents Accredited to the American Commission to Negotiate Peace," n.d., Swope Papers; the *Chicago Tribune* also had seven, perhaps a sign of competitiveness. See also Mowrer, *House of Europe,* 245–52, 338–39; Zobrist, "Edward Price Bell," 236.

"GERMAN BOLSHEVIK REVOLUTION" Heald, *Transatlantic Vistas,* 244.

"considerably exceed $200,000" Victor Lawson to Edward Price Bell, July 21, 1916; August 9, 1918, Bell Papers; Startt, *Unofficial Ambassador,* xii; Zobrist, "Edward Price Bell," 270; Zobrist, "How the Chicago Daily News Covers the War," 5–7. The statistic on the average number of foreign stories in 1921 is from Cole and Hamilton, "A Natural History of Foreign Correspondence," 155.

169 **"dumped into a great strange city"** Paul Scott Mowrer to Edward Price Bell, June 4, 8, 1910, Bell Papers.

"Although it made me feel inferior" Mowrer, *House of Europe,* 140, 147, 270.

170 **foray into serious reporting** Ibid., 202–3, 349.

"small, weak, jealous" Paul Scott Mowrer, *Balkanized Europe: A Study in Political Analysis and Reconstruction* (New York: Dutton, 1921), 3. For details on this book and Mowrer's accomplishments during the 1920s, see Mowrer, *House of Europe,* 320, 349, 390, 419, 423, 431; Heald, *Transatlantic Vistas,* 54.

Did Mowrer coin the term "Balkanization"? Citing a 1922 comment by British historian Arnold J. Toynbee, William Safire, in the *New York Times,* April 21, 1991, attributed the term to German socialists describing "what was done to the western fringe of the Russian Empire by the Peace of Brest-Litovsk." Mowrer's book appeared the year before.

"I have visited the unknown Riff" Paul Scott Mowrer, *Chicago Daily News,* November 11, 1924.

171 **"dark zeal"** Recollections of Mowrer appeared in two separate prefaces, by Carl Sandburg and by Donald Colors Peat, to Paul Scott Mowrer, *Poems between Wars* (Chicago: Louis Mariano, 1941), v, ix; Alice Hunt Sokoloff, *Hadley: The First Mrs. Hemingway* (New York: Dodd, Mead, 1973), 96; Gioia Diliberto, *Hadley* (New York: Ticknor and Fields, 1992), 272.

"the newest of the great public professions" Heald, *Transatlantic Vistas,* 253; Mowrer to Bell, February 19, 1913, Bell Papers; Mowrer, *House of Europe,* 345–47.

"the greatest correspondent" Casey, *Such Interesting People,* 288; Paul Scott Mowrer, "Report on American Press Situation," in Mowrer to Charles Dennis, October 3, 1917, Bell Papers. Wood deserves more attention than he gets in the annals of foreign correspondence. A revealing and endearing example of Wood's independence while in Russia, where he wrote highly critical reports, is in Mowrer, *Triumph and Turmoil,* 170; Zobrist, "Edward Price Bell," 236.

172 **"If public opinion"** Paul Scott Mowrer, "Suggestions for Reorganizing the Foreign Service," May 6, 1920, Bell Papers.

"Edgar and Paul" Lilian T. Mowrer, *Journalist's Wife* (New York: William Morrow, 1937), 118–19. Edgar Mowrer's daughter, Diana Beliart, offers similar recollections. Diana Beliart, interview by author, June 2, 2004.

"The Reorganization of the British Empire" Mowrer, *House of Europe,* 566. Mowrer describes his ideas for this column in an undated draft letter to Charles Dennis, a copy of which is in the Bell Papers.

"most closely approximate the ideals" Charles P. Cooper to Nicholas Murray Butler, March 15, 1929; W. P. Beazell to Butler, March 16, 1929; A. H. Kirchhofer to Cooper, March 12, 1929, all in the files of the Office of the Administrator, The Pulitzer Prizes, Columbia University. The creation of the current single international category is outlined in "Confidential Report of the A.S.N.E. Jury on International Telegraphic Reporting Nominations for 1947 Pulitzer Prizes in Journalism for Work done in 1946," March 12, 1947, Pulitzer Prize files; and in Bud Kliment, deputy administrator, Pulitzer Prizes, to author, June 16, 2004. One of the signers of the "Confidential Report" was Carroll Binder. For a sampling of Pulitzer Prize–winning reporting, see the five-volume series of books edited by Heinz-Dietrich Fischer, *Outstanding International Press Reporting: Pulitzer Prize Articles in Foreign Correspondence* (New York: Walter de Gruyter, 1984–2000).

175 **the machinery of diplomacy** Creelman, *On the Great Highway,* chap. 18. Smalley's diplomacy can be found in Mathews, *Smalley,* chap. 10. Scali's involvement is documented in Aleksandr Fursenko and Timothy Naftali, *"One Hell of a Gamble": Khrushchev, Castro, and Kennedy, 1958–1964* (New York: W. W. Norton, 1997); Dino A. Brugioni, *Eyeball to Eyeball: The Inside Story of the Cuban Missile Crisis* (New York: Random House, 1991); Debra Gersh Hernandez, "An 'Accident' of History Remembered," *Editor and Publisher,* November 19, 1994.

Scali was not the only journalist involved. Warren Rogers of the *New York Herald Tribune* was too, although in a less direct way. A KGB informant who worked as a bartender at the National Press Club reported Rogers's off-hand comment that President Kennedy's military threats were to be taken seriously. Upon getting this report, the Soviets arranged for someone else to have a "casual" conversation with Rogers to confirm his view, which was then passed all the way to Khrushchev.

On Koppel's diplomacy see Jonathan Alter, "America's Q & A Man," *Newsweek,* June 15, 1987, 50–53, 55–56. On Friedman's diplomacy, see John Bebow, "Journalist or Diplomat?" *American Journalism Review,* April 2002, 10–11. The literature on media diplomacy has become extensive. A summary of the various types of media diplomacy is found in Eytan Gilboa, "Global Communication and Foreign Policy," *Journal of Communication* 52 (December 2002): 731–48.

176 **"The right kind of foreign correspondent"** Dennis, *Lawson,* 273; Desmond, *Windows on the World,* 108–9; Constantine Brown to Charles Dennis, January 10, 1927, Dennis Papers. Brown previously worked for the *Times* (London). He was hired on the suggestion of James Keeley. Dennis noted in a letter to Paul Mowrer that Brown "had been of very great service to the American government" while in Constantinople. Dennis to Mowrer, December 27, 1923, Dennis Papers.

"More than any other writer of his time" Startt, *Unofficial Ambassador,* 91; Jaci Cole and John Maxwell Hamilton, introduction to Bell, *Journalism of the Highest Realm,* xxx.

"If the reader thinks" Victor Lawson to Edward Price Bell, July 9, 1915, Bell Papers; Startt, *Unofficial Ambassador,* 79, 91, 99, 159–60. The *Daily News* published Bell's interviews in Edward Price Bell, *World Chancelleries* (Chicago: Chicago Daily News, 1926), with an introduction by Calvin Coolidge; and in Edward Price Bell, *Europe's Economic Sunrise* (Chicago: Chicago Daily News, 1927), with an introduction by Charles Gates Dawes.

177 **diplomatic roles** Swing, *Good Evening!* chaps. 16 and 23; Mowrer, *Triumph and Turmoil,* chaps. 29–30; Dixon Wecter, "Hearing Is Believing," *Atlantic Monthly,* July 1945, 39; Carroll Binder, "The Shadow of Global Censorship," *Saturday Review of Literature,* March 24, 1951, 8–9; and Carroll Binder, "Draft Convention on Freedom of Information," *Vital Speeches of the Day,* March 1, 1951,

310–12. Information on Binder is from his entry in *Current Biography: 1951* (New York: H. W. Wilson, 1952), 39–41. Richard Mowrer, interview by author, June 28, 2004; David Binder, interview by author, August 2, 2004.

Edgar Mowrer had a far more volatile, argumentative personality than his brother. The different Mowrer temperaments are described in George A. Brandenburg, "Chicago's Mowrer Trio Has Gained Journalistic Distinction," *Editor and Publisher,* October 9, 1943, 13.

178 **Paul Ghali** Ghali obituaries are in the *Chicago Daily News* and the *New York Times,* June 4, 1970. For background on the Ciano diaries, see Ray Moseley, *Mussolini's Shadow: The Double Life of Count Galeazzo Ciano* (New Haven, Conn.: Yale University Press, 1999), 248–51; James H. Walters, *Scoop: How the Ciano Diary Was Smuggled from Rome to Chicago Where It Made Worldwide News* (Self-published, 2006).

"never forgets his country" Dennis, *Lawson,* 273. The reparation proposal is discussed in Heald, *Transatlantic Vistas,* 101.

Our Foreign Affairs Mowrer, *Our Foreign Affairs,* 8, 61, 78, 212, 307, 344–45; Heald, *Transatlantic Vistas,* 207.

"See that glint!" Arthur Conan Doyle, *When the World Screamed and Other Stories* (San Francisco: Chronicle Books, 1990), 14; Villard, *Disappearing Daily,* 145–46; Startt, *Unofficial Ambassador,* 127; Mowrer, *House of Europe,* 533.

179 **"a journalist panjandrum"** "Mr. Mowrer Remembers," *Time,* September 24, 1945, 62; Smith, "'It's the Way It's Written' and 'Writing Versus—Everything Else,'" 18–19; Paul Scott Mowrer, "The Press and the Public," in *The Educational Role of the Press* (Paris: International Institute of Intellectual Co-Operation, 1934).

"There are more romances" Jacob and Cahan, *Chicago under Glass,* 11.

"the attached cable" For an example of the form letter, see communication of Edward Price Bell to Charles Dennis, n.d., Bell papers. This story, about a Swedish professor who was charged with falsifying railway tickets, clearly did not deserve to be cabled. Many examples of complaints by correspondents and their bosses can be found in the Newberry Library collections related to the *Chicago Daily News.* Examples include Dennis to Bell, February 6, 1918; Paul Scott Mowrer to Dennis, August 21, 1918; Mowrer to Bell, February 28, 1922; Bell to Dennis, March 8, 1922, all in Bell Papers.

On the comparative costs of cabling, salaries were $19,235.00 in 1899, and payments for work, which were paid on a space basis, came to $10,184.18—a total of $29,419.18. Cable costs were $66,492.41. Victor Lawson to A. H. Belo Messrs., February 9, 1900, Lawson Papers.

excluding "stop" Junius Wood to Edward Price Bell, March 15, 1917; Bell to Charles Dennis, February 26, April 1, 1918, all Bell Papers.

180 **"I had a single room"** Junius Wood, "Memo to Mr. Dennis," February 23, 1922; Charles Dennis to Victor Lawson, February 15, 1922, both in Lawson Papers.

"Mr. Lawson's efficiency man" Charles Dennis to Paul Scott Mowrer, March 12, 1924, Dennis Papers; Mowrer to Victor Lawson, May 15, 31, 1924; and Edward Price Bell to Lawson, May 11, 1924, all in Bell Papers. In his resignation letter, Mowrer said Rogers was only part of the reason for quitting, but in his memoirs he puts the blame entirely on Rogers. Mowrer, *House of Europe,* 438–39.

"Mr. Lawson's last order" Paul Scott Mowrer to Edward Price Bell, April 15, 1920, Bell Papers; Charles Dennis to Mowrer, October 29, 1923, Daily News Records; Heald, *Transatlantic Vistas,* 102.

"the man on the spot is always right" Mowrer, *Triumph and Turmoil,* 176. Edgar Ansel Mowrer also commented on being left alone by *Daily News* editors in a speech he gave at the University of Michigan, April 10, 1969, E. Mowrer Papers, Newberry. For a similar expression, see Mowrer, *House of Europe,* 525; and Diana Beilard, Edgar Mowrer's daughter, interview by author, June 2, 2004. Bell's statement on Lawson's genius is in Startt, *Unofficial Ambassador,* 168–69.

181 **"My deep conviction"** Edward Price Bell to Walter A. Strong, memorandum, December 26, 1925, Dennis Papers; Mowrer, *House of Europe*, 525–26.

"despite the fact" "The Chicago Daily News, Inc.," Edwin G. Booze Surveys, 1926, n.p., Lawson Papers. This report provides a practical inside look at the *Daily News*. See also Dennis, *Lawson*, 453–59; "Service," *Chicago Daily News*, June 10, 1929 (an editorial that describes the new building and the *Daily News* tradition); Walter A. Strong, "General Memorandum," May 7, 1926, Dennis Papers, in which he calls "attention to the keynote of this memorandum which is—*ECONOMY*." In a cable to Adolph Ochs, Strong says he owns 60% of the *Daily News*, that 16% is owned by associates at the newspaper, and that the balance is owned by prominent Chicagoans. Strong to Ochs, May 10, 1929, NYT Archives. Lawson's wife was the cousin of Walter Strong's father. David Strong to author, e-mail, August 6, 2007.

"The Chicago Daily News" This part of Strong's will is found in a document that does an excellent job of describing the financial transactions involved in this and later purchases of the newspaper. It is written by a Chicago banker who was a classmate of Strong and involved in sales to Frank Knox and John Knight: Holman D. Pettibone, "The Chicago Daily News—For Sale," 3, unpublished manuscript, Daily News Records. Also see a description of Strong's will in a "Confidential" memorandum written by Paul Scott Mowrer, June 16, 1931, Binder Papers; *New York Times*, August 13, 1931, had a news story and an editorial, whence the quotes; editorial in *Daily News*, August 12, 1931. The financial situation of the *Daily News* at the time of Knox's purchase is discussed in Norman Beasley, *Frank Knox: American: A Short Biography* (Garden City, N.Y.: Doubleday, Doran, 1936), chap. 11.

182 **"I should like to have word"** John Gunther to Carroll Binder, June 11, 1931, Gunther Papers; Mowrer, *House of Europe*, 594–95; Startt, *Unofficial Ambassador*, 161–62; Constantine Brown, *The Coming of the Whirlwind* (Chicago: Henry Regnery, 1962), chap. 20. A discussion of Depression cutbacks is in Paul Scott Mowrer to Binder, February 12, 1931, Binder Papers. Lawson's claim about not voting in primaries is in Robert Lloyd Tree, "Victor Fremont Lawson and His Newspapers, 1890–1900: A Study of the Chicago *Daily News* and the Chicago *Record*" (Ph.D. diss., Northwestern University, 1959), 308.

limited to the battlefield Villard, *Disappearing Daily*, 138; Frank Knox to Edward Price Bell, December 18, 1931, Bell Papers.

"to deflect me" On Bell's final years at the *Daily News*, see Knox to Bell, September 29, 1931, Bell Papers; Mowrer, *House of Europe*, 595; Startt, *Unofficial Ambassador*, 160–67; Beasley, *Frank Knox*, 134–35. Bell quickly passes over his departure from the *Daily News* in his memoir, saying it was a function "of a new management with notions and purposes of its own"; for several oblique references that he made to pressure from Knox, see Bell, *Journalism of the Highest Realm*, 152, 309, 323.

183 **"Bell's attitude"** Startt, *Unofficial Ambassador*, 165.

"an almost fanatical stickler for accuracy" Mowrer's passion for accuracy is in Brown, *The Coming of the Whirlwind*, 213. Also see, on this period and on Knox generally, Mowrer, *House of Europe*, 595, 607, 624–27; Mowrer, *Triumph and Turmoil*, 224, 234, 264, 275; Raymond Gram Swing, "Knox—Publisher into Candidate," *Nation*, February 19, 1936, 219.

impose "his will" John Whitaker to Leland Stowe, April 12, 1939, Stowe Papers. Almost reverential examples of *Daily News* correspondents' positive feelings about Binder and the support he gave reporters are reflected in interviews for Stacy M. Powell, "The Chicago Daily News Foreign Service during World War Two and the Men Who Made It Great" (honors thesis, University of Michigan, 1984). For an example of Binder's internationalism, see "The United States in a War Minded World," *Annals of the American Academy of Political and Social Science* 192 (July 1937): 42–50; and "Since September 1, 1939," *Survey Graphic*, November 1941, 560–63, both by Binder. Binder wrote a spirited and memorable critique of bias in the distribution of Pulitzer Prizes, concentrating especially on foreign reporting: "The Press and the Pulitzer Prizes," *Amer-*

ican Mercury, April 1948, 462–71. His criticism attracted considerable press attention at the time.

"Just as soon as I know a deal" Frank Knox to Annie Reid Knox, July 18, 1931, Knox Papers.

184 **"easily among the first half-dozen"** Frank Knox to wife, July 18, 1931, Knox Papers; Villard, *Disappearing Daily,* 146. Mowrer's Republican voting is from Richard Mowrer, his son, interview by author, November 3, 2004.

"our chief competitor" Frank Knox to John Gunther, November 11, 1931; Paul Scott Mowrer to Knox, April 30, 1942, both in Knox Papers; Edwards, *McCormick's Tribune,* 202; Wendt, *Chicago Tribune,* 580–81; Donald A. Ritchie, *Reporting from Washington: The History of the Washington Press Corps* (New York: Oxford University Press, 2005), 22. For examples of the *Daily News* cartoons that drew attention to mounting international problems in the years leading up to World War II, see Vaughn Shoemaker, *1940 A.D: Cartoons by Vaughn Shoemaker* (Chicago: Chicago Daily News, 1941).

185 **"delighted to be a member"** Leland Stowe, "Memo regarding—L.S. 'Too Old to Cover a War,'" February 17, 1975, Stowe Papers; Quentin Reynolds, *Only the Stars Are Neutral* (New York: Random House, 1942), 187; Leland Stowe, *No Other Road to Freedom* (New York: Knopf, 1941), 5.

Holman Pettibone took the view that Knox's Washington appointment "required considerable sacrifice of the independence, quality, and operating results of the News." Pettibone, "The Chicago Daily News—For Sale," 10. For an example of the pride the newspaper continued to take in its foreign service, see the fortieth- and sixtieth-anniversary issues, the former on December 31, 1915, and the latter with no date, early March 1935.

It was widely reported that Stowe was denied an overseas post because the editor said he was too old for the assignment, even though he was only thirty-nine. As his memorandum on the subject notes, the real reason is more complicated. The editor who denied him the assignment was Wilbur Forrest, with whom he had tangled in the past. Among other points of contention was a scoop that Stowe got in Paris at the expense of his colleague. In any event, the *Herald-Tribune* owner, Helen Reid, did not think Stowe was too old, and she intervened. She pleaded with him to take back his resignation, but by that time he had committed to the *Daily News.*

"I want to congratulate you" Frank Knox to Carroll Binder, December 4, 1943, Binder Papers.

"IN MY ANNOUNCEMENT" Stephen Becker, *Marshall Field III* (New York: Simon and Schuster, 1964), 391–93; "Knight Acquires Control of Chicago Daily News," *Editor and Publisher,* October 21, 1944, 5, 62; Smith, *The Colonel,* 460; Whited, *Knight,* chap. 10, for description of the purchase and changeover. The cable is Carroll Binder to Richard Mowrer, October 19, 1944; for the speed with which people departed, see two other cables from Binder to foreign service staffers, October 21, 1944, and November 7, 1944, files of Richard Mowrer. The Mowrer quote on incompatibility with Knight is in Paul Scott Mowrer to Ted Thackrey, December 3, 1944, Schiff Papers.

"It seemed to us" The comments from Binder's wife are in an undated eulogy provided by Binder's son. The Hutchins quote is in "Cancelled Check," *Time,* June 2, 1961, 51.

186 **"fully and intelligently"** William Stoneman to Carroll Binder, January 17, 1945; May 19, 1946, Binder Papers.

"So, mighty Casey went under" M. W. Newman, "Adieu, Adieu, Kind Friends, Adieu," *Chicago Daily News, Panorama,* March 4, 1978, 2. Basil Walters and Binder are described in Bradley L. Morison, *Sunlight on Your Doorstep: The Minneapolis Tribune's First Hundred Years, 1867–1967* (Minneapolis: Ross and Haines, 1966), 66–67, 76–77, 99–100. On the *New York Post* and its recruitment of *Daily News* staff, see Marilyn Nissenson, *The Lady Upstairs: Dorothy Schiff and the New York Post* (New York: St. Martin's Press, 2007), 70–77; Julia Edwards, *Women of the World: The Great Foreign Correspondents* (Boston: Houghton Mifflin, 1988), 113–14. Also Edgar Ansel Mowrer to Paul Scott Mowrer, October 28, 1922; Edgar Mowrer to Helen Kirkpatrick, cable, December 2, 1944, E. Mowrer Papers, LOC. A discussion of Cowles's use of the *Daily News* foreign service is in a two-part article that provides a good portrait of John Knight at the time of the sale: Kenneth Stewart, *PM,* October 29, November 5, 1944. Walters is described in these articles as a "promotion expert and stunt man," although the thrust is generally favorable to Knight.

187 **"He booted out most of the foreign service"** Casey, *More Interesting People,* 51; William Stone-man to Carroll Binder, September 12, 1955, Binder Papers; Georgie Anne Geyer, *Buying the Night Flight: The Autobiography of a Woman Foreign Correspondent* (New York: Delacorte Press, 1983), 39–48; Donald R. Shanor, "CDN: What We'll Miss about the Chicago Daily News," *Columbia Journalism Review,* May–June 1978, 35–37. The Tokyo correspondent was Ernie Hill, writing in *The Foreign Correspondent: His Problems in Covering the News Abroad* (Iowa City: State University of Iowa, 1954), 27.

"editors, copyreaders" Edward Price Bell to Victor Lawson, February 6, 1915, Bell Papers. Walters is quoted in "The Editor and His Foreign Correspondent," *I.P.I Report,* March 1953, 5. His dispute with Sevareid is mentioned in Basil L. Walters to Ralph Casey, January 13, 1954; and Casey to Eric Sevareid, January 21, 1954, Sevareid Papers. The statistics on subscribers to the *Daily News* foreign service and the comparative amount of news is in International Press Institute, *The Flow of the News: A Study* (Zurich: International Press Institute, 1953), 18, 219–21.

188 **"it is a question"** Paul Scott Mowrer to Ted Thackrey, December 8, 1945; Thackrey to Mowrer, February 4, September 21, 1948, Schiff Papers. For additional background, see Antonia Felix et al., *The Post's New York: Celebrating 200 Years of New York City as Seen through the Pages and Pictures of the New York Post* (New York: HarperResource, 2001), 136; and Nissenson, *The Lady Upstairs,* 74–77.

love, poetry Paul Scott Mowrer, *On Going to Live in New Hampshire* (Sanbornhill, N.H.: Wake-Brook House, 1953), 27. Among Mowrer's writings at the end of his life, in addition to other books of poetry, are his aphoristic *School for Diplomats* (Francestown, N.H.: Golden Quill Press, 1964) and *Six Plays* (Boston: Branden Press, 1967).

189 **forces worked against afternoon newspapers** For a discussion of the final days of the *Daily News* and the forces working against it, see the paper's last issue, which bore the front-page headline "So Long, Chicago," *Chicago Daily News,* March 4, 1978; also "Chicago Daily News to Die on March 4," *Editor and Publisher,* February 25, 1978; Haynes Johnson, *Washington Post,* February 8, 1978; Gary Cummings, "The Daily News Looks Homeward," *Columbia Journalism Review,* March–April 1977, 60–61. On early circulation, see Abramoske, "The Chicago Daily News," 24–25. To celebrate its centennial, the newspaper staff assembled an anthology of some of its best work: Dick Griffin and Rob Warden, eds., *Done in a Day: 100 Years of Great Writing from the Chicago Daily News* (Chicago: Swallow Press, 1977).

decided to sell the *Daily News* Whited, *Knight,* 198–99.

190 **"It seemed like we had"** Georgie Anne Geyer, interview by author, April 13, 2005. Especially helpful for details on the final years were Joe Geshwiler to author, e-mail, November 16, 2007; Robert A. Signer to author, November 10, 2007; Larry Green to author, e-mail, January 31, 2005; and the author's interviews of Milt Freudenheim, August 23, 2004; Donald Shanor, August 23, 2004; James Hoge, September 14, 2004; and Green, January 28, 2005. On the honor by the Society of Professional Journalists, then called Sigma Delta Chi, see *Chicago Daily News,* May 8–9, 1971.

"Even should it change hands" Will Irwin, "The American Newspaper," *Collier's,* July 8, 1911, 15–16.

191 **"May the spirit"** This quote is found in M. W. Newman's lead article in the final edition, "So Long, Chicago," *Chicago Daily News,* March 4, 1978.

CHAPTER 13

192 **"About eight o'clock one evening in April 1927"** Root, *The Paris Edition,* 3.

"planned only a vacation jaunt" Hallett Abend, *My Life in China: 1926–1941* (New York: Harcourt, Brace, 1943), 3; Tillman Durdin quoted in MacKinnon and Friesen, *China Reporting,* 32; Cecil Brown, untitled typewritten autobiographical essay, January 14, 1940, Brown Papers; Howard K. Smith, *Events Leading Up to My Death: The Life of a Twentieth-Century Reporter* (New

York: St. Martin's, 1996), 27–30; F. McCracken Fisher, interview by author, December 13, 1980; Mary Knight, "Girl Reporter in Paris," in *We Cover the World: By Sixteen Foreign Correspondents,* ed. Eugene Lyons (New York: Harcourt, Brace, 1937), 277; Robert St. John, *Foreign Correspondent* (Garden City, N.Y.: Doubleday, 1957), 13–23; Haldore Hanson, *Fifty Years around the Third World: Adventures and Reflections of an Overseas American* (Flint Hill, Vt.: Fraser, 1986), chap. 1; Haldore Hanson, *"Humane Endeavour": The Story of the China War* (New York: Farrar and Rinehart, 1939), chap. 1; Ken Cuthbertson, *Nobody Said Not to Go: The Life, Loves, and Adventures of Emily Hahn* (Boston: Faber and Faber, 1998); Emily Hahn, *China to Me* (Garden City, N.Y.: Doubleday, 1944); Helen Foster Snow, *My China Years* (New York: William Morrow, 1984), 19–20; Edna Lee Booker, *News Is My Job* (New York: Macmillan, 1940), 5–6.

The student group with which Fisher went to China was under the direction of Upton Close, who had a colorful career as a spy, a newspaperman, and a radio commentator. "Upton Close" was a pen name derived from reporting he had done for the China *Weekly Review,* which had been signed "Up Close." His real name was Josef Washington Hall. For details on Hall, see Irving E. Fang, *Those Radio Commentators!* (Ames: Iowa State University Press, 1977), 121–30.

"Prices in Europe" Albion Ross, *Journey of an American* (Indianapolis: Bobbs-Merrill, 1957), 14.

193 **"began to roll up in waves"** Laney, *Paris Herald,* 76; Eric Sevareid, *Not So Wild a Dream* (New York: Knopf, 1946), 84; Raymond A. Schroth, *The American Journey of Eric Sevareid* (South Royalton, Vt.: Steerforth Press, 1995), 117–19; Taylor, *Awakening from History,* 75; Weber, *News of Paris,* 234–35.

194 **"verse, short stories"** Burton Bernstein, *Thurber: A Biography* (New York: Quill, 1985), 139–40; Kenneth Stewart, *News Is What We Make It: A Running Story of the Working Press* (Boston: Houghton Mifflin, 1943), 55–59; William L. Shirer, *Twentieth Century Journey: A Memoir of a Life and the Times,* vol. 1, *The Start, 1904–1930* (New York: Simon and Schuster, 1976), 23–24, 59–62, 217–21.

"In a click of time" Vincent Sheean, *Personal History* (Boston: Houghton Mifflin, 1935; reprint, with new introduction, 1969), 36–37; Sheean's journal entry is noted in Carl Edward Johnson, "A Twentieth Century Seeker: A Biography of James Vincent Sheean" (Ph.D. diss., University of Wisconsin, 1974), 494. Johnson's dissertation is an extremely valuable source of information on Sheean, who has never had a published biography. In addition to drawing together archival materials, Johnson interviewed Sheean, his wife, and others who have since died.

golden age The term *golden age* is thrown around a good deal. Phillip Knightley has dated the golden age for war correspondence as running from 1865 to 1914 "because of the rise of the popular press, the increasing use of the telegraph, and the tardy introduction of organized censorship." *The First Casualty,* 43. Among those who consider the interwar years the golden age is Heald, in *Transatlantic Vistas,* xi. In researching for this book, I was struck by the number of people who thought their own age, whenever it was, was a golden age. But the best case, I believe, can be made for the 1920s and 1930s.

Six newspapers Background for this section on newspapers can be found in Robert W. Desmond, *Crisis and Conflict: World News Reporting between Two Wars, 1920–1940* (Iowa City: University of Iowa Press, 1982), chaps. 12, 14.

"not expecting them to publish it" Martha Gellhorn, *The Face of War* (New York: Simon and Schuster, 1959), 12–13. Background for this section can be found in Frank Luther Mott, *A History of American Magazines,* vol. 5, *1905–1930* (Cambridge, Mass.: Harvard University Press, 1968), chap. 4; Joseph C. Goulden, *The Curtis Caper* (New York: Putnam's, 1965), 29; Robert S. Lynd and Helen Merrell Lynd, *Middletown in Transition: A Study in Cultural Conflicts* (New York: Harcourt Brace Jovanovich, 1965), 386 (a follow-up to the Lynds' original study, which was published initially in 1937); Carl G. Ryant, "From Isolation to Intervention: The Saturday Evening Post, 1939–42," *Journalism Quarterly* 48 (Winter 1971): 680; Johnson, "Twentieth Century

Seeker," 385; Theodore Peterson, *Magazines in the Twentieth Century* (Urbana: University of Illinois Press, 1964), 57–64; "Among the Publishers," *Publishers' Weekly,* May 10, 1941, 1935.

195 **"the terrible political intrigues of Geneva"** Stephen A. Schuker, "American Foreign Policy: The European Dimension, 1921–1929," in *Calvin Coolidge and the Coolidge Era: Essays on the History of the 1920s,* ed. John Earl Haynes (Washington, D.C.: Library of Congress, 1998), 299; Mowrer, *Our Foreign Affairs,* 308.

"Oriental luxury" Graham Peck, *Through China's Wall* (Boston: Houghton Mifflin, 1940), 12; Peter Rand, *China Hands* (New York: Simon and Schuster, 1995), 264–67; S. J. Taylor, *Stalin's Apologist: Walter Duranty: The New York Times's Man in Moscow* (New York: Oxford University Press, 1990), 228. Haldore Hanson lived on seventeen dollars a month. Hanson, *Fifty Years around the Third World,* 27. Cecil Brown's expense account is in Cecil Brown to Paul W. White, May 6, 1941, Brown Papers.

196 **"The phenomenon of contemporaneity"** Vincent Sheean, *Not Peace but a Sword* (New York: Doubleday Doran, 1939), 343.

"J.V. Sheean" byline Vincent Sheean, *Personal History,* 42. Details on Sheean's early life are drawn from Sheean, *Personal History,* chap. 1; Vincent Sheean, *This House against This House* (New York: Random House, 1946), 50–51; Vincent Sheean, *First and Last Love* (New York: Random House, 1956), chap. 1. The obituaries of Sheean's mother and father are in their local Pana newspaper, the *Daily Palladium,* January 18, August 22, 1921, and were supplied by Susan Elaine Sheean Wheeler along with other family background. Susan Wheeler to author, January 11, 2005. Interviews by author with Sheean's daughters, Ellen Sheean, November 17, 2004, and Linda Sheean, April 15, 1992.

"In those days" Malcolm Cowley, *Exile's Return: A Literary Odyssey of the 1920s* (New York: Viking, 1951), 79.

197 **"Extraordinary adventures in African deserts"** Quote from *Chicago Daily News* promotional notice, November 1924. See also Mowrer, *House of Europe,* 497; Vincent Sheean, *An American among the Riffi* (New York: Century, 1925). Sheean's articles appeared in the *Chicago Tribune* in February 1925—the quote is from February 10, 1925. Shirer's reaction is in *Twentieth Century Journey: The Start,* 34–35, although his memory may have been muddled. Shirer suggests that he read the *Chicago Tribune* stories in mid-1925, but Sheean had left the paper by that time.

198 **"a liar, disloyal and dishonorable"** Robert McCormick to Joseph Patterson, May 5, 1928, Patterson Papers. Sheean, *Personal History,* 116; Smith, *The Colonel,* 304; Seldes, *Tell the Truth and Run,* 167–70; Shirer, *Twentieth Century Journey: The Start,* 227–28. The *Tribune* story on the assumption of the Virgin Mary, December 27, 1923, is quoted in Johnson, "Twentieth Century Seeker," 88.

"the first graphic, face-to-face story" "The Riff! Morocco! Barbary Gun-Runners! And a Crisis in France!" *Asia,* August 1925, 712.

again slipped into the Riff Vincent Sheean, "Peace in Morocco," *Asia,* March 1926, 210–11+; Sheean, *Personal History,* chap. 4, as well as subsequent chapters for summaries of his activities during these years; Wythe Williams, "African Interlude," in *The Inside Story: By the Members of the Overseas Press Club of America,* ed. Robert Benjamin (New York: Prentice-Hall, 1940), chap. 20; Webb Miller, *I Found No Peace: The Journal of a Foreign Correspondent* (Garden City, N.Y.: Garden City, 1938), chap. 13.

199 **"Jimmy"** Shirer, *Twentieth Century Journey: The Start,* 253. For a lively discussion of the merits and demerits of the *Paris Times,* see Hillel Bernstein, "The Golden Age of Journalism," *Esquire,* June 1934, 36+.

200 **"is, I suppose, a hybrid form"** Sheean, *Personal History,* xvii.

"Even if I took no part" Ibid., 398. The word "interesting" appears often in Davis's book, including twice in one paragraph. Richard Harding Davis, *A Year from a Reporter's Note-Book* (New York: Harper, 1897), 59.

"**a large, calm man**" Sheean, *Personal History,* 203–4.

"**I was not, to begin with, a 'sympathizer'**" Ibid., 211–13.

202 "**I believe it to be fear**" Henry Seidel Canby, "The Threatening Thirties," *Saturday Review of Literature,* May 22, 1937, 3.

"**A remarkable achievement**" R. L. Duffus, *New York Times Book Review,* February 3, 1935, 1; Mary McCarthy, "One Man's Road," *Nation,* March 6, 1935, 282; Malcolm Cowley, "The Long View," *New Republic,* February 20, 1935, 50–51.

fourth-best-selling nonfiction book Michael Korda, *Making the List: A Cultural History of the American Bestseller, 1900–1999* (New York: Barnes and Noble, 1992), 69; "Vincent Sheean," *Wilson Library Bulletin,* May 1935, 464–65; "Booksellers Make First National Book Awards," *Publishers Weekly,* May 16, 1936, 1948; William McWhirter, "When Jimmy Told It Like It Was," *Life,* April 18, 1969, 8; Michael Arlen, "The Air," *New Yorker,* January 6, 1975, 53.

203 "**Sheean established**" Stewart, *News Is What We Make It,* 198, 204; Canby, "The Threatening Thirties," 4. With a touch of journalistic cynicism "to hide our sentiment," Stewart noted, correspondents joked, "Into each life some Rayna must fall."

"**full of adventure**" On Duranty, see Oswald Garrison Villard, "A Great Press Writer," review of *I Write as I Please, Nation,* November 27, 1935, 627. Duranty's book appeared at the end of 1935, not soon enough to be a top seller that year; the next year it was. Duranty gave a highly favorable review to *Personal History* when it appeared. *New York Herald Tribune,* February 10, 1935.

On Farson, see Frank Knox to Negley Farson, February 8, 1935, which Farson transcribed in a letter to Leland Stowe, April 19, 1957, Stowe Papers. Twice Farson publicly told his story of leaving the *Daily News,* in *The Way of the Transgressor* (New York: Literary Guild of America, 1936), 600; and in *A Mirror for Narcissus* (Garden City, N.Y.: Doubleday, 1957), 26. Farson was described in the *Chicago Daily News,* May 8–9, 1971.

Gunther's book is described at length in chapter 14 of this volume.

Best sellers are noted in Korda, *Making the List;* and Keith L. Justice, *Bestseller Index* (Jefferson, N.C.: McFarland, 1998).

"**No other American correspondent**" Leland Stowe, "Vincent Sheean as I Knew Him," typewritten note, n.d., Stowe Papers; Marquis W. Childs, *Sweden: The Middle Way* (New Haven, Conn.: Yale University Press, 1936), xi; "Childs, Marquis," in *Current Biography,* ed. Maxine Block (Bronx, N.Y.: H. W. Wilson, 1943), 126–28.

204 "**joined the parade**" The quote on Mary Knight's book is from *New York Times,* April 24, 1938; the quote by Gunther is from his review of the book, "Potential Battlegrounds," *Saturday Review of Literature,* November 14, 1936, 7; "only Vincent Sheean's prose" is from Eugene Lyons, "Looking at Trouble," *Saturday Review of Literature,* January 28, 1939, 5; Stewart's comment is in his *News Is What We Make It,* 198.

"**It has now been 30 years or more**" Norman Cousins, "Editor's Page," *Saturday Review,* January 22, 1977, 4.

205 "**is the father of us all**" John Gunther's quote is in "Two Countries Shot under Him," review of *Not Peace but a Sword,* by Sheean, *Saturday Review of Literature,* July 29, 1939, 5.

"**I say there, correspondent**" Sevareid, *Not So Wild a Dream,* 498–99. While I was doing research for this chapter, a number of people commented on the power *Personal History* had for them when they were young, among them Michael Bessie and Marvin Kalb. The information that *Personal History* was required at Dartmouth is from Roy Rowan, *Chasing the Dragon: A Veteran Journalist's Firsthand Account of the 1949 Chinese Revolution* (Guilford, Conn.: Lyons Press, 2004), 75.

broadened his contacts still further Vincent Sheean, *Between the Thunder and the Sun* (New York: Random House, 1943), 27–34, 171–72.

Hollywood Donald Spoto, *The Dark Side of Genius: The Life of Alfred Hitchcock* (New York: Da Capo Press, 1999), 222–40, 248; Donald Spoto, *The Art of Alfred Hitchcock* (New York: Hopkinson and Blake, 1976), chap. 9; and Gene D. Phillips, *Alfred Hitchcock* (Boston: Twayne, 1984), 98–100.

206 **"It is not much better"** "New Play in Manhattan," *Time,* April 15, 1940; Vincent Sheean, *New York Times,* March 31, 1940. Sheean's 1940 earnings are in Johnson, "Twentieth Century Seeker," 381.

"You must go for the Herald *Tribune*" Vincent Sheean, *Dorothy and Red* (Boston: Houghton Mifflin, 1963), 286–87.

danger just the same Sheean, *Not Peace but a Sword,* 331; Sheean, *This House against This House,* 348.

207 **Sequels** Malcolm Cowley, "Personal History, Cont'd," *New Republic,* March 28, 1943, 450. Edmund Wilson's comment appeared first in *Nation* in 1952 and was reprinted in a collection of his essays, *The Shores of Light* (New York: Vintage Books, 1952), 744. Ellen Sheean mentioned Sheean's wish to number the books *Personal History II,* etc. Ellen Sheean, interview by author, November 14, 2004.

"a petty thing" Sheean, *Between the Thunder and the Sun,* 144, 365–70. Sheean mentions visiting Fisher and says that he (Sheean) and Mowrer worked as a team, although the suggestion is that they teamed up for reporting purposes. Mowrer provides the same inference in *Triumph and Turmoil,* 323–24. Mowrer received his invitation to work in government information while in Chungking.

"I was quite ready to do any job" Sheean, *This House against This House,* 176, 303.

"celebrating his recall" Seldes, *Tell the Truth and Run,* 168.

208 **"Sheean is perhaps the most remarkable"** John Gunther, "London on Edge," *Atlantic Monthly,* April 1937, 395–96; Ellen Sheean, interview by author, November 17, 2004; Peter Kurth, *American Cassandra* (Boston: Little, Brown, 1990), 273; Johnson, "Twentieth Century Seeker," 467.

"a socialist materialist" Sheean, *This House against This House,* 320; Johnson, "Twentieth Century Seeker," 175–76 (Johnson extensively uses Bernstein's recollections); Ellen Sheean, interviews by author, January 27, 1991; November 17, 2004. For an example of Sheean's expressing shame over living comfortably, see Sheean, *This House against This House,* 183. Diana Cooper mentioned her friendship with Sheean in Diana Cooper, *Trumpets from the Steep* (London: Rupert Hart-Davis, 1960).

"I see her, Bernie" Johnson, "Twentieth Century Seeker," 195; Louis Fischer, *Men and Politics: An Autobiography* (New York: Duell, Sloan, and Pearce, 1941), 157.

"could not go on" Sheean, *Personal History,* 374; Sheean, *Not Peace but a Sword,* 305. For other examples of Sheean's ambivalence about journalism, see *Personal History,* 52, 82, 187–88, 238, 246, 251, 379; and *Not Peace but a Sword,* 11, 78–80, 245, 344.

209 **"I have come down to save you"** Johnson, "Twentieth Century Seeker," 269–74 (which draws on Dinah Sheean's recollections of her husband's illness); Sheean, *Between the Thunder and the Sun,* 60; *New York Times,* August 19, 1936; "Transitions," *Newsweek,* March 6, 1937, 38; Sarah R. Shaber, "Hemingway's Literary Journalism: The Spanish Civil War Dispatches," *Journalism Quarterly* 57 (Autumn 1980): 422.

"in heroes, saints, and prophets" Vincent Sheean to Frances Gunther, May 14, 1949, Gunther Papers; Sheean, *Personal History,* 141–42; Kurth, *American Cassandra,* 400, 403, 531.

"I'd have been a fish out of water" Vincent Sheean, *The Tide: A Novel* (Garden City, N.Y.: Doubleday, Doran, 1933), 303; Arthur Ruhl, "Reporter's Record of the Post-War Years," *Saturday Review of Literature,* February 2, 1935, 458.

"If some people really are psychic" Eric Sevareid commentary on CBS, March 17, 1975, Sheean Papers; Dinah Sheean to Eric Sevareid, June 17, 1970, Sevareid Papers.

210 **"Are you a Christian?"** John Gunther, "John Gunther Interviews Vincent Sheean," *New York Herald Tribune Weekly Book Review,* July 31, 1949, 2.

Sheean's emotional state Johnson, "Twentieth Century Seeker," 453, 498, 601; John Keats, *You*

Might as Well Live: The Life and Times of Dorothy Parker (New York: Simon and Schuster, 1970), 251. The post-party bender is recounted in Sheean's diary, June 11, 1947, Sheean Papers.

"charm and gaiety" For background on Sheean's relationship with his wife, see Dinah Sheean to Leland Stowe, August 25, October 12, 1949; Stowe to Diana Sheean, October 17, 1949, all in Stowe Papers. On the musical comedy part, see Vincent Sheean to Dinah Sheean, September 5, 1943, Sheean Papers.

"I am at the end of my tether" Johnson, "Twentieth Century Seeker," 400; William L. Shirer, *Twentieth Century Journey: A Memoir of a Life and the Times,* vol. 3, *A Native's Return, 1945–1988* (New York: Simon and Schuster, 1990), 326–27. His prediction to *Holiday*'s editor is mentioned in an editor's note to Vincent Sheean, "Victory to Mahatma Gandhi!" *Holiday,* June 1948, 81. For a brief discussion of *Holiday* and the editorial genius that pulled it together, see Kathryn News, "Edwin Hill ('Ted') Patrick," in *American Magazine Journalists, 1900–1960* (Detroit, Mich.: Gale Research, 1994), 218–23.

On Sheean's efforts to become "denicotinized," see Vincent Sheean, diary, November 6, 1947; January 13, 1948, Sheean Papers. In another diary entry, January 21, 1948, he spells out his premonition about Gandhi: "The fact that he is so uncannily able, by the instinct of genius, to assist the operation of fate, merely makes this climax inevitable. I have believed since last summer that if he is to be killed it must be (for India's sake) by a Hindu and not by a Muslim. This is the logic of every sacred drama in the entire history of religion, and I believe it will take place."

211 **"What would the Master think of me"** Serge Fliegers reminisced about Sheean in *Off the Record: The Best Stories of Foreign Correspondents,* ed. Dickson Hartwell and Andrew A. Rooney (Garden City, N.Y.: Doubleday, 1953), 152.

"Considering the strength of my premonition" Vincent Sheean, diary, January 14, 19, 1948, Sheean Papers; Snow, *Journey to the Beginning,* 399, 412.

"You can move into the house" Vincent Sheean, *Lead, Kindly Light* (New York: Random House, 1949), 191.

"I've lost my only *guru*" Sheean, *Lead, Kindly Light,* 207, 212; *New York Herald Tribune,* February 8, 1948; Margaret Parton, interview by author, April 12, 1981; Snow, *Journey to the Beginning,* 399. Sheean's diary entries from this time are useful in understanding what happened; the "pain and suffering" quote is from his diary, February 8, 1947, Sheean Papers.

212 **"Up to a few months ago"** Jonathan Schell, *The Real War* (New York: Da Capo, 1988), 59; Jonathan Schell, interview by author, February 1, 2005. *The Real War* is a reissue of Schell's two books on Vietnam. The impact of his Vietnam reporting is mentioned in Neil Sheehan, *A Bright Shining Lie: John Paul Vann and America in Vietnam* (New York: Random House, 1988), 687.

"always became quests" David Carr, *New York Times,* February 22, 2005; Wolfe is quoted in Robert Love, "A Technical Guide for Editing Gonzo," *Columbia Journalism Review,* May–June 2005, 63. See also Paul Perry, *Fear and Loathing: The Strange and Terrible Saga of Hunter S. Thompson* (New York: Thunder's Mouth Press, 1992), 46–49, 68, 74, 213–15. The continuing potential for landing a job on an overseas English-language newspaper is discussed in an article by *Chicago Daily News* correspondent Ernie Hill, "You Can Be a Foreign Correspondent," *Writer's Digest,* August 1951, 47–49+.

"Rio was the end" Peter O. Whitmer, *When the Going Gets Weird: The Twisted Life and Times of Hunter S. Thompson* (New York: Hyperion, 1993), 133.

213 **"can only be admired"** Vincent Sheean, *The New Persia* (New York: Century, 1927), 130.

"Anti-Americanism" Peter G. Peterson et al., *Finding America's Voice: A Strategy for Reinvigorating U.S. Public Diplomacy* (New York Council on Foreign Relations, 2003), 5; Andrew Kohut and Bruce Stokes, *America against the World: How We Are Different and Why We Are Disliked* (New York: Henry Holt, 2006), 25; Sheean, *Not Peace but a Sword,* 345. See also Melvin L. DeFleur and Margaret H. DeFleur, *Learning to Hate Americans* (Spokane, Wash.: Marquette Books, 2003), 57; Molly Moore, conversation with author, October 4, 2008.

"My approach" Finnegan's comment is in an unpublished essay by Judith Paterson, who interviewed him in 1992; Peterson, *Magazines in the Twentieth Century*, 64, 80, 151. Technically speaking, the *Saturday Evening Post* still exists, but as a bimonthly health magazine.

"I was indeed lucky" Eric Sevareid to Kate Holliday, December 28, 1977, Sevareid Papers; Melissa Ludtke Lincoln, "The Free-Lance Life," *Columbia Journalism Review*, September–October 1981, 49–54; "Grub Street Revisited," *Time*, April 10, 1978, 75–77; Deborah Baldwin, "Paris Blues," *American Journalism Review*, May 1995, 40–43. The National Writers Union report is "Report on Pay Rates for Freelance Journalists," found at www.nwu.org/nwu/index.php?cmd=showPage&page _id=1.5.2.6.1 (accessed August 13, 2008).

214 **"There is probably a limit"** Laura A. Scofea, "The Development and Growth of Employer-Provided Health Insurance," *Monthly Labor Review* 117 (March 1994): 6; *Statistical Abstract of the United States* (Washington, D.C.: Department of Commerce, 1993), 115; Aileen Gallagher, "Dateline Baghdad, Capital of Chaos," www.blacktable.com/gallagher040714.htm, July 14, 2004.

"in at least one significant respect" Leo Bogart, "The Overseas Newsman: A 1967 Profit Study," *Journalism Quarterly* 45 (Summer 1968): 305; Elisa Tinsley, interview by author, February 2, 2005.

"It's a corporation" The safety policy, supplied by Elisa Tinsley, is dated September 16, 2002. Tinsley to author, e-mail, March 27, 2005.

215 **"In domestic news"** Carleton Beals, "Color in Our Foreign News," *Outlook and Independent*, February 25, 1931, 300.

"In the reporting of foreign news" Curtis D. MacDougall, *The Press and Its Problems* (Dubuque, Iowa: William C. Brown, 1964), 188.

approached real science This alternative view of scientific objectivity is inspired in part by the comments of Tom Rosenstiel at the 2005 annual meeting of the American Society of Newspaper Editors, Washington, D.C., April 12–15, 2005. Another example of such thinking is found in Mitchell Stephens, "We're All Postmodern Now," *Columbia Journalism Review*, July–August 2005, 60–64; Mitchell Stephens, "Beyond News," *Columbia Journalism Review*, January–February 2007, 34–39; and in Michael Massing, "Iraq, the Press, and the Election," *New York Review of Books*, December 16, 2004, 26–32.

Modern newspaper correspondents still can develop a "body of work" that is far-reaching and anticipatory, as *Washington Post* veteran correspondent Michael Getler pointed out to me in an interview on March 16, 2005. Without a doubt, Getler is one of those seasoned, reliable correspondents. But the example he used of drawing on that experience is revealing of the waffling that plagues correspondents. Getler's example is a paragraph from a December 25, 1979, *Washington Post* story in which he predicted that Germany would eventually reunify: "Looking eastward, where East Germany also outperforms its neighbors within the Soviet bloc, one also senses here in the West a suppressed pride, a feeling that there will be an irresistible tug ultimately leading to reunification of 80 million Germans under a world political alignment different—admittedly very different—from what we now have."

aftermath of the *Anschluss* Vincent Sheean, *New York Herald Tribune*, July 5, 1938.

216 **"One wonders"** Homer Metz, *Christian Science Monitor*, March 30, 1946; Korda, *Making the List*, 97.

strong sales Johnson, "Twentieth Century Seeker," 649; "Objective—Red China," *Newsweek*, June 1, 1959, 88; Ellen Sheean, interview by author, November 17, 2004. Sheean's travails with his biography of King Faisal are recounted in Vincent Sheean to Seyyid Ahmad abd el-Wahhab, November 25, 1970; and Dinah Sheean to John Glubb, December 7, 1979, Sheean Papers. The book was published as Vincent Sheean, *Faisal: The King and His Kingdom* (Tavistock, UK: University Press of Arabia, 1975).

"Jesus of Nazareth" Ellen Sheean, interview by author, January 27, 1991; Johnson, "Twentieth Century Seeker," 662.

217 **"Communist fellow-traveler"** "The Stage and Screen," *Commonweal*, April 19, 1940. The Lawrenceburg trial is mentioned in the Sheean obituary: Paul L. Montgomery, *New York Times*,

March 17, 1975; Ellen Sheean, interview by author, November 17, 2004. Examples of Sheean's name turning up in connection with colleagues under scrutiny are in Herbert Mitgang, *Dangerous Dossiers: Exposing the Secret War against America's Greatest Authors* (New York: Donald I. Fine, 1988), 66, 82.

Sheean was a burden Johnson, "Twentieth Century Seeker," 644, 672, 703–4; Vincent Sheean to Eric Sevareid, June 23, 1968, Sevareid Papers; Jane Gunther, interview by author, June 23, 1992. The FBI report is in G. H. Scatterday to A. H. Belmont, May 21, 1959, FBI Files. On Alice Roosevelt's views of drinking and her wit, see Stacy A. Cordery, *Alice: Alice Roosevelt, from White House Princess to Washington Power Broker* (New York: Viking, 2007), 294, 453–54.

"India is a country of the soul" Ellen Sheean, interviews by author, January 27, 1991; November 17, 2004; Gilbert Harrison, *The Enthusiast: A Life of Thornton Wilder* (New Haven, Conn.: Ticknor and Fields, 1983), 373.

"played in orchestras" Dinah Sheean to Leland Stowe, January 10, 1976, Stowe Papers; Ellen Sheean, interview by author, November 17, 2004. Sheean's plans for his last book discussed in Johnson, "Twentieth Century Seeker," 714.

CHAPTER 14

218 ***Who's Who in America*** "John Gunther," in *Who's Who in America* (Chicago: Marquis, 1956), 1046.

"At about this time" Cass Canfield, *Up and Down and Around: A Publisher Recollects the Time of His Life* (New York: Harper and Row, 1971), 121–22. Other details on this episode can be found in John Gunther, *A Fragment of Autobiography: The Fun of Writing the Inside Books* (New York: Harper and Row, 1961), chap. 1; and Ken Cuthbertson, *Inside: The Biography of John Gunther* (Chicago: Bonus Books, 1992), chaps. 17–19. Like all good stories, this one about the inception of the *Inside* books is told by different people in different ways. Canfield says nothing about Gunther's novel-in-progress and claims that he had to pursue Gunther for some years. I have made extensive use of Cuthbertson's biography for details about Gunther's life. The dust jacket referred to was on Drew Pearson and Robert Allen, *Washington Merry-Go-Round* (New York: Blue Ribbon Books, 1932); Richard L. Strout discussed the impact of their book in "Rediscoveries," *Washington Post Book World,* July 22, 1984.

"the largest sum I had ever heard of" Gunther, *A Fragment,* 7.

"Attitude to sex" Ibid., 10–12.

219 **"A hulking (6 ft. 1 in., 238 lbs.) legman"** "The Insider," *Time,* April 14, 1958, 44.

cover of *Time* Ernie Pyle was *Time*'s cover story on July 17, 1944, Dorothy Thompson on June 12, 1939, and Ernest Hemingway on October 18, 1937 and again on December 13, 1954.

"the highest indices" Vilfredo Pareto, *A Treatise on General Sociology,* trans. Andrew Bongiorno and Arthur Livingston (New York: Dover, 1935), 3:1423; Pareto's *Treatise* was originally published in Italian in 1916. Seldes, *Lords of the Press,* 291. For a brief discussion of elite media, see Kathleen Hall Jamieson and Karlyn Kohrs Campbell, *The Interplay of Influence: News, Advertising, Politics, and the Mass Media* (Belmont, Calif.: Wadsworth, 2001), 14–15.

220 ***Specialization and education*** T. B. Connery, "Great Business Operations—The Collection of News," *Cosmopolitan,* May 1897, 32; Mowrer, *House of Europe,* 113; John Gunther, *Chicago Revisited* (Chicago: University of Chicago, 1967), 92; George Anthony Weller, *Not to Eat, Not for Love* (New York: Smith and Haas, 1933), 113; Brown, *The Coming of the Whirlwind,* 13. Ray Stannard Baker recalled how he embarrassed himself by bringing his college diploma with him when he applied for a position at the *Daily News.* Baker, *Native American,* 262.

221 ***Compensation*** "How We Get Our News," *Harper's New Monthly Magazine,* March 1867, 518; Casey, *Such Interesting People,* 280–81; Williams, *The Baltimore Sun,* 341; Carleton Beals, "Life at the Full," unpublished autobiography, n.d., 204, Beals Papers. Beals had many titles for this

memoir besides "Life at the Full," which I have used here, and the manuscript in his collection of papers is a hodgepodge with really no title at all. The Clurman anecdote is in William Prochnau, *Once upon a Distant War* (New York: Random House, 1995), 116. The *Herald Tribune* anecdote is from Stuart Loory, interview by author, January 13, 2005.

Further on the matter of expense accounts is this: "I had never spent fifty cents for a cab ride without fearing the [*Baltimore*] *Sun* would reprimand me for squandering money," said Russell Baker of his experience as a local reporter. When he was named London bureau chief in the early 1950s, he was "told to squander freely." Forced to reveal that he couldn't afford to buy luggage, Baker was told by his editor to get a new suitcase and send the bill to the newspaper. Baker realized that he was now "a prince of journalism." Russell Baker, *The Good Times* (New York: William Morrow, 1989), 166–67.

Autonomy Williams, *Dusk of Empire*, 9; Paul Scott Mowrer, "An Ocean Away," *Atlantic Monthly,* July 1950, 93; Patrick Skene Catling, *Better Than Working* (New York: Macmillan, 1960), 183.

222 *Lifestyle* Leo C. Rosten, *The Washington Correspondents* (New York: Harcourt, Brace, 1937), 239; Sidney Whitman, *Turkish Memories* (New York: Scribner's, 1914), 11; John Gunther, "Dateline Vienna," *Harper's Monthly Magazine,* July 1935, 202. The need to socialize as an equal is also discussed in Wolf Von Schierbrand, "Confessions of a Foreign Newspaper Correspondent," *World's Work,* April 1903, 3355–58.

Dress Williams, *Dusk of Empire*, 11; Raymond Clapper, *Watching the World,* ed. Mrs. Raymond Clapper (New York: Da Capo Press, 1976), 18–19; James A. Mills, "Scoop Hunting around the World," in Lyons, *We Cover the World,* 371–88. For other such comments, see J. C. Oestreicher, *The World Is Their Beat,* 234.

223 *Honors* Russell's diary comment is from a March 25, 1856, entry, Russell Papers. His handwriting is a nightmare to read, and the word *portrait* in the quote is a best guess. Hohenberg, *Foreign Correspondence,* 27; Max Hastings, introduction to *William Russell: Special Correspondent of the Times,* ed. Roger Hudson (London: Folio Society, 1995), xix, xxvi–xxvii; Harrison Salisbury, "China Reporting: *Red Star* to Long March," in *Voices of China: The Interplay of Politics and Journalism,* ed. Chin-Chuan Lee (New York: Guilford Press, 1990), 216; Robert A. Rosenstone, *Romantic Revolutionary: A Biography of John Reed* (New York: Vintage Books, 1981), 384–85; Tracy B. Strong and Helene Keyssar, *Right in Her Soul: The Life of Anna Louis Strong* (New York: Random House, 1983), 349; Ruth Price, *The Lives of Agnes Smedley* (New York: Oxford University Press, 2005), 418; Walker, *Januarius MacGahan,* 328–30; Mowrer, *Triumph and Turmoil,* 125; by a foreign correspondent [the byline], "Your Mirror of Europe," *Saturday Evening Post,* December 9, 1922, 149; Gibbons, *Floyd Gibbons,* 112–14, 182, 192, 330, 348–49. William Stoneman laments his "tin medal" in a letter to Carroll Binder, February 18, 1954, Binder Papers. The Beijing street named after Morrison was renamed after the Communists took over in 1949.

Information on the naming of Liberty Ships can be found at www.fiu.edu/~thompsop/liberty; this Web site does not say whether it is James Gordon Bennett Sr. or Jr. who is being honored. Being a foreign correspondent probably helped Irwin Cobb in the award department, although he was also a versatile writer in many homespun forms and was considered a hero for chairing the Authors and Artists Committee of the Association against the Prohibition Amendment. In addition to the Liberty Ship recognition, he had a fancy hotel named after him in his whiskey-loving state of Kentucky as well as an Ohio river, a cigar, a flower, a bass fish, a hunting shirt, an Oregon canyon, and many other things. See Anita Lawson, *Irwin S. Cobb* (Bowling Green, Ohio: Bowling Green State University Press, 1984), 212–13.

225 **"The executive heads"** J. Lincoln Steffens, "The Business of a Newspaper," *Scribner's,* October 1897, 447. The costs of newspapering are discussed in William S. Solomon, "The Site of Newsroom Labor"; and Marianne Salcetti, "The Emergence of the Reporter," both in *Newsworkers: Toward a History of the Rank and File,* ed. Hanno Hardt and Bonnie Brennen (Minneapolis: University of Minnesota Press, 1995), 53, 113; Nasaw, *The Chief,* 97–98.

"**Newspaper proprietors**" Salmon, *The Newspaper and the Historian,* 68; Larry Heinzerling, "Foreign Correspondents: A Rare Breed," in *Breaking News: How the Associated Press Has Covered War, Peace, and Everything Else* (New York: Princeton Architectural Press, 2007), 265; Tifft and Jones, *The Trust,* 67; Turner Catledge, *My Life and the Times* (New York: Harper and Row, 1971), 165; Jacob and Cahan, *Chicago under Glass,* 18. For another study of bylines on the *New York Times* front page, see Christine Ogan, Ida Plymale, D. Lynn Smith, William H. Turpin, and Donald Lewis Shaw, "The Changing Front Page of the New York *Times,* 1900–1970," *Journalism Quarterly* 52 (Summer 1975): 340–44.

An interesting twist on the prevalence of bylines for correspondents, as opposed to stay-at-home reporters, comes from Tifft and Jones in *The Trust,* 175: The Ochs family was sensitive about being Jewish and having their newspaper viewed as a Jewish newspaper. Jews on the editorial staff "were convinced they got out-of-town assignments less frequently than Gentiles because such stories were more likely to merit bylines." Bylines began to flourish on the sports page of the *Times* in the mid-1920s. Berger, *Story of the New York Times,* 191–92.

"**They are trying to get**" Lubow, *The Reporter Who Would Be King,* 130, 137.

"**sell the goods**" Irwin, *Making of a Reporter,* 235; Richard Harding Davis, *With the Allies* (New York: Scribner's, 1917), 53–54. One of Davis's reports on what it was like to be a correspondent was Richard Harding Davis, "Our War Correspondents in Cuba and Puerto Rico," *Harper's New Monthly Magazine,* May 1899, 938–48.

"**seemed to me**" Irwin, *Making of a Reporter,* 234; Lubow, *The Reporter Who Would Be King,* 2, 297.

226 "**was one of those magnetic types**" Van Wyck Brooks, *The Confident Years: 1888–1915* (New York: Dutton, 1952), 103, 106; Mencken, *Newspaper Days,* 239; H. L. Mencken, *Prejudices: Second Series* (New York: Knopf, 1920), 43.

228 "**In all the history of inventing**" Susan J. Douglas, *Inventing American Broadcasting: 1899–1922* (Baltimore: Johns Hopkins University Press, 1987), xv, 303. On the number of radios owned, see David Holbrook Culbert, *News for Everyman: Radio and Foreign Affairs in Thirties America* (Westport, Conn.: Greenwood Press, 1976), 15.

"**The microphone**" Swing, *"Good Evening!"* 190.

"**Did my broadcast about India**" Cuthbertson, *Inside,* 226.

"**His fan mail**" Gibbons, *Floyd Gibbons,* 195–97, 214–15, 220–21, 224, 233; Fang, *Those Radio Commentators!* 45–63, Stookie Allen, *Men of Daring!* (New York: Cupples and Leon, 1933). Estimates of Gibbons's maximum word count vary; I have used the number in the hagiographic Douglas Gilbert, *Floyd Gibbons: Knight of the Air* (New York: Robert M. McBride, 1930), 17.

229 "**The air raid is still on**" Edward R. Murrow, *This Is London* (New York: Schocken, 1989), 159, 167.

a brief encounter with the new medium Richard Harding Davis, "Breaking into the Movies," *Scribner's Magazine,* March 1914, 275–93; Lubow, *The Reporter Who Would Be King,* 282–83.

a movie metropolis Mae D. Huettig, "Economic Control of the Motion Picture Industry," in *The American Film Industry,* ed. Tino Balio (Madison: University of Wisconsin Press, 1985), 266; Joshua Gamson, *Claims of Fame: Celebrity in Contemporary America* (Berkeley: University of California Press, 1994), 25–27; Taylor, *Stalin's Apologist,* chap. 17; Rand, *China Hands,* 212. For a physical description of Hollywood, see John Kobal, *Hollywood: The Years of Innocence* (London: Thames and Hudson, 1985), 50–51. On the Hollywood Foreign Correspondents Association, later renamed the Hollywood Foreign Press Association, see Stephen Hess, *Through Their Eyes: Foreign Correspondents in the United States* (Washington, D.C.: Brookings Institution, 2005), 51.

230 "**Come to Hollywood**" Mowrer, *Triumph and Turmoil,* 294; Strong and Keyssar, *Right in Her Soul,* 204; Hecht, *A Child of the Century,* 467; Lawson, *Cobb,* 226.

Foreign Correspondent For a summary of movies about foreign correspondents, see Alex Barris, *Stop the Presses!* (South Brunswick, N.J.: A. S. Barnes, 1976), chap. 5; Matthew C. Ehrlich,

Journalism in the Movies (Urbana: University of Illinois Press, 2004), 80–81. Hecht also worked on screenplays for *Viva Villa!* and *China Girl.*

231 **"The public's taste"** *Variety Film Reviews,* March 7, 1933; May 2, 1945. On George Weller, see *Chicago Daily News,* May 8–9, 1971.

"a la Floyd Gibbons" The *Variety* description of Ralph Graves, which appeared on August 23, 1932, is in *Variety Film Reviews,* vol. 4 (New York: Garland, 1983), n.p.; the book identifies reviews by date. On Gibbons's reporting, see Gibbons, *Floyd Gibbons,* chap. 20.

232 **Real correspondents' love lives intertwined** Stanley Cloud and Lynne Olson, *The Murrow Boys: Pioneers on the Front Lines of Broadcast Journalism* (Boston: Houghton Mifflin, 1996), 110, 197, 248, 269, 315, 335–36, 378.

"ORGANIZE AND EQUIP CAMEL CARAVAN" Gibbons, *Floyd Gibbons,* 160; Smith, *The Colonel,* 299. Later, when sending his INS newspaper dispatches from China, Gibbons used the expensive urgent rate no matter what he was reporting: as his editors saw it, Gibbons did this because he thought his reputation demanded it—see J. C. Oestreicher, *The World Is Their Beat,* 18–19.

233 **anything CBS's Eric Sevareid wanted to write** Cloud and Olson, *The Murrow Boys,* 104, 184; Schroth, *The American Journey of Eric Sevareid,* 191; Eric Sevareid to Robert E. Sherwood, February 19, 1943, Sevareid Papers.

"The lecturer was, *ipso facto,* a 'celebrity'" Sheean, *Personal History,* 326–27; Sheean, *Between the Thunder and the Sun,* 271; Heald, *Transatlanatic Vistas,* 148–49.

"autograph was valued like that of a film star" Sheean, *Between the Thunder and the Sun,"* 216; Reynolds, *By Quentin Reynolds,* 211–12, 268. The biography of Reynolds is F. E Rechnitzer, *War Correspondent: The Story of Quentin Reynolds* (New York: Julian Messner, 1943).

234 **"The book clubs were a vital point"** Leonard J. Leff, *Hemingway and His Conspirators: Hollywood, Scribners, and the Making of American Celebrity Culture* (Lanham, Md.: Rowman and Littlefield, 1997), 45, 117. For further background on book clubs, see Janice A. Radway, *A Feeling for Books: The Book-of-the-Month Club, Literary Taste, and Middle-Class Desire* (Chapel Hill: University of North Carolina Press, 1997), 187–90; Robert E. Spiller, Willard Thorp, Thomas H. Johnson, and Henry Seidel Canby, eds., *Literary History of the United States: History* (New York: Macmillan, 1963), 1267.

Book-of-the-Month Club favorite Gunther, *A Fragment,* 90. In *A Fragment,* Gunther notes that all seven of his *Inside* books were BOMC selections; he had yet to write *Inside South America.*

"It is not in me to be profound" Jay Pridmore, *John Gunther: Inside Journalism* (Chicago: University of Chicago Library, 1990), 21; Canfield, *Up and Down and Around,* 124.

235 **"a hashed breast of goose"** John Gunther, "The Coarse Feeder," *Esquire,* January 1935, 134; Truman Capote, *Too Brief a Treat: The Letters of Truman Capote,* ed. Gerald Clarke (New York: Random House, 2004), 169. On Gunther's amorous interests, see Cuthbertson, *Inside,* 97, 114, 191, 198, 352. Gunther's first wife, Frances, had her own sexual history. She may not have slept with Nehru, but she certainly tried to get him sexually interested in her. Also on food, see "The Insider," *Time,* April 14, 1958, 49; John Gunther, "Cabbages for Kings," *Saturday Evening Post,* April 22, 1933, 14–15+.

"famosity" Ellen Sheean to author, e-mail, May 5, 2005; Ellen Sheean, interview by author, November 17, 2004. On celebrity friends and Sheean, see Cuthbertson, *Inside,* 76, 307. Other comments on Gunther's personality come from Jane Gunther, interview by author, June 23, 1992; Gunther, *A Fragment,* 4. Gunther mentions the *Vanity Fair* photo spread in two places, in John Gunther, "Autobiography in Brief," *Story,* May 1938, 94–95; and in his novel *The Lost City* (New York: Harper and Row, 1964), 365; the *Vanity Fair* photo spread, "Our Fourth Estate Abroad," appeared August 1932, p. 37.

"the inner and outside life" John Gunther to Carl Brandt, July 10, 1936, Gunther Papers.

236 **"INSIDE ENGLAND"** John Gunther, "*Inside* England," *Atlantic Monthly,* March 1937, 266 78.

238 **Gunther's "*Inside*" brand name** Richard Rovere, "Profiles," *New Yorker,* August 23, 1947, 30;

Cuthbertson, *Inside,* 344, 356. The relationship between Gunther and Waugh's character is mentioned in W. F. Deedes, *At War with Waugh: The Real Story of Scoop* (London: Pan, 2003), 112, but the intent of Waugh's comment was clear to all at the time.

239 **"I have eaten every book"** Cuthbertson, *Inside,* 309.

"Being a journalist" Pridmore, *John Gunther;* 21, Cuthbertson, *Inside,* 337.

240 **Greta Garbo** Cuthbertson, *Inside,* 223, 252, 309.

suited to broadcasting Ibid., 86, 181, 123, 224–27, 304, 344–46; "The Reminiscences of A(bel) A(lan) Schechter, Oral History Collection, Pickler Library, Columbia University, New York.

"virtually a semi-official status" Gunther, *A Fragment,* 37, 73; Cuthbertson, *Inside,* 170–72, 199, 263.

241 **"Guntherize"** Pridmore, *John Gunther,* 28; Cuthbertson, *Inside,* xvii, 95; Gunther, *A Fragment,* 94.

"before things changed" Jane Gunther, interview by author, June 23, 1992; John Gunther, *Inside Africa* (New York: Harper, 1955), 923.

"which was to sympathize" Gunther, *Inside Africa,* 464, 891. Gunther, *A Fragment,* 18, 29–30, 112; H. B. Elliston, "Chicagoans as Cicerones," *Atlantic Monthly,* August 1939.

"My kind of book" Gunther, *A Fragment,* 39–40; Pridmore, *John Gunther,* 28.

"someone ought to show him up" Richard H. Rovere, *Arrivals and Departures: A Journalist's Memoirs* (New York: Macmillan, 1976), 181; Rovere, "Profiles," 30. Rovere's congratulatory letter is undated, Gunther Papers.

242 **"Twice as many foreign correspondents"** Hess, *International News and Foreign Correspondents,* 12–14. The quote on the Sundance Channel's *Iconoclasts* series was in a *New Yorker* advertisement, November 26, 2005.

"Doomed Europe" "Doomed Europe" is mentioned in an undated, typewritten book blurb in Gunther Papers. Alexander Cockburn, "How to Earn Your Trench Coat," *[MORE],* May 1974, 1+.

243 **"They've been on a cruise in the Volga"** Georgie Anne Geyer, interview by author, April 13, 2005.

"magic to the moniker" "Foreign Correspondent," *Nation,* March 29, 1975, 357–58.

"Aristocracies do not last" Pareto, *A Treatise on General Sociology,* 1430.

CHAPTER 15

244 **"By 1925 there remained"** Sullivan, *Our Times,* 1:64.

"Never before" Joseph Wood Krutch, "Still Innocent and Still Abroad," *Harper's Monthly,* April 1931, 533; James Devine, "Everybody Is Going Abroad," *Educational Review,* May 1928, 306; Cindy S. Aron, *Working at Play: A History of Vacations in the United States* (New York: Oxford University Press, 1999), 3–4, 184.

"designed to give practical information" Arthur Warner, "Travel for a Song," *Nation,* March 22, 1933, 315. The *New York Times* travel section startup is mentioned in an unpublished, looseleaf book assembled for internal use by the *Times,* "Facts about the New York Times."

National Geographic Society Poole, *Explorers House,* 85, 223.

245 **"Clipper Ships"** Annie S. Peck, *Flying over South America* (Boston: Houghton Mifflin, 1932), 251–52. Background on Peck is found in Marion Tinling, *Women into the Unknown: A Sourcebook on Women Explorers and Travelers* (New York: Greenwood, 1989), 209–16; and in Elizabeth Fagg Olds, *Women of the Four Winds* (Boston: Houghton Mifflin, 1985), 5–70.

"flying as now in the day's work" Peck, *Flying over South America,* 3. Barrett, *Joseph Pulitzer,* 296–97; Thompson, *The Tour de France,* 17; Irwin, *Propaganda and the News;* Crockett, *Caliph of Baghdad,* 5; Pound and Harmsworth, *Northcliffe,* 300–301; Mott, *American Magazines,* 4:487–88; Lewis, *Man of the World,* 37–38; A. Scott Berg, *Lindbergh* (New York: Putnam's, 1998), 91–96;

Shepard, *The Paper's Papers*, chap. 22; Poole, *Explorers House*, 131, 159–61; Larry Rue, *I Fly for News* (New York: Albert and Charles Boni, 1932).

The newspaper executives on the *China Clipper* were Roy W. Howard of Scripps Howard, Paul Patterson of the *Baltimore Sun*, and Amon Carter of the *Fort Worth Star-Telegram*. See Robert L. Gandt, *China Clipper: The Age of the Great Flying Boats* (Annapolis, Md.: Naval Institute Press, 1991), 107–9.

European journals, as the above references noted, joined in the travel fun. *Le Matin*, among the many French periodicals that got into the act, created the Tour de France automobile race in 1899, a Paris-London dirigible race in 1906, the Circuit de l'Est airplane race in 1910, and a long-distance horse trek in 1911. The *London Daily Mail*'s Lord Northcliffe offered a £10,000 prize for a flight from London to Manchester, a £50,000 prize for the first flight in less than seventy-two hours between North America and the British Isles, and a £75 prize for a contest involving model planes propelled by elastic bands. Although the victor in the model-plane competition went on to start a successful aviation company, not everyone took these aerial challenges seriously. The satirical *Punch* offered a large reward for a flight to the moon.

246 **these locomotions** Dennis, *Lawson*, 302–8; Farson, *Way of the Transgressor*, 455; Negley Farson, *Sailing across Europe* (New York: Century, 1926). Farson's original agreement with Lawson is in Negley Farson to Victor Lawson, March 2, 1925, Lawson Papers. Wellman's comments on the uncertain possibilities for the flight are in an undated memorandum, NYT Archives. Several years after the ill-fated transatlantic flight, Wellman, worried that his landlord would evict him, asked *Times* owner Adolph Ochs for a $500 loan while he "worked on an invention which will revolutionize rapid transit in all large cities of the world." Ochs gave him $100. Wellman's request for a loan is in Walter Wellman to Adolph Ochs, June 15, 1921, NYT Archives.

Around-the-world antics Carroll V. Glines, *Round-the-World Flights* (New York: Van Nostrand Reinhold, 1982), 12–13; Mathews, *Reporting the Wars*, 125; Bryan B. Sterling and Francis N. Sterling, *Forgotten Eagle: Wiley Post, America's Heroic Aviation Pioneer* (New York: Carroll and Graf, 2001), chaps. 5, 6; J. Gordon Vaeth, *Graf Zeppelin: The Adventures of an Aerial Globetrotter* (New York: Harper, 1958), 9, 83; Lowell Thomas, *The First World Flight* (Boston: Houghton Mifflin, 1925), 196–208; Linton Wells, *Blood on the Moon* (Boston: Houghton Mifflin, 1937), 206, 232–33, as well as chaps. 13 and 16 for background.

Again around-the-world travel involved foreign journals as well. At the turn of the century, reporters on two French journals raced each other around the world. A one-legged French newspaperman named Andre Jaeger-Schmidt was a record-setter around the same time.

"reduce the girth of the globe" Linton Wells, *Around the World in Twenty-Eight Days* (Boston: Houghton Mifflin, 1926), 9–10, 37, and passim. In this latter book, Wells says the cost of the trip was $32,000; in *Blood on the Moon*, his autobiography, he says it cost $42,000. The editorial comment on the trip by the *New York World* appeared on July 15, 1926. An obituary for Fay Gillis Wells is in the *New York Times*, December 9, 2002; obituaries for Linton Wells are in the *New York Times*, February 1, 1976, and the *Washington Post*, February 2, 1976. Wells, an inveterate traveler, once visited 402 towns and cities to test the quality of Prohibition whiskey and, with a colleague, made the first nonstop automobile drive from Los Angeles to New York City.

247 **GALLANTLY IGNORING STOMACH ACHES** H. R. Ekins, "A Reporter Aloft," in Lyons, *We Cover the World*, 371–88; H. R. Ekins, *Around the World in Eighteen Days: And How to Do It* (London: Longmans, Green, 1936); Lee Israel, *Kilgallen* (New York: Delacorte, 1979), chaps. 3–6; *New York World-Telegram*, October 2, 1936; *New York Times*, September 27, October 10, 14, 16, 26, 1936. A retrospective on Kilgallen's feat appeared in the *New York Post*, April 26, 1960. Here is an example of Kilgallen's references to her sister: "Nellie Bly did the world in 72 days, but she wore a bustle and she didn't have airplanes." Dorothy Kilgallen, *Girl around the World* (Philadelphia: David McKay, 1936), 30. While this three-way race was on, Jean Batten became "the first woman to have flown solo from England to New Zealand and I have lowered the previous best time for crossing the Tasman Sea." *New York Times*, October 17, 1936.

248 **escape literature** Allen Churchill, *The Literary Decade* (Englewood Cliffs, N.J.: Prentice-Hall, 1971), 256–75. Burton Holmes is described in "Holmes (Elias) Burton," in *Current Biography*, ed. Anna Rothe (New York: H. W. Wilson, 1945), 302–4. For details on Powell, see E. Alexander Powell, *Adventure Road* (Garden City, N.Y.: Doubleday, 1954); and his obituary, in the *New York Times*, December 14, 1957.

"the world's foremost globe trotter" "They Stand Out from the Crowd," *Literary Digest*, March 17, 1934, 11; Joel C. Hodson, *Lawrence of Arabia and American Culture: The Making of a Transatlantic Legend* (Westport, Conn.: Greenwood Press, 1995), 78 and passim; Fang, *Those Radio Commentators!* 78; Lowell Thomas, *European Skyways* (Boston: Houghton Mifflin, 1927), 3. A collection of profiles of Thomas is found in Norman R. Bowen, ed., *Lowell Thomas: The Stranger Everyone Knows* (Garden City, N.Y.: Doubleday, 1968). Lowell Thomas's autobiography is *So Long until Tomorrow: From Quaker Hill to Kathmandu* (New York: William Morrow, 1977).

An example of embroidering his experiences is that Thomas overstated his academic accomplishments. So the Valparaiso University archivist informed Carolyn Pione, my coauthor for a profile of Thomas in *American National Biography* (New York: Oxford University Press, 1999): "It distresses me to point out inaccuracies in his autobiography, but I feel I must for the sake of your research. This school was never officially known as the University of Northern Indiana at Valparaiso. . . . While Lowell may have believed he was doing the equivalent of two years' work in one, the hand-written Student Registers . . . indicate that he was not taking any more courses than most other students at the time. Finally, he did not receive a master's degree here, although later he was granted an honorary doctorate." Mel Doering to Carolyn Pione, December 20, 1995.

fashion the odd escapade Mary Knight, "Girl Reporter in Paris," in Lyons, *We Cover the World*, 276; Will Rogers, *There's Not a Bathing Suit in Russia and Other Bare Facts* (New York: Albert and Charles Boni, 1927), 52, 54; Ray Robinson, *American Original: A Life of Will Rogers* (New York: Oxford University Press, 1996), 119–73; Ben Yagoda, *Will Rogers: A Biography* (New York: Knopf, 1993), 243; Richard Patience and John Abbe, *Around the World in Eleven Years* (New York: Frederick A. Stokes, 1936); Michael Korda, *Making the List: A Cultural History of the American Bestseller, 1900–1999, as Seen through the Annual Bestseller Lists of Publishers Weekly* (New York: Barnes and Noble, 2001), 70; and J. Fred MacDonald, *Don't Touch That Dial!* (Chicago: Nelson-Hall, 1979), 296.

"A trip to Europe" Francis F. Miller and H. D. Hill, "Europe as a Playground," *Atlantic Monthly*, August 1930, 226; Harvey Levenstein, *We'll Always Have Paris: American Tourists in France since 1930* (Chicago: University of Chicago Press, 2004), 46–47.

249 **"When the diploma was safely clutched"** William Harlan Hale, "Grand Tour, New Style," *Atlantic Monthly*, December 1932, 567.

"that hardy perennial" Corey Ford, "The Adventure Racket," *Vanity Fair*, July 1929, 35. Halliburton's wide appeal is noted throughout Ford's article and discussed, among other places, in Churchill, *The Literary Decade*, chap. 16.

250 **"the pleasantest country club in America"** F. Scott Fitzgerald, *This Side of Paradise* (New York: Macmillan, 1986), 36; references to Davis and Brooke can be found on 106, 231, 147. Background on Fitzgerald's book is found in André Le Vot, *F. Scott Fitzgerald: A Biography*, trans. William Byron (Garden City, N.Y.: Doubleday, 1983), 54, 71.

"The *romantic*" Richard Halliburton, *The Royal Road to Romance* (Indianapolis: Bobbs-Merrill, 1925), 4; Richard Halliburton to Gilbert Grosvenor, July 9, 1921, National Geographic Archives.

"I can actually spit a mile" Halliburton, *Royal Road*, 19. See also Jonathan Root, *Halliburton: The Magnificent Myth* (New York: Coward-McCann, 1965), 74–77, 82, 92. This is the best biography of Halliburton, although it leaves room for something grander with, among other things, footnotes. I make extensive use of Root's book for background. Another biographical work is James Cortese, *Richard Halliburton's Royal Road* (Memphis: White Rose Press, 1989).

***National Geographic* did not use** In *Royal Road*, Halliburton says that *National Geographic* bought one of his articles. It is suggested in the National Geographic Archives that the magazine did buy one article; see editor to Wesley Halliburton, Richard Halliburton's father, November 10, 1922, a letter accompanied by a typewritten article on Tibet and sixteen related photographs. The archives also contain a September 1, 1922, letter from Wesley Halliburton, which seems to refer to an Andorra story that was rejected. Acceptance is one thing, however, and publication another. Halliburton implies that the magazine used the story and the photographs—several photos in *Royal Road* have the credit line "Photo. by Richard Halliburton, copyright National Geographic Magazine." Halliburton's chief biographer says outright that the magazine published a story on Gibraltar. Root, *Halliburton*, 97. But I found no article by Halliburton in the magazine, nor any Halliburton photographs. No doubt Halliburton thought it was good publicity to suggest that *National Geographic* had an interest in his work.

The Royal Road to Romance Root, *Halliburton*, 114, 139–40; Korda, *Making the List*, 51. Irvine Hockaday Jr., Mike Hockaday's son, interview by author, October 17, 1990. Hockaday's adventure with Halliburton was periodically recounted in local newspapers in later years, e.g., Ed Shook, *Kansas City Star*, September 14, 1958; Laura Rollins Hockaday, *Kansas City Star*, October 23, 1977. As an indication of how many young people were traveling at the time, Hockaday met up with his brother and another Princeton classmate during the trip. Halliburton's 1930 royalties are listed, along with those from other years, in an undated document in Bobbs-Merrill Mss.

251 **"gorgeous, clean-cut, 110 per cent red-blooded"** *Chicago Tribune*, March 13, 1979. Descriptions of Halliburton's talks and the importance of the word "romance" are from *Chicago Tribune*, October 13, 1926; Root, *Halliburton*, 101–5, 123, 133; Richard Halliburton to parents, November 9, 1935, Halliburton Papers; Richard Halliburton, *Richard Halliburton: His Story of His Life's Adventure as Told in Letters to His Mother and Father* (Indianapolis: Bobbs-Merrill, 1940), 385; Richard Halliburton, "A Glorious Adventure among the Booksellers on the Royal Road to Best Selling," typescript, n.d., 2; and Richard Halliburton to Hewitt Hanson Howland, May 11, 1925. The latter two are found in Bobbs-Merrill Mss.

"an adventure not in the air is obsolete" Root, *Halliburton*, 179.

"one of the greatest press-agents of his time" "Last Adventure," *Time*, June 19, 1939, 59; Root, *Halliburton*, 143–44, 156.

The Panama Canal was perfect "Holmes (Elias), Burton," 303; "Panama Tourist Mecca," *Pan-American Magazine*, March–April 1928, 4; Root, *Halliburton*, 109–11, 149; "Panama Canal Stunt Swims Began Early," *Panama Canal Review*, August 1966, 6–8.

253 **"undeniably pretty"** Richard Halliburton, *New Worlds to Conquer* (Indianapolis: Bobbs-Merrill, 1929), 104.

255 **"Armed with my omnipotent letter"** Ibid., 112–19.

"oblivion" Ford, "The Adventure Racket"; John Riddell, "New Ladies' Clubs to Conquer," *Vanity Fair*, September 1928, 73; "We Nominate for Oblivion," *Vanity Fair*, June 1930, 49; Root, *Halliburton*, 157–58. John Riddell's spoof on Halliburton also appeared in his *Meaning No Offense* (New York: John Day, 1928), a volume full of spoofs on travel.

256 **"clean and clear"** Richard Halliburton, *The Flying Carpet* (Indianapolis: Bobbs-Merrill, 1932), 270; *Chicago Tribune*, July 13, 1928; David M. Schwartz, "On the Royal Road to Adventures with 'Daring Dick,'" *Smithsonian*, March 1989, 170. Halliburton was singled out as a hoaxer in a book on the subject, Curtis D. MacDougall, *Hoaxes* (New York: Dover, 1958), 134.

slathered on the color Olds, *Women of the Four Winds*, 17; Halliburton, *New Worlds to Conquer*, 25.

"the foremost historian in Panama" Halliburton, *New Worlds to Conquer*, 136. For a discussion of Balboa's sighting of the Pacific Ocean, see Kathleen Romoli, *Balboa of Darién: Discoverer of the Pacific* (Garden City, N.Y.: Doubleday, 1953), 158–62. The conclusions about Halliburton's failure to reach the summit of Cerro Pirre come from my own 1992 ascent to the top, which is now clearly identified by a geodetic marker. My climbing party included an Indian who had made the climb before but nevertheless became temporarily lost en route. Although Halliburton made the trip in about the same amount of time as we did (three days), he came in the rainy season, when the going should have been harder, and climbed with an ocelot on his shoulder. We had enough trouble ducking under vines and fallen trees with just our packs on our backs; extra weight, even to make for a good story, seems excessive even for the most hard-bitten romantic. Although Halliburton might have come another way, the only other route, via the ranger station in Boca de Cupe, is just as long and just as difficult, according to experts I interviewed.

257 **"Burning current events are poison in book form"** Richard Halliburton to William L. Chambers, June 20, 1935, Bobbs-Merrill Mss; Richard Halliburton, *Seven League Boots* (Indianapolis: Bobbs-Merrill, 1935), 358; Halliburton, *Royal Road*, 255–56; Fitzgerald, *This Side of Paradise*, 76. Halliburton had his own check-dodging experience in Monte Carlo, but he later repaid with casino winnings. *Royal Road*, 107–10.

Two Richard Halliburtons The *Philadelphia Inquirer* article is in the Bobbs-Merrill file; it has no author or date but carries a copyright of 1938. Richard Halliburton, "Where I'll Spend My Honeymoons," unpublished, probably written around 1935, judging from a note written on the manuscript; Richard Halliburton to Wesley Halliburton, November 27, 1936, both in Halliburton Papers. The "regulations mould" portion of the letter is reprinted in Halliburton, *Halliburton Letters*, 386. The divorce case is mentioned in Root, *Halliburton*, 31. The woman who remembers his expressing interest in marriage is Helen P. Halsey. Halsey to author, January 18, 20, November 6, 1993.

258 **"behind the mask"** John Loughery, *The Other Side of Silence: Men's Lives and Gay Identities: A Twentieth-Century History* (New York: Holt, 1998), 44. The Harvard story is in William Wright, *Harvard's Secret Court: The Savage 1920 Purge of Campus Homosexuals* (New York: St. Martin's, 2005). The rudeness at the book signing is in Elizabeth Jameson to author, n.d., 1991. Halliburton's dismay about Princeton appears in many letters; this quote is from one to his editor at Bobbs-Merrill, Halliburton to David L. Chambers, January 3, 1933, Bobbs-Merrill Mss.

"my first and last love" Richard Halliburton to Marchesa Capponi, May 17, 1927, McClure Mss. Halliburton to David L. Chambers, April 10, 1933; Halliburton to Chambers, telegram, April 22, 1937, all in Bobbs-Merrill Mss. See Root, *Halliburton*, 129, 133, 181, 204, 275, for details on the Brooke biography, which was ultimately done by novelist Arthur Springer from Halliburton's notes. It is not the definitive biography and is as purple as anything Halliburton was capable of writing. Springer opens with a long section on Halliburton, not Brooke, explaining the reticence of Brooke's mother about Halliburton's writing a biography of her son: "With all his fineness of feeling and his wind-harp responsiveness to the urges of the flesh, he had not escaped those human frailties which according to Saint Luke could even win the piety of God. There was a chapter or two in his book of life that called for silence. But this second Richard the Lion-Hearted, who claimed that he always liked resistance, was not easily discouraged." Arthur Springer, *Red Wine of Youth: A Life of Rupert Brooke* (Indianapolis: Bobbs-Merrill, 1948), 16. Subsequent Brooke biographers give little heed to Springer and less still to Halliburton.

259 **The make-believe world of Hollywood** Root, *Halliburton*, 174, 204–5, 210–16, 254.

"cancer of the throat" Halliburton, *Seven League Boots*, 99–100, 105. The Stoneman quote is in Anthony Summers and Tom Mangold, *The File on the Tsar* (New York: Harper and Row, 1976), 181. Interesting details on the czar's death are found in Edvard Radzinsky, *The Last Tsar: The Life and Death of Nicholas II* (New York: Anchor, 1993), especially part 3. William R. Maples headed a team that studied the remains when they were unearthed, which he describes in his *Dead Men Do Tell Tales: The Strange and Fascinating Cases of a Forensic Anthropologist* (Garden City, N.Y.: Doubleday, 1994), chap. 15. Maples had read Halliburton's account when he was a young man and suggests that the Ermakov interview helped him piece the story together in the early 1990s.

"Freedom!" Halliburton, *Seven League Boots*, 227.

260 **"regular Captain Bligh"** Root, *Halliburton*, 25. Discovery of the rudder is in the *Chicago Tribune*, July 6, 1940.

"HIGH SPIRITS" Richard Halliburton to Bobbs-Merrill, March 5, 1939.

"Perhaps we're wrong" "Talk of the Town," *New Yorker,* December 14, 1929, 14.

261 **"just an accommodation for publicity"** "Panama Canal Stunt Swims Began Early," 6–8. Albert Oshiver's quest to get his ten-cent refund is vividly described in Willie K. Friar, deputy director of public affairs, Panama Canal Commission, to Oshiver, January 15, 1988; Oshiver to Dennis P. McAuliffe, administrator, Panama Canal Commission, March 7, 1988; Oshiver to Steny H. Hoyer, U.S. representative, October 13, 1988; Hoyer to McAuliffe, October 20, 1988; Michael Rhode Jr., assistant to chairman and secretary, Panama Canal Commission, to Hoyer, November 14, 1988—all in the files of the Panama Canal Commission, Balboa, Republic of Panama. Michael Rhode, interview by author, November 26, 1991; John Eberenz, interview by author, March 1992. Eberenz was at the time chief of the canal unit that assessed tolls. The best explanation for Halliburton's toll, Eberenz said, is that he was charged one-half of the one-ton rate prevailing at the time. I was the freelance public radio reporter.

not the only journalist-adventurer to perish Robinson, *American Original,* 167, chap. 17; Susan Butler, *East to the Dawn: The Life of Amelia Earhart* (Reading, Mass.: Addison Wesley, 1997), 201, 206, 219, 353–54.

"Few careers afford a better cartoon" George Weller, "The Passing of the Last Playboy," *Esquire,* April 1940, 58, 112. On Weller's Stanley trip, see *Daily News* story on its foreign service, May 8–9, 1971.

"Gone are the holidays abroad" Paul Fussell, *Abroad: British Literary Traveling between the Wars* (New York: Oxford University Press, 1980), 218–19.

a transitional figure Jennifer Cox, *Around the World in Eighty Dates* (New York: Downtown Press, 2005). Mount Everest climbing is discussed in *New York Times,* May 27, 2003. A study showing the proliferation of travel sections is Larry Wood, "Is Travel Writing a Growing Profession?" *Journalism Quarterly* 54 (Summer 1977): 761–64. For an interesting discussion of what is left to discover today, see "A World to Explore," *Economist,* December 23, 1995–January 5, 1996, 56–58. The Atlantic Ocean walker is mentioned in the *New York Times,* March 6, 2000. Mihir Sen's entry was included along with such feats as the longest swim using the butterfly stroke (40.6 miles). See *Guinness Book of World Records* (New York: Sterling, 1989), 416–17. Neither of those swims is included in more recent editions of the book. Data on the financial contribution of travel and tourism can be found in William F. Theobald, ed., *Global Tourism,* 3rd ed. (Maryland Heights, Mo.: Elsevier, 2004). Josep Areny i Fité, one of the descendants of the Andorran innkeepers, interview by author, May 27, 1993.

262 **"with some of the young writers"** Miriam Lyman, "Richard Halliburton's Letters," typewritten report, n.d., Bobbs-Merrill Mss. The book was published as *Richard Halliburton: His Story of His Life's Adventure as Told in Letters to His Mother and Father* (Indianapolis: Bobbs-Merrill, 1940). See also William Hale obituary in *New York Times,* July 1, 1974; John Maxwell Hamilton, *Edgar Snow: A Biography,* rev. ed. (Baton Rouge: Louisiana State University Press, 2003), 11; Root, *Halliburton,* 93; Susan Sontag, "Homage to Halliburton," *Oxford American,* March–April 2001, 120. After Snow's death, his travel writings were collected in *Edgar Snow's Journey South of the Clouds,* ed. Robert M. Farnsworth (Columbia, Mo.: University of Missouri Press, 1991).

"From the beginning" *The Second Fifteen: Class of Nineteen Hundred and Twenty-One, Princeton University* (n.p.: Progress, 1951), 497. As examples of what was written about Halliburton in magazines, see Guy Townsend, "Richard Halliburton: The Forgotten Myth," *Memphis Magazine,* August 1977 and April 2001 (article available at memphismagazine.com/backissues); R. C. Phelan, "Halliburton's Banana Peel," *Vogue,* February 1, 1960, 64; and, of course, Schwartz's *Smithsonian* article, "On the Royal Road to Adventures with 'Daring Dick.'" A description of the computer game is found at www.adventureclassicgaming.com/index.php/site/reviews/161/ (accessed August 19, 2008).

263 **"The late (?) Richard Halliburton"** Schwartz, "On the Royal Road to Adventures with 'Daring Dick,'" 177–78; Root, *Halliburton,* 268–69; Irvine Hockaday Jr., interview by author.

CHAPTER 16

264 **Edith Lederer** Details of the party, her expulsion, and her return home are from Edith Lederer, interviews by author, November 2, 2003; May 17, 2004. She writes poignantly about the challenges she faced as a woman reporter in Vietnam in Edith Lederer, "My First War," in *War Torn: Stories of War from the Women Reporters Who Covered Vietnam*, ed. Denby Fawcett et al. (New York: Random House, 2002).

"Peru Meets Match" *Washington Post*, July 22, 1975.

265 **"Nowadays the expulsion"** Sheean, *Dorothy and Red*, 249.

Those who did stood out For a discussion of these and other women correspondents, see Edwards, *Women of the World*; Nancy Caldwell Sorel, *The Women Who Wrote the War* (New York: Arcade, 1999); Joyce Hoffman, *On Their Own: Women Journalists and the American Experience in Vietnam* (Cambridge, Mass.: Da Capo, 2008).

266 **"This was the first real story"** Williams, *Dusk of Empire*, 208.

"the *Manchester Guardian* of America" Wile, *News Is Where You Find It*, 415; Edward Price Bell to Victor Lawson, October 3, 1922, Lawson Papers. Villard, *Disappearing Daily*, chap. 22, offers an interesting picture of Curtis and his newspaper, as does Villard's *Some Newspapers and Newspapermen* (New York: Knopf, 1923), chap. 9. On the *Guardian* as a model, Seldes said, "I think that every publisher who starts as a reporter has the same dream—the hope of equaling or even outdoing the *Manchester Guardian* in America." Seldes, *Lords of the Press*, 183. Curtis's interest in buying the *Daily News* is in Charles R. Miller to Adolph Ochs, December 18, 1925, NYT Archives.

"a warehouse fire" Goulden, *The Curtis Caper*, 37.

"We had *carte blanche*" Williams, *Dusk of Empire*, 207.

"buzzing into the office" Ibid., 209; Kurth, *American Cassandra*, 71. Much of the detail in this chapter about Thompson is from Kurth's excellent biography.

267 **"was Richard Harding Davis"** Kurth, *American Cassandra*, 50.

"full of promise" Ibid., 92; Mowrer, *Triumph and Turmoil*, 196; Dorothy Thompson, *New York Times*, August 27, 1934. Mowrer paints a vivid picture of Berlin in the 1920s.

268 **"*Dove* Seldes?"** Seldes, *Tell the Truth and Run*, 196; George Seldes, *You Can't Print That! The Truth behind the News, 1918–1928* (Garden City: N.Y.: Garden City, 1929), 9, 427. Seldes tells the story of his expulsions from Russia and Italy slightly differently in various books.

"may throw the republic" Dorothy Thompson, "Poverty De Luxe," *Saturday Evening Post*, May 9, 1931, 144.

"stupidity of their demagogic leadership" Ibid.

"I Saw Hitler!" Dorothy Thompson, "I Saw Hitler!" *Cosmopolitan*, March 1932, 32+; Dorothy Thompson, *"I Saw Hitler"!* (New York: Farrar and Rinehart, 1932).

271 **"new records"** Roy Howard recounted the experience in a chapter that UPI correspondent Webb Miller invited him to write in Miller, *I Found No Peace* (chap. 7). See also Hohenberg, *Foreign Correspondence*, 116–17; Emery and Emery, *The Press and America*, 246–47.

Years later, a similarly embarrassing experience occurred in Africa. Correspondents covering the civil war in the Congo mistakenly reported the arrival of an airplane carrying UN secretary general Dag Hammarskjöld. Hammarskjöld's plane had crashed. David Halberstam, a fledgling *New York Times* correspondent, rejoiced that he had been unable to reach the airport to cover the story. "Had I made that mistake," he said, "I would have gone down in *Times* annals as 'Old Airport Halberstam.'" An AP reporter on the scene told him it was "the greatest gaff of the age." Halberstam described the experience in his *The Making of a Quagmire* (New York: Random House, 1965), 13, 15.

"more like a call to arms" Sheean, *Dorothy and Red*, 260; John Gunther, "A Blue-Eyed Tornado," *New York Herald Tribune Magazine*, January 13, 1935, 7.

"Germany safe for war" Dorothy Thompson, "Back to Blood and Iron: Germany Goes German

Again," *Saturday Evening Post,* May 6, 1933, 70; Dorothy Thompson, "The Militant Disarmed," *Saturday Evening Post,* September 17, 1932, 13.

"Jews as Hitler's unique target" The *Times* editor who rued his paper's lack of coverage of Jewish persecution is Max Frankel, writing in a special section devoted to celebrating the 150th anniversary of the *Times. New York Times,* November 14, 2001. Thompson's articles for the *Jewish Daily Bulletin* appeared on May 7, 14, 21, 1933. One of the few libraries (for all I can tell, the only library) that has the *Bulletin* from this period is the Klau Library, Hebrew Union College–Jewish Institute of Religion, Cincinnati.

Jewish affairs had been of interest to Thompson since her initial voyage to Europe in 1920 aboard a ship packed with Zionists headed for a conference on the future of Palestine. One of her first International News Service assignments in London was to cover the conference. Afterward the Jewish Correspondence Bureau in London offered to hire her as a reporter, a job she turned down. For another example of her interest in Nazi treatment of Jews, see Dorothy Thompson and Benjamin Stolberg, "Hitler and the American Jew," *Scribner's Magazine,* July 1933, 136–40.

A useful discussion of American coverage of Nazi terror against Jews is found in Deborah E. Lipstadt, *Beyond Belief: The American Press and the Coming of the Holocaust, 1933–1945* (New York: Free Press, 1986); the examples of reporting by the *Baltimore Sun* and the *New York Journal American* are on 154. On skepticism about atrocity propaganda and general lack of coverage, see Vernon McKenzie, "Atrocities in World War II—What We Can Believe," *Journalism Quarterly* 19 (September 1942): 268–76; and Arlene Rossen Cardozo, "The American Magazine Coverage of the Nazi 'Death Camp Era,'" *Journalism Quarterly* 60 (Winter 1983): 717–18.

272 **"No one less like"** Thompson, "Back to Blood and Iron," 3–4; Dorothy Thompson, "What This Country Needs," *Saturday Evening Post,* August 30, 1933.

"no fewer than fourteen hundred" William L. Shirer, *The Rise and Fall of the Third Reich: A History of Nazi Germany* (New York: Simon and Schuster, 1960), 248; John Gunther, "Dateline Vienna," *Harper's Monthly Magazine,* July 1935, 199. *Zuckerbrot und Peitsche* mentioned in Joy Schaleben, *Getting the Story out of Nazi Germany: Louis P. Lochner* (Austin, Tex.: Association for Education in Journalism, 1969), 26. Also see Louis P. Lochner, *Always the Unexpected: A Book of Reminiscences* (New York: Macmillan, 1956), 251; and Oestreicher, *The World Is Their Beat,* 48–49.

273 **"gallant fighter"** Mowrer, *Triumph and Turmoil,* chap. 20; Mowrer, *Journalist's Wife,* chap. 22; *Times* (London) dispatch published in *New York Times,* September 1, 1933. Mowrer in his own way belittled Hitler, writing, "Subjectively, Adolf Hitler was, in my opinion, entirely sincere even in his self-contradictions, for his is a humorless mind that simply excludes the need for consistency that might distress more intellectual types." Edgar Ansel Mowrer, *Germany Puts the Clock Back* (New York: William Morrow, 1933), 251. Also like Thompson, Mowrer underestimated Hitler, predicting in one of the *Chicago Daily News* articles that helped him win a Pulitzer that, as a result of the poor Nazi showing in late 1932 elections, Hitler "seems to be a remote issue, at least as possible boss of Germany." Quoted in Edgar Ansel Mowrer, "The Optimism for the Following Year and Its Reasons," in Fischer, *Outstanding International Reporting,* 120.

274 **"Dorothy Thompson Emergency Squad"** Bella Fromm, *Blood and Banquets: A Berlin Social Diary* (New York: Birch Lane Press, 1990), 170; Frederick T. Birchall, *New York Times,* August 26, 1934; Kurth, *American Cassandra,* 202.

"Hitler is a big stiff" Kurth, *American Cassandra,* 200.

"In view of your numerous anti-German publications" Birchall, *New York Times,* August 26, 1934. The episode is discussed in some detail in Kurth, *American Cassandra,* 198–204. Thompson's description of being presented with the expulsion order is in Dorothy Thompson, "Goodby to Germany," *Harper's Monthly Magazine,* December 1934, 51. On Hanfstängl's possible role, see William L. Shirer, *Berlin Diary: The Journal of a Foreign Correspondent, 1934–1941* (New York: Knopf, 1941), 12.

"gave her a great bunch" Birchall, *New York Times,* August 26, 1934. Also see "Little Man," *Time,*

September 3, 1934; Sorel, *The Women Who Wrote the War,* 7–8; Sheean, *Dorothy and Red,* 250. In the early days of National Socialist power, according to Birchall, the Nazis became suspicious of a Paris correspondent in Germany and threatened expulsion. The French government responded in turn that "four German correspondents would be immediately expelled from France as reprisal, and that would continue as long as a German was left in France." The French correspondent remained in Germany. In February of 1933, following the Reichstag fire, the Nazis expelled two Russian correspondents representing official Soviet newspapers but allowed them reentry after the Russian government "immediately expelled every German correspondent in Russia." Birchall, *New York Times,* August 26, 1934.

"My offense" Thompson, *New York Times,* August 27, 1934. A report on her radio broadcast is in *New York Times,* August 30, 1934. Also see "Little Man," *Time,* September 3, 1934, 23; "The Newsweek in Transition," *Newsweek,* September 1, 1934, 27.

275 **"a heroine"** Sheean, *Dorothy and Red,* 207, 251, 263; George Seldes, *Witness to a Century: Encounters with the Noted, the Notorious, and the Three SOBs* (New York: Ballantine, 1987), 291.

"She is read, believed and quoted" "Cartwheel Girl," *Time,* June 12, 1939, 47; Kurth, *American Cassandra,* 262.

"conceited ass" Dorothy Thompson, *Listen, Hans* (Boston: Houghton Mifflin, 1942), 172.

"liberal conservatism" Kurth, *American Cassandra,* 221; Lynn D. Gordon, "Why Dorothy Thompson Lost Her Job: Political Columnists and the Press Wars of the 1930s and 1940s," *History of Education Quarterly* 34 (Fall 1994): 280. Thompson's work on behalf of the Jews in Germany is found in Lipstadt, *Beyond Belief,* 192, 241.

"Quite possibly" Sheean, *Dorothy and Red,* 281; Kurth, *American Cassandra,* 66–67, 159. For a discussion of the *Saturday Evening Post* during this period, see Jan Cohn, *Creating America: George Horace Lorimer and the Saturday Evening Post* (Pittsburgh: University of Pittsburgh Press, 1989).

arrived by rail a couple of hours after Thompson left William L. Shirer, *Twentieth Century Journey: A Memoir of a Life and the Times,* vol. 2, *The Nightmare Years, 1930–1940* (Boston: Little, Brown, 1984), 118.

276 **"I ought to send the whole bunch"** Ernst Hanfstaengl, *Hitler: The Missing Years* (London: Eyre and Spottiswoode, 1957), 256; Shirer, *The Nightmare Years,* 138–39. On the Soviet habit of expelling correspondents, see Desmond, *Crisis and Conflict,* 30–47.

In time "Putzi" Hanfstängl had his own problems. His qualifications for working with the foreign press included having a Harvard education and an American mother. In addition to his press work, he played Wagner on the piano to cheer up Hitler. Over time Hitler apparently came to care less and less for his services. Arranging the Thompson interview seems to have been one of many irritants. Upon being reminded of it, Hitler commented that he would "let the fellow have it!" Before he could follow through, Hanfstängl fled Nazi Germany and became an adviser to the U.S. government. Hanfstängl apparently asked many journalists for job recommendations when he offered his services to the United States. Reynolds, *By Quentin Reynolds,* 128. The "I'll let the fellow have it!" quote is from a memoir by an American Nazi, Kurt G. W. Ludecke, *I Knew Hitler: The Story of a Nazi Who Escaped the Blood Purge* (New York: Scribner's, 1938), 531.

"real or imagined compulsion" "27 Correspondents Leave Germany under Pressure of Nazi Regime," *Editor and Publisher,* April 6, 1935, 10. On Schultz, see Edwards, *Women of the World,* 69; and Sigrid Schultz, interviews by Alan Green, 1971 and 1972, American Jewish Committee Oral Histories, New York Public Library. On Flanner, see Sorel, *The Women Who Wrote the War,* 10–11. On the Hottelet case, see Harnett and Ferguson, *Unipress,* 138. The Birchall book-burning story is in *New York Times,* May 11, 1933. On Bouton, see S. Miles Bouton, "A Particular People," in Benjamin, *The Inside Story,* 116. According to an in-house written history of the *Baltimore Sun,* its American correspondent in Germany (probably Miles Bouton) started out being pro-Hitler, while another reporter also used by the newspaper, a German, favored the Weimar constitution. As Hitler acquired more power, the German changed sides and so did the American, who was expelled. A *Sun* correspondent in the Far East was not allowed into Japan. Gerald W. Johnson, Frank R. Kent, H. L. Mencken, and Hamilton Owens, *The Sunpapers of Baltimore* (New York: Knopf, 1937), 415.

277 **"Oedipus complex"** Gunther, *A Fragment,* 19; *New York Times,* January 18, 1940. For an example of Sheean's pride over being banned, see Sheean, *First and Last Love,* 142.

"divine Dictator" On Steffens's reaction to Mussolini, see Justin Kaplan, *Lincoln Steffens: A Biography* (New York: Simon and Schuster, 1974), 286. On Tarbell's see Ida M. Tarbell, "The Greatest Story in the World Today," *McCall's,* December 1926, 83.

"sword of Damocles" From autobiographical note, January 14, 1941, Brown Papers.

"knew that the Seldes affair still smoldered" David Darrah's expulsion is recounted in his *Hail Caesar!* (Boston: Hale, Cushman, and Flint, 1936), 21, 291–329; See Edwards, *McCormick's Tribune,* 96. Precise calculations of expulsions are difficult to come by. Robert W. Desmond says two correspondents were given the heave-ho from Italy between 1922 and 1936; see his *Tides of War,* 55. He does not give a source or say who the two were, but by deduction they must be Seldes and David Darrah, who left in 1935. Other background came from Richard Mowrer, interview by author, June 28, 2004; Taylor, *Awakening from History,* 200–209; and Neil MacNeil, *Without Fear or Favor* (New York: Harcourt, Brace, 1940), 129. MacNeil says twenty-five correspondents were expelled from Italy between 1936 and 1939; he doesn't cite a source. The mention of AP photographers jailed in Austria is from Robert F. Schildbach, Vienna bureau chief, AP, in a typed note, "Requested by General Manager of meeting of Managing Editors," n.d., received at headquarters in New York on August 24, 1934, AP Archives. On Seldes's problems publishing *Sawdust Caesar* and on press support for Mussolini, see John P. Diggins, *Mussolini and Fascism: The View from America* (Princeton, N.J.: Princeton University Press, 1972), chap. 3.

278 **"continuing hostile attitude"** Cloud and Olson, *The Murrow Boys,* 126.

"The basic point" Nate Polowetzky, "Changes in Coverage by the Associated Press," in *Third World News in American Media: Experience and Prospects,* ed. Donald Shanor and Donald H. Johnston, Columbia Journalism Monograph No. 4 (New York: Center for Advanced Study of Communication and Public Affairs, Graduate School of Journalism, Columbia University, 1983), 25. Polowetzky often admonished correspondents about covering every sparrow. George Krimsky, interview by author, April 5, 2004. As another example of this attitude, which was constantly reinforced within the AP, see the *Service Bulletin of the Associated Press,* April 24, 1923, 3: "Somebody, somewhere must have the function of furnishing the really important news of the day, and it is for this that The Associated Press is maintained by the newspapers of this country." The AP's emphasis on facts, not opinion, is found, among many other places, in *Service Bulletin of the Associated Press,* May 1, 1920, 26: "The introduction of a news story should cover the four 'W's'— What, Where, When, Who. (And never 'Why' unless authority is given.—NEWS EDITOR.)"

"after nineteen ejections" Louis P. Lochner, *What about Germany?* (New York: Dodd, Mead, 1942), 311; Lochner, *Always the Unexpected,* 252. A similar comment came from another AP reporter, this time one stationed in Italy, on the need to avoid "being kicked out of any important news center." See Diggins, *Mussolini and Fascism,* 45.

"Believing as I do" Schaleben, *Getting the Story out of Nazi Germany,* 8.

279 **"If I had had a three-year lease"** Seldes, *You Can't Print That!* 82.

"discovered only too soon" Pierre van Paassen, *Days of Our Years* (New York: Hillman-Curl, 1939), 163; Lipstadt, *Beyond Belief,* chap. 11. On Barnes's concerns, see Shirer, *The Nightmare Years,* 550–51.

"The difficulties under which we work" Schaleben, *Getting the Story out of Nazi Germany,* 37. The final chapter of Schaleben's monograph paints an interesting picture of Lochner's socializing in the interest of gathering news.

"to wipe out any traces" Ibid., 8, 21–22, for Lochner's recollections on covering Nazi Germany.

280 **"I always knew I was hostage to them"** Marvin Kalb, interview by author, January 8, 2004.

prodigious drinking Warren Hoge, *New York Times,* May 13, 2004. The apology is described in a May 17, 2004, "News Alert" from the Committee to Protect Journalists, cpj.org/news/2004/brazil17may04na.html (accessed August 17, 2008). The correspondent who committed journalism was Barry Bearak, who told of his imprisonment in *New York Times,* April 27, 2008.

myriad of horrors Prochnau, *Once upon a Distant War,* 113; David M. Alpern, "Beating the Press," *Newsweek,* August 29, 1977; Judith Matloff, "Unspoken," *Columbia Journalism Review,* May–June 2007, 22–23.

"A common device" David Lamb, *Washington Post,* February 15, 1978.

281 **"AP had one mission"** George Krimsky, "A Life So Far," unpublished memoir, provided to author in 2004.

282 **"How many journalists"** Nora Boustany, *Washington Post,* March 30, 1986; Eason Jordan, *New York Times,* April 11, 2003.

"an excellent example" Hohenberg, *Foreign Correspondence,* 180. For a discussion of how expulsion can backfire, see C. Anthony Giffard and Lisa Cohen, "South African TV and Censorship: Does It Reduce Negative Coverage?" *Journalism Quarterly* 66 (Spring 1989): 3–10. For a discussion of how the threat of expulsion continues to shape reporting, see William A. Hachten and Brian Beil, "Bad News or No News? Covering Africa, 1965–1982," *Journalism Quarterly* 62 (Autumn 1985): 626–30.

"unreal and offensive" The story with the quote is from a dispatch dated June 19, 1970, according to Susan James of the AP staff. Background on this episode is from Joseph McGowan, interview by author, June 3, 2004. The "womanhood" sentences that may have irked officials were in a story that he wrote on June 18: "Prostitutes are out in force. One hotel employe [*sic*] said, however, girls hanging out in the lobby were college girls 'thinking that if they can marry a flier, they'll get to the United States.'" McGowan believes the Spanish-language version, rewritten in New York from his dispatch and used by the military-leaning newspaper in Lima, was more damning of Peruvian womanhood. One reason for believing that it was the government's concern over his inside source that accounted for his expulsion was that a Peruvian general casually said so to his successor.

"Edie" Edith Lederer, interview by author, November 2, 2003. I worked in Peru shortly after Lederer's expulsion and, wary of the same fate, kept a briefcase full of material I wanted to take out of the country should I be expelled. The UPI reporter at the time expressed concern about going too far in his reporting lest he get the boot as well. He had a particular reason for wanting to stay: his wife was Peruvian. Yet another example of the AP's not wanting its reporters expelled is provided by Peter Arnett, who worked in Indonesia for the AP in the 1960s. "The wire service was not eager for a public confrontation over press freedom in a peripheral place such as Indonesia. It was more concerned about building up its coverage for regional clients." Nevertheless, Arnett did press forward with his reporting, was expelled, and his career took off. For details, see Peter Arnett, *Live from the Battlefield: From Vietnam to Baghdad, 35 Years in the World's War Zones* (New York: Simon and Schuster, 1994), 66–70.

CHAPTER 17

283 **"unparalleled in the history of journalism"** *New York Herald,* October 1, 1899. Douglas, *Inventing American Broadcasting,* 19 and all of chap. 4 in that volume, contains a thorough discussion of the navy's early lack of interest in Marconi's wireless. Before teaming up with Bennett, Marconi tried a similar experiment with the *Dublin Daily Express.* In that instance, the news story was the Kingstown Regatta. On this, see Carolyn Marvin, *When Old Technologies Were New: Thinking about Electric Communication in the Late Nineteenth Century* (New York: Oxford University Press, 1988), 214.

"the great banking and business houses" Ray Stannard Baker, "Marconi's Achievement," *McClure's Magazine,* February 1902, 298; *New York Times,* November 5, 1897.

284 **"looked forward to the day"** Douglas, *Inventing American Broadcasting,* 80–82, 145, 154–57, 167, 172, 293; Gavin Weightman, *Signor Marconi's Magic Box* (Cambridge, Mass.: Da Capo, 2003), 209–10. Again, Douglas's book is good on background for this period.

"Home Stuff" Douglas, *Inventing American Broadcasting,* 102, 276–80; Erik Barnouw, *Tube of Plenty: The Evolution of American Television,* 2nd rev. ed. (New York: Oxford University Press, 1990), 17; MacDonald, *Don't Touch That Dial!* 3–4. During the war, Marconi was back in his home country, Italy, as a general staff officer responsible for organizing wireless service.

285 **"prove positively offensive"** John W. Spalding, "1928: Radio Becomes a Mass Advertising Medium," *Journal of Broadcasting* 8 (Winter 1963–1964): 38; Barnouw, *Tube of Plenty,* 43.

"You are quite right" Dennis, *Lawson,* 390–91. At first the Lawson station had the call letters MGU, but they were changed to WMAQ later in the decade.

The Political Situation in Washington Tonight Wile's experience is described in his *News Is Where You Find It,* chaps. 28–29. See also Barnouw, *Tube of Plenty,* 41.

"The radio can never be" Aylesworth's speech is mentioned in B. J. Hauser, "NBC History," "Draft B.," typescript, n.d., NBC Papers, LOC; this history seems to have been written in the early 1930s. Schechter is quoted in David H. Hosley, *As Good As Any: Foreign Correspondence on American Radio, 1930–1949* (Westport, Conn.: Greenwood Press, 1984), 17.

"in easy communication" David Fraser, *A Modern Campaign; or, War and Wireless Telegraphy in the Far East* (London: Methuen, 1905), 4; Douglas, *Inventing American Broadcasting,* 123; Culbert, *News for Everyman,* 70. Fraser's travail erecting a tall antenna on the Shantung coast is amusing.

286 **"If radio is to be the means"** H. S. Davies to J. M. Patterson, December 18, 1924, AP Archives.

"the suppression of legitimate news" E. H. Harris, "Radio and the Press," *Annals of the American Academy of Political and Social Science* 177 (January 1935): 166. For background on the radio-press war, see Giraud Chester, "The Press-Radio War: 1933–1935," *Public Opinion Quarterly* 13 (Summer 1949): 252–64; MacDonald, *Don't Touch That Dial!* 282–85. A discussion about concern over radio's ability to propagandize is in Gwenyth L. Jackaway, *Media at War: Radio's Challenge to the Newspapers, 1924–1939* (Westport, Conn.: Praeger, 1995), 131–35.

287 **"The idea of broadcasting"** César Saerchinger, *Hello America! Radio Adventures in Europe* (Boston: Houghton Mifflin, 1938), 225.

"the first transatlantic" Wile, *News Is Where You Find It,* 455; Culbert, *News for Everyman,* 37.

"The actual sounds" "Radio Milestones of 1935," December 3, 1935, NBC Papers, LOC; Hosley, *As Good as Any,* 9–10, 22–25; Cloud and Olson, *The Murrow Boys,* 455.

288 **"Broadcasting has no role"** Joseph E. Persico, *Edward R. Murrow: An American Original* (New York: McGraw-Hill, 1988), 113; A. M. Sperber, *Murrow: His Life and Times* (New York: Fordham University Press, 1998), 98–104; Shirer, *The Nightmare Years,* 284; Hosley, *As Good as Any,* 28–29.

"the most important story of my life" Shirer, *The Nightmare Years,* 298. Shirer's hiring and subsequent reporting on the *Anschluss* for CBS is found in this book, chap. 11, and in many other accounts, including Persico, *Murrow,* 119, 129–34.

"The crisis has done one thing" Shirer, *Berlin Dairy,* 91, 97, 100; Hosley, *As Good as Any,* 54–55; Persico, *Murrow,* 143; H. V. Kaltenborn, *I Broadcast the Crisis* (New York: Random House, 1938); Lenox R. Lohr to David Sarnoff, October 23, 1938, NBC Papers, LOC.

289 **"Radio's performance"** "War in the Living Room," *Newsweek,* September 11, 1939, 4; Frederick Lewis Allen, *Since Yesterday: The Nineteen-Thirties in America* (London: Hamish Hamilton, 1940), 265.

"For the first time history" James Rorty, "Radio Comes Through," *Nation,* October 15, 1938, 372–74. This article mentions midwestern advertising interest in crisis coverage.

"Passionately though we may desire detachment" Martin Gilbert, *A History of the Twentieth Century,* vol. 2, *1933–1951* (New York: William Morrow, 1998), 267.

290 **"knocked around considerably"** "Jimmy Tells the World," *Time,* December 25, 1939, 50. For other skimpy details about Bowen and this entire episode, also see George N. Gordon and Irving Al Falk, *On-the-Spot-Reporting* (New York: Julian Messner, 1967), 113–16; and Louis L. Snyder and Richard B. Morris, eds., *They Saw It Happen: Eyewitness Reports of Great Events* (Harrisburg, Pa.: Stackpole, 1951), 398–401. The excerpt is taken from the latter book. Bowen did broadcasts prior to those on December 17, including one on December 14, the day after the battle that damaged the *Graf Spee,* which described witnesses on the beach who saw "guns flashing, cannons booming, everything pertaining to war at sea was right in front of them." The story of the *Graf Spee* is told in Dudley Pope, *Graf Spee: The Life and Death of a Raider* (Philadelphia: Lippincott, 1957).

"Hello, New York!" I have used the quote from the *Time* article. The *Newsweek* article has Bowen saying, "Hello, New York! Hello, New York! Give me the Air! The ship has exploded!"

"major war episode" "NBC's War Beat," *Newsweek,* December 25, 1939.

292 **"telephoned in"** "Matters for the Information of the Board of Directors," December 22, 1939, NBC Papers, LOC; "NBC's War Beat," 36; *Washington Post,* December 18, 1939; Lenox R. Lohr to John F. Royal, September 9, 1939, NBC Papers, LOC.

"We are cutting our coverage" Culbert, *News for Everyman,* 20; John T. Royal to Niles Trammell, September 5, 1939, NBC Papers, LOC.

"It is unfortunate" James Rowland Angell to John F. Royal, n.d. but received December 18, 1939; Royal to Angell, December 19, 1939; Royal to James Bowen, letter and telegram, December 23, 1939, all in NBC Records, Wis.

293 **"American clerk"** John T. Royal to Robert W. Sarnoff, January 5, 1960, NBC Papers, LOC; Barbara Raab, NBC producer, to author, e-mail, February 9, 2004.

"Your name is as well-known" H. V. Kaltenborn to Edward R. Murrow, November 24, 1939, Kaltenborn Papers.

"it is a topic" Everett M. Rogers, *A History of Communication Study: A Biographical Approach* (New York: Free Press, 1994), 270, 279. Chapter 7 of Rogers's book, from which I have drawn, is devoted to Lazarsfeld and his contributions. In advancing mass communication research, Lazarsfeld married quantitative and qualitative research, a technique that scholars should welcome but, alas, often don't, preferring in their own provincial ways to seek divorce on the grounds of incompatibility.

"In the European crisis" Paul F. Lazarsfeld, *Radio and the Printed Page* (New York: Duell, Sloan, and Pearce, 1940), 259–60; Edwin Muller, "Radio v. Reading," *New Republic,* February 19, 1940, 236; Dixon Wecter, "Hearing Is Believing," *Atlantic Monthly,* June 1945, 54; Hadley Cantril and Mildred Strunk, *Public Opinion, 1935–1946* (Westport, Conn.: Greenword Press, 1978), 524; Persico, *Murrow,* 180, 276.

294 **"Ed didn't know"** Persico, *Murrow,* 137. Background on Murrow at Washington State University is found in chaps. 4 and 5.

"A searchlight just burst into action" This quote is taken from a compact disk that accompanies Mark Bernstein and Alex Lubertozzi, *World War II on the Air: Edward R. Murrow and the Broadcasts That Riveted a Nation* (Naperville, Ill.: Sourcebooks, 2003).

295 **"This is London"** Persico, *Murrow,* 145.

the model Murrow adopted Persico, *Murrow,* is a good source for background on the "Murrow Boys." For a good overview of the evolution of radio, as well as the comment on the growth of the CBS News staff, see Ronald Garay, "News Reporting, Radio," in *Encyclopedia of International Media and Communications* (San Diego: Elsevier Science, 2003), 299–313.

296 **"gained a six-hour best"** "Collingwood's Beats," *Newsweek,* February 1, 1943, 61; Cloud and Olson, *The Murrow Boys,* 202–3; William S. Paley, *As It Happened: A Memoir* (Garden City, N.Y.: Doubleday, 1979), 374; "Dr. Max Jordan Adds Flash of War's End to His List of Historic NBC 'Firsts,'" NBC Press Department, August 17, 1945, NBC Papers, LOC.

corrected the false statements Persico, *Murrow,* 180.

"There were no precedents" Cloud and Olson, *The Murrow Boys,* 2; Jeff Alan and James M. Lane, *Anchoring America: The Changing Face of Network News* (Chicago: Bonus Books, 2003), xiv.

"In twenty years" Muller, "Radio v. Reading," 236; Richard S. Salant, *Salant, CBS, and the Battle for the Soul of Broadcast Journalism,* ed. Susan and Bill Buzenberg (Boulder, Colo.: Westview, 1999), 24.

297 **"about as absurd"** Cloud and Olson, *The Murrow Boys,* 288, 291; Sig Mickelson, *The Decade That Shaped Television News: CBS in the 1950s* (Westport, Conn.: Praeger, 1998), 124. For examples of resistance to television, see Reuven Frank, *Out of Thin Air* (New York: Simon and Schuster, 1991), 30, 35.

"spotty" Sig Mickelson to Van Volkenburg, August 26, 1953; Frank F. Donghi to Mickelson, January 11, 1954, Mickelson Papers.

Stanton assembled his correspondents Cloud and Olson, *The Murrow Boys,* 298–300; Mickelson, *The Decade That Shaped Television News,* xv. Useful background on the proposal for two news departments is found in Van Volkenburg to William Paley and others, February 4, 1954, and Mickelson's notes on what needed to be done, April 27, 1954, Mickelson Papers.

"It was an invaluable opportunity" Mickelson, *The Decade That Shaped Television News,* 196–97; Grant Tinker and Bud Rukeyser, *Tinker in Television: From General Sarnoff to General Electric* (New York: Simon and Schuster, 1994), 182.

298 **"Bill"** Marvin Kalb, who was CBS correspondent in Moscow when the Paris meeting took place, interview by author, January 8, 2004. As yet another example of this attitude, a CBS executive is credited with saying, "The entertainment end of the network business did its worst so that CBS News could do its best." Salant, *Salant, CBS,* 147.

"I believe the coverage" Bill Wheatley to author, e-mail, April 24, 2006.

"When a story breaks" Marcy McGinnis, interview by author, May 26, 2006; McGinnis to author, e-mail, August 15, 2006.

299 **"techno-producer"** Sid Bedingfield, interview by author, February 24, 2006; Andrew Tyndall to author, e-mail, May 23, 2006.

"advertising, research, or show business" Mickelson, *The Decade That Shaped Television News,* 150; Sperber, *Murrow,* 613. Stanton's "carpet" remark is in his obit, in *New York Times,* December 26, 2006. On Rather's angry resignation, see CBS News Release, June 20, 2006; "Statement Released by Dan Rather to Jim Romenesko, June 20, 2006"; and *New York Times,* June 17, 2006.

300 **"the only full-time, on-air correspondent"** Bittermann, "The Best of Times . . . ," in Foote, *Live from the Trenches,* 78; Bill Wheatley, interview by author, May 3, 2006. For additional background, see "Network TV," in *The State of the News Media 2004* (Washington, D.C.: Project for Excellence in Journalism, 2004), 8; Lucinda Fleeson, "Bureau of Missing Bureaus," *American Journalism Review,* October–November 2003, 32–34; Daniel Riffe and Arianne Budianto, "The Shrinking World of Network News," *International Communication Bulletin* 36 (Spring 2001): 1835.

"From Murrow to Mediocrity?" Shanor, *News from Abroad,* 69; Salant, *Salant, CBS,* 142.

301 **"is the most expensive medium for news"** Garrick Utley, "The Shrinking of Foreign News," *Foreign Affairs,* March–April 1997, 6; Fleeson, "Bureau of Missing Bureaus," 34. The change in the number of CBS news bureaus is from Scotti Williston, "Global News and the Vanishing American Foreign Correspondent," *Transnational Broadcasting Studies,* 2001, www.tbsjournal.com/Archives/Spring01/Williston.html, which is quoted without attribution in Tom Fenton, *Bad News: The Decline of Reporting, the Business of News, and the Danger to Us All* (New York: Regan Books, 2005), 65.

302 **"I have been far too occupied"** Howard K. Smith's complaint is in Cloud and Olson, *The Murrow Boys,* 292.

television has become better and better These points are made in Andrew Tyndall, "Climbing

Down from Olympus," *Media Studies Journal* 12 (Fall 1998): 135; Matthew A. Baum, "Sex, Lies, and War: How Soft News Brings Foreign Policy to the Inattentive Public," *American Political Science Review* 97 (March 2002): 105.

"When I hear some character" Robert St. John's comment is from an anonymous, untitled, undated typewritten profile of him in St. John Papers; Larry McGill and András Szántó, *Headlines and Sound Bites: Is That the Way It Is?* (New York: Freedom Forum Media Studies Center, April 1995), 11, 28.

"Ideas are not easy to translate" Sig Mickelson, "General Orientation of CBS News," typewritten notes for CBS Foundation Fellows Dinner, September 24, 1957, Mickelson Papers; Mickelson, *The Decade That Shaped Television News,* 126; Cloud and Olson, *The Murrow Boys,* 376; Tyndall, "Climbing Down from Olympus," 141. The point about television not producing great photojournalism is found in Frank, *Out of Thin Air,* 407.

"Today's correspondents" Stanley Cloud and Lynn Olson, "The Murrow Boys—Broadcasting for the Mind's Eye," *Media Studies Journal* 11 (Spring 1997): 5. Arnett's quote is from Felicity Barringer, *New York Times,* July 8, 1998.

303   **"the dramatic and the emotional"** Lazarsfeld, *Radio and the Printed Page,* 213. For background on the evolution of audience measurement, see Barnouw, *Tube of Plenty,* 133, 503–4.

"became the Holy Grail" Mickelson, *The Decade That Shaped Television News,* xviii; Ted Koppel, *New York Times,* January 29, 2006; Shanor, *News from Abroad,* 119.

"when something important" Hamilton, *All the News That's Fit to Sell,* 103; *Global Perspectives in Local Television News Coverage* (Washington, D.C.: Radio and Television News Directors Foundation, 2004), 15.

James T. Hamilton has found that television pays more attention to subjects given a high priority by the public, or, to put it another way, gives them what they want more than what they need; see his "The Market and the Media," in *The Press,* ed. Geneva Overholser and Kathleen Hall Jamieson (New York: Oxford University Press, 2005), 355–56. For an example of an early demographic study showing male preferences for foreign news on radio, see William S. Robinson, "Radio Comes to the Farmer," in *Radio Research 1941,* ed. Paul F. Lazarsfeld and Frank N. Stanton (New York: Arno, 1979), 238–42. Hadley Cantril and a colleague elucidated an elemental truism about the power of advertising in a 1941 study: "When a manufacturer decides to advertise his product over the radio, he knows that his chief problem is to find a program his prospective customers will enjoy. A 'good' program, like a 'good' movie, is, from the point of view of the man who puts it on, one that brings satisfactory financial returns." Hadley Cantril and Gordon W. Allport, *The Psychology of Radio* (New York: Peter Smith, 1941), 66.

304   **"Soft-news media"** Baum, "Sex, Lies, and War," 94; Matthew A. Baum, *Soft News Goes to War: Public Opinion and American Foreign Policy in the New Media Age* (Princeton, N.J.: Princeton University Press, 2003), 81.

"Unlike every newspaper in America" Tinker and Rukeyser, *Tinker in Television,* 181.

"from the Paley-Stanton era" Salant, *Salant, CBS,* 146.

"While I think" Niles Trammell to Sidney N. Strotz, September 23, 1941, NBC Papers, LOC.

"We must" Mickelson, "General Orientation of CBS News"; Barnouw, *Tube of Plenty,* 383; Cloud and Olson, *The Murrow Boys,* 331; Mickelson, *The Decade That Shaped Television News, 177;* Salant, *Salant, CBS,* 142.

305   **"expected to generate profits"** Ken Auletta, "Sign-Off," *New Yorker,* March 7, 2005, 57.

"A ninety-six-hour-late film story" Mickelson, *The Decade That Shaped Television News,* 28. The comment on television's losing hegemony over images is from CBS News president Andrew Heyward in a talk given at the Shorenstein Center, October 17, 2002. John T. Royal at NBC reported a similar dynamic about hegemony when it came to the use of BBC radio material in the early years. The material was desirable when only NBC and CBS had access to it; when Mutual acquired the right, the programs became "commonplace.... There was a falling of interest on the part of all three Networks." Royal to Robert W. Sarnoff, January 5, 1960, NBC Papers, LOC.

"Television is just a toaster" Janice Hui and Craig L. LaMay, "Broadcasting and the Public Interest," in *The Business of News: A Challenge for Journalism's Next Generation,* ed. Cynthia Gorney (New York: Carnegie Corporation, 2002), 40; "Network TV," in *The State of the News Media 2004,* 35. A useful, succinct discussion of these regulatory changes is found in Ronald Garay, "News Reporting, Radio," 299–314.

"You'll often see individuals" Marcy McGinnis, interview by author, May 26, 2006; McGinnis to author, e-mail, August 15, 2006.

"The higher circles of radio" Dixon Wecter, "Hearing Is Believing," *Atlantic Monthly,* July 1945, 37; Persico, *Murrow,* 344–46; "The Reminiscences of A(bel) A(len) Schechter," Oral History Collection, Pickler Library, Columbia University, New York.

306   **"a fully rounded correspondent"** Dan Rather, *The Camera Never Blinks: Adventures of a TV Journalist* (New York: Ballantine, 1978), 173, 186.

"YOU'LL GET USED TO IT" Cloud and Olson, *The Murrow Boys,* 61.

"The networks" Fenton, *Bad News,* 64, 383.

"Showbiz invokes showbiz" Tunku Varadarajan, "Geraldo's War," *Wall Street Journal,* December 10, 2001.

"Time spent in developing reporters" James T. Hamilton, discussion paper published in *News in the Public Interest: A Free and Subsidized Press* (Baton Rouge: Reilly Center for Media & Public Affairs, Manship School of Mass Communications, Louisiana State University, 2004), 84. The institutional or brand name recognition of anchors is discussed in P. David Marshall, *Celebrity and Power: Fame in Contemporary Culture* (Minneapolis: University of Minnesota Press, 1997), 124. The point on anchors covering head-of-state deaths is in Bittermann, "The Best of Times…," 81. Reuven Frank's comment is in his *Out of Thin Air,* 412.

"That's generous, even noble" Fenton, *Bad News,* 156–57; Meryl Gordon, "Koppel's Therapy," *New York Magazine,* December 5, 2005, retrieved from www.nymag.com/nymetro/news/media/features/15198/index.html. For anchor salaries, see Hamilton, "The Market and the Media," 363.

307   **"everything but authority"** Smith, *Events Leading Up to My Death,* 346; Persico, *Murrow,* 219.
    The gradual decline in the foreign experience of anchors is told in the careers of others. Chet Huntley, of the Chet Huntley–David Brinkley pair at NBC, was CBS editor of war information during World War II and had several assignments overseas; after the war, CBS sent him to cover the Berlin airlift. To get away from the office "and see something of the world I was reporting on every night," Brinkley made some of the first travel documentaries on television in the 1950s. In the 1960s, he did documentaries on Vienna and Hong Kong, which he showed were on the sidelines of the cold war but nevertheless unable to escape its consequences. Before he anchored ABC's *Nightline,* British-born Ted Koppel was chief diplomatic correspondent and bureau chief in Hong Kong and Miami, from the latter location covering Latin America. *Nightline* began in 1979 to cover the ongoing Iranian hostage crisis and afterward devoted considerable time to thoughtful foreign news. Its early promotion line was "Bringing people together who are worlds apart." Harry Reasoner was with the *Minneapolis Times,* the U.S. Information Agency in the Philippines, and CBS radio and television before joining ABC as coanchor with Howard K. Smith. Woodruff's foreign experience involved teaching law in China during the 1989 crackdown at Tiananmen Square and working for CBS as a translator at the time.
    Background on anchors is found in Lyle Johnston, *"Good Night, Chet": A Biography of Chet Huntley* (Jefferson, N.C.: McFarland, 2003), 32–34; David Brinkley, *Brinkley's Beat: People, Places, and Events That Shaped My Times* (New York: Knopf, 2003), 101, 124–25; Ted Koppel and Kyle Gibson, *Nightline: History in the Making and the Making of Television* (New York: Times Books, 1996), xiii; "Brian Williams," biography found at MSNBC Web site, www.msnbc.msn.com/id/3667173 (accessed August 22, 2008); television review on ABC anchors in *New York Times,* January 9, 2006.
    More than half of the editors at the fifteen highest-circulation newspapers in early 2004 had experience as foreign correspondents. Of the four newspapers that stood out for foreign cover-

age—the *New York Times,* the *Washington Post,* the *Los Angeles Times,* and the *Wall Street Journal*—only the editor of the last of these had not been a foreign correspondent. But the chairman and CEO of the parent company, Dow Jones, had been a foreign correspondent.

"very hard to recruit" Fenton, *Bad News,* 194–95. When ABC aired a special on Jennings's career after his death in 2005, nearly forty-five minutes of the two-hour program related to his overseas reporting. It was as though the network was mourning the passing of the era of network foreign correspondence. The Jennings retrospective aired on August 10, 2005.

CHAPTER 18

308   **"This is probably my last message"** This dispatch, which became a story in *Time,* May 11, 1942, is reprinted in the form in which it arrived to *Time* in Gordon Carroll, ed., *History in the Writing: By the Foreign Correspondents of Time, Life, and Fortune* (New York: Duell, Sloan, and Pearce, 1945), 101–3.

     "Your number's about up" Jack Belden, *Retreat with Stilwell* (New York: Knopf, 1943), 243–44.

     "We had to break through" Belden, *Retreat with Stilwell,* 150.

309   **"I claim we got a hell of a beating"** Barbara W. Tuchman, *Stilwell and the American Experience in China, 1911–45* (New York: Macmillan, 1971), 300.

     "caught in the fog of war" Belden, *Retreat with Stilwell,* 243; Carroll, *History in the Writing,* 102–3.

     "attempted to lighten the yoke" Belden, *Retreat with Stilwell,* 4.

     "The best description" Theodore H. White and Annalee Jacoby, *Thunder out of China* (New York: William Sloan, 1946), 88; Hallett Abend, "Giant among Political Pygmies," *Saturday Review,* March 13, 1943, 7; John Paton Davies Jr., *Dragon by the Tail: American, British, Japanese, and Russian Encounters with China and One Another* (New York: Norton, 1972), 240.

     "This sort of thing" Jack Belden to his mother, November 2, 1943, files of Sandra Kearney, Belden's niece.

310   **"Sports"** Joe James Custer, *Through the Perilous Night: The Astoria's Last Battle* (New York: Macmillan, 1944), 79; Desmond, *Tides of War,* 244.

     More journalists went in harm's way Hohenberg, *Foreign Correspondence,* 246; other estimates can be found in Desmond, *Tides of War,* 451–53. Hohenberg puts the number of casualties in the field at 1,647. Casualties for the army, the navy, and the marine corps are from Hannah Fischer, Kim Klarman, and Mari-Jana Oborceanu, *American War and Military Operations Casualties: Lists and Statistics* (Washington, D.C.: Congressional Research Service, June 29, 2007).

     "My own motto" Berger, *Story of the New York Times,* 450; Angus M. Thuermer, *Editor and Publisher,* June 6, 1942, 3. This issue of *Editor and Publisher* summarizes the internment of correspondents during the early part of the war. Denny told his story in *Behind Both Lines.* On Powell, see J. B. Powell, "I Was a Prisoner of the Japanese," *Reader's Digest,* November 1942, 63–66; Hamilton, *Edgar Snow,* 155, 170.

     "the story of a lifetime" Larry Heinzerling, "The Execution of Joe Morton AP War Correspondent," typescript, February 23, 1995, AP Archives.

     One of the most harrowing escapes This story is told in two books by Robert St. John, *Foreign Correspondent,* chap. 10; and *From the Land of the Silent People* (Garden City, N.Y.: Garden City, 1942), which is devoted entirely to the escape.

312   **"beer and cigarettes"** Desmond, *Tides of War,* 302, 451.

     Like the GIs they covered Desmond, *Tides of War,* 453. Details on Larry Allen can be found in *"Larry Allen,"* AP Archives; as well as in Elizabeth A. Brennan and Elizabeth C. Clarage, *Who's Who of Pulitzer Prize Winners* (Phoenix: Oryx, 1999), 592. In 1952 Allen also received the French Croix de Guerre from the French High Command in Indochina.

     "Norway's capital" Knightley, *The First Casualty,* 248; Mathews, *Reporting the Wars,* 182–84;

Homer Bigart, *Forward Positions: The War Correspondence of Homer Bigart,* ed. Betsy Wade (Fayetteville: University of Arkansas Press, 1992), 41.

"surrender your license" Major C. R. Fisher to C. B. Brown, January 8, 1942, Brown Papers; Cloud and Olson, *The Murrow Boys,* 152; A. J. Liebling, "The Press and the Military," in *Reporting World War II* (New York: Library of America, 1995), 2:737. George Weller's stories were found years later and recently published in George Weller, *First into Nagasaki: The Censored Eyewitness Dispatches on Post-Atomic Japan and Its Prisoners of War,* ed. Anthony Weller (New York: Crown, 2006).

313 **"You can't say"** Clare Boothe, "Burma Mission: Part II," *Life,* June 22, 1942, 93; Belden, *Retreat with Stilwell,* 275.

"The worst form of censorship" A. J. Liebling, "The Press and the Military," 737; Knightley, *The First Casualty,* 299–300, 313–14, 323; Mathews, *Reporting the Wars,* 190.

"Correspondents acquired the habit" Mathews, *Reporting the Wars,* 194; John Steinbeck, *Once There Was a War* (New York: Penguin, 1986), xii–xiii. Steinbeck was with Belden in North Africa and described him as "dour" (190–94).

"Anybody here from Wisconsin" Robert W. Wells, *The Milwaukee Journal: An Informal Chronicle of Its First 100 Years* (Milwaukee, Wis.: Milwaukee Journal, 1981), 328–29; Will C. Conrad, Kathleen F. Wilson, and Dale Wilson, *The Milwaukee Journal: the First Eighty Years* (Madison: University of Wisconsin Press, 1964), 157; James Tobin, *Ernie Pyle's War: America's Eyewitness to World War II* (Lawrence: University Press of Kansas, 1997), 15; Ernie Pyle, *Here Is Your War* (Cleveland: World, 1945), 87, 179. Pyle's book is a collection of his dispatches.

315 **"the Ernie Pyle bill"** "Ernie Pyle's War," *Time,* July 17, 1944, 65, 72; Martin Sommers, "The War to Get War News," *Saturday Evening Post,* March 25, 1944, 102; Knightley, *The First Casualty,* 336, 357.

"I have to fight an inner depression" Tobin, *Ernie Pyle's War,* 85, 201, 220.

316 **"The American way of writing about war"** Sheean, *This House against This House,* 360; Fletcher Pratt, "How the Censors Rigged the News," *Harper's Magazine,* February 1946, 99. Although Sheean thought Pyle could not be "spoiled for good," he believed Pyle's acclaim went to his head. Once, when Pyle was "boiling drunk," he told Sheean, "Have you any idea how famous I am, Jimmy? I'm more famous than you are. Hell, I'm more famous than Dorothy Thompson is!" Vincent Sheean to Dinah Sheean, January 30, 1944, Sheean Papers.

Pratt observed of correspondents' courage: "Their losses were proportionately greater than those of any combat service, and they were men who for age or for physical infirmity had been rejected as unfit to take part in combat. Some of them—Pyle, Hersey, Tregaskis, Trumbull— were very able writers. But if physical courage is the basic criterion, the Japanese of Attu are entitled to still higher praise than the correspondents; their losses were 99.5 per cent. The fact is that with a few exceptions the writers, like the Attu Japanese, failed to achieve their objective." "How the Censors Rigged the News," 104.

"I'm going to use you fellows" Reynolds, *By Quentin Reynolds,* 271–72.

"Our conclusion is that we're Americans first" Reynolds, *By Quentin Reynolds,* 293–94; Knightley, *The First Casualty,* 344, 349–50. Knightley's version differs slightly from that told by Reynolds, who was an eyewitness to the meeting with Eisenhower. Another player was the AP's Edward Kennedy, who reported the story from the war zone after Pearson took it public in a broadcast. Kennedy's account is in *Reporting World War II,* 1:665–71. The week before the slapping incident, Patton assailed another enlisted man he suspected of being a malingerer, hitting him in the face with his gloves.

Background on Pearson's retaliation is in Richard W. Steele, "News of the 'Good War': World War II News Management," *Journalism Quarterly* 62 (Winter 1985): 713–15. Background on Pearson himself is in Ritchie, *Reporting from Washington,* 136.

"As I am writing this" Canham, *Commitment to Freedom,* 303–5. Edward Marshall's accounts are in "A Wounded Correspondent's Recollections of Guasimas," *Scribner's,* September 1898, 273–76, and in "How It Feels to Be Shot," *Cosmopolitan,* September 1898, 557–58.

317 **"What a story!"** Reynolds, *By Quentin Reynolds,* 279; Knightley, *The First Casualty,* 323–24; E. J. Kahn Jr., "The Men behind the By-Lines," *Saturday Evening Post,* September 11, 1943, 19.

with the word *I* The news stories are found in Jack Stenbuck, ed., *Typewriter Battalion: Dramatic Frontline Dispatches from World War II* (New York: William Morrow, 1955), 90, 133, 226, 456; *Reporting World War II,* 1:456. Larry Allen's report, dated January 10, 1941, is among the materials submitted for a Pulitzer Prize, Pulitzer Prize files, Columbia University. St. John, in *Foreign Correspondent,* 7, describes his success retelling his story in other places.

"came to adore the whole business" Knightley, *The First Casualty,* 345; Sperber, *Murrow,* 176–77, 233–34; Cloud and Olson, *The Murrow Boys,* 202–3; Bernstein and Lubertozzi, *World War II on the Air,* 101; Caroline Moorehead, *Gellhorn: A Twentieth-Century Life* (New York: Henry Holt, 2003), 172.

318 **autobiographical notes** As noted in the introduction to this book, Belden has not received full biographical treatment. The biographical details used for the personality sketch of his early life here were mostly found in notes that he left behind, which were in files held by his niece, Sandra Kearney, and his son, David Belden, especially these: Jack Belden, "PERSONAL AND CONDITIONS IN CHINA in 30's and 40s," n.d.; "*Jack Belden,* 1910–1989," n.d. The latter document seems to have been compiled with the assistance of Beatrice Weber, who also helped prepare a similar narrative, "Sequel to the Razz-berry of Jack Belden, Foreign Correspondent (1901–1989)," n.d., files of Beatrice A. Weber. Other bits of information used here come from a short biographical note in Carroll, *History in the Writing,* 388; MacKinnon and Friesen, *China Reporting,* 34. Belden's accounts are a bit muddled; when quoting, I have cleaned up typographical errors.

319 **"gained an encyclopedic knowledge"** Tillman Durdin to author, July 20, 1990; "Gas!" *Time,* November 10, 1941, 26. Belden's relations with Stilwell and his work on the Shanghai underground are mentioned in MacKinnon and Friesen, *China Reporting,* 39, 45; his Shanghai work also is mentioned, in passing, in Frederic Wakeman Jr., *The Shanghai Badlands: Wartime Terrorism and Urban Crime, 1937–1941* (Cambridge: Cambridge University Press, 1997), 178. Belden's map drawing is apparent in the personal papers he left behind, Belden Papers.

"he was the only foreign newspaperman" Other such stories can be found among newspaper clippings in the Belden Papers at the Hoover Institution, for example:

> "I am retreating with the Chinese army along the Peiping-Hankow Railway toward the Yellow River after one of the most disastrous defeats the Chinese have suffered in this war." *Newark Star-Eagle,* October 1, 1937.
>
> "I have seen a full-grown city die before my eyes, and it is a sight that remains engraved upon the memory." *New Orleans Item,* November 19, 1937.
>
> "I walked through fire and water last night and through the dead today. I started without official permission and had to go with a guard. The soldiers cared for me." *Valparaiso (Ind.) Vidette,* March 4, 1938.

320 **"the man who knew"** Owen Lattimore, introduction to Jack Belden, *China Shakes the World* (New York: Monthly Review Press, 1970), ix; Snow, *Journey to the Beginning,* 383; Tuchman, *Stilwell,* 182; David Crook to author, May 1, 1992; MacKinnon and Friesen, *China Reporting,* 57–58; Rand, *China Hands,* 194; Tillman Durdin to author, July 20, 1990.

"often ruffled feathers" Tillman Durdin to author, July 20, 1990; Rand, *China Hands,* 198–99.

"gangster imperialism" Belden, *Retreat with Stilwell,* 4, 327.

"a sort of emotional drug" Belden, *Still Time to Die* (Philadelphia: Blakiston, 1944), 4.

"Down below us on the river" These accounts of the air war in China are found in *Time,* "Rough on Rabbits," August 3, 25; and "Flight to the Rising Sun," August 24, 1942, 34. Belden's billing as eyewitness and other biographical notes are in *Time,* "A Letter from the Publisher," September

21, 1942, 2; "Across Wadi Zigzau," April 5, 1943, 17; and "The Fall of Troina," August 23, 1943, 30. Desmond, *Tides of War,* 291.

"a soldier's eye view of war" Whitehead's recollection is in Don Whitehead, *Combat Reporter: Don Whitehead's World War II Diary and Memoirs,* ed. John B. Romeiser (New York: Fordham University Press, 2006), 229. For more of Whitehead's reporting, see his *Beachhead Don: Reporting the War from the European Theater, 1942–1945,* ed. John B. Romeiser (New York: Fordham University Press, 2004).

321 **"on the battle field alone and in pain"** Belden, *Still Time to Die,* 304. The details on his cold and recurring malaria are mentioned in "Letter from the Publisher," *Time,* September 27, 1943, 15.

"HEY, SOLDIER, I'M WOUNDED!" Jack Belden, "Hey, Soldier, I'm Wounded," *Life,* September 27, 1943, 27–32; and "The Beaches of Salerno," *Time,* September 1943, 28–29. World War II war reporting has been substantially anthologized. The best effort is the two-volume *Reporting World War II,* previously cited, along with Stenbuck, *Typewriter Battalion.* The *New Yorker* has a volume of its own staff's work, *The New Yorker War Pieces,* published originally in 1947 and reissued (New York: Schocken, 1988). The Belden article here does not appear in any of these, nor in *Time-Life*'s own *History in the Writing,* edited by Carroll. It is also worth noting that the aforementioned World War II anthologies print original articles without providing any background to help the reader understand them, which is a pity.

324 **"press her lips against mine"** Jack Belden, "Sequel to Salerno," *Life,* March 20, 1944, 101, 113; Beatrice Weber, interview by author, April 22, 1990.

"a long cry" Erma Hanneman to Jack Belden, September 27, 1943; Karl F. Amaila to Belden, December 7, 1943, both in Belden Papers.

325 **"I should like to write about War"** Jack Belden to Edwin Hunt, n.d., Belden Papers. Belden told Hunt he did not write "it is hell on the front," but of course he had written just that way in China, albeit with his characteristic emotional intensity.

"I was very lonely" Jack Belden, "A Synopsis," unpublished, undated note, provided by Lois Snow; Belden, *Still Time to Die,* 3, 15, 307. Reviewing the book—"Lessons of War," *Time,* September 25, 1944, 99—*Time* mixed praise with criticism, saying it was "often frankly bitter, often overemotional, occasionally theatrical (in phrases such as 'Battles are merely the flashing, seductive garments that hide the passionate but terrible whore's body of war')."

"The rush of battle" Chris Hedges, *War Is a Force That Gives Us Meaning* (New York: Anchor Books, 2003), 3. The narcotic aspects of war are mentioned by others, e.g., CNN's Walter Rodgers: "But it is the greatest adrenalin rush in the world. We came out of Afghanistan once, and we were in some hairy situations. I was on the ceiling for four day afterwards. I don't care if this generation uses drugs. Forget it. There is nothing like war for a high." Foote, *Live From the Trenches,* 129. For what it is worth, Hedges coincidentally graduated from Belden's alma mater, Colgate.

"Everything was bathed in a blurry radiance" Belden, *Still Time to Die,* 145.

"Casual encounters" Hedges, *War Is a Force,* 101.

"I plunged into that" Moorehead, *Gellhorn,* 408; Arnett, *Live from the Battlefield,* 312; John Laurence, *The Cat from Hué: A Vietnam War Story* (New York: Public Affairs, 2002), 32–33, 71, 817; Anthony Loyd, *My War Gone By, I Miss It So* (New York: Penguin, 2001), 58; Jon Steele, *War Junkie* (London: Corgi Books, 2002), 541–42; Robert D. Kaplan, "Get Me to Vukovar," *Columbia Journalism Review,* September–October 2004, 11–12. Loyd has a second book on this theme, Anthony Loyd, *Another Bloody Love Letter* (London: Headline, 2007).

326 **"embedded" reporting** Anna Husarska, "News from Hell," *New Yorker,* October 5, 1992, 99; Michael Weisskopf, *Blood Brothers: Among the Soldiers of Ward 57* (New York: Henry Holt, 2006). The Farnaz Fassihi email, dated September 29, 2004, can be found at Poynter.org/column.asp?id=45&aid=72659 (accessed August 28, 2008). The death rate statistics are from *Wall Street Journal,* April 9, 2003.

With regard to having the spotlight on the men and women in the trenches, Oliver North, a Marine Corps officer who became a Fox News war correspondent, observed of the Iraq War, "The American people are much more interested in knowing how their kids are doing than whether some grumpy general got enough bran flakes for breakfast." North, *War Stories: Operation Iraqi Freedom* (Washington, D.C.: Regnery, 2003), 245. A discussion of first-person reporting in Iraq is found in Julia R. Fox and Byungho Park, "The 'I' of Embedded Reporting: An Analysis of CNN Coverage of the 'Shock and Awe' Campaign," *Journal of Broadcasting and Electronic Media* 50 (March 2006): 36–51.

327 **"on the psychological health"** Anthony Feinstein, John Owen, and Nancy Blair, "A Hazardous Profession: War, Journalists, and Psychopathology," *American Journal of Psychiatry* 159 (September 2002): 1570–75; Anthony Feinstein, "The Psychological Hazards of War Journalism," *Nieman Reports* 58 (Summer 2004): 75–76; panel discussion in "Dealing with the Trauma of Covering War," *Nieman Reports* 53 (Summer 1999): 24–26; Judith Matloff, "Scathing Memory," *Columbia Journalism Review,* November–December 2004, 19–21; Anthony Feinstein, *Journalists under Fire: The Psychological Hazards of Covering War* (Baltimore: Johns Hopkins University Press, 2003).

On training for war correspondents, see Ian Fisher, "How Not to Get Killed on Deadline," *New York Times Sunday Magazine,* January 31, 1999, 36–37; Yael Danieli, ed., *Sharing the Front Line and the Back Hills: International Protectors and Providers: Peacekeepers, Humanitarian Aid Workers, and the Media in the Midst of Crisis* (Amityville, N.Y.: Baywood, 2002), part 5; Kaethe Weingarten, *Common Shock: Witnessing Violence Every Day* (New York: New American Library, 2003), chap. 5.

For a discussion of trauma generally among journalists and the lack of counseling and other specialized support by media companies, see Roger Simpson and James Boggs, "An Exploratory Study of Traumatic Stress among Newspaper Journalists," *Journalism and Mass Communications Monographs* 1 (Spring 1999): 1–26. Another study that looks at correspondents' physical and emotional safety is Howard Tumber and Frank Webster, *Journalists under Fire: Information War and Journalistic Practices* (London: Sage, 2006).

"the consequences of such coverage" Information on the Dart Center can be found at www.dartcenter.org/.

"not to be hurt if I am gloomy" Belden to his mother, Nov. 2, 1943, Kearney files.

"first sun seen in weeks" This dispatch, in Belden Papers, is undated but from around mid-October 1944. The comment that Belden was a "prima donna" is in Rand, *China Hands,* 198.

328 **"A ravishing blond"** Belden's experiences in liberating Paris are in an undated dispatch in Belden Papers, as is an autobiographical note, "Halle," n.d., which describes his tryst with the German girl. Other details on this period of his life are from Belden, "*Jack Belden*"; Belden, "PERSONAL AND CONDITIONS IN CHINA." For a couple of examples of women appearing in his stories, see Jack Belden, "The Girl Partisan of Chartres," *Life,* September 4, 1944, 20–23; and "Where Is the Front?" *Life,* December 4, 1944, 28–29.

"a neglected masterpiece" Lattimore, introduction to *China Shakes the World,* xiv. Belden wrote his publisher saying he was returning the check. The uncashed check, however, is among his papers along with the copy of the letter, suggesting that he did not send it. Jack Belden to Cass Canfield, n.d., Belden Papers. His papers contain an earlier angry letter to Canfield detailing his frustration with earnings, July 23, 1950, which he also may not have sent. The title Belden chose for the book is a nod to John Reed's *Ten Days That Shook the World* (1919; reprint, New York: Penguin Books, 1977).

"There is nothing out there any more" Keyes Beech, *Tokyo and Points East* (Garden City, N.Y.: Doubleday, 1954), 30; Theodore H. White, *In Search of History: A Personal Adventure* (New York: Harper and Row, 1978), 260.

Bessie at Harper offered Belden Conversation between author and Michael Bessie, February 23, 2006.

329 **"I believe I know more"** Belden, *Still Time to Die,* 308. Belden's "Retreat in Belgium" story was in *Time,* January 1, 1945, 22. His jobs after dropping out of journalism are listed in a handwritten sheet that he apparently prepared with an eye to drafting a résumé. It is in the files of Sandra Kearney. The "archaic" comment is in Belden to Lois Snow, January 10, "some year," a letter provided by Lois Snow.

"a great set of notes" Durdin's observations about the China story are in Durdin to author, July 24, 1990.

"a nice echoing whistle" Robert McCabe to author, March 27, 1990; Jack Belden to Sandra Kearney, October 16, 1979; undated 1985; May 11, 1987; and January 1, 1988, Kearney files; interviews by author with Sandra Kearney, May 10, 1990; Jack Egle, April 17, 1992; and David Belden and Jacques Boni, November 9, 2006. Belden to Lois Snow, January 10, "some year"; and December 5, 1976; "Transcript of Louis Wheeler Snow's taped comments on Jack Belden," n.d., both letters and the transcript provided by Lois Snow.

"I wouldn't mind" Belden, "PERSONAL AND CONDITIONS IN CHINA." James Greenfield, interview by author, March 14, 2006; Greenfield was chief trustee of the Correspondents Fund.

"He still needs me" Beatrice Weber, interviews by author, April 14, 22, 29, 1990; Belden, "*Jack Belden.*"

CHAPTER 19

331 **"Should I sacrifice my life"** Lee Finkle, *Forum for Protest: The Black Press during World War II* (Rutherford, N.J.: Fairleigh Dickinson University Press, 1975), 112. This book and John D. Stevens's *From the Back of the Foxhole* (Lexington, Ky.: Association for Education in Journalism, 1973) are seminal for anyone wishing to understand African American reporting of World War II. Also useful is Stevens's "Black Correspondents of World War II Cover the Supply Routes," *Journal of Negro History* 57 (October 1972): 395–406.

I appreciate my colleague Jinx Broussard's help in understanding something of the black press. This chapter draws from our article, Jinx Coleman Broussard and John Maxwell Hamilton, "Covering a Two-Front War: Three African-American Correspondents during World War II," *American Journalism* 22 (Summer 2005): 33–54. Dr. Broussard is doing important research in this understudied area.

The work of Vincent Tubbs, a correspondent for the *Baltimore Afro-American;* Roi Ottley for *PM,* the *Pittsburgh Courier,* and *Liberty;* and Denton J. Brooks for the *Chicago Defender* appears in the two-volume anthology *Reporting World War II.* The names of Tubbs, Ottley, and Brooks, as well as those of such prominent African American reporters as Edgar Rouzeau, David Ortiz, Scoop Jones, Fletcher Martin, Thomas W. Young, Lem Graves Jr., and John "Rover" Jordan are not found in Hohenberg, *Foreign Correspondence;* Emery, *On the Front Lines;* Knightley, *The First Casualty;* or Roth, *Historical Dictionary of War Journalism.* Nor do African American correspondents appear in the recent PBS documentary and accompanying book, Michelle Ferrari and James Tobin, *Reporting America at War* (New York: Hyperion, 2003).

"Double V" Finkle, *Forum for Protest,* 112. A fascinating account of the Double V activities that sprang forth is in Patrick Washburn, *The African-American Newspapers: Voice of Freedom* (Evanston, Ill.: Northwestern University Press, 2006), chap. 6.

"We must stand united" *Chicago Defender,* December 13, 1941; *Norfolk Journal and Guide,* April 25, 1942.

"close ranks" W. E. B. Du Bois wrote the "Close Ranks" editorial in *Crisis,* July 1918. On the victory parade, see Harvey Levenstein, *Seductive Journey: American Tourists in France from Jefferson to the Jazz Age* (Chicago: University of Chicago Press, 1998), 231. On lynchings, see Finkel, *Forum for Protest,* 44; on not being able to wear uniforms, *Norfolk Journal and Guide,* January 31, 1942.

332 **"Tokio is as heartless"** Finkle, *Forum for Protest,* 203; Charles A. Simmons, *The African-American Press: A History of News Coverage, with Special Reference to Four Black Newspapers, 1827–1965* (Jefferson, N.C.: McFarland, 1998), 74–75.

"We cannot defend America" *Afro-American,* December 20, 1941. Alternative interpretations of the Double V campaign have been advanced. Finkle, *Forum for Protest,* 10, views the Double V as militant in rhetoric but conservative in dealing with the government; the goal was to encourage blacks to fight for their country. On page 101 he comments on the domestic riots during the period. Earnest L. Perry Jr., "It's Time to Force a Change," *Journalism History* 28 (Summer 2002): 85–96, views the press as more militant in practice by resisting government pressure to tone down exposure of "American apartheid during the war while at the same time negotiating ways to change the system." On the number of blacks in the Army in 1940, see David P. Colley, *Blood for Dignity: The Story of the First Integrated Combat Unit in the U.S. Army* (New York: St. Martin's, 2004), 25.

"Golden Age" Brenda Gayle Plummer, *Rising Wind: Black Americans and U.S. Foreign Affairs, 1935–1960* (Chapel Hill: University of North Carolina Press, 1996), 103.

"It is a peculiar sensation" W. E. B. Du Bois, *The Souls of Black Folk* (New York: Modern Library, 2003), 5.

"five hundred thousand free people of colour" Simmons, *The African-American Press,* 9–11; Bernell Tripp, *Origins of the Black Press: New York, 1827–1847* (Northport, Ala.: Vision Press, 1992), chap. 1.

333 **"The *Sun* shines for all white men"** William G. Jordan, *Black Newspapers and America's War for Democracy, 1914–1920* (Chapel Hill: University of North Carolina Press, 2001), 14–15; Finkle, *Forum for Protest,* 27. A discussion of newspaper names is found in Cedric Larson, "American Newspaper Titles," *American Speech* 12 (February 1937): 10–18.

"The press" Gunnar Myrdal, *The American Dilemma: The Negro Problem and Modern Democracy* (New York: Harper, 1944), 909–11. Discussion of the growth and power of the black press is found in Finkle, *Forum for Protest,* 10; Perry, "It's Time to Force a Change," 88; Harry McAlpin, "The Negro Press and Politics," *New Republic,* October 16, 1944; Villard, *Disappearing Daily,* 24.

334 **navigate crosswinds** A discussion of the black press's balancing of interests is found in Jordan, *Black Newspapers,* chap. 1; Finkle, *Forum for Protest,* 53, 58, 71–72; Simmons, *The African-American Press,* 39.

"Oh, Africa, sweet Africa!" The poem is quoted in Frederick G. Detweiler, *The Negro Press in the United States* (Chicago: University of Chicago Press, 1922), 185. Detweiler notes the strong orientation toward African topics.

"I must confess" Willard B. Gatewood Jr., *"Smoked Yankees" and the Struggle for Empire: Letters from Negro Soldiers, 1898–1902* (Urbana: University of Illinois Press, 1971), 279; Gatewood's introduction discusses press coverage of the Spanish-American War by black media; Willard B. Gatewood Jr., *Black Americans and the White Man's Burden: 1898–1903* (Urbana: University of Illinois Press, 1975), chap. 1, pp. 100–101; George P. Marks III, "Opposition of Negro Newspapers to American Philippine Policy, 1899–1900," in *Race and U.S. Foreign Policy in the Ages of Territorial and Market Expansion, 1840 to 1900,* ed. Michael L. Krenn (New York: Garland, 1998).

"equal to anything in the slave trade" John Hope Franklin, *George Washington Williams: A Biography* (Chicago: University of Chicago Press, 1985), 201, 208, 321; John Hope Franklin, "George Washington Williams: The Massachusetts Years," *Proceedings of the American Antiquarian Society* 92 (October 1982): 262; Adam Hochschild, *King Leopold's Ghost: A Story of Greed, Terror, and Heroism in Colonial Africa* (Boston: Houghton Mifflin, 1999), 102; Pagan Kennedy, *Black Livingstone: A True Tale of Adventure in the Nineteenth-Century Congo* (New York: Viking, 2002). The latter book is a biography of Sheppard.

"Open Letter to His Serene Majesty" Franklin, *George Washington Williams,* 253.

335 **"somehow never got beyond"** Roi Ottley, *The Lonely Warrior: The Life and Times of Robert S.*

Abbott (Chicago: Henry Regnery, 1955), 135, 152; Alfred Lawrence Lorenz, "Ralph W. Tyler: The Unknown Correspondent of World War I," *Journalism History* 31 (Spring 2005): 2–12.

"dis" and "dat" Irwin S. Cobb, "Young Black Joe," *Saturday Evening Post,* August 24, 1918, 7–8+; Irwin S. Cobb, *Exit Laughing* (Garden City, N.Y.: Garden City, 1942), 436–37.

"a sense of freedom" J. A. Rogers, "The American Negro in Europe," *American Mercury,* May 1930, 1; David Levering Lewis, *W.E.B. Du Bois: The Fight for Equality and the American Century, 1919–1963* (New York: Henry Holt, 2000), 117; Levenstein, *Seductive Journey,* 231–32, 264.

336 **During these interwar years** Stevens, *From the Back of the Foxhole,* 2, 57–60; Lawrence D. Hogan, *A Black National News Service: The Associated Negro Press and Claude Barnett, 1919–1945* (Rutherford, N.J.: Fairleigh Dickinson University Press, 1984), chap. 5; Laurie F. Leach, *Langston Hughes: A Biography* (Westport, Conn.: Greenwood Press, 2004), 21, 101; Michael B. Salwen, *Evelyn Waugh in Ethiopia: The Story behind Scoop* (Lewiston, N.Y.: Mellen, 2001), 172; Andrew Buni, *Robert L. Vann of the Pittsburgh Courier: Politics and Black Journalism* (Pittsburgh, Pa.: University of Pittsburgh Press, 1974), 141, 222, 244, 248, 258, 381; John D. Stevens, "A Black Correspondent Covers the Ethiopian War, 1935–36," *Journalism Quarterly* 49 (Summer 1972): 349–51; Homer Smith, *Black Man in Red Russia* (Chicago: Johnson, 1964). On the African American attachment to Ethiopia, see William R. Scott, *The Sons of Sheba's Race: African-Americans and the Italo-Ethiopian War, 1935–1941* (Bloomington: Indiana University Press, 1993); Robinson is discussed at length in chap. 6 and Smith briefly on 217–18.

Smith is largely overlooked. He does not figure into Whitman Bassow's *The Moscow Correspondents: Reporting on Russia from the Revolution to Glasnost* (New York: Paragon House, 1989). He is briefly mentioned in Langston Hughes, *I Wonder as I Wander* (New York: Hill and Wang, 1956), 101–2; in Harrison Salisbury's *A Journey for Our Times: A Memoir* (New York: Harper and Row, 1983), 226; in C. L. Sulzberger's *A Long Row of Candles: Memoirs and Diaries, 1934–1954* (New York: Macmillan, 1969), 808–9; and in "Americans in Ethiopia," *Ebony,* May 1951, 79–83. When Salisbury met Smith during the war (before Smith went to work for the AP), Smith was surviving "largely through help from foreign correspondents." He became disillusioned with the Soviet Union and its lack of true equality. After the war, when Haile Selassie returned to his throne and relations with Russia were restored, Sulzberger wrote, "The Ethiopians were pressed by the Russians to accept a small aid mission of four persons. Smith persuaded" an Ethiopian diplomat in Moscow "to specify his name." Smith subsequently worked for the Editorial Department of the English section of the Ethiopian Government's Press and Information Office and occasionally reported for the AP and *Time.* One can find Homer Smith's byline in an AP article in the *Washington Post,* October 15, 1950. Smith became as unhappy in Ethiopia, where he found that the dark-skinned upper class looked down on him as not of their race, as he had been in Russia. He asked to be readmitted to the United States. He died in Chicago in 1972 (see obituary in *Chicago Tribune,* August 18, 1972). Although Homer Smith criticized the Soviet Union in his memoir, his newspaper dispatches from Moscow were typically along the lines of "Nowhere in the world did or could workers have met the New Year with as great happenings, optimism, and hope as did the Soviet workers." *Chicago Defender,* January 11, 1936.

In a curious parallel to the title of Smith's memoir, Gary Lee, a black correspondent who covered the Soviet Union for the *Washington Post,* wrote an article on his return home called "Black among the Reds," *Washington Post,* April 21, 1991. Whereas Smith had received special treatment as a way to show that the Communists were not racist, Lee experienced racism, even being asked to go to the back of a Moscow bus.

"Before a Negro could get to Geneva" Ottley, *The Lonely Warrior,* 347–49. The description and photo of Operative 22 are in the *Defender,* February 15, 1935.

337 **"I shall be a crusader"** *Norfolk Journal and Guide,* July 22, 1944; Stevens, *From the Back of the Foxhole,* 9–10; Henry Lewis Suggs, *P. B. Young, Newspaperman: Race, Politics, and Journalism in the New South, 1910–1962* (Charlottesville: University Press of Virginia, 1988), 135–36. It is Ste-

vens who estimates that twenty-seven correspondents covered the war for black newspapers; I use the number, even though it does not include Roi Ottley, who is described elsewhere as having worked as a war correspondent for the *Courier* as well as other publications. *Reporting World War II,* 1:855.

Indicative of its middle-of-the road approach, a *Journal and Guide* editorial (July 4, 1942) criticized the "increasingly militant campaign" waged by some African American newspapers and organizations. The *Guide* complained that the "ineptness" and "inexperience" of "the men at the head of several movements" and the owners of "two or three newspapers" created the impression they wanted to integrate blacks into the "intimate social life of the American white people." Such actions played into the hands of "bigots and disciples of intolerance." At the same time the *Journal and Guide* pressed for equality for race members. An August 19, 1944, editorial pointed to postwar inequities and criticized the U.S. Senate's acceptance of the "states rights doctrine" regarding distribution of public funds in recovery efforts. The editorial maintained that it would be a "sorry" event if "an army of black veterans who've been fighting for democracy" would "return and be forced through such devices, into virtual or actual serfdom." The newspaper expressed similar concerns in subsequent weeks. Myrdal described the *Journal and Guide* as "highly respected and respectable." *American Dilemma,* 927. The newspaper had a national edition as well as Virginia and Carolina editions.

338 **"I'm not the kind of reporter"** Suggs, *P. B. Young, Newspaperman,* 136; Stevens, *From the Back of the Foxhole,* 15. Jordan discussed his experience in an oral history, Wallace Terry, *Missing Pages: Black Journalists of Modern America* (New York: Carroll and Graf, 2007), 80.

Those front lines lay stateside *Norfolk Journal and Guide,* May 1, 1943; September 9, 1944; Patrick S. Washburn, *A Question of Sedition: The Federal Government's Investigation of the Black Press during World War II* (New York: Oxford University Press, 1986), 59, 89; Finkle, *Forum for Protest,* 106–7, 164; Stevens, *From the Back of the Foxhole,* 6.

339 **"an overnight revolution"** Virginius Dabney, "Nearer and Nearer the Precipice," *Atlantic Monthly,* January 1943, 94, 99; Washburn, *A Question of Sedition,* 8, 66, 82, 154–55; Finkle, *Forum for Protest,* 71–72, 77; Simmons, *The African-American Press,* 83; Ulysses Lee, *The Employment of Negro Troops: United States Army in World War II* (Washington, D.C.: Office of the Chief of Military History, 1966), 383–87.

"No black sonofabitch" Stevens, *From the Back of the Foxhole,* 14, 32; Enoch P. Waters, *American Diary: A Personal History of the Black Press* (Chicago: Path Press, 1987), 272–73.

"Tan Yanks in Navy blue" *Norfolk Journal and Guide,* September 2, 1944.

340 **"Twenty six of the intrepid sky warriors"** Ibid., September 11, 1943. On Dorie Miller, see Finkle, *Forum for Protest,* 94; Stevens, *From the Back of the Foxhole,* 8.

negative news about their race *Norfolk Journal and Guide,* November 13, 1943; April 18, 1945; Stevens, *From the Back of the Foxhole,* 29.

"genuine war correspondents" Suggs, *P. B. Young, Newspaperman,* 134; *Norfolk Journal and Guide,* June 19, 1943; August 26, September 2, 1944.

344 **"The record of the Negro war correspondents"** Stevens, *From the Back of the Foxhole,* front matter, n.p.

"League to Maintain White Supremacy" Dabney, "Near and Nearer the Precipice," 95; the media section of the National Advisory Commission on Civil Disorders report is in Tom Goldstein, ed., *Killing the Messenger: 100 Years of Media Criticism* (New York: Columbia University Press, 1989), 205. Finkle, *Forum for Protest,* 66, comments that black leaders often complained that "the daily press was a 'white' press." For a discussion on the failures of balance and objectivity in covering the lynching of blacks, see David T. Z. Mindich, *Just the Facts: How "Objectivity" Came to Define American Journalism* (New York: New York University Press, 1998), chap. 5.

345 **"there were no Negroes in this war"** *Norfolk Journal and Guide,* January 15, 1944.

"African natives" *Norfolk Journal and Guide,* August 29, 1942; Brenda Gayle Plummer, *Ris-*

ing Wind: Black Americans and U.S. Foreign Affairs, 1935–1960 (Chapel Hill, N.C.: University of North Carolina Press, 1996), 105–6.

346 **"The United States, Great Britain"** Walter White, *A Rising Wind* (Garden City, N.Y.: Doubleday, Doran, 1945), 155; Horace R. Clayton, "The Negro's Challenge," *Nation,* July 3, 1943, 10; Myrdal, *American Dilemma,* 915. For a discussion of the interconnection of decolonization abroad and the civil rights movement at home, see Thomas Borstelmann, *The Cold War and the Color Line: American Race Relations in the Global Arena* (Cambridge, Mass.: Harvard University Press, 2001).

"Almost everything in the Negro press will be new" Thomas Sancton, "The Negro Press," *New Republic,* April 26, 1943, 559.

"Survey of Racial Conditions" Washburn, *A Question of Sedition,* 179.

"are well-informed" Myrdal, *American Dilemma,* 48.

"By the war's end" Eric Foner, *The Story of American Freedom* (New York: Norton, 1998), 239; Finkle, *Forum for Protest,* 220.

347 **"the most successful employment of Negro units"** Colley, *Blood for Dignity,* 207; Terry, *Missing Pages,* 83.

"When the white Southern editors" Sancton, "The Negro Press," 558; Ritchie, *Reporting from Washington,* 33; Washburn, *A Question of Sedition,* 134, 202, 192–93.

"the tranquilizing drug of gradualism" This phrase is from King's 1968 "I Have a Dream" speech, which can be found many places including www.usconstitution.net/dream.html; Gene Roberts and Hank Klibanoff, *The Race Beat: The Press, the Civil Rights Struggle, and the Awakening of a Nation* (New York: Knopf, 2006), 54, 75–76, 150. William Finnegan showed how the black press in apartheid South Africa played a role similar to its role in the United States. One black reporter told him, "We are black before we are journalists. Facts are sacred—we certainly have no need to exaggerate the situation—but the only journalism worth doing in our situation is crusading journalism, work that will help to advance our struggle." See "Getting the Story," *New Yorker,* July 20, 1987, 40, 51.

hiring practices Bendixin & Associates, "Ethnic Media in America: The Giant Hidden in Plain Sight," New California Media, www.ncmonline.com/polls/executivesummary.pdf, released June 7, 2005; Sally Lehrman, *News in a New America* (Miami: Knight Foundation, 2005), 8, 47. A useful history of newspaper efforts to hire more blacks is Orayb Najjar, "ASNE Efforts Increase Minorities in Newsrooms," *Newspaper Research Journal* 16 (Fall 1995): 125.

Estimates of the number of contemporary African American foreign correspondents are difficult to make with confidence because all data on the size and composition of foreign correspondents are shaky. In the absence of a central database of foreign correspondents, researchers must piece one together. And no matter how good today's database may be, tomorrow it will be out of date because of the constant comings and goings of correspondents. The 15 percent figure cited here for the share of nonwhite foreign correspondents is from H. Denis Wu and John Maxwell Hamilton, "US Foreign Correspondents: Changes and Continuity at the Turn of the Century," *Gazette* 66 (December 2004): 523–24. A contrasting and lower estimate of about one in ten correspondents being nonwhite is found in a survey done several years earlier. Hess, *International News and Foreign Correspondents,* 132.

A discussion of coverage of blacks after the war is found in Carolyn Martindale and Lillian Rae Dunlap, "The African Americans," in *U.S. News Coverage of Racial Minorities: A Source Book,* ed. Beverly Ann Deepe Keever, Carolyn Martindale, and Mary Ann Weston (Westport, Conn.: Greenwood Press, 1997), 87–103. On the impact of television on civil rights, see Roberts and Klibanoff, *The Race Beat,* 376–77.

348 **"In a fully integrated society"** Roland E. Wolseley, *The Black Press, U.S.A.: A Detailed and Understanding Report on What the Black Press Is and How It Came to Be* (Ames: Iowa State University Press, 1972), 323. Circulation figures for black newspapers are sketchy, although the num-

bers have continued to climb. An estimate of black newspaper readership in 2004 is 12.7 million. allied-media.com/Publications/african_american_publications_html (accessed August 23, 2008). Data on black reliance on mainstream media for political and government news is in "Ethnic/ Alternative," in *The State of the News Media 2006* (Washington, D.C.: Project for Excellence in Journalism, 2006), 16. The Gordon Jackson quote is from an interview by Shearon Roberts, one of my research assistants, November 15, 2005.

"The Negro makes up" Thomas A. Johnson, "The U.S. Negro in Vietnam," in *Reporting Vietnam* (New York: Library of America, 1998), 1:620; Shearon Roberts, "The Iraq War and Beyond: The Future of War/Foreign Correspondence in the Black Press," 2005, unpublished research paper in author's collection. Curry's reports can be found on http://nnpa.org.

349   **"to offer tortured explanations"** Keith Richburg, *Out of America: A Black Man Confronts Africa* (San Diego: Harcourt, 1998), 92, 141, 144. Also see Richburg, "Continental Divide," *Washington Post Sunday Magazine,* March 26, 1995. One of Richburg's black predecessors in Africa wrote a similar article about the tensions of being black and part of the establishment media: Neil Henry, "A Stranger in Africa," *Washington Post,* Outlook section, August 18, 1991. Another black-correspondent memoir of working in Africa is Howard W. French, *A Continent for the Taking: The Tragedy and Hope of Africa* (New York: Vintage Books, 2005). The first full-time black female journalist at the *Post* was Dorothy Gilliam, who had previously sent stories to the newspaper from Africa, where she was in the Peace Corps. Ritchie, *Reporting from Washington,* 266.

"a roots tour" Keith Richburg, interview by author, April 12, 2005.

Jerelyn Eddings Jerelyn Eddings, interview by author, September 6, 2007.

CHAPTER 20

350   **"one great event"** Walter Lippmann and Charles Merz, "A Test of the News," *New Republic,* August 4, 1920, 1. Lippmann and Merz carried their study further in a subsequent article, "More News from the Times," *New Republic,* August 11, 1920, 299–301. Background on how Lippmann and Merz came to do this study is in Steel, *Walter Lippmann and the American Century,* chap. 14.

"was nothing short of a disaster" Lippmann and Merz, "A Test of the News," 3.

"No less than ninety-one times" Ibid., 10–11, 39.

351   **"magnified the Revolution's meaning"** Peter G. Filene, *Americans and the Soviet Experiment, 1917–1933* (Cambridge, Mass.: Harvard University Press, 1967), 10–13. Leonid Strakhovsky, *American Opinion about Russia* (Toronto: University of Toronto Press, 1961), is especially good on the press during this period.

"I have seen the future" Among the variants of Steffens's line were these: to colleagues gathered in a Paris parlor, "By God, it works!"; to Bernard Baruch, "I have been over to the future and it works"; and on another occasion, "I have seen the future, and by God, it works!" In 1953 William Bullitt told a scholar that Steffens practiced the line before arriving in Moscow. John M. Thompson, *Russia, Bolshevism, and the Versailles Peace* (Princeton, N.J.: Princeton University Press, 1966), 175–76. One source claims that Bullitt came up with the phrase first: Will Brownell and Richard N. Billings, *So Close to Greatness: A Biography of William C. Bullitt* (New York: Macmillan, 1987), 90. For more background, see Irwin, *Making of a Reporter,* 151; Steffens, *The Autobiography of Lincoln Steffens,* 799; Kaplan, *Lincoln Steffens,* 250; Kahn, *World of Swope,* 222.

"the days of the present Bolshevik regime are numbered" Lippmann and Merz, "A Test of the News," 30; William G. Shepherd, "The Road to Red Russia," *Everybody's Magazine,* July 1917, 11.

352   **"Eleven British and U.S. reporters"** Desmond, *Crisis and Conflict,* 30, 230. The "softening euphemisms" quote is from *Christian Science Monitor* reporter William Henry Chamberlin in "Soviet Taboos," *Foreign Affairs,* April 1935, 431. For a general discussion of the problems of covering So-

viet Russia, also see Knightley, *The First Casualty,* chap. 7; Desmond, *The Press and World Affairs,* 273–74; Desmond, *Windows on the World,* 359; Bassow, *The Moscow Correspondents,* 63–65; and Murray Seeger, *Discovering Russia; 200 Years of American Journalism* (Bloomington, Ind.: AuthorHouse, 2005), chap. 14, which deals with Harrison. The latter two books are extraordinary. One author was a correspondent for UP and the other for the *Los Angeles Times,* both organizations that care about such things as attribution; yet neither book has notes. Citations are available, Bassow says, "on request." Seeger says they would "break the flow of the text." On Donald Day, see Edwards, *The Foreign Policy of Col. McCormick's Tribune,* 60–61; and Day himself in Donald Day, *Onward Christian Soldiers* (Torrance, Calif.: Noontide Press, 1982).

John Reed Knightley describes John Reed, along with Philips Price of the *Guardian* (Manchester), as "head and shoulders above any other war correspondent of the time"; "his description of the events in Petrograd in November 1917 is unequalled." Knightley, *The First Casualty,* 151, 158–59. For a similar view, see A. J. P. Taylor, introduction to Reed, *Ten Days That Shook the World,* vii: "Reed's book is not only the best account of the Bolshevik revolution, it comes near to being the best account of any revolution." Also see Hohenberg, *Foreign Correspondence,* 107; and Bassow, *The Moscow Correspondents,* 21. Price was the only correspondent to report the Allied intervention from the Russian side. He was sympathetic to their cause, although his reporting is still better than others. See Knightley, *The First Casualty,* 163–68. For Reed's problems with the law in America and writing his book, see Rosenstone, *Romantic Revolutionary,* chap. 19; Stone, *Perilous Times,* 164–70.

353 **wrapped in mystery** Dash wrote in his first story (*Washington Post,* August 7, 1977): "From the time I walked across the Angolan border Oct. 4 until I recrossed it back into Zambia May 22, I traveled 2,100 miles on foot through the UNITA-occupied areas of southern Angola. Traveling through five provinces. . . . I concluded that the UNITA guerrillas effectively occupy the southern half of Angola, an areas the size of Texas." The UNITA story was complicated. The rebels fought against a government that was backed by the Soviet Union and Cuba; their leader, Savimbi, who had U.S. support, was a socialist and some of his forces had been trained in Communist China. Dash's exploit was highlighted in Kim Willenson, "Angola: Behind the Lines," *Newsweek,* August 22, 1977, 38–39.

"HIGH HOUR COLD NIGHT" Carleton Beals to "Press Kirchwey," February 10, 1928, Beals Papers. The story was published as Carleton Beals, "With Sandino in Nicaragua," *Nation,* February 22, 1928, 204–6. Background on the encounter with Sandino is in John A. Britton, *Carleton Beals: A Radical Journalist in Latin America* (Albuquerque: University of New Mexico Press, 1987), chap. 5.

Edgar Snow's "discovery" Hamilton, *Edgar Snow,* 61–63, 79; Edgar Snow, *Red Star over China,* rev. ed. (New York: Random House, 1938), 8; Edgar Snow, "I Went to Red China," *Saturday Evening Post,* November 6, 1937, 98. In describing Snow's work in this chapter, I have drawn heavily from my biography of him. Among the other sources available on Snow are his autobiography, *Journey to the Beginning,* and two biographies that concentrate on his work during the early part of his life: S. Bernard Thomas, *Season of High Adventure: Edgar Snow in China* (Berkeley: University of California Press, 1996); and Robert M. Farnsworth, *From Vagabond to Journalist: Edgar Snow in Asia, 1928–1941* (Columbia: University of Missouri Press, 1996). Peter Rand devotes a long section to Snow and his first wife, Helen, in *China Hands.* Also useful is the memoir by his first wife, Helen Foster Snow, *My China Years.*

"the China equation" John S. Service, "Edgar Snow: Some Personal Reminiscences," *China Quarterly* 50 (April–June 1972); 211; Malcolm Cowley, "Red China," *New Republic,* January 12, 1938, 287. For background on Snow's reporting immediately after his return from the Communist areas, see Hamilton, *Edgar Snow,* 80. On Luce and communism in China and the Soviet Union, see Swanberg, *Luce and His Empire,* 3, 94–103.

354 **"an event in modern Chinese history"** John K. Fairbank, foreword to Edgar Snow, *Random*

Notes on Red China, 1936–1945 (Cambridge, Mass.: Harvard East Asian Monographs, 1957), v. On Snow's seeing youngsters carrying *Red Star,* see Edgar Snow, *The Battle for Asia* (New York: Random House, 1941), 259.

"Brooding over my stereotype style of living" Edgar Snow to Anna and J. E. Snow, February, July 9, 1928, Snow Papers. The similarities between Millard, Powell, and Snow are discussed in John Maxwell Hamilton, "The Missouri News Monopoly and American Altruism in China: Thomas F. F. Millard, J. B. Powell, and Edgar Snow," *Pacific Historical Review* 55 (February 1986): 27–48. When Snow left the *Review* to work for the Consolidated Press in 1930, he still harbored Halliburtonesque aspirations and wrote numerous travel articles that appeared in the *New York Sun,* the *Chicago Daily News,* and other clients of the Consolidated Press. These were posthumously collected in *Edgar Snow's Journey South of the Clouds.*

"Strange, isn't it" Edgar Snow, "Lifting China out of the Mud!" *China Weekly Review,* October 10, 1928, 84–91.

"Lift China out of the Mud" Snow to Howard Snow, July 20, 1935, Snow Papers.

355 **"liberal and progressive"** Owen Lattimore, *China Memoirs: Chiang Kai-shek and the War against Japan,* compiled by Fujiko Isono (Tokyo: University of Tokyo Press, 1990), 155.

"rather Lincolnesque" Snow, *Red Star,* 66, 215.

"rural egalitarianism" Ibid., 211, 167, 433; Hamilton, *Edgar Snow,* 72–73.

356 **"developed a new"** Gerald W. Johnson, "The Average American and the Depression," *Current History,* February 1932, 672; Walter Duranty, *I Write as I Please* (New York: Simon and Schuster, 1935), 340; Osgood Nichols reviewed Duranty's book in the *Washington Post,* November 10, 1935; Eric Homberger, "Proletarian Literature and the John Reed Clubs, 1919–1935," *Journal of American Studies* 13 (August 1979): 233; Edmund Wilson, "An Appeal to Progressives," *New Republic,* January 14, 1931, 238. Also see George Soule, "Hard-Boiled Radicalism," *New Republic,* January 21, 1931, 261–65; Hamilton, *Edgar Snow,* 83–84.

357 **"The news of this war"** Miles Vaughn, *Covering the Far East* (New York: Covici Friede, 1936), 294–95; Arthur S. Link, *American Epoch: A History of the United States since the 1890s,* vol. 2, 3rd ed. (New York,: Knopf, 1963), 476; Hadley Cantril and Mildred Strunk, eds., *Public Opinion: 1935–1946* (Princeton, N.J.: Princeton University Press, 1951), 1156.

"was a Communist agent" Lattimore, *China Memoirs,* 154–55; Snow, *Red Star,* 374, 378; Hamilton, *Edgar Snow,* 87.

"The 'Red bandits'" R. L. Duffus, *New York Times,* January 9, 1938; *Milwaukee Journal,* January 9, 1938; John Gunther, *Inside Asia* (New York: Harper, 1939), 219. Gunther called Snow's book "one of the best books of historical journalism ever written" (215).

358 **"YENAN, A CHINESE WONDERLAND CITY"** *New York Times,* October 6, 1944; Mackinnon and Friesen, *China Reporting,* 154–55; Kenneth E. Shewmaker, *Americans and Chinese Communists, 1927–1945: A Persuading Encounter* (Ithaca, N.Y.: Cornell University Press, 1971), 171. Shewmaker provides a thorough discussion of coverage of the Chinese Communists. George Seldes expressed a comment similar to Arch Steele's, in *Lords of the Press,* 292: newspaper proprietors viewed Bolshevism "as a threat to possessions and profits and every newspaper worker who could see on which side his bread was buttered 3000 miles away, knew how to handle that subject. If he was so dumb as to think he could treat Bolshevism as fairly as other European phenomena, . . . he soon found out better."

"merely reformers" Mao's interview and Snow's impressions are found in Snow, *The Battle for Asia,* 290–93, 335.

"so-called Communists" Edgar Snow, *The Pattern of Soviet Power* (New York: Random House, 1945), 140; Snow, *Random Notes,* 125–30; Barbara W. Tuchman, *Stilwell and the American Experience in China, 1911–45* (New York: Macmillan, 1971), 486; Hamilton, *Edgar Snow,* 168–69.

"first and way in the lead" Hamilton, *Edgar Snow,* 152–53.

359 **"the man of the year"** Ralph B. Levering, *American Opinion and the Russia Alliance, 1939–1945*

(Chapel Hill: University of North Carolina Press, 1976), 104–5, 145; Martin Kriesberg, "Soviet News in the *New York Times,*" *Public Opinion Quarterly* 10 (Winter 1946–47): 560; Melvin Small, "How We Learned to Love the Russians: American Media and the Soviet Union during World War II," *Historian* 36 (May 1974): 464–65.

"Let us not be deceived" Kahn, *World of Swope,* 404. Well-explained background on the spiraling distrust in the cold war is found in John Lewis Gaddis, *The Cold War: A New History* (New York: Penguin, 2005), chap. 1.

"smash across the Pacific Islands" Louis Francis Budenz, "The Menace of Red China," *Collier's,* March 19, 1949, 23; John T. Flynn, *While You Slept: Our Tragedy in Asia and Who Made It* (New York: Devin-Adair, 1951), 59–61, 73–74, 82.

"external peace" Edgar Snow, *Stalin Must Have Peace* (New York: Random House, 1947), 142; Edgar Snow, "Will Tito's Heretics Halt Russia?" *Saturday Evening Post,* December 18, 1948, 22–23.

362 **"is no longer a child"** Jonathan D. Spence, *The Search for Modern China* (New York: Norton, 1990), 514; for discussion of relations with the Soviet Union, see 524, 544, 560–61, 577, 584–89.

"seems to have been looking over my shoulder" Steel, *Walter Lippmann and the American Century,* 440–46; Edgar Snow to Martin Sommers, March 29, 1947, Snow Papers.

"strongly slanted Leftie articles" Martin Sommers to Jack Belden, January 14, 1948, Belden Papers. Sheean's feelings are reflected in *This House against This House,* part 3.

"Strange Case" Freda Utley, "Red Star over Independence Square: The Strange Case of Edgar Snow and *The Saturday Evening Post,*" *Plain Talk,* September 1947, 9–20.

363 **"contacts with representatives"** Robert St. John describes his passport problems in his unpublished memoir "Stories of a Century," chap. 13, St. John Papers; J. C. Strickland to D. M. Ladd, May 25, 1945, FBI files. A discussion of the measures to limit travel by left-leaning Americans is in Stanley I. Kutler, *The American Inquisition: Justice and Injustice in the Cold War* (New York: Hill and Wang, 1982), chap. 4.

364 **loyalty oaths** Sally Bedell Smith, *In All His Glory: The Life and Times of William S. Paley* (New York: Random House, 2002), 307; Robert M. Hutchins's speech may be found in *Problems of Journalism: Proceedings of the American Society of Newspaper Editors, 1955* (Washington, D.C.: ASNE, 1955), 25. When the Federal Communications Commission talked about the Fairness Doctrine, it did not mean giving all sides a chance to speak out; the FCC was clear in saying that it had no intention of making time available to Communists. Edward Jay Epstein, *News from Nowhere: Television and the News* (New York: Vintage Books, 1974), 64.

"a plain, unmitigated liar" Alfred Kohlberg to E. Otterbourg, August 27, 1945, Kohlberg Papers; Edgar Snow to R. B. Shipley, director of the Passport Office, June 11, 1953; Snow to "Mickey," March 27, 1956, Snow Papers; "Edgar Parks Snow," June 4, 1951; director, FBI, to New York SAC, April 7, 1966, both in FBI Files; Hamilton, *Edgar Snow,* 180, 204. Discussion of book removal and burning is in Walter LaFeber, *America, Russia, and the Cold War, 1945–1966* (New York: Wiley, 1967), 137–38; and *New York Times,* June 11, 22, 1953.

"how deeply indebted" Henry Luce to Edgar Snow, February 25, 1941, Snow Papers; "'Getting Tough' with Russia," *Life,* March 18, 1946, 36; Swanberg, *Luce and His Empire,* 266–67, 297–98; James Reston's article appeared in the *New York Times,* December 9, 1952. When Snow threatened a libel suit, Reston called to apologize and wrote a retraction. The vague accusation lived on. When Snow's wife ran for the school board, the Reston article was resurrected as evidence of her unsuitability. She lost by a narrow vote. For details, see Edgar Snow to Arthur Hays Sulzberger, December 10, 1953; Snow to Amory Bradford, January 4, 1954, NYT Archives; Hamilton, *Edgar Snow,* 201–4.

McCarthyism silenced Britton, *Carleton Beals,* 202–9.

365 **"From 1954 to 1972"** White, *In Search of History,* 391; Reynolds, *By Quentin Reynolds,* chap. 18; Powell's story is told in Neil L. O'Brien, *An American Editor in Early Revolutionary China: John William Powell and the China Weekly/Monthly Review* (New York: Routledge, 2003). Although

his charges about American use of germ warfare in Korea were not substantiated, it did emerge that the military used Japanese biological warfare officers to conduct experiments during World War II.

Snow's editors Ben Hibbs to author, December 8, 1974.

career went into a tailspin Hamilton, *Edgar Snow,* 206–9, 214–15.

366 **"hysterical anti-Sovietism"** George F. Kennan, *Memoirs: 1925–1950* (New York: Pantheon, 1983), 354–67, 558–59; Steel, *Walter Lippmann and the American Century,* 440–49. On Acheson's views, see James Chace, *Acheson: The Secretary of State Who Created the American World* (New York: Simon and Schuster, 1998), 216–24.

"McCarthyism was never decisively rejected" George F. Kennan, *Memoirs: 1950–1963* (New York: Pantheon, 1983), 227; Margaret Macmillan, *Nixon and Mao: The Week That Changed the World* (New York: Random House, 2007), 104.

"I cannot" Spence, *The Search for Modern China,* 553.

367 **"There are many reasons for this"** John Foster Dulles to Arthur Sulzberger, April 30, 1957, NYT Archives; William W. Alfeld, "Newsgathering and the Right to Travel Abroad," *Journalism Quarterly* 36 (Fall 1959): 401–30; Charles C. Alexander, *Holding the Line: The Eisenhower Era, 1952–1961* (Bloomington: Indiana University Press, 1976), 86–87; Smith, *In All His Glory,* 370–71; Steven M. Goldstein, "Dialogue of the Deaf? The Sino-American Ambassadorial-Level Talks, 1955–1970," in *Re-examining the Cold War: U.S.-China Diplomacy, 1954–1973,* ed. Robert S. Ross and Jiang Changbin (Cambridge, Mass.: Harvard University Asia Center, 2001), 217–18; A. T. Steele, *The American People and China* (New York: McGraw-Hill, 1966), 156–57; John Roderick, *Covering China* (Chicago: Imprint Publications, 1993), 122–36.

"the American people had a right to know" Gardner Cowles, *Mike Looks Back: The Memoirs of Gardner Cowles, Founder of Look Magazine* (New York: Gardner Cowles, 1985), 190–93. The Cowleses' attitude toward Dulles is discussed in George Mills, *Harvey Ingham and Gardner Cowles, Sr.: Things Don't Just Happen* (Ames: Iowa State University Press, 1977), 98–100. Edmund Stevens's article appeared as "Inside Red China," *Look,* April 16, 1957, 33–52. He later wrote a shorter piece, "Red China Clings to Ancient Medicine," October 1, 1957, 75–79. Also see John Strohm, "An American in Red China, *Look,* April 28, 1959, 49–54. Strohm was the Wisconsin farm editor who went to China. Lancashire's work is described in his obituary, *Toronto Globe and Mail,* September 15, 2007.

368 **"writer"** Edgar Snow, *The Other Side of the River: Red China Today* (New York: Random House, 1962), 22, 77. This book subsequently was published with the title and subtitle switched.

largely misunderstood Arch Steele provided an excellent analysis of news coverage in his mid-1960s book *The American People and China,* chap. 8.

"At formal interviews" Snow, *The Other Side of the River,* 22, 58, 293.

"The limits of education by travel" Ibid., 620–24. For modern estimates of the shortfall in grain, see Roderick MacFarquhar, *The Origins of the Cultural Revolution: The Coming of the Cataclysm, 1961–1966* (New York: Oxford University Press and Columbia University Press, 1974–97), 13. On the number of deaths, see Jasper Becker, *Hungry Ghosts: Mao's Secret Famine* (New York: Free Press, 1996), xi; see p. 95 for Becker's comment on the difficulty of getting information on the famine: "Those inside the country knew as little as those outside. All mail was controlled by the local authorities and checked to prevent news of the famine spreading."

369 **"Who cared?"** Snow, *The Other Side of the River,* 77.

"no longer interested in writing" Ibid., 395, 402.

"In so far as the Mao 'cult' is reminiscent" Ibid., 145–52.

"China's most remarkable achievement" *China: Socialist Economic Development,* vol. 1, *The Economy, Statistical System, and Basic Data* (Washington, D.C: World Bank, 1983), 11; Snow, *The Other Side of the River,* 86–92, 100; Edgar Snow, "Red China's Leaders Talk Peace—On Their Terms," *Look,* January 31, 1961, 85–104.

"You have made China practically a monopoly!" Harrison Salisbury to Edgar Snow, February 3, 1965, Snow Papers; Hamilton, *Edgar Snow,* 256. For a case of Mao possibly giving Snow bad information—although the matter is still debated—see MacFarquhar, *The Origins of the Cultural Revolution,* 431–32.

Salisbury had a high regard for Snow. After reading *Red Star* when it came out, Salisbury said, he and other journalists "immediately fixed on an image of Ed Snow and his exploits in our mind and wanted to model ourselves after this romantic pattern." Salisbury, "China Reporting: *Red Star* to *Long March,*" in Lee, *Voices of China,* 219–20. Salisbury labels Snow a romantic realist. He adds intriguing, although unattributed, color to the Chinese Communist invitation to Snow in 1935. He suggests that the leadership was urged by Moscow to invite him. A standard view explaining why the Chinese Communists wanted a Western visitor was that they were ready to explain their cause to the West. Journalist-historian Philip Short has noted that the Chinese Communists were aware that Britain and the United States were increasingly concerned about the Japanese and thus likely to welcome Mao's reversal of policy by declaring resistance against the Japanese as a priority over defeat of the Nationalists. Philip Short, *Mao: A Life* (New York: Henry Holt, 1999), 344–45.

370   **"The interviews"** Edgar Snow to James Greenfield, March 3, 1971, NYT Archives.

"friendly personage" Edgar Snow, diary, October 7, 1970, Snow Papers; Hamilton, *Edgar Snow,* 272. The use of interview material and Snow's dislike of the label "friendly personage" or, variously, "friendly American," were discussed by Lois Snow, interview by author, July 9, 1981; and Lois Snow's undated written response to questions from author, circa 1985.

"In this international cataclysm" Hamilton, *Edgar Snow,* 229.

"my place in relation" Sheean, *Personal History,* 398; Shewmaker, *Americans and Chinese Communists,* 221; Tuchman, *Stilwell,* 476–77; Steele, *The American People and China,* 23–30; Harold R. Isaacs, *Scratches on Our Minds: American Images of China and India* (New York: John Day Co., 1958), 187–88; Hamilton, *Edgar Snow,* 117–23.

371   **"Snow Job"** "Snow Job," *Time,* July 25, 1960, 60; Harold C. Hinton, "Red China through Rose-Colored Glasses," *Commonweal,* January 11, 1963, 417; Cowles, *Mike Looks Back,* 190–99; *New York Times,* December 9, 1962. Gardner Cowles said that *Look* sent Snow because of the magazine's editor Dan Mich, "a great friend and admirer" of Snow; Cowles knew Snow only moderately well. Gardner Cowles to author, June 22, 1978.

the election of John Kennedy Hamilton, *Edgar Snow,* 237–38, 247; Lawrence O. Houstoun, interview by author, April 4, 1982.

"return to political life" Rosemary Foot, "Redefinitions: The Domestic Context of America's China Policy in the 1960s," in Ross and Changbin, *Re-examining the Cold War,* 274, 283; James C. Thomson Jr., "On the Making of U.S. China Policy, 1961–9: A Study in Bureaucratic Politics," *China Quarterly* 50 (April–June 1972): 220–43; Senate Committee on Foreign Relations, *Nomination of Chester Bowles: Under Secretary of State-Designate,* 87th Cong., 1st sess., January 19, 1961, 8. Chester Bowles tells of his approach to the hearings in his memoir, *Promises to Keep: My Years in Public Life, 1941–1969* (New York: Harper and Row, 1971), 391–403.

372   **"The United States fought in Vietnam"** Robert D. Schulzinger, "The Johnson Administration, China, and the Vietnam War," in Ross and Changbin, *Re-examining the Cold War,* 238–39.

"Too much going on" Edgar Snow to Rewi Alley, January 15, 1967, Snow Papers. For a general discussion of this period in Snow's life, see Hamilton, *Edgar Snow,* 254–60.

was ironic Macmillan, *Nixon and Mao,* 255, 334.

373   **"He can just get on a plane and come"** Edgar Snow, "Notes on Chairman Mao's Talk," December 18, 1970, Snow Papers. Background on the interview is in Edgar Snow, *The Long Revolution* (New York: Random House, 1972), chap. 24.

374   **"our crude Occidental minds"** Henry Kissinger, *White House Years* (Boston: Little, Brown, 1979), 698; Patrick Tyler, *A Great Wall: Six Presidents and China: An Investigative History* (New York:

Public Affairs, 1999), 86; Gong Li, "Chinese Decision Making and the Thawing of U.S.-China Relations," in Ross and Changbin, *Re-examining the Cold War,* 339–40; MacMillan, *Nixon and Mao,* 181.

"unparalleled opportunity" Seymour Topping to James Greenfield, memorandum, January 27, 1971, NYT Archives; Seymour Topping, interview by author, September 26, 2002; Topping to author, e-mail, October 3, 2007; Lois Snow, interview by author, July 9, 1981; Edgar Snow, "The Open Door," *New Republic,* March 27, 1971, 20–23. In his book *Journey between Two Chinas* (New York: Harper and Row, 1972), ix, Topping commented, "Like so many of his colleagues in the field, I am bereaved by the death this year of Edgar Snow, and I salute his pioneer research and his reporting, which have been of so much value to all of us." For further discussion, see Harrison E. Salisbury, *A Time of Change: A Reporter's Tale of Our Time* (New York: Harper and Row, 1988), 240.

rapprochement Edgar Snow, "A Conversation with Mao Tse-tung," *Life,* April 30, 1971, 46–48; the editorial is titled "Reopening the Door to China," 52.

"gave us a great encouragement" John H. Holdridge, *Crossing the Divide: An Insider's Account of the Normalization of U.S.-China Relations* (Lanham, Md.: Rowman and Littlefield, 1997), 41, 49.

"he would get it for you from *Life*" Ralph Graves to Edgar Snow, July 31, 1971, Snow Papers; Hamilton, *Edgar Snow,* 274–75.

375 **"that every President has been against Red China"** Jerald F. ter Horst, "And How It Was Covered," *Quill,* April 1972, 10.; J. F. ter Horst, "Peking," and Robert L. Keatley, "Shanghai," in *The President's Trip to China,* ed. Richard Wilson (New York: Bantam, 1972), 17–18, 130.

"Your handshake" MacMillan, *Nixon and Mao,* 30, chap. 19; James Mann, *About Face: A History of America's Curious Relationship with China, from Nixon to Clinton* (New York: Knopf, 1999), 48–51; *U.S.-China Relations: An Affirmative Agenda, A Responsible Course* (New York: Council on Foreign Relations, 2007), 3.

"more fresh but no less superficial" Brantly Womack, "The Dilemma of Centricity and Internationalism in China," in Lee, *Voices of China,* 239. Reston's comments are in Harry Harding, "From China, with Disdain: New Trends in the Study of China," *Asian Survey* 22 (October 1982): 938. A similarly thoughtful discussion of overly bright views of China is Sheila K. Johnson, "To China, with Love," *Commentary,* June 1973, 37–45. On Reston's travel to China, see John F. Stacks, *Scotty: James B. Reston and the Rise and Fall of American Journalism* (Boston: Little, Brown, 2003), 306–13.

In *Scratches on Our Minds,* Harold Isaacs divided American attitudes toward China into six ages: the Age of Respect (the eighteenth century), the Age of Contempt (1840–1905), the Age of Benevolence (1905–1937), the Age of Admiration (1937–1944), and the Age of Hostility (1949–). This concept of ages has become a common metric for thinking about China and is seen, for instance, in Steven W. Mosher, *China Misperceived: American Illusions and Chinese Reality* (New York: Basic Books, 1990), 20. Mosher identifies three ages since Isaacs's last one. Harding is among those who use the term *euphoria* to describe feelings toward China during the Nixon period.

"has changed" *New York Times,* February 4, 1973; Joseph Alsop, "Has China Changed?" *Foreign Policy* 10 (Spring 1973): 73–76; Robert W. Merry, *Taking on the World: Joseph and Stewart Alsop— Guardians of the American Century* (New York: Viking Press, 1996), 507. For additional discussion on Alsop's complicated attitudes toward China and China hands, see Edwin M. Yoder Jr., *Joe Alsop's Cold War* (Chapel Hill: University of North Carolina Press, 1995).

"The danger is" Snow, *The Long Revolution,* 188. He began the book before his cancer operation and did some work on it afterward. His wife, along with editor and longtime friend Mary Heathcote, finished it after his death.

376 **"I can only hope"** Richard Nixon to Edgar Snow, January 31, 1972, printed in *New York Times,* February 20, 1972. Snow's views of Nixon were expressed by Lois Snow in various interviews by author, including November 7, 1984.

"**so-called Communist China**" *Washington Post,* April 22, 1984. Oksenberg is quoted in Harding, "From China, With Disdain," 939.

"**It was not possible to be dispassionate**" Orville Schell, *Mandate of Heaven* (New York: Simon and Schuster, 1994), 88. The analysis of coverage is in Michael J. Berlin, Marvin L. Kalb, and the Shorenstein Center, *Turmoil at Tiananmen: A Study of U.S. Press Coverage of the Beijing Spring of 1989* (Cambridge, Mass.: Shorenstein Center, John F. Kennedy School of Government, Harvard University, 1992), 95. On the live-coverage milestone for television, see Lewis A. Friedland, *Covering the World: International Television News Services* (New York: Twentieth Century Fund Press, 1992), 3–4.

377 "'**Loyal follower**'" Bruce Gilley to author, October 21, 2005; Bruce Gilley, "In China's Own Eyes," *Foreign Affairs,* September–October 2005, 151. In publishing his "correction," Gilley wrote that Snow should be called "a loyal servant of the U.S. Communist Party." Gilley, letters to the editor, *Foreign Affairs,* January–February 2006, 169.

"**to please Moscow**" Jonathan Mirsky, letter to editor, *New York Review of Books,* November 16, 2006, 55; also Mirsky, "The Mark of Cain," *New York Review of Books,* February 5, 1998, 31; and Mirsky, "Getting the Story in China: American Reporters since 1972," 2000, Working Paper 2000-11, Shorenstein Center, Cambridge, Mass., 30. The American Communist Party documents can be found in Harvey Klehr, John Earl Haynes, and Kyrill M. Anderson, *The Soviet World of American Communism* (New Haven, Conn.: Yale University Press, 1998), 336–46. For suggestions that Snow was capable of lying, see Mosher, *China Misperceived,* 111–13; and Fang Lizhi, "The Chinese Amnesia," trans. Perry Link, *New York Review of Books,* September 27, 1990, 31. Also see Anne-Marie Brady, *Making the Foreign Serve China: Managing Foreigners in the People's Republic* (Lanham, Md.: Rowman and Littlefield, 2003), 42–50, 121–22, 177–79. The recycling of criticism of Snow is apparent in Robert Service, *Comrades! A History of World Communism* (Cambridge, Mass.: Harvard University Press, 2007), 206, which exaggerates the already tendentious: Jung Chang and Jon Halliday, *Mao: The Unknown Story* (New York: Knopf, 2005), 190–95.

"**discuss the contribution**" Hsinhua, October 18, 2000. I discuss the Chinese use of Snow at greater length in Hamilton, *Edgar Snow,* xxii–xxiii.

"**I cannot and will not remain silent**" Kyodo News Service, April 6, 2000; Lois Snow to author, September 21, 2002; Lois Snow, interviews by author, September 10–11, 2003. The story of Snow's involvement in the December 9th Movement is told in Hamilton, *Edgar Snow,* 55–59. Dingxin Zhao noted the parallels between the December 9th Movement and the 1989 Tiananmen demonstrations in *The Power of Tiananmen: State-Society Relations and the 1989 Beijing Student Movement* (Chicago: University of Chicago Press, 2001), 268–96. The Shorenstein study *Turmoil at Tiananmen* notes the parallels between Millard, Powell, and Snow in relation to demonstrations.

378 "**Human habits**" Crane Brinton, *The Anatomy of Revolution,* rev. ed. (1938; New York: Vintage, 1965), 262; Salisbury, "Red China Reporting," 227. In this vein, Leon Dash has noted that he was too hopeful about Savimbi when he covered Angola in the 1970s:

> Savimbi's one-man control over UNITA, his anti-communist rhetoric and his leading position among his Ovimbundu people, Angola's largest ethnic group, shaped the U.S. decision to make him our man in Angola. In the 1970s, he got great press from most of us in the Western media—including me. He seemed the epitome of a new kind of African visionary, one who was tough enough to prevail, yet idealistic enough to truly favor pluralistic politics and democratic government. But revelations in recent years . . . show Savimbi to be ruthless and limitlessly cruel. . . . The gruesome incidents reportedly include the live burial of two persons in March and two mass burnings of dissidents in the 1980s. *Washington Post,* August 30, 1992.

379 "**Luck broke my way**" On Walter Duranty's approach to the Soviet Union, see his *I Write as I*

Please, 103, 278. For an analysis of coverage of Russia and the 1930s famine, see David C. Engerman, *Modernization from the Other Shore: American Intellectuals and the Romance of Russian Development* (Cambridge, Mass.: Harvard University Press, 2003), chap. 9. Also thoughtful is an analysis of Duranty's work by historian Mark von Hagen, which was commissioned by the *New York Times.* It can be found at http:hnn.us/articles/printfriendly/1754.html (accessed August 6, 2008). Duranty and Louis Fischer, a colleague in Moscow who reported for the *Baltimore Sun* and the *Nation,* are examined in James William Crowl, *Angels in Stalin's Paradise: Western Reporters in Soviet Russia, 1917 to 1937, a Case Study of Louis Fischer and Walter Duranty* (Washington, D.C.: University Press of America, 1982). Pulitzer Prize problems for Duranty were discussed by Sig Gissler and Bud Kliment in interviews by author, May 21, 2004.

"one of the great institutions of Moscow" Whitaker, *And Fear Came,* 143.

"the Bolshevik system" Berger, *Story of the New York Times,* 328; Adolph Ochs to A. O. Sulzberger, August 28, 1933, NYT Archives; Harrison Salisbury, *Without Fear or Favor: The New York Times and Its Times* (New York: Ballantine, 1980), 462. The entire chapter in which this quote appears analyzes Duranty.

"Behind the facade of communism" Walter Duranty to Adolph Ochs, December 27, 1924, NYT Archives.

"the grand old man" Taylor, *Stalin's Apologist,* 237; also Salisbury, *Without Fear or Favor,* 462. In his mea culpa, Duranty wrote in *I Write as I Please,* 277:

> In 1928 here began for me a period which lasted nearly four years upon which I look back with mingled regret and pride. During much of that time I was in a position of seeing the wood so well that I did not distinguish the trees well enough. What I mean is that I gauged the "Party Line" with too much accuracy and when my opinion and expectations were justified by events, as they frequently were, I was so pleased with my own judgment that I allowed my critical faculty to lapse and failed to pay proper attention to the cost and immediate consequences.

380 **"self-image"** James C. Thomson Jr., "On Reporting Revolutions," *Nieman Reports,* Summer 1975, 2.

"Marxist-Leninist" Anthony DePalma, *The Man Who Invented Fidel: Cuba, Castro, and Herbert L. Matthews of the New York Times* (New York: Public Affairs, 2006), 190–91. Matthews did not do himself any favors by insisting after the 1961 announcement that Castro really wasn't a Communist.

"Newspapers" Walter Lippmann, *Public Opinion* (New York: Macmillan, 1922; New York: Free Press, 1965), 19. A decade after *Public Opinion,* Lippmann was still pondering the role of the press: "Thus this press, escaped from the tutelage of government, fell under the tutelage of the masses. It was not a free press in the sense that it was moved by the conviction of its writers, but a kind of freedmen's press, which, lacking the positive qualities of a liberal existence, found support and profit in serving the whims and wishes and curiosity of the people." Walter Lippmann, "Two Revolutions in the American Press," *Yale Review* 20 (March 1931): 436.

381 **his optimism began to fade** Rosenstone, *Romantic Revolutionary,* 373–79.

"'guested' to death by the Chinese" Edgar Snow, diary, August 15, 1970, Snow Papers. Snow did not want to be in the situation of journalist Anna Louise Strong, who lived in China and died there in 1970. She was aware of the predicament that arose by her accepting help from the Chinese. She once commented that she "very much did not want Snow to know how much I get for free here, for he is not discreet with facts that seem to him to make a good story." Strong previously was expelled from the Soviet Union for being a "Titoist" in her support of the Chinese. Strong and Keyssar, *Right in Her Soul,* 244, 304.

For an analysis of Snow that compares him with and contrasts him to Strong and Agnes Smedley, see David E. Apter, "Bearing Witness: Maoismas Religion," *Copenhagen Journal of Asian Studies* 22 (2005): 5–36. As Apter notes, Snow was more reserved than the other two journalists, though still committed to a hopeful outcome of the revolution. He held a view of objectivity "that included partisanship as a means of rectifying widespread and prevailing distortion of fact and interpretation."

"Different reporters" A. J. Liebling, *The Press* (New York: Ballantine, 1961), 72. Some have argued that one could cover China in the 1950s and 1960s better from Hong Kong than inside the country. As Arch Steele noted, covering China from Hong Kong was not nearly as problematic as covering the Soviet Union from Riga in an earlier period. Steele, *The American People and China*, 144. There was more expert information to be gleaned in Hong Kong. But Steele and others also saw the need for direct observation inside the country. This view is echoed by Richard Hughes, a *Sunday Times* of London correspondent, who wrote frequently for the *New York Times* in the 1950s:

> It is true, therefore, that a diligent reporter in Hong Kong can report, review and discuss Chinese affairs if he is not troubled by reservations over writing about events he never witnesses, people he never sees and a country he cannot enter, if he is prepared to devote himself to mountainous research conduced by other persons and if he has been blessed with an objective mind and good eyesight for day and night reading.
>
> It can also be argued that in Hong Kong he escapes the suffocation of an unnatural hermit like existence in a Communist community, which—for all Peiping's difference from dark and sullen official Moscow—tends insensibly over a period to turn his mind against the good human qualities of the people.
>
> At best, however, this line of argument is surely rationalization. The correspondent working on the spot inside China has the immeasurable, essential advantage of seeing things for himself. Richard Hughes, "What 'Dateline Peiping' Means," *New York Times Magazine*, June 23, 1957, 43.

"Edgar Snow" John K. Fairbank, "Mao and Snow," *New York Review of Books*, April 27, 1989, 60.

CHAPTER 21

382 **On Liberty** John Stuart Mill, *On Liberty*, ed. Alburey Castell (New York: Appleton-Century-Crofts, 1947), 45.

"a small Communist force" Prochnau, *Once upon a Distant War*, 52–53, 85. This story is told elsewhere, for example, David Halberstam, "Portrait of an Outsider," *MORE*, August 1972, 6–8+; Salisbury, *Without Fear or Favor*, 38–39; Bigart, *Forward Positions*, 216–17; Neil Sheehan, "Life during Wartime, Vietnam, 1966," *New Yorker*, June 12, 2006, 50–52. Prochnau's book is useful for coverage of Vietnam in the early 1960s, and I have made extensive use of it. The book's endnotes are sketchy, which makes checking his facts difficult; his rendition of the Sheehan-Bigart story has several errors in it. Sheehan's report and Bigart's ran in the *New York Times* on May 13, 1962. Sheehan filed a correction, but it did not run in the *Times*, which instead used a story by Bigart that clarified: "The first reports of 300 guerrillas, or Vietcong, dead were drastically reduced this morning." It ran the next day, May 14, 1962. On the new challenges presented by this war, see Michael S. Sweeney, *The Military and the Press: An Uneasy Truce* (Evanston, Ill.: Northwestern University Press, 2006), 138; Daniel C. Hallin, *The "Uncensored" War: The Media and Vietnam* (New York: Oxford University Press, 1986), 127–28.

383 **"minimized"** Prochnau, *Once upon a Distant War*, 57; Behr, *"Anyone Here Been Raped and Speaks English?"* 250.

"S---kick and Motherf---er" Michael Herr, "The War Correspondent: A Reappraisal," *Esquire*, April 1970, 95, 160. This article appeared in what has become a minor classic of reporting on the Vietnam War, Michael Herr's *Dispatches* (New York: Knopf, 1977). In yet another example of Vietnam War New Journalism, novelist Norman Mailer reported on an antiwar demonstration at the Pentagon for *Harper's*. His report plus another in *Commentary* became a book, *The Armies of the Night,* which won a National Book Award and a Pulitzer Prize in nonfiction.

Tom Wolfe, onetime Latin America correspondent for the *Washington Post* and a leader of the New Journalism, said it was time to violate "what Orwell called 'the Geneva conventions of the mind.'" Tom Wolfe, "The New Journalism," in *The New Journalism,* ed. Tom Wolfe and E. W. Johnson (New York: Harper and Row, 1973), 21. For a good discussion of changes in journalists' attitudes, see James L. Aucoin, *The Evolution of American Investigative Journalism* (Columbia: University of Missouri Press, 2005), chap. 2.

"Our worst enemy" William M. Hammond, *Reporting Vietnam: Media and Military at War* (Lawrence: University Press of Kansas, 1998), ix. An example of the continual rethinking of the Vietnam War is Melvin R. Laird, "Iraq: Learning the Lessons of Vietnam," *Foreign Affairs,* November–December 2005, 22–43.

"This," he said Homer Bigart, "Heave Ho, Vietnamese Style," in *The Working Press: Special of the New York Times,* ed. Ruth Adler (New York: Bantam Books, 1970), 157.

"a benchmark" On Lippmann and Merz's farsighted scholarly work, see Hanno Hardt, "Reading the Russian Revolution: International Communication Research and the Journalism of Lippmann and Merz," *Mass Communication and Society* 5 (February 2002): 26.

A considerable body of scholarship argues that the government shapes media coverage. A landmark 1973 study by Leon Sigal found that U.S. and foreign officials were a primary source of information in 88.3 percent of staff-written foreign-dateline stories in the *New York Times* and the *Washington Post.* Nongovernmental Americans and nongovernmental foreigners each were a primary source in less than 3 percent of the stories. Leon V. Sigal, *Reporters and Officials: The Organization and Politics of Newsmaking* (Lexington, Mass.: Heath, 1973), 125. A subsequent study of the Vietnam War pointed the way to the concept of indexing: Hallin, *The "Uncensored" War.* Hallin argues, "Structurally the American news media are both highly autonomous from direct political control and, through the routines of the newsgathering process, deeply intertwined in the actual operation of government" (8).

An excellent discussion of indexing is found in W. Lance Bennett, Regina G. Lawrence, and Steven Livingston, *When the Press Fails: Political Power and the New Media from Iraq to Katrina* (Chicago: University of Chicago Press, 2007). An early study of indexing is in W. Lance Bennett, "Toward a Theory of Press-State Relations in the United States," *Journal of Communication* 40 (Spring 1990): 103–25. Substantiating Bennett's argument, while offering nuance (it noted a "tendency of reporters to be more hawkish than official sources when the United States faced a Communist foe and more dovish when the United States suffered a military setback"), is John Zaller and Denis Chiu, "Government's Little Helper: U.S. Press Coverage of Foreign Policy Crises, 1945–1991," *Political Communication* 16 (October–December 1996): 385–405. Another example of fine-tuning Bennett, in this case showing how the media can challenge the dominant power of the government, is Robert M. Entman, "Cascading Activation: Contesting the White House's Frame after 9/11," *Political Communication* 20 (October–December 2003): 415–32.

These are only a few of the studies that examine the ties between policymakers and the news. For a sampling of others, see Martin Kriesberg, "Soviet News in the *New York Times,*" *Public Opinion Quarterly* 10 (Winter 1946–47): 540–64; T. McCoy, "The New York Times Coverage of El Salvador," *Newspaper Research Journal* 13 (Summer 1992): 67–84; Edward S. Herman, "The Media's Role in U.S. Foreign Policy," *Journal of International Affairs* 47 (Summer 1993): 23–45; Nicholas O. Berry, *Foreign Policy and the Press: An Analysis of The New York Times' Coverage of U.S. Foreign Policy* (New York: Greenwood Press, 1990); Jonathan Mermin, *Debating War and Peace: Media Coverage of U.S. Intervention in the Post-Vietnam Era* (Princeton, N.J.: Princeton University Press, 1999).

384 **"Once officials engage"** Bennett, Lawrence, and Livingston, *When the Press Fails,* 100. I am indebted to Regina Lawrence for helping me understand this concept. The phrase "bias toward power" is hers.

"essentially accepted the consensus" Steel, *Walter Lippmann and the American Century*, 490. **only full-time correspondent** Knightley, *The First Casualty*, 410; Prochnau, *Once upon a Distant War*, 37.

385 **"naked aggression"** Robert Mann, *A Grand Delusion: America's Descent into Vietnam* (New York: Basic Books, 2001), 3; Daniel Ellsberg, *Secrets: A Memoir of Vietnam and the Pentagon Papers* (New York: Penguin, 2003), 12, 50; Sweeney, *The Military and the Press*, 143.

386 **"a miserable fucking performance"** Stanley Karnow, *Vietnam: A History* (New York: Viking, 1983), 262. Vann's sentiments were picked up in the press, but with the language cleaned up. Hammond, *Reporting Vietnam*, 8. The casualty figures are discussed in Prochnau, *Once upon a Distant War*, 241.

"seized on the Buddhist crisis" Sheehan, *A Bright Shining Lie*, 346; Halberstam's report was in the *New York Times* on June 22, 1963.

"embittered confrontation" Sheehan, *A Bright Shining Lie*, 314–15; Prochnau, *Once upon a Distant War*, 171–72, 244; Halberstam, *The Making of a Quagmire*, 156.

"Don't believe any official statement" Prochnau, *Once upon a Distant War*, 59, 120, 168, 324.

387 **different route from Bigart's** Arthur Gelb, *City Room* (New York: Putnam's, 2003), 350–51; Prochnau, *Once upon a Distant War*, 34, 45, 175. Bigart's impatience with editors erupted when he was denied military transportation in Vietnam that was given to Joseph Alsop, who was visiting. Bigart cabled home: "IF NYKTIMES CANNOT SAFEGUARD ITS CORRESPONDENTS AGAINST THIS KIND OF FAVORITISM EYE WANT TO QUIT." The cable is in the Catledge Papers; it is misquoted in Prochnau, *Once upon a Distant War*, 45.

"We regarded the war" Sheehan, *A Bright Shining Lie*, 271; Halberstam, *The Making of a Quagmire*, 144; Salisbury, *Without Fear or Favor*, 37; Hammond, *Reporting Vietnam*, 4; *New York Times*, June 22, 1963.

"advisors" Prochnau, *Once upon a Distant War*, 43–46; Hammond, *Reporting Vietnam*, 2–3.

388 **"how Homer used his ammunition"** Sheehan, *A Bright Shining Lie*, 352–57; Prochnau, *Once upon a Distant War*, 138, 327–30, 365.

"The Vietcong simply refused to panic" *New York Times*, January 4, 1963.

"get cracking" Prochnau, *Once upon a Distant War*, 194–95, 203, 208, 213; Halberstam, *The Making of a Quagmire*, 164.

389 **"young and inexperienced"** Malcolm W. Browne, *Muddy Boots and Red Socks: A Reporter's Life* (New York: Random House, 1983), 155; Morley Safer: *Flashbacks: On Returning to Vietnam* (New York: Random House, 1990), 107; Prochnau, *Once upon a Distant War*, 266–68; Richard Tregaskis, *Vietnam Dairy* (Lincoln, Neb.: iUniverse.com, 2001), 5, 380–81.

"just little boys" Stuart Loory, interview by author, August 10, 2007; *New York Herald Tribune*, August 26, 1963.

"a political time bomb" Prochnau, *Once upon a Distant War*, 401–42, 415–16; Yoder, *Joe Alsop's Cold War*, 15.

"Look, I don't even have to talk to you people" William Small, *To Kill a Messenger: Television News and the Real World* (New York: Hastings House, 1970), 102; Hammond, *Reporting Vietnam*, 5; Knightley, *The First Casualty*, 427–28.

"Vietnam is a graveyard" Halberstam, *The Making of a Quagmire*, 271–72; "Report on the War," *Time*, September 20, 1963; Prochnau, *Once upon a Distant War*, 259, 433–35, 452; "Foreign Correspondents: The View from Saigon," *Time*, September 20, 1963, 62; "Foreign Correspondents: The Saigon Story," *Time*, October 11, 1963, 55–56.

390 **"A great newspaper"** Prochnau, *Once upon a Distant War*, 450; Tifft and Jones, *The Trust*, 312–15; Tad Szulc, "The New York Times and the Bay of Pigs," in Brown and Bruner, *How I Got That Story*, 328. Kennedy made a similar comment to Orvil Dryfoos, the publisher at the time. Shepard, *The Paper's Papers*, 188. Regarding the *Times'* distaste for crusading, see Berger, *Story of the New York Times*, 259.

On deference to the administration, Turner Catledge said that Arthur H. Sulzberger, the

Times' publisher in the mid-1950s, was "so great an admirer of Eisenhower that he would not have dreamed of going against the administration's wishes on what it claimed was a highly sensitive issue of foreign policy." Turner Catledge, *My Life and the Times* (New York: Harper and Row, 1971), 292.

Not all *Times* reporters have found *crusading* a wormwood word. A good discussion of the *Times* anticrusading attitude by one of its crusading-minded reporters (and a former *Times* foreign correspondent) is John L. Hess, *My Times: A Memoir of Dissent* (New York: Seven Stories Press, 2003), 29–30. Hess admired Salisbury.

"soap box" Prochnau, *Once upon a Distant War,* 358, 360, 378–79, 398, 402, 416–17, 451, 453–55; Sheehan, *A Bright Shining Lie,* 350–51. On Reston, see Salisbury, *Without Fear or Favor,* 91, and Stacks, *Scotty,* 243–51. An example of Reston's criticism of the government for its secrecy in Vietnam was in the *Times* on February 14, 1962.

Halberstam's experience of having his story paired with a contradictory one was not unique. The *Times* staff was sharply split over the Spanish Civil War of the 1930s. Herbert Matthews covered the Loyalists, and Catholic William Carney covered Franco's side. Editors used rulers to make sure each side received equal attention. Matthews discusses this in Herbert L. Matthews, *A World in Revolution: A Newspaperman's Memoir* (New York: Scribner's, 1971), chap. 2; so does Harrison Salisbury in *Without Fear or Favor,* 452–53.

Salisbury had his own dose of this treatment. When reporting from the Soviet Union in the 1950s, he endured the old problem of writing stories in ways that would pass the censor, which he believed made him appear sympathetic to the Communists. To avoid that impression, he wanted his stories to run under a note informing the reader that they had "passed through the hands of the Soviet Censorship." This the *Times* would not do. Instead, to Salisbury's consternation, it hired Harry Schwartz, a former analyst in the OSS and the State Department, to provide "balance" by covering the Soviet Union from New York. The use of Schwartz is discussed in Talese, *The Kingdom and the Power,* 524–25. For an example of the back-and-forth on this issue between Salisbury and New York, see Harrison Salisbury to Turner Catledge, November 15, 1951; and Catledge to Salisbury, January 10, 1952, Salisbury Papers. This issue is discussed in Don Grierson, "Battling Censors, Chiding Home Office: Harrison Salisbury's Russian Assignment," *Journalism Quarterly* 64 (Summer–Fall 1987): 313–16.

391 **"For a while"** Prochnau, *Once upon a Distant War,* 360; Halberstam, *The Making of a Quagmire,* 267; William L. Lunch and Peter W. Sperlich, "American Public Opinion and the War in Vietnam," *Western Political Quarterly* 32 (March 1979): 22, 27.

"We missed the big one" Neil Sheehan, "Not a Dove, but No Longer a Hawk," *New York Times Sunday Magazine,* October 9, 1966, 27; Prochnau, *Once upon a Distant War,* 282, 483. Halberstam's book is *The Making of a Quagmire;* Browne's is *The New Face of War* (Indianapolis, Ind.: Bobbs-Merrill, 1965). Sheehan, thought Halberstam, should have won a Pulitzer Prize too, but working for the lesser service, UPI, and being in Tokyo at the outset of the coup did not help. Sheehan's 1966 magazine article clearly outlined the underlying failure of the South Vietnamese government to win support from its people.

"unemployable" Prochnau, *Once upon a Distant War,* 193; Leslie H. Gelb with Richard K. Betts, *The Irony of Vietnam: The System Worked* (Washington, D.C.: Brookings Institution, 1979), 213–17.

392 **expelled Harrison Salisbury** Salisbury, *A Journey for Our Times,* 86–87.

"gulped down" Salisbury, *A Time of Change,* xi, 200; Hamilton, *Edgar Snow,* 189. Talese, *The Kingdom and the Power,* 522. Salisbury, *A Journey for Our Times,* 69, 300–303. Salisbury talks about meeting Bigart in his foreword to Bigart, *Forward Positions,* xi–xii. An important aspect of Salisbury's personality was that he had many journalistic heroes against whom he measured himself. In his quickie book *Heroes of My Time* (New York: Walker, 1993), he wrote chapters on Edgar Snow, Homer Bigart, and David Halberstam. He noted in the book that he especially liked "antiheroes" who did not seek to "win the applause of the multitude" (vii). For another one of his references to heroes, see *A Time of Change,* xi, 289.

"**Also, let me add**" Turner Catledge to Harrison Salisbury, December 8, 1954, Salisbury Papers; Talese, *The Kingdom and the Power*, 526–27. Salisbury's view on Snow and the *Saturday Evening Post* was conveyed by Salisbury in an interview with the author, circa 1985.

"**steel-rimmed glasses**" Talese, *The Kingdom and the Power*, 38, 136, 138, 236, 505, 513, 567. Salisbury's prowling was once described to the author by a neighbor who observed it firsthand.

In the quest for promotions and power, *Times* journalists develop sharp elbows and sensitive ribs. Arthur Gelb later recalled a slight by Salisbury, whom he believed to be a rival of future editor Abe Rosenthal. During the 1964 Democratic party convention in Atlantic City, Salisbury booked rooms for Rosenthal and Gelb at "a kosher boardinghouse some distance from the principal hotels near the convention center, where he himself was staying" along with the publisher and executive editor. Gelb, *City Room*, 394–95.

393 "**We have never bombed their population**" "Civilians Weren't the Target, but...," *Newsweek*, January 9, 1967, 17. Background on the lost invitation is in Salisbury, *A Time of Change*, 143. Many of the details of Salisbury's trip recounted here are from this memoir and from Salisbury's book written after returning home, *Behind the Lines, Hanoi, December 23, 1966–January 7, 1967* (New York: Harper and Row, 1967). A discussion of administration comment in December on the *possibility* of having bombed civilian areas, as well as a reprise of Salisbury's trip, is in William M. Hammond, *Public Affairs: The Military and The Media, 1962–1968* (Washington, D.C.: Center of Military History, 1988), 273–79.

"**A VISITOR TO HANOI**" *New York Times*, December 25, 1966. Details on the handling of the story are from Clifton Daniel's draft memorandum, untitled and undated, NYT Archives; it is not possible to determine whether the memorandum was distributed.

395 "**no visible military objectives**" Quotes from Harrison Salisbury, *New York Times*, are in this order: January 8, 1967; December 28, 27, 1966; January 4, 8, 1967. Salisbury's reporting raised other issues, such as the independence of the Communist National Liberation Front in South Vietnam from Hanoi, which are not discussed in this chapter.

"**the most careful, self-limited air war**" Karnow, *Vietnam*, 490.

"**Hanoi-picked correspondent**" *New York World Journal Tribune*, January 20, 1967; Phil G. Goulding, *Confirm or Deny: Informing the People on National Security* (New York: Harper and Row, 1970), 79; Salisbury, *A Time of Change*, 147.

396 "**Strictly one-dimensional**" "Flak from Hanoi," *Time*, January 6, 1967, 13–14; *San Diego Union*, January 28, 1967; *St. Louis Globe-Democrat*, January 4, 1967; *Washington Star*, January 3, 1967; Knightley, *The First Casualty*, 457–58. An assessment of heavily negative coverage of Salisbury is found in Mark Atwood Lawrence, "Mission Intolerable: Harrison Salisbury's Trip to Hanoi and the Limits of Dissent against the Vietnam War," *Pacific Historical Review* 75 (August 2006): 447–53; and James Boylan, "A Salisbury Chronicle," *Columbia Journalism Review*, Winter 1966–67, 10–14.

"**careless, erratic, and misleading**" A. J. Langguth, *Our Vietnam: The War, 1954–1975* (New York: Simon and Schuster, 2002), 436; Joseph Kraft, *Minneapolis Tribune*, January 9, 1967.

397 "**nearly boundless confidence**" The comment on Salisbury's "boundless confidence" is in his obit, *New York Times*, July 7, 1993. See also *New York Times*, December 27, 1966; Clifton Daniel to Turner Catledge, January 4, 1967, NYT Archives. Topping's urgings are mentioned in Lawrence, "Mission Intolerable," 453. Salisbury gives his source for the Nam Dinh statistics in *A Time of Change*, 147. Salisbury's comments on writing hastily are in Senate Committee on Foreign Relations, *Harrison E. Salisbury's Trip to North Vietnam*, 90th Cong., 1st sess., 1967, Committee Print, 14.

"**This reporter cannot say**" *New York Times*, December 31, 1966. In his memoir, Phil G. Goulding, a Defense Department spokesman, wrote an analysis of Salisbury's reporting: *Confirm or Deny*, 52–92. Although the memoir has its own bias, that of the government, it is thoughtful. Commenting on Nam Dinh, Goulding said the city's primary industry was textiles; these plants were not targets. A thermal power plant and a petroleum-oil storage plant near them were. Also

Nam Dinh had a large railroad yard. Salisbury apparently was unaware of the power plant, but he did speculate that there was a railroad and "presumably" freight yards and depots that qualified as military targets. On Daniel, Talese, *The Kingdom and the Power,* 534.

Salisbury also wrote on December 27, 1966, "Another target in Nam Dinh has been the Dao (Black) River Dike." Hitting dikes was contrary to U.S. policy. Goulding insists they were "not deliberately attacked at any time," but were hit accidentally. Salisbury would have been on safer ground to write, as he did in a subsequent story, that local officials believed the dikes were targeted on purpose.

Salisbury was incorrect in reporting on December 31, 1966, that the government had never mentioned Nam Dinh as a target. It had been mentioned, three times in nightly briefings in Saigon months before, although this was done in such a way that the announcements were scarcely noticed. Salisbury, *Behind the Lines,* 97–98.

"intelligence sources" *Washington Post,* January 1, 1967; *Wall Street Journal,* January 6, 1967. This episode and others showing the attacks on Salisbury are discussed in James Aronson, *The Press and the Cold War* (New York: Monthly Review Press, 1990), 253–61.

398 **"Now he is using another weapon"** *Washington Post,* January 2, 1967. Karnow, *Vietnam,* 490, mentions that Roberts took government cues.

"admiration" for Salisbury Walter Lippmann to Arthur Sulzberger, January 7, 1967, NYT Archives; Steel, *Walter Lippmann and the American Century,* 557, 572, 576–79. Lippmann's defense of Salisbury is found, among other newspapers, in *Washington Post,* January 10, 1967.

399 **"Obliquely but perfectly clearly"** See Salisbury, *A Time of Change,* 159, 161, and passim, for general discussion of this aspect of his trip. For other details, see Kraft, *Minneapolis Tribune,* January 9, 1967; William P. Bundy, "Secretary Rusk's Appointment with Harrison Salisbury," memorandum of conversation, Department of State, January 13, 1967; and Dean Rusk, "Highlights of Harrison Salisbury Private Report to Me," memorandum for the president, January 14, 1967, both available in the Virtual Vietnam Archive, Texas Tech University; retrieved in October 2007 from www.virtual.vietnam.ttu.edu; and William Gibbons and Patricia McAdams, "Interview with Harrison Salisbury," typescript, January 9, 1979. This later document was prepared by the Congressional Research Service for a study on American involvement in Vietnam; a copy is located in Salisbury Papers.

"a clever, carefully prepared piece of propaganda" The Department of State cable (in Salisbury Papers) warning embassies to give little credence to Salisbury's dispatches was sent January 10, 1967. For a discussion of the administration's follow-up on Salisbury's interview with the premier, see the full congressional study of which the Salisbury interview is a part: Senate Committee on Foreign Relations, *The U.S. Government and the Vietnam War: Executive and Legislative Roles and Relationships,* part 4, July 1965–January 1968, 103rd Cong. 2nd sess., June 1994, 498–524; also see Karnow, *Vietnam,* 494–95. Salisbury was so willing to help that he wrote a follow-up letter to William Bundy to reiterate his suggestions. Salisbury to William Bundy, January 16, 1967, Salisbury Papers.

"It isn't necessary" Clifton Daniel to Robert L. Simpson, January 17, 1967, NYT Archives; Gay Talese, "The Public and Private Wars of Harrison E. Salisbury," *Esquire,* May 1967, 172. A discussion of the *Times'* editorial policy at the time is in Salisbury, *Without Fear or Favor,* 44–46; Hallin, *The "Uncensored" War,* 61; Matthews, *A World in Revolution,* 425–27.

Max Frankel, then a Washington correspondent and later executive editor, thought that Salisbury "pulled a few punches to maintain access to communist countries." Lawrence, "Mission Intolerable," 434. James Greenfield did not like Salisbury's "fawning" letters to Communist leaders (and did not like Salisbury's reports from Vietnam). Greenfield, interview by author, March 14, 2006. Greenfield, a *Time-Life* correspondent who served as an official in the State Department during the Kennedy and Johnson administrations, was hired by Rosenthal and later became foreign editor. Thanks to his government experience, Greenfield's "Rolodex bulged with government sources." Gelb, *City Room,* 498. Rosenthal later expressed a similar concern over the tone of the letters Salisbury wrote to get an invitation to Cambodia and North Korea. See Edwin Diamond, *Behind the Times: Inside the New New York Times,* rev. ed. (Chicago: University of Chicago Press, 1995), 184. In fact, it is not unusual for journalists to flatter foreign governments of all persuasions in order to get access or avoid being expelled. When the Diem regime booted a visiting NBC correspondent, the network tried to get the decision reversed by telling Diem of their efforts to show "your valiant efforts to stop the spread of Communism in Southeast Asia." Prochnau, *Once upon a Distant War,* 179.

400 **"congratulate" Salisbury** Arthur Sulzberger to Harrison Salisbury, December 28, 1966, Salisbury Papers; Clifton Daniel to Turner Catledge, January 4, 1967, NYT Archives. Also see untitled, undated Daniel draft memorandum mentioned above. Salisbury says he received a congratulatory cable from Sulzberger on December 30, 1966. Salisbury, *A Time of Change,* 142. By mid-February, the mail was 179 in favor, 66 against, and 42 "comments"; this tally, dated February 16, 1967, is in Salisbury Papers.

"Dear Clif" Hanson Baldwin to Clifton Daniel, December 27, 1966; Daniel to Baldwin, December 28, 1966, NYT Archives. Baldwin's sentiments on the war are clear also from his 1966 letter to Arthur Sulzberger and editorial page editor John B. Oakes to protest editorial policy on Vietnam: "In all sincerity I feel we are wrong and that we are hurting the country and ourselves needlessly." Baldwin to Sulzberger and Oakes, January 10, 1966, Catledge Papers. On the same day Baldwin wrote a "personal" note to Sulzberger, also in the Catledge Papers, protesting treatment of his stories from Vietnam. Salisbury was tasked with reviewing the editing of Baldwin's stories, which he concluded "was handled with intelligence." Harrison E. Salisbury to Clifton Daniel, January 17, 1966, Catledge Papers. If Baldwin had reported what he knew about U-2 overflights, Salisbury thought, the United States might have avoided a diplomatic disaster, Salisbury, *Without Fear or Favor,* 512–13.

"military officials in the Pentagon" *New York Times,* December 30, 1966.

401 **"do everything we can"** Daniel's memorandum is quoted in Langguth, *Our Vietnam,* 436; *New York Times,* January 2, 10, 1967.

"the circumstances of Salisbury's visit" Catledge, *My Life and the Times,* 292–93; Catledge speech to the "Little Forum," Bronxville, New York, March 27, 1967, Catledge Papers.

"despite minor technical flaws" Aronson, *The Press and the Cold War,* 260–61; John Hohenberg, *The Pulitzer Diaries: Inside America's Greatest Prize* (Syracuse, N.Y.: Syracuse University Press, 1997), 169–77, 322.

"I love Harrison" Marvin Kalb to Seymour Topping, arrival date in *Times* office, January 5, 1967, NYT Archives. Marvin Kalb to Harrison Salisbury, May 2, 1967, Salisbury Papers. Marvin Kalb, interview by author, February 27, 2008.

"Over 75 percent" Hammond, *Reporting Vietnam,* 96; "The Effectiveness of the Air Campaign against North Vietnam, 1 January–30 September 1966," Central Intelligence Agency memorandum, December 1966, declassified in July 1985, 14, available in the Virtual Vietnam Archive, Texas Tech University, retrieved in October 2007 from www.virtual.vietnam.ttu.edu. Also available at the Texas Tech archive are Central Intelligence Agency Intelligence Information Cable, "Statement That One Faction in North Vietnam Feels Food Situation Is So Difficult That War Should Stop," January 30, 1967 (I appreciate help from Mark Lawrence in securing a copy of this document); "The Rolling Thunder Mission in North Vietnam," Central Intelligence Agency Memorandum, November 1966, declassified 1986, 3; "Background to Current North Vietnamese Refusal to Allow Newsmen into North Vietnam," Intelligence Information Cable, April 4, 1967. This last document reported "a big debate" among North Vietnamese officials about Salisbury's articles, which some deemed too unfavorable to the Communist side.

402 **"Success appears dubious"** The Mohr story appeared in the *New York Times,* May 28, 1984. The CIA document is "The Vietnam Situation: An Analysis and Estimate," May 23, 1967, part 5, p. 37; part 4, p. 1, Virtual Vietnam Archive, Texas Tech University; retrieved in December 2007 from www.virtual.vietnam.ttu.edu.

"looked at primarily as news" Boylan, "A Salisbury Chronicle," 14. Also arriving in Vietnam about this time was John Gerassi, who wrote as a freelance journalist; his book-length account, which reaches many of the same conclusions as Salisbury did, is *North Vietnam: A Documentary* (Indianapolis: Bobbs-Merrill, 1968). A brief discussion of *Guardian* coverage is in Melvin Small, *Covering Dissent: The Media and the Anti-Vietnam War Movement* (New Brunswick, N.J.: Rutgers University Press, 1994), 66. At the time, Salisbury did not draw attention to his travels with Burchett, possibly to avoid guilt-by-association with an avowed left-leaning journalist. Later Salisbury wrote an introduction to Wilfred Burchett's autobiography, *At the Barricades: Forty Years on the Cutting Edge of History* (New York: Times Books, 1981). Harry Ashmore and William Baggs traveled to Hanoi as representatives of the Center of the Study of Democratic Institutions; they returned in 1968. The pair wrote *Mission to Hanoi: A Chronicle of Double-Dealing in High Places* (New York: Putnam's, 1968). In it they expressed frustration with the U.S. government's expansion of the war.

"surgical precision" Goulding, *Confirm or Deny,* 52; Senate Committee on Foreign Relations, *The U.S. Government and the Vietnam War,* 553–54. An example of credit being given to Salisbury for galvanizing "the peace movement" is in Langguth, *Our Vietnam,* 436. The Fulbright hearing is in Senate Committee on Foreign Relations, *Harrison E. Salisbury's Trip to North Vietnam;* in this Senate testimony, p. 3, Salisbury suggested that the United States should engage in secret negotiations with the North Vietnamese, but he advanced this as his own idea, not something proposed by Pham Van Dong.

"embarrass the administration" Mann, *Grand Delusion,* 433; "Civilians Weren't the Target, but . . . ," *Newsweek,* January 9, 1967, 18; *New York Times,* September 1, 1967; McGeorge Bundy, "The End of Either/Or," *Foreign Affairs,* January 1967, 195, 197.

403   **"We face more cost"** Mann, *Grand Delusion,* 521; Senate Committee on Foreign Relations, *The U.S. Government and the Vietnam War,* 555–56; Lunch and Sperlich, "American Public Opinion and the War in Vietnam," 25–26.

correspondents for network television Hammond, *Public Affairs,* 197–98; Small, *To Kill a Messenger,* 15–16, 94; Laurence, *The Cat from Hué,* 481; *Los Angeles Times,* January 7, 1967.

404   **"consensus medium"** David Halberstam, *The Powers That Be* (New York: Knopf, 1979), 507; Epstein, *News from Nowhere,* 206–7: Gans, *Deciding What's News,* 261.

"The main source for hard news" Daniel Hallin, "The Media, the War in Vietnam, and Political Support: A Critique of the Thesis of an Oppositional Media," *Journal of Politics* 46 (February 1984): 9–10; Hallin, *The "Uncensored War,"* 146, 161–62; Lawrence W. Lichty, "Comments on the Influence of Television on Public Opinion," *Vietnam as History: Ten Years after the Paris Peace Accords,* ed. Peter Braestrup (Washington, D.C.: University Press of America, 1984), 158–59.

"Vietnam Perspective" Hammond, *Reporting Vietnam,* 56; Barnouw, *Tube of Plenty,* 378–80, 393; Hallin, *The "Uncensored" War,* 139.

a separate table Fred W. Friendly, *Due to Circumstances beyond Our Control* (New York: Random House, 1967), 214–15; Halberstam, *The Powers That Be,* 438–39.

"Communist Broadcasting System" Safer: *Flashbacks,* chap. 12; Gary Paul Gates, *Air Time: The Inside Story of CBS News* (New York: Harper and Row, 1978), 122; Hallin, *The "Uncensored" War,* 132; Barnouw, *Tube of Plenty,* 383.

405   **"The Johnson administration"** Hallin, *The "Uncensored" War,* 157. For background on Cronkite's views and change of heart, see Don Oberdorfer, *Tet! The Turning Point in the Vietnam War,* rev. ed. (Baltimore: Johns Hopkins University Press, 2001), 248; Walter Cronkite, *A Reporter's Life* (New York: Ballantine Books, 1997), 242, 252; Hammond, *Public Affairs,* 277; Walter Cronkite to Pulitzer Prize Advisory Board, February 1, 1967, Salisbury Papers; Halberstam, *The Powers That Be,* 514. An example of the esteem in which Cronkite was held is in a cover story on him, "The Most Intimate Medium," *Time,* October 14, 1966, 56–64, which also mentions his hesitation on using the Safer footage.

406   **"What the hell is going on?"** Knightley, *The First Casualty,* 436; Oberdorfer, *Tet!* 250; Mark Kur-

lanshy, *1968: The Year That Rocked the World* (New York: Ballantine, 2004), 57–63; Gates, *Air Time*, 210; Cronkite, *A Reporter's Life*, 254–58. Cronkite also gave a personal history of his broadcast on *All Things Considered*, August 7, 2002.

"personal observations" Walter Cronkite, "Report from Vietnam," *CBS Evening News*, February 27, 1968.

407 **"If I've lost Cronkite"** There are several versions of this comment by LBJ: Kurlanshy, *1968*, 61; Cronkite, *A Reporter's Life*, 258; Halberstam, *The Powers That Be*, 514; Small, *To Kill a Messenger*, 123.

Only seven objected "Cronkite Takes a Stand," *Newsweek*, March 11, 1968, 108; Cronkite, *A Reporter's Life*, 258; Karnow, *Vietnam*, 548; Gates, *Air Time*, 211; Charles DeBenedetti, *An American Ordeal: The Antiwar Movement of the Vietnam Era* (Syracuse, N.Y.: Syracuse University Press, 1990), 210–11; Zaller and Chiu, "Government's Little Helper," 398. The argument that Cronkite and other critics might not have spoken out if the administration had had a clear policy line to present is in Hallin, *The"Uncensored" War*, 169.

408 **"Stalemate"** Oberdorfer, *Tet!* 86–92; James Landers, "Specter of Stalemate: Vietnam War Perspectives in *Newsweek, Time*, and *U.S. News & World Report*, 1965–1968," *American Journalism* 19 (Summer 2002): 13–38.

"that the enemy has not yet" Oberdorfer, *Tet!* 244–46; Peter Braestrup, *Big Story: How the American Press and Television Reported and Interpreted the Crisis of Tet 1968 in Vietnam and Washington*, abridged ed. (Novato, Calif.: Presidio, 1994), 133; Reston column, *New York Times*, February 7, 1968. For an example of matter-of-fact press reaction on Cronkite's broadcast, see the *Washington Post* radio and television reporter's comment: Lawrence Laurent, *Washington Post*, March 8, 1968. A good discussion on Vietnam reporting in general—and Tet in particular—is in Charles Mohr, "Once Again—Did the Press Lose Vietnam?" *Columbia Journalism Review*, November–December 1983, 51–56.

"In short" Oberdorfer, *Tet!* 272–74. The television critic's comment on McGee's program is by Jack Gould in *New York Times*, March 11, 1968.

two divisions Roberts, *In the Shadow of Power*, 374, 383–85, 393–95; David Wise, *The Politics of Lying: Government Deception, Secrecy, and Power* (New York: Random House, 1973), 283; Halberstam, *The Powers That Be*, 528–30, 534, 548; Katherine Graham, *Personal History* (New York: Knopf, 1997), 375–76; 397–402.

409 **"Everything's okay"** Herbert Block, *Herblock: A Cartoonist's Life*, updated and expanded (New York: Random House, 1998), 201. Block began his career as a cartoonist on the *Chicago Daily News* in the 1920s.

"into open political debate" DeBenedetti, *An American Ordeal*, 211–12. The meeting with LBJ is discussed in Walter Isaacson and Evan Thomas, *The Wise Men: Six Friends and the World They Made* (Boston: Faber and Faber, 1986), 698–706. James Reston, *The Artillery of the Press: Its Influence on American Foreign Policy* (New York: Harper and Row, 1967), 63.

"bound to be a revulsion against war" Small, *To Kill a Messenger*, 96, 129; Robert Elegant, "How to Lose a War: Reflections of a Foreign Correspondent," in *Vietnam Reconsidered: Lessons from a War*, ed. Harrison E. Salisbury (New York: Harper and Row, 1984), 145–50.

410 **"bang-bang"** Laurence, *The Cat from Hué*, 811; Hallin, *The "Uncensored" War*, 129–30; Lichty, "Comments on the Influence of Television on Public Opinion," 158; Epstein, *News from Nowhere*, 17–18; Judith Sylvester and Suzanne Huffman, *Reporting from the Front: The Media and the Military* (Lanham, Md.: Rowman and Littlefield, 2005), 17. Additional analysis can be found in Michael Mandelbaum, "Vietnam: The Television War," *Daedalus*, Fall 1982, 157–69; and George Donelson Moss, "News or Nemesis: Did Television Lose the Vietnam War?" in *A Vietnam Reader: Sources and Essays*, ed. George Donelson Moss (Englewood Cliffs, N.J.: Prentice Hall, 1991), 245–300.

draw their own conclusions George A. Bailey and Lawrence W. Lichty, "Rough Justice on a Saigon Street: A Gatekeeper Study of NBC's Tet Execution Film," *Journalism Quarterly* 49 (Summer 1972): 238; Knightley, *The First Casualty*, 434. Similarly, viewers tended to see their views reflected in the network anchor; 75 percent of hawks in a 1968 survey thought Cronkite a hawk; see, for instance, Hallin, *The "Uncensored" War,* 107.

"small appetite" Safer: *Flashbacks,* 107–8; Small, *To Kill a Messenger,* 96; Lichty, "Comments on the Influence of Television on Public Opinion," 158; James David Barber, *The Pulse of Politics: Electing Presidents in the Media Age* (New York: Norton, 1980), 289.

411 **"largely meaningless scraps"** Clarence R. Wyatt, "The Media and the Vietnam War," in *The War That Never Ends: New Perspectives on the Vietnam War,* ed. David L. Anderson and John Ernst (Lexington: University Press of Kentucky, 2007), 280–81; Knightley, *The First Casualty,* 422–23. Ward Just's comment is in his book *To What End: Report from Vietnam,* quoted in *Reporting Vietnam,* 1:360. The latter two-volume anthology usefully collects reporting on Vietnam.

I knew and admired Reed when I worked at the *Milwaukee Journal.* Lucas had been a marine lieutenant and a correspondent in World War II. He wrote a book during the war, *Combat Correspondent* (New York: Reynal and Hitchcock, 1944). Indicative of his feelings is this passage: "The Japanese were still resisting on Apamama, eighty-five miles to the south, and I was to go with a battalion from the Sixth Marines to wipe them out" (201).

"Goyaesque" Michael J. Arlen, "The Effect of the Vietnam War on Broadcast Journalism," in Salisbury, *Vietnam Reconsidered,* 101–2; Michael J. Arlen, *Living-Room War* (New York: Viking, 1969), 7–8. Arlen's view is affirmed by a study that examined anchor reporting from mid-1965 to mid-1970, George Bailey, "Interpretive Reporting of the Vietnam War by Anchormen," *Journalism Quarterly* 53 (Summer 1976): 323: "The network anchormen, in their daily summaries of the war, read short stories of events without much interpretation, certainly without challenging, adversary interpretation. The combat news—except when a network crew shot film—generally came from the wires which covered the daily military press briefings. Although many criticized the statistics as a measure of progress of the war, the anchormen, when they read off the body counts, did not call them estimates, which they were at best."

"Hey, hey, LBJ" Barnouw, *Tube of Plenty,* 385–87; Schroth, *The American Journey of Eric Sevareid,* 373; Hammond, *Reporting Vietnam,* 173–75, 211–12; Gans, *Deciding What's News,* 121, 135–36, 187; DeBenedetti, *An American Ordeal,* 264; Stacks, *Scotty,* 249.

"As protest moved" Todd Gitlin, *The Whole World Is Watching: Mass Media in the Making and Unmaking of the New Left* (Berkeley: University of California Press, 1980), 205. This volume contains thorough analysis of media attitudes toward protestors.

412 **"seemed more in agreement"** Epstein, *News from Nowhere,* 210–11; Halberstam, *The Powers That Be,* 514; Hallin, "The Media, the War in Vietnam, and Political Support," 9; Hammond, *Reporting Vietnam,* 126.

"Westmoreland Requests" Wise, *The Politics of Lying,* 283; Oberdorfer, *Tet!* 266–71.

"reputation was on the line" Diamond, *Behind the Times,* 118; Shepard, *The Paper's Papers,* 189; Tifft and Jones, *The Trust,* 481; David Rudenstine, *The Day the Presses Stopped: A History of the Pentagon Papers* (Berkeley: University of California Press, 1996), 100, and, on the *Washington Post* decision, 129–32. The *Times* series was published later in book form, *The Pentagon Papers: As Published by the New York Times* (New York: Bantam Books, 1971). On the Pulitzer Prize, see Hohenberg, *The Pulitzer Diaries,* chap. 31. The trustees also were unhappy about an award to muckraking columnist Jack Anderson, who exposed faulty policymaking with regard to the Indo-Pakistan War. The trustees no longer have authority to approve or disapprove the votes of the Pulitzer board.

The *Washington Post* viewed its publication of the Pentagon Papers as a sign that it had become a force in American journalism. The risk factors for the *Post* included pending applications for renewed licenses for radio and television properties. It also had just "gone public" with an offering of its shares; management was not sure whether an injunction would force cancellation. Among the journalists on the staff who tipped the balance was Chalmers Roberts, who threatened to retire early if the papers were not published.

"plausibly deniable covert" Hammond, *Reporting Vietnam*, 202, 204–5; Wise, *The Politics of Lying*, 342.

413 **"nattering nabobs of negativism"** Hammond, *Reporting Vietnam*, 192, 215–18; Gelb, *City Room*, 567; Gitlin, *The Whole World Is Watching*, 228–29; Corydon B. Dunham, *Fighting for the First Amendment: Stanton of CBS vs. Congress and the Nixon White House* (Westport, Conn.: Praeger, 1997), 92, 101. A discussion of the "nattering nabobs" comments, as they relate to the Bush administration's efforts to curb the press after U.S. military intervention in Iraq, is in David Remnick, "Nattering Nabobs," *New Yorker*, July 10, 2006, www.newyorker.com/archives/2006/07/10/060710ta _talk_remnick.

"as good as if we had done it ourselves" Paley, *As It Happened*, 305–7; Salant, *Salant, CBS*, chap. 10; Rudenstine, *The Day the Presses Stopped*, 127. In recounting the episode in his memoir, William Paley noted one weakness in the documentary. The editing made it look as though several comments were made in response to a single question, which they were not. Although this did not change the meaning of the interview, it led Paley to strengthen network editing policies. The step was taken to become more responsible, not to knuckle under to the government, but it reflected the intense self-reflection that goes on when a network is at odds with officials. A similar point can be derived from the comment of a CBS executive who said Agnew's crusades "made us more cautious," adding that that "might not have been a bad thing: where we would have double-checked a fact before, we would triple-check it now." Gitlin, *The Whole World Is Watching*, 278. Triple-checking is always good, but it should apply to officials as well as those who have a different point view. In an affidavit tied to the contempt citation, CBS Washington bureau chief William Small pointed to the chilling effect of congressional investigations. "Courage," he said, "is an essential ingredient of my craft. It will be replaced with caution."

"peace with honor" Karnow, *Vietnam*, 654, 668; Langguth, *Our Vietnam*, 661, 664; Salisbury, foreword to Bigart, *Forward Positions*, xii.

414 **Ochs's first attempt overseas** Shepard, *The Paper's Papers*, 343–44; Tifft and Jones, *The Trust*, 66–68; Berger, *Story of the New York Times*, 132–34; Adolph Ochs to James W. Alexander, April 22, 1899, NYT Archives.

idea flickered again Details on efforts in the 1920s to create a foreign edition come from the NYT Archives, specifically, Robert R. McCormick to Charles H. Grasty, April 15, 1922; Grasty to Adolph Ochs, May 3, 1922; Ochs to Grasty, May 6, 1922; Edwin L. James to Ochs, May 23, June 22, 1923; March 20, May 5, 1924; August 1925; May 28, July 6, August 10, 1926; Ochs to James, June 4, July 28, 1926; Ochs to family members ("Dear Ones All"), May 21, 1926.

The details of the planned weekly are outlined in various memoranda, including one probably written by James in 1923, "THE NEW YORK TIMES EUROPEAN EDITION"; another called "CONCERNING THE EUROPEAN EDITION" is unsigned, and dated July 13, 1926. In 1940, when Ochs's heirs sought once again to create a European edition, James was asked for his recollections, which he provided in James to Lang, October 10, 1940—this also is found in a NYT Archives file, "European Edition, 1940." James believed that Carl Van Anda, the managing editor, made the case for abandoning the European weekly. Criticism for being unpatriotic was not a theoretical issue to Ochs. He had had a chastening experience toward the end of World War I. When Austria held out the possibility of peace, a *Times* editorial advocated "non-binding" discussions, a suggestion that was widely criticized for "running up the white flag." A furious President Wilson worried about the reaction to the editorial in Europe. Ochs's unpleasant experience is recounted in Berger, *Story of the New York Times*, 221–25.

"THE NEW YORK TIMES" The quote is found in an untitled, unsigned memorandum, probably written by James in 1925, in the NYT Archives.

"indefinitely postponed" Ochs to James, July 28, 1926, NYT Archives.

"The Publisher" Turner Catledge to A. H. Sulzberger, September 7, 1965, NYT Archives; Shepard, *The Paper's Papers*, 347–48; *New York Times*, June 12, 1967.

415 **with the Paris *Herald Tribune*** Wade Green, "C'est la Guerre!" *Madison Avenue,* November 1960, 29–30+; Walter B. Kerr, "The War of the Paris Editions," *Saturday Review,* November 12, 1966, 104–5; *New York Times,* May 12, 1967; Susan Paterno, "International Intrigue," *American Journalism Review,* February–March 2006, 50–55. See also Robertson, *The International Herald Tribune.*

"European paper for Europeans" Anthony Bianco, "The Future of the New York Times," *Business Week,* January 17, 2005, 68.

"handmaiden" Salisbury, *Without Fear or Favor,* 14; William Rivers, *The Other Government: Power and the Washington Media* (New York: Universe Books, 1982), 229, 231; Wise, *The Politics of Lying,* 342.

run-up to the Iraq invasion Brent Cunningham, *Columbia Journalism Review,* July–August 2003, 26; Michael Getler address, "Lesson from Iraq: The News Media and the Next War," Lucius W. Nieman Symposium, Marquette University, Milwaukee, October 29, 2003, 78; Michael Massing, "Now They Tell Us," *New York Review of Books,* February 26, 2004, 43–49; *New York Times,* May 26, May 30, August 13, 2004. The *Washington Post*'s acknowledgement of mistakes came in an article on coverage by its reporter Howard Kurtz, August 12, 2004. The article is instructive in its list of problems in coverage that are similar to those in the Vietnam era, such as concern with being seen as a crusader, deference to officials, and editorial support for the administration, to wit, "It is hard to imagine how anyone could doubt that Iraq possesses weapons of mass destruction." The *New Republic* also apologized: "Were We Wrong?" June 28, 2004, 8.

Considerable research, exemplified by the Bennett, Lawrence, Livingston volume, *When the Press Fails,* supports the contention that the media covered the Iraq War from the point of view of the administration. For another example, see Susan D. Moeller, *Media Coverage of Weapons of Mass Destruction* (College Park, Md.: Center for International and Security Studies at Maryland, March 9, 2004). The use of former military officers with ongoing Pentagon ties for network analysis was revealed in *New York Times,* April 20, 2008.

416 **"During the four years"** *New York Times,* April 25, 2007.

paradoxically, are rare A discussion of the need to crusade on issues of war and peace is found in a volume that critiques the "fifty-year habit at the *Times* of undermining or ignoring international law in its coverage of US foreign policy." Howard Friel and Richard Falk, *The Record of the Paper: How the New York Times Misreports US Foreign Policy* (New York: Verso, 2004), 250, 256.

Seymour Hersh Hersh and My Lai are discussed in Hammond, *Reporting Vietnam,* 188–89. CBS broke the Abu Ghraib scandal, but Hersh gets credit. At the request of the government, the network held back for two weeks. It changed course when it learned that Hersh's investigative pieces were on the way. The issue of coverage of Abu Ghraib is discussed at length in Bennett, Lawrence, and Livingston, *When the Press Fails.* The administration, they argue, managed to shape the story as one of abuse, not torture, which was a plausible alternative that received little attention at the time: "The photos may have driven the story, but the White House communication staff ultimately wrote the captions" (107).

"seemed to make more sense" Ellsberg, *Secrets,* 140; Richard Moose, interview by author, January 28, 2008; Seib, *Headline Diplomacy,* 22; Langguth, *Our Vietnam,* 438. Langguth's book does not give a source for his statement that Salisbury's reports from Hanoi distressed McNamara, but in e-mail to Raluca Cozma (February 5, 2008), he says the information came from his talks with McNamara. Paul Warnke, who worked with McNamara, remembered that Salisbury's trip had an impact on McNamara. Melvin Small, *Johnson, Nixon, and the Doves* (New Brunswick, N.J.: Rutgers University Press, 1988), 96. Hersh and My Lai are discussed in Hammond, *Reporting Vietnam,* 188–89.

417 **"seems to be growing"** Harrison Salisbury to Herb Klein, February 9, 1967, Salisbury Papers. Talese, "The Public and Private Wars of Harrison E. Salisbury," 89; Diamond, *Behind the Times,* 184. The press critic comment about the op-ed page is from Edwin Diamond, "Who Is the 'Enemy'?"

Columbia Journalism Review, Winter 1970–71, 39. Copies of many of the cartoons on Salisbury can be found in his papers at Columbia University.

Salisbury remained interested in North Vietnam after his retirement. In early 1975, when the North Vietnamese were about to take over the south, Salisbury—working as a Sunday special correspondent for the *Times*—tried to engineer a visit to Hanoi. Rosenthal squelched the attempt. Salisbury also proposed a trip to North Vietnam in 1970, which Rosenthal also scotched. He wanted "to give another person a crack at North Vietnam, to apply the expertise that comes with experience in South Vietnam and to have different eyes looking at the same subject." A. M. Rosenthal to Harrison Salisbury, memorandum, February 1970, NYT Archives. Salisbury describes his sometimes-tense relationship with Rosenthal in *A Time of Change,* chap. 28.

Salisbury continued to have his critics; see, for instance, Norman Podhoretz, *Why We Were in Vietnam* (New York: Simon and Schuster, 1982), 117–20. Another critique may be found in Guenter Lewy, *America in Vietnam* (New York: Oxford University Press, 1978), 398–404. Although most New Journalism was antiwar, Tom Wolfe projected a different point of view when writing on the inner workings of pilots who flew bombing missions over North Vietnam. The pilots, wrote Wolfe, in an admiring account of their bravado, considered Salisbury a "blessing" for Hanoi, "a weapon that no military device known to America could ever get a lock on"; see Tom Wolfe, "The Truest Sport: Jousting with Sam and Charlie," in *Mauve Gloves and Madmen, Clutter and Vine,* by Tom Wolfe (New York: Farrar, Straus and Giroux, 1988), 43.

"The true and the crusty ingredients" Salisbury, *A Time of Change,* 168; Harrison Salisbury, typewritten, undated speech, Salisbury Papers.

CHAPTER 22

418 **"doss down"** Evelyn Waugh, *Scoop* (Boston: Little, Brown, 1999), 153–54.

"patron saint" Behr, *"Anyone Here Been Raped and Speaks English,"* vi. Others have tried to show the zany side of foreign reporting and in doing so harked back to Waugh. For another example, there is Rosenblum's glib *Coups and Earthquakes,* 19: "Inspiration for this [chapter] is from Evelyn Waugh's *Scoop,* a preposterous but real novel published in 1938 based on Waugh's experiences in Ethiopia. Some correspondents still study *Scoop* regularly as a handbook for such skills as wastebasket rifling, expense account padding and myth weaving." The best effort at finding *Scoop* in real life, however, is also Waugh's—in his first-person account of his time in Ethiopia as a correspondent for the *London Daily Mail.* That book—highly amusing field notes for *Scoop*— is virtually unknown among correspondents. For a discussion of the book, see John Maxwell Hamilton, introduction to Waugh's *Waugh in Abyssinia* (Baton Rouge: Louisiana State University Press, 2007). Also for background, see Deedes, *At War with Waugh.* Novels along the lines of *Scoop* are Christopher Wren, *Hacks* (New York: Simon and Schuster, 1969); and Neil MacFarquhar, *Sand Café* (New York: Public Affairs, 2006). For a discussion of such novels, see Christopher Dickey's review of *Sand Café* in *New York Times,* May 7, 2006. One correspondent, Christopher Hanson, took as his pen name the name of the hero in *Scoop,* William Boot. Boot-Hanson's article on Scoop's popularity with the correspondent crowd is "Scoop Redux: The Press Goes to Boot Camp," *Columbia Journalism Review,* January–February 1991, 19–22.

"In all that miserable city" Catling, *Better Than Working,* 79.

"the New and Honorable Fraternity" Rudyard Kipling, *The Light That Failed* (New York: Airmont, 1969), 23; Webb Miller, "Webb Miller Tells of Hardships of News Men in Ethiopia," *Editor and Publisher,* November 9, 1935, 11; Forrest, *Behind the Front Page,* 190–91; Behr, *"Anyone Here Been Raped and Speaks English?"* 158; Arnett, *Live from the Battlefield,* 225. The comments about press conditions in El Salvador draw from an article by correspondent Joanne Omang in *Washington Post,* February 28, 1982.

419 **"The Lost Legion"** Irwin, *Making of a Reporter,* 124–26.

"We had no place to go" Farson, *A Mirror for Narcissus,* 266; Walker, *Januarius MacGahan,* 191–

92; Cuthbertson, *Inside,* 104; Haverstock, *Fifty Years at the Front,* 121; Rand, *China Hands,* 207–10; Salisbury, *A Journey for Our Times,* 255. Carleton Beals devotes an entire chapter, "Newspaper Men," to journalists and the Hotel Regis in his unpublished autobiography, "Life at the Full," 194–211, Beals Papers.

420 **"never to take this stuff too seriously"** G. Jefferson Price, interviews by author, February 11, 2004; May 12, 2006.

"venerable Maryland institution" Villard, *Some Newspapers and Newspapermen,* 134. For background on the *Sun,* I made particular use of Williams, *The Baltimore Sun.*

421 **"it speedily appeared"** Villard, *Some Newspapers and Newspapermen,* 135. For a description of the *Sun*'s nascent interest in foreign news at this time, see Johnson, Kent, Mencken, and Owens, *The Sunpapers of Baltimore,* 407–13. Also for background from this period I appreciate the observations of *Sun* alumnus James H. Bready in his letter to me, November 5, 2006.

"absolutely core" Tony Barbieri, interview by author, February 17, 2005. This idea of using the foreign service to lure good reporters arose in interview after interview with *Baltimore Sun* veterans, including Ernest B. Furgurson, March 15, 2005. Another example of foreign services helping with recruitment is that of the *Boston Globe.* John Yemma to author, e-mail, November 10, 2002.

422 **"are chosen with care"** Johnson, Kent, Mencken, and Owens, *The Sunpapers,* 415; Williams, *The Baltimore Sun,* 341.

"All was fair" Kipling, *The Light That Failed,* 23; Weightman, *Signor Marconi's Magic Box,* 166; G. Jefferson Price, interview by author, May 12, 2006.

"The two met" Beech, *Tokyo and Points East,* 167–83; Kluger, *The Paper,* 448. Higgins discusses her rivalry with Bigart in a memoir but never mentions "My colleague" by name; see Marguerite Higgins, *War in Korea: The Report of a Woman Combat Correspondent* (Garden City, N.Y.: Doubleday, 1951), 56–58, 99, 116.

423 **"the stories"** Richard Severo, in his *New York Times* obit for Bigart, reprinted in Bigart, *Forward Positions,* 224; Higgins, *War in Korea,* 97.

"Radical" Waugh, *Waugh in Abyssinia,* 52. Waugh's attendance at a banquet for Phillips is recounted in Noel Monks, *Eyewitness* (London: Frederick Muller, 1955), 44.

424 **"I was bowled over"** Bradley Martin to author, e-mail, February 23, 2005; Michael T. Kaufman, interview by author, September 30, 2008.

expression of the Golden Rule Casey, *More Interesting People,* 256; Seldes, *Lords of the Press,* 286. Ryszard Kapuscinski's comment is from a radio interview by *Fresh Air* on WHYY, aired January 26, 2007. Kaufman interview by author, September 30, 2008.

efficient Catling, *Better Than Working,* 194; Gilbert Lewthwaite, interview by author, April 12, 2004; G. Jefferson Price, interviews by author, February 11, 2004; May 12, 2006. A laudatory obituary of Wise was written by Edith Lederer of the Associated Press, May 22, 1998. Wise was a World War II military hero before going abroad for the *Mirror;* he later reported for the *Far Eastern Economic Review.* Lederer quoted a colleague of Wise who said, "He was the David Niven of journalism. He had a similar wit, was similarly successful with women, and bore an uncanny resemblance to the actor." On Wise's willingness to work with others, see Jon Swain, *London Observer,* March 16, 2003.

425 ***adds value*** Waugh, *Scoop,* 127; Whitaker, *And Fear Came,* 90–91. Ulf Hannerz provides an anthropologists'-eye-view of the way correspondents cooperate in *Foreign News: Exploring the World of Foreign Correspondents* (Chicago: University of Chicago Press, 2004), chap. 5. A similar examination of correspondents' collective enterprise is in Mark Pedelty, *War Stories: The Culture of Foreign Correspondents* (New York: Routledge, 1995), especially chap. 1.

"I worked regularly" Whitaker, *And Fear Came,* 91. Such collaboration is particularly useful in wartime, as Sir Harry P. Robinson observed during World War I. "For the public good," he noted, "we have stifled that primitive instinct of the journalists to 'beat' the other man. . . . It has taken us some time to organize this system. . . . I do not believe that ever before has the public come so near to getting the full truth from the battlefield." Robinson is quoted in Salmon, *The Newspaper and the Historian*, 215–16.

Arthur Krock Krock, *Memoirs*, 56–57.

"In an environment" John Schidlovsky to author, e-mail, May 11, 2005.

added power against authority Eugene Lyons, "Foreign Correspondent," in Benjamin, *Eye Witness*, 304.

426 **Foreign Correspondents Club of Japan** Steven Hunziker and Ikuro Kamimura, *Kakuei Tanaka: A Political Biography of Modern Japan* (Singapore: Time Books International, 1996), 121–22.

"I guessed" Murray Fromson, *New York Times*, December 11, 2006.

a measure of physical safety Williams, *The Baltimore Sun*, 229.

maintains sanity Prochnau, *Once upon a Distant War*, 177; Richburg, *Out of America*, 70; G. Jefferson Price to author, e-mail, June 26, 2006.

427 **joined forces with Neil Sheehan** Prochnau, *Once upon a Distant War*, 152–53, 272–75.

428 **"We were all outsiders"** Interviews by author of Marvin Kalb, January 8, 2004; Ernest B. Furgurson, March 15, 2005; and Stuart Loory, March 16, 2005; June 8, 2006.

"You're all in it together" Interviews by author of G. Jefferson Price, February 11, 2004; Curtis Wilkie, May 1, 2006; and Vaughn Smith, November 17, 2004. Knightley, *The First Casualty*, 333.

"fraternity or the club system" Sheean, *Not Peace but a Sword*, 241–42; Sheean, *Between the Thunder and the Sun*, 216; Reynolds, *By Quentin Reynolds*, 297.

"tripe" *Variety Film Reviews*, September 5, 1942.

"me by sending cables in my name" Huddleston, *In My Time*, 222, 259; Linda H. Davis, *Badge of Courage: The Life of Stephen Crane* (Boston: Houghton Mifflin, 1998); Irwin, *Making of a Reporter*, 428. Marshall became a model for correspondent Rufus Coleman in Crane's *Active Service*; see J. C. Levenson, introduction to *The Third Violet and Active Service*, by Stephen Crane, ed. Fredson Bowers (Charlottesville: University Press of Virginia, 1976), xlvii. Crane's lack of urgency in writing his own dispatches may have contributed to his estrangement from the *World*; he subsequently went to work as a correspondent for Marshall's newspaper, the *Journal*. The estimate of four reporters who helped their colleague on the Hoover trip is from a letter written by *Chicago Daily News* editor Charles Dennis, who noted disapprovingly to a newspaper friend that the correspondent "spent nearly the entire two days in bed" and that "at least four other fellows fil[ed] stories to his paper and sign[ed] his name to them." Charles Dennis to Samuel Harrison, January 18, 1928, Daily News Records.

429 **"to go to xxxx"** William Schmick to author, e-mail, November 17, 2002.

"I'm feeling like a million dollars" Duff Hart-Davis, *The House the Berrys Built* (London: Hodder and Stoughton, 1990), 9; Stanley Morison, *The History of the Times*, vol. 2, *The Tradition Established* (New York: Macmillan, 1939), 295.

430 **"always being astonishingly well informed"** Hart-Davis, *House the Berrys Built*, 124–25, 172. The quote on Bennet Burleigh is from Burnham, *Peterborough Court*, 65–66.

"Bill, we are going to have a good story" William F. Schmick III, interviews by author, 2003–6. Also see his story on the demolition of the Arab dwellings in the *Baltimore Sun*, June 16, 1969; and a Reuters story on his treatment by Israeli officials the same day. In reprinting Wallis's story, I inserted a couple of commas that the editors did not put in as they should have.

432 **"WHERE WERE YOU YESTERDAY?"** Reyonlds, *By Quentin Reynolds*, 85.

"One of the rules" Milt Freudenheim, interview by author, August 23, 2004. Correspondents, especially bureau chiefs, have other jobs besides reporting. AP correspondents, for instance, try to sell their service to foreign newspapers, and there is office work—and dossing with the bosses. According to one old study, 38 percent of full-time correspondents spent at least one-quarter of their time on nonjournalistic activities. Leo Bogart, "The Overseas Newsman: A 1967 Profile Study," *Journalism Quarterly* 45 (Summer 1968): 300.

"friends, political counselors, and interpreters" Mowrer, *Triumph and Turmoil*, 274–75; Swanberg, *Luce and His Empire,* 279. The comment on how much more fun it is not to have the boss around is from Gordon Mott to author, e-mail, September 14, 2007.

"nervous dread" Dennis, *Lawson,* 345–46; Startt, *Unofficial Ambassador,* 37–38, 125, 213.

433 **"Never fire that man"** Root, *The Paris Edition,* 65.

"assigned to rent a special Pullman" Shirer, *Twentieth Century Journey: The Start,* 351; Hart-Davis, *House the Berrys Built,* 173.

Katherine Graham Keith Richburg, interview by author, April 12, 2005; Elizabeth Hylton, interview by author, February 1, 2005; Graham, *Personal History,* 372–77, 605–9.

434 **"Our futures"** Baker, *The Good Times,* 187. Schmick and Black are described in Williams, *The Baltimore Sun,* 319–28, 343; and in two articles by G. Jefferson Price, *Baltimore Sun,* April 28, 2002; April 25, 2004. The anecdotes also draw on aforementioned interviews of Schmick, Martin, Lewthwaite, and Price as well as e-mail correspondence from Hideko Takayama, who was the news assistant in the *Sun* Tokyo bureau.

435 **Trips by the boss** Brad Martin interview by author, February 20, 2005.

"peaceful coexistence" Hohenberg, *The Pulitzer Diaries,* 39–41.

"The workings of the great newspaper" Waugh, *Scoop,* 14.

"I don't want our correspondents helping" David Shaw article in *Los Angeles Times,* July 8, 1986.

"It is almost impossible to miss" Catling, *Better Than Working,* 182; Peter Copeland, interview by author, November 5, 2003.

436 **"The *Sun* has died"** Todd Richissin, interview by author, October 10, 2006.

"The Chicago *Tribune* wants synergy" G. Jefferson Price, *Baltimore Sun,* April 28, 2002.

CHAPTER 23

437 **"the principal 'post office'"** London as the *Times*' "post office" is in *Around the World . . . with the New York Times,* a booklet published by the Times in 1950, NYT Archives. Ochs's rationale for London, also in those archives, is in Adolph Ochs to Edwin James, June 30, 1925. General background on the processes during Anthony Beard's career is from Beard, interview by author, November 18, 2004.

438 **"The French telegraph system"** "Your Mirrors of Europe," *Saturday Evening Post,* December 9, 1922, 146. The author—"By a Foreign Correspondent"—was anonymous. Thomas Stevens, "Telegraph Operators in Persia," *Electrical Review,* August 18, 1888, 6.

"end up with the wrong bits and bobs" Beard interview.

439 **"Dear Mr. Bell"** Charles H. Dennis to Edward Price Bell, August 24, 1904, Bell Papers. The problems with cablese are discussed in Knightley, *The First Casualty,* 188.

Because the subject is so important, this book gives considerable attention to the concerns of editors and owners about the cost of transmitting news from afar. The *Times* was not immune to this. After a visit to the *Times* London bureau in 1925, Edwin James estimated that 10 percent of the words could be eliminated from its cables, saving $750 a month. A quarter of a century later, a *Times* foreign editor argued that cable costs could be "cut down, by the way, if 'the's,' 'a's' and 'an's' were omitted in places where their omission is obvious. . . . This does *not* mean a return to complicated cablese. It does mean that we ought to try to avoid expenditures adding up to thousands of dollars a year on unnecessary words." These communications are found in the NYT Archives: Edwin James to Adolph Ochs, March 8, 1925; and Henry Lieberman to Emanuel Freedman, "about 1951" (memo is not signed or dated, but a note on top suggests this is the author and date).

440 **"Speed in transmission"** Williams, *Dusk of Empire,* xii.

"Every age" Robert Darnton, "Paris: The Early Internet," *New York Review of Books,* June 29, 2000, 42. Darnton, it so happens, is the son of *New York Times* war correspondent Byron Darnton, who died in the conflict, and brother of a John Darnton, who became a *Times* correspondent. For a brief time, Robert Darnton worked at the paper.

Venice from London Fernand Braudel, *The Structures of Everyday Life: The Limits of the Possible* (New York: Harper, 1981), 424–27; Pred, *Urban Growth and the Circulation of Information*, 38; Schwarzlose, *The Nation's Newsbrokers*, 1:37.

"200 or 300 pigeons" The late-in-life interview is with Moses Beach, *New York World*, Sunday Supplement, January 20, 1884. For a discussion of steamships, railroads, and pigeons, see Hudson, *Journalism in the United States*, 432, 596–97.

441   **"What hath God wrought?"** Tom Standage, *The Victorian Internet* (New York: Berkley, 1999), 46–47; Hudson, *Journalism in the United States*, 596; Blondheim, *News over the Wires*, 31–33. Before a bill funding Morse's experiments narrowly passed in 1842, senators joked that it made as much sense to appropriate money for the study of mesmerism, which was actually proposed (and failed). Seventy congressmen abstained from the Morse vote on the grounds they could not spend "public money for a machine they could not understand."

"The railroad, the telegraph" Edward W. Byrn, "A Century of Progress in the United States," *Scientific American*, December 29, 1900, 402–3.

"At present" W. J. McCambridge, "A.P. Transmits News by Eleven Methods, *"Service Bulletin of the Associated Press*, May 1, 1920, 27–28.

"Despatches" Joseph E. Sharkey, "Gathering News in the Far East," *Service Bulletin of the Associated Press*, June 14, 1919, 9. On the amount of time for *Times'* stories to reach New York from Europe, see "Wireless as a New Carrier," *Electrical Review and Western Electrician*, April 6, 1912, 668.

442   **"listless"** J. B. Powell, "The American Correspondent in China," *Asia*, May 1927, 380–82; "Work of the Foreign Newspaper Correspondent in China," *China Weekly Review*, September 15, 1928, 50–54; Stanley Washburn, *The Cable Game* (Boston: Sherman, French, 1912), 51. The *China Weekly Review* article was signed "By One of Them," who is most probably Powell.

"virtually impossible" Henry Bradsher to author, e-mail, October 27, 2006.

443   **"Rarely"** Mickelson, *The Decade That Shaped Television News*, 28; Gans, *Deciding What's News*, 128.

444   **cost of a telephone call** "Going Cheap," *Economist*, July 20, 1991, 117.

"Once we landed" Fred Francis to author, e-mail, March 16, 2005; Jim Rosenberg, "Tech from Gulf War to Gulf War," *Editor and Publisher*, March 31, 2003, 23–24; Susan E. Reed, *New York Times*, January 31, 2002. Sites's work is described in *New York Times*, September 12, 2005. A good description of the equipment available to correspondents during Operation Desert Storm is found in Molly Moore, *A Woman at War: Storming Kuwait with the U.S. Marines* (New York: Scribner's, 1993). Moore, a *Washington Post* correspondent, found that the equipment worked well and helped her file when the switchboards were jammed. The problem was that she did not have the equipment with her in the field when she needed it.

"were ready to present a story" Michael Murrie, "Communication Technology and the Correspondent," in Foote, *Live from the Trenches*, 97; for background on these changes, see Murrie's entire essay.

"A man's outfit" Richard Harding Davis, "A War Correspondent's Kit," in his *Notes of a War Correspondent* (New York: Scribner's, 1914), 239.

445   **"A WAR CORRESPONDENT'S KIT"** Richard Harding Davis, "A War Correspondent's Kit," 253–61.

446   **"The flags are to warn bullets"** Stallings is quoted in "Correspondents Trek to Africa," *Literary Digest*, August 24, 1935, 24.

"an enormous cart" Davis, "A War Correspondent's Kit," in his *Notes of a War Correspondent*, 243.

"enough writing materials" Miller, *I Found No Peace*, 243; Wells, *Blood on the Moon*, 371. For an example of a story on packing, see "REPORTERS: Why Auditors Grow Gray Checking 'Swindle-Sheets,'" *Newsweek*, December 7, 1935, 22.

"When foreign correspondents gather" Eugene Robinson's article is in *Washington Post*, April

14, 1990; James P. Sterba's article is "Vested Interest: The Snugli for Gear Nuts," *Wall Street Journal,* January 2, 1990; Nicholas D. Kristof's is in *New York Times,* September 24, 1998.

447 **"What to pack"** Juan Tamayo, *Miami Herald,* November 29, 1987.

450 **"will be—as perhaps he is now"** Smith, *"It's the Way It's Written" and "Writing Versus—Everything Else,"* 50.

"We now live in a nanosecond news cycle" David Hoffman, interview by author, April 14, 2005. Governale is quoted in *New York Times,* March 24, 2003.

John Hughes coped with John Hughes, interview by author, February 27, 2007.

451 **day-to-day travel plans** Drew Middleton to Harrison Salisbury, February 11, 1971, Salisbury Papers; Williams, *The Baltimore Sun,* 333–32; 341. On Francis and editing, see *New York Times,* March 24, 2003. An enthusiastic discussion of the benefits of this kind of editorial supervision is in John Yemma, "Instant Connection: Foreign News Comes in from the Cold," in *From Pigeons to News Portals: Foreign Reporting and the Challenge of New Technology,* ed. David Perlmutter and John Maxwell Hamilton (Baton Rouge: Louisiana State University Press, 2007), 110–29.

452 **"I try to be in voice contact"** Elisa Tinsley, interview by author, February 2, 2005; David Shaw, *Los Angeles Times,* July 6, 1986.

"the newspaper reader" Hudson, *Journalism in the United States,* 601.

"time is everything in journalism" George Smalley to Whitelaw Reid, March 3, 1870, Reid Papers, LOC. The Russell quotes are in W. H. Russell, *The Atlantic Telegraph* (1866; reprint, Brimscombe Port, UK:, Nonsuch, 2005), 105; Walker, *Januarius MacGahan,* 20; and William Howard Russell to John Delane, March 24, 1876, Delane Papers.

"The very improvement" Huddleston, *In My Time,* 211; John Hohenberg, "The New Foreign Correspondence," *Saturday Review,* January 11, 1969, 115. Descriptions of Huddleston are found in George Slocombe, *The Tumult and the Shouting* (New York: Macmillan, 1936), 63–64; Canham, *Commitment to Freedom,* 212–14.

"I think" Marvin Kalb, interview by author, January 8, 2004.

453 **"Like executions"** Bernard Kalb, "In the Days of Carrier-Pigeon Journalism," *Media Studies Journal* 7 (Fall 1993): 75–78; Garrick Utley, *You Should Have Been Here Yesterday: A Life Story in Television News* (New York: Public Affairs Press, 2000), 242–43; Fred Francis, interview by author, March 11, 2005.

"Going live" Tom Rosenstiel, *Washington Post,* September 12, 2004; Michael Schudson and Tony Dokoupil, "The Limits of Live," *Columbia Journalism Review,* January–February 2007, 63. See also "Cable TV," in *The State of the News Media 2004* (Washington, D.C.: Project for Excellence in Journalism, 2004), 19.

"stories they would expect" These quotes came in Byron Calame's *Public Editor* column, *New York Times,* November 19, 2006.

454 **"Almost every American correspondent"** Hess, *International News and Foreign Correspondents,* 65; Roger Cohen, interview by author, September 3, 2003; Foote, *Live from the Trenches,* 111.

"Any appraisal" The report on Kelley's fraudulent reporting is Bill Hilliard, Bill Kovach, and John Seigenthaler to Craig Moon, memorandum, "Re: The Problems of Jack Kelley and USA Today," April 12, 2004, author's files.

"Rarely does the telegraph editor" John L. Given, *Making a Newspaper* (New York: Henry Holt, 1907), 224–25. On Dorsey, see Williams, *The Baltimore Sun,* 341; on *Collier's,* Reynolds, *By Quentin Reynolds,* 246. In the early 1970s *Chicago Tribune* Moscow correspondent James Yuenger received a phone call from the home office once a year; see Alicia C. Shepard, "An American in Paris (and Moscow and Berlin and Tokyo...)," *American Journalism Review,* April 1994, 23.

"Some people work better" Talese, *The Kingdom and the Power,* 274–75; Tifft and Jones, *The Trust,* 255. Turner Catledge's letter is from November 7, 1957; Craig Whitney to Arthur Gelb, April 4, 1983, both in NYT Archives. Tony Beard described the process in London for keeping track of correspondents in Beard to author, e-mail, September 3, 2006.

Not all *Times* editors were so gentle in communicating with correspondents about their freedom. While Warren Hoge was the *Times* foreign editor in 1983, he sent "a letter of holiday good wishes" in which he said, "Don't call to complain about conditions, unkept hotel reservations, flights that don't exist, etc. I know from personal experience what it's like, and I sympathize with you. But I also know that with energy, resourcefulness and an occasional deft application of maliciousness they can be overcome." Warren Hoge, "Memorandum to ALL FOREIGN CORRESPONDENTS," December 19, 1983, NYT Archives.

455 **"much more subject"** Leon V. Sigal, *Disarming Strangers: Nuclear Diplomacy with North Korea* (Princeton, N.J.: Princeton University Press, 1998), 227.

"International journalism" Sheean, *This House against This House,* 94.

"top brass" Jonathan Randal, "The Decline, but Not Yet Total Fall, of Foreign News in the U.S. Media," Working Paper 2000-2, fall 1998, Shorenstein Center, Cambridge, Mass., 17, 19. For a survey of correspondents' attitudes toward technology, for good and ill, see H. Denis Wu and John Maxwell Hamilton, "US Foreign Correspondents: Changes and Continuity at the Turn of the Century," *Gazette* 66 (December 2004): 517–32.

"the one predictable component" Steven Livingston and W. Lance Bennett, "Gatekeeping, Indexing, and Live-Event News: Is Technology Altering the Construction of News?" *Political Communication* 20 (October–December, 2003): 363–80; George F. Kennan, *American Diplomacy: 1900–1950* (Chicago: University of Chicago Press, 1951), 19. For a good discussion of the acceleration of decision making as a result of improved communications, as well as of the telegraph's erosion of diplomats' autonomy, see Nickles, *Under the Wire,* conclusion. See also Eytan Gilboa, "Television News and U.S. Foreign Policy: Constraints of Real-Time Coverage," *Harvard International Journal of Press/Politics* 8 (Fall 2003): 97–113; and Nik Gowing, "Real Time Television Coverage of Armed Conflicts and Diplomatic Crises: Does It Pressure or Distort Foreign Policy Decisions," Working Paper 1994-1, spring 1994, Shorenstein Center, Cambridge, Mass.

456 **"nothing will change"** Some editors, of course, acknowledge the loss of independence. As an example, see comment from Simon Li, a *Los Angeles Times* foreign editor, in Hannerz, *Foreign News,* 149.

make themselves compelling David Hoffman, interview by author, April 14, 2005. Foisie's lack of communication was mentioned by Michael Getler in interview by author, March 16, 2005. A discussion of Foisie's influence is found in Roberts, *In the Shadow of Power,* 359. Foisie was a consummate editor, very dedicated and far from passive, even if correspondents did not hear much from him. At a small seminar in a woody retreat in New England that I attended, Foisie sat down when it was his time to make a presentation, a role he did not relish. When others spoke, he stood up, as if at a press conference, taking notes and firing questions.

"I ask them" David Hoffmann to author, e-mail, May 25, 2005; R. W. Apple, "Gone Forever. . ." *Nieman Reports,* Spring 1991 (reprinted from *Times Talk,* June 1991), 26. NBC's Richard Valeriani made much the same comment: "Technology has ruined the life of the foreign correspondent." David Gergen, "Diplomacy in a Television Age: The Dangers of a Teledemocracy," in Serfaty, *The Media and Foreign Policy,* 51.

457 **"When young men ask me"** Sulzberger, *A Long Row of Candles,* xiii. Sulzberger was not the only *Times*man who had such views. Longtime Washington correspondent Arthur Krock, at the end of his career, made similar comments about "over-organization; the second-guessing treatment applied to highly qualified reporters by a growing horde of editors in the New York office; a mechanization of the personal relations between management and staff on which depend the pride of individual and devoted achievement." Krock, *Memoirs,* 93.

CHAPTER 24

458 **"The Natural History of the Newspaper"** Robert E. Park, "The Natural History of the Newspaper," in *Mass Communications,* ed. Wilbur Schramm (Urbana: University of Illinois Press, 1960), 8–9, 19.

459 **"The struggle for existence"** Ibid., 9. On the possible disappearance of classified advertising

from newspapers, see Steven Rattner, *Wall Street Journal,* February 15, 2007. The NBC executive, Jeff Zucker, chief executive of NBC's Universal television group, is quoted in an Associated Press story published on its Financial Wire, October 19, 2006; it can be found at www.msnbc.msn .com/id/15327437/. The data on decreases in paid circulation is in Murali K. Mantrala, Prasad A. Naik, Shrihari Sridhar, and Esther Thorson, "Uphill or Downhill? Locating the Firm on a Profit Function," *Journal of Marketing* 71 (April 2007): 28. On television audience declines, see "Network TV," in *The State of the News Media 2004* (Washington, D.C.: Project for Excellence in Journalism, 2008), 12.

eras in the natural history For a discussion of these eras, see Jaci Cole and John Maxwell Hamilton, "The History of a Surviving Species: Defining Eras in the Evolution of Foreign Correspondence," *Journalism Studies* 9 (October 2008): 798–812.

460 **"We should not expect"** Harrison E. Salisbury, memorandum, "Foreign News Coverage," March 1, 1965; and Seymour Topping to Emanuel Freedman, November 7, 1966, both in NYT Archives. **"How to make the best use"** Terrence F. Smith to Abe Rosenthal, January 18, 1977, NYT Archives; Bernard Gwertzman, "Memo to the *Times* Foreign Staff," *Media Studies Journal* 7 (Fall 1993): 33, 40. The Gwertzman article was disseminated as a memorandum to staff in 1992. On Topping's power as foreign editor, see Talese, *The Kingdom and the Power,* 337–38, 246, 553.

"On-going" experimentation has varied from newspaper to newspaper, medium to medium. By way of example, the *Chicago Daily News,* before its demise, initiated a two-thousand-word front-page *Insight* report along the lines of Topping's "takeout." Under Buck Dorsey and other editors at the *Baltimore Sun,* the philosophy was that correspondents should not let the wires beat them with a breaking story destined for the front page. Otherwise, they concentrated on context pieces. Ernest B. Furgurson, interview by author, March 15, 2005. In 2006 the *Wall Street Journal*'s publisher described a two-pronged approach: "As the print Journal moves even more toward exclusive, 'what it means' journalism, WSJ.com will be the place to go for 'what's happening right now.'" L. Gordon Crovitz, *Wall Street Journal,* December 4, 2006. In a communication to the author in September 2006, former *Chicago Daily News* correspondent Donald Shanor explained the value of the *Insight* column:

> I tried to be aware of the day to day news not to repeat it to my readers but to use it as information for trend and interpretive pieces I would write. . . . I was helped enormously in this mapping out of trends by the Daily News' invention in 1967 of Insight, a 2,000 word daily takeout from abroad, Washington, or the nation that began on the front page and jumped inside. I tried to write two of these every week, and to my surprise, almost all were used. The generous wordage allowed me to start out with an anecdote or description of a bleak steel town and to sandwich in good evidence in the form of statistics or (usually not for attribution) quotes.

461 **paid and supported** Networks do not divulge salaries of foreign correspondents; rough estimates here are provided as background by network sources. Newspapers are more forthcoming. The $250,000 figure was mentioned, for instance, by Roy Gutman, foreign editor for McClatchy newspapers, in an interview by author, September 27, 2008; and John Yemma, deputy managing editor of the *Boston Globe,* in an e-mail to author, October 23, 2002. At that time the *Globe* had five bureaus. The *Dallas Morning News* had the same number in that period, some with television reporters who worked for other properties owned by the parent company, Belo; costs for single bureaus with newspaper reporters were closer to $200,000. Bob Mong, editor, *Dallas Morning News,* to author, e-mail, October 27, 2002. Both the *Globe* and the *Morning News* have pulled back from foreign reporting since.

twice as well Terry Atlas, interview by author, February 11, 2004.

"Then, by God" Villard, *Some Newspapers and Newspapermen,* 99; van Paassen, *Days of Our Years,* 109.

"If it is terrorism" Atlas interview. Russell F. Anderson, "News from Nowhere: Our Disappearing Foreign Correspondents," *Saturday Review of Literature,* November 17, 1951, 11; Don Cook,

"Trench Coats for Sale: The Eclipse of the Foreign Correspondent," *Saturday Review of Literature,* June 24, 1978, 13–14.

"The reason that we'll be challenged" Jack Fuller, speech, annual dinner of the International Center for Journalists, Washington, D.C., October 8, 2002. Fuller also cited the $250,000 figure for maintaining foreign correspondents.

462 **A CASE STUDY** Topping's analysis of the shortcomings of competing with broadcast and of running ponderous diplomatic news is in "Memorandum for the Foreign News Staff," June 20, 1968, NYT Archives. This memorandum also outlined the new guidelines for correspondents, including his description of the "takeout." Additional background on his approach to reshaping the foreign news is from Topping, interviews by author, September 17, 2003; February 3, 2005. The *Times'* tradition of being the newspaper of record and publishing cables of official texts is highlighted in *America's Most Distinguished Newspaper,* a booklet prepared in the early 1940s (no exact date) for the business and advertising staffs and now found in NYT Archives. Alfred Friendly is quoted in Leon V. Sigal, *Reporters and Officials,* 187. Sulzberger is discussed in Shepard, *The Paper's Papers,* 169.

Sulzberger's fondness for the famous is apparent in this passage from his memoir, *A Long Row of Candles,* xiv:

It has been my fortune to play bad golf, bridge or chess with Eisenhower, Harriman, Nixon, Bohlen and Couve de Murville. I have lunched in Dulles' honor at the Quai d'Orsay and heard him obfuscate the French language. I have interpreted between Turkish officers and Soviet diplomats and, for that matter, at a most private luncheon between an American ambassador and future prime minister of France. By chance I have become acquainted with diverse famous men from de Gaulle (whom I have known a quarter of a century) to Tito, Chiang Kai-shek, Khrushchev, Nasser, De Gasperi, Castro and the Duke of Windsor, a clutch of Communists and a wallet of kings.

Topping was proud of making the foreign editor position more powerful than it had been. In an earlier era, authority had been highly diffuse. As chief foreign correspondent, for instance, C. L. Sulzberger held considerable sway over who was hired as a foreign correspondent. One of those whom he nixed was Topping in 1947. At the time Topping was a young AP correspondent making a name for himself by covering the war in Indochina. *Times* man Henry Lieberman, who was posted in the region, marked him as a strong talent. Topping thought he had the job sewn up until Lieberman received a cable from Sulzberger, "Negative on Topping." Not until ten years later did Topping make it onto the *Times* staff. Topping, interview by author, March 28, 2007.

463 **"the genre known as 'foreign correspondent'"** Marvin Kalb, foreword to Serfaty, *The Media and Foreign Policy,* xiv; Michael Emery, "An Endangered Species: The International Newshole," *Gannett Center Journal,* Fall 1989, 151–64. A similar statement is made in Peter Arnett, "Goodbye, World," *American Journalism Review,* November 1998, 52. On declines in magazine bureaus, see "Magazines," 17.

For other studies of the number of foreign correspondents abroad, which show increases and decreases in the numbers, see Theodore Edward Krulak, *The Foreign Correspondents: A Study of the Men and Women Reporting for the American Information Media in Western Europe* (Geneva: Librairie E. Droz, 1955); John Wilhelm, "The Re-appearing Foreign Correspondent: A World Survey," *Journalism Quarterly* 40 (Spring 1963): 147–68; Ralph E. Kliesch, "A Vanishing Species: The American Newsman Abroad," *1975 Overseas Press Club Directory,* 1975, 18–19+; Ralph E. Kliesch, "The U.S. Press Corps Abroad Rebounds," *Newspaper Research Journal* 12 (Winter 1991): 24–33.

Details on the cutback in foreign correspondents at the *Inquirer* came from John Brumfield, on its then existing foreign desk. Brumfield, conversation with author, 2007. The "hyperlocal" quote is from John Yemma, interview by author, February 28, 2007. (At the time, Yemma was assistant managing editor at the *Boston Globe;* he subsequently became editor of the *Christian Science Monitor.*) See also Howard Kurtz's comments in the *Washington Post,* November 27, 2006.

The Fenton quote is in his *Bad News,* 65. The absence of bureaus in South America, India, and South America, save ABC's in Nairobi, is from an article by former foreign correspondent Pamela Constable, *Washington Post,* February 18, 2007.

"was rapidly losing ground" "Changing Content," in *The Changing Newsroom* (Washington, D.C.: Project for Excellence in Journalism, 2008), 1. In 2007 only about 13 percent of the news in *U.S News & World Report* and *Newsweek,* and 16 percent of the news in *Time,* was international. See "Magazines," 2, ibid. On networks, see *Washington Post,* October 11, 2008. Details on *Time* bureaus are from Adi Ignatius, deputy managing editor, *Time,* to author, e-mail, October 1, 2008. On *Newsweek* bureaus, Mark Miller, assistant managing editor and chief of correspondents, interview with author, October 13, 2008.

My thanks to Madeline Casey for carrying out the somewhat arcane but interesting calculations about the size of *World* in *U.S. News & World Report.* Even more arcane is that the area of the *W* was 92 percent of the area of the *U* in 1948 but only 5 percent in 2008.

464 **civic virtue** Seymour Topping, interview by author, February 4, 2005.
"would have been totally out of character" Roberts, *In the Shadow of Power,* 214; Connie Bruck, "Rough Rider," *New Yorker,* November 12, 2007, 54.

465 **"I think we need to continue to do more locally"** The anonymous reporter's comment is from an interview by author.
basis for improvement This discussion is drawn from John Maxwell Hamilton and Eric Jenner, "Redefining Foreign Correspondence," *Journalism* 5 (August 2004): 301–21; and John Maxwell Hamilton and Eric Jenner, "The New Foreign Correspondence," *Foreign Affairs* 82 (September–October 2003): 131–38.
Foreign Foreign Correspondent H. Denis Wu and John Maxwell Hamilton, "US Foreign Correspondents: Changes and Continuity at the Turn of the Century," *Gazette* 66 (December 2004): 521–24; Tom Kent, interview by author, April 7, 2008. Details on the *New York Times* use of local reporters are in David S. Hirschman, "'NYT' War Reporter; 'Anarchy' Curtails Reporting in Iraq," published by *Editor & Publisher* online as www.editorandpublisher.com/eandp/article_brief/eandp/1/1003122985, September 16, 2006.

467 **"fixer"** Stephen Kinzer, *Blood of Brothers: Life and War in Nicaragua* (Cambridge, Mass.: David Rockefeller Center for Latin American Studies, Harvard University, 2007), 155–56. Ofusa obit is in *New York Times,* March 20, 1994; Junnosuke Ofusa, "A Journalist's Memoir: Fifty Years' Experience in an Eventful Era," NYT Archives. Dith Pran's obit is in *New York Times,* March 31, 2008. Nancy Youssef, annual meeting of American Society of Newspaper Editors, Washington, D.C., March 30, 2007. Elizabeth Witchel, "The Fixers," found at the Committee to Protect Journalists Web site, www.cpj.org/Briefings/2004/DA_fall04/fixers (accessed November 5, 2004). A discussion of fixers also can be found in Jerry Palmer and Victoria Fontan, "Our Ears and Our Eyes," *Journalism* 8 (February 2007): 5–24. Michael Massing, "As Iraqis See It," *New York Review of Books,* January 17, 2008, 17. Information on *Washington Post* fixers getting training is from a talk by Molly Moore, Manship School of Mass Communication, Louisiana State University, October 4, 2008.

Because fixers are often used as reporters in dangerous countries, they are often at risk. A poll of correspondents in Iraq found that 57 said at least one Iraq in their staff had been killed or kidnapped in the previous year. "Journalists in Iraq: a Survey of Those Reporting from the Front Lines," 2007, Project for Excellence in Journalism, Washington, D.C., 1.
"they do not require" Bittermann, "The Best of Times . . . ," in Foote, *Live from the Trenches,* 81. For a discussion of newspapers more inclined to use foreign news that comes from their own reporters, see John B. Adams, "What the Foreign Correspondent Does for a Newspaper's Readers," *Journalism Quarterly* 43 (Summer 1966): 304. The study compared the *Minneapolis Tribune,* the *St. Louis Post-Dispatch,* and the *Toledo Blade,* which had two or three correspondents abroad, with the *De Moines Register,* the *Kansas City Star,* and the *Akron Beacon-Journal,* which had none, during early 1965.
Nearly one out of five Wu and Hamilton, "US Foreign Correspondents," 524.

468 **"through the wreckage"** Ruslan Musayev, AP dispatch, December 16, 1999, AP Archives.
"'Near East' and 'Far East'" Sheean, *This House against This House,* 96. For background on the evolution of interdependence, see John Maxwell Hamilton, *Entangling Alliances: How the Third World Shapes Our Lives* (Cabin John, Md.: Seven Locks Press, 1990), introduction. Oberdorfer quoted in Dwight L. Morris and associates, "America and the World: The Impact of September 11 on U.S. Coverage of International News," 2002, Pew International Journalism Program, Washington, D.C., 15.

A revealing study by the Congressional Research Service in the late 1980s examined federal government activities that aided foreign countries but were not financed through the regular international affairs budget. Of the 85 governmental entities queried, 78 reported having their own foreign-aid activities. Among these governmental bodies were the Bureau of Engraving and Printing, the Disability Research Center of the Education Department, the National Park Service, the Federal Railroad Administration, and the Supreme Court. The CRS report, which was never published, concluded that these initiatives were uncoordinated and in the case of some countries possibly not consistent "with U.S. foreign policy, national security and economic interests." See Theodor W. Galdi, Carol Kuntz, Erin Day, and Robert Shuey, "U.S. Government Activities Not Directly Financed through the International Affairs Budget Account Yielding Benefits to Foreign Nationals or Foreign Governments: 1983–1986," 1989, Congressional Research Service, Washington, D.C., 2–22.

In later Senate testimony, an official from the U.S. General Accounting Office underscored the proliferation of agency activity abroad, noting among other things, "In 1995 we found that 23 departments and independent agencies were implementing 215 aid projects in the former Soviet Union." See U.S. General Accounting Office statement of Benjamin F. Nelson, director, international relations and trade issues, National Security and International Affairs Division, U.S. General Accounting Office, before Task Force on International Affairs, in Committee on the Budget, U.S. Senate, *International Affairs: Activities of Domestic Agencies* (Washington, D.C.: GAO, 1998).

469 **"Global Atlanta"** Stephen Seplow, "Closer to Home," *American Journalism Review,* July–August 2002, 26; Charles Layton, "It's a Small World," *American Journalism Review,* June 2000, 56–57. The survey is *Global Perspectives in Local Television News Coverage,* 11. See also Bill Kirtz, "Local Stories Far from Home: 'Globalizing' Brings World Affairs into Focus," *Presstime,* September 2002, 26. Information on the *Atlanta Journal-Constitution* is from former "World Section" editor Raman Narayanan, interview by author, January 17, 2007. Such experiments are far too many and too episodic to list fully, but two other examples are worth mentioning. The *Spokane Spokesman-Review* has run a full page of international and national news called "connections" in its Sunday editions, with each main story having a sidebar explaining the local connection. In 1986, the *Wisconsin State Journal* announced it would henceforth produce two four-page tabloids, one called *World Outlook* and the other *Outdoor World* for sportsmen and -women. The only one that existed in 2008 was the latter.

approaches for making foreign news local Joyce Barnathan, interview by author, September 22, 2008. The resulting book in the Society of Professional Journalists' project is Hamilton, *Main Street America and the Third World;* Hamilton directed the project. The ASNE book is by George Krimsky, *Bringing the World Home: Showing Readers Their Global Connections* (Reston, Va.: American Society of Newspaper Editors, 1999).

Parachute Foreign Correspondent This section draws from Emily Erickson and John Maxwell Hamilton, "Foreign Reporting Enhanced by Parachute Journalism," *Newspaper Research Journal* 27 (Winter 2006): 33–47; Erickson and Hamilton, "Happy Landings: A Defense of Parachute Journalism," in Perlmutter and Hamilton, *From Pigeons to News Portals,* 130–49. Typical critiques of parachute foreign correspondence are in Hohenberg, *Foreign Correspondence,* 307, 323; Rosenblum, *Coups and Earthquakes,* 11–12; Pedelty, *War Stories,* 109–12; Tunku Varadarajan, "Parachute Journalism Redux," *Wall Street Journal,* November 12, 2001. The *Wall Street Journal* stories were by James P. Sterba, November 29, 1984; and Joe E. Hilsenrath, April 9, 2003.

"**Mike Hanna of CNN**" Hannerz, *Foreign News,* 42–50, 63–64. On travel by foreign correspondents, John Yemma, interview by author, March 10, 2005; on the *Los Angeles Times,* foreign editor Simon Li, interview by Emily Erickson, November 4, 2004.

470 "**to explore and research situations**" On the *Minneapolis Tribune,* see Charles W. Bailey, "Foreign Policy and the Provincial Press," in Serfaty, *The Media and Foreign Policy,* 185. On the *Milwaukee Journal,* George Lockwood to author, May 6, 2007; Thomas Blinkhorn to author, e-mail, April 7, 2008. The newspaper survey was carried out by Erickson and Hamilton; see their "Foreign Reporting Enhanced by Parachute Journalism." Of the six newspapers that said they did not do parachute journalism, only two said none of its reporters had ever reported outside the country. A 2002 survey of foreign editors found that 39 of the 81 larger newspapers at least occasionally used parachute journalists: Morris and associates, "America and the World," 4. The local television news directors' study is *Global Perspectives in Local Television News Coverage,* 16.

"**blessed invention**" Frederick T. Birchall, *The Storm Breaks* (New York: Viking, 1940), 5; Erickson and Hamilton, "Happy Landings," 133; Topping, "Memorandum for the Foreign News Staff"; Seymour Topping to Robert Semple, August 21, 1981, NYT Archives. An example of parachuting during Topping's time is that the *Times* sent its art editor to cover a flood in Florence in 1966. Michael E. Bishop, "An Analysis of How the New York Times Gathers and Disseminates International News," *Gazette* 13 (1967): 345. The calculation on the decreasing cost of air travel is from the Air Transport Association, July 18, 2005, www.airlines.org/. The charges are expressed as yield, "an industry term denoting the price . . . a revenue passenger pays to fly one mile."

471 "**There are examples [of this] all the time**" Timothy McNulty, interview by author, March 23, 2005.

472 "**We went all over the world**" Bob Mong, interview by author, October 27, 2005; and Brooks Egerton, Reese Dunklin, and Brendan Case, interviews by author, October 26, 2006.

473 **managed flood control** Information on the work of the *Eugene Register-Guard* is from Kevin Miller, interview by Emily Erickson, June 2, 2005. KRON is mentioned in Shanor, *News from Abroad,* 81.

"**some relationship to Portland**" Richard Read, interview by author, September 8, 2007.

rarely happen where you have a bureau Marcy McGinnis, interview by author, May 19, 2004. On the ABC expansion, see Jennifer Dorroh, "Armies of One," *American Journalism Review,* December 2007–January 2008, 12–13.

transnational issues as much as places Author interviews of John Yemma, March 10, 2005; Eliza Tinsley, February 2, 2005; Keith Richburg, January 27, 2006; David Hoffman, April 14, 2005, and September 22, 2008.

474 "**firefighters**" Author interviews of Eliza Tinsley, February 2, 2005; James Cox, senior assignment editor, world, *USA Today,* February 2, 2005. On the outsourcing of *Globe* financial jobs, see Adam Reilly, "Morrissey Boulevard Melancholia," *Phoenix,* accessed on its Web page, http://thephoenix, February 2, 2007.

Reuters was the first large media company to outsource journalism and data processing, when it opened an office in Bangalore in 2004 to assemble reports on companies' earnings and filings with the Securities and Exchange Commission. Reuters outsourcing is described in the *Guardian,* October 7, 2004. In a disturbing twist on this, a Web site—pasadenanow.com—used five contributors overseas to cover Pasadena, California, city council meetings using Web casts and citizen volunteers. See www.copydesk.org/news/08_singleton_says.php.

interest in international news For an example of the attention paid to local foreign news, see John Mauro, "Readers Care," in Hamilton, *Main Street America and the Third World,* 164–82.

International Reporting Information Systems Details on IRIS come from two sources. The first is from a series of articles about IRIS by John de St. Jorre, one of the journalists recruited to join IRIS, after it folded. The series appeared in the *Washington Post,* April 10, 11, 12, 13, 1983. The second is the author of this book, who worked as chief U.S. foreign policy reporter for IRIS. The creation of Reuters has been discussed earlier in this book. Background on Havas is in Fenby, *The International News Services,* 27–30; and Desmond, *The Information Process,* 134–40.

475 **"It's a laudable objective"** *Washington Post,* April 13, 1983.

Dow Jones Newswires Economist Intelligence Unit Web page, www.eiu.com (accessed January 19, 2007). Author interviews of Rob Rossi, February 13, 2007; Paul Ingrassia, February 15, 2007; and Chaz Repak, March 8, 2007, and September 30, 2008. For a discussion of the growth of the Dow Jones Newswires, see *NewsCorp Annual Report, 2008,* 14, which can be accessed from the News Corporation home page.

476 **"see which bonds were cheap"** Michael Bloomberg, *Bloomberg by Bloomberg* (New York, John Wiley, 2001), 73. Bloomberg's autobiography is billed as coauthored by Matthew Winkler, who thus becomes to his boss what Frederic Hudson was to his, James Gordon Bennett, in *Journalism in the United States.* The big difference between Bloomberg and Bennett is that the latter, as evidenced by his self-promotion in the pages of the *Herald,* could make fun of himself and had a sense of irony.

branched into traditional media Matthew Winkler, interview by author, February 1, 2007; e-mails to author from Gregori Reto, September 29 and October 1, 2008. The Bloomberg count, as noted, included support staff such as television technicians. For pure journalists, Reto noted, the total count would drop about 270, but the percentage outside the United States would still be greater than inside. "The Secret World of Modern Slavery" article is in *Bloomberg Markets,* December 2006, 46–66.

478 **"It's all about 'I've got news'"** The BP operation is described by Jeffrey E. Borda, interview by Mary Schoen, September 6, 2005. The other examples and the quote are from attendees at the Global Public Affairs Institute conference, New York City, February 26, 2004: Thomas Mattia, vice president, Global Communications, EDS Inc.; Michael Reilly, president, Hally Enterprises; Eric Jackson, vice president, Corporate Communications, FedEx Corporation.

"the eyes, the ears" Beech, *Tokyo and Points East,* 42.

"Today and in the future" Garrick Utley, "The Shrinking of Foreign News," *Foreign Affairs,* March–April 1997, 9. Data on cellular telephone sales can be found in Steven Livingston, "The Nokia Effect: The Reemergence of Amateur Journalism and What It Means for International Affairs," in Perlmutter and Hamilton, *From Pigeons to News Portals,* 52.

SALAM PAX Salam Pax, *The Clandestine Diary of an Ordinary Iraqi* (New York: Grove Press, 2003), 123; Clark Boyd, "Iraqis Seek a Voice via Blogs," BBC News, http://news.bbc.co.uk/2/hi/technology/3632614.stm, posted September 8, 2004.

L. T. SMASH "The New Ernie Pyles: Sgtlizzie and 67cshdocs," www.Washingtonpost.com, posted August 12, 2005.

WAN YANHAI Committee to Protect Journalists, News Alert, September 5, 2002.

479 **MARK RANKOV** The LiveJournal account of the hostage crisis is reported on in a *Wired News* article by Sergey Kuznetsov, www.wired.com/news/culture/0,1284,56073,00.html.

THE ENVIRONMENTAL ORGANIZATION GREENPEACE These stories could be found at www.greenpeace.org/international/news/greenpeace-shuts-down-esso, posted October 25, 2002.

Google-searching Indian stories *New York Times,* March 5, 2009.

"When you come right down to it" Edwin O'Connor, *The Last Hurrah* (Boston: Bantam, 1970), 224. The same point was made by Robert Park in a scholarly way: "As long as there are people in this country who have common racial or nationalist interests, they will have papers to interpret events from their own peculiar point of view." Robert E. Park, *The Immigrant Press and Its Control* (New York: Harper, 1922), 12–13. For detail on the reach of the Iranian media available to Iranians living in the United States, I am grateful to my colleague Foad Izadi, a doctoral student at the Manship School of Mass Communication, Louisiana State University.

480 **"Today's immigrants to the United States"** Stanley A. Renshon, *The 50% American: Immigration and National Identity in an Age of Terror* (Washington, D.C.: Georgetown University Press, 2005), 26. Shakuntala Rao, "Adding Al Jazeera," *American Journalism Review,* August–September 2007, 16–17.

available nowhere else Discussion of these uses of citizen media by main street media is in Allison Romano, "Why Everybody Is a Reporter," *Broadcasting and Cable,* August 22, 2005, 14; *Wall*

Street Journal, January 3, 2005; *New York Times,* December 4, 2006; Geoffrey A. Fowler, *Wall Street Journal Online,* September 28, 2007. Discussion of the use of terrorist-monitoring sites by journalists is in *New York Times,* June 18, 2006. Saddam Hussein's execution video is described in *New York Times,* January 1, 2007. The rate of Twitter postings with the word "Mumbai" during the terrorist attacks is reported in *New York Times,* November 30, 2008.

481 **"Many of these"** Melissa Wall, "'Blogs of War': Weblogs as News," *Journalism* 6 (May 2005): 165; *New York Times,* October 6, December 20, 2006. Discussion of camera use at the pope's funeral is in Livingston, "The Nokia Effect," 52.

"What will happen" Peter Maass, "War Stories: Salam Pax Is Real," *Slate,* posted June 2, 2003. The Salam Pax quote on Bush is in his *The Clandestine Diary of an Ordinary Iraqi,* 121.

"a very recent manifestation" Park, "The Natural History of the Newspaper," 11. On the origin of the term *weblog,* see Kaye D. Trammell and David D. Perlmutter, "The New 'Foreign' Foreign Correspondents: Personal Blogs as Public Affairs," in Perlmutter and Hamilton, *From Pigeons to News Portals,* 72.

"We have a very large global independent laboratory" John McQuaid, "Charles Lewis on the Future of Investigative Journalism on the Web," posted on http://newassignment.net, November 20, 2006.

482 **"It is my heartfelt view"** Arthur Sulzberger's quote was on the *New York Observer*'s Web page, www.themediamob.observer.com, accessed February 13, 2007; Bill Wheatley, interview by author, May 3, 2005.

"felt-covered table" Campbell, *The Year that Defined American Journalism,* 15; Seymour Topping, interview by author, March 28, 2007.

MTV News A thoughtful discussion of the power of soft media to reach broader audiences is in Matthew A. Baum, "Sex, Lies, and War: How Soft News Brings Foreign Policy to the Inattentive Public," *American Political Science Review* 96 (March 2002): 91–109. See also his book *Soft News Goes to War.*

high-quality reporting about the world is not over John Walcott and Roy Gutman, bureau chief and foreign editor, respectively, in the McClatchy Washington bureau, interviews by author, February 13, 2007. Gutman had previously been with *Newsday,* whose foreign service was defunct. AP changes are discussed in *New York Times,* June 20, 2005; Judith Matloff, "Can the AP Go Global?" *Columbia Journalism Review,* May–June 2004, 16–17; Sherry Ricchiardi, "Covering the World," *American Journalism Review,* December 2007–January 2008, 32–39; AP's 2006 Annual Report, titled "Essential Leadership," Associated Press, New York City. Naturally, such changes at the AP, including substantial personnel changes, have generated concern, including an open letter to the chair of AP's board that floated around the Internet from retired foreign correspondent Mort Rosenblum. Rosenblum to Burl Osborne, January 31, 2006. A discussion of the increase in front-page foreign news in the *Wall Street Journal* before and after its sale is in press release from the Project for Excellence in Journalism, April 23, 2008, which can be accessed at http://journalism.org/node/10769.

483 **"In a world that is so big and complex"** David Hoffman, interview by author, April 14, 2005.

help it get "meat" Jacqueline Leo, interview by author, May 10, 2006. *Vanity Fair*'s international coverage is discussed in "Vanity Fire," *Columbia Journalism Review,* January–February 2007, 41–46. Originally *Reader's Digest* was a reprint magazine that culled stories from other publications. Because the Internet is far better at such aggregation, the *Digest* now commissions foreign news stories.

"an ad-supported video network" AP video network described in its 2005 annual report, *Essential Solutions* (New York: Associated Press, 2006), 16. On Kevin Sites, see *New York Times* story, September 12, 2005; Peter Copeland, interview by author, January 22, 2007. Another Iraq-related blogger who landed a book deal is Colby Buzzell, who also wrote for *Esquire* after his military experience in the country. The *New York Times* paid only a small premium of a few hundred dollars a month over and above the normal subscription fee to publish Bloomberg News in its pages. Because the newspaper, unlike the Internet, is finite, the *Times* could not take much of the Bloomberg fare. As a result, Bloomberg allowed the *Times* to use in the newspaper anything Bloomberg sent out; but on its Web site, the *Times* could only use what it published in the newspaper. This prevented it from offering the entire Bloomberg service to its customers. In this transaction, the *Times* acquired news and Bloomberg got a good advertising boost. On the number of Bloomberg stories in the *New York Times,* see Felix Gillette, "All the Bloomberg News That's Fit to Print," *Columbia Journalism Review,* August 8, 2006; retrieved online on April 16, 2008, from www.cjr.org/the _audit/all_the_bloomberg_news_thats_f.php.

484 **"measure the impact"** GlobalPost press release, October 16, 2008; David Cook, www.csmonitor .com/2008/1029/p25s01-usgn.html; Rick Byrne, interview by author, October 22, 2008; Charles Sennott, interview by author, November 3, 2008.

excel at foreign news Seymour Topping, interview by author, February 4, 2005.

"take the view" Matthew Winkler, interview by author, February 1, 2007.

485 **"Sending those reporters overseas"** Charles Lewis, "The Nonprofit Road," *Columbia Journalism Review,* September–October 2007, 33; Carol Guensburg, "Nonprofit News," *American Journalism Review,* February–March 2008, 27–33; Geneva Overholser, "On Behalf of Journalism: A Manifesto for Change," 2006, Annenberg Public Policy Center, University of Pennsylvania, Philadelphia, 8; Shanor, *News from Abroad,* 214; Jon Sawyer, executive director of the Pulitzer Center, interview by author, January 18, 2007. Overholser's report provides an excellent outline of the changing landscape for traditional models of news. On Hersh's support from the Fund for Investigative Journalism, see Knightley, *The First Casualty,* 428–32.

486 **government support** An excellent article on the various government-supported possibilities is Bree Nordenson, "The Uncle Sam Solution," *Columbia Journalism Review,* September–October 2007, 37–41. I thank James Hamilton for helping me think this through. For a groundbreaking discussion of historical government support for news, see Timothy E. Cook, *Governing with the News: The News Media as a Political Institution* (Chicago: University of Chicago Press, 2005), especially chap. 3.

old Fitwarari "Nine Months of Reporting This War," *Newspaper World,* April 25, 1936, 2.

487 **"All the reporters in the world"** Lippmann, *Public Opinion,* 214.

"comparatively new" Charles A. Dana, "Journalism: A Lecture Delivered to the Students of Union College," *McClure's,* May 1895, 555.

A NOTE ON SOURCES

In writing this history, I have drawn from journalists' memoirs and personal papers, from secondary sources, from interviews I have conducted, and from personal correspondence carried out over many years. In an effort to make endnotes useful but not cumbersome, I have grouped citations at appropriate points and sometimes included with those notes amplification and additional observations. To further simplify matters for the reader, some of the more important sources for this book are listed below.

First is a list of archives and collections of papers, which includes the abbreviated forms used in the endnotes. I also have had access to papers held privately. The provenances of these private papers can be found where they are cited.

A second set of sources is bibliographic. This list is divided into primary sources—books by foreign correspondents as well as by news media owners and editors—and secondary sources of particular value. The large number of memoirs in the former group is instructive. In the argot of the newsroom, foreign correspondents make "good copy"; correspondents have not been shy about taking advantage of this fact, in the process augmenting their celebrity.

AP Archives	Associated Press Corporate Archives, Associated Press, New York.
Beals Papers	Carleton Beals Papers, Howard Gotlieb Archival Research Center, Boston University, Boston.
Belden Papers	Jack Belden Papers, Hoover Institution Archives, Stanford University, Stanford, Calif.
Bell Papers	Edward Price Bell Papers, Midwest Manuscript Collection, Newberry Library, Chicago.
Binder Papers	Carroll Binder Papers, Midwest Manuscript Collection, Newberry Library, Chicago.
Bobbs-Merrill Mss.	Bobbs-Merrill Manuscripts, Manuscript Department, Lilly Library, Indiana University, Bloomington.

Brown Papers	Cecil Brown Papers, State Historical Society of Wisconsin, Madison.
Catledge Papers	Turner Catledge Papers. Special Collections, Mitchell Memorial Library, Mississippi State University, Starkville.
Daily News Records	Chicago Daily News Inc. Records, Midwest Manuscript Collection, Newberry Library, Chicago. (The Newberry has since reorganized collections relating to the *Daily News*.)
Delane Papers	John Delane Papers, News International Archives, London.
Dennis Papers	Charles Dennis Papers, Midwest Manuscript Collection, Newberry Library, Chicago.
E. Mowrer Papers, LOC	Edgar Ansel Mowrer Papers, Manuscript Division, Library of Congress, Washington, D.C.
E. Mowrer Papers, Newberry	Edgar Ansel Mowrer, Midwest Manuscript Collection, Newberry Library, Chicago.
FBI Files	Federal Bureau of Investigation, Washington, D.C.
Gunther Papers	John Gunther Papers, Special Collections Research Center, University of Chicago Library, Chicago.
Halliburton Papers	Richard Halliburton Papers, Manuscript Division, Department of Rare Books and Special Collections, Princeton University Library, Princeton, N.J.
Kaltenborn Papers	H. V. Kaltenborn Collection, State Historical Society of Wisconsin, Madison.
Knox Papers	Frank Knox Papers, Manuscript Division, Library of Congress, Washington, D.C.
Kohlberg Papers	Alfred Kohlberg Papers, Hoover Institution Archives, Stanford University, Stanford, Calif.
Lawson Papers	Victor Fremont Lawson Papers, Midwest Manuscript Collection, Newberry Library, Chicago.
McClure Mss	S. S. McClure Manuscripts Department, Manuscripts Department, Lilly Library, Indiana University, Bloomington.
McKinley Papers	William McKinley Papers, Manuscript Division, Library of Congress, Washington, D.C.
Mickelson Papers	Sig Mickelson Papers, State Historical Society of Wisconsin, Madison.
National Geographic Archives	Archives, National Geographic Society, Washington, D.C.
NBC Papers, LOC	National Broadcasting Company History Files, 1922–86, Manuscript Division, Library of Congress, Washington, D.C.

NBC Records, Wis.	National Broadcasting Company Records, State Historical Society of Wisconsin, Madison.
NYT Archives	New York Times Archives, New York Times, New York. (Many of these files have since been moved to the New York Public Library.)
Patterson Papers	Joseph Patterson Papers, Special Collections, Donnelley and Lee Library, Lake Forest College, Lake Forest, Ill.
P. Mowrer Papers	Paul Scott Mowrer Papers, Midwest Manuscript Collection, Newberry Library, Chicago.
Random House Papers	Random House Papers, Rare Book and Manuscript Library, Butler Library, Columbia University, New York.
Reid Papers	Whitelaw Reid Papers, Manuscript Division, Library of Congress, Washington, D.C.
Russell Papers	William Howard Russell Papers, News International Archives, London.
Salisbury Papers	Harrison Salisbury Papers, Rare Book and Manuscript Library, Butler Library, Columbia University, New York.
Schiff Papers	Dorothy Schiff Papers, Manuscript Collection, New York Public Library, New York.
Sevareid Papers	Eric Sevareid Papers, Manuscript Division, Library of Congress, Washington, D.C.
Sheean Papers	Vincent Sheean Papers, State Historical Society of Wisconsin, Madison.
Snow Papers	Edgar Snow Collection, University Archives, University of Missouri–Kansas City, Kansas City, Mo.
St. John Papers	Robert St. John Papers, Howard Gotlieb Archival Research Center, Boston University, Boston.
Stowe Papers	Leland Stowe Papers, State Historical Society of Wisconsin, Madison.
Swope Papers	Herbert Bayard Swope Papers, Howard Gotlieb Archival Research Center, Boston University, Boston.

PRIMARY SOURCES

Abend, Hallett. *My Life in China: 1926–1941.* New York: Harcourt, Brace, 1943.
Adams, Henry. *The Education of Henry Adams.* New York: Modern Library, 1931.
Adler, Ruth, ed. *The Working Press: Special of the New York Times.* New York: Bantam Books, 1970.
Arnett, Peter. *Live from the Battlefield: From Vietnam to Baghdad, 35 Years in the World's War Zones.* New York: Simon and Schuster, 1994.
Ayers, Chris. *War Reporting for Cowards.* New York: Atlantic Monthly Press, 2005.
Baker, Ray Stannard. *Native American: The Book of My Youth.* New York: Scribner's, 1941.

Baker, Russell. *The Good Times.* New York: William Morrow, 1989.

Beals, Carleton. *Glass Houses: Ten Years of Freelancing.* Philadelphia: Lippincott, 1938.

———. *The Great Circle: Further Adventures in Freelancing.* Philadelphia: Lippincott, 1940.

Beech, Keyes. *Tokyo and Points East.* Garden City, N.Y.: Doubleday, 1954.

Behr, Edward. *"Anyone Here Been Raped and Speaks English?": A Correspondent's Life behind the Lines.* London: New English Library, 1985.

Belden, Jack. *China Shakes the World.* New York: Monthly Review Press, 1970.

———. *Retreat with Stilwell.* New York: Knopf, 1943.

———. *Still Time to Die.* Philadelphia: Blakiston, 1944.

Bell, Edward Price. *Europe's Economic Sunrise.* Chicago: Chicago Daily News, 1927.

———. *Journalism of the Highest Realm: The Memoir of Edward Price Bell.* Ed. Jaci Cole and John Maxwell Hamilton. Baton Rouge: Louisiana State University Press, 2007.

———. *World Chancelleries.* Chicago: Chicago Daily News, 1926.

Benjamin, Robert Spiers, ed. *Eye Witness: By Members of the Overseas Press Club of America.* New York: Alliance, 1940.

———, ed. *The Inside Story: By Members of the Overseas Press Club of America.* New York: Prentice-Hall, 1940.

Bigart, Homer. *Forward Positions: The War Correspondence of Homer Bigart.* Ed. Betsy Wade. Fayetteville: University of Arkansas Press, 1992.

Birchall, Frederick T. *The Storm Breaks.* New York: Viking, 1940.

Bloomberg, Michael. *Bloomberg by Bloomberg.* New York: John Wiley, 2001.

Bonsal, Stephen. *The Real Condition of Cuba To-day.* New York: Harper and Brothers, 1897.

Booker, Edna Lee. *News Is My Job.* New York: Macmillan, 1940.

Brinkley, David. *Brinkley's Beat: People, Places, and Events That Shaped My Times.* New York: Knopf, 2003.

Brown, Cecil. *Suez to Singapore.* New York: Random House, 1941.

Brown, Constantine. *The Coming of the Whirlwind.* Chicago: Henry Regnery, 1962.

Browne, Malcolm W. *Muddy Boots and Red Socks: A Reporter's Life.* New York: Random House, 1983.

———. *The New Face of War.* Indianapolis: Bobbs-Merrill, 1965.

Burchett, Wilfred. *At the Barricades: Forty Years on the Cutting Edge of History.* New York: Times Books, 1981.

Burnett, John F. *Uncivilized Beast and Shameless Hellions: Travels with an NPR Correspondent.* New York: Rodale Press, 2006.

Canfield, Cass. *Up and Down and Around: A Publisher Recollects the Time of His Life.* New York: Harper and Row, 1971.

Carroll, Gordon, ed. *History in the Writing: By the Foreign Correspondents of Time, Life, and Fortune.* New York: Duell, Sloan, and Pearce, 1945.

Casey, Robert J. *Baghdad and Points East.* New York: Robert M. McBride, 1928.

———. *I Can't Forget.* Indianapolis: Bobbs-Merrill, 1941.

———. *More Interesting People.* Indianapolis: Bobbs-Merrill, 1947.

———. *Such Interesting People.* Garden City, N.Y.: Garden City, 1945.

———. *This Is Where I Came In.* Indianapolis: Bobbs-Merrill, 1945.

———. *Torpedo Junction: With the Pacific Fleet from Pearl Harbor to Midway.* Indianapolis: Bobbs-Merrill, 1942.

Catledge, Turner. *My Life and the Times.* New York: Harper and Row, 1971.

Catling, Patrick Skene. *Better Than Working*. New York: Macmillan, 1960.

Chamberlin, William Henry. *The Confessions of an Individualist*. New York: Macmillan, 1940.

Childs, Marquis W. *Sweden: The Middle Way*. New Haven, Conn.: Yale University Press, 1936.

Clapper, Raymond. *Watching the World*. Ed. Mrs. Raymond Clapper. New York: Da Capo Press, 1976.

Cobb, Irwin S. *Exit Laughing*. Garden City, N.Y.: Garden City, 1942.

Cooper, Anderson. *Dispatches from the Edge: A Memoir of Wars, Disasters, and Survival*. New York: HarperCollins, 2006.

Cowles, Gardner. *Mike Looks Back: The Memoirs of Gardner Cowles, Founder of Look Magazine*. New York: Gardner Cowles, 1985.

Cowley, Malcolm. *Exile's Return: A Literary Odyssey of the 1920s*. New York: Viking Press, 1951.

Cox, Jennifer. *Around the World in 80 Dates*. New York: Downtown Press, 2005.

Creelman, James. *On the Great Highway: The Wanderings and Adventures of a Special Correspondent*. Boston: Lothrop, 1901.

Critchfield, Richard. *Villages*. Garden City, N.Y.: Anchor/Doubleday, 1981.

Cronkite, Walter. *A Reporter's Life*. New York: Ballantine Books, 1997.

Crow, Carl. *China Takes Her Place: A Story of Struggle and Achievement*. New York: Harper, 1944.

———. *Four Hundred Million Customers: The Experiences—Some Happy, Some Sad—of an American in China, and What They Taught Him*. New York: Harper, 1937.

Custer, Joe James. *Through the Perilous Night: The Astoria's Last Battle*. New York: Macmillan, 1944.

Darrah, David. *Hail Caesar!* Boston: Hale, Cushman and Flint, 1936.

Davis, Richard Harding. *Cuba in War Time*. 1897. Reprint, Lincoln: University of Nebraska Press, 2000.

———. *Notes of a War Correspondent*. New York: Scribner's, 1914.

———. *With the Allies*. New York: Scribner's, 1917.

Day, Donald. *Onward Christian Soldiers*. Torrance, Calif.: Noontide Press, 1982.

Decle, Lionel. *Three Years in Savage Africa*. 1900. Reprint, Bulawayo, Zimbabwe: Books of Rhodesia, 1974.

Deedes, W. F. *At War with Waugh: The Real Story of Scoop*. London: Pan, 2003.

Dennis, Charles. *Victor Lawson: His Time and His Work*. Chicago: University of Chicago Press, 1935.

Denny, Harold. *Behind Both Lines*. New York: Viking Press, 1942.

Dillon, E. J. *The Inside Story of the Peace Conference*. New York: Harper, 1920.

Douglas, Ab. *On Foreign Assignment: The Inside Story of Journalism's Elite Corps*. Calgary, Alberta: Detselig, 1993.

Duranty, Walter. *I Write as I Please*. New York: Simon and Schuster, 1935.

Ekins, H. R. *Around the World in Eighteen Days: And How to Do It*. London: Longmans, Green, 1936.

Farson, Negley. *Behind God's Back*. New York: Harcourt, Brace, 1941.

———. *Black Bread and Red Coffins*. New York: Century, 1930.

———. *Caucasian Journey*. London: Evans Brothers, 1951.

———. *Last Chance in Africa*. New York: Harcourt, Brace, 1950.

————. *A Mirror for Narcissus.* Garden City, N.Y.: Doubleday, 1957.

————. *Sailing across Europe.* New York: Century, 1926.

————. *Transgressor in the Tropics.* New York: Harcourt, Brace. 1938.

————. *The Way of the Transgressor.* New York: Literary Guild of America, 1936.

Fawcett, Denby, et al. *War Torn: Stories of War from the Women Reporters Who Covered Vietnam.* New York: Random House, 2002.

Fenton, Tom. *Bad News: The Decline of Reporting, the Business of News, and the Danger to Us All.* New York: Regan Books, 2005.

Filkins, Dexter. *The Forever War.* New York: Knopf, 2008.

Finnegan, William. *Crossing the Line: A Year in the Land of Apartheid.* Berkeley: University of California Press, 1994.

Fischer, Louis. *Men and Politics: An Autobiography.* New York: Duell, Sloan, and Pearce, 1941.

Forrest, Wilbur. *Behind the Front Page: Stories of Newspaper Stories in the Making.* New York: Appleton-Century, 1934.

Fox, Paula. *The Coldest Winter: A Stringer in Liberated Europe.* New York: Henry Holt, 2005.

Frank, Reuven. *Out of Thin Air.* New York: Simon and Schuster, 1991.

Fraser, David. *A Modern Campaign; or, War and Wireless Telegraphy in the Far East.* London: Methuen, 1905.

French, Howard W. *A Continent for the Taking: The Tragedy and Hope of Africa.* New York: Vintage Books, 2005.

Friendly, Fred W. *Due to Circumstances beyond Our Control.* New York: Random House, 1967.

Fromm, Bella. *Blood and Banquets: A Berlin Social Diary.* New York: Birch Lane Press, 1990.

Fuller, Margaret. *Margaret Fuller's New York Journalism: A Biographical Essay and Key Writings.* Ed. Catherine C. Mitchell. Knoxville: University of Tennessee Press, 1995.

————. *These Sad but Glorious Days: Dispatches from Europe, 1846–1850.* Ed. Larry J. Reynolds and Susan Belasco Smith. New Haven, Conn.: Yale University Press, 1991.

Gannett, Frank. *Winging 'Round the World.* Rochester, N.Y.: Gannett Newspapers, 1947.

Gelb, Arthur. *City Room.* New York: Putnam's, 2003.

Gellhorn, Martha. *The Face of War.* New York: Simon and Schuster, 1959.

Geyer, Georgie Anne. *Buying the Night Flight: The Autobiography of a Woman Foreign Correspondent.* New York: Delacorte Press, 1983.

————. *Waiting for Winter to End: An Extraordinary Journey through Soviet Central Asia.* Washington, D.C.: Brassey's, 1994.

Gibbons, Floyd. *"And They Thought We Wouldn't Fight."* New York: George H. Doran, 1918.

Graham, Katherine. *Personal History.* New York: Knopf, 1997.

Gunther, John. *Chicago Revisited.* Chicago: University of Chicago, 1967.

————. *A Fragment of Autobiography: The Fun of Writing the Inside Books.* New York: Harper and Row, 1961.

————. *Inside Africa.* New York: Harper, 1955.

————. *Inside Asia.* New York: Harper, 1939.

————. *Inside Europe.* New York: Harper, 1936.

————. *Inside Latin America.* New York: Harper, 1941.

————. *Inside Russia Today.* New York: Harper, 1958.

Hahn, Emily. *China to Me*. Garden City, N.Y.: Doubleday, 1944.

Halberstam, David. *The Making of a Quagmire*. New York: Random House, 1965.

Halliburton, Richard. *The Flying Carpet*. Indianapolis: Bobbs-Merrill, 1932.

———. *The Glorious Adventure*. Indianapolis: Bobbs-Merrill, 1927.

———. *New Worlds to Conquer*. Indianapolis: Bobbs-Merrill, 1929.

———. *Richard Halliburton: His Story of His Life's Adventure as Told in Letters to His Mother and Father*. Indianapolis: Bobbs-Merrill, 1940.

———. *The Royal Road to Romance*. Indianapolis: Bobbs-Merrill, 1925.

———. *Seven League Boots*. Indianapolis: Bobbs-Merrill, 1935.

Hanson, Haldore. *Fifty Years around the Third World: Adventures and Reflections of an Overseas American*. Flint Hill, Vt.: Fraser, 1986.

———. *"Humane Endeavour": The Story of the China War*. New York: Farrar and Rinehart, 1939.

Hartwell, Dickson, and Andrew A. Rooney, eds. *Off the Record: The Best Stories of Foreign Correspondents*. Garden City, N.Y.: Doubleday, 1953.

Hawkins, Eric, and Robert N. Sturdevant. *Hawkins of the Paris Herald*. New York: Simon and Schuster, 1963.

Hearn, Lafcadio. *Editorials from the Kobe Chronicle*. Ed. Makoto Sangu. Tokyo: Hokuseido Press, 1960.

———. *Lafcadio Hearn's America: Ethnographic Sketches and Editorials*. Ed. Simon J. Bronner. Lexington: University Press of Kentucky, 2002.

———. *Lafcadio Hearn's Japan: An Anthology of His Writings on the Country and Its People*. Ed. Donald Richie. Rutland, Vt.: Charles E. Tuttle, 1997.

———. *Life and Letters of Lafcadio Hearn*. Ed. Elizabeth Bisland. Boston: Houghton Mifflin, 1923.

Hecht, Ben. *A Child of the Century*. New York: Simon and Schuster, 1954.

Hedges, Chris. *War Is a Force That Gives Us Meaning*. New York: Anchor Books, 2003.

Herr, Michael. *Dispatches*. New York: Knopf, 1977.

Higgins, Marguerite. *War in Korea: The Report of a Woman Combat Correspondent*. Garden City, N.Y.: Doubleday, 1951.

Hoberecht, Earnest. *Asia Is My Beat*. Rutland, Vt.: Charles E. Tuttle, 1961.

Horwitz, Tony. *Bagdad without a Map*, New York, N.Y.: Dutton, 1991.

Huddleston, Sisley. *In My Time: An Observer's Record of War and Peace*. New York: Dutton, 1938.

Hughes, Langston. *I Wonder as I Wander*. New York: Hill and Wang, 1956.

Irwin, Will. *The Making of a Reporter*. New York: G. P. Putnam's Sons, 1942.

———. *Propaganda and the News*. New York: McGraw-Hill, 1936.

———. *Warrior the Untamed: The Story of an Imaginative Press Agent*. New York: Doubleday, Page, 1909.

Isaacs, Harold R. *Scratches on Our Minds: American Images of China and India*. New York: John Day, 1958.

Iyer, Pico. *The Global Soul: Jet Lag, Shopping Malls, and the Search for Home*. New York: Knopf, 2000.

Johnston, H. H. *The Kilimanjaro Expedition: A Record of Scientific Exploration in Eastern Equatorial Africa*. London: Kegan, Paul, Trench, 1886.

Keim, De B. Randolph. *Sheridan's Troopers on the Border: A Winter Campaign on the Plains*. Philadelphia: David McKay, 1885.

Kendall, George W. *Narrative of an Expedition across the Great Southwestern Prairies, from Texas to Santa Fé.* Vol. 1. London: David Bogue, 1845. Republished, Ann Arbor: University Microfilms, 1966.

———. *The War between the United States and Mexico, Illustrated.* Austin: Texas Historical Association, 1994.

Kilgallen, Dorothy. *Girl around the World.* Philadelphia: David McKay, 1936.

Kinzer, Stephen. *Blood of Brothers: Life and War in Nicaragua.* Cambridge, Mass.: David Rockefeller Center for Latin American Studies, Harvard University, 2007.

Knight, Mary. *On My Own.* New York: Macmillan, 1938.

Koppel, Ted, and Kyle Gibson. *Nightline: History in the Making and the Making of Television.* New York: Times Books, 1996.

Krock, Arthur. *Memoirs: Sixty Years on the Firing Line.* New York: Funk and Wagnalls, 1968.

Lattimore, Owen. *China Memoirs: Chiang Kai-shek and the War against Japan.* Comp. Fujiko Isono. Tokyo: University of Tokyo Press, 1990.

Laurence, John. *The Cat from Hué: A Vietnam War Story.* New York: Public Affairs, 2002.

Lesueur, Larry. *12 Months That Changed the World.* New York: Knopf, 1943.

Lochner, Louis P. *Always the Unexpected: A Book of Reminiscences.* New York: Macmillan, 1956.

———. *What about Germany?* New York: Dodd, Mead, 1942.

Loyd, Anthony. *Another Bloody Love Letter.* London: Headline, 2007.

———. *My War Gone By, I Miss It So.* New York: Penguin Press, 2001.

Lyons, Eugene, ed. *We Cover the World: By Sixteen Foreign Correspondents.* New York: Harcourt, Brace, 1937.

Marx, Karl. *Dispatches for the New York Tribune: Selected Journalism of Karl Marx.* Ed. James Ledbetter. New York: Penguin Press, 2007.

Marx, Karl, and Friedrich Engels. *The American Journalism of Marx and Engels.* Ed. Henry M. Christman. New York: New American Library, 1966.

Massing, Michael. *Now They Tell Us: The American Press and Iraq.* New York: New York Review Books, 2004.

Matthews, Herbert L. *The Education of a Correspondent.* New York: Harcourt, Brace, 1946.

———. *A World in Revolution: A Newspaperman's Memoir.* New York: Scribner's, 1971.

Mauldin, Bill. *Up Front.* New York: Norton, 2000.

Mencken, H. L. *Newspaper Days: 1899–1906.* New York: Knopf, 1941.

———. *Prejudices: Second Series.* New York: Knopf, 1920.

Mickelson, Sig. *The Decade That Shaped Television News: CBS in the 1950s.* Westport, Conn.: Praeger, 1998.

Miller, Webb. *I Found No Peace: The Journal of a Foreign Correspondent.* Garden City, N.Y.: Garden City, 1938.

Monks, Noel. *Eyewitness.* London: Frederick Muller, 1955.

Moore, Molly. *A Woman at War: Storming Kuwait with the U.S. Marines.* New York: Scribner's, 1993.

Morgan, Ted. *My Battle of Algiers: A Memoir.* New York, HarperCollins, 2005.

Mowrer, Edgar Ansel. *The Dragon Wakes: A Report from China.* New York: William Morrow, 1939.

———. *Germany Puts the Clock Back.* New York: William Morrow, 1933.

———. *The Nightmare of American Foreign Policy.* New York: Knopf, 1948.

————.*This American World.* New York: J. H. Sears, 1928.

————. *Triumph and Turmoil: A Personal History of Our Time.* London: Weybright and Talley, 1968.

Mowrer, Lilian T. *Journalist's Wife.* New York: William Morrow, 1937.

Mowrer, Paul Scott. *Balkanized Europe: A Study in Political Analysis and Reconstruction.* New York: Dutton, 1921.

————. *The House of Europe.* Boston: Houghton Mifflin, 1945.

————. *On Going to Live in New Hampshire.* Sanbornhill, N.H.: Wake-Brook House, 1953.

————. *Our Foreign Affairs: A Study in National Interest and the New Diplomacy.* New York: Dutton, 1924.

————. *Poems between Wars.* Chicago: Louis Mariano, 1941.

————. *The Poems of Paul Scott Mowrer: 1918–1966.* Francestown, N.H.: Golden Quill Press, 1968.

————. *School for Diplomats.* Francestown, N.H.: Golden Quill Press, 1964.

————. *Six Plays.* Boston: Branden Press, 1967.

Murrow, Edward. R. *This Is London.* New York: Schocken, 1989.

Neuharth, Allen H. *Confessions of an S.O.B.* Garden City, N.Y.: Doubleday, 1989.

————. *Nearly One World.* New York: USA Today Books / Doubleday, 1989.

————. *Window on the World: Faces, Places, and Plain Talk from 32 Countries.* Washington, D.C.: USA Today Books, 1988.

Neuharth, Allen H., Jack Kelley, and Laura E. Chatfield. *World Power Up Close: Candid Conversations with 31 Key Leaders.* Washington, D.C.: Gannett, 1989.

The New Yorker War Pieces. 1947. Reprint, New York: Schocken, 1988.

North, Oliver. *War Stories: Operation Iraqi Freedom.* Washington, D.C.: Regnery, 2003.

O'Donovan, Edmond. *The Merv Oasis: Travels and Adventures East of the Caspian.* London: Smith, Elder, 1882.

Paley, William S. *As It Happened: A Memoir.* Garden City, N.Y.: Doubleday, 1979.

Palmer, Frederick. *With My Own Eyes: A Personal Story of Battle Years.* Indianapolis: Bobbs-Merrill, 1932.

Patience, Richard, and John Abbe. *Around the World in Eleven Years.* New York: Frederick A. Stokes, 1936.

Pax, Salam. *The Clandestine Diary of an Ordinary Iraqi.* New York: Grove Press, 2003.

Peck, Annie S. *Flying over South America.* Boston: Houghton Mifflin, 1932.

Peck, Graham. *Through China's Wall.* Boston: Houghton Mifflin, 1940.

Powell, E. Alexander. *Adventure Road.* Garden City, N.Y.: Doubleday, 1954.

Powell, J. B. *My Twenty-five Years in China.* New York: Macmillan, 1945.

Pyle, Ernie. *Here Is Your War.* Cleveland: World, 1945.

Rather, Dan. *The Camera Never Blinks: Adventures of a TV Journalist.* New York: Ballantine, 1978.

Rea, George Bronson. *Facts and Fakes about Cuba.* New York: George Munro's, 1897.

Reaves, Joseph A. *Warsaw to Wrigley: A Foreign Correspondent's Tale of Coming Home from Communism to the Cubs.* South Bend, Ind.: Diamond Communications, 1997.

Reed, John. *Ten Days That Shook the World.* 1919. Reprint, New York: Penguin Books, 1977.

Reporting Vietnam. 2 vols. New York: Library of America, 1998.

Reporting World War II. 2 vols. New York: Library of America, 1995.

Reston, James. *The Artillery of the Press: Its Influence on American Foreign Policy.* New York: Harper and Row, 1967.

Reynolds, Quentin. *By Quentin Reynolds.* New York: Pyramid, 1964.

———. *London Diary.* New York: Random House, 1941.

———. *Only the Stars Are Neutral.* New York: Random House, 1942.

Richburg, Keith. *Out of America: A Black Man Confronts Africa.* San Diego: Harcourt, 1998.

Roderick, John. *Covering China.* Chicago: Imprint, 1993.

Rogers, Will. *There's Not a Bathing Suit in Russia and Other Bare Facts.* New York: Albert and Charles Boni, 1927.

Rosenblum, Mort. *Back Home: A War Correspondent Discovers America.* New York: William Morrow, 1999.

———. *Coups and Earthquakes: Reporting the World to America.* New York: Harper, Colophon, 1981.

———. *Who Stole the News? Why We Can't Keep Up with What Happens in the World and What We Can Do about It.* New York: John Wiley, 1993.

Ross, Albion. *Journey of an American.* Indianapolis: Bobbs-Merrill, 1957.

Rovere, Richard H. *Arrivals and Departures: A Journalist's Memoirs.* New York: Macmillan, 1976.

Rowan, Roy. *Chasing the Dragon: A Veteran Journalist's Firsthand Account of the 1949 Chinese Revolution.* Guilford, Conn.: Lyons Press, 2004.

Rue, Larry. *I Fly for News.* New York: Albert and Charles Boni, 1932.

Safer, Morley. *Flashbacks: On Returning to Vietnam.* New York: Random House, 1990.

Salant, Richard S. *Salant, CBS, and the Battle for the Soul of Broadcast Journalism.* Ed. Susan and Bill Buzenberg. Boulder, Colo.: Westview Press, 1999.

Salisbury, Harrison. *Behind the Lines: Hanoi, December 23, 1966–January 7, 1967.* New York: Harper and Row, 1967.

———. *Heroes of My Time.* New York: Walker, 1993.

———. *A Journey for Our Times: A Memoir.* New York: Harper and Row, 1983.

———. *A Time of Change: A Reporter's Tale of Our Time.* New York: Harper and Row, 1988.

———, ed. *Vietnam Reconsidered: Lessons from a War.* New York: Harper and Row, 1984.

———. *Without Fear or Favor: The New York Times and Its Times.* New York: Ballantine, 1980.

Schell, Jonathan. *The Real War.* New York: Da Capo, 1988.

Seldes, George. *Lords of the Press.* New York: Julian Messner, 1939.

———. *Tell the Truth and Run.* New York: Greenberg, 1953.

———. *Witness to a Century: Encounters with the Noted, the Notorious, and the Three SOBs.* New York: Ballantine Books, 1987.

———. *You Can't Print That! The Truth behind the News, 1918–1928.* Garden City, N.Y.: Garden City, 1929.

Sevareid, Eric. *Not So Wild a Dream.* New York: Knopf, 1946.

Sheean, Vincent. *An American among the Riffi.* New York: Century, 1925.

———. *Between the Thunder and the Sun.* New York: Random House, 1943.

———. *Dorothy and Red.* Boston: Houghton Mifflin, 1963.

———. *Faisal: The King and His Kingdom.* Tavistock, UK: University Press of Arabia, 1975.

———. *First and Last Love.* New York: Random House, 1956.

———. *Lead, Kindly Light.* New York: Random House, 1949.

———. *The New Persia.* New York: Century, 1927.

———. *Not Peace but a Sword.* New York: Doubleday, Doran, 1939.

———. *Personal History.* 1935. Reprint, with new introduction, Boston: Houghton Mifflin, 1969.

———. *This House against This House.* New York: Random House, 1946.

———. *The Tide: A Novel.* Garden City, N.Y.: Doubleday, Doran, 1933.

Sheehan, Neil. *A Bright Shining Lie: John Paul Vann and America in Vietnam.* New York: Random House, 1988.

Shirer, William L. *Berlin Diary: The Journal of a Foreign Correspondent, 1934–1941.* New York: Knopf, 1941.

———. *Midcentury Journey: The Western World through Its Years of Conflict.* New York: Farrar, Straus, and Young, 1952.

———. *The Rise and Fall of the Third Reich: A History of Nazi Germany.* New York: Simon and Schuster, 1960.

———. *Twentieth Century Journey: A Memoir of a Life and the Times.* Vol. 1, *The Start, 1904–1930.* New York: Simon and Schuster, 1976.

———. *Twentieth Century Journey: A Memoir of a Life and the Times.* Vol. 2, *The Nightmare Years, 1930–1940.* Boston: Little, Brown, 1984.

———. *Twentieth Century Journey: A Memoir of a Life and the Times.* Vol. 3, *A Native's Return, 1945–1988.* New York: Simon and Schuster, 1990.

Shoemaker, Vaughn. *1940 A.D.: Cartoons by Vaughn Shoemaker.* Chicago: Chicago Daily News, 1941.

Simpson, John. *News from No Man's Land: Reporting the World.* London: Pan Books, 2003.

Sites, Kevin. *In the Hot Zone: One Man, One Year, Twenty Wars.* New York: Harper Perennial, 2007.

Small, William. *To Kill a Messenger: Television News and the Real World.* New York: Hastings House, 1970.

Smalley, George W. *Anglo-American Memories.* New York: Putnam's, 1911.

Smith, Henry Justin. *Deadlines: Being the Quaint, the Amusing, the Tragic Memoirs of a News-Room.* Chicago: Covici-McGee, 1923.

———. *"It's the Way It's Written and "Writing versus—Everything Else."* Chicago: Chicago Daily News Reprints, 1923.

———. *Josslyn: The Story of an Incorrigible Dreamer.* Chicago: Covici-McGee, 1924.

Smith, Homer. *Black Man in Red Russia.* Chicago: Johnson, 1964.

Smith, Howard K. *Events Leading Up to My Death: The Life of a Twentieth-Century Reporter.* New York: St. Martin's, 1996.

———. *Last Train from Berlin.* New York: Knopf, 1942.

Snow, Edgar. *The Battle for Asia.* New York: Random House, 1941.

———. *Edgar Snow's Journey South of the Clouds.* Ed. Robert M. Farnsworth. Columbia: University of Missouri Press, 1991.

———. *Journey to the Beginning: A Personal View of Contemporary History.* New York: Random House, 1958.

———. *The Long Revolution.* New York: Random House, 1972.

———. *The Other Side of the River: Red China Today.* New York: Random House, 1962.

———. *The Pattern of Soviet Power.* New York: Random House, 1945.

———. *Random Notes on Red China, 1936–1945.* Cambridge, Mass.: Harvard East Asian Monographs, 1957.

———. *Red Star over China*. Rev. ed. New York: Random House, 1938.

———. *Stalin Must Have Peace*. New York: Random House, 1947.

Snow, Helen Foster. *My China Years*. New York: William Morrow, 1984.

Stanley, Henry M. *The Autobiography of Sir Henry Morton Stanley*. Ed. Dorothy Stanley. Boston: Houghton Mifflin, 1909.

———. *How I Found Livingstone: Travels, Adventures, and Discoveries in Central Africa*. London: Sampson Low, Marston, 1872.

———. *Stanley's Dispatches to the New York Herald, 1871–1872, 1874–1877*. Ed. Norman R. Bennett. Boston: Boston University Press, 1970.

Steele, Jon. *War Junkie*. London: Corgi Books, 2002.

Steffens, Lincoln. *The Autobiography of Lincoln Steffens*. 1931. Reprint, New York: Harcourt, Brace, 1958.

Steinbeck, John. *Once There Was a War*. New York: Penguin Press, 1986.

Stenbuck, Jack, ed. *Typewriter Battalion: Dramatic Frontline Dispatches from World War II*. New York: William Morrow, 1955.

Stevens, Thomas. *Around the World on a Bicycle*. 1889. Reprint, Mechanicsburg, Pa.: Stackpole, 2001.

———. *Scouting for Stanley in East Africa*. London: Cassell, 1890.

Stewart, Kenneth. *News Is What We Make It: A Running Story of the Working Press*. Boston: Houghton Mifflin, 1943.

St. John, Robert. *Foreign Correspondent*. Garden City, N.Y.: Doubleday, 1957.

———. *From the Land of the Silent People*. Garden City, N.Y.: Garden City, 1942.

———. *Once Around Lightly*. Garden City, N.Y.: Doubleday, 1969.

———. *This Was My World*. Garden City, N.Y.: Doubleday, 1953.

Stone, Melville. *Fifty Years a Journalist*. Garden City, N.Y.: Doubleday, Page, 1921.

Stowe, Leland. *No Other Road to Freedom*. New York: Knopf, 1941.

———. *While Time Remains*. New York: Knopf, 1946.

Sullivan, Mark. *Our Times: The United States, 1900–1925*. Vol. 1, *The Turn of the Century, 1900–1904*. New York: Scribner's, 1926.

Sullivan, Walter. *Quest for a Continent*. New York: McGraw-Hill, 1957.

Sulzberger, C. L. *A Long Row of Candles: Memoirs and Diaries, 1934–1954*. New York: Macmillan, 1969.

Swing, Raymond. *Good Evening! A Professional Memoir*. New York: Harcourt, Brace, 1964.

Sylvester, Judith, and Suzanne Huffman. *Reporting from the Front: The Media and the Military*. Lanham, Md.: Rowman and Littlefield, 2005.

Taylor, Edmund. *Awakening from History*. Boston: Gambit, 1969.

Thomas, Lowell. *European Skyways*. Boston: Houghton Mifflin, 1927.

———. *The First World Flight*. Boston: Houghton Mifflin, 1925.

———. *So Long until Tomorrow: From Quaker Hill to Kathmandu*. New York: William Morrow, 1977.

Thompson, Dorothy. *"I Saw Hitler!"* New York: Farrar and Rinehart, 1932.

———. *Listen, Hans*. Boston: Houghton Mifflin, 1942.

Thompson, Hunter S. *The Great Shark Hunt: Strange Tales from a Strange Time*. New York: Simon and Schuster, 2003.

Tietjens, Eunice. *The World at My Shoulder*. New York: Macmillan, 1938.

Tinker, Grant, and Bud Rukeyser. *Tinker in Television: From General Sarnoff to General Electric*. New York: Simon and Schuster, 1994.

Topping, Seymour. *Journey between Two Chinas*. New York: Harper and Row, 1972.

Tregaskis, Richard. *Guadalcanal Diary*. New York: Random House, 1943.

———. *Invasion Diary*. New York: Random House, 1944.

———. *Vietnam Diary*. Lincoln, Nebraska: iUniverse.com, 2001.

Tyler, Patrick. *A Great Wall: Six Presidents and China: An Investigative History*. New York: Public Affairs Press, 1999.

Utley, Garrick. *You Should Have Been Here Yesterday: A Life Story in Television News*. New York: Public Affairs Press, 2000.

van Paassen, Pierre. *Days of Our Years*. New York: Hillman-Curl, 1939.

Vaughn, Miles. *Covering the Far East*. New York: Covici Friede, 1936.

Vizetelly, Edward. *Reminiscences of a Bashi-Bazouk*. London: Bristol, 1878.

Washburn, Stanley. *The Cable Game*. Boston: Sherman, French, 1912.

Waters, Enoch P. *American Diary: A Personal History of the Black Press*. Chicago: Path Press, 1987.

Waugh, Evelyn. *Waugh in Abyssinia*. Ed. John Maxwell Hamilton. Baton Rouge: Louisiana State University Press, 2007.

Weisskopf, Michael. *Blood Brothers: Among the Soldiers of Ward 57*. New York: Henry Holt, 2006.

Weller, George. *First into Nagasaki: The Censored Eyewitness Dispatches on Post-Atomic Japan and Its Prisoners of War*. Ed. Anthony Weller. New York: Crown, 2006.

———. *Not to Eat, Not for Love*. New York: Smith and Haas, 1933.

———. *Singapore Is Silent*. New York: Harcourt, Brace, 1943.

Wells, Linton. *Around the World in Twenty-Eight Days*. Boston: Houghton Mifflin, 1926.

———. *Blood on the Moon*. Boston: Houghton Mifflin, 1937.

Wells, Linton, and Nels Leroy Jorgensen. *Jumping Meridians*. Garden City, N.Y.: Doubleday, Page, 1926.

Whitaker, John T. *And Fear Came*. New York: Macmillan, 1936.

White, Theodore H. *In Search of History: A Personal Adventure*. New York: Harper and Row, 1978.

White, Theodore H., and Annalee Jacoby. *Thunder out of China*. New York: William Sloan, 1946.

White, Walter. *A Rising Wind*. Garden City, N.Y.: Doubleday, Doran, 1945.

White, William Allen. *The Autobiography of William Allen White*. New York: Macmillan, 1946.

Whitehead, Don. *Beachhead Don: Reporting the War from the European Theater, 1942–1945*. Ed. John B. Romeiser. New York: Fordham University Press, 2004.

———. *Combat Reporter: Don Whitehead's World War II Diary and Memoirs*. Ed. John B. Romeiser. New York: Fordham University Press, 2006.

Whitman, Sidney. *Turkish Memories*. New York: Scribner's, 1914.

Wile, Frederic William. *News Is Where You Find It: Forty Years' Reporting at Home and Abroad*. Indianapolis: Bobbs-Merrill, 1939.

Wilkie, Franc B. *Personal Reminiscences of Thirty-five Years of Journalism*. Chicago: Schulte, 1891.

Williams, Wythe. *Dusk of Empire*. New York: Scribner's, 1937.

———. *The Tiger of France: Conversations with Clemenceau*. New York: Duell, Sloan, and Pearce, 1949.

Wilson, Richard, ed. *The President's Trip to China*. New York: Bantam, 1972.

SECONDARY SOURCES

Alan, Jeff, and James M. Lane. *Anchoring America: The Changing Face of Network News.* Chicago: Bonus Books, 2003.

Allen, Margaret Vanderhaar. *The Achievement of Margaret Fuller.* University Park: Pennsylvania State University Press, 1979.

Ames, William E. *A History of the National Intelligencer.* Chapel Hill: University of North Carolina Press, 1972.

Andrews, J. Cutler. *The North Reports the Civil War.* Pittsburgh: University of Pittsburgh Press, 1955.

Arlen, Michael J. *Living-Room War.* New York: Viking Press, 1969.

Aronson, James. *The Press and the Cold War.* New York: Monthly Review Press, 1990.

Atkins, John Black. *The Life of Sir William Howard Russell.* 2 vols. London: John Murray, 1911.

Baehr, Harry W., Jr. *The New York Tribune since the Civil War.* New York: Dodd, Mead, 1936.

Bailyn, Bernard, and John B. Hench, eds. *The Press in the American Revolution.* Worcester, Mass.: American Antiquarian Society, 1980.

Baker, Ray Stannard. *Woodrow Wilson and World Settlement.* Vol. 1. Garden City, N.Y.: Doubleday, Page, 1922.

Barnouw, Erik. *Tube of Plenty: The Evolution of American Television.* 2nd ed., rev. New York: Oxford University Press, 1990.

Barrett, James Wyman. *Joseph Pulitzer and His World.* New York: Vanguard Press, 1950.

Barris, Alex. *Stop the Presses!* South Brunswick, N.J.: A. S. Barnes, 1976.

Bassow, Whitman. *The Moscow Correspondents: Reporting on Russia from the Revolution to Glasnost.* New York: Paragon House, 1989.

Baum, Matthew A. *Soft News Goes to War: Public Opinion and American Foreign Policy in the New Media Age.* Princeton, N.J.: Princeton University Press, 2003.

Beasley, Norman. *Frank Knox: American: A Short Biography.* Garden City, N.Y.: Doubleday, Doran, 1936.

Becker, Stephen. *Marshall Field III.* New York: Simon and Schuster, 1964.

Bennett, W. Lance, Regina G. Lawrence, and Steven Livingston. *When the Press Fails: Political Power and the New Media from Iraq to Katrina.* Chicago: University of Chicago Press, 2007.

Berger, Meyer. *The Story of the New York Times, 1851–1951.* New York: Simon and Schuster, 1951.

Bernstein, Burton. *Thurber: A Biography.* New York: Quill, 1985.

Bernstein, Mark, and Alex Lubertozzi. *World War II on the Air: Edward R. Murrow and the Broadcasts That Riveted a Nation.* Naperville, Ill.: Sourcebooks, 2003.

Berry, Nicholas O. *Foreign Policy and the Press: An Analysis of The New York Times' Coverage of U.S. Foreign Policy.* New York: Greenwood Press, 1990.

Bierman, John. *Dark Safari: The Life behind the Legend of Henry Morton Stanley.* New York: Knopf, 1990.

Blackbeard, Bill. *The Yellow Kid: A Celebration of the Kid Who Started the Comics.* Northampton, Mass.: Kitchen Sink Press, 1995.

Blondheim, Menahem. *News over the Wires: The Telegraph and the Flow of Public Information in America, 1844–1897.* Cambridge, Mass.: Harvard University Press, 1994.

Bowen, Norman R., ed. *Lowell Thomas: The Stranger Everyone Knows*. Garden City, N.Y.: Doubleday, 1968.

Brady, Anne-Marie. *Making the Foreign Serve China: Managing Foreigners in the People's Republic*. Lanham, Md.: Rowman and Littlefield, 2003.

Braestrup, Peter, ed. *Big Story: How the American Press and Television Reported and Interpreted the Crisis of Tet 1968 in Vietnam and Washington*. Abridged. Novato, Calif.: Presidio, 1994.

———. *Vietnam as History: Ten Years after the Paris Peace Accords*. Washington, D.C.: University Press of America, 1984.

Britton, John A. *Carleton Beals: A Radical Journalist in Latin America*. Albuquerque: University of New Mexico Press, 1987.

Brown, Charles H. *The Correspondents' War: Journalists in the Spanish-American War*. New York: Scribner's, 1967.

Brown, David, and W. Richard Bruner, eds. *How I Got That Story*. New York: Dutton, 1967.

Bullard, F. Lauriston. *Famous War Correspondents*. Boston: Little, Brown, 1914.

Buni, Andrew. *Robert L. Vann of the Pittsburgh Courier: Politics and Black Journalism*. Pittsburgh: University of Pittsburgh Press, 1974.

Burnham, Lord. *Peterborough Court: The Story of the Daily Telegraph*. London: Cassell, 1955.

Campbell, W. Joseph. *The Year That Defined American Journalism: 1897 and the Clash of Paradigms*. New York: Routledge, 2006.

———. *Yellow Journalism: Puncturing the Myths, Defining the Legacies*. Westport, Conn.: Praeger, 2001.

Canham, Erwin D. *Commitment to Freedom: The Story of the Christian Science Monitor*. Boston: Houghton Mifflin, 1958.

Cantril, Hadley, and Gordon W. Allport. *The Psychology of Radio*. New York: Peter Smith, 1941.

Capper, Charles. *Margaret Fuller: An American Romantic Life: The Public Years*. New York: Oxford University Press, 2007.

Carlson, Oliver. *The Man Who Made News*. New York: Duell, Sloan, and Pearce, 1942.

Clark, Charles E. *The Public Prints: The Newspaper in Anglo-American Culture, 1665–1740*. New York: Oxford University Press, 1994.

Cloud, Stanley, and Lynne Olson. *The Murrow Boys: Pioneers on the Front Lines of Broadcast Journalism*. Boston: Houghton Mifflin, 1996.

Cohen, Bernard C. *The Press and Foreign Policy*. Princeton, N.J.: Princeton University Press, 1963.

———. *The Public's Impact on Foreign Policy*. Boston: Little, Brown, 1973.

Cohn, Jan. *Creating America: George Horace Lorimer and the Saturday Evening Post*. Pittsburgh: University of Pittsburgh Press, 1989.

Conrad, Will C., Kathleen F. Wilson, and Dale Wilson. *The Milwaukee Journal: The First Eighty Years*. Madison: University of Wisconsin Press, 1964.

Cook, Timothy E. *Governing with the News: The News Media as a Political Institution*. Chicago: University of Chicago Press, 2005.

Copeland, David A. *Colonial American Newspapers: Character and Content*. Newark: University of Delaware Press, 1997.

Copeland, Fayette. *Kendall of the Picayune*. Norman: University of Oklahoma Press, 1943.

Cortese, James. *Richard Halliburton's Royal Road*. Memphis: White Rose Press, 1989.

Cott, Jonathan. *Wandering Ghost: The Odyssey of Lafcadio Hearn.* Tokyo: Kodansha International, 1992.

Creel, George. *How We Advertised America.* New York: Harper, 1920.

Crockett, Albert Stevens. *When James Gordon Bennett Was Caliph of Baghdad.* New York: Funk and Wagnalls, 1926.

Crouthamel, James L. *Bennett's New York Herald and the Rise of the Popular Press.* Syracuse, N.Y.: Syracuse University Press, 1989.

———. *James Watson Webb: A Biography.* Middletown, Conn.: Wesleyan University Press, 1969.

Crowl, James William. *Angels in Stalin's Paradise: Western Reporters in Soviet Russia, 1917 to 1937, a Case Study of Louis Fischer and Walter Duranty.* Washington, D.C.: University Press of America, 1982.

Crozier, Emmet. *American Reporters on the Western Front, 1914–1918.* New York: Oxford University Press, 1959.

Culbert, David Holbrook. *News for Everyman: Radio and Foreign Affairs in Thirties America.* Westport, Conn.: Greenwood Press, 1976.

Cuthbertson, Ken. *Inside: The Biography of John Gunther.* Chicago: Bonus Books, 1992.

———. *Nobody Said Not to Go: The Life, Loves, and Adventures of Emily Hahn.* Boston: Faber and Faber, 1998.

Dabney, Thomas Ewing. *One Hundred Great Years: The Story of the Times-Picayune from Its Founding to 1940.* Baton Rouge: Louisiana State University Press, 1944.

Dallas, Gregor. *At the Heart of a Tiger: Clemenceau and His World, 1841–1928.* New York: Carroll and Graf, 1993.

Danieli, Yael, ed. *Sharing the Front Line and the Back Hills: International Protectors and Providers: Peacekeepers, Humanitarian Aid Workers, and the Media in the Midst of Crisis.* Amityville, N.Y.: Baywood, 2002.

Davis, Elmer. *The History of the New York Times: 1851–1921.* New York: New York Times, 1921.

Davis, Linda H. *Badge of Courage: The Life of Stephen Crane.* Boston: Houghton Mifflin, 1998.

DeBenedetti, Charles. *An American Ordeal: The Antiwar Movement of the Vietnam Era.* Syracuse, N.Y.: Syracuse University Press, 1990.

Dell'Orto, Giovanna. *Giving Meanings to the World: The First U.S Foreign Correspondents, 1838–1859.* Westport, Conn.: Greenwood Press, 2002.

Denis, Brian. *Pulitzer: A Life.* New York: John Wiley, 2001.

DePalma, Anthony. *The Man Who Invented Fidel: Cuba, Castro, and Herbert L. Matthews of the New York Times.* New York: Public Affairs, 2006.

Desmond, Robert W. *Crisis and Conflict: World News Reporting between Two Wars, 1920–1940.* Iowa City: University of Iowa Press, 1982.

———. *The Information Process: World News Reporting to the Twentieth Century.* Iowa City: University of Iowa Press, 1978.

———. *The Press and World Affairs.* New York: Appleton-Century, 1937.

———. *Tides of War: World News Reporting, 1931–1945.* Iowa City: University of Iowa Press, 1984.

———. *Windows on the World: World News Reporting, 1900–1920.* Iowa City: University of Iowa Press, 1980.

Detweiler, Frederick G. *The Negro Press in the United States*. Chicago: University of Chicago Press, 1922.

Diamond, Edwin. *Behind the Times: Inside the New New York Times*. Rev. ed. Chicago: University of Chicago Press, 1995.

Dicken-Garcia, Hazel. *Journalistic Standards in Nineteenth-Century America*. Madison: University of Wisconsin Press, 1989.

Douglas, Susan J. *Inventing American Broadcasting: 1899–1922*. Baltimore: Johns Hopkins University Press, 1987.

Dunham, Corydon B. *Fighting for the First Amendment: Stanton of CBS vs. Congress and the Nixon White House*. Westport, Conn.: Praeger, 1997.

Edwards, Jerome E. *Col. McCormick's Tribune: 1929–1941*. Reno: University of Nevada Press, 1971.

Edwards, Julia. *Women of the World: The Great Foreign Correspondents*. Boston: Houghton Mifflin, 1988.

Ehrlich, Matthew C. *Journalism in the Movies*. Urbana: University of Illinois Press, 2004.

Emery, Michael. *On the Front Lines: Following America's Foreign Correspondents across the Twentieth Century*. Washington, D.C.: American University Press, 1995.

Emery, Michael, and Edwin Emery. *The Press and America: An Interpretive History of the Mass Media*. Englewood Cliffs, N.J.: Prentice-Hall, 1992.

Engerman, David C. *Modernization from the Other Shore: American Intellectuals and the Romance of Russian Development*. Cambridge, Mass.: Harvard University Press, 2003.

Epstein, Edward Jay. *News from Nowhere: Television and the News*. New York: Vintage Books, 1974.

Fang, Irving E. *Those Radio Commentators!* Ames: Iowa State University Press, 1977.

Farnsworth, Robert M. *From Vagabond to Journalist: Edgar Snow in Asia, 1928–1941*. Columbia: University of Missouri Press, 1996.

Fay, Bernard. *The Two Franklins: Fathers of American Democracy*. New York: AMS Press, 1969.

Feinstein, Anthony. *Journalists under Fire: The Psychological Hazards of Covering War*. Baltimore: Johns Hopkins University Press, 2003.

Felix, Antonia. *The Post's New York: Celebrating 200 Years of New York City as Seen through the Pages and Pictures of the New York Post*. New York: HarperResource, 2001.

Fenby, Jonathan. *The International News Services*. New York: Schocken, 1986.

Ferguson, Billy G. *UNIPRESS: United Press International Covering the 20th Century*. Golden, Colo.: Fulcrum, 2003.

Ferrari, Michelle, and James Tobin. *Reporting America at War*. New York: Hyperion, 2003.

Filene, Peter G. *Americans and the Soviet Experiment, 1917–1933*. Cambridge, Mass.: Harvard University Press, 1967.

Finkle, Lee. *Forum for Protest: The Black Press during World War II*. Rutherford, N.J.: Fairleigh Dickinson University Press, 1975.

Fischer, Erika J., and Heinz-Dietrich Fischer. *American Reporter at the International Political Stage: Herbert Bayard Swope and His Pulitzer Prize-Winning Articles from Germany in 1916*. Bochum, Germany: Studienverlag Dr. N. Brockmeyer, 1982.

Fischer, Heinz-Dietrich, ed. *Outstanding International Press Reporting: Pulitzer Prize Articles in Foreign Correspondence*. 5 vols. New York: Walter de Gruyter, 1984–2000.

The Flow of the News. Zurich: International Press Institute, 1953.

Foote, Joe S., ed. *Live from the Trenches: The Changing Role of the Television News Correspondent.* Carbondale: Southern Illinois University Press, 1998.

Ford, Edwin H., and Edwin Emery. *Highlights in the History of the American Press.* Minneapolis: University of Minnesota Press, 1954.

The Foreign Correspondent: His Problems in Covering the News Abroad. Iowa City: State University of Iowa, 1954.

Franklin, John Hope. *George Washington Williams: A Biography.* Chicago: University of Chicago Press, 1985.

Frederic, Harold. *The New Exodus.* New York: Putnam's, 1892.

French, Paul. *Carl Crow: A Tough Old China Hand.* Hong Kong: Hong Kong University Press, 2006.

Friedland, Lewis A. *Covering the World: International Television News Services.* New York: Twentieth Century Fund Press, 1992.

Friel, Howard, and Richard Falk. *The Record of the Paper: How the New York Times Misreports US Foreign Policy.* New York: Verso, 2004.

Gans, Herbert J. *Deciding What's News: A Study of CBS Evening News, NBC Nightly News, Newsweek, and Time.* New York: Vintage Books, 1980.

Gates, Gary Paul. *Air Time: The Inside Story of CBS News.* New York: Harper and Row, 1978.

Gatewood, Willard B., Jr. *Black Americans and the White Man's Burden: 1898–1903.* Urbana: University of Illinois Press, 1975.

———. *"Smoked Yankees" and the Struggle for Empire: Letters from Negro Soldiers, 1898–1902.* Urbana: University of Illinois Press, 1971.

Gibbons, Edward. *Floyd Gibbons: Your Headline Hunter.* New York: Exposition Press, 1953.

Gilbert, Douglas. *Floyd Gibbons: Knight of the Air.* New York: Robert M. McBride, 1930.

Giles, Frank. *A Prince of Journalists: The Life and Times of Henri Stefan Opper de Blowitz.* London: Faber and Faber, 1962.

Gitlin, Todd. *The Whole World Is Watching: Mass Media in the Making and Unmaking of the New Left.* Berkeley: University of California Press, 1980.

Given, John L. *Making a Newspaper.* New York: Henry Holt, 1907.

Global Perspectives in Local Television News Coverage. Washington, D.C.: Radio and Television News Directors Foundation, December 2004.

Gordon, George N., and Irving Al Falk. *On-The-Sport-Reporting.* New York: Julian Messner, 1967.

Gordon, John Steele. *A Thread across the Ocean: The Heroic Story of the Transatlantic Cable.* New York: Walker, 2002.

Gorney, Cynthia, ed. *The Business of News: A Challenge for Journalism's Next Generation.* New York: Carnegie Corporation, 2002.

Goulden, Joseph C. *The Curtis Caper.* New York: Putnam's, 1965.

Goulding, Phil G. *Confirm or Deny: Informing the People on National Security.* New York: Harper and Row, 1970.

Griffin, Dick, and Rob Warden, eds. *Done in a Day: 100 Years of Great Writing from the Chicago Daily News.* Chicago: Swallow Press, 1977.

Halberstam, David. *The Powers That Be.* New York: Knopf, 1979.

Hallin, Daniel C. *The "Uncensored" War: The Media and Vietnam.* New York: Oxford University Press, 1986.

Hamilton, James T. *All the News That's Fit to Sell: How the Market Transforms Information into News*. Princeton, N.J.: Princeton University Press, 2004.

———. *Channeling Violence: The Economic Market for Violent Television Programming*. Princeton, N.J.: Princeton University Press, 1998.

Hamilton, John Maxwell. *Edgar Snow: A Biography*. Rev. ed. Baton Rouge: Louisiana State University Press, 2003.

———. *Entangling Alliances: How the Third World Shapes Our Lives*. Cabin John, Md.: Seven Locks Press, 1990.

———. *Main Street America and the Third World*. Cabin John, Md.: Seven Locks Press, 1986.

Hammond, William M. *Public Affairs: The Military and the Media, 1962–1968*. Washington, D.C.: Center of Military History, 1988.

———. *Reporting Vietnam: Media and Military at War*. Lawrence: University Press of Kansas, 1998.

Hannerz, Ulf. *Foreign News: Exploring the World of Foreign Correspondents*. Chicago: University of Chicago Press, 2004.

Hapgood, David. *Charles R. Crane: The Man Who Bet on People*. Self-published, 2000.

Hardt, Hanno, and Bonnie Brennen, eds. *Newsworkers: Toward a History of the Rank and File*. Minneapolis: University of Minnesota Press, 1995.

Harnett, Richard M., and Billy G. Ferguson. *Unipress: United Press International, Covering the 20th Century*. Golden, Colo.: Fulcrum, 2003.

Hart-Davis, Duff. *The House the Berrys Built*. London: Hodder and Stoughton, 1990.

Haverstock, Nathan A. *Fifty Years at the Front: The Life of War Correspondent Frederick Palmer*. Washington, D.C.: Brassey's, 1996.

Heald, Morrell. *Transatlantic Vistas: American Journalists in Europe, 1900–1940*. Kent, Ohio: Kent State University Press, 1988.

Henrick, Ellwood. *Lafcadio Hearn*. New York: New York Public Library, 1919.

Hero, Alfred O. *Mass Media and World Affairs*. [Boston]: World Peace Foundation, 1959.

Hess, Stephen. *International News and Foreign Correspondents*. Washington, D.C.: Brookings Institution, 1996.

———. *Through Their Eyes: Foreign Correspondents in the United States*. Washington, D.C.: Brookings Institution, 2005.

Hilderbrand, Robert C. *Power and the People: Executive Management of Public Opinion in Foreign Affairs, 1897–1921*. Chapel Hill: University of North Carolina Press, 1981.

Hodson, Joel C. *Lawrence of Arabia and American Culture: The Making of a Transatlantic Legend*. Westport, Conn.: Greenwood Press, 1995.

Hoffman, Joyce. *On Their Own: Women Journalists and the American Experience in Vietnam*. Cambridge, Mass.: Da Capo Press, 2008.

Hogan, Lawrence D. *A Black National News Service: The Associated Negro Press and Claude Barnett, 1919–1945*. Rutherford, N.J.: Fairleigh Dickinson University Press, 1984.

Hohenberg, John. *Foreign Correspondence: The Great Reporters and Their Times*, 2nd ed. Syracuse, N.Y.: Syracuse University Press, 1995.

———. *The Pulitzer Diaries: Inside America's Greatest Prize*. Syracuse, N.Y.: Syracuse University Press, 1997.

Hosley, David H. *As Good as Any: Foreign Correspondence on American Radio, 1930–1949*. Westport, Conn.: Greenwood Press, 1984.

Huber, Leonard Victor, and Clarence August Wagner. *The Great Mail: A Postal History of New Orleans.* State College, Pa.: American Philatelic Society, 1949.

Hudson, Frederic. *Journalism in the United States from 1690 to 1872.* New York: Harper, 1873.

Hudson, Roger, ed. *William Russell: Special Correspondent of the Times.* London: Folio Society, 1995.

Israel, Lee. *Kilgallen.* New York: Delacorte, 1979.

Iyengar, Shanto. *Is Anyone Responsible? How Television Frames Political Issues.* Chicago: University of Chicago Press, 1991.

Jackaway, Gwenyth L. *Media at War: Radio's Challenge to the Newspapers, 1924–1939.* Westport, Conn.: Praeger, 1995.

Jacob, Mark, and Richard Cahan, *Chicago under Glass: Early Photographs from the Chicago Daily News.* Chicago: University of Chicago Press, 2007.

Jeal, Tim. *Stanley: The Impossible Life of Africa's Greatest Explorer.* New Haven, Conn.: Yale University Press, 2007.

Johnson, Gerald W., Frank R. Kent, H. L. Mencken, and Hamilton Owens. *The Sunpapers of Baltimore.* New York: Knopf, 1937.

Johnston, Lyle. *"Good Night, Chet": A Biography of Chet Huntley.* Jefferson, N.C.: MacFarland, 2003.

Jordan, William G. *Black Newspapers and America's War for Democracy, 1914–1920.* Chapel Hill: University of North Carolina Press, 2001.

Kahn, E. J. *The World of Swope.* New York: Simon and Schuster, 1965.

Kaplan, Justin. *Lincoln Steffens: A Biography.* New York: Simon and Schuster, 1974.

Karnow, Stanley. *Vietnam: A History.* New York: Viking Press, 1983.

Keever, Beverly Ann Deepe, Carolyn Martindale, and Mary Ann Weston, eds. *U.S. News Coverage of Racial Minorities: A Source Book.* Westport, Conn.: Greenwood Press, 1997.

Kennedy, Pagan. *Black Livingstone: A True Tale of Adventure in the Nineteenth-Century Congo.* New York: Viking Press, 2002.

Kielbowicz, Richard B. *News in the Mail: The Press, Post Office, and Public Information, 1700–1860s.* New York: Greenwood Press, 1989.

Kluger, Richard. *The Paper: The Life and Death of the New York Herald Tribune.* New York: Knopf, 1986.

Knight, Oliver. *Following the Indian Wars: The Story of the Newspaper Correspondents among the Indian Campaigners.* Norman: University of Oklahoma Press, 1960.

Knightley, Phillip. *The First Casualty.* Baltimore: Johns Hopkins University Press, 2002.

Knudson, Jerry W. *Jefferson and the Press: Crucible of Liberty.* Columbia: University of South Carolina Press, 2006.

Koizumi, Kazuo. *Father and I: Memories of Lafcadio Hearn.* Boston: Houghton Mifflin, 1935.

Kornfeld, Eve. *Margaret Fuller.* Boston: Bedford Books, 1997.

Kovach, Bill, and Tom Rosenstiel. *Warp Speed: America in the Age of Mixed Media.* New York: Century Foundation Press, 1999.

Krimsky, George. *Bringing the World Home: Showing Readers Their Global Connections.* Reston, Va.: American Society of Newspaper Editors, 1999.

Kroeger, Brooke. *Nellie Bly: Daredevil, Reporter, Feminist.* New York: Times Books, 1994.

Krulak, Theodore Edward. *The Foreign Correspondents: A Study of the Men and Women*

Reporting for the American Information Media in Western Europe. Geneva: Librairie E. Droz, 1955.

Kunst, Arthur E. *Lafcadio Hearn.* New York: Twayne, 1969.

Kurth, Peter. *American Cassandra.* Boston: Little, Brown, 1990.

Laney, Al. *Paris Herald: The Incredible Newspaper.* New York: Appleton-Century, 1947.

Langguth, A. J. *Our Vietnam: The War, 1954–1975.* New York: Simon and Schuster, 2002.

Lasswell, Harold D. *Propaganda Technique in the World War.* New York: Garland, 1972.

Lawson, Anita. *Irwin S. Cobb.* Bowling Green, Ohio: Bowling Green State University Press, 1984.

Leach, Laurie F. *Langston Hughes: A Biography.* Westport, Conn.: Greenwood Press, 2004.

Lee, Chin-Chuan, ed. *Voices of China: The Interplay of Politics and Journalism.* New York: Guilford Press, 1990.

Leonard, Thomas C. *News for All: America's Coming-of-Age with the Press.* New York: Oxford University Press, 1995.

———. *The Power of the Press: The Birth of American Political Reporting.* New York: Oxford University Press, 1986.

Lewis, Alfred Allan. *Man of the World.* Indianapolis: Bobbs-Merrill, 1978.

Linn, James Weber. *James Keeley: Newspaperman.* Indianapolis: Bobbs-Merrill, 1937.

Linsky, Martin, Jonathan Moore, Wendy O'Donnell, and David Whitman. *How the Press Affects Federal Policymaking: Six Case Studies.* New York: Norton, 1986.

Lippmann, Walter. *The Phantom Public.* New York: Macmillan, 1927. Reprint, New Burnswick, N.J.: Transaction, 1999.

———. *Public Opinion.* New York: Macmillan, 1922. Reprint, New York: Free Press, 1965.

Lipstadt, Deborah E. *Beyond Belief: The American Press and the Coming of the Holocaust, 1933–1945.* New York: Free Press, 1986.

Lubow, Arthur. *The Reporter Who Would Be King: A Biography of Richard Harding Davis.* New York: Scribner's, 1992.

Lynch, Lawrence. *Jules Verne.* New York: Twayne, 1992.

Lyon, Peter. *Success Story: The Life and Times of S. S. McClure.* New York: Scribner's, 1963.

MacDonald, J. Fred. *Don't Touch That Dial!* Chicago: Nelson-Hall, 1979.

MacKinnon, Stephen R., and Oris Friesen. *China Reporting: An Oral History of American Journalism in the 1930s and 1940s.* Berkeley: University of California Press, 1987.

MacNeil, Neil. *Without Fear or Favor.* New York: Harcourt, Brace, 1940.

Mann, Robert. *A Grand Delusion: America's Descent into Vietnam.* New York: Basic Books, 2001.

Mansfield, Stephanie. *The Richest Girl in the World: the Extravagant Life and Fast Times of Doris Duke.* New York: Pinnacle Books, 1994.

Marks, Jason. *Around the World in 72 Days: The Race between Pulitzer's Nellie Bly and Cosmopolitan's Elizabeth Bisland.* New York: Gemittarius Press, 1993.

Marvin, Carolyn. *When Old Technologies Were New: Thinking about Electric Communication in the Late Nineteenth Century.* New York: Oxford University Press, 1988.

Mathews, Joseph J. *George W. Smalley: Forty Years a Foreign Correspondent.* Chapel Hill: University of North Carolina Press, 1973.

———. *Reporting the Wars.* Minneapolis: University of Minnesota Press, 1957.

May, Ernest R. *American Imperialism: A Speculative Essay.* New York: Atheneum, 1968.

———. *Rethinking International Relations: Ernest R. May and the Study of World Affairs.* Ed. Akira Iriye. Chicago: Imprint, 1998.

McCombs, Maxwell E., Edna Einsiedel, and David H. Weaver. *Contemporary Public Opinion: Issues and the News*. Hillsdale, N.J.: Lawrence Erlbaum, 1991.

McCombs, Maxwell E., David L. Shaw, and David H. Weaver, eds. *Communication and Democracy: Exploring the Intellectual Frontiers in Agenda-Setting Theory*. Mahwah, N.J.: Lawrence Erlbaum, 1997.

McLynn, Frank. *Stanley: The Making of an African Explorer*. Chelsea, Mich.: Scarborough House, 1990.

Merry, Robert W. *Taking on the World: Joseph and Stewart Alsop—Guardians of the American Century*. New York: Viking Press, 1996.

Milford, Nancy. *Savage Beauty: The Life of Edna St. Vincent Millay*. New York: Random House, 2001.

Mills, George. *Harvey Ingham and Gardner Cowles, Sr.: Things Don't Just Happen*. Ames: Iowa State University Press, 1977.

Milton, Joyce. *The Yellow Kids: Foreign Correspondents in the Heyday of Yellow Journalism*. New York: Harper and Row, 1989.

Mindich, David T. Z. *Just the Facts: How "Objectivity" Came to Define American Journalism*. New York: New York University Press, 1998.

Mock, James R. *Censorship 1917*. Princeton, N.J.: Princeton University Press, 1941.

Mock, James R., and Cedric Larson. *Words That Won the War: The Story of the Committee on Public Information, 1917–1919*. Princeton, N.J.: Princeton University Press, 1939.

Moorehead, Caroline. *Gellhorn: A Twentieth-Century Life*. New York: Henry Holt, 2003.

Morison, Bradley L. *Sunlight on Your Doorstep: The Minneapolis Tribune's First Hundred Years, 1867–1967*. Minneapolis: Ross and Haines, 1966.

Mosher, Steven W. *China Misperceived: American Illusions and Chinese Reality*. New York: Basic Books, 1990.

Moss, George Donelson, ed. *A Vietnam Reader: Sources and Essays*. Englewood Cliffs, N.J.: Prentice Hall, 1991.

Mott, Frank Luther. *American Journalism: A History of Newspapers in the United States through 250 Years, 1690 to 1940*. New York: Macmillan, 1947.

———. *A History of American Magazines*. Vol. 1, *1741–1850*. Cambridge, Mass.: Harvard University Press, 1966.

———. *A History of American Magazines*. Vol. 2, *1850–1865*. Cambridge, Mass.: Harvard University Press, 1967.

———. *A History of American Magazines*. Vol. 3, *1865–1885*. Cambridge, Mass.: Harvard University Press, 1967.

———. *A History of American Magazines*. Vol. 4, *1885–1905*. Cambridge, Mass.: Harvard University Press, 1957.

———. *A History of American Magazines*. Vol. 5, *1905–1930*. Cambridge, Mass.: Harvard University Press, 1968.

Nasaw, David. *The Chief: The Life of William Randolph Hearst*. Boston: Houghton Mifflin, 2000.

Nevins, Allan. *American Press Opinion: Washington to Coolidge: A Documentary Record of Editorial Leadership and Criticism, 1785–1927*. Vol. 1. New York: Kennikat Press, 1928.

———. *The Evening Post: A Century of Journalism*. New York: Boni and Liveright, 1922.

Nickles, David Paull. *Under the Wire: How the Telegraph Changed Diplomacy*. Cambridge, Mass.: Harvard University Press, 2003.

Nissenson, Marilyn. *The Lady Upstairs: Dorothy Schiff and the New York Post.* New York: St. Martin's Press, 2007.

Oberdorfer, Don. *Tet! The Turning Point in the Vietnam War.* Rev. ed. Baltimore: Johns Hopkins University Press, 2001.

O'Brien, Neil L. *An American Editor in Early Revolutionary China: John William Powell and the China Weekly/Monthly Review.* New York: Routledge, 2003.

O'Connor, Richard. *The Scandalous Mr. Bennett.* Garden City, N.Y.: Doubleday, 1962.

Oestreicher, J. C. *The World Is Their Beat.* New York: Duell, Sloan, and Pearce, 1945.

Olds, Elizabeth Fagg. *Women of the Four Winds.* Boston: Houghton Mifflin, 1985.

Ottley, Roi. *The Lonely Warrior: The Life and Times of Robert S. Abbott.* Chicago: Henry Regnery, 1955.

Park, Robert E. *The Immigrant Press and Its Control.* New York: Harper, 1922.

Pedelty, Mark. *War Stories: The Culture of Foreign Correspondents.* New York: Routledge, 1995.

Perlmutter, David. *Photojournalism and Foreign Policy: Icons of Outrage in International Crises.* Westport, Conn.: Praeger, 1998.

Perlmutter, David, and John Maxwell Hamilton, eds. *From Pigeons to News Portals: Foreign Reporting and the Challenge of New Technology.* Baton Rouge: Louisiana State University Press, 2007.

Perry, James M. *A Bohemian Brigade: The Civil War Correspondents.* New York: John Wiley, 2000.

Perry, Paul. *Fear and Loathing: The Strange and Terrible Saga of Hunter S. Thompson.* New York: Thunder's Mouth Press, 1992.

Persico, Joseph E. *Edward R. Murrow: An American Original.* New York: McGraw-Hill, 1988.

Peterson, Theodore. *Magazines in the Twentieth Century.* Urbana: University of Illinois Press, 1964.

Poole, Robert M. *Explorers House: National Geographic and the World It Made.* New York: Penguin Press, 2004.

Pound, Reginald, and Geoffrey Harmsworth. *Northcliffe.* London: Cassell, 1959.

Pray, Isaac. *Memoirs of James Gordon Bennett and His Times.* New York: Stringer and Townsend, 1855.

Pred, Allan. *Urban Growth and the Circulation of Information: The United States System of Cities, 1790–1840.* Cambridge, Mass.: Harvard University Press, 1979.

Price, Ruth. *The Lives of Agnes Smedley.* New York: Oxford University Press, 2005.

Pridmore, Jay. *John Gunther: Inside Journalism.* Chicago: University of Chicago Library, 1990.

Prochnau, William. *Once upon a Distant War.* New York: Random House, 1995.

Rand, Peter. *China Hands.* New York: Simon and Schuster, 1995.

Read, Donald. *The Power of News: The History of Reuters.* Oxford: Oxford University Press, 1992.

Rechnitzer, F. E. *War Correspondent: The Story of Quentin Reynolds.* New York: Julian Messner, 1943.

Rieff, David. *A Bed for the Night: Humanitarianism in Crisis.* New York: Simon and Schuster, 2002.

Ritchie, Donald A. *Reporting from Washington: The History of the Washington Press Corps.* New York: Oxford University Press, 2005.

Rivers, William. *The Other Government: Power and the Washington Media*. New York: Universe Books, 1982.

Roberts, Chalmers M. *In the Shadow of Power: The Story of the Washington Post*. Rev. ed. Cabin John, Md.: Seven Locks Press, 1989.

Roberts, Gene, and Hank Klibanoff. *The Race Beat: The Press, the Civil Rights Struggle, and the Awakening of a Nation*. New York: Knopf, 2006.

Robertson, Charles L. *The International Herald Tribune: The First Hundred Years*. New York: Columbia University Press, 1987.

Robinson, Elrie. *Biographical Sketches of James M. Bradford: Pioneer Printer*. St. Francisville, La.: St. Francisville Democrat, 1938.

Robinson, Piers. *The CNN Effect: The Myth of News, Foreign Policy, and Intervention*. London: Routledge, 2002.

Robinson, Ray. *American Original: A Life of Will Rogers*. New York: Oxford University Press, 1996.

Rogers, Everett M. *A History of Communication Study: A Biographical Approach*. New York: Free Press, 1994.

Rogers, Jason. *Newspaper Building: Application of Efficiency to Editing, to Mechanical Production, to Circulation and Advertising*. New York: Harper, 1918.

Root, Jonathan. *Halliburton: The Magnificent Myth*. New York: Coward-McCann, 1965.

Root, Waverly. *The Paris Edition, 1927–1934*. San Francisco: North Point Press, 1987.

Rosenau, James N., ed. *Domestic Sources of Foreign Policy*. New York: Free Press, 1967.

Rosenstone, Robert A. *Romantic Revolutionary: A Biography of John Reed*. New York: Vintage Books, 1981.

Rosten, Leo C. *The Washington Correspondents*. New York: Harcourt, Brace, 1937.

Roth, Mitchel P. *Historical Dictionary of War Journalism*. Westport, Conn.: Greenwood Press, 1997.

Rudenstine, David. *The Day the Presses Stopped: A History of the Pentagon Papers*. Berkeley: University of California Press, 1996.

Salmon, Lucy Maynard. *The Newspaper and the Historian*. New York: Oxford University Press, 1923.

Salwen, Michael B. *Evelyn Waugh in Ethiopia: The Story behind Scoop*. Lewiston, N.Y.: Mellen, 2001.

Sandweiss, Martha A., Rick Stewart, and Ben W. Huseman. *Eyewitness to the War: Prints and Daguerreotypes of the Mexican War, 1846–1848*. Washington D.C.: Smithsonian Institution Press, 1989.

Schaleben, Joy. *Getting the Story out of Nazi Germany: Louis P. Lochner*. Austin, Tex.: Association for Education in Journalism, 1969.

Schell, Orville. *Mandate of Heaven*. New York: Simon and Schuster, 1994.

Schlesinger, Arthur M. *Prelude to Independence: The Newspaper War on Britain, 1764–1776*. New York: Knopf, 1958.

Schroth, Raymond A. *The American Journey of Eric Sevareid*. South Royalton, Vt.: Steerforth Press, 1995.

Schudson, Michael. *Discovering the News: A Social History of American Newspapers*. New York: Basic Books, 1978.

———. *The Good Citizen: A History of American Civic Life*. New York: Free Press, 1998.

———. *The Power of News*. Cambridge, Mass.: Harvard University Press, 1995.

Schwarzlose, Richard A. *The Nation's Newsbrokers*. Vol. 1, *The Formative Years, from Pre-telegraph to 1865*. Evanston, Ill.: Northwestern University Press, 1989.

———. *The Nation's Newsbrokers*. Vol. 2, *The Rush to Institution, from 1865 to 1920*. Evanston, Ill.: Northwestern University Press, 1990.

Scott, William R. *The Sons of Sheba's Race: African-Americans and the Italo-Ethiopian War, 1935–1941*. Bloomington: Indiana University Press, 1993.

Seeger, Murray. *Discovering Russia: 200 Years of American Journalism*. Bloomington, Ind.: AuthorHouse, 2005.

Seib, Philip. *Headline Diplomacy: How News Coverage Affects Foreign Policy*. Westport, Conn.: Praeger, 1997.

Seitz, Don C. *The James Gordon Bennetts*. Indianapolis: Bobbs-Merrill, 1928.

Serfaty, Simon, ed. *The Media and Foreign Policy*. New York: St. Martin's Press, 1990.

Shanor, Donald R. *News from Abroad*. New York: Columbia University Press, 2003.

Shepard, Richard F. *The Paper's Papers: A Reporter's Journey through the Archives of the New York Times*. New York: Random House, 1996.

Shewmaker, Kenneth E. *Americans and Chinese Communists, 1927–1945: A Persuading Encounter*. Ithaca, N.Y.: Cornell University Press, 1971.

Sigal, Leon V. *Disarming Strangers: Nuclear Diplomacy with North Korea*. Princeton, N.J.: Princeton University Press, 1998.

———. *Reporters and Officials: The Organization and Politics of Newsmaking*. Lexington, Mass.: Heath, 1973.

Simmons, Charles A. *The African-American Press: A History of News Coverage, with Special Reference to Four Black Newspapers, 1827–1965*. Jefferson, N.C.: McFarland, 1998.

Small, Melvin. *Covering Dissent: The Media and the Anti–Vietnam War Movement*. New Brunswick, N.J.: Rutgers University Press, 1994.

Smith, Albert E. *Two Reels and a Crank*. Garden City, N.Y.: Doubleday, 1952.

Smith, Jeffery A. *Printers and Press Freedom: The Ideology of Early American Journalism*. New York: Oxford University Press, 1988.

Smith, Richard Norton. *The Colonel: The Life and Legend of Robert R. McCormick, 1880–1955*. Boston: Houghton Mifflin, 1997.

Smith, Sally Bedell. *In All His Glory: The Life and Times of William S. Paley*. New York: Random House, 2002.

Snyder, Alvin A. *Warriors of Disinformation: American Propaganda, Soviet Lies, and the Winning of the Cold War*. New York: Arcade, 1955.

Snyder, Louis L., and Richard B. Morris, eds. *They Saw It Happen: Eyewitness Reports of Great Events*. Harrisburg, Pa.: Stackpole, 1951.

———, eds. *A Treasury of Great Reporting*. New York: Fireside, 1962.

Sorel, Nancy Caldwell. *The Women Who Wrote the War*. New York: Arcade, 1999.

Sperber, A. M. *Murrow: His Life and Times*. New York: Fordham University Press, 1998.

Stacks, John F. *Scotty: James B. Reston and the Rise and Fall of American Journalism*. Boston: Little, Brown, 2003.

Standage, Tom. *The Victorian Internet*. New York: Berkley, 1999.

Starr, Louis M. *Bohemian Brigade: Civil War Newsmen in Action*. Madison: University of Wisconsin Press, 1987.

Startt, James D. *Journalism's Unofficial Ambassador: A Biography of Edward Price Bell, 1869–1943*. Athens: Ohio University Press, 1979.

Steel, Ronald. *Walter Lippmann and the American Century.* New York: Vintage Books, 1980.

Steele, A. T. *The American People and China.* New York: McGraw-Hill, 1966.

Stevens, John D. *From the Back of the Foxhole.* Lexington, Ky.: Association for Education in Journalism, 1973.

Stevenson, Elizabeth. *The Grass Lark: A Study of Lafcadio Hearn.* New Brunswick, N.J.: Transaction, 1999.

Stewart, Donald H. *The Opposition Press of the Federalist Period.* Albany, N.Y.: State University of New York Press, 1969.

Stone, Geoffrey B. *Perilous Times: Free Speech in Wartime.* New York: Norton, 2004.

Strobel, Warren P. *Late-Breaking Foreign Policy: The News Media's Influence on Peace Operations.* Washington D.C.: United States Institute of Peace Press, 1997.

Strong, Tracy B., and Helene Keyssar. *Right in Her Soul: The Life of Anna Louis Strong.* New York: Random House, 1983.

Suggs, Henry Lewis. *P. B. Young, Newspaperman: Race, Politics, and Journalism in the New South, 1910–1962.* Charlottesville: University Press of Virginia, 1988.

Swanberg, W. A. *Luce and His Empire.* New York: Scribner's, 1972.

———. *Pulitzer.* New York: Scribner's, 1967.

Sweeney, Michael S. *The Military and the Press: An Uneasy Truce.* Evanston, Ill.: Northwestern University Press, 2006.

Tagg, James. *Benjamin Franklin Bache and the Philadelphia Aurora.* Philadelphia: University of Pennsylvania Press, 1991.

Talese, Gay. *The Kingdom and the Power.* New York: Dell, 1986.

Taylor, Carson. *History of the Philippine Press.* Manila: Self-published, 1927.

Taylor, S. J. *Stalin's Apologist: Walter Duranty: The New York Times's Man in Moscow.* New York: Oxford University Press, 1990.

Thomas, S. Bernard. *Season of High Adventure: Edgar Snow in China.* Berkeley: University of California Press, 1996.

Tifft, Susan E., and Alex S. Jones. *The Trust: The Private and Powerful Family behind the New York Times.* Boston: Little, Brown, 1999.

Tinker, Edward Larocque. *Lafcadio Hearn's American Days.* New York: Dodd, Mead, 1924.

Tobin, James. *Ernie Pyle's War: America's Eyewitness to World War II.* Lawrence: University Press of Kansas, 1997.

Tripp, Bernell. *Origins of the Black Press: New York, 1827–1847.* Northport, Ala.: Vision Press, 1992.

Tucher, Andie. *Froth and Scum: Truth, Beauty, Goodness, and the Ax Murder in America's First Mass Medium.* Chapel Hill: University of North Carolina Press, 1994.

Tumber, Howard, and Frank Webster. *Journalists under Fire: Information War and Journalistic Practices.* London: Sage, 2006.

Tye, Larry. *The Father of Spin: Edward L. Bernays and the Birth of Public Relations.* New York: Crown, 1998.

Vaughn, Stephen L. *Holding Fast the Inner Lines: Democracy, Nationalism, and the Committee on Public Information.* Chapel Hill: University of North Carolina Press, 1980.

Villard, Oswald Garrison. *The Disappearing Daily: Some Chapters in American Newspaper Evolution.* New York: Knopf, 1944.

———. *Some Newspapers and Newspapermen.* New York: Knopf, 1923.

Walker, Dale L. *Januarius MacGahan: The Life and Campaigns of an American War Corre-spondent*. Athens: Ohio University Press, 1988.

Walsh, Justin E. *To Print the News and Raise Hell! A Biography of Wilbur F. Storey*. Chapel Hill: University of North Carolina Press, 1968.

Washburn, Patrick S. *A Question of Sedition: The Federal Government's Investigation of the Black Press during World War II*. New York: Oxford University Press, 1986.

Weber, Ronald. *News of Paris: American Journalists in the City of Light between the Wars*. Chicago: Ivan R. Dee, 2006.

Weightman, Gavin. *Signor Marconi's Magic Box*. Cambridge, Mass.: Da Capo, 2003.

Weisberger, Bernard A. *The American Newspaper Man*. Chicago: University of Chicago Press, 1961.

Wells, Robert W. *The Milwaukee Journal: An Informal Chronicle of Its First 100 Years*. Milwaukee, Wis.: Milwaukee Journal, 1981.

Wermuth, Paul C. *Bayard Taylor*. New York: Twayne, 1973.

Wendt, Lloyd. *Chicago Tribune: The Rise of a Great American Newspaper*. Chicago: Rand McNally, 1979.

Whited, Charles. *Knight: A Publisher in the Tumultuous Century*. New York: Dutton, 1988.

Whitmer, Peter O. *When the Going Gets Weird: The Twisted Life and Times of Hunter S. Thompson*. New York: Hyperion, 1993.

Wilcox, Denis L. *English Language Newspapers Abroad: A Guide to Daily Newspapers in 56 Non-English-Speaking Countries*. Detroit: Gale, 1967.

Wilkerson, Marcus. *Public Opinion and the Spanish-American War*. Baton Rouge: Louisiana State University Press, 1932.

Williams, Francis. *Transmitting World News: A Study of Telecommunications and the Press*. Paris: UNESCO, 1953.

Williams, Harold A. *The Baltimore Sun, 1837–1987*. Baltimore: Johns Hopkins University Press, 1987.

Wisan, Joseph E. *The Cuban Crisis as Reflected in the New York Press, 1895–1898*. New York: Columbia University Press, 1934.

Wolseley, Roland E. *The Black Press, U.S.A.: A Detailed and Understanding Report on What the Black Press Is and How It Came to Be*. Ames: Iowa State University Press, 1972.

Woodward, Julian Laurence. *Foreign News in American Morning Newspapers: A Study in Public Opinion*. New York: Columbia University Press, 1930.

Yagoda, Ben. *Will Rogers: A Biography*. New York: Knopf, 1993.

Yoder, Edwin M., Jr. *Joe Alsop's Cold War*. Chapel Hill: University of North Carolina Press, 1995.

Zelizer, Barbie, and Stuart Allan, eds. *Journalism after September 11*. New York: Routledge, 2002.

INDEX

Page numbers in italics refer to illustrations and captions.

NBC (National Broadcasting Company)
(*continued*)
   compared with newspapers, 301–5; current
   changes in, 459; early broadcasts of, 285–93,
   296–99; foreign correspondents for, 464; on
   genocide, 106; and Gibbons, 228, 233; and
   Iraq War (2003), 415–16; and new platforms
   for television, 482; news anchors at, 305–7,
   551*n*; overseas bureaus of, 298, 473; ownership
   of, 464; and Dorothy Thompson, 275; and
   Vietnam War, 403. *See also* Radio; Television;
   and specific radio and television journalists
Negro Digest, 339
Negro World, 334
Nehru, Jawaharlal, 216–17, 535*n*
Nerone, John C., 49*n*
Neuharth, Allen, 4, 489–90*n*
Nevins, Allan, 5, 7
New Deal. *See* Roosevelt, Franklin
New Journalism, 383, 572*n*
New Masses, 356
New Mexico, 48, 54
New Orleans, Battle of, 27–35, 48, 56, 440,
   493–94*n*
New Orleans Crescent City, 52
New Orleans Gazetteer, 29
New Orleans Item, 114
New Orleans Picayune, 47–56, 50, 224
New Orleans Times-Democrat, 114, 115, 116, 473
New Orleans Times-Picayune, 96
The New Persia (Sheean), 200
New Republic: on black newspapers and
   correspondents, 344, 346; book reviews
   in, 202; on Chinese Communists, 354, 372,
   374; contributors to, 199, 344; founding of,
   194; and Halliburton, 262; Lippmann-Merz
   critique of *New York Times* in, 350–52, 359,
   379, 380, 383; on race relations, 347; on radio,
   296; on Versailles Peace Conference, 152; on
   Vietnam War, 391. *See also* specific foreign
   correspondents
New Worlds to Conquer (Halliburton), 251, 253
New York American, 127
New York Call, 352
New York Courier and Enquirer, 37, 38, 45
New York Daily News, 196
New York Enquirer, 332
New York Evening Journal, 247
New York Evening Post: on Battle of New Or-
   leans, 27; and cost of foreign news-gathering,
   125; on Cuba, 99; Curtis's ownership of, 266;
   and public opinion, 103; and Pulitzer Prize,
   173; staff of, 193; and syndication, 194. *See also*
   specific foreign correspondents
New York Evening World, 93, 95, 279
New York Guardian, 238*n*
New York Herald: and Arctic exploration,

85–86; attacks against rival editors by, 43–45;
and Bennett Jr., 76–88; and Bennett Sr., 34,
36–47, 49, 54; and *Chicago Daily News,* 161;
collaboration between other newspapers and,
52; on coronation of Queen Victoria, 38–43;
criticisms of, 45, 82; on Cuba and Spanish-
American War, 95, 97, 99, 104; economic
news in, 37, 46–47, 476, 482; expulsion of
foreign correspondents from, 276*n*; foreign
correspondents for, 37–38, 46, 157; foreign
news in, 46–47; founding of, 36; interview of
Pope Leo XIII in, 83*n*; London office of, 166;
merger of, with *New York Tribune,* 112, 157;
on Mexican War, 52; Paris edition of, 112; and
penny press, 36, 46, 49; readers' price for, 36;
salary for foreign correspondents of, 221; staff
of, *77,* 88; on Stanley's search for Livingstone
in Africa, 76, 78–82, 88, 138, 153, 225; steam-
powered press for, 36; and Stevens's assignment to find Stanley, 84; and syndication, 95;
and telegraph, 283, 285, 452; travel articles for,
83. *See also* specific foreign correspondents
New York Herald Tribune: and air travel, 246;
competition among foreign correspondents
of, 422–23; decline and closing of, 156; excellence of, 156, 219–20, 519*n*; expense accounts
for foreign correspondents of, 221; expulsion
of foreign correspondents of, 277; foreign
news in, 127; on Hitler, 277; and Lippmann,
362; merger producing, 112, 157; Millard at,
121; Moscow office of, 59*n*; Paris edition of,
415; and Pulitzer Prize, 173; resignations from,
185; and Sheean, 206, 209–10, 215–16; Steele at,
186; and syndication, 194; Dorothy Thompson
at, 275; on Vietnam War, 389; Whitney's
purchase of, 415; on World War II, 312. *See
also* specific foreign correspondents
New York Journal: on air travel, 247; on Boxer
Rebellion in China, 168; on Cuba and
Spanish-American War, 89–90, 93–95, *94,*
96–97*n*, 98, 99, 106; end of, 458; on Hitler's
persecution of Jews, 271–72; McKinley as
reader of, 103; and public opinion, 102; and
Spanish-American War, 428; on World
War II, 316; and Yale-Princeton Thanksgiving
football game (1895), 225–26. *See also* specific
foreign correspondents
New York Journal of Commerce, 37, 43–44, 47, 52
New York News, 139
New York Post, 186–88, 275
New York Press, 92
New York Sun: Bennett on, 44; and cable
dispatches, 55–56; on Chinese Communists,
353; collaboration between other newspapers
and, 51–52; London office of, 166; Martí as
contributor to, 90; on Mexican War, 51–52;
as penny newspaper, 36, 44, 129, 440–41; and

Nixon, Richard, 277, 365, 372–76, 383, 412–14
NNPA. *See* National Newspaper Publishers Association (NNPA)
Nobel Peace Prize, 177
Noel, Percy, 168, 276*n*
Nolting, Frederick, 386
Nonprofit models for financing, 485–86
Norfolk Journal and Guide, 331, 332, 337–47, *338,* 560*n*
North, Oliver, 556*n*
North Africa, 320–21, 340–44
North American Newspaper Alliance (NANA), 194, 198, 199, 206, 208, 209, 213, 240, 246, 446
North-China Daily News, 193
North Pole, 85–86, 246
Northcliffe, Lord, 84, 86, 131, 169, 537*n*
Northwest Passage, 85, 85*n*
Norway, 312
Not Peace but a Sword (Sheean), 206–7
Noyoe Vremya, 86
NPR (National Public Radio), 483, 485
Nuremberg war crimes trials, 178, 275
Nusbaum, Don, 470

Oakes, John, 400, 577*n*
Ochs, Adolph: and bylines, 225, 534*n*; Byrd's naming of places after family of, 88; on communication between New York and London, 437; and Duranty, 379; family of, 7, 88; and foreign news-gathering operations at *New York Times,* 4, 156, 162*n*; honors for, 224; and International edition of *New York Times,* 414–15; and joint foreign news service with *Chicago Daily News,* 161; and Lawson, 160, 518*n*; lifestyle of, 222; and Paris bureau of *New York Times,* 4, 6; personality of, 4; purchase of *New York Times* by, 160; rewards for, as newspaper publisher, 464; and Strong's purchase of *Chicago Daily News,* 522*n*; and Wellman, 537*n*; and World War I, 581*n*
O'Connor, Edwin, 479–80
Office of Strategic Services (OSS), 177, 178, 210
Office of War Information, 177, 207, 262, 333
Official Gazette, 112
Ofusa, Junnosuke, 467
Ohio State Journal, 103
Oksenberg, Michael, 376
Olasky, Marvin N., 505*n*
Olivette, 93, 102
Olney, Richard, 91
Olson, Harry, 131, 137–39
Olympics games, 3, 337
Omaha World-Herald, 98, 127
Onis, Juan de, 474
Op-ed page, 151
Opera News, 216
Organization of American States, 126, 176

Ortiz, David, 557*n*
Orwell, George, 572*n*
Oshiver, Albert H., 260
Osnos, Peter, 70
OSS. *See* Office of Strategic Services (OSS)
Ottley, Roi, 557*n*, 560*n*
Our Foreign Affairs (Mowrer), 10, 178, 195
"Our Horse" (*New Orleans Picayune*), 50, 51
Outcault, Richard, 92
Outing, 84, 437
Outlook, 228, 266
Outsourcing, 594*n*
Overseas bureaus. *See* Foreign news-gathering; and specific newspapers and countries
Overseas Weekly, 508*n*
Owen, Russell D., 88
Owens, Jesse, 337
Oxford-Cambridge boat race, 71
Oxford-Harvard boat race, 61–62, 64–69, *64,* 75, 287

Pahlavi, Reza, 198
Pakistan, 280
Palestine, 128, 199, 208, 275, 429–32, 470
Paley, William, 288, 296–98, 304, 404, 581*n*
Palmer, Frederick, 144, 145
Pan-American Magazine, 114
Panama, 256–57
Panama Canal, 251, 253, 256, 260–62, 541*n*
Panay sinking, 357
Pandora, 85
Parachute foreign correspondents, 466, 469–74, 594*n*
Pareto, Vilfredo, 219, 243
Paris. *See* France
Paris Comet, 111
Paris Evening Telegram, 111
Paris Herald, 112, 147, 193
Paris Herald Tribune, 188, 415
Paris Moniteur, 19
Paris Post, 187, 188
Paris Times, 111, 199, 208
Paris Tribune, 193–94, 197, 198, 414
Park, Robert, 458–59, 481, 487, 595*n*
Parker, Dorothy, 210
Parker, James, 14
Parton, Margaret, 211–12
Patria Libre, 90
Patten, William, 115
Patterson, Donald H., 420
Patterson, James, 139–41
Patterson, Joseph, 194–95, 198
Patterson, Paul, 420–21, 537*n*
Patton, George, 316, 316*n*, 553*n*
Paul, Elliot, 240*n*
Pax, Salam, 478, 481, 483, 484
PBS (Public Broadcasting Service), 485
Peale, Norman Vincent, 216

ABOUT THE AUTHOR

John Maxwell Hamilton, the Hopkins P. Breazeale Foundation Professor of Journalism and founding dean of the Manship School of Mass Communication, Louisiana State University, began his journalism career at the *Milwaukee Journal* and reported from abroad for the *Christian Science Monitor* and ABC Radio. He was a longtime commentator on public radio's Marketplace. His work has appeared in *Foreign Affairs, The Nation,* the *New York Times,* and many other newspapers and magazines.

Hamilton was a political appointee in the Agency for International Development during the Carter administration and served on the staffs of the House of Representative's Foreign Affairs Committee and the World Bank. He held a fellowship at Harvard University in the Joan Shorenstein Center on Press, Politics & Public Policy, Kennedy School of Government, and was a visiting professor for two years at the Washington Program of the Medill School of Journalism, Northwestern University.

Hamilton is a member of the Council on Foreign Relations and is on the board of directors of the International Center for Journalists. He is the author or coauthor of five other books, as well as editor of the LSU Press book series From Our Correspondent.

DATE DUE

GAYLORD   PRINTED IN U.S.A.